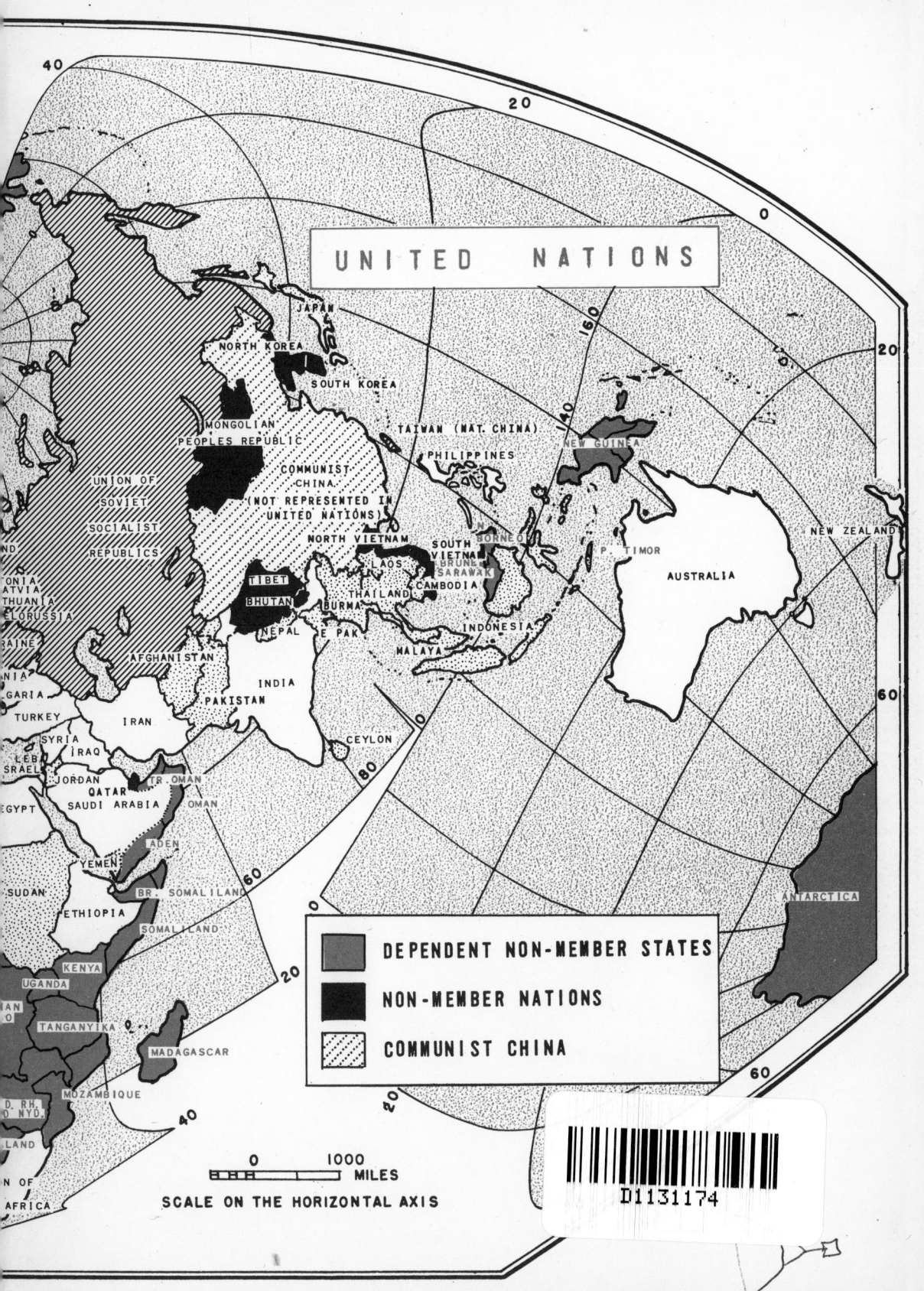

UNITED NATIONS

DEPENDENT NON-MEMBER STATES

NON-MEMBER NATIONS

COMMUNIST CHINA

0   1000 MILES

SCALE ON THE HORIZONTAL AXIS

GEOGRAPHY
AND WORLD POLITICS

LUCILE CARLSON

Western Reserve University

Allen K. Philbrick, cartographer

Michigan State University

PRENTICE-HALL, INC.   *Englewood Cliffs, N.J.   1958*

To the Memory
OF
My Beautiful and Beloved Mother

ANNA CATHERINA

Preface

Political geography is old—the philosophers of ancient Greece and Rome pondered the relation of states to their physical settings, and history records the geopolitical problems that plagued men even in the days of Babylonia. Political geography is controversial and, as brought out in the following pages, scholars in many disciplines have contributed thought.

The original contribution of this book lies particularly in the arrangement of the regional material. The immense and fragmented body of materials in a regional survey must be organized before the totality of the subject can be comprehended. The author has long felt that most regional presentations in political geography have lacked genuine coherence. This book offers a challenging presentation: it is integrative and based on the power blocs into which the world is presently broken—Western, Communist, and Neutral. Although some small readjustments may occur to somewhat alter the alignment of nations, no major change in the basic motif of the political world is likely to take place in the near future.

While the various aspects of the political geography of each of the many states are in most instances examined individually, the book retains the international scene in a total mosaic. The integrated picture has never been lost sight of; it has, in fact, been continuously and purposefully stressed. Only in such a perspective can a regional presentation of political geography define existing conditions and relationships. Areal differentials are presented, but always within the broader focus of the alignment of nations and the world as a whole. Not all of the elements of political geography are stressed equally; rather, those aspects of each state that weigh most heavily in the balance of geopolitical relationships are given emphasis.

The author has attempted to select those ideas that have survived critical scrutiny and been demonstrated valid, and to consider the ideas of those who have discerned most clearly the realities of political geography. Outstanding among these is Derwent Whittlesey's *The Earth and State,* regarded by the author as a near-classic in political geography. It has served as an inspiration and a source of ideas, interpretation, and information. The writings of Isaiah Bowman have likewise provided an understanding of basic philosophies and a wealth of information.

Western Reserve University L. C.

Acknowledgments

I extend my thanks to the many publishing companies, the several industrial firms, agencies of the United States Government, and the United Nations for their respective permissions to reprint extracts and to reproduce maps and photographs. Quotations of generous length were permitted by the editors of the American Geographical Society; American Statistical Association; Appleton-Century-Crofts; The Association of American Geographers; Carnegie Endowment for International Peace; Charles Scribner's Sons; *The Christian Science Monitor;* Columbia University Press; Cornell University Press; *Foreign Affairs; Fortune;* Harcourt, Brace & Company; Harper and Brothers; Henry Holt & Company; John Wiley & Sons; The Macmillan Company; *New York Herald Tribune; New York Times;* Oxford Book Company; Prentice-Hall, Inc.; Simon and Schuster, Inc.; United Nations; United States Department of Agriculture; University of California Press; University of London Press; William Morrow & Company, Inc.; World Book Company. Map and photograph credits are listed separately below each illustration.

I wish also to thank the academic colleagues—strangers and friends—from whom I received generous assistance. For valuable criticisms of the manuscript, my deepest gratitude to Professor Stephen B. Jones of Yale University, Professor Saul B. Cohen of Boston University, Professor Huey Louis of the University of California at Los Angeles, and Professor Merle C. Prunty Jr. of the University of Georgia. To my associates at Western Reserve University, my sincere appreciation for their advice and opinions on problems of international law and the United Nations to Edgar I. King, Assistant Dean of the Law School, and John R. Williams, lecturer in Law, School of Law; for their help in the derivation, meaning and usage of words to Professor Raven I. McDavid and Professor Joseph H. Friend, Department of English; for advice on data relative to political science to Professor Felix Rackow, Political Science Department; for checking on certain historical concepts and data contained in the manuscript to Professor Arvel S. Erickson, History Department; for assistance on problems of sociology to Professor Henry M. Busch, Professor William E. Lawrence, and Professor Newbell N. Puckett, all of the Department of Sociology. To Dr. Carl F. Wittke, Dean of the Graduate School, my deep gratitude for his wise and kindly counsel on many matters pertaining to the book.

To Professor Allen K. Philbrick, Michigan State University, I extend my utmost gratitude for his excellent design and execution of many of the maps contained in the volume, and his aid in the selection of others. The cartographer wishes to acknowledge assistance in the drafting of the maps of the faithful services of his wife, Mrs.

Eugenie Philbrick, and two graduate assistants at Michigan State University's Department of Geography—Miss Hannelore Sadezky, and Mr. Robert G. Janke. Lastly, my deep appreciation to Frances M. Goff, secretary to the Dean of the Law School, Western Reserve University, the typist who untiringly stayed with the manuscript until it was completed.

The authority used for the spelling of the place names was *Webster's Geographical Dictionary, Revised Edition.*

Contents

PART ONE. THE PRINCIPLES OF POLITICAL GEOGRAPHY

Section A. Interpretation and Growth of Political Geography

1. What Is Political Geography? **3**

The Dimensions of Political Geography, 4. The Differentials of State-Areas, 6. The Equation of Power, 8. The Geography of Power, 9. The Political Area: In Space and Time, 10. The Compartmentalization of the Continents by Barrier Boundaries, 11. The Role of Political Geography, 12

2. The Development of Geopolitical Thought **13**

The Contributions of the Germans to Geopolitical Thought, 14. The Growth of Political Geography in Other Countries, 22

Section B. The Primary Factors in Political Geography

3. The Space Factors: Location, Size, and Shape **24**

The Location of States, 25. Size, 36. Shape, 38

4. Population **40**

Race and National Policy, 44. The Ethnic Integrants, 44. Population Trends (The Dynamics of Population), 44. Movement of Population, 51. The Changing Balance of Power as Expressed in the Human Element, 54

5. Resources and Industry, Transportation and Trade **55**

Resources and Industries, 55. *The Land Resource,* 56. *The Extractive Resources: Minerals,* 58. *Laws and Resources,* 66. *Industry and the Power of a State,* 67. *Transportation and Trade,* 68. *Trade as a Political Weapon,* 71. *Transportation and Communication in an Air-Age,* 72

6. The State **75**

The Structure of a Political Unit, 76. *The Nuclear Area,* 76. *The Ecumene,* 76. *The Capital,* 77. *The Constituent Units of the State,* 78. *Problem Areas,* 78. *Territorial Interests: Colonies, Mandates, and Other Dependent Territories,* 79. Political and Geopolitical Maturity and Immaturity, 84. Government and Habitat, 86. Laws and the State, 86. Foreign Policy and the State, 87

7. Boundaries **89**

Natural Boundaries, 90. *Water Boundaries,* 90. *Mountains as Boundaries,* 95. Cultural Boundaries, 96. Geometrical Boundaries, 97. Complex Boundaries, 98. Steps in Establishing the Location of a Boundary, 99. Boundary Function and Surveillance, 104. The Open Versus the Closed Sky, 106. Inter-Realm Boundaries, 106. In Conclusion, 107

8. The Concept of Power in a Bi-Polar World **109**

The Political Alignments of the Present Day, 110. The Western Bloc, 110. The Communist Bloc, 118. The Neutral States, 124. What is a Great Power? 131. Trends for the Future, 132

PART TWO. WORLD REGIONAL SURVEY

Section A. The Communist Bloc

9. The Soviet Union **137**

Physiography, 138. Climate, 139. Unity, Pre- and Post-Revolutionary, 142. Pulsations in the Growth of the State, 142. Bones of Instability: Boundaries, 153. Role of Transportation and Communication, 158. Political Structure of the Soviet Union, 160. The Economic System, 163. Industrial and Power Resources: Soil—and Agriculture, 164. People and Population, 167. Industrial and Power Resources: Minerals, Power, and Industry, 172. *Power Resources,* 173. *Mineral Resources Other than Fuel: Iron,* 175. *Alloy Metals.* 176. Industry, 178. Foreign Trade, 182

10. Communist States of Central Europe and the Balkans **183**

The Physical Setting, 184. The Ethnic Structure, 187. Boundaries, 192. Cohesive and Disruptive Forces in Central Europe and the Balkans, 202. Political and Economic Structures, 206. Problem Areas, 213. The Communist Frontier in Europe, 216

11. The Continental States of East and Southeast Asia **217**

China, 219. *Communication for Coherence and Development,* 224. *Population,* 226. *The Contemporary History,* 227. *Chinese Territories not Yet Re-Incorporated,* 227. *The Economic Structure,* 229. Korea, 232. *People and Population,* 235. *The Historical and Political Background,* 235. *The Postwar Issue of Korea,* 237. Indochina, 240. *Divided Vietnam,* 243

Section B. The Atlantic Basin States

12. The United States **246**

Population and People, 248. *Location, Size, Shape,* 250. *The American Domain,* 253. *Boundaries,* 256. *Resources and Industry,* 256. *The Geopolitical Power of the United States,* 259. *Foreign Policy,* 260. American Territories: Alaska, 262. *Resources and Resource Development,* 265. *Geopolitical Considerations,* 266. Pacific Interests: The Hawaiian Islands, 267. *People and Population,* 267. *Physical Elements,* 268. Other Pacific Possessions, 269

13. Canada and the Arctic **271**

Population and People—and Nationalism, 272. The Canadian Economy, 275. Location, 276. Canadian Problems, 276. Anglo-American Relations, 276. The Canadian Northland, 277. Geopolitical Considerations, 278. The Significance of the North American Arctic, 279. The Arctic Mediterranean, 279

14. Latin America **284**

The Two Americas, 284. Hemispheric Relations, 286. Political Stability and Instability in Latin America, 287. Population and People, 289. Latin American Economy, 289. Communication, 290. Central America, 291. The Panama Canal and Panama, 291. The Strategic Canal, 295. The Plateau States: Mexico, Peru, and Bolivia, 296. Northwestern South America, 298. Southern South America, 301. Brazil: Portuguese America, 305

15. Western Europe **309**

Eastern Versus Western Europe, 313. Great Britain, 315. Transportation and Coherence, 319. France, 326. Population and People, 328. The Empire, 329. The French Economy, 331. Disputed Areas, 333. The Benelux Countries: Belgium, Netherlands, and Luxembourg, 335. Germany, 343

16. The European Neutrals **351**

Scandinavia, 353. Norway, 355. Denmark, 355. Sweden, 357. Scandinavian People and Population, 359. Finland, 360. The Mountain States of Austria and Switzerland, 361. Switzerland, 362. Austria, 364

Section C.   The Mediterranean-African World

17. The Mediterranean **366**

Geopolitical Considerations, 366. Historical Summary, 367. The Mediterranean Environment, 368. The Iberian Peninsula: Spain and Portugal, 369. Portugal, 371. Spain, 372. Italy, 374. The Italian Empire, 376. Geopolitical Considerations, 376. Greece, 377. Turkey, 380. Historical Background, 380. The Geographic Character of Anatolia, 381. Problems of the Republic, 384. Strategic Considerations, 384. Turkey and the Dardanelles, 386. The Political Geography of the Straits, 389. The Mediterranean and the Middle East, 391. Mediterranean North Africa, 393. Aspects of the Physical Geography and Economy, 395. Population and People, 397. The Mare Mediterranean: Its Importance, 398. In Retrospect—to Gain Perspective, 398

18. The Middle East **400**

Importance of The Middle East, 401. Middle East Unrest, 402. The Character and Impact of Islam, 404. Resources of The Middle East, 405. The Oil of the Middle East, 406. Strategic Concerns, 409. Problems of the Middle East, 410. The Arab League, 412. Contributions of the Middle East to Modern Civilization, 414. Egypt, 415. Egypt in the Modern Era, 417. Problems of the Egyptian Republic, 419. The Nile River, 419. Population and People, 420. Sudan, 420. Libya, 421. Saudi Arabia, 422. The Boundary Problems of Saudi Arabia, 422. The States of the Syrian-Palestine Mandates: Lebanon, Syria, Israel, and Jordan, 423. Lebanon, 423. Syria, 424. Boundary Problems of the Former Mandate States, 424. Israel, 426. Jordan, 430. Iraq, Iran, and Afghanistan, 431. Iraq, 431. Iran, 433. Afghanistan, 436

19. Africa: Continent in Ferment **439**

History of the Continent, 440. Natural Features, 443. People and Population, 444. Colony Evaluation, 444

Section D.   Western and Neutral Lands of Asia and the Pacific

20. East Asian Offshore Islands and the Pacific **457**

The Attitude of the East Toward the West, 458. East and South Asia in World Economy, 459. Japan, 460. *Geopolitical Considerations,* 463. Formosa, 465. Thailand, 466. Malaya and Singapore, 468. The Philippine Republic, 470. Oceania, The Pacific World: The Trust Territories, 473. Australia and New Zealand, 473. *Geography,* 475

21. South Asia **478**

India and Pakistan, 478. *The Two Republics,* 483. *Pakistan,* 486. *The Dominion of India,* 489. *India versus China,* 492. Ceylon, 493. Burma, 494. *Background to Burmese Problems,* 495. Indonesia, 497. *Emergence of the Political Structure of the State,* 499. The Colombo Plan, 501

**Section E.   The Changing Character of
Geopolitical Patterns and Concepts**

22. The Geography of Future World Politics **504**

The Evolution of the Supra-National Organization, 504. The Character of War, 506. Strategy and Tactics for Lasting Peace, 508. The Need for the "Voluntary Subordination of National Policy," 509. *International Law,* 509. *Nationalism and Neutralism,* 510. *The Supra-National Concept,* 511. *The Need for a Supra-National Organization,* 514. Geography and the Way of the Future, 515. *The Changing Dimensions of the Globe,* 515. *The Concept of "the Hemispheres,"* 517. *The significance of the Shrinking Globe,* 519. *Geography as a "Weapon" of Planning,* 519

Bibliography **521**

Index **525**

PART ONE

THE PRINCIPLES OF
POLITICAL GEOGRAPHY

INTERPRETATION AND GROWTH OF POLITICAL GEOGRAPHY

1

What Is Political Geography?

In all eras of history, political geography is theoretically challenging, but in periods of insecurity such as have prevailed since the beginning of World War II, the study of geography —and particularly the "power aspect" of political geography—becomes critical. The experience of the two world wars and of the more recent ideological warfare did much to quicken the recognition of the contribution of geography to an understanding of world affairs.

Why? How are geography and international relations associated? Or geography and war— the latter, one of the major manifestations of the inter-relations between states? Walter Lippmann, correspondent of the New York Herald Tribune, gave a partial answer when he wrote:

It must have seemed to many a crude oversimplification of the problem when they read . . . that the great ideological conflict of our age, the contemporary form of the wars of religion, could be and should be translated into a contest over territory.

It does . . . define the problem in far simpler terms than it is now the fashion to use in speaking of the ideological war, but to define the problem simply and concretely is not to say and to suggest that the problem can be solved easily or cheaply. On the contrary, nothing is so rare in human history as a peaceable change in the sovereign control of disputed lands. . . .

. . . unless ideology can be translated into geography, the conflict cannot be dealt with by diplomats and military strategists. . . . if they mean to deal with the conflict, not merely to agitate it and talk about it, then they must come down to geography. . . . every treaty or agreement which settles or purports to settle a mortal conflict is essentially a map. Every war has a geographical objective which is to be defended or captured or destroyed.

Dynastic wars, religious wars, nationalist wars, wars of independence, imperialist wars, all have had to be fought for and settled in terms of territory. They have been fought to enlarge or to reduce the domain of this king or that one. The great religious conflict between the Greek and the Latin church, between Christendom and Islam, between Protestantism and Catholicism, all ended in a division of territory. The nationalist wars and the wars of independence have ended in the fixing of national frontiers. The imperialist wars have ended in the recognition of colonies, dependencies, protectorates, and spheres of influence.

The rivalry of kings, of churches, of nations, and of empires has continued. But insofar as the rivalry led to war, or could be regulated by diplomacy, the issue that had to be decided was the control of territory. What could not be settled by the conquest or the defense of territory, or by treaties fixing the boundaries of powers and sovereignty over the territory, was beyond the diplomats and the strategists. . . .[1]

Geography is deeply involved in almost every side of national life and international affairs whether the aspect in question is the evaluation of the potential and actual resources of combatants engaged in a war (and this would involve the estimation not only of the resources of allied nations, but of the opposing side as well); whether it concerns the peace, with all its problems of reconstruction—on a local, national, and international scale; or simply the normal day-to-day affairs of the nation. Each boundary adjusted, each parcel of land exchanged, each transfer of displaced persons, each reparations' settlement becomes an experiment in the geo-political[2] field. Whether the design of the frontiers recommended and laid down will satisfy local and national needs and promote international stability has deep ramifications in the geography of the regions involved.

To ignore the geographic factor in national and international affairs is to overlook one of the most important sources of intelligence on the subjects of economics, development, and security.

No future settlement of human affairs can claim to be valid unless it is based upon the intelligent knowledge and use of the physical properties of the world in which we life. This proposition is simple enough to express in principle, but it is infinitely difficult to apply in practice because of the lag that exists between the time that the need for conscious social direction is perceived and the time at which it is achieved. This . . . defines the essential problem in the relationship of geography and politics. The political geographer uncovers and displays for the information and use of his fellow men those features of the physical world

that are related to the life of man and to his collective social effort.[3]

With economics and ethnography, geography should serve as a frame within which political agreements are made.

THE DIMENSIONS OF POLITICAL GEOGRAPHY

The scope of political geography is great, the base broad, for it ramifies into at least four fields of research: geography, history, political science, and international relations. Being the study of the inter-relationship of the earth and state, it contributes a geographical interpretation of the international relationships between states. But it goes farther than mere interpretation: it offers an approach to a sound appraisal of national enterprise and international relations, and can play a part in pointing the way toward political agreements that promote peace.

Defined thus, political geography might be said to be the culmination of geographic thought and research. The physical setting, geographic location and the other space relations of size and shape, resources, populations and people, political ability nationally and internationally, and other such factors are reviewed—*in time* as well as *in space* and *in their inter-relationships with human living*. All of these elements have had important influences on the accomplishments of men and states in the past, and must inevitably have an enormous bearing in the future.

The function of geography in political geography. Geography provides the expert with knowledge of the earth environment itself, including an inventory of the physical and cultural possessions. Bowman calls these the "existing realities." Nor does the scientific research of geography stop with material things; it includes man himself. Thus, geography furnishes a component in the "sought-for understandings of the world"—places, and

---

[1] Walter Lippmann, "Geography and the Ideological Conflict," *New York Herald Tribune,* June 21, 1951, page 21, columns 1-2.

[2] This adjective is a portmanteau word used occasionally throughout the book in place of the cumbrous terms political-geographic or politico-geographic. It implies involvement of both political and geographic factors.

[3] H. Arthur Steiner, "The Relation Between Geography and Politics," *Global Politics,* edited by Russell H. Fitzgibbon (Berkeley, California: The University of California Press, 1944), pp. 3-4.

their relation to other places—that are necessary to lessen "tension by a process of rational change in the existing realities."

Our widening knowledge of the earth has shown us a far greater number of relationships, finer and closer here, less obvious there. Each refinement of technique of measurement and analysis of regional association gives us a deeper or at least a more vivid understanding of the complexities of life and the difficulty of "explaining things" or of making reasoned decisions. This fuller equipment for understanding is akin to the astronomer's growing depth of vision as he perfects and enlarges his telescope. . . .

If we desire to quicken choice and action with respect to our neighbor, widen the range of experience, and trade knowledge for mutual benefit, then our study of realities must now sweep through the whole interrelated earth with all its regional divergencies.[4]

The earth science of geography, then, takes stock of the "existing realities"—the physical and cultural attributes—of states, and unfolds the relationship of human activity and culture and organization to the environment provided by nature. The core of geography is "the study of places," that is, the analysis of the important dissimilarities that differentiate the various regions of the world from one another. It delineates and analyzes the regional differences between state-areas and thereby provides for the political geographer the necessary knowledge of the actual and potential material and human resources.

Geography often furnishes a first logical approach to the technological examination of a region because it outlines the extent of recognizable natural resources in terms of known needs, provides a rational explanation of the physical framework to which the resources are tied, puts into relation the principal distributional facts of production and population, and thus helps indicate the scope of national limitations and possibilities. It supplies the deficiencies of purely technological results by revealing the relationships of a national group of regions to the rest of the world.[5]

The role of history in the interpretation of political geography. Just as the political geography of no state can be understood without recourse to a study of the geographic environment, so few, if any, areas can be profitably studied without resorting to a review of the past. Therefore, the contemporary political scene must be set within and against whatever residuum of history as survives in the patterns of the present.

History provides a means of discerning what man's achievements within an area have been. However, for political geography, the historic occurrences that have influenced the advance or decline of the political state tend to be given the stress.

Only as the present is set in perspective against the historic record of the past can the political geography of any region be completely interpreted for, as Whittlesey states: "The emotional character of political thought holds communities and states to traditional patterns and practices long after their original connections with the natural environment have been forgotten. Sound political geography therefore must trace these relict forms and procedures to their source . . . When once the data from the past have been collected and the locale has been intimately studied, the significant geopolical pattern is likely to appear. Where political events have repeatedly occurred in unmistakable relationship to the natural, the role of nature in human affairs can be clearly read. Elsewhere the data may warrant only a tentative sketching of the geopolitical design."[6]

How the field of international relations contributes to political geography. The liaison between the area under consideration and other parts of the world is provided by the field of international relations, for international relations attempts to explain the policies and conduct of states relative to other political units. The problems of international relations and their geographical implications are manifold

[4] Isaiah Bowman, *Geography in Relation to the Social Sciences* (New York: Charles Scribner's Sons, 1934), p. 210.

[5] *Ibid.,* p. 205.

[6] Derwent Whittlesey, *The Earth and the State* (New York: Henry Holt & Company, Inc., 1939), p. 591.

and complex, and they lift political geography out of the more restricted realm of internal national policy and practice and thrust it into the broad arena of world relationships—with all of the complications of power politics, of imperialism, and of the struggle for the survival of nations and peoples.

The contributions of political science. Political science examines the form, principles, and mechanisms of government that lie at the base of the political functioning of the domain, both in matters of internal and external affairs. The political structure is most successful when it harmonizes with the physical environment in the area where it obtains. It is, ideally, a means of expediting the economic and social life of the group. It has the dual role of at once adapting to and modifying the natural environment. Thus, political concepts and forms have power and vitality.

There is another side in the relationship of government to the physical environment, however—nature unceasingly qualifies the effectuation of all human efforts. Political theories and structures are, therefore, directly or indirectly "modified by the compulsion to function within the limits set by nature. As technology advances or recedes, the scale of political operations changes and the incidence of conditioning nature alters. It never disappears."[7]

Political geography closely relates to political science. The two fields resemble each other in that the object of both is the analysis of the state. Political science, however, concerns itself with the policy and sovereignty of the nation whereas political geography deals with its power and space relations.

THE DIFFERENTIALS OF STATE-AREAS

The static and dynamic elements of political geography. Since political geography is concerned with the interplay of law and region, there are both dynamic and static elements involved. The human factors—people, group motivations, ideas—are the dynamic aspects

___
[7] *Ibid.*, pp. 556-57.

while the factors of natural resources, space, location, and the like—the earth factors—are the static, or relatively static, elements.

The potence of any country depends upon the available resources, potential and actual. Each state is equipped with actual and potential resources and power. The potential assets and power of a nation are primarily determined by the natural resources found within the domain of the state. The actual resources and potence are the product of human ingenuity and achievement working within the bounds of the physical possibilities.

Independent states vary greatly in size. There are some eighty sovereign states on the earth occupying spaces quite disparate in size. In the Netherlands, for example, live ten million people crowded together on 13,025 square miles whereas in Australia a smaller population (8,696,000) spreads widely over a vast area of 2,974,581 square miles. The United States and Canada each occupy more than three million square miles of the earth's surface whereas little Luxembourg covers but 998 square miles. The colossus of the world, the Soviet Union with its 8,600,000 square miles of land area, stands in diametrical contrast to Vatican City, a mere dot of sovereign territory, 0.2 square miles in size.

Space is relative. The examples presented make it apparent that there are striking differences in the way in which space has been apportioned to the various nation-states. However, *space as such* is of relatively minor importance. It is the resource-base found within that space that really counts, and the contrasts in quantity, quality, and variety of natural resources are as marked as are the dissimilarities in area: some areas are rich in mineral or other resource reserves—as the vast basin of the Congo and the small valley of the Saar; others are meagerly endowed. The large spaces of the French Sahara, Libya, Pakistan, and Mongolia (as far as is known at present) belong in the latter category.

The achievements of human groups contrast sharply. Contrasts in man's economic, political, intellectual, and social accomplishments, however, stand out even more strikingly from area to area and from state to state than do the contrasts in space and resources. While the achievements—and even the ideas and group motivations—of a people usually reflect to a more or less marked degree the type and potential of the environment in which the group resides, nevertheless the above statement holds true. By way of example, Western civilization, peopled from and including Europe and inventive of mechanical things, in general developed a highly mechanized society in the many and varied habitats where it established itself, whereas others have not shown the same genius and initiative—as the African and Asian.

The economic structures of Asia and Africa have continued to depend largely on manpower, utilizing to only a minor degree the resources that form the base of national power in a modern mechanized world. In Asia, only Japan developed an industrial system at all comparable to that of the West previous to World War II. In those parts of Africa where industrial development has taken place, it has been done by Western enterprise and with Western money.

On the continent of Europe there is considerable disparity in the way in which the various groups have utilized the physical potential of their habitats. The reclamation and development of *the netherlands* within the Dutch state, for instance, is an outstanding example of man's skill in improving a marginal area; the Irish, on the other hand, in an environment of similar handicaps and possibilities have achieved much less. The present-day Swiss and Spanish show contrasting use of domains that possess differing potentials: the Swiss, in a rugged mountain environment lacking mineral resources other than water and with a minimum of arable land, have built a nation whose prosperity is perhaps second to none; the Spanish, inheriting a land richly endowed with minerals and with a varied agricultural base, have a poverty-stricken population. Of European peoples who colonized the Americas, the accomplishments of the Anglo-Americans north of the Rio Grande and of the Latins, occupying the area southward, likewise stand in marked contrast.

The character of the society evolves as a result of the interplay of the physical environment and human initiative. From the illustrations cited, it is to be seen that when peoples with differing cultures and backgrounds occupy environments that are strikingly alike in certain respects, great dissimilarities in utilization often result. Further, differences not easy to explain may develop among the peoples occupying such relatively comparable regions. Note how the doctrines of pacifist Christianity and Judaism, and of militaristic Islam, all developed within the same environment and even within the same area, among homogeneous pastoral peoples; how, in mountain environments, Swiss national policy eventuated into one of extreme pacifism, Turkish history unfolded as an almost opposite extreme of militarism, and the Tibetans developed as a seclusive and cloistral society. Modern Germany has stood for aggression—plunging the globe into a series of disastrous wars; Scandinavia has represented peace, spending its efforts in negotiating for world concord; China until 1910 remained isolated from international affairs—a nation living to itself.

Human dissimilarities characterize these differences—variations in the culture, impulsions, and philosophies of the groups. The variety among human societies is as pronounced as is the diversity in the natural habitats, and the interplay between the human and the physical factors is so close that one cannot generally discern where the influence of one begins and the other ceases. Both have an impact upon the character of the total pattern that unfolds and upon the kind of development that takes place within a given area. Neither works alone, nor in a determinative fashion. The play of habitat and human upon each other traces and fills in the outline of the evolving state or society.

THE EQUATION OF POWER

The security of nations in the international world is closely related to the allocation of resources—the base of *power*.

The essential components of the political world have been the independent states, these states acknowledging no superior authority in the conduct of their internal or international relations. Although international organizations are being set up to care for special aspects of the problems with which states are faced, and although the states govern themselves in accord with the recognized conventions concerning their relationships with each other, ultimately the safekeeping of each nation rests with itself —rests on the strength that it can command and the alliances it can make to assure its security. For the effectuation of a defense the state must consider the factors that determine power.

Changes in the power equation of the world. Few nations have the potential "to play the game of power politics." The nineteenth century saw a number of states that were powerful enough to be termed great. However, as power came more and more to mean industrial might, the number that could so qualify became smaller. At the beginning of World War I there were eight great powers. But, by the end of the global struggle, only five strong states emerged. Russia had folded internally during the war period, Germany and Turkey were defeated, and Austria-Hungary was carved up into several pieces. Italy, France, Great Britain, the United States, and Japan remained.

Within twenty years, however, a defeated Germany had revived, rearmed, and had reassumed the position of a great power while Russia, as the Union of Soviet Socialist Republics, had reasserted and tightened its authority over Russian lands and, building rapidly under the Communist form of government, likewise emerged as one of the mighty nations of the earth.

With the end of World War II, only three great powers remained—the United States, the Soviet Union, and the United Kingdom. France? It was still a power to be reckoned with. Due, however, to disturbances and uprisings in colonial holdings and to the inability of any elected government to remain in office for any length of time in Metropolitan France itself, France has lost much of its former potency. It is, nevertheless, considered one of the Western "Big Three."

Another power—or two, even three—are appearing in the East, namely, Communist China, India, and Japan. If tendencies persist, the power equation of the world, in a few years, may have to be quoted somewhat differently than at the present moment.

Of the great post-World War II powers, the United States and the Soviet Union have the greatest actual and potential wealth. However, the United States has been using its resources intensively over a longer period of time than has the USSR, and it has acted as the "arsenal" for the Allied Nations in two highly mechanized world wars as well as in the more recent Korean conflict. Though its resource potential is still great, the United States has used its minerals and forests, its soil and grasslands recklessly, holding, until recently, the *laissez faire* attitude of limitless reserves. However, the American nation possesses a commanding position, not held by the Soviets, with regard to access to the ocean lanes—*i.e.* access to ice-free and politically non-restricted waters. On the other hand, the Soviet Union has certain advantages of location that the United States lacks—namely, the advantages of close contact with the Eurasian peoples and states. Air power, with its great mobility, minimizes the handicaps implied above. Both the United States and the Soviet Union possess great air strength. Potentially, the Soviet Union is perhaps the most nearly self-sufficient nation in the world. It has a large and growing industry based on one of the greatest reserves of mineral resources (almost untouched) found within the bounds of any one state. It has, as well, the advantage of population numbers, the latter being nearly as great as those of the United States and Great Britain combined—and a population still in the stage of active population growth.

The Commonwealth of Nations has had several severe setbacks since 1945 that have weakened, somewhat, its power position in the world. In the first place, Great Britain was left in straitened economic circumstances at the close of the war. Secondly, many colonial territories demanded—and were given—sovereign status: Burma disassociated itself from the Commonwealth; the Union of South Africa, struggling internally with the bitter animosities that reared themselves over race policies, has at times hinted separation from the other dominions; the Sudan is gone and, with it, whatever influence the British were formerly able to exert in that part of Africa; the Suez Canal Zone was rather suddenly and completely removed from British jurisdiction; India and Pakistan, becoming republics within the Commonwealth, have been on the verge of war ever since partition in 1948; Ceylon and Malaya have become sovereign states within the Commonwealth, while the colony and protectorate of the Gold Coast became the independent state of Ghana in March, 1957. Is the power of the Commonwealth weakening? Diplomacy and time will decide. To date, however, the Commonwealth of Nations is the only effective league of nations of its kind that the modern world has seen.[8]

THE GEOGRAPHY OF POWER

Power—and the geography of power—is a component of the world situation in any age, and especially in the present era when power is represented by industrial might. The problems of power and space—area, resources, population—deeply involve political geography. Today, more than ever before, the earth is a power world where the political balance shifts somewhat with every passing month. National potency is dependent upon economic and military

strength which, in turn, rests upon the bases of economic and human resources.

For this reason, through the exploration and assumption of control of the unclaimed lands of the globe, various European states (and, in time, their political progeny) built up colonial empires to augment national power. There followed successive periods during which the balance of colonial power was shifted and rearranged. The addition of such dependencies, spheres of influence, or economic rights of exploitation of resources, extends the physical base of the territorial domain of the state. When the resources of a nation are found in variety and quantity, there is a tendency for the newly-discovered materials to be carried to the centers where trade and manufacture are already established. This also magnifies the national power potential, and makes available an increase in capital for investment in the areas just opening up, both at home and abroad. By such methods of production and exchange, the world is tied together, and a delicate mesh of world relationships has developed that is sensitive to impulses from every part of the globe.

Political power posits responsibilities. To assure a just and peaceful world, the possession of political power implies certain obligations. In the first place, as long as states exist, the national security must be maintained. Increasingly, this must be accomplished through the mutual collaboration of all nations on a global basis. Retreat into national, continental, or hemispheric solidarity no longer assures the integrity of a country. Second, international relations must rest upon a spirit of justice and right rather than only upon force and strength. It likely follows, then, that some international—supra-national—organization, invested with the power to enforce right throughout the world, must be erected to assure the peace. The League of Nations and the United Nations are preliminary steps in the accomplishment of the latter goal. Both, however, have lacked the power to function effectively.

---

[8] The ancient Greek leagues and the Holy Roman Empire are examples of effective alliances of the more distant past.

THE POLITICAL AREA: IN SPACE AND TIME

Political areas are not foreordained divisions of the earth's surface.

They may expand or shrink with the passage of time. Military conquests, folk migrations, discoveries of new lands, and changes in material technology have more than once altered the size, shape, and character of political areas. They may even lose their identity, although regions which have once stood out as leaders in political affairs are likely to reappear after longer or shorter eclipse. In the long view it must be conceded that the political significance of any area bears a well-defined relation to its climate, landforms, and natural resources. This relation remains unchanged, with the momentous exception that human ability to utilize and cope with nature advances or recedes and by so much alters it.[9]

In the political, social, and economic evolution of the human race, the adaptation of man to his habitat is in a process of continuous change. This adaptation is not entirely a matter of the influence of the environmental elements but is, in part at least, an intelligent selection by man of the alternatives of opportunity offered by the habitat. Thus man assists in limning his own environment. He does this in the light of his knowledge of the experience of the past and of his appraisal of the possibilities offered by nature. The state of culture attained by the group is a factor of no small importance in shaping the character of the adjustment.

The time variable influences man's response. The contrasting uses that were made in pre- and post-colonial days of the territory that now makes up the United States provides a forceful example of the importance that the level of technology—*i.e.* the time variable—has in influencing the mode of adjustment. The primitive Indian societies, spread thinly over much of the three million square miles of territory in numbers not exceeding 850,000, left almost untouched the great potential of resources that furnished the base of the industrial society that was developed by European immigrants and their posterity. Except for occasional truces declared for the purpose of

exchanging such products as flint for war purposes, no trade existed between the various Indian tribes. Their contacts with each other were characterized by hostility. As a consequence, the Indians remained in primitive states of progress and secured, at best, but a meagre subsistence.

The environment to which the Europeans came was the same as that of the Indians. Only two things were different. In the first place, the Europeans brought with them domesticated animals (there were no domesticable animals, except the dog, among the indigenous fauna of North America) and "proven" seeds for the growing of crops; second, they had the benefit of the accumulated knowledge and technology of all of the civilized peoples of the Old World, including that of Asia and North Africa.

The differing use made of a particular environment *by a particular group with the passage of time* illustrates even more clearly the time variable. The whole history of man, from the simple beginnings of his occupancy of the earth to the complex contemporary economies that utilize the whole habitat, bears out the influence of time in varying the response. Two other specific examples are cited to illustrate further, namely: the differing use of the United States domain in colonial and contemporary America, the former largely agricultural, the latter, industrial; Czarist pre-revolutionary Russia and the Communist post-revolutionary Soviet Union, the former likewise agricultural as against the mechanized and industrialized present state.

Different groups, then, according to the stage of technology, vary greatly in their modes of response to environments—as do also particular societies with the passage of time. Why is this so? Density of population and custom in most instances determine the choice—or mode—of adjustment. This accents the fact that the human element is generally more important as a determinant of the character of the adjustment than is the physical element.

The conquest of space recants spatial isolation. "The inter-relations of states become closer" (although "not necessarily more sym-

9 Whittlesey, *op. cit.*, pp. 585-86.

pathetic") as man surmounts the obstacles of distance, climate, and topographic barriers. Today, "political isolation is impossible."[10] Contrast the lengthy and hazardous voyages of the Polynesians as they slowly spread throughout Oceania in their hand-hewn wooden vessels, guided only by the stars, drifting seaweed and the like, as against the speedy passage of jet aircraft which span a 3000-mile distance in less than four hours. Though nations might desire neutrality, or strive to remain aloof from entanglements of the world, such apartness is now impossible to maintain, even in those countries with seemingly peripheral location.

THE COMPARTMENTALIZATION OF THE CONTINENTS BY BARRIER BOUNDARIES

Of the wide range of problems that falls within the scope of political geography, that of boundaries comes up for closest scrutiny. Neighboring nations—some friendly, some hostile—face each other across some 100,000 miles of international boundaries. What are boundaries? How do they work? What are the current boundary problems of the world, and how can they be solved?

"Frontiers are indeed a razor's edge on which hang suspended the modern issues of war or peace, of life or death for nations," wrote Curzon. Wars may come from economic rivalries or military threats, but it should not be overlooked that they have often sprung from disputed frontiers. At times of political readjustment, as in the postwar years following 1945, the "geographical basis of frontiers and their justification" comes in for unusually careful scrutiny and study. In such periods men recognize that the boundaries which separate one nation from another are "instruments of regional partition" that have few if any sanctions in geography.[11]

Sharp frontiers in geography are rare. Rather, there is a transitional blending from one type of physical environment—such as climate, vegetation, and even landforms—to another region with dissimilar characteristics. Nor is the transitional character limited to nature. The activities in which man engages in one area or state will tend likewise to merge gradually with those human activities carried on in adjacent regions or countries. Thus, in crossing from France to Belgium, Switzerland to Italy, Germany to Denmark, etc., except as one is required to show a passport, one would be unable to tell when he left one state and entered the other. *Frontier zones tend to be zones of blending. Even on boundaries that are marked by sharply defined natural barriers, the barrier-region itself will form the transition zone between one area and another.*

Except in rare instances, the term natural frontier is not geographically valid. There is seldom, if ever, any sanction for frontiers (boundaries) in geography. Mountain ranges and crests of mountains, river valleys, ringing-deserts, were long considered superlative "natural" boundaries. But with the advent of modern warfare, and of aircraft that can conquer the mightiest ranges and cross the broadest deserts in a minimum of traveling time, such barrier boundaries lost much of their protective character. As for rivers, though there are numerous examples of streams that have served and serve as political boundaries, throughout history they have tended to be fluvial centers of trade and unification rather than zones of separation.

Frequently, more "natural" than the natural boundary as instruments of political separation are the various types of ethnic and cultural boundaries where language, religion, custom, and the like serve as a basis of drawing people apart. The Saar, the Sudeten, Carinthia, and Istria are boundary problems that can be permanently settled only by recognizing that the ethnic factor must be a major consideration in the final drawing of national boundaries if lasting peace is to be achieved along these international frontiers.

The search for satisfactory lines of defense is one of the most fruitless to which national statesmen are still committed. It is inevitable under

---

[10] Walter Fitzgerald, *The New Europe* (New York: Harper and Brothers, 1945), pp. 2-3.

[11] *Ibid.*, p. 2.

existing conditions that every State will demand for its own security a frontier which nature has made defensible, the assumption being, almost invariably, that the neighboring State is potentially hostile, and liable to any time convenient to itself to go to war. Yet it must be obvious that no one State can acquire a frontier advantageous for defense without at the same time placing its neighbor at a corresponding strategic disadvantage.

Political history offers very few instances of a frontier drawn with such equity of purpose that neither of the States affected has received an unfair strategic advantage . . .

As the world is a whole made up of inter-related parts, political frontiers—however "natural"—are artificial lines of division which obstruct inter-regional co-operation, their purpose being to partition what to Nature is indivisible. Through their influence adjacent peoples are turned away from association with each other, and are led to exaggerate the usually small ethnological and cultural differences which distinguish them. Moreover, as they correspond more with political ideals than with geographical realities they may be opposed to a satisfactory economic and social adjustment of the community to its environment.[12]

The arbitrary division of Indochina along the Seventeenth Parallel is a case in point.

THE ROLE OF POLITICAL GEOGRAPHY

Political geography embodies change; it is not static. Though the potential of regions may not change except as technology offers new ways and uses, the pattern of possession of these earth resources is in a constant state of flux, as is also the use-pattern. Political geography is particularly dynamic today when the whole world is like a stage—where plot and counterplot emerge in succession—and the game of power politics is played, tipping the balance of the bipolar world first in favor of one side, then the other.

"Interest in geography's contribution to an understanding of the basis of civilization has been much stimulated by the experience of war. In the recent world conflict our military effort had to be calculated on a careful estimate of the actual and potential resources of all the belligerents, friendly and hostile . . . in the preva-

lent mood for national as well as international reconstruction the planning of community life in its proper relation to environment is now accepted as deserving serious study. The statesmen of postwar Europe are undertaking a great experiment in political geography. The framework of frontiers [and of federations of economic union, as the Schumann Plan and others] which they recommend will prove" their worth insofar as they both satisfy local needs and promote international equilibrium.[13]

Geographers are not agreed among themselves as to the services that political geography can render. The views of Derwent Whittlesey, however, express those held by most men in the field. In his words:

The study of geography, more than any other discipline, should inculcate a sympathetic understanding of political groups inhabiting all the varied regions of the earth. It emphasizes the long view, the persistent conditioning of human life by nature-made surroundings, and the difficulty any group of humankind has of seeing beyond its geographical horizon. . . .

Among the cross-currents of political, social, and economic streams the only fixed points for guidance are found in the natural environment. Within broad limits human society must always shape its political order so as to facilitate economic life. As man's skill in utilizing earth resources improves, his political horizon must widen. The alternative may be the destruction of the material technology which carries group interests beyond local regions. To reshape the political world wisely requires all man's ingenuity. Success is to be measured by the degree to which states harmonize with the regional pattern of the earth. Political geography provides the needed facts. Its calm outlook in the world of governance can provide salutary release of the high emotional charge which politics usually carries. If it is to function effectively, its practitioners must hold to the impartial study of political groups in their regional distribution. Otherwise they will drift into the mystical realm of propaganda, serving only the selfish ends of narrow national emotions. Sound political geography must always take the long view afforded by history and archeology, because in the political realm much of the past coexists with all the present.[14]

---

12 *Ibid.*, pp. 4-5.

13 *Ibid.*, p. 1.
14 Whittlesey, *op. cit.*, pp. 592-93.

2

The Development of
Geopolitical Thought

The recognition of the geographical factor in history and politics has its roots deep in the historical past. Of the ancient philosophers and historians the Greeks were apparently the first who gave verbal acknowledgment to the interaction between society and the geography of an area. Herodotus (485-425 B.C.), a historian, suggested in his writing a causative tie between the two; the philosopher, Plato (427-347 B.C.), in his *Republic* raised certain questions regarding the relationship of the state to its area that are even today of interest to political geographers; Strabo (63 B.C.-A.D. 24), Greek historian and geographer, attempted to indicate how the culture and the political subdivisions of a state were determined by the natural environment.

Among the Romans Julius Caesar (100 B.C.-44 B.C.), statesman and soldier, stands out for his contributions to early geopolitical thought. In his writing of *Gallic Wars* he weaves political geography in with his history, and thus indicates his recognition of the limitations imposed by the natural environment upon his conquests. In fact, this cognizance of the importance of the geographic factor is often cited as the reason for his successful expansion of the Roman state: he never overstepped the limits imposed by geography but, with geopolitical discernment, envisioned and conquered a compact area bounded by strong frontiers. While Alexander was stopped just within the gateways to India and Napoleon was starved out at Moscow because they overlooked the geographic factor of space (long lines of supply) in their attempts to conquer the world, Caesar succeeded by retreating of his own will from those areas where geography seemed to indicate that such a course was best. Other thoughtful observers, as Ptolemy, Pliny the Elder, and Cicero, contributed to the nascent unfoldment of political geography. In every instance, however, this early development of the subject was obscure, an unnamed part of philosophical or geographical thought.

People from many countries and many professions contributed to the development of political geography with the passage of the years. Not only geographers, but philosophers, biologists, mathematicians, historians, educators, statesmen have added ideas relating to the governing of territories by states, and to international relations. Among the French, Montesquieu (1689-1755), jurist and philosopher, was interested in the effect of geography upon political change and human conduct. Much of Book XIV of his *Esprit des Lois* was devoted to this subject.

THE CONTRIBUTIONS OF THE GERMANS TO GEOPOLITICAL THOUGHT

But it was the Germans who, centuries after the Greek and Roman contributors, first gave recognition to political geography as a separate discipline: it was Immanuel Kant (1724-1804), a German, who won the title "father of political geography," and is even known as the founder of modern geography itself. He defined geography, dignifying it "not only as the 'summary' of nature but also as the basis of history," outlined the fields of geography, one of which was political geography, and, in his lectures on physical geography, laid the theoretical groundwork for the political geography of modern times.

His geographic thinking found few adherents outside of Central Europe and Germany, but, among his countrymen, there arose a number of followers whose contributions are noteworthy in one way or another. They include Friedrich List, Karl Ritter, Alexander von Humboldt, Heinrich von Treitschke, Georg Friedrich Wilhelm Nietzsche, and Friedrich Ratzel. These Germans wrote and developed ideas concerning the relationship of the *geography* of the world to the *states* of the world. Ratzel published the first methodical treatise on political geography and thus became the actual originator of that branch of the discipline.

The concept of *lebensraum* developed in Germany. Political geography developed differently in different countries, a reflection of the realities of the political and geographic conditions obtaining within and around the national states. In Germany the idea of expansion (of "living-space") from the first became associated with geopolitical thought. Germans from many walks of life contributed to this idea, some unwittingly, some directly. A number lived long before the terms "geopolitics" or "Nazism" were coined, but their ideas nevertheless concurred with the concepts and gave verve to the propaganda that advanced them. Nietzsche, with his concept of the super race, was one of these men. Heinrich von Treitschke, expounding his venomous doctrines of expansion by war, thought the acquisition of territory by war was the only elixir for devitalized nations, and he was first to use the term *Lebensraum,* living-space. "The state is power," he said and he extracted from Machiavelli the idea that the state is not bound by the restraints of morality as are individuals.

Ritter and the development of geographic determinism in Germany. Humboldt and Ritter held to the principle of the unity of the globe, and to the idea that geography had a directive and determinative influence upon man. While the ideas of von Humboldt had little effect upon German geopolitical thought, those of Ritter did. Ritter extended his geographical theories into the realms of history and archaeology. He held, on the one hand, that the movements of man and the history of states are greatly affected by topography and climate, and he thought that the day might come when geography could "furnish the directives of political life as a whole." The historical element in geography he viewed as the varied functions of the same natural region in different areas of progress. Though he saw the natural environment as highly directive upon the course of history and civilization, he recognized that, to man, the relative value of the geographical element constantly changes with the development of his arts and the unfolding of history.

The theories of Ritter are complex and often vague, but in his massive writings can be discovered the formulation of the idea of the *living globe,* the continents being conceived as the primary organs of the great organism. Though Ritter did not set forth the idea of the organic state, the suggestion is there for others to draw out. Such ideas undoubtedly had an influence upon the thinking and philosophy of the men who, first, under the Hohenzollern and then the Nazi, led Germany into two aggressive wars of expansion. As stated before, expansionism was a dominant theory throughout the thinking of most of these Germans—and this meant accretion at the expense of other nations, for Europe was taken up at this time and there were no empty spaces on that continent as the United States had found in North America.

The contributions of List and Ratzel to the political philosophy of Nazi Germany. The ideas of Friedrich List and Friedrich Ratzel must also be examined briefly before the full meaning of Haushofer's geopolitics and the geopolitical thinking and actions of Nazi Germany can be understood. Friedrich List was trained as a political scientist, a field which he later abandoned for economics. Both disciplines, however, flavored his writings and theories. He was raised and educated in a disunited Germany made up of petty principalities that spent their strength in quarreling over rival claims to tiny pieces of territory. In 1825, he visited the United States and was much impressed by the vast space possessed by the young nation, by the arrangement of the several states banded together in a customs union, and by the protectionist doctrines of Alexander Hamilton. On his return to Germany some years later he carried with him a deep admiration for these ideas, and hoped that they might be applied to his country. He urged the expansion of German industry and trade through protective legislation, a customs union within the state and, to further the economic development of Germany, "an extended and conveniently bounded territory reaching from the North and Baltic Seas to the Black Sea and the Adriatic." Thus, though he did not coin the term *Lebensraum,* he did originate the theory of living-space.

Friedrich Ratzel (1844-1904) was influenced by Darwin's thinking, and extended the latter ideas into the fields of political science and political geography. His theories carried political geography to a point where geopolitics could materialize. "A large space maintains life," he stated, and he felt that the state is in the same relation to its environment as is any biological organism to its habitat. He accepted from Darwin's theory of evolution the concept that although isolation is very important in producing a new species, "largeness of area" is on the whole more necessary for the evolution of a long-lived species that will be capable of spreading abroad. He viewed the state as comparable to an organism with the biological necessity of growth, that growth to take place, if necessary, by force. He laid out laws governing the spatial growth of states. They were:

1. The space of states grows with culture. (That is, as populations disperse and spread the culture of the state over other territories, new areas are added to the state, enlarging its territory.)
2. The growth of states enlarges following other manifestations of the spread of peoples, and these manifestations must, of necessity, come before the state will grow. (That is, the flag follows the spread of commercial and missionary activity, ideas, and the like.)
3. States grow through the amalgamation and absorption of smaller units.
4. The frontier is the peripheral organ of the state and reflects, therefore, the strength, growth, and changes in the state.
5. In their growth, states seek to absorb politically valuable areas (as plains, river valleys, coasts, regions rich in natural resources as ores, oil, soils for food production, etc.).
6. The first impetus for territorial growth comes to the primitive state from without. (States with higher levels of progress bring their ideas to backward peoples who, due to increasing population with bettered conditions, need to expand their territory.)
7. The general trend toward territorial annexation and amalgamation transmits the trend from state to state, and intensifies the tendency (*i.e.* history has proven that expansion whets appetites).

In brief, according to Ratzel, the state is a growing organism and if it does not feed on something, it withers and dies. This was good propaganda for Ratzel's day—which coincided with the period of German amalgamation and colonial expansion under Bismarck. The seventh "law" opened up unlimited possibilities for state aggrandizement. To make this law clear, Ratzel enlarged on the meaning of it in the following manner: "There is on this small planet sufficient space for only one great state."

Ratzel's theories, which define *Lebensraum* and the means by which that space can grow, relate closely to the ideas of Karl Haushofer and the practices of the Nazi dictator. However, Ratzel elevated his theories to the realm of science, many of which carry over into the field of political geography today.

Kjellen and Haushofer and the theory of geopolitics. Haushofer drew heavily from Ratzel in formulating his concepts of German *Geopolitik*. He considered Ratzel's statement, "a large space maintains life," as "the state-biological rule of life put into classic form." This phrase was the inspiration that brought such catch phrases as *Lebensraum* and *grossraum* into the every-day semantics of Nazi Germany; it may also have contributed to the ideology that characterized National-Socialist Germany.

The *Geopolitik* of Haushofer has not been accepted among political geographers of other Western states. It met its most violent criticism from American geographers whose antipathy to the theory first found voice in Isaiah Bowman's *The New World*. This work, growing out of Bowman's association with the State Department and his participation in the Versailles Conference as one of President Wilson's aides, struck out at the theory in these words:

In all times large and small states have existed side by side, and their inequalities of size, strength, and function are the result of many forces and conditions—varying topographic layout, unequal resources, different stages of development, inequality with respect to dominant economic centers. Curiously enough, it is the large states that require the most elbow room and seek most aggressively for increase of space and power, often to the point of weakening the central state and government. There is no such thing as an "organic boundary" in a territorial sense. The philosophy of *Lebensraum* is open to abuse like the arguments based on history and military necessity. Even if boundaries were adjusted to national needs and if proper economic advantages were given to every nation, the equilibrium would last but for a moment. Inequalities would at once appear just as they would among a whole population in case of an equal distribution of wealth. National power, like individual power, is composed to a marked degree of intangibles not susceptible of statistical expression.[1]

Haushofer also drew ideas from men other than Ratzel, and accorded credit to them for their contribution to his thinking. Two of the outstanding contributors to his *Geopolitik* were Rudolf Kjellen, a Swede, and Sir Halford Mackinder, an English geographer who advanced the *heartland theory* of power politics. Though the geopolitics of Haushofer has long since passed into disrepute with the passing of Hitler, the geopolitical ideas of Mackinder have caused recurrent discussion.

The Geopolitik of Rudolf Kjellen. Rudolf Kjellen was the first to use the term *Geopolitik* and to make the distinction between geopolitics and political geography. A definition of *Geopolitik,* worked out by the editors of *Zeitschrift für Geopolitik*[2] as follows, may be accepted as closely expressing the views of both Kjellen and Haushofer. "*Geopolitik* is the science dealing with the dependence of political events upon the soil. It is based upon the broad foundations of geography, especially political geography, which is the doctrine of political organisms of space and their structure . . . *Geopolitik* aims to furnish the armature for political action and guidance in political life . . . *Geopolitik* must come to be the geographical conscience of the state."

Rudolf Kjellen, professor of history and government at the University of Göteborg, Sweden, turned from the study of these two fields of thought to geography for a deeper

---

[1] Isaiah Bowman, *The New World* (Yonkers-on-Hudson: World Book Company, 1921), p. 266.

[2] Haushofer, *et al.*, editors (published in Munich from 1924 to 1941).

insight into world problems for he felt that the geography of a state was more significant to the understanding of that state than was the form of government. Pro-German, Kjellen forecast that several great superstates would rise in Europe, Africa, and Asia and that, in Europe, that state would be Germany. His concepts of the state he borrowed in part from earlier German thinkers: the state is a living organism; its continuance (life) depends upon its people, culture, government, economy, and soil; and, power is its most necessary characteristic. He forecast the passing of the power of the great maritime empires into the hands of the compact land nations which would in time also control the sea lanes. Kjellen's ideas greatly influenced the geopoliticians at Munich who, after his death, revised and published some of his writings.

German *Geopolitik* versus the concept of the status quo. German geopolitics is neither political science nor political geography in the strictest sense of the word. Its theorists really attempted to present a geopolitical plan that might serve as a blueprint for the measurement and harnessing of the forces that make for growth of the state. It is concerned with power politics. During the latter part of the nineteenth century the concept of foreign relations had centered around two ideas, namely, the concert and the balance of powers. These policies grew out of the practice in international politics that was dominant in that day, *i.e.* that national policy should and could be accordant with maintaining an international equilibrium where diplomacy, employing negotiation and compromise, was looked upon as the method of securing political advantage with the least possible risk of war.

Geopolitics was a revolutionary departure from these old concepts for it premised instability as the basic tenet of international relations, regarding states as organisms that must grow or decline; they could not keep the status quo. According to Kjellen, a state, to be considered a great power, must have three basic attributes: 1) spaciousness; 2) freedom of movement; 3) internal cohesiveness. Looking

at three of the powerful nations of his day he wrote that "Russia barred from outlets to the seas, lacks the second, the British Empire the third, Germany, with her small and dispersed colonial possessions, lacks all three."

The *Geopolitik* of Haushofer. Karl Haushofer (1869-1946) was the intellectual heir of Kjellen upon the death of that scholar. In life, they had collaborated on their geopolitical ideas, and upon Kjellen's death, Haushofer took over many of Kjellen's concepts, including his terminology. He went on from there, adding his own ideas and extracting from those of others, notably Mackinder. Geopolitics is the product of the minds of many men, not one; but whereas the forerunners of Haushofer were merely formulating or amplifying theories, Haushofer elaborately verbalized and publicized the geopolitical concepts. Haushofer has been called the prophet of *Geopolitik;* this concept is inseparably linked with his name.

Karl Haushofer was born in Bavaria. Entering the army as a young man, he served in the artillery and was sent, in 1908, to Japan as an artillery instructor in the army of that country. He made many friends in Japan, learned the language, and acquired knowledge of the Pacific Ocean. He was impressed with the Far East and, on his return to Germany, advocated the establishment of cordial relations between the German and Japanese states. By 1925 he had come to look upon the Pacific area as the most important in the world, geopolitically.

During World War I he fought in the German Army with a rank of Major General having, as his aide-de-camp, Rudolf Hess. Returning to civilian life in a defeated Germany, he attempted to determine the reasons for its collapse. He was appointed to the Chair of Geography and Military Science at the University of Munich in 1919, and shortly thereafter organized the *Institut für Geopolitik* in Munich, from which he and his followers propounded their ideas on geopolitics in a number of books and scores of articles and papers. Through Hess, it is said, Haushofer met the imprisoned Hitler after the failure of the Bierhallen-Putsch of 1923.

It is not known to what extent, if any, Haushofer's ideas were used by Hitler, but, upon attaining power, he appointed Haushofer to the presidency of the German Academy. Chapter XIV of *Mein Kampf,* in which Hitler outlined the objectives of Nazi foreign policy and presented his conception of *lebensraum,* is said to have been inspired by Haushofer's theories.

Nowhere in his writings (or in the vast quantity of material put out by the *Institut für Geopolitik,* where were gathered together many of the political scientists and geographers in Germany) does Haushofer set forth in clear, concise language his conceptions of geopolitics. "Vast space" is necessary for the greatness of a state—so necessary, he thought, that if states decline it is invariably due to a "declining space conception." With Ratzel, he held that a state must continue to expand its territory or it would decay (*i.e.* he concurred in the concept of the organic state), and with this doctrine all of the German geopoliticians also agreed. The Monroe Doctrine—conceived in terms of a hemisphere—was greatly respected by Haushofer, but he thought the United States should stay in the Western hemisphere, and he anticipated that after World War I it would. The concept of the Monroe Doctrine, he felt, might serve as a model for blocking out the share of the world's territories over which Germany should exert high influence. Economic self-sufficiency was another of the precepts of German geopolitics, economic self-sufficiency because economic control of vital materials and industries is necessary for power. Such self-sufficiency and power implied control over large spaces of the world's lands.

Flexibility was the *foundation* of Haushofer's doctrine: the expansive urge of the state must know no limits. Political geography is static and descriptive, said Haushofer, but geopolitics is a dynamic science—probing the "dynamics of world change," vivifying space. According to his theories the "first and indispensable attribute of national greatness" is "living space."

From Mackinder he took the idea of the struggle of land-locked *versus* oceanic peoples, and held that the conflicts in policy between states derive from this basic antagonism. He went to great lengths in his attempts to develop this idea.

It is difficult to evaluate Haushofer's work, or to know to exactly what extent he influenced, directly or indirectly, the policies of Nazi Germany. His rise to recognition coincides with the ascent to power of Hitler, and Haushofer's decline and death with the fall of the Nazi *Führer.* His work in general covers several areas. He exerted great influence—as the head of the *Institut für Geopolitik* and the German Academy—upon the intellectuals of Germany, and the dissemination of his beliefs was immensely facilitated by the opportunities that these two organizations provided. As stated before, though he was the voice and the prophet for German geopolitics, that doctrine emerged under him as the product of many minds. Though some of the concepts involved are twisted and unsavory, some will have challenging and lasting import for political geography. The unwholesome character is the lack of morality which the doctrine predicates, *i.e.* the expansion of the strong state without regard for the rights of other nations.

The Heartland Theory of Sir Halford Mackinder. A number of the ideas basic to German *Geopolitik,* and publicized by the *Institut* at Munich, were drawn directly from the writings of Sir Halford Mackinder. This English geographer presented his "Heartland" thesis under the title of "The Geographical Pivot of History," in 1904, before the Royal Geographical Society in London. The original paper presented most of the principal ideas involved in his theory, though he modified the original version twice, in 1917 and in 1943, in light of world developments. The 1917 revision was a significant one for it expanded the "Heartland" to include Eastern Europe up to the Elbe River, thus furnishing a new criterion for evaluating the "Heartland," namely, the European plain and its resources. His latest thoughts on the subject reiterated his early thesis on the geopolitical organization of the world and its implications.

Though the Heartland is the "pivot" around which he organized all the rest of the land and water areas of the globe, his premise is perhaps more easily grasped if his organization of the continents and oceans is first understood. He notes that three-quarters of the area of the world is water, one-quarter land. The oneness of the several oceans and the unity of the land masses are better comprehended if thought of in terms of a *World-Ocean* and a *World-Island*.

"There is one ocean covering nine-twelfths of the globe; there is one continent—the World-Island—covering two-twelfths of the globe; and there are several smaller islands, whereof North America and South America are, for effective purposes, two, which together cover the remaining one-twelfth."[3] The World-Island consists of Europe, Asia, and Africa. But, of these three, only two are of continental proportions for Europe is, in actuality, merely a peninsula thrust out from Asia and separated from it by the relatively low Urals, even as India is a peninsula blocked off from the rest of the Asiatic continent by the high Himalayas. Eurasia and Africa are essentially one continent, however—not divided but united at Suez and Gibraltar. The name *Mediterranean* (from the Latin) was aptly chosen to designate the sea that lies "in the middle of the land—Europe, Asia, and Africa." From the point of view of land mass, the World-Island has unity, though man throughout history has tended to settle along the edges. In spite of this high concentration, fourteen-sixteenths of the world's population inhabit the World-Island, another sixteenth live on the *Offshore-Islands, i.e.* those islands lying off-shore from the World-Island, and another sixteenth are distributed over North and South America and Australia.

Within the World-Island there lies the "Heartland," the pivot area, geopolitically speaking. It stretches from the Russian Volga in Europe to eastern Siberia, and from the frozen Arctic seas south to the plateau of Iran, Afghanistan, and Baluchistan (the Iranian Up-

land). The north, central, and western portions of the pivot area are a vast plain ("the Great Lowland"), broken only by the ranges of the Ural Mountains, and a region of interior and Arctic drainage. Politically the Heartland is largely Russian territory though western China and Mongolia, Afghanistan, and all but the coastal strips of Iran and Baluchistan are included. Why this definition in terms of territory?

According to Mackinder, here is a great plains' unit, with interior drainage, surrounded by barriers that make it impregnable to attack from the outside. It is a center in which great land power can develop and from which it can spread.

The northern edge of Asia is the inaccessible coast, beset with ice except for a narrow water lane which opens here and there along the shore in the brief summer owing to the melting of the local ice formed in the winter between the grounded floes and the land. It so happens that three of the largest rivers in the world, the Lena, Yenisei, and Obi, stream northward through Siberia to this coast, and are therefore detached for practical purposes from the general system of the ocean and river navigations. South of Siberia are other regions at least as large, drained into salt lakes having no outlet to the ocean; such are the basins of the Volga and Ural Rivers flowing to the Caspian Sea, and of the Oxus and Jaxartes to the Sea of Aral. Geographers usually describe these inward basins as "Continental." Taken together, the regions of Arctic and Continental drainage measure nearly a half of Asia and a quarter of Europe, and form a great continuous patch in the north and center of the continent. That whole patch, extending right across from the icy, flat shore of Siberia to the torrid, steep coasts of Baluchistan and Persia, has been inaccessible to navigation from the ocean. The opening of it by railways—for it was practically roadless beforehand—and by aeroplane routes in the near future, constitutes a revolution in the relations of men to the larger geographical realities of the world. Let us call this great region the Heartland of the Continent . . .

Southward the Great Lowland ends along the foot of a tableland, whose average elevation is about half a mile, with mountain ridges rising to a mile and a half. This tableland bears upon its broad back the three countries of Persia, Afghanistan, and Baluchistan; for convenience we may describe the whole of it as the Iranian Upland.

---

[3] Sir Halford Mackinder, *Democratic Ideals and Reality* (New York: Henry Holt & Company, Inc., 1919, reissue 1942), pp. 64-65.

The Heartland, in the sense of the region of Arctic and Continental drainage, includes most of the Great Lowland and most of the Iranian Upland; it extends therefore to the long, high, curving brink of the Persian Mountains, beyond which is the depression occupied by the Euphrates Valley and the Persian Gulf.[4]

Around the Heartland is the arc of coastlands, the Inner Crescent of amphibian states whose unifying characteristic is the fact of drainage that empties into navigable seas. It consists of three sections: the coastlands of Europe, the Arabian-Middle East desert lands, and the monsoon lands of Asia. It is an area that looks both to the land and the sea, an intermediate belt lying between the Heartland (from which it is separated—and protected—by a series of barriers along the whole contact line, except where the Russian plain blends into the European lowland) and the waters of the World-Ocean. Except for the Mid-East deserts, this is an area of generally navigable rivers, of plentiful rainfall and fertile soil, and, in general, of dense population. The powers of the pre-World War period were numbered among these coastland states, or were located in the Offshore Islands. (Britain and Japan belong to these latter states.)

Beyond the Inner Crescent are the World-Ocean and the widely separated lands of the Outer (Insular) Crescent. The Offshore Islands, the outlying islands (including North and South America, and Australia), and Africa south of the Sahara comprise this belt of territories. Among the states of the outlying islands only the United States is a power on a world scale. Mackinder, in 1904, placed little importance on these outer lands as compared to those of the World-Island. By 1943, he had somewhat modified this view.

What is the significance of this geopolitical organization of world regions as Mackinder viewed it? He feared an overbalancing of power in favor of the pivot area that might result in "its expansion over the marginal lands of Euro-Asia," which in turn would "permit

of the use of vast continental resources for fleet-building," and that then "the empire of the world would be in sight" (1904). In 1904, he did not anticipate Russia (which occupies the pivot area) as the nation to fear, but visualized instead that Germany might attempt to conquer the Heartland and thus become master of the World-Island and, from there—using the Heartland as the base—eventually conquer the world. He notices that it was by way of the European plain that the Heartland was pregnable. In the past, Mongol and Tartar hordes had swept out of the Heartland to invade the coastlands. Why couldn't the process reverse itself? Wrote Mackinder:

"Who rules East Europe" (and thus the gateway to the Heartland) "commands the Heartland;
"Who rules the Heartland commands the World-Island
"Who rules the World-Island commands the World."[5]

But, as stated previously, by 1943 Mackinder found it necessary to revise somewhat his original organization of states and his interpretation thereof. In that year, as both the USSR and the United States continued to prove their increasing power and strength, he: 1) changed somewhat his ideas of what constituted the Heartland by excluding Lenaland; 2) recognized that the fulcrum of world power rested not only in the World-Island but in the industrial might of the United States as well; and 3) began to realize that the threat of domination of the World-Island and of the world could come from the pivot area itself, namely, the USSR. He wrote:

All things considered, the conclusion is unavoidable that if the Soviet Union emerges from this war as conqueror of Germany, she must rank as the greatest land Power on the globe. Moreover, she will be the Power in the strategically strongest defensive position. The Heartland is the greatest natural fortress on earth. For the first time in history it is manned by a garrison sufficient both in number and quality.[6]

4 *Ibid.*, pp. 73-74.

5 *Ibid.*, p. 150.
6 Sir Halford Mackinder, "The Round World and the Winning of the Peace," *Foreign Affairs,* Vol. 21, No. 4 (July, 1943), p. 601.

He regarded, in 1943, the Heartland thesis as "more valid and useful today than it was either twenty or forty years ago."

Variations of the Heartland Theory of Mackinder: Fairgrieve and Spykman. It was another Englishman and an American, James Fairgrieve and Nicholas John Spykman respectively, who, as students of the geopolitical ideas of Mackinder, worked out revisions that were in part the same, in part different, from the organization presented by the original drafter. Fairgrieve presented his ideas in 1915 in his book, *The Geography of World Power,* and revised somewhat his thesis with the passage of the years. The following excerpt from his writings presents his plan of the geopolitical organization of world states and his reasons for them:

With the organization of the heartland and the sea powers a crush zone of small states has gradually come into existence between them. These states are largely survivals from an earlier time when political and economic organizations were on a smaller scale, and each has characteristics, partly acquired in that earlier time and partly natural. With sufficient individuality to withstand absorptions, but unable or unwilling to unite with others to form any larger whole, they remain in the unsatisfactory position of buffer states, precariously independent politically, and more surely dependent economically. This zone of states, with small populations, has varied in position from time to time with changing conditions, but it has included Finland, Sweden, Norway, Denmark, Holland, Belgium, Luxemburg, Switzerland, Poland, the Balkan States, Iran, Afghanistan, Siam and Korea. . . .

In some sense Germany and even China belong to this belt. Central Europe, unorganized and broken into small and antagonistic communities, essentially belongs to the crush zone, but organized and powerful, is in a very different position. In touch with the sea and tempted on to the ocean Germany is one of the sea powers, while her situation on the western and most populous margin of the great heartland makes her, at any rate, a possible centre from which that heartland might be organized.

The larger China, the land of the Chinese, roughly corresponds to the Chinese Empire at its greatest extent. This China, again, a world in itself, is far too great and homogeneous to be crushed, though parts of it may be exploited by men of other lands. Unwilling, and quite naturally as we have seen, to become seamen in any numbers, the Chinese are yet in touch with the sea, and reap advantages, which they are ready to take from that position; and again, like Germany, and to an even greater extent than Germany, China is in a position to dominate the heartland with little possibility of interference from others . . .

The conceptions of the central heartland, the sea powers and the crush zone, do correspond to actual facts. There is order, but it is an order which comes from growth, and with changing conditions the heritage of the past is knit into the present scheme. There is no rigid arrangement.[7]

Spykman's first published material on the subject of geopolitics came out in 1938 and 1939. He was much interested in the problems of power in international relations, and of the place of geopolitical analysis in the formulation of a security program. This was perhaps natural for in the late pre-World War II period a policy of hemispheric defense was strongly favored in the United States. His version of the heartland theory discredits the Heartland of Mackinder as a possible center of communication, mobility, and power potential in the near future. ". . . the distribution of climate in the world," he states, "makes it certain that, in the absence of revolutionary developments in agricultural technique, the center of agrarian productivity will remain in western Russia rather than in the central Siberian region." He notes also that the iron and coal deposits of the world, and the oil and water power ("essential elements of industrial power") are largely located west of the Ural ranges. Further, though he grants that modern means of transportation have created a "new mobility in the center of the Eurasian land mass," he adds that this area is nevertheless surrounded on most of its boundary by some of "the greatest obstacles to transportation in the world."[8] For these, and other reasons, he concludes that the Heartland becomes less significant than the Rimlands (his term for Mackinder's Inner Crescent), and that

---

[7] James Fairgrieve, *Geography and World Power* (London: University of London Press, 1941), pp. 329-333.

[8] Nicholas John Spykman, *The Geography of the Peace* (New York: Harcourt, Brace & Company, Inc., 1944), pp. 38-39.

"it is the co-operation of British, Russian, and United States land and sea power that will control the European littoral and, thereby, the essential power relations of the world." [9]

The contributions of geopolitics to geopolitical thought. Geopolitics, which includes not only German *Geopolitik* but also the Heartland thesis (and all modifications of it), has made an outstanding contribution in that it has demonstrated the significance of geography in international affairs, a factor that, in the past, has been frequently overlooked. Though many elements enter in to affect the relations between nation and nation, the geography of states is basic to the assessment of the power potential of a country. It must, therefore, be taken into consideration in any evaluations of states, or negotiations of any sort between them. The emphasis given to geography in international relations is the greatest contribution of geopolitics to politics and geopolitical thought and, because of this, it deserves recognition and study.

THE GROWTH OF POLITICAL GEOGRAPHY IN OTHER COUNTRIES

Geopolitics, in countries outside of Germany, received little recognition even though men from several nations contributed to its theses. We have noted how, in England, Mackinder (and later Fairgrieve) developed their ideas of the importance of geography in the politics of the world. Mackinder, when he originated his thesis, was trying to warn England of the possible rise of Germany. His ideas, discussed and criticized by other geographers of that country, were given no heed by the designers of English foreign policy. And political geography itself received only slight attention among other Englishmen in the profession.

The development of political geography in the United States. In the United States the situation was much the same: political geography was almost ignored. A politician, Theodore Roosevelt, and an officer of the United

States Navy, Alfred Thayer Mahan, were among the first Americans to recognize the importance of geography to state-planning and to foreign policy and relations.

Mahan and his concepts of sea power. Thinking in geopolitical fashion long before a term was coined to designate that concept, Mahan's writings on the theory of sea power[10] were among those from which the German geopoliticians drew their ideas. A naval man of long standing, he was an advocate of the importance of sea power and an interpreter of naval history. The Navy was his profession, and, living in a day when Britain was queen of the seas and when the great states of the world were the sea powers, it is not surprising that he should maintain the belief that the first requisite of world power was dominance over the seas. This Britain held, and he felt that state would continue to hold it for a long time.[11] Only one country in the world, he contended, had the potential to supersede Britain in her position of dominance: this nation was the United States. Like Britain, the United States had the advantage of insularity and possessed, besides, sure access to the resources of a continent. Mahan envisioned the United States as a world power, and pleaded not only for a great fleet but for overseas expansion as well. He advocated the possession of Hawaii as a strategic and vital "outpost" of the United States against invasion from Asia. He also

---

[9] *Ibid.,* p. 44.

[10] See Alfred Thayer Mahan, *The Influence of Sea Power Upon History* (Boston: Little, Brown & Company, 1890).

[11] Only by taking into account the sea power of his day is it possible truly to appreciate the geopolitical thinking of Mahan. The fact of British sea power arose from the command of the "narrows" (that connected the world oceans and seas) through which most ocean-borne traffic must pass. At the turn of the nineteenth century Victoria's Britain was in control of all of the water gateways between the three continents of the eastern hemisphere and of all of the navigable waterways of the commercial oceans (Atlantic, Pacific, and Indian): under her jurisdiction were the entrances to the Mediterranean—Gibraltar and Suez, and the Strait of Bab-el-Mandeb which leads to the Red Sea; Dover Strait between England and France; and the Strait of Malacca, separating Malaya and Sumatra and controlling the trade routes to the East.

THE PRIMARY FACTORS IN
POLITICAL GEOGRAPHY

3 ───────────────────────────

'he Space Factors: Location,
ize, and Shape

n all eras of history, countries of diverse
racter, large and small, have co-existed side
side, the disparities in size, potency, and
ction being a product of many forces and
ditions. The varying patterns of topogra-
, the dissimilarities in shape, the inequali-
in natural resources, the differences in
ation relative to dominant centers of eco-
nic activity, and the unequal degrees of
elopment are many and varied, and are
ne of the more important factors that have
tributed to the divergent roles that states
 in world affairs. There are several ele-
nts that are basic to any discussion of geo-
itical relations. Of these, some form the
es of the power-potential of the state. They
: the space factors of location, size, and
pe (and climate and topography are in-
led here); population, resources, and in-
try; and social and political structure.
Another factor basic to such analyses is that
frontiers—boundary problems which are

an aspect of involvement between states often
critically important in determining the type of
relations that exist between the nations concerned, whether peaceful or otherwise.

A state can be understood only in the light
of human adjustment and achievement "at a
certain location in a certain space."[1] *Space* is

[1] Derwent Whittlesey states further: "Because
every infant is born into a state, mankind grows up
with an unreasoned conviction that his country or
people is immutable, a force inseparably linked to a
specific portion of the earth's surface. This feeling
transformed into argument underlies many attempts
to make political geography serve the purposes of this
or that particular state—emotional efforts which have
been rationalized into the dogma known as Geopolitics. The brutal, temporary dissection of territory
incidental to warfare, and the more permanent and
hardly less rude dismemberment produced by dictated peace terms do not dislodge this faith that the
state is inherently entitled to its proper place, to its
'place in the sun.' Even the stubborn fact that two
different states may lay equal claim to the same
border zone fails to undermine the devotion of the opposing nationals to their respective articles of faith."
From *The Earth and State* (New York: Henry Holt
& Company, Inc., 1944), p. 8.

24

stressed the need for a canal across the isthmus between North and South America—a canal to connect the waters of the Atlantic and Pacific Oceans and, hence, the United States fleets of those two seas.

Bowman led the way among American geographers. Isaiah Bowman was the first American geographer to write a text on political geography, but up until World War II, political geography was scarcely recognized in American universities. However, during the years of conflict, it suddenly appeared in the curricula of universities across the country—though spottily.

In 1939 Derwent Whittlesey wrote, in the preface to his text on political geography, *The Earth and State,* the following which indicates the stage of development in geopolitical thought in this country even at that late date:

Political geography is perhaps the oldest kind of geography. Paradoxically, there is even yet

neither a universally accepted subject nor a consensus as to it therefore indulged in the pleasu of pioneering along lines that se nant.[12]

Political geography was achieving the attention it des world wars and, even more, th dition of international affairs the last decade have made field of study will be recogniz for its vital application to strategy of the national and lations of every state on the can be expected that more co be accorded the geopolitical fa world affairs in the days to true in the past.

---

[12] Derwent Whittlesey, *op. cit.,*

the integrating factor in geography just as *time* is for history. The national economies of powerful countries clearly reflect the significance of advantageous space relationships, and an examination of the great states, both those of the present day and those of the past, will reveal that they owe their commanding positions in no small part to favorable location, size, and form. All of the historic empires of the past were, each in turn, the largest states within the then-known world.

When found in effective combination, the space factors *promote* the growth of a great nation, such as the United States. It is difficult to fully assess the significance of the location of this country. As one writer points out, the United States is far better off than it would be with a landlocked position such as has the Soviet Union, where all outlets to ice-free seas can be blocked in time of war. Located in a temperate climate, the United States spreads through nearly twenty-five degrees of latitude, is bounded to the north and south by friendly neighbors, and faces upon the world's two most important oceans. The latter, in turn, offer cheap and easy access to the highly industrialized countries of Europe on the one hand and to Asia, Africa, and South America —with their vast resources and expanding markets—on the other. The location of the United States cannot be matched by that of any other nation of the present day. The one drawback is its physical separation, by the oceans, from the Afro-Eurasian land mass where the two greatest population agglomerations of the world are found. This "isolation" makes it difficult for peoples of other nations to know and understand Americans and the American way of life, and vice versa. In the past, however, this separation by ocean barriers was an advantage for it meant that the young and struggling state did not become easily embroiled in the power struggles of Europe and the East.

The space components must be seen in association with all of the other elements of the state, however, because it is impossible to isolate any one geopolitical factor while trying to rate its importance. For example, agricultural development and production, though highly dependent upon climatic conditions as such, cannot be wholly separated from such things as soil fertility, availability of market, and plant and animal resources each of which, in turn, is related to the other. All of the geographic and economic (and, at times, even political) elements are so tied in with successful productivity that it is affected by them all. Yet, some one inhibitive element—as isolated location, unfavorable climate, lack of mineral or fuel resources—may at times loom far above the other elements (human and natural) in its effective influence, and seem to limit and even restrict man's opportunities.

THE LOCATION OF STATES

Location is a fundamental geographical and political consideration. *Where is it?* is perhaps the primary query to be raised when a place is mentioned. The question can be answered in a number of ways for the geopolitical location of an area has several different connotations. The location of a state may bear reference to: astronomical factors, position relative to land and water masses, vicinal location, central *versus* peripheral accessibility, and strategic location. All are relevant and significant to the meaning of the term, and all have implications for political geography.

Astronomical location. Astronomical location establishes the locus of an area in terms of its position in the globe, *i.e.* in degrees of latitude and longitude. Such a description has greater significance than appears on the surface for, by implication, the astronomical position also defines locus relative to hemispheres, climatic regions, time belts, and, in the United States, the land survey system. To illustrate: it is usually with reference to the equator that latitudinal location comparisons are made. Within the bounds of what parallels are the great powers? Today, they are mid-latitude states, largely, if not entirely, outside of the tropic, subtropic, and polar areas of the earth.

True, this was not always so. Early civilizations grew up in subtropical and tropical-desert regions, and for several reasons. Chief among these were the facts that: 1) natural barriers (desert barriers surrounding river-valley civilizations) were necessary for protection, and 2) it was necessary for the people (in an early state of material technology) to live within a climatic environment that presented no serious problems for the provision of shelter and warmth. With advance in technical knowledge and, hence, in ability to cope with environment, people moved into the more temperate latitudes.

Tropical climates produce certain conditions that tend to inhibit human progress. States with tropical locations typically attain their greatest achievements in upland areas or under the incentive of mid-latitude enterprise. It may be, however, that even as improvements in technology and science permitted advance into the more rigorous areas of the middle latitudes, so further progress in scientific and technical knowledge may make the tropical and polar lands more usable and habitable. Thus far, white men appear to fare well only where altitude alleviates the tropical conditions.

Polar lands have a climate restrictive to normal living, and hence, to great economic or political achievement. The lands of the high latitudes (polar and subpolar regions) provide very feeble bases for the support of human life. Usually, like the tropics, they must be developed from the mid-latitudes if they are to be exploited beyond the bare subsistence level that has characterized the way of life of the small groups of indigenous peoples, such as the American Eskimo and the Nentsi of Soviet Siberia.

All of the circumpolar territories that surround the North Pole are held by states whose domains lie entirely, or in great part, within the middle latitudes but which have frontage on the Arctic Mediterranean.

The astronomical location of an area gives some indication of the expected effectiveness of man within that region. Tropical and polar areas are generally marginal in terms of human energy; such lands, for development, apparently require the drive of *entrepreneurs* from more favorable climes. In the tropics the environment is lush, in the polar and subpolar lands meagre; both areas are, however, monotonous in the extreme, and have an enervating effect. For strategic purposes, and for the exploitation of the mineral, vegetable, and animal resources, these lands will be sought after and inhabited, to an extent. But, except in cases where climatic conditions are somewhat ameliorated (as previously indicated), or the nations incorporate more temperate lands within their bounds, they will never become the locus of powerful states.

Astronomical location largely determines climate. Climate, in turn, partially sets the limits of agricultural and other resource[2] production *and* the establishment of transportation lines. Astronomical location, therefore, acting indirectly through climate, exerts a powerful influence upon the economic structure of the nation and, consequently, upon its international policy. Both astronomical location and continental and maritime location are influential in determining whether a state is in proximity to production (power) centers, to nets of communication and transportation, and to zones of contention.

Maritime versus continental location. Location with reference to land and water masses helps to determine the character and interests, economic and political, of the state. Countries located in or on oceans are described as maritime; those not adjacent to large water bodies, as continental. Most of the world's great powers, from the time when man first set sail upon the seas, have been and are, in varying degrees, maritime states possessing access to the lanes of ocean trade. Among the powerful states of today only the Soviet Union stands out as non-maritime: though the USSR has a longer coastline than any other country, it does

_____

[2] As forests and grasslands, and even the distribution of certain minerals, as coal and nitrates.

not have close contact with the sea. The ice-blocked character of the bordering waters and the interior location, within a ring of mountains and high plateaus on the world's largest land mass, make it continental in the extreme.

The other large powers of the pre- and post-war period are, to a degree, maritime. China and Japan, rising nations of the East, face the Pacific which carries approximately ten per cent of the world's sea trade. The remainder of the great states face on, or have free access to, the Atlantic, that vast water-carrier of the globe which bears nearly eighty per cent of the world's ocean traffic. Aside from the Soviet Union, which stretches from Pacific to Atlantic, of the great powers only the United States is so fortunate as to front upon both oceans.

Maritime location may be designated in one of several ways depending on the position of the state on the land mass in relation to the adjacent water body. It may be: 1) littoral, such as Chile or Venezuela, which lie on a continent along the seacoast; 2) peninsular, such as Italy, India, and Scandinavia; or 3) insular, *i.e.* an island location such as the British Isles and Japan. Note must be taken of the fact, however, that maritime location, as peninsular or insular or coastal, does not necessarily imply close contact with the sea: a seacoast may be regular, lacking indentations and, therefore, natural harbors; the coastal waters may be made difficult by heavy surfs, ice floes, or shelves—or be blocked by ice part of the year; or the interior may be cut off from the coastlands by natural barriers—mountains, deserts, and the like. It is notable that Europe, a peninsula of peninsulas with many deep and protected indentations, nurtured the most intrepid sailors and the greatest merchant marines and navies of the early world and, therefore, of the Eastern Hemisphere. On the other hand, aside from the Arabs who crossed the Indian Ocean to the Far East long before the Europeans, the Chinese who traded locally with the East Indies, and the Japanese and Malayans, Asian peoples historically have not taken to the sea. The Euro-Asian contrast

undoubtedly lies, at least in part, in the facts that, whereas much of the Asiatic coast is smooth and unindented and vast areas are hundreds of miles from the sea, all of Europe lies close to the oceans. Only the eastern side of Italy appears to be markedly lacking in natural harbors, and only interior Plateau Spain is difficult of access from the shore. Further, no great part of the long coastlines of Europe is unduly plagued by storms[3] as are parts of southeast and southern Asia where the coastlands and fringing waters are beset by tropical typhoons.

The relative richness and scope of the resources of land and sea usually influence the economic orientation and political course of the state with maritime location. Maritime location may, at times, be the dominant factor in determining the character of the state; in other instances, the role a nation plays appears to be less directly affected by situation-on-the-sea, and its interests are diverse, divided between maritime and continental opportunities. The insularity of Britain and Japan, with all of the concomitants that insularity can imply, has undoubtedly been a significant factor in the building up and welding together of a political and economic world empire in the case of the former state, and of the policies of aggression on the part of the latter. The rise of British industry into the colossus that it was to become was dependent, it is true, upon the imagination of the technologists and scientists who invented the first basic industrial machinery beginning with the steam engine. But, it was also dependent upon the British merchant marine—for raw materials had to be brought in from, and markets had to be sought and served, across the seas. Further, insular confinement, which left no room for territorial expansion for the growing populations, *and* favorable coastlines made the sea inviting to the peoples of both island-states and induced them to seek out the opportunities offered by

---

[3] The North Sea and those lands fronting upon it, especially the Netherlands, are harassed by severe storms, however.

the marine location.[4] Both have been great sea, rather than land, powers.

Peninsular Italy, Greece, and Iberia were, historically, sea-minded. Today the Greeks and Italians are still maritime, at least in part. Called "the carriers of the Mediterranean," their merchant fleets are growing larger, and are no longer confined to the waters of the *Mare Internum;* they sail the highways of the world oceans. On the other hand, the former maritime glory of Iberia is no longer reflected in the economies of the nations of that peninsula: empires dwindled as the mother countries became impotent and impoverished and, with impoverishment, came a withdrawal from maritime activities. Portugal has remained closer to the sea than has Spain, the products of its fishing industry being the largest single export. Spain is non-maritime; it looks landward.

Norway and Sweden, located side by side on the same peninsula, display interesting divergences in the characteristic economy each has developed. The control apparently lies in the physical nature and setting of the two states. Norway is a mountainous, inhospitable land, but possessed of a long coastline deeply indented with fiords facing upon rich fishing grounds and fronting on the world's greatest

sealanes. This small nation has the greatest per capita merchant marine in the world and one of the largest fishing and whaling fleets. In opposition, Sweden, occupying the eastern portion of the peninsula, has extensive flat and fertile farmlands, accessible forests and minerals. To further direct the interests landward, the Swedish shore is characterized by a relatively smooth coastline on seas that are ice-blocked for a portion of each year and that, further, are a bit offside of the great traffic routes of the world's oceans. Sweden is land-minded. In no sense is it a maritime state. The only Swedish fleet of any size is the ore-fleet that carries the Arctic iron to foreign ports—largely through the Norwegian port of Narvik.

China also is, in general, continental. There are areas, however, where the land environment of the Oriental state, like that of Norway, is so restrictive, and the sea made so inviting through the incidence of good harbors, that the Chinese have become sailors and fishermen. Such an area is the southeast-coastal region.

Whether a state with a maritime location is both land- and sea-minded or not depends largely upon the opportunities offered by the two diverse realms: if the land base is rich and varied, offering numerous opportunities for development, the state will be "continental" in character. If the sea, likewise, is made inviting by the presence of protected natural harbors, adjacent fishing grounds, etc., it is likely that the state will also take to the sea. A number of such dual-character states are found: Greece and Italy are maritime-continental; France and the United States are outstanding examples. France, having a land base that incorporates a portion of each of the three broad natural divisions of Europe—northern plains, mountains, and Mediterranean coastal lowlands—also has frontage on two seas, the Atlantic Ocean and the Mediterranean Sea. It is nearly unique among European states in this. The "entanglement" of the land and sea (both favorable) has led to an economy that is broad and diverse, partaking of both the

---

[4] Though island location may be an advantage in time of war (*i.e.* insular states are less likely to be drawn into a war on the continent) as well as advantageous economically in that it induces the inhabitants to take to the sea, it has the disadvantage of having a tight boundary. In other words, a state is literally confined within the limits of the island area. For a rapidly growing population such as Britain had a few decades ago, this posed a problem for which there were but two alternatives: 1) a lowered standard of living; 2) new means of livelihood or new frontiers. The expanding English colonies provided one outlet, and the industrial revolution opened up another. In the case of Japan, the pinch of restricted territory began to be felt soon after the Meiji restoration (1869) when what might be called a "population explosion" took place. Instead of using peaceful, legitimate means of solving the problem of over-population, the Japanese began a program of aggression and encroachment that ended only with their defeat in 1945. Over-population, and a rapidly-expanding population, are Japan's most critical problems even today.

land and the sea as has that of the United States.

Countries not bordering on a sea are handicapped in that they are dependent upon land transportation (which is expensive transportation). To send goods into the channels of ocean trade, they must utilize the ports of a foreign nation. Few truly continental states are well located with regard to trade. Some, however, have made an advantage out of a seemingly adverse situation—as Switzerland, landbound, but controlling several of the major mountain passes between northern and Mediterranean Europe.

Maritime and continental location bias the style of defense. Continental *versus* maritime location exerts an important influence upon the security policies of a state: for the most part, aside from air power, land powers depend upon armies whereas oceanic states construct navies and merchant marines. Maritime England, with its naval and merchant ships, assembled and held together the greatest empire on the globe; the continental Russian state spread over and incorporated the largest contiguous land area within the bounds of one nation—but it has never held lands off the Eurasian land mass.[5] There is not always so sharp a distinction, however. Within Japan— and Britain as well—there have developed both maritime and continental schools of thought relative to strategic and expansion policies. In fact, Japan has developed commercially as a seapower but, militarily, has placed most of its faith in land forces. This is because the Japanese expansionist program has been directed against the close-lying lands of the Asiatic continent, and, aside from the short lines of sea-connection between the island-state and the mainland, subjection and control have depended upon land-mobility rather than upon a large navy.

Geopolitical advantages and disadvantages of maritime and continental location. Non-contiguous boundaries, as a long coast-

line, may have political advantages in that there is less danger of international misunderstandings becoming fighting quarrels where the boundaries of one nation do not touch those of another. To carry it further, intervening seas may be, and usually are, a handicap to invasion. Britain has not been invaded since the days of William the Conqueror; no enemy force had ever successfully made landings on the Japanese main islands until the Americans did so in 1945, and then only after a long and arduous campaign of approach and with the aid of the atom bomb.

On the other hand, a long land boundary is often a threat. That this is so is illustrated by the existence of buffer states—weak countries whose integrity is guaranteed in order that the interests of two powerful nations may be separated from each other, and thus minimize possible trouble. It is well known that Afghanistan has acted as a buffer between Russian interests and those of British India and that Siam has stood between French and British spheres of influence in Asia. Where nations are friendly, however, as in the case of the United States and Canada and, to a lesser degree, Mexico and the United States, the long land boundary may be an advantage to both countries. This thought leads, then, to the next category of location, namely, vicinal location.

Vicinal location. Who are the neighbors of a state? What are the circumjacent countries like? Are they large or small, populous or sparsely inhabited, powerful or weak? Vicinal location defines position relative to countries immediately bordering upon any state. Because it specifies location with reference to relations of the one state with the contiguous nations, issues of territorial security are implied. In times of peace, proximity may be an asset. The United States and Canada have already been cited in this instance. The flow of goods, especially in the form of raw materials from Canada to the United States, is tremendous; in the other direction move American capital and enterprise for the development of

[5] Except Alaska.

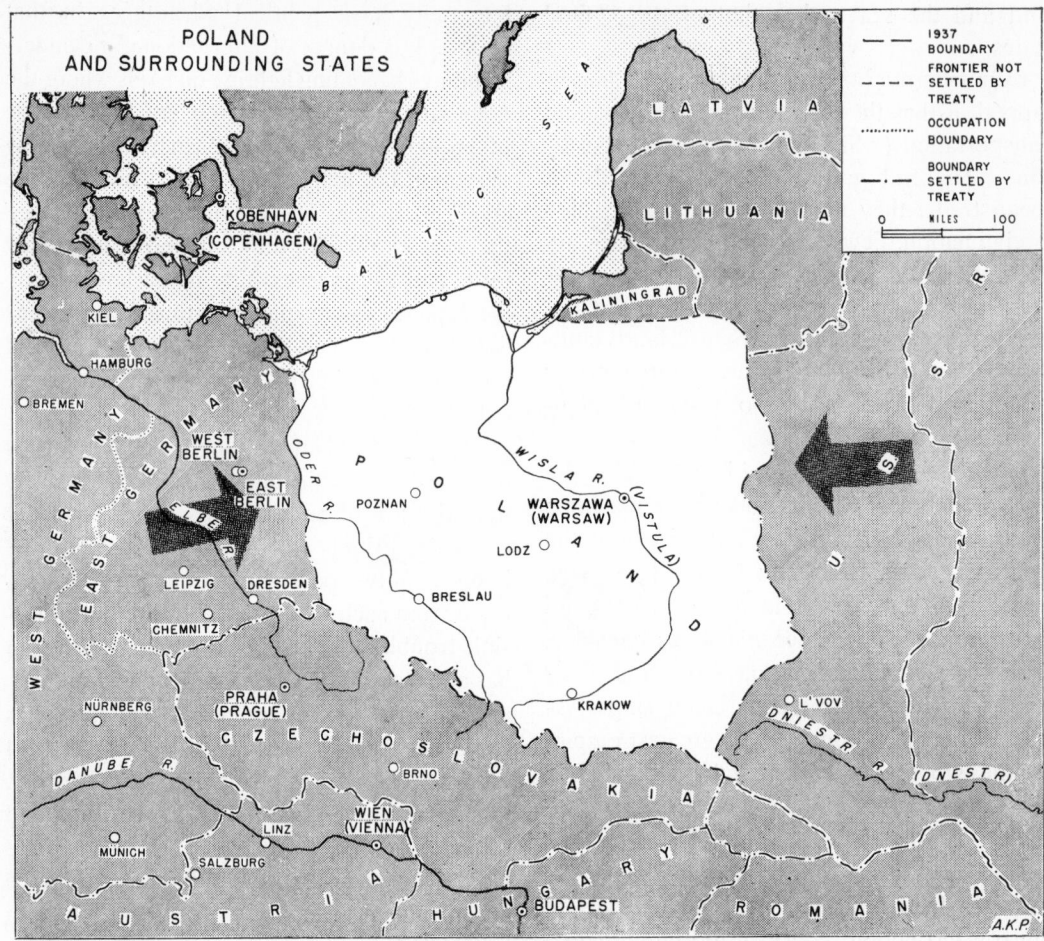

Figure 3.1. Today Poland is conscious of pressure from states on two sides—Germany and the USSR. In the past, before the Austro-Hungarian Empire was broken up, pressure was also exerted from the south. Because of vicinal location, there have been few years when the Polish nation has been constituted as a sovereign political entity.

the rich resources of the virgin northern land, and manufactured goods. The Netherlands and Germany likewise benefit by being neighbors, particularly in the close association they have through the Rhine waterway—the one nation controlling the outlet to the sea, the other providing the great flow of goods outward and, in its industrial cities, the markets for the agricultural and dairy products and the precision-manufactures of the smaller state.

Where countries, disparate in size, lie side by side, "vicinity" has frequently meant subjection of the smaller state. It would be impossible to recount all of the instances where contiguity has led to mutual cooperation, and where the latter, in turn, has been a source of strength and development to both countries. On the other hand, this very frequently is not the case. History is full of instances where the big neighbor has taken advantage of or overrun the smaller. Population differences between states are very great and these differ-

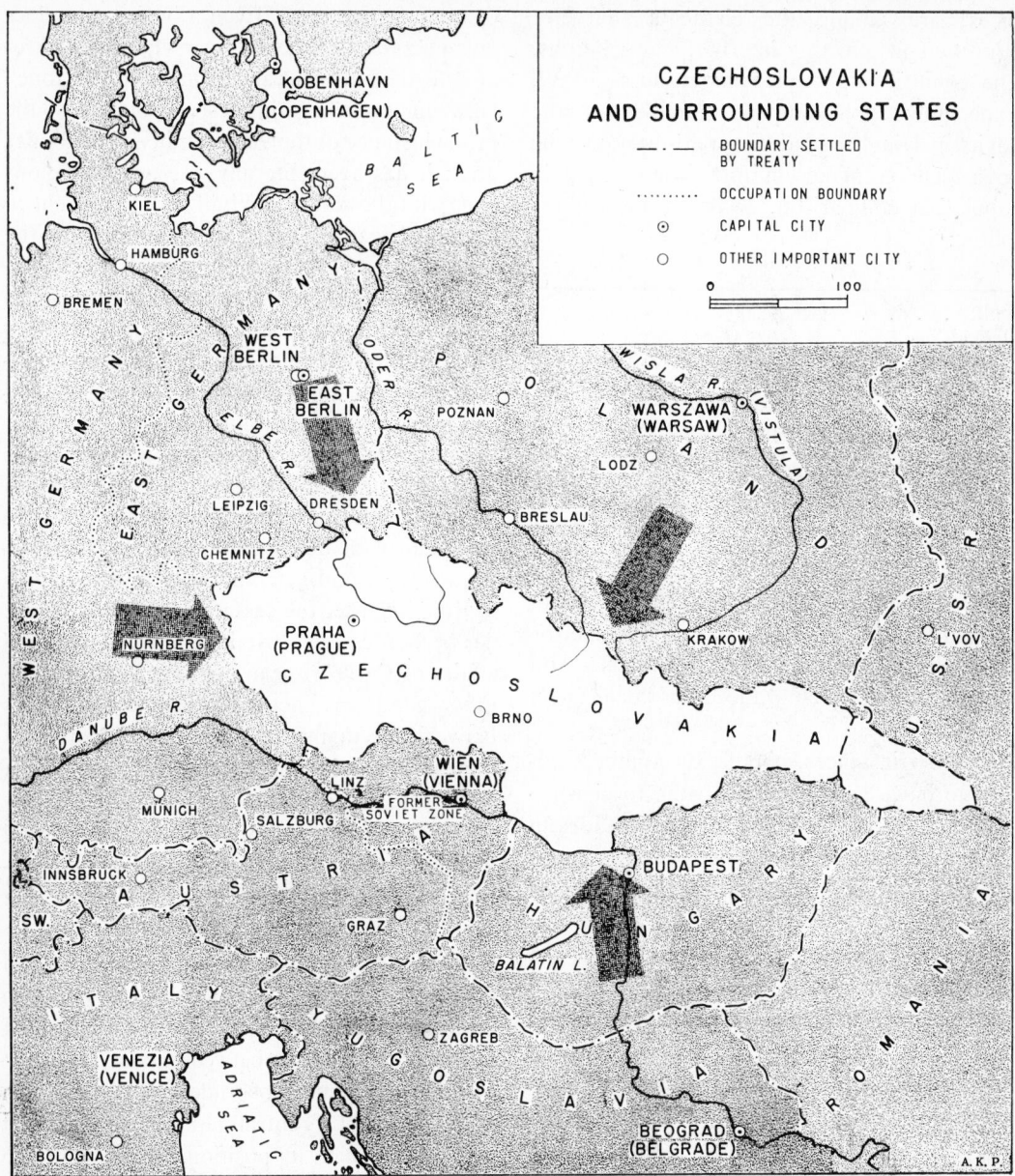

Figure 3.2. Pressures—aside from those exerted by the USSR, which secured Ruthenia after World War II—are and have been felt from several directions. Though nearly surrounded by mountains along its frontiers, Czechoslovakia is pregnable because of the elongate shape and the passes, in the form of broad lowlands, that give easy access into the country.

ences[6] are among the elements that are important in affecting international relations. The countries (all independent up to 1939, some now subject to or satellites of the Soviets) lying around the periphery of the Soviet Union make an interesting study in population comparison. Some of the figures follow:[7]

USSR	. . .	.	198,600,000
Finland	. .	.	4,216,000
Estonia	. .	.	1,131,000 (1953 ed.)
Latvia	. .	.	2,000,000 (1953 ed.)
Lithuania	. .	.	2,500,000 (1953 ed.)
Poland	. .	.	27,100,000
Hungary	. .	.	9,750,000
Rumania	. .	.	17,400,000
China	. .	.	585,000,000 (excluding Formosa)

Does it not appear significant that Finland, the three Baltic republics of the USSR, Poland, Hungary, and Rumania all are, to a greater or lesser degree, pawns of the Russians? And that, on the other hand, the latter "deal" with the Chinese?

In other instances, population numbers appear to have less relevance to the foreign relations of vicinal states: Germany made an attempt to conquer the Soviet Union, a country whose population is three times greater than its own.

As already noted, one of the reasons for the setting up of the great number of small independent states in Central Europe after World War I was to separate German and Russian spheres—actually to protect the Russians from German imperialism. Even a buffer zone does not necessarily prevent war, however. Frequently the buffer area becomes a "crush zone" between opposing interests. Poland is the prime instance of the vulnerability of the buffer area: it has been, literally, a pawn of nations and, with the rest of the buffer zone of Central Europe, became a crush zone again during the past war.

Vicinal location is relative location. As illustrated above, the location of a country relative to other states usually has deep implications in the formulation of its foreign policies and in the determination of historical events. The former isolation policy of the United States can be explained in terms of vicinal location. The profound change wrought by the airplane did much to alter this policy— though the country temporarily reverted again to isolation after the cessation of World War I. The aloofness of Britain from the political affairs of the European continent and, on the other hand, the incessant disputes and wars between the mainland states of that continent are explained in the location of these states relative to each other.

Central versus peripheral location. Central location means accessibility; peripheral location, relative inaccessibility. Where are the central locations of the world? They must be defined in terms of land mass, population, and economic activity. Central location tends to imply, because of ease of contact, growth of commercial relations between states. The tremendous movement of trade across the North Atlantic, most "central" of all of the great oceans, is due to its position between the two great population centers of the world most advanced technologically. Peripheral Australia and New Zealand, on the other hand, could not compete in world markets (which for them are largely British markets) were it not for, first, the preferential trade agreements between England and the two dominions; second, the development of refrigerated ships; and, third, the type of commodity exported, namely, high value goods of little relative weight.

---

[6] Of course, other factors also enter in, such as national ideology and character. France, though about equal in population to Germany, has for decades feared the latter state because of the aggressive tendencies of the Prussians; the Russian Slav seems always to have pushed outward to the detriment of its neighbors. In the Balkans, proximity has meant almost constant squabbling between Slav and Slav, Slav and Greek, and the like. It is not without reason that the Balkan Peninsula is known as "the powderkeg of Europe." Land boundaries between states have frequently led to repeated wars and are, therefore, at times a handicap rather than an advantage.

[7] From *Goode's World Atlas*, Edward B. Espenshade, Jr., ed. (Chicago: Rand McNally & Company, 1957 ed.).

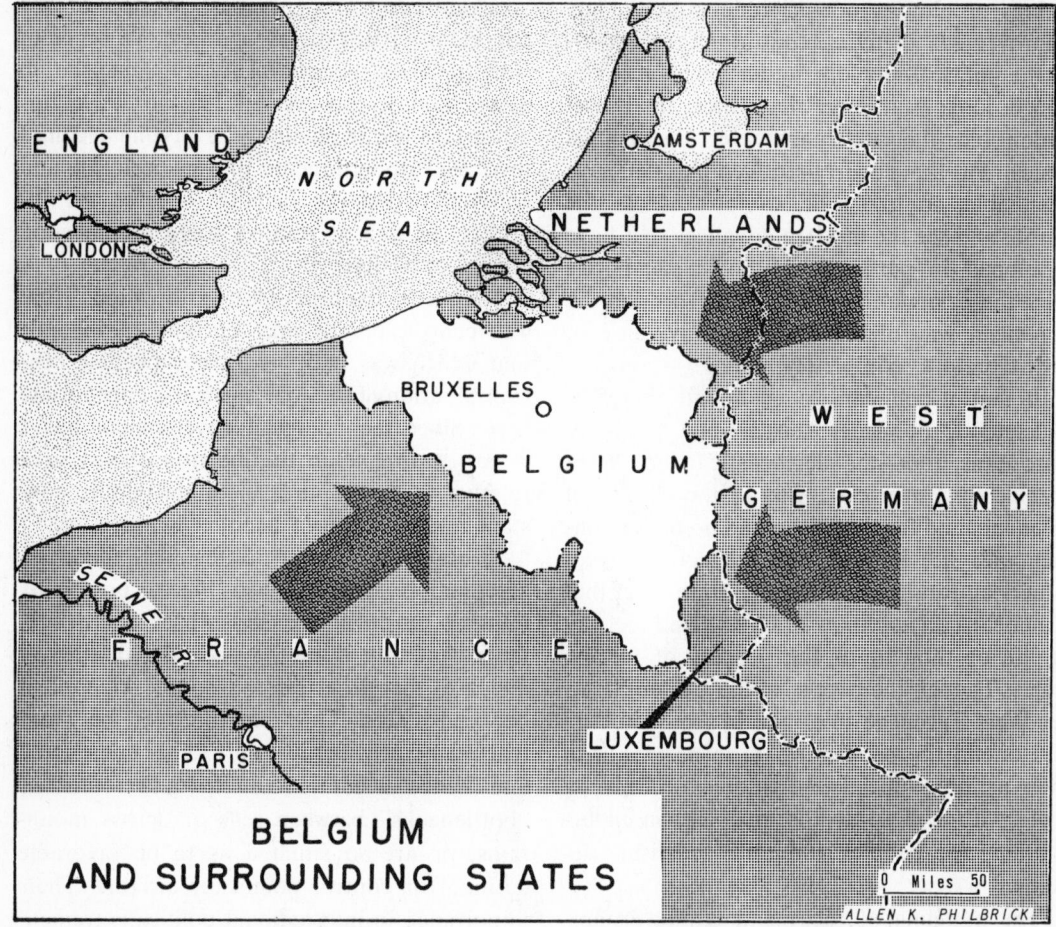

Figure 3.3. Little Belgium, providing the route of easiest access between two generally hostile states, has often been overrun because of her "crush" position.

Proximity fosters the transfer of ideas. The interchange of ideas, upon which the condition of technology and the arts is highly dependent, is another advantage of centrality. The states of the Western World, actively exchanging the skills among themselves and borrowing from others, achieved a unique progress from a primitive base within a short time. The art of the Greeks, the mathematics of the Arabs, the law of the Romans, the industrial techniques of the British (and later others) have disseminated throughout the West. In the Orient, while Europeans were still rude, the Chinese and others of the Asians had already reached a high level of achievement in the arts. There was, for a period, a ready exchange of ideas among the peoples of the East. But the East closed its doors to Western ideas and people. The result was that Oriental life and art and technology, until today, have remained as medieval in character as in centuries past. To a degree, the Japanese emancipated themselves, but only partially.

Contact, coupled with ease of intercourse, aids understanding. Ready exchange of ideas implies also ease of propagandization. During the past quarter century, when ideologies have struggled for the minds of men and spawned wars—military and verbal—the relative proximity of nations has spelled, very directly, advantage or disadvantage. For people such as the vast majority of the Asians who live in conditions of almost indescribable poverty, any improvement in living conditions, regardless of the political ideology under which it is obtained, looks attractive. Here, then, the Soviet Union has the advantage over the United States, for the poverty-stricken Asians have been able, so to speak, to look across the border and see the modern advances that have developed in parts of the Soviet territories since the Communists took over. How can the American way of life—so far away, unseen, and therefore completely foreign—compete with that which can be seen and therefore understood? For most Asians—and for many Europeans, too—the democratic (and, more specifically, American) way of life is difficult to understand for they have had no direct contact with it.[8] In part, the ineffectiveness of American foreign policy is due to the fact that Americans do not know or understand the way of life or thought of the peoples of foreign states. Though the people of the United States are West European in origin, in the main they still offend the peoples of those nations with their actions, official and unofficial. Only by living with or close to other peoples can understanding for peoples and their idealisms develop.

The mingling of races and ethnic groups, with the resultant mingling of languages and ideas, arts and technology, results in enrichment of language and culture. Without such mingling and interchange sterility sets in. The postwar travel of Americans abroad and of foreigners in the United States, the exchange student-and-teacher programs and the like, should have a leavening influence—*i.e.* Americans should understand the other peoples of the world better, and vice versa.

Location peripheral to centers of population and activity hinders contact. Peripheral location is usually a handicap. In terms of

accessibility, Europe is best located of the continents, Australia the poorest. In times of war, however, peripheral location may be an asset. Today, however, it has not even this advantage for, in an air age, everyone becomes involved. Modern means of transportation and communication are helping to erase the ill-effects, as well as remove some of the good effects, of periphery.

Time can change relative location. What was central before may become peripheral; that which was peripheral, may become central. Mention of the Arctic world is appropriate here. Since technological development has a direct bearing upon the location of any area relative to other portions of the globe, constant re-evaluation of location is necessary.

Strategic location. "Strategic" is the characterization that is given places possessing military or economic advantage. Such locations generally offer the potential of control and are, therefore, often a source of conflict between states. They are likely to be areas where land or water ways are either constricted and hence become foci of trade routes or "bottlenecks" between seas or across mountains, or are so situated as to be favorable terminal or control points for aircraft. Their importance in international politics is tremendous: in peacetime such strategic locations are likely to influence the flow of trade, while in wartime they may take on an acute significance from several aspects.

This has been true in any given period of the world's history. At Thermopylae, narrow mountain pass between Thessaly and Attica, the Persian tide of Xerxes was held back. Copenhagen and Helsingör historically occupied strategic positions on the water route between the Baltic and North Seas, particularly in the day when Denmark also held the Swedish coast opposite the Danish Peninsula. Rotterdam, at the mouth of the Rhine, is strategic in situation as is Istanbul at the head of the Dardanelles-Marmara-Bosporus waterway. The Virgin Islands were purchased from Denmark (1917) because they occupy a position

---

[8] This, of course, is not true for the states of Northwest Europe where the democratic way of life actually had its birth—in France and England. As a matter of fact, a great part of the problem of France's "many governments" is the independent thinking of the individual Frenchman.

of control to the approaches to the Panama Canal. Gibraltar, Malta, Cyprus, Suez, Aden, the Socotra Islands, all strategic, are (or were) British-controlled to protect the vital "lifeline" of the Empire. Since the relinquishment of Suez to Egypt that narrow but important waterway has become—in peacetime—a "bottleneck" to the free flow of trade for at least some peoples of the world.

In the present day of modern weapons and aircraft, the military importance in time of war of such decisively-located points may be lessened because of the ease with which the limited installations can be crippled or destroyed. But economically—and for as long as they can be kept operating in time of war—they are highly critical. The demand for air bases in Morocco, bases in Japan, control of the Ryukyus, the selection of Cyprus as the British base of operations in the Eastern Mediterranean when Suez had to be given up, and any number of other such instances that could be cited, all indicate the value of such areas relative to the safety and defense of the Western World.

Location as a factor in history. "No phenomenon on the earth surface may be considered for itself; it is understandable only through the apprehension of its location with reference to other places on the earth," stated Hettner.

Today the earth is small. But in the days before 1492 the world was large. The continents across the sea that later became known as the New World did not exist for Europeans. For hundreds of years before that time, the people of China had regarded their land as the "Middle Kingdom," *i.e.* the state occupying the center of the earth—a world that showed on the periphery a mere fringe of land and water surrounding China, the core. India existed as a world apart.[9] Europe, the Eastern

Mediterranean lands, and North Africa were essentially one world, isolated from the other worlds, but themselves united through the cohering influence of the Mediterranean. Africa south of the Sahara did not exist; nor did Antarctica. What happened in China had no effect upon India, or Europe, or the Americas. When sailing vessels and caravans began to connect the Orient with the Occident, the influences thus disseminated were largely cultural, interfused through brief contacts of trade and the products exchanged. At this period in history there were at least three— and possibly four or five—distinct worlds, some completely unknown to any of the others. Some of the worlds were vaguely aware of the existence of other ones but there was a minimum of contact, and one area of the globe felt little or no concern about any other. Each lived to itself.

With the discovery of America by Columbus, the world grew smaller. And with the circumnavigation of the globe by Magellan (establishing the fact of a round world), with the conquest and exploitation of the newly-discovered lands of the earth by the Spanish, Portuguese, English, French, and others, and the consequent steady flow of riches from the New to the Old World, the oceans of the globe became familiar highways and the round earth grew yet smaller. Knowledge and time cut distance. The Western Hemisphere and the Orient were still peripheral in location, however, and Australia and New Zealand were unknown and unheard-of. Not until the late eighteenth century did the "world" embrace these latter lands.

The political and economic center of the globe has moved with advance in geographic enlightenment and the passage of history. With the rise and fall of empires, centricity changed. At one period in history, the Near and Middle East and Egypt were "central" and all other lands peripheral. As power shifted from Asian to Greek to Roman dominance of the known world, the Mediterranean gradually became the center and every other

---

[9] Western Asia, to the eastern borders of India, was a part of the known world very early, for conquests of the Persians by the Greeks, and vice versa, were recurrent until the fourth century A.D. Essentially, however, there had been little contact between India and the lands farther to the west.

land lay on the outskirts. Even within the centripetal Mediterranean the focus moved, however, so that by the era of Spanish and Portuguese glory the Eastern Mediterranean had fallen into eclipse and was, so to speak, backwater. Centricity had shifted from those that were purely Mediterranean to those that were Atlantic-Mediterranean. Gradually, as technology advanced, Europe north of the Alps became more populated. The center had again shifted, this time to the northwest.

Except for an enlargement of the core, which has spread to encompass Eastern United States, the North Atlantic nations have remained the focus of the world until the present time. Though the "arsenal" of the Occident is located in the United States, the centricity of the world has not altered. It remains in the North Atlantic where the concentration of production and markets, transportation and trade make this area the most "central" of world regions. Another shift could come, however, as the buying power of the European— and the production of raw materials and manufactured goods—declines relative to increases elsewhere, as in the Orient where one-half of the world's population is massed.

Militarily, the Arctic seas—formerly offside —are now central. This is due to the advance of transportation. Because of the airplane, no part of the world is as peripheral in location as it was at any period in the past. However, for the earth as a whole, weight of land and people make—and will make—the Northern Hemisphere focal.

Ultimately, although certain aspects of locus are inherent in the natural environment, the position of one part of the world relative to another depends largely upon time with its implication of technological development.

SIZE

The most apparent spatial factor of a state is its size. Although it should be evident that there can be no absolute relationship between area and the power and vigor of the state, yet it is likewise obvious that the greater the extent of a nation the more likelihood that a large population and a varied and abundant base of natural resources will be contained therein— and therefore, also, the greater will be the possibility for an economically and politically strong nation. We may say then, that, other things being equal, the greater the size, the greater the probability of an important state.

Other things, however, are never equal and there are many instances that can be cited where small states are outstandingly more important than certain large ones. Compare the resources and productivity—and therefore the importance—of the Ukraine (217,062 square miles) with that of the entire Soviet Union (8,600,000 square miles).

The "great" state in ancient times was small in size. In an ancient day, the small state represented the unit of political, social, and economic power. This was true because small protected areas, such as the Nile Valley set in the midst of a desert, served to nurture and transform a society. In fact, the small state held an advantage over the large one. In the first place, populations were nowhere large— actually, they might be characterized as sparse as compared to populations today, but, living in usually constricted and relatively isolated areas, people quickly integrated into communities with strong group feelings, and often developed strong economies and great political strength (for that day). Sparta, Athens, and Troy are outstanding examples of such early communities. Mesopotamia, the fertile and irrigated desert plain of the Tigris and Euphrates rivers, was divided into three powerful states: Assyria, Babylonia, and Chaldea. Today Iraq, though it embraces all of Mesopotamia as well as territory to the north, east, and west—a domain possibly ten times greater in size than any one of the early Mesopotamian nations—has not compared in power nor commanded the respect of nations (to the present time) as did the ancient states. Nevertheless, all great contemporary powers have commensurately great areas—for power in a modern world tends to be coupled with large rather than insignificant size.

Although size is relative, large size is a necessary attribute of a great power in the modern era. Space is an essential in time of peace for great space is likely to carry with it the raw material resources that are necessary for the building of a modern industrial state as well as a climate sufficiently varied to provide a broad and varied agricultural base. Also, large space will generally offer a greater variety and multiplicity of opportunity for its people than will small size.

Space is also essential in time of war, the size of a nation having an important relation to its ability to resist or absorb attackers. Great size allows for "defense in depth." China has never yet been conquered. Nor has Russia ever been overpowered. Would-be conquerors have become mired in the depths of space and endlessly resisting population, and have eventually been expelled. On the other hand, Belgium and the Netherlands have been battle-grounds for stronger nations and the Central European zone—made up of a shattering of peoples and nations—has been the "crush zone" of the continent for centuries.

"Depth in space" is equally applicable to a state possessing vast expanses of water (with bases distributed throughout) into which it can withdraw in the face of attack—as did Japan during World War II. It was an arduous task that the American forces undertook when they fought their way through the seemingly interminable, island-strewn ocean waters to strike at the Japanese islands themselves.

Great size can be a handicap. Large size, then, appears to be a necessary concomitant to power. But can a state be too large? It might be said that the ideal size of a state varies with the resources, the standard of living of the people, the level of technological and scientific maturity, and the effectiveness of the transportation and communication system. The major handicap of the Soviet Union today, aside from its lack of warm water ports, ap-

pears to be its unwieldy size and the large number of problem areas that great space makes unavoidable: swamps impassable except in winter; land communication in terms of days-of-distance between east and west; vast deserts, great barren mountain barriers within as well as around it. Likewise Brazil, politically and economically speaking, is essentially plateau Brazil, vast Amazonia remaining an almost empty, disease- and poverty-ridden area except for the one sparkling city of Manaus. Canada is a fringe of population along the southern border with a few small spurs thrust into the more northern lands wherever mineral and water resources, mid-west farm lands, and easily exploited forests beckon the intrepid. As for the rest, Canada is a huge trackless area of taiga or tundra—where mounted police must travel on foot or horseback or by canoe in order to bring law and justice into the wastes. Because of the problems they pose, these immense but marginal Canadian lands (like those of the USSR) are a handicap to the country—despite their wealth in resources. Greater China is an example of another political giant loosely hung together—Mongolia, Tannu Tuva, China Proper, Tibet, and Sinkiang, the two first-mentioned units no longer a part of the Chinese domain.

The ideal size of a state varies with the status of material technology and communications. Insufficient and backward means of transportation and communication make the size of the above-named states far from ideal. In the case of some of these nations, this condition reflects the long years of hesitancy in accepting the advances of modern science and technology. However, as the USSR has expanded water, rail, and air communications to the interior and peripheral parts of the Union, the nation has spread itself more comfortably to fit within its great proportions. Brazil, China, India and others are also advancing along these lines.

Size—including weight of land, and, in the case of India and China, weight of population

—may, in the not too far distant future, serve as a centrifugal force to shift the market and industrial center of the economic world from its present locus in the North Atlantic. Size, therefore, may have a vital bearing upon relative location within the world of men, but it is *size made effective through technology and science.*

SHAPE

A chunky form has advantages over attenuation, protuberance, fragmentation, etc.: compactness generally minimizes the amount of transportation needed and produces internal coherence more readily than does elongation, perforation, or fragmentation of the territory of a state.[10] In general, also, the compact state will have the advantage of a shorter boundary to defend in case of attack and, relatively, greater depth for retreat. A striking example of attenuation is found in the case of Chile, 2600 miles long and extending but 100 miles inland from the coast. Such awkward form can be a marked disadvantage for it may serve to create a serious military handicap, usually implies long transportation lines and, further, adds to the expense of the ordinary administration of the state. The major advantage of such north-south attenuation is the variety of climate that the domain embraces.

Cohesiveness refers not only to the binding together of the land physically, but idealistically as well. The compact state has a better chance of becoming a *nation of people,* unified in purpose, *i.e.* of possessing, as a people, the "emotion of nationality." Such national cohesiveness is more than mere political or material unity: it develops only after decades and even centuries of living together, and is a phenomenon growing out of a "political pattern engendered in a world geared to making a

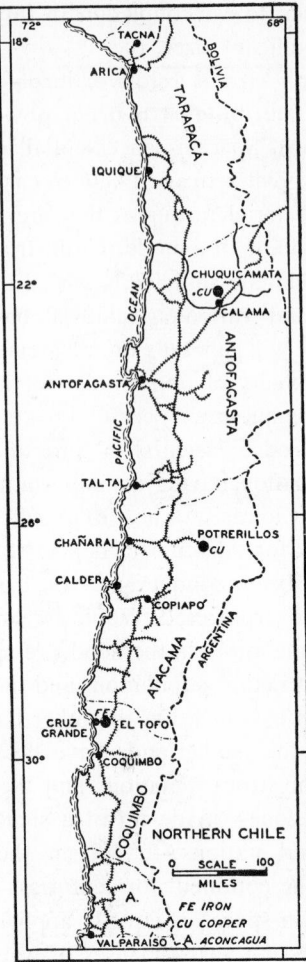

Figure 3.4. Transportation pattern of Chile. (Courtesy Odyssey Press, Inc. From Preston E. James, *Latin America.*)

livelihood in small units . . ." according to Whittlesey. "During the past century," however, "these small units have been overtaken by material advancement which has redoubled the ideal size of states and placed a premium on natural resources from beyond established national boundaries. Traditional loyalties have thereby been brought into collision with economic welfare."[11]

France, which in the minds of many politi-

---

[10] Unity and internal cohesiveness are also affected by the physical structure (topography) of the land, the latter thereby having a bearing upon the strength of a state. For example, while plains and river valleys foster unity, mountains often have an opposite effect, hindering transportation and separating one region of the country from another.

[11] Whittlesey, *op. cit.,* p. 23.

MAP OF THE FRENCH NATIONAL RAILROADS

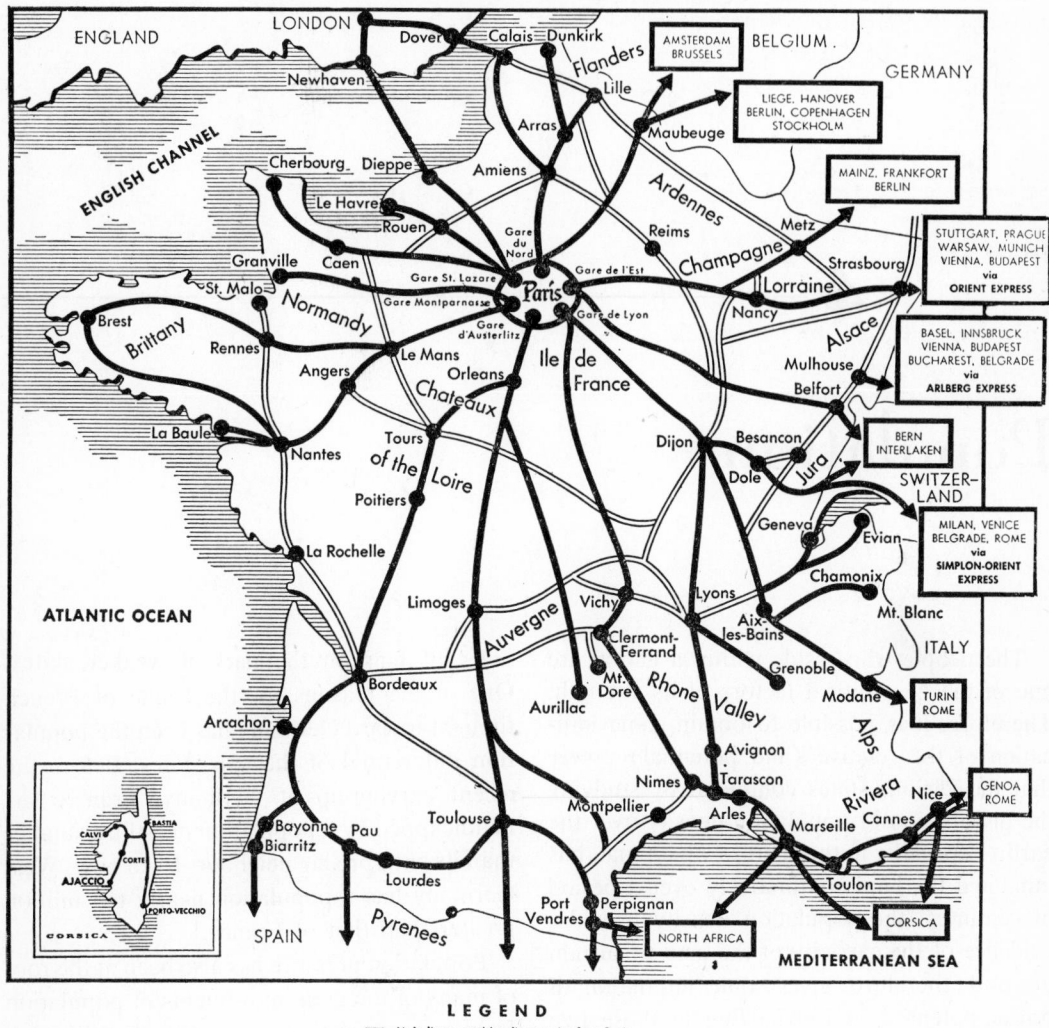

LEGEND

▬▬ Main line served by direct trains from Paris
═══ Main cross-country lines

Figure 3.5. Transportation pattern of France.

cal geographers represents the "ideal state," is a nation that is—and has been for about two decades—going through just such a crisis. French national, and world-international welfare have time and again been jeopardized by the intense nationalism that every Frenchman feels. The rejection of EDC[12] was one of the relatively recent manifestations of this extreme emotion of national feeling.

[12] EDC (European Defense Community) included both economic and military aspects and incorporated the Benelux countries, West Germany, Italy, and France; it also specified a unified command.

4

Population

The people who reside within a nation are one of the geopolitical factors of its strength. Therefore, it is possible to obtain some indication of the relative (and potential) power that the various states command by studying the distribution of population density over the earth. Especially in those areas where man has inhabited the land continuously over a period of centuries, the population density provides evidence of the capacity of the area to sustain life and, therefore, gives some intimation of power potential. It is true that in those two countries where are found the highest concentrations of people on the globe—namely, China and India—the standard of living has been so low as to keep these states from ranking as first-rate powers up to the present time. The teeming millions, however, offer a potential of manpower unequalled by any other area.

Population problems are often interrelated with international problems. Population pressure has often been the impulsion that has moved powerful states to intrude on the territories of other nations; conversely, it, also, has been instrumental in the development of atti-

tudes of fear on the part of weaker states. One of the reasons for the frame of French thought toward Germany has been the population differential of the two states. Before the recent carving-up of Germany, France was handicapped by a population one-third smaller than its enterprising neighbor. Even now, West Germany has a population nearly ten million greater than that of France.[1]

Population pressure has also been at the root of many of the great movements of population from one part of the world to another. Though the greater part of the world's people will live out their entire lives within the same political unit, large numbers of others will move, such migrations often creating serious national and international problems.

The distribution of land area and population within the world climatic regions is unequal. The two and one-half billion of man-

---

[1] During the Napoleonic period the populations of the two countries were about equal and France, then, held an advantage over Germany in that the former state had attained political unity whereas Germany still remained merely a "geographical expression."

kind are spread very unevenly across the land masses of the globe. However, a comparison of the map of population-distribution with the distribution charts of rainfall and temperature shows that density of population is correlated with these two aspects of climate. Siberia and the forest and tundra lands of Canada are almost empty. So, also, are the too wet and the too hot lands of the tropics, and the desert regions of Asia, Africa, and Australia in those areas where irrigation is not possible. Only where wells or streams (fed by the snows or rains of extra-desert areas) bring life-giving water to the arid soils, do we find the desert cultivated; and only where cultivation or mineral extraction is possible are these marginal lands populated, either densely (as in the Nile Valley oases) or sparsely, as in the Soviet-Siberian mineral fields. In contrast, the bulk of humanity lives in those places where precipitation is moderate (between fifteen and sixty inches) or seasonal and where temperatures change to bring seasons about equal in length.

The distribution of land and population among the continents is likewise disparate. A large proportion of the world's people live in regions where densities reach 500 or more per square mile whereas, on the other hand, over forty-three per cent of the total land area of the earth (including the Antarctic and Greenland icecaps) is inhabited by mankind in densities of less than one person per square mile. The *concentration of population in certain places* is a fact of tremendous geopolitical significance. About half of all the world's people are crowded together in east, southeast, and south Asia and the adjacent islands on about 12 per cent of the total land area of the globe. It is seldom realized that well over two and a quarter billion of mankind live *outside* of the United States! The following table bears out the uneven population distribution among continents and articulates the fact that the two Americas are but sparsely populated as compared with Asia and Europe.

	Per cent of land area of the globe	Per cent of world's population[2,3]
Africa	22.5	8
North America	18	9
Asia	32	55.5
Australia	5.5	.003
Europe	7	18
South America	13	4.5

On the continents, the pattern of population-distribution is closely related to the distribution of industry, topography, and land use, the latter two reflecting climatic and soil differences to a degree, also.

As the population distribution is irregular among continents so it is among countries. China, with upwards of 600 million[4] inhabitants, and India, with 376 million[5] people, are the giants of the world; the populations of the USSR, comprising some 200 million, and of the United States with 168 million[6] are next largest. The Commonwealth of Nations incorporates within its territories more people, how-

[2] The United States and the Soviet Union have, respectively, about 6 and 16.5 per cent of the land area, and 7.4 and 8.2 per cent of the population of the globe.

[3] Computed from statistics cited in the *United Nations' Demographic Yearbook, 1955.* The population figures used had a percentage margin of possible errors ranging from one to five per cent in most instances and in the case of East Asia, of 10 per cent.

[4] In November 1954, the Statistical Bureau of the People's Republic of China announced that, according to the June 1953 census, the mainland population totaled 582 million. This figure sounded unexpectedly high to students of China who had placed the population of Communist China somewhere between 400 and 500 million. Ta Chen (director of the Institute of Census Research, Tsing Hua University) in 1944* placed the population at about 400 million, and the 1948 census figures (the last published by the Nationalist government of China) announced a total of 452 million. The latter figure was subsequently revised to 468 million.
[* "The Newest Estimate of China's population," *Quarterly Review of Social Sciences,* Institute of Social Sciences, Academia Sinica, Peking, Vol. 6, 1935, pp. 191-266. In Chinese, referred to in Ta Chen, *Population in Modern China.*]

[5] Mid-1954 estimate.

[6] September 1956 Bureau of Census report.

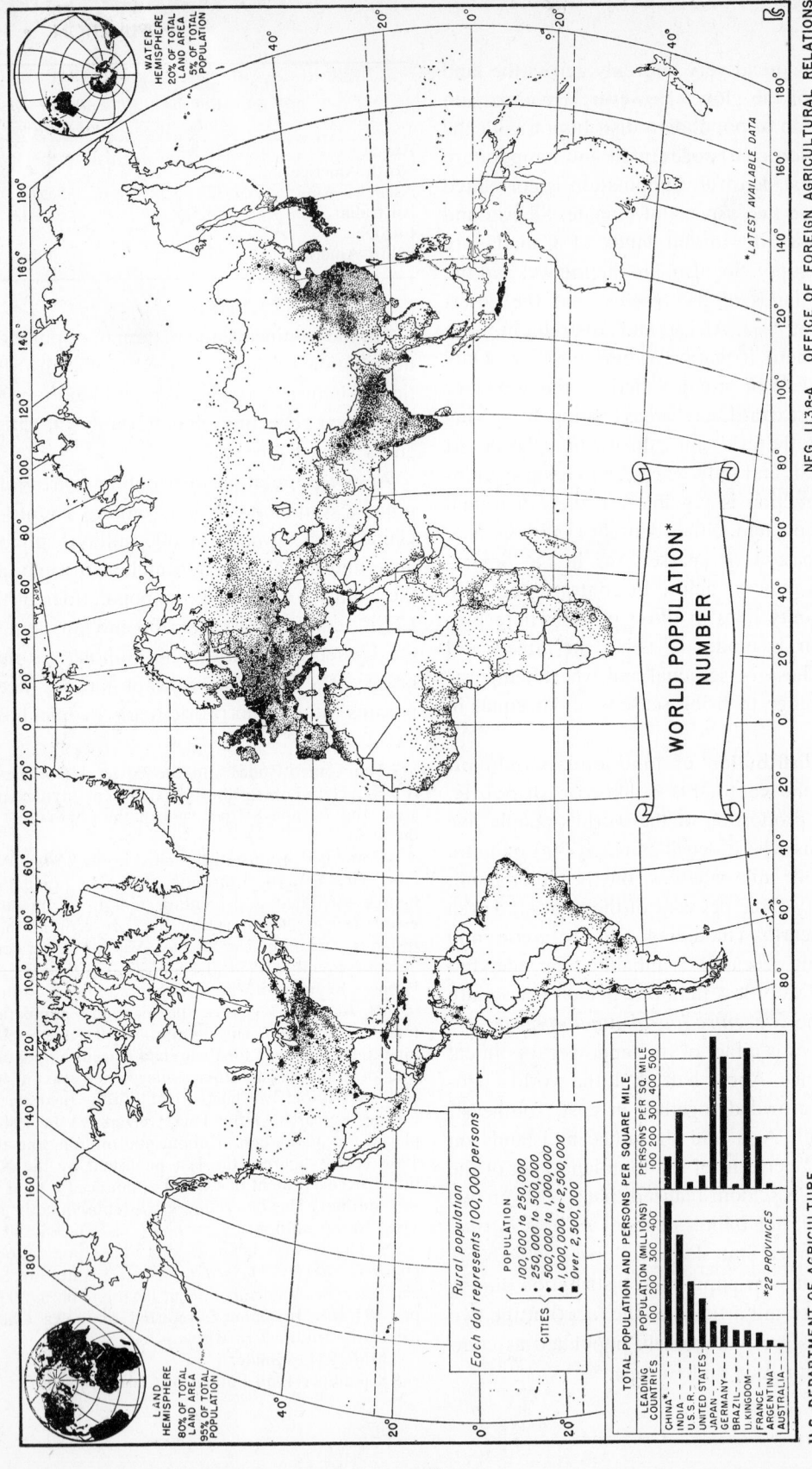

Figure 4.1. World population distribution.

ever, than any of the above countries, over 620 million people. But it must be taken into account that each state within the Commonwealth is an independent nation.

The geopolitical implications of a large population within a state present a striking picture of international strength (in numbers) according to alignment. Free Europe has less than 275 million people within its several states whereas Communist Europe (including all of the Soviet Union) has authority over some 390 million, exclusive of Finland. Were we to estimate comparative figures representing the populations of the Communist World as against those of the West, the contrast would be even more striking—the Soviet Bloc populations total about 900 million.

In speaking of *size* of population, however, an aspect other than mere numbers must be taken into account. This is the *potential for growth* that any group possesses.

The relationship between population size and effectiveness is relative. Although "the military strength of a nation is usually related to the size and composition of the population," mere numbers of people cannot be considered a prime factor of geopolitical strength—for population numbers and manpower are not always one and the same thing. "Large populations can be a source of national weakness as well as of strength."[7] For example, a larger population might make Brazil stronger—both politically and economically; fewer people might produce the same results in India.

Effectiveness is a further aspect of population that must be taken into account, therefore. Where standard of living is low and caloric intake below that which is requisite for good health, the energy of a people will be below par, and the vitality of the group is likely to spend itself in the primary task of making a living. Likewise, where the level of the culture and the development of technical skills has

remained static and the organization of the group has not advanced to a point to bring social benefits to its population, the bulk of the nation will remain at a subsistence level of existence. Again, the time of the people will be spent in merely securing the essentials of life—with little or no leisure to devote to scientific, inventive, or educational activities. In either instance, the actual output of the manpower as against the possible potential productivity under better living conditions is, relatively, unimportant. (Compare the effectiveness of the 376 million Indians living on the subcontinent of Asia with that of the 168 million Americans in the United States.) On the other hand, where the industrial development of two nations is roughly equal, the size of the population may be critical.

The relationship, then, between population-size and the power of a state is not direct or simple: manpower potential is to be assessed in terms of many interrelated factors,[8] some of which are not even directly related to population size, trend, or composition.

The population composition has implications on the effectiveness of the population. Is the group as a whole young, old, or middle-aged? The vitality and fertility, outlook and productiveness of a people are significantly affected by age-composition. So, too, is the growth potential. Further, is the nation largely agrarian, or both rural and urban? A population-analysis in terms of rural urban distribution gives at least some indication of the industrial and commercial importance of a state, for extensive urbanization usually goes hand-in-hand with industrialization and the development of commercial enterprise. These varied characteristics, in turn, reflect the internal effectiveness of a state as well as have reference to the creation of some of the acute geopolitical problems that develop between states. Further, they provide insight into some of the reasons for the interdependence of one region (or nation) with another. They point up the fallacy

---

[7] Frank W. Notestein, "Fundamentals of Population Change in Europe and the Soviet Union," from *Compass of the World* (New York: The Macmillan Company, 1947), p. 429.

[8] As morale, political unity, technological progress, resource development, etc.

of reliance on statistics alone in making geo-political analyses of population.

RACE AND NATIONAL POLICY

In but few instances does race stand at the root of geopolitical problems. Race and such ethnographic factors as religion and language are important variants of the population factor. Race does not generally enter into the structure of a state, however, nor is it, basically, at the root of geopolitical problems that arise between states. There are countries, however, where race does enter into the structure of the population, and others where race both enters into the structure of the population as well as dictates national policy. In the first instance, Liberia and Sierra Leone, countries set up by the United States and Great Britain as homelands for freed slaves, are striking examples; Australia, which holds out for a "white nation," is another. Of the second case, that of racial attitudes prescribing the political structure and law, the Union of South Africa is an egregious example. Although nationality is intermingled in this highly complex situation, the major conflict is between Caucasian and Negro: the apartheid policy of the Malan government (and of the subsequent governments which have carried out the same policies) converted the race question from a relatively dormant problem into an acute and burning enigma.

The term "race" is often misused. Race may be defined as a group of people having similar physical characteristics distinguishing them from those of other groups. The lay interpretation generally places the distinction in terms of color while science characterizes the various races on the basis of head dimensions, texture of the hair, etc., as well as color. The most generally accepted classification lists four stocks: Caucasoid, Mongoloid, Negroid, and Australoid. Geopolitically, ethnographic factors of population are far more important than are racial, and political boundaries generally overlap racial divisions. It is not the fact of race itself but "what people think about race" that raises this question to the status of a geopolitical problem.[9]

THE ETHNIC INTEGRANTS

The ethnographic factors of religion and language are often pregnant with geopolitical implications. Ethnic ties are both more valid and enduring than are those of race for when people are linked ethnically it means either that they have experienced a period of living together for a sufficiently long time to establish ties—such as language (and this predicates some common background, historical and cultural)—or it means a communion of thought and ideology, as in the case of religion. Language is usually the more potent as a unifying or divisive force but, at times, religion exerts a powerful influence. Both have great potency.

POPULATION TRENDS (THE DYNAMICS OF POPULATION)

The problems of population are variable—and this changing character is, in itself, one of the inherent geopolitical forces that affects international stability. The growth in the world's population is about twenty-five to thirty million persons annually. In general, the population of any region or state is either increasing or declining—it is rarely static. And it is this ever-changing regional differential—in rates of growth and population composition—that is geopolitically very significant.

An increase in the world's population may lead to several alternative conditions. It may: 1) bring about closer cooperation among peoples, the wide differentials in population density between varied regions leading to exchanges beneficial to both groups and, therefore, to the development of interdependence; 2) leave international relations unchanged—but, unless the environment is rich and not over-populated, and the population inventive and enterprising, it may bring about a lowering

---

[9] Anthropologists assert that, according to their findings up to the present time, no physically or intellectually superior race exists as such.

in the standard of living within that state; 3) be the cause of mass migrations—as that of the Irish to the United States during the potato famine of the middle nineteenth century; 4) be the cause of great tensions and frictions and, eventually, lead to aggression and even war. A state possessing a rapidly growing population pressing against the resources of the land may begin a series of aggressions—as did Japan beginning about the turn of the century. On the other hand, two nations with large differentials of size, density, and growth may live side by side in peace.[10]

The last three centuries have marked a unique period of growth in the world's population. Not very much is known regarding population growth throughout the world up to the beginning of the nineteenth century. However, it is thought that during the past three hundred years the population of the world has about doubled and that of Europeans and their descendants has increased five-fold. The latter scattered to all parts of the globe. This multiplication and dispersal of Europeans, with the broadening of cultural and trade contacts consequent to it, brought about changes in the economic and political relations of the entire world.

What was the source of this unparalleled period in the demographic history of mankind? It lies largely in the revolutionary changes that have taken place in the ratio between birth and death rates.[11] Before the explosive rise in population, high birth rates almost canceled high death rates, the near-equation of fertility and mortality yielding a small natural increase.

The *vital revolution* typically takes its course with the industrialization of an area. It commenced first in the industrial West where the high birth and lowered death rates of the first phase of the population cycle were, in time, replaced by low birth and death rates which, as in the pre-industrial phase, nearly canceled each other to yield but little increase. The period of growth came between these two phases of the population cycle—between the transition from high to low birth and mortality rates. Death rates decreased first, and it was in the lapse of time before birth rates also declined that the rate of growth swung sharply upward, often in spectacular fashion.

Mortality rates may be lowered for a number of reasons but, in general, this occurs as soon as technological and social improvements raise the standard of living.[12] A marked decline in birth rates has usually been associated with the change from rural to urban environments. Typically this, in time, has brought the transition from the large to the small-sized family—the former having none of the advantages under

---

[10] Rarely does international friction arise as the result of only one factor; usually such disturbances are due to the interaction of a number of variables, of which population pressure is but one—though at times it may be paramount.

[11] The increase or decrease of a population is due to the balance between births and deaths, immigration and emigration.

[12] "No simple laws can suffice to predict the response of population trends to changing social and economic conditions. The social and economic factors are linked in complex relations to one another and to each of the components of population change—*viz.,* fertility, mortality, and migration—and these components are functionally interrelated. The age structure of the population is a further complication; its form at any time is shaped by the trends of fertility, mortality and migration over a long period in the past, and it influences the trend of population over many decades in the future.

"It may be in some situations that population growth stands in a fairly simple relation to economic factors. According to one view, where the population is near the maximum that can be supported (at the standard of living upon which the people insist), and given the existing technology and available resources, the role of population increase over long periods is governed by the rate at which the production of economic goods is expanded through development of resources and technology. That is to say that mortality, fertility and migration are joint functions of economic development, so that a change in any one of these components of population growth, unless balanced by the expansion or contraction of production, will bring about a compensating change in the other components. The manner in which the compensation is effected may depend on the characteristics of the culture; in some societies a tendency for population to grow beyond the 'means of subsistence' may be corrected by emigration or the reduction of fertility; in others, rising mortality rates may restore the balance." (*Determinants and Consequences of Population Trends,* United Nations Population Study, No. 17, 1953, p. 149.)

urban living that it had under rural conditions. It has been recurrently observed that, in the city, the high cost of rearing a child—along with the shedding of family responsibilities—brought a marked drop in the number of children per family unit which eventually reduced the total natural increase and checked the formerly rapid growth tendencies induced by the lowered rate.

The transition-cycle did not begin simultaneously in all parts of Europe. It commenced in the northwest and spread slowly from the west to other portions of Europe and the globe—as the revolution in industry, commerce, and science slowly broadened its base. While in Northwest and Western Europe, the United States, Canada and Australia, the population-cycle had, in the pre-war years, advanced into the third (declining rate of growth) phase, in certain other regions, as Central, Eastern, and Southern Europe, the populations were and are still in the transition period of rapid growth.[13] And in many parts of the world, notably the densely populated lands of the Far East, of Africa, and of Latin America, the vital revolution has scarcely begun. What are the prospects of population change in these various areas where fertility and mortality show such marked differentials?

Prospects in countries well-advanced in the population cycle. It is, in general, agreed that the conditions affecting possible population changes during the next few decades in countries where both death and birth rates are now relatively low differ from those where either (or both) fertility and mortality are high.[14]

Although future gains in life-expectancy (lowering of mortality) are to be expected in those countries well-advanced in the cycle, these increases are likely to be smaller and achieved with greater difficulty than during the

past century. The future of fertility rates is not as bright either, and though the long-continued, previous downward trend in birth rates in these countries was recently interrupted during the war and postwar periods, there is no unanimity of opinion that the long-range trend to smaller families has been checked.[15] "Explanations for a larger average number of births per completed family are to be found in changing attitudes regarding the desirable size of family rather than in short-term fluctuations which are only temporarily reflected in the annual number of births."[16]

---

[13] Those regions that are in the transition phase of the vital revolution will have a more youthful population than will those in either of the other two phases.

[14] *Determinants and Consequences of Population Trends, op. cit.,* p. 153.

[15] In the middle 1930's, the end of the notable period of growth was thought to be in sight for much of Europe as well as for the English-speaking European political-progeny—namely, the United States, Canada, Australia and New Zealand. As noted, demographers, watching the pattern of population growth and decline within industrialized areas, had plotted the last phase of the population cycle as one of decreasing growth. In 1935, for example, a number of the countries of the West were showing steadily declining growth patterns: the Swedish population was not replacing itself; the United States reached the lowest percentage-increment in its entire history; France and other of the West European states displayed the same trend.

However, in the decade and a half between 1935 and the late 1940's, a reversal of this trend toward decline took place with startling rapidity, and a renewed reproductive vitality has continued to characterize the populations of the Western nations.

Just what the implications of this reversal in population-growth trend are cannot be forecast. Whether this upsurge in population of the last few years will be a permanent trend or is just an irregular phase or fluctuation within the pattern of growth slowdown (predicted by the demographic cycle) remains to be seen. The recent percentage increases in the population of the United States have been large although they have declined somewhat from the 1947 level—which registered the largest percentage increase in the history of the nation. So persistent has been the trend of high percentage increments that demographers are now in doubt as to the validity of the industrial-cycle thesis.

However, regardless of what the trend is in the West, the over-all picture of world population is one of an increasing differential in population growth between the states of the West and that of most other parts of the earth—many areas of the latter having not only larger bases on which to multiply growth, *but* also being in the early or the pre-industrial stages of the industrial cycle.

[16] *Determinants and Consequences of Population Trends, op. cit.,* p. 153.

ESTIMATED AGE DISTRIBUTION OF WORLD POPULATION BY REGIONS, 1947[17]

Region	Per cent of Population			
	Under 15 years	15-59 years	60 years and over	Total
World Total	36	57	7	100
Africa	40	55	5	100
America:				
Northern America*	25	64	11	100
Latin America	40	55	5	100
Asia:				
Near East	40	54	6	100
South Central Asia	40	56	4	100
Japan	37	55	8	100
Remaining Far East (except Asian USSR)	40	55	5	100
Europe:				
Northwest Central Europe	24	62	14	100
Southern Europe	30	59	11	100
Eastern Europe (including Asian USSR)	34	59	7	100
Oceania	28	62	10	100

* "Northern America" includes all countries north of the Rio Grande; "Latin America" comprises the remainder of America, including the Caribbean region.

The increasing age of the population is another important factor that may tend to retard the growth rate in these countries during the next several decades. Unless the large increases in fertility rates continue, a constantly larger part of the total population will be made up of persons past middle age. Under these circumstances, not only will the birth rates be cut but the death rate will also rise, and rise high enough to counteract any possible gains in age-specific mortality that may be won. The implications are clear: the rate of natural increase of Western Europe, America north of the Rio Grande, and the British dominions in the Pacific, will probably be distinctly lower, on the average, during the last half of the twentieth century than they were during the first fifty years—unless the recent trend continues.

According to a set of growth-curve projections issued recently by the United Nations the indications are that the average rate of increment in the populations of these countries between 1950 and 1980 is not likely to exceed one per cent *per annum* and, further, that the total populations will increase from 486 million in 1950 to somewhere between 548 and 655 million in 1980. The *rate* of growth may not be steady but may fluctuate according to large cyclical variations as the fertility rates rise or drop with world conditions. It is unlikely that migrations will have much effect on the pattern of growth though emigration may be significant in some countries, as Italy; in others, immigration may add materially to the total population, as in such areas as Canada and Oceania.[18]

Prospects in countries in the transition stage of the population cycle (incipient decline). Areas where fertility is lowest are often adjacent to regions where birth rates are still high

[17] United Nations, *Demographic Yearbook 1949-50*, p. 15.

[18] *Determinants and Consequences of Population Trends, op. cit.*, p. 153.

but have shown a recent trend toward decline. Eastern Europe (including the Soviet Union), Japan, and parts of Latin America belong to this category. In all of them there have been marked reductions of mortality in recent decades bringing the death rates to moderate levels while birth rates have remained high. This has meant rapid growth. Further reductions in death rates are expected in these countries. It is quite possible that the life-expectancy of peoples in these areas will, before long, reach the level found in those states having the present lowest mortality rates: "the prospects are generally not unfavorable" for the further development of industry and a rising standard of living and these conditions, along with the emphasis that is being put upon public health and education, are expected to bring considerable savings in life, particularly among infants.[19]

It may be expected that birth rates will also continue to drop in these countries if they take the pattern of demographic evolution found among the peoples where low fertility and mortality obtain. The curve of the population trend will depend upon the relative rapidity of decline in death and birth rates but, if these states repeat the history of the above-mentioned regions, the number of births will eventually reach a near-balance with the number of deaths. Nonetheless, the present imbalance between birth and death rates makes a transition period of rapid increase seem inevitable—unless the growth-tendency is checked by calamities which increase the mortality or by adverse economic conditions resulting from an attempt to absorb the additional numbers into the population.

Prospective population increases of, on the average, "not less than one per cent nor more than 1.9 per cent" *per annum* are expected, with the aggregate population of this group of states rising from 533 million in 1950 to between 718 million and 938 million by 1980. Relatively, the population of this group of nations will rise in proportion to that of the world.[20] Population analysts of Eastern Europe and the Soviet Union (including Lorimer, Notestein and others) imply that, though a future decline in the populations of these states is expected, during the next few decades a more rapid growth than that anticipated for the Western nations will take place. Between 1940 and 1970 an increase in the aggregate populations of Poland, Lithuania, and the Balkan states of from 87.7 million to 105 million is indicated. These analysts do not hold to the possibility that economic necessity can seriously limit the population increase in these Central European states in the near future. In the other Central European countries, where population increases are also expected, the increased numbers may "hinder progress toward a higher level of living" but such growth will not be economically impossible. As for the Soviet Union, that nation has an immense potential for both economic development and population growth.[21]

Large increases of population in Japan have been viewed in a somewhat different light. It is thought likely that rapid growth, continued over a long period of time, will be prevented either by emigration or by a rising mortality or falling fertility rate (or both), the latter following upon the adverse economic conditions that would develop as a concomitant to the increasing numbers of people. These conclusions are drawn because of the geographic realities of the tight little island-location where, already, there is a high density of population relative to available cultivable soil and other natural resources. It is doubted that an average growth-rate of one or more per cent "would, or could, occur in Japan." Self-containment is impossible. Only by the development of foreign trade to provide food and raw materials—and markets—*and* emigration along with a sharp decline in birth rate, can Japan

[19] *Ibid.,* p. 157.

[20] United Nations, "The Past and Future Growth of World Population: a Long-Range View," *Population Bulletin,* No. 1, Document No. ST/SOA/Series N/1, December, 1951, pp. 1-12.

[21] *Determinants and Consequences of Population Trends, op. cit.,* pp. 157-58.

"avoid disaster."[22] England is, and has been for long, in a similar situation.

Population growth in Latin America (where industrial development is not as advanced as in Japan) is often viewed as an asset to increased economic activity and the development of potential resources. The populations of Latin America are increasing more rapidly than those of any other major region in the world today: the rate of increase is more than double the rate for the world as a whole. Between 1920 and 1940 these populations rose in numbers by an average of 1.7 per cent *per annum*. If this trend continues, the number of people in 1980 will be twice that of the present time and, by the year 2000, would mount to above 373 million.[23]

The countries just discussed are areas of incipient decline. The decline, however, cannot be anticipated for a number of decades but must be projected into a relatively distant future. Population increase is, among this group of states, an immediate and long-term prospect.

Prospects in countries in the early period of the population cycle. Birth rates are generally high throughout Asia, much of South America, and among the indigenous peoples of Africa. In these regions (except for Japan and some of the states in South America) fertility rates have shown little, if any, trend toward decline whereas, according to the somewhat sketchy data that is available, notable reductions have been achieved in the mortality rates of some of these countries. This has meant an increasing growth at a quickening rate, at times reaching and even exceeding three per cent *per annum*. In other areas

[22] F. W. Notestein, "The Population of the World in the Year 2000," *Journal of the American Statistical Association,* Vol. 45, No. 251 (September, 1950), pp. 342-43.

[23] According to: Earl P. Hanson, "The Amazon: a New Frontier," *Headline Series,* No. 45, March, 1944, pp. 5-88; K. Davis, "Future Migration into Latin America," *The Milbank Memorial Fund Quarterly,* Vol. XXV, No. 1 (January, 1947), pp. 44-62.

within this group of states decreases in mortality have been less marked. The overall picture is a mixed one with large increments in population showing in some parts and slowly-increasing (or even stationary) populations in others. According to population analysts, the lack of adequate information on population tendencies and uncertainties with regard to possible economic developments make any predictions on population trends, of necessity, hypothetical. Uncertainty is especially great in areas where population density is low, as in most of Africa and the islands of the Pacific and Indian Oceans. Further, in the densely populated areas, such as portions of China and India, the maximum density of population that the regions will carry—under existing social and economic conditions—has possibly been reached, and only by an increase in economic productivity can greater numbers of people be supported.

However, even in areas where the mortality rate has been reduced, still further reductions are possible, particularly in those countries where there has been less progress in disease and epidemic control. But the extent to which such gains will last is questionable unless social improvements better the living conditions of the populace. It is further possible that, with improvements in economic and social conditions, the fertility rate will drop. Despite all of these things, the outstanding implications remain: *i.e.* in those regions of high fertility, the present high rate of birth is likely to remain high for at least several decades and, it follows, that where mortality continues to decline, an accelerating growth in population can be anticipated. Percentage increases in population in East, South and Southwest Asia, and Africa will not rise above 1.2 per cent on the average nor fall lower, on the average, than 0.7 per cent *per annum,* with the assumed mean being one per cent. If the populations of the states of these Afro-Asiatic regions increased at this assumed rate they would rise from the 1,387 million of 1950 to between 1,710 million and

2,048 million in 1980 (mean 1,869 million).[24, 25]

The rate of population growth in India and China, whose aggregate populations comprise nearly half of the present world total, are particularly critical in any geopolitical analysis. What are the prospects in these states? A variety of estimates has been made with reference to India-Pakistan, all implying large absolute increases although the predicted percentage increases do not run very high; figures (maximum) of 550 million and 650 million by 1970 have been predicted by two writers.[26, 27, 28] The estimates regarding population trends in China are quite contradictory to each other. One writer (Ta Chen)[29] expresses the view that population growth has tended to run in cycles in China and that the end of such a cycle, with population increases almost at a standstill, has been reached. Thus, he anticipates a decline in population rather than an increase. Other writers hold to the view that the economic capacity of China has not yet been fully developed and that future population increases "commensurate with the carrying capacity of the country may be anticipated."[30, 31, 32]

Summary. The probabilities for future population growth have been analyzed with reference to three regional groups: those where both birth and death rates are relatively low; those where, though birth rates are still moderately high, a decline has set in; and those where fertility remains high with little or no indication of declining. What does this evidence mean in terms of the power blocs into which the political world has aligned itself?

It is a hazardous undertaking to attempt to make forecasts in demography for it has been amply proven that population trends are susceptible to considerable reversals within periods of a few decades or even a few years. Nevertheless, certain indications emerge: the West, with its small proportion of the earth's present population, cannot anticipate any great growth to compare with that of the communist world. In the areas of communist control, where are found at least one-third of the people of the globe, a substantial population increase can well be expected, within the next decades, as the benefits of Western science and medicine, technology and industry thrust some of

[24] United Nations, "Past and Future Growth," etc., *op. cit.*

[25] "Future population estimates for a number of countries in Asia and Africa where great progress in public health work has been made indicate that, in the absence of major catastrophes, large increases will result from the rapidly declining mortality accompanied by little or no immediate decline in fertility. The estimates for some of the poorest and most heavily populated countries in these continents, however, are generally more conservative." *Determinants and Consequences of Population Trends, op. cit.,* p. 159.

[26] K. Davis, *The Population of India and Pakistan* (Princeton: Princeton University Press, 1951), p. 89.

[27] K. Davis, "Demographic Fact and Policy in India," *The Milbank Memorial Fund Quarterly,* Vol. XXII, No. 3 (July, 1944), p. 257.

[28] A. V. Hill, "Health, Food and Population in India," *International Affairs,* Vol. XXI, No. 1 (January, 1945), p. 45.

[29] Ta Chen, *Population in Modern China* (Chicago: The University of Chicago Press, 1946), pp. 4-5.

[30] The great reduction of death rates in the West during the nineteenth century has been credited largely to the development of industry and commerce, the rising trend of per capita income, and the spread of education. (Though not previously mentioned, the abandonment of traditions, which formerly bound peoples to the ways of their ancestors, should also be included.)

[31] K. Sun, *La Chine de Demain* (Paris, 1946), pp. 269-70.

[32] If it is accepted that the industrial revolution in Europe initiated a series of social and economic changes which, in time, lowered the birth rates of many European countries to a near balance with the greatly reduced death rates, the presumption might be supported that a corresponding industrialization of the Far East might have a similar effect. However, on the presumption that it is possible to reduce the birth rates appreciably in the radically different social and economic setting of the Orient, the timing might conceivably be very different. Thus, the degree of expansion of the Oriental populations before reaching the third phase of demographic equilibrium might be greater or less than that observed in Europe. According to some authors, the whole pattern of demographic changes which may be expected to result from such a change in economic activities depends upon the form of the social order and is entirely different in capitalistic and communistic societies. *Determinants and Consequences of Population Trends, op. cit.,* p. 150.

these states into the growth-phase of the vital revolution. Since they already have a broader population-base on which to begin this increase, the prospects in actual numbers are great. With the passage of time, the differential in population size must widen in favor of the presently more-retarded areas (which include the great proportion of the neutral states, some of which have huge populations) while, simultaneously, the margin of industrial advantage (held presently by the West) narrows as the Communist and neutral states take on the advances of the machine-civilization.

MOVEMENT OF POPULATION

Although the relationship between fertility and mortality is the primary factor affecting population growth and decline, movements of people—internal and international—offer an indispensable approach to the understanding of demographic tendencies and geopolitical affairs.

Migrations appear to have gone on almost continuously since the history of mankind began for, if man were not mobile, his exploitation of the natural resources of the earth and his capacity to make room for his growing numbers would be greatly hampered. During the modern period, the great movement of Europeans overseas into the Western Hemisphere, the colonization of Siberia by the Russians, and other migrations into empty or sparsely-populated areas has produced a better proportion of population to resources. Migration, therefore, "has had the general effect of raising the rates of natural increase in the world as a whole, over long-time periods, above the levels that would have been possible without migration."[33] On the other hand, such movements have at times been the cause of great hardship to the receiving group and have, as well, served to develop international tensions and strife.

Migration and population growth or decline. The effects of migration upon general increase in population in particular areas of immigration and emigration depend upon several things: 1) permanence of residence in the area of immigration; 2) the sex and age structure of the migrant group; 3) the fertility and mortality rates of the migrants (after their arrival) and of their descendants; 4) the effects of the migration upon the fertility and mortality rates of the indigenous people in the country of immigration and of the population remaining in the land of emigration.

The permanence of the migration is important. That is to say, the effects depend upon how large a proportion of the migrants make their new habitation their permanent home and how long those who subsequently return home or migrate elsewhere remain in the area to which they immigrated. It is obvious that migrants who return to the country of emigration, taking with them any children who were born to them during their stay, can have but a passing influence on the population of the land to which they immigrated. Much of the migration between neighboring European states, or between areas in Africa and Asia, or parts of Europe (as Italy) and South America, has been made up of laborers seeking employment for a period of weeks, a season, or a few years. Thus, such persons have had relatively little effect on population increase. On the other hand, the immigration of Europeans, from the period of early colonization until the present, to North and South America, Oceania, and parts of Africa, has been to a large extent permanent and has established large and increasing populations of European extraction in these newer lands of the world. In many instances, as in the West Indies, Australia, New Zealand, and America north of the Rio Grande, the immigrants and their descendants remained in numbers large enough to form the base of nations and of increasing population; in others, as in Latin America, Africa, and parts of Oceania, they have formed minorities within a large indigenous population. At times, immigration on a permanent basis can easily add to the population growth in proportions that exceed the in-

---

[33] *Ibid.,* p. 136.

crease of the native population. This is true because of the sex and age composition of most migrant groups: they generally are made up, in large part, of young adults who are at the reproductive age and of an age when the death rate is low.[34]

Emigration seldom solves the problem of over-population. A low rate of natural increase may produce a situation that is favorable to immigration whereas, on the other hand, emigration may be induced by a high rate of population growth—or by population pressure on the natural resources of the land as of the period of emigration. It is difficult to predict what effect emigration will have upon the population tendencies of the land from which the people departed; it may be favorable or adverse. Although emigration is offered by some as a solution to the problems of over-population in certain countries, it is to be questioned whether or not migration, in the long run, will alleviate the population pressure to any great extent, particularly in areas with high densities and numbers. Such a large group would have to be drained off that it would become physically impossible to carry out a population move on so vast a scale. It is likely that, in terms of a permanent relief, emigration can play only a subsidiary part to reduction of fertility through birth control, industrialization, and improved techniques of agriculture in easing the pressure—emigration providing, so to speak, a breather during a period of transition.

Political authority and migration. Unrestricted international migration has seldom prevailed during the period of man's history. Even among such groups as the nomadic pastoralists of semi-arid and desert regions, the migrations (which may be nearly continuous or on a seasonal basis) are controlled to the extent that one group respects the territory of another and does not encroach upon it. However, where central governing authority is weak and local interests dominant, people may move (or sweep) in almost unrestricted fashion across international boundaries. In the past, this was true of the periodic movements of the Lapps in northern Europe; it was true of the peoples along the Great Wall of China where, in good times (periods of favorable rainfall), the Chinese farmers might make their way across the man-made barrier to encroach upon the lands of the Mongols, whereas during periods of great and enduring drought the opposite situation obtained—Mongol hordes crossed the walls to pillage settled inhabitants of China.[35] The wave after wave of barbarians that swept out of Central Asia into Europe and the Far East during the period of the "dark ages" were migrants who were evidently impelled to move outward into the surrounding lands either because of crowding, within what were then lands of meagre resources (meagre because the low level of technology did not permit the inhabitants to make full use of all of the natural wealth that was present), or purely for aggressive reasons.

The effects upon the economies and populations of the several countries into which these different migrants have made their incursions varied. The movements of the Lapp peoples, in general, bring no changes in either the economy or the population trends of the several states across whose territories they migrate—for theirs is a seasonal movement. The migrations of the Asiatic "barbarians," on the other hand, were invasions of pillage and plunder, the effects of which had a tremendous impact upon the population, culture, and economy of all of the lands through which they passed—an impact that showed its effects for centuries. Where the invaders settled permanently, they either formed the base for a future political

---

[34] According to a study of the contribution of immigration (and the natural increases of immigration groups) to the growth of population over long periods of time in the United States, it was estimated that, during the period 1790-1920, descendants of early immigrants and survivors of recent immigrants during this period totaled 53.5 millions by 1920, a number larger than that of descendants of the colonial white populations despite rapid increases among the latter.

[35] An antipathy seems always to have existed between the nomadic pastoralist and the settled cultivator.

state, as in Hungary (Magyars), or minority groups that, though they generally kept their character, were drawn into the political units of the indigenous population.

It would require a volume to trace the effects—demographic, cultural, economic, and political—of the migrations of the Moslems, from their center on the Arabian Peninsula, eastward across southern Asia into the Philippines and the Indies, westward across North Africa into European Spain and, via Turkey, into the Balkans. The significance of this migration of a religious group is only realized and understood by an examination of the impact of Islam upon the politics and economies, the culture and state of the arts of the numerous Moslem states and the role these Islamic nations play in international affairs today.

Nations set up machinery to regulate the entrance and departure of travellers into or from their territories. National restraints— political, economic and social—have limited and frequently prohibited immigrations (and in some cases, emigrations) of people who desire to enter, or leave, a country to settle permanently or even to visit. In some nations, groups of temporary laborers are prevented from entering because of the protests of certain labor groups, or government policy. Australia prohibits any immigrant laborers, other than Caucasian, from entering the country on either a permanent or itinerant basis. Such restrictions may express attitudes of a social or nationalistic nature, or may lead to their development.

Internal migration in Eurasia since World War II has been one of the outstanding phenomena of the postwar period. The post-World War II migrations within the Eurasian continent have been of various sorts and for varied reasons. The movement of eight million Germans from the former German territory east of the Oder-Neisse River boundary (now Polish) into West Germany was a migration forced as an aftermath of the transfer of territory by treaty to the communist state. This was part of the spoils of war. It worked extreme hardship on both the migrants and the population of the German Republic, the latter finding great difficulty in absorbing so many persons within so short a period of time into the war-weakened economy. Another move was the return of the Dutch colonists from the East Indies to the Netherlands.

A third and fourth migration were: 1) the return of Jews from *all* parts of the world— notably from Nazi-dominated European states during the war and from poverty-stricken Near Eastern lands, such as Yemen and Iraq— after Israel became an independent state set up as a homeland for the Jewish people; and 2) a semi-reciprocal emigration of Arabs from Israel. In the Jewish state, the resource-bound economy of the young nation has slowly attempted to assimilate the newcomers; in Arab countries, such as Jordan, the displaced migrants have been unwanted and great numbers have continued to live under unsatisfactory conditions, supported by the United Nations.

Another dramatic migration of the postwar period was the voluntary transfer of populations that took place upon the division of India into the states of India and Pakistan. Again, as in all of the other instances cited, great hardships attended the move—hardship for the migrants as well as for the immigrant-states, the economies of which were seriously strained to make room for the millions who exchanged places.

Population density influences national policy toward immigrants and emigrants. In certain parts of the world the signs of population-saturation stand out clearly. Many areas of Western Europe reflect this condition in the standard of living maintained by the majority of their people. Some countries of the world have virtually closed their doors to immigrants, as the United States where all incomers are carefully sifted on a strict quota basis. As for the emigrating-lands, these "countries do not want their surplus populations to stay home, and yet they do not want to lose contact with them. Countries of immigration," on the other hand, "may want new populations, but they also desire to have full control over them, if not to assimilate them."[36] Some states, as Canada and Australia, are so in need of more people that they hold out inducements to those of selected countries in order to encourage immigration.

Tensions frequently develop when immigrants remain as unassimilated minorities. In some cases, the immigrants assimilate themselves easily and quickly into the society and economy of their new land; in other instances, the settlers remain as small islands of foreign populations within the nation—minority groups that may or may not become sore spots of internal and international tension.[37] Such groups may become persecuted minorities, socially or politically. The Jews in most parts of the world exemplify the former; the Germans, who settled in eastern European Russia, the latter. Or the immigrants may become irredentist, i.e. though subject to the immigrant state, they may desire incorporation into the emigrant-country. Numerous instances of this have obtained in the past and present—the Trieste-Italians and Yugoslavs to cite two recent examples.

THE CHANGING BALANCE OF POWER AS EXPRESSED IN THE HUMAN ELEMENT

Power in relation to population means manpower. Manpower may be seen in several categories. First, it is seen in its physical nature —as used for economic production, and, when the necessity arises, for war and military purposes. Secondly, it is manifested in its intellectual nature: i.e. manpower as represented by people, educated and intelligent, who can apply the experiences of the past to the problems of the present and future; who can anticipate the problems of their populations and economy, and of international affairs; and who manifest their intellectual power on a national level in the social, political, and economic structure of the state and, on an international plane, in wise diplomacy and negotiation. Thirdly, manpower may be seen in its philosophical nature, equally important to the physical and intellectual in the geopolitical aspects of life for, as are the philosophies of the people, so will be the spirit and the nature and the morale of the group.

As these several powers—or categories of manpower—change within each of the various population groups of the numerous political states of the globe, the trends toward peace or war will change. Sheer physical productivity, stage of technology and science, intellectual and moral level, and "nature" and morale are all weighting factors. Manpower—or population—as thus defined, comprises a large proportion of the actual power of any state because it is man who develops the resources, produces the goods, and otherwise provides for the needs of the state. Without progressive, intelligent people the resources of the land will lie largely idle or be exploited by other nations. Therefore, on this basis, the larger the population the greater the potential strength of any state—provided that the population increase is not more rapid than economic, social and scientific development, or beyond the means of continued support of the growing population at a good living standard.

---

[36] Bowman, *The New World, op. cit.,* p. 16.

[37] Though there is mixing at the Slav-Teuton border, neither Slavic nor German infiltrates, in either direction, have assimilated with the populations of the states of immigration but have remained as distinct minorities even after the passage of decades.

5

Resources and Industry, Transportation and Trade

RESOURCES AND INDUSTRIES

Location, size, and relief, which form the physical structure within which a state functions, are elements that affect not only internal policies and national well-being but foreign policy and international position as well. However important as these elements are, the power and latitude of any nation is largely determined by the physical and population resources and the industrial development of that state. A comparative examination of the resources, potential and actual, and of the stage and scope of the technology of nations, is necessary to comprehend the position of any particular country as a world power. Such a study also provides a key to an understanding of its external policies—the *geography of power* is an important factor in determining foreign policy and international status.

The resources of the earth are not equitably distributed. World resources are highly local-ized, with the result that some nations are well supplied while others are not. Especially is this true of cultivable soils and mineral deposits. Further, man's ability to avail himself of these resources is limited by the stage of technological progress: the greater the advance in technology and science, the greater will be the capacity for utilization of the potentials of the environment. However, though man may drain swamps or irrigate arid places, though he can convert coal into gas or oil and, at times, substitute one mineral for another, it is only within very narrow limits that he is able to "change" the distribution of these useful and necessary resources.

The potential and actual resources of a state vary from place to place and from age to age. Some nations have a rich resource base, physically and technologically speaking; others have not. The distinctions between states stood out more clearly in the past than they do today for, in an earlier period, the utilization of resources was more nearly commensurate with the localized reserves and culture than is true at present. For example, people in some parts of the world were so handicapped by resource lacks that they remained at a low level of culture until the advent of the European. This was true both of the American Indian and of the Australian aborigine: domesticable animals (with the exception of the dog in America) were absent in both environments and, in Australia, there were no domesticable plants. In such regions as the low latitude forests of the Amazon and Congo, and the tundra lands of the Arctic, the limits of both resources and climate kept the people from advancing beyond a primitive stage. Today, transportation and communication, commerce and war, have obscured some of the differences. However, they still stand out: mark how the machine civilization of the West contrasts with that of the Orient where human labor is still dominant; or the near-empty tropical Amazon Basin with the industrialized society of Northwest Europe and the United States. Thus we see that the utilization of natural resources differs widely from one region of the world to another.

The time element in resource-utilization is strikingly illustrated by the various stages of resource-use through which certain regions of the earth have passed. The United States offers a dramatic illustration of this differential use of environment in the changing pattern of land occupance. It shifted from: 1) the pre-European (Indian) utilization of the continent—varying from place to place, but providing only a meagre living for the less than one million inhabitants then spread throughout the land—to 2) the European era which combined an imported agricultural technique with the extraction of the indigenous resources—the former supplementing the native plants and fauna with imported seeds and domesticated animals—to 3) the present complex and highly industrialized society that utilizes every type of resource offered by the environment and that, further, through exchange and trade with outside areas, enriches this environment by im-

porting those things which are lacking. Today, with a population exceeding 170 million, the nation (*i.e.* territory that in the pre-European period provided but a poor existence to relatively few Indians who were spread over the three million square miles) is not over-populated, and Americans live at a higher standard than the nationals of any other state in the world.

The continent of Africa is another area where time and technology have brought a remarkable change in resource utilization. To cite a specific example: the "peculiar" characteristics of the land occupance of the indigenous people and of the Europeans in the Belgian Congo are distinct. This region, occupied by primitive native societies making superficial use of surface resources only, has, under European development, become one of the mineral source-centers of the industrial world. Likewise, Russia under the Czarist regime and the Soviets: the natural resources of the USSR were there at the time of the Czars but very few were developed, and Czarist Russia remained backward until its last years; under the Soviets, the same resources form the base for one of the industrial and political giants of the globe.

As Whittlesey points out, "It is unsafe to assume that economic and political regimes are tied to fixed regions determined by the distribution of resources. On the contrary, novel utilization of natural resources may shift the emphasis as well as alter the structure of economic and political life." . . . Nevertheless, at "any stage of technology the force a state can exert [and the extent and interrelations of economic life from which its political strength comes] are limited by the available natural resources —available in the primary sense of existing within the state boundaries, and available in the relative sense of being physically accessible and technologically usable."[1]

The Land Resource

The land resource is the first essential to any state. The natural resources of a state and

[1] Whittlesey, *op. cit.*, pp. 25 and 27.

its industrial capacity are a manifestation of a nation's economic strength. Without access to needed resources, therefore, a state is not in a position to become a world power. The first requirement is arable land, and control over the production and distribution of agricultural products has been one of the long-known motivations toward international contention.

In a former day, the mere process of exchange—trade—tended to exert this control for the state that held sway over the major routes of commerce, whether on land or on the sea, exercised a dominant role over resources and the products thereof. In a modern day, however, *entrepreneurs* have not been satisfied with controlling merely the lanes of commerce; they have gone to the sources of production and have secured control over the productive process itself. One of the resources in which this has been done is soils, and the means has been the establishment of the system known as *tropical plantation agriculture*. As complex as industry, plantation agriculture carries on research and employs the most scientific methods of plant culture. From these plantations in the tropics, a "stream of raw materials flows from the ends of the earth toward the great market centers of the industrial powers."[2] One of the major values of colonial possessions—and one of the reasons for their being greatly sought after during the nineteenth century—was found in this indirect form of benefit which obtained in peace and war. The worth of colonies was measured not according to the deficits which were incurred but in terms described above.

From the beginning of the system, plantation agriculture has been involved in politics. Although arable land is less localized than are mineral resources, the geographical distribution of cultivable soils in association with suitable climate is disparate. Further, the inadequacies (or adequacy) of the resources—land, mineral or animal—had usually not been ascertained at the time when the territorial domain of a state was being assembled and "territorial rights" established. Hence, if conditions suitable for fulfilling all of the economic (and political needs) of the state do not obtain within the territories of the nation itself, then the state must look to lands that are not yet taken up, or to the lands of less powerful, or perhaps more backward, countries. These nations desire the right of exploitation and development with as little discriminatory regulation as possible, whether in the cost of securing concessions, port dues, and the like. "Out of this difficulty power beats its way by laying down the terms under which the stronger nation will exploit raw materials"; ... demanding "access to new resources or to increased territory with sufficient raw materials to form a complement to the home country. The tendency to do this is strengthened ... by the geographical fact that the resources of greatest concern in the vegetable world are to be found in the tropics, where control is exercised by the white man not by settlement and crowding out of other populations, but by supervision and administration of natives through a limited numbers of whites."[3]

Exploitation of the richest resources of a land by a colonial or foreign power—with less benefit accruing to the nationals themselves than to the exploiting nation—may lead to protests on the part of other world powers (as in the case of the Belgian Congo in the late nineteenth century) or of the country itself. The exploited state or subject territory may try to drive out the foreign power (or interests). This happened recently in Guatemala with reference to the United Fruit Company and it is a continuing condition in French Algeria and British Kenya, all areas of concern to Western security.

Another aspect of "land" that may find its way into international politics is land-distribution. Where poverty and striking inequalities of living conditions exist within a state, there is always a breeding ground for malcontent leading, perhaps, to the acceptance of extremist ideas. Basically an internal problem, it may become international, due to the effect upon the

---

[2] Bowman, *The New World, op. cit.,* p. 12.

[3] *Ibid.,* p. 13.

world balance of power. The land problem of Italy—one of the Western states where communism has its strongest hold—is a case in point. Here, communism—or anything that holds out promise of a change from present conditions—becomes attractive. It is for this reason that, in areas where blocks of the population are discontented, the West feels least secure. The power of the Western Bloc could be considerably weakened, and even threatened, by a change of government in the above-named country—a change of government that might entail also a change of policy in international affairs.

Since World War I there has been an attempt within many European states to divide large land holdings (acquired by the state through the expropriation of crownlands, private and church estates, and the like) and distribute the land more equitably among the agricultural population. Such division of landed estates took place rapidly after 1918 in Central and Eastern Europe; more slowly in the Southwest. With the imposition of communism in the former areas, however, the small plots awarded the peasants were taken away as government leaders collectivized private holdings.

Not always is the economy of a country necessarily bettered by the division of large landed properties into small peasant holdings. Large acreage generally allows the use of more efficient methods. Further, not only is the agricultural problem within countries one of land tenure; it also involves the application of science to agriculture. The measure of productivity must, in the last analysis, be understood in terms of *output per working unit* and this depends upon a number of factors, including the application of modern techniques to agriculture and a vital people.

Land—and industrial resources—are the economic foundation for the role a state will play in world politics. As previously pointed out, where large populations press upon the land, either for reasons of population increase or because of lack of available area or suitable soils or both, the country may seek several means of alleviating the difficulty. These may

include, among others, migration, industrialization, improvement in agriculture, birth control, or aggression on other less-crowded or more fertile territories. Whatever the "land" situation within any state—whether as a base of power or a critical economic problem—directly or indirectly there is involvement in the geopolitical relations of the world.

Certain areas, because of the character of the climate that obtains within them (as the too hot and humid, too dry, or too cold areas), are eliminated as possible zones of great power. This is true because of their unsuitability to agricultural production on a scale that can support a large population; true, even though they may contain valuable mineral, forest, or fish resources—also foundations of power.

The material integrants of agricultural and industrial production do not determine entirely the power potential of a state. As stated before, population is also a factor. But a large population cannot be supported where it is not possible to carry on the basic means of subsistence, namely, cultivation of the soil. The two great belts of land stretching around the globe in the intermediate zones of the northern and southern hemispheres, where climatic conditions are suitable to great and continuous production and thus to the support of large populations, are also the two zones of the globe that contain all of the great powers of the modern world. The political *centers* of powerful state units are found within *these* belts while the extra-territorial regions of colonial and foreign exploitation are found within the climatically-marginal areas.

The Extractive Resources: Minerals

The substance of mineral resources cannot be increased. Minerals are in fixed supply due to the length of geologic time necessary to concentrate the ores and rocks within the earth's crust. Mankind's life on the globe is transient by comparison with this slow process which involves millions of years. Minerals are expendable resources. Circumscribed limits of supply give rise to intense and unmitigated striving on the part of political powers for the

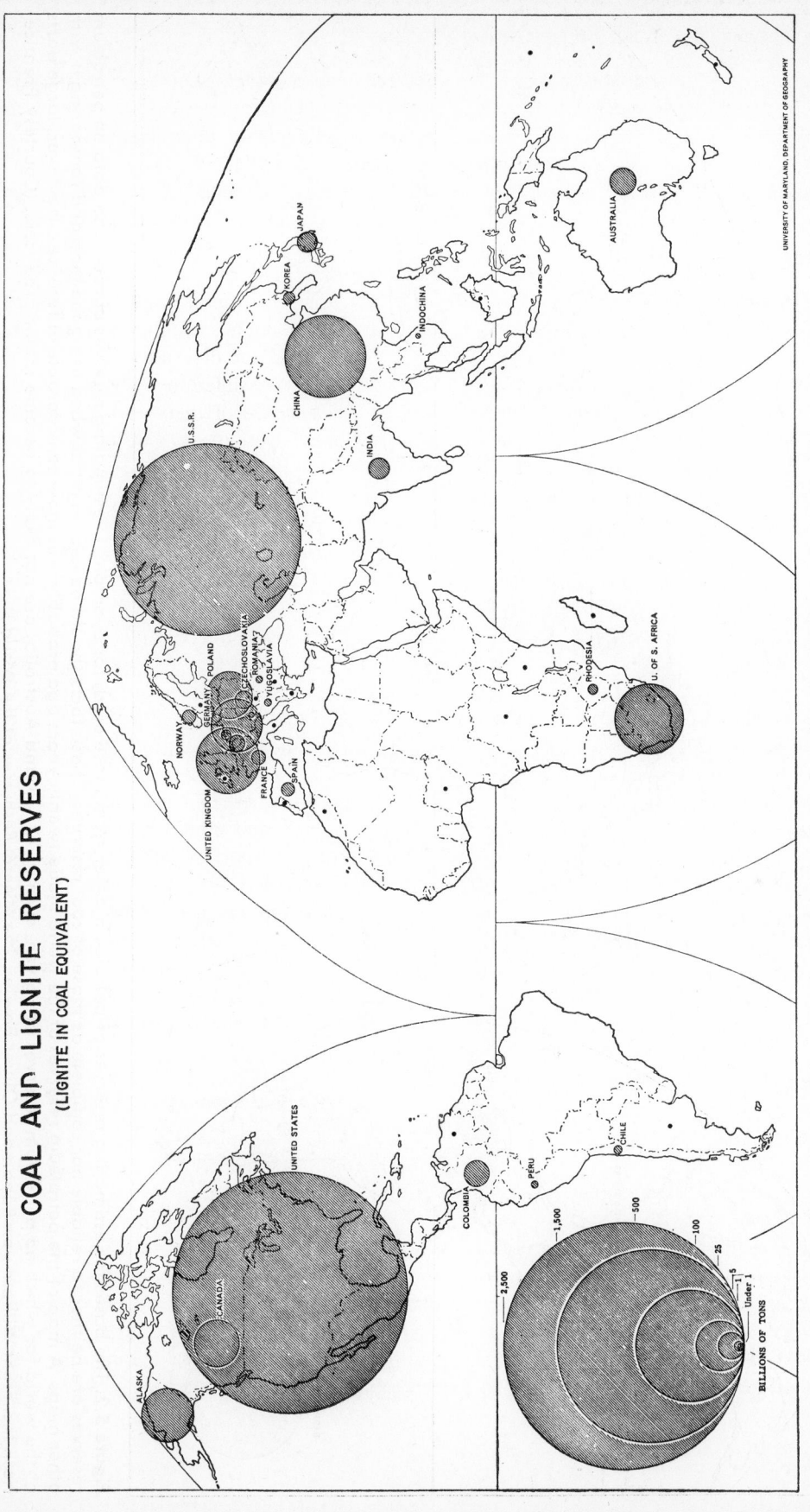

COAL AND LIGNITE RESERVES
(LIGNITE IN COAL EQUIVALENT)

UNIVERSITY OF MARYLAND, DEPARTMENT OF GEOGRAPHY

Figure 5.1. Coal reserves are distributed very inequably over the world, with North America, the USSR, western Europe, and China having most. While the extents of the reserves are not known exactly, there is no possibility of the upset of the world pattern because of new discoveries. The regions of known small reserves (Latin America, most of Africa, the countries of the Middle East, and areas such as the Canadian and Scandinavian shields) offer no such hope. (Courtesy Prentice-Hall, Inc. From William van Royen and Oliver Bowles, *The Mineral Resources of the World*.)

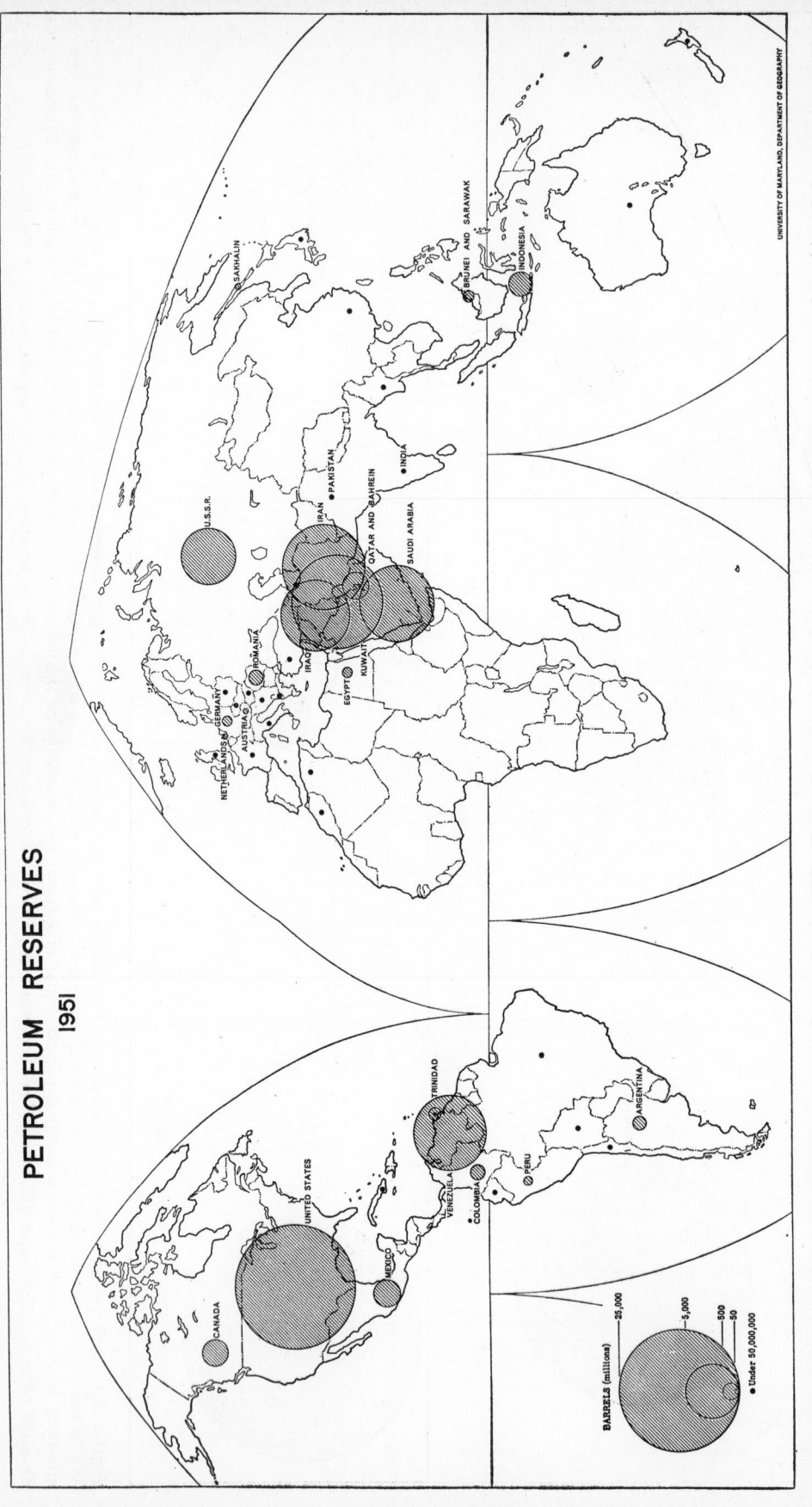

Figure 5.2. The bases for estimating reserves of petroleum differ from those used, for example, in estimating reserves of coal, and data on petroleum reserves are neither so reliable nor complete as those of coal reserves. These facts should be kept in mind when using the map and comparing it with other maps. A map of the petroleum reserves of the world made twenty years ago probably will show considerable differences. However, large parts of the world for which no petroleum reserves are given, such as Africa and Australia, are not likely to become major producers. (Courtesy Prentice-Hall, Inc. From William van Royan and Oliver Bowles, *The Mineral Resources of the World.*)

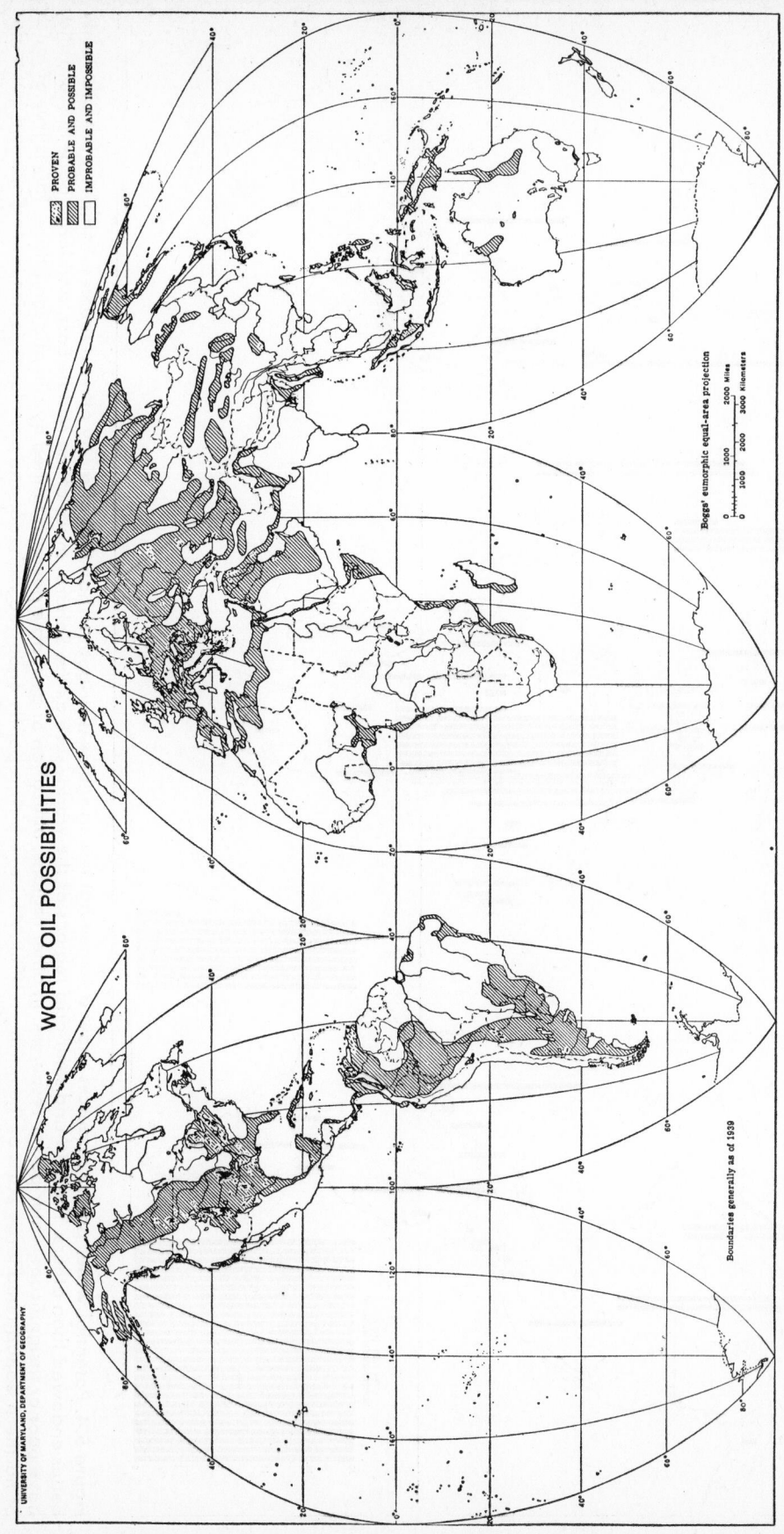

Figure 5.3. While data on world petroleum reserves are subject to constant revision, it is possible to make a map projecting possible petroleum occurrence. (Courtesy Prentice-Hall, Inc. From William van Royen and Oliver Bowles, *The Mineral Resources of the World.*)

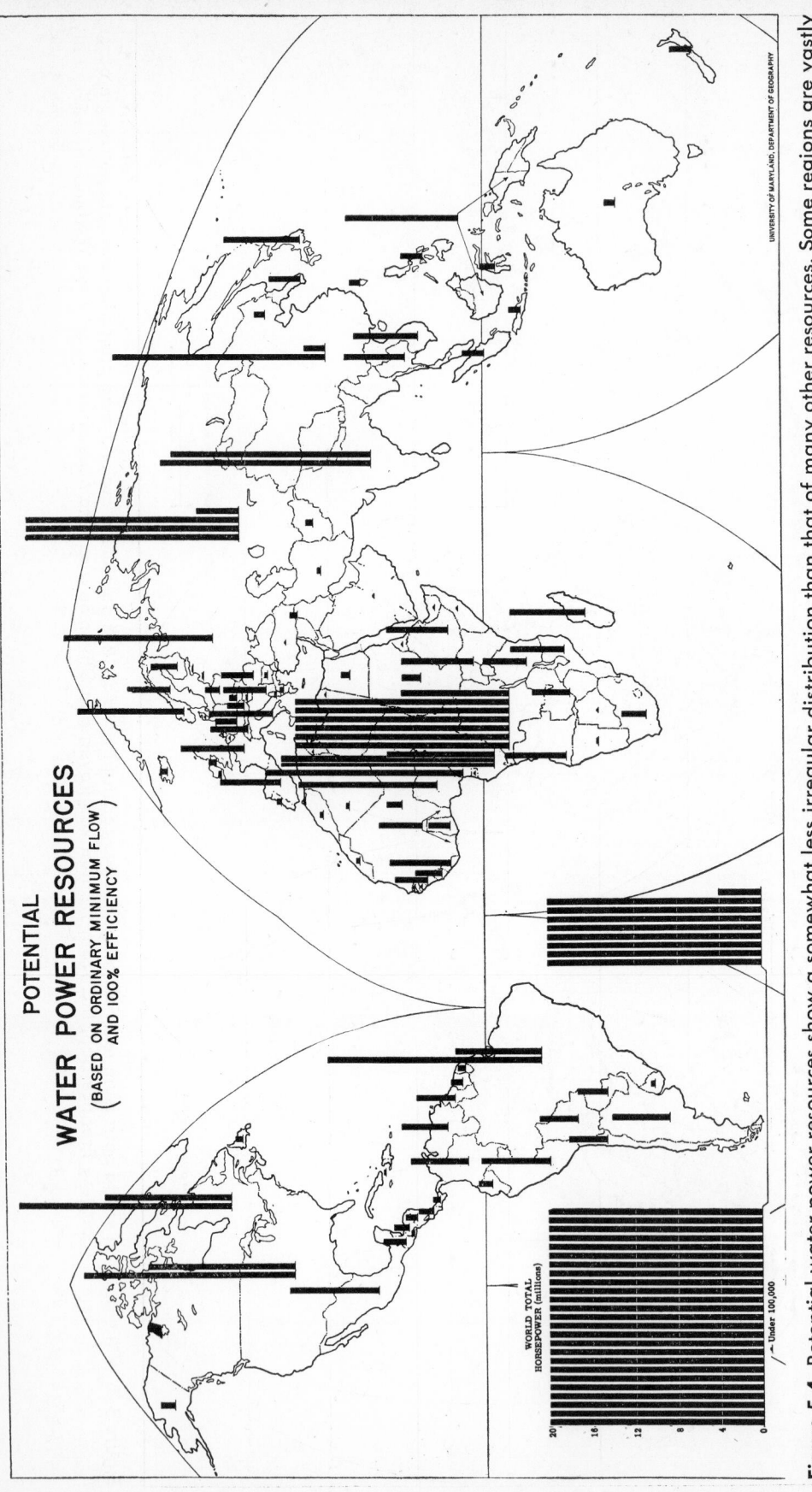

Figure 5.4. Potential water power resources show a somewhat less irregular distribution than that of many other resources. Some regions are vastly better endowed than others. The arid and semi-arid regions of the world, such as the Sahara, much of the Middle East, and large parts of Australia, have poor or insignificant water power resources. In other regions, utilization of available power is limited by climatic conditions. This is true of much of northern Canada and large parts of the northern USSR. Africa, which is poorly endowed with coal and petroleum, is rich in water power; but major resources are located in the equatorial portions of the continent where, up to the present, demand for power has been negligible. Latin America has important water power resources. The estimate for Brazil is probably on the low side. (Courtesy Prentice-Hall, Inc. From William van Royen and Oliver Bowles, *The Mineral Resources of the World.*)

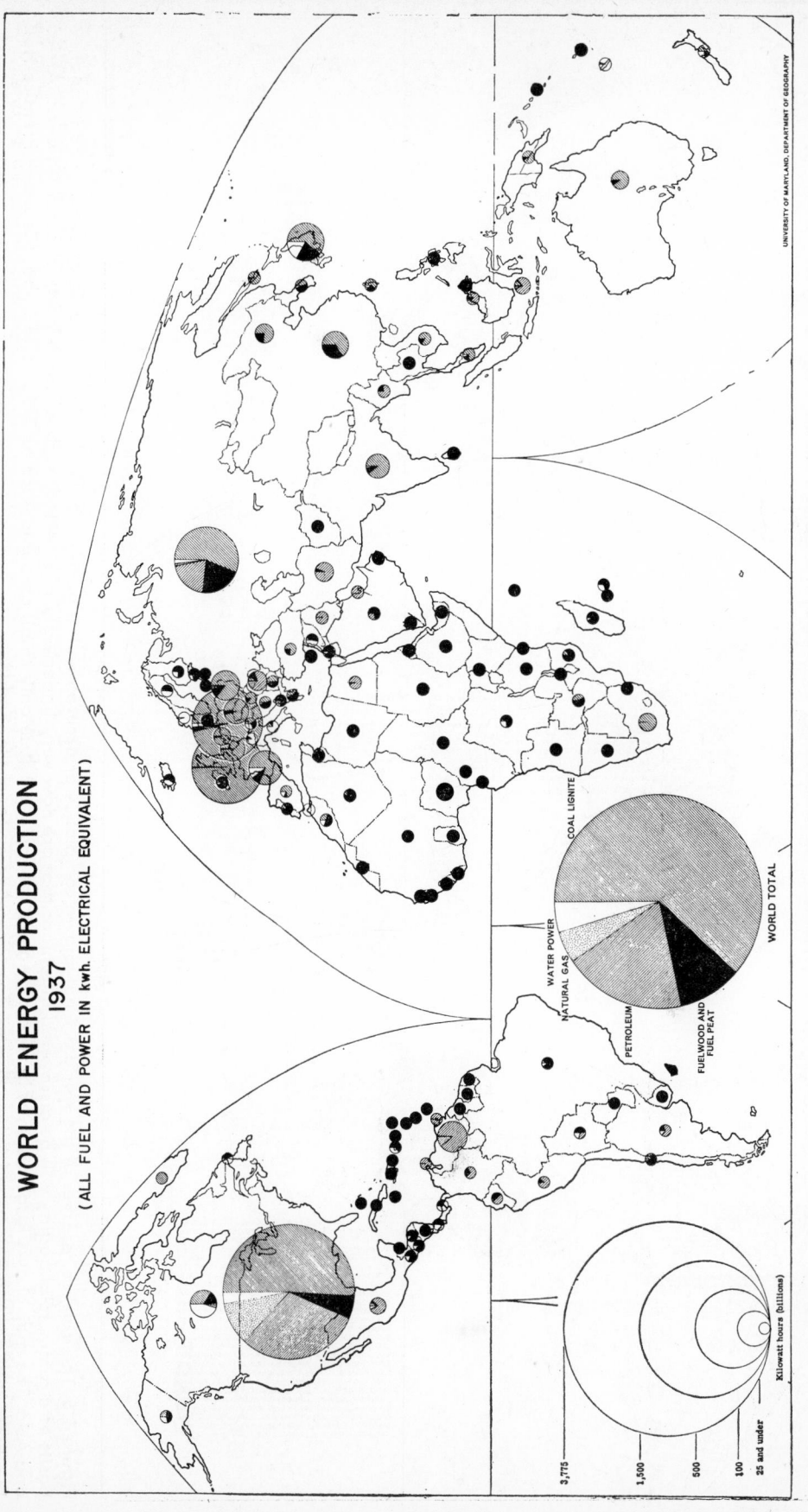

Figure 5.5. In many parts of the world, production of power still depends largely upon wood. In the more advanced countries, coal, petroleum, natural gas, and water power are used. The dominant positions of coal, petroleum, and natural gas in the world power picture is very evident. In only a few sections does water power represent any appreciable percentage of the total power generated. Examples are Norway, Switzerland, Sweden, Italy, Canada, Japan, and the Belgian Congo. (Courtesy Prentice-Hall, Inc. From William van Royen and Oliver Bowles, *The Mineral Resources of the World*.)

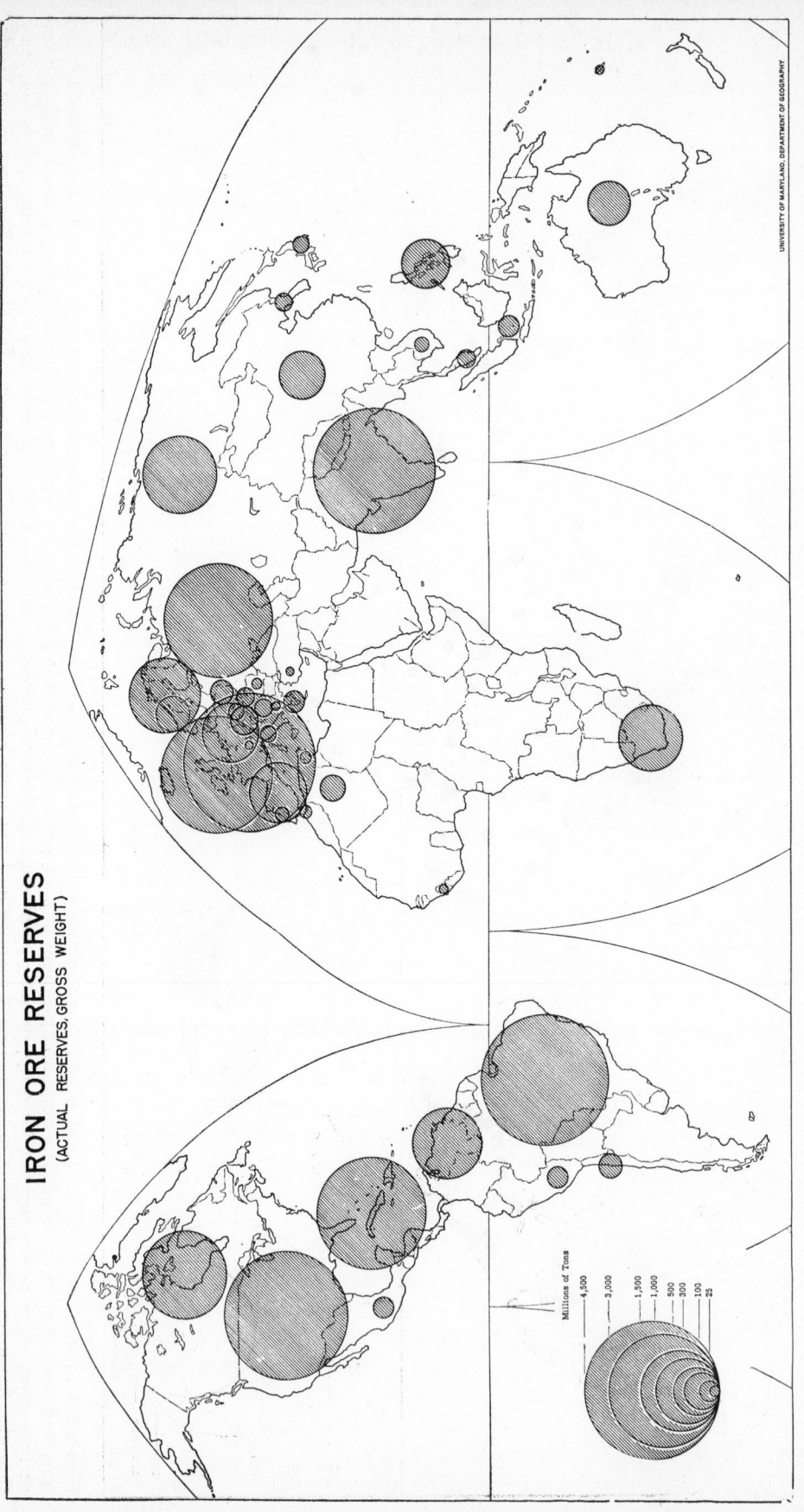

IRON ORE RESERVES

(ACTUAL RESERVES, GROSS WEIGHT)

Millions of Tons

4,500
3,000
1,500
1,000
500
300
100
25

UNIVERSITY OF MARYLAND, DEPARTMENT OF GEOGRAPHY

Figure 5.6. The iron ore reserves of the world are not known completely or accurately. It is quite likely that in the coming decades many additional deposits of a commercial quality will be discovered in regions that are now very imperfectly prospected, such as large parts of Latin America, Africa, and Asia. The map shows large reserves in several regions that now produce only small amounts, such as Brazil and Cuba. (Courtesy Prentice-Hall, Inc. From William van Royen and Oliver Bowles, *The Mineral Resources of the World*.)

64

territories where ore deposits are known—or thought—to exist, or for rights of exploitation. Owing to their character as the materials of foremost importance in the production of tools for industry and weapons for war, minerals have figured more conspicuously and continuously in world politics than have any other of the earth-resources: control of the minerals "in vogue"[4] at the time places a state in a superior position of potential power, making possible a rapid material progress and putting it, as well, in a position to build up military strength.

Fully half of the minerals ever mined have been brought to the surface in the past thirty-five years; further, the rate of utilization increases constantly. Fortunately, the earth is rich in useful resources—and man's ingenuity for searching them out and mining them grows greater every day.

Minerals play a unique role in the affairs of man, a condition accented by their extreme localization. The above statement becomes most obvious in the case of certain rare minerals such as nickel, 90 per cent of which is produced in one small area—the Sudbury district of Ontario, Canada; as tin, the greater proportion of which is derived from the Malay-Indonesian mines and from plateau Bolivia; as manganese, critical alloy-ore required for every ton of steel manufactured; as *commercial* (and therefore economically-exploitable) deposits of iron and copper, petroleum and coal.

The sharp localization of minerals is one of the peculiarities of this class of extractive resources. Because of this, many states have been unable to establish any large-scale manufacturing enterprises. Brazil's tremendous reserves of high-grade iron lie almost entirely undeveloped, used neither within the country nor, to any degree, for export because of their location. About three hundred miles in from the coast and separated from it by difficult terrain, the ore has been uneconomic to mine. At present Bethlehem Steel, which began exploitation

in 1949, takes out about one to three million tons annually.

At times, mineral deposits may lie outside of the ecumene but not too far distant to warrant development. In such instances, transportation lines will be put in serving not only to economically strengthen a nation but to integrate and tie together the state-territories as well. In this instance, the Lake Superior iron ore-Appalachian coal combine, on which is based much of United States steel production, is relevant—the Great Lakes Waterway carries more tonnage than any inland water route in the world and makes possible the huge production of the heavy-industrial products for which this nation is known.

The occurrence of minerals bears little relationship to the distribution of population. In fact, the disparity between population and mineral distribution is greater than is that of any other natural resource. The outstanding example is the incidence of industrial minerals relative to population in the Atlantic and Pacific basins: the North Atlantic is bounded on both sides by countries richly endowed (the United States, Britain, France and the Saar, Belgium, Germany) whereas those countries facing on the Pacific are much less fortunate, generally speaking. The reasons for this are to be found in the age of the mountain groups that border the two ocean basins; "young" mountains, such as are found along the Pacific, are relatively devoid of minerals.

No great contemporary power is supplied, within its own territories, with all of the essential—or even most vital—minerals. Certain states, as the United States and the USSR, approach most nearly the ideal of self-sufficiency. In order to achieve economic well-being and, even more especially, international power and prestige, a relatively adequate resource base is necessary, either to supply the natural resources themselves or to provide the capital for their purchase. Self-sufficiency for any state in this modern world is a false hope for modern society has many and complex needs. No single state possesses a territory sufficiently large and

---

[4] Whittlesey, *op. cit.*, p. 28.

environmentally varied to supply all of these needs.

The power of the modern state derives from its industrial strength. Directly important to the political and military strength of a nation are the industrial resources and development of that state. Tools produced from iron and steel are the essentials of Western machine civilization. Since iron and coal represent the basic fuels and raw materials for the manufacture of machines, their distribution is important. Both coal and iron ore are quite generally spread over the earth, but not always in commercial deposits and not always in combination: the raw materials for the modern iron-worker—large ore deposits within working range of huge deposits of good coking coal —are rarities. Those states in which they are found in combination have become the world's industrial leaders and those same states are the great powers of the geopolitical globe. Whether new mineral ores, as titanium, magnesium, bauxite, or new energy sources such as atomic power, will ever replace the two basic raw materials in the manufacture of machines no one can say. There is a new panorama of minerals that are presently coming into "vogue" and only time will tell how decisive and vital a role they will play.

Laws and Resources

Resource control includes both protection and scientific management—both functions of government. It is reasonable that any government should try to govern the exploitation of resources so that they will be utilized to best advantage for conservation and development. Where resource development is the internal affair of only one state, law provides the regulation; where there is more than one interested nation, treaty agreements establish the rule of law. The extractive industries subject themselves quite readily to such direction; agriculture presents more problems. It is usually only in the sale of agricultural products that government management (or direction) can be effectively introduced except in those nations where a dictatorship exists—as in the Communist states—and, even in these countries, the regulation of agricultural production appears to be the outstanding "management" problem.

Successful government direction of resource development requires that there be "harmony between the law and the environment."[5] Dutch law regulating commerce at the mouth of the Rhine River stimulates trade by establishing free ports, subsidizing shipping lines, encouraging international banking, and the like. The discriminatory rulings of the Egyptian Government over the Suez Canal, on the other hand— denying use of that strategic and necessary waterway to the shipping of Israel—was out of harmony with the geographic and economic realities of the Eastern Mediterranean area. Friction is inevitable under such circumstances.

Internal disharmonies between law and environment are to be observed in any number of instances in the regulation of resource use within the United States. The Homestead Laws of 1862 provided for the distribution of public lands in homesteads of one hundred sixty acres in an area that was marginal to anything but extensive grain-farming or ranching. The weaknesses of the law were soon displayed in the number of homesteaders who pulled up stakes and abandoned their homesteads. Humid-type agriculture cannot be practiced in areas where dry-farming methods should obtain. Later the size of the homestead was increased to three hundred and twenty acres, in 1877, for "desert" land and for "dry farming" land in 1910; to six hundred and forty acres in the "sand hill" country of Nebraska (1904), and for "stock-raising" homesteads in 1916. Some of the laws levying taxes on farm woodlots are also contrary to the best interests of this valuable source of timber supply, as was the lack of law at the time of the early uncontrolled and destructive exploitation of the white pine forests of New England and the upperlake states.

The need for "consonance" between law and natural habitat has become increasingly ap-

---

[5] *Ibid.,* p. 53.

parent during the past fifty years of high demand and consumption. It has led to the gradual shift from a policy of *laissez faire* in internal and international exploitation of natural resources to one of government (or international) supervision and control. Within nations evidence of this is to be observed in the enactment of conservation and land-planning programs. International conservation and planning is more difficult. Resource-grabbing usually predicates waste, and as long as the political world engages in a power struggle, the great states of the world are going to attempt to gain control over vital raw materials by one means or another—and these nations may be intransigent to regulation.

International cooperation must eventuate if the mineral resources of the globe are to be equitably divided among the earth's inhabitants. The necessity for international cooperation in the utilization of natural resources is a real one and will become more acute with time, particularly where the minerals are basic to key industries. Minerals "are diminishable assets; and their geographical distribution cannot be altered." Since no country is wholly self-sufficient in minerals, all states "ought to recognize both the immediate and ultimate advantages—and certainly the fairness—of the principle of agreement respecting their ownership and use"; and, since "a constant and basic source of supply" is a necessity to the maintenance of the modern type of civilization and present standard of living, it may be necessary, at some future date, to work out a pooling and rationing system to assure every nation its needed share of those basic resources that are most vital. The United States is by far the largest consumer of minerals in the world, and this country "has no more severe test of character to meet than that which it will face when it comes into real conflict with other powerful industrial nations over the sources of basic supplies of imported raw material, whether minerals or others. By the same token there is no more important question for the United States to watch in the conduct of others toward

itself."[6] The high demand of certain minerals by this country, which often causes a shortage to other importing states, has stirred up bitterness. With less than 10 per cent of the world's population, American industry consumes more than half of the world production of, among other minerals, petroleum, sulphur, manganese, iron ore, zinc, tin, and copper.

Industry and the Power of a State

Today, the effectiveness of national power is measured largely by capacity for the development of industry. In comparison to industrial might, any other single factor—population, precious metals, territory—becomes subordinate. Every political giant of the world is also an industrial giant. The political talkers of the world are heard because they are backed by the industrial might of their nations. The capacity for industrial development lies, basically, in the raw materials that are essential to that industry.

Raw materials are classified as strategic, critical, and essential to any country. Because the classification of any raw material is based on two factors—need to industry and source of supply—the same mineral may be classed differently in different states. Strategic materials (of which most are of mineral origin) are defined as those that are indispensable to the national defense, and which are supplied, in whole or in part, by sources outside the national domain. For these, during wartime, rigid conservation and distribution control are necessary. On the strategic list for the United States are antimony, manganese, tin, tungsten, chromium, mica, mercury. Those materials termed critical are characterized as those that are indispensable to national defense but the procurement of which in war is less of a problem than is that of strategic materials. Aluminum, asbestos, vanadium are among those placed on the critical list of this country. Essential materials are defined as those in which procurement is not a problem in time of war. For the United States, copper, iron and steel, mag-

6 Bowman, *The New World, op. cit.,* pp. 738-39.

nesium, and molybdenum, among others, belong on this list. These products are procurable within the state, the only obstructions to obtaining them being the manufacturing process or distribution agency.

A study of the maps of mineral occurrence indicates the dissimilarity in the distribution of strategic and critical minerals with that of the world industrial nations. Since industry is the key to power in the present day, it becomes obvious why the free flow of trade—founded on international concordance—is vital in this machine age.

Transportation and Trade

Communication facilities are inherent to the utilization of earth resources and, therefore, closely associated with the industrial centers of the world are the lines of transportation—the ocean routes, the airways, the internal waterways, railroads, and systems of highways—that link raw material to factory and finished product to market.

Ocean highways are of first magnitude within this system of connections. The North Atlantic Route between Northwest Europe and Northeastern United States is the busiest of the oceans' highways for it connects the most commercial and industrialized continents and, at present, the greatest market centers on the globe. It is probable that one-fourth of all of the world's merchant tonnage shuttles back and forth across the North Atlantic and, as for the movement of mail and passengers, the volume that moves along this route is greater than that of all of the other seaways combined. The Mediterranean-Asiatic-Australasian Route is second in importance passing, as J. Russell Smith puts it, "through the heart of the world."[7]

[7] It passes through the heart of the world in two senses: "First, in point of land mass served by it. . . . Second, because it reaches lands containing most of the world's population. . . . This great trade route connects America and Europe with Asia by way of the Mediterranean and Red Seas. . . ." J. Russell Smith and M. Ogden Phillips, *Industrial and Commercial Geography* (New York: Henry Holt & Company, Inc., 1946), p. 852.

A permanent basis for trade is found in the differing climates and differing cultural levels of various regions of the earth. The state whose economy is largely agricultural needs the products of the industrial world and vice versa; mid-latitude areas seek to exchange subtropical and tropical crops for grains, cotton, tools, etc.

Desire for trade led to the eventual opening of the oceanways. Once the waterways were traced, many nationalities quickly made commercial contacts which grew with the years. Although these enterprises were private, the governments of the marine states contributed to the enlargement of trade ventures by subsidizing exploration expeditions, chartering trading companies, providing protection to their nationals in foreign lands, and laying claim to the unclaimed territories on which their ships touched shore. In the latter regions, attempted domination by the outsiders almost inevitably touched off friction but the Europeans, more advanced in the use of weapons, were able to impose their power. Friction not only arose between the Europeans and the indigenes but also between the great colonial powers themselves—for possession of the untaken lands and resources of the new world that ocean navigation opened up.

The unfolding of the oceans through navigation and the discoveries of the vast new worlds beyond re-oriented the political world. States formerly oriented toward the interiors of land masses along roadways and rivers and canals now turned to face the seas. Those states unfortunate enough to lack ocean frontage or facing ice-closed waters became second-rate powers, and they have continued to be handicapped for the oceanways are the international "lifelines" that make possible the industrial civilization of our day.

Because seapower was an essential to exploration and acquisition of colonies during the four centuries preceding the present, seapower and colonial empires came to be inseparably linked: the great colonial powers were the seapowers of the past—Portugal, Spain, Nether-

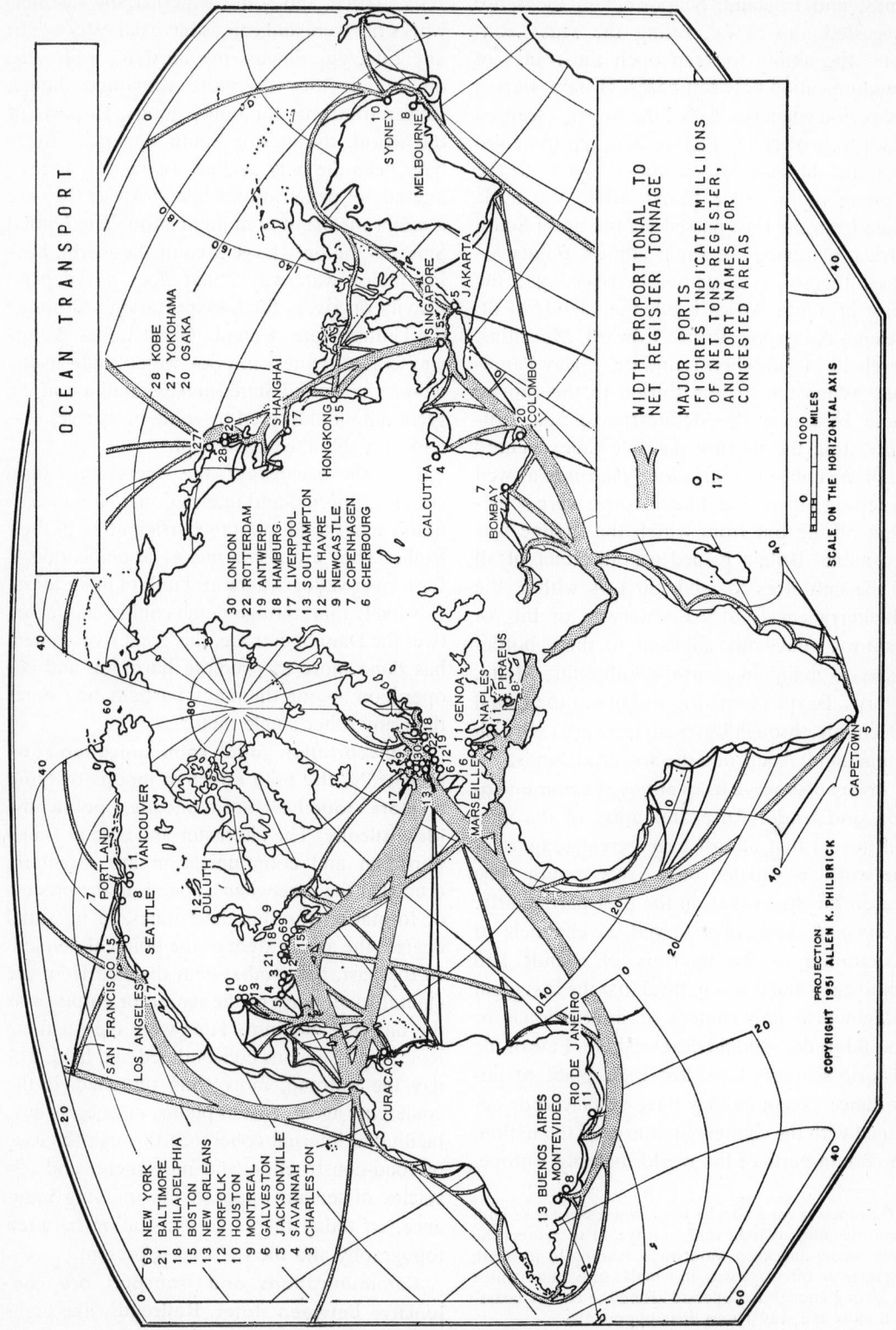

Figure 5.7.

lands, and England. Seapower[8] in the sense suggested above—*i.e.* ruling the seas—connotes the ability to keep open the routes of communication between bases. Britain, during the period when she "ruled the waves," secured bases to protect the lifeline between the colonies and the mother country. Previous to the opening of the Suez Canal, when the trade route from the East passed via the tip of South Africa, a number of small control points assured the ships of unmolested passage: the coast of South Africa itself, the islands of St. Helena, Ascension, Prince Edward, Mauritius, Seychelles (and others), and the Malay Peninsula. When the lifeline shifted to the shorter route, by way of the Mediterranean Sea, Britain, within the shortest possible time, secured *all of the control points along the route* as well as certain others that, like Socotra, were somewhat offside but from which the lifeline was pregnable. Britain gained a hold either of all of the entrances to, and narrows within, the Mediterranean-Red Sea waterway or bits of territory sufficiently adjacent to these bottlenecks to maintain control—Gibraltar, Malta, Cyprus, Egypt (virtually, and hence the Canal which runs through Egyptian territory), British Somaliland, Aden, and the Socotra Islands.

Rivers also serve as avenues of communication and trade. An examination of the map will reveal that almost every great seaport of the world is situated on a river mouth. The reason for this is that, in the past particularly, rivers and waterways served as channels of penetration to the interiors of islands and continents, and it was natural that the first great settlements—and centers of international or coastal trade—should develop here. Few of the historic seaports have lost their place of importance except as they have advanced or declined with the changing patterns of the nation. In certain parts of the world, notably Europe,

Asia, Africa, and South America, the vast networks of rivers and canals have delayed—or at any rate, cut down—the need for railroads, offering as they do more economic though slower transport for bulky goods. In parts of the world, as interior South America, rivers have been the only avenues (except by foot or animal) of penetration while in Africa they are a major means of communication. The United States is the only large area of the world, having major waterways, that does not depend heavily on rivers for transportation. Although the United States-Canada Great Lakes Waterway is the greatest interior water route in the world, the United States makes small use of the great potential offered by some of its river systems, notably the Mississippi.

Like the oceanways, the river- and canal-systems, internal and international, are an economic asset to all nations participating in their traffic. They are also a means of unification—for a river valley is a natural unit of integration. It is likely that, though much conflict has arisen over the Danubian trade, this great river system has done more to promote harmony and cooperation among the many participating states than any other single factor.

Transportation and communication are, physically, the only effective means of tying a state together—economically, politically, idealistically. The character and ease of transportation and communication are singularly crucial at the time when a state is in the process of formation for this determines, in no small degree, the areal extent of the political domain. In the past, the road-system that led from the capital to all parts of the nation or empire was the unifying medium. Thus were the far-flung Roman possessions consolidated and held. Today the railroad, more than the road, is the coalescing agent. Just as plains, in an early day, facilitated internal coherence through the ease of road-construction and movement, and obstacles of terrain opposed the unifying influence, so today the same association between topography and the railroad is present.

Communications and transport are conjunctive between states. Railroads, like high-

---

[8] Seapower may also be used in a lesser sense with dual meaning, as indicating ability: 1) to protect the home coast and keep waterways, leading to it, open; 2) wage an offensive war, in which sense a navy must be strong enough to "operate along the enemy coast" and close the seaways to their opponents.

ways and oceanways, serve to foster the need of cooperation between states and, therefore, international collaboration and understanding. They may also present obstacles not found in any of the other means of transportation and communication—namely, the "gauge" of the railroad in one state may not be the same as that in another. Although not an insurmountable barrier, the differing gauges, at times, require transshipment of goods at frontiers, an unnecessary and wasteful expense. The problem of varying railroad gauges has been greatest in Europe but, as time passes, the European railroad system is becoming more integrated. Nations have come to realize that the expeditious flow of trade between states is far more conducive to national well-being than are political and technological restrictions and barriers.

Modern methods of communication and transport annihilate distance. As the means of transportation and communication have increased the speed with which goods, people, and ideas can be transferred from one place to another, they have amplified their cohesive powers, nationally and internationally. It took months for the Russian princes to ride to the seat of their Mongol overlords in Eastern Asia to pay the demanded tribute; it was an often death-dealing journey to go by boat from the United States Atlantic seaboard, via the Isthmus of Panama, to the Pacific Northwest—and one that nearly caused secession of the Western territory from the Union; it took months of stupendous effort and ingenuity on the part of Hannibal to enter Italy via the Alps. It took, in other words, extensive time, tremendous effort, at times nearly unbearable cost and, frequently, many lives to accomplish in the past what today is expedited, by modern means of transportation and communication, with a minimum of effort in minimal time. With the telephone, telegraph and cable, radio and television, and the airplane surmounting all barriers, the final necessary link to complete unification has been forged. This can act as a promise or a threat, internationally.

Trade as a Political Weapon

In peacetime the great powers are engaged continuously in an armaments race or in a struggle over economic objectives. These contests for power represent international rivalries for economic and industrial dominance. For the achievement of their ends, states frequently use trade as a political weapon. It was for the attainment of economic superiority that the concept of the closed seas persisted and that the scramble for "exploitable"[9] colonial holdings took place. To be "exploitable" a territory must be dependent rather than independent. As the colonies of European states emancipate themselves from their positions of dependence to the status of independent countries, the natural resources of the areas yet available for exploitation become generally minor by comparison with what obtained at the commencement of World War II. This condition undoubtedly will accentuate the trend toward using trade as a political weapon. For example, the power of the neutral, oil-rich states of the Middle East lies in the potential of petroleum as a bargaining weapon.

Trade barriers, such as tariffs, frequently cause ill-feeling among nations. Although it is true that import duties may be needful to protect minority economic groups within a state, it may well be that the aroused emotions offset the advantages. Further, such obstructions to commerce may be "used" by a rival country: the latter may remove its own trade barriers and negotiate to draw up mutual trade agreements that permit the free flow of materials between itself and other states. All this acts not only to the economic detriment of the former nation but may lower it in the regard of otherwise-friendly powers as well. This, undoubtedly, has been part of the idea behind the trade proffers of the USSR to the many states with whom it has negotiated commercial treaties and to whom it has offered economic assistance.

---

[9] Whittlesey, *op. cit.*, p. 78.

Transportation and Communication in an Air-Age

The significance of air power, in peacetime and in war, cannot be disputed. It is well, however, to examine its importance not only in terms of the strategy but also in the light of economics and geography (the latter qualifying the exercise of all power).

From the time when man first began to make the sea his roadway, the geopolitical roles of the various maritime areas—Atlantic, Pacific, Indian and Polar—have differed the one from the other. For almost five hundred years, the Atlantic has been the great thoroughfare between Europe and America. The Pacific and Indian Oceans have opened lanes of ocean traffic among the states bordering on their waters for an even longer period. Although heroic attempts were made by men of several nationalities to find the Northeast Passage by sailing the ice-blocked Arctic seas, climate and the limits of technological knowledge and science kept that maritime zone one of the greatest hindrances to the conquest of the globe. Along with Antarctica and the Sahara Desert, the Arctic lands and waters have remained the most extensive barriers on the earth. Although Soviet ice-breakers and freighters push their way through these northern seas in increasing numbers to connect the western and eastern portions of that vast nation, the Arctic passageway can never have the significance of a Panama or a Suez Canal because climatic obstructions are too formidable. The Arctic, in place of acting as another bond between the Old and the New Worlds (as have the Atlantic and Pacific Oceans), has functioned until the present as a nearly insurmountable obstacle to man's ingenuity.

Air transportation provided man with a new means of overcoming the barrier-nature of the marginal places on the globe. And yet it is unlikely, except in terms of military strategy, that air power can ever give the polar maritime "front" the importance of the other two great waterfronts—the Atlantic and Pacific. Population numbers and a rising standard of living and technology might well bring a change in the relative importance of the Atlantic, Pacific, and Indian Oceans as roadways of commerce, but that air transport can place the air or sea routes of the Arctic wastelands economically on a plane with either those of the Atlantic or the Pacific is not to be expected. Nor can the freight-plane, likely, ever compete with the great ocean freighters or railroad carriers as a means of transporting the millions of tons of goods that move between countries and continents in a single year.

In the most conservative view, it will be years before Arctic airborne trade will be able to compete with the sea-borne traffic of the two great commercial oceans—if ever. There are several reasons for this. While it is a fact that 1) the shortest distance between two points in the northern hemisphere follows a great circle route (and at times directly over the pole) and 2) that stratospheric flying conditions in polar areas are little, if any, more severe than over mid-latitude regions, nevertheless, climate still remains a tremendous obstacle. Airplanes must have bases, for "air power" is not planes alone but planes plus bases, and bases must be supplied by auxiliary land and sea routes. Therefore, it is highly unlikely that transportation across the poles will ever equal anything but a small proportion of that which moves over the oceans in time of peace *and* war. The relative cost of transportation and quantity of goods transportable per surface carrier unit counterbalances the advantages of speed and distance in air-freight haulage. As for small products of light weight and high value, and passenger travel, this is quite another matter. Atomic-powered planes, if they become feasible, could take away the relative advantage that surface-carriers now possess, however.

Planes follow the pressure patterns of the earth's atmosphere instead of the great circle. It is customary to expect that—granted political obstacles are absent—air transport routes will take the great circle routes, *i.e.* the shortest lines of travel between the two points. Instead, navigators try to find the level where the winds are favorable—where there are "tail winds."

Although aircraft are still limited as to the upper level at which they can fly, usually they are able to find a flow of air at some level that will be favorable to their flight even if the surface flow of air is unfavorable. In other words, they seek ribbons of wind in which the aircraft can drift, and which have the dual advantage of increasing the flight speed—at times markedly—and of saving on fuel. With the growing importance of jet aircraft, the latter is of untold significance because of the "strict fuel limitations of the jet engine." Weather bureaus now plot, several times daily, the pattern of the flow of air throughout the atmosphere up to 25,000 feet elevation and send this information out by teletype and radio for the use of not only the pilots of commercial and military aircraft, but private navigators as well.

The most dramatic of the ribbons of wind are the high altitude phenomena known as "jet streams," veritable "rivers of wind." These fast-moving streams of air "are usually encountered between 15,000 and 40,000 feet. They are characterized by the *jet stream* [which is] normally embedded within an already fast-flowing stream of winds. The jet stream is the 'ribbon' where the air flow has the greatest velocity, normally about 115 to 175 miles per hour.

"Pan American World Airways has already begun using the jet stream for non-stop Stratocruiser flights from Tokyo to Honolulu during the winter months . . . Here the jet stream is as much as 300 miles wide and six miles deep, and its use at 25,000 feet . . . has already eliminated a refueling stop and saved Pan American over eight hours of flying time for the 4000-mile trip."[10]

In no country today is air power self-sufficient in terms of transporting all needed materials by air. The areas of densest rail and ocean nets have also the densest network of airlines. The planes are tied, in a direct sense, to their bases and, indirectly, to the oil fields that supply their fuel. They are able to rise from the earth only because trucks and ships and

railroads have moved fuel and lubricants and supplies from depots and docks. It is necessary to accept "land power" as a fundamental fact in continental or naval warfare; air power is an auxiliary employed to clinch decisions on land and on the sea. It must, it would appear, play the same role in peacetime affairs. The three aspects of conveyance—land, water, air—however, should be welded into one cohesive system of effective transportation.

The telegraph, cable, and radio are indispensable adjuncts to the modern transportation system. Just as the telegraph developed to aid the railroad in dispatching trains, and the cable in maintaining contact between ship and shore, so the radio is a requisite to the dispatching and contacting of airplanes. Further, as the telephone and telegraph become the communication connection between people close to telephone facilities or railroads, so the radio has become the means by which people in remote areas are able to communicate with each other.

Transportation and communication facilities represent elements of power, and are implements of government. Among these, the radio functions uniquely as a "weapon" for it is utilized by all of the great powers as an instrument of propaganda and, not infrequently, as a means of undermining the position of a rival state.

The full importance of air transport and such newer means of communication as radio, television, radar, etc., has not yet been told. The future will gauge this. Spaceships are a coming reality, to mention but one anticipated future development now in the blueprint stage. The importance of communication and transportation—including air power—to the states of the world is demonstrated in the fact that these aspects of state development take precedence over many other national efforts in the powerful nations. Whatever the relative role of any particular medium of transportation or communication, the power of the state will always be closely identified with these indispensable, cohesive forces.

Aviation has changed the world's outlook. The airplane has attained a position of great

---

[10] *Air Navigation,* Air Science 3, Vol. VII (AROTC), pp. 128-29.

military importance since 1940 and, with the end of the war, as a vehicle of passenger transport—undoubtedly because of the speed and convenience of air passage. It is necessary to go back to the days of Columbus to find a like revolution within the geographical context. The discovery of the New World turned the faces of nations from the interior of continents toward the sea; the airplane has turned them from the seas that lie to the east and the west toward the north—and skyward.

The coming of aircraft has completely re-oriented man's thinking in reference to the size of the world and the physical relationship of one part of the globe to another. Already important effects have been felt upon the orientation of national defense, economics, politics, outlook. The year 1955 saw the first (SAS) passenger plane fly from the Pacific Northwest to Scandinavia via the polar route. It took the airplane to direct man's attention to the lands to the north and to make nations realize the proximity of other peoples in the northern half of the globe.

6

The State

The characteristic unit of the political pattern of the earth is the sovereign state, the supreme authority[1] in the conduct of its internal affairs and its relations with other nations. Although international bodies are created for the purpose of dealing with certain aspects of inter-state problems, it is the national unit that bears the final responsibility—and right—for the security and development of its own territories.

It appears that, because a human is born within a country—and is usually reared within the same political unit—he grows up with a strong feeling of "nationality." Even the postwar urge toward the coalescence of political units, observed in so many facets of international relations in the last decade (Benelux, NATO, etc.), at times chills as certain states draw back from this possible relinquishment of national authority into shells of non-participation.

The tendency toward the international integration of political units constantly advances, nonetheless. It may be that the airplane and recent innovations in communication have been instrumental in this trend for, throughout history, periods of political unification or disintegration have, in the main, been coincident with those eras when transportation and communication were either well developed, or backward, hazardous, and expensive. The status of political units is constantly in flux, diminishing or expanding, changing form, coalescing, even disappearing. Nevertheless, the state is still the unit of highest political authority.

The state is distinctive in that it has a territorial base. The territory of a state is that portion of the globe within the bounds of which it exercises supreme authority, administering the people and resources therein. So dependent

---

[1] When two or more nations enter into a treaty, they each agree that the provisions of the treaty shall be the rule of law among them. This may mean giving up a certain amount of sovereignty, but such forfeiture of rights arises out of the consent of the states. The Constitution of the United States is an excellent example stating that it—and "treaties made pursuant thereto"—shall be the law of the land.

It is to be seen, then, that sovereignty does reside in the state but that, out of the consent of the state, international law becomes superior to national law.

is the welfare of a state upon maintaining un-questioned authority over this particular sec-tion of terrain that to have another nation infringe upon it may menace national existence as an autonomous political unit.[2] Thus is ex-pressed the *concept of territoriality*.

The character of the territorial base exerts a strong influence upon the nature of the political unit itself and, also, upon its ex-ternal relations with other states. The charac-ter of a national entity is directly contingent upon the physical traits of the domain. Size influences relative power; and natural re-sources bear a relation to potential population density and the economic framework, both factors affecting the formulation of national and international policies. Latitudinal location and position with reference to maritime and continental masses contribute not only the basic climatic pattern, with all of the attendant influences upon the many facets of national living that this implies, but also determine to a large degree proximity to industrial and trans-portation centers (and hence, foci of power), zones of international friction, and vicinal loca-tion (which characterizes the locale in terms of potentially hostile neighbors). Such location, therefore, bears directly upon the economic welfare and territorial security of the nation.

Along with size and location, climate and topography enter in to exert several peculiar effects upon state relations. Topography contri-butes to the strength or weakness of a nation by its influence upon the usability of the terrain for agriculture and upon the internal coherence and unity. Climate circumscribes the cultivabil-ity of the territorial base and, along with topog-raphy, effects coherence and unity in the limits it may set upon transportation. More than any other physical factor, climate exerts an effect upon agricultural productivity and, to a lesser degree, qualifies the structure that the economy of the state may take. Thus, unmistakably though indirectly, it also conditions foreign relations.

---

[2] "Integrity over the land," therefore, would seem to define national security.

THE STRUCTURE OF A POLITICAL UNIT

The geopolitical pattern that the many states of the world combine to impose over the earth is patchy in design—in the variety of sizes, shapes, and locations; in the realities of power —potential and actual; in economies, popula-tions, etc. But, anatomically speaking, each of the states bears resemblance to every other in the pattern of the interrelated and overlapping parts of which it is composed. They include the nuclear area, the ecumene, the capital, the constituent units, the frontier, boundaries, and colonial possessions and dependencies.[3]

The Nuclear Area

All states that evolve naturally germinate in and about nuclear areas. Italy grew from Rome which was cradled in the valley of the Tiber; China spread from a tiny zone in the Wei Ho area around the present city of Sian;[4] the United States grew from the several nuclei of the Atlantic coastal region; and England and France expanded, respectively, from the Thames Basin and the Île de France, centers where the nations where born and nurtured, and from which they spread.

The Ecumene

The ecumene is defined as that section of the country that is most densely settled and has the closest network of transportation and commu-nication (and, hence, is generally also the most industrialized). It usually includes the nuclear area within its bounds as is true of France where the Paris Basin, including the Île de France area, is the major center of national ac-

---

[3] In an extended sense, *Raum* can also be in-cluded. This reveals the state in its many varied and intricate associations with other portions of the earth, those economic and geopolitical interrelationships of state to state, and state to region: *i.e.* the manifesta-tion of state through economic contacts, missionary efforts, diplomatic alignments, etc., whereby it extends its influence.

[4] The *ecumene* of China, however, is a broken one composed of three river valley regions: the Si Kiang delta area in the south, the valley of the Yangtze Kiang from its mouth along the whole course up to and including the Red Basin in which Chungking is located, and the lower Hwang Ho district.

tivity; it holds in the United States, for the eastern region of the nation is the commerical and industrial leader; it obtains in England, the ecumene of which spread from the nuclear center to include the Liverpool-Manchester district and the Apennine littoral. Nevertheless, such is not always the case: the ecumene of modern Italy is not the peninsular portion but the heavily industrialized and cultivated Po Valley in the north. (The administrative center, however, has not shifted from Rome.) In such an instance, we say the ecumene has migrated. The ecumene may also shift or spread as a state expands its territory. For example, the ecumene of the United States has enlarged from the seaboard area to include virtually all of the region east of the Mississippi.

Because it supports a relatively dense population, there is the implication that the ecumene is also the most richly endowed. This is true in most instances. At times the base may consist of a single resource or be favorable to the carrying on of only a limited number of activities—as in the La Plata Basin of Argentina, where terrain, climate, and vegetation make cultivation and animal-raising the paramount adjustments. On the other hand, the natural potential of the ecumene may include a number of favorable factors that contribute to the carrying power of the area. The physical attributes of the American northeast—the fuel potentials in water power, coal and oil, the rich soils combined with a climate suitable for agriculture, the forests, and a favorable situation for commerce—make it one of the most highly endowed regions in the world.

The Capital

Since the capital is the administrative center of the state, accessibility is an advantage. The capital is usually found within the nuclear area or ecumene—or both. Where the ecumene has migrated from the original nuclear core, as in the case of Italy and Yugoslavia, the capital is likely to remain in the "cradle" area of the state, offside from the contemporary center of activity. The contemporary ecumene of Yugoslavia, and the capital, Belgrade, are both far

removed from the original nucleus in the Serbian mountain fastnesses. Or the capital may shift with the ecumene to the richer, more populous district. Occasionally, the capital will take an atypical location, as that of Canberra, in Australia, where the governmental center is located midway between two nuclear areas; or Ottawa, Canada, placed centrally between discordant nationality groups. At other times, an effort may be made to locate the capital in a place having centrality of area (rather than of population as it would have if situated within the ecumene) so as to be conveniently accessible from all parts of the country, as Madrid, Spain. There are many instances where the nuclear area has remained within the ecumene and hence, the capital is located in both, as in the cases of London, Moscow, Paris. There is a tendency for a capital to adhere to the nuclear area.

Occasionally the relative location of the capital shifts, with change in the territory of the nation, without an actual change in the site. Thus Vienna, formerly quite centrally located within the Austro-Hungarian Empire, occupies a pregnable location in the northeast corner of Austria. In a few instances a change in regime or policy in government may move the seat of administration from one place to another—for reasons of prestige (of a regime), or security, or centrality of location, etc. Peter the Great built St. Petersburg on the mouth of the treacherous Neva River as his "window to the west"; China, during the past war with Japan, shifted the capital several times—from Peking to Nanking to Chungking and back to Peking again—for security reasons.

The functions performed within the capital cities vary from country to country. Where the city was built to serve primarily as a center of national government—as Versailles, Washington, D.C., St. Petersburg, and Canberra—huge sums of money have been spent to beautify the city, and the cities reflect the benefits that their favored political position gives to them. Vienna, reconstructed by Franz Josef as the capital of his great empire, has one of the most impressive avenues in the world in the Ringstrasse, located on the site of the old walls that formerly surrounded the inner town.

Usually the sole function of such capitals will be that of government. This is not true of Vienna, however, which carries on the important functions of industry and commerce. St. Petersburg is also an exception to this for the Russian city was conceived by Peter the Great not only as his governmental center (and a monument to himself) but as the first port of Russia—first in the sense of time, for until then Russia had had no outlet to the sea. Though a port and industrial center today, it still is reminiscent of its former glorious days as the Russian capital in the magnificent structures that made up the palaces and churches of the early era. Numerous other capital cities have government as only one of several functions performed—as London, which is a world port and manufacturing center as well as capital, as are Paris and Moscow.

The Constituent Units of the State

The state is comprised of constituent parts that divide and subdivide into smaller and smaller entities each of which, like the nation itself, embodies space. These units range in size and authority all the way from districts (that are entirely administrative) to independent states such as the dominions of the Commonwealth of Nations. Between these two extremes are intermediate types with varying degrees of legal power, as: the states of the United States of America and the cantons of Switzerland, both at one time sovereign units, now members of a federal union wherein, although they still hold some authority, the degree and kind has changed with the passage of time; the counties of England and provinces of France, subordinate to their central governments, but divisions full of tradition and cultural unity. The former still exist, but the French *province* has been superseded by the contemporary *department* which cuts across provincial boundaries. However, to the Frenchmen, the provinces remain: a Frenchman from Brittany is still a Breton, from Normandy, still a Norman, and thus it will likely always be, for these political subdivisions grew up out of cultural cores that had developed in homogeneous environments.

The ancient French provinces corresponded more or less with units of the natural environment. Political subdivisions that conform to such regional alignments of nature will tend to retain their individual character longer than will those showing no such coincidence; individuality will likewise be more pronounced. For example, Kentucky with its bluegrass country, California of the dry subtropical climate, semi-tropical Florida, all stand out with an individuality that gives each of them a character distinctive from that of any other area in the United States. In other sections of regional unity, as in the northwest or the northeast, where the political components are small and clearly subdivisions of the more extensive region, the people are likely to regard themselves as being from the Pacific Northwest or New England.

Problem Areas

From the nuclear area and the ecumene extends the remainder of the "territory" of the state. It is, except in the case of very small countries, composed of a number of differentiated geographical regions. This outer portion of the nation is usually less well integrated in terms of transportation, and the feeling of "nationality" may be less strongly felt. The maintenance of such regional diversity within the unity of the state is made possible by a transportation and communication system that integrates the differentiated regions without obliterating their distinctiveness.

Diversity between regions usually has its base in contrasts in the physical environment or in natural barriers that produce a degree of isolation. Some regions are so unlike the other portions of a state or present such difficulties to effective development and utilization as to constitute "problem areas." The desert regions of Australia, the Amazon Basin of Brazil, the North Country of Canada and of the USSR, all are so vast and so handicapped by nature as to constitute, in a certain sense, dilemmas rather than assets—or areas with latent assets—to the particular states within whose territories they lie.

Sometimes the proximity (within a state) of a region of meagre resources to one more richly endowed will act to retard the development, accentuate the marginal condition, or even create a problem area in the poorer district. The most striking examples of this are perhaps to be found in the American Midwest. The trek of people to the Pacific Northwest was made up in large part of those from the Great Plains area, a region of marginal farming country. Although the "dust bowl" became a problem area through careless utilization by man, the marginality became accentuated when thousands abandoned their land during the drought period of the mid-thirties for regions where less risk obtained.

Another problem area is that associated with zones of friction where thorny political issues arise constantly or intermittently to harass the government. Such trouble spots are likely to be found where islands of discontented minorities —racial, religious, or of foreign nationality— reside within the state, or in the frontier and boundary regions along the margins of the country. Here, more than one nation is involved for periphery zones are typically regions of population mixing rather than zones of sharp separation. Further, deposits of minerals, streams potential to water power development and irrigation and the like, will at times cause friction and even hostilities between states— as between Germany and France over Alsace and Lorraine—or require endless negotiations to keep the problems in hand. The United States-Mexican Commission, that is at all times on hand to deal with problems relative to the disposition of the waters of the Rio Grande River, is a case in point in the latter instance.

Because the frontier-boundary areas are along the peripheries of the state they are usually less well integrated with—and therefore possibly less securely held than—the rest of the country. The extent to which the national government is centralized and holds authority over the various portions of its territory reflects in the degree of security that the boundary areas provide as well as in their character.

Territorial Interests: Colonies, Mandates, and Other Dependent Territories

For as long as political history has obtained, the great powers of the world have tacitly agreed among themselves on the right of states to carve out and maintain empires of colonial territories in the "backward" and "unclaimed"[5] areas of the globe. Every European nation with frontage on the Atlantic Ocean, as well as states of other continents (notably Japan, the United States, and Australia) had a part in the territorial expansion that took place during the four centuries preceding World War II. When, toward the end of the last century the last, and more marginal, of the unclaimed fragments of the earth were partitioned among three great European powers—Germany, France, and Italy—there could have been and was no real objection.

No less than twelve European states have, or have had during the past one hundred years, vast colonial domains on other continents. The wars between Old World nations inevitably involved their colonial territories— if in no other way, in the writing of peace and armistice terms at the cessation of hostilities. With slight disguise, the empires of the defeated have been divided among the victors almost as spoils of war. Thus were the colonial domains of Turkey and Germany distributed among the Allied powers, as mandated territories, after World War I and the dependencies of Japan and of the state of Germany itself, after 1945. A process of shuffling out the more impotent contenders in this contest for territory has gone on from the inception of the colonial period.

Spain created the first and most spectacular of world empires, built upon the base of precious minerals extracted in the subject lands. It melted away, however, with the seizure of trade initiative by England, and by insurrection within the colonies themselves. The Common-

---

[5] Thus characterized by the states who desire to control them, not by the indigenous peoples.

COLONIAL POWERS - TERRITORIES, DATES OF ACQUISITION AND CHANGE OF STATUS

BELGIAN TERRITORIES
BELGIAN TERRITORIES......1896-1898
CONGO STATE......1885

BRITISH EMPIRE
ANGLO-EGYPTIAN SUDAN
CONDOMINION......1896-1898
BECHUANALAND......1885,1895
BRITISH EAST AFRICA
(KENYA)......1885-1895
BRITISH GUIANA......1796
BRITISH NORTH BORNEO......1881
BRITISH SOMALILAND......1884
BRUNEI......1846
BURMA......1826
......1852
......1886
CAPE COLONY:......1806
CEYLON:......1796
EGYPT: TURKISH DEP.......1517
BR. OCCUPIED......1882
BR. PROTECTORATE......1914
GAMBIA......1882
GOLD COAST......1898
HONG KONG......1842
INDIA......1803
MALAYA......1874
NEW GUINEA
NIGERIA......1886
NYASALAND......1891
ORANGE FREE STATE......1902
RHODESIA......1889-1890
SARAWAK......1888
SIERRA LEONE......1787
TRANSVAAL (SOUTH AFRICAN
REPUBLIC)......1884
BRITISH......1902

DENMARK
DANISH WEST INDIES
(VIRGIN ISLANDS) ACQUIRED
AT FOUR DATES......1666,1672
......1684,1733
FAEROES......1380
GREENLAND......1815
ICELAND......1380

DUTCH TERRITORIES
NETHERLANDS INDIES......1885-1895
SURINAM......1796

FRENCH TERRITORIES
ALGERIA   TURKISH DEP.......1519-1710
TUNISIA   FRENCH......1830
DJIBOUTI......1862
FR. EQUATORIAL AFRICA......1886
GUINEA COAST TERRITORIES......1873-1905
SAHARA......1806
FR. GUIANA......1893-1898
INDOCHINA......1884
(CAMBODIA)......1863
KARIKAL,MAHE,PANDICHERRY,......1517
MOROCCO (FR. PROTECTORATE)......1912
MADAGASCAR......1843,1896
YAUAON......1874

GERMAN TERRITORIES
CAMEROONS......1884
GERMAN EAST AFRICA
(TANGANYIKA)......1885
S.W. AFRICA......1884
TOGOLAND......1884

ITALIAN TERRITORIES
TRIPOLI   TURKISH VILAYET 1835
CYRENAICA   TO ITALY......1912
LIBYA
ERITREA......1885
ITALIAN SOMALILAND......1889

JAPAN
FORMOSA (TAIWAN)......1895
KOREA (CHOSEN)......1910

PORTUGUESE TERRITORIES
ANGOLA......1510
PORTUGUESE GUINEA   BEFORE......1650
MOZAMBIQUE......
GOA......1510
MACAO......1520,1557
PRINCE'S IS.......1484
ST. THOMAS IS.......
TIMOR......ABOUT......1511-1525

SPANISH TERRITORIES
ANNOBON ISLANDS......1778
FERNANDO PO ISLANDS......1778
RIO DE ORO
RIO MUNI
SPANISH MOROCCO......1912

TURKEY
ARMENIA......1520-1566
COASTLANDS OF ARABIA......1517
CYPRUS(NOT TURNED OVER TO THE
BRITISH UNTIL 1914)......1517
LEASED TO BRITISH......1878

EUROPEAN TURKEY......1361,1453
MESOPOTAMIA......1520-1566
SYRIA AND PALESTINE......1512-1520

UNITED STATES
ALASKA......1867
HAWAII......1898
PANAMA CANAL ZONE......1903
(UNDER PERMANENT LEASE)
PHILIPPINE ISLANDS......1898
PUERTO RICO......1898

Figure 6.1a.

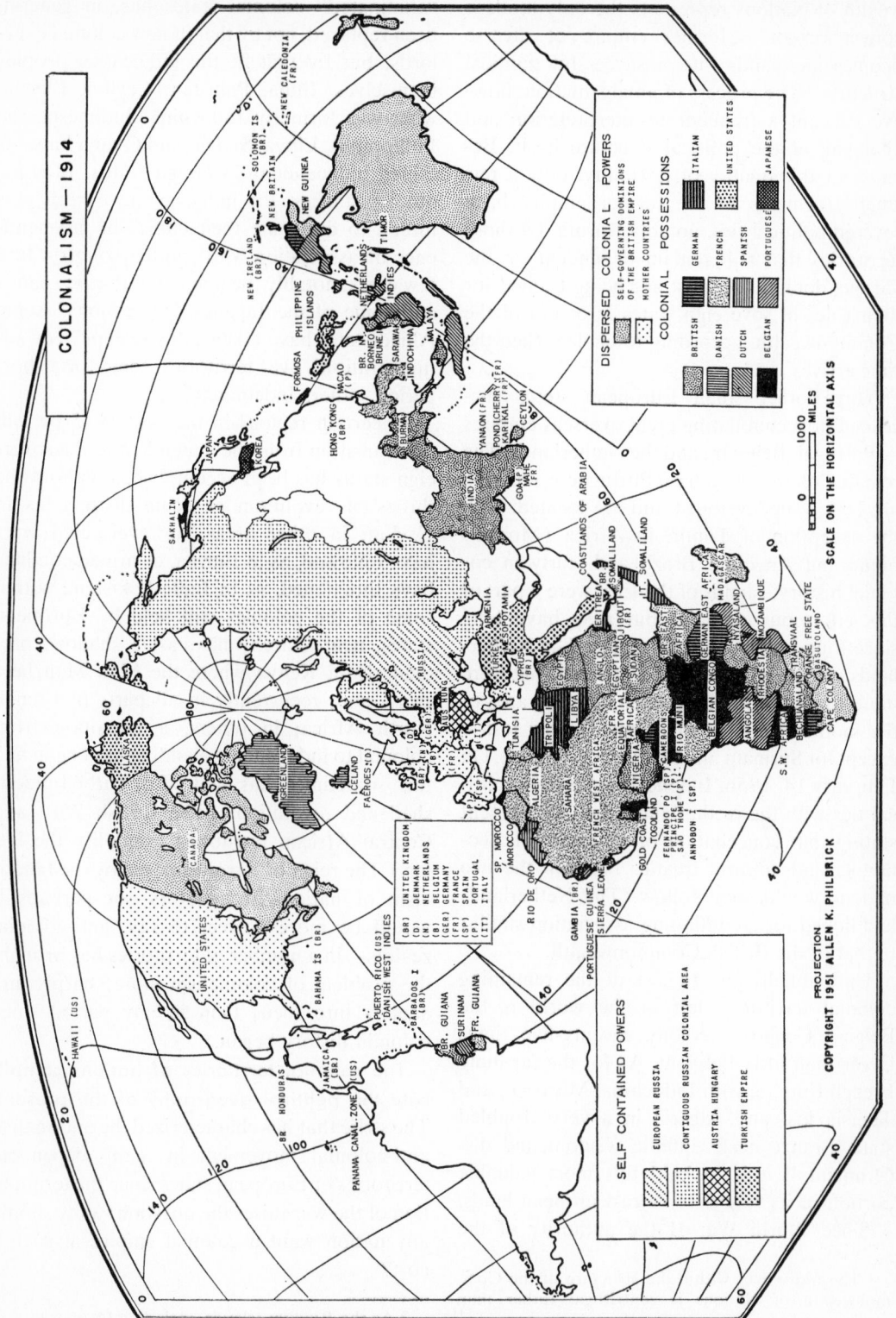

Figure 6.1b.

COLONIALISM—1914

COPYRIGHT 1951 ALLEN K. PHILBRICK

PROJECTION

SCALE ON THE HORIZONTAL AXIS

DISPERSED COLONIAL POWERS

SELF-GOVERNING DOMINIONS
OF THE BRITISH EMPIRE

MOTHER COUNTRIES

COLONIAL POSSESSIONS

BRITISH
DANISH
DUTCH
BELGIAN

GERMAN
FRENCH
SPANISH
PORTUGUESE

ITALIAN
UNITED STATES
JAPANESE

SELF CONTAINED POWERS

EUROPEAN RUSSIA

CONTIGUOUS RUSSIAN COLONIAL AREA

AUSTRIA HUNGARY

TURKISH EMPIRE

(BR) UNITED KINGDOM
(D) DENMARK
(N) NETHERLANDS
(B) BELGIUM
(GER) GERMANY
(FR) FRANCE
(SP) SPAIN
(P) PORTUGAL
(IT) ITALY

wealth of Nations represents the only modern conversion of a former empire of diverse peoples and lands into a successful political structure.[6] The process of amalgamation, however, meant a frequent re-interpretation and changing of the political structure itself. Because of this quality of flexibility, only a few small fragments of the former empire have severed political ties, notably Burma. Of those territories that still remain dependent on the various dominions, most are being trained for their roles of sovereign states in or out of the Commonwealth, according to choice when the time arrives.

Three other small European states succeeded in accumulating great overseas empires—Portugal, Belgium, and the Netherlands. The remains of the once vast Portuguese colonies are largely undeveloped and are located, with the exception of Timor, in Africa (Mozambique and Angola). Brazil and, early in colonial history, islands of the East were a part of this enormous domain, but they have long since found other political status. The Netherlands empire incorporated territories that were more than sixty times greater than the area of the mother state. Most of this is now lost—except for Surinam and Dutch New Guinea. On February 14, 1956, Indonesia cut its last political ties with the Netherlands, the Government stating that concellation of all financial, economic, and cultural treaties between the two nations would soon follow. The Netherlands had hoped for a continuing association similar to that of the British Commonwealth.

Undoubtedly the richest of the remaining colonial territories left in the world is the Belgian Congo, a colony seventy-five times larger than little Belgium. As for the far-flung French Empire, with Indochina, Morocco, and Tunisia lost and Algeria in a very troubled state, France needs infinite wisdom and discernment if it is to hold this most valuable portion of its extensive extra-European lands.

Since World War II the authority of the "eliminated" colonial states has, in general, been replaced, not by that of new colonial overlords, but by that of the indigenous peoples themselves. India, Pakistan, Ceylon, Burma, what was formerly Indochina, Indonesia, the Philippines, Libya, Sudan, and Ghana have attained independent sovereign status. In some other instances, the indigenes have been permitted to designate their choice of independence or association with another country. In a few cases, notably the mandated Pacific islands and some of the Japanese possessions,[7] some Allied states have taken "trusteeships" (or administration) over territories, some for a short period, others indefinitely.

In certain regions in the post-1945 period, the transition from the dependent to the sovereign status has been accomplished without the throes of revolution or acute distress, as in Ceylon; in other areas, however, civil wars have followed, as in Burma, or armed conflicts have threatened, as in India-Pakistan. Within some of the colonies still held by European states, near-anarchy has cast a shadow, particularly in Kenya where the Mau Mau held sway, and, recurrently in all parts of French North Africa; in others, a transition from colonial to independent standing has begun and this, sometimes, has held off or curbed bloodshed and revolution. (The British West and Central African territories exemplify the latter.) The reign of terror imposed by the fanaticism of nationalist agitators—or perhaps it would be more correct to say, anti-colonial zealots—in a number of territories has brought the problem of colonialism more sharply and acutely into focus than in any period since colonial history began.

The colonial territories of nations complicate the political geography of the present. The strife that has characterized the nationalist, anti-colonial movement in many dependent territories of European states since the termination of the war raises the question: Why should any nation want a colonial empire at such a cost?

---

[6] The movement within the structure of the Commonwealth of Nations is centrifugal rather than amalgamative.

[7] As the Ryukyu Islands, including Okinawa.

One of the major incentives to colonial expansion was economic. To a large extent, the industrial and commercial structures of the colonial powers were built on their empires—on the exploitation of (and trade with) territories which have not been and are not populated by majorities of their own nationals. This is not true of the United States, Russia, possibly France, or Germany, even though the mining and agricultural possibilities offered by the German Cameroons and Tanganyika territories in Africa were very attractive to the latter nation. A dominant aim of the colonial powers in this world-wide territorial expansion has been to free themselves of dependence on other states for foodstuffs and the raw materials of industry; and in the vast, largely tropical and subtropical, undeveloped dependencies of their empires they found these. In the last scramble for colonial possessions, which took place in the latter part of the nineteenth century, prestige was also an incentive.

The foremost problem in colonialism today is the definition of rights and powers. The leading question in colonialism in the present period is: "how are we to define and reconcile the rights and powers" of colonial[8] and indigene? That question must be answered adequately first for the European and native inhabitants of the territories, and then for the colonial powers. Until this question is resolved in each dependency, the larger geopolitical problems of world import—as security and the like—cannot safely be worked out. Security is highly dependent upon trustworthy colonial territories not only for their resources but for their use as land, air, and sea bases as well.

The administration of the "people of darker skins" was termed, in the past, the "white man's burden." It was perhaps a picturesque phrase—and a convenient one for it more or less gave acquiescence to the holding and exploitation of extra-national territories and peoples on the supposition that they were unable to rule themselves. In the modern phase of economic and political development, where all portions of the globe are integrated into the commercial and security patterns, this is undoubtedly true for many backward areas—at least up to the present. In viewing the colonial problem, however, one cannot take heed only of a *white* man's burden; one must also recognize the burden that the foreigner has laid upon the indigene—even in the best efforts at bringing the benefits of western technology, science, and medicine to the latter peoples.

European exploitation of colonial territories has usually disturbed the way of life of the native by: 1) employing—and even conscripting—native labor to perform the tasks of the mines, the plantations, and the like, and 2) by drawing (through the attractions of city life and work opportunities) the natives[9] from their traditional homes to urban centers of industry and commerce. As a consequence, in most colonial territories there has been a large displacement of native people. This change of living pattern and the accompanying throw-off of the moral restraints of the native social group has brought confusion to the natives for the new has been incompatible with the old. The rural-to-urban migrations have replaced the security of the simple pattern of rural and village living with the complexity of western urban life—at times with the evils of slum life for in the cities the natives most frequently live in *bidonvilles,* tin-can and shanty slums that become breeding places for discontent and unrest. It is among these displaced persons, who have witnessed and tasted some of the advantages and blights of western civilization, *and* among the western educated, that the nationalist and anti-colonial movements have arisen.

In subtropical areas, the colonial indigenes are displaying an energy for self-determination that is frustrating European control and in-

---

[8] The word "colonial" is used in the connotation of the agricultural-colonist from the mother country (or, in some cases, from other European states) who settled in the territory years ago, or were born there, and consider it their home.

[9] In order to carry the costs of colonial government, a tax is usually laid upon the natives "in metal currency"—another factor that forces the latter, very often, to leave their homes and secure work.

tention. This is a different elimination of colonial powers than took place when dependencies changed hands due to the outcome of war. Imitating principles and practices of western government (although perhaps not always fathoming the spirit of such government and life), colonial peoples are slipping away from the domain of colonialism into the world of sovereign states. Since this is a post-World War II development, the colonial problem of today is very different from that of 1930. It is no longer merely one of administration, development, and exploitation, but rather of appeasing native peoples by according varying degrees of sovereignty to them, attempting at the same time to hold these peoples and territories by some sort of political relationship to the colonial power if possible.[10] The white man's burden is being lightened, not by the wish of the colonial powers but by native resolution, as subject peoples renounce the white man as a guardian of their political estate. Colonial responsibility, decimated, is restricted almost entirely to minor island groups and tropical lowlands—and the transition has begun even in the latter regions. In Asia and Africa, the move toward nationalism has started and advanced to a point where it is irreversible.

A burden of commitment rests with the colonial powers. A responsibility still remains with the colonial powers to relinquish authority gradually enough so that the native peoples are able to take over control without going through the spasms of radical change that often result in the imposition of injustices on a part, or the mass, of the people by their own leaders, or without the danger of usurpation of power by other nations. These territories have all been fitted into the world economic and security pattern from which, even if they so desired, it is impossible to retreat. Therefore, adjustment must take place within a modern and a global connotation. On the other hand, an acceleration of the granting of sovereignty in the areas where colonialism still exists is needed. There are many difficulties in this process of transition to independence in reasonably good order. Involved are the dilemmas of constitutional formulae for each stage and the deeper and more important problems of achieving increased competence and responsibility among the native populations.

The promise of ultimate independence must be made persuasive. The Indochina and North African situations have made clear that substantial injury can be done by permitting a delay to action on the demands of colonial peoples. The bitter but enlightening lesson of the postwar years is that it is safer for the colonial powers to move sooner rather than later.

POLITICAL AND GEOPOLITICAL MATURITY AND IMMATURITY[11]

Many of the colonial holdings are, politically, not ready to take the reins of government and act as independent states within the world of nations. For this reason, a period of training usually precedes the granting of autonomy. The Gold Coast—now the independent state of Ghana—went through such a training period; Nigeria and (Italian) Somaliland are being prepared for sovereignty, the latter promised to the natives within a stated interval. The Philippines were given much practice in government while they still held the status of dependency because the declared purpose of the United States was independence when the island group was politically ready. In a number of colonies, however, the colonial government

---

[10] A further complicating factor are the "colonials," who oppose these independence moves, fearing to live as white minorities within the native states.

[11] States may be defined as *geopolitically* mature when: population has reached a level of density so as to be commensurate with the resources; the growth of resource-use has reached full development; and when the means of transportation and communication have reached a stage where the ecumene is fully served, and the marginal areas and border regions are also effectively tied into the ecumene. Geopolitical immaturity in a state represents a condition of underpopulation and development relative to resources, and incomplete coherence in terms of transportation and communication. The period of geopolitical old age approaches as population outruns resources and the standard of living of the population accordingly goes down.

has been such that it was difficult for facility in self-government to develop.

Political maturity would likely be accorded all sovereign states by other nations of the world even though a number of countries display evidence of immaturity.

However, not all states are *geopolitically mature*. Some countries are not populated to the degree that the resource-base of the domain would allow or have not fully integrated all parts of the domain through a cohering system of communication and transportation. Among the giant states of the earth—the USSR, Brazil, Canada, the United States, China, India, Australia—only the United States can be characterized as geopolitically mature.

The political re-alignment of Europe that followed the first world war segmented or snipped off the ends of the transportation systems of a number of countries. Although many welds were made, it left communication badly articulated within and between a number of states so that, during the inter-war period, several of the Central European states were unable to reorganize themselves so as to attain accordance with their new dimensions and unitary character. World War II, which disjointed and repatterned the communication systems for the second time within a few decades—*and* the dropping of the "Iron Curtain" between Western and Communist countries—again left Europe with many links to be woven together.

In other parts of the world, geopolitically immature countries are those who are still trying to fit themselves to their resource and space dimensions. Some large states—like China, India, the USSR, Brazil, and Canada—belong to this group as do also a number of smaller ones in Asia and on the continents of North and South America, Australia, and Africa. In South America and Africa, for example, in almost every instance boundaries are remote from the ecumene. Where boundary troubles arise, the disputed territories are often so peripheral to the areas where populations are most heavily concentrated as to make defense of the frontier zone difficult.

In the greater number of these immature nations the ecumene makes up only a small proportion of the entire country, or it may be fragmented—*i.e.* distributed in several parts of the nation, at times the various portions separated one from the other by difficult physiographic obstacles. As long as integration is in terms of river navigation and animal traction, the state will remain relatively impotent politically; even the railroads and telegraph have been unable to compensate entirely for natural handicaps, except locally. However, the railroads and wireless have done much to emancipate out-of-the-way and frontier areas from positions of isolation and marginality inflicted by nature.

Transportation and communication are, physically, the integrative media. Communication has been the instrument of political unification during the past hundred and twenty-five years, but not since the days of the Romans —until the present highway development in the United States—have roads become major transportation links. A characteristic of the road pattern as an integrative force is that frequently highways parallel rather than feed into the other transportation media: in deserts, roads and camel caravan trails interknit for the paths between waterholes and oases are definitive; in heavy forest areas a trail, slashed through forest growth, will usually be widened to allow for a road; through mountain valleys, roads and railroads typically interweave although roads are able to traject farther up precipitous slopes, reaching into remote recesses where railroads cannot penetrate; similarly, for swampy terrain where an elevated zone provides the best and easiest passageway, roads will tend to parallel the rails. Such paralleling of transportation lines is costly for several reasons. In the first place, this constitutes an expensive duplication of facilities, especially where topographic or vegetation barriers make road and railroad building difficult, because similar problems of construction and upkeep are posed for both. Second, traffic must be shared by two routes in a region that ordinarily is unable to make even one economic. Further, the double means of communication serve to open up relatively less new territory than would be true if the lines followed separate paths. On the other hand, in instances where roads have been constructed supplementary to and feeding into the railroad-waterway pattern, development and unification have been accelerated. Telegraph and telephone lines are likely to follow highways into virgin lands.

Air service and radio have been especially opportune in opening up—and tying into the national integrating system—regions of extreme environment for these facilities are not tied to the earth in the sense that ground and water communications are. They have the further advantage of direct, swift, and continuous interlinkage. It is, therefore, in some of the least developed areas of the globe where air transport and radio are most prized. The dream of a Cape-to-Cairo railroad in Africa was abandoned with the entry of the commercial airplane. In the USSR, with its millions of square miles of coniferous forest, tundra, desert, and steppe, the airplane brings medicine and portable hospitals, quick transport to replace tedious travel, and dozens of other advantages to the people of these enormous areas that must always remain marginal to the rest of the state. Canada's North Country depends heavily upon air service, particularly in the winter season.

In large states the airplane, radio, and television have advanced integration more rapidly within the past two or three decades than was possible to accomplish over the centuries using the land-bound connections. However, in certain countries—small ones, where all parts of the state are within a short time-distance from each other—the airplane has less use except as a means of linking up the various parts of an empire or making international connections.

Air transport, oceanways, and radio perform the same integrative function between the mother country and dependencies as do roads, railroads, telegraph, and telephone between the parts of the metropolitan domain. Further, the newer types of transport and communication are the means of shortening the distances between states—they have the effect of erasing all barrier boundaries except the political, which are man-raised. However, by thus further narrowing the frontier zone between states, the danger of international friction mounts. Any deficiency in adequate and ready means of interconnection is an element of political weakness in a state, whatever the area or population density.

GOVERNMENT AND HABITAT

The progress of any political unit is affected by its areal pattern. The areal pattern is comprised, it has been noted, of nuclear core and ecumene, component—or administrative—regions, capital, problem areas, strategic points, and boundaries. These integrants acquire their character through the interaction of the political structure with the conditions of the physical setting and the tendency is strong, once constituted, for them to endure indefinitely. For the most part, they accord with the earth environment. But in cases where a political feature is misadapted to the circumstances of the natural environment, the maladjustment may become accentuated over many passing generations before being finally corrected. Such misadaptations of political patterns to the natural habitat, which require that people adjust to them, cause discontent. At times, when government forms persist unchanged for too long a period, the political structure may actually interfere with the natural intention of geography.

The most enduring states are those that show the greatest flexibility—altering their laws and institutions as the need becomes apparent. Where discordancies continue and political structures petrify, violent overthrow of the government by revolution, conquest, or gradual disintegration may be necessary to rectify the incongruity.

LAWS AND THE STATE

Law is the instrument through which the political structure of any state functions. As with other devices of man, laws are not always adequate to their intended purpose: at times, they are so greatly at variance with the realities of the physical conditions of the political area that they must be revoked—or are simply forgotten through disuse; in other instances, they may function without being completely accordant. The greater part of law, however, is passably acceptable to the conditions of the earth environment and, with the passage of time, the basic statutes of a state will mutate to fit the few compulsions of the natural habitat.

Successful law must be harmonious with nature. At times, the insistency of nature is able to force laws into conformity with the physical environment; on the opposite side, laws may, by their effects, make changes in natural conditions. There is a constant interplay between law and habitat—each influences the other and is thereby altered to a greater or lesser degree. Laws that are in accord with the physical conditions of the habitat are the most successful; however, the temper of geography is such that the natural setting allows for a broad scope of legal forms in most areas.

Contrasts in the utilization of similar habitats may be created by varying legal structures. For example, the dissimilarities of culture in similar natural regions found on two sides of national frontiers are not unusual and they demonstrate that, through laws, it is possible to modify and adapt the physical environment.

Resources may utimately be laid waste by the operation of laws—or policies of government—inappropriate to the nature of the region, or, conversely, because of the lack of legal means of control. Almost any tampering with "nature" is likely to have repercussions in one form or another: the laying bare of hillslopes through lumbering increases flood danger, soil erosion, and a whole string of attendant results; the conservation of certain wild fauna may destroy the balance of nature and make a pest out of a normally harmless species; the introduction of a new species of flora or fauna into a highly suitable environment may have a like effect; the construction of barrages and dams to hold and conserve water for regu-

lated use can eventuate in a whole chain of reactions—beneficial and otherwise.

The attempts of government policy to make changes in—or improve on—the natural environment illustrate the conflicting beneficial and detrimental consequences that are often attendant on such interference with nature. The barrages on the Nile have, within a matter of decades, made necessary the use of commercial fertilizer by the Egyptian farmers on land that for six thousand years retained its fertility through the natural process of silt-import by the annual floods of the river; at the same time, they guarantee a sure supply of water when it is needed and make possible year-round cultivation. As yet very little is known about the way in which law and nature react to synchronize with or oppose each other.

FOREIGN POLICY AND THE STATE

International economic relations have become widespread and complex. With the accelerated rate of agricultural production in many parts of the world, with the rapidly increasing rise of urban populations intent upon enlarging industrial output and commerce, with the rising demand on the part of large masses of people—in industrially virgin lands—for the products of modern industry, with the competitive demand for strategic materials for stockpiling and for the building of weapons for security, international trade has extended to all parts of the globe and has reached enormous proportions. Although the process is not new, the pace has been greatly quickened and the scope enlarged in the past decade. These phenomena, along with others such as the investment of money, the provision for financial and technological aid to foreign states, the lending of ships or planes in exchange for bases, airfields, ports, etc., make apparent how intricate and diverse are the international relations of the present day, how broad are the extra-national transactions of governments. To take the United States as an example: American economic and political exploits and responsibilities extend from beyond the Arctic

Circle in Alaska south to Antarctica; they engirdle the earth east and west, from Japan and the Philippines to Liberia and the Mediterranean. Though the territorial *possessions* of the United States are not as far-spread and extensive as those of certain other nations, the economic and commercial relations, and the political power, are perhaps the greatest on the globe.

The swift development in the past century of industrial power, and the concomitant spread of economic and political interests to encompass the entire globe, have brought a quality of precariousness to international relations. This has led certain nations to seek some means other than force to assure the security of states. However, international policy can not be entirely a matter of cooperation and mutual agreement for the primary realities of the organization of the political world are inimical to this. In the first place, states differ as to the "sets of values" that are regarded as fundamental to their national way of life, and usually will not hesitate to defend these values—if necessary, even engaging in armed conflict. Further, there are few states, except those not sufficiently powerful, who will not resort to pressure to achieve what they consider legitimate objectives.

The area of international relations is the most trying and frustrating in the geopolitical arena. Most attempts to solve the perplexities of international relations seem only to involve nations more deeply in an ever more complex web of events. The much tried and seemingly expedient use of force, war, has not solved international disputes. Treaties and international law have likewise seemed to fail; both continue to be abrogated by aggressive powers who impose their strength on weaker peoples. International organizations, also, as the League of Nations and the United Nations, have, to the present time, proven innately impotent both in their organization and in their powers.

If and when a new scheme of world organization is worked out—or the present one revised—to succeed, it must vouchsafe security and immunity from injustice to all states, allow for the participation of all of the peoples of the globe, and have the flexibility to be applicable to the immense variety of economic and social structures of which the world political mosaic is composed.

It is impossible to return to "international disorganization." Today, nations have no alternative but to accept each other for the world is getting smaller. However, with this shrinking world that the realities of change have brought about, the mutual relations between nations become not only closer but more complex. This is the enigma that states must face in attempting to resolve international problems and in individually formulating their own foreign policies.

7

Boundaries

It is likely that boundaries generate more friction among states than any other factor of international relations. This is true because almost any inter-state clash involves the adjustment of territory, almost any aggressive action upon the lands or rights of one nation by another is motivated by the desire for additional space—moves which presuppose changes in boundaries.

The extent of the territories of a state are defined in terms of boundaries.[1] Because linear boundaries are more precise than the zonal type and are more convenient to administer, in the contemporary period, the linear boundary is the habitual pattern. Not until fairly recent times was this the case, however, for most international frontier areas were separated from each other by *zones* that were in the nature of barrier boundaries: those barrier zones that have most continuously defied easy transit—and hence have remained persistent

fractures in the movement of peoples and goods—have typically been the boundaries of least friction. However, as improvements in transportation and communication reduced the width of these "barriers," the zonal aspect was gradually pinched out and replaced by the line.

Nevertheless, the zonal boundary is in harmony with the conditions of the social and natural habitats more exactly than are "lines." Though lines, in marginal[2] regions, designate the separation of the territories of one nation from those of another, actually, in practice, many such boundaries are zonal in character— at least in certain respects. For example, the Tibetan-Butanese boundary recognizes a "zone," an upper and lower tree limit within which Butanese can take bamboo and Tibetans, pine; the Pyrenees are used by both French and Spanish herdsmen as pastures during the summer period; traditionally, the Lapp peoples of Northern Europe have moved across the mountains and tundras with their reindeer

---

[1] The state exercises its legal authority, *i.e.* its sovereignty, not only over its land areas but also over its territory in the wider sense—the marginal waters, the air above the domain (at least as far as air transportation is concerned), and the rocks and minerals beneath the surface of the ground.

[2] Those areas of the globe that are not easily adapted to human use are considered "marginal." Included are the climatically difficult zones, most mountain regions, swamp lands, etc.

herds despite the boundaries laid down by the four states concerned—Norway, Sweden, Finland, and the USSR; and the folk of the Asiatic Kirghiz and Kazak groups have crossed and recrossed the Russo-Chinese frontier in their cycles of movement.

When lines are drawn through such frontier areas, where the people of both states have been accustomed to commingle in the course of their daily living, many difficulties are created for the border peoples, particularly if the two governments concerned are not on friendly terms—as in East and West Berlin.

"There are no intrinsically good or bad boundaries."[3] Any and all international frontier areas have the potential of becoming critical: while at one period they may be stable, at another they are as likely to become unstable without any alteration in the position of the boundary itself. Whether a boundary is good or bad results as much from the general international situation at the time as it does upon such aspects as delimitation and demarcation. "Back of a boundary are not only national interests and ambitions but a philosophy of international relations."[4]

An international boundary is a line marking an outer definition of the territory within which a state exercises sovereignty. Neighboring states face each other across the more than 100,000 miles of international boundaries that separate each nation from the other. These boundaries may be of various sorts—natural, cultural, mathematical, or complex. When a boundary conforms to some feature of the physical terrain—as streams, seas, mountains, deserts, watersheds, lakes, marshes and the like—it is said to be a *natural boundary*. The *mathematical* (or *geometrical* type), *i.e.* straight lines, arcs of circles, etc., has become prevalent in recent times. Such lines may, of course, be drawn within natural boundary zones in which case the character of the boundary is related to the physical feature. *Cultural* (*or anthropo-geographic*) boundaries are related to some aspect of human occupance while the *complex* (*or compound*) type represents a compromise between several features.

NATURAL BOUNDARIES

Because of its former "barrier" aspect, there has remained prevalent a belief that the natural boundary is superior to other kinds. In the past—and even today—*natural barrier* frontiers have had a very real defensive value. Although natural boundaries have lost some of their defensive utility with the growth of modern technology, yet, as long as they retain their barrier aspect (*i.e.* act as zones of separation), they make good boundaries[5]—on the assumption that to decrease the amount of possible contact between people is to reduce, as well, the possible amount of friction. At times, this has been given as an excuse for expanding into some region that a state desires. The Soviet absorption of the western (Polish) portion of the Pripet Marshes, at the end of World War II, is a case in point.

Natural barrier features are usually so broad that the actual boundaries are really lines *within the zones.*

How adequate are the several types of physical features as frontiers?

Water Boundaries

Rivers as boundaries. Among the natural features that may act as *water boundaries* are rivers, oceans, and lakes. In the older civilizations rivers rarely served to separate; they were, instead, regions of unity. This is typical of their character even today (although the contemporary period can point to a number of river boundaries): "Egypt is the Nile," and the valley of the Tigris-Euphrates rivers is Iraq. At an early date, the latter valley nurtured three important civilizations—not, however, sepa-

[3] Stephen B. Jones, *Boundary-Making* (Washington, D.C.: Carnegie Endowment for International Peace, 1945), p. 3.

[4] Isaiah Bowman, "Foreword," *International Boundaries* by S. Whittemore Boggs (New York: Columbia University Press, 1940), p. v.

[5] Such a view is actually negative rather than positive: to view a "zone of separation" as a good frontier is to regard your neighbor as a potential enemy. If it serves as a barrier in time of war it may act as an economic barrier in peacetime equally well.

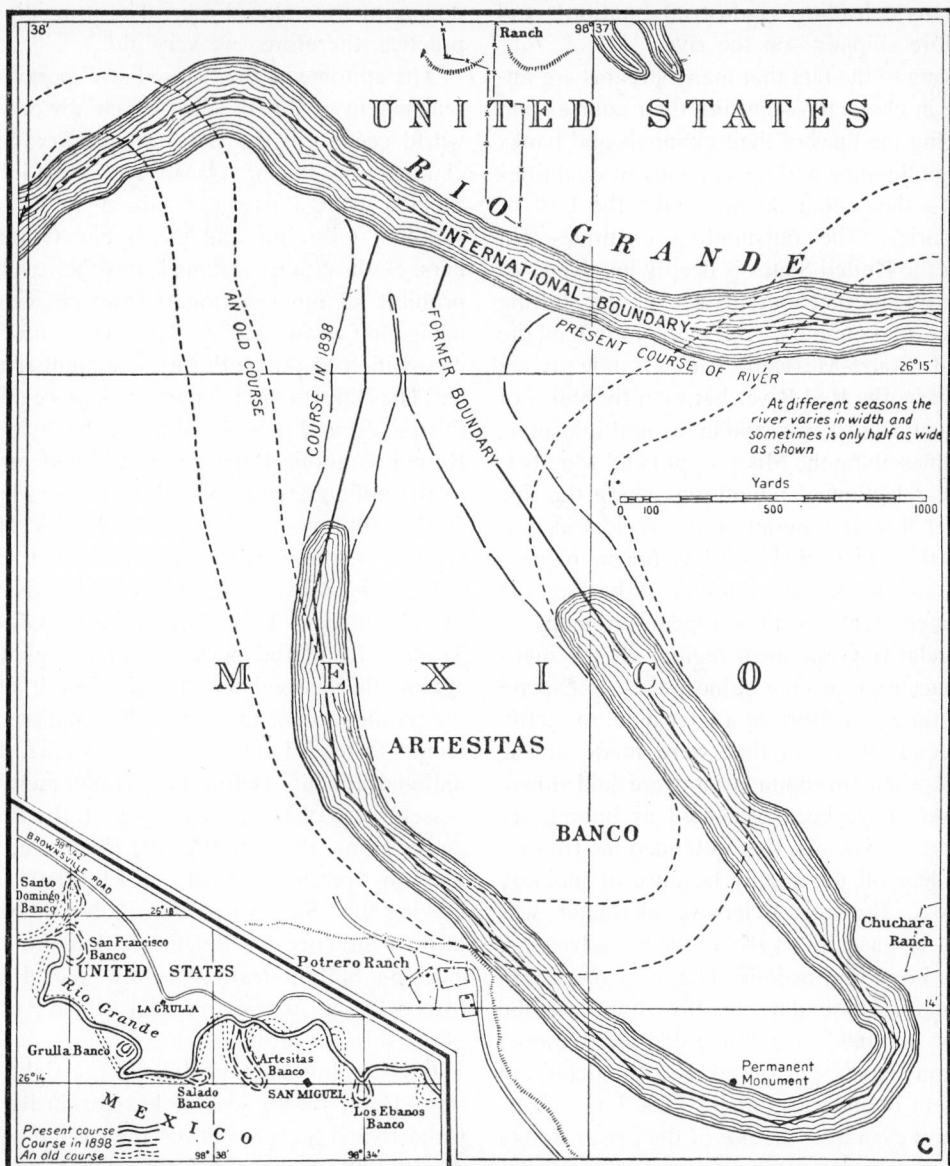

Figure 7.1. The wanderings of the Rio Grande and the old and new boundaries about Artesitas Banco.

rated from each other by the river. Chaldea grew up in the south, Babylonia in the central portion, and Assyria in the north.[6] Although

[6] Later, however, beginning in the last century before the birth of Christ, the desert-Upper Euphrates frontier did serve as a boundary between the East Roman and Parthia-Sassanian empires for several centuries.

the Rhine and the Danube appear to be outstanding examples of rivers as boundaries, in the past there were notable periods of valley unity and, today also, these rivers serve to draw together the states that border upon them. Note the necessity of close association between the Netherlands, controlling the Rhine outlet, and

Germany, leading industrial nation—and therefore shipper—on the river.

Owing to the fact that many streams are unstable in character—shifting their courses and changing the lines of their channels and banks through flooding and the carrying of quantities of silt—they often do not make the best of boundaries. The outstanding examples (in which the United States is deeply involved) of the problems that may arise over the shifting courses of boundary rivers are found in the United States-Mexican Rio Grande River boundary, the Red River between the states of Oklahoma and Texas, and in the multiple interstate lines along the Mississippi (Old Muddy).

The selection of boundaries along the line of river flow is generally more typical in new lands than in settled sections for in pioneer areas, rivers (or mountains) may be the only prominent features that appear on maps of such relatively unknown regions. If the maps are inaccurate, it may be necessary to expend much time and effort, at a later date, to rectify the technical errors that were made at the period when the boundaries were laid down.

Rivers have been esteemed as boundaries because, as barriers, they defended the frontier —holding off the enemy because of inability to cross. But this defensive character was largely lost as military technique has advanced.

The bounding oceans. The most unmistakable natural boundary features on the globe are the *oceans*. Yet innumerable international questions have been raised over the definition of ocean boundaries, inland seas, large lakes, etc., and even over the use of the ocean waters themselves.

The concept of closed and open seas. The principle of the open sea obtains today except in very restricted areas. But the seas of the world were not always free and open. Seafaring began in small restricted waters which were controlled by those states that held the entrances—and closed to all others except a privileged few. When seamen emerged from such protected water bodies (as the Mediterranean-Red Sea and Persian Gulf areas) into the open oceans, they carried with them this

dogma of the "closed sea." The principle and practice, therefore, are very old.

The epitome of the "closed sea" period was reached in a Papal edict which divided the world oceans in the sixteenth century; Spain claimed the Pacific Ocean and the Gulf of Mexico while Portugal regarded the Atlantic south of Gibraltar and the Indian Ocean as hers. Both nations assumed it as their right to prohibit all other nationals from entering or navigating these waters. However, enforcing recognition of this authority was another matter. The Reformation (which took place during this period and repudiated the authority of the Roman Catholic Papacy) contributed further to the difficulties of controlling the sea lanes.

In 1608 a young Netherlands lawyer, Hugo Grotius, wrote a treatise entitled, "The Freedom of the Seas, or the Right Which Belongs to the Dutch to Take Part in the East Indian Trade." It offered such vigorous arguments against the "closed sea" that in time it led to the termination of these incredible national attempts to regard entire oceans as a part of the national domain. Before long Dutch merchant vessels were offering a challenge to the Portuguese along the Afro-Asiatic route and the English "pirates" of Queen Elizabeth were making the "Spanish seas" (the North Atlantic) so insecure for Spaniards that the ships carrying bullion from the New World were forced to sail in convoys with a heavy escort of warships to protect them.

Grotius, however, postulated the right of a state, facing on the seas, to have exclusive and protective jurisdiction over the ocean waters directly off its coastline. In such a manner began the development of international recognition of a zone of offshore water where the state along the shore has the right to claim sole authority for defending itself against attack, giving protection to merchant ships coming into or departing from its ports, keeping watch over coastal fisheries, etc.

Three and a half centuries of historic argument and interpretative legal development lie in back of the concept of the marginal sea. The *marginal sea* is generally regarded as "the three-mile limit." Very early after navigation began, the need for such a marginal zone was generally conceded by most states. However, some three hundred years after the time of Grotius, the width of the zone of *territorial waters* is still disputed. It was again a Dutchman, Cornelius von Bynkershoek, a judge of the Supreme Court of Holland, who, in 1703, provided some standard by which to mark out the bounds of the marginal sea. He held that the littoral state should have dominion over as much of the sea as it could control from the land, *i.e.* the range across which shore-based cannon could hurl projectiles. Since such a range was about three miles, the marginal waters were given a corresponding breadth.

Logically, as armaments became more powerful and able to dominate an area of greater width, the three-mile offshore zone likewise should have been broadened. Although many states claim authority over a marginal area greater than three miles, none do so on the basis of this reasoning; further, to keep up with such armaments' advances would mean a constant re-definition of the marginal seas. To be specific, the Scandinavian states, whose coastlines are very irregular, have claimed jurisdiction over four-mile zones. This is an arbitrary but historic claim. A number of the Latin-American nations maintain they hold authority over at least a six-mile zone of marginal seas while Peru, Chile, and Ecuador declared a 200-mile limit to their zone of territorial waters under the 1952 Santiago agreement;[7] the Soviet Union claims 12 miles of offshore waters.

At The Hague Conference for the Codification of International Law in 1930, much time was spent in studying this problem in the hope that possible agreement might be reached among nations for setting up "a universal standard for measuring the marginal seas." There was no disagreement on the minimum breadth of three miles for the offshore area, but no agreement on the maximum width could be reached. Most of the countries favored an extension to four or six miles, but no unanimity was attained on either the current or future width of the zone.

The status of the marginal waters remains about the same: international law confirms the right of every nation to a "protective" zone of coastal waters and recognizes the width of such zone to be at least three miles. After several centuries the question of marginal waters still remains a provocative problem, and one that causes contention. The United Nations' International Law Commission has been exploring the issue with a view toward working out a codification of the existing international law on territorial waters.

The problems involved are many. Among them is the fact that the "shoreline" is *not a line but a zone* of varying width, high and lower tides marking the limits. Further, the impracticability of paralleling the shoreline, in all its sinuousness, three (or more) miles seaward has been substantiated. Where a circuitous coast runs across the frontier of two states, the problem of rights to territorial waters must be solved by intricate mathematical studies. Even the *median line* (which was the boundary affixed along the Great Lakes-United States-Canadian border) is usually a complicated geometrical problem to work out. For lakes, however, it is the most desirable boundary; for rivers, less so. Many interesting—but touchy—problems can also arise when water boundaries are defined with reference to their landward margins, for shore lines change both vertically and horizontally with tides, melting snow, the action of streams and rills, droughts, etc., and they further alter their profiles with erosion and accretion.

No phase of resource exploitation illustrates more fully the need for international agreements and regulations than do fisheries. All of the extractive resources are inevitably

---

[7] This treaty was subsequently ratified. In September–October 1955, officials of the United States met with representatives of the three treaty nations in an attempt to negotiate an agreement relative to the conservation of fishery resources in the Eastern Pacific, and proposed a return to the three-mile maritime zone. Although Peru had seemingly accepted in principle the American proposal, the treaty is apparently still in force. The protocol was signed by the three Latin American states in 1955 and was adhered to by Costa Rica also.

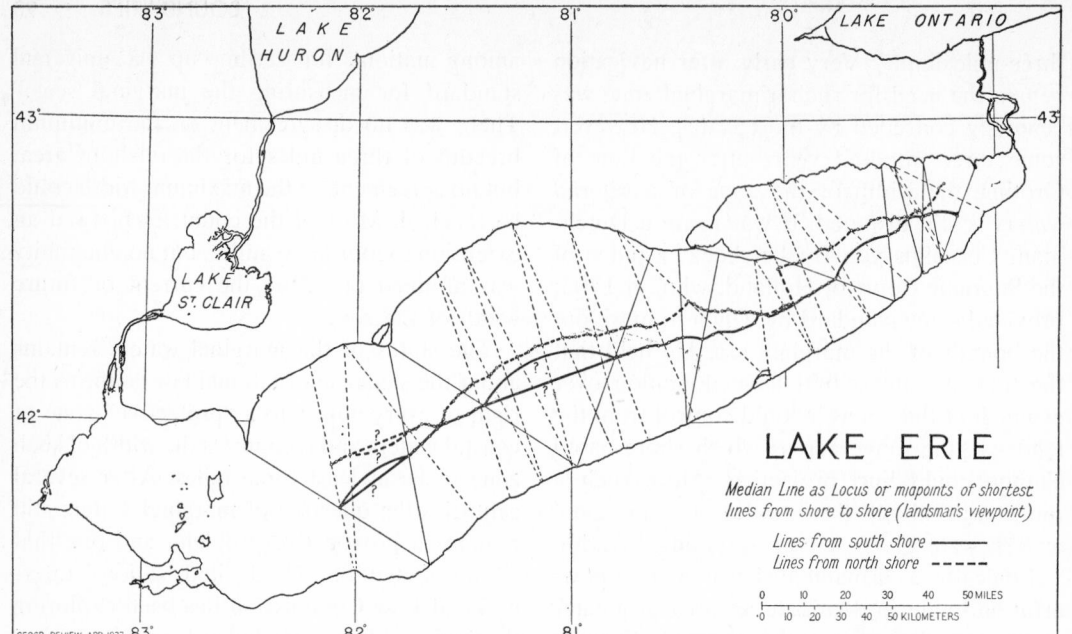

Figure 7.2.

Impractical and practical concepts of the median line. In Figure 7.2 (the impractical concept) the median line is located at the midpoints of all lines drawn from points on one shore to the nearest point on the opposite shore. The line differs as drawn from the north or the south shore, the two versions only occasionally being coincident. In Figure 7.3, the median line connects points placed equidistant from the nearest points on the opposite shore. (Courtesy American Geographical Society. From Boggs, "Problems of Water-Boundary Definition: Median Lines and International Boundaries Through Territorial Waters," The Geographical Review, XXVII.)

Figure 7.3.

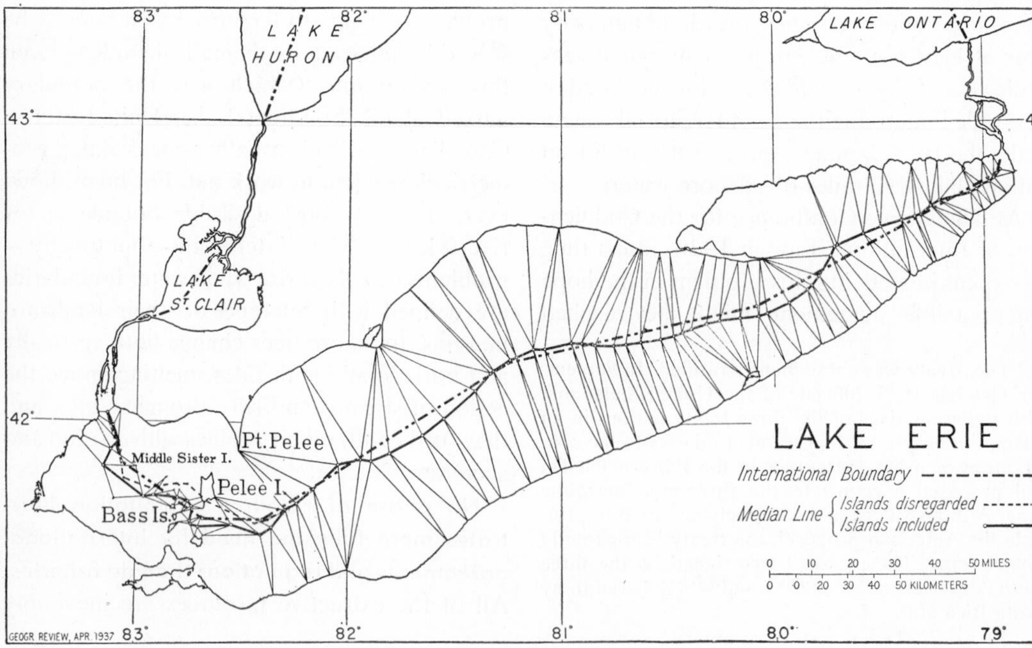

mixed up with the ambitions of government, and wherever resources are exploited without possibility of replacement—or where replacement is difficult—governments and men have tried either to assume control of the resource area or to secure an abundant share of the product.[8] Especially is this the case in deep-sea fishing. Centuries before international agreements established the three-mile limit as the zone of territorial waters over which a nation holds jurisdiction, men had become accustomed to fishing in the offshore zone—for, as soon as man had conquered his fear of the sea, he began to use those nearby waters and, eventually, the farther "deeps" as his fishing grounds.

Cooperation between nations is inevitably involved in the exploitation of deep-sea and coastal fisheries. The major fishing banks of the world lie on either side of the North Atlantic and North Pacific oceans, and here some of the most important international treaties have been made governing fishing in those waters. As Martin points out:

One of the still unsolved problems of fishery management is that of jurisdiction over marine grounds extending beyond the three-mile limit. Under the generally accepted usages of international law it is permissible for aliens to operate fishing boats in coastal waters just outside that limit. Many disputes have arisen in the past over the interpretation of this rule, but it was not until the rapid increase in the use of floating canneries, particularly by Japanese interests, that the problem became acute. During the summer of 1937 Japanese canneries of this type entered the red salmon area of Bristol Bay, Alaska, catching and

canning part of the inbound salmon run. Using deep curtain nets it is possible to remain outside the three-mile limit and still intercept part of an anadromous fish run on the continental shelf.

Alaskan salmon abundance has so far been carefully preserved by conservation measures ... It is a question whether alien interests which have borne none of the cost and are not bound by the 50 per cent escapement rule of the Fish and Wildlife Service should be allowed to share in the catch and perhaps nullify the conservation work.

. . . . .

There is a growing sentiment in favor of abandoning the three-mile limit for fisheries, substituting in its place the continental-shelf limit. Since the continental shelf is actually a highly productive underwater extension of the land area, it may become necessary for nations to assert jurisdiction over it in order to preserve their hardwon fisheries. President Truman's proclamation of September 28, 1945, claiming control over areas of the high seas contiguous to the coasts of the United States wherein fishing activities have been or may in the future be developed, is an assertion of continental-shelf sovereignty.[9]

Fisheries of many sorts, including (besides those already mentioned) shellfish in the Gulf of Mexico and pearls off northern Australia, have been the source of the development of international friction. The question of fishing rights is sure to arise wherever a remunerative industry can be carried on outside of the territorial waters—in other words, on all of the important fishing banks of the world—for advanced techniques of taking and preserving the catch send fishing boats even into remote areas of the globe.

Mountains as Boundaries

Mountains are relatively permanent and visible features, both assets in boundary-making. Like rivers, mountain areas may at times be zones of unity, as in low latitude regions where heat and humidity drive people to the uplands. Usually, however, because in colder climes they are areas relatively inhospitable to

---

[8] A controversy over the ownership of territorial waters took place recently, in the dispute between the United States federal government and certain states possessing frontage on the seas, over "oil rights": when the majority of the Supreme Court prevented Alabama and Rhode Island from challenging the constitutionality of the Submerged Lands Act of 1953, Justice Douglas wrote a dissenting opinion. This opinion pointed out that the Justice considered more to be at stake than the ceding of federal offshore oil lands to a few states by stating that "the marginal sea is not an oil well: it is more than a mass of water; it is a protective belt for the entire nation over which the United States must exercise exclusive and paramount authority."

---

[9] H. H. Martin, "Fisheries of the Future," Conservation of Natural Resources, edited by Guy-Harold Smith (New York: John Wiley & Sons, Inc., 1950), p. 437.

human occupance, they are sparsely settled and, therefore, suitable as frontiers.

As separators, some mountain boundaries are unsurpassed. The Indian-Tibetan frontier in the Himalayas and the Andean border between Chile and Argentina are outstanding examples of defensive frontiers. Here the mountains impose severe natural barriers— high, rugged, snow-covered, and glaciated. As barriers, however, (and "barrier" signifies "barrier-to-movement"), the character of mountains varies. Not always does rugged appearance negate easy passes; nor is a high pass necessarily more difficult than a low one. The mountains of western United States probably constituted no more serious a barrier to the pioneer movement than did the deserts for the Rockies are cut through in several places by long, low-slung gaps. The very ruggedness of the Italian-Swiss Alps has aided rather than hindered movement between north and south Europe. Here, steepness of slope has meant less tunneling in the construction of railroads. In some mountains the ridges make better passes than the valleys—as in the Himalayas where valleys are so deep and sheer that it is almost impossible to emerge from them once they are entered, and in the dissected plateau area west of Sydney in Australia where the Blue Mountain passes run along ridge-tops that separate abrupt canyons.

The boundary *line* in mountains may be delimited in terms of the highest crests (summits), the watershed (or divide), along points some place below the highest portions, or along the foot of the slopes. Several boundary commissions may be required to work at the setting up of such a mountain border, employing detailed surveying and mapping information, before the involved states are satisfied.

The nomenclature used in describing mountains and mountain boundaries is often very deceiving and, therefore, frequently great care has been necessary by boundary commissions in delimiting such frontiers. The water parting, crest, and highest peaks do not always form synonymous lines; actually, they may be separate lines, widely spaced. The classical example of the difficulties that reliance on such terminology may involve in the setting up of a borderline in mountain areas is that of the southern Andes: here the precipitous west-flowing streams eat headward to spread their drainage systems into the eastern flanks of the mountains. Three centuries of disturbed inter-state relations, and long and tedious negotiations by boundary commissions, preceded the final acceptance of the present Chilean-Argentine border.

Every mountain area has its own character, and its effectiveness or lack of effectiveness as a hindrance to circulation—and therefore as an effectual barrier frontier—varies from that of other mountain groups. However, as pointed out, some mountains may present less serious obstacles to surface movement than do deserts, swamps, tropical forests, and the like. Though high peaks and the hazard of cloud-coverage may interfere with even air transport, yet, typically, desert routes follow the base or seek mountain trails for water; man settles in mountainous regions for reasons of safety, or to exploit the resources—power, pastures, timbers, minerals.

CULTURAL BOUNDARIES

A cultural boundary is one laid down to delimit two areas of differing anthropo-geographic characteristics. In a sense, all international boundaries are cultural for their purpose is to separate the human groups known as "nations." The states of Central Europe were defined in terms of "nations" or culture. The boundaries of these new states roughly followed lines of separation between the ethnic traits of the several nationalities involved: language figured most prominently but was not the only trait considered. The Soviet Union is another example where the cultural boundary was prominently employed: the USSR is actually a federation of ethnic groups for every culture group that is comprised of a fairly large number of people representing a distinctive cultural pattern has been given its own political unit within the federation. Such factors as language, religion, tribal affiliation, nationality, historical background, economic unity, etc., may be the basis for delineating cultural frontiers.

Areas of cultural or national separation are usually not sharply defined. Cultural frontiers tend to be zones of blending where ethnic groups merge and intermix. In the definition of a boundary through such a zone, it is usually necessary to be very detailed with respect to towns, railroads, features of the terrain, etc. Even so, few cultural boundaries have been, or can be, drawn so as not to include minority cultural groups within the bounds of either state. At times, such groups assimilate readily into the nation into which they have been incorporated; in other instances, however, they seem unable to reconcile themselves and become festering sores of international difficulty. Some states, to rectify such a condition, have carried out exchanges of peoples—as Turkey and Greece several decades ago, and more lately, Hitler and Mussolini in the Tyrol, and India and Pakistan. Such minority exchanges usually improve relations between the states. Forced evacuation or transfer, or forced assimilation, of minority groups readily become instruments of oppression and are likely to give rise to more problems than they resolve.

GEOMETRICAL BOUNDARIES

Geometrical boundaries make use of straight and curved lines of various kinds. Generally, geometrical boundaries disregard culture and the natural features of the landscape. For the most part, the use of this type of frontier demarcation testifies to "armchair" rather than field boundary-making, and is usually employed either when the area being divided is considered of marginal value or when the negotiators are not familiar with the region. Hence the geometrical type boundary is quite prevalent in newly explored and settled areas of the globe. It was used extensively in Africa, Australia, and the Americas during the early periods in the history of those states.

To say that a boundary disregards cultural or physical features does not always imply that it is unsatisfactory. The two geometric lines

selected to separate Canadian territory from that of the United States—namely, 49 degrees North Latitude between the two countries proper and the 141st meridian West Longitude between Canada and Alaska—have proven very satisfactory as boundaries. There are, however, strong possibilities that a mathematical boundary *may* be out of harmony with the realities of the region. Many instances could be cited that would indicate that boundary lines were laid down regardless of culture groups, economic units, etc., doing violence to established settlement, and creating hardship and bitterness. The Togoland boundary that divides the former German territory into French and British trusteeships (mandates until 1946) though not by any means a straight line, cuts right through the midst of the Ewes tribe, a centuries-old culture group.[10]

It would appear that to lay a rule on a map and draw a line is one of the simplest means of defining a boundary. For the demarcators (people who mark the boundary on the ground), however, the geometrical boundary may give more trouble than almost any other sort. The demarcators of the Canada-Alaska and Canada-United States frontiers "were forced to scale mountains and ford rivers, wherever their line led. Holdich says the meridian boundary of South West Africa was demarcated through a howling wilderness, at great cost of time, money, and even life, though the land was almost worthless. The north end of the meridian boundary between Anglo-Egyptian Sudan and French Equatorial Africa could be reached only by a hazardous dash through a waterless desert."[11] It is almost impossible to mark out a geometrical boundary

---

[10] In 1953, leaders of the Ewes tribe (a group of about 800,000) appealed to the United Nations to be unified. The years of partition, however, had already done much to complicate even the problem of unity: the natives of the British Mandate, attached to the Gold Coast, desired unification with that British territory. When Gold Coast independence was granted in March, 1957, British Togoland was incorporated into the new state of Ghana (as the Gold Coast is now called); the French area remains a trusteeship.

[11] Jones, *op. cit.,* p. 151.

Figure 7.4. The Boundaries of Libya. (Courtesy Columbia University Press. From Boggs, International Boundaries.)

exactly as it has been delimited but once it has been demarcated, surveillance is generally easier than over, say, an unstable river frontier.

COMPLEX BOUNDARIES

Boundaries, it has been noted, may be established on the basis of terrain or ethnic features, or be mathematically defined. However, to delineate a frontier on the basis of any one of these factors will often mean ignoring others that may be nearly or just as important. It is rarely, therefore, that a purely cultural or physical or geometric boundary is laid down; usually boundaries are *compound* in type. Such complex boundaries are compromise lines adjusted to a number of factors. For a short distance the boundary may attempt to strike a balance between the divergent views of the resident people, at another point some physical feature may be the locating factor, at still another some aspect of the economies of the states, etc. When the boundaries of the world states are examined along their entire lengths, it will be seen that most are compound, although single adjustments along frontier segments may reflect the resolution of particular problems. Thus, the United States-Mexican frontier is a physical-geometric boundary.

STEPS IN ESTABLISHING THE LOCATION OF A BOUNDARY

There are three steps in establishing the location of a boundary—territorial *allocation* through political decision, *delimitation* by a treaty, and *demarcation* at the site. In terms of chronology, these steps may take place either simultaneously, or may follow each other in uninterrupted succession, or may be separated from each other by periods of many years. For example, frequently allocation and delimitation are settled at a single meeting; on the other hand, the delimitation of the territory may not take place until long after the area has been acceded. Demarcation may be delayed along all or part of the boundary. In fact, even today, many delimited boundaries have never actually been demarcated. This is especially true of some of the Inner Asian Chinese frontiers.

Allocation is effected by the transfer of a given territory to a given state; and, since the area of a territory is defined by its bounds the second step, delimitation, necessarily follows. Delimitation, which defines the limits of the territory in a treaty, generally takes place at the conference table. The third step—the actual surveying and marking of the boundary on the ground—is carried out by a mixed commission made up of representatives from the interested states.

In principle, there is a strong continuity in boundary-making, regardless of gaps or overlaps in the chronological history. In territorial allocation, nowadays, it is seldom possible to ignore the question of boundary site. A treaty of delimitation involves the choice of site and the choice of words with which to define the site. Also it may include

provisions for demarcation and administration. Demarcation is not solely an engineering task, for almost inevitably there are fine decisions on site to be made. The treaty cannot define the line as exactly as surveyors can run it. In their fine decisions, the demarcators should consider ease of administration. In the placing of monuments and the cutting of vistas through forests, the demarcators are aiding administration. Their final report may contain suggestions on the future management of border affairs.[12]

Territories of varying size may be involved in the allocation of land. Territories allocated may range in area from a few to many thousands of square miles. Such territory may be either forcibly acquired or with the acquiescence of the ceding nation because war and negotiation are the time-honored methods of securing territory. Territorial settlement through negotiation, first practiced in Europe during the seventeenth century, has, since that time, spread throughout most of the world. European states have generally attempted to settle questions of colonial-territorial ownership through negotiation, and thus was the final partitioning of Africa carried out—without hostility except from the Turks and the indigenous peoples themselves, the latter not always yielding peaceably to foreign domination.

Other than direct seizure by war, various types of negotiation are employed for accomplishing the assignments of territory. Included among the ways in which territory may be allocated by negotiation are outright purchase, arbitral award, allocation by some international body, and the plebiscite. Purchase is most frequently used by states in the acquisition of colonial territories (aside from war), and the United States has employed this method of extending the national domain more prominently than has any other nation. On a number of occasions arbitration—or similar processes—have successfully solved perplexing problems of territorial allocation. Two relatively recent and outstanding examples come to mind—the settlements of boundaries between Iraq and Turkey by a League of Nations' Commission, and the union of Italian Eritrea with

12 Jones, *op. cit.*, p. 5.

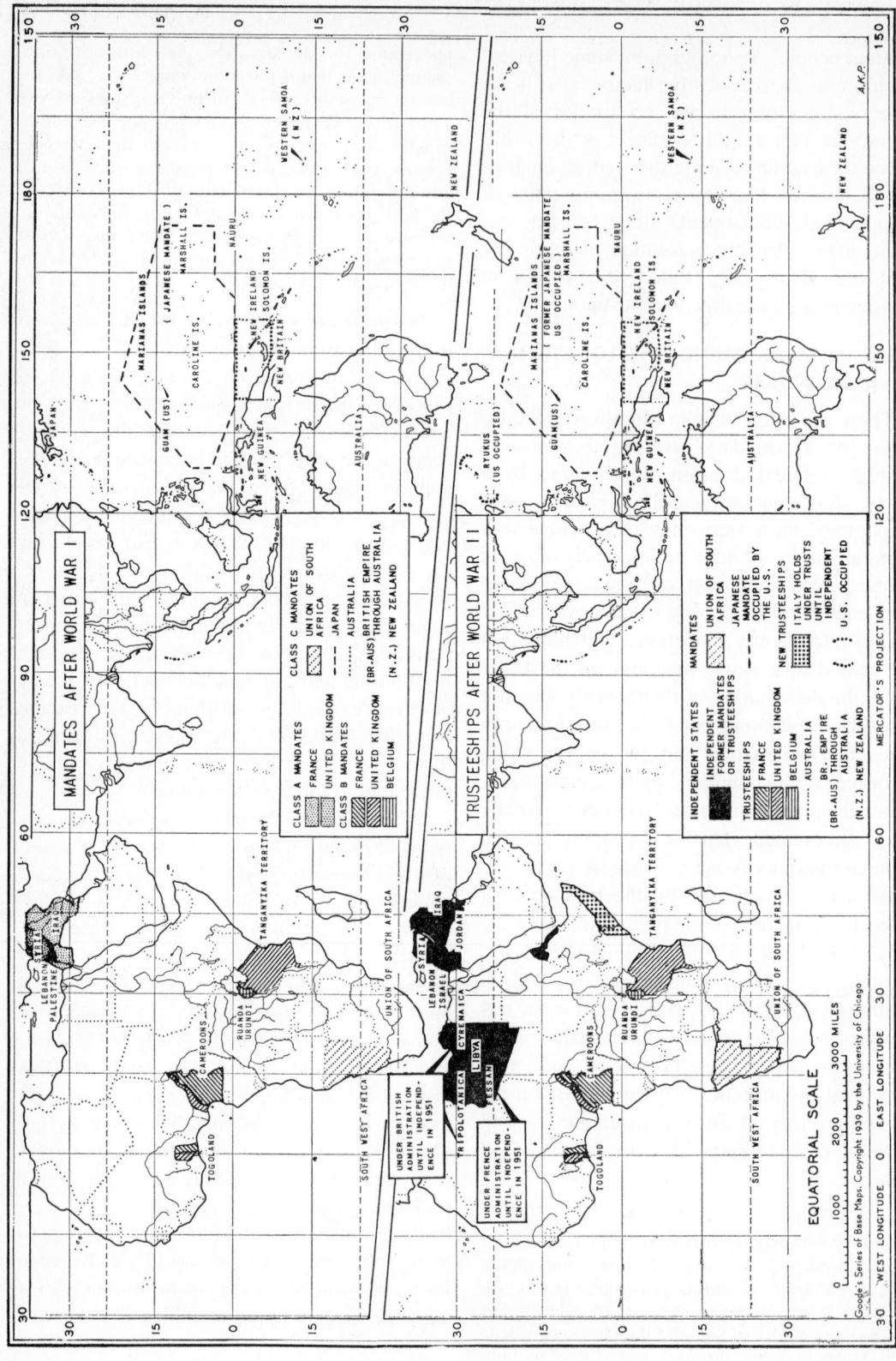

Figure 7.5.

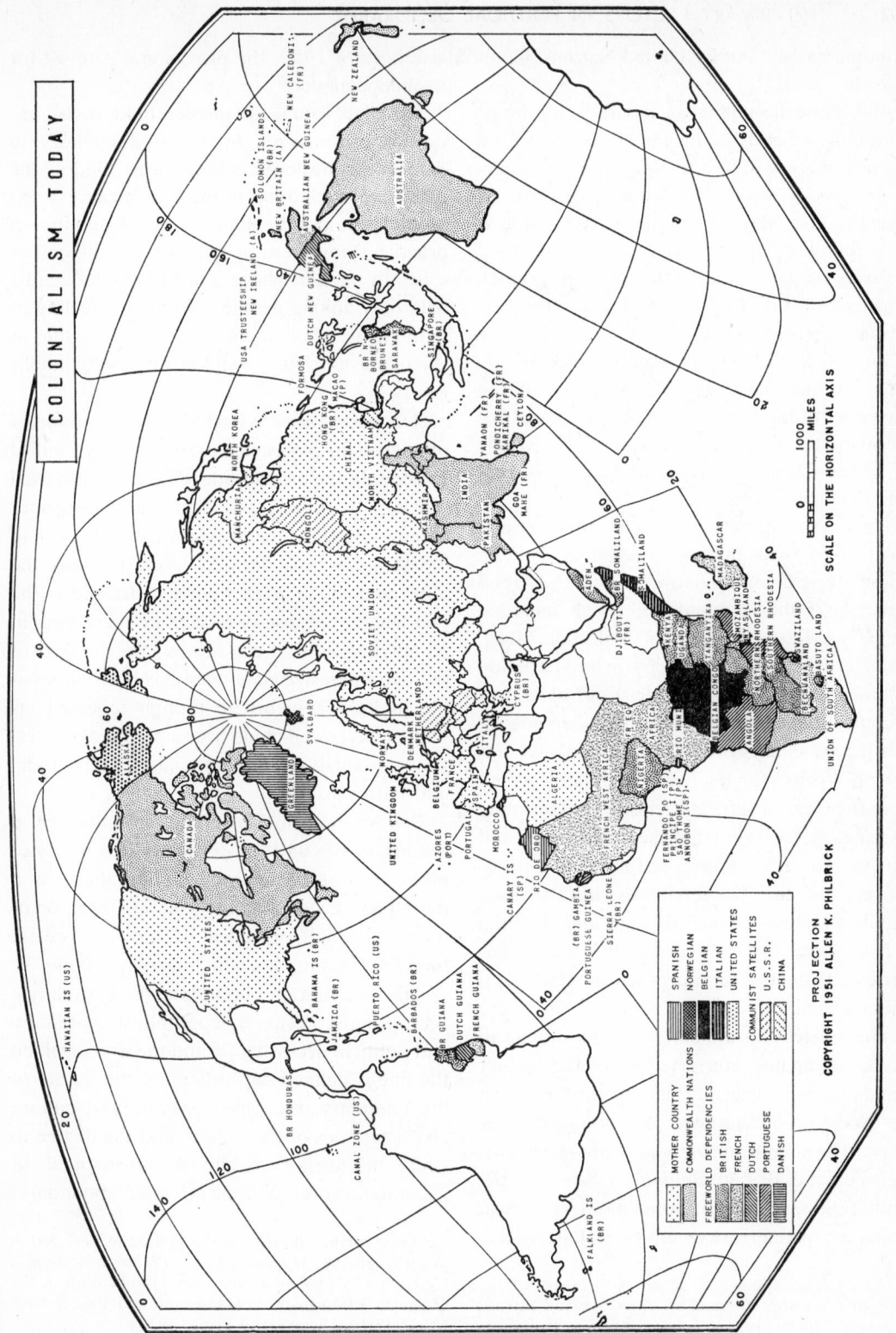

Figure 7.6. (Most small island possessions have been omitted.)

101

Ethiopia carried out by United Nations' Commission.

The apportionment of territory by international bodies is of recent origin. Not until the termination of World War I was an international body, with power to allocate territory, created. The *mandates* of the League of Nations following the World War I armistice and the *trusteeships* of the United Nations (which organization followed on the heels of the cessation of World War II) are the most notable examples of the consignment of territory by such international bodies. Article 22 of the Covenant of the League of Nations established the mandate system and Chapter XII, Article 75 of the Charter of the United Nations, created the "trust" territories.

Under the mandates system, the colonial holdings of Germany and the former Turkish Empire were committed to various of the Allied Powers. Of the A mandates, which included the Near Eastern states of Palestine, Iraq, Transjordan (now Jordan), Syria and Lebanon (French and British Mandates), all have now become independent states; of the C mandates, the Japanese territories were re-assigned following World War II. The B mandates, which were the Central Africa territories of Germany —Tanganyika, Togoland, the Cameroons, and Ruanda-Urundi—have posed more of a problem because they are territories that the three mandate-states—France, Britain and Belgium —have wished to hold along with their other African Colonies for purposes of trade and military security.

The trusteeship system,[13] a plan similar to that of mandates, converted all of the former mandates not receiving independence—with the exception of Southwest Africa—to trusteeships. The administering states are Australia, New Zealand, Britain, Belgium, France and the United States. Italian Somaliland was also made a trust territory, under Italian super-vision, until 1959, the provisional date set for its independence.

The plebiscite is an election held, by an impartial commission, in disputed territory to determine national allegiance. Under the plebiscite, each adult in the region can express an opinion, and the majority ballot obtains. In practice, however, a number of difficulties arise. In the first place, a fair plebiscite can be held only among people who have a feeling of national attachment and to whom the issues at stake are sufficiently well known to vote intelligently.[14]

The period after World War I saw a number of successful plebiscites carried out in Central Europe. In the past decade it has also been used but largely in Asia and Africa among former colonial peoples; the dispensation of Istria and Trieste was thus decided, also. Perhaps the most interesting contemporary instance is the one where, because of lack of cooperation (in complying with all conditions) on the part of the two interested nations, it has been impossible to hold a plebiscite though repeated attempts have been made over a period of several years—namely, in Kashmir, disputed by India and Pakistan.

Delimitation involves the selection of a boundary site and "its definition in a treaty or other formal document." Delimitation "is a more precise step than the general allocation of territory which preceded it, but less precise than the demarcation which usually follows."[15]

The selection of a boundary site is usually a "compromise between geographical suitability and political necessity,"[16] and the way in which the line is defined depends upon the nature of the boundary, the physiographic and culture characteristics of the region, and the degree to which the territory is known and mapped. In general, however, a "treaty *defines* a boundary;

---

[13] For an excellent treatise on the Charter of the United Nations see: Leland M. Goodrich and Edvard Hambro, *Charter of the United Nations, Commentary and Documents* (Boston: World Peace Foundation, 1949).

[14] For further details on the plebiscite, see: Sarah Wambaugh, *A Monograph on Plebiscites, with a Collection of Official Documents* (Publication of the Carnegie Endowment for International Peace, New York: Oxford University Press, 1920).

[15] Jones, *op. cit.,* p. 57.

[16] *Ibid.,* p. 57.

Oil pipeline across the Iranian mountains.

The Rio Grande at El Paso, Texas (Ewing Galloway).

Facing page. Top: A big flock of sheep in a valley on the Georgian Military Road in Dzherakhavakyae Gorge, near Balta, the gateway between Europe and Asia. Most of the population live by sheep-raising, and a little agriculture. Pelts from this region are widely used in the fur trade. (Ewing Galloway.) Center, left: The "Christ of the Andes," Argentina (Ewing Galloway). Center, right: Boundary markers at El Paso, Texas, for the international boundary between the United States and Mexico (Ewing Galloway). Bottom: British forts on the Persia-Baluchistan frontier (Ewing Galloway).

A twenty-foot clearing that marks the line of boundary between the United States and Canada. This is one of the boundary markings which have been erected and kept in repair by the U.S. Section of the International Boundary Commission. (Ewing Galloway).

the final report of the demarcation commission *describes* it . . ."[17] In the location of geometrical boundaries the treaty may define the boundary-site completely, leaving little leeway to the judgment of the demarcators; in other instances, however, only major alignment points may be designated, and the running of the boundary between these selected spottings is up to the demarcation commission. Treaty-definitions, therefore, vary all the way from descriptions of great exactitude to those where the line is characterized in principle only. In the latter instance, the demarcators are left with a wide latitude in which to exercise their judgment. Usually several variations of definition—relative to different sections of the boundary—are found within one treaty. The usual practice is for delimitation to take place at the conference table instead of in the field, and maps are the instruments of definition. The delimitation committee ordinarily does not have detailed or first-hand knowledge of the area, hence the "latitude" allowed to the demarcators who perform their work in the field.

Serious mistakes may creep into the delimitation—errors either in the choice of unsuitable sites, or of suitable sites inaccurately defined. Either type of mistake may be the cause of major international friction and even armed strife. The errors may be the result of unfamiliarity with the frontier being considered or "with the peculiar properties of the geographical features, human and natural, adopted as boundary sites,"[18] inaccurate maps, or a lack of knowledge of the mechanics of boundary definition. An expensive set of errors that resulted from the use of an inaccurate map in the defining of a boundary was that which followed on the Treaty of 1783 which established the independence of the United States and defined its borders. Mitchell's map was the chart employed and (although some of the mistakes were errors of demarcation rather than delimitation), as a result of the map inaccuracies, a series of sixteen negotiations—in the form of

conventions, treaties, and the like—were necessary before the northern frontier was correctly defined and demarcated.

The demarcation of a boundary is, by its very nature, a field operation. Much of the work of demarcation is strictly technical: control by astronomy, triangulation, or aerial photography, projection of the line, mapping a boundary strip, and erection of monuments. However, an element of delimitation enters into the activities of a demarcation commission. Many treaties leave, and all should leave, to the demarcators the final adjustment of the line to local needs and the realities of the terrain. These final adjustments may be of great importance to the smooth functioning of a boundary.

In a thickly settled and highly developed region, the delimitation phase of a commission's work may consume more time than does the physical demarcation. It may prove necessary to make traffic counts, to study marketing areas and school and church attendance, to make or examine maps of mines and public utilities. Interviews, preferably guided by some form of sampling, and public meetings may be required.

A demarcation commission has also a third function, seldom, if ever, explicitly stated. That function is, according to Clifford, the improvement of frontier relationships. A demarcation commission often is the first international civil body to enter a disputed region after a war or period of tension. If the commission is itself harmonious and if good relations are maintained with the populace, international relations may be improved and the new boundary have a better chance of stability.[19]

The actual marking of the boundary is the work of the demarcation commission. Demarcation may be done either through monumentation or linear markings as boundary fences or hedges, or by a swath (vista) through a forest or prairie land. Since it is advantageous that a boundary can be seen along the entire frontier, the latter method is employed in areas of high vegetation where a path, varying usually from four to eight metres in width, is cut. Along the Canada-United States frontier, the two states maintain a "twenty-foot clear skyline" which may require a path more than that width on the ground.

Boundary and property-line monumentation

[17] *Ibid.,* p. 57.
[18] *Ibid.,* p. 57.

[19] *Ibid.,* p. 165.

and marking is an ancient custom; and the respect in which such property lines were held is demonstrated by the fact that ancient markers often bore the likenesses of the gods. In modern times, boundaries that are not marked by natural features may be indicated by cairns, signs, pillars, monuments, beacons, and the like. Naturally marked boundaries may also have markers or monuments. According to approved practice, markers should be so spaced as to be visible from the next nearest marker. To make markers thus "intervisible," it may be necessary to cut brush or intervening vegetation "to keep the boundary vistas open" (as was provided in the 1925 United States-Canada treaty).

BOUNDARY FUNCTION AND SURVEILLANCE

The present political period, which has seen the rapid industrialization and the attendant urbanization of nations, has also witnessed the entrance of government, in increasing amounts, into the affairs of its citizens. The increased government intervention has redounded in "boundary functions" so that along certain frontiers nationalism—or perhaps more accurately, the restraint of intercommunication between states—has become pathological in degree: the Iron and Bamboo Curtains reached the epitome of boundaries functioning as barriers. Although the near-future may see a lessening of such absolute restraint to international intercourse, it also will undoubtedly evidence the retainment by governments of the many and complex functions for which boundaries are set up.

The lives of people are intimately affected by such policies which often determine the potentials for war or peace. Although the moving —or the cutting down in the number—of boundaries does not necessarily promise harmony, nevertheless problems tend to lose their sharpness when the number of functions of international boundaries can be reduced. It is likely that it would prove more feasible to "*change boundary functions* than to *change boundaries themselves.*"[20]

20 *Ibid.,* p. 11

A boundary's suitability and its meaning to the peoples it limits change with changes in ideas, in methods of production, in modes of warfare, in ways of life. That the bombing plane has revolutionized the relationship of men to space hardly needs stating. Less explosive but no less fundamental a change has been the replacement in many lands of relatively immobile peasants by more restless urban and commercial-farm populations. In respect to boundaries, the major changes of modern history have been the replacement of feudalism by nationalism as the dominant political ideal and the related growth of commerce, industry, and cities. The geographical expression of nationalism perhaps reached its ultimate in the territorial clauses of the Paris Treaties of 1919. That the general situation of boundaries has changed since then is obvious. How and when these changes will reach geographical expression lies in the realm of prophecy.[21]

A list of boundary functions of today would almost duplicate a list of human activities. The increasing play of government in all phases of life has made international boundaries sharp and severe barriers. Few natural obstacles restrict the movement of persons, things, and even ideas as completely as do the boundaries of some states. A boundary impinges on life in so many ways that it becomes an important part of the environment. Vested rights and interests develop about it and peaceful change becomes difficult. A peaceful boundary, no matter how queerly located, had best be left alone. It is usually in a period of flux associated with war that sweeping boundary changes have been made. A federal government usually finds it difficult to force boundary changes upon its constituent states. The rigidity of even short-lived boundaries is a reason for ignoring temporary for permanent aims in territorial allocations and for accumulating complete and objective information in advance of territorial settlements.[22]

It is usually not difficult to bring about a change in boundary function relative to such matters as shipment of goods between nations: this does not imply any direct diminution in sovereignty. It is, however, difficult even for political units within nations—as the states and counties of the United States—to agree to a reduction in their political powers—let alone a reduction in national sovereignty over national boundaries. One of the historic political

21 *Ibid.,* p. 4.
22 *Ibid.,* p. 11.

controversies in the United States has been states' versus national rights.[23]

Boundary functions are viewed differently by countries according to the national philosophy of states. Boggs, formerly Chief of the Division of Geography and Cartography, United States Department of State, listed as follows the functions of modern boundaries;

(1) *In respect of persons:* restriction or even total exclusion of immigrants, visitors, and workingmen from foreign countries, because their competition for work and bread is not desired, because their race, their religion, or their political ideas are unwelcome, or for any other reason; restriction or even prevention of contact of a state's own nationals with the nationals of other nations, for any reason; examination and detention of persons with communicable diseases, both of domestic and foreign citizenship; apprehension of criminals and fugitives from justice; and apprehension of persons engaged in illegal movement of things, especially in smuggling;

(2) *In respect of things:* the collection of duties and taxes of legally imported or exported goods; the prevention of illegal movements of goods; prevention of the influx of foreign goods in competition with those of domestic production; control of the movement of money and the precious metals across the frontiers; control of the flights of airplanes across any portion of the national territory; the exercise of sanitary measures, such as plant and animal quarantine.[24]

Another more general analysis of boundary functions breaks them down into: 1) military; 2) non-military. This division is somewhat similar to the interpretation given by Spykman, who wrote:

The boundary is . . . not only a line of demarcation between legal systems but also a point of contact of territorial power structures. From the long-term point of view, the position of that line may become an index to the power relations of *the contending forces.*[25]

Modern warfare, due to its "total" character, has lessened the differences between military and non-military boundary functions; however, the distinction between North American and European frontiers has continued to be the importance placed on the military function on the latter continent.

Regardless of which interpretation is major, the boundary between nations is the expression of the limit of the sovereignty of any state, and it is for this reason that it is so difficult to decrease the rigidness of the boundary, functionally speaking. The international boundary is a more effective barrier in halting the movement of people, goods, and machines than are the widest oceans, highest mountains, most arid deserts.

Boundary functions vary according to the purposes of the state. In general, the functions of boundaries are "negative rather than positive."[26,27] Depending on the administration of the frontier, boundaries restrict the movements of goods and people to a greater or lesser degree. If they are simple administrative boundaries, as between minor internal political units, they scarcely have a limiting function. But, since international boundaries are set up to preserve the integrity of a nation's people in various ways, by their very character they are unable to promote trade or communication as is sometimes held.

Surveillance of the frontier varies with function. An unusual number of boundary restraints obtains in some parts of the modern political world. It is possible for problems to arise in connection with any or all of the functions: they may cause friction and administrative difficulties that often call for diplomatic negotiation. In the case of water boundaries, not only functional difficulties, but the surveillance and control of fishing, navigation, water for irrigation and domestic and industrial sup-

---

[23] It still goes on, actually, today in such matters as the setting aside of forest lands within states as national forest reserves, etc.

[24] S. Whittemore Boggs, *International Boundaries* (New York: Columbia University Press, 1940), p. 10.

[25] Nicholas John Spykman, "Frontiers, Security, and International Organization," *Geographical Review,* Vol. 32 (1942), p. 437.

[26] Boggs, *op. cit.,* p. 11.

[27] From the viewpoint of the nation concerned, however, the functions of national boundaries are considered "positive"; boundaries set up to preserve national homogeneity are also regarded as positive.

ply, pollution, etc., make their administration particularly complex.

THE OPEN VERSUS THE CLOSED SKY

Under conditions of peace, in order to cut down on the number of incidents that might cause friction between states, flying restrictions limit the national boundary zones across which commercial craft may move. Usually they enter by way of specified gateways. There is a dual reason for this: first, it permits a check on all vehicles and persons entering or leaving a country; and, secondly, it safeguards the border zones from being spied upon by unfriendly parties. In certain states, large areas are banned to planes. Even the leasing of airbases on the territories of friendly states does not give the nation that is the leaseholder the right to use the bases for commercial aircraft: in the interest of security it may be deemed best not to allow access to commercial planes.

International law on commercial air transport prescribes to two related principles: 1) that every state has jurisdiction over its own "air"; 2) the "closed port" system. Under the first tenet, legally, the planes of no nation can navigate over the territory of another country without permission: the only "free air" lies over the oceans and international seas beyond the three-mile limit.[28] The second principle holds with the right of a state to open or close its airports to the aircraft of any other nation, as it sees fit. A state, therefore, may grant the right of free transit without permitting planes to land; or, contrawise, may grant planes the right to land at designated airports to discharge and take on cargo and passengers, but not allow complete transit over its territories.

The core of international commercial aviation is, of course, the open port: in lieu of internationalization of airports and air—which would allow planes of every nation to fly at will over all territories—are agreements made between nations regulating transit and the use of airports. Although only a few states engage in international commercial flying, every country in the world has interests in the laws and regulations relative to such traffic for all nations are served by commercial planes, whether their own or those of another nationality. Because of trade interests and the maintenance of national security, policies of international air commerce have necessarily become a part of the state problems of every country.

INTER-REALM BOUNDARIES

Of profound importance to the two-world situation that has obtained in international politics almost from the cessation of World War II has been the change that was brought about by the gradual emergence of a third force—the force of neutralism. The character of the political globe has been altered in the strategic and political aspect by this new tripartite division, for the group of uncommitted states is doing much to balance the power of the world as expressed in the power blocs—Communism and the West. The political world today is a three-power world—although the power of the three forces differs considerably, due to (besides other factors) the degree of integration found within the several blocs. *The new alignment has raised new boundaries—multinational boundaries—some of which are more impenetrable than any national frontier has ever been;* in other cases, it has broken their rigidity.

Due to the mass of accumulated power that both the Western and Communist blocs represent, these realm boundaries are likewise more formidable than the frontiers of any individual state. On either side of the realm boundaries, however, between the states within the two power-blocs, boundary restrictions have been lowered considerably to the movement of goods, people,[29] and ideas—in the case of certain Western states, lowered to a degree where closer international integration has been ac-

---

[28] Some states hold to the twelve-mile limit even as it pertains to the air.

[29] One of the sources of greatest discontent among the Western states are the trade barriers (in the form of tariffs), the restrictive immigration laws, and the high cost of visas of the United States. Americans travel in most Western countries without a visa; only a passport is necessary.

complished than has been known between sovereign states not joined in a union or federation. Individually for the Communist bloc and the West, this has been advantageous for it has meant, to the states *within each bloc,* increased international trade, greater equalization of resources and wealth and technological knowledge, the exchange of ideas, and the contribution of aid to one another in the form of finances, skilled technicians, and even military advice and weapons. Thus, the economies of the states have, in general, prospered; and the security of the boundaries has been more surely guaranteed.

The neutral force, however, has raised no new boundaries nor changed the degree of function of old ones, for this is not a close group of nations. Rather, they are a force only because they adhere to like ideas—*i.e.* they maintain a status of neutrality, aligning themselves with neither the West nor the Communist nations.

The multi-state frontier is a new political phenomenon. But the political-realm boundaries are uneasy borders—in places, they have been zones of hot and cold wars and pressures, and of much diplomatic maneuvering. The boundary has a different significance for each of the three power-forces according to their view of the functions of these frontiers: the Communist bloc regards it as a (potentially) moving frontier along which Communism spreads; the West is putting all of its efforts into keeping the status quo; the neutral states are spending much of their diplomatic energies in attempting to decrease the friction along the several frontiers lest they flare into frontiers of war—or lest the states themselves become involved or engulfed within the struggle.

As with the national frontier, within the bounds of the inter-realm borders there is a feeling of identity through common ideology, connoting at the same time a sense of "foreignness" to areas outside the boundary. This feeling is present and persistent within each bloc even though customs and languages differ. The rigidity of the multi-national borders have accentuated the sense, to those inside the boundary, of "outside" nations and this, coupled with internal restraints, indoctrination, aggressiveness (toward the countries of the other bloc), even fear, has led to frontier incidents, the building up of "bloc" defenses, wars hot and cold. Boundary incidents have been used by all of the three forces for the purpose of manipulating their populations. The policy of the USSR—in seeking to extend the zone of uncommitted states in Europe by neutralizing Austria, by attempting to accomplish the same stratagem in Yugoslavia and by advocating a "united Germany"—has been for the purpose of *deepening* the frontier zone between itself and the Western states, temporarily at least, and, in the future, of possibly expanding the Communist frontier to the outer edge of these neutral nations.

In a political world that seems, at present, to be moving toward the partial supplantation of the political unit known as the state with international alignments of various sorts, the multinational (or inter-realm) boundary must be recognized. On the way these frontiers function will depend the future international relations of the world—more so than upon the individual national frontier.

IN CONCLUSION

In the words of Isaiah Bowman, "One is inclined to say that the chief defect of any boundary is its *definition,* a quality that is indispensable in the modern world with almost every square mile of land occupied and desirable for production or site."[30]

Boundaries that have been relatively permanent and frictionless provide no clue to an easy principle for the setting up of satisfactory and unsatisfactory boundaries. Desirable and undesirable boundaries do not run to type and it is impossible to say in advance which boundaries will or will not prove frictionless. ". . . boundary problems in Europe are largely due to the fact that too much history is remembered, in contrast to the genesis of boundary problems in the Americas where too little

---

[30] Isaiah Bowman, "Foreword," from Boggs, *op. cit.,* p. v.

geography was known when the boundaries were first defined."[31] For this reason it is hard for Americans to understand the frontier problems of European countries. "The boundaries are set as perimeters of areas of separate nationalities, and, because the essence of national consciousness is sentiment, each nation builds upon those periods in history and those grander limits of territorial extent which reflect the accomplishment of great things in the past and which serve as earnest [guides] of equally great achievement in the future."[32]

Plans of international economic affiliation and political integration that would link European states into closely associated groups have been disfavored in Europe due to a reluctance to relinquish any degree of national sovereignty and to an apprehension that the accumulated power might be usurped by one of the participating states. It is this latter fear—that France holds with regard to Germany—that has held France from participating fully in the Monnet plan for economic integration although the

[31] *Ibid.,* p. 118.
[32] *Ibid.*

draft of this international cooperative venture originated with one of her own nationals.

For the pacific resolution of international boundary problems it is vital that the issues themselves be not dramatized, and that the emotions of the citizens of the involved states are not excited. Boundary questions should be resolved with as little publicity and in as cool an atmosphere as it is possible to obtain.

Every factor related to the frontier should be considered when a boundary is being defined or boundary questions reopened, and the greatest care should be exercised to place the line where the least possible friction is likely to occur and where administration expenditures can be held to a minimum. Once the frontier has been established, the states should try to avoid creating a barrier, but should attempt instead to keep the functions simple so as to facilitate international movement rather than to curb it. Simplification of boundary functions is one of the greatest needs in those areas where friction is recurrent. When disputes and incidents do arise, they should be handled at once —impartially to both sides.

8

The Concept of Power in a

Bi-Polar World

Historically, and without exception, the great powers of the world from the Persians on have been those that have, by one means or another, expanded their territories either into contiguous areas so to enlarge the nation itself or into extra-continental regions to develop great colonial empires. As justly as we label the early Romans, in the days of empire, imperialistic we must name Russia and early United States in the same manner. Ruins of temples and other structures, uncovered in the farthest reaches of the Roman Empire, indicate that peoples from the southern peninsula migrated into the wildernesses of Europe to populate colonial holdings. Rome, therefore, was not merely an empire built on marching legions; its colonists followed the armies; the United States and Russia pushed their borders outward, across millions of square miles of territory held by other peoples, in the wake of

colonists from the nuclear areas of the mother states.

Following the unveiling of the Orient and the virgin world in the West to European intelligence, the new lands were looked upon as regions ripe for exploitation by European peoples, and individuals and governments made it a common venture, complementing each other. With the development of the resources of the Western Hemisphere, the East, and Africa, there evolved the interconnected structure of world economy, grounded on international trade, that typifies the global relations in the present era. A primary motivation in this exploitation of extra-European territories was profit although other motives entered in. As time went on, national prestige became increasingly important for to gain a position of political importance seemed to demand an empire. This, then, provoked the last wild scramble for even the most marginal of the "exploitable,"[1] unclaimed lands of the earth.

As the globe opened up to the energetic ambitions of Europeans, power became distributed among a number of states, those making the most extensive conquests of territory attaining the greatest strength. However, as one part of the world after another continued to unfold, some of the new lands earlier held by European powers were successful in freeing themselves from the rule of the mother country. These territories were largely within the belt of the mid-latitudes, in those climates where Europeans found an environment most similar to the one from which they had migrated. In time, as colonies liberated themselves from the hold of the colonial powers, certain of the West European nations waned in power while, concomitantly, outside of Europe, certain other countries increased in strength.

Throughout the interval of centuries between the days of the Romans, who conquered nearly all of the then-known world,[2] and up until the post-World War II period, no possibility of world domination by one power became imminent.[3] After 1945, however, Communist USSR posed this threat. It was to counteract the menace of world domination that the Western powers built up their military strength—to balance that of the Communist bloc of states. And with this dual build-up in territory (through consolidation), resources, industrial and agricultural production, etc., *two poles of world power* arose—the Western and the Communist.

THE POLITICAL ALIGNMENTS OF THE PRESENT DAY

Up until mid-1954 there were essentially two power blocs, and it was customary to refer to the political globe as a *bi-polar* world, giving polarity to the United States and the USSR, each with their respective allies or satellites. A third force has gradually emerged, however, that may have the power to alter profoundly this global strategic and political picture, namely, neutralism. Two Great Powers—and two "poles" of power—still survive, but the greater part of the human race lies outside the frontiers of both the United States and the Soviet Union—and approximately one-half of the world's population remains outside of the two polar blocs. The future political and economic policies of the states within this huge intervening belt of territories is important: the relative areas, populations, resources, and industrial strength of the Western and Communist blocs are not the only factors that are going to be decisive in the relations of the two great centers of power. A number of other developments in Europe and Asia have stimulated the growth of the third force, variously termed neutralism, fence-sitting, the uncommitted bloc, the pacifists—sometimes, the restoration of the balance of power. The implications of this growth, although still speculative and subject entirely to future events, are profoundly significant to a two-world situation. A complete global realignment and major shift in United States and Soviet strategic policies is the possible outcome. Neutralism presents Western diplomats with one of their most difficult problems; conversely, it plays into the hands of the Soviet Bloc.

There are, therefore, two "*poles of power*" but *three* political *forces* in the world today—the Western, the Communist, and the Neutral—each hung together more or less loosely, consciously or unconsciously.

THE WESTERN BLOC

The Western Bloc is physically fragmented, connected only through effective means of transportation and communication. The United States and the other countries of the Americas, Africa, Australia and New Zealand are insular (in strategic terms), occupying positions "external" to the central land and

---

[1] Whittlesey, *op. cit.*, p. 78.

[2] *I.e.* known to Europeans.

[3] Except by the Holy Roman Empire which, through the subservience of kings to the Pope (as Charlemagne and the Germanic rulers), held sway and *extended its power* up into the middle of the 18th century. The parallel is somewhat different, however, than with the purely political state.

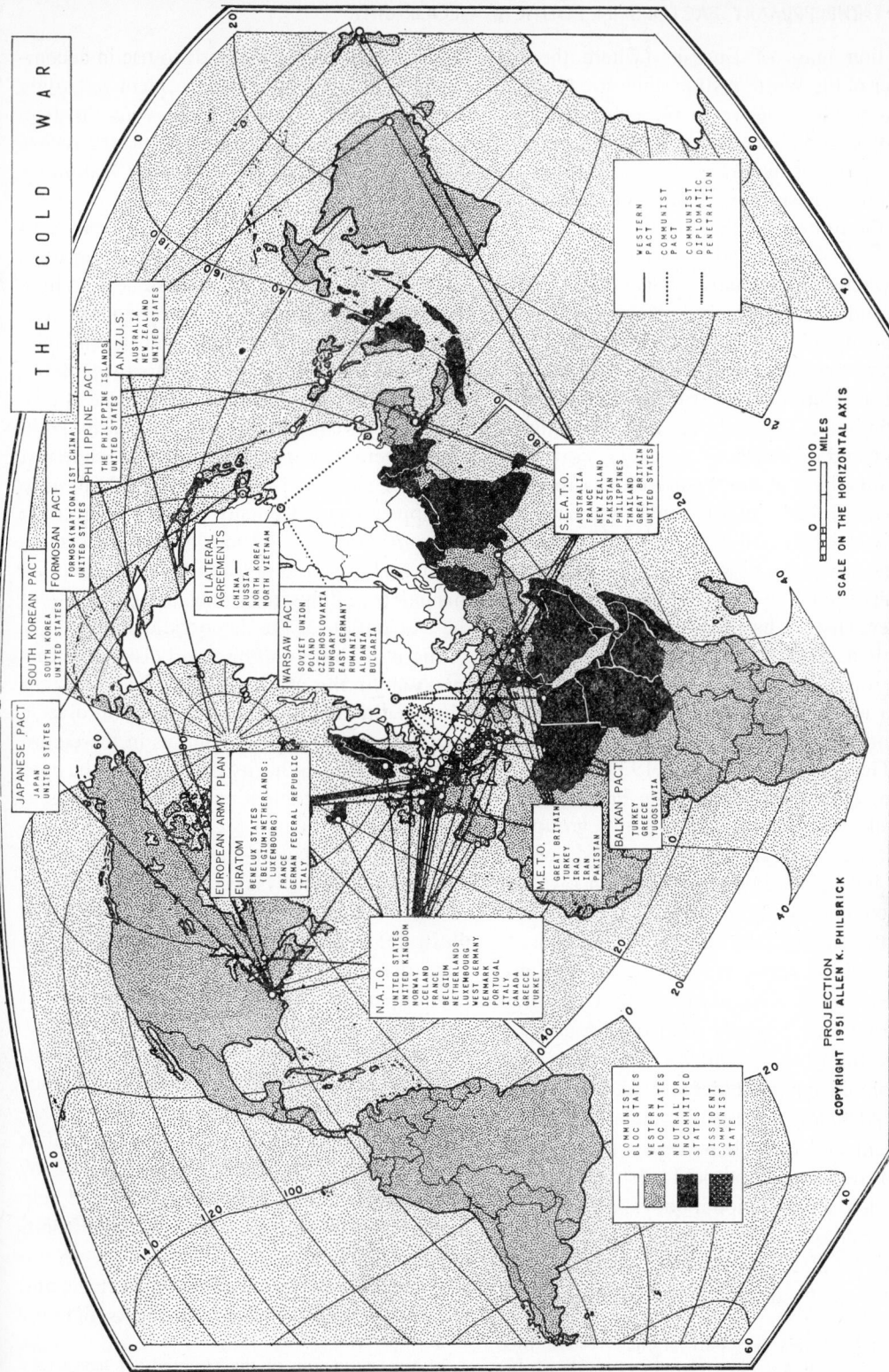

Figure 8.1. As the Cold War has progressed, two of the three power blocs—Western and Communist—have set up a series of interlocking defense pacts to further strengthen ties within the blocs among the bloc-states. This map shows the more important of these alliances along with a listing of the member states.

population mass of Eurasia (where the remainder of the Western Bloc states are found). They are able to move to the coastal fringelands of Europe and Asia only over long distances by sea or by air.

With few exceptions, a common philosophy unites the nations of the West.[4] The states of the Western Bloc are, in most instances, nations where "individuals" have dignity and status, and where collective opinions represent government opinion. Currently, the most binding force is negative in character: i.e. security against the Communist world, and a halting of the continuing spread of the Communist ideology and influence.

The members of the Western Bloc are variously crosslinked. International organizations of various kinds and with varying purposes bind the several nations together. The West has staked much in its comprehensive defense alliances. History has demonstrated, however, that reliance on mere formal agreements is treacherous; to bear this out, it is necessary only to recall Italy's shift in the First World War and the quick turnabout of relations between Germany and Russia in 1939 and 1940. On the other hand, during the last war, the most effective alliance among any group of nations was one compacted not by law or treaty, but by the bonds of common loyalties and a common body of values, i.e. the tie between the United States and Great Britain.

Some of the states in the Western Bloc are former enemies. Several of the Western Allies have been only recently antagonistic and aggressive to the very countries with whom they now join in common defense and economic effort. At times, some of the members are intransigent and difficult to deal with—usually due to reluctance to yield certain national powers to the international body. At times even the overall objectives of the Western states seem to be at variance with each other. But more frequently discordance is due to a lack

of agreement on the methods to use in accomplishing the aims. The disagreement regarding the kind and amount of trade with the Iron Curtain countries is a case in point; the recognition of Red China by the United Nations is another.

Democracy[5] cannot utilize any means—and remain a democracy—to attain an end as does Communism. Democracy is more flexible than dictatorship, but it is also slower to act; it is more volatile and sometimes less dependable. The ideal of freedom and democracy of the Western Bloc is its greatest asset, but it is also its greatest weakness. This is necessarily so in the democratic way of doing things. Frequently, however, slow and contentious methods give the appearance—to many peoples both inside and outside of the Western group—of disharmony and even the outright hostility, creating misunderstandings regarding the closeness of the association of the democratic states.

There are both unifying and disruptive factors within the Western Bloc. The Western Bloc is literally, "an aggregation of diverse voluntary associations." And, as in the democratic state, the authority derives from the consent of the participating parties (the governed); hence, behind *the law* of the Western Bloc stands the law of the cooperating states. The accent on *means* is clearly another essence of the ideology and practice of the West. To illustrate: could one of the Communist states have dissented from joining the Communist counterpart of NATO, the Warsaw Pact? It took but half an hour to pass this measure, complete in all details. Where, on the other hand, but in a democratic alliance could France have turned down the European Defense Project (EDC) as it did in November 1954, after months of tedious work and acceptance by other powers? And then turn around and help to work out an alternate plan to hold the bonds of western unity?

A common danger, a common heritage, and a common objective have forged links that now

---

[4] Most of Africa is a part of the Western Bloc simply because it is a "dependency" of the West. No common philosophy unites the indigenes with the controlling Europeans or the mother country.

[5] For a discussion of the essentials of democracy see: William Ebenstein, *Today's Isms* (Englewood Cliffs, N.J.: Prentice-Hall, Inc., 1958), pp. 119–192.

bind the United States more tightly to the other states of the Western Bloc than at any time in the history of the republic. The *danger* was and is Communism (aggression, specifically by Russia and China); the *heritage* is European civilization, transmitted to the United States by millions of colonists and immigrants—English and Poles, Italians and Germans, Scandinavian and Irish; the long-range *objective* is peace.[6] The depth and importance of the ties behind the current relationship of the United States and Western Europe are often overlooked in the debate over free world policy.

Regarding the common danger, there is general political agreement among the states of the Western Bloc not only that defense measures must be taken that will raise barriers to Communist expansion, but that Soviet diplomatic maneuvers must be met in *concert*. Further, the combined forces of the West, political and military, must find some means of lessening the hold of the Soviets upon the center of Europe—and keep it from advancing farther. However, the *means*[7] by which this is to be done are perhaps the foremost divisive factors threatening to separate the states of the Western Bloc.

Another factor that has been—and is—a source of much strain between European nations and the United States are the colonial connections of the West European powers with various overseas territories. Because the United States has interfered—naturally, perhaps rightfully, but frequently indiscreetly—in colonial affairs, it has been harshly criticized: it is part of Dutch dogma that the United States was responsible for the loss of the Indies. On the other hand, the American state is frequently criticized by others for non-interference when the country refrains from participating in the colonial affairs of other nations.

There is a strong and evident economic interdependence among the states of the Western alliance. Today, however, because West Europe is prosperous, this mutual economic dependence is less obvious than it was a few years ago. Nevertheless, observers of the economies of Great Britain, Italy, Belgium, the Netherlands, France, and Germany indicate an increased intricacy and strength in the relationship between great industries and trade on both sides of the Atlantic Ocean. This relationship raises its own stresses and tensions, however—in the competition of the United States, England, and Germany for world markets, and in the tariff barriers of the American state. A further dispute over the economic aspect has been East-West trade—the European states have been eager to renew and enlarge such trade relations; the United States has held out against it.

In working toward the resolution of all of these differences and disputes, both Europe and the United States are assisted by the common heritage. However, this heritage must be viewed in its broadest terms: for example, it is apparent that a Scandinavian Socialist minister can have little in common politically with the government of the Spaniard, Francisco Franco. Although the cradle of American culture lies in Europe, the common heritage is less effective as an adhesive within the Western Bloc than it should be.

Above all these historical bonds and present stresses is a general concordance on peace and the need for halting Communist expansion. Even here, however, there are "hot" and "lukewarm" moments: whenever American policy seems to be gambling with peace, the ties between the United States and West European nations are weakest; when American leaders speak out firmly for peace, the links are strongest.

The ties that bind the Western Bloc together are complex, and the coalition is only as strong as the will of the cooperating states to work together. Herein is the Achilles' heel of the West. However, the disruptive influences are likely not as strong as those that link the

---

[6] In the United States—and more lately in Canada —the European civilization has been *Americanized,* creating what might almost be called an American civilization, an offshoot of, but distinct from, the European.

[7] *A propos,* the Eisenhower Doctrine and the British-French attack on Egypt for possession of the Suez Canal.

states together—a common descent, culture, and idealogy, a common peril, and a common purpose.

The states of the Western Bloc rim the Communist Euro-Asian core. They are represented by three separated land-masses that extend out from the center almost like three great lobes: non-Communist Europe and Africa; Australia-New Zealand, Japan, and the Pacific isles; North and South America. In contrast to most of the Communist Bloc, which is continental in character, the Western Bloc is by nature dual in character—maritime and continental. With the West, mobility on the oceans is a necessity for without it the parts cannot hang together and it loses its power. The West is—and must be, therefore—amphibious; the Communist Bloc is not—need not be—and will not be truly amphibious unless it moves across Western territory to the sea, encompassing maritime lands within its embrace in the process.

It becomes increasingly more difficult to say which of the three lobes of the Western Bloc is the most important for each is significant in its own way. Of the major land masses, South America would appear the least important strategically as to location and raw materials. Yet, adjacent to it is the Panama Canal, and from this continent the West secures bauxite, petroleum, copper, tin, and iron, to list only a few of the natural resources.

Parts—though not all—of the Western Bloc are highly developed in contrast to the Communist states which, relatively, are under-developed in spite of the large industrial build-up that has characterized the Soviet state and some of the satellite countries. The two most important regions of industrial development, as well as significant "power" source-areas, are located in the West, namely, northeast United States and northwest Europe. Although ocean trade has been an advantage in the development of many of the Western nations and serves, as well, the function of holding the sections physically together, nevertheless, the physical unity of the Communist Bloc places the West at a disadvantage.

Since the cessation of hostilities in 1945, the West has been faced with the difficult task of working out policies that would be most likely to afford security and maintain the peace. During the previous century, "keeping of the peace" rested largely on the British Empire which operated with mobility and flexibility through its large navy and its network of naval bases spread across the world. The two world wars of the twentieth century, however, decimated the resources and strength of the individual states that had in the past been the world powers and created an entirely new international situation: 1) to the United States fell the leadership of the free world that had previously been held by several states; 2) the aftermath of the wars created the condition where no one power, however great, could by itself maintain the peace and security of the world against the new aggressive force of Communism for no single state had sufficient power or reach.

The changed conditions of national and world economic and political strength have enhanced the role of the dependent territories. To a greater degree than in any period of the past, dependencies have become significant, and, with the loss of most of the European holdings in Asia, the role of Africa has steadily advanced in importance. Phosphates, tin, copper, cobalt, uranium, radium, iron ore, diamonds, gold, manganese, lead, zinc, oils and other agricultural and forest products now flow "West"-ward to supplement national resources and replace those that could previously have been expected to come from other colonies. The significance of Africa extends beyond its role as a source of raw materials. It is also critical because of its position of strategic importance: effective control of the Mediterranean Sea and Gibraltar, of Suez, of the lifeline between northwest Europe and East Asia and the Pacific, of Europe, and even of the entire Western Bloc depends to a great degree upon the position of the West in Africa—hence, the great concern of Western nations (aside from French national considerations) with the problems of the North African territories. Whether or not Western security could be maintained without Africa is a question.

The structure of Western economic and political unity. The collective-security, defense, and economic concepts are still in the process of evolution and are represented by a wide variety of pacts, alliances, and agreements in various stages of development and acceptance. The *Inter-American Treaty of Reciprocal Assistance* (Rio Pact) of 1947 was among the first of a series of international agreements designed to help secure national security and world order. It was a collective security pact and bound the participating nations as follows: "an armed attack against one [nation] would be considered as an attack against all." The *North Atlantic Treaty Organization* (NATO) is a regional alliance premised on somewhat the same formula. It goes much further in organizing the combined military forces and facilities —but it falls short of the commitments made by nations that participate in collective security agreements. NATO makes provision for essential air and naval bases as well as for the planes and ships and weapons that will operate from these bases; however, each member-state "can contribute—according to its means and capabilities."

One of the idealistic things that made NATO distinctive was the intention to develop an Atlantic Community. That community was to have no formal political institutions—at least at the beginning—but was to be an association of nations growing together naturally through day-to-day cooperation: military, economic, and political. Economic rebuilding was stimulated through financial aid extended by the United States.[8] In contrast, political cooperation has been elusive and disappointing in cases where it has not been absent. The political arrangements of NATO are unusual in that they govern a military organization on the principle of unanimity.

The heart of the alliance is military and lies in Article Five of the North Atlantic Treaty:

The Parties agree that an armed attack against one or more of them in Europe or North America shall be considered an attack against them all; and consequently they agree that, if such an armed attack occurs, each of them, in exercise of the right of individual or collective self-defense recognized by Article 51 of the Charter of the United Nations, will assist the Party or Parties so attacked by taking forthwith, individually and in concert with the other Parties, such action as it deems necessary, including the use of armed force, to restore and maintain the security of the North Atlantic area.

Any such armed attack and all measures taken as a result thereof shall immediately be reported to the Security Council. Such measures shall be terminated when the Security Council has taken the measures necessary to restore and maintain international peace and security.

As a deterrent against the spread of Communist control in Europe, NATO has been successful. However, the Korean War brought out the fact that Communist ambitions were not confined to European territories. Accordingly, NATO was broadened to include countries in the Eastern Mediterranean (Greece and Turkey), and the United States and Great Britain began to set up a system of defense pacts—bilateral and multilateral—with and between Asian and Pacific states that might act to insulate Outer Asia and Africa against Communism. The Southeast Asia Treaty Organization (SEATO) and the Middle East Treaty Organization (the Bagdad Pact) evolved.

Of these pacts SEATO is the most extensive (though not necessarily the most consequential).[9] Signed at Manila on March 19, 1955, by eight nations (and later ratified), the pact is an instrument of mutual defense under which the party states signified their collective determination to stand together against Communism—considered as a common threat to their freedom and political ideals. The Manila Pact is not a counterpart of the European defense commitments; it merely pledges the signatory powers to immediate consultation in case of a threat to any by either aggression or subversion, and

---

[8] Through the Marshall Plan, ECA, MSA, the International Bank, etc.

[9] Bi-partite pacts entered into between the United States and single Asian countries have tended to have a highly explosive character—as the pacts between this country and 1) Korea; and 2) Formosa.

to take required action within the limitations of their constitutional processes. *Anzus,* another in the series of Pacific defense treaties, is subscribed to by the United States, Australia, and New Zealand. In South and Southwest Asia, other security pacts have also been set up: the *Balkan Alliance* between Greece, Turkey, and Yugoslavia; the *Turkey-Iraq Pact;* and the *Turkey-Pakistan defense agreement.* Thus, a whole chain of interlacing treaties and pacts links the Western nations of Canada, the United States, and Great Britain with allies in Asia and the Pacific areas.

As a concomitant of these defense alliances, some beginnings of international economic planning and unification within the Western Bloc have been made, largely in Europe. *Benelux* is perhaps the most successful of Western European economic unity plans; it was the trail-blazer of European integration. Opposition to the completion of the economic union between Belgium, the Netherlands, and Luxembourg[10] has almost disappeared in private industry and agriculture. However, the objection of some private interests (which thought they might be injured by competition) have frequently forced the postponement of new moves to establish a common market among the three countries. In spite of this, private interests have never succeeded in diverting the three governments from the goal of full economic union.

The final phases of Benelux will move more slowly than the early ones because they are more difficult. But they are going forward with the support of, and even on the initiative of, the affected private interests, not against their opposition. Most of the remaining obstacles to full union are in agriculture. These are to be removed by 1962 under a program of mutual adjustment already under way.

The *Coal-Steel Community* (Schuman Plan) is an economic integration plan on a larger scale than Benelux and embraces the three

states of the latter Union as well as France, West Germany, and Italy. Under the materialized plan, established by treaty April 18, 1951, the six nations are not only removing tariffs and import quotas on coal and steel, but are giving up their traditional rights to impose such trade barriers: they are replacing national controls with controls exercised by the supranational High Authority of the Community. Technically it is a plan for linking the two basic industries, regardless of political frontiers, in what is called a coal and steel "community"— the latter to be governed by a single set of policies.

In May 1955, the Benelux countries, with approval from West Germany and Italy, called for an extension of the Schuman Plan principle of integration into other economic facets, notably transportation and atomic energy, but the French cabinet indirectly rejected the proposal. At the same time it issued a general statement of endorsement to the European integration idea in principle.

However, a later move toward the further integration of Western Europe came when two treaties were signed in Rome on March 25, 1957, by the same nations that make up the Coal and Steel Community. The plans are called the European Economic Community (Euromarket) and the Atomic Energy Community (Euratom). The two treaties are economic and provide for a common market and a nuclear pool among the six participating nations, the latter sometimes referred to as Little Europe.

Euromarket sets up the common (or free) market for the member states and their overseas territories with the plan that, over a 17-year period, all tariff barriers are to be gradually eliminated and a uniform tariff plan for imports on foreign goods established. It is envisioned that, in time, labor and capital will move as freely throughout Little Europe as do goods, and that other benefits, such as standardized social security systems and wage rates will emerge. Euromarket is to function through the Council and Assembly of the Coal and Steel Community.

---

[10] Integration began early in 1951 but was planned from 1949 in a "pre-union" which lifted all controls on more than one-third of the trade between the three countries.

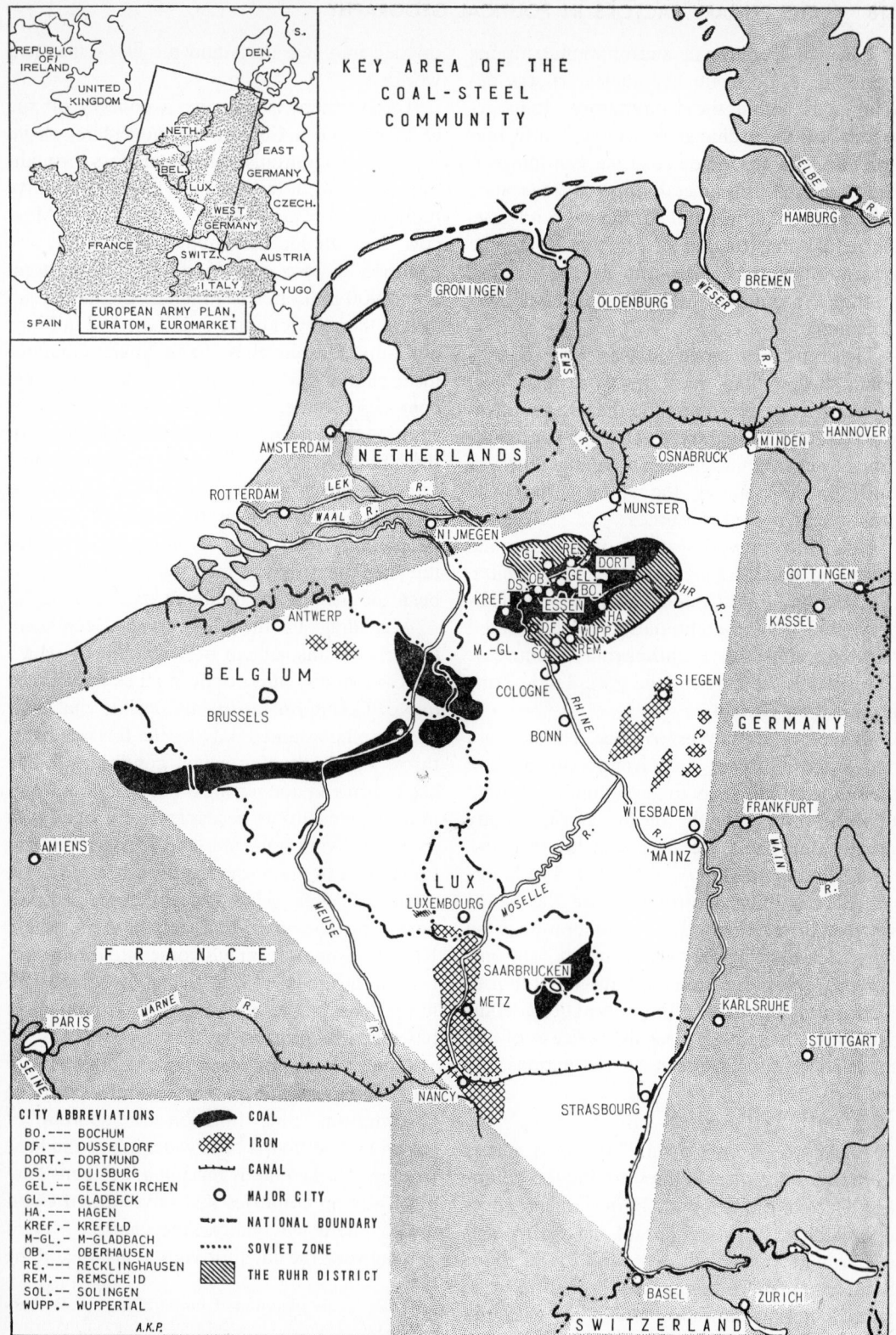

Figure 8.2.

Through Euratom a supranational atomic agency is set up to further nuclear energy development within the Community. Joint research and the exchange of technical information and help are indicated. Like Euromarket, Euratom establishes a common (or free) market for raw materials and equipment but leaves the actual construction of reactors up to the separate countries. Euratom is to function through Euromarket and the Coal and Steel Community.

These treaties move further toward economic fusion than does the Coal and Steel Community at the same time that they are less supranational in character. All three communities, however, through the breaking down of tariff barriers among the states, affirm the principle of pooled resources.

Other integrative programs of an economic nature include the *European Payments Union,* the *Marshall Plan Council,* and *Uniscan* (abbreviation for the combination of the United Kingdom and the Scandinavian countries). The latter is the core for the Free Trade Zone proposed by Britain.

The future of the Western Bloc. The strength and indivisibility of the Grand Alliance are factors that will help to determine the trend of world history for the future, and the many interlocking pacts are necessary to the continued unity and vitality of NATO. The Western Bloc is only as strong as are the bonds between the member states—cooperation is the one effective policy for "containment" of Communism. But concessions of national authority made in the interests of the international communities are necessary to the success of the association of the Western Bloc of nations.

THE COMMUNIST BLOC

When the "Iron Curtain" dropped across Communist frontiers in the west and the "Bamboo Curtain" in the east, both had the effect of shielding, from the rest of the world, any disharmony that might be found inside those borders. A more significant sequel in geopolitical terms, however, was that, with the drawing of the Iron Curtain, Europe was divided into two parts and the *globe* into two worlds.

Today, there is scarcely a country on the earth without a Communist movement—legal or illegal. Communist party members throughout the world, however, total fewer than thirty million, according to figures published in Moscow. Yet, under Communist *sway* today are countries whose combined populations total about 900 million. They include the more than 200 million Soviet citizens and the 582 millions of China. Despite these facts, Soviet Communism cannot lay claim to a single ideological conquest outside of its borders—save perhaps China—that has not been achieved by force or the threat of force. Most of the Communist satellites are bound to the USSR by power—physical power—not by the free will of a free people in a free society. Communism[11] *has* influenced the minds of men, but often force has been the persuasive argument.

According to the *Communist Manifesto,* force is the instrument of operation by which the Communist philosophy shall be spread. To quote: Communists "openly declare that their ends can be attained only by the forcible overthrow of all existing social conditions." The use of force in converting a nation into a Communist state is more necessary in Europe (with its higher living standards and Western civilization) than in Asia, characterized by poverty-stricken masses, grinding want, depressed millions, and backward cultures. In Asia, where Russian Communism has come into direct contact with areas whose living standards are lower than in the Soviet Union, Communism has taken its greatest hold.

Communism has elements of both strength and weakness. There are several aspects to Communism that function as sources of strength. The first is the "widening of the base from which the elite is recruited." (Ebenstein) Typically, in countries that have turned Communist there was, before the change, a great gap between the small privileged group and the

---

[11] For a discussion of Communism, see William Ebenstein, *Today's Isms,* Second edition (Englewood Cliffs, N.J.: Prentice-Hall, Inc., 1958), pp. 3–80.

mass of the people. The revolution swept away distinctions in race, sex, nationality and, supposedly, society (at least in the first impulse) and opened up opportunities to those who showed abilities.

The second source of Communist strength in government comes from its rapid industrialization. Communist states were, as a whole, outstandingly agricultural under their previous governments. To use Russia again as an example, in pre-revolutionary days that country ranked seventh in the world as an industrial power instead of second as at present. In figures of absolute production, the Communist states are thought to fall considerably below the West; but, due to the fact that their industrial effort concentrates heavily on production for military purposes, and due to the rapid rate of industrial *growth,* Communist production is growing, percentage-wise, more rapidly than that of the West.[12]

The early traditional patterns of industrialization—as found in Great Britain, France, and the United States—established "strong middle classes independent of the state" whereas "*industrialization in politically backward societies*" could have "*the opposite tendency of strengthening the state,*" since the programs are, more frequently than not, set up and developed by the government. Thus—and this is a paradox—Point IV, carried out to assist in the development of industry in backward areas by advancing money and "knowhow" to *states,* "strengthens *collectivism* rather than individualism, even if the receiving government is explicitly anti-Communist."[13]

A third—and perhaps the most salient and threatening—source of Communist strength is its military power. The vigor of that power is perhaps best demonstrated in its successes. Since 1939 the Soviet Union has built up an empire, through imperialistic acquisition of territory of adjacent states, equal in size to all of New England and the Middle-Atlantic states of the United States. The following table presents a list of these territories and area and population statistics for each.[14] Additionally, the Russians communized or aided in communizing all of Central Europe from Poland south through Bulgaria, Rumania, and Albania, as well as East Germany, Manchuria, Outer Mongolia, China, North Korea, and Northern Indochina.[15] History has never in the past witnessed the acquisition of so great a control "through imperialistic expansion . . . in so short a time" (Ebenstein). For a build-up of immediate power and quick action, Communism holds great advantages over the West for it has but to dictate orders—not await the long legislative approvals of many states, a prerequisite in the democracies. It is, further, able to operate more secretively.

But the role of a dictatorship—and the Communist states are dictatorships—is never smooth; there is always the danger of intrigue. To meet such conspiracy (actual or imagined), a huge police force, that operates openly and under cover, must be maintained: the spy system and treachery are the bulwark of control. Herein lies the most direct strength and weakness of the Communist state: control by absolute power is always accompanied by the fear that tomorrow which may bring a purge.

A second source of weakness lies in the accent on conformity which steals the initiative of leaders and stultifies literary and other artistic ventures by curbing originality and circumscribing ideas.

Its greatest failure, however, lies in the disparity between the ideals of theoretical Communism and reality. Its most powerful appeal to humanity lies in its call for social justice but, where Communism has gained power, the

---

[12] The percentage growth is greater in the Soviet Union than in the United States. However, the greater the production becomes, the more difficult to raise that production percentage-wise. The United States could not absorb the kind of percentage-wise production that characterizes Soviet industry today.

[13] Ebenstein, *op. cit.* (first edition, 1954), p. 45.

[14] *Ibid.,* p. 45.

[15] Although outright annexation has not taken place the satellite states of Europe are so integrated, economically, politically and militarily, with the Soviet Union as to have a status almost comparable to direct acquisition.

Territory	Acquired from	Area (square miles)	Population
Lithuania		24,058	3,029,000
Latvia		20,056	1,950,000
Estonia		18,353	1,120,000
Petsamo	Finland	4,087	4,000
Karelia	Finland	16,173	470,000
East Poland	Poland	68,290	10,150,000
Bessarabia and Bukovina	Rumania	19,360	3,748,000
Moldavia	Rumania	13,124	2,200,000
Königsberg area of East Prussia	Germany	3,500	400,000
Carpatho-Ukraine	Czechoslovakia	4,922	800,000
Karafuto (South Sakhalin)	Japan	14,075	415,000
Kurile Islands	Japan	3,949	4,500

most oppressive means of uncompromising dictatorship have been put to use. Not only within the USSR, but also within all other Communist states, the gulf between ideology and reality (promise and performance) emerges. The pledge of Communism is international brotherhood and equality to all peoples, yet the Soviets—the primary exponents of this ideology—have pursued a course of foreign relations that is manifestly and ironically imperialistic.

The definition of Communism. Communism stresses that the point of opposition dividing the world of nations into two camps is the collision of "individual, capitalist enterprise with public, collective ownership of the means of production." This cannot, however, be the basic issue of international clash for socialism, too, predicates collective ownership, and a number of the firmest allies among the Western states practice varying degrees of socialism within their governments, as Great Britain, Norway, New Zealand, Australia, and Scandinavia (and the United States).

Nor can the Communist states be distinguished from those of the Western Bloc on the basis of being un- or anti-democratic although, in practice, Communist regimes are dictatorial and harsh: many countries, tied by alliances with other Western states, have anti-democratic political structures, as Spain, Portugal, and certain Latin American states. However, a third and dual factor that weighs heavily as an issue of conflict is that of human freedom

and the dignity of man as against suppression and bondage: Communism remains wide open to the latter charge.

Communism has taken divergent paths in the several countries where the Russian influence is not direct. Undoubtedly with the passage of time Communism, if it continues to operate as the political, economic, and social structure of many states, will be modified as the social and physical environments of the various states determine. Already there is a perceptible disparity between Yugoslav and Russian Communism in the patterns developing. It is to be imagined that an even greater dissimilarity will likely evolve in the Far Eastern states.

The Communist body of nations is made up of the USSR and China, and their satellites and allies. Physically, the Communist nations are closely associated for the Communist World is essentially a bloc of states that extends from Central Europe in the west through China and northern Korea and Indochina in the east, a vast land that stretches from the Baltic and Adriatic seas to the Pacific Ocean. It encompasses a population of close to a billion—nearly half of the peoples of the world. The Communist states possess the advantage of contiguity—an advantage that the Western bloc does not have—and this character of space is opportune to the Communists for purposes of both administration and propagandization.

The efficacy of the Soviet situation, contiguous to a great ring of nations, is demonstrated in the rapidity with which the Communist state has enlarged the Communist realm at the expense of other states. The "crush zones" of Europe and Asia—that dual crescent of states that touches on the heartland in the west and in the east—are Communistic. Where it has not succeeded in doing so already, Communism is attempting to break through to the rimlands of the two continents. Political focus tends to center upon lands where Communist and independent rimland countries touch, as: East and West Germany with the conflict high-pointed in Berlin; 38th parallel in Korea, which essentially divides the north from the south; the Burma-Chinese boundary; and the North and South Vietnam (together formerly French Indochina) border. More recently, Communist pressures, in the guise of economic overtures, have been focused on countries of the marginal crescent not contiguous to Communist territories—namely, the Moslem lands of the Middle East and North Africa.

The states of the Communist Bloc are interwoven through trade, treaties, and direct military and political control. A system of trade pacts links the Soviet Union with its European satellites and the satellites with one another. Communist China is also, by degrees, entering the picture as an important element.

In general, the Soviet Union looks to the satellite countries for manufactured goods and machinery and, in exchange, exports raw materials, foodstuffs, and producers' goods (heavy machinery for the manufacture of other goods). The series of trade pacts embrace every national unit inside the Communist Bloc. For example, a Bulgarian-Soviet pact, signed in February 1955, provides for the delivery of Bulgarian non-ferrous metals, tobacco, tugboats, and barges in exchange for agricultural machinery, chemicals and fertilizers, cotton, and rubber; a Polish-Soviet agreement specifies the export of Polish coal, coke, rolled steel, zinc, ocean-going vessels, railroad cars and engines for Russian cotton, iron and chromium ore, manganese, oil, industrial equipment, ball bearings, cars and corn; from Albania goes crude and refined oil and copper in trade for corn, drugs, chemicals, and semi-finished iron products; between the USSR and Rumania flow Soviet industrial items for Rumanian oil, timber, and fishing boats.

Thus, a network of Soviet-Satellite trade is formed—a pattern that calls for the exchange of goods, raw materials, and semi-finished products in such a way that each satellite nation performs the specific functions of supplier and producer. The *Communist Organization for Economic Cooperation* probably laid the design; it also controls the internal trade relations within the Bloc between the satellite countries.

Communist China forms a separate trade chapter. Until 1952, all transactions affecting that state were negotiated through the Soviets. Since that time, however, transactions have been made directly between China and the Communist European states, giving the latter almost unlimited outlets for their goods in the populous and under-industrialized areas of the Far East. An agreement reached in March 1955 between the Asian state and Poland arranged for the supplying of machinery, railroad and automobile stock, and textiles and three complete cold-storage units to the Chinese; in 1954, Poland supplied China with two fully-equipped sugar refineries. On the other side of the trade pact, Chinese iron ore, asbestos, non-ferrous metals, cotton and silk, and small amounts of rice and tea move westward to Poland.

The economic ties among the Communist Bloc countries are strengthened by a policy of specialization of production in each of the satellite states—a division of responsibility: Poland is looked upon as the center of coal and coke production as well as the major center of the smelting industry; Czechoslovakia specializes in heavy machinery and industrial equipment; in East Germany are concentrated the manufacture of precision instruments and types of heavy machinery; Hungary and Bulgaria function as suppliers of raw materials.

Strong political ties bind the states of the Communist Bloc together. Beside the control exerted over the satellite states through economic integration and the hold exercised through domination of the Communist national leaders of the various states, Soviet influence was tightened over the satellite states in May 1955 through the effectuation of the Communists' European 'NATO'—the *Warsaw Pact*.

In a sense, this pact "ratified the obvious," as one writer aptly put it, for since World War II, on the basis of international agreement, Soviet forces have been present in four of the Central European states—Poland, Hungary, Rumania, and East Germany. Under the Warsaw Pact the Russians were given the right to garrison troops in three more satellite states, Albania, Bulgaria, and Czechoslovakia. In each of the latter countries, Soviet forces occupy positions of great strategic importance, internationally speaking: Bulgaria puts them within easy distance of the Black Sea Straits (the Dardanelles) and the Aegean Sea; in Albania they are at the outlet to the Adriatic Sea directly across from the heel of the Italian "boot"; and in Czechoslovakia, they face West Germany.

The *Warsaw Pact* had further political implications of major importance. The agreements reached seemed to provide a legal basis for retention of Soviet troops and forward bases in Hungary and Rumania, which, theoretically, would have had to be evacuated with the signing of the Austrian peace treaty. The Warsaw Pact legalizes the unification of forces that have long been integrated under Russian command. Bilateral military treaties have linked the satellites with the Soviet state, and three general area-commands are believed to have been in existence for some time—one for the Baltic area, one for the German-Polish-Czechoslovak region, and one for the Balkans. The Warsaw treaty formalized and constituted as a unit the already existing military and political arrangements, establishing a "high command."

Ethnic, locational, and resource patterns contributing to political and economic integration. There are a number of socio-geographic patterns persisting within the Communist Bloc that have a bearing on the economic and political ties that have developed. Among the European Communists, language is a common tie within a large segment of the population—*i.e.* the Slavic—despite the fact that the Slavic peoples divide into three quite distinct groups linguistically—the Western, the Eastern and the Southern. Although the Communist front and the forward boundary of Slav peoples along the West are not one and the same thing, it is nevertheless of interest that all of the governments representing Slavic peoples are Communist. There are non-Slavic states, on the fringes of the Slavic bloc, that are within the Communist Bloc, however—the Baltic Republics, East Germany, Hungary, Albania, and Rumania; and there is one neutralist Communist state, Yugoslavia. Otherwise, the westward thrust of Slavism also represents the westward frontier of Communism. Religion is another ethnic tie, but similarities are less extensive throughout the bloc than in the case of language, and perhaps more divisive where differences exist: Poland, Czechoslovakia, and Hungary are Roman Catholic while the other states are dominantly Orthodox; Moslems also are found.

In the nature of the economic ties is reflected the varying or corresponding patterns of resource potential and development—and, hence, the economic needs—of the several Communist states. Reciprocal movement of goods has been the pattern of trade that has developed although, in some instances, there has been less than reciprocity in the supplying of soviet needs by the satellite states.

The method of Communism. The Soviet policy of infiltration and aggression that has built up the bloc of Communist states is a form of colonialism. With a central location that is vicinal to about twenty countries along the perimeter (measuring some 20,000 miles) and with an advantageous location on the Arctic Mediterranean, this bloc of nations holds a tremendous advantage—propaganda-wise, militarily, and strategically—over the Western Bloc nations. The propaganda operation is not merely local along the rim of the bloc, however, for the Communists have introduced across the globe the machinery of international Communism.

The future of Communism. In 1831 de Tocqueville made the following observation regarding the United States: "The more I see of this country the more I admit myself penetrated with this truth: that there is nothing absolute in the theoretical value of political institutions, and that their efficiency depends almost always on the original circumstances and the social conditions of the people to whom they are applied."

To apply de Tocqueville's words to current conditions, institutions that have applicability for people living in a particular country under the existing conditions may in no sense be appropriate to peoples and conditions at another time or in another land. Or, to draw the meaning even closer, there can be social and governmental structures, in no sense like those of any particular state of the West, that do not warrant censure. "Forms of government are forged mainly in the fire of practice, not in a vacuum of theory. They respond to national character and to national realities." (George Kennan) Carrying these thoughts further, there are aspects of Communism—internal, national aspects—that may not have implications for other nations; on the other hand, there are certain other elements of Communist policy that are of wide import to the rest of the world —but they do not include "the form of government" itself *except as the government extends itself beyond certain recognized limits*.

What should the rest of the world be able to expect from the Communist states? Since a review of each of the nations within the Communist Bloc would require more space than can be given to such a study, the analysis will be confined to the Soviet Union, the most powerful state of the Communist group and the one where Communism has been practiced for the longest period of time. If the governmental structures of the other Communist nations continue to be the same as at the present time, most of the statements made below will hold also for them.

What not to expect—and to expect. Looking at the economic system, it is obvious that private enterprise, as the West knows it, scarcely exists. Thirty-eight years have passed by since the Revolution, and Russian youth "has no comprehension or concept of anything but the *state capitalism* that the Soviet regime has enforced . . . there is no Russian national understanding which would permit the early establishment in Russia of anything resembling the private enterprise system as we know it. This is not to say that understanding will not some day develop. It may, if circumstances are favorable. But it will never be a system identical to our own. And no one will usefully be able to force the pace, particularly no one from the outside."[16]

"Large sections of economic life known to us as the normal provinces of private enterprise will almost certainly remain in national hands for a long time to come in Russia, regardless of the identity of the political authority."[17,18] Agriculture is the weak link in the Soviet system. If, under Communism, it is permitted to remain in (or return to) private hands, then Communism is conceding to "human freedom and individual initiative." Collectivized under force, the peasant is burdened by the machinery of direction and compulsion necessary to keep him on the land and producing. This forced collectivization of the peasant is perhaps "the greatest single cause of discontent" in Communist countries, states Kennan. It "may be taken for granted that one of the first acts of any future progressive authority in Russia would be to abolish this hated system of agricultural serfdom and to restore to the farmers the pride and incentives of pri-

---

[16] George F. Kennan, "America and the Russian Future," *Foreign Affairs*, Vol. 29, No. 3 (April, 1951), p. 354.

[17] Kennan states that even in "pre-Revolutionary times the government always had a close hold on a number of economic activities, notably transportation and the armament industry. There were, to be sure, in the earlier period of Russian history, distinguished families of private Russian entrepreneurs, famous for their bold commercial pioneering in the undeveloped areas of the realm. But by and large indigenous private capital remained more conspicuous in the exchange than in the production of commodities."

[18] Kennan, *op. cit.*, p. 354.

vate land ownership and free disposal of agricultural commodities." However, a development during the past decade has led to a further tightening of controls—namely, the collectivization of the collectives[19] and the attempt to abolish the small plots of land hitherto worked by the collective farmers as their own.

On the political side, it is unlikely that a liberalized form of democratic government, along the pattern of American democracy, can emerge, either in the USSR or in China—perhaps not even in the majority of the Central European countries. This statement does not necessarily predicate illiberal regimes, however. Many elements of the present system will undoubtedly hold tenaciously if "only for the reason that everything has been destroyed which might seem to have constituted an alternative to them"—and it must be kept in mind that the young adults and growing generations know only Soviet power and ideology.

These features of the social, economic, and political system relate to the internal affairs of the USSR and the other Communist states. But what are the features of the Soviet system—

and Communism in general—that are external, and, therefore, that have a bearing for the rest of the world?

In the first place, although it is to be legitimately expected that the national interests of each Communist Bloc states will continue to be pushed vigorously (as in the case with all political units), just as legitimately should the political world be able to expect that, in the accomplishment of national purposes and aspirations, other states will not have their rights infringed on, or be superseded and in time overthrown. "Tolerant, communicative, and forthright" relations with other states and peoples should be assumed, including conventional contacts with the outside world.

Second, when any segment of mankind is enslaved—as is true under the totalitarian systems of Communism—it becomes the business of the world community. Such a government is likely to become unsocial and aggressive in its international policies. Therefore, granting that the "form of government (provided it keeps within certain well-defined limits)" is not the affair of the outside world, a totalitarian structure of government within any state generally becomes the concern of other nations.

Thirdly, it should be expected that the Communist states will desist from imperialistically extending their domain, and will, as well, release from the status of colonialism and restore to sovereignty those peoples—now satellites—who "have the instinct and capacity for national self-assertion." However, as Kennan remarks, "there is no more difficult and treacherous [subject] in the entire lexicon of political issues" than colonialism. It is, even among the Western states, one of the most critical issues of the present day.[20]

THE NEUTRAL STATES

It is scarcely accurate to call the neutral group of states a "bloc" though portions of it— the more integrated parts—recognize them-

---

[19] "The crowning manifestation of intensive collectivism under Stalin was a campaign beginning in 1950 and spearheaded by Krushchev to create super-collectives by merging and enlarging the existing collective farms, thus widening the gap between management and the rank and file membership. The campaign was carried out throughout the country in regions with most diverse natural and economic conditions, and in those where farms were already large as well as where they were small.

"As a result, the number of collectives were more than cut in half, decreasing from over 250,000 at the beginning of 1950 to less than 90,000 in 1955. The average sown area per collective farm in 1955 was 4,200 acres—or nearly 3½ times larger than in the prewar period.

. . . . .

"In March 1956 the basic collective farm charter was revised. In many cases the size of the peasants' little personal plots and the number of livestock they could own were reduced. A later decree used the weapon of taxation and compulsory deliveries at low fixed prices to have the increased number of cattle privately owned by urban population transferred to the collectives." (From Lazar Volin, "Twenty Years of Soviet Agrarian Policy," *Foreign Agriculture,* Vol. XXI, No. 1, (January, 1957), p. 10.

[20] Section on "Toward a Balanced View" summarized and quoted from George F. Kennan, "America and the Russian Future," *Foreign Affairs,* XXIX (April, 1951), pp. 351-370.

selves as such. This is a relatively new element in the present world of power politics and one that is holding out against both Communism and the West. It is largely South Asian–North African and includes India, Indonesia, Israel, most of the Arab lands of the Middle East and Africa, as well as certain historically "neutral" European states, such as Switzerland, and the Scandinavian nations. What is the impact of this neutral group of countries upon the rest of the world? How much power does it possess in terms of location, resources, manpower to make itself felt and effective? What is—and will be—its role?

The weakness and vulnerability of this group of states lies in the fact that the countries are not tied together in any manner except in terms of *the middle course* that all have chosen to take in international affairs. India is impartial and views itself as a mediator, refusing to take sides although the state is vulnerable to Communism due to the extreme poverty of the mass of Indian people and the proximity of the Chinese (in Tibet). The oil states of the Arab lands use their neutrality as a bargaining weapon to squeeze out from the countries holding oil concessions (all Western nations) the best terms possible. Though the Moslem religion is antithetical to Communistic philosophies, undoubtedly the Arab World will bargain with the Communists whenever the Western powers are considered at all niggardly in the terms of their contracts or show favoritism to Israel. Israel, though at swords points with many peoples of the neutral group, is nevertheless a part of it. Israeli interests are bound up with those of the West; yet, the state is somewhat antagonistic because of the feeling that Western nations are sacrificing Israel to keep the Arab states friendly. Morocco and Tunisia, former colonial holdings of France (and still theoretically a part of the West) and Algeria, in French eyes part of Metropolitan France, offset much of their worth in the uncertainty they engender through their anti-French and anti-West sentiment and violence. It is an uneasy "alliance" that the Western Bloc maintains with these latter territories.

The neutral states and the balance of power. Can the neutral states, dissident among themselves and in the purposes for which neutrality is maintained, act to balance the power and keep the peace?[21] This does not appear even to be their intention.[22] Yet they hold within their power strategic oil and human resources, and strategic situation—so that to swing their influence in one direction or the other can markedly tip the scales of world power. With at least half the oil reserves in the world concentrated in their lands, they have a powerful bargaining weapon and one that commands respect. As to location—to take only two examples—without North Africa, Europe could not be held by the West and the Suez Canal is one of the vital trade links on the globe.

On the other hand, it is perhaps wise to recognize that most of the neutral states have greater or lesser ties with the West. This is, in part, due to the fact that these countries fear the penetration of the Communists. In case of a broadly spread conflict of the nature of World War II, involving many or most of the countries of the world, they might or might not remain neutral depending upon the contingencies of the conflict. If fighting developed to a point where they were forced to take sides, undoubtedly most of the neutrals—if permitted a free choice—would align themselves with the West. A "fringe" position—*i.e.* rimming either the Communist or Western bloc states—would help also to determine the choice, for such vicinal location could force certain countries to one or the other side.

A factor influencing ties with the West is *colonialism*. In many instances the former—or present—close associations would incline the

---

21 The concept of balance of power as a means of keeping world peace was discarded as outmoded at the close of World War I, and Wilson's principle of collective security advanced to take its place. (For a discussion of these two concepts see: Claude, *Swords Into Plowshares.*)

22 The Scandinavian states of Norway, Sweden, and Denmark act somewhat as a bloc themselves to forward their objective of peace although Norway and Denmark are members of NATO.

neutrals to a Western alliance; where deep bitterness is felt, however, as in Indonesia, Egypt, parts of Atlas Africa, and Syria, the reverse might be true.

The neutral alignment, therefore, must be regarded as somewhat fluid, the ebb and flow of events perhaps subtracting from or adding to it. Yet there is great relevance in viewing the noncommitted separately. The nature of the neutral states, however, must be understood.

Backgrounds of neutralism. Neutralism is an old idea in the lexicon of world politics. But not until 1950 has it, contemporarily, represented a force strong enough to have telling effect upon the bi-polar political situation.

The neutralist group (sometimes called "the third force") is not subject to exact definition. Included are such states as Finland, economically linked to the USSR and under the pressure of the geographical adjacence of the Soviet state and its military force, but politically non-Communist and with strong bonds to the West. In the case of Finland, neutralism is dictated by geography. Swedish neutrality is, in part, the result of geography, but to a degree, also, of a chosen international policy that has become traditional to the Swedish state: Sweden has been a neutral for a long time. Even more than in the case of Finland, however, Swedish interests are tied to the West. Like Sweden, Swiss neutrality[23] is very deeply established. A neutral Austria,[24] however, is a new political phenomenon, required at present by treaty—possibly necessary for a small state, economically not too strong and certainly unable to defend itself against larger states by its own resources and action.

Iran? Hanging on the fringes of Soviet territory and, in the past, closely adjacent to areas of British and Russian domination, Iran long has been subject to the pressures of the great powers. The Iranians have no deep convictions that would influence them toward one side or the other; but the country has warm water ports and oil which make it a valued ally—or a rich prize of conquest. At present Iran, a member of the Middle East Treaty Organization, is associated with the West. Its "political complexion" can alter quickly, however, as has been discovered—and Iran must be characterized as a "fence-sitter."

The neutralists of Asia are considerably less antagonistic toward Communism than are those of Europe. Many factors have contributed to this growth of neutralism—some historic, some deeply philosophic, some geographic. Included are anti-colonialism, anti-Westernism, the racial problem, the enigmatic but opinionated leadership of Prime Minister Nehru in India, proximity to the great Communist Chinese state, the influence of Communism in Vietnam, the "bandwagon complex" of many Asians, and the need to concentrate their attention upon internal matters because of the backward state of most of the Asian countries.

As yet the "third force" does not compare in strength with the other power blocs. In physical terms, perhaps the neutrals can never compare with the West or the Communist Bloc because these uncommitted states are—basically—independent, isolationist, distrustful of alliances. Their geopolitical strength rests in moral and political influence rather than in physical power.[25] It lies in the significance of their geographic location, their strategic resources, and in the "strategic changes" that would follow as a result of the further development of neutralism: the withdrawal of Ameri-

---

[23] In 1815 Switzerland was neutralized by declaration of the European powers and they, in return, guaranteed the inviolability of the Swiss domain. This neutralization was expedient to the then-existing balance of power, a condition which all of the signatory nations desired to maintain.

[24] In the case of the neutralization of Austria (also prescribed), there was not the slightest semblance of mutuality.

[25] This is true largely because of the fragmentary and disunited character of the neutral bloc. An analysis of the military *potential* of these combined states would reveal a great latent power—in the control of strategic locations (land and water passageways and approaches), fuel and mineral resources as bases for industrial, and hence military potential and manpower. If they ever decide to "get together"—and the Bandung Conference heralded such a tendency on a partial scale—the force of the neutral group of states could undoubtedly match that of either Russia or the West.

can troops from Germany would mean a major realignment of defense forces. Such was not the case for the Soviets, however, because they have great depths beyond the frontiers of Germany; for the Western nations, the situation is quite the reverse—it is likely that there would be no place, on the continent or England, where these American personnel could be comfortably accommodated. On the other side of the world, Japanese nationalism is forcing United States troops out of the territories of Japan. This means a withdrawal to Okinawa, the Philippines, and other smaller Pacific islands— and already the Japanese are pressing for the return of the Ryukyu's and the Bonins.

India has, for a number of years, been following an impartial course and, more recently, has sought the role of mediator and pacificator for the world. In the neutral belt that appears to be taking form across the vast territories of Southeast Asia and the Middle East, India is, naturally, the nucleus. At one end lies Indonesia, at the other, Egypt, the Near East, and indigenous North Africa—all favoring, to a degree, a foreign policy similar to that of India.

The purposes of neutralism vary. Indian neutralism and that advocated by the Soviets differ widely both in origin and purpose. Whereas India and the Scandinavian states look upon a neutral force as a means of achieving a balance between the two ideologically opposed power groupings (as a means of insuring peace and preserving good relations with all states), the Soviets use neutralism as a buffer, or "pad," to protect their borders. The Soviet purpose of neutralism, in other words, is to hold anti-Communist forces at a distance —and, perhaps, in the long view, to use it as a means of "preconditioning" for later Communist ingression.

Neutralism seems certain to be a central issue in inter-bloc dealings between the West and the Communists. It is already a powerful force on the continent of Europe and in the Mediterranean area. In the East, the fear of alienating the neutrals in Asia is believed to have played a part in Communist China's decision to negotiate with the United States to ease the tensions over Formosa Strait and in the favorable response of the American state to that overture.

The neutral states characterize three types of neutrality. In the first place, small states have taken, historically, the neutral way, as in the case of Sweden and Switzerland. Second, there are those that have had neutrality forced on them by circumstances, as in the case of Finland, or by outside dictation, as with Austria. In the third place, there are those neutrals that, as in the case of those Afro-Asian countries, have chosen the middle way for the dual reason that they do not concur with Communist ideology and/or practice—and fear its expansionist policies. But, at the same time, having held a colonial or dependent status for a long time, regard the latter as being as great a menace— if not more so—than Communism. All of the peoples of the latter countries belong to what the Westerners loosely term "colored races," although the color of some, like that of the Arabs, is the deep burn of the sun.

The European neutrals. Little nations have frequently tried to maintain positions of neutrality because of the handicap that small size imposes in the arena of international politics. At times, the Great Powers have upheld and honored that neutrality, but not always. Because France is vulnerable through the Belgian-Netherlands lowland, Belgium has been twice invaded during the past forty years, the Netherlands once. Switzerland was not a combatant in either of the great wars, but it would be a mistake to assume that this was so because of its neutrality. It part, the mountain location and a valiant people under wise leadership have supplied the means for establishing a firm and formidable defense against would-be aggressors. However, Swiss neutrality has been compromised: because of the economic dependence of Switzerland upon the Germans for such commodities as coal, the state was, in a sense, subservient to Germany during World War II and not truly neutral.

The Scandinavian countries have sought to function internationally as pacificatory nations, but all have not successfully preserved their neutrality in time of war, *nor* do all choose the neutral role in the present power struggle. Denmark and Norway, however, have continued their pacific policies.

Norway and Sweden, in particular, have formed their national programs of international relations in terms of non-aggression. This has been wise for, although the natural environment and location act, somewhat, as deterrents to invasion, the three million nationals of Norway and the six million of Sweden would be powerless against aggressors. For nearly a century and a half, they have used peace as a resource; and, since they are a little off the beaten path, they have "played" their geographical position. Finland, less favorably located, has taken more precautions for defense than have the other three countries. Although, in the past, the Scandinavians were some of the fiercest fighters and raiders of the world—Norsemen, Dane, and Viking are appellations that call up this former epic—in the modern era they wish to be considered *nationally pacific* and to act as world leaders in achieving and maintaining international peace. The efforts of the Swedes in the Palestine-Arab dispute that led to the division of territory creating the present Middle East boundaries between Israel and its neighbors, and the successful endeavors of the Norwegians and Swedes through the United Nations organization to promulgate harmony among the Great Powers, are monuments to their plan of action in international relations.

The political documents of all four of the Scandinavian states reflect their pacific intentions: Norway and Sweden divided into independent states and remained friendly; the Aland Islands were transferred from Sweden to Finland without disrupting relations; though Denmark was offered all of Schleswig-Holstein through the Versailles Treaty, that state requested a plebiscite in the two most non-Germanized sections and accepted only the northern third of the territory (which had voted to be attached to Denmark). It is one of the few instances in history where "offered" territory was rejected.

For the last fifty years the Scandinavian countries have played their international politics very carefully. The sincerity of all of these states in their advocacy of pacification is perhaps epitomized in their relatively recent treaties which contain a clause signifying that there is "no question on which we will go to war."

By nature, however, the Finns are not neutral—they face the West and turn away from the East for historical reasons. Ethnic ties have been with both the East and West: the first Finns, the Finno-Ugrians, migrated northward from the lower Volga area; on the other hand, for years Finland was a part of Sweden and today 10 per cent of the population is Swedish, and the religion, culture, etc., are more Scandinavian than Asian or Russian. Idealistically bound to the West, Finland necessarily must remain neutral for it is politically and economically tied to the Soviets.

For Austria this is not the case. In the change of diplomatic strategy by which the Soviets are attempting to create a neutral belt of nations around the periphery of the USSR—either for "buffer" reasons, or to insure that these vicinal territories will not turn "Western"—Austria was accorded independence and, for the time being, evacuation of foreign troops from its territory. This is a "protected" neutralism: Austria—impotent and located along the fringe of the Communist Bloc, a small remnant of a once great empire and now the home of only seven million people, without resources for defense and barred from alliance with friendly nations—needs protection. Neutrality is likely assured on the theory of "dog watch dog," or else Austria becomes a crush zone between the two power forces. This is not positive or constructive neutrality. The treaty of independence, however, enjoined complete neutrality.

The neutrals of South, East, and Southeast Asia. The career of India as a conciliator is of long standing, and the passive resistance advocated by Gandhi (and adhered to by his followers) indicates that the pacific way is deeply inbred in the Indian. However, though neutralist, not all of the Afro-Asian portion of the neutralist bloc are pacifically inclined: there is belligerence and fighting among the neutral states themselves, and the territories of these countries have the potential of a Pandora's box—there are many spots where the tinder lies smoldering for all of these states have spent most of their time in modern history as political and/or economic dependencies of the great Western powers. The Bandung Conference,[26] sponsored within this bloc but overlapping to include both Communists and Western sympathizers and allies (all nonwhite, however) was, in a sense, an attempt to gather together nations with common interests—*i.e.* anti-colonialism, and a new nationalism desirous of making itself heard. It made the world uneasily aware of the political reality of neutralist Free Asia and Africa.

With the exception of Japan, which is highly industrialized, highly literate, and enjoys relatively high standards of health and living, these neutrals share many problems that shape their political attitudes. Especially in the newly-independent states, nationalism is intense and goes hand in hand with resentment against colonialism and a general suspicion of the white man. All of the states are ambitious to industrialize and to raise the standards of living of their people. Western ideas of democracy are handicapped in many of these countries: first, because they are represented mainly by Europeans; second, because they are slow and complex to function; and third, because the political and material standards of the West seem beyond attainment. The Asians blame the Europeans, to whom they were formerly subject, for their lack of development in industry and trade and for their dependence on raw materials exports to uncertain Western markets —jute, cotton, tin, rubber, copra, kapok, etc. The average per capita income is (as a whole)

low, and the rapid increase of population in stagnant economies has actually lowered standards of living in many of the countries since pre-war days. Illiteracy and disease are heavy burdens.

From many viewpoints, the focal neutralist states of the East are Japan, India, and Indonesia. Japan is the only country where industry, prior to the war, had developed to any degree. Hence—advanced as it is above the other Asian states—Japan could function to supply tools and techniques for the development of industry in the latter nations. Further, because of dependence on manufacturing, this state must export products in order to exist, for Japan is a small country, handicapped by a forbidding physiographic environment, and over-populated. The United States regards Japan as its most necessary ally in Asia, but Japan undoubtedly belongs to the neutralist group.

Indonesia is one of the neutrals' great purveyors of raw materials—tin, rubber, and petroleum make it a valuable source-area—and one of the naturally best-endowed regions of the Far East. However, since the islands were relinquished by the Dutch the economy of the country has retrogressed as the uncertainties, demands, and waste of internal dissension have continued. Dissentient groups in various parts of the island state—West and Central Java, Northern Sumatra, Celebes—have kept Indonesia from returning to a condition of political stability. Although a Communist insurrection was suppressed in 1948, the Communists were allowed to continue operations in the guise of supporters of the coalition government. They are so influential and the Government is so weak that neutralism becomes the only possible policy.

By far the most heavily populated of the neutral countries—and hence the greatest potential market—is India, with 380 million and more people. Near the end of the first five-year plan to develop the diversified and wide resource potential of the country, the politico-economic experiment had mixed results: steady

---

[26] One of the salient features of the Bandung Conference was the "fluidity of relationships" among the twenty-nine participating nations. Countries in agreement on certain issues differed on others with the result that few clear-cut groupings of states were produced. (The same condition holds within the Neutral Bloc.) However, Free Afro-Asia emerged from that conference as a force to be reckoned with.

progress was achieved in food production but industry lagged; millions (one authority states 20 million) were unemployed, and half of the rural population were idle except during the growing season. The possibilities of achieving the aim of doubling the per capita income by 1977 do not look very bright. India bears a heavy military burden, undoubtedly due to the continuing disputes with Pakistan over Kashmir and water rights.

In 1948, when given the opportunity of political choice Burma chose independence, rejecting association within the Commonwealth. However, with 2000 miles of common boundaries with Communist China, Burma has been acutely aware of the danger to which that country is exposed. The only course is neutrality.

These several states are neutral because (though they represent, politically, the democratic way) their past is replete with experiences of exploitation and domination by the European—historical facts that make them avoid any attachments that might once again induce subservience to the Westerner.

Among the neutralist states of the Far East, there is the potential for an active trade but, so far, economic interchange of a regional character is only in its nascent stages.

Neutral states of the Middle East. The "magic catalyst" that has brought ferment, activity, and modern life to the Arab world is oil. This vast subterranean wealth of the Near East—comprising one-half to two-thirds of the known petroleum reserves of the globe—has lured no fewer than 22 American oil companies, as well as British, French, and Dutch concerns into the area. With the oil boom, nationalism has been stoked. The Iran flare-up under the former Premier Mossadegh in 1951, when the Iranian oil industry was nationalized and the Anglo-Iranian Oil Company closed down,[27] was one of the most dramatic episodes of militant nationalism.

At the center of the Middle East stage—as almost continuously since 1948—are the recurring flare-ups of trouble over the Suez, and the flashes of hatred between the Arabs (who have long considered the Middle East "their own" part of the world) and the Jews, whose new state of Israel perches precariously on the very rim of the Arab lands. Focus of the Arab-Jewish strife has been over the Jordan-Syria-Israeli border and the sun-scoured Gaza strip between Israel and Egypt, and the right of transport through the Gulf of Aqaba and the Suez Canal. In the two former areas, hundreds of thousands of Arab refugees are crowded—in the bleak desert strip of Gaza they are administratively under Egypt, to the east under Jordan. These refugees further complicate the troubled Middle East picture.

In the long sweep of land from the Atlantic coast of North Africa to the borders of Iran live sixty million people of common tongue, religion, general racial background, and way of life—but of more than fifteen nationalities. So divisive is the latter factor that numerous attempts at unity within the area have failed: the rival ambitions of the Arab countries stand in the way of coherence.

The *Arab League* was the first attempt at integration. Established in 1945, it was set on uneven and untested foundations for its base consisted of a group of unstable governments. Although there was every ethnic, cultural, and strategic reason for establishing the League, the organization itself was a maze of conflicts and contradictions. Within three years, when subjected to the strains and stresses of the war in Palestine, the League fell apart.

For some time after that such bitterness existed among the states of the League that even a meeting of its council was impossible. Recurrent attempts at cooperation were made by the member states—Egypt, Libya, Jordan, Syria, Lebanon, Saudi Arabia, and Yemen—but they failed to accomplish a coalition, either

---

[27] Iranian oil is now produced by an international consortium of eight companies: British Petroleum Co. (formerly Anglo-Iranian), Standard Oil Company of California, Texas Co., Standard Oil of New Jersey, Socony Mobil Oil Co., Gulf Oil, Royal Dutch Shell Group, and Cie. Française des Petroles.

as a whole unit or in small groupings,[28] until the spring of 1955, when Egypt, Saudi Arabia, and Syria reached agreement on most points of a defense pact between their countries. It included: 1) the establishment of a special council charged with working out a common foreign policy; 2) a proposed unified command of the forces of the three states with headquarters at Damascus; 3) in the economic field, the unification of markets—as well as a proposed economic planning council and a united Arab bank. The member states of the pact agreed to negotiate with other powers in unity. Since then, community of attitude toward Israel and the Suez crisis has drawn most of the Moslem states closer (Turkey, Pakistan, Iran, and Iraq excepted). Whether this unity will continue and grow—or fall by the wayside, a casualty of intense nationalism—will be told only in the future. Egypt has spearheaded the cohesive movement, and is striving for the place of leadership and direction among the Arab states.

WHAT IS A GREAT POWER?

To answer that question, the best technique is to hold up for analysis one or two current examples—and, in the present world, there are two nations that stand out above all others: one is, of course, the United States; the other, the Soviet Union. What does "being a Great Power" mean to these two states? Toynbee, in a metaphorical context, brings out the contrasting views of "power," as held by the West and Communism, in these words:

Undoubtedly America is a Great Power, yet it is equally clear that being a Great Power does not mean being omnipotent—as Americans know from their experiences in Europe since the Second World War. The task of trying to induce America's European allies to cooperate for their common defense against the grave threat of a Russian attack has proved as baffling as that nightmare game of croquet that Alice had to play in Wonderland, with a curled-up hedgehog for a ball and a straightened-out flamingo for a mallet. Each time that Alice has just got both her living implements into position for playing a stroke, the flamingo curls up its head and the hedgehog at once takes the opportunity to uncurl its body and waddle off the lawn. What game could be more exasperating?

But the baffled American Alice gets no sympathy from her Russian opponent; for, in the Russian player's eyes, Alice's tender-handedness is contemptible folly. The Russian croquet-player stands no nonsense. When his Czech flamingo dares to curl up its head at him, he just thrusts a ramrod down its throat to keep its neck properly stiff; and when his Rumanian hedgehog dares to begin to uncurl itself, he just wires it up to keep it properly bunched into a ball. In this way the Russian can play his strokes whether his living implements like it or not; and, in consequence, he wins some points in the game at Alice's expense. . . .

Here are two ways of playing the Great Power game that are as different as they could be; and this difference between Russia's and America's conduct is one, not of necessity, but of choice.[29]

A "Great Power" can be defined as a state that has the strength to play a decisive role in any struggle for influence and control within the society of which that nation is a member. A large ingredient of power is force—a large part of the essence of being a Great Power is *the command of effective physical force;* it is the primary factor that admittedly singles out the United States and the Soviet Union as the uncontestably great powers of the moment. On the one hand, however, coercion is the weapon that is used for enforcing and reinforcing that strength; on the other, cooperation. This is a brutal definition, but it has, nonetheless, a hard core of truth.

While power undoubtedly means effective strength, that strength is not exclusively physical. Military force, today more than ever, requires "economic and political sinews, and

---

[28] The effectuation of the Turkey-Iraq Pact constituted a break in Arab neutrality. Since Turkey was already allied with Pakistan (an ardent Moslem member of the Western Bloc), as well as a member of the North Atlantic and Balkan alliances, this links Iraq with the West. As a result, Iraq is regarded by other Arab states almost as a traitor. The Egypt-Saudi Arabia-Syrian Pact was undoubtedly in part an answer to the Turkey-Iraq Treaty, though the Arab League states denied this.

[29] Arnold J. Toynbee, "What Makes a Great Power Great," *The New York Times Magazine,* May 29, 1955, p. 10.

these sinews, in their turn, moral fibre." (Toynbee) One of the constituent elements of the present power of the United States is the goodwill of its allies, and the conclusion would seem to be that moral factors have played an appreciable, and even significant, part in the rise of the United States to political and military greatness —as well as in Japan's and Nazi Germany's fall from it.

But not even the mightiest of the great powers can today stand alone, regardless of how strong may be the temptation in moments of bafflement and perplexity. The United States and the USSR are the only two unmistakably great powers of the moment—but the greater part of the human race lies outside American and Soviet frontiers, and the future of this huge intervening belt of territories is important. The relative areas, populations, resources, and war potentials of the United States and the Soviet Union are not the only factors that will be decisive in the present relations between these two states: the "cold war" is a missionary war as well as a technological one. It is a battle for winning the goodwill, cooperation, support and trade of the non-American and non-Russian majority of mankind.

TRENDS FOR THE FUTURE

There are at least three realities of the contemporary world militating against freedom and acting to favor authoritarianism: the pressure of population in certain parts of the globe, the deadliness of the high-powered weapons with which man has now equipped himself, and the demand for social justice.[30] All three are driving the political world toward the regulation and regimentation of life.[31]

To enlarge on this, in the fields of economics and politics the opportunities for freedom seem likely to diminish, for, to meet the demands of population pressure, there is a tendency for governmental planning and regulation to step in—the more effectively and quickly to alleviate the problem. Further, the control of war, or rather, the necessity to control war, appears to mean a continuing maintenance of military forces by the West—a condition that in itself is antagonistic to the democratic way that these forces would defend for the military structure is highly authoritarian. This trend is strong in spite of the fact that the new destructive instruments of war act in opposition to the opening of military hostilities. (Formerly, war seemed a reasonably sound method of settling problems because it was possible to assume that, first of all, the fighting man—by risking, and if need be, sacrificing his life—at least had a chance to effectively defend what was behind the front; secondly, there was a consensus that it is better to win a war than to lose it. But the weapons of today have obliterated distinctions between soldier and civilian, front and rear, victor and vanquished; they have created the possibility of something new and different in the historic institution of war, namely, mass suicide; further, today, wars are not won—fighting simply ceases when the contestants reach a "draw," a stalemate.)

Mankind is living through a revolutionary era. Not only has war changed its tactics, endangering all of the human race, but the improved means of transportation and communication have decimated distances. This decimation of distance and atomic weapons have, together, literally set all of mankind within close quarters—within shooting range of each other. The world has the choice of destroying itself, or of making the globe a com-

[30] The latter seems antithetical to the idea of authoritarianism. However, it may, nonetheless, be a factor promoting dictatorship—and it has been in the current era: in groping to find a means toward attaining social justice, the social movement has often been captured and the people fallen victims to greater injustices than characterized their societies and governments before—at least in certain aspects of daily living.

[31] The purpose of socialism is to spread wealth and opportunity more evenly. However, in the process of this apportionment of riches, it likewise regiments life

in that it curtails free enterprise and sets the pattern in other aspects of the society: to a greater and greater degree, government steps in to perform functions formerly left to private undertaking or the lesser political components of the state. Illustrative of this regulation and regimentation are the trend of education in the United States, and the nationalization of utilities in certain socialist and pro-socialist countries.

mon home for mankind on which to live peaceably and closely.

The present change involves a third difference from past ages, a difference in kind: *i.e.* the acceleration of the pace of social alteration. The present revolution is perhaps not the greatest in human history to date. But earlier changes were diffused over so many successive generations that no one person was ever able to apprehend the mutation that he and society were experiencing. In contrast, in the current era the rate of transmutation has become so rapid that mankind is conscious of being hurried to keep up with it.

PART TWO

WORLD REGIONAL SURVEY

THE COMMUNIST BLOC

9

The Soviet Union

The political colossus of the world, in terms of territory, is the Union of Soviet Socialist Republics. Its area, more than 8,600,000 square miles, spreads over one-sixth of the land surface of the globe. Occupying the eastern half of Europe and the upper third of Asia, its position is one of contact with three-fourths of the world's population; it has common frontiers with a dozen foreign states that lie as far distant from each other as Norway and China. Extending through over 170 degrees of longitude, it reaches nearly half way around the globe in its more than 6000-mile east-west breadth. Its northeastern peninsula extends many degrees farther east than any other part of Asia being, at one point, only five miles from United States territory. On the west it projects into Central Europe. In a north-south direction it extends through more than 45 degrees of latitude, 3000 miles—a distance as great as the east-west breadth of the United States. Its northernmost islands reach farther poleward than the most northern tip of Alaska, and its southern frontiers along the Afghan border dip farther southward than Mediterranean Algeria, or, in relation to the United States, would touch approximately at the place where the Ohio River flows

into the Mississippi at Cairo, Illinois. The United States could be fitted nearly three times within the Soviet Union.

Size is, and has been, an important element in the history and development of the state. The huge extent of territory makes possible the large population and the diversified economy which form the base of the nation's power. It also permits of the trading of "space for time" in case of attack, the vast Russian expanses being used to weaken and eventually defeat the invaders. Napoleon and his army in 1812 and Hitler's force in the mid-1940's both became mired in "space" as the Russians retreated into the interior, drawing the invaders after them and thus lengthening (and enfeebling) the enemy supply lines.

As has been pointed out in an earlier chapter, large size does not necessarily signify strength. In the case of the Russian state, the vastness of territory makes integration difficult and expensive, and lack of transportation and communication has been—and is—next to climate, the greatest handicap of the Soviet Union. Until the present regime, although the Russian Empire controlled vast land areas, for generations the state did not participate in

European or world affairs in a fashion commensurate with its extensive territories. Though the large dimensions have contributed diversity and multiplicity of peoples and resources, factors other than size are responsible for the power and affluence of the Soviet Union.

Location has influenced the history and development of the Russian state. The location of the Soviet Union—in Mackinder's "pivot area" on the "world island"—has been a significant element in the history of the state and in the development of Russian foreign policy and power. Location places the nation in a position to aggress on many peoples at its very borders; on the other side of the picture, if the state were not sufficiently large and powerful, inroads on Russian lands could as easily be made, from the east or the west, by vicinal nations: land boundaries leave no space for "cushioning" as do thousands of miles of ocean waters bordering a state's frontiers. The concentration of industries behind the Urals and the bands of buffer states fronting the west and east peripheries both represent efforts to strengthen the strategy of selling space for time in case of war.

PHYSIOGRAPHY

The Russian plain, extending from the Yenisei River to the Carpathians and into Central and Northern Europe, is the largest single physical unit of lowland in the world, and the greatest natural unit on the globe to be brought under the jurisdiction of one state. It is surrounded by borders and barriers of considerable depth—mountains with no really easy passes, arid regions, and forbidding ice-blocked seas. To the east of the plain is Central Siberia, oriented around Lake Baikal. Notice how chains and blocks of mountains, swinging northeastward, seal off the interior from the Pacific; southward and southwestward rise the Sayan, Altai, and the Tien Shan; and to the east of these spread the great desert areas of Mongolia and Sinkiang. Between the Altai and the Tien Shan lies the Dzungarian Depression which affords lowland gateways between

Chinese and Soviet territory in the river valleys which open out toward Russian lands. To the south, the Pamirs, the Iranian Plateau and associated ranges, and the Anatolian Block buttressed to the north by the Caucasus Mountains, tie together to form a system of circumferential obstruction. As in the east, passes and valleys open up toward the interior making access to the countries and seas that lie to the south difficult. Long, arduous journeys are involved to pass from Russian territory to the waters of the Indian Ocean and the Arabian Sea, or vice versa. The Black Sea–Dardanelles route and the European Plain are the only two effective outlets to the ocean for the USSR. Catherine the Great opened up the window to the south by obtaining frontage on the Black Sea; Peter the Great developed St. Petersburg (Leningrad) on the Baltic, but this path is blocked by ice during part of the year; Murmansk faces on year-round, ice-free waters but it is far from population and industrial centers.

In the west, however, there is no barrier and, along with the European Plain, the Danubian Gate opens up another passageway between the Soviet Union and Europe. The Ural Mountains, which lie in the midst of the plain, do not constitute a barrier: in the region where transportation lines cross them, the approaches are gentle and they rise to an elevation of only about 2000 feet. However, these mountains brought noteworthy mineral wealth to the Russians because, for their size, they are one of the most heavily mineralized areas in the world.

In the Soviet expanse, then, is a great lowland brought together politically, and functioning as a tremendous economic and trade unit. It was just such a combination—of plain and size and customs union—that made the United States great. Here, too, is one of the most significant areas on the globe for the growth of political unity: that is, the setting does not defeat unity. In fact, in terms of political geography, the natural scene seems to be conducive to political integration.

The possibilities of the Soviet Union are great. Southward, natural and political barriers serve to stop Russia; but to the east and west, where passes are easier, Russian influence has spread: Tannu Tuva is now a part of the Soviet Union; Mongolia is Communist (though perhaps incompletely) and close to the Union, though not one of the states; China has accepted the Communist way of life; and a frontal zone of Communism has formed along the western margins, *i.e.* the European states that border the USSR.

CLIMATE

Since much of the Soviet Union is a vast, flat, unbroken land mass, the climatic pattern is characterized by large zones with one type of climate running for thousands of miles east and west. Climate is important for several reasons. To a great degree, it influences—and even controls—agriculture and the structure of economic life in general; it affects, also, the vitality of the people.

There is no single Soviet climate. Though, by reputation, "Russian climate" tends to be thought of as synonymous with Siberian cold, the climates of the Soviet Union range all the way from those of extreme cold, in the taiga and frozen tundra areas of the polar north (where it also becomes quite warm in summer) to Riviera-like along the Crimean coast, and the humid subtropics of the Batum district where citrus and tea and silk are raised (though the latter lies in a latitude that corresponds to some point located midway between San Francisco, California, and Portland, Oregon, in the United States).

Immense as is the area of the Soviet Union, there are large parts of it that are marginal for human use. One-third of the country can be considered potentially for agricultural use. "The remainder of the country is covered by forests, tundra, deserts, mountains, and marshes, which will probably never be developed agriculturally because of the forbidding climatic and soil conditions."[1]

There are a series of concentric climatic bands that run lengthwise across the country.

[1] Theodore Shabad, *Geography of the USSR* (New York: Columbia University Press, 1951), p. 54.

If one could look down upon the Soviet Union from a height great enough to view the whole of the nation in a glance, zones of vegetation (which correspond closely to climatic and soil zones) would stand out as belts of color extending, somewhat irregularly, from west to east. Just south of the Arctic seas lies the *tundra,* a land of mosses, lichens, and brush, but no trees. It is a negative area as far as timber and agriculture are concerned, and there is little in the way of other resources: a few reindeer, some minerals, and a little ivory dug from the frozen wastes where the mammoths of another era lie buried. Relative to the whole country, it composes a small region—the Arctic fringe. There is not much political power here, but there is strategic value.

South of the tundra stretches the *taiga,* the great northern coniferous forests of the USSR —the largest commercial forest area left in the world by many times over. Here is a rather untouched reservoir of softwood. Europe especially, but also other parts of the world, need wood, and so the timber has potential for trade —and therefore political advantage.

The Siberian climates of the northeast are the most severe of the polar regions and have the greatest variations in temperature; they are dry and cold—bitter in winter, hot in summer. Included within them are portions of both the tundra and taiga. The coldest towns in the world are situated in northeastern Siberia, Verkhoyansk and Oimyakon. At the latter station, January temperatures average −59 degrees while at Verkhoyansk an extreme minimum of −90 degrees was recorded. It is continentality—*i.e.* location on the leeward side of the world's largest land mass—that subjects northeastern Siberia to such extremes of heat and cold. These extreme climatic conditions of the east and north make life difficult and, therefore, the centers of population concentration are in the western and southern portions of the country, notably in the Moscow–Leningrad district and in the Ukraine. In Siberia, the larger part of the population lives in a wedge that widens in the west and narrows to a point near Lake Baikal, the wedge being bordered along the south and north by the desert and the taiga.

To the south of the taiga is the belt of continental climates, widest in the west where it extends from the Danube River to the Gulf of Finland, narrowing into a wedge some 3000 miles distant to the east. This is a humid continental region comparing with the United States grain belt of North Dakota, Minnesota, Wisconsin, and Kansas. It is the most extensive and best farming region in the Soviet Union and is often referred to as "the agricultural wedge." Because of the climate and the levelness of the topography, extensive farming is most suitable here—and extensive agriculture is the important thing under the Soviets. Extensive agriculture, in turn, is one of the bases for the development of cooperative enterprises, such as *collective farms,* and this region, along with the steppelands of the southern Ukraine, are the areas where the cooperative farm has had its greatest development.

To the south of the humid continental regions lies the land of the dry *steppes,* the area with a semi-arid climate where agriculture carries major risks. This is the real wheat climate, however, and here is the area where Russian wheat first grew. Because of the risks involved, the *state farm* predominates; here, too, animal industries achieve their greatest importance. The region includes the southern and the southeastern portions of the Ukraine and the Kirghiz Steppes.

Deserts with their oases extend between the steppe grasslands and the mountains or the political borders, at the extreme south. They stretch from the great salt deserts that arc themselves around the northern portion of the Caspian Sea eastward to the Pamirs and the associated mountains. The oases are small as compared with the desert, and are possible only because of the mountains from which rivers disgorge to supply the life-giving water. None of these rivers reaches the sea; all lose themselves in the desert sands of Russian Turkestan except the Syr Darya and the Amu Darya (Oxus River) which succeed in flowing across the southern desert to the interior Aral Sea.

Along the foot of the mountains and spreading up over the slopes are many climates that range all the way from the deserts at the base through grassland and forest climates to lands of eternal snow. Around the Caucasus, which are parallel ranges of mountains that extend for 700 miles between the Black and Caspian seas, is a grouping of climates. The north is humid continental; the western valleys include the "corn belt" type, (as in the Kuban Valley which is a corn-producing area) and the humid subtropics of the Batum district. Between the central portions of the ranges and the valleys at the eastern end (as around the oil city of Baku) desert prevails.

Some of the climates of the USSR are highly productive, some are not. Summers are very warm for their latitude, a fact that is often forgotten: summer days are long because of the latitude, and summer days are warm because of the great land mass; the long hours of summer sunshine make it possible to push crops much farther north than would otherwise be possible.

The problem of closed seas. In another respect, important to both economic and political affairs, the difficulties imposed by climate handicap the country. Since the sea is the unrivaled medium of global transport, major powers depend upon access to the sea and open sea-routes for fullest national development. However, with the most extensive coastline of any country in the world, the USSR has a littoral that is rendered essentially useless by ice-locked seas and waterlogged shores: the longest area of seacoast faces the Arctic Ocean and is tributary to sparsely inhabited or unpopulated lands. Only the Murmansk coast on the northerly Kola Peninsula, kept open by the warm waters of the Gulf Stream, offers year-round and direct access to the world's oceans.

In those parts where coast and hinterlands are more densely settled, the seas are, in many parts, ice-blocked for portions of the year—as in the case of the northern Caspian—or controlled politically by another power, as with the

Black Sea outlet. In the Black Sea the Soviets face warm waters, but the natural and political bottleneck of "the Straits" intervenes to close off the Black Sea coasts from the world trade routes of the Mediterranean. The legendary names of the Bosporus and the Dardanelles are almost synonymous with international contention. Since long before the time when Catherine the Great secured the foothold on the Black Sea, in 1774, the Turks have controlled the Straits. Today, under modifications of the terms of the 1936 Montreux Convention, Turkey still nominally holds authority over and administers these narrows, but with the support of the Mediterranean fleets of the British and the United States navies. Although the Montreux Convention provides, in peacetime, for the free movement of the merchant ships of all nations, the Soviets feel that the Black Sea is politically hemmed in: the Dardanelles have been the subject of long and bitter disputes between the Russians and the Turks, with other European states stepping in to exert their influence in one way or the other. It was for the purpose of securing a direct route to the Mediterranean, that would by-pass the Straits, that the Soviets sponsored the Bulgarian demands for parts of Greek Macedonia shortly after the termination of World War II.

For four centuries, this lack of ice-free and politically-free access to sea routes has frustrated the Russians, and has been one of the major causes for the tensions and conflicts that have developed between the Russian state and other nations, as well as for the temper of its foreign policy.

Between the Black and the Baltic Seas the Soviet frontiers diverge from the coasts to cut across the central portions of Europe; but, on the Baltic, the Soviets have acquired a number of harbors that can be kept open the year around by means of ice breakers. Again, however, the outlets to the ocean lanes are controlled by foreign states, in this instance the Scandinavian countries. Nevertheless, the Baltic Sea is of primary importance to the Russians for this sea includes, in its portion, the Gulf of Finland and the Gulf of Riga, large inlets within Soviet territory. The Baltic, providing the shortest avenue to the Atlantic Ocean and the world sea routes, is bordered by the principal ports of the Soviet Union, most of which were acquired as the result of the acquisition of the three Baltic republics.

Arctic waters that extend along Soviet territory from Finland to Alaska are now regularly navigated. Navigation conditions throughout the northern seas are difficult, but through the construction of ice-breakers, weather reports and predictions made possible through Arctic meteorological study and exploration, and the navigation of aircraft above these polar regions, the Soviet Arctic seas have been opened up as a navigation lane of major importance to the country. Ships now pass along the entire Northern Sea Route from the Pacific via the Bering Strait and through the Arctic seas "to Archangel in the White Sea two months of the year [August and September]; . . . the western portion of the Arctic Ocean is navigable for a longer period of time. During the summer the three great northflowing Arctic rivers are likewise navigable. It provides a good and economic water outlet for the Arctic hinterlands of the Ob, Yenisei, Lena, and Kolyma with their important natural resources. However, the 'open' season is short, lasting 70 to 120 days (usually from July to October); for the other months of the year the ice pack renders it unnavigable. The ice conditions in different sections of the route are dissimilar. The Barents and Kara Seas, which are protected on the north by islands, have a longer ice-free period than the Laptev Sea, and especially than the East Siberian and Chukotsk Seas. The latter are open to the heavy Arctic ice pack, which accumulates over many years, driven down by the north winds."[2] Nevertheless shipping grows larger with every year, and the Northern Sea Route has already become an integral and important part of the communication network of the Soviet Union.

---

[2] S. S. Balzak, V. F. Vasyutin, and Ya. G. Feigin, *Economic Geography of the USSR* (New York: The Macmillan Company, 1949), pp. 492-4.

UNITY, PRE- AND POST-REVOLUTIONARY

During the Empire, the vast Eurasian holdings of the Russian state were not organized into a political entity as they are at the present time. Asian and European Russia, in fact, were never named as a unit until after the revolution: they were always called Siberia and Russia. After the revolution, the Russians brought these extensive lands into a politically integrated whole and, with their amalgamation by the Soviets, there was formed a federation of states into a union—something that had not been done in the Old World before. Soviet influence now extends from the Atlantic to the Pacific, and the division between European and Asiatic Russia has disappeared. This fact should be borne in mind. The extension of modern means of transportation and communication make this ever more true.

PULSATIONS IN THE GROWTH OF THE STATE

The Russian Revolution and the consequent development of a Communist state was a very complex phenomenon, with origins rising from deep in the past. The history of Russia is largely the narration of territorial expansion and contraction—and expansion again. But also woven into its fabric is the development of numerous forces and occurrences that have impressive connotations in the present, as, for example, the subservient role of the Russian masses and the autocracy of the ruling class under the Czars; the unity—and disunity—of the Slavic peoples; the national and multinational character of the state; the ever-continuing pressure on amphibious lands; the pioneering spirit of the Russian people. The historical effects upon the contemporary pattern of Soviet action and life are almost numberless. Some of the effective clues will be found in the next few brief pages of selected Russian history.

Russia, the state, was not brought into being in any particular year as was the United States in 1776. The nation formed gradually as early city-states (notably Kiev, Novgorod, and Moscow) evolved into the nation.

The first portion of Russian history describes the spreading of the Slavic peoples. From the steppes lying to the north and east of the Carpathian Mountains in Central Europe into the forests and plains of this eastern land, the Slavs probably began moving into what is now Russian territory in the sixth century A.D. Rivers played a historic role in the settlement and development of the country for it was along the rivers that the Slavs penetrated the interior (and it was by means of the waterways that the Czars, later, ingressed the wildernesses of the Asian East, to extend their empire, in a remarkably short time, all the way to the Pacific shores). The Finnish tribes of the north and the Slavs seem to have had no conflicts for the advance of the Slavs was one of interpenetration, not conquest. Slavic colonies began to dot the river courses and, by the ninth century, their settlements stretched across the countryside from the Black Sea north to the Baltic. Using river connections, they established the trade route that later came to be known as "the road from the Vikings (Scandinavia) to the Greeks (Constantinople)."[3] Towns grew up along the rivers—Kiev, Chernigov, Smolensk, Polotsk, Novgorod—and around them, farm communes developed.

The Vikings, known to the Slavs as Varangians, played a notable role in Russian history. The Varangians began to descend from Scandinavia, via the rivers, in the middle of the ninth century, quickly subjecting a number of the Slav settlements. The first traditional ruler of Russia was a Varangian—Ryurik, who set himself up as ruler of Novgorod about 862 A.D. The following ruler, Oleg (also Viking), while still holding Novgorod, made Kiev, farther south and located on the Dnieper, the seat of his government.

By the middle of the tenth century the domains of Novgorod and Kiev had expanded eastward to the Volga River and the Ural Mountains, and northward to the White Sea

---

[3] Between the Baltic and the Black Sea, along a line from the Dnieper to Lake Ladoga, the Russian Plain narrows, so that there is a short line of communication from north to south.

and the Pechora River. Kiev had become a beautiful and powerful city and the territories of the princes of Kiev were known as "Kievan Russ." Kiev is still regarded as the "mother of Russian cities."

The introduction to Christianity came from the Greeks. It was during this period that the Christian religion was officially introduced into Kiev—under Vladimir Svyatoslavich in 1015 A.D. The beginning of Christianity marked a turning point in the cultural development of the country, for, with the new religion came Greek priests who introduced the alphabet—an adaptation of the Greek alphabet to the Slavic language. These religious and language ties had the effect of binding the Eastern Slavs to a culture that was much older and much more advanced that its own—namely, the Byzantine; at the same time, they served to separate the Eastern and Western Slavs in the matter of religion for, concurrent with the acceptance of the Greek Orthodox faith by the Slavs of the East, those of the West were embracing the Catholicism of the Church of Rome. This was apparently the first really divisive force among the Slavs for, at the beginning of the ninth century, all of the Slavic tribes were closely associated.

The decline of Kiev. The territory of the Russ was extended in the north along the Baltic shore and in the upper Volga region by a descendant of the Viking Ryurik, Yaroslav the Wise (1019-1054), so that, by the eleventh century, Kiev-Russia was the largest state in Europe. But the expansion of the Kiev state presented new problems. The feudal system, developed and expanded around the royal family, the courtiers, and the "boyars" (independent large landholders) and monasteries growing up under Christianity, required serf labor for the operation of their extensive holdings. As time went on, all of these groups acquired more and more of the land previously worked by a free peasantry, with the result that the peasants became tenants, and serfdom developed. The peasantry resisted both the loss of land and attachment to the estates.

Kiev had also become a large and prosperous trading center but, by the end of the eleventh century and the beginning of the twelfth, the state became torn with endless feuds: the oppressive rule of the princes and the usuries of the rich set the population to revolt; and factions of the heirs of Ryurik began to fight among themselves for "seats" and seniority; nomads from the Asian steppelands were hired to help this side or that, and frequently roved throughout the country at will. This general breaking-up of the state constrained the population to migrate to the west and north where dense forests had acted as an obstacle to the horse-riding nomads. There, far from Kiev, a new center grew up around the cities of Rostov, Vladimir, and Suzdal. Increased importance was given to the new center when the Metropolitan of the Greek Orthodox Church moved north, abandoning the devastated southern city. Moscow was first mentioned in 1147. It was described as a princely state located on the river of the same name.

The era of the Golden Horde. In all parts of the land a constant strife between central authority and feudal separatism was characteristic. This rivalry for power in part accounts for the helplessness of the people against the advance of the Mongols, under Genghis Khan, in the thirteenth century.

The Golden Horde, as the mighty army of Genghis Khan was called, swept westward into the heart of Europe all the way to the Danube. Having overrun and laid waste central Asia with its centuries-old cities, the Mongol proceeded westward to take Azerbaijan, Armenia, and Georgia, and, in 1223, advanced into the Russian steppes. He dealt the Slav army a crushing defeat, and then proceeded up the Volga to be turned east, at this time, by the Volga Bulgars.

The devastation of the Mongols was carried on, after the death of Genghis Khan (1227), by his grandson, Batyi, who had been willed "all the lands west of the River Irtysh in Western Siberia 'as far as the hoofs of Mongol horses could travel.' " Invading again the lands of the Volga Bulgars (1236), Batyi wiped out that culture and people so that they disappeared from future pages of history. The following year northwest Russia was entered, and, in one month, Moscow and thirteen other cities were set to the torch. Moving south, the Mongol horde captured the Crimea and, in 1240, destroyed the city of Kiev. Handicapped in the mountainous terrain of the Carpathians when they moved westward (for they rode horses), they were defeated, and, turning to the east, established themselves in the southern Russian steppes. At the mouth of the Volga, near the site of the present port of Astrakhan, they founded the city of Sarai as the provincial capital of the Golden Horde.

For Russia there began the period of the so-called Tatar Yoke. The country was devasated, and it is claimed by some historians that the population was reduced by one-half. The cultural level of the nomadic conquerors was low, but they knew how to make use of the latest developments in military technique, which they took over from the Chinese. The Tatar rulers adhered to a rather loose type of empire organization but were interested in efficient tribute collection from all parts of their vast domain . . . Toward all religions and clergy the conquerors demonstrated a remarkable degree of tolerance and even encouragement, provided, of course, the particular church helped them to enforce their rule. Local rulers, among them the Russian princes, were also encouraged, provided they obeyed and produced the tribute. What two centuries before was the largest state in Europe (Kiev Russia), with dynastic ties all over the continent, was now not only split into many little principalities and devastated, but was also only a very minor part of a vast empire stretching all the way to the Pacific.[4]

The Mongols instituted an oppressive way of life in Russia, for, as rulers, they were absolute masters. It might have been expected that, after the hold of the Mongols was thrown off, the despotic social order established by the Orientals would be replaced by one more just. But such was not the case. The tyranny was carried on by a handful of Russians who held dominion over and exploited the mass of the population. In this fashion, autocracy became well-established in the Russian state.

The Lithuanians expanded rapidly during the fourteenth century, taking over many Russian lands. The Lithuanians and Poles were Roman Catholic in religion and, when they united in 1385, the Russian principalities that remained were fronted on the west by Roman Catholic powers that held large areas of formerly Russian-Greek Orthodox lands. What was left of Russia, during the Tatar reign, became more and more encircled by antagonistic powers: the Swedes were to the north, the Polish–Lithuanian state and the Prussian knights to the west; when, in 1453, the southern Turks captured Constantinople from the Greeks, the encompassment was complete. As far as the rest of Europe was concerned, Russia receded from the scene of international affairs for about three hundred years, and the Western advances in the arts and sciences were almost unheard of in that state, where culture and economic standards declined. The economy was largely one of subsistence. Since land was plentiful and labor at a premium, it was to the advantage of the landholders to attach the peasants to their land, and so semi-serf conditions, already in evidence, became more widely established.

The re-integration of Russian lands and the emergence of the three Russian nationalities. It was the system of peasant taxation, imposed by the Russian princes to meet the high tribute demands of the Mongols, that eventually led to the breaking-down of the economic isolation of the fragments of the realm and opened the way to integration once again. Enforcement of this taxation led to the formation of alliances between the various principalities with the result that, during this period, the princes set up uniform customs duties for their provinces.

During this period also, the three great Russian nationalities that exist today began to emerge as separate and distinct groups, each with its own culture and language: the Eastern Slavs, living around Moscow between the Oka and Volga rivers, developed into the Great Russian nationality; the Belo-Russian nationality arose among those living under Lithuanian rule; while, in the south, those Slavs residing under Polish jurisdiction, in and

---

[4] Ernest J. Simmons, *USSR* (Ithaca, N.Y.: Cornell University Press, 1947), p. 42.

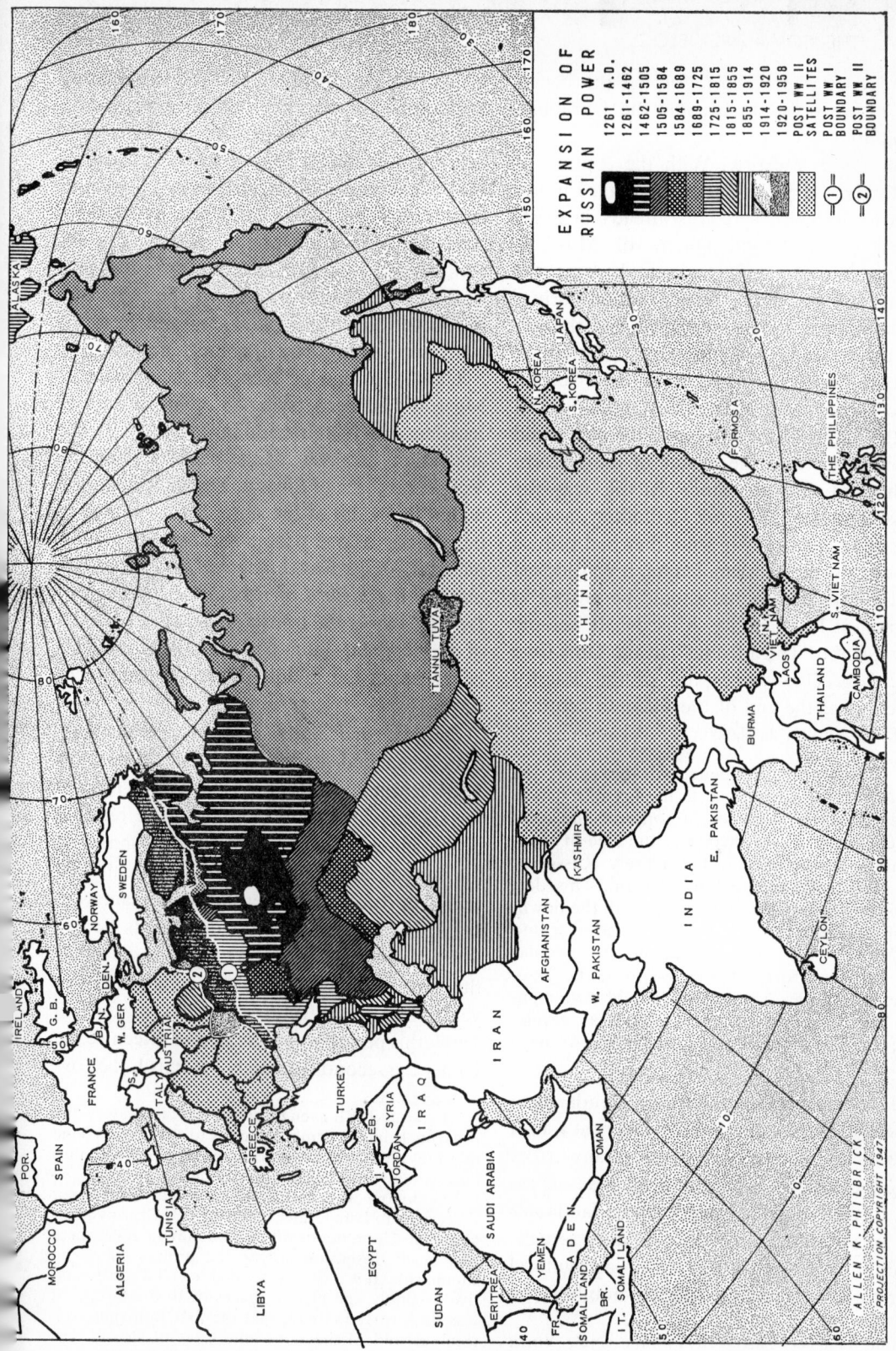

Figure 9.1. The Moscow Principality was founded in 1295 around the village of Moscow, first mentioned in Russian chronicles in 1147 A.D. From here, the small Russian state expanded. The European territories were taken first over a period of several centuries. The moving frontier of Russia eastward the Asiatic territories to the coasts of the distant ocean has been likened by certain historians to the westward movement of the American frontier to the Pacific shores. Lands of the indigenous peoples were taken over in both instances.

around Kiev and Galicia, formed the beginnings of what was to become the Ukrainian nationality.

The rise of Moscow. With the capture of Constantinople by the Turks, the Tatar Empire began to decline. There was already in existence a strong Grand Duchy of Muscovy (which, in a few years, was to become the nucleus around which Russia would form). Constantinople was the spiritual and the administrative center of the Greek Orthodox Catholics who recognized it as the "Second Rome." However, when Constantinople fell into the hands of the Moslems, the city could no longer serve as the center of the Eastern (Orthodox) Church. Since Russia was the "eldest daughter" of Greek Orthodoxy, as well as a strong and growing state that had proved itself against the Moslem Tatars, it was logical that the religious capital should be moved to the greatest Russian city, Moscow. It became known as the "Third Rome"; at the same time the city became the capital of the country (which, near the end of the fifteenth century, was to be known as Russia).

In Moscow, the residence of the ruler, the Kreml (or, as we now call it, Kremlin), was sanctified by the presence of some of the most holy churches . . . we encounter the idea of sanctification; the country is not merely Russia or even 'Mother Russia,' but 'Holy Russia.' This idea, it must be emphasized, did not die with the downfall of the Czarist regime; it was carried over into the ideology of Soviet Communism, in a secular (non-religious) form. Russia was to be the fountainhead of a new creed which would save mankind. The new creed had its own prophets, revelations, dogmas, rewards, and punishments for non-believers.[5]

Russia becomes multi-national. Under Ivan IV (whose armies defeated the Tatars at Kazan in 1552 and subjected, as well, many tribes along the Volga), a regular army was organized, formed of petty royalty whose landholdings were contingent on their military service. In order to furnish a supply of agricultural labor to this increasing military nobility (on

which Ivan depended), a new law was enacted which made it more difficult for a peasant to change residence: the decree set aside only one day a year (St. George's Day in November) when peasants might move[6]— and then only if all debts were paid. Thus, at the same time that unification of the country was advancing and feudalism *as a barrier to that unification* was being broken down, the feudalistic bonds between the landowners and peasants were being strengthened, namely, serfdom.

Until the reign of Ivan IV, the princes of Moscow had been trying to create a state of Russians—a "single-national" state. With the subjection, however, of the peoples along the Volga and parts of Siberia, and their inclusion within the realm of the state, Russia ceased to be a nation of one people and became "multi-national." *This was a new and important element in the history of Russia for the reign of Ivan IV marks the transition between two eras of development—uni- and multi-national.* This began about the middle of the sixteenth century.

Serfdom and early peasant revolts. Serfdom expanded under Ivan's successors. In 1584, freemen, working longer than six months for shelter, food, and clothing, were reduced to the status of house serfs. The harshness of the system, along with famine, eventually led to an uprising of the enslaved peasantry in 1603. House serfs and bond-peasants fled to Poland and the Ukraine by the thousands. At this time, a runaway serf, if caught within five years, had to be returned to his master; in 1607, this period was increased to fifteen years. Under the second Romanov,[7] Alexis I, the gov-

---

[5] Emil Lengyel, *The Soviet Union* (New York: Oxford University Press, 1951), p. 34.

[6] Later, in 1581, even this right was taken away, the peasants being so firmly attached to the owner's land that they were prohibited from moving. Serfdom thus became universal, legal, and complete.

[7] Godunov, who had acted as regent for Fyodor (successor to Ivan), later made himself Czar by proclamation. Upon the death of Godunov in 1605, there was much dissension among the princes over who should rule. It was finally decided to call a representative assembly and elect a successor to the throne. It was thus, early in 1613, that the first Romanov, sixteen-year-old Michael, became Czar of Russia. His successors ruled the Empire until its fall in 1917.

ernment appeared to concentrate on an effort to expand serfdom still farther: in 1649, it was decreed that a serf could be forcibly returned to his master regardless of when he was caught. Though legally different from slavery, serfdom, under Alexis I, in practice came to resemble slavery very closely.

The accomplishments of Peter the Great (1672-1725). The first break to the open sea was attempted early—under Ivan during the 25-year war (1558-83) waged against Poland and Sweden. Ivan was unable to break through, however, and it was not until a century later, under Peter (1700-1), that the Eastern Slavs succeeded in reaching the Baltic and gaining a foothold on the sea. Peter moved his capital from Moscow to the head of the Gulf of Finland, building, on the swamp lands around the Neva River, the city of St. Petersburg. (Later, the name was changed to Petrograd and, today, is known as Leningrad.) St. Petersburg was Peter's "window to the west"; it opened the doors to foreign contacts and ideas. A naval victory in 1720 made certain Russian mastery of the Baltic and broke the power of Sweden. With the occupation of the ports of Viborg (Viipuri), Narva, Reval, and Riga, Russia was firmly established on the sea. The attempts of Peter to secure a window in the south on the Black Sea were frustrated. It remained for Catherine II to accomplish this objective decades later.

Peter made the country into a first-rate naval and military power. In 1721, he took the title of Emperor and established the Russian Empire. Russia once more became active in the affairs of Europe as in the period of Kiev's ascendancy, and Peter revolutionized many of the customs of the country, *forcing* western manners and dress upon the court whether they concurred with the idea or not. Peter (and Catherine later) looked toward Europe, and some of their most driving efforts were to increase and strengthen the ties—cultural, political, economic—between Russia and other European states. Under Peter, trade, shipbuilding, industry, and mining were encouraged and their development begun. It was during his

reign, also, that the building of canals to connect the interior waterways was initiated.

But serfdom was expanded under Peter. "Factory-serfdom," which permitted merchants to buy serfs, was initiated, and the condition of the enserfed peasants became more severe than ever. A further hold over the rural inhabitants was insured by the poll tax which Peter imposed upon all of the population of the land: since such a tax had to be paid by the landowners for their peasants, the bondage of the latter was increased.

Developments under Catherine II (the Great). When Catherine[8] ascended the throne of Russia (1762-1801), the internal affairs of Russia and Poland were in a state of disintegration. In Russia, she reinstated the rigorous and aggressive policies of Peter—expanding the empire and thrusting Russia into a very active role in European affairs. In the Polish state, within a year, the Russian Empress had an openly pro-Russian king upon the throne and, in five years, Russia was practically dictating to the rulers of Poland. To weaken the influence of their eastern neighbor, Austria and Prussia stepped into Polish affairs with the result that the first partition of Poland was made: Austria took Galicia, East Prussia became part of Prussia, and large parts of Belo-Russia went to Russia. This was the first of the three partitions of Poland that placed large parts of that state under the Eastern Slavs. The final absorption of the Ukraine by Russia was accomplished at this same time. The third partitioning gave Russia frontage on the Baltic Sea so that, under Catherine, the Great Russians were at last firmly established on both the Baltic and the Black Seas, for, during her reign, Catherine wrested from the Turks the northern littoral of the Black Sea and the Crimea. Thus, she completed the plan of Peter the Great. The Black Sea conquests, the first move toward the accomplishment of a long-standing Russian ambition to obtain the strategic Dardanelles-

---

[8] A number of rulers followed Peter after his death in 1725, until, with the assassination of the Czar in 1762, Catherine, Empress of the Czar and a former petty German princess, ascended the throne.

Bosporus waterway which remained under Turkish sovereignty, initiated the ever-continuing attempts of Russia to control the straits. At times, in this effort, the state has sought out-and-out annexation; at times, merely preference for Russian warships navigating the straits.

The social institution that was the foundation of the empire was serfdom, and when, between 1773-75, peasant revolts again occurred, the outbreak was in the nature of an open challenge to the entire economic and social structure. Therefore, Catherine took measures to strengthen the landowning class. Her reign became known as the "golden era" of the serf-owning nobility: she added to the landholdings of the nobles and "gave away some 800,000 serfs"; landowners were given the right "to exile peasants into chain gangs for 'impertinence' "; the right of filing complaints against landholders, by serfs, was prohibited; serfs were treated like chattel—sold on the open market, exchanged for animals; some nobles even exercised the right of life and death over their peasants;[9] factory serfs were forced to put in as much as 16 hours a day. All of the peasants of Russia were by this time serfs—half of them being attached to the lands of noblemen; the remainder were the property of the state or the imperial family, or the church. Serfdom reached its height in Russia during the reign of Catherine the Great.

Innovations during the reign of Alexander I; the Great Fatherland War. During the 24 years that Alexander I (grandson of Catherine) was on the throne, a number of changes were introduced into the social and economic system. First, noblemen were accorded the right (1803) to liberate their serfs. However, since only a handful were given their freedom (one-half of one per cent were freed), the problem of serfdom was scarcely touched. Alexander gave merchants and non-nobles the right to buy unsettled land—formerly forbidden (1801).

In 1809 Finland became a part of the Russian Empire—through diplomatic subterfuge.[10] Russia was invaded by Napoleon in 1812. The significant aspect of this war, so far as political geography is concerned, was the attitude exhibited by the peasants: *they rose up against the invaders for the expulsion of Napoleon* so that the war took on the nature of a "national liberation"[11] movement. This has always been known as the "Great Fatherland War." However, the emancipation of the serfs did not follow.

The penetration of the lands beyond the Urals. The Russians did not begin to penetrate eastward beyond the Urals until the latter part of the sixteenth century. The colonization of Asian territory was spontaneously carried out by the Russian people. Although there is no evidence either of an organized plan or of imperialistic design on the part of the Czars, the government lost no time in claiming the land thus gained. The primary interest of those who went into Asia was trade—trade in furs, especially—backed by Russian merchants residing in the Urals. Outside of the convoying of the fur "caravans" by Cossack freebooters, there was no military aspect to this invasion.

The first penetration took place in the westernmost lowlands of Central Siberia, namely, those of the upper and middle Ob–Irtysh River system. The first Russian settlements in Siberia were fortified trading posts, and the dates of their establishment mark the historic eastward march of the Russian Slav. In 1625 Tomsk, on the upper Irtysh, was founded and, seven years later, Yakutsk, more than 1500 miles eastward in the Siberian Lena River district. The latter post acted as the outpost for the further expansion toward the eastern coast. By the latter part of the seventeenth century, traders and settlers had reached the far Pacific and Russia's hold on those shores was assured. The distances

---

[9] Simmons, *op. cit.*, p. 72.

[10] At Sweden's refusal to help Russia effect a blockade against England, Finland (then controlled by Sweden) sided with Russia. Freed from the Swedes, the Finns were guaranteed a constitution by the Russ. However, the Czar made himself Grand Duke of Finland, the country "joined" the Empire, and the Czar became the new monarch of the Finnish state.

[11] Simmons, *op. cit.*, p. 76.

covered were tremendous. As the crow flies, it is a thousand miles from the Urals to Tomsk, once and a half again as far from Tomsk to Yakutsk, and from Moscow to Vladivostok (established in 1860) 4500 miles.

There was little opposition to the Russian infiltration for the area was so rigorous that population was sparse. The natives were of a different physical type than the Russians— Mongoloid in features, skin color, shape of eyes, and straightness of hair—and were related to the peoples of Central and Eastern Asia. Many of the groups were of Turki-Tatar origin, descendants of the followers of Kublai Khan and Genghis Khan who, during the thirteenth century, invaded this area with their armies. The present geographical distribution of these scattered groups still holds the same pattern as when the Russians made their first entry beyond the Urals. A variant, however, is the rather large element of Russian in the population resulting from colonization by the Slav.

The eastward advance held closely, as far as Lake Baikal, to what later was characterized as the *agricultural wedge*—that is, the grassland wedge between the taiga on the north and the semi-arid plateaus on the south. It was the path along which the Trans-Siberian Railroad was later routed. East of Lake Baikal the advance moved forward in two directions: one went eastward to explore the northern territory along and Arctic-ward of the Amur River; the other bent southward into the Vitim Plateau, the water divide of the Amur and Lena Rivers.

Russo-Chinese contacts in the Far East. On the plateau, the Russian traders made first taction with outposts of Manchu China. It became necessary for the two powerful states to define the limits of their respective territories, and, in 1689, the first Sino–Russian treaty was contracted, at Nerchinsk on the upper Amur (Vitim Plateau area).

Not until the last century was colonization of the Asian lands entered into with any real seriousness by the Russians; and, until the middle of the century, the Czars showed scant interest either in the economic or strategic aspects of the Siberian holdings. However,

largely due to the frustration of Russian attempts to gain control of the Dardanelles-Bosporous outlet to the seaways, the Russians began to look eastward to the Pacific Asian coasts with determination. Russian pressure on China increased, particularly in Manchuria, with Slav colonization of this Manchu territory.

Russo-Japanese conflicts of interests. With the construction of the strategic single-track Trans-Siberian Railroad during the decade 1891 to 1901, settlement was furthered in the east, the latter leading to more intensive economic development. The exploitation of Chinese weakness brought Russian ambitions into conflict with the interests of Japan, then a rising power in the East. Notwithstanding, in 1898, Russia seized the Liaotung Peninsula (with Port Arthur) and extorted from China permission to construct a railroad across Manchuria—an extension of the Trans-Siberian that cut the distance to Vladivostok; between 1900 and 1905, Russia occupied Manchuria. These moves provoked the Russo-Japanese War of 1904-1905 as a result of which Russia was excluded from southern—but not northern —Manchuria. The defeat and loss of territory, however, compelled the Russians to give up Port Arthur, the southern part of the South Manchurian Railroad, and Karafuto, the southern half of the island of Sakhalin. In 1935, Japan bought Russian rights in the Chinese Eastern Railroad, but, after World War II, Russia regained these and other former concessions through the 1945 Yalta agreement. (Karafuto and the Kuriles were returned to the USSR.)

The penetration of Central Asia and contacts with the British sphere of influence. Russian imperialism brought a spread of Slav influence in another direction during the second half of the nineteenth century, namely, southward into the Turkestan area. This region, which stretches from the Caspian to the Pamirs and to where the lands of China, India, and Russia run together, embraces two highly contrasted geographical zones: the arid desert steppes and the irrigated oases that string along the intermontane river valleys—oases historically known for their rich subtropical cultivation and equally famous culture centers, Samarkand, Bukhara, Tashkent, to name only the most outstanding.

This region, though spottily populated, held greater concentrations of people than any of the other Asian Russian spheres, and the arid grasslands were inhabited by virile, nomadic pastoralists. There was less opportunity here, therefore (because of the pattern of living and the high density of population in irrigated areas), for Russian settlement, and the annexation of Turkestan was not followed by any great ingress of Russian settlers, except in the Kazakh plateau. Ethnic and cultural unity were strikingly developed within the various peoples.

The conquest of Turkestan brought the Russians dangerously close to the borders of Persia, Afghanistan, and India, lands considered by the British to be within their sphere, and English distrust of Russian intentions cooled relations between these two states. Nowhere on the globe do the frontiers of the Russians and British actually touch. But Russian interests along the boundaries in the south have often run counter to those of Britain: Russia, as a continental power, has bid for an outlet on the Persian Gulf or through the Dardanelles, while Great Britain, a sea power, has resisted these Russian aspirations. However, Russian-British rivalry in the Middle East was lessened by the *entente* of 1907, under which Persia was divided into three spheres of influence, the Russian north, the British south, and the Central portion "open to both." Afghanistan was recognized as outside of the Russian sphere. Thus, Persia was set up as a buffer separating the spheres of influence of the two great European powers.

Outside of Turkestan, prior to the Soviet regime, there were no really "national" groups within the Russian Asiatic zone. The Caucasus peoples, incorporated into the Empire in the nineteenth century, had, however, developed a feeling of *nationality*. The latter was sufficiently strong so that attempts at Russification by the Czarist regimes failed to stamp it out—in fact, Russian oppression strengthened it.

Sovietization of the Asian territories. The Central Asian territories, lying east and southeast of the Urals, were added to the empire at a rather late date; some were not fully subdued until just prior to the outbreak of World War I. It could well have been expected that when the chaos of revolution laid hold of the Russian state, these Asiatic groups would sever their union with the Slavs. However, this did not occur, and one of the achievements of the Russians is to be found in the federation of these foreign peoples into the Russian-constituted Soviet Union, accomplished within the short period of one to two years. The task of restoring Russian authority over Siberia and Turkestan involved a four-fold aim: 1) to complete the pacification of the vast Asian holdings and unite these fully into the Soviet state; 2) to further cultural and political development among those groups who desired and were capable of an autonomous status; 3) to survey the potential resources and initiate a development commensurate with the latent wealth; 4) to introduce scientific and technological "know-how" in the persons of trained Russians who would be capable of carrying through the planned economic development.

Although secession has at times threatened, these peoples are today all incorporated into the Union, each group holding a political status in accordance with the level of cultural and "national" development. (In the case of the five Trans-Caspian republics, it is geopolitically noteworthy that they hold to the Moslem religion.)

Decline of the empire: background for revolution. Russian defeat in the Crimean War (1853-56) marked the beginning of the decline of the Empire. Although the reign of Alexander II (1855-81) is known as "the era of great reforms," and the Czar himself as the "Great Liberator," his rule was marked by trouble. He initiated many changes, probably the most important of which was the abolition of serfdom in February, 1861. However, during this same period, in the extra-Russian territories of Central Europe, Poland revolted and, in Lithuania and Belorussia, the peasants rose up.

To build up the military prestige of the Empire once again, Alexander entered into a series of conquests in Central Asia with the result that, by 1885, all of Central Asia was subdued. Under slogans of pan-Slavism, further expansion was attempted in the west, but failed. Within the Russian Empire, also, there was discontent and dissatisfaction: strikes increased; intellectuals moved about the land in peasant garb preaching anti-Czarist ideas; terrorists concentrated on attempts to assassinate the Emperor. The latter was accomplished in March, 1881.

The new Czar, Alexander III (1881-94), determined to stop the tide of revolution rising in all parts of the realm through repressive measures. Within the decade of the eighties, the following steps were taken to put down the revolt by force: agricultural laborers who quit their jobs became subject to criminal prosecution; special judges were installed for the peasants; local self-government was curtailed; a surge of Jewish pograms was instituted in the Ukraine and, throughout the empire, educational restrictions for Jews were introduced.[12] In non-Russian areas, intensified efforts at Russification were applied—all of which served only to foster further insurrection. Initiated among the intellectuals, the revolutionary movement spread to the working class.

Karl Marx's *Capital* had been translated into Russian in 1872, but it was not until 1883 that the first circle of Russian Marxists was formed. Vladimir I. Lenin helped to organize the first Marxist societies for the working class, and, in 1898, the Russian Social Democratic Labor Party was formed.

The last Czar, Nicholas II, ascended the throne in 1894. He began his reign with a continuation of the policy of imperialism—in this instance, an expansion in the Pacific area. As noted before, he obtained rights to construct the Manchurian railroad and, in 1898, took

over the warm water port of Lushunkow (Port Arthur) on the China Sea. The railroad soon connected this outlet with the rest of the empire. Public sentiment was against the Russo-Japanese War that followed upon the heels of this expansion and unrest within the empire began to rise almost from the beginning of hostilities. Strikes spread, and the peasants began to revolt. In Finland, in the Ukraine, in Warsaw, in Kazan, in Georgia—throughout the empire—the people rose in rebellion. To stem the movements which were, in one form or another, beginning to merge and take on the aspect of revolution, the government attempted to stir up animosities against certain groups (as the Jews), hoping thus to divert the revolutionary ardor. The revolution failed because the many facets of rebellion were not sufficiently coordinated. However, from that period on until the overthrow of the Empire and the usurpation of power by the Communists, revolts and strikes and discontent were written into the history of Russia.

With the overthrow of the Czar, a struggle for power ensued and the Bolsheviks emerged in the ascendency within a short period of time. Gradually the Communists assumed complete control. But the foreign policies of the nation did not change, nor did the tactics for accomplishing the aims—although, for several decades, all foreign policy seemed to be held in abeyance.

The post-World War I domain. On the heels of the defeat of Czarist Russia by the Germans and while in the throes of revolution and political weakness, some changes in the territorial jurisdiction of certain Russian European lands were contrived—to the impairment of the Russian frontier holdings in the west. On March 2, Russia at Brest–Litovsk, Poland, relinquished all claims to the territory of Finland, Estonia, Livonia, Kurland, Lithuania, Poland, and the Ukraine. However, with the eventual defeat of the Germans, Finland, Latvia, Estonia, Lithuania, and Poland were made sovereign, and the Ukraine was handed back to Russia. In the southeast, Rumania had taken Bessarabia, part of former Czarist Russia, while farther north, a

---

[12] A century earlier action against the Jews had been instituted. In 1796, a "pale of settlement" for Jews was established which excluded Jews as traders from most of the country; in 1823, the Jewish people were driven from the villages of Belorussia.

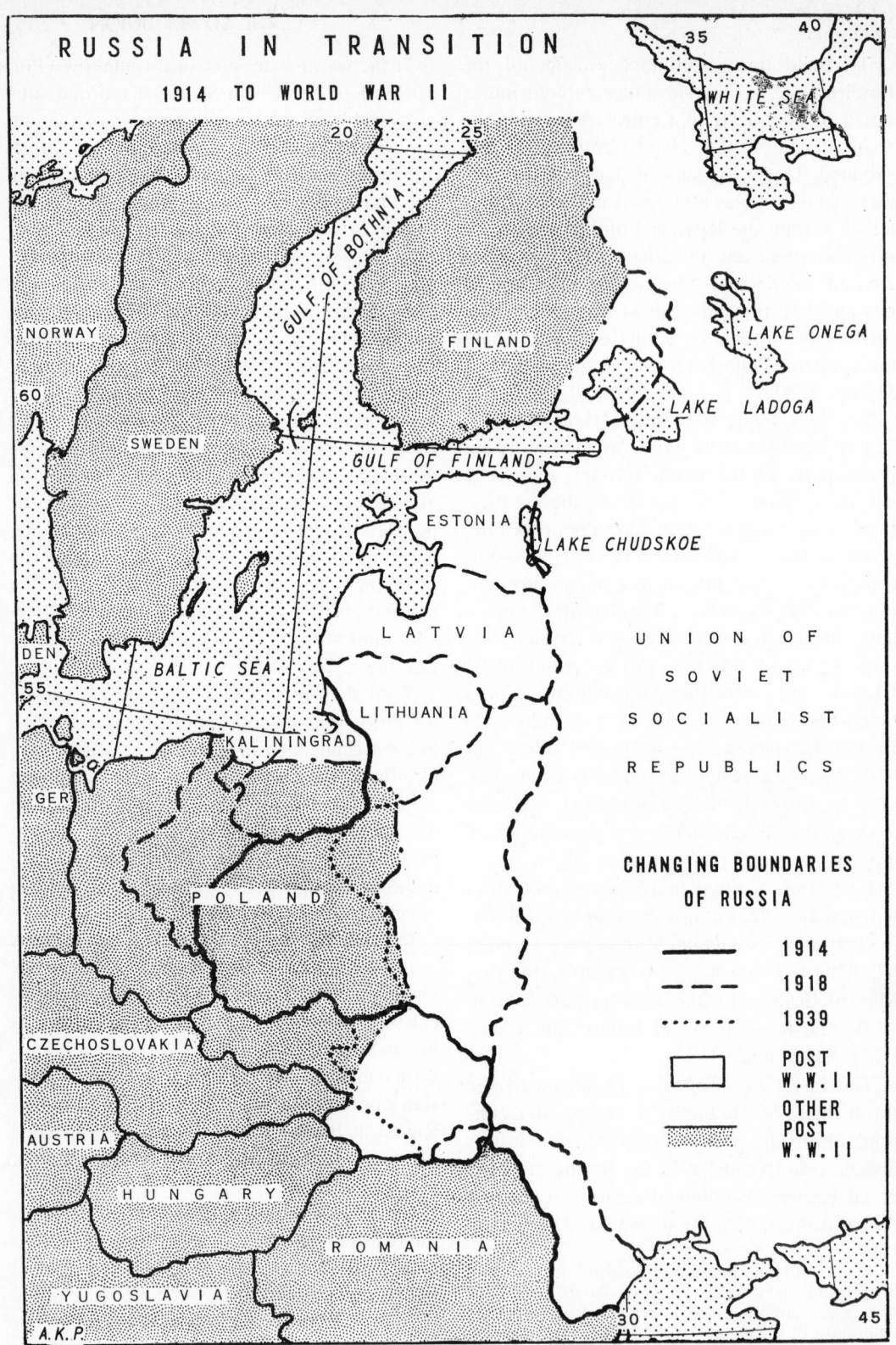

Figure 9.2.

large parcel of Russian lands—populated by White Russians—fell to the Polish Republic when the Soviet-Polish War resulted in a Polish victory in 1920.

Although these losses in territory left Russia much reduced after World War I, the Slav state came out of the struggle indisputably the nation with the largest contiguous domain on the globe. The lands that were lost, along the western frontier, stretched from the Baltic to the Black Sea and included the lumber resources of the eastern Baltic states, the flax lands of Latvia and Estonia, the wheatlands of Bessarabia, the industries of the Warsaw district, and, perhaps more important, all but one of the Baltic ports. The Dardanelles outlet to the sealanes of the Mediterranean and world oceans was more of a political "bottleneck" than before, closely watched by powers that wanted to restrict Russia. To the east, Vladivostok was still hemmed in by Russia's long-standing foe, Japan; in the west, Leningrad lay exposed.

The repossession of former Russian lands. Just before the outbreak of World War II (1939), the Russian Soviets began to repair their "boundary fences." A fourth partition of Poland (See Fig. 9.2, p. 152) ceded 75,000 square miles of territory and 14 million people to the Soviet Union. Most of this territory had been Russian previous to World War I. Pressing on the three small Baltic states to concede air and naval bases, the Soviets, in 1940, reembodied these lands into the growing Communist state. The Finno–Soviet war (November, 1939—March, 1940) followed the refusal of Finland to accede bases to the USSR. The outcome of these hostilities led to Finnish surrender of some of Finland's most valuable territories: the Karelian Isthmus with its renowned Mannerheim Line, Viipuri (Viborg) and the western half of Lake Ladoga, and part of the mineralized Petsamo district on the northeast frontier. A 35-year lease on Porkkala Peninsula gave a strategic site for a naval base to the Soviets. Two months later (June, 1940), with the occupation of Rumanian Bessarabia and northern Bucovina, the Union of Soviet Socialist Republics had extended the western boundaries to approximately the same position

as were the Czarist borders in 1914. Mastery of Finland and the three Soviet Baltic republics improved the Russian position strategically in the north, while the seizure of the Rumanian provinces gave command of the main outlet of the Danube River. Furthermore, the Soviet Union had *regained a significant buffer area* along the west where it was most pregnable. With the spread of Communism across the wide swath of the Central European republics in the west and Outer Mongolia and China in the east, the Soviets have cushioned their state with buffer frontiers against foreign states. It might be possible, however, for the Soviets to contend that the incorporated lands are justly Russian—"integral" parts of the state as are Texas or the (Confederate) South "integral" to the United States.

Except for Murmansk on the far northern Kola Peninsula and Latvian Lepaya, the extended nation *has not yet acquired ice-free ports with easy access to the trade lanes of the world oceans.* As in the past, the USSR is hemmed in by land barriers, frozen seas, or politically closed waters along the whole of its long frontier.

ZONES OF INSTABILITY: BOUNDARIES

For many decades Americans, looking across their frontiers, have seen amiable, "uncoveted" countries on their northern and southern borders, and vast water expanses, essentially under United States influence, beyond their eastern and western shores. In more recent years, as the cold war with the Soviet Union—in Europe, Africa, the Middle and Far East—has become more involved, Americans have come to recognize the possible menace of air attack from across the Arctic seas. To most Americans these views are a commonplace. However, not as apparent to them are their notions as to what the Soviet citizen sees when he looks outward across his borders toward the world. An attempt is being made here to reconstruct the Soviet picture.

The USSR is a huge state with frontiers nearly equalling in length the global circumference. As with the United States, frontiers are about equally divided between land and sea; in contrast to this country, the waterfronts of the Soviet Union face upon icy seas and offer poor access to the navigable oceans of the world. This reality of physical geography has been instrumental in determining the foreign policy of the state: externally, Russia and the Soviets have been interested primarily with the areas immediately adjacent to the national domain, and less directly with areas beyond, at least up to the present.

From the standpoint of Soviet strategy, the border zones of the USSR have a dual aspect. The Soviet boundaries may function as the moving front of Russian expansion from the inside or they may constitute barriers against contraction and invasion from without. Because of the vast spaces comprehended within the Soviet state, it is to be expected that different sectors of the boundary will vary greatly in their defensive or offensive character. With respect to this, Soviet frontiers may be blocked out into six fairly precise divisions: 1) Afghanistan-West China; 2) North China and Korea; 3) Pacific Coast; 4) Arctic Coast; 5) Europe; 6) Black Sea-Middle East.

The Afghan-West China border zone is one of the most impregnable frontiers on the globe. Lofty highlands, barrier deserts, a sparse population, and a cultural development (among the bordering peoples) relatively static for ten centuries give this boundary something of a fortress character. The probability of outward aggression here is slight, and the possibility of an outside attack upon the USSR is negligible. Only in the south, and then only if Chinese and Russian Communists should decide to move upon India, would there seem to be any danger of expansion outward along this zone. Although, in the past, Russian agents have operated in the Khyber Pass area this route, except for local trade—or for purposes of military encroachment—does not have the importance that it formerly held. Present United States and inherent British interests in India are likely strong enough to act as a deterrent. In the Russian-Chinese Turkestan area, however, the Russians are carrying out some economic plans that could, strategically, be very important to both (or either) China and the Soviet Union:

the Russian-West China border apparently took on a new significance to the Soviets with the Communization of China and the discovery of strategic mineral resources just across the Chinese frontier. The shorter southern route of the Trans-Siberian Railroad, now in construction (and connecting with a Chinese line working westward) confirms this. This is the area within which caravan trails have historically provided intercourse between East and West.

Section two of the periphery straddles parallel 40 degrees north, extending from China's western frontier to the Sea of Japan at Vladivostok. This region has long been characterized by political fluidity. In the west is Mongolia, a distant, marginal, and underdeveloped land, politically a sovereign Communist state in satellitic relationship to the Soviet Union. Tannu Tuva, formerly Chinese, has been incorporated into the Soviet Union as the Tuva Autonomous Oblast. In the east, Manchuria and North China are parts of the Chinese Communist nation; North Korea is one of the Asian Communist states. For decades this sector as a whole has offered, to the Russians, great possibilities for political, military, and economic expansion. What the possibilities will be, with an increasingly strong and increasingly independent Communist China in control, is a question; but the two states are allies. While providing some technical and military assistance and guidance to the Chinese it is likely that, in this sector, the Russians themselves will remain quiet for the moment. Nevertheless, though centering attention on the west, the USSR constantly lends moral and material support to strengthen the newly-founded Chinese Communist state and its policies of expansion. (The Chinese gave aid in Indochina, and more recently, turned their attention upon Formosa.) In the long view, sector two is one of the three major areas for possible Russian (or communist) expansion.

Segment three faces the Pacific Ocean across the Sea of Japan, the Sea of Okhotsk, and the Bering Sea. Extreme climatic conditions limit the value of this waterfront as an exit to the

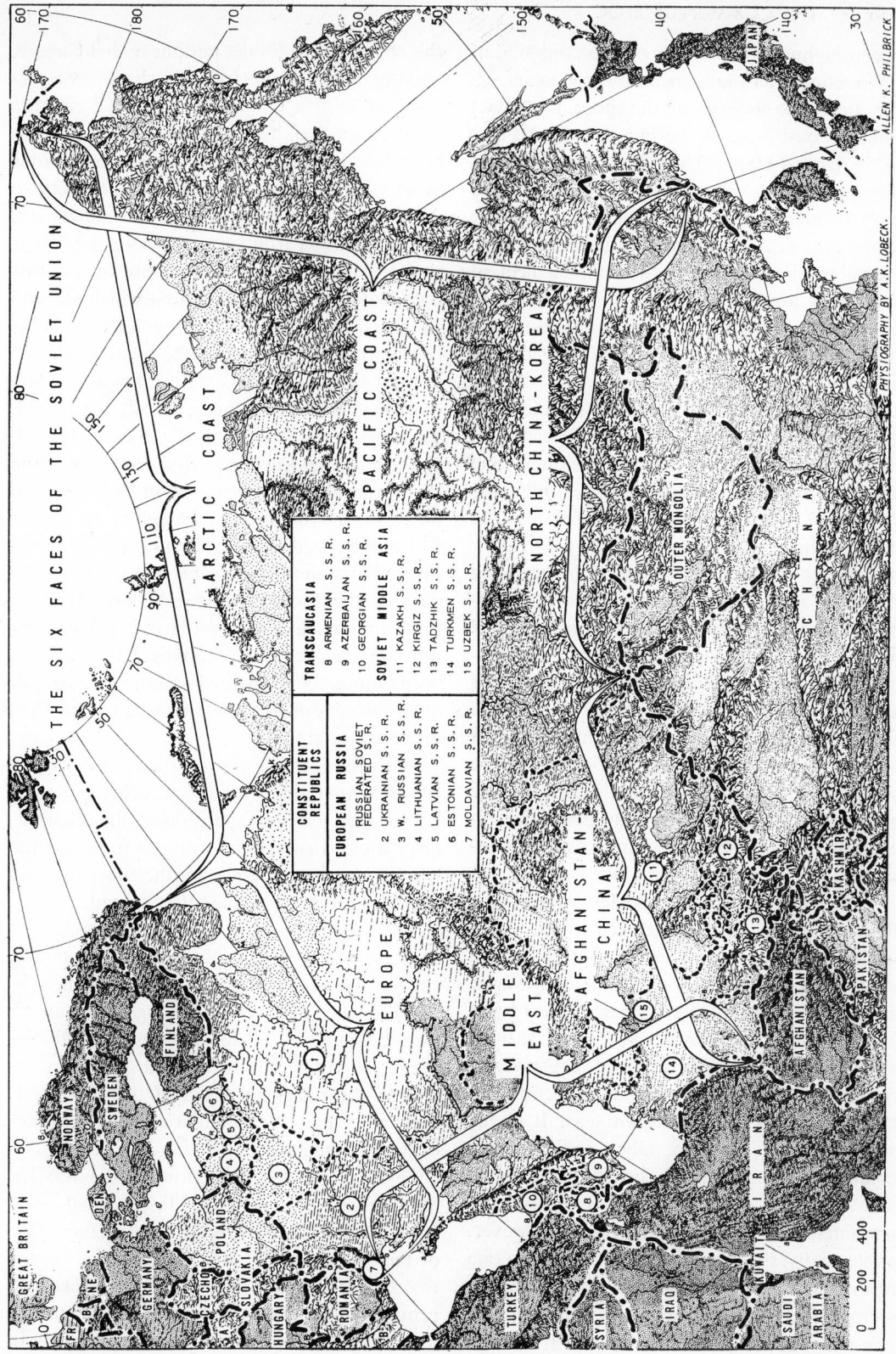

THE SIX FACES OF THE SOVIET UNION

ARCTIC COAST

PACIFIC COAST

NORTH CHINA – KOREA

CHINA

AFGHANISTAN – CHINA

MIDDLE EAST

EUROPE

CONSTITUENT REPUBLICS

EUROPEAN RUSSIA

1 RUSSIAN SOVIET FEDERATED S.S.R.
2 UKRAINIAN S.S.R.
3 W. RUSSIAN S.S.R.
4 LITHUANIAN S.S.R.
5 LATVIAN S.S.R.
6 ESTONIAN S.S.R.
7 MOLDAVIAN S.S.R.

TRANSCAUCASIA

8 ARMENIAN S.S.R.
9 AZERBAIJAN S.S.R.
10 GEORGIAN S.S.R.

SOVIET MIDDLE ASIA

11 KAZAKH S.S.R.
12 KIRGIZ S.S.R.
13 TADZHIK S.S.R.
14 TURKMEN S.S.R.
15 UZBEK S.S.R.

GREAT BRITAIN

FRANCE

GERMANY

NORWAY

SWEDEN

DEN

FINLAND

POLAND

CZECHO SLOVAKIA

HUNGARY

ROMANIA

TURKEY

SYRIA

IRAQ

KUWAIT

SAUDI ARABIA

IRAN

AFGHANISTAN

PAKISTAN

KASHMIR

OUTER MONGOLIA

JAPAN

PHYSIOGRAPHY BY A.K. LOBECK

ALLEN K. PHILBRICK

0   200   400

Figure 9.3.

155

ocean highways: far north on the cold side of the continent and influenced by the polar current that slips down along the shore, the Soviet Pacific Coast is not to be compared with that of the United States. Though relatively unsuitable as an area for the development of a surface navy or merchant marine, it has nevertheless, in the past decade, become an important base for submarine operations. Whether a fleet of surface or undersurface craft (or both) could be operated from there in sufficient strength to take control of the North and West Pacific is questionable.

The southern portion of the Pacific area gives access to Japan—which the Soviets will likely consider as barred for expansion as long as the island state continues to be under the "strategic" protection of the United States. The northern half provides the base for possible air maneuvers between the Soviet Far East and Alaska, Canada and, perhaps, even the American Pacific Northwest. The great circle Pacific air and shipping routes of the world pass adjacent to these northern lands and, from this standpoint, it is, strategically, a powerful zone. Segment three is likely of limited importance as an avenue for expansion in the future, but the same conditions that make that statement true give the area defensive strength. From the Pacific, the USSR may be regarded as nearly invulnerable.

In segment four—the Soviet Arctic—the Russians could be daunted. Icebound except in the west, the polar area has only a limited value for navigation and was, until almost now, a near- "insurmountable barrier, outward and inward." The Northern Sea Route (kept open by the ice-breakers which precede every vessel that goes through) has partially overcome the barrier aspect of these frozen seas. It opens an all-Russian sea lane, albeit difficult, that connects the Far East with the European sector and also breaks down, to an extent, the extreme marginality of the Soviet Arctic. However, strategically, the Soviet Arctic has become one of the most important defensive and offensive sectors of the nation. Long-range aerial warfare can and will surmount this barrier. It is from this sector of the Soviet periphery that Canada and the United States feel most directly vulnerable.

Segment five, fronting on Europe, is the boundary zone that marks the western border of Soviet territory. It extends from the Arctic to the Black Sea. Soviet leaders view, however, not the Russian frontier as the bounds of their territory in the west but the westward limit of the Communist controlled area which already stretches from the eastern bounds of West Germany southward along the western edge of Central Europe to outliers on the Adriatic Sea (Albania). Looking outward at the world, Moscow views this sector as the most critical. In the past, the European lands constituted the Russian avenue for pressures on the West. Via the western boundary came much of the impact that modernized Russia; across it came the supreme Russian triumphs and defeats. Since the days of the Mongol conquests, only through this frontier has Russia been invaded. During the last decade, Soviet political activity has been more concentrated—and, in general, more successful—in the European zone than in any other area.

In Europe, where many issues arising out of World War II are as yet unresolved, the Soviets hold hopes for the expansion of the Communist system. However, it is on this front that the USSR, likewise, encounters the most resolute stand by the West against that spread.

The western frontier is the most pregnable of the several segments of the Soviet boundary. In fact, this sector—and the Black Sea area—provides the only avenues along which an effective thrust by outside nations is feasible—because it is the only sector that gives easy access to the industrial heart of the state. It is here, also, that the boundaries have most repeatedly changed.

Segment six faces out toward the Eastern Mediterranean and the Middle East, and stretches from Rumania to Afghanistan. One of the "physical and strategic features" is the Black Sea, forming the western one-third and providing the outlet for the Russians to the Mediterranean Sea through "the Straits." In the Modern era, the Russians have focussed more attention on this Europe-Asian segment than on any other except the Europe-USSR frontier. Here in the south, Russian czars attempted repeatedly to make the push to the sea—in this case to the warm waters of the Mediterranean and the Persian Gulf. More recently, the vast oil reserves in the possession of the impotent and retarded Middle East countries has given a new emphasis to this urge.

For a hundred years British sea power and diplomacy blocked Russia in this region. Shortly after World War II, when British power began to decline, the USSR again put out a few aggressive feelers in the Middle East. However, the concern of all of the great Western powers in the strategic Middle East lands appeared to make the Soviets somewhat cautious in the area for a while. But in 1955 they boldly entered into the arena of Near East politics by providing arms to states that had been turned down by the West, as well as by giving moral and verbal support to the Arab cause. In this instance, they overleapt the border countries; but these moves were, nevertheless, relative to this boundary sector.

As for encroachment on Soviet lands from this side, the barrier character of much of this sector and its location—somewhat offside as compared with the European segment of the periphery—secure it more surely against attack than the western frontier but less than the Asian and polar regions. Caspian oil and the rich wheat lands of the Ukraine are vulnerable to attack along this frontier.

The Soviets, looking beyond their frontiers in six directions, view the world across six segments of boundary—segments that show great variety in their potential for expansion and defense. Along most of their 20,000-mile length, natural barriers and non-aggressive (or subservient) neighboring peoples make incursions on Soviet territory a remote possibility. The natural boundaries—as mountain masses, deserts, Arctic seas—have the effect of keeping other nations at arms' length. In some places, however, frontiers are close, as in the east where

Siberia is separated from Alaska by only a 36-mile strip of water; in Bering Strait, two islands—Big and Little Diomede—are under Soviet and United States authority respectively, and lie only five miles apart. One of the reasons for the Monroe Doctrine in 1823 were the Russian moves toward northern California—the clause relative to "future colonization" in the New World had particular application. This boundary has been a peaceful one, however, for in 1867, Russia sold Alaska and the Aleutian Island group to the United States. The purchase was the subject of much controversy in the United States but the Senate at length gave approval to "Seward's Icebox" in deference to the "friendship of Russia to the Northern cause in the Civil War."

Farther to the south Russian and Japanese territories adjoin, and this frontier has not been a quiet one: wars, interchange of land, frictions have punctuated the history of the relations between these two states. The Kuriles, that volcanic island chain that arcs between the tip of Kamchatka and northwestern Hokkaido Island, were ceded to Japan by the Russians in 1875, and further cessions of the Russian domain were accorded the Island Empire when, in 1905, the southern half of Sakhalin Island (Karafuto) was turned over. The largest oil reserves were located in the Russian half, but Japan forced concessions for working these reserves out of the Czarist government. This became a source of strife between the two countries for the Russian inhabitants wanted to make use of this resource themselves.

A second resource that has led to contention are fisheries—prolific in these northwestern Pacific waters. The disputes arose after the Japanese obtained, through the Treaty of Portsmouth, fishing rights in Russian waters. Since 1936, the fishing agreements have been made on an annual basis, and, as Soviet diplomatic and military power has increased, the Soviets have driven better bargains. After World War II, with the defeat of Japan (and due to the fact that the Soviets entered the war just in time to share in the fruits of victory), all fishing concessions to the Japanese were withdrawn, and the Kuriles and Karafuto were returned to the Russians.

Neighboring states are also accessible along the Western border where the European plain blends with the Russian. As stated before, one of the objectives in the foreign relations of the Russians has been the setting up of "buffer areas" along frontiers. The present Soviet attempts to extend a neutral belt around its periphery—as in Austria, Germany, Yugoslavia, etc.—is an interesting commentary on this historic aim.

ROLE OF TRANSPORTATION AND COMMUNICATION

Size has been one of the handicapping elements of the nation, and the spread and development of the Russian and Communist states have been—and are—acutely dependent upon transportation. Compactness is an advantage, but the favorableness of shape is largely defeated by the physical handicaps of terrain imposed by climate, and by the difficulties encountered in integrating this immensity of space.

Early settlement of European Russia was accomplished by the utilization of the rivers as avenues of penetration, while the exploration and pioneering conquest of the Asiatic lands was achieved by recourse to an amazing combination of river navigation and portage that carried the settlers all the way across the continent to the Pacific shore. In the days of the Czarist Empire there was less need for the linking of the Asiatic territories (and the northern half of European Russia) with the ecumene by railways and other man-made communications than there is today. The Siberian–North European territories are still marginal to the ecumene, although under the Communist regime integrant outliers of industry and population have been built up in these otherwise marginal and sparsely populated regions. The nuclear area (which might be considered as either the Kiev or Moscow nucleus, or both) lies within the ecumene of the modern state, a roughly rectangular area stretching westward from the Volga River and from the shores of the Black Sea northward to the Leningrad-Moscow-Gorki district. It is an ecumene with great scope, like that of the United States; the total population is not much larger and is spread somewhat more uniformly, although in the past two decades the tendency has been for great urban cores of population to develop at industrial sites—as is even more true in the ecumene of the American state.

The Soviet ecumene lacks direct frontage on any of the commercial oceans. The outlets are embedded to great depths in back of other states, as the outlets on the Black Sea and the Gulf of Finland, or lie far outside the ecumene to be reached only by long overland lines of transportation, as the Murmansk or the Vladivostok coasts. Even here they lie offside the major trade routes, and, in the case of the Asiatic outlet, are encased within inland seas by the Japanese Isles.

In general, the transportation system of the USSR has been developed with the view to providing access to seaports and to raw materials. The web of the communications' network is coarse, for the arms reach out in all directions across the great Russian domain to seek sea-frontage and to join together the widely separated but supplementary regions of the Soviet Union—as between industrial centers and districts of raw material production and between farming and grazing lands and industrial population nodes. (For example, the steppelands of the south exchange grain for the lumber of the forested north; Magnitogorsk in the Urals, and Karaganda and the Kuznets Basin about 500 and 1200 miles distant eastward, interchange iron ore and coal to complete the base of heavy industry; the oil of the Caspian area is 1500 miles to the south of its major market center in the industrial areas of Moscow and Leningrad.) Suitable transportation connections are indispensable.

When the sparsely populated lands lying outside of the ecumene are added to the core, the combined area is more than two times greater than that of any other political state; to straddle the east-west extent of the Soviet Union, the Trans-Siberian Railroad becomes the longest on the earth. Riverways, canals, and the Northern Sea Route, roads, branch lines of railroads, telegraph, telephone, radio, and air routes interconnect throughout the domain to make communication between the parts possible. The pattern that the transportation system has taken has been influenced by a number of features peculiar to the geography of the Soviet Union: the huge size and, therefore, the tremendous distances; the low average density of population, along with the uneven distribution of people; the location of natural resources and, hence, of industry. The latter is undoubtedly the most determinative factor in the extension of the system under the Soviets.

Rivers provided the first routes of travel and communication. As has been noted, these internal waterways were very important in the early development of the nation. Long before

there was anything that corresponded to a Russian state, the major river arteries of both the European and Asian portions were connected by "portages" across the low divides that separated the oppositely flowing streams. Later an important system of canals was constructed so that now it has become possible to send goods or people, along these internal waterways, from the Black and Caspian areas in the south all the way to the White Sea. The Volga–Don Canal, which has the effect of opening the Caspian Sea to the Mediterranean, is the latest addition to the canal system. The importance of waterways relative to Russian development is shown by the fact that the first railroads that were constructed were "clearly subordinated to the waterways and merely served as links over portage routes."[13]

---

[13] Shabad, *op. cit.*, p. 82.

Figure 9.4. Siberian Railway expanded, as of May, 1955. (Courtesy *The New York Times.*)

The role of railroads. The railways assumed an importance of their own when industry became more prominent and began to spread. The first major line ran between Moscow and St. Petersburg (Leningrad) on the Gulf of Finland, and subsequent pre-revolutionary railroads formed a pattern of radiating lines: 1) out of Moscow, to other parts of the empire, particularly to the grain-producing regions (which supplied food to the industrial centers and required, in return, the products of manufacture); and 2) to outlets that led to the ocean trade routes, on the Black and Baltic Seas.

When the Soviets took over, there were but 36,300 miles of railroads. Under the Communist state the rail pattern was altered. Dropping almost completely out of world trade, the necessity for transportation to the seaports and the western frontier was lessened while shipping with the east markedly increased. Secondly, appreciating the significance of railroads to the industrial development of the state, a program of extensive railway construction was initiated that more than doubled the mileage within less than 25 years. The Russian ecumene is now much better linked in terms of transportation and communication than in any previous period but the interlacing network still does not have the fineness of those of the United States and the Western European nations. As for the lands that lie marginal to the ecumene, the discriminate importance of the various outlying industrial nodes has largely determined where connections are most dense. One of the most recent developments—and, according to the best sources, still in the process of completion—is the southern rail connections between the Soviet Union and China via Alma Ata and Lanchow. This shortens the rail route between the two states by 200 miles and gives an alternate rail line to the Trans-Siberian. Strategic and political in significance, it is not accidental that it traverses richly mineralized areas of Chinese territory. The line follows the old silk route of the days of Marco Polo. Its strategic significance lies in the fact that it is so deeply hidden in the recesses of Inner Asia as to be virtually invulnerable as compared with other rail lines.

POLITICAL STRUCTURE OF THE SOVIET UNION

The component unit of the Soviet Union is the *republic,* each of which, in turn, is subdivided into smaller and smaller political components representing ethnic groups of peoples. Soviet policy toward ethnic and racial minorities was one of the unique principles of Communist development in the Russian state. The Soviet Union was set up as an *ethnic democracy.* The very name—"Russia" was rejected so that none of the minority peoples would feel "subordinate" to the large Russian majority group—carries implications of this policy, Union of Soviet Socialist Republics. "Russia" became one of a number of sovereign and equal republics—now 15—within the union, *i.e.* the republic of the Russian people. With a federative structure, which resembles that of the United States, it left the way open for the affiliation of new republics.

The basis for the determination of the component units was "the principle of national cultural autonomy." In practice, the actual autonomy is very slight. The *Union Republics* are the largest of these political subdivisions. Each represents a specific territory inhabited by a large population group with strong national and cultural associations. The Union Republics redivide into smaller units, the *Autonomous Republics* being the next larger component in the "nationalities' ladder." They each represent an ethnic people not as large as in the case of the Union Republic, or as integrated culturally and economically; yet some of these peoples have lived under a single government for centuries. The *autonomous oblasts* (autonomous regions) and *national okrugs* (national districts) are representative of still smaller ethnic groups less closely unified in a cultural, historical, and economic sense. The national okrugs, fourth among the major classes of autonomous units, are found only within the RSFSR. They are peopled by minor Siberian groups in the main.

REPUBLICS OF THE SOVIET UNION

Republic	Area (Square Miles)	Population In 1,000's (Est. 1947)	Year Formed	Predominant Ethnic Strain	Titular Group: Per cent of Population	Russian: Per cent of Population	Capital
Russian Soviet Federated Socialist Republic	6,501,500	111,000	1917	Eastern Slav	73	73	Moscow
Ukrainian Soviet Socialist Republic (SSR)	222,600	40,500	1917	Eastern Slav	80	9	Kiev
Byelorussia SSR	80,100	7,220	1919	Eastern Slav	81	7	Minsk
Estonian SSR	17,400	1,000	1940	Ugro-Finnic	91	7	Tallin
Latvian SSR	24,600	1,800	1940	Slavonic-Baltic	76	12	Riga
Lithuanian SSR	31,200	2,700	1940	Slavonic-Baltic	80	3	Vilnius
Moldavian SSR	13,100	2,660	1940	Moldavian	65	7	Kishinev
Georgian SSR	29,400	1,345	1921	Japhetic	61	4	Tbilsi (Tiflis)
Armenian SSR	11,500	3,555	1920	Japhetic	84	2	Yerevan
Azerbaijan SSR	33,100	3,100	1920	Turkic	63	10	Baku
Kazakh SSR	1,061,600	6,000	1936	Turkic	57	20	Alma-Ata
Uzbek SSR	157,400	6,000	1924	Turkic	76	6	Tashkent
Turkmen	187,200	1,170	1924	Turkic	72	8	Ashkhabad
Tadzhik	54,900	1,455	1929	Iranian	78	1	Stalinabad
Kirghiz	76,100	1,490	1936	Turkic	67	12	Frunze
Total USSR	8,570,600	190,995	1922				Moscow

Regional economic planning was another major motif. The second basic principle adhered to in the development of the Communist state structure in Russia was that of economic regionalism. The dominant motive in the creation of these components is the establishment of "well-integrated economic units." The main administrative divisions of these economic integrants are the oblast and the kray; each are delineated in such a way "as to include in it a well-coordinated economic region centering on an important industrial and commercial center and specializing in the production of some particular commodity, while striving for regional self-sufficiency in the greatest possible degree."[14]

There are both strengths and weaknesses in this form of collocation: the "territorial organization, at least within the nonautonomous sphere, is . . . entirely subordinated to the requirements of an economy which is itself extremely dynamic";[15] on the other hand, it means an approach to the economy that is responsive to the changes that time and circumstances demand. As new developments occur—as the opening up of new industrial regions, new mining developments (as railroad construction opens up areas to exploitation), and as reclaimed lands are made available for cultivation—adjustments are made within the administrative structure. The adaptability of the Soviet system has been proven; and the Russian regime has been stabilized and its strength increased by the accordance of cultural autonomy to the many varied peoples, and the centralization and synthesis of political and economic authority.

The policy on minorities is a central thesis in the constitution and in the political structure of the state. According to both the old and new constitutions, the right of minority groups is upheld. The Union of Soviet Socialist Republics is a federation of autonomous peoples. Stalin, himself a member of one of the persecuted minorities under the Czars (Georgian), was Soviet Commissar of Nationalities, from 1917 to 1923. However disparate policy and practice may be, the New Constitution makes

[14] *Ibid.*, p. 46.
[15] *Ibid.*, p. 47.

RUSSIA'S MINORITY PROBLEM — PEOPLES OF SOVIET UNION

THE GEOGRAPHICAL DISTRIBUTION
(Shadings explained on chart below)

ESTONIAN S.S.R.
KARELO-FINNISH S.S.R.
LATVIAN S.S.R.
LITHUANIAN S.S.R.
BYELORUSSIAN S.S.R.
UKRAINIAN S.S.R.
MOLDAVIAN S.S.R.
GEORGIAN S.S.R.
ARMENIAN S.S.R.
AZERBAIJAN S.S.R.
TURKMEN S.S.R.
UZBEK S.S.R.
TADZHIK S.S.R.
KIRGIZ S.S.R.
KAZAKH S.S.R.

RUSSIAN SOVIET FEDERATED SOCIALIST REPUBLIC

0   Miles   1,000

THE BREAKDOWN BY ETHNIC GROUPS

Balts 6 mil.
Byelorussians 10 mil.
Russians 107 mil.
Ukrainians 42 mil.
Moslems 20 mil.
Others 21 mil.
Caucasians 6 mil.
Moldavians 2.5 mil.
Karelo-Finns 0.5 mil.

Figure 9.5. (Courtesy *The New York Times.*)

explicit provisions for the respect of minorities in Article 123, which reads:

Equality of rights of the citizens of the USSR, irrespective of their nationality or race, in all spheres of economic, state, cultural, political, and social life, is an indefeasible law. Any direct restriction of the rights of or conversely any establishment of direct or indirect privileges for citizens on account of their race or nationality, as well as any advocacy of racial or national exclusiveness or hatred or contempt, is punishable by law.

According to the 1917 Declaration of Rights of the Peoples, the constituent national bodies within the USSR also have the right to independence, even to the point of secession from the union and the setting up of independent states. The right of secession is one of the most crucial questions in the history of federative states. The record of Great Britain in granting independence to dominions is well known; the northern states of the United States went to war to hold the South within the union. It must, therefore, be doubted whether any of the republics of the USSR would be permitted to separate themselves from the federation to form independent states. The designers of the governmental structure of the Soviet Union were undoubtedly appreciative of the fact that the strength of the Union depended upon its unity. In 1944 the constitutional rights of the republics were broadened to grant to them some of the rights enjoyed by independent states—namely, "Full power to enter into relations with foreign states and to make treaties with them." If carried through as stated, this is a very desirable thing for most of the republics have common frontiers with foreign states. In practice, however, the change has not been one of independence of action in such matters but of the consulting by Soviet officials of the Central government with the republics about foreign relationships.

The Soviet Union, however, achieves certain advantages by the mere announcement of such constitutional reforms and of independence of action by the republics. It not only builds the morale of the people within the state but—and both aims have undoubtedly been in the minds of the Soviet officials—it increases the "moral" position of the Soviet Union in the world of nations. If such independence of action were accorded the republics, much of the criticism that is leveled against the USSR by the outside world would be silenced. The disparity between words and actions (or intentions) has fostered distrust of Soviet diplomacy.

THE ECONOMIC SYSTEM

The entire economy of the USSR is state controlled, including land and the important means of production. Five successive Five-Year Plans have worked to change the backward agrarian economy into one with an industrial power capable of producing goods in quantity second only to the United States. The Soviet aim, as expressed by Stalin in 1925, was to transform this agricultural state "into an industrial giant . . . as quickly as possible."

In this respect, impressive progress has undeniably been made by the Soviets. In industry, the main emphasis has been placed on the production of capital goods and defense materials. The output of coal and steel, the two most basic and important elements in heavy industry, has mounted ten times above that of the past and the Soviet Union has moved up from a position of a minor producer to second in the world. Quite in contrast to industry, which continues to expand rapidly, in agriculture the achievements have been anything but spectacular: food production has not kept up with population increase since the revolution and cattle production remains below the 1928 pre-collectivization level. Particularly during the past decade has agriculture been the weak element in the economy.

State planning is the fundamental characteristic of the Soviet economic structure. With the private *entrepreneur* gone, all enterprise—agricultural and industrial—is directed by the State. This government management means, on the negative side, absolute control over all production and the smothering (or voiding) of private initiative; on the positive side, it manifests itself in the state planning—regionally planned but nationally integrative—that is possible within such an economic pattern; initiative of the non-capitalist kind is possible.

The central planning has led to such advances as the introduction of new crops and the redistribution of old ones to new regions; the reconstruction of the industrial location pattern so as to bring raw material and factory, and factory and consumer, closer together; and attempts at something approaching self-sufficiency in consumer goods within regional units. Some quite remarkable results in crop introduction and adaptation to marginal environments have taken place under the Soviets.

The Soviet system has exploited the peasant. A flaw in the system—that has resulted in the rapid growth of Soviet industry and the near-confounding of official efforts in agriculture—is the exploitation of the peasantry. Industrial development has been financed by state requisition of large proportions of the peasants' produce at prices far below their worth. The bitterness resulting from this unreasonable exaction explains much of the hostility of the peasantry toward the Communist system during the decades it has been in operation. Only in the fall of 1953 were the first attempts to alter this pattern made. As incentives to the peasants, farm taxes were halved, and prices for livestock and other products—although not grain, the essential crop—were raised.

A collective system of working the land was put into practice. In the densely populated areas of rural European Russia the *collective farm* was put in operation; in sparsely populated regions, as the marginal European lands and the Asian areas, *state farms*—owned and operated by the state—were set up. Former grazing lands were planted to wheat and cotton, or organized into great animal-producing farms. On the collective, the State is given an annually prescribed proportion of the produce, after which the rest is divided among the collectivized farmers; under the state farm system, workers are paid in wages—which may be "in kind" and not always in money. The state farms are typically large, usually comprising at least 5 to 6000 acres of land, whereas the collectives—until recently[16]—rarely exceeded a thousand acres in size.

INDUSTRIAL AND POWER RESOURCES: SOIL—AND AGRICULTURE

Traditionally, Russia and its people have lived close to the soil. Before 1939, more than half of the population of the Soviet Union lived on the land; today the figure is probably somewhat less. But in comparison to the United States—where about one-sixth of the total population are farmers—this is high. Yet, as in other countries undergoing the industrial revolution, the proportion of the people in the USSR directly dependent upon agriculture for

a living has fallen. Concurrent with this has been the increase—actual and proportional—in both the non-agrarian population and the population as a whole.

A statement by Beria, in 1951, placed the annual population increment at about three million, and this figure is taken by demographers as a fairly reliable indication of the rate of growth. Although this figure indicates that Soviet population is increasing at a reduced rate, it nevertheless means that every three years, to the already more than 200 million Soviet citizens, are being added upwards of ten million more. Whatever the growth in the next few decades, the needs of a large and increasing number of people must be met. Therefore, the demands for agricultural produce are large and increasing. These needs would be even greater if the Soviet authorities were to attempt to carry out their expressed intention of measurably raising the standard of living of the mass of its people.

At least three factors make agriculture of central importance in the Soviet Union: 1) the large proportion of the population that depends on agriculture for a livelihood; 2) the present low level of farm production—inadequate to provide the population with anything but a minimum diet consisting largely of cereals and other starches; 3) the indifferent production of industrial products and crops—wool, hides and leather, and flax—creating a shortage in the raw materials necessary for the production of consumer goods.

It is necessary to guard against either exaggerating or minimizing the resources of the USSR. The Soviet resources, agricultural and otherwise, are often over- or under-estimated: the huge area makes it easy to overestimate the potential and to minimize the handicaps. Holding to facts, much of the Soviet's vast territory is unsuitable for cultivation. The outstanding physical element restricting agriculture is, directly or indirectly, climate; the second, terrain. The climatic handicaps are due to two critical elements of the Soviet Union—location in the high latitudes and shape—*i.e.* the great longitudinal extent. The size, combined with the

---

[16] As time has passed, the design of the "collective" has been altered somewhat. The latest change (1951) has been the creation of the huge *agro-collectives* under which *the collectives were collectivized,* all individual ownership of land and buildings withdrawn, and the rural population housed in great rural apartments. This was so vigorously resisted that in certain areas the plan had to be abandoned, but the movement has started and the agro-collective obtains in parts of the Union. The collectivization of farm lands has been the most persistently resisted aspect of the Communist program, and agriculture is—and has been—the weakest part of the Soviet economy.

other two space elements, makes it continental in the extreme. Among the marginal lands are the tundra wastes and the forest and marsh lands of the north, and the deserts and mountains in the east and south, altogether comprising more than two-thirds of the total area. About 10 per cent of Soviet land is classified as tillable; 2.5 per cent as grasslands and pastures, some of which might be made cultivable; 15 per cent as pasture. In other words, about 27.5 per cent of the country may be classified as agricultural or potential agricultural land—as compared to Germany and France where 40 per cent is tillable and 60 per cent agricultural, and to the United States with comparable figures of 27 and 65 per cent.

Cultivated acreage in the Soviet Union and the United States are approximately equal, but recent agricultural trends in the two states have shown marked contrasts; whereas in the United States farm production has increased 40 per cent since 1940, in the same period Soviet output has lagged and the per capita production of milk and meat declined by about 30 per cent in a 25-year period.

Aside from the increase in the total acreage of all crops, many changes have taken place in the distribution of acreage among various crops and groups of crops. Wheat acreage has expanded at the expense of rye; the percentage of grains in the total acreage cultivated decreased but there was an attendant rise in the more "intensive" food and industrial crops, such as sugar beets and cotton, and in forage crops including grasses and sown hay. These changes have been accompanied by a rise in productivity.

Agriculture is concentrated within an elongated wedge. The cultivated land lies in a triangle—*the agricultural wedge*—broadest in the west, where it extends from the Gulf of Finland to the Black Sea, and narrowing to a blunt point in the east near Lake Baikal. There are only two major agricultural outliers beyond the margins of this wedge—both are to the south: one, the Caucasus region; the other, Russian Turkestan. The northern limit is a frost-line, in combination with infertile podozolic soils,

poor drainage, the taiga, and permafrost (frozen subsoil), the latter all climatically induced. Cultivation in the south is stopped by drought; in the east, by mountainous topography.

Climate is restrictive even within the agricultural triangle, and the growing season, even in the most southerly republics, is short. If Soviet Europe were placed over central United States in corresponding latitudes, Yalta (Russian Riviera on the southern side of the Crimea) would lie over a point somewhat north of Minneapolis, Minnesota, and Odessa, Black Sea port in the Ukraine, approximately over Duluth. Kharkov and southern Minnesota have a corresponding frost-free period—about 151 days—while the frost-free period of Moscow (130 days on the average) is similar to that of northern North Dakota. (Volin) The short growing season naturally restricts the choice and variety of crops that can be grown, as well as concentrates cultivation within a short period. The brevity of the growing season is somewhat compensated for by the longer hours of sunshine in the northern lands during the warm months. It is this fact that permits a small variety of crops to be grown in latitudes that would ordinarily be thought of as prohibitive to agriculture. The areas of marginal rainfall include the fertile black earth regions of the steppes. As with the "dust bowl" of the United States, this is a risk area. Wheat, normally accounting for about three-fifths of the acreage in these lands, is heavily concentrated here. In the pre-war period, estimates indicated that this black earth district accounted for three-fourths of the tillable acreage.

Average crop yields in the USSR are lower than in either Western Europe or the United States. It is difficult to quote figures of Soviet production because they often do not represent just what they purport to. For example, 1933-37 average crops yields were quoted as a little more than 13 bushels to the acre, but these figures are the "pre-harvest, so-called biological" yields and do not account for the heavy grain losses incurred in harvesting. Production can undoubtedly be raised, particularly as fer-

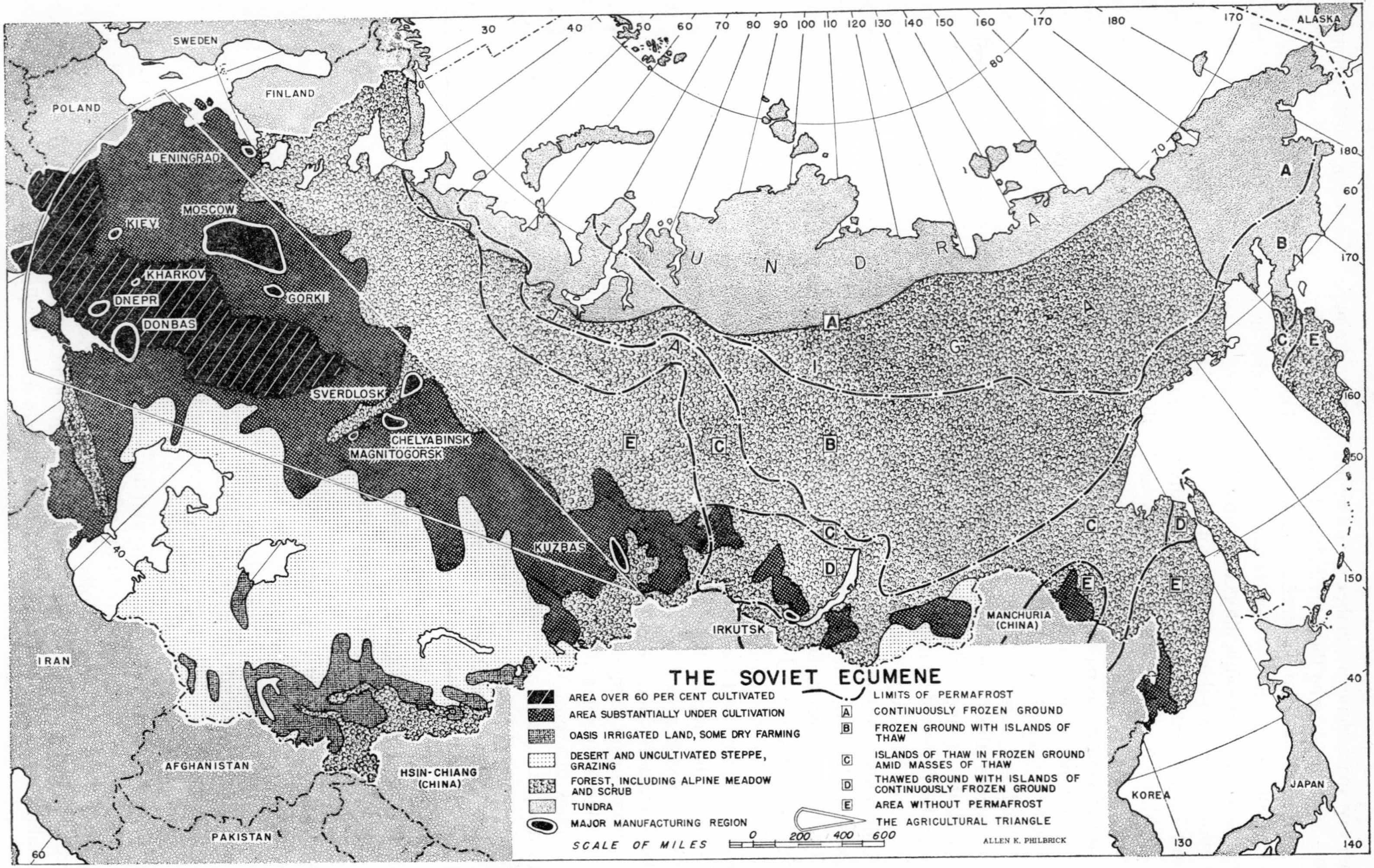
THE SOVIET ECUMENE
AREA OVER 60 PER CENT CULTIVATED
AREA SUBSTANTIALLY UNDER CULTIVATION
OASIS IRRIGATED LAND, SOME DRY FARMING
DESERT AND UNCULTIVATED STEPPE, GRAZING
FOREST, INCLUDING ALPINE MEADOW AND SCRUB
TUNDRA
MAJOR MANUFACTURING REGION
SCALE OF MILES
0 200 400 600
LIMITS OF PERMAFROST
A CONTINUOUSLY FROZEN GROUND
B FROZEN GROUND WITH ISLANDS OF THAW
C ISLANDS OF THAW IN FROZEN GROUND AMID MASSES OF THAW
D THAWED GROUND WITH ISLANDS OF CONTINUOUSLY FROZEN GROUND
E AREA WITHOUT PERMAFROST
THE AGRICULTURAL TRIANGLE
ALLEN K. PHILBRICK
SWEDEN
FINLAND
POLAND
LENINGRAD
MOSCOW
KIEV
KHARKOV
GORKI
DNEPR
DONBAS
SVERDLOSK
CHELYABINSK
MAGNITOGORSK
KUZBAS
IRKUTSK
MANCHURIA (CHINA)
IRAN
AFGHANISTAN
PAKISTAN
HSIN-CHIANG (CHINA)
KOREA
JAPAN
ALASKA
T U N D R A
T A I G A

Figure 9.6.

tilizer (very essential on northern agricultural lands) is used in increasing amounts; and the rise in the fertilizer industry, along with the discovery of important deposits of potash and phosphate, should open the way to such improvements.

The significance of agriculture—particularly grain cultivation—to the Soviet Union cannot be over-emphasized. Before the revolution Russia had a long, though sporadic record as an exporter of grain, at times leading the world. An increase in acreage, states Volin, "may make it even more a competitor with the United States in the world market." The "Battle for Grain," a slogan of the early days of the Soviet regime, epitomized not only the struggle to increase production but also the struggle, referred to before, that has persisted between the peasantry and the government; it has been at the core of the major shifts in Soviet economic policy from the first.

Grain, being the "bread" of the people, has always been the most critical item of the Soviet economy. The shift from numerous experiments in agro-technique to the extension of acreage into risk areas is taken by observers as further evidence of the failure to make "plan" and "achievement" synchronize.

The importance attached to the new grain areas was underlined by the addition to the existing railroad system, in the fall of 1955, of a series of narrow gauge lines to form a close network of transportation for the distribution of the (hoped-for) increased amounts of grain. "An initial 700-mile system of feeder lines" was to be ready by harvesting time, 1955, this to be expanded by 1957, to 1300 miles length.[17]

Plant introduction and adaptation. One of the more spectacular—and important—sides to Soviet developments in agriculture has been the introduction of new industrial crops to supply the state with needed raw materials for which, because of latitude, it ordinarily would be dependent upon outside areas. Some of

these are indigenous wild plants that have been domesticated, as *kendyr,* a variety of fiber from Central Asia which produces a long-wearing fabric, *kok-sagyz* and *tau-sagyz,* rubber-bearing plants from the Tien Shan Mountains, discovered in 1930-31. Soviet plant scientists have combed the world for plant varieties that will adapt successfully to conditions within some portion of Soviet territory, and a number of foreign plants have been introduced and are cultivated, as: *ramie,* a Chinese nettle which produces a durable cotton substitute; *kenaf,* a fiber that can be used as an alternative to jute from the Indian subcontinent; the Chinese tung tree, oil-producing and valuable as an ingredient of paints and varnishes; the soybean from Manchuria, indigenous to the Far East and now grown extensively in the Ukraine and neighboring Moldavia; the cork oak from Algeria, citrus fruits, and a wide variety of other useful and necessary plants.

PEOPLE AND POPULATION

The Soviet Union is a nation of many peoples. While the Russian plains have always had some mingling and blending of other nationalities and races, the marginal lands—as the mountains and deserts and polar areas—have generally kept their cultures aloof from intruders and have fostered peculiar peoples. More than one hundred separate divisions compose the eleven largest ethnic groups of the USSR. The Eastern Slavs—the Great Russians, Belorussians, and Ukrainians—form the largest ethnic group, accounting for three-fourths of the total population. Turkic strains comprise the second most important group followed by the Ugro-Finnic (Mongoloid from the lower Volga region), the Slavonic-Baltic group, several peoples speaking the Japhetic languages, and Iranians; Moldavians and Jews each number about two million. The most numerous of the lesser groups are the Buryat-Mongols of Eastern Siberia. Although the Slavic element outnumbers by several times the combined populations of all of the other ethnic groups, the multi-national character of the

---

[17] Theodore Shabad, *New York Times,* May 15, 1955, p. 26.

people of the Soviet Union is clearly reflected in the political structure.

The USSR is basically European. Because there are in the USSR large numbers of ethnic groups that are of Asian origin, there is a tendency to erroneously think of "Russia" (the Soviet Union) as Asian. Another fact that prompts this fallacious association is that 6,460,000 of the 8,570,000 square miles of Soviet territory lie in Asia.

But the USSR is not Asian; it is East European for several reasons. In the first place, the Russians have shared with the West the heritage of Christianity: for over a thousand years the religious tie has united the Slavs of Eastern Europe with the people to the West, even though the Christian traditions of the former were inherited from Greece and not from Rome. During the past two and a half centuries the Russians have turned westward, not to the Orient, for their cultural ties. It is obvious that their technology comes from the West. From the West they also adopted the idea of universal education. They have steeped themselves in Western philosophical and political thought: the revolutionaries borrowed the Marxist cult not from the Orient but from the West. "A study of Oriental thought, no matter of what school, will not help you to understand Russia . . . For the Chinese, the Russian is a European white man speaking a European language . . ."[18]

The Russian Slav. It is generally accepted that the Slav peoples originated as an ethnic group in the Dnieper lowlands and the grasslands lying to the west. Here, all of the Slav peoples—Eastern, Western, and Southern— were cradled, and from here spread to the far parts of the eastern two-thirds of Europe where they are found today. The Russian Slavs, therefore, are directly descended from the nuclear Slav group that developed in the original steppe core-area during the early centuries after Christ.

The Ukrainian peoples (Little Russians or

Ruthenes are alternative names for this group or portions of it) number about 40 million. They spread northward from the Black Sea shores to the Pripet Marshes (which stopped their advance about 80 miles north of Kiev) and extend westwards into Bessarabia, Bukovina, and Eastern Galicia, grasslands that are continuous with the Ukrainian steppes.

The Ruthenes are a "detachment" of Little Russians who moved into the Carpathians and, in places, beyond the crests to the opposite slopes. The Carpatho-Ruthenes were, at the time Czechoslovakia was created, incorporated within that Western Slav state; since World War II, however, they are again a part of the Ukraine. The Carpatho–Ruthenes are a united group, numbering more than half a million. Having lived for centuries in an isolated mountain environment, they are very backward in their ways, and formed the least-advanced portion of Czechoslovakia while they were a part of that state. Ethnically close to the Ukraine, the Ruthenes are now politically associated with these people—a tie which they had long desired.

Eastern Galicia, politically a part of the Ukraine since 1945, held a majority group of about five million Ruthenes (forming 60 per cent of the total population of that area) living under Polish rule. They tended to form the rural population while Poles and Jews, who made up the other 40 per cent, were urban dwellers. Thus, geographically and socially, the Ruthenes were a group apart. A further cleavage ran along religious lines because the Little Russians, like the other Eastern Slavs, are Orthodox Christians, the Poles Roman Catholic. On ethnic and national grounds it is logical that Eastern Galicia become a part of Little Russia. In Bessarabia and Bukovina, the Ruthenes did not constitute a majority group, however. These territories were, nevertheless, annexed to the USSR on the basis of the Russian minority.

Great Russians make up the bulk, not only of the Russian Slav population, but of the total Soviet population as well. There is no basic difference between the Little and the Great Russians, and such distinctions as exist are the

---

[18] R. Gordon Wasson, "Are the Russians As Well Off as They Were under the Czar?" *U.S. News and World Report,* March 16, 1951, p. 33.

result of the evolution of changes, in differing environments, that have taken place over the thousand year period that the two groups have inhabited their respective lands. They could not help but develop a differing "outlook" and certain unique characteristics. The fact that both Slav peoples have assimilated small bodies of Tatar or Mongol peoples makes the resemblance between the Great and Little Russians even more close.

The first phase of the spread of the Great Russians was completed with the establishment of Moscow as their most important center. Their migration had carried them from the Slav cradleland in the Dnieper steppes northward into the forest zones of north-central Russia where they established themselves as agricultural colonists. When the second phase of their migrations—movement into the north European and Siberian *taigas*—began, they had to modify their economic pursuits in conformity to the more restrictive environment and they became fishers and hunters. The exploitation of the forest resources of this great northern belt of conifers was scarcely begun until the early part of this century, although the timber of the southern European fringes of the taiga has been cut for decades.

When the Tatar yoke was thrown off, unification of the country was carried out from Moscow, we have noted, not Kiev, and the former city has, during most of the following centuries, been the seat of the central government.

The reincorporation of the non-Slav Baltic territories—that for centuries had been a part of Imperial Russia (Estonia and Latvia became a part of Russia under Peter over two centuries ago, and Lithuania during the last half of the eighteenth century) but which experienced political independence during the brief interwar period of the twentieth century—indeed raises a geopolitical problem. The Slavs themselves touch the Baltic waters only in the Leningrad area, a spearhead of Great Russians thrust through by Peter when he built St. Petersburg—but, along the north shore of the Gulf of Finland, 20 miles from the outskirts

of Leningrad, Finns are in a majority; on the south shore, Esths predominate only 50 miles distant. The southern portion of the Finno-Russian border—both pre- and post-World War II—is a zone of mixing where language is the basis for determining nationality. Although the earlier boundary, drawn after World War I satisfied neither state, it was a more reasonable frontier, ethnically speaking, than is the present boundary gouged westward in places by the Russians during the past two decades.

The spread of the Great Russians into Asia was accelerated by the development of industry beyond the Urals under the Communists. It is estimated by some writers that so great has been this eastward movement that in all parts of Russian Asia, except possibly Turkestan, Russians equate non-Slavs in number, and, further, that, in time, Russians will be in the ascendency in the Asian sector, numerically speaking. The Russians make good pioneers: they have, throughout their history, shown a remarkable adaptability to varying physical environments and an outstanding capability for getting along with foreign groups.

The White Russians occupy the area to the north of the Pripet Marshes, along the western frontier of the Soviet Union adjacent to northern Poland and Lithuania. The Pripet Marshes, found in the southern portion of the Republic, somewhat segregate this group of Eastern Slavs from the Little Russians. Although under the Czars they were the most persecuted of the Russian Slavs, they are nevertheless closely related to the Great Russians linguistically and in other ethnic factors.

Under the Communist regime, they have been accorded their own Soviet republic. A wedge of higher ground (that narrows across White Russia and has its apex at Warsaw in Poland) stretching between the Pripet and Baltic Marshes, marks the population center of Belorussia; the heaviest concentration is around Minsk, their cultural center and nuclear area. The numbers of this group are difficult to gauge because they are spread out from this center into the former Polish territories, Lithuania, and Latvia; they possibly number about 7.5 million.

The White Russians are largely rural, Poles, Jews, and Germans making up most of the urban populations. Until the revolution, more than half of the land in the territories where White Russians formed the majority group was held by Polish landlords and the Russian peasants existed under almost serf-like conditions. It is little wonder that development of White Russia has been slower than in the other Russian republics, and that rectification of the economic structure was desired.

The USSR is demographically a young country. The Soviet population is larger than that of the United States, but smaller than that of China or India. Territorial changes, from 1939 on, have markedly affected the population data, increasing the total by several million; a high annual national increment—estimated to be about 1.3 per cent—has increased the figure still more. The rate of increase is far above that characteristic of the West European nations.

The spread of the population is very uneven over the Soviet Union. In the black earth region of the Ukraine, the density averages as high as 250 per square mile, while throughout European Russia the average density figures are only 65, and in portions of the Asian region —as in the East and Central Siberia—density averages from but three to five persons per square mile. Along the Trans-Siberian Railway, however, these figures may rise to 50, indicating the importance of transportation in affecting the settlement pattern. In the southern desert areas, the irregularities are even more glaring, with vast nearly uninhabited spaces being relieved by fertile oases where population densities reach 350 and 400 per square mile. The same condition obtains in the extreme northeast.

As in the United States, where population has been characterized by a continuing expansion into virgin territory, the Russian population has pioneered outward from the nuclear-center ever since the middle of the sixteenth century. Since the reign of Peter, the fertile black earth regions have gradually been settled;

and the extension of agriculture, the development of the rich mineral resources, and the consequent industrialization have made the southern steppeland over-all the most productive region in the Soviet Union. Climate and distance shielded the north and Siberia against Russian penetration, although, as pointed out in the historical review, Russians reached the Arctic and Pacific littorals at an early date. The arid south, where ancient civilizations of oases and nomad peoples had persisted for centuries, remained culturally and economically sacrosanct against Russian settlement. Not until the 1930's was the resistance of the nomadic Kazakh peoples broken under the enforced sedentarianism of Soviet policy. Russian settlement, to the east of the Urals, was confined to a narrowing wedge of colonization circumscribed by the formidable subpolar forest zones to the north and steppe and bleak desert lands to the south.

Under the Soviets the pattern of Russian colonization remained much the same—a filling-in of the already settled regions and a thin spreading into the marginal districts north, east, and south. In contrast to the expansion of population into the virgin territories in the United States, the peopling of the frontier Russian lands beyond the European ecumene was, under the Empire, superficial. Those Russians who were attracted to the Siberian areas centered their attention almost entirely on the potential for agricultural utilization. Not until the planned regional economy, under the Communist structure, did the development of the full resource potential begin. As pointed out, even now accessibility to transportation facilities determines relative development.

Changes in demography due to population relocation under the Soviets. In 1926 the relocation of Soviet nationals from European areas eastward into the Ural Mountains, Siberia, and the East, constituted a migration of 2.7 million people; into the Kazakh SSR and other sections of Central Asia, 910,000 persons. Similar movements west of the Urals concentrated over half a million into the Leningrad and Central industrial regions, and more than a million persons into the mining and industrial districts of the Ukraine and the new agricultural area in the northern Caucasus.

Population relocation, begun before World War II and accelerated during that period of conflict, effected major changes in the population pattern, for the threat of invasion by the Germans sent not only people but industry into the safer recesses of the Volga, Ural, and Asian areas of the domain. In the Volga region, the Ural Mountain area, western Siberia, Kazakh, Central Asia, and the Arctic lands, the rise in population was accompanied by a sharp and concomitant upswing in industrial production and cultivated area. New industrial and mining centers mushroomed where only villages or forts or barren spaces had formerly marked the spot.

Undoubtedly the most striking change in the population pattern of the Soviet Union—from the days of the Czarist Empire—is that which took place in the rural-urban ratio. The urban population, listed in 1897 as only 12,969,000, had risen to 61 millions in 1940, representing nearly one-third of the total. As a result of the programs for industrialization, large numbers of rural people were required to lease the farms and move to the growing and multiplying industrial centers, so that, beginning in 1928, urban population increased rapidly. This growth of new urban centers in areas of industrial development—began during the first Five-Year Plan and continuing into the present—is the most significant factor altering the pattern of distribution of the Soviet population.

In general, the redistribution of population has been pointed toward the economic development of the different regions and the exploitation of their resources. "The principal population movements," writes Lorimer, "have been complementary to the transition of Russian economy from a diffuse, largely agrarian order to an integrated national economy with an effective balance between agriculture, industry, commerce, and social services. As industrial activities increase, and as agriculture becomes technically more advanced, the latter, which in 1939 supported about 55 per cent of the Soviet

population, will eventually require a much smaller proportion of the total labor force. The transition to a balanced, industrial economy in the USSR is still in its initial stages."[19]

The effectiveness of the Soviet people. The productive capacity of a people has a far-reaching impact on the conversion of potential resources into actual resources—*i.e.* it does much to determine the "power" of any state. How does the "population effectiveness" of the Soviet Union compare with that of other great nations?

In the small space of about three decades the Soviets have undertaken to transform their large, multi-national, largely illiterate population into a unified literate people in a modern socialist state—the latter concept involving the conversion of a capitalist economy, largely agarian, into one with a communal, Communistic structure balanced between industry and agriculture. The population distribution (largely rural) and the pattern of peasant farming (in densely populated areas, as in the Ukraine and around Moscow, of the usual European system of small plots of land individually worked)—both an inheritance from Czarist days—had to be radically changed for it was necessary to transmute rural peasants and pastoralists into modern urban factory workers.

One of the first steps undertaken was to set up a collective form of agrarian structure. Under the first design of the communal system, each farmer had a garden plot and his own buildings, but the fields were collectivized and communally tended. The Government Central Tractor Station supplied the modern machinery under a rent system. Excess rural populations were brought into industrial centers. Those who resisted communization (as the kulaks) were redistributed to other districts of the domain—mostly Siberia—to form a large body of slave labor used to construct the many and huge public works (power and irrigation dams

---

[19] Frank Lorimer, "Population Movements in Imperial Russia and in the Soviet Union," *Compass of the World* (New York: The Macmillan Company, 1947), p. 459.

and canals, etc.) and industrial plants—projects owned and directed by the Communist state. Thus was the population reconditioned by the Communists for the "new State."

Population projections. Several population projections of significance to political geography can be deduced on the basis of certain realities and trends in the population conditions now prevalent in the USSR. First, it can be expected that the population will increase rapidly for many years (in contrast to most of the states of the West) but in slowly decreasing proportions relative to the total population. As clear—and more important to the mass of the people of the Soviet Union—is the evidence that the resources, if properly developed and allocated, will be able to support a rising standard of living for the growing population. A rise in the living standard was arrested during the 1940's by the emphasis placed upon the development of basic industry and defense needs. However, large advances took place in the fields of education, health, and social services.

The advance made, culturally and technologically, in the Soviet republics will, without doubt, have an impact upon development in neighboring Eurasian nations—if in no other way than to expand the volume of trade, particularly between the industrially retarded Asian countries and the more technologically advanced Russian state. The recent trade agreements already negotiated between the USSR and other Eurasian and South American states —both Communist and Western Bloc countries —make an imposing array. Communist trade ties have developed so swiftly and dramatically as to have almost the appearance of a trade "offensive."

INDUSTRIAL AND POWER RESOURCES: MINERALS, POWER, AND INDUSTRY

One side of any nation's production is its agricultural output, the other half is the industrial strength—based on power and mineral resources. Being an agricultural country, the development of industrial fuels and minerals had scarcely been begun when the Soviets took over. The basic aim of the Communists—as stated before, to transform agrarian Russia into a world industrial power—was accomplished by two means: 1) socialization of all forms of production, a measure which permitted government control; and 2) the introduction and carrying through of Five-Year Plans, each with a stated goal and placing the stress on industry, particularly heavy industry.

The program of intensive industrialization, initiated in the middle 1920's, has produced changes of great magnitude in the economic and industrial geography of the domain. One of the most impressive effects has been the emphasis given certain types of industry: heavy industry has received the stress, particularly the production of machine tools and machines. A second trend was the gravitation of industry from the Moscow-Leningrad and Ukraine centers in European Russia eastward into and beyond the Urals. Some industry had developed in the Urals during the Empire but not in terms commensurate with the mineral resources of the area.

When the first Five-Year Plan was begun, in 1928, industry accounted for 58.7 per cent of the total production in the country and, of the total industrial output, 39.7 per cent came from heavy industry. Immediately preceding Soviet entry into World War II in 1940, industry's share in the state's production had risen to 84.7 per cent, 61.2 per cent of the total industrial production coming from basic industry, and the demands of the war had raised this latter figure to 76.1 per cent by 1945.

Two major principles controlled the location of industry under the Soviets. Proximity to raw materials and fuels and proximity to markets largely controlled the distribution pattern of industry, although this was somewhat modified by the trend to place industry in the interior, safer recesses of the nation. Not always can the three aims be harmonized and, further, regional and national interests must also be considered. Another very interesting— and significant—development was the formation of the great fuel-mineral combines (*kombinat*), as the Magnitogorsk–Kuznetsk Combine of iron ore and coal. Industries expanded and were modernized in the old industrial centers, and, in newer areas, industrial output multiplied by several times over: between 1941-45, production (through manufacture) increased in the Urals 3.6 times, in Siberia 2.8, and in the Volga Basin 3.4 times.

Industry produces commodities never manufactured in the country during the Empire. Former imports, now fabricated at home, include "automobiles, tractors, textile, printing and paper-making machinery, steel-rolling mills, powerful hydraulic turbines, excavators, and internal combustion engines. New technical processes have been developed, such as hydraulic cutting techniques in peat-working, the use of peat as fuel for electric power stations, the underground gasification of coal, and the manufacture of synthetic rubber."[20]

Power Resources

Industry requires power and, in terms of fuel resources, the USSR is potentially one of the richest countries in the world; however, in terms of development of some of these fuels, the Soviets are surpassed by other industrialized countries. Exclusive of water power, coal represents over 75 per cent of the fuels consumed, wood 9.7 per cent, peat 6.2, petroleum 6.3, gas 1.4, and shale .4 per cent.[21]

Official estimates of Soviet coal reserves place the USSR second only to the United States. As is the case with so many of the mineral resources of the Soviet Union, most of the commercial coal deposits (over 90 per cent) are in Asia, far from the industrial and population nodes of the nation which are in the European portion. Lack of transportation, sparse population, and lack of a local industrial market mean that most of these fields are "inaccessible or economically unexploitable"—at least for the present. Coal production is concentrated in those areas convenient to industrial centers or with transportation facilities to such centers.

Compared with the reserves, total coal production is low, as is also the per capita output (compared to some countries). The principal coal producers are the Donets Basin in the Ukraine, the Kuznetsk Basin in Central Asia, the Ural Mountains and the Moscow vicinity (both mostly lignite and hence inferior or unusable for industry, though not for power plants), and Karaganda.

The USSR is supplied with all of the coal that it is going to need in the foreseeable future —looking generations ahead; the stop-gap is transportation and not cost because, in a Communist state where all means of production are under the same central control, deficits in one area (as transportation costs for needed raw materials) can be made up from others that are showing a profit. This immense reserve of coal, as one of the two basic requirements in heavy industry, is a tremendous power resource to the Soviet Union.

How does production compare with other nations? When the first Five-Year Plan was put into operation in 1928, coal output in the USSR was only 34 million metric tons, "less than one-tenth that of Germany and the United Kingdom together"; by 1953 the production had been raised to 320 metric tons, "nearly equal to the combined total for these two highly industrialized countries, and not far below the output of the United States (440 million metric tons)."[22, 23]

The water power potential is large. It is difficult to state what the hydroelectric power potential of the Soviet Union is because estimates vary from 35 per cent of the world's total, the

---

[20] Shabad, *Geography of the USSR, op. cit.,* p. 69.
[21] The USSR—Summary of Basic Economic Information, International Reference Service, U.S. Department of Commerce, Vol. VII, No. 122, December, 1950.

[22] The breakdown of lignite, bituminous, and anthracite is not available for 1953, but in 1948 (the last year in which the breakdown was available for the USSR) about 20 per cent of Soviet coal was lignite, and the remainder bituminous, whereas of United States production, less than one-half of one per cent was lignite, about 90 per cent of the remainder bituminous, and 10 per cent anthracite.
[23] *Focus* (New York: American Geographical Society, Feb., 1955.)

Soviet claim, to 12 per cent as estimated by American observers. Whichever is correct, the latent resources are large. Again, however, only a small proportion of the potential is found in the European section—five-sixths of the total is concentrated in Asia. Of the European share, more than one-half lies far south and east of the major power market centers in the Caucasus Mountains.

Though the potential resources are great—the USSR ranking first (or possibly second to the Belgian Congo)—the developed hydroelectric power is relatively small. Most of the power stations constructed before the war were in the Caucasus, the northwest, and on the Volga, although the largest single station, at Zaporozhe, was on the Dnieper River. The fourth Five-Year Plan specified a greatly extended program of hydroelectric power construction, calling for the rehabilitation of six stations including the Dneproges (destroyed during the war), "30 stations to be completed, the first phase of 8 others to be put into operation, and work on five others yet to be begun."[24] These included extensive developments at Begovat (Farkhad) on the Syr Darya, at Mingechaur on the Kura River, a series of stations on the Zanga River, the Ust-Kamenogorsk on the upper Irtysh River, the Sevan and Kram in the Caucasus, at Gorki on the Volga, Molotov on the Kama, and several in the Urals. A still greater program is projected by the Soviets for the decade ending in 1960. The irrigation and hydroelectric stations at Kuibyshev and Stalingrad on the Volga and the Kakhovka on the Dnieper, along with three big canals (the Main Turkman, the South Ukrainian, and the North Crimean) are to increase the hydroelectric capacity by four million kilowatts and the annual output by 22 billion kilowatt hours.

Petroleum resources of the USSR. As in the case of waterpower, there is a huge disproportion between the production and the reserves (as well as in the estimates of the actual petroleum potential) of the USSR. The Soviet

Union, at the 17th International Geological Congress in 1937, announced an estimated reserve of 3,866.2 million metric tons or nearly 55 per cent of the total world reserves. Other estimates are not so extravagant; Eugene Stebinger suggested an ultimate output of 168 billion barrels of oil as against 100 billion for the United States.[25, 26] Whatever the exact figures, the petroleum reserves of the USSR are large and form a significant proportion of the total global oil resources.

The Soviet Union is the third largest petroleum producer in the world, exceeded only by the United States and Venezuela. However, the discrepancy between the output of the two world powers is enormous: in 1951 (for which the latest comparative figures are available), the USSR produced 292 million barrels of oil as against the over 2.2 billion barrels of the United States. Although new American discoveries annually disclose reserves two times greater than the amounts consumed by the United States in a year's period, these new fields are uncovered through greater efforts by more people using more scientific techniques than ever before—and there are fewer and

---

[24] The USSR—Summary of Basic Economic Information, *ibid.,* p. 9.

[25] Eugene Stebinger, "The USSR," from *World Petroleum Geography,* Wallace E. Pratt and Dorothy Good (New York: American Geographical Society, 1950), p. 238.

[26] The justification for the higher projected production in the USSR is geological, and is explained by Stebinger in these words: there are "many similarities in the geologic settings of the petroleum basins of the two countries: all of the great types of petroleum occurrence are well represented in each, and the complete age range of the productive formations is also the same. The average thickness of the sedimentary series is roughly equal, with the result that in each case total volume of sediments is proportional to area. Counterparts of the high-yield areas of California and the Texas–Louisiana–Gulf Coast are readily found in the USSR. Counterparts of the great interior basins of the United States, with deep Paleozoic production, are also represented in Russia.

"With no fundamental differences as to the types of occurrence, there is, however, a considerable difference in the size of the effective areas available to each, as indicated by the square miles of effective sedimentary area . . . the Russian total, selected on the same basis, is 4.3 million square miles, compared to 2.6 million for the United States; giving a ratio of 1.7 to 1.0 in favor of Russia." *Ibid.,* p. 238.

fewer "gushers." Stebinger estimates that (up to ten years ago and "taking account of the difference in total area") American scientists had exerted 150 times the effort of Soviet scientists in the search for petroleum. The disproportionate consumption of oil in the two states is somewhat startling: by 1951 less than 7 billion barrels had been drawn from Soviet resources whereas nearly 40 billion (of the 100 billion estimated reserves) had been pumped in the United States. It does not take much discernment to understand why the tremendous reserves of the Middle East are so strategic and significant to the West. The Communist Bloc would undoubtedly like to gain control of these oil lands adjacent to their own, also—not so much because of need of further reserves as to keep them out of the hands of the Western nations where they contribute a necessary and important power factor. The obstacle blocking greater production in the USSR is not lack of oil wells but of equipment, according to the best evidence obtainable. The "critical" oil fields in global geopolitics, however, are neither the Soviet nor the American but those in other parts of the world, as in Saudi Arabia, Kuwait, and Venezuela. The West is highly dependent upon them as a fuel resource.

The oldest and most productive petroleum fields are located in the Caucasus and Caspian area at Baku (Apsheron), Grozny, and Maikop; newer, but also very productive, is the field known as the Second Baku, located between the Volga River and the Urals. Other developed fields include the Emba, northeast of the head of the Caspian Sea along the Emba River; Ukhta in the Pechora River basin in the European Arctic; the Bukhara–Fergana field in Central Asia; and the reserves in the northern part of Sakhalin Island in the Far East.

Current production is well below the industrial, agricultural, and military needs of the nation. "Indicative of the shortage are the constant warnings to industry and agriculture to economize fuel oil and to change over to other fuels whenever possible and the modest place assigned to petroleum by the Soviet Government in the balance of fuels for 1950."[27]

Despite the deficit,[28] the Soviet Union exports petroleum and petroleum products to Afghanistan, Bulgaria, Czechoslovakia, Finland, and Poland, through trade agreements consummated in 1950. As a trade item, petroleum thus becomes a weapon of power also.

Mineral Resources Other than Fuel: Iron

Industry is based, first on power, secondly on raw materials. Of the total resources of world energy (fuel and water power) 23 per cent are found in the Soviet Union, 29 per cent in the United States. This means that more than one-half of the global energy resources are divided between the two present political giants—another reason for the centrality of their positions at the two power poles.

Supplies of iron ore are adequate. In the second base of heavy industry—minerals—the USSR is likewise well supplied: it has substantial amounts of all of the needed minerals—including the alloy ores—with surpluses in some.

The single most important mineral for industry is iron and the USSR is adequately supplied with excellent quality ore, well distributed. The proven reserves are sufficient to last a century under current conditions of technology and economy at present rates of use. About 66 per cent of these reserves are located at Krivoy Rog, Magnitogorsk, and Kerch which together produce over 80 per cent of the ore output. The Krivoy Rog, located in the industrially developed Ukraine, has provided the bulk of the Russian requirements for a great

27 The USSR—Summary of Basic Economic Information, *op. cit.,* p. 8.

28 Exact figures on Soviet petroleum consumption are not available, but since World War I (contrary to the policy of Czarist Russia), practically all of the petroleum produced in the Union has been consumed at home. Accordingly, since Soviet 1953 production was 365 million barrels, it can be assumed that consumption was approximately the same; in that year, the United States consumed approximately 2,848 million barrels (or three-fifths of the world production).

number of years. This is a large reserve of high-grade ore, although, because of the continued use, the better ores are being exhausted. The same condition is beginning to obtain at Magnitogorsk. The Kerch ores in Crimea are the largest reserves in the Soviet Union but indications are that this field is not a large contributor due to the fact that the ores are low grade—35 per cent ore content. The Magnitogorsk deposit, located in the southern Urals, is a large scale development dating from the early 1930's. The reserve is about one-third the size of that at Krivoy Rog; the predominant ore is magnetite and the iron content of industrial ores varies from 30 to 67 per cent.

There are approximately 600 known iron ore deposits of which some 100 are exploited, the latter mostly in the older industrial centers. The others are scattered deposits, in the Urals and beyond—some estimated to be large and important—but so far they are small contributors to the ore output.

Alloy Metals

As far as is known, the world's largest manganese reserves are in the USSR. Up to 1948, the Soviet Union supplied 80 per cent of the manganese consumed in the world, and India most of the rest. The continuing tension between the Communist states and the West made it expedient for the latter to look in other parts of the world for manganese with the result that today the USSR, while still the leading producer, no longer holds a near-corner on the market. Ghana and the Union of South Africa are now significant producers, as is Morocco.

The significance of manganese to industry—and hence as a strategic mineral in international trade—lies in its role as an alloy metal: manganese is important in the fabrication of high-grade steel, and every ton of steel produced requires from 10 to 40 pounds. Small amounts remove impurities; larger amounts impart great toughness to steel and make it resistant to abrasion. No substitute for manganese in steel manufacture has been found, and 95 per cent of all of the ore is used in the metallurgical industries.

Other nonferrous metals have an essential role in the production of steel with varying qualities suitable to particular purposes, as chromium, tungsten, antimony, molybdenum; others (also used as alloys) are useful not only as alloys, but are individually important in the production of such products as electrical supplies and precision instruments, aircraft, automobiles, and the like, namely, aluminum, copper, lead, zinc, and nickel.

Soviet chrome resources rank second in the world. Steels alloyed with nickel and chromium are hard and strong, and suitable to the manufacture of armor plate, projectiles, heavy guns, ball bearings, and the like. Such steels also are corrosion-resistant. No official figures on Russian chrome production have been available since 1934 but estimates place Soviet production second in the world, with Turkey ranking first by the slight margin of 2000 tons. Furthermore, it has chrome in such quantities that it is an important item of trade. Chrome production-distribution underwent a change after new important discoveries of the mineral were made at Donskoye and Khrom–Tau in the Aktyubinsk oblast in Kazakhstan. The latest available (1952) chrome production figures for the world leaders are as follows.[29]

Country	Metric Tons
Turkey	635,000
USSR	600,000 (est.)
Union of South Africa	580,024
Philippine Republic	543,514
Southern Rhodesia	322,666
Yugoslavia	107,700
World	3,200,000

It is significant to note that the greater proportion of the output of this alloy metal, so important in the manufacture of steels used for military and defense purposes, is within lands of the Western Bloc, although these deposits are handicapped in that they lie far from the steel-producing centers of the West.

Soviet nickel reserves are second only to those of Canada. In nickel production the

29 *Minerals Yearbook,* 1952.

USSR also ranks second—but a poor second to the outstanding world producer, Canada, a Western Bloc state; the reserves are, nevertheless, the world's second largest. Production in metric tons of contained metal, 1952, was as follows: Canada, 127,021; USSR, 25,000; New Caledonia, 10,500. In the Soviet Union nickel is mined principally in the Norilsk region near the mouth of the Yenisei River; the Monchegorsk and Pechenga regions of the Murmansk Oblast (also in the Arctic); and in the south and central Urals.

The USSR is the world's second largest producer of tungsten. Steel is alloyed with tungsten and cobalt to produce a product of great hardness: tungsten and cobalt steels retain their hardness and cutting qualities under "red heat of great friction" and, therefore, are used in the fabrication of metal-working machines, lathes, and high-speed tools. Cobalt also improves the electrical qualities, and is used in permanent-magnet steel. After China, the USSR ranks as the world's second producer of tungsten, only small quantities of which are required. World production, in 1952, was 55,-400 metric tons: China produced 20,000 tons; the USSR, 7,500;[30] and the United States, 5,905 tons. The fourth largest producer is Bolivia. Russian tungsten (wolfram) ores are usually found in combination with molybdenum; tungsten occurs in the Urals, Kazakhstan, and Transbaikalia. The greatest share of Soviet cobalt comes from the nickel deposits of Norilsk and from the Baku district.

Molybdenum requirements are supplied from national sources. The estimated 1952 world production of molybdenum was 22,200 metric tons, which indicates that only small quantities of this alloy are required by industry. Although figures are not available on Soviet output, it appears that the Russian mines satisfy the needs of state industries. Sixty per cent of the production comes from the tungsten-molybdenum deposits in the Urals, Akchatau in Kazakhstan, and the Dzhida River area near Lake Baikal.

Copper is in moderately good supply in the Soviet Union. There is enough copper to last at least several decades at the present rate of use. Like the copper found in the United States, the metal content of the major ore deposits is low. Nevertheless, the USSR ranks fourth in world production (according to estimates not based on actual output figures), Soviet mines producing about one-tenth of the world's total copper. Half of the known Russian reserves are in Kazakhstan (at Kounradskiy and, to the west, at Dzhezkazgan), and it is believed that this republic will become the principal center for the production and refinement of copper in the USSR. However, until a short time ago most of the copper was produced in the Urals at the old copper-mining and smelting center at Sverdlovsk. As recent as 1942, the Sverdlovsk Oblast accounted for 31.4 per cent of the total output while the Urals area, as a whole, supplied 46 per cent.

Aluminum (and bauxite). Aluminum "logistics" is complex for the principal ore from which aluminum is made is a non-metallic clay that requires an electrolytic process to convert it to a metal. The clay is bauxite.[31] Aluminum is produced in those nations where hydroelectric power is abundant, whether the raw material lies within the national boundaries or not; however, the Soviet Union has both the raw material and the power for conversion. Soviet reserves of bauxite are moderate, the total resources estimated at 56.6 million metric tons. Nearly 80 per cent of this is in the Urals. Considering that the United States mines nearly 2 million tons of bauxite annually, and imports sizable amounts as well, this figure looks small. A significant part of the bauxite requirements of the USSR are supplied from the satellite states, however, as from Hungary where there are extensive deposits of high-grade "ore." Aluminum-producing plants are

---

[30] 1951 estimates; 1952 figures not available.

[31] This is not the only "ore" from which aluminum can be obtained although it is the most economic up to the present time. However, both alumina and aluminum are produced at Kandalaksha on the Kola Peninsula from nephelite mined in the Khibiny Mountains to the north.

located in a number of localities extending from the Volkhov plant near Leningrad and the one at Kandalaksha on the Kola Peninsula, to Zaporozhe in the Ukraine, into and beyond the Urals to Stalinsk in Siberia. The large hydroelectric constructions on the Volga River and tributary system will likely also produce this light-weight, strategic metal in construction where weight and strength are important, as in aircraft.

At the present rate of use, the known lead and zinc reserves of the Soviet Union will soon be exhausted. Imports supplement the national production. Over one-half of the reserves of lead and nearly 50 per cent of the zinc deposits are found in the Altay Mountains in Kazakhstan; these reserves produce 80 per cent of the total lead output and one-half of the zinc. Tin also exists in the Soviet Union, and in amounts that apparently take care of the national demand.

The extensive Soviet reserves of nonmetallic minerals are of special significance and interest. Among some of the spectacular deposits of non-metallic minerals are the nephelite of the Khibiny Mountains on the Kola Peninsula used, as stated, as a source of aluminum ore and also as a raw material for the manufacture of glass, enamel, and dyes. In association with the nephelite are huge deposits of mineral apatite used to make phosphoric acid and superphosphate fertilizer. This deposit placed the USSR first in world phosphate reserves. Superphosphate is now exported. Other phosphate deposits found in the Kirov and Moscow oblasts, in Kazakhstan and in the Ukraine increase the total reserves; all are producing superphosphate, one of the world's most needed and prized fertilizers. Nearly as proportionately large—and actually more vast —are the deposits of more than 18 billion tons of potash in the USSR, 80 per cent of the world's known supply. These give the Soviets another powerful item of exchange and provide an abundance of natural fertilizers for the agricultural industries.

Precious minerals. Although not useful in the creation of machines, the precious metals constitute power in the hands of a state in their capacity as weapons of trade. Shipments of gold went out from the USSR, in 1955, to Britain and other nations in exchange for manufactured articles and raw materials. The Soviet Union has for a long time been an important producer and exporter of platinum and gold. Rich gold deposits, that regularly compete with the Union of South Africa for first place in world production, are found in Siberia and the Far East, in Kazakhstan, and in the Urals; platinum is confined to the Urals area.

INDUSTRY

The natural reserves of energy and mineral resources in the Soviet Union are adequate for many decades of production, and, it would appear, are sufficient in variety, quantity, and quality to make that state nearly independent of other countries, if the Soviets so desire. There are several problems—relative to the richness of the ore, in certain instances, and to the distribution of the deposits in others—that hamper easy exploitation, and the development of industry.

The enormous size of the domain is one of the aspects of Soviet geography that raises a noteworthy problem for industry. Large areas of the Soviet domain do not have access to cheap water transportation which means that heavy and bulky materials—of low value according to weight and space requirements— must be sent long distances by land. This constitutes relatively expensive haulage. The thousands of miles of interconnections means, also, that an unduly large proportion of the fuel— estimated to be about one-third of the total— has to be used as energy for this transportation. This compares unfavorably with most other European states where fuel use for transportation runs about one-third of the Russian, due to shorter distances. An attempt at partially solving this problem of the tremendous intercommunication distances has been sought by stressing regional self-sufficiency to as great a degree as is feasible in regional planning.

There are four major industrial core-regions. The most highly developed is that centered around Moscow and spread over the provinces of Moscow, Ivanovo, Yaroslavl, Vladimir, Kostroma, Ryazan, and Tula. The Russians call it *The Industrial Center,* and the significance of this region cannot be over-estimated. It is a relatively small sector of the domain comprising, prior to World War II, only a little over one per cent of Soviet territory, but 9.5 per cent of the total population (20 per cent of the total urban population) and nearly one-third of the industry.

It was not due to the natural resources of the area—lignite, peat, phosphorus, and some iron and coal—that the Moscow center attained this importance, but rather to the fact that it was the historic nave of old Russia. Here is the nerve center—politically and economically—of the Soviet Union.

The district is fairly coincident with the watershed of European Russia, and a number of large rivers—or their tributaries—begin here to flow outward in several directions. Through a system of canals that interlaces the river systems, Moscow, the transportation hub of the country, is connected with the seas. Traditionally, textiles, machines, and chemicals (in that order) were the leading manufactures. With the shift in emphasis to heavy industry, the order of importance changed although the three same manufactures continue to be outstanding—specialized machines, chemicals, and textiles. Today this is the key center for machine tools, precision instruments, and automobiles, and, along with Leningrad, the Moscow center leads in the production of electrical equipment. The influence of the Moscow region is felt throughout the Union for it is an engineering center: engineers are trained here and sent to all of the other industrial areas. Over one-sixth of the total Soviet industrial output is from the Moscow region.

From the standpoint of available resources the *Donbas* is ideally located. This is the most heavily-industrialized sector of the Ukraine and one of the principal Soviet centers. Donets coal, Krivoy Rog iron ore, Nikopol manganese, and Zaporozhe power make it a natural center for heavy industry and chemical manufactures. The industrial district is not large, extending east and west between the bend of the Donets–Don Rivers, where the coal basin is located, to Krivoy Rog, about 235 miles distant. Coal moves west and ore moves east so that the industrial basin is characterized by a great number of industrial centers where iron and steel are processed, and steel products manufactured. This is in contrast to "The Industrial Center" where most of the plants are centered in and around Moscow. Most of the large mills of the Donbas go through the entire process of metallurgical production—from pig iron and coke to steel ingots and rolled steel, with the heavy machine industries completing the picture. The Donbas dips southward in the east as Kerch ore moves north in exchange for Donets coal. Stalino is the largest city in this area of heavy industry, and is surrounded by smaller centers—Makeyevka, Kramatorsk, Gorlovka; Mariupol (now Zhdanov), Rostov-on-Don, and Taganrog, all on the Sea of Azov, form manufacturing nodes to the south. The Donbas has been, and should remain, the outstanding metallurgical center of the USSR—because of its favorable geography.

As early as the era of Peter the Great, the mineral resources of *the Urals* provided the base for the development of industry, notably pig iron. The district stretches north-south through the central Urals from approximately 60 degrees north to Magnitogorsk in the south at 53 degrees north latitude. This is not a belt of continuous industry but rather "a series of independent industries" centered in or around several urban centers, the most important of which are Sverdlovsk, Molotov, Chelyabinsk, Ufa, and Magnitogorsk. The major problems of the Urals' industries are insufficiency of transportation facilities and inadequate supplies of industrial fuels. The energy to run the plants is still supplied, in the main, by coal from Karaganda (and, for Magnitogorsk, from the Kuzbas as well) and oil from the Emba River area. Despite these handicaps, the Urals area has become "one of the largest industrial and mining regions in the world."[32]

The *Kuzbas,* outstanding industrial region of Siberia, is primarily identified with coal: on the extensive fuel deposits of the Kuznetsk Basin, ferrous and nonferrous industries and machine manufacture have arisen. Local coal and iron ore (in part local and in part Ural ore) form the bases for the industries. The Kuzbas is part of the famous Kuznetsk–Urals (Magnitogorsk) Combine whereby coal and iron ore were exchanged so that heavy industry could develop at both terminals. This Combine is gradually losing its importance as Karaganda coal replaces that from the eastern basin, and local iron supplants the Urals ore—but both terminal industrial nodes are steadily growing greater and more important. Like other interior regions, Western Siberia, of which Kuzbas is a part, was stimulated to greater activity during World War II by the gain of enterprises evacuated from the west.

Of the four major industrial regions, two are situated in European Russia, one on the border between the Asian and European divisions, and only one in the vast Asian territories; or, to look at the distribution somewhat differently —in terms of political subdivisions—three of these centers are within the Russian Republic (RSFSR) and one in the Ukraine. If the Soviet objective of regional development, commensurate with the resource potential of each area, were to be carried out (along with the objective of regional semi-selfcontainment) then these four massive industrial concentrations would not meet the requirements. Hence, a great number of smaller but very significant centers of industry, scattered from the western and northernmost European frontiers to the southeastern and Far Pacific borders, are developing. Some have been centers of industry from the historic past—as the Leningrad district— and have merely expanded in size and, perhaps, in variety; many are completely new developments that have mushroomed (and this is the appropriate phrase) since the five-year

plans were begun in 1928. Geopolitically, they are very significant, both internally and externally. Concomitant with the industrial growth has been a population increase in these still sparsely populated districts, for the Soviet Union has offered inducements—and at times used force—to locate people in these new industrial nodes.

The *Northwest* industrial center is composed of two rather widely separated districts, the Leningrad and the Murmansk. Like Moscow, Leningrad is a center for the manufacture of machine tools, precision instruments, electrical equipment, etc., but adds, as well, shipbuilding, the chemical industries (as synthetic rubber from potato alcohol), phosphate fertilizers from Khibiny apatite, plastics, lumber and wood products, to mention only some of the great variety of fabricated items produced here. To generate the electric energy required for the industries, it is necessary to import large amounts of Donbas coal, and oil from the Baku fields. These fuels are transported northward via the river and canal systems that now connect the northern and southern seas bounding the country. Leningrad is the chief port for the export of raw materials from the entire national domain, and of imports, likewise for the whole nation. Murmansk, the largest city of the northern area and the only Russian port located in the north that is open to year-round shipping, is an outlet to ocean shipping as well as the western terminus of the Northern Sea Route. Among its industries are shipbuilding and fish-processing.

The *lower Volga* (approximately between the Kama tributary and the Caspian Sea) is destined to become industrially very significant, according to projected developments. Resources include part of the oil reserves of the "Second Baku," iron ore, oil shale, natural gas, chemical salts, and gypsum. The development of the area is part of the "Greater Volga" plan. The latter scheme was projected before World War II, and called for the construction of a series of dams along the river for: 1) the establishment of a deep-water course along the entire length of the river; 2) the irrigation of

---

[32] Shabad, *Geography of the USSR, op. cit.,* p. 99.

the semi-arid lands of the lower Volga region; and 3) the generation of hydroelectricity. The projects on the upper Volga were first completed, and the Kuibyshev and Stalingrad dams were finished in 1956. A part of the project to develop the lower Volga–Caspian area is the Volga–Don Canal (now in use) that opens up the landlocked Caspian Sea and Volga River to connect them with the Black and Mediterranean, and hence, with the world sea lanes.

A second canal (as far as known, not yet constructed although the objective was completion by 1955 or 1956), that ties in with the Volga-Don-Caspian system, extends the waterway into the southern heart of Russian Asia, namely, the Turkmen Canal. It is part of the development of another industrial center, namely, that in *Russian Turkestan.* Extending from the Fergana Valley (a historic caravan route of the past), from the Zeravshan Valley which cradles the mosques and bazaars of Tamerlane's Samarkand and Bukhara, past Tashkent and its surrounding cotton fields to Krasnovodsk on the eastern shores of the Caspian Sea, lie the industries of Russian Turkestan. Particularly in the southeastern half of this region have mineral and manufacturing developments of some importance taken place. The Fergana–Bukhara oil fields are the principal area of petroleum production east of the Urals; second in importance are the Turkmen fields to the east of the Caspian. Local coal has been used to develop industry, sulphur forms the base for a chemicals development at Shorsu in the Fergana Valley, zinc and copper are mined and plants are being erected for refining the minerals, and tungsten and molybdenum are exploited. Desert country, the population is concentrated on oases lying either at the base of the mountains and along the valleys of perennial mountain streams that flow out of the lofty and snow-covered Tien Shan—as the Fergana and Zeravshan oases—or along oases that stretch across the flat desert sands irrigated by streams that lose themselves in deserts or inland seas— as the Syr Darya and Amu Darya oases. It is a lush garden spot, and among the industrial

crops produced are cotton and silk. The Tashkent area carries on both heavy and light industry, and the city has the largest cotton manufacturing plant in Eurasia, according to the Soviets. Heavy industry includes the manufacture of agricultural machinery at Tashkent, chemicals and nitrate fertilizer at Chirchik, and, very important, the steel plants at Begovat which are the only metallurgical developments in the Central Asian area.

The remainder of the Central Asian–Far Eastern industrial developments have grown up, on natural resources, along the Trans-Siberian Railroad. The Irkutsk Oblast, to the west of *Lake Baikal,* while little developed at present, holds out important prospects in the Cheremkhovo–Irkutsk coal fields, the Ilim–Angara iron deposits (very rich), the manganese on Olkhon Island in Lake Baikal, the tremendous waterpower potential of the Angara River, and the lumber reserves of the area, to mention only the outstanding resources. Plans for this development are said to be in blueprint form. To the north lie the gold fields of the Vitim–Lena River area. Ulan-Ude, in Buryat Mongolia and east of Lake Baikal, has developed rapidly as an industrial center since the 1930's. Produced are locomotives and railroad cars, glass and lumber, and meat is packed.

Certain centers in the *East* developed rapidly. Komsomolsk, known as the "youth city," Khabarovsk, and Nikolayevsk are centers of heavy metallurgy and engineering industries (built on Amur River deposits of coal and iron), and shipbuilding. Vladivostok, eastern outlet of the Trans-Siberian Railroad and leading Pacific port, is also found here. Heavy industry, food-processing, cement manufacture, shipbuilding are industries of the Maritime Kray of which Vladivostok is the capital. North Sakhalin produces oil and coal, the former in sufficient amounts to take care of the needs of the Soviet Far East.

Other *Arctic areas,* besides the Kola Peninsula, are the sites of important mineral and forest resources and industrial developments are progressing rapidly and, in some cases, with great secrecy. The coal deposits of the Vorkuta district, in the Pechora River area, are some of the largest in the Soviet Union while at Ukhta are petroleum deposits. The north Pechora Railroad, built in 1942, greatly stimulated the development of these fuel resources which are vital to industries in Leningrad, and, it is anticipated, to Ural industrial centers when rail connections are made. East of the Urals, near the mouth of the Ob River, are fisheries; near the outlets of the Yenisei, particularly the Norilsk–Dudinka area, are exploited deposits of nickel, platinum, copper, coal—and, according to latest unofficial reports, uranium. The ores are refined near the mines and shipped via a 60-mile narrow gauge railway to the port of Dudinka.[33]

FOREIGN TRADE

The total world trade of the USSR appears to be low—about 2.2 per cent of global commerce. Soviet foreign trade is, like all other enterprise, a monopoly of the government; the right to enter into "foreign commercial transactions on behalf of all agencies and institutions in the USSR is reserved to the Ministry of Foreign Trade." East-West trade, particularly, has been sought by the Communist Bloc

of late. Like the preceding year, both 1954 and 1955 were distinguished by the signing of new trade agreements and for the renewal of former pacts which had lapsed. By this means, literally a web of bilateral trade agreements between Western nations and the Communist Bloc has been set up. Out of 127 separate trade pacts made in 1954 between Communist and Free World states, 28 were entirely new—that is, previous to 1954 there had been no trade agreements between the two states involved. The Soviet Union was very active in contracting such pacts, and, as in 1953, was expanding its trade agreements to countries outside of Europe, although the majority are still with West European nations. Though the Soviet Union is looking for markets for some of its surplus products, and, even more, requires goods produced in other states, a further objective of the state is purely geopolitical— namely, to attract attention to the USSR and to extend its influence and prestige.[34]

Prior to World War II and up through 1948, the greater portion of the foreign trade passed through ports—the Soviet's former customers were overseas or at a distance away, namely, Great Britain, the United States, and France. Since then, however, the larger part of the international trade has been with East European or Far Eastern Asian states and, hence, is transported by railway. Of the overseas shipping, more than half passes through the Black and Sea of Azov ports which tap the rich Ukraine grainlands, the Donbas industrial district, and the Caucasus and Caspian oil fields.

---

[33] Nothing has been said regarding uranium resources and the production of atomic products because, aside from the knowledge that such enterprises are developed to some extent, nothing is known. The reason for supposing possible uranium deposits at Norilsk is the secrecy that was suddenly imposed concerning the mining activities of the area. Further, from a mere town, it has suddenly seemed to climb in population. Shabad wrote in the *New York Times* for January 16, 1955, "Soviet failure to explain the recent rapid growth of a large urban center in environmentally so adverse an area as northernmost Siberia seems to indicate an economic development of a sensitive nature."

[34] Harold E. Stassen, *Soviet Bloc Economic Activities in the Free World,* Sixth Report to Congress, Second Half of 1954. Washington, D.C.: U.S. Government Printing Office, 1955, pp. 13-24.

10

Communist States of Central Europe and the Balkans

The Communist nations of Central Europe —Poland, Czechoslovakia, Hungary—make up the western sector of that crescent of states that swings around the USSR from Finland to Korea; countries that are subject to the influences of both the Russian state and the amphibious lands of the "inner crescent." This arc of nations bordering upon the Soviet Union is an old historic pressure zone that has felt the impact of aggressive forces, from the continental and oceanic sides, over a period of centuries in many instances. In the south, the pressures have resulted in the creation of spheres of influence set up by opposing powers in Iran (Persia), Afghanistan, and Tibet; in the west and southwest, in a crush zone—and a shatter zone—most particularly in the Polish lowlands;[1] in the east, in two new "crush"

areas, namely, Korea and Indochina. Even the giant state of China has suffered through the centuries from the hegemonical moves of states on both sides, inner and outer. All of the lands of the crescent are zones of uneasy political tenure, and their political fortunes have fluctuated largely as a result of the imperialistic designs of vicinal and amphibious nations.

This is to be undertsood, in part at least, in the light of a diverse physical environment that varies greatly in topography and economic usability. This is in marked contrast with the ethnic and natural conditions of the USSR which, physically and politically, dominates all of the broad eastern half of continental Europe. Although the areal "bulk" of Soviet Europe is enormous, the USSR has a unified plains' environment, with transitions of climate, that has resulted in ethnic homogeneity and a Russian "pattern" of social and economic living rather than in diversity.

[1] It should be noted that the west and southern sectors of this arc (notably Poland and Iran) did not become crush zones until after the Industrial Revolution. Prior to that period, both states had been strong bases of independent power.

183

THE PHYSICAL SETTING

Topographic diversity characterizes Central and Southeastern Europe. Just to the west of the USSR, the mass of the continent contracts sharply between the Baltic and Mediterranean Seas. Here, in the north, the Russian plain adjoins the lowland of northern Europe, where, becoming narrower, it continues uninterruptedly to the Belgian low country, nearly pinching out before it widens again in the Paris Basin of France. Westward from the Ukraine, however, the Carpathian-Transylvanian Alps elbow their way across the Russian and Middle European lowlands to act as a barrier, diverting all communication north or south—north to the plains corridor or south to the restricted passageway along the Danube River that leads to the interior Hungarian lowlands.

Two zones of marshland have influenced the pattern of history in this area. Although an examination of a physical map would seem to indicate that the low country to the north of the Carpathians presents no obstacle to east-west passage, in actuality this is a marshy region that has been prohibitive to transportation and settlement. By the same token, however, at times these marshes have acted positively—as a natural obstruction to protect groups of people against cultural and political extinction, particularly among the more ancient inhabitants. The southern sector, northward of Kiev in the region where the headwaters of the Dnieper River rise, is the largest area of marsh country in all Europe—the Pripet Marshes, involving a territory half the size of England. These marshlands constitute a real barrier frontier between the Russian and Polish nationalities, whereas, elsewhere across the northern lowlands, there are no physical barriers to keep these two Slavic peoples apart.

Farther to the north, in the Baltic lowlands fronting the sea, is a second widespread but disconnected area of shallow lakes and swamps traced from eastern Estonia southwestward through Latvia and Lithuania past the Masurian Lakes of East Prussia. This northern swampland likewise has impeded movement in the past, protecting coastal settlements along the Baltic for a long time against German and Slav infiltration.

Separating the two regions of waterlogged countryside a westward thrust of the Russian platform, in the form of an elevated triangle of higher ground that has its apex at Warsaw, provides an intervening corridor of drained surface. Within the limits of this wedge are found the most important urban centers and the major communication connections.

To the south of the Pripet Marshes rise the foothills of the Carpathians, a low and fertile plateau that slopes gradually from the north. By nature this is steppeland, a continuation of the steppe-grasslands of the Ukraine, but now, like that Soviet area, mostly planted to wheat. The plateau extends along the whole front of the north Carpathian slopes, thrusting into South Poland a spur of rich soil with good drainage that contrasts markedly with the ill-drained Polish lowlands of the north; it continues along the Sudeten and Ore Mountains around the blunt end of Czechoslovakia into Bohemia.

Historically, the Carpathian Mountains have had a barrier function. The Carpathians, being a part of the same folded structure as the Alps, are high and complex mountains that, along with their covering of forest vegetation, have acted as an effective obstruction to most movement and settlement.

The mountain system divides rather readily into three parts: the Tatra Plateau buttressed on the north by the western Beskids; the eastern Beskids; and the Transylvanian Alps. In the eastern Beskids, the folds of the Carpathians are tightly compressed, and the water divide marks the southward bounds of Polish language and people. The Beskids have acted advantageously as a barrier between groups; however, the highlands do not constitute a real hindrance to transmontane communication for there are several passes, some of which, like the Jablonica, are historically famous, facilitating movement and allowing good connections between Galicia and the Hungarian lowland. It was through the Jablonica Pass that the Magyar horsemen, riding from the Asiatic interior grasslands during the eighth century, passed from the steppelands to settle in the Central Danubian Plain where they remained to form the state of modern Hungary.

The Transylvanian elbow of the Carpathian arc partially encircles an upland, the Transylvanian Plateau. On the east and south the Transylvanian Alps overlook, from a relatively abrupt height, the lowlands of Moldavia and Walachia cut through by the Danube and encased on the south by the Balkan Mountains. The inner slopes descend into the plateau which, in turn, slopes in a general westerly direction toward the lowland of the middle Danube. The Mures River, tributary of the Tisza (in turn, tributary to the Danube), has formed the passageway between the mountains and plateau and carries off drainage of most of the area. The north-south front of the Transylvanian Plateau ends sharply, commanding the Great Alfold (Great Plain) of Hungary that stretches from the plateau base to the Danube River. The Danubian lowland is one of the most concisely defined physical regions in Central Europe. The arc of the Carpatho-Transylvanian Mountains encloses this depression, clearly outlining the sweeping lowlands of the interior prairie shared by Hungary, Rumania, and Yugoslavia.

River valleys provide access within the rugged Balkans. South of the Danubian depression, the complex Balkan Peninsula bulges into the Mediterranean Sea. The Balkans have a ragged mountain structure, struck through here and there by narrow, penetrating river plains. This latter character, combined with the general north-south, northwest-southeast trend of the tight folds of the ranges, has opened the continental mass of Europe to the recesses of the peninsula in contrast to the sharp divides that the Alps and Pyrenees form between northern Europe and the peninsulas of Italy and Iberia, respectively. Longitudinal river corridors connect to provide natural transit lanes, in the clefts of the Morava–Vardar Rivers, between the Danube lowland and the Aegean Sea; and tributaries of the Danube finger out of the mountains to descend, as widening valleys, to the Sava–Danubian flats. Access, therefore, from either the Danubian or Aegean side has been easy, but, due to the fact that the trend of the peninsular structure is north-south, there are no natural east-west passageways that cut across the grain to permit transverse movement.

Geopolitically, the most decisive geographic features of the Balkans have been, first, the numerous impenetrable mountain recesses that have served as centers where cultures were nurtured and as strongholds against invaders; and, second, the Morava–Vardar portal. Within this " 'corridor' much of the tragic history of the Balkans has been enacted. Along it, from one end or the other, have moved a long succession of migrating peoples, of advancing or retreating armies. Without control of it—as the Ottoman Turks experienced—the maintenance of political authority throughout the Balkans proved impossible. People have, from time to time, crowded into its narrow limits, so that cultural and ethnic complexity is to be expected. In war its inhabitants have been forced to abandon their farms and seek mountain refuge from aggressors entering the 'corridor' behind them. As the main highway of southeastern Europe its record is one of almost unending population movement, conflict, and political instability."[2]

East of the Morava–Vardar Valley the trend and part of the structure of the mountains changes. At the Iron Gate, the gorge where the Danube River cuts through the mountains, the Transylvanian Alps describe a turn, concave to the sea. The southern portion of this arc of folds forms the Balkan Mountains that thrust eastward across central Bulgaria, playing out just short of the sea. The folded ranges of the Balkan Mountains retreat from the Rhodope Massif, a firm block of ancient rock against which they apparently crushed. Although elevations of 9,000 feet are attained in the Balkan Mountains, they do not constitute

[2] Walter Fitzgerald, *The New Europe* (New York: Harper and Brothers, 1945), p. 57.

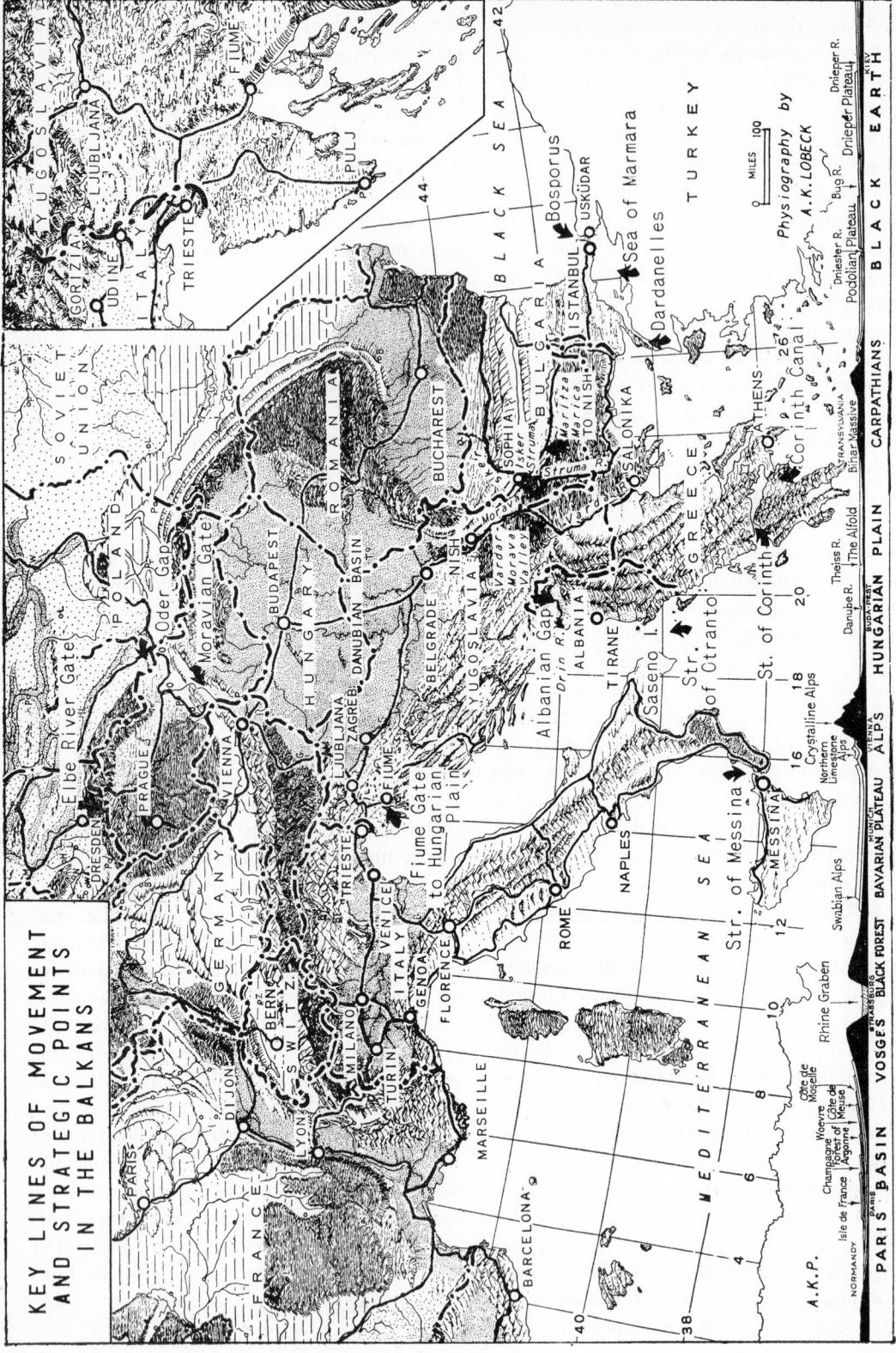

Figure 10.1. Movement in the Balkans and south central Europe, historically and in the present, has been along the natural passes—through breaks in the mountains and via river valleys.

a hindrance to movement between the lower Danube Basin and the Maritza Valley for the average height is only 3,000 feet and the range is cut through by a number of low passes, easily approached, especially from the north—as demonstrated in the southward Bulgar invasion during the seventh century. It is to be noted that railroads cross the mountains and not the seemingly easier coastal plains. The Isker River, tributary to the Danube, cuts through to provide a passage to Sofia, the capital of Bulgaria.

In a region of meagre plain, the fertile Maritza valley, protected by the bordering ranges and massif, has the further advantage of a moderate climate. Here is the ecumene of Bulgaria and the nucleus of settlement. It is to be noted that the Maritza turns south, to flow, not into the Black Sea but into the Aegean. A depression between the folded Balkan mountains and the massif in the southwest provides a relatively easy passageway across the divide between the headwaters of the Maritza and the Morava tributaries (the Dragoman Pass). Along here, between Nis (Nish) on the Morava and Sofia—and dropping from there to the Maritza Valley—the transcontinental express (Orient Express between Belgrade and Istanbul) has been routed.

The longitudinal structure of the northwestern folds, known as the Dinaric Alps, run parallel with the Yugoslav coast and have no easy transverse corridors or passes from Adriatic Dalmatia to the interior. The Dinaric Alps, of limestone structure, are a greatly dissected mountain mass involving all the features of dissolved limestone that are characteristic of *karst* regions—forbidding both to movement and settlement. While, historically, the Adriatic coast, fragmented with islands and inlets that provide excellent natural harbors, had several ports that were prosperous in medieval times, then, as now, contacts of the littoral with the interior were barred by the difficult limestone terrain.

The fragmentation of cultures and the difficulty of national coherence in Yugoslavia is largely explained in this physical structure of the state. Lines of communication between Dalmatia and the Yugoslav ecumene in the Danubian lowland mostly swing around the main ranges. In the north the Fiume gate, east of the Istrian Peninsula, offers a break in the form of a gulf that penetrates deeply into the land giving ready connection with the Hungarian plain. At the extreme south, where the Dinaric Alps abut the arcuate folds of the Pindus ranges, the Albanian Gap, along the precipitous and winding Drin Valley, opens up another entrance, albeit circuitous and difficult.

South of the Drin River and fronting the northwest arc of the Pindus Mountains lies the broad coastal plain of Albania. Although the widest of the west Balkan lowlands, the Albanian plain is but sparsely settled, due partly to the malarial character of the ill-drained flats, partly to the character of the Albanian people who, historically, are of a mountaineering type. Major foci of population are found in the cities—as Tirana, the capital—which are situated in the foothill country between the plain and mountains.

THE ETHNIC STRUCTURE

Ethnic diversity is the dominant geopolitical characteristic. Even as Central Europe and the Balkans represent a complex of topography so also this area holds a complexity of peoples. Linguistically, it describes the eastern and southernmost thrust of the Slavic peoples. German drives toward the east have pushed into Slav territory and settled, but these Germans represent simply three intrusive fingers of Germanic culture within the Slavic realm: 1) down the Danube to Vienna; 2) later, eastward into Rumania; and 3) up the Oder River into Silesia and eastern Bohemia. The Slavs spread over the eastern European territories from the Urals to the Oder-Neisse, Ore Mountain-Bohemian Forest, and westernmost Yugoslav frontier in Istria, and extend north-south between the Baltic and Adriatic Seas. The three East Baltic republics lie outside of the Slav block, and Austria and Hungary constitute ingresses of non-Slavic peoples in other-

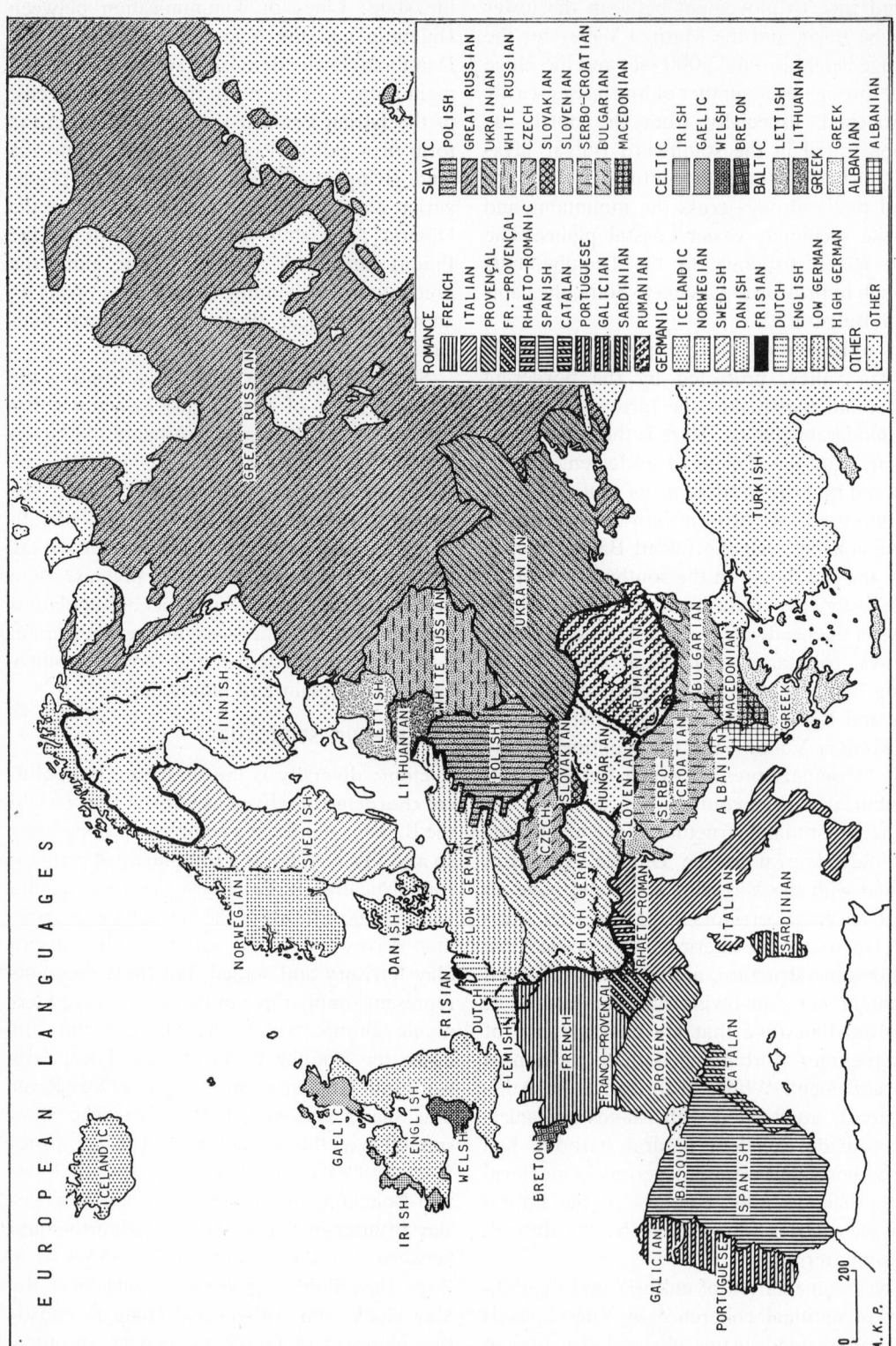

Figure 10.2. Distribution of dominant languages in Europe.

wise solidly Slav country: Austria is Germanic, the Hungarians, Magyar. Albania, too, is non-Slav.

Within central and southeast Europe more than twenty nationalities, distinct from each other, lay claim to the right of political self-expression for the Slavic peoples themselves are divided into a number of different groups each clinging to "national" loyalties. For centuries, this region was a transit land across which continuous movements of people took place along fairly well-defined passages, resulting in a certain amount of interchange and blending of cultures. In the Balkans this tide of population movement was expressed both in the form of pulsations of immigration from the outside and of a more local transmigration—a movement between the mountain refuges and the plains, as the security of the era demanded.

Physically, the Balkan Peninsula is that section of southeastern Europe that extends between the Adriatic Sea on the west, and the Black and Aegean Seas in the east, dropping southward into the Mediterranean; on the north, the margins are less easily determined. Traditionally, the northern limit of the Balkan Peninsula has been set to conform to the course of the lower Danube as far westward as the Sava, the latter stream providing the recognized northern extremity in the northwestern half. Such a division of southeast Europe, on a physical basis, is hardly valid when cultural considerations are taken into account, however. In an ethnic sense, the Balkans comprise not only Yugoslavia, Bulgaria, and Albania—and Greece occupying the southern extremities of the peninsula—but also Rumania, whose peoples are very similar to the Southern Slavs and the Bulgars. Here, also, are the last distinguishable Asian elements—and blends—that remain on European soil as a result of the Great Migrations.

The antipodal processes of scattering and segregation lie at the core of many of the geopolitical problems of this historically uneasy peninsula.

The Slavs spread outward from a central nuclear area. The spread of the Slavic peoples took place between the fourth and seventh centuries A.D., apparently set in motion by the onward sweep of the Asiatic nomads. The original nuclear center of the Slavic peoples is disputed but it was evidently someplace along the western frontier of the present Soviet steppe, probably toward the south. From this nuclear area where Slav character was cast, the Slavs moved outward into the varying physical environments of Central, East, and Southeast Europe.

In spite of great population dislocations due to later migrations and invasions of foreigners, the distribution pattern of Slavic peoples has changed little since their first spread. The westernmost Slav thrust was to a north-south line somewhere along the Elbe and Saale Rivers near Magdeburg, and for some time the Germanic peoples were compacted west of this frontier. However, in the twelfth century, the Germans were able to press the first Germanic intrusion into Slav territory.

To the south of the Elbe–Saale sector, the westward fringe of Slav territory extended to the mountain confines of Bohemia while still farther south, the Slavs had pushed out the bounds of their territory from the steppelands, up the Danube corridor to the Hungarian grasslands (where they were later displaced by the Magyars), southward across most of the Balkan Peninsula, and eastward across what later became the Russian Slav lands.

Differentiation among the Slavic peoples. As previously stated, the Slav groups during this early period bore far more ethnic and cultural resemblance to each other than later was the case, for, the farther they migrated from their original homeland, the more differentiated they became—as new environments and new contacts slowly mutated their customs and ideas. Especially distinctive are: 1) those Slavic groups that were most directly contiguous with the more technologically advanced people of the west, as the Czechs and western Poles, and 2) those Slavs that penetrated the northern forest sections of European Russia to absorb into their body a few Asian peoples.

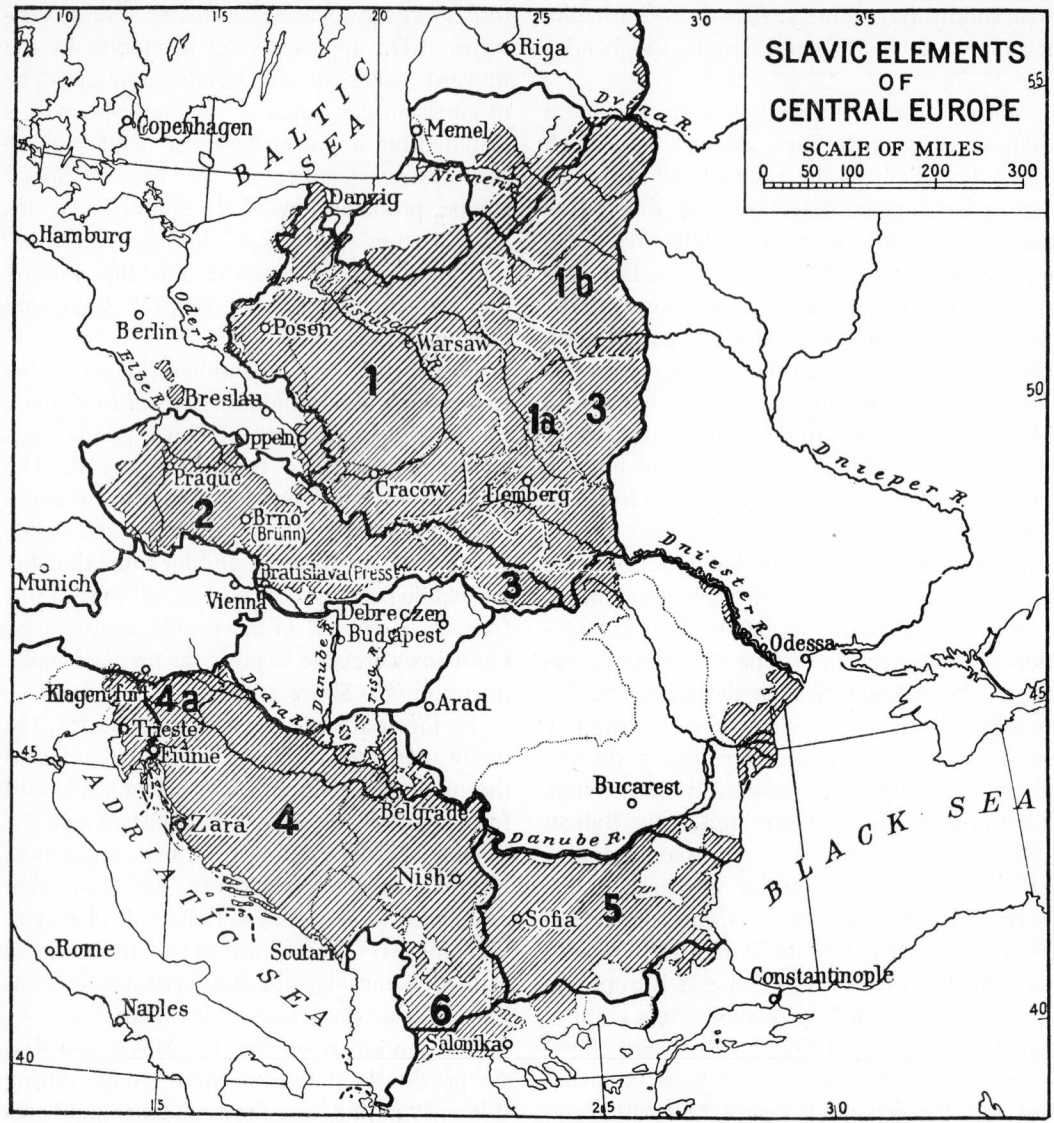

Figure 10.3. Slavs in Europe outside Russia. The key to the numbers is as follows: (1) Poles; (1a) mixed Poles and Ruthenians; (1b) White Russians; (2) Czechs, Moravians, Slovaks; (3) Ruthenians; (4) Serbo Croats; (4a) Slovenes; (5) Bulgarians (originally Finno-Ugrian but now principally Slavic); (6) Macedonians. Boundaries of 1914 shown by fine dotted lines. (Courtesy World Book Company. From Bowman's *The New World.*)

Linguistically related, the Slavs divide into three major groups on the basis of geographic location—the Eastern, the Western, and the Southern Slavs—each of which again subdivide. An earlier reference indicated the approximate period when the Eastern Slavs became recognized as the three distinct Russian nationalities; the Czechs, the Slovaks, and the Poles constitute the Western Slavs; while the Slavic populations of the Balkan Peninsula make up the Southern group.

The East Baltic republics are non-Slavic and

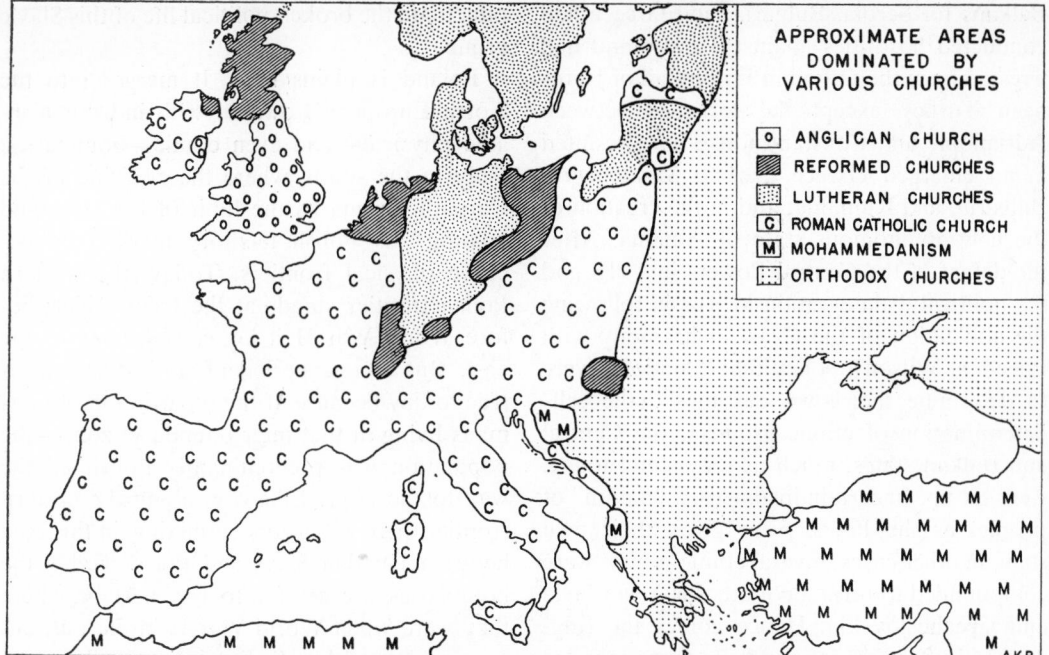

Figure 10.4. Distribution of dominant religions in Europe.

non-Germanic. The Finns and the Esths show ethnic affinity but the duality of the Finnish peoples modifies the relationship. Linguistically both groups are Finno-Ugrian, a Mongoloid people from the lower Volga that early migrated into the northern Baltic territories. Both nationalities are alike in the physical contrast they present to the Scandinavians living to the westward: the latter are of the tall, blond, Nordic type while, except along the littoral of Finland, the former belong to the broad-headed, shorter-statured folk. In the Finnish lowland, where the Swedes are found, the physical type reflects Nordic mixtures, and the Finnish culture and outlook show such a marked Scandinavian influence as to justify classifying that eastern state as one of the "four" Scandinavian countries. The Letts and Lithuanians are an East Baltic group—Aryan—and ethnically alike, but they differ from all of the other surrounding peoples.

Diversity of religion further entangles the ethnic pattern. To complicate the already complex and varied ethnic pattern that was developing, influxes of Jews spread into Poland and the Teutonic territories. Add to this the religious differences among the Slavs: early, Greek Orthodox, later Roman Catholic, and still later, Protestant. The long era of Turkish domination in the south left its traces in the oriental character of some of the cultures of the Balkans, and in the rather large body of Moslem believers. Return again to the character of the physical environment—which, broken into many fragments by the isolating effect of the mountains, fostered individualism and distinctness of cultural development—and some of the complexity of the geopolitics of central Europe and the Balkans becomes clear.

The political pattern has been transient. Until 1912 most of the lands of central and southeastern Europe were under the control of a few large states, namely, the Russian, German, Austro-Hungarian, and Turkish empires; there were, besides, the small states of Serbia, Montenegro, Rumania, Bulgaria, and Greece. By the time the war broke out in 1914, the political pattern had changed somewhat in the

Balkans for Serbia, Bulgaria, and Greece had conducted hostilities against Turkey and had wrested from the Ottoman Empire all of European Turkey except the territory between Adrianople and Constantinople. This resulted in an enlarged Greece, Serbia, Montenegro, Bulgaria, and Rumania, and in the creation of the new autonomous state of Albania. After the defeat of the Central Powers in 1918 and the political disintegration in Russia following the abdication of the Czar, in harmony with President Wilson's policy that " 'nations' were to determine their own destinies" (the self-determination of ethnic groups), the Central and Balkan states, much as they stand today, were set up. In certain instances, a "nation" of people, as the Poles, were given their own state; in other cases, several ethnic groups were compounded to form a country, as Yugoslavia and Czechoslovakia. Hence comes the fragmented buffer-zone of countries that separates the USSR from the West.

BOUNDARIES

Polish political sovereignty has waxed and waned with the passage of history. The nuclear area of the Polish people was in the basin of the Vistula River, around the historic city of Krakow. Despite the centuries that the Polish "nation"[3] has existed as a distinct ethnic group, Poland has, for periods of its history, ceased to exist as a sovereign, geopolitical entity. Even when it did have political status as a self-governing unit, its position was remarkably insecure and unstable. The history of its peoples is written in the acquisition and re-acquisition of its lands by one foreign nationality after another. It would be presumptuous to even suggest that the ebb and flow of Polish political existence was due entirely to the physical environment. And yet, the topographic setting of the Polish state is such that it has influenced the course of events that

punctuate the broken political life of this Slavic group.

Poland is plains land. It merges into the North European Lowland with indistinguishable physical—and even ethnic—boundaries. Only in the south, where the crestline of the Carpathians marks the limit of the state and "nation," is Polish territory marked by decisive physical frontiers. Today, the western Polish frontier stands at the Oder River; before World War II it lay considerably to the east. But at one period of its history—as is true to day because of the repatriation of Germans living in that inter-boundary[4] zone—the population was predominantly Polish all the way to the river. Likewise, along the eastern frontier there was a zone of mixing, in this area between Russian Slavs and Poles. Today the boundaries are set far to the west of where they were when World War II broke out, encompassing within Soviet bounds all of the Pripet Marshes and many cities that were formerly considered Polish, not Russian. Within the inter-boundary zone were many Poles and many Russians, but, from here, as in the west, the dispossessed people were largely repatriated.

Undoubtedly the monotony of the landscape, along with the intricate tracing of the domain by the rivers Oder, Warta, Vistula, Bug, and their tributaries, invites movement and discourages stable political boundaries. At any rate, whatever the cause, the physical environment of Poland has provided a setting that seemed to invite transgression by vicinal powers. Following the last of the three partitionings in 1795, Poland, as a state, disappeared from the political scene for more than a century. It was reinstated as a sovereign nation only after the Treaty of Versailles.

Minority groups within the political bounds have frequently served as the excuse for interference in Polish political affairs. Space does not permit historical analysis of this problem but it is of interest to point out the approximate

---

[3] The term "nation" is used with two different connotations: when enclosed with quotation marks, as above, it refers to an ethnic group of people (a "nation" of people); when used without quotation marks, it is used synonymously with state, country, etc., that is, in terms of a political territory.

[4] The *inter-boundary zone* refers to that territory on both sides of an international frontier where the nationalities mix.

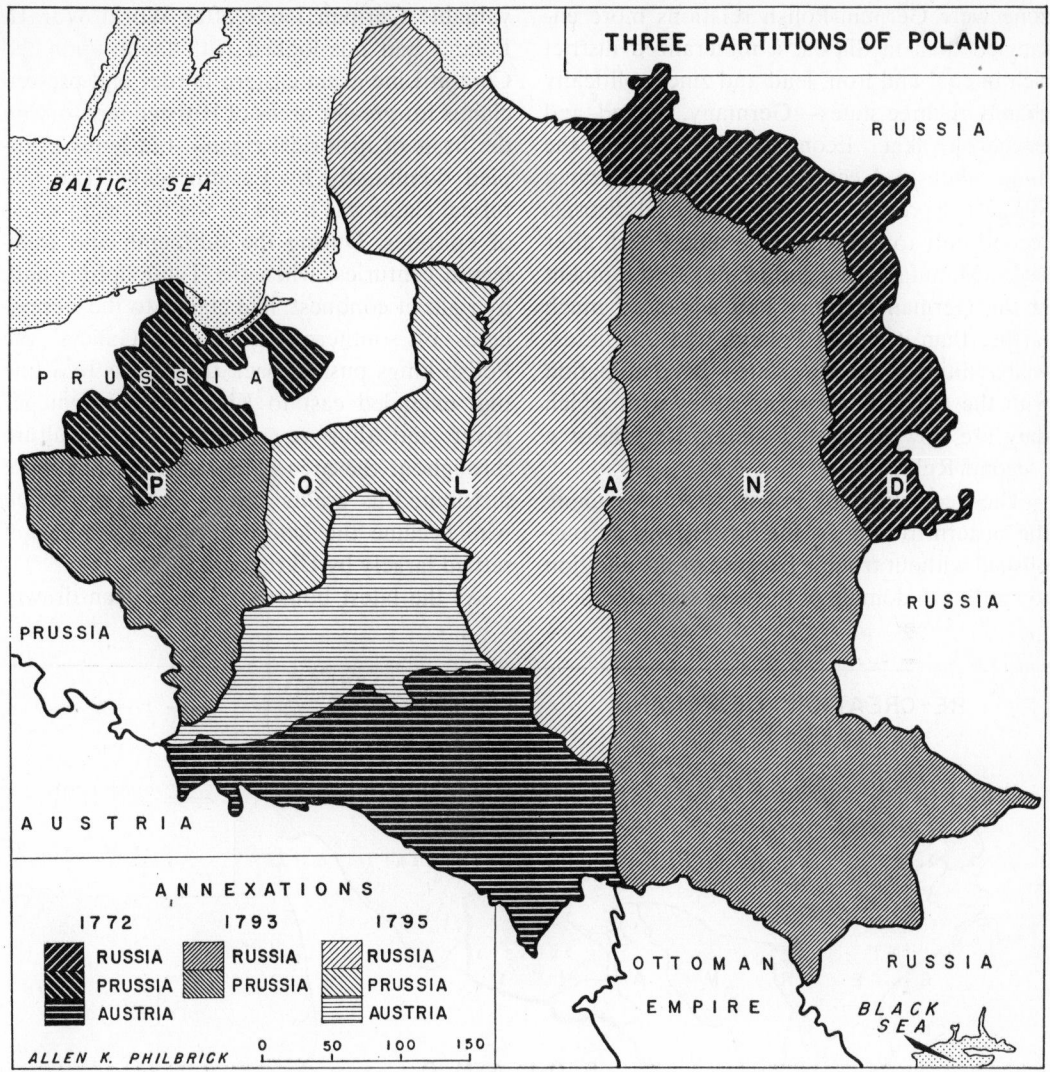

Figure 10.5.

proportions of populations, in pre-World War II days, within what have been termed the inter-boundary zones along the east and west: in those areas contiguous to the USSR (the Vilna–Pinsk region of the eastern half of the Polish marshland) less than 25 per cent of the population were Poles; from there (midway through the former Polish lands) to the present eastern Polish frontier, Poles comprised from 25 to 75 per cent of the people; while along the west about one-third of the territory was less than 25 per cent Polish (*i.e.* between Danzig

and Königsberg where the population was overwhelmingly German—in what was known as East Prussia, a Germanic territory separated from the German state by the Polish Corridor); the rest of the state was over 75 per cent Polish. It is easy to see, with such minority conditions obtaining, why the USSR and Germany might feel they had a right to lay claim to these districts; at the same time, however, the historical justification for the Oder-Neisse boundary also becomes apparent.

In no part of the western inter-boundary

zone were German-Polish relations more entangled than in Silesia, a mineralized district rich in coal and iron, lead and zinc, politically shared by three states—Germany, Poland, and Czechoslovakia. Economically one of the major industrial centers of Europe, German Silesia (of pre-war German industrial districts second only to the Ruhr) became Polish after 1945. Manufacturing and mining development in the German territory had advanced much farther than it had in Poland, and this industrial addition to the Slav state—in combination with the Czech Silesian industries with which they are now integrated—comprise almost a "second Ruhr."

The acquisition of Polish territories along the eastern frontier by the Soviets was accomplished without trouble because of the addition to the Polish domain of the economically more valuable German lands after World War II. Poland had not looked with favor upon the Curzon Line as an eastern border and pressed claims for greater areas of Russian territory on the basis of historical rights—but lands occupied dominantly by Eastern Slavs. The historical claim was based on the following series of episodes. During the thirteenth and fourteenth centuries, when the Tatar hordes had, by right of conquest, laid claims to the steppe-lands of southern Russia and Galicia, the Polish kings pushed back the Asians to a line that extended east to Kiev and the Dnieper River and thus re-established Slav culture throughout the area. The lands retaken were distributed as grants among Polish noblemen who became the landowners within a region settled largely by Ukrainians.

As the latest boundaries have been drawn,

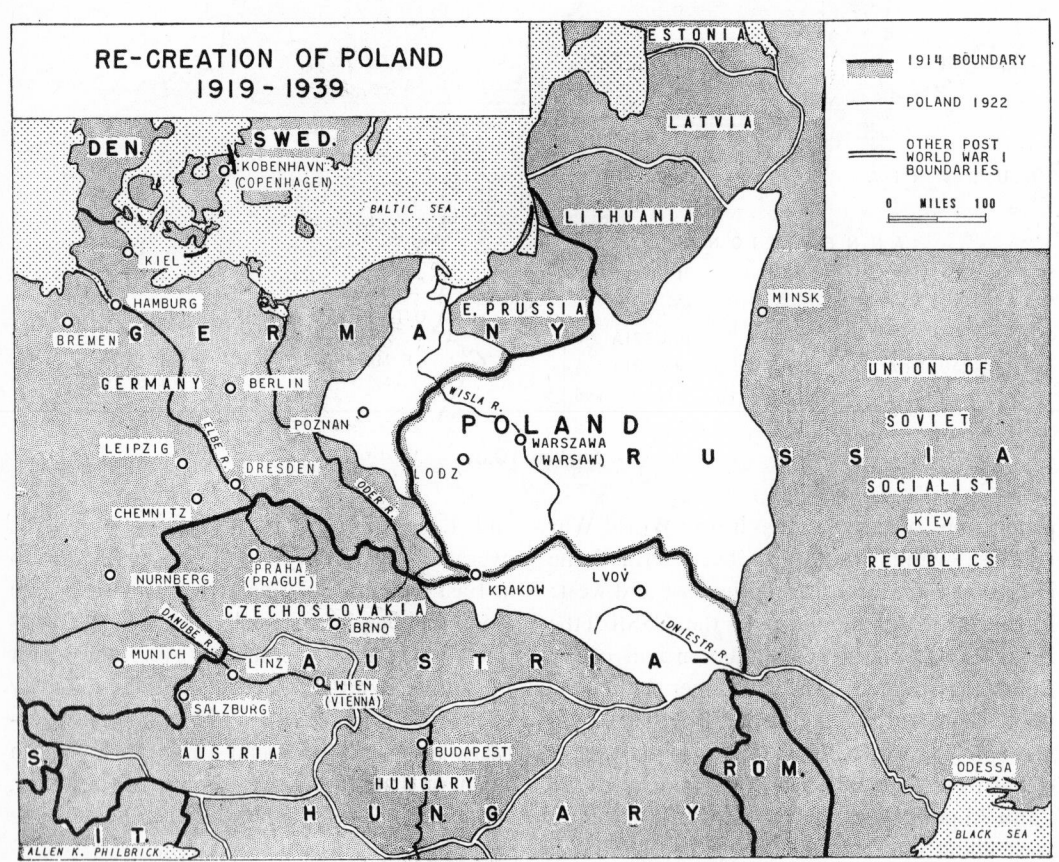

Figure 10.6.

there has been a constricting of those territories where foreign nation minorities made up a large proportion of the population, or, as in the newly added, former German lands, minorities have been completely expelled and replaced by Slavs. Before the war the latter territories held about eight million Germans, but by 1951 the Germans had been ejected and some five million Poles resettled from other parts of Poland and the now-Soviet eastern lands. Completion of the population transfer was vigorously sought by Poland to justify the Oder–Neisse River line as a permanent Polish frontier.

The population movements of postwar Poland constitute one of the greatest demographic translocations in the history of the world. While minority peoples made up nearly one-third of the total Polish population before 1945, the ethnic composition of Poland today is nearly homogeneous. The Oder-Neisse line cuts off Upper and Lower Silesia, Eastern Pomerania, and East Prussia from Germany, and the area is divided between Poland and Russia. Although the United States, Britain, and France refused to recognize Poland's territorial claims, maintaining they gave consent only to temporary Polish occupation, the western boundaries of Poland have stood. Physically, this frontier translocates the state 150 miles westward so that Poland now reaches far into Middle Europe; the new territories in the west compose nearly one-third of the present national domain. In the east, the state lost 45 per cent of the prewar territory. Poland today, therefore, corresponds but little to prewar dimensions and definition.

The Balkan Peninsula and Central Europe are full of just such instances of "justifiable" claims and counter-claims to territory, with the background of history to back up the rights of the various nations—or the clamor of minority groups living under a foreign flag, or the rankling of dispossession to keep geopolitical conditions unstable, and rival states agitated.

The boundaries of Czechoslovakia. Physically, Czechoslovakia is almost the antithesis of Poland for it is completely fenced in by high mountain barriers except in the south-central portion where the Danube plain extends into Moravia to open a wide lowland gateway between the highlands of Bohemia and the western Beskids. Northward, this Moravian Corridor narrows abruptly as it passes between the Carpathian and Sudeten Mountains to connect the North European Plain with the Danube Basin. Access from the south is controlled by Vienna, on the north by Krakow. (The commercial and strategic importance of these two cities is in large part explained by their commanding positions relative to the "corridor.")

For Czechoslovakia this transverse passageway, bisecting the elongated territories, has been a political handicap, in a sense, because it connected two portions of Teutonic territory across the Slav nation. Another notable passageway through the mountain wall, the narrow Dresden Gateway is formed by the Elbe River which rises in Bohemia and flows into the German state. This is a strategic and significant break in the mountain boundaries that has had important geopolitical implications.

The Czechs form the most westward thrust of the Slavic peoples, in Bohemia sending a promontory far into Germanic territory. This state, therefore, is perhaps the most percariously located of all of the Slav nations: however, with Austria "neutralized" and East Germany a Communist ally, the Czech position is somewhat better than it was previously.

The state was created, after World War I, by the Allies through the union of two ethnic peoples, the Czechs and the Slovaks, with some Ruthenes also incorporated within the domain. Though politically united, the country has remained divided into two parts along ethnic lines, the Czechs occupying Bohemia and Moravia in the west, the Slovaks the eastern portion; Ruthenia reverted to the USSR after World War II. These divisions are given further accentuation by the respective degree of economic development—the Czech end being highly industrialized (although still dominantly agricultural), Slovakia relatively backward and entirely agricultural except as the

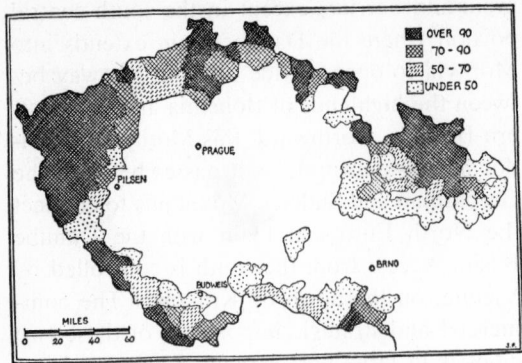

Figure 10.7. Western Czechoslovakia (year 1931): Proportion of Germans to total population. (Courtesy Harper and Brothers. From Walter Fitzgerald, *The New Europe.*)

Communist regime has made initial attempts at industrialization.

The Czechs entered Bohemia early and by the early thirteenth century occupied that basin right up to the mountain rim, having expanded outward from the Elbe-Vltava Valley. Although the topography rises to a plateau toward Moravia, the elevation of Bohemia is not great nor is the plateau rim a barrier; hence, the Czechs moved westward at an early date. German penetration of Bohemia and Moravia, via the Elbe Gateway, also began early and, from the thirteenth century on, continued almost unceasingly. This German penetration and settlement was not disfavored by the Czechs and, in time, the Germans had planted a solid arc of settlement along the three sides of the inner mountain rim. By the 1930's, the Czechs were largely set back from the bordering mountains, and throughout large parts of the rim-area, German population proportions ran to 90 per cent. In 1938, Germans comprised 30 per cent of the total Bohemian population.

Within the interior of Bohemia and Moravia, however—and especially in the nuclear valleys of the Elbe and Vltava—Czechs made up nearly all of the population. They occupied the areas of low elevation, generally below 1,500 feet. Nevertheless, German penetration was "deep" in places here, also, as in the north-

western corner. On the other hand, the German rim held large Czech minorities that often ran as high as 45 per cent of the total population—in contrast to Central Bohemia where German minorities were usually slight compared with the Czech population. In Moravia, Germans constituted a large proportion of the population (three-tenths) and, as in Bohemia, this was largely a fringe colonization—in Silesia in the north, along the Austrian border in the south. Certain of the Moravian cities, as Brno, held large numbers of Germans.

A Czech language had become distinguishable by the sixth century but the Czech "nation" was slower to develop. In the late Middle Ages the Kingdom of Bohemia was an expression of Czech nationalism, but, with the military defeat in 1620, the Czech state ceased to exist and did not reappear until reconstructed by foreign nations—as Czechoslovakia—in 1918. However, Czech nationalism was a vibrant force throughout the period of Austrian authority. It was not, however, antagonistic toward the Empire within which, until 1914, the Czech people would have been content to remain if accorded an autonomous position within the state political structure. Nor was the Austrian dynasty hostile to the development of individualism in Czech culture—the literary arts, in particular, flourished under the Hapsburgs.

Religion was not a cohesive factor among the Czechs, for, although the majority hold to the Roman Catholic faith, since the days of John Huss both Bohemia and Moravia held many Protestants. However, religion was not a disruptive element—the well-defined geographical setting seeming to foster the growth of the Czech "nation" and counteract any ethnically induced disruptions.

The frontiers of the Hungarian state. The Magyars were an Asiatic people, related linguistically and racially to the Finno-Ugrians and the Turkic populations who settled in parts of eastern Europe. For a thousand years they have retained a group individuality that is unusual even among Europeans. They originated in the steppelands of Central Asia, but, abandoning their nuclear area, moved westward during the ninth century as a part of the last Great Migration to settle in the lowlands of the Danube. In this environment, which somewhat resembled their homeland, they found conditions suited to their pastoral life. Absorbing the Avars, an Asiatic element that had preceded them, and driving out the Slavs who had inhabited the lowland during the centuries of the Asiatic migrations, they firmly established themselves in the Hungarian plain.

By their occupance of the Central Danubian lowland, contacts between the Western and Southern Slavs were cut off, and the Magyars, thus, stood in the way of any Pan-Slavic movement or political aims. It was the purpose of the Magyars to embody into their political realm all of the peoples and territories within the mountain ring that surrounded the Danubian lowland: this ambition was frustrated, however, by the Yugo-Slavs who, in time, acquired portions of the Hungarian plain.

Except for three outliers, the Magyar peoples are confined essentially within the bounds of the Hungarian state. In the south, the frontiers are far from the mountain rim that the Magyars earlier strove to establish. Along this boundary the Southern Slavs and the Magyars are neighbors—more than that, the post-World War I boundary was so drawn that a quarter million Magyars were cut off from Hungary and incorporated into Yugoslavia—the first outlier. In the east, a large body of Magyars was placed under the Rumanian flag when Transylvania was given to that country. A part of this group, the Szeklers, living far in the interior of the plateau basin (where they had maintained themselves formerly as a front guard against invasion of the Magyar plains) are completely surrounded by Rumans. A persistent desire for union with Hungary makes this outlier of Magyars a problem for the Ruman state. To the north the Magyars spread, as a third outlier, into the Moravian lowland of Czechoslovakia where they are left unmolested by the Slovaks who cling to their mountain homes. On the west the Magyar and Austrian touch along an ethnic boundary and, as

the frontier drops south, Magyar, Austrian, and Yugo-Slav meet. Eastward along the southern borders, in the Tisza River area—*i.e.* the Banat, which is the region where the boundaries of Yugoslavia, Hungary, and Rumania run together—there is a great intermixture of these three nationalities, so much so that it would be impossible to draw national boundaries along ethnic lines.

It can be seen from this brief analysis of Hungarian frontiers that, not only is the Magyar nation located, landbound, within the heart of Europe, but also that it is encircled by many nationalities, the majority of whom are Slav who retain memories of long and oppressive subjugation by the Magyars. Linguistically, the Hungarians are completely unrelated to any of the vicinal peoples. The unique character of the Hungarian language has acted at times as a handicap in international affairs.

Had ethnic self-determination been rigidly adhered to in the delineation of the Central European and Balkan states after World War I, Hungary would have been considerably larger in both area and population. Three vicinal countries—Czechoslovakia, Rumania, and Yugoslavia—gained considerably because Hungary had been one of the Central Powers: the boundaries laid down by the Treaty of Versailles showed discrimination against the Magyars. As in a number of other instances at Versailles, the basic principles of self-determination for ethnic groups[5]—which constituted the justification for partition—were discarded in order to favor a friendly nation. The new Hungarian frontiers cut off more than half of the domain of the former Magyar state in some areas of which Magyars were a distinct majority. (The short-lived Hungarian possession of much of Transylvania after the Vienna Award, by the Germans, in 1940 actually was

---

[5] Throughout this chapter stress has been laid upon ethnic boundaries, and the principle of ethnic boundaries seemingly embraced. It ought to be pointed out, however, that often (perhaps usually) where one factor in the boundary consideration has been satisfied, others are violated. In this instance the redrawing of the frontier along more definitive ethnic lines would propagate economic resource problems.

a more equitable adjustment of territory than was the 1919 allocation by the Allies. It perhaps favored the Magyars to some extent, because, in order to embody a large part of the Szeklers within Hungary, a triangular wedge was withdrawn from Rumanian territory. However, Germany tried to be impartial because both states at that time were allies.)

Despite the territorial and population losses that the Magyar nation suffered due to the division of the Austro-Hungarian Empire at Versailles, Hungary came out considerably better as an economic unit than did Austria which was left a little mountain state with a large urban population. Hungary embraced the fertile Danube lowland. One of the most favorable wheat and corn-growing areas in Europe, the Hungarian plain more than feeds its population; the Austrian people, on the other hand, faced many precarious years because, within the mountain state, it was simply not possible to produce enough food to supply the population. However, Hungary (except in its bauxite and agricultural products) has practically no base for manufacturing, and is unlikely to develop industrially to any appreciable degree. Austria, on the other hand, is advancing through the development of new industries.

The geopolitical problems of the Rumanian frontiers. The belief that the Rumans are of non-Slavic origin stems entirely from a linguistic legacy of Latin, a remnant of the Roman era. During the first century after Christ the legions of Imperial Rome conquered territories in the region of the lower Danube (present Walachia) and, intermarrying with the local population (Dacians), Latinized them somewhat. Two centuries later, after the Romans had evacuated the region, Slavs and Asiatic peoples invaded the area and laid waste the Roman installations. The population fled into the mountains of Transylvania where, living in isolation, they clung to their Latin language. Later, the highlanders returned to the region of the lower Danube to recolonize the lowlands. The ethnic group known as the Rumans, who form the base of the Rumanian nation, was made up of the amalgamation of the Transylvanian highlanders and the Walachian lowlanders, the latter remnants of the invaders among whom the Slav element was most prominent. However, though Slav traits are dominant, the language of Rumania preserves its ancient Latinity.

Since the Rumanian peasants still cling to the ancient language, in this respect—linguistically—they are distinct from their neighbors. But the Slav element, which made up a large part of their composition at an early period, has with the passage of the centuries become increasingly strong: except in manner of speech there is little, ethnically, to distinguish the Ruman from the Slav. In religion, the Rumanians are Orthodox.

The nuclear area of the Rumanian state was in Moldavia and Walachia; there, too, is found the ecumene of the modern nation. These lands lay under Turkish domination for over three and a half centuries. In 1822 the Ottoman control was thrown off, however, and hence, during the latter three-quarters of the nineteenth century, while the rest of the Balkans remained under the domination of the Turks, the Rumanians (safe behind the lower Danube and the adjacent wide margin of marshland in Walachia and Moldavia) grew strong.

Post-World War II Rumania encompasses not only Walachia and Moldavia, but also all of mountain and plateau Transylvania, part of the Banat, and most of Dobrudja; two valuable portions of the pre-World War state were Bessarabia and Bukovina. In Bukovina, the Rumans were not in the majority; Ruthenes formed nearly half of the total population, and Germans and Jews formed large groups. This territory and Bessarabia were annexed by the Soviet Union on the basis of a majority of Russian Slavs after World War II. The Prut River now forms the north-south frontier between Russia and Rumania whereas the easterly Dniester marked the former border.

Rumania had laid claim to Bessarabia in 1919 although, again, Rumans did not constitute a majority group. Like Bukovina, the composition of the population is complex: Rumans and Ruthenes each formed about one-third of the inhabitants. In the north, Rumans far outnumbered any other group; in the south, the same held true for the Ukrainians; in the south, also, there are large numbers of Tatars, remnants of the Asiatic hordes who swept through this area in an earlier century.

Dobrudja, in the southeast, is divided between Bulgaria and Rumania. Along the Danube the land is too marshy for settlement, but away from the river-swamplands, Dobrudja becomes dry steppe country and here the Bulgars outnumber any other group; only in the extreme north are Rumans in the majority. Although, early in this century, extensive areas of land were appropriated from Bulgars to allow Rumanian colonists to settle, the Bulgarians have remained in this Rumanian territory. To many, the granting of Dobrudja to Rumania appeared to have done violence to Bulgar claims on the basis of people and history, but through it, Rumania has acquired its only Black Sea port.

When World War I broke out, the Rumanian state included Walachia and Moldavia, whose bounds were clearly marked by the Prut and Danube Rivers along the east and south; the Transylvania mountain elbow distinctly defined the physical limits of the national territories along much of the west and north. Like some sort of appendage to this naturally defined region, the Dobrudjan arc, between the Danube bend and the Black Sea, was also a part of the state. As the war ended, Rumania made territorial demands that more than doubled the former holdings. In none of the annexed territories, however, did Rumans form a majority group. The lands of the neighboring states were acquired (1919) at a time when Austria, Hungary, Russia, and Bulgaria were militarily impotent—and they were taken with the consent of Allied Powers.

At this period Rumania embraced within its boundaries all Rumanian nationals with one exception—but the state likewise incorporated large minorities of foreign nationality in order to do this. Just before the outbreak of World War II the population of Rumania was nearly 20 million; of this, 28 per cent were foreigners. The geopolitical situation was explosive, particularly with relation to Hungary and Russia for Magyars and Russians made up 8 and 6 per cent of the *total* population, respectively. The minority peoples, in places, formed as much as 75 per cent of the total population. Tension was heightened by the acquiescence of the Western powers to this territorial arrangement, Britain going so far as to guarantee Rumanian integrity—as a means of stopping German aggression. However, the USSR interpreted the move as directed equally against the Russian state, and this did not lessen the Soviet intention to reincorporate Bessarabia at the earliest convenient period.

Bulgars, residing in Dobrudja, formed two per cent of the population of Rumania. This territory had been wholly in Rumanian hands since the close of the 1912-13 Balkan wars, but the northern portion had been Rumanian since 1878 when the Rumans secured this territory from Russia in exchange for southern Bessarabia. Ethnically, at least southern Dobrudja was Bulgarian, and the expropriation of this territory meant a loss of 2,000 square miles and nearly 300,000 Bulgarian nationals to the Bulgarian state. Redistribution of these annexed lands of Rumania gave the latter area back to Bulgaria after World War II, but the intervening period between annexation (of Dobrudja and Bessarabia–Bukovina) and reallocation had drawn Bulgaria and Russia close together, and Bulgaria looked to the latter state as the only one on whom she could lean for understanding and aid. Cooperation of the Bulgarians with Soviet aims is more understandable in the light of twentieth century history.

The period of the 1940's saw a shifting and reshifting of Rumanian boundaries as large parcels of territory passed back and forth between neighboring states. In 1940, when the Western powers were not in a position to aid Rumania, her three historically hostile neighbors—Russia, Hungary, and Bulgaria—subjected Rumania to a "political squeeze": the USSR took northern Bukovina and Bessarabia;

Hungary seized portions of Transylvania to again incorporate the Szeklers within the Magyar state; and Bulgaria moved into Southern Dobrudja. Germany had occupied Rumania, and the latter state was compelled to aid Germany in the attack on Russia. Germany, in payment for this assistance, promised the return of Bessarabia and Bukovina—and even additions of Soviet territory—to Rumania. For a short period during the war Rumania did again hold the lost territories but in 1944, with the arrival of Soviet armies, the eastern lands were again surrendered to the Russians—who magnanimously gave back Hungarian Transylvania to the Rumanians. However, the Rumanian state had to cede South Dobrudja to Bulgaria.

The Paris Treaty of 1947 formally recognized the approximate 1944 boundaries which embrace an area of 91,600 square miles, four-fifths as large as 1938 Rumania and with a population of 16 million. The restoration of the annexed territories to Russia and Bulgaria have lessened tensions in the Balkans although there are still a number of areas where complex ethnic populations and changing political alignments make future claims and counterclaims a certainty. The crossroads location of Rumania, between eastern Europe and the central Balkan states, has not made the geopolitical role of this country any easier. It is an area in which the interests of many states merge and conflict. The political instability of the Balkan states has undoubtedly been one of the determining factors in retarding economic progress.

The definition of the Bulgarian state. Although the capital of a minor, backward agricultural nation today, Sofia occupies a position of strategic importance that compares with that of Vienna on the Danube—but to a lesser degree. The influence of both reaches out through easy gateways to command neighboring valleys and basins. Sofia stands at a nodal point of inland routes. For two-thirds of its history, Sofia was dominated from Constantinople. The Byzantine and Ottoman Empires both used it as an "advance base" to the lands of the Danube and those beyond. For the rest of its history it has been a part of the Bulgarian state, and, for portions of that period, the capital.

Important though the Sofia basin has been, strategically, throughout the known history of the eastern Balkans, it was not the nuclear center of the Bulgarian nation. The nucleus was in that strip of lowland that lies between the Danube River and the Balkan Mountains. Throughout this portion of its course, the Danube is wide—from a half to three-quarters of a mile—and the river, after it leaves the Iron Gate, has formed one of the most persistent boundaries that can be found. Although, during certain periods of history, the lands on either side of the river have changed hands, the river has always marked the frontier *between* states.

From approximately the seventh century on, the Bulgars (a Mongoloid group related to the Finnic people) have inhabited this territory. They entered from the north across the low and sterile plateau of Dobrudja, historically a transit land for these and other even larger groups, mostly Slavic. From their center in the Danube Basin and Pontic Bulgaria, Bulgar colonists moved across the Balkan Mountains to Inner Thrace, and, in the first part of the ninth century, took the Sofia basin. By this move, they not only established a precedent for territorial accretion which they used later, but they also increased their power for political unity and expansion by the taking of this strategic spot. Within approximately a hundred years they had extended their lands to form an empire including not only the nuclear area but Inner Thrace, the Struma Valley as far as the Macedonian lowland, most of the Morava basin, the upper Vardar, and the karst lakeland (mingling zone of Southern Slavs, Greeks, Albanians and Bulgars). At the height of its power, the Bulgarian nation occupied territories from the Black Sea to the head of the Adriatic.

But the Bulgarian state was the first to be overthrown by the Ottoman Empire and the last to wrest its freedom from the Turks. It was a Russian army that, in the 1870's, forced the

Turks out of Bulgaria and the Russians, acting as the defenders of Orthodox Christianity as well as of Slavism, obtained for the Bulgarians the right to have their own church leader independent of the Greek Church. Although Russia had planned to re-establish Bulgaria as a great state, other powers of the day—Austria–Hungary, ambitious in the Danube region, and Britain, afraid of Russian domination of the Bosporus—interfered with these aims; and Bulgaria, as reconstituted, was an autonomous principality, incorporating only the Danubian nucleus, half of Pontic Bulgaria and the Sofia basin within its limits. Sofia became the capital, replacing the one in the cradleland area, Tirnovo.

The history and the changes in territory are very complicated, too complex to review in full. After having early established a large empire, Bulgaria struggled for four and a half centuries to throw off the yoke of the Turk. According to the Treaty of San Stefano (1878), Bulgaria would have recovered most of the territories held during the period of its great expansion in the ninth century; but the subsequent Treaty of Berlin in the same year reduced the empire to a tiny state. Three times since then they have almost succeeded in their dream of restoring the empire, and as many times they have failed—in 1912, during World War I, and during World War II. The loss of the frontage on the Aegean was the most bitterly resented, and the recent post-1945 agitation to push through to the Aegean coast, under the urging of the USSR, and thus by-pass the bottleneck of the Bosporus indicates the presence of old ambitions and resentments.

The territories of Yugoslavia. Yugoslavia represents a variegated pattern of peoples, languages, and religions—the union of which has constituted one of the most difficult geopolitical problems ever faced by a sovereign state. Further, in a ring around its periphery are a number of regions under the administration of other governments in which Yugoslavs constitute minority and, at times, majority populations—regions of highly volatile geopolitical conditions.

Born of the World War which in 1914 started in an area now within its borders, chunks of the former Austro-Hungarian and Turkish empires were thrown together and called Yugoslavia, "country of the Southern Slavs." But the chunks hold a great diversity of nationalities, customs, religions, and physical regions, and the task of welding these parts into a nation has been a formidable one.

A little larger than the British Isles, and first in area among Balkan states since the dismemberment of Rumania, Yugoslavia is still a small country. Its area is about equal to that of Ohio and Michigan combined; its population is somewhat larger than that of the two midwestern states. Three-fifths of its territory is mountainous. It rises out of the Adriatic Sea in the bold buttresses of the jagged, limestone Dinaric Alps, an island-studded coast—including the irregularities of the shoreline, almost 1200 miles long and facing Italy. In the northwest these mountains extend into the Alps.

The mountains separate the western Adriatic shore from the interior sections, forming physical obstacles almost insurmountable in terms of land transportation. Not only are the highlands rugged but the eroded character of the limestone accentuates the difficult relief. Due also to the karst nature of the area, only dispersed and scanty spots are capable of being utilized. Historically, the coastal dwellers along the Adriatic littoral of Yugoslavia, like all of the other Adriatic peoples, have been maritime and have tried to dominate these inland waters. Although the Adriatic coast has a number of excellent ports, they are unavailable to the Yugoslavs, in the main because of their isolated location relative to the ecumene. Historically, and through political agreements today, the port of Thessalonika serves as the outlet for the Danubian plains region and old Serbia of the Morava Valley.

In the north and northeast, and forming two-fifths of the national domain, the Danube lowland and the tributary lowlands of the Sava, Drava, Morava, and other rivers constitute a level fertile region of black soils that forms the economic—and political—center of the state.

The nuclear area of Yugoslavia lies in the Morava Valley (which continues southward to form a corridor, with the valley of the Vardar, extending through Macedonia and Greece to the Aegean). The area, long under Turkish domination, reflects the rule of the Moslem in the minarets and customs and costumes of many of the people. The Moslem women of Serbia wore the veil until the introduction of Communism.

Between the Morava–Vardar valley, the Danube lowland, and the Adriatic coast lies the "bastille" of Yugoslavia—the highlands of inner Croatia, Bosnia–Herzegovina, and Montenegro, rugged lands where living is difficult. But to these mountains, in times of adversity, the people fled, the highland recesses acting as a sanctuary and fortress for the people of the plains. Montenegro, in the southwesternmost corner of these mountains, was the one portion of Yugoslavia that never fell under the domination of the Turk. During the past war, Bosnia–Herzegovina and Montenegro formed the base of armed resistance.

Few places in the Balkans are more impenetrable and obscure than Albania. Albania, a country of rugged mountaineer peasants and craftsmen, small cattle breeders and hunters, base for Mussolini's legions in the Italian attempt to restore to Rome its ancient supremacy over the borderlands of the eastern Mediterranean, is today Communism's advance front on this inland sea. Albania's role as an enclave, first of Italian, then of Russian power, could not have been possible without its isolation among the Balkan nations. The only predominantly Moslem country in Europe, its little more than one million people speak a language which predates that of their Slavic neighbors and is more archaic than modern Greek.

Geography had little to do with the Albanian position of isolation. Had it not been for the peculiar social and cultural conditions, for the backwardness of its hinterland (the Balkans), and the absence of a really strong power on either side of the Adriatic, Albania would long ago have become what it was in the past—an important bridgehead and transit area between the Mediterranean, the Danube, and the Black Sea. It is still possible to see the remnants of the paved Roman roads extending out from Durres (Durazzo—but famous to the Ancients as Dyrrachium) to the lower Danube, and from Valona to Salonika. During World War II, when all of the Balkans lay under German control, tank trucks rode over the foundations of these ancient roads carrying Rumanian oil to Albanian ports, from where it was ferried across the Adriatic to Italy.

COHESIVE AND DISRUPTIVE FORCES IN CENTRAL EUROPE AND THE BALKANS

Several factors have fostered unification among the Poles. Language, religion, and topography often act as singularly cohesive or disruptive forces in the development of nationalism among peoples. In central and southeastern Europe they have had both roles. In Poland the Roman Catholic Church, holding complete authority, has done much to unify the Polish people, and has identified itself consistently with the struggle for national survival. However, although religion served as a strong cohesive politically, the Church did little or nothing to breach the social and economic cleavages that existed within the state. The aristocracy, representing the few, owned half of the land in Poland; the remainder of the population was comprised, generally speaking, of a largely illiterate, poverty-stricken mass of humanity—and between the two classes there was a wide social and economic gap with no middle group to bridge it.

A common language also aided in the fusion of the Polish peoples into a "nation" and the ease of communication, provided by the plains-like character of the landscape, likewise facilitated coherence and negated sectionalism. Among Slav languages, the Polish more closely resembles that of the Russian than any other; this has not, however, acted to bring the two nations close together—in fact the relationship, until the present postwar era, has been, rather, one of hostility, maintained as long as the Poles were held in subjection and denied proper representation in government.

In Czechoslovakia, two ethnic groups form the population base—similar in certain respects, dissimilar in others. Language and religion act as unifying forces between the Czechs and the Slovaks, both peoples belonging to the great family of Slavs; they are even more closely related in that both are a part of the Western Slav group. The divisive features appear to have developed out of dissimilarities in the geographic environments of the two peoples so that in their economic and political interests and outlook, of necessity modified by the differing habitats, they are counterposed.

Slovakia is largely a mountainous, forested land, occupying the western end of the high Carpathian arc; to the west and south the mountains merge into plains. Traditionally, the Slovaks are hillsmen; the two areas of lowland are populated by Magyars in the majority. For many centuries the Slovaks have been tyrannized by this Hungarian group and the antagonism felt by each nationality for the other would have prevented Slovakian autonomy under a Hungarian seigniory. Not even a common Catholic religious belief has been able to overcome the long-standing hostility.

On the other hand, because of the character of the Slovakian people, it is unlikely that they would have been drawn into close association with the Czechs except for the feeling of greater animosity toward the Magyars. The geographic detachment of Slovakia from Bohemia is almost complete in the Moravian lowland. Overlooking, as Slovakia does, the Moravian corridor, and due to the fact that the Slovakian valleys open southward to the Danube, the natural economic orientation is to the south; the contrasting environments—the Slovakian productive of timber and ores, the Hungarian of agricultural products—would further suggest economic reciprocity. Such has not been the case.

Other contrasts tend to accentuate the differences between Czech and Slovak. Economically, Slovakia is a marginal area—farming is difficult, and both agriculture and industry are backward as compared with that of Moravia and Bohemia; Slovakia is isolated, set off from

the currents of economic, political, and historical events; fairly well mineralized, the area has been little developed. The population is thin and scattered: covering approximately a third of the territory of the nation, Slovakia holds perhaps one-seventh of the people—a conservative, mountain population. Bohemia and Moravia, on the other hand, are constituted in large part of plains land and are rich agricultural regions more advanced and more westernized than Slovakia. The Czech–Moravian territory was the portion of the old Empire where industry had been developed and, when Austria-Hungary was broken up, Czechoslovakia inherited 80 per cent of the industry of the former state.

Although Czechoslovakia was considered by many to be the "bright spot" in Central Europe because to it were allotted territories that held the potential for a well-balanced and varied state economy, politically, it was not very successful. The constitution of the Republic granted equality of political rights to Czech and Slovak alike, but in practice the Czechs held political control and the Slovaks were given a status of inferiority. The choice of Prague, Bohemia, as the national capital, was another fundamental handicap to unity for it stressed the political ascendancy of the Czechs: Prague is far from Slovakia—and has always been. In March, 1939, when the government fled in the face of German occupation, the Slovaks favored the reorganization of Czechoslovakia into two states when and if sovereignty could be re-instituted. Under the Communist regime, however, the two parts function again as a unit, welded together by the authority of dictatorship.

In Rumania the physical disruption of the state into well-nigh hostile geographical regions has made both political coherence and economic development a problem. Transylvania faces west, and is physically cut off from the ecumene of the country which lies in Moldavia and Walachia, river lowlands draining to the Danube; secondly, Dobrudja, a region very significant to Rumania geopolitically and economically, is separated from the rest of the state by the Danube River and the frontal swamp areas.

Despite the Oriental origin of the Bulgars, the Bulgarians are, ethnically and by blood ties, very close to the Slavonic peoples. Ingressions of Slavs into Bulgaria were much greater than were those of the Asians. Furthermore, Bulgarian Christianity is Orthodox; linguistically, the Bulgars are Slav because their Finnic language was replaced by a Slav dialect shortly after the Danubian lowland was inhabited.

This triple relationship of blood, religion, and language has not drawn the Bulgarians any closer to the vicinal peoples. It is the political and military support that the Russians have historically given the Bulgars that has drawn these nationals closer to the great Slav state. Russian advocacy of pan-Slavism and pan-Orthodoxy was the means of expanding Russian influence. The feeling between the Serbs and the Bulgars has been hostile, and antagonisms are acute and long-standing against the Greeks and Rumanians over territorial and minority problems. Within the country, minority problems have largely disappeared except in remoter areas, as in the Rhodope Massif in the south. Here a group of Bulgar Moslems, the Pomaks, are found. Today woodcutters and charcoal burners, during the period of Turkish rule they helped persecute the Christian Bulgarians. Here also are a Rumanian group, the Vlachs (from Walachia), and the Macedonians. The latter have been a troublesome minority in any country where they are found, but the Bulgars claim them as close relatives, and have had less difficulty with them than has Yugoslavia because the Bulgarians accorded the Macedonians an autonomous status in contrast to the policy of persecution that the Serbians followed until recent years.

Physiographically, Yugoslavia is anagonistic to political coherence. Blood ties and language should favor unity but geography has engendered hostility among the Southern Slavs. The Yugoslavs, federated under Serbian leadership (because the Serbs were the largest group), include, among other peoples, the Serbs, Croatians, and Slovenes—the Southern Slavs.

The Serb tribe grew into a nation within and around the Morava Valley. The Croatians and Slovenians germinated as strong and distinct ethnic groups in areas separated from the Serbian lands by difficult terrain; their orientation has been westward toward the Adriatic or northward to the Danubian plains while Serbia focused on the Morava. While contrasting environments separated the groups physically from each other, historical events widened the differences induced by the natural environments. First, because of location, Croatia was only indirectly subjected to Turkish rule, Serbia occupied; secondly, the Croatians, early arrivals in the Balkans, were influenced by a Christian Italy to accept Roman Catholicism while the Serbs, living close to the culture of the Byzantine Empire from about 1700 on, adopted the Greek Orthodox interpretation of Christianity.

Turkish domination, although it interfered little with the agricultural life of the Serbian peasant, did arouse a militant nationalism so that, when liberation came in 1878, Serbian ambitions concentrated on a "Greater Serbia" —for all Slavs who spoke Serbian, including not only those who used conventional Serbian but also those who used slightly different versions, as the Croatians and Montenegrins.

The question of union in Czechoslovakia and Yugoslavia was somewhat similar except that, in the latter case, the attempt was made to unite a greater number of peoples with attachments and qualities that were distinctly individualistic in several basic ways. Although linguistically similar, elements of marked contrast occur in traditions that have created differences even in language. Since the Serbians are members of the Orthodox Church (until 1917 headed by Russia), the Serbs use the Russian alphabet whereas the Croatians, following the Roman Church, adhere to the Latin characters. This basic difference in language makes contact difficult between these two factions of Yugoslavs and leads as well to variance

In cultural outlook, the latter likewise influenced by the difference in religion. A further contrast between the two peoples is fostered by the fact that the Serbs dwell inland while some of the Croatians are maritime, residing along the Adriatic Sea. However, since a large proportion of the Croatians are also inlanders, centering around the city of Zagreb as their focal point, there is a division even among the Croatians in point of view. Such bivalent interests should really be a source of strength within a state if they do not serve to breed hostility between groups as apparently they have here.

The maritime Croatians have, since the days of the Roman Empire, had large numbers of Italian colonists as neighbors. The Italians came as traders, settling in numbers in all of the port areas along the Dalmatian coast. The binational character of the population has eventuated in a bitter struggle over territory. Istria is about equally occupied by Italians and Croatians—the Italians concentrated in Trieste but spreading, especially in urban centers, from Trieste to Pola; the Slavs, on the other hand, occupying the rest of Istria in slight majority, are largely rural or village dwellers. Excluding Trieste, which was largely Italian, Slavs were definitely in a majority throughout all of Istria when Italy annexed the city about 40 years ago. Further south, the Italians made up only small scattered groups. The Istrian— or Trieste—territorial problem came to a head after World War II.

Although Croatian territory is located in the far west on the Balkan Peninsula, Turkish cultural influence is evident, particularly in Inner Croatia. The Turkish impact was largely religious and through it, many of the Croatians turned Moslem. In South Serbia, even greater numbers of Serbs accepted Islam. So inculcated did the latter become in Turkish and Islamic customs that it is difficult to distinguish Moslem Serbs from the Turks that remain in the Balkans.

The Slovenes are the smallest and spatially most compact of the Yugoslavs. Culturally and linguistically they are farther apart from the Serbs than are the Croatians; like the latter,

they are Roman Catholic. Because of their location next to Austria, they have been brought into close contact with that state. In fact, just across the Austrian border, in the Klagenfurt Basin (Carinthia), live large numbers of Slovenes, a factor that has led Yugoslavia twice to demand the area. In 1920, therefore, a plebiscite was held to decide the preference of the people of the basin. The Slovenes indicated that they preferred to remain under Austrian rule. Again, after World War II, the Yugoslav demand was repeated and quite a political stir made but no official action was taken.

The Klagenfurt Basin (actually the basin of the Drava River, tributary to the Danube) is the focus of important railways. In this and in its function as the outlet for the Austro-Hungarian lands to the Adriatic and the port of Trieste lies its greatest significance.

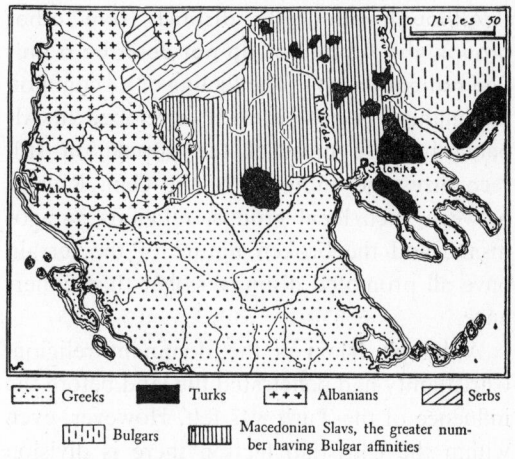

Figure 10.8. (Courtesy Harper and Brothers. From Walter Fitzgerald, *The New Europe.*)

Besides Serbs, Croatians, and Slovenes, there are the Montenegrins and the Macedonians as well as a number of minorities representing other nationalities scattered throughout and along the borders of Yugoslavia—Hungarians, Rumanians, and Albanians are the most numerous. The major political controversy has been betweeen the Serbs and the Croatians who have vied for dominance in Yugoslav politics. Leadership of the new state of Yugoslavia did not fall to the majority people, the Serbs, however, but to Croatia, when Tito took over as dictator.

Yugoslavia is organized as a federal republic along the same lines as that of the Soviet Union. There are six People's Republics—Serbia, Croatia, Slovenia, Bosnia–Herzegovina, Macedonia, and Montenegro. The Voivodina district, in the northeast, is an Autonomous Province, while the Kosovo and Metohija districts, near the Albanian frontier, are together administered as the Oblast of Kosmet. Thus, Yugoslavia represents the union of ethnic groups into a federal system, by this means according autonomy to the largest and most unified groups and, hence, reducing tension. However, Yugoslavia's problem is still one of harmonizing its several peoples—and this requires time—*and* of working out a strong and integrated economy based on all of its varied regions and resources.

Although ethnically distinct from other groups, the Albanians do not describe a unified national entity. The feeling of a "common nationality" is not yet well developed in Albania because most of the population still recognizes the authority of the clan. Rivalry between such local groups, religious antagonisms, and the broken nature of the terrain have all promoted disunity rather than coherence.

Although Islam is the dominant religion, Christianity had penetrated the land before the influence of the Turk was felt. However, even within the Christian faction there is division because there are adherents of both Roman and Orthodox Christianity. In fact, the collision of creeds is sharper in Albania than elsewhere in the Balkans. To widen the gap between Moslems and Christians (though this can scarcely be widened because, to the traditional Moslem, the Christian is a heretic and an inferior), the majority of the landowners have been Moslem, and those Albanians who clung to Christianity were dispossessed of their lands and made, virtually, peasant serfs. Albania was Europe's last stronghold of primitive feudalism.

POLITICAL AND ECONOMIC STRUCTURES

Although territorially smaller, the post-World War II Poland gives the country a more favorable domain than the one that was created after World War I. Under the latest allocation of territory, the Corridor was eliminated to give Poland a more continuous Baltic coastline; the east and west boundaries were smoothed by the removal of the vulnerable "Vilna prong" and "Poznan bulge"; and readjustments of territory incorporated several important rivers within Polish domain. Today Poland encompasses 120,359 square miles of territory and a population of about 25 million.

Economically, there was an even greater transmutation. An economic revolution, that began in 1948, has changed the backward agrarian nation into a semi-industrial state in the Communist pattern. "Although heavy stresses are apparent, especially in the agricultural sector, the achievements as well as the goals . . . cannot be discounted. Already in 1949, it appeared that the mines and factories of Poland were producing almost twice as much as they had in 1937; and the present rate of production foreshadows for 1955 a fourfold increase over prewar years."[6]

Such fundamental economic changes would not be possible were it not for the fact that, due to the readjustments of boundaries, Poland now incorporates within the domain a large base of natural mineral resources. Poland today is one of the most richly endowed, minerally speaking, of the European states. Although, with the transfer of the eastern territories to the Soviet Union went also the transfer of Poland's former most valuable fuel and chemical resources, the nation appears to have been more than compensated by the German acquisitions in the west. Poland lost the Jaslo-Krosno oil fields (which, however, have since declined in output by nearly three-fourths) as well as the Polish potash reserves. Stern says, "It is not possible at present to judge whether

---

[6] Peter M. Stern, "Poland," *Focus* (New York: American Geographical Society, Vol. III, No. 2, November, 1952), p. 1.

this serious loss has been made up by the recently reported discovery of extensive potassium salts in the Kolo–Konin region. It is hardly a coincidence, however, that the current Six-Year Plan calls for the establishment of a new chemical industry in this district."[7] In the west, Poland gained the rich Silesian ore beds and industrial district. It is an area of great industrial concentration developed on excellent local coal and other mineral resources. This district, which has a population of 3 million and six urban centers of over 100,000 people each, has become the economic core of the Communist state.

Silesia has long been a disputed area. Up to 1914 it was divided among Germany, Austria–Hungary, and Russia; after the 1921 plebiscite, it was split up among Germany, Poland, and Czechoslovakia; at present, Poland and the Czech Republic jointly hold ownership, Poland acquiring the former German and Polish portions. The 1921 division was not very desirable in either a physical or economic sense. The territory, as allocated, gave to the Slav state the major mines and to Germany the greater proportion of the industrial plants—coke ovens, steel furnaces, and by-products plants for chemicals. "In places the boundary was so arbitrary that workers living in one country found themselves at work underground in another."[8] Under such conditions, it was inevitable that industrial development was handicapped.

At present Poland holds all of the Silesian coal mines except those in one district in Czechoslovakia. The Silesian reserves are estimated at 135 billion tons, which, if correctly assessed, are larger than those of the Ukraine's rich Donbas and the Franco–Belgian basin. In 1953 the combined Polish–Czech Silesia produced 99 million tons of coal to the German Ruhr's 125.5 million, and about half as much steel as the German district—8 million tons to the Ruhr's 15.5 million tons. The margin of difference betweeen the two "Ruhrs"

has likely widened somewhat because the Ruhr production has, during the past decade, increased, actually and proportionately, more greatly than that of the Silesian districts of the two Slav states. Although iron mines are found adjacent to the coal beds, the ore has a low mineral content and, therefore, the Silesian industries depend heavily on foreign sources (Sweden and the Ukraine) for this basic metal. It is expected, however, that local ores can eventually provide about a third of the needs. Nonferrous minerals are found in Silesia—in fact, the most productive lead-zinc mines in Europe are those of Polish Silesia.

Current industrial plans lay stress on the output of steel, chemicals, and electricity. The major center of production is in Upper Silesia, the triangular minerals area just west of the city of Krakow. Here are the largest and best coal fields, and the valuable lead-zinc mines. Lower Silesia (farther west in the Sudeten Mountains) is the second most productive district. If not already, the chemicals and synthetic-fuel industries of this region will soon be the second largest in Poland.

But important as industry is becoming, Poland is still an agricultural country—farming its leading occupation. The best of the agricultural lands lie in Central Poland in the higher and better drained sections of the southern half of the country. More than 50 per cent of the country is cultivable; forests cover about one-fifth; only 10 per cent can be listed as not productive. Formerly a leading European producer of flax and sugar beets, the eastern lands on which these crops were grown passed into Russian hands. Among European states, Polish agricultural yields rank among the poorest, the peasantry is typically backward and poverty-stricken, and agriculture is hard put to supply the food requirements of its large and increasing urban industrial populations. The discrepancy in achievements between industry and agriculture highlights what is undoubtedly the weakest part of the Polish economy—its farm production. The reasons are much the same as in the Soviet state to the east: peasants have resisted collectivization.

---

[7] *Ibid.*, p. 2.
[8] *Ibid.*, p. 2.

The economy of Czechoslovakia. Czecho–Slovakia, 600 miles long and, on the average, about 100 miles wide, is, in area, about the size of the state of New York; in population, some 2 million less (Czechoslovakia, 14.3 million). In location, it is handicapped for the state is landlocked, and hence, dependent upon other nations for transit to the sea lanes. In natural resources, it is richly endowed, however: forests cover one-third of the country, providing a valuable timber reserve—with distance east, the proportion of land in timber increases; the mineral resources are large and industrial development has gone far—one-third of the population is employed by industry (38 per cent are engaged in agriculture). Hard and soft coal, iron, uranium, graphite, silver, lead, copper, garnets, and salt make up the minerals; coal and lignite provide most of the power, although the production of electricity (generated largely with coal as fuel) ranks high.

Total coal reserves are large, exceeding those of France and Belgium; the most important beds of industrial coals are located in adjacence to those of Poland's upper Silesia, the Ostrov–Karvinna field. Three-fourths of the hard coal production is from this area. Total reserves of iron ore also are large, equalling those in Spain and central Sweden. Production is small, however, and the ore—to supply a heavy industry that compares favorably with that of Poland, the Saar, or Luxembourg—is imported, mostly from Sweden. Information on uranium supplies is held highly confidential, but, according to reports, Czechoslovakia has been the major source of uranium ore for the Soviet nuclear industry in the USSR. The mines are located almost directly south of the Polish-German border and near the frontier.

Soil resources are generally good and, in several areas, such as central Bohemia, Moravia, and the "corridor," they are rich and black over wide areas. Forty per cent of the country is in cultivation, 16 per cent in pastures and meadows.

The Communist pattern of agriculture in Czechoslovakia is different from that in the other satellite states, the distinguishing features being the lack of wide collectivization, the extensive "individual" land holdings that persist, and the system of "contracting," the device chosen as the "bridge between individual and socialist production," as the Czech Communists have stated it, for some device had to be found to make private farming "compatible with over-all planning." The reasons for the slight collectivization are found in the fact that, in Czechoslovakia, 1) peasants were not pressed by a shortage of land, 2) the interwar years brought some good agarian reforms, 3) agricultural techniques are good (though deteriorating eastward in Slovakia), 4) there was no poverty-stricken peasantry clamoring for reform—the farmers were well-fed and moderately prosperous, and 5) grain farming is not dominant.[9]

However, as in other Communist states, with the inception of the Five-Year Plan (1949), "government direction of the economic life of Czechoslovakia assumed the characteristics of all-inclusive central planning," and, although farming is largely on an individual basis, "decision-making on purchases, production policies, and marketing" are all in the hands of the government.[10]

Czech agriculture is well balanced. Although cereals occupy over half of the cultivated acreage, the proportion of land thus used is small compared to that of other Slav states. Nor does any one grain stand out dominantly above all the others: rye, oats, wheat, and barley lead, but all have nearly the same production. Fodder crops are important and potatoes occupy almost as much acreage as does barley. Thus, monoculture does not pose the danger, economically, that is true in certain areas, as in Rumania and the Far East. Sugar beets are important and Czechoslovakia ranks

[9] Experience has demonstrated that large units devoted to grain farming are best adapted to collectivization.

[10] Ernest Koenig, "Planning in Czechoslovak Agriculture," Foreign Agriculture, Vol. XVI, No. 9, September, 1952, pp. 157-8.

second only to Germany as a European producer.

The industrialization of Czechoslovakia, under the planned Communist economy, is linked with that of Poland, as indicated before. Under a treaty signed by both states in 1947, communication and transportation facilities between the two countries were to be developed and extended, and the industrial and agricultural programs somewhat coordinated; particularly with regard to the Silesian industries was this true—they were to be developed as a unit evidently along the lines under which the coal-steel community in Western Europe functions. This program of unification in industry has evidently been carried out.

The economy of Czechoslovakia, despite its well-balanced character, is highly dependent on foreign trade both as an outlet for manufactured products and for imports of raw materials. In prewar days, three-fourths of the exports were manufactures, more than one-half of the imports, raw materials. The present pattern is much the same. Iron and steel products, machinery, textiles, glass, timber, pulp and paper, and shoes are the leading exports; raw cotton and wool, iron ore and other metals, oil, and chemicals head the import list.

Hungary is, geographically, quite an effective political unit. Compact in shape and relatively level, coherence is facilitated; supplied with a fertile soil that produces a substantial surplus and with minerals that furnish the base for some industry, the economic base is good. The economy is further strengthened by the Hungarian position on the Danube River; Budapest is almost centrally located on this important water route. Hungary's major geopolitical problem appears to be that of relations with the neighboring states. Although hostilities are held in abeyance under the unification brought about by the Soviets, the antagonisms are too basic and long-standing to have disappeared.

Not until the early years of the last century did the pastoral, semi-nomadic Magyar way of life undergo a change and the people take up a sedentary existence with agriculture as the base. Since then, however, cereals have largely replaced animals, although, so deeply ingrained is pastoralism in the traditions of the Magyar, that transhumance still obtains to a degree.

One of the gravest weaknesses of the Hungarian economy throughout the past century and up until the postwar years was the medieval system of land tenure which had remained unchanged even though measures to change and democratize such conditions were taking place in most of the states around Hungary after World War I. In 1944, from one-third to one-half of the land was still held by large estates, and there had been no effort on the part of the government to redistribute the land or to cut down on the number of landless peasants. This throbbing problem of "land" is always the basic appeal of Communism to the masses; therefore, the Magyars were pregnable.

Hungary is an agricultural country. More than two-thirds of the total area is arable, about 12 per cent in forests. Since the war, Hungary has attempted (Communist-wise) to secure a better balance between agriculture and industry, and hence industry has been pushed. Resources on which to base such a development are not entirely lacking but they have little variety, and, except in the case of bauxite, are very minor deposits. The bauxite reserves are estimated to equal those of France and Yugoslavia, but production has been sporadic; what it is at present is unknown. However, according to published statistics, more than 50 per cent of the bauxite now mined in Hungary is processed within the country; formerly, nearly all of it was exported as taken from the mines, and aluminum was imported. To broaden the industrial base, Hungary has expanded the manufacture of iron and steel; the small ore reserves, however, can never supply the industrial needs of the state.

Although a "poor" country with a backward and poverty-stricken peasantry, paradoxically Rumania is relatively rich from the standpoint of undeveloped and developed resources. This paradox is difficult to explain, for the state might best be described, perhaps, by defining it as overwhelmingly backward. The land problem—with most of the arable districts in the hands of a few large landowners while the mass of the people was composed of a largely landless peasantry—was particularly acute until the agrarian reforms introduced during the inter-war years. Through expropriation of land from such landowners as the church and aristocracy, 90 per cent of the farm lands again passed to the farmers.

The Rumanian economy is agrarian. Agricultural methods were still relatively primitive when the Communists gained power. Gradually, a collectivization of agriculture took over, although this was not as easily introduced as in some countries for the reform of the prewar years had taken care of land distribution. In 1949 the first collectives were formed, and, within a year to a year and a half, one thousand collective farms, embracing about 1.8 million acres of land, had been established. Gradually mechanization of agriculture was introduced in the Soviet pattern, but per acre production is still the lowest in Europe. Eighty per cent of the population belong to the farming peasantry, a high proportion as compared to other parts of the world.

Aside from soil, forests and oil are the major resources. Forests cover the Transylvanian slopes, and the timber business is quite significant. The oil fields are found in two areas, around Ploesti along the base of the mountains and east of the Carpathians. Although the petroleum output is but a small part of world production, Rumania is nevertheless Europe's leading producer, in 1953 bringing up three times as much as the nearest European competitor, Austria, and ranking tenth in the world (but with a small one-seventieth of the total output). Pipelines take the oil from the Ploesti fields to Constanta on the Black Sea. A second fuel resource is found in the natural gas reserves which rank next to those of the Russians on the continent. Coal in the Banat and local iron ore feed a small iron and steel industry that has an annual production of 300,000 tons of steel; this will be increased to

perhaps 450,000 tons, it is expected. Manufacturing, however, except for steel, local food-processing and native home-crafts, is almost undeveloped.

Bucharest is the capital and the traditional cultural center of the Ruman people. The one metropolis of the country, its population numbers about a million and a half inhabitants. Except for the ports—Constanta on the Black Sea, and Galati and Braila on the Danube—urban centers are represented in small local market-towns. Since the Danube flows in the wrong direction (*i.e.* away from the most productive areas of Europe) and through economically retarded lands, the Danubian ports of Rumania, although they are the outlets to the river, are of minor importance and will never compare in importance with such a port as Rotterdam on the Rhine.

As an agricultural country, Bulgaria has a good economic base. In size (42,796 square miles), Bulgaria has approximately the area of the state of Ohio; in population, the two units are also close, Bulgaria numbering 7.2 million, about a million less than the American state.

The nation is small, but topography helps provide environments that vary, somewhat, from steppe-like plateaus where wheat and corn predominate to better watered and climatically sheltered valleys that permit the cultivation of fruits and vegetables of many sorts. Although production is not spectacular, because muscular labor—human and animal—still provides most of the agricultural "power," Bulgaria exports grain and other products, including fruits and tobacco, to the states of Central Europe.

From a purely agricultural country, Communist-controlled Bulgaria is gradually becoming a source of semi-finished industrial products. Manufacturing can still be described as in its beginnings. However, there is little doubt that industry has advanced greatly in postwar years. Before the war, coal production was two million tons; in 1953 this had been increased to eight million, and by 1957 it had reached 14 million tons. Estimates of reserves are impossible, but, beside the increase in coal production, there has been started the manufacture of coal products: a synthetic gasoline plant and a chemical plant for reprocessing coal. The nonferrous industry is also being developed. Manganese ore is mined at several centers; copper is extracted up to 30,000 tons annually; chromium deposits are said to have been discovered; lead and zinc are mined in several areas; and uranium ore reserves are found northeast of Sofia and mining has begun. Oil and steel production are two other aspects of the same trend. Bulgaria still depends on oil products imported from Rumania, but, according to the system of trade within the Soviet Bloc, it can receive no more than 100,000 tons of crude oil and oil by-products a year. Therefore, Bulgaria has begun prospecting for oil near the Black Sea southeast of Stalin (formerly Varna).

Thus the change from a strictly agrarian economy to one that balances more favorably with industry is slowly taking shape. Burgas, on the Black Sea, is the leading port surpassing, in volume of trade, Varna, farther north.

Productive as is the state, it is not easy to assess how significant the agricultural and industrial output is—to the Communist Bloc or within the world of nations. It is likely that the major international importance of Bulgaria lies not so much in its productive capacity as in its strategic position in the midst of the Balkan–Black Sea states.

Like Bulgaria, traditionally, the region now represented in Yugoslavia has been agricultural. The most productive area is in the north lowland plain, a part of the fertile central Danubian breadbasket. This surplus food region helps make up the shortages in other parts of the state for part of the country is unable to supply its own food needs. This area, and even more, the more mountainous regions are plagued with a climate in which the rainfall is so variable that, within a period of a few years, crop yields may vary as much as 50 to 60 per cent. During dry years, the more marginal mountain farmers face near-disaster but for distribution of grains. The problem posed by undependable climatic conditions is accentu- ated by backward methods of cultivation. Further, several parts of the country are already over-populated in terms of supporting the present population through agriculture.

Under the Communist system of economic planning, the government tried to improve these conditions and raise production—and, at the same time, gain control over "the means of production," is the aim in all Communist states. Cooperatives and collective farming, with grain collections and other Communist concomitants, were introduced and functioned side by side with private farming. But food production did not meet expected schedules and farmers resisted collectivization. For these reasons, beginning in 1951, the government has gradually eased up on the drive for the socialization of agriculture and has permitted a much wider latitude of individual ownership and operation than has been accorded under any other Communist regime.

The planned economy calls for the development of industry commensurate with the resources and the regional needs and potentialities. But industrialization has moved ahead slowly and stumblingly although Yugoslavia has a number of mineral resources. Two reasons for this are: 1) the relatively minor resources in fuel, and 2) the dependence of Yugoslavia upon foreign sources for "producer's goods"—turbines, generators, machines for manufacturing, etc. The extent of the coal reserves are not known but production has more than doubled since 1939; in oil output, the production of crude petroleum rose from 1000 tons in 1939 to 171,700 tons in 1953; in its mountains, Yugoslavia has a large potential for hydroelectric power development. The country is a producer of several minerals— copper, chrome, manganese, lead, bauxite, zinc, iron, and antimony. Production has been hampered by lack of machinery, however, and, though some installations have been completed, Yugoslav ore production remains low as compared to that of central and west European nations.

Yugoslavia is a politically controversial area in an international context. After its separation from close association with the states of the Communist Bloc, it was gradually drawn into the folds of the West in spite of its Marxian doctrines. With the re-opening of Yugoslav–Soviet relations in the summer of 1955, Yugoslavia acquired a strategic place in international politics that was quite unique. However, by 1957 Soviet–Yugoslav relations had again cooled.

The future alone can ascertain the real Yugoslav position in the international scene. But it is likely that Yugoslavia must be regarded as a neutral. There are several reasons why Yugoslavia is a valuable component of the West, or of the Communist Bloc, or of the neutrals. In the first place, due to the location of the state, Yugoslavia controls a portion of the Danube, the leading river system of southeast Europe. Secondly, all railways connecting the Danube Basin with the Mediterranean Sea pass through Yugoslav territory, and, "except for one minor line, all rail transport between Bulgaria and the Soviet sphere has to depend on the Yugoslav railroad system."[11] Further, the Adriatic ports of Rijeka (formerly Fiume), Split, and Dubrovnik are all linked with Yugoslav transportation lines, and the ports of Pula and Kotor offer excellent anchorage and protection for large fleets—in case of hostilities. Thirdly, Yugoslavia isolates Albania from all other Communist Bloc states, making the position of that strategic little country extremely untenable if Yugoslavia were hostile toward the Communist nations. It was this that seriously frustrated Soviet attempts to make Albania a major naval base because the only other connections are by air or by the Black Sea–Mediterranean Sea route—long, and pregnable at the Straits.

In a broader view, a Western-allied Yugoslavia—as through the Balkan Pact—would keep watch over the USSR on the south and stand as a sentinel, with Greece and Turkey, over the Dardanelles. In this way, it also controls the outlet to the Ukraine, the major agricultural and industrial region of the Soviet Union. Thus, says Kish, "while the open plains of northern Yugoslavia may well be helpless before an invader, the positional advantages of Yugoslavia, and of its neighboring states, are likely to balance that threat in the continental strategy."[12] In other words, the location of Yugoslavia and of all of the other Balkan states is such that, regardless of the period, they hold the potential of a "live fuse."

It is in its strategic location that Albania is of interest to the nations of the world. Geopolitically, the Albanian resource and power potential are small for Albania is a rugged and rather arid highland country whose chief wealth is found in its soils and mountain pastures. Most of the people have subsisted on pastoral activities. They have avoided agglomeration and have, rather, spread widely and thinly over the highland interior leaving the coastal lowlands relatively empty for the Italians to occupy, particularly in the ports of Durres and Valona. In character, the Albanian people are like other mountaineers—independent and often turbulent. In their fortress environment, they have resisted incursions by the Turk and Slav alike, although contact with the latter peoples has affected their language and ethnic composition, and the Turks gave them their religion.

After World War II, for several reasons this independent and individualistic people voted to become Communist. It would appear that this was a rather unrealistic solution to the problems of Albania because the whole setting —people, terrain, philosophy—are against Communism. However, under Communism, and under the direction of the Soviets, the resources of Albania are being explored and the country developed as never before. Railroads leading into the interior from the ports have been extended by several hundred miles, mineral production has been pushed and industry developed. Oil, Albania's most valuable export, has reached prewar levels of output (only about a million and a half barrels annually, however), and a small refinery has been

11 George Kish, "Yugoslavia," *Focus,* Vol. I, No. 6 (March 15, 1951), p. 4.

12 *Ibid.,* p. 4.

constructed; hydroelectric plants are being put in to increase power resources; whatever mineral resources have been discovered—coal, copper, chrome, asphalt—are being developed.

The Albanian location gives it control of the Strait of Otranto and, hence, of the Adriatic Sea. In this, rather than in the inherent wealth of the state, lies the geopolitical importance of the small country.

PROBLEM AREAS

The Macedonian problem. Macedonia has been called the "vortex" of the political whirlpool that is the Balkan Peninsula. Areally, it centers on Salonika, its chief city and principal port, to spread eastward halfway to the Turkish border across northern Greece, northward to encompass the southwest portions of the Bulgarian Rhodope region, westward across Yugoslav territories to the Albanian borders as far north as Skoplje and Vranje, and south into Greek lands to and beyond Phlorina and Kastoria. The region is drained by two important rivers, the Vardar and the Struma, which have cut valuable outlets for the inner Balkans. Thus, Macedonia runs counter to the political structure of the Balkans. Essentially, it comprises the combined valleys of the Vardar and Struma rivers in Yugoslavia, Bulgaria, and Greece.

Since prehistoric times, Macedonia has been a crossroads and a battleground. In the early fifth century B.C., Macedonia was subdued by Persia, and during the fourth century it knew the rule of the Macedonian conquerors, Philip and Alexander the Great, the latter extending the sway of Macedonian power eastward into India. Later, it fell under the Romans, Byzantines, barbarian Slavs, and Turks. Saint Paul established the first Christian churches in Macedonia, and Saints Cyril and Methody, creators of the Slavic alphabet still used throughout Eastern Europe, went north from Salonika to teach the barbarians. Hence, the cultural and political influence of ancient Macedonia was great.

Modern Macedonia is, generally speaking, Slavic in character and the Macedonian generally bilingual, speaking Bulgar or Serb (with a small minority knowing Greek) although the majority prefer the Bulgar language. The center of population gravity, however, is in Yugoslavia. The Macedonians have been claimed by both Serbs and Bulgarians, though they have not been treated as equals by either nationality. When viewed in its details, the Macedonian population is not simple but is a variegated one, made up, among others, of Serbs, Bulgarians, Greeks, Vlachs, Albanians, Turks, Gypsies, and Jews, and the inhabitants speak a dozen different languages and are divided into several rival religious groups. Like so much of the Balkan peninsula, Macedonia— the epitome of Balkanism—is a land of many tongues, a veritable Babel, for it has been a dropping-off place for many peoples. The Macedonians number about two million of which perhaps 100,000 reside in Greece. Traditionally, Bulgaria has been looked upon by the Macedonians as a political harbor when troubles cropped up for them elsewhere.

The Macedonians are unable to identify the Slavic tribe from which they are in part descended and as which they entered the Balkans, apparently in the ninth century. Actually, they do not form a special racial or ethnic group. In the main of Caucasian-Slav origin and linguistically Slav, they incorporate Mongol elements; in looks and literature, the Bulgar influence predominates. Volatile as is—and has been—the Macedonian problem, it is only very recently that the Macedonians have begun to display any feeling of nationalism. When their cause has been supported by outsiders, it has been not so much for the sake of the Macedonians as for what some other state could gain out of the struggle.

The Treaty of San Stefano gave to Bulgaria almost all of the area known as Macedonia— the exception being the three-pronged peninsula on which Salonika is located. In the same year, however, the Congress of Berlin reversed the San Stefano agreement (designed by Russia) and returned Macedonia, with other territories, to the Turks. During the Balkan Wars of 1912-13, Macedonia was again taken from Turkey, this time by Serbia, Greece, and Bulgaria; the present disposition of Macedonian territory was made after World War I when the Balkan boundaries were assigned by the Allied Powers. In 1949, the Soviet Union backed the formation of a free Macedonian state, which, in actuality, would have functioned as a part of a Greater Bulgaria.

The Macedonians have been "used." The Serbs exploited them as ruthlessly as did the Turks; the Bulgarians took advantage of their resentment against the Serbs to promote their own aims for a Greater Bulgaria (and thus to oppose a Greater Serbia). When the fanatical IMRO group (Independent Macedonian Revolutionary Organization) began working for independence in the late 1940's, the Bulgars began to support them in the hope that they could eventually take over Macedonia—and the Soviets supported both the IMRO and the Bulgarians because of the advantages that would accrue to the USSR.

Trieste. Trieste, a natural harbor at the head of the Adriatic, has been a bone of international contention since the break-up of the Roman Empire. Italians from Dante to the present have called it "ours," and the Hapsburgs built it into a "port of empire." When the Austro-Hungarian Empire collapsed and the Slavs achieved sovereignty in Yugoslavia, they looked on Trieste as theirs; but by 1924 Italy had gained control of the vital Istrian area. Since that time, the Yugoslav government continued to remind the world that the disposition of the territory was not to its liking.

Istria is the keystone in the arch of the North Adriatic, and its two flanking ports are the best trade outlets in the north and east reaches of that sea. To the Yugoslavs, it is the outlet to one of the two passageways from the interior; to the Italians?—after acquisition, colonists in great numbers from the western state filed in, forming local majority groups. Further, the port of Trieste is better than that of Venice and has been used somewhat by the Italians as the Adriatic outlet of the Po Valley. However,

Trieste is not naturally an Italian port—it is a *port of Italians, serving an area almost entirely non-Italian*. Its true hinterland is landlocked Austria, Hungary, and northern Yugoslavia; Genoa, on the Mediterranean, is the more natural outlet for the Italian Po district.

In the Italian Peace Treaty of 1946, the Allied powers agreed to make Trieste a free territory under a Governor to be appointed by the United Nations Security Council. The Powers, however, were not able to agree on a Governor, and the Free Territory of Trieste remained divided along the lines of military occupation in effect at the end of the war. In the north was Zone A, including the city of Trieste, with an Italian majority population and occupied by Anglo–American troops; in the south, Zone B, which included much of the rural area, held most of the Slav population and was occupied by Yugoslav troops. Both Yugoslavia and Italy laid claim to the entire territory; Anglo–American policy vacillated with the changing stresses of the cold war.

In 1948, when the Italian Communists made a strong bid for election in the peninsula, Great Britain and the United States jointly declared themselves in favor of ceding the territory to Italy; but after Belgrade broke off relations with the Soviets, the Western Powers proposed bilateral talks between Italy and Yugoslavia. When, in 1952, these failed to bring a settlement, the United States and Britain entered the picture again.

The area was one not only of mixed peoples but of supercharged national emotions. An effort, in October, 1953, to bring about agreement on the basis of an Anglo–American declaration was belligerently rejected by both Rome and Belgrade on the grounds that they had not been consulted. One year later (October 10, 1954), after eight years of mounting tension, an agreement was reached. Under its terms, Yugoslavia received Zone B, Italy Zone A; American and British troops were withdrawn. Italy was pledged to operate the city of Trieste as a free port without discrimination against Yugoslav interests. A small section of Zone A, predominantly Slavic in population, was also ceded to Yugoslavia. "Equality of rights and treatment" is guaranteed for both "the members of the Yugoslav ethnic group in the area administered by Italy, and the members of the Italian ethnic group in the area administered by Yugoslavia."[13]

The Danube River. The Danube is one of Europe's most important waterways, touching on more countries than any river in the world. It rises in Germany's Black Forest not far from the Rhine, and flows through and past eight nations to its delta. All but 150 of its 1750 miles are navigable. However, although over twice the length of the Rhine, the Danube carries less than half the volume of trade. Danubian commerce has never been great in a continental sense for the river rises just outside the continent's most highly industrialized section and flows in the wrong direction, in terms of markets and world sea lanes, to empty 1725 miles away in the nearly landlocked Black Sea. Nevertheless, it is a commercially important river.

For over 2000 years this stream has carried the trade of the riparian states. In Roman days, the Danube countries formed the outlying provinces of the Empire. At Vienna the Danube is crossed by the north-south corridor of cultural interchange and, under the Austro-Hungarian Empire, the river formed a connection between its different parts.

Rivers—and their interconnecting canals—are one of the primary components of the European transporation system and, for a century, a canal (the Main-Ludwig canal) has connected the upper Rhine and the Danube, making the bi-river traffic route one of some importance. Commerce from central and southeastern Europe has flowed along its sur-

face;[14] at times, however, the natural flow of trade has been tampered with.

Because of its multi-national character, the Danube is an international river, and all considerations regarding traffic, handling of shipping, channel and port upkeep, and improvement must be internationally agreed to. Traditionally the control of the Danube has changed with the increase or decline of Russian power. From 1812 to 1856 Russia administered shipping through control of the river mouth, the delta at Vilcovo (which it once again holds as a result of the latest annexation of Bessarabia). After 1856, however, various degrees of international control tended to overcome boundary obstacles. Between World Wars I and II the entire navigable channel, from the delta to Ulm, Germany, was open to all Danubian states on a basis of complete equality. An International Commission, authorized by three separate treaties (in 1856, 1878, 1918 under various titles), greatly improved navigation conditions on the river—dredging the central channel (particularly in the delta area), canalizing the section of swift rapids at the Iron Gate between Rumania and Yugoslavia, removing unnecessary customs restrictions, etc. The Commission established by the Treaty of Versailles excluded Russia and Rumania but included three non-Danubian states—Great Britain, France, and Italy.

During the last war, control of the river passed, first, to the Nazis and then to the Soviets. In 1945, the Danube was cut in two as effectively as though it were, in fact, two separate rivers. The short upper section in Bavaria and Austria came under American occupation and the long, long fall downstream from Linz to the Black Sea completely under Soviet control. Between the two there was no interchange of commerce. In 1948 the Belgrade Conference once more set up an International Commission for the regulation of river traffic. Seven of the ten members of the Com-

---

[13] The Trieste settlement was a major diplomatic achievement for the West, because for five years Italian–Yugoslav rivalry over this territory had been a major obstacle to the planning of a unified defense against Communist advance in southeastern Europe. With the settlement, the West was in a position to coordinate defense in the area through NATO (which includes Italy, Greece, and Turkey) and the Balkan Pact (which links Yugoslavia with Greece and Turkey).

[14] Important as is the canal as a link between northwest and eastward moving traffic, due to the shallowness of the canal, roads and railroads are far more important as carriers of cargo.

mission—Rumania, Hungary, Bulgaria, Yugoslavia, Czechoslovakia, the USSR, and the Ukrainian SSR—adopted a convention. It left only 200 miles of the Danube open to Western traffic—the stretch between Ulm, Germany, and Linz, Austria. The Russians insisted the Danube be open to the shipping of Danubian states only—but to them on a basis of equality. In reality, under this convention there was little transport on the river. The situation worsened after the Yugoslav break with Moscow. Until then, there had been a substantial passage of goods along the satellite-held stretches of the river. But within a year these had come to a standstill. In their anxiety to strangle Yugoslavia economically, the Soviets brought about a virtual closure of the 450-mile Yugoslav section—the biggest stretch within the borders of any one Danubian country and the biggest shipper—which had hitherto carried a million tons of postwar Yugoslav trade. Then, in 1953, by unanimous election a Yugoslav, representing the first non-Russian in five years, became secretary of the Commission, and once more free navigation was re-established and the Danube made an international river.

Since 1953, both Austrians and Yugoslavs have greatly increased their shipping tonnage. Although figures are not obtainable for the Soviet Bloc countries through which the river flows, there is little doubt that, throughout its navigable length, the over-all movement of goods is greater than at any postwar period. It has the potential of an increase that will surpass anything in the past as mines and industries open up more and more in these formerly backward areas.

THE COMMUNIST FRONTIER IN EUROPE

The frontiers of Communism in Europe are seen to extend in a north-south line that stretches from the Gulf of Bothnia to the mouth of the Adriatic Sea. Behind this boundary there are no non-Communist or isolated "islands" of democratic, completely sovereign states remaining. Austria indents the frontier for a space in tracing the eastern half of its border. During occupation, however, this penetration did not exist, and the notch in the frontier made by a neutral Austria is less significant to the West than is the western tail of Austria, trailing between Germany and Italy, to the USSR. Austria reverses the frontier trend, but the breach is plugged—by neutrality—and the neutral role robs Austria of political initiative in international affairs. Greece, behind the line, is nevertheless exempt from the pressures that states in back of the frontier would feel because it dips south as a peninsula, open on three sides and touching the Communist frontier along only the northern border. The western front of Communism is a solid front—up to this line.

Beyond this frontier, however, there are some Communist intrusions into Western territory. One is found in East Germany, two others in the strong elements of Communism that obtain in Italy and France. A study of the map of Europe will reveal that, spatially, the design of expansion was, until 1956, one of an even, outward spread—not one of leaping across intervening areas to form outliers from the Communist core. This was a very interesting pattern of accretion and one that, as a map of Asia will also reveal, was also used on the eastern continent. This pattern of spread to *contiguous regions, advancing always as a solid front of Communism,* was due not only to intent (and this must have been by intent), but also to several geopolitical factors already discussed, such as "vicinity" and all of its implications. A change of policy, however, begun largely in the late fall of 1955, saw the Soviets employing the strategy of spanning contiguous lands in order to exert influence—if not control—over certain lands in the Middle East and Asia. This policy of leaping beyond the bounds and advancing—like a dart from a blow-gun—is high-pointed in the Suez Canal Zone and the Arab countries at the eastern end of the Mediterranean Sea. It represents a change in strategy, not purpose.

11

The Continental States of East and Southeast Asia

One part of the world where Western foreign policy has been seriously ineffective is in East and Southeast Asia. The failure on the part of the Western world to effect an understanding with the literate Asians who largely guide the course of Asian politics has had broad reverberations in China and Indochina. There appear to be four key issues on which the Asian outlook differs significantly from the Western—in principle, or stress, or both. These have frustrated a meeting of minds. They are 1) imperialism and colonialism; 2) economic development; 3) the nature of Communism; and 4) the nature of democracy. It is necessary to examine the contrasting points of view of Asian and the Westerner in order to understand Asia today, as well as the failure of the West to gain an effective understanding with the nations of Asia.

The force of the colonial heritage upon the contemporary literate Asian is very complex.

One of the outstanding impacts is reflected in the high level of priority that Asians place on the uprooting of colonialism (from those places where it still clings), and in their attitude of impatience—and even intolerance—with the process of metastasis to independence. A second effect is found in the inclination of Asians to accept, in whole or in part, Lenin's conception of imperialism, and to define the motives of the Western states in these terms—which give credence to the idea that the West has been forced to build and retain colonial holdings *by the inevitable working of capitalist states*. In short, the Asians—having passed or passing through a transition from dependent to independent action and status—have been disposed to lay the blame for all of their difficulties on the colonialism of the past, and to be hypersensitive to fosterage of any sort from Western nations and nationals. The whole complex problem of East–West relationships has been further intensified by profound, often unrealized, antagonisms of race and color.

To the educated Asian, the profound but intrinsically non-material aims have seemed beyond attainment until a transformation has been brought about in the economic structure —until Asia has been transformed from the archaic systems of the past to a modern industrial economy with all of the accruing benefits. But to bring about a condition of economic change and growth by continuous and automatic process is neither easy nor quick. Such mutations as took place in those countries now characterized by an industrial economy have, historically, required decades and achievement of self-sufficiency was long and arduous. The most recent attempt at such transformation was in the USSR and the European Communist-satellite states. In the Soviet Union this change has been going on for over thirty years and the economy still has weak elements.

This determination for economic transformation and betterment has undoubtedly been at the base of the feeling among many Asians that American concern with Communist expansion in Asia has been greatly exaggerated and has distorted emphasis and priority in the terms that the Asian views his own problems, interests, and ambitions. According to the Asians, they have sought, by whatever means as were open, to preserve the peace so that their energies could be exerted to develop the resources of their respective states and to better the social and economic standards and the political status of their people. Most Asians have felt the need of devoting themselves to pressing domestic problems. The transition from an agricultural to an industrial economy was accomplished years ago in most Western states and without a sense of urgency. The economic and social revolution now underway in most parts of Asia—in many instances captured in a political revolution that, at least temporarily, submerged the first-mentioned aspects of change —represents the desire of the Asian to be free of the suffocating poverty of the centuries and to share in the benefits of modern Western technology.

The attitude toward Communism found generally among Asians is complex and frequently ambivalent. In the simple, broad collection of Marxist principles setting forth an interpretation and prediction of the course of societies, the educated Asian, including non-Communists, has found great appeal. Particularly has the Lenin doctrine of capitalist imperialism impressed those who have been in responsible positions of government, for, almost without exception, these intellectuals grew up under a colonial system and spent their formative years struggling against foreign rule. Hence, from youth, the Communist doctrine (as practiced by the Soviets, imperialistic but seemingly not so recognized by many Asians) has seemed pertinent and well-founded. Further, the Asian leaders have been greatly impressed by the failures of the West in the East—in China, Indonesia, and Indochina—by the rocketing of Communist China to a position as a major power in the world, and, finally, by the possibility that Communism may be the way of the future for Asian states.

Notwithstanding the strong attraction of Communism—and there are, among a number of Asian peoples, ancient traditions of communalism—many Asians have been deeply drawn to the doctrines and practices of the democratic way. In fact, democracy should have deeper implications for most Asians than for many of the Western peoples for, in Asia, democracy has been related to the discontinuance of colonialism and to the lifting of the individual from a position of subservience and subjection to one of dignity and freedom.

There are important and basic differences between the Asian and Western conceptions of democracy. These differences are founded on the differing political and social environments in which the two broad groups of people developed. One of the bases for these differences is found in the illiteracy of the Asian masses which fosters a role of influence and power *among the literate few* for whom there are no counterparts among the Western democracies. Leadership—and innovation— originate at the top and work down. A second factor in creating the discrepant attitudes has deep roots in the system of private capitalism —under which there exists, in the West, a large and responsible middle class capable of carrying out such matters as investment, management, tax payment, and initiative. Since such a middle class is nearly everywhere absent in Asia, it is to be expected that a more authoritative and direct system of state economies will take over in most of that area, at least for a time. Full political expression would seem to them less necessary than the correction of flagrant social and economic derelictions.

Further, democracy was not native to this continent, and, in no state except the Philippines was it practiced until the post-World War II period. Therefore, the assumption that the democratic way is, or should be, preferred and accepted by Asian peoples cannot be inferred. As Romulo of the Philippine Islands stated, "Asian society, for long ages, has rested on a solid authoritarian base, heavily overgrown with custom, tradition, and ritual. The appeal of democracy . . . is not general in Asia . . . by any means . . . To peoples who have known little or no freedom for centuries, who have lived for ages in a state of poverty and hunger, the high shine and polish which our propaganda has given to democracy can hold no special attractions. These peoples will judge political and economic systems only in terms that have a concrete bearing on their daily lives: first, on what they have to do with the freedom movements among the still subject peoples of Asia . . .; second, on what they are disposed and able to do to help raise the living standards of the Asian . . . peoples."[1]

Three forces are pulling at Asia. One is international Communism; the second force is the meaning and capacity of democracy, largely centered in the West; the third, Asia's own nationalism and neutralism. The latter has an immeasurable influence. Which way the balance of forces in Asia will move the ma-jority of Asian populations is perhaps the decisive question of our time.

CHINA

Communist China is a massive and powerful political fact. During the years that have passed since the Communists proclaimed the People's Republic of China on October 1, 1949, the nation has been transformed from a divided and war-torn country into a coherent political unit with a strong central government. Historically, "the parts" of Greater China—China, Manchuria, Sinkiang, Tibet, and Mongolia—have been so loosely hung together as to scarcely justify the term nation; today central control reaches into the remote regions of Tibet and Sinkiang and Mongolia, to every village and hamlet and farm; in fact, government control embraces virtually every facet of Chinese life. Not only has the regime established central control over a population of more than 582 million, but there is strong evidence that it commands a wide acceptance.

Territorially, China is the second largest state in the world. The Chinese domain, over 3.75 million square miles, is nearly half as great as that of the USSR and one-fifth greater than that of the United States. It occupies one-fifth of the Asian continent, stretching nearly 3000 miles east and west, and spreading almost an equal distance north and south across the northern middle latitudes. Its borders touch on those of almost every other state in the eastern two-thirds of Asia. The USSR arcs around it on three sides—west, east, and north, sharing the frontier with the Mongolian People's Republic; the peninsula of Korea attaches itself on the east; while along the southern side, common boundaries are shared with North Vietnam, Burma, India, and Afghanistan. At China's most southern point, Thailand borders lie only a few miles distant; and, in the east, a relatively small portion of the Pacific (Sea of Japan) separates it from Japan.

Although all of China's frontiers are drawn along natural features, not all of them constitute good boundaries in terms of protection.

---

[1] Carlos P. Romulo, "What the Asians Expect of Us," *New York Times Magazine*, June 19, 1955, pp. 55, 60.

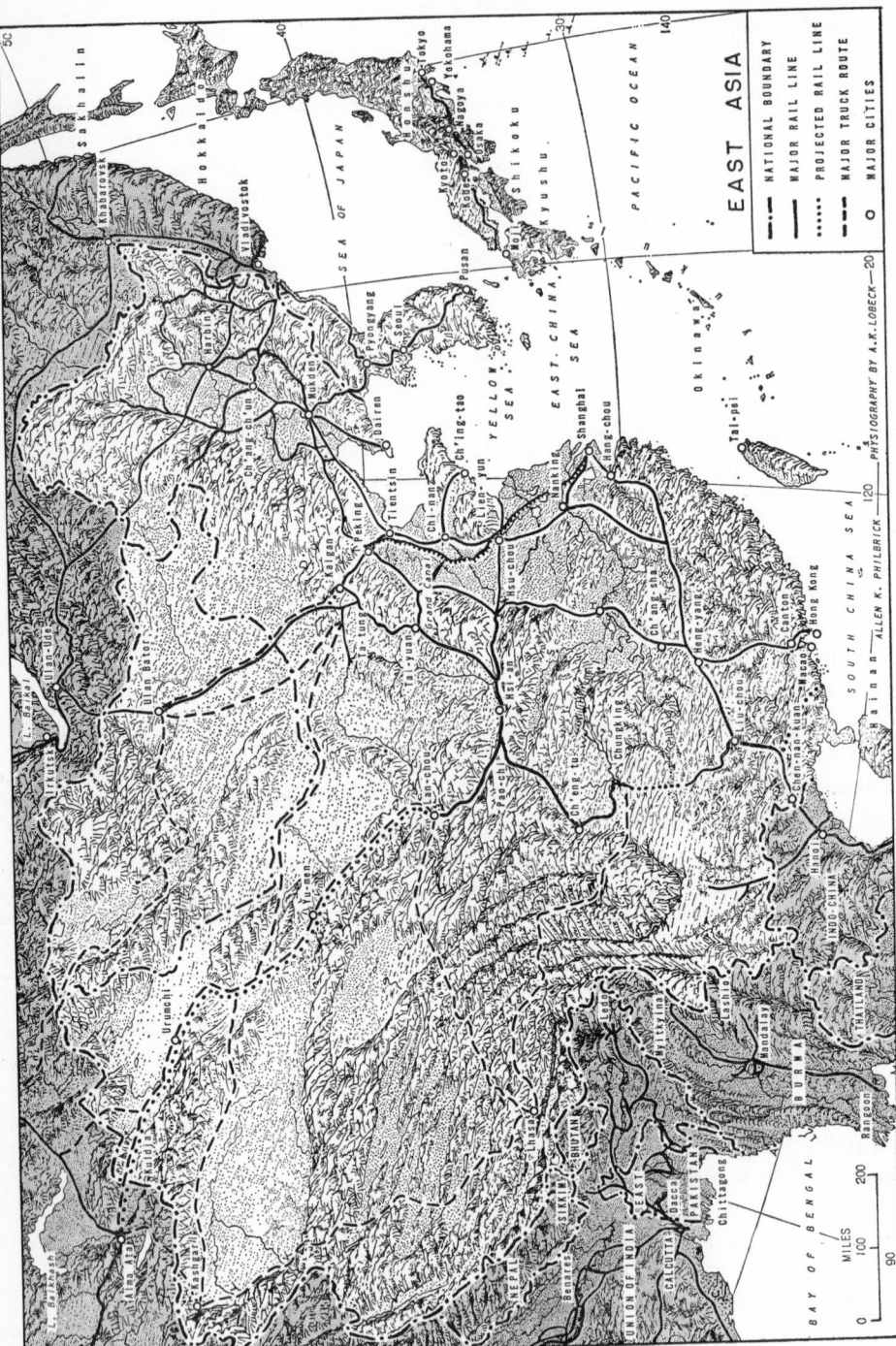

Figure 11.1. Physiography and major transportation lines of East Asia. One of the outstanding handicaps to the economic development in East Asia is the lack of adequate transportation facilities. A study of the map indicates that large sections are completely without modern means of transportation, even in terms of roads; in the seaboard areas, where the rail connections are most dense, railroads serve only major cities. Attention is called to two new rail routes: 1) that running from Kalgan to Ulan Bator and northward into Soviet territory to connect with Ulan-Ude, already completed; 2) the projected railroad, as yet only partially laid, that will run from Lan-chow in China to Alma Ata in Soviet Asia.

Further, the airplane has diminished the importance of the mountain barriers that once shut China off, to a large extent, from the neighboring countries. The Himalaya Mountains, between India and China, mark the most clearly defined frontiers, and, for China, are the most defensible. Along the west and north are the deserts of Sinkiang and Mongolia, constituting a frontier *zone* rather than delineating the bounds of the state. Throughout the whole of the desert political control has been loose and ill-defined, although the major east-west Eurasian transportation routes historically pass through these wastes from Chinese to Russian Turkestan.

This region has been one of the major centers of Russian interest and development within Chinese territory. Chinese pressures have pushed outward, and Russian interests eastward, in this desert zone; and, when the Mongolian People's Republic declared its independence (which eventually the Chinese were forced to recognize), a great chunk of the empire fell away. Tannu Tuva, northwest of Outer Mongolia, was taken by the Soviets and absorbed into the Russian Federation, but the Mongolian Republic maintained its sovereignty though it has remained a satellite of the Soviets. In the northeast, Manchuria thrusts upward into Russian territory and isolates, from the rest of Soviet territory, the port of Vladivostok and the highland spur of the Sikhote Alin Mountains. Here the Russians gained concessions to construct a railroad to the Soviet port, thereby cutting off a distance of several hundred miles.

The portions of the 9500-mile overland frontier where the Chinese have concentrated their most recent pressures have been along those of Korea and Indochina. Here, through military assistance to the Communists of North Korea and North Vietnam, they have appreciably spread Chinese influence outward along two fronts during the Communist Chinese period of political incubation. It was a rather remarkable accomplishment for a government not yet firmly established within its own country, and one which aided in raising Chinese prestige among other Asians.

Not accounting for irregularities, the coastline of China extends 4000 miles along the Pacific front. This long doorstep on the sea makes China both a maritime and continental power—an amphibious nation. Historically the Chinese traded by sea, more so than in the modern era; in the main, the state is—and has been—continentally directed. One reason for this may be found in the fact that China does not have unrestricted access to the world sea lanes. All of the China shore is bordered by offshore islands, some of the groups representing strong political empires in the past and modern eras. However, these same fringing islands created a border of inland seas that provided sheltered routes for the early trade between China and the islands of the Indies, Philippines, and Ceylon as early as the Christian era. Although the delta regions of the three greatest Chinese rivers do not provide good harborage, China has fairly adequate port facilities and a populous hinterland to back them up. Coastwise trade between Chinese ports has always been important.

Along this ocean frontier, east and south, is the region where China has felt most of the political pressures exerted by West European states—in the nature of "treaty ports" where China had to concede not only territory for restricted foreign "colonies" within her port cities and concessions along the waterfront but, also, to forfeit the right to hold jurisdiction over these same European nationals. These concessions, exacted from the state when it was politically unable to refuse, were one of the major factors underlying the feeling of Chinese bitterness toward the West in postwar years, including even the United States, despite the fact that, traditionally, America has been the guardian of Chinese integrity and independence.

It is to be seen that China's strategic location, which in a sense is that of a "heartland" in the Far East, has created both opportunities and problems for the state. In a global sense, the location of China is not—has not been—

among the best relative to the lanes of world trade; but the position is very good with respect to a large local commercial area within which there is a growing potential of natural resources and markets. With half of the people on the globe living within or around its frontiers, China possesses the best potential market, within a limited area, of any region in the world. The potential market will become "actual" when the standards of living of the Asians have been raised sufficiently to create a demand for many more products than are needed under the current subsistence economies.

As with the USSR, nature has not favored China to the degree that size seems to suggest. Much of the country is mountainous or desert, the climate one of extremes in most parts, with great aridity, or undependability of precipitation, or short growing season and dust erosion—as in the northern half. The climatically favored areas are, in general, in the south where a subtropical climate prevails along the shoreward regions, decreasing, with distance north and west, in its subtropical characteristics and becoming continental. The hilly topography over much of the south restricts the amount of cultivation that can be carried on, and determines, in part, the type of crops that are suitable. This is China's great tea-growing region; the delta of the Si Kiang is one of the great rice bowls of China, a surplus food area. Northward, the delta of the Yangtze and upstream, the Red Basin of Szechwan where Chungking and Chengtu are located, are also favored areas. But, whereas it is possible to grow three crops annually in the south, in the Yangtze Basin two are the maximum. The delta and the Red Basin, however, are two of the most productive regions in the entire country.

Still farther northward, within the basin of the Hwang Ho (Yellow River), single cropping is generally the pattern, and many vicissitudes plague the farmer in this marginal area of uncertain precipitation: drought, floods, wind, locusts, uncertain and fluctuating yields, and the like. Yet, here too is one of the great river basins of agricultural production—wheat, maize, soybeans, and millets largely replace rice, and in the loess region (westward within the big bend of the Hwang Ho) is a marginal but remarkably productive area—when rainfall is right—for the growing of wheat, cotton, and opium poppies. The lowlands of Manchuria, too, are highly productive of soybeans, maize, and the like.

Although little ribbons of cultivation string along every available river valley or hillside, or small plots of rice or tea or mulberry dot the countryside wherever it is possible to make use of the land, much of China is either too mountainous or hilly, or too dry, to carry a very dense population. Hence, China's 582 million people, in general, are found agglomerated within the basins and deltas of the three great rivers.

Areal greatness has acted, geopolitically, both to advantage and disadvantage. Size has actually been a handicap to the political unification and effective control of the widespread domain throughout most of the centuries of China's history. And size, personified in the outlying provinces of Tibet, Sinkiang, and Mongolia, has not really added to the power or resource wealth of the state until the present era, for China has concentrated largely on the exploitation of the agricultural resources and not the industrial potential. However, size has been effective as a weapon of defense. One of China's greatest military assets has been "defense in depth," greatest in the west, adjoining the Soviet Union. In using "defense in depth" as a weapon, the Chinese have been ingenious; in retreating before the Nipponese advance, they changed the course of the outlet of the Hwang Ho and flooded great areas of land to delay the invaders; they moved the capital from Peking to Nanking to Chungking; and carried their factories, literally, on the backs of coolies into the Red Basin of Szechwan, where, behind river gorges and mountain fastnesses, the government and industrial production "holed in"—but did not give in. Without this capability for trading space for time, it is unlikely that the Chinese could have held out. Whether planned or not, space becomes a factor of strategy in war.

Another aspect of size having the same swallowing effect as vast space is enormous population. No invader has conquered China and maintained its identity; the Manchu successfully took over the government and established the Manchu dynasty which ruled China for 269 years (1643-1912), but, except in remote areas where small contingents of Manchurians and their families went out to border regions to protect frontiers (as along the Amur River in the north, and in the remoter districts of Western Sinkiang) Manchus, as such, do not survive. They, as a nation, have been absorbed into the Chinese bloodstream.

The climates of China are varied and extreme. Size has given China diversity of climate. But, compared to total area, it is an adverse diversity, the climate growing more and more marginal with distance west, north, and northwest, for China lies on the leeward side of the most continental of continents—Eurasia, the world's largest land mass. China is located on the side that feels the least effect of mid-latitude moderating and rain-bearing winds. Size, then, contributes a compound of assets and liabilities.

In shape, China is compact. China has no great attenuations of territory that make possession difficult, except in Manchuria. Here such an attenuation does exist. Manchuria is a thick projection, however, comprising a large area apparently not easily trespassed. But, as already indicated, this one attenuation of the Chinese domain—with its own smaller attenuation in the Liaotung Peninsula to the south—has been subjected to foreign ingression more than has any other single portion of China. The Manchurian attenuation is not so extreme as to interfere with internal coherence, however. In fact, transportation facilities are more extensive to and within Manchuria than in any other part of the empire.

Topography is, generally speaking, adverse. The shape of China, then, should facilitate coherence and unification of the state. But another element of political geography enters in to counteract the positive factor of compactness, namely, adverse topography. Towering mountains in Western Szechwan and the high plateau character of Tibet, buttressed by mountains or deserts or both, made it impossible to assert strong Chinese control over these two provinces in the past. Tibet has gone its own, isolationist way, scarcely recognizing even a tie to China; Szechwan is inhabited by little-known and often lawless tribes. China has claimed these territories, but, unable to impose its rule, the resident peoples have simply ignored—or have been unaware of—the political attachment throughout most of the centuries.

Outer Mongolia (now the Mongolian People's Republic), encompassing the great Gobi Desert and Sinkiang (the latter comprising the two desert basins of Tarim and Dzungaria), were as loosely held. As a matter of fact, it was necesary to build the Great Wall as a protective barrier between parts of the Empire—between Mongolia with its virile and marauding nomadic peoples and the peaceful, settled, agricultural populations of North China. As in the instance of the southwestern provinces these western and northwestern territories were claimed, but so loosely held as to scarcely feel "Chinese." The way of life, too, in all of these outlying regions was incompatible with Chinese agrarian habits, a factor which further separated the Chinese from their subject peoples—and made the latter populations incomprehensible to the conservative Chinese.

Not until the Manchu established their sovereignty over China did Manchuria become Chinese territory. However, during the first centuries of Manchu rule, from 1643 until the beginning of the twentieth century, Manchuria was maintained as an Imperial Reserve of the royal family. No Chinese were permitted to migrate into Manchuria; from there, the rulers drew their military personnel and retainers. The interesting—and significant—thing is, that, in spite of two centuries of attempted Manchurian "distinctness" from the Chinese masses, when Manchuria was opened to Chinese colonists, the pattern of immigration was such that the Manchurian "nation" became lost in the Chinese. In the first influx, mostly Chinese men entered. They married Manchurian women, and, at present, the Manchurian population is Chinese; the Chinese immigrants absorbed the indigenous stock so that Manchuria is as Chinese as China Proper. Undoubtedly, the similarity of environments and the eastward trend of the migration and communication routes between the two areas account for the likeness of the peoples and cultures. There are no physical barriers to separate the densely populated migration areas of North China and the fertile river plains of Manchuria; nature has facilitated movement and mixing. On the other hand, the peoples in the outer provinces have remained distinct in culture and aloof from Chinese mixture and infiltration.

Communication for Coherence and Development

From the above discussion, the conclusion can be drawn that environmental contrasts, fostering cultural contrasts, have partly nullified Chinese attempts to unify their large domain. But even within China Proper, where a more uniform culture obtains, the state has lacked internal coherence. During this century, from the overthrow of the Manchu dynasty until the Communists took over power, China was the essence of political cleavage. Inadequate transportation caused, in part, by the inaccessibility of some regions, the unfavorable topography in others, and a static society that clung to antiquated transport and communication, were largely responsible. Before 1950, the only areas of political unification were in the Si Kiang Basin and the Red Basin in the Upper Yangtze. Here, navigable waterways and scantily populated surrounding hill regions that circumscribed the basins fostered unity. Elsewhere, disruption and fragmentation have been characteristic; even the basins of the Hwang Ho and Yangtze were segmented.

The Chinese ecumene lies in the eastern lowland region where the deltas of the Hwang Ho and the Yantze blend and merge, extending upstream along the Yangtze to include the industrial Wuhan Basin and up the Hwang Ho to include the productive hill country of the loess area. In the delta region, canals and rivers have provided the needed transportation. Through here, across the full length of the double delta, the Grand Canal formed the major route of transportation until railroads largely replaced it in the present century. Rivers and canals have been much used in China to provide transportation. But, beyond collecting tribute, the Chinese rulers were not much interested in providing facilities to connect the several parts of the country. For this reason, China has been a land of disaster and starvation—because, when floods struck or food shortages developed, there did not exist adequate means for bringing rice from surplus areas to the stricken peoples. Instead, in times of flood or drought (both of which have been the cause of devastating famines in China) great migrations left the disaster areas for the south where they subsisted until conditions at home had righted themselves. The Hwang Ho, river of floods and famines, is known as "China's sorrow." Flood control and utilization of the river for controlled perennial irrigation could eliminate most of such misfortunes.

Railroads have been built in those areas already best supplied with canal and river transportation, as in the delta regions of the three large rivers; or, if they strike inland from the coast, they almost invariably parallel a river which already provides fairly adequate, though slow, transport. The great weakness of the Chinese road and railroad system is this "paralleling" of existing transportation routes rather than the construction of lines of railway and highway that transverse the east-west flowing rivers. There is, of course, a reason for the existing pattern, and that is population: rail lines have supplemented water transportation in those areas where population is dense.

Except in the ecumene, in the Si Kiang Basin, and in Manchuria, transportation was by river, or, where that failed, by animal or coolie carrier. South China is criss-crossed with narrow, steep, and often "stepped" roads, paved with stone—indicative of the beast of burden, *man*. Through the Szechwanese mountains, the plateau and desert spaces of Tibet and Sinkiang and Mongolia, caravan trails connecting the better watered and better populated sections led out from Peking to the far corners of the domain. Beyond the borders of Chinese territory, these caravan routes led, through passes, into Russian territory along the west: the Semipalatinsk gate, following the headwaters of the Irtysh, and the Ili and Chuguchak gateways leading to the Lake Balkhash district, connected Chinese Turkestan with Russian territory. Caravan trails that converged around the Koko Nor carried goods betwen China and forbidden Tibet, the caravans meeting in that region at a specified time and exchanging products; two routes skirted the Tarim Basin along the mountain edges, converging at Kashgar to pass westward into West Asia, and later, European territory. By the southern sector of the latter routes, Marco Polo "discovered" the Orient.

Except for the innovation of railroads along the eastern seaboard areas, the pattern of transportation has not changed in a thousand years. Man is still a beast of burden, competing with the animal for living space. Under the Communists, one of the first problems attacked was that of transportation and communication, for the sake of both political coherence and the furtherance of economic development.

Two kinds of transportation connections have received emphasis under the construction program of the Communists, namely, highways and railroads. In railroad building, three areas appear to have been the focus of Communist efforts: 1) in the south, where a short rail line linked Hanoi and Haiphong with a spur line connected to China's Grand Trunk Line; 2) in the northwest, where tracks have been laid from Alma Ata on the Russian side and from Lanchow in Kansu Province, the two projects to connect; 3) in Mongolia, where a line has been constructed from Tsining to Ulan Bator in the Outer Mongolian People's Repub-

lic from where it has been extended to link up, eventually, with the Trans-Siberian Railroad of the Soviets. The strategic importance of such railway extensions is immediately apparent. On later examination, the economic significance will also stand out.

The connection in the south runs between Linhsien (Linchow) and Nanning. The Nanning–Hanoi–Haiphong Railroad had been constructed by the French, and the spur from the Chinese trunkline had also been in existence; but the gap between the two, which would give all of East China access to North Vietnam, and vice versa, had never been filled. In 1955 that line was completed. The chief significance of the new rail link between the Red River delta and the South China province of Kwangsi lies in the fact that it opened up a new major sea outlet for South China, a region where communications by sea have been, normally, very much restricted. From the standpoint of immediate needs at the time of completion, the Haiphong connection provided an opportunity to bring vital imports into South China by sea without having to go through Hongkong or run the risk of a Nationalist blockade around Formosa. There has been no indication as to what sort of agreement Peking made with Vietnam for the joint use of the railway and port-head of Haiphong. But it is fairly obvious that, considering the vital strategic importance of the port outlet for all of South China, this is likely a part of the price the Vietminh were required to pay for Peking's assistance in the Indochinese civil war.

In China's vast northwest, three major railway projects emphasize Chinese determination to build an industrial-agricultural base far from its exposed coastline. The railways link Lanchow with Urumchi in Sinkiang—and with Kuldja where the Russian and Chinese lines join, and Chungking, China's wartime capital on the Yangtze, with Paotow in Inner Mongolia.

China's outer territories are predominantly settled by non-Chinese peoples. The outer territories embody a large region, sparsely populated, but equalling in area half of the United

States. Sinkiang (Chinese Turkestan) is larger than Alaska, but its population is only 4.8 million; Tsinghai has only a little under 1.7 million people. Tibet is larger than Texas and California combined yet under 1.3 million people inhabit its large domain; Inner Mongolia, wrapping itself from Ningsia to the Amur River around the edges of Outer Mongolia, has but 6.1 million inhabitants.

To the Chinese Communists, therefore, this whole area is the frontier into which, eventually, they hope to settle some of the surplus population of China Proper where the overwhelming bulk of China's millions are now crowded. From the vast unsurveyed stretches of this land, they hope to extract the coal, iron, oil, and other resources on which to build their ambitious industrialization program. Through the building of dams and irrigation projects, they expect to turn some of its unproductive wastelands into rich farmlands and pastures.

However, without a better communication network than the centuries-old caravan routes provided, none of the reputed and hoped-for resources could be developed. Hence the extreme haste with which the railway and highway program was pushed. For China, the opening of the entire Lanchow-Sinkiang Railroad means not only better connections with the Soviet Union but the speeding of Sinkiang's economic development. Crude oil already is in production in Sinkiang under the auspices of the Sinkiang Petroleum Company; the Yümen oil fields in upper Kansu province have also become more directly accessible.

Some observers have found interesting parallels between present Communist activity in the northwest and that of previous Chinese regimes. The great dynasties of the former Han and T'ang both had their capitals at Sian (the nuclear area of the Chinese Empire) in the northwest, and from there ruled an empire stretching eastward to the China seas and westward across the Kansu corridor to Turkestan and the shores of Lake Balkhash. By contrast, dynasties such as the Sung and Ming, which based themselves in the central plains, were weaker and ruled little more than China Proper.

Nationalist China, according to these observers, had based itself (like the weaker regimes in the past) in the coastal plains with the capital at Nanking. Meanwhile, the Communists, after the "Long March" of 1934, had established themselves in Yenan in the northwest and were building up a solid basis of power in the Shensi–Kansu–Ningsia border region. When the Communists came to power and established Peking (close to their newly won industrial complex in Manchuria) as their capital, perhaps they did not forget the lesson of history. And so, while, on one hand, the Communists reached out across the Formosa Strait toward the island base of Nationalist China, with the other they have pressed the agricultural and industrial development of their own Inner Asian frontiers. This strategic development in the northwest is, geopolitically, highly significant.

The new railway from Ulan Bator to Tsining near Kalgan (converging center for the old caravan routes) is, presumably, to provide transport for steel and pig iron manufactured in the Suiyuan plant to be sent to Siberia for Soviet consumption. It has far greater economic and geopolitical implications than this, however, as can be readily seen.

To this ambitious railway building program has been added a no less significant and ambitious road construction plan. Highways from Sikang and Tsinghai into Tibet have been completed providing an efficient link between China and this outer, isolationist territory. The rapid and planned development of the outer provinces underlines the determination of the Communists to unify the state, and, in accordance with the basic principles of Communist economic regional planning, to open up the great frontier along its inner borders.

Population

China's population is its most impressive geopolitical element. The Chinese population numbers, by recent Communist count, 582.6 million—almost triple that of the Soviet Union, more than three and a half times that of the United States. And it is a rapidly expanding population; one recent set of data suggested an annual increment of 12 million. Western population analysts have been dubious of this figure, however, as well as of the totals that have been officially released. Regardless, however, of the controversy over statistics, the basic and all-important demographic fact remains that the Chinese population is almost as great as that of the two next largest states combined, a geopolitical fact of a significance that cannot be overlooked. In general, also, though poverty-stricken and plagued (in places and at times) by famine, the Chinese are a sturdy, strong people used to hard labor. Further, given the opportunity—even a slight opportunity—for bettering themselves, economically and otherwise, they have invariably shown themselves capable of immediate emergence from the lower level of living.

In the past, the Chinese considered their state "the Middle Kingdom." They have the population potential for again achieving this dominant position—and to an even greater degree than formerly—in East Asia. All indications, however, point to the emergence of China as one of the world's five or six great powers if a government like the present one, with strong capabilities for centralization and unification, remains in power. Weak, decadent, and corrupt administrations made pre-Communist China the impotent state it was earlier in the modern period of history.

Population is highly concentrated. The population is concentrated in four main nodes: the loess region of North China; the Hwang Ho–Yangtze delta plain; the Red Basin of Szechwan; and the Cantonese region in the Si Kiang delta.

In religion, a number of doctrines are represented. The Mongolian–Sinkiang–Tibet outer provinces are Buddhist; throughout the rest of the country Buddhism, Taoism, Christianity, and the Moslem religion are professed. Confucianism, not a religion but a way of life, has dominated the pattern of living throughout China Proper for centuries, stamping Chinese society with a static pattern of values, personal relationships, and ritual of living that has given Chinese culture its distinctiveness. Like a common religion, this common ritual-of-living found among the Chinese acts as a cohesive force.

The Contemporary History

The postwar history of China divides into three periods: first, the conquest of China by the Communist Chinese forces, from V-J day until 1949. Given a strong initial position in Manchuria, which was occupied at the war's end by Soviet forces, the Communists, from there, swept like a flood over the rest of the country. The second phase came between 1949 and late 1954. During this period, the Communists consolidated their hold and increased activities. The village gentry and urban merchant classes were liquidated; the vast land reform program was initiated; the process of indoctrination of the youth along the lines of the Communist ideology occupied the propaganda and education systems; reconstructon of damage resulting from the long years of civil war and Japanese invasion was carried through; and those outer territories, not yet consolidated under central control, were brought under Communist sway. Tibet was the last to succumb.

The latest period began in the last months of 1954 and has extended through to the present. With consolidation complete, the Communists adopted a new constitution—symbolic of the conviction that they were moving toward permanent rule, and transition to full socialism; and they began to participate in international affairs with the confidence of a great power.

Chinese Territories Not Yet Re-Incorporated

Formosa, Hongkong, and Macao press like three thorns against the side and underbelly of China. Formosa (the Second China), an island separated from the Chinese mainland by a 100-mile channel, is the base and domain of

Nationalist China. The obvious determination of the Chinese Communists to bring Formosa under Peking authority, either by political or military means, underlines the importance which the Communist state attaches to this Nationalist-held territory. In the hands of the Nationalists, particularly if American backing is maintained, Formosa represents a standing threat to the security of Communist China. Perhaps to an ever greater degree, the island is desired for the sake of prestige. Thirdly, in the hands of the Communists, it would constitute another useful base for extending the Communist advance in Asia and in undermining the position of the West on the Asian continent and in the Pacific.

On the other side, Formosa lies within the American defense-line in the West Pacific, formed by the Philippines, the Ryukyus, Japan, and some of the lesser island groups. According to General Douglas MacArthur, the Formosan location is such that, if the island were held by an unfriendly country, it would constitute an enemy intrusion almost centering the defensive island arc that strings along the periphery of Asia; further, the island is 100 to 150 miles nearer to the lifeline than is any part of the Asian mainland.

In the past, Formosa served as a base for military operations against areas to the south, and historically, it was used by other Chinese regimes as a stronghold for attempted returns to the mainland. When Nanking fell, in 1644, under the onslaught of the Manchus, the remnants of the Ming Dynasty withdrew to Southeast China and later to Formosa from where they carried on the fight against the invaders from the north. For 38 years, until 1683, Formosa served as an anti-Manchu operational base. During one period of these four decades the Ming followers recaptured Amoy, retook large portions of South China, and, in 1657, actually attacked the capital, Nanking. So formidable was this force on Formosa that, in 1661, the Manchu decreed the evacuation of the entire coastal area of China Proper to a depth of ten miles. Not until their fleet was destroyed off the Pescadores Islands by the Manchus did the Ming cease to harass the usurpers.

What parallelism—if any—will appear between the historic and the present situation remains to be seen. Certainly the seventeenth century problem was not the same as the current one although there are common features. The latest and most consequential of military action based from Formosa was that made by the Japanese during World War II in their campaign against Southeast Asia and the Indies. The air forces supporting the Japanese army and navy in these moves were based in southern Formosa and, from 1942-44, Formosa was an important connection in the Japanese transportation and communications system that led from Japan southward through the Ryukyus and Philippines to the southeast. As American forces advanced toward the Japanese homeland, the military role of Formosa in Japanese strategy became more vital. Should Formosa ever fall into the hands of an enemy nation, stated MacArthur, "history would repeat itself."

Although small, Formosa would be a valuable addition to China economically, for Formosa is a surplus food area. Militarily and psychologically, the Nationalists on Formosa are the last hindrance to a clean sweep of Chinese territory by the Communists. Further, the Nationalists on small Formosa have been made members of the United Nations while the powerful Communist regime smarts under exclusion. These are the major reasons behind the determination of the Peking regime to obtain the island. On the opposite side, from here the Nationalists hope to regain a hold on the continent again.

The most penetrating thorn on the underside of China is Hongkong and the adjacent mainland territory of Kowloon,[2] Crown Colony of Great Britain. The island of Hongkong and the three-mile mainland strip known as Kowloon were obtained by the British from China as "spoils of the Opium War." It was not much of a cession, the one made in 1841—

----

[2] At the same time, it is as great an asset to China as it is a thorn.

simply a barren island inhabited by some 2000 fishermen. But, when Victoria's reign ended in 1901, the colony had been enlarged by a 390 square-mile area above Kowloon, known as the New Territories (and leased from the Chinese in 1898 for 99 years), and Victoria on Hongkong Island had grown into one of the great ports of the world. The latter has, at present, a population of over two million.

Victoria is a city with a quality all its own— British, Oriental, international—and its geographical position is such that it cannot escape from the forces that impinge upon it. Beside being a great commercial entrepôt, eclipsing Canton on the mainland delta opposite, it is a haven for political refugees, an important center for secret agents, and a listening post for the West for developments in China and the Far East. From the time of the invasion of the Chinese mainland by the Japanese, and more particularly after Communist forces began to envelop China, the importance of Hongkong as a listening post has been enhanced many times over. Much of the news that has seeped out from Communist China has passed to the outer world via Hongkong.

Before the war, 70 per cent of Hongkong trade was Chinese. Since the end of World War II, the British have attempted to diversify the trade of the port by strengthening ties particularly with Southeast Asia. However, during the first half of 1950, nearly 50 per cent of the island's transshipped goods continued to be exported to China and Macao, and these two political units supplied nearly one-fourth of the Hongkong imports marked for re-export. As an international port, its importance has increased greatly in the last decade; it has become a clearing house for much Asian trade. As a world port, it currently ranks eighth. All these things considered, it does not require much imagination to understand why China wants Hongkong back.

Across the delta mouth from Hongkong is a third small thorn pressing into Chinese territory—Portugal's tiny possession of Macao. Macao is a city-colony of only six square miles. It was given, by China, to the Portuguese in 1557 as a reward for assistance in suppressing the pirates that infested the South China coast. Now, however, no official relations exist between Macao and China; Portugal, far from recognizing "the people's government" in China, has not yet acknowledged a Communist regime anywhere, not even in Soviet Russia.

Nevertheless, the colony has remained on peaceful—if not cordial—terms with Peking. Apart from several incidents which occurred when Communists were clearing Nationalists from the neighborhood of Macao, no important difficulties have arisen between the Chinese and Portuguese authorities. The Macao policy must, of necessity, be one of avoiding disputes. Therefore, while attempting to avoid international involvement, the minute colony has given most of its attention to internal affairs. It huddles, however, between China and the sea—a very precarious position.

The Economic Structure

The central fact of Chinese economics is the pressure of people on the cultivable soil. The overwhelming majority of Chinese are peasants who patiently and painstakingly work the most minute pieces of land to achieve even a minimum subsistence. Conditions of crowding are difficult for the Westerner to comprehend, but, even in remote and inhospitable areas, wherever a workable spot of land is found, the diligent, plodding peasants are working the soil to the limit of their abilities. Essentially no usable land is idle. If additional acres are made arable, it will be through the application of irrigation or similar measures of conservation. In general, China is not an exporter of food products. The total agricultural picture is one of subsistence production.

Known mineral reserves in China are moderate in amount. Coal is the greatest fuel and mineral resource, and the reserves reportedly are the fourth largest in the world. Although there are coal beds in every province of China, Shensi and Shansi hold 80 per cent of this fuel reserve. Since, however, these fields lie outside the areas of greatest demand, the more accessible deposits have been exploited. The two leading producing mines are at Fushun, in Manchuria, and the Kailan reserves north of Tientsin. The Shensi–Shansi deposits remain as a great reserve for future development, and the coal is good enough for any industry the Chinese might wish to develop there.

Tungsten and antimony, two of the world's rare minerals, are found in major quantities, and, normally, China has been the world's leading producer of both ores. However, though valuable alloy metals, the world requires such small amounts of these metals that the export of these two ores will never be a source of much revenue.

Iron ore is China's most important mineral resource. The most usable iron deposits are near the Wuhan cities in the lake basin along the Yangtze, and here, the iron and steel industry of China Proper has developed. Hainan Island also has iron. The largest deposits, however, are those of Southern Manchuria, and, because of the importance of the developments of heavy industry in this area, the Anshan–Fushun district is known as China's Ruhr. In 1942, 50 per cent of Chinese iron ore was produced in this region, about one-third from the Yangtze deposits, and the rest from Hainan Island (about one million tons from the latter area).

New additions to former installations have added considerably to the capacity of the Manchurian center of heavy industry, and the Soviets have assisted in the expansion of a second center of heavy industries in the Yangtze Valley near the principal iron ore deposits of China Proper. Here was developed, in the past, what heavy industry as existed in that portion of the empire.

China's most important reserves of tin, the second ranking metallic mineral in the country, are located in Yunnan and Kwangsi provinces. In the proportion of world output China's production is small, equalling but seven per cent. Other minerals—copper, salt, mercury, and sulphur—are also found in scattered but minor deposits. Tibet has long been known for its gold and borax.

Under the Communist regime, explorations are being pushed that may lay open new reserves, but, contrary to what the world has been inclined to believe (taking into consideration present known resources), China is not the fabulously rich country that Marco Polo and other travellers have portrayed it to be. However, the future may open up new finds.

Future industrial development is difficult to predict. In the past, the manufactures of greatest importance were food-processing and textile production. At present, the population pressure on the soil is so great that, after the needed food has been raised, not much space is left for the production of industrial crops. Note has already been taken of the expansion of the iron and steel industry, but supplies of industrial minerals are moderate. It would appear, however, that China has adequate resources for the development of quite an important chemical industry, based on coal, salt, and sulphur. In general, however, indications are that China lacks the ores needed to supply a modern industrial state.

Rapid industrialization is one of the Communist goals in China; and, in achieving this goal, Peking has depended heavily on the USSR. The aim is to convert the Chinese economy into the same kind of centrally planned industrial structure, based on collectivized agriculture and government directed manufacture, that is found in the Soviet Union. Industrial and communications expansion have progressed rapidly. Old industrial nodes, as Anshan, are crowded with great numbers of newly arrived workers, fresh from the rural areas, as are also the new industrial centers that are rising. And yet, despite the great effort and importance placed on industrial development, the industry and commerce of such great cities as Shanghai and Canton are still only marginal phenomena in Chinese life; steel production is less than that of Brazil or Spain, the coal and electric power used are but fractions of the consumption in the United States despite the immense population.

The ratio of resources to population is very acute. At least in past years, the discrepancy between population and resources has been increasingly reflected in China's foreign trade. Since 1877, imports have, annually, shown an excess over exports although such items as remittances from abroad have helped to balance the deficit. What does this mean geopolitically? It means that China, in general, lacks "weapons of trade" with which to increase the nation's power and influence in the international scene. Tungsten and antimony are strategic minerals but China does not hold a monopoly on the supply, and, as stated before, these minerals are used in very small amounts—merely a few thousand tons annually supplies all of the industrial needs of the world.

The great proportion of China's trade is carried on with the Soviet Union or other Communist states. Whereas in 1950, only 26 per cent of Chinese commerce was with the Communist Bloc, today 75 per cent of the commerce is carried on with these nations. If tension betweeen the Western and Communist Blocs eases, these proportions will undoubtedly change because the Chinese market is one that is eyed by a number of Western states. Formerly, China traded heavily with the United States and Japan, followed by Great Britain, Germany, and France; a large commerce was also carried on with Southeast Asia —Indochina, Thailand, Malaya, Indonesia, and the Philippines—areas to which large numbers of Chinese have emigrated.

China has the products of the fields, the mines, and "cheap" labor to sell. Before World War II, the major exports were soybeans and bean products (from Manchuria), raw silk, wool, hides, furs, egg products, tin, antimony, tungsten, and tung oil. Not all of these can achieve again their former importance: whereas Manchuria formerly had a monopoly on the soybean market, this is no longer true; synthetic fabrics have largely replaced natural silk; Chinese hides and raw wool have been of an inferior quality and purchasers have preferred to buy them elsewhere. However, as with the Soviet Union, there may be a period of years during which China will not attempt to export much, retaining domestic products to build up the economic might and raise the living standards of the poverty-stricken people. One cannot assume, however, that this will be the pattern followed. China may need to sell in order to buy.

The foreign policy of Communist China. The international policy of Communist China falls into three spheres according to the differing relations with the states of the three power blocs of the world, Communist, Neutral, and Western.

With Moscow and the Soviet satellite states, Chinese relations have been cordial, even warm; and both the USSR and China have reaffirmed their close ties at relatively frequent intervals. But, notwithstanding this outward, and undoubtedly sincere, relationship, China has slowly but continuously loosened the links that have bound her to the Soviets. From October, 1954, when an agreement between Moscow and Peking was signed, an increasing independence of Chinese diplomatic action has been noticeable. Since then it has become evident that, within the Communist world, the Asian state is an ally with unusual bargaining powers, able to extract from Moscow very considerable concessions to the advantage of China.

The territorial remittals made at Peking by the Soviets were significant. According to the terms of the Peking Agreement, the Russians withdrew from Port Arthur in May, 1955. This was perhaps the most spectacular cession, but the pact further confirmed Chinese sovereignty over the interior province of Sinkiang which had been the object of Russian interest over many decades. Equally significant, the Soviets concurred on the readmission of Chinese influence in Outer Mongolia, a former Chinese province that had, under Russian pressure on China, been accorded an independent status.

The Peking document has now been implemented to the end that there has been a major withdrawal by the Soviets on the Soviet–Chinese frontier, one of the very few territorial retreats in the entire history of the Russian state, and a very substantial one. There was a period, not very far removed, when Moscow seemed to be adding to its domain a vast semi-circle of Chinese territory, including Sinkiang, Tannu Tuva (still Soviet), Outer Mongolia, and Manchuria. At that time American diplomacy could, and did, call Chinese attention to the fact that the USSR was the nation that was making the imperialistic encroachments upon the ancient territories of the Chinese nation. The movement of the Sino–Soviet frontier, at Peking, was in the opposite direction and China expanded at the expense of the Russians.

China and the Soviet Union are bound by a mutual defense alliance and by economic agreements which form the base of the rapid industrialization of the Asian nation and equip its army with modern weapons. The economic compact, signed by the Russians, involves financial aid and technical assistance characteristic of the American Point Four program in underdeveloped areas.

It is difficult to state just what the concessions that the Chinese were able to extract from the Soviets indicate. One thing is obvious, however—China is rapidly gaining stature as a power to be reckoned with, and, like the Soviet state, has its own satellites—North Korea and North Vietnam, and Chinese economic planning and developments indicate that these two states have apparently been drawn as closely into the Communist Chinese orbit as the European satellites have been bound to the Soviet state.

Toward the Asian and African neutrals, the Peking attitude is one of courtship. The Chinese have obviously done everything in their power to win the friendship and influence the peoples of these uncommitted and apprehensive states—by emphasizing the Chinese desire for peace and Chinese support of the independence of these peoples.

Communist Chinese policy toward the Western powers has been so vacillating that it is difficult to characterize. There are, however, certain reactions that have, to date, remained sufficiently constant as apparently to reflect basic attitudes. One of these has been a spirit of harsh and continuous hostility toward the United States. As for relationships with Britain, these have fluctuated from friendly to unfriendly at different times; always, however, there has been an element of uncertain standoffishness; at times efforts appear to have been concentrated on an attempt to bring a split in Anglo–American relations. The gesture of apparent cordiality displayed by the Chinese to the United States in the summer of 1955, in an announced willingness to discuss inter-state problems, appeared to be a slight shifting in policy. As for the present, the temper of Sino–Western relationships is unpredictable.

The unanswerable future. Many questions regarding Communist China remain unanswered—as, for that matter, do questions relative to the future policies of all of the Communist states. Will China and the USSR remain close allies? Will China, in time, become so increasingly demanding of the Soviets that the latter will break with this Asian state and seek ties with the West? Will India and China vie with each other for a place of dominance in Asia? What is the role of Japan with reference to this big neighbor? Will China eventually dominate the Communist Bloc?

No one can say with assurance what the geopolitical position of China will be in the world of nations, or what geopolitical power that nation can summon or will command.

KOREA

Korea makes an interesting study in political geography because the Korean War and the events that followed on that war brought the country to the forefront of world attention, and very close to every American. Within the decade, Korea was cut up into two small political units, each sovereign, and the boundary between the two newly created states has fluctuated back and forth across a frontier set up, by outside powers, as a temporary line along which no permanent division was initially intended. The present boundary is the result of a military stalemate—as is also the line that separates the two states of the former French territory of Indochina, namely, Vietnam and North Vietnam.

An analysis of the two Asian peninsular units brings out a parallelism that is quite unique—although there are obvious differences as well. Among the parallelisms are the facts that: both have been torn by a civil war in the last ten years that tore the national domain into two almost equal parts; both were assisted in the conflict by outside powers that prolonged the war, and, in a sense, made the countries themselves the innocent pawns of power politics; the two parts of both peninsulas are divided, not only by political barriers in the form of new divisive boundaries, but are rent apart—and drifting constantly farther away from each other—on the basis of imported political ideologies, antipodal in character—Communist and Western. The Communist states of both peninsulas occupy positions of dependence on Communist China—are, in fact, Chinese satellites (these are the portions of the former states that are Communist territory). The other parts are, theoretically, within the folds of the Western Bloc—though both South Korea and Vietnam have been restive under restraints that irritate them. Both are critical areas within the Western Bloc; Vietnam may fall away to the North, South Korea is like a small, sputtering, lighted fuse.

In order to view the Communist divisions of these new peninsular states, it is necessary to set them in the context of the whole of the former domain; hence, both North and South Korea, and North and South Vietnam will be taken up at this time.

The boundaries of Korea have remained remarkably stable. The historical Japanese name of Korea is *Chosen,* which means "Land of the Morning Calm." The name is, figuratively, descriptive of the little state for, although its political *status* has altered several times, the frontiers of Korea have not changed since the eleventh century. Throughout its long history Korea has maintained a political conti-nuity such as very few nations can claim.

The historical and political backgrounds are relatively simple. Only three dynasties (the Silla, Koryu, and Yi) ruled Korea from the year 669 A.D. until 1910. Periods of invasion and strife over the peninsula have alternated with eras of isolation during which the Koreans attempted to withdraw their little kingdom from the political arena—not always successfully. In 1910, conflicts between Russia, Japan, and China over Korea climaxed in the formal annexation of the peninsular nation by Japan. This dependent status was maintained until the defeat of Japan in 1945. The Cairo Conference promised independence to Korea; instead, the post-World War II period has been characterized by a civil war that tore the country into two parts—a war that was actually the manifestation of the struggle between the Communist and Western worlds.

In location, Korea lies on the periphery of Asia. Korea is a peninsula bounded on the north by Manchuria and the Soviet Far East, separated from China Proper by the Yellow Sea to the west, and, from the islands of Japan, on the southeast, by the Straits of Shimonoseki. The country occupies a buffer position. This fact dominates the political geography of the peninsula for, with China, Russia, and Japan as its neighbors, lying between and among them, Korea has either held a status of nervous independence or has been dominated politically by one of these powers.

More particularly, Korea hangs on the margins of China, a position that has meant its subjugation, in varying degrees at different periods in the past, to China—politically, economically, and ideologically. Though it has been a political entity during various periods in its history and though the mountain barriers that form the boundary between Korea and the larger state partially counteract the proximity of the two countries, this physical contiguity to China has had important effects upon the history, culture, and progress of the nation.

Korea is peninsular and insular. In area, Korea is a little larger than the state of Minnesota, 85,239 square miles. The country is essentially an elongated peninsula that extends 600 miles in a southeastward direction from the broad continental base of eastern Asia. It is not only peninsular, however, but insular as well, including within its territory over 3000 islands.

The breadth of the continental attachment and the elongation of the peninsula both have had effects on several aspects of Korean geography and geopolitics. First of all, on the climate, the semi-insularity of the portion lying south of the 40 degree parallel gives the southern half a subtropical or modified subtropical climate, whereas north of the line, the climate is continental as is that of East Asia to which Korea so broadly attaches. Secondly, on coherence, the attenuation in two directions— that is, the long narrow peninsula *and* the attenuated continental region bordering the northern frontier (in hand with the ruggedness of the terrain)—combine to make communication more difficult and expensive than would be true if the state were compact; political unification is also more difficult to achieve. Thirdly, on its defensive ability, Korea is vulnerable to attack because of its elongation, although mountainous frontiers and water boundaries help greatly to counteract this geopolitical feature.

Despite small size, Korea is characterized by physical diversity—diversity of climate, resources, land forms. It is from such diversity that a state gains strength. A united Korea made a "nice" geopolitical unit for, in its variety, it possessed most of the requirements of a modern industrial state, albeit small; divided, each part is less varied, for the resources of the North and South are, generally speaking, complementary.

Korea is "a land of mountains." Though mountains have in many parts of the world been the birthplace of political units—due to the protection from interference that such areas give for the cradling and development of group life—in Korea the mountains have never taken this role. The barrier aspect of the boundaries gave protection, however, for the nurturing of the growing state in the more habitable areas.

At first glance, Korea appears to be a great tangle of lofty mountains and valleys and hills. However, closer examination reveals a pattern in the topography, with well-marked differences from north to south and from east to west. The north and east have a great deal more mountainous land than the south and west, the latter being formed essentially of alluvial river plains with tongues of hills and lower mountains interposing themselves here and there.

Separating Korea from its northern neighbors are two rivers (the Yalu and the Tumen) that run in opposite directions, and ranges of mountains, the Chang Pai Shan. The principal mountain backbone of the peninsula runs south from the Chang Pai Shan close to the east coast where the slopes fall steeply and abruptly toward the sea, for Korea is a plateau block tipped higher in the east than in the west. The eastern edge, therefore, is characterized by precipitous inclines and fault escarpments separated from the sea only by a narrow coastal plain that is interrupted here and there by rocky projections as highland spurs reach down to the water's edge. To the west, it slopes off more gradually to become lowlands and river plains. The same pattern holds from north to south, *i.e.* the north is rugged, mountainous, relatively high while toward the south, mountains gradually become lower to lose themselves as hills in extensive alluvial lowlands. The divisive character of the mountains is reflected in communications and unity. While the lowland ecumene is joined by railroad, road, and water transportation, some other portions are less well served.

The west and south have virtually all of the richer alluvial lands so valuable for cultivation. On the other hand, the mountains of the north contain most of the mineral deposits and lumber reserves. These mountains, volcanic in origin and rising to elevations of 9000 feet, contain few open valleys. Hence, a great part of this northern frontier zone is uninhabited.

None of the rivers of Korea are long and most of them rise near the eastern edge of the plateau block. Those that flow west or southward are the largest and have relatively gentle gradients whereas those that course in an eastward direction disgorge abruptly down the steep slope into the Sea of Japan. For this reason there are only a few good harbors along the eastern shore while the west and south have deeply embayed coasts that, with their numerous protective islands, provide greater shelter for fishing craft and modern vessels.

People and Population

The Koreans are an ancient and homogeneous people. Although Mongolian in race and thus related to the Chinese and Japanese, the Koreans are nevertheless distinct from them. The distinctive ethnic character is found in the language. It is similar, however, to the Altaic languages of Central Asia and related as well as to the Chinese. "Korean" has borrowed many Chinese words. The alphabet might be called modified Chinese for the form of the characters was taken from those of the Chinese language. The characters, however, have been simplified and greatly reduced in number.

The racial origins of the people are veiled in antiquity, but they are thought to have migrated early into the peninsula from Central Asia. The Korean was probably the result of the admixture of people who came in a succession of waves out of Central Asia, northern China, and Manchuria. The old culture, copied from China, has declined; the present culture has become an incredible hodgepodge of the old and the new as Japanese customs were imposed upon the country and, later, the ideas of Western civilization made their encroachments.

Latest population statistics indicate that Korea, as a whole, has over 30 million inhabitants. This means a natural increase in population of about a half million annually (two to two and one-half per cent), an increment greater than that of any European country except the Soviet Union. Two-thirds of the population is found in the southern half.

In Korea, an old country and densely populated, such an increase is not desirable for it accentuates an already serious problem—how to raise the living standard to one that is acceptable with so many people crowded on so little useful land. The problems of scarcity of land and over-population are further heightened by the fact that about 80 per cent of the people are peasants, deriving their living directly from the soil. Nor does the density figure of 350 tell the whole story for by far the larger part of Korea is mountainous, with good cultivable land occupying but a minimum of the total area. The density figures are, therefore, doubled and even tripled in certain areas, as in the south and west, while the north and east tend to be but sparsely settled.

The Historical and Political Background

Korean civilization is one of the oldest in the world. Accounts take Korean history back over 4000 years to Tan Gun, the mythical founder of Korea.

The peninsula was called Ch'so Hsien (Chosen) by Ki-tze, the Chinese scholar and noble who, dissatisfied with a change in dynasty, emigrated from China to Korea in 1122 B.C. with 5000 followers. They brought with them the Chinese arts and crafts which they taught to the Koreans—the techniques of agriculture, the raising of silkworms, the construction of houses. The dynasty of Ki-tze ruled until about the fourth century B.C.

In the fourth and fifth centuries A.D., the Koreans accepted Buddhism. This new religion and other innovations introduced from the Middle Kingdom greatly influenced Korean civilization. Korea had already developed an art of its own but under Chinese influence

Korean craftsmen produced creative works of great beauty and imagination.

Historically, Korea acted as a migration-bridge. Though the Chang Pai Shan provide a formidable barrier-boundary between the mainland and the peninsula, at either end (and particularly in the northeast) two river lowlands have invited the movements of people. It is thought that the Japanese migrated to their island home from the Asian continent, in the dim past, via the Korean peninsula; the Tatars and Manchus moved in and out; and the Mongols passed across, from north to south, to use the extreme tip of the country as the jumping-off place for their attempted invasions of Japan. Transit lands have difficulty in maintaining independence, and even in cohering. In the case of Korea, which is fragmented into compartments of densely occupied plains separated from each other by areas of mountainous relief, this has been particularly true.

Korea has known only intermittent periods of independence. Thus, even during its early history, the peninsula was not free from invasion. With the overthrow of the Mongols by the Chinese and the establishment of the Ming Dynasty in the latter part of the fourteenth century, revolt against the existing authority in Korea took place and, in 1392, the Yi Dynasty was established. For two centuries after this the peninsula was comparatively free from invasion. Then, in 1592, under the command of Hideyoshi, Japan's feudal leader, the Japanese invaded Korea. Seoul and several other cities were captured. Although, upon the death of Hideyoshi in 1598, the Japanese withdrew from the peninsula, they exacted heavy tribute, thereby incurring the intense and lasting enmity of the Korean people.

The last invaders of the peninsula, until the modern era, were the Manchus. By 1644, they had overthrown the Ming rulers in China and established themselves as the reigning dynasty of the Middle Kingdom. In order to stop any aid to the Mings from Korea, the Manchus invaded that country in 1627 and again in 1631.

Relations between the Korean ruler and the Manchus were friendly, however, for Korea had, in the past, recognized Chinese suzerainty. In fact, in Chinese political thought, Korea was looked upon as a "younger brother"; its kings had obtained investiture from the Chinese Emperor. However, the Koreans now came to the conclusion that the only safeguard against invasion was retreat into isolation and so, for a period of more than two hundred years after the Manchu conquest, Korea maintained a policy of isolation from other countries, and the peninsular state became known as the "Hermit Kingdom." The only foreign contacts maintained were with the Chinese Court and some commercial contacts with Japanese merchants through Pusan. Not until 1875-80 was Korea made fully accessible to the world.

Political independence has been difficult for Korea. So closely has the political fortune been tied to China in the past that when the Middle Kingdom was weak, Korea has suffered most heavily and when China was strong the peninsular state has shown the greatest prosperity and advancement.

The Sino–Japanese War of 1894-95, waged mainly on the peninsula of Korea, forced China to accede its rights of suzerainty and recognize Korea as an independent state. Following the war, Russia, Japan, and certain European nations requested and acquired concessions of various sorts, and the period of isolation for the "Hermit Kingdom" was definitely at an end. Russian influence continued to increase until Japan went to war to check it. The Treaty of Portsmouth (September, 1905), signed at the conclusion of the Russo–Japanese War, in effect made Korea a protectorate of Japan. In less than five years the Emperor of Korea made "complete and permanent cession to His Majesty, the Emperor of Japan, of all rights of sovereignty over the whole of Korea," and, in 1910, Korea was annexed by Japan. Korea as an independent nation disappeared.

The Japanese ruled Korea with a heavy hand. And yet, under Japanese direction, the country became more modernized as Japan developed the resources and industries. The cultivated acreage increased and the production of rice, cotton, and other crops reached new highs; extensive reforestation and control of soil erosion were begun. Railroad mileage was extended, new roads built and old ones improved. The production of such minerals as copper, gold, iron, and coal was expanded, and large-scale hydroelectric projects were installed to harness the potential water power. New industries, mostly of the heavy basic type, sprang up.

The Japanese dominated the economic and political life of the country; in the main, Koreans were permitted to hold only minor positions in government and business. This lack of self-government—the deprivation of any political self-expression—hindered the development of political maturity. Also, in spite of the continuing desire for liberation and self-determination, there was a surprising amount of disunity among the Koreans. It was only natural, therefore, that the Cairo Declaration, in December, 1943, only promised independence "in due course."

The Postwar Issue of Korea

The story of Korea as an issue in global and domestic politics started with the Cairo Conference in 1943. That conference adopted the policy that "in due course, Korea shall become free and independent."[3] The second chapter was written on July 26, 1945, at the Potsdam Conference where the United States, Great Britain, and China set forth the terms for the unconditional surrender of Japan and reaffirmed that "the terms of the Cairo Declaration shall be carried out." The Soviet Union declared war on Japan on August 8, 1945, stating at that time that it "joined in the declaration of the Allied Powers of July 26," thus indicating the adherence of the Moscow regime to the Potsdam Declaration to support Korean independence.

Japan's offer of unconditional surrender and request for an armistice came on August 10, 1945, at a time when Soviet troops already had penetrated Manchuria almost to the Korean border. During the next four days the 38 degree parallel was chosen as the dividing line between the zones of American and Russian authority. North of this line the Japanese were to surrender to the Russians and south of it they were to lay down their arms to the forces of the Unied States. The decision originated in Washington[4] and was transmitted to General MacArthur.

The international boundaries have remained unchanged. The boundaries that separate Korea from its three neighbors are natural frontiers, sufficiently "barrier" in character to have been tacitly agreed upon in the early historical period. There are no records of boundary disputes. The Chinese, though they claimed a loose sort of allegiance from the Koreans, made no attempts to overstep the mountain and river divide and place the boundary farther south. And the Japanese, separated by water barriers from the Korean homeland, made but one early attempt to incorporate the territory of that country into their state.

From its earliest past Korea has had a "buffer" capacity, the whole peninsula serving as a boundary zone between more powerful states. This buffer capacity, seen in terms of a middle zone between spheres of influence and power, became especially marked in the latter part of the nineteenth century when China and Japan, and Russia and Japan, fought wars over Korea. However, in spite of intrigue, the frontier boundaries of Korea have not changed.

Because it is barrier in character, the land boundary that follows the Chang Pai Shan

---

[3] In the Cairo Declaration President Roosevelt, Prime Minister Churchill, and Generalissimo Chiang Kai-shek stated that their governments, "mindful of the enslavement of the people of Korea, are determined that in due course Korea shall become free and independent."

[4] Arthur L. Grey, Jr., "The Thirty-eighth Parallel," *Foreign Affairs*, Vol. 29, No. 3 (April, 1951), p. 483.

along the north is a sparsely settled region where there has been little inclination on the part of the peoples on either side of the line to interpenetrate the territory of the other state. It is, therefore, a peaceful segment of the frontier. Less so has been the river valley portions to the southwest (the Yalu River) and the northeast (the Tumen River). These, as was indicated, have been corridors of migration, of penetration, and invasion.

The whole of the northern frontier zone is strategic as far as the resource potential is concerned. The Yalu River provides hydroelectricity; the Chang Pai Shan are rich in forest reserves, the best remaining in Korea; and the northeast is endowed with large iron ore and coal deposits. In an era when the powerful states of the world are those that are heavily-industrialized (and when the industrialized powers are those that have iron ore and coal in combinations and in quantity), this makes the northeast a choice bit of land to dominate through alliance or to hold.

The 38 degree parallel has been the Korean boundary of greatest interest in the postwar era. Isaiah Bowman once wrote: "Frontiers are indeed a razor's edge on which hang suspended the modern issues of war and peace." In the case of the 38 degree parallel in Korea this has most certainly been true. As a wartime decision prompted by military considerations to effect the defeat and surrender of Japanese forces in Korea, the directive governing the surrender did not provide a permanent political division of the peninsula at the 38 degree parallel. During the early days of the occupation, the American commander initiated negotiations for relaxation of travel restrictions and the unification of the economy and administration of Korea. The strict interpretation by the Soviet authorities of their responsibilities over the northern zone, however, changed *into a barrier* the line that was agreed upon solely to carry out the surrender of the defeated foe.

According to plans, the occupying powers were to meet and arrange the peaceful unification of Korea. But Soviet–American negotiations collapsed. In November, 1947, the General Assembly of the United Nations established a commission to hold elections throughout the country. The Soviets, however, did not allow the commission to enter the northern zone. Elections were held in the south, and the government of the Republic of Korea was established in August, 1948. While this Government was being organized there was set up in the Soviet zone a Communist regime, the Democratic People's Republic of Korea. In December, 1948, the USSR announced that Russian occupation forces had been withdrawn from the peninsula; the United States completed withdrawal of American occupation troops in June, 1949. Just one year later there came the "blitzkrieg" invasion by North Korea. These events had the effect of freezing the zone roughly in the vicinity of the 38 degree parallel[5] into the international boundary that it has since become—a part of the borderland between the two power blocs into which the globe has been divided.

Both Korean governments claim the right to exercise authority over all of the country; each appears to adhere to the most extreme doctrines of the political philosophies of its supporters. Thus Korea, unified for many centuries, was, upon being liberated from Japan, divided along a geodetic parallel of latitude, a line found on maps and globes but one not apparent in the geographical landscape. Therefore, it is of interest to look at this line—this boundary—and examine both its geographic character and its function, present and future.

Why was this particular line chosen?

Two days after the Japanese surrender the Soviets began operations on the territory of Korea. On August 12, they made amphibious landings at Unggi and Najin, two Korean seaports in the extreme northeast just one hundred

---

[5] The present boundary between North and South Korea does not run along the 38th parallel, but along a truce-line that marks the area along which the fighting stalemated.

miles from the main Soviet base at Vladivostok.

With the Soviets already on Korean soil, it was recognized that the acceptance of the surrender of all of the Japanese forces in Korea could not be made by American troops alone. Further, while the surrender document was being prepared, other amphibious landings were being carried out by the Soviet forces at Wonsan, east coast port located much farther south than the August 12 landings. "Yet," wrote Grey, "there was still the possibility of American forces getting possession of Seoul" which was not only the capital but also by far the largest city. Therefore the 38 degree parallel of north latitude was chosen, this line passing somewhat north of the city of Seoul and south of the farthest penetration of the Russian forces on the peninsula.[6]

As a further advantage, the 38 degree parallel was a geodetic line and one that as nearly bisected Korea into two equal parts as could any regular boundary thrown across the peninsula. But, outside of that, it had little to recommend it for the line cuts across the country near the point of its greatest breadth and, at one point on the west coast, it slices off and isolates an important peninsular area from the rest of the territory of South Korea; in addition, a number of important cities are dangerously near the boundary.

Undoubtedly the most important factor influencing the choice of the parallel as the dividing line was that the boundary was set up with a purely military objective in mind, the most limited of tactical considerations, namely, the surrender of the Japanese forces to the Russian and the American troops. Therefore, it was taken for granted that the boundary would erase itself once the surrender had been accomplished. For such a limited purpose, the more obvious and clear the line the better it would be. And a parallel—a geodetic line already laid down, easily read on maps and diffi-

cult to misjudge—offered a demarcation that would be subject to fewer confusing interpretations than would any other. Although a slight adjustment of the line here or there would have made administration by the civil government less difficult, this was not within the scope of the commission's work.

As a permanent boundary division, however, the truce line that resulted from the 38 degree parallel division has a number of disadvantages. In the first place, it cuts through many minor political units. Political administrative boundaries in Korea evolved, historically, over a long period and usually were quite "natural," following river valleys, crests of ridges, etc., defining, generally, the limits of trading centers. The boundary slashes across all the main roads, railroads, and air routes, all of the main telephone and telegraphic lines of the peninsula. It does not form a boundary between differing peoples: North and South Koreans are about as different as Vermonters are from those New Englanders who live in Maine. There is, however, some cultural, physical, and economic diversity between the North and South—and this was, formerly, one of the greatest strengths of the state; today, it jeopardizes the well-being of both units, acting like a schism to keep each section weak and relatively impotent. Since this is true, the longer the line of separation persists the stronger will grow the differences between North and South. The wedge may be so widened that, in time, it becomes an unbridgeable gap—for the regional diversity that, in unity, had elements of strength for the nation, will function increasingly as a highly divisive force.

The two Koreas. The differences to the north and south of the 38 degree parallel make the two Koreas, to a remarkable degree, complementary to each other. There is contrast in topography and there are notable climatic contrasts between the two parts of the peninsula.

These variances in climate and topography bear their imprint upon the land use and population distribution patterns. Variations in

---

[6] Grey, *op. cit.*, p. 484.

length of growing season are responsible for the single cropping in the north and the double cropping of many fields in the milder, more humid south. Because of the greater extent of level—and therefore cultivable—land in South Korea, this portion of the country produces the greatest quantities of food and is capable of supporting the larger population.

But it is in the distribution of industrial resources—mineral, power, and forest—that the most striking regional disparity is to be observed. Not only are these resources concentrated in the North but, within this region, there is an extraordinary localization of those minerals needed for heavy industry, namely, iron and coal. The first of these concentrations is found around the city of Pyongyang where, within a radius of 50 miles, some of the most usable reserves of coal and iron ore on the whole peninsula are found. This is the major center of Korean heavy industry. The second concentration is far up in the northeast near the Manchurian border where estimates place the reserves of iron ore at a billion tons; in proximity, there is abundant and good coal. Scattered through the north, also, are sizable deposits of gold, graphite, copper, and tungsten while, along the northern boundary, the Tumen and Yalu Rivers have a large waterpower potential.

By comparison, the mineral resources of the southern portion of the country are meagre. The coal is, in general, of low grade, the sites of waterpower development few and scattered. Manganese, tungsten, and copper, however, occur in considerable quantity and will undoubtedly become increasingly important as the industry of the South develops. In the latter section, the products of manufacture are, in the main, light consumer goods, as textiles and processed food. The production of a recent year points up the relative position of the two regions. In 1944, northern production of coal was four times greater, iron ore 300 times, and electric power 23 times greater than in the south. In limestone and magnesite production the North also was overwhelmingly ahead.

Northern Korea produced 85 per cent of all the minerals mined while the South manufactured 90 per cent of all of the textile products.

The best forests, and by far the greatest reserves, remain far north along the Manchurian border.

As Shannon McCune states, however, it would be a misleading over-simplification to call North Korea industrial and South Korea agricultural for industry and agriculture are found in both sections.[7] Nevertheless, the fact remains that there are significant economic differences between the North and the South. This dissimilarity of economic production provided the basis for the brisk exchange of goods that was typical until 1948, for, although both portions carry on agriculture and industry, the stress is sufficiently different so that the surplus products are disparate. Hence, the North and South are economically reciprocal.

With the North and South united, there was a "jointure of strongly contrasted and reciprocal resources." (Whittlesey) This was economically advantageous for there was no barrier to trade, political or otherwise, between the two parts. Though the cleavage was not sharp, there was a variant resource and agricultural base in each portion. This gave strength and needed diversity to the state.

INDOCHINA

French relations with the territories of Indochina—Tonkin, Laos, Annam, Cochin China, and Cambodia—have varied over nearly a century of association. The ties have been those of conqueror and vanquished, mother country and colony, a loose relationship as equals within a commonwealth, and, finally, severance of all political connections between France and the greater portion of the former dependency.

It was through Catholic missionaries that

---

[7] Shannon McCune, "The Thirty-eighth Parallel in Korea," *World Politics,* Vol. 1, No. 2 (January, 1949), p. 227.

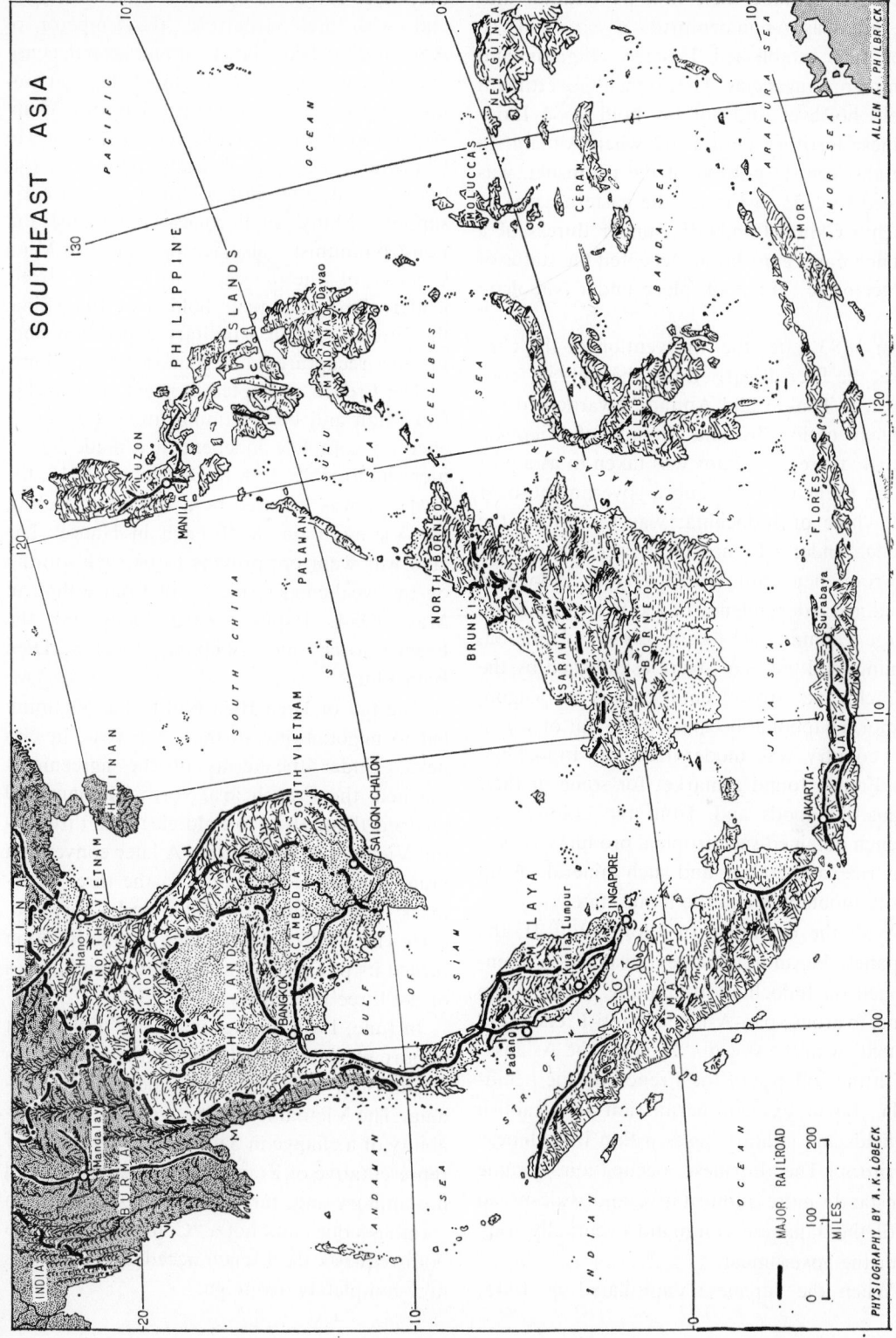

Figure 11.2. Physiography, political boundaries, and major rail lines of Southeast Asia.

the French made their first penetration into the Southeast Asian peninsula; as early as 1615 they had established Eastern religious and commercial agencies. The French Government itself, however, did not lay hold upon Indochinese territory until 1862 when Annam, in the east central portion of the peninsula, was forced to cede to France the eastern areas of Cochin China; Cambodia, under duress of a French naval expedition, accepted the status of protectorate. This took place under Napoleon III.

In 1883, after the intervention of the Chinese, the French carried out the military conquest of Tonkin and Annam, awarded to the French nation by the Treaty of Tientsin. Shortly thereafter, Laos was taken in as a part of the French Empire and a government, over the whole of Indochina, was set up by the French under a French Governor.

From then until World War II Indochina remained a dependency of the European state. Large commercial enterprises—plantation, mining, and the like—were established by the French, and urban centers, such as Saigon, Hanoi, Haiphong, became nodes out of which the country was modernized. In Indochina, the French found a market for some of their industrial goods and, from the colony, the French obtained such tropical products as rubber, rice, and cotton, and such minerals as tin —all unobtainable in the home state.

With the beginning of World War II, the Japanese began to indicate a disposition to encroach on Indochina attempting, at the same time, to arouse pan-Asian and anti-French sentiments with the slogan, "Asia for the Asians." With the collapse of the French on the peninsula, Japan exacted permission to establish airfields and military bases within Indochinese territory. The Japanese occupation became constantly more authoritative and widespread until the Japanese command eventually took over the government.

When the Japanese capitulated in 1945, they were forced to evacuate these territories and, with their departure, the Emperor of Annam, Bao Dai, abdicated and an independent government was set up under the Communist-trained resistance leader, Ho Chi Minh. At the inception of his insurrectional reign, Ho Chi Minh asked the former Emperor to act as his personal counselor; he thereby won early support. Many intellectuals—nationalist but non-Communist—also accepted Ho Chi Minh because of the absence of another strong leader. To regain their hold over Indochina, the French sent in a military expedition that, in time, recaptured a large part of the colony.

The French attempted to negotiate with Ho Chi Minh and his Vietminh forces but insistence on complete independence made agreement impossible, and, in December, 1946, the civil war was initiated by a surprise attack of the Vietminh on the French in Hanoi. The civil war went on, proving to be such a drain on the weakened resources of France that, in May, 1954, despite United States' aid, the French forces met complete defeat at Dien Bien Phu.

The fall of Dien Bien Phu to the Vietminh led to negotiations, in the same year, in Geneva. Under the terms of the agreements reached, the French lost North Vietnam and pledged themselves to hold elections throughout Vietnam in June, 1956. A later convention granted internal autonomy to the three provinces of Vietnam, Cambodia, and Laos, and, early in 1955, the French administration turned its powers over to the native authorities of the three territories.

In June, 1955, France made one of the most important political and diplomatic moves in its relationship with the newly independent Vietnam. The Vietnamese had suggested the desirability of a change in Saigon whereby the chief representative of France should be civilian and not military and, further, that he should be an "Ambassador" and not a "Commissioner." To both requests the French acceded. Vietnam is now completely sovereign.

Divided Vietnam

At least temporarily, there are two countries in Vietnam. This elongated tropical peninsula became the third country to be divided by the struggle between the Communist and anti-Communist forces of the world. The process of splitting Indochina into a Communist North and non-Communist South was completed in the late spring of 1955 by the evacuation of French forces from above and at least the acknowledged Vietminh forces from below the 17 degree parallel, the line finally agreed upon by both parties as the dividing boundary. Since that time two Vietnamese Governments have functioned with full authority in their respective domains, and the distinct characteristics and potentialities of the two political units have become ever more sharply apparent. As a result of the evacuation of enemy forces from the territories of each of the two newly created states, the French had to give up an important region they held in the North while the Vietminh were required to withdraw from large areas in Central and South Vietnam in some of which they had been established and in control for eight years. A population exchange of those Vietnamese who wished to move from Communist or non-Communist-held lands further crystallized the differing characters of the two states and consolidated authority by withdrawing what might have proven to be troublesome minorities. The provision for the balloting in 1956 supposedly laid the groundwork for the eventual reunification of the whole country. Cambodia and Laos were to take part in this plebiscite. However, it was never held.

The Geneva agreement gave the North (the Democratic Republic of Vietnam) slightly less territory but more population than the South (the State of Vietnam in the South). Although no reliable census has been taken for decades in Indochina, estimates set the population of the southern state at 10 million, of the northern unit at perhaps 13 million. The northern Vietnamese are generally regarded as the more energetic.

Both territories have big rice bowls—the Red River Valley and Cochin China. In a picturesque fashion Indochina as a whole has often been likened to two baskets of rice suspended at the opposite ends of a bamboo pole, Annam. The two rice areas are not quite comparable, however; they are, instead, more or less reciprocal for the Red Valley of the North is overpopulated and unable to supply its food needs whereas the southern bowl in Cochin China is less densely populated and is a surplus food area. In the latter region, because food is so plentiful, the land is not used to its fullest capacity; double and triple cropping are possible but seldom done. Indochina has been one of the three rice surplus areas of Asia (along with Burma and Siam). The surplus for export has always gone out from the South.

Politically and economically, the North is undoubtedly the stronger. The political structure of the North is that of an authoritarian regime dominated by the Vietnamese Communist Party and supported by the Chinese Communists. Although there are nationalist non-Communists in the North Vietnamese government—which is officially called a "coalition," responsible to an Assembly elected nearly ten years ago—the non-Communists have little power.

Economically, the Communist state has the larger and more varied economic resources for practically all of the industrial minerals are located in the northern half. However, the most important agricultural cash crop, rubber, comes from the South where all of the rubber plantations are located. (More than half of the total European cash investment in Indochina went into plantation rubber in northeastern Cochin China.)

Tonkin and Northern Annam (essentially North Vietnam) are rich in ores—coal, tin, tungsten, gold, zinc, iron, manganese, chromium, and antimony. All are well located with regard to the available labor in the Red River lowland, but only coal and tin have been exploited to date. The others remain, however, as a potential for industrial development or exchange in world trade. As far as is known, the South has only some gold and zinc. Industry—except for cotton textiles in the North based largely on imported cotton, and processing and manufacture to supply local needs—has not been developed. It was French policy to keep Indochina as a market for French manufactures and a source of raw materials for the homeland.

The topographic pattern makes coherence of the peninsula difficult. The backbone of the country, the Annam Chain, stretches almost the full length of the peninsula. Elevations reach up to 8000 feet to fall abruptly to the very narrow and interrupted coastal plains along the east, and more gently toward the Mekong lowland in the west. The mountains have been a formidable barrier to east-west communication of all kinds—people, ideas, goods; and jutting spurs of rock eastward to the coast interrupt that attenuated but constricted plain, and long stood in the way of a complete railway connection between the north and south. In the northwestern part of the peninsula and up to the Chinese border are the mountains of northern Tonkin and Laos. So difficult is the terrain in this portion of Indochina that Laos, which stretches from here southward along the inner side of the Annam Chain, has been a state almost isolated from the rest of Indochina.

The two nodes of population are found in the lower Red River Valley of Tonkin (and spreading down the narrowing coastal lowland of Annam) and in Cochin China in the south. One end of the colony was the political and plantation nucleus, the other, the industrial (such as there was). Twenty million of the 23 million Vietnamese are Annamite, the group that is also the strongest politically. Annamites led the nationalist movement which finally wrested the northern portion of the colony from France. The only minority group at all influential are the Chinese, four-fifths of whom are concentrated in the Saigon–Cholon district in the south. As in other countries of Southeast Asia, the Chinese are predominant in trade—internal and export—money-lending, and the like; the other fifth, who live in the Hanoi–Haiphong area, control most of the banking and commerce in that part of the country.

Under the French, the development of the dependency was steadily expanded—on a resource base not too great. Over-populated in the North, which apparently was the nuclear area of the Vietnam, the history of the Vietnamese has been one of gradual extension, from the north, southward. This was a slow process, because, being a people closely attached to their homes and land, they have been unwilling to migrate to new areas. Although settlement of northerners in Cochin China, on small, individually owned farms or for plantation labor, was opened up by the French, it was extremely difficult to induce the people to move. The South has been, and is, the frontier (in the sense of land not over-crowded) of Indochina and it can be imagined that no effort will be spared to encompass these uncrowded lands into Communist Vietnam. This is true despite the fact that the lands of the South are, in general, highly leached and poor except along the major streams. Poorer methods of land and water management prevail in the South than in the North.

The parallel with Korea, formerly made, is further extended in the "complementary" economic character of the two new countries. Each can survive alone; but, as in Korea, the North is the better endowed for industrial development. Population densities are reversed in the two states on the two peninsulas. The relationship of the North dependent on the South for food holds true. Both Vietnamese states can undoubtedly exist as fairly prosperous little Asian units, but united the possibilities for a well-rounded economy would be much better. According to Asian standards, the Vietnamese as a whole live rather well.

Cambodia. Occupying, with Vietnam, the southern portion of the peninsula, Cambodia is at present a separate political unit that may or may not integrate with the Vietnam. Present indications would appear to signify that it will not.

The significance of the 17 degree parallel. Trends in the political world are bound up in Vietnam and what happens there. The Communists view the 17 degree parallel of latitude as the frontier along which their ideology will advance; the West, as the boundary beyond which Communism must be confined for Western diplomats are apprehensive that, if South Vietnam falls to the North, Siam and Burma will be the next to go. The 17 degree parallel has thus come to function as a "holding line."

In the creation of the two Vietnams, France lost a colony from its large but gradually disintegrating empire. It is controversial whether or not the 200-year holding of Indochina was an asset or a loss financially speaking, probably a loss. But in the present political struggle—both between the dependent peoples and colonial states, and between the two power blocs of the world—the loss of all of the peninsula would be a blow to the West (which includes South Vietnam in its Pacific strategy).

THE ATLANTIC BASIN STATES

12

The United States

For a century and a quarter after the beginning of its history as a nation, the United States remained on the fringes of the world political arena. This was the period during which the United States wrote and implemented its Constitution, expanded its territories from the seaboard nucleus to encompass all of the lands of North America from the Atlantic to the Pacific between the 49 degree parallel and the Rio Grande. It took on the responsibility, besides, of a few outlying possessions—Alaska, the Hawaiian Islands, and the Philippines; leased the Panama Canal Zone and built the connecting waterway; and fought a civil war to keep a large part of its territory from seceding. In this way, and by other means, the young state spread, strengthened, consolidated, and unified its domain. It needed this period for growth; and, it was fortunate, in a day when transportation was relatively slow, to have been located between the two greatest oceans of the world, a position that offered security and isolation from the turbulent affairs of the Old World. Bordered on the north and south by two other young and struggling states occupied with their own "growing" problems, the United States was left relatively free to develop.

However, during this period, it went to war several times to protect the interests and rights of its nationals, as in 1812;[1] or to bring aid to other weak states that were oppressed by European powers, as in the Spanish–American War. It also ventured into the Mediterranean to suppress the pirates of the Barbary Coast who were harassing American and other shipping.

In the main, however, domestic or hemispheric affairs were considered the rightful scope of American activities: let the Old World stew in its own squabbles—the United States was far away and had no business to meddle. Many Americans objected to the taking on of extra-continental territories—as the Hawaiian Islands—and even of the purchase of Alaska, separated from the national domain by Canada.

From the cessation of the war for independence and for a long time thereafter, Americans regarded foreign affairs as an unjustifiable encroachment into their appropriate concerns, or, conversely, as unwarranted meddling abroad—and the mass of Americans were backed up in their thinking by the statements

---

[1] The Canadians call this an aggressive war.

and policies of some of the most outstanding of American political leaders. George Washington announced a policy of neutrality; Jefferson expressed gratification that the country was "kindly separated by nature from one quarter of the globe" and "too high-minded to endure the degradations of the others," and he advocated abstinence from entangling alliances. Monroe formulated a "policy of mutual exclusiveness" for the eastern and western hemispheres and succeeding Presidents further developed this strategy of national political conduct.

However, to keep the record straight it is well to point out that there were no objections raised at home to American intervention in the affairs of the territories lying adjacent to the domain of the state as then constituted nor to incorporating such areas into the domain of the United States.

An interesting parallel can be drawn between the westward expansion of the American state across the east-west extent of the continent and the eastward extension of Russian control across Asia. Both, beginning in the nuclear areas where the states had their birth, expanded the political realm *on the heels of agricultural colonists* who preceded the political extension of the state. Both continued the Pacific-ward march *until the ocean shores were attained;* both experienced *great difficulties in unifying the far-flung empires* due, not only to distance, but to difficult physiographic barriers (acting as obstacles to easy transportation) as well. Both *encountered opposition to their moving frontiers* among the resident peoples— Russia among the various Mongolians who occupied the lands east of the Urals; the United States among the Indians (handful that they were), and the Spanish and Mexicans. As the Czarist regime in Russia followed settlers into virgin lands, so many Americans felt likewise that "where the folk went the flag should follow" (Ratzel). For many Americans it was "written in the stars" that the United States should extend its sovereignty over most of the North American continent, particularly those parts that were not separated from the territories of the United States by physiographic barriers—the American people should achieve their "physiographic destiny." Illustrative of this is a quotation from the February 27, 1819 issue of *Niles' Weekly Register:*

Every man, the least acquainted with the geography of our country, must have seen that the Floridas would certainly pass into the possession of the United States. They as naturally belong to us as the country of Cornwall does to England; and, besides, the sovereignty of them was found by experience to be indispensable to the safety of our citizens—they have been to us as an enemy's country . . . and . . . ought to have been seized upon many years ago.[2]

Some Americans regarded this outward push of American power and control as inevitable and, historically, it is referred to as the *policy of Manifest Destiny.* Obviously, the onward drive of the American pioneers was not to be stopped. The governmental policy of "the flag following the folk" reached its height about the middle of the nineteenth century under Polk. In 1844 the Democratic convention that selected James K. Polk as its presidential nominee stated its platform in the following words:

That our title to whole of the Territory of Oregon is clear and unquestionable; that no portion of the same ought to be ceded to England or any other power, and that the re-occupation of Oregon and the re-annexation of Texas at the earliest practicable period are great American measures, which this Convention recommends to the cordial support of the Democracy of the Union.[3]

The Trist Treaty with Mexico, approved on March 10, 1848, under the Polk administration "must be read in the light of Manifest Destiny—'the great American disease'—which . . . was rampant in the forties. Early in 1846 William H. Seward testified that 'The popular passion for territorial aggrandizement is irre-

---

[2] *Niles' Weekly Register,* XIV, February 27, 1819, p. 4. (Published in Baltimore, Maryland).

[3] K. H. Porter ed., *National Party Platforms* (New York, 1924), p. 6.

sistible.' Under the spell of the Mexican War Senator Dickinson of New York offered this toast at a Jackson Day dinner: 'A more perfect Union, embracing the Whole of the North American continent.' Several years later one editor prophesied that before the end of the century 'every sea that laves the shores of North America will mirror the stars and stripes.' "[4]

Yet, as the United States stood on the brink of its first major intervention in global affairs, Woodrow Wilson was able to exclude from his inaugural address anything touching upon foreign policy; Franklin Delano Roosevelt, who led the nation right into the center of the arena of power politics, was able to act similarly. Only within the last generation has the United States held a position of centrality in world affairs. The move that put the nation there was one of the most striking and unequivocal changes in national policy in the history of the world.

It would, however, not be correct to say that during this era of non-intervention the United States lacked a foreign policy; and it would be just as incorrect to label that policy one of isolationism. But it must be acknowledged that, for a century and a quarter, most Americans held the feeling that the further the United States stayed out of international politics, the better—except in the case of those countries whose independence movements we backed. Americans also felt that there was a neat line of distinction between foreign and domestic affairs, and that anything that obscured the separation was unwise.

Today foreign and domestic policy are interdependent. Not only does the foreign policy of the United States determine much of the national policy but it has become decisive for the whole of the Western World as well. The conversion to the present condition was brought about only a short time ago, and before the American people were ready for it—

---

[4] Thomas A. Bailey, *A Diplomatic History of the American People* (New York: Appleton-Century-Crofts, Inc., 1950), pp. 276-77.

in a technical, intellectual, or psychological sense. The United States did not have the opportunity of a training period to get ready for this position of world leadership whereas Britain, the former helmsman of world politics, had a century in which to prepare for the role. Not only has the United States been called on to take a position of leadership in global affairs but has, as well, had to lead in the organization, and largely support, a great alliance of countries. Perhaps no state in the world has been as amazed as has the United States by its own display of strength and the part it plays in international affairs. What is the basis of American power?

Population and People

Its people are one of the most decisive forces of United States' strength. With only six per cent of the world's land area and but seven per cent of the world's population (171 million plus), the people of the United States have the highest living standards, are better nourished, and rank among the few national groups on the globe with an almost complete incidence of literacy. "Of all the great industrial nations, the only one that clings most tenaciously to private capitalism"—*i.e.* the United States—"has come closest to the socialist goal of providing abundance for all in a classless society." (*America's Needs and Resources,* Twentieth Century Fund) As employment and incomes have expanded, so have leisure and the standard of living. The general economic trend, viewed over the years, has carried the United States into a level of abundance beyond anything other industrial states have ever dreamed of. American per capita income is probably five times the average for the world as a whole.

The increase in economic production has been little short of phenomenal. According to the findings of the "Fund" publication quoted above, the American economic output has increased, since 1900, by twenty-five times while the population doubled (in 1900, the population was 76 million persons). Today the

United States produces and consumes over one-third of the world's goods and services.

Behind the exceptional economic advancement of the United States is the productivity and effectiveness of the American people. According to one source, the average increase in labor productivity, per decade, is about 18 per cent, and, according to economists, this "input" will go even higher by the time the decade of the 1950's is over, probably to 25 per cent. This production increment has been coincidental with the lowering of the number of hours worked per week per man. In productivity, there is no worker in the world that has surpassed the American; it may be equalled in some instances, as in the case of Germany.

Two aspects of the population picture have been a matter of concern to the nation. One is the declining family size (leading to a decline in the total increase); the other, the increasingly higher age-average. According to the Federal Security Agency, "since 1900, the population of the United States has doubled, but the number of persons 45 to 64 years has tripled, while the number 65 years and older has quadrupled. In early 1952 there were 13 million men and women 65 years of age or older. This number is increasing currently at the rate of about 400,000 a year." While every modern nation attempts to advance the longevity of its people, a concomitant decrease in the number of births means a population of gradually declining numbers, and one less virile. Between 1940 and 1950, the nation's population 65 years of age and older increased by 36 per cent. During the same decade, the number of births increased markedly as a result of the war. This increase will produce another "peak" about 1965 when the "war babies" become adults. But the United States belongs to that group of nations (all Western and industrial) where low fertility and low mortality rates are prevalent, and, according to the United Nations Survey, "the rate of natural increase . . . will probably be distinctly lower, on the average, during the second half of the twentieth century than it was during the first half." It is interesting to note, however, that in the first half of the present century, the United States population gained more, proportionately, than did any other part of the world. The following percentages indicate the comparative gain, during those five decades, in population: United States, 100 per cent; USSR, 93 per cent; the world, 55 per cent; Asia (exclusive of the USSR), 49 per cent; and Europe (exclusive of the USSR), 31 per cent.

The population pattern in the United States has been changing in other respects. A drop in the foreign-born reflects the steady decrease in immigration that once contributed so substantially to the growth. Compensating for the decline in immigration has been, as a whole, the better health of Americans: infant mortality has dropped from 162 per 1000 to 31 per 1000 since 1900; longevity has risen 20 years to 71 for women, 67 for men.

Different parts of the country show vastly differing population increases—indicating where the "frontier areas" of the United States have been as well as the resource and living potential. The population has moved steadily westward—a migration into sparsely populated areas. Since 1940, the population of the Pacific Coast area increased by 49 per cent, the Rocky Mountain states by 22 per cent, the East (south of New England and east of the west end of Lake Erie) by 19 per cent although the latter region is the most densely settled region in the Western Hemisphere. The Great Plains states and New England recorded the smallest increments ranging from 4 per cent in the northern portion of the Great Plains to 10 and 11 per cent in New England and the southern Great Plains (through Texas), respectively.

A second migration, in the past 50 years, has been one from rural to urban areas. In 1900, some over 60 per cent of Americans were rural and some under 40 per cent urban (39.7); in 1950, this had been reversed and 58.7 per cent of the population were classed as urban. Among those counted as rural were not only the 7 million families living on farms but another 7 million, also, who lived in villages classed as rural. The cityward movement, since World War I, was accompanied by a counter-trek—that to the suburbs. Decentralization of industry has tended to follow the latter migration pattern to the suburbs.

Americans are a multi-national people—but they are also a "breed." Culturally, Americans have become quite a smooth blend with characteristics that stamp them immediately as "American" regardless of where they travel; they are made up of all colors and races, but the stamp "American" is on all of them. It is undoubtedly because of the great mixture of strains—the drawing on the multi-national cultures, backgrounds, and blood—that the American heritage is so rich.

Location, Size, Shape

It is difficult to fully appraise the location of the United States. The geopolitical value of the protected position, behind dividing oceans, in the early history of the American nation has been touched on. The continuing friendship and reciprocal economic benefit accruing from the peaceable borders has permitted all of the people of the North American continent to live under conditions free from strain unprecedented in any other part of the world. Vicinal location, therefore, is highly favorable. A further aspect of vicinity is found in the fact that the United States touches on only two nations and hence, compared with many countries, is fortunate—if one holds to the premise that international frontiers are potiential trouble areas. In the case of the Canadian–United States boundary—3,987 miles in length—is found one of the most pacific border regions within the political world. In Canada, the United States finds its greatest customer for American goods, and, in turn, buys more from Canada than from any other single state. In international affairs, the history of the two states has been, in general, that of seeing eye to eye.

The location is continental and maritime, an unusual combination not true of many states. This has led, in turn, to the development of a dual national interest—continental and maritime—and a broadened economy and economic outlook.

The United States faces on the world's two greatest and most travelled oceans in a latitude where the seas are free from ice the year around, and in the northern hemisphere which means proximity to people and therefore to trade. And American trade is worldwide. The maritime interests are further evidenced in the fact that the United States has the world's second largest merchant marine, exceeded by Britain, followed by Norway. It has also one of the largest of the world's fishing fleets, and the fish caught annually by United States fishermen reach, perhaps, the highest value of any national catch in the world today (although in the pre-World War II period, Japan ranked first and the United States second).

Its continentality is demonstrated in a number of ways. It occupies a central position on North America, covering one-third of the continental area. Climatically, the different regions reflect its position on a large land mass for the climatic contrasts, from east to west, are as marked—and really more so—than those induced by latitude. Differences in climate from north to south, and from west to east, however, have provided a varied setting for a highly diversified agriculture; no country in the world has such diversification because the climates of the United States range from the subtropical wet and dry, and desert regions, to mid-latitude semi-arid and arid to humid continental (corn belt type) to the almost constantly moist marine regions of the northwest. Only a nation with a wide west-east span *and* a broad band of latitude (the United States stretches from 24.33 degrees north, at Key West, Florida, to above 49 degrees in its northernmost point at Lake of the Woods) could possess such potentials for agricultural diversity. In fact, so diverse were the farming conditions in the early South and North that two contrasting systems of agriculture developed—mixed farming in the North, plantation-slave agriculture in the South—that almost rent the Union in two in later years.

A further indication that the United States is continental as well as maritime is shown in the interest displayed in developing the "land" resources. It looks to the sea—and its coastal people are, at least in part, maritime—but the major national economic effort is with the development of the domain. Several superlative examples of this development of the land are found in its tremendous agricultural production, in the close network of land communications of all sorts, in the exploitation of its mines and forests, the raising of millions of animals on the grasslands of the state, and, perhaps above all else, in its vast development of manufacturing industries. Although its largest and most important cities are coastal or Great Lakes' ports (with the dual function, generally, of port and manufacturing industries), the whole of the American domain is dotted with urban centers; there are ten cities over 800,000 in size (ranging from Boston, at about the latter figure, to New York with over 7.8 million); and the 1950 census showed 874 centers with a population greater than 15,000. Each of these is an industrial or trading center (or both) of greater or lesser importance.

The United States is the fourth largest nation on the globe. The American state is not quite two-fifths as large as the Soviet Union and but slightly smaller than Canada, China, and Brazil. However, from the standpoint of usability, the American domain, percentagewise, is better off than any of the four larger states. It has tillable land about equal in amount to that of the USSR (farm land in the United States comprised 1.14 billion acres in 1950); nearly one-third of its territory is in forest (and while its timberland acreage does not equal that of three of the larger nations, the forests are, generally speaking, of good commercial timber and relatively more accessible); it is richly endowed with mineral resources, and grazing lands; it has nearly 5000 miles of oceanfront indented with many large natural harbors. Although both Canada and the USSR have more miles of ocean frontage, compared to that of the United States, theirs is relatively much less usable. The United States is, furthermore, large enough to have defense in depth—although this geopolitical feature of size has never been tested out in the United States; and, secondly, one might well ask, does any nation have defense in depth in an air and atomic age?

In form, the United States is compact. The American domain is comprised of over three million square miles of contiguous land area. Only in Florida is there a protuberance that might have proven unwieldy. However, physical features of the terrain stood in the way to easy and early national coherence and unity. At one period the Pacific Northwest threatened secession due to its position of isolation on the western fringe of the continent and the time consuming and dangerous sea-and-land travel that was necessary to make connections with the core in the east. The route consisted of a sea voyage to the Isthmus of Panama, portage through the malarial jungle to the opposite side and, from thence, travel again by ship. In fact, had the people of the United States spread across the wide American territories with only animal traction, rough trails, and mail to bind them, it seems likely that variations in physical conditions would have created great differences in culture and interests—eventuating also in differences in dialect and the like. The difficulties and inconveniences encountered in making the journey to the capital to attend the sessions of Congress would have become so taxing with distance westward that the Union would inevitably have fallen apart into a disjunct league of almost independent and dissimilar countries.

The river steamer, the railroad, and the telegraph appeared in time to prevent political distinctiveness and disunity. The populating of the country was hastily completed through the use of modern means of communication. The United States became the prototype of the modern "transport" nation, more aware of its coherence than any state the world

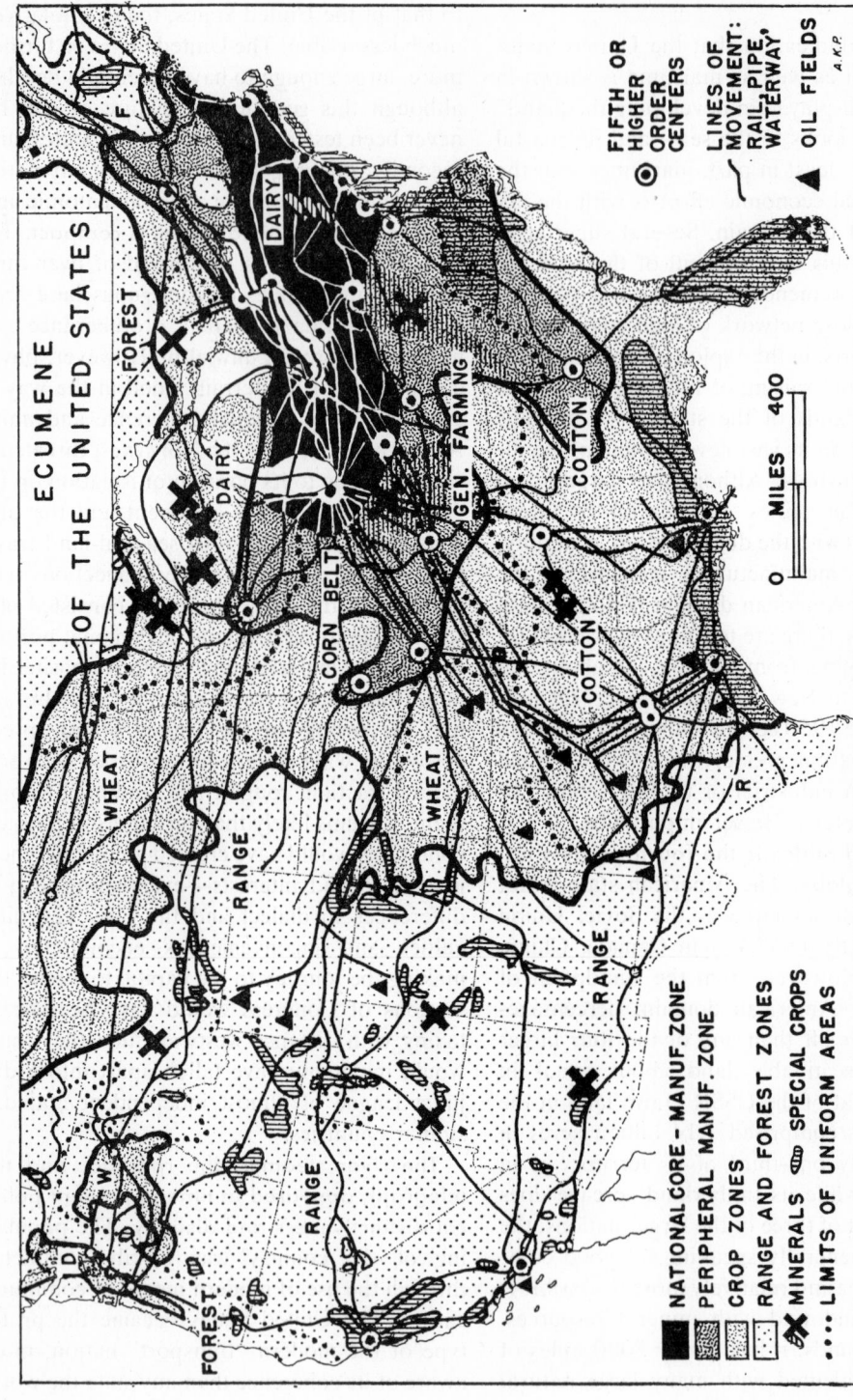

Figure 12.1 United States east of the Mississippi River and, the Northeast particularly, comprises the ecumene of the country. More than two-thirds of the industrial production and workers are amassed here. The may also indicates the high concentration of urban centers and transportation connections in half of the nation. The heart of American production is here, the Northeast, and of farming and dairying in the eastern (Courtesy *Economic Geography*.)

had seen up to that time. Until the past quarter century, perhaps only the British Empire has made such efforts to draw the parts of the state into a unified whole. For the past near-hundred years, the impulsion in the united American states has been not to drift apart but to draw always more closely together, assimilating the individual states into an ever more closely coherent national whole; instead of differences between the different regions becoming more distinct, the peoples of the United States grow more alike. It was through the cohering influence of the most closely knit communication system in the world that this has been achieved.

Regional divergences of interests have developed differing outlooks. Even so—with several transcontinental railways crossing the country from east to west, with air and highway connections tightening the transportation web, and telephone and telegraph adding intricate interconnections—because of the size of the state and the barrier aspect of the Rocky Mountains, the United States falls into two (or three) divisions with differing viewpoints and outlook. The area east of the mountains faces east; its trade and interests look to the East Coast and across to Europe. (From the foothills of the Rockies to the Atlantic this holds true, exemplified in the fact that Chicago acts as the great market and entrepôt center for all of the Great Plains and Corn Belt regions.) On the other hand, the Pacific Coast states—Washington, Oregon, and California—look west and northwest to Alaska, the Hawaiian Islands, and the Orient. For those living on the West Coast, there is a "feeling of separateness" from the problems of Europe, and "the Coast" is wrapped up in the dilemma and challenge of the Pacific area; contrariwise, in the East, Pacific problems receive relatively less stress than do the European, although, because the national capital is located in the East, the outlook, as a whole, is broader.

Both the Pacific and Great Lakes–Atlantic coastal regions are, however, *urban-maritime*—hence, international and cosmopolitan—in their outlook, as are also the Gulf Coast states. Against this urban-maritime division is another that bears reference—a region quite distinct in viewpoint due to the continentality of its location, namely, the midwest, or the *farmcontinental,* comprising the eastern and western highlands regions and the interior plains. In this area are concentrated what "isolationist" sentiments as remain in the United States. Facing the shores of neither ocean, the view is circumscribed and reflects itself in the political point of view of the people. Interests are local or national—rarely international; here is the most conservative section of the nation.[5]

The third of the three major regional divisions is "the South," conservative, and distinct, because of the heritage that plantation and slave agriculture left to it. This section is perhaps not comparable to the East and West with their differing international interests but is perhaps more similar to the Mid-West. It is not, however, isolationist.

The American Domain

The United States has developed into one of the greatest "power" centers in the world. It is likely that the United States is at—or on its way to—the peak of its achievements; the American nation might be likened, today, to Rome in its day of glory. Economic and political tentacles stretch out from the nerve center of the state, in the eastern ecumene, to every portion of the globe.

The nuclear center of the nation was in the thirteen original colonies. The colonies were grouped along the eastern seaboard between the Appalachians and the shore. Royal grants of territory—which were the base on which the colonies developed—extended inland, however, at times well beyond the mountains. The logical expansion, therefore, was inward across the mountains, and, concurrently, the consolidation of territory among the colonies. The new state followed this pattern.

---

[5] From the outbreak of the Korean War, which centered the attention of all Americans on the Orient, these distinctions (highly generalized) have been somewhat blurred and the international outlook of the American people, as a whole, has broadened in scope.

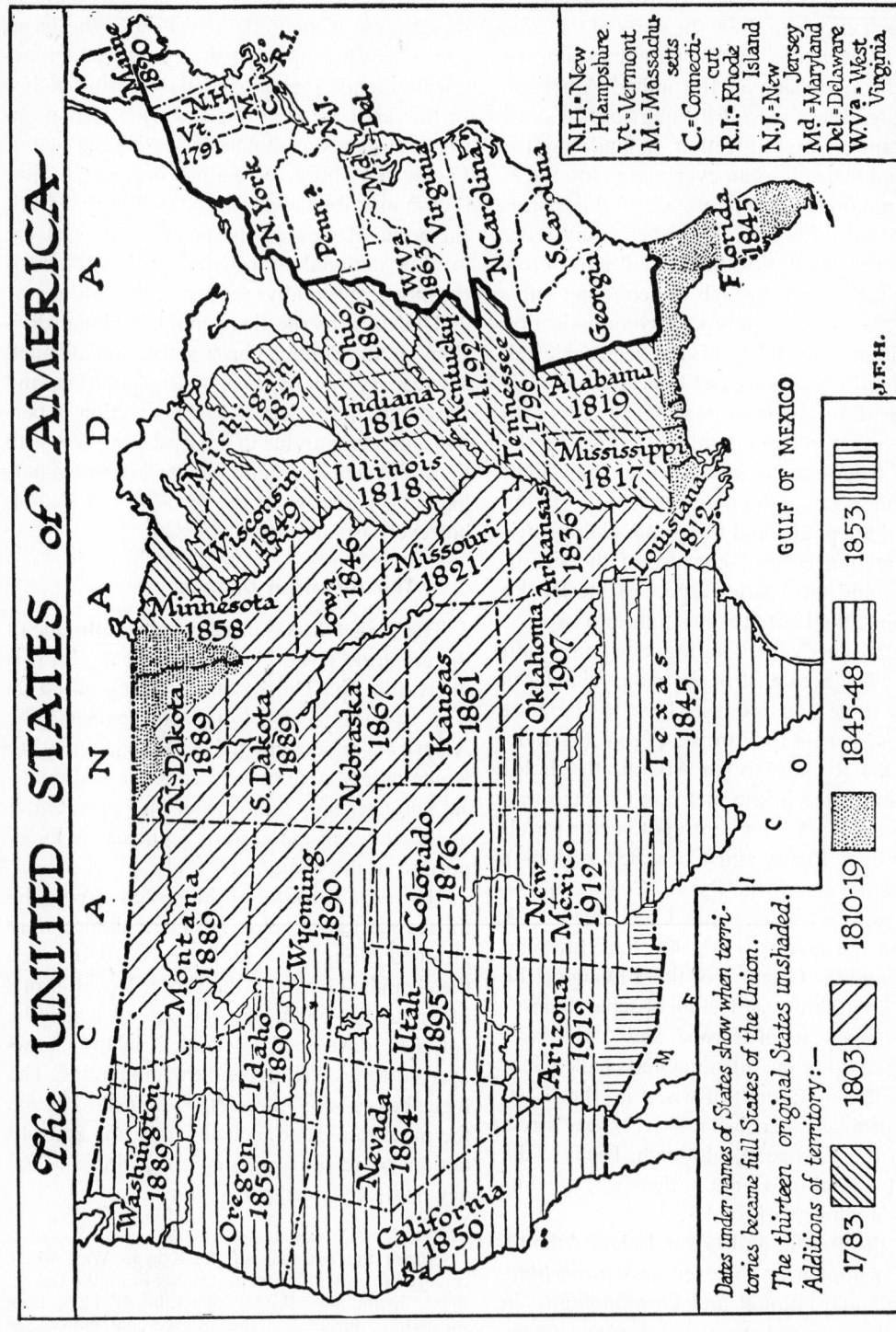

Figure 12.2. Territorial Extensions of the United States. (By permission of J. F. Horrabin.)

The combined area of the original thirteen states at the time of their union, in 1790, was 850,000 square miles, the population, 3.9 million (Indians on reservations not included). New York, Virginia, Massachusetts, Connecticut, South and North Carolina, and Georgia had extensive claims to western lands as far as the Mississippi River. By 1802, these claims were all resigned to the United States Government which organized them into "preparatory" states, or territories.

The remainder of American territorial acquisitions has been made in a number of ways. The nation has acquired territory by: 1) purchase (and the United States has acquired more territory by purchase than has any other nation); 2) right of discovery, exploration, and settlement, as in the case of the Pacific Northwest; 3) annexation upon request of the territorial inhabitants, as the Texas annexation in 1845; and 4) cession from foreign states following military conflicts.

Louisiana was purchased from France in 1803 for 15 million dollars. The area comprised 1.2 million square miles, embracing essentially the region between the Rocky Mountains and the Mississippi River and extending from Canada to Texas. In 1819, Spain ceded Florida to the United States for the nominal price of 5 million dollars—an area of 59,268 square miles. In the Florida Treaty, a settlement was made for the area now embracing the whole of Oregon, Idaho, and Washington, and small parts of western Montana and Wyoming (on the basis of previously mentioned claims). Texas, having seceded from Mexico and for a time an independent country, was, in 1845, annexed to the United States. The annexed territory included 375,239 square miles and now forms the states of Texas, eastern New Mexico, and portions of Oklahoma, Kansas, Colorado, and Wyoming. Through the Mexican Cessions of 1848 and 1850, the United States acquired 545,783 square miles of land now comprising California, New Mexico, Utah, Nevada, part of Colorado, and the northern part of Arizona. In payment the United States gave Mexico 15 million dollars, and, for settling the claims of private citizens against Mexico, 3.2 million dollars. In 1854, the Gadsden Purchase secured 45,535 square miles of territory for the United States at a cost of 10 million dollars. The area of this purchase is located in southern Arizona and New Mexico. Thus the American state, in 75 years, had extended its frontiers—except for a few boundary adjustments—to those of the present.

After the consolidation of the continental domain, the United States gradually acquired several territorial dependencies. The first, Alaska, was ceded by Russia in 1867 for 7.2 million dollars—an area of 590,884 square miles. For 20 million dollars—and as an aftermath of the Spanish-American War—the United States purchased the Philippine Islands, some 3000 in number and with a combined area of 115,026 square miles. In 1898 and 1899, Spain also turned over Puerto Rico (3,455 square miles) and Guam (210 square miles). In 1900, the Territory of Hawaii, an independent republic that had applied for admittance to the Union over a period of years, was annexed. The total area was 6,449 square miles. Tutuila Island, Samoa, was acquired in 1900.

Thus, by the turn of the century, the United States had purchased, roughly speaking, 2.9 million square miles of territory for 85.4 million dollars. Since that time, several further additions have been made—the Virgin Islands, the Pacific Trust Territories, etc. Today, the United States proper covers an area of over 3 million square miles; with its possessions, the domain equals about 3.7 million square miles, an area larger than Brazil.

However, large though the American territories are, the expression of the domain of the United States goes beyond land holdings. It is represented in the new frontiers of activity that Americans are pushing in all parts of the world—naval, air, and military bases, technical aid, dollar grants and loans, and investments—private and public. In Europe, the country is deeply entrenched. These new frontiers, however, are of a different nature than the frontiers that bound the territorial domain. The latter delimit the regions within which American political authority obtains; the former mark the limits of American influence and aid.

In Europe and Asia, Africa and South America, the American capability for shaping the local political scene is limited. However, as demonstrated in many areas, complete non-interference is an illusion. American power and its degree of involvement around the globe makes the United States a more significant force in local politics than is normally true of the techniques and practices of conventional diplomacy.

Boundaries

To say that American boundaries have been some of the most peaceful and politically stable frontiers in the world is not to imply that they did not hold all of the explosive potiential that characterizes many international border areas. On the United States-Canada boundary alone, "at least seventeen treaties, conventions, and protocols," between 1782 and 1925, were necessary in order to lay down the frontier as it stands today. There were two arbitrations, and a number of international commissions were appointed "to settle details in dispute relating to interpretation of treaty provisions." The boundary dispute in the Oregon Territory, which had aroused the slogan "Fifty-four forty or fight," was settled in 1846 between Britain and the United States with the boundary set at the 49 degree parallel. The strongest claim the United States had to the territory was the presence of about a thousand settlers. Most disputes, however, arose as a result of the discrepancy between the actual physical conditions at the site and the inaccurate maps and information on which the territories were allocated. "The making of the boundary between Canada and the United States provides many illustrations of the difficulties encountered by treaty-makers in defining 'paper boundaries based upon insufficient surveys.' The controversies regarding this boundary, much of which was established antecedent to settlement, origi-nated in the difficulties of finding on the face of the earth the rivers, highlands, and divides which corresponded with the terms of treaties and other diplomatic instruments."[6]

On the United States–Mexico boundary, most of the recent problems have been those deriving from water rights and water diversion, and the changing course of the Rio Grande whose waters mark the international frontier. The stabilization of the demarcation line has required the establishment of a permanent boundary commission that handles all problems that arise. However, this southern boundary was a product of conquest. The United States and Mexico waged several wars over it —in fact, not until the second quarter of this century did Mexico and the United States do a diplomatic turnabout and fight on the same side. Although money was paid for territorial allocations, the cessions were forced on Mexico as the result of the unfavorable outcome of military conflicts. These wars were not, however, the devastating, lengthy, and continuous conflicts that have characterized the settling of some European boundaries.

Resources and Industry

The United States is rich in natural resources—soil, minerals, forests, water, wild life. Varied and plentiful as have been—and are—American resources, the "abundance" has been carelessly applied; in fact, there has been what might be called a disquieting destruction of the resources of this nation. In many countries populated by Europeans, the "intensity" of resource waste has been as great, but in none does the scope and immensity reach the proportions found in the United States. Although, in certain aspects, other parts of the world have destroyed existing reserves as ruthlessly as was the handling in this nation —as the grass, soil, and water resources of South Africa, or the deforestation in parts of Canada—the destruction was generally confined to a smaller area or to one resource.

The primeval abundance of colonial America engendered the fallacious impres-

[6] Boggs, *op. cit.*, pp. 31-54.

sion that the resources were inexhaustible. The forests stretched out so endlessly as to be a nuisance; cultivable land seemed unbounded. No individual could begin to take inventory of even one resource and it was not until late in the first quarter of the twentieth century that a systematic survey of the natural reserves of the United States was inaugurated. The inventory indicated the extent of the wanton destruction. In hardwoods and white pine,[7] the former were cut to clear the corn belt lands for farming, the latter exploited for commercial timber. Large areas were despoiled of topsoil, washed into the rivers and sea by water erosion, through deforestation of slopelands, over-grazing, and such farming malpractices as single cropping in the cotton and tobacco belts. Vast wind-eroded dustbowl areas resulted where plowed grasslands laid the soil open to the devastating action of strong winds. The decrease, or extinction, of bird, animal, and fish life in the offshore waters and the often wanton exploitation and use of minerals seriously impaired the resource base of the country. Today, the "myth of inexhaustibility" has been eradicated to a large degree for the conditions that fostered it have altered.

It is fortunate for the American state that the natural abundance was so great. Despite use and misuse, the United States is still one of the most naturally rich areas in the world. It adds nothing to a geopolitical analysis to say "the richest" for any such statements are hypothetical in the face of the fact that, all over the globe, new and potential resources are being uncovered by exploration and *by science*. It is sufficient to say that, with judicious use and by supplementing the American supplies from foreign sources through exchange of surpluses, the United States still has the resources—mineral, forest, soil, fauna, and human—to maintain a position of great power for a long time to come. Only a few areas in the world are abundantly supplied with minerals. One of

these is the United States' domain; the others include the USSR, middle Africa, and Canada. Although there are other regions of small, highly concentrated mineral deposits, as Bolivia, Kuwait, Indonesia, the Ruhr, etc., the four areas previously mentioned are on so vast a scale, spatially speaking, and so rich and varied in resources that, at present, no comparable areas under one power are known.

The United States has excellent reserves of all of the traditional fuels as well as the raw material for that new source of power, the atom. Including lignite—which as yet remains almost untouched in this country—the United States is supplied with *coal* to last, at the present rate of use, for 3500 years. Much of this is good industrial coal, bituminous or anthracite. The United States produces annually about 525 million tons of coal, a production nearly twice as great as the world's next largest producer, the USSR, and more than twice as great as that of West Germany, ranking third. Twenty-seven per cent of the world's coal is supplied by the United States.

In the production of crude petroleum the United States also ranks first, the annual output since 1950 comprising over 50 per cent of that produced in the world. Although the output continues at a tremendous pace (succeeding annual outputs exceeding previous ones), new finds more than make up for the "take"; the December, 1951 reserves exceeded the December, 1950 reserves by 2000 million barrels. However, petroleum is an exhaustible resource, and, at the present high rate of consumption, the lifetime of American reserves are, of course, limited.[8] However, new sources of energy—as atomic—will help to alleviate any shortage that may develop or serve as items of exchange for petroleum and petroleum products. Further, private American enterprise has more capital invested in foreign oil proper-

---

[7] The present policy of balanced timber-cutting, the replanting of forests, and the like, indicates how much progress conservationists—beginning about the turn of the century—have made.

[8] There are two contrasting schools of thought regarding the extent and life of the petroleum resources of the United States. One is represented in "the philosophy of abundance" held by Eugene Holman and other domestic petroleum leaders, the other in "the philosophy of scarcity" as subscribed to by William Vogt.

ties than that of any other nation. Improved methods of bringing the oil out of the ground mean that a greater percentage of recovery is constantly possible.

In natural gas the United States is well supplied, although this may be the first of the fuel resources to run out for there has been extravagant waste, both in the amount that escapes in association with oil drilling, and in unknown seepage from vents in the earth. It is colorless and odorless, and hence can escape unnoticed. Today, however, the United States is storing or using 95 per cent of released natural gas. Although the American domain is estimated to have but a little more than five per cent of the world's potential of water-power, it has made better use of this important fuel resource than any other state (with the exception perhaps of Switzerland), having 28 per cent of the world's developed hydroelectricity.

It is not possible to state just where the United States stands in uranium resources and atomic development in comparison with the few other states engaged in atomic research and development. Up until mid-1955, all such mineral reserves and developments were highly secretive. However, the United States is well toward the front, if not the outstanding possessor, of atomic mineral resources and developed power. Atomic weapons' research and production received the major emphasis for the first decade of development; however, the present trend is the "atom for peace"—without neglecting the former defense aspect. Nuclear power is one of the most critical factors in the possible success of inter-planetary research. It is a new power field just unfolding and, at present, the potentialities look so great as to justify the term "possibilities unlimited." How far it will replace traditional energy sources remains to be seen.

The United States is the world's leading producer of iron and steel. "Power," in the political world, depends to a large degree on the industrial capacity of a nation, and industrial capacity, to a large degree, is roughly equivalent to the iron and steel production of a state—for on the production of steel depends the output of machines that make industry (and hence, power) possible. The basic metal for steel production is iron ore. Of this mineral the United States produces from 40 to 50 per cent of world output, this production being more than twice greater than the next largest producer, the USSR, and many times over that of the next near competitors. The same condition holds true for pig iron and steel production.

In the United States there are three major steel producing areas and three or four minor districts. The Pittsburgh–Youngstown–Upper Ohio River district in Western Pennsylvania and Eastern Ohio normally accounts for about 40 per cent of United States production; the Chicago–Gary–Indiana Harbor and the East Pennsylvania–Baltimore–Sparrows Point districts each produce about 22 per cent of American steel; the Lake Erie ports (Cleveland–Buffalo–Toledo–Detroit) and the Birmingham, Alabama, areas put out about 8 and 5 per cent of the steel, respectively. In the west, there are several scattered, small producing centers that, combined, account for approximately 5 per cent of United States steel (in Colorado, Utah, California, and Seattle). Of the four eastern industrial centers, all but the East Pennsylvania–Baltimore–Sparrows Point district use local coal and Lake Superior or East Canada ore; the Baltimore center depends entirely upon foreign ore for its supplies—Canada, Brazil, Chile, and Venezuela, principally.

Of the alloy metals necessary to produce quality steel, the United States has supplies of some, must import others. Some of the most conspicuous lacks are manganese and tin, nickel and cobalt. However, within the Western Bloc, large quantities of all four of these minerals are found, and, in the case of nickel, the most extensive deposits in the world lie in Canada, a few miles away from the eastern United States industrial centers. Some other alloys, as tungsten and antimony, are also almost absent within the American domain but such small quantities are required that the supply of these does not constitute much of a problem. However, in time of war, the supply of all of these strategic minerals becomes critical for long "supply" lines are necessary to transport them to American shores.

In copper, lead, zinc, molybdenum, bauxite, sulphur, the mineral fertilizers and chemical minerals, the United States is well supplied as the following figures—representing United States percentages of world production—indicate.

Mineral	Per Cent of World Production	World Rank
Molybdenum	84 per cent (mostly from Climax, Colorado)	1
Copper	32 per cent	1
Lead	20 per cent	1
Zinc	22 per cent	1
Bauxite	18 per cent	3
Sulphur	91 per cent	1
Phosphate	50 per cent	1
Magnesium	47 per cent	1
Nitrogen compounds	30 per cent	1
Potash	27 per cent	1

(West German production of potash is almost as great as, and the combined production of East and West Germany would exceed, that of the United States.)

Like steel, aluminum is another structural product of high value, actually competing with steel in certain fields, as in the aircraft industries. Out of a total world production of 1.8 million tons, the United States produces about .75 million tons; Canada is the next larger producer, followed by the USSR.

The United States holds an outstanding position in power resources, basic industrial minerals, and industrial output. As the world's largest producer *and* consumer of industrial goods and agricultural produce, the United States is again in an enviable position, for, in a day when most other industrial nations are clamoring and competing for markets, the United States, with its tremendous continuing and increasing production, has in the high-living American public its own best and sure market. "Market" is another reason why living standards should be raised in other parts of the world, for high living standards, by creating a high demand, increase the productivity, prosperity, and power of a state.

The Geopolitical Power of the United States

The physical characteristics of the American domain are a source of geopolitical power to the nation. Once the divisive aspect of natural barriers had been surmounted in the efficient network of communication and transportation, the marked contrasts in the environments of the several regions provided a diversity that gave a strength possible only in a territorially great nation. The addition of the outside possessions further contributed to this diversity for they spread from the tropic to the Arctic realms. The influence of climate reflects in a varied occupational and produce pattern.

The geopolitical power stemming from location, shape, space, and population is to be observed in several aspects of the present state. The long period of incubation and development, not without internal stresses and strains, was relatively free from foreign interference due to the isolating effects of the oceans. Had the United States occupied a position to vicinal countries comparable to Poland, let us say, the century-long period of growth might have been cut short—or, at least, sporadically interrupted by imperialistic moves by the world political powers. Although occupying the central position on a continent, the location—at least, the early location—was in effect insular. Just as invasion of England or Japan is premised on amphibious capacity—an effective landing and consequent inland push, lengthening the lines of supply and requiring several transshipments—so would attempted conquest of the United States have to be patterned. Although the United States carried out a miraculously effective amphibious war in the 1940's, waged on two fronts widely separated from the "arsenal" on the American continent, nevertheless the principle always holds true that the greater the length of the supply line, the less effective the operation. To effect success in the Asian and European sectors and in the offshore bases (as England and Australia) required planned and executed logistics on a scale never before attempted. Perhaps Hannibal, when he crossed the Alps to invade the Italian Peninsula, performed a comparable feat considering the stage of technological and scientific knowledge of that period.

However, the location is not invulnerable particularly with developments in land, sea, and air communication nullifying, as they do, the isolation factor. Flying time from one part of the globe to another is short. Air power, it has been pointed out, has changed the geopolitical function of the Arctic Ocean, reversing its role from that of an impassable barrier to a "mediterranean."

The position of the United States is vulnerable on a further point. Indispensable to the functioning of the two ocean navy of the United States, and hence to national security, is the Panama Canal, a pinpoint on the globe and highly vulnerable in the present era. Strategically and economically, as a unifier of the American East and West and as an essential part of the foreign supply route of the nation, its destruction could have serious crippling effects. The position of the United States as a Pacific power rests, to a large extent, on the Panama Canal—or some other connecting waterway across the divisive isthmus of Central America—because of the fact that the industrial core of the nation lies from 2000 to 3000 miles distant from the Pacific Coast and is separated from it by high mountains.

The social and political structure of the United States has advanced the geopolitical strength of the state. The individualism of the thirteen original states and the tenacious clinging to states' rights, the divergent interests of geographic regions developing into strong feelings of sectional coherence, led to expressions of separatism several times, reaching a culmination in the Civil War. But so adaptive was the Constitution, so representative the flag, that, difficult as was the history through which the young state passed, it gradually cohered as a strong union populated by a people with firm ties of "nationality." Those powers that could be left with the states remained as "states' rights"; those that touched on the welfare of the whole country were allocated to the federal government.

The government "of the people, by the people, and *for* the people" extended benefits of a semi-socialist character when, in the mid-thirties, the "welfare" state was introduced. In the field of economics the federal government has also shown certain socialist tendencies—in state-owning of power and munitions plants, in granting personal loans, in controlling production (instituted during the war period and retained), in sponsoring scientific research, and by encroaching on education (long considered a function of the separate states). In general, however, it is a capitalist nation—more so than any nation in the world—and the policy of government is not to compete with or stand in the way of individual enterprise. The social and political structure of the United States meets the ideal of "equality for all" as well as—perhaps better than—that of any other country.

Foreign Policy

Some of the indecision that has characterized American foreign policy stems from certain aspects inherent in the political structure. Although "the conduct of foreign relations is a function of the President" acting through the Secretary of State, and, although this right of the President allows broad powers, in certain respects presidential action is limited by legislative review. Treaty ratification, for example, requires a two-thirds vote of the Senate or it is automatically rejected. Conduct of American foreign policy, therefore, is limited by this "security check" as well as by the attitudes and responses of other nations. This latter behind-the-scenes check puts the United States, as the designer of present-day Western international policy, in a difficult position.

The foreign policy of the United States, both global and regional, has a strong geographical and economic base. Just as there are few features of the American economy and society that do not affect the military strength and few military decisions that do not have economic and social repercussions, so there are

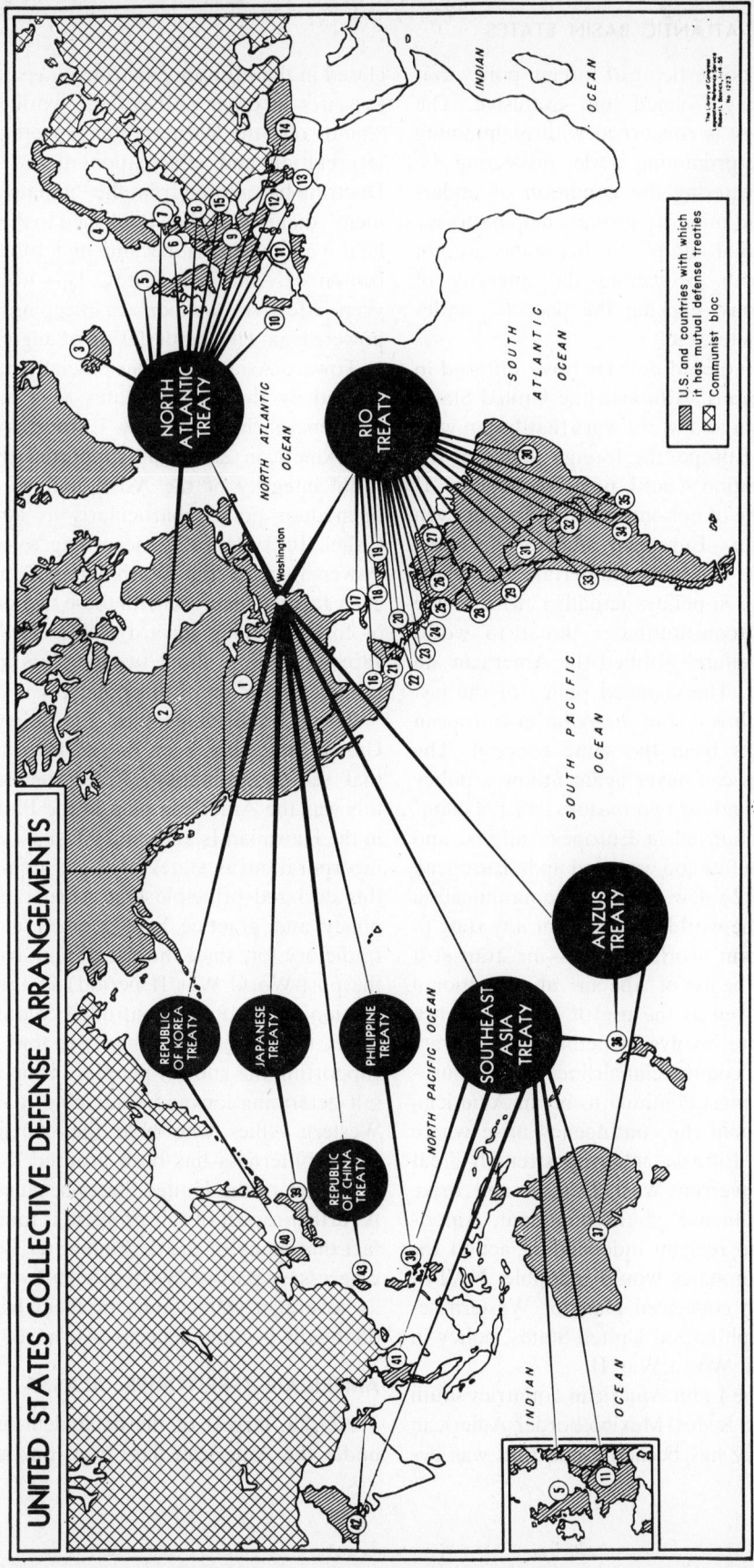

Figure 12.3.

few areas of domestic or of foreign policy that are completely isolated and exclusive. The global strategy is concerned with maintaining world peace, promoting trade, protecting the rights and bettering the condition of under-privileged and minority groups, helping to see that the internal affairs of other states are not interfered with, protecting the integrity of smaller nations, backing the peaceful settlement of disputes, etc.

Its world regional policies have differed in different regions. Although the United States participated in two world wars that began with incidents in Europe, the foreign policy of the American nation (until post-World War II days) was one of non-intervention in—or even isolation from—European affairs. The interference in the two wars (undertaken previous to this change in policy, actually), which were regarded as constituting a threat to world peace and welfare, justified the American aid to the Allies. The changed policy of the last decade, which is one of *direction* in European affairs, results from the same concern. The United States can never again follow a policy of isolation, and for two reasons: 1) the country is too entangled in European affairs, and American welfare too wrapped up in European welfare; and 2) new means of communication have made the world too small for *any* state to withdraw from world affairs—air transport necessitates the use of "the air" above national domains as well as the use of airports, hence all nations are involved whether they operate international commercial airlines or not. European affairs must continue to be an American concern. Should the contingency arise where a power on Eurasia achieved strength great enough to overrun West Europe and drive American influence off the continent, American efforts to reclaim independent action for the European states would redouble. NATO, an American conceived plan for Western security, has epitomized United States' policy in Europe since World War II.

Toward the Latin American countries south of the United States–Mexico border American foreign policy has been the one that was de-clared in the Monroe Doctrine—*i.e.* a warning to states in other parts of the world to keep "hands off" the Western Hemisphere. The interpretation and effectuation of the Monroe Doctrine has altered from the "unilateral statement" that it was when published to the "multilateral agreement" it became under the Organization of American States. This has been a very effective weapon in keeping foreign powers from either interfering or aggressing.

Toward Asia, which has officially been considered by the United States as a backward area encroached upon by European powers, the American state has supported the territorial integrity of the Asian nations and the open door policy, particularly as applied to China. In 1921-1922, according to the Nine Power Pact of the Washington Conference, even Japan concurred with these two principles of foreign policy toward China. Reversal of Japanese action about twenty years later was in direct violation of this policy.

Toward subject peoples, the policy of the United States has been one of favoring eventual self-determination. From the beginning this was the American plan in the Philippines; in the Hawaiian Islands and Alaska, the goal is incorporation as states of the Union. It is in this declared principle that American foreign policy and practice have seemed most contradictory for, since the rise of nationalism (in the post-World War II period) in the greater portion of European controlled colonial territories, the United States has been torn between supporting the subject peoples in their bid for self-determination and remaining loyal to its Western Allies who hold the dependencies. Much bitterness has been aroused from both sides toward the United States because of this. A further aspect of this problem is found in the fact that many of the dependent territories are a necessary part of Western security planning; as sovereign states some of them would undoubtedly become neutrals—or have.

AMERICAN TERRITORIES: ALASKA

Alaska, largest of the dependent territories under the American flag, faces on the Arctic

Mediterranean. Formerly in a marginal location, in the present air age it lies at the potential crossway of the world. A part of the Western security system, the radar installations and polar air flights—and the territories facing on the Arctic seas—are looked upon as the first line of defense for the Western Hemisphere, and Alaska, along with northern Canada and Greenland, is being turned into one of the sentinels beyond the nation's frontiers. In this strategic role, Alaska is becoming ever more critically valuable to the United States.

Since Seward's purchase of Alaska from Russia, in 1867, the territory has had an uneven development. Temporary booms, subsequent to the discovery of gold and the intensive exploitation of such extractive resources as furs and fish, failed to bring about a steady economic growth in the territory. With the establishment of the Matanuska Valley development (agricultural) in the 1930's, the first manifestation of sound economic growth became apparent. World War II and the 1.5 billion dollars of defense spending started another boom. The question Alaskans have been asking is: What will happen when this lush boom period is also over?

Alaska is the one remaining pioneer frontier within the American domain. Its greatest need is people. However, until it can offer steady employment and economic opportunities somewhat comparable to those "outside," permanent residents will not be drawn to the territory. For example, in 1951, "fewer than one-half of those employed in Alaska at the peak of the summer season had jobs there during the following winter. The construction, canning, and mining industries are almost entirely seasonal, attracting from the Western states thousands of migrant workers whose interest in Alaska is limited to wages (which are high) and housing conditions (which are substandard)."[9] With inadequate capital and labor, and distant from markets, the peacetime economic development of Alaska—a necessity

[9] Peter M. Stern, "Alaska," *Focus* (American Geographical Society, Vol. IV, No. 1, September, 1953), pp. 1-2.

if the region is to build any degree of strength —is seriously handicapped.

However, it is not lacking in resources; these are diverse, relatively abundant, and useful. Once variously termed Seward's Folly, Seward's Icebox, Icebergia, Walrussia, in output of gold alone it has several times over repaid the seven million dollar purchase price.

Alaska is big. The area of Alaska, 586,000 square miles, is 477 times larger than Rhode Island, twice the size of Texas, or, compared with the United States, one-fifth the size of the mother country. At its longest and widest parts it is longer and wider than the United States proper, and its coastline of 26,000 miles exceeds that of the United States by 3000 miles. A blocky peninusla with many protuberances, including the string of the strategic Aleutians looping westward to enclose the Bering Sea and Strait (outlet to the Arctic Ocean between the Asian and North American continents), its shape—all parts of the territory considered— is a disadvantage from the viewpoint of defense. It projects out from the body of Canada, and has no defense in depth. Long supply lines connect it across Canadian territory or Pacific waters with the United States. Despite its large size, it lacks diversity except that offered by maritime and interior location. Here, however, marked contrasts are found—the more marked because of coastal mountains—so that panhandle, southern, and southwestern Alaska are relatively mild, partaking of many of the characteristics of the marine climate as found in the Puget Sound area and Coastal West Canada. North of Bering Strait and in the interior, Arctic climates take hold. Except in south and west coastal lowland littorals and river valleys, much of Alaska is a land of taiga, tundra, and, in the extreme north around Point Barrow and eastward, of ice and snow.

Location must be regarded from two points of view. The Alaskan location must be viewed, first, from Alaska alone; and secondly, from its relation to the United States. From the first standpoint, Alaska's location is relatively unfavorable. The Arctic Circle crosses the peninsula about three-fifths of the way northward,

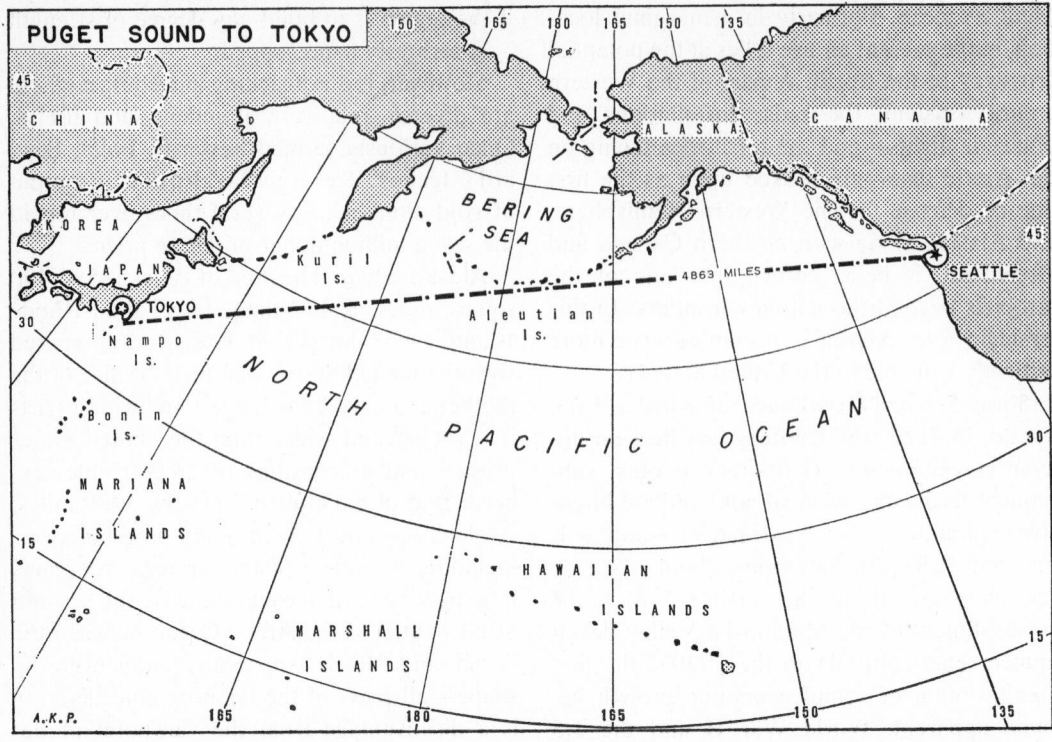

Figure 12.4. Two things should be noted on this map: the close association of Soviet and American territories at the Bering Strait; and the straight-line relationship of Western United States and East Asia. This projection clearly brings out the important fact that the northern Pacific route is far shorter than the one that passes the Hawaiian Islands across the central Pacific.

and, although it occupies a west coast location (in the southern portion, in the belt of the westerly winds), the northern half lies in the lee of the Asian continent which cuts off some of the ameliorating effects. Further, the whole of the west coast lies north of the wall of the lofty Aleutians facing the icy Bering Sea waters. Little moderation of temperature is felt from those seas.

Alaska, however, has some physical peculiarities that contradict somewhat its Arctic aspect. One of these is climatic: because of its peninsular character, projecting into western waters with onshore winds the year around, it is not the land of eternal snow that location might suggest. Less than three per cent of the entire territory is continuously covered with snow and ice—despite the fact that its top third lies within the Arctic Circle. Neverthe-

less, the small proportion of lowlands having a suitable climate limits seriously the area that can be cultivated, and one of the handicaps of living in Alaska is the meagerness of the fresh fruits and vegetables and of dairy products that can be obtained by the population.

A second aspect of location, from the point of view of Alaskans, is its proximity to Soviet territory. In both the westernmost tip of the peninsula and of the Aleutians, the Asian continent lies but a few miles distant. In the past, according to some scientists, Alaska served as the natural bridge across which the American indigenes migrated to this continent from Asia; during the middle of the nineteenth century, it functioned as a lane of access for the economic and political penetration of the Russians; in the modern era it offers as convenient a gateway to the North American continent. In case of war—which would be an air and atom war to a large extent—Alaska is destined (with northern Canada) to become a crush and shatter zone area as the first line of defense for the American industrial arsenal.

It is the strategic aspect of location that touches the American nation most closely, although the natural resources—forests, fish, and minerals—are such that it is a valuable piece of land to hold, economically. However, looking northward the American state sees Alaska as, locationally speaking, its most vulnerable piece of territory, and, strategically, as one of the most valuable for it is the only United States' frontage on the critical Arctic Mediterranean. It is a territory that must be developed and held at all costs.

With the completion of the Alcan highway the United States joined this outside territory to the domain proper. Former connections were confined to air transport and the inland water passageway, vulnerable to submarines.

Coherence within the territory is largely dependent on air travel. Three rail lines have been constructed. The longest runs from Seward inland to Fairbanks, the second from Cordova into the copper country—both tap important mineral areas, the third runs between Haines and Whitehorse. The Alaska Highway supplements the rail lines and sends feeders into areas exploited for their resources. Two of the rivers are navigable, the Yukon and the Kuskokwim. The major, or "working," mines are served by one or more means of communication or lie on the coast where ocean transport is available. Although south-central Alaska and parts of the interior are well served with transportation, the territory urgently needs additional facilities to cohere its large area as well as to open it up to tourists and development. A huge base—the United States Naval and Petroleum Area No. 4—stands guard over hundreds of square miles of territory south of and out from Point Barrow. The only connections to this base are by air for along the northern coast the shipping season is only one month long.

Development of the American Arctic has been slow as compared with that carried out in Eurasia. Although exploratory expeditions have undertaken and navigated the Arctic passage above North America, nothing in the way of an established route, comparable to that of the northern route of the Soviet Union, has been effectuated by the United States and Canada. Up to the World War II period and since that time, Arctic exploration and studies have been minimal as compared with those of the Europeans and Russians. Now extensive research on land and sea is being carried on by both American states (of weather and climate, ice conditions, geologic exploration, etc.), and defense installations reach from Pacific to Atlantic and beyond into Greenland where the United States has naval and air bases.

Resources and Resource Development

Ever since the establishment of the first cannery in Alaska in 1878, fishing and canning have been the outstanding industries of the territory. Facing the North Pacific, one of the world's two most important fishing grounds, fish constitute a replaceable resource that annually nets a catch valued at about 100 million dollars, and supplies nearly two-thirds of the world's salmon as well as seafood of other varieties, such as halibut, herring, and shellfish. At times over-fishing threatens to hurt the industry, but, with careful management and cooperation between Canada and Alaska and other nations taking part of the catch, fishing promises to be a continuing source of wealth to the territory.

Another replaceable resource is found in the forests of Alaska which, if handled rightly, are capable of producing a billion board feet of lumber annually in perpetuity in the Tongass and Chugach regions alone. The interior also has forests, of less importance commercially although of great local value. Little exploited now, the forests await development and appear to offer one of the most immediate of the economic opportunities offered in the territory.

The waterpower potential exceeds any foreseeable local needs. A reconnaissance survey by the United States Bureau of Reclamation in 1949 reported a potential of hydroelectric development in Alaska of more than 8 billion kilowatts (half the capacity of waterpower installation in the United States proper at present). Alaskan hydroelectricity is regarded as a potential source of power for extensive developments in the electrometallurgic and electrochemical industries.

It was the gold of the Yukon that brought Alaska spectacularly to world attention, and it was mineral wealth that drew the greatest numbers of people into the territory—that is until the war and post-war defense boom. Since gold was discovered in 1898, ores and metals valued at about one billion dollars have been sent out of Alaska. And yet any estimates of the mineral wealth of the territory are largely speculative for only a very small proportion (.3 per cent in 1953) of Alaska has been mapped on a scale suitable for detailed analysis of geologic features. According to several government publications, however, all of the 33 minerals classed in the United States as critical or strategic (except bauxite and industrial diamonds) are existent in Alaska in "significant quantities." Today, gold, copper, lead, coal, zinc, platinum, chromite, and tin are mined, and reserves of copper, copper-zinc, and petroleum are known to exist. In comparison to the potential, development is light.

Remoteness, seasonality of industries, the eccentric population distribution (concentrated in three areas with the rest of Alaska almost void of people), and "the oneway payload traffic have contributed to the excessive ocean freight rates which have discouraged risk capital and slowed further economic expansion," states Stern.[10]

Geopolitical Considerations

In view of the present state of economic development, the greatest importance of Alaska lies in its location and strategic value. With the long Aleutian island arc, Alaska flanks the great-circle shipping routes across the Pacific. Planes, ships, and submarines based on Kodiak and elsewhere in the Aleutians, and working with forces on Hawaii and the West Coast, protect these vital supply lines between the United States and the East. Such bases could control the Northeastern Pacific while fields of operation in the Western Aleutians tend to neutralize the strong Soviet naval centers at Petropavlovsk, on Kamchatka, and in the Kuriles—the only Russian bases on the open oceans.

Important as is Alaska to American maritime strategy, it is even more significant in terms of the strategy of the air for Alaska is "the springboard" for the so-called Polar Concept of the Air Force. Across the polar sea lies the shortest route to any point in Asia and Europe east of the Baltic Sea. The polar concept, however, is still a subsidiary one in American offensive-defensive strategy for the United States has bases more easily supplied and climatically more favored than those in the North American North, as those in West Europe, England, Africa, and the Middle and Far East. Nevertheless, as air defense against possible attack from the Eastern Hemisphere, the Arctic defenses are indispensable.

Statehood for Alaska and Hawaii has found strong opposition. Each time that bills proposing the admittance of 49th and 50th states to the Union have been presented on the Senate floor, they have been defeated. Opposition has come largely from the South and from certain Eastern states; both Hawaii and Alaska have native and polyglot populations living in an atmosphere where there is little racial feeling. It is believed by the Senate opposition that their legislators would add support to the northern bloc that is historically liberal in racial and civil rights issues. Opposition also comes from those who, in the case of Alaska particularly, do not want to grant statehood to a comparatively few thousands of people (Alaska's population is about 208,000) while some states, as New York and Pennsylvania, for example, with a combined population of 25 million, still have but two senators each. Statehood for Alaska still pends.

---

[10] *Ibid.,* p. 6.

PACIFIC INTERESTS: THE HAWAIIAN ISLANDS

Hawaiian statehood also pends. In the case of the Hawaiian Islands there is more economic reason for the granting of statehood than in the case of Alaska; however, from a strategic point of view, Alaska is the more valuable. Hawaii has a population greater than four of the present states of the Union (about 500,000) and it pays federal taxes that are higher than those levied in ten of the states.

A major argument used by those against Hawaiian statehood (and this has also been directed against Alaskan statehood) is that Hawaii is non-contiguous and, hence, outside of the pattern of the present union of states. A Senate minority report, in 1952, stated that "if statehood is granted, it will represent a radical departure from all-over traditions and previous policies in admitting states to the Union."

Two other lines of opposition to Hawaiian statehood have been taken. One comes from the South which, as stated before, is opposed on the basis of the racial and ethnic issue. Further, southern sugar interests fear they would suffer if statehood were granted since the present sugar quota system tends to favor the South over Hawaii.

In the minority report (formerly quoted) dissenting Senators made the statement that "with so-called Caucasians outnumbered, political control will be in the hands of groups alien to the American way of life." However, no Hawaiian citizen is an alien. Hawaii's mixed population—one of the most cosmopolitan in the world—has lived within the American framework for sixty years, and, as the Senate majority committee reported, "Hawaii's American institutions and school system have produced American citizens worthy to stand on a basis of full equality with the best citizens of any state in the Union." The "alien" argument is a refutation of the sound American doctrine (not always well implemented in American territory) of equal rights regardless of race. Supreme Court action in 1954 under-

lined this policy of "equal rights" in the decision handed down on discrimination against Negroes.

It is likely that statehood would be to the national interest. It would, in the first place, give dynamic expression to the principle of self-government upon which the United States was founded and upon which an important part of American foreign policy is based. Further, it would produce federal economies by lifting the cost of administration off the federal government; and thirdly (but by no means least), it would enhance the prestige of the United States among the hundreds of millions of newly independent peoples of the world where American prestige has suffered some severe setbacks. Economically, the Hawaiian "star" would make a rich addition to the Union. Eighteen other areas have been admitted to the Union as states since Hawaii first sought political attachments with the United States about the middle of the nineteenth century.[11] None of these had to serve so long an apprenticeship: none was better qualified to become a state from the standpoint of economy and law, and loyalty to American democracy. None of the reasons put forward opposing statehood for Hawaii is valid. In area—nearly 6500 square miles—the Territory of Hawaii is larger than the combined territories of three of the present states (Connecticut, Rhode Island, and Delaware); in population, except for Oklahoma, Hawaii (over 540,000) is larger than that of any state upon admission; in wealth and economic significance, it outranks several states.

People and Population

Hawaii, the mid-Pacific American territory, has a wide reputation for its multiracial population and for the ease with which its numerous immigrant stocks adjust to one another and to the emerging Hawaiian–American culture. By

---

[11] The islands were not annexed, however, until 1898; in 1900, Hawaii was organized as a territory. But as early as 1875 a reciprocity agreement was negotiated and achieved with the United States; hence, there have been close economic ties for more than three-quarters of a century.

virtue of its mid-ocean detachment from the major points of racial tension and its well-established tradition of tolerance and objectivity on such matters, Hawaii provides a unique laboratory of the processes involved in the meeting and fusing of various ethnic groups and as a working example of an effective community living on an interracial basis. Hawaii is a meeting place of the East and the West, probably unparalleled anywhere else on the globe.

The indigenous Hawaiians, who are Polynesians related to most of the other South Sea island peoples, came to this archipelago probably 1000 to 1500 years ago. In 1778, the Sandwich Islands (as Cook named them) were "discovered" by Captain James Cook, English navigator; and soon thereafter, white traders and then white missionaries moved into the Polynesian archipelago. In the relations of these first-comers with the native Hawaiians, there was little consideration of skin color. However, this racial equality was almost upset when the sugar planters imported immigrant laborers who settled as separate racial groups on the plantations, thereby initiating occupational stratification on the basis of race.

The largest immigrant groups in Hawaii are the Chinese, the Japanese, and the Filipinos; they arrived in that order. Honolulu, an urban and commercial center, provided an outlet for plantation workers who sought free competition for jobs. Compulsory education, with the emphasis on democracy in the schools, appeared for a time to be a threat to plantation labor and that pattern of life. Thus, the public schools have had an important acculturating influence. In the past ten years, rapid unionization of plantation labor has further undermined the character of the plantations as determinants of race relations, breaking down residential and cultural segregation; mechanization and the consequent displacement of labor further contributed toward this trend.

In addition to the historical elements, several other factors have helped to determine race relations in Hawaii in contrast with race relations elsewhere. In the first place, slavery

never existed in these islands; and, secondly, contract labor has enjoyed considerable freedom. Another factor was the relative size of the racial groups: no one ethnic group in Hawaii has represented a numerical majority of the population. A fourth factor was Hawaii's expanding economy—the Caucasians have never been sufficient in number to fill all of the preferred jobs in the developing economy; hence, other groups could rise without causing tension. The development of an interracial consumer group, along with interracial capital and enterprise, was also important.

All of these factors combined to contribute to favorable race relationships exemplified, perhaps, in the interracial marriages that are so commonplace that one out of every three marriages today is "mixed." Each year the problem of race classification becomes more difficult due to the growing proportion of the population of racially mixed ancestry. The Japanese make up the largest racial or ethnic element, composing about 40 per cent of the total Hawaiian population of over 540,000; part-Hawaiians comprise 17 per cent; Caucasians, 15 per cent; Filipinos, 14 per cent; Chinese, 7 per cent; Hawaiians, 3 per cent; Koreans, 1 per cent; all others, about 4,000 persons. As indicated above, however, such statistics are becoming less meaningful because of the change in the racial structure of the population: children of interracial marriages are classed as though they belonged to a "pure" racial classification, and this system becomes even less satisfactory as offspring of "outmarriages" increase.

Physical Elements

The location of the Hawaiian Islands is one of near-centrality in the great Pacific Ocean and, hence, strategic. The Hawaiian archipelago, about 2400 miles southwest of San Francisco, lies in the Pacific trade wind tropics between latitudes 10° 55′ and 22° 15′ North and longitude 150° 50′ and 160° 30′ West. It covers a 1590-mile span. Because of its central position whalers and traders, early after the English discovery, began using Hawaii as a port of call, and soon ships of many nations were crowding its harbors. Great circle routes from the West Canadian ports to New Zealand–Australia and from Singapore to Panama touch the Hawaiian archipelago. The increased interests—and land holdings—of the United States in the Pacific area have increased the cultural, geographical, and political importance of Hawaii. Military and naval bases dot the islands, centering around the Pearl Harbor base; the establishment of the Trust Territory (in Micronesia and in the Ryukyus) and the increasingly important role of the United States —politically and economically—in East and Southeast Asia, enhance the value of the strategically placed islands. They are, literally, the crossroads of the Pacific. As a frontal defense outpost for the Pacific Coast of the North American mainland the Hawaiian Islands are not strategically too important, for, from East Asia, the shortest line of air and sea travel is by way of the northern great-circle routes. It is to be recalled, however, that Mahan envisioned the islands as a "vital strategic 'outpost' against a 'wave of barbaric invasion' from the Far East." The islands are like a string of oases in the vast "desert" of the Pacific. They must not be underrated; their possession gives the United States a strong position in the Pacific, and, despite the catastrophic attack on Pearl Harbor, they are readily defensible—except as any spot is vulnerable in an air and atom age.

The archipelago consists of seven inhabited islands and a number of small unpopulated islets. The inhabited islands are, from northwest to southeast, Niihau, Kauai, Oahu, Molokai, Lanai, Maui, and Hawaii. Hawaii is the largest of the group (4030 square miles); however, Honolulu, the capital and political center, is on Oahu. They are a group of mountainous, volcanic islands that have been built up from the seafloor, with elevations rising to a maximum of 13,784 feet in Mauna Kea, on Hawaii. Approximately only 8.5 per cent of the total area is under cultivation.

Generally characterized as tropical islands, the climates range, altitudinally, from tropical shores to snow-capped mountains; due to the alignment of the mountains, there is also a wet and a dry side to the islands—that side facing the trades (the northeast) being lush and green and tropical, the side on the lee of the winds (southwest) having semi-arid and arid characteristics of climate. In general, the climate is mild and free from extremes.

Although fragmented, lines of communication of various sorts join the archipelago into an economic and political unit. With the advent of newer means of transport, however, the communication pattern underwent a change in "the nature of the transport agencies." According to Otis Freeman, "Railroads have almost ceased to function, most of the mileage on Oahu and that on the Hamakua Coast of Hawaii have been torn up, and only a few short railways on plantations are in operation. Abandoned rail lines have been replaced by trucks and busses . . . The six principal islands are well served by paved highways, and these islands also have good airports. Early in 1949 passenger service by steamship between islands was discontinued, and the inter-island ships and barges carry freight only. Airplanes transport the passengers, mail, and some of the package freight."[12]

OTHER PACIFIC POSSESSIONS

Although Alaska (with the Aleutians) and the Hawaiian Islands give the United States a strong position in the Pacific and in Pacific affairs, tiny islets in the western half of the great ocean act as stepping stones between the mid-Pacific archipelago and the Asian mainland, and, secondly, act as the first line of American defense in those waters. Wake Island and Guam, 2018 miles and 2700 miles from Hawaii respectively (and the intermediate bases at Johnson Island and Kwajalein), are the links in the vast ocean spaces that carry American influence more safely toward the Asian extremity, shortening the gaps.

In the pre-World War II period all of the intermediate islands between Hawaii and the

---

[12] Otis Freeman, *Geography of the Pacific* (New York: John Wiley & Sons, Inc., 1951), p. 361.

Philippines (then a dependency of the United States) and Asia were in German—and later, Japanese—hands. Painfully slow and costly fighting pushed the Japanese back to their national base in and around the four major islands of Japan, and, as a result of their repossession by American troops, numbers of small islands in the southwest portion of the North Pacific became Trust Territories of the United States; others, upon the demand of the United States—because of the heavy loss of American lives—were also turned over to the United States, as Iwo Jima and Okinawa. Hence, the United States now has a closely knit network of air and naval bases, radar, radio, and cable stations that places it in a strong position not far off the Asian mainland. Leased bases in the Philippines and Japan further bulwark this position. Samoa is another link in the series of Pacific possessions and defenses.

During World War II, for the first time in the history of the world, the powers engaged in a struggle for the control of a major *ocean*. When conflicts for control of maritime areas had been engaged in at earlier periods of history, they had been for possession of small inland water bodies or connecting waterways; the United States might be described today as in possession of most of the Pacific. The following statement, made by Douglas MacArthur before a meeting of the Veterans of Foreign Wars in Chicago in 1950, gives a clear appraisal of United States' Pacific strategy relative to these islands—and Chinese Nationalist-held Formosa—and highpoints some of the reasons for postwar American policy on Formosa.

Prior thereto the Western strategic frontier of the United States lay on the littoral line of the Americas with an exposed island salient extending out through Hawaii, Midway, and Guam to the Philippines. That salient was not an outpost of strength but an avenue of progress along which the enemy could and did attack us . . .

All of this was changed by our Pacific victory. Our strategic frontier then shifted to embrace the entire Pacific Ocean . . . We control it to the shores of Asia by a chain of islands extending in an arc from the Aleutians to the Marianas held by us and our free allies. From this island chain we can dominate with airpower every Asiatic port from Vladivostok to Singapore and prevent any hostile movement into the Pacific . . . Our line of defense is a natural one and can be maintained with a minimum of military effort and expense. It envisions no attack against anyone nor does it provide the bastions essential for offensive operations, but properly maintained it would be an invincible defense against aggression. If we hold this line we may have peace—lose it and war is inevitable.

13

Canada and the Arctic

"Stephen Leacock once remarked that Canadians were so busy explaining to the British that they weren't Americans and assuring Americans they weren't British that they had precious little time left to be Canadians. World War II and its aftermath have helped change all that. Today Canadians are so busy being Canadians they've little time for anything else."[1] Perhaps more conscious than the United States is of being American, Canada is now conscious of being Canadian—for Canada is experiencing a boom that has made that state a "nation."

During the past decade, Canada has economically mushroomed. Canada is the third largest country in the world—with but 14.5 million people. Since the war, despite the handicap of a small population, Canada has gone into a rapid development of industry and her rich natural storehouse of raw materials.

The war forced the great state of the North American North to take immense economic strides. Within little more than a decade, many

Canadian industries more than doubled their production. New discoveries indicate that within the Canadian borders huge reserves of oil, natural gas, iron ore, uranium, and other basic minerals lie buried. These provide the foundation for an expansion comparable to that experienced by the United States in the middle of the nineteenth century.

The economic spiralling brought a self-confidence, a feeling of national pride, and a resolution to be independent of both the United States and Great Britain. The rise of *nationalism* is not an indication of United States–Canadian disharmony. Quite to the contrary, relations between the two American states have never been more friendly nor their destinies more closely tied; and, along the four thousand miles of unfortified frontier, never has there been less need for defenses. As a matter of fact, the economic developments have had two effects quite contradicory to each other: on the one hand, they encouraged political nationalism; on the other, they *increased Canadian economic dependence on the United States*. In some years the United States has taken nearly two-thirds of Canadian exports.

---

[1] Keith Munro, "Now Canada Comes of Age," *The New York Times Magazine,* March 30, 1952, p. 13.

In the current developments, American capital is pouring into the northern country to help finance industries whose primary market lies to the south, and it appears that the two nations are destined to be economically integrated even more closely.

As for British–Canadian relations, the last perceptible link with Great Britain was broken in 1950. In that year, the Canadian Supreme Court became the highest court of justice: since then it has no longer been necessary to carry judicial appeals to the Privy Council in London. When, in 1952, Vincent Massey became the Dominion's new Governor-General another milestone was reached for he was the first native-born Canadian to be appointed to that office by the Crown.

Despite what has been said above, Canadian nationalism is of long standing. For 85 years Canadian nationalism has represented "one of the world's major triumphs of politics over economics."[2] It might be said with great elements of truth that Canada, as represented on the map, is a state *in spite of* geography and economics.

Political independence poses handicaps. Canada is made up of the ten provinces that string along the 4000-mile southern boundary —plus the territories in the north. Seventy per cent of the people reside within a hundred miles of the American frontier. Each of the provinces would undoubtedly be benefited if permitted to trade freely with the United States. Since they are not a part of Union to the south and since trade restrictions pose inhibitions, the provinces must carry on much of their commerce east and west—across the wide and sparsely populated Canadian shield. Added to this is the fact that, throughout the country as a whole, the per capita income is about one-third lower than in the United States.

The economic history of Canada is the story of a dogged, even heroic insistence on paying this high price for independence, for not being a part of a North American market. Canada paid the price in the form of expensive transportation. The Intercolonial Railway was built at great expense and no hope of profit to provide the Maritime Provinces with a market in Ontario and Quebec and vice versa. The Canadian Pacific was built at even greater expense to keep British Columbia in the Confederation. Many of the lines that now make up the Canadian National were built to serve a destiny that has not even yet arrived.[3]

Population and People —and Nationalism

When the federation was formed in 1867, it was predicted by the *Almanac of Canada* that by 1941 the population would reach 42.6 million people. However, when that date arrived Canadian population totaled but 11 million. During the century from 1850 to 1950 only 7.2 million persons entered Canada as immigrants—and during the same period, 6.6 million persons *emigrated* from the northern nation, large numbers to the United States. Many of those who left were numbered among the ablest and best educated.

The "pull to the south" could not be withstood. Higher wages and lower prices, greater opportunities and greater freedoms drew the Canadians to the United States. Says one writer in discussing the settlement of the Canadian West, "The list [of advantages in the United States] becomes so impressive that one wonders why anyone went to the Canadian Northwest . . . the blunt truth was that the Canadian West had to wait until the American West had filled up."[4]

However, the contemporary boom has manifested itself also in substantial population increments. Since the war population has risen by more than 20 per cent, from 11.6 million to over 14.5 million. Large as was the gain, the Canadian population—which spreads over an area one-third greater than that of the United States—is still less than that of New York State, and less than twice as large as that of New York City.

In addition to being small, the population is

---

2 Gilbert Burck, "The Boom That Made Canada," *Fortune*, August, 1952, p. 91.

3 *Ibid.*, p. 92.

4 Arthur R. M. Lower, *Colony to Nation* (Toronto: Longmans, Green & Co., 1946), p. 420.

divided linguistically. One-third of the people, of French descent, cling tenaciously to the customs and tongue of their forebears. It has been said, and with much truth, that the French Canadians are more French than the French themselves because here is an archaic relic of old French culture. One hundred and ninety-two years of British rule has not changed them —in fact, Americans and British Canadians are far more alike than are British and French Canadians. The duality of language does not make Canada bilingual: Canada is a nation of two languages.

Peculiarly, Canadian character and cohesion grew out of three foreign nationalistic forces—French Canada, the United States, and "British tradition and temper." The part that French Canada played toward integration was, in actuality, negative. In 1774, to keep the French in Quebec from aiding the American colonies in their fight for independence, George III guaranteed their laws and religion in the Quebec Act. The Act that essentially granted Canada its constitution (the British North America Act of 1867) confirmed these rights to the French Canadians and recognized two official languages—still used in Federal and Quebec affairs. The Canadian French have never given up any of these rights—and Canada has not asked them to. A distinct group that has grown in power over the years, they are a part of Canada—at the same time that they do not amalgamate with it. "They are Canadian nationalists because no setup in the world can better preserve their particularism."[5]

From a core of 60,000 original French settlers their numbers have risen to over four million, and, with the passage of time, they have spread beyond the confines of Quebec into the other provinces. Although "the rights" acceded to them originally applied to the French in Quebec, French Canadians have carried these rights, as well as their language and customs, into the other parts of Canada to which they have gone. Into whatever region they have spread they have remained a group

apart. The *particularism* of the French Canadian is a particularism indeed for French Canada is—and has been—"isolationist, anti-free-trade, anti-intellectual, anti-British, anti-U.S.-capital, and anti-immigration."[6]

About one-half of the Canadians are of British stock, and British *tradition* is a large part of what might be characterized as "Canadian." The Englishmen who immigrated to Canada, contrary to what was true of the American colonists from the British Isles, brought over to the new land the institutions of the mother country and transposed them without much change on to the Canadian scene. For example, the parliamentary and judiciary systems are those of the British. Further —and again unlike what happened in the United States, where floods of immigrants from all parts of Europe mixed with the original stock until the American state became a veritable melting-pot—British traditions and temperament largely persisted in Canada. Since the end of World War II, however, this "pure" character of Canadian stock has begun to change. Like Australia, Canada has been chronically short of manpower, particularly so since the increased postwar industrial development. Hence, Canada like Australia has opened its doors and invited in immigrants from all European countries. Therefore, in large population centers such as Toronto, one is as likely to hear a European tongue as English spoken. There is also a large Chinese element in some centers.

Perhaps the outstanding British influence reflected in the Canadian scene is that of the "British temper—that pervasive moderation, that undefined but clearly visible respect for the rights of others, that innate, wire-drawn sense of proportion that now and then manifests itself as hypocrisy and Puritanism. As Emerson said about the English, 'They never let out all the length of the reins . . . there is no abandonment or ecstacy of will or intellect . . . like that which intoxicated France in 1789.' The

---

[5] Burck, *op. cit.*, p. 95.

[6] *Ibid.*, pp. 95-96.

habit of holding on to the reins is embedded . . . deeply."[7]

Americans make up about 18 per cent of Canadian population. But, small though the proportion is, in the blend of the three national elements that have contributed most greatly to the Canadian character, the American influence is winning out. However, it was not the American *settler* in Canada that was instrumental in helping to forge the unity of the state. Quite the contrary. As with the French, the American contribution to Canadian national coherence was negative. With the cessation of fighting after the Civil War, there were those in the North (of the United States) who contrived the idea of "Manifest Destiny" with reference to Canada—referring to the annexation of Canada by the United States as a revenge against the British for their pro-South sympathies during the war. The Canadians resisted the idea, formulated the British North America Act which was passed by the British Parliament, and Canada became a dominion. Later, when the Canadian Prime Minister proposed trade reciprocity, the United States turned it down.

However, Canada and the United States are inextricably bound together by scores of visible and invisible ties. Despite the rejection on the part of both states of closer legal connections, it is likely that there cannot be found on the globe two states that live more harmoniously side by side and are more dependent on each other.

Population—generally, of low density—is concentrated in four nodes. The four principal cores in which population concentrates are separated from each other by physical barriers of such magnitude that, at times, Canadians have felt closer to Americans across the border than to their own countrymen. The most densely populated block is found in the industrial district along the St. Lawrence River and eastern Great Lakes in Ontario and Quebec. The other three are found in the three Maritime Provinces, in the prairie provinces of

Alberta, Saskatchewan, and Manitoba, and in British Columbia.

Dividing the two eastern nodes from each other is the American state of Maine and great stretches of barren rocky land and forests. Between the industrial core and the agricultural center in the prairie provinces lies the expanse of the Laurentian Shield, an ancient rock upland covering nearly one-third of Canada. Formerly considered valuable only for its timber and furs, recent geological exploration has uncovered a vast store of mineral wealth here—most of the state's gold, silver, nickel, iron, and uranium. Westward, effectively sealing off the populated Pacific portions of British Columbia from the rest of the country, are the Canadian Rockies.

The nuclear center of the Canadian state was in the St. Lawrence–Great Lakes district of Quebec and Ontario where today is found the ecumene—the greatest population node and the greatest concentration of industry and transportation as well as the political center of the nation.

Canada's prairie provinces make the state one of the world's great producers and exporters of food for here is raised Canada's great wheat crop. The prairie population—largely rural, or agglomerated in centers that serve the rural districts, and numbering about three million—is one of many nationalities for into these extensive farmlands many of the post-war immigrants have streamed. Winnipeg, leading market center for the entire area, numbers about 350,000 persons, and publishes newspapers in *23 languages*.

Growth in urbanization has been impressive. Under the incentive of development another change in the population pattern has taken place that has changed the character of the country, namely, agglomeration in urban centers. Wilderness towns have risen: Burnt Creek—a spot in the desolation of Labrador that few white men had seen less than a decade ago—has grown apace; Kitimat, but recently an Indian village, likewise has burgeoned; Seven Islands and Eskimo Point have mushroomed from tiny fishing villages to cities; in

[7] *Ibid.*, p. 174.

1951 materials for the construction of a town were hauled by sled to the locale of a great nickel mine in Northern Manitoba while at the site of the largest North American uranium mines, Uranium City has sprung up in the northern part of Saskatchewan.

Old urban centers have grown, also, and concomitant with this growth, in some cities like Toronto, a counter-movement to the suburbs has begun, dispersing not only people but industry as well.

The Canadian Economy

Canada has risen to the rank of fourth among the world's commercial nations, and sixth among industrial states. The base of this spectacular economic revolution lies in its extensive forests and in the vast store of mineral wealth that has been uncovered. Further, Canada's resource potential, largely untouched, is only partially measured. What reserves of iron ore lie buried in the Labrador hills, in the barren lands of Northern Ontario, and in the islands off Newfoundland is not known. Already, in the Ungava district, 500 million long tons of high-grade ore have been proven, and it is thought that the deposits at **Steep Rock** may be even greater. These lie north of Lake Superior. At Burnt Creek in Labrador, drillings to 350 feet down failed to reach the end of the ore body.

Nor is it known how much oil is contained in the "tar sands" and oil deposits of the prairie provinces. It has been estimated that the Athabaska area alone contains 300 billion barrels of oil. According to Colin A. Campbell, Canadian engineer and oil expert: "Besides deep wells of oil, Alberta has fabulous surface deposits of bituminous tar sands containing potential reserves of oil exceeding in quantity all the world's known resources." Although Canada has the highest per capita output of hydroelectric power in the world, not even a fifth of the potential has been developed.

Canada is three dimensional. Until recently it was said that Canada had but one dimension —breadth between its eastern and western seaboards. But with the opening of the North by polar exploration and development, and the development and exploitation of the vital underground mineral reserves, Canada now has all three dimensions in major proportions.

Many of the mining and manufacturing enterprises are so recent that the latest available statistics on production do not give an accurate picture of the place of Canadian mining and manufacturing industry in the world. Whatever the production is—and it is substantial—it can be expected to increase steadily for many decades. Some scientists have estimated that comparable mineral reserves are to be found in only one other national area, namely, in the vast recesses of the USSR.

Why then the lag in Canadian development? There are three answers: climate, physiography, and population—and the latter factor is the most important. Canada has lacked manpower—and many of the most capable Canadians were lured away to the United States by the opportunities offered there. As to the first and second reasons, climate in many areas is, by its severity, a distinct handicap. The large proportion of rugged terrain and wasteland has likewise discouraged development.

The industry is widespread. Among the larger installations that are included within the industrial expansion are the Kitimat aluminum plant in British Columbia; the uranium mine, owned by the government, near Great Bear Lake in MacKenzie Territory; the oil fields in Alberta and the associated pipelines that extend to Vancouver on the Pacific and eastward to the lakes. Hundreds of lesser plants have sprung up in southern Ontario and Quebec and in the maritime provinces; and the pulp and paper industry has greatly expanded. The St. Lawrence Waterway—a joint Canadian–United States undertaking—has made the new developments even more significant because, with its completion, world markets will be closer for the waterway essentially extends the oceanways into the heart of the North American Continent and, coincidentally, right up to the door of Canada's greatest industrial district. Since more than one-third of every

Canadian dollar is earned from exports, the possible significance of the St. Lawrence Seaway to Canada becomes apparent.

A few miles to the east of Seven Islands, on the St. Lawrence River, is the world's largest body of titanium ore, a new metal now being experimented with and producing a "steel" as tough as steel but, because of the decreased thickness required to get this toughness, lighter in weight. It is worked by the Kennecott Copper Corporation and the New Jersey Zinc Company who have also built, at Sorel, the largest titanium plant in the world.

Ninety per cent of the world's nickel and most of the asbestos comes from Canada. In the production of radium and platinum, and the basic nonferrous metals, Canada is also the leader while the country ranks second in production of gold, zinc, cadmium, and silenium and is the third largest producer of silver, copper, and lead. Three-fifths of all newspapers of the world are printed on Canadian newsprint. The cod and mackerel fisheries in the Atlantic Banks are the most productive on the globe while two-thirds of all of the lobsters are taken from Canadian waters.

Location

Like the United States, Canada fronts on the world's two most travelled oceans, the Atlantic and Pacific. Up to the present the location with long maritime frontage has not had the effect upon the Canadian economy and outlook that it did in the United States. Canada is not maritime but continental in outlook; the state looks not to the sea but to the land. This is true despite the importance of trade to Canadian economic welfare. Only in the extensive development of the fishing industries has Canada faced seaward.

One of the reasons for this undoubtedly lies in the small population; another in the fact that the eastern shores—which face the busiest trade lanes—are treacherous, ice-infested, fog-bound coasts for much of the year. Hudson Bay, one of the greatest natural sea inlets in any land, is icebound most of the year while the one railroad that makes its way to Churchill

on the western side of the bay passes through sparsely populated and desolate country in the main.

In the air age, Canadian location becomes better for the Great Circle air routes spanning five continents stretch across Canadian territory.

Canadian Problems

Canadian progress has its concomitant of problems. As already brought out, the most pressing need of Canada is manpower. To efficiently develop the economy, Canada needs twice as many people as the country has at present. In the post-World War II period, immigrants have come into the country in greater numbers than in any period since 1913. But this influx of new nationalities has brought its own problems to the nation for the newcomers tend to group together instead of spreading out and assimilating with the Canadians.

A second problem almost equally critical to that of population deficiency is the lack of risk capital. Canadian progress is seriously curbed by the conservatism—typically British—of local *entrepreneurs*. Foreign capital develops most of the enterprises, particularly American capital. While a tremendous amount of Canadian capital has been invested in the industrial expansion of the nation, Canadian money has tended to go into "safe portfolio investments" whereas most American capital has been invested in "the more dynamic" but riskier development projects.[8] The iron fields at Ungava and Steep Rock, the titanium, waterpower, and nickel ore are all largely financed by money from the United States. Even the great Alberta oil developments are backed by no more than 20 per cent Canadian financing.

Anglo-American Relations

Canada has been characterized as "two countries in one" because of the close relationship and likeness it bears to the two other great English-speaking states, Britain and the United States. Traditions tie Canada to Britain while

---

[8] Burck, *op. cit.*, p. 94.

geography, culture, certain ethnic factors, and economics weld the two American states into close associations. It has been estimated that possibly one-seventh (about 25 million) of the United States' population were either born in Canada or are directly descended from Canadians. To cross the Canadian–United States boundary is like moving from one state of the United States to another.

Although all three of these English-speaking states have the strength and character to stand alone on international issues in which they feel strong convictions, generally they stand together—partly because they wish to cooperate, partly because they think alike and hold common ideals.

The Canadian Northland

Aside from the expeditions of the Vikings, the first European penetration of the Canadian North began about 400 years ago with the three voyages of Martin Frobisher to Baffin Island in his fruitless search for gold and the Northwest Passage to the Orient. No permanent settlements were established until 1670 when the Hudson's Bay Company set up trading posts along the western shore of Hudson Bay. A century later Samuel Hearns trekked, with a group of Indians, to the headwaters of the Coppermine River from whence he followed the river course northward to Coronation Bay on the Arctic Sea; in 1789 Alexander MacKenzie canoed 600 miles down the great river (that later took his name) to its delta on the Arctic Coast.

During the next 100 years a number of Britishers went in search of the fabled Northwest Passage, which they later plotted, and they and others moved so widely over the northern wastes of Canada that that portion of the huge country actually became better known, during that early period, than did much of Canadian territory farther south. The only Arctic explorations carried on during the twentieth century (until recent years)—comparable in scope to those of the nineteenth century—were those of Stefansson who, sailing in the Arctic waters, came upon islands never before reported by Europeans.

Throughout all of these centuries, however, the only economic pursuit, aside from whaling in the northern waters, was the fur trade. And the Canadian Northland remained a storied country of furs and Indians, snow and dogsleds —until gold was discovered in the Klondike in 1897. The next few years saw a surge of people into the Alaskan and Canadian Yukon. Gradually, beginning about 25 years later with the discovery of oil on the Mackenzie River, a few hundreds of people were attracted into the north to make permanent settlements. The outcome of this was the establishment of the Northwest Territories and the Yukon Branch of the Federal Department of the Interior which handled the legislative, scientific, and native welfare work in the territories. The decade 1921-31 saw mining laws and game conservation legislation passed as well as the setting aside of game preserves and sanctuaries; a herd of Alaskan reindeer was bought by the Government to aid the Canadian Eskimos.

But Northern Canada is still an empty land. Above 60 degrees north latitude live, in all, about 6000 Eskimos and 5000 Indians— fishers and hunters. A few medical practitioners, scattered across the vast areas between the Yukon and Baffin Island, care for their medical needs; educational and hospital facilities are largely in the hands of missionaries, Catholic and Church of England. The Hudson Bay Company is still dominant, retaining hold on the natives particularly in the east.

In the years since the war, however, Canada has begun to awaken to the opportunities and the needs of the Far North. The awakening began during the war when the aspect of Arctic Sea changed from that of a frozen barrier to a mediterranean lake as new and powerful aircraft raised the possibility that the Canadian Northland might well become a crush zone between forces in Eurasia and the United States. Continental defenses, set up during and, more particularly, after the war by both Canada and the United States, exist in the radar and "air" lines that extend in triplicate across Canada from west to east.

Opportunities lie in the vast natural reserve of resources found in the North. In 1951, Canada's agricultural frontiers were pushed farther Arctic-ward into Alberta's northern wilderness as three large tracts of virgin land were opened up for homesteading in the Peace River area. All three tracts lie north of the 56 degree parallel, one of them extending beyond the 57 degree parallel of latitude. This is undoubtedly marginal farming land but it is no more marginal than are many of the near-Arctic frontiers of agriculture that the Soviets have opened up east of the Urals. The Peace River region is, however, generally looked upon as the Canadian West's last frontier for settlement.

The opening up of these tracts to homesteading was made possible largely through the work of oil exploration crews who were extending their search for petroleum into the northern part of the province. This suggests the second potential resource of the Northwest Territories, namely, minerals. The significance of the wilderness reserves has already been alluded to and two of the problems (insufficient manpower and the lack of risk capital) discussed. A third factor has entered in to retard the development of the north country, namely, transportation.

Lack of transportation facilities handicaps development of the North. A study of the map of communication and transportation connections of Canada indicates that, if Canada is to move northward, the transportation net—one of the finest in the world along the southern fringe of the country—must be extended into the north. Under existing transport conditions, full development cannot take place. In the east, rail facilities have been rapidly pushed into the Labrador fields. During the war, a major link for both the United States and Canada was the Alcan Highway that was built, under difficult conditions and with great speed, diagonally across the prairie provinces from the United States border into Alaska. Further developments, however—or the extension of

present mining activities—await better and extended facilities for taking the ores out.

On the other hand, so long as large economically exploitable reserves of ores exist in regions where rail service is more accessible, it may be that many of the known deposits of the Far North will remain relatively untouched.

Geopolitical Considerations

Like the USSR, Canada faces a tremendous problem in cleaving the vast territories, a problem that is accentuated beyond the factor of mere size by the terrainal difficulties induced largely by climate—namely, vast forest and brush lands, and swampy or snow-covered ground. Until the war and postwar era there appeared to be little reason for even attempting to integrate the whole of these territories. As in the Soviet state and Africa, air transport has done much to open up inaccessible parts and will undoubtedly be the major means of rapid communication throughout great portions of the North. As a matter of fact, the vehicle that was most valuable to Canadians in the exploration of the mineral resources in this wilderness territory was the airplane. It permitted the surveying of vast areas, the air-lifting of machinery, food, and the like into remote districts using pontoons in summer and skis in winter in lieu of landing strips. Air, rail, and highway communications alone can unlock the rich interior of the North.

Canada is a surplus nation. Canada, a large country rich in natural resources and productive power and but a small population, has a small national market. It produces, therefore, a great surplus of commodities. This surplus becomes a political and economic weapon with which: 1) to secure products in limited supply at home, 2) to win friends, and 3) to increase its power position within the world of nations. In addition to the mineral ores and agricultural products already referred to, Canada raises great numbers of animals—dairy and beef cattle, hogs, and poultry. Canada is, in fact, one of the world's major food-exporting countries. Besides wheat, Canadian beef, bacon, cheese, and eggs play an important role in feeding the peoples of many lands. In the past, Canada's markets have traditionally been in Europe, the United Kingdom, and the United States; the future pattern of Canadian exports will depend on a number of factors, including international currency exchange.

THE SIGNIFICANCE OF THE NORTH AMERICAN ARCTIC

The North American Arctic and Subarctic stand now in much the same relation to the rest of the continent as did the Far West a century ago. It is a vast frontier little known and almost entirely undeveloped. It has recently become accessible by means of long-range aircraft to a degree undreamed of a few years ago. The resources of its lands and seas, particularly its mineral wealth, hold promise of economic benefits for the entire continent. In addition this area, covering all of Alaska and Greenland and eighty per cent of Canada, has become within the past few decades an internationally significant region.

There is in this situation a challenge to modern science. For here is the opportunity, perhaps for the first time, to provide a scientific basis for the orderly development of a new land. It is a challenge to the seasoned scientist to employ his experience and talents to insure the broadest interpretation of the raw facts collected. It is a challenge to the young scientist to seek the rewards promised by a region daily increasing in importance for government and industry. It is a challenge—we must not overlook—already being met on a broad front by the other great powers which circle the Arctic Ocean.

But beyond this and of greater concern to the scientist is the unexcelled opportunity afforded in the Far North to add significant data to man's knowledge of his environment and himself. This area constitutes a huge laboratory, a natural "experimental set-up" not to be matched in temperate zones. The extremes of temperature, the perennially frozen ground, the alternating periods of constant daylight and darkness, the remnants of glaciation, the Aurora, the biological adaptivity of plants and animals, the profusion of life in the Arctic seas, the indigenous peoples—all are features inviting alike to studies in the natural, biological, and social sciences.[9]

THE ARCTIC MEDITERRANEAN

The increasing attention that Arctic regions have received in the past 75 years has been focused at times on one aspect of Arctic geography, at other periods on other features. Along both the Eurasian and North American Arctic waters explorers have sought a passageway from the Atlantic to the Pacific side. Nordenskjöld blazed the trail for the now regularly used Russian waterway; a number of explorers took part in plotting the Northwest Passage in the North American Arctic, a water route that has been navigated but a few times.

Meteorological exploration was a second interest that drew people Arctic-ward. A number of nations took part in these scientific pursuits but undoubtedly the Scandinavians led in the early weather observations, the continuance of which are adding so much to man's knowledge of the complex atmosphere that envelops our globe. Begun relatively early, the Soviets recently stepped up their Arctic weather research being particularly interested because of the great areas of the Russian domain that are "polar" in climate and because of their resolution to establish an Arctic Ocean passage that would link—by water—the two widely separated coasts. Today a vast network of weather, radar, and air stations—on land and on the sea—ties the Soviet Arctic together.

Compared to the Russian state, Canada and the United States have until very recently given little attention to Arctic research, use, or development.[10] The Japanese occupation of the Aleutian Islands—with the threat to the two states that this posed from the north—led the American nations to institute Arctic studies of many sorts as well as to begin the construction of the defense lines, facing the threatening Arctic. Through the government meteorological programs of both Alaska and Canada, significant data are being assembled; meteorological research is also being carried on by such private organizations as the Arctic Research Laboratory at Point Barrow. Research is

---

[9] "Pressing Scientific Problems of the North," New York: The Arctic Institute of North America, p. 1. (Mimeographed.)

[10] This statement holds true despite the work of Mackenzie (already referred to), Perry, Schwatka, and others.

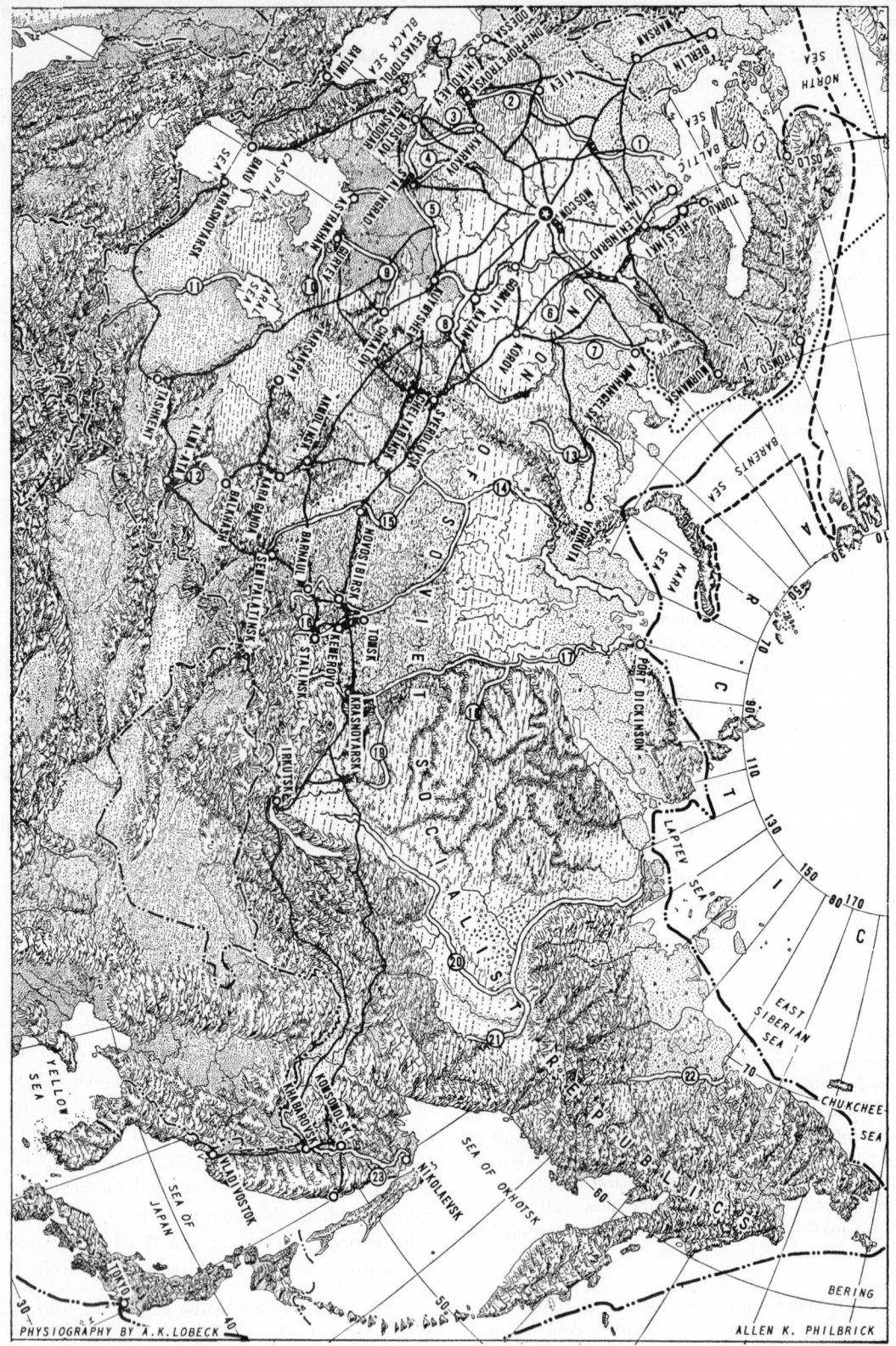

Figure 13.1.

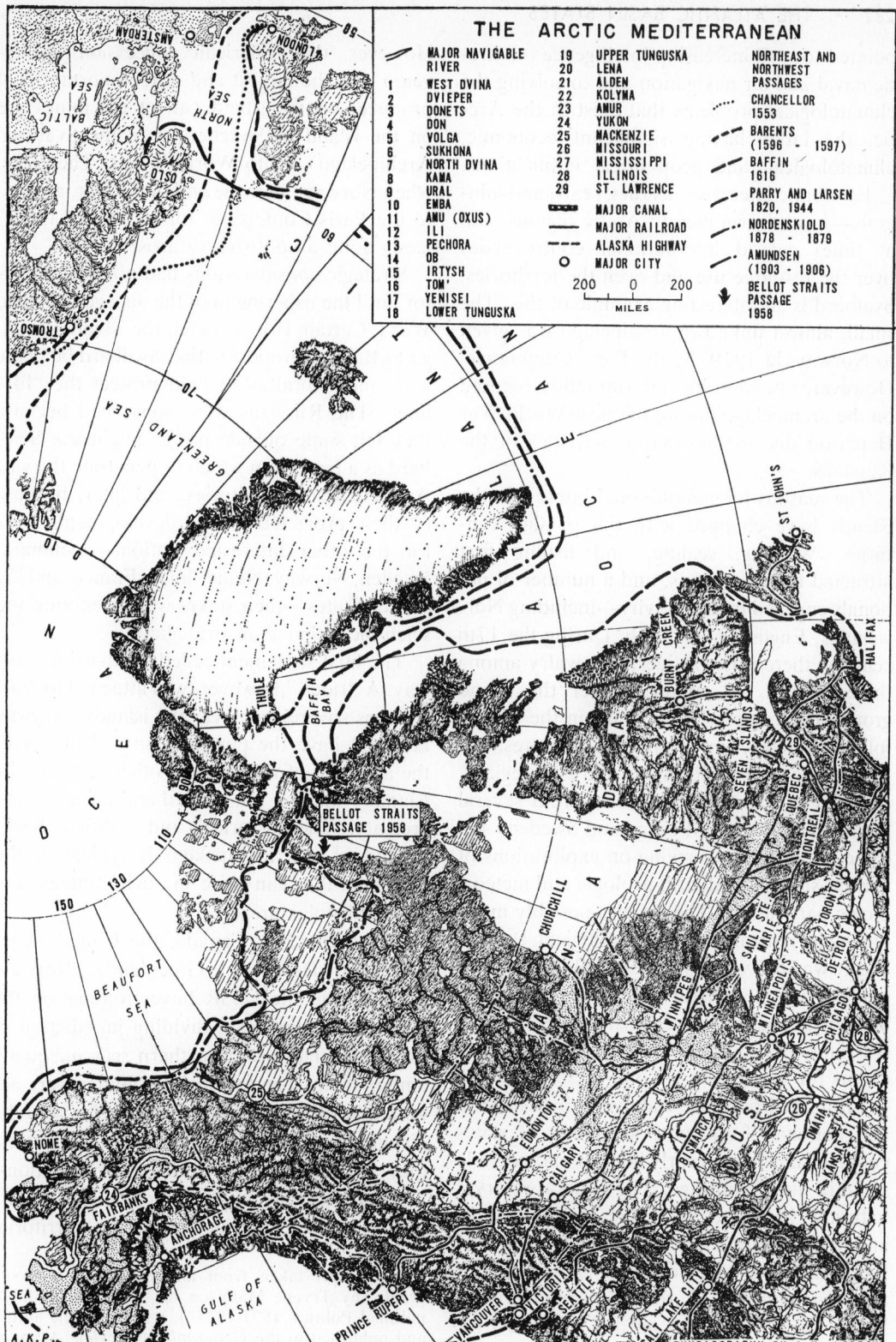

THE ARCTIC MEDITERRANEAN

	MAJOR NAVIGABLE RIVER	19	UPPER TUNGUSKA
1	WEST DVINA	20	LENA
2	DVIEPER	21	ALDEN
3	DONETS	22	KOLYMA
4	DON	23	AMUR
5	VOLGA	24	YUKON
6	SUKHONA	25	MACKENZIE
7	NORTH DVINA	26	MISSOURI
8	KAMA	27	MISSISSIPPI
9	URAL	28	ILLINOIS
10	EMBA	29	ST. LAWRENCE
11	AMU (OXUS)		MAJOR CANAL
12	ILI		MAJOR RAILROAD
13	PECHORA		ALASKA HIGHWAY
14	OB		MAJOR CITY
15	IRTYSH		
16	TOM'		
17	YENISEI		
18	LOWER TUNGUSKA		

NORTHEAST AND NORTHWEST PASSAGES

CHANCELLOR 1553
BARENTS (1596 - 1597)
BAFFIN 1616
PARRY AND LARSEN 1820, 1944
NORDENSKIOLD 1878 - 1879
AMUNDSEN (1903 - 1906)
BELLOT STRAITS PASSAGE 1958

200   0   200
MILES

BELLOT STRAITS PASSAGE 1958

PHYSIOGRAPHY BY A.K. LOBECK

pointed toward increasing intelligence on Arctic naval and air navigation and to solving the climatological problems that exist in the Arctic, the latter having significant economic, climatological, and geopolitical implications.

Economic interests—as furs, seals, and minerals—have drawn men to Arctic regions, and at times caused international controversies over the resource use and even the territories. Svalbard is an interesting example of this. The small, almost unknown archipelago was given to Norway, in 1919, by the Paris Conference. However, attention has intermittently focused on the archipelago during the post-World War II period due to the mining activities of the Russians.

The reasons for international interest in the islands have changed with the passing centuries. Whaling, sealing, and fishing first attracted the Europeans, and a number of nationals engaged in the activity—including Norwegians, English, and Dutch. During the 17th century, there was considerable rivalry among these nations for authority over the island group. The trapping of animals on the islands followed closely on the marine ventures, engaged in largely by Russians and Norwegians. As early as the 1860's scientists from several nations (particularly France and Sweden) became interested in carrying on explorations of various sorts in Svalbard, geologic and meteorologic particularly. The Swedes possibly made the most outstanding meteorological studies, and it was a Swede (Nordenskjöld) also who made the first mineral discoveries, in 1864. Shortly thereafter Norwegians, Swedes, British, Russians, Germans, and Americans staked out claims for the mining of coal.

From the brief review above, it is to be seen that nationals from quite a number of states could lay claim to an early interest and possible stake in the archipelago. The mineral reserves naturally increased the value of the islands, and to two states Svalbard coal was extremely significant—namely, Norway who needed it for the development of the coal-impoverished North, and Russia who needed it for fuel for the newly constructed Murmansk railroad.

However, the American concession (Longyear) was the largest and only important coal producer on the island (all of the mines are on the island of Spitzbergen in the Svalbard Archipelago) up to World War I. Therefore, when Norway, after the end of the war, applied to the Paris Conference for control of the islands quite a controversy arose.

Strategic considerations had not been a factor until the ushering in of the air-age in World War I. Certain Britishers felt the islands should go to Britain, proposing that Svalbard be made a second Gibraltar to help protect the "lifeline." The Russians were concerned because they felt some outside power might use Svalbard as a base from which to penetrate the vast Arctic Russian territories, and later, because of their projected Arctic developments. "As for the other interested nations—Denmark, Sweden, Norway, Netherlands, France, and the United States—their stakes were economic and scientific rather than strategic."[11]

The final settlement ceded Svalbard to Norway. A "rider," however, was attached to Norwegians sovereignty over the islands: Norway does not have the power of surveillance over the activities of nationals of other states in the islands—making it a limited and peculiar sovereignty. The historical and political background of this archipelago is typical of the problems that can arise in such strategic but marginal polar areas.

The Arctic Sea. Canada, the United States (Alaska), Denmark (Greenland), Norway, Iceland, and the USSR have frontage on the Arctic Mediterranean, dividing jurisdiction of the littoral lands and northern seas unequally among them. The territorial holdings were acquired in various ways, but, except for periodic disputes over fishing rights in territorial waters, they are today uncontested by other nations.

Somewhat by implicit agreement among most of the countries involved, "territorial

[11] Excerpts taken from an analysis of a monograph (by Trygve Mathison on "Svalbard in International Politics, 1871-1925"), written by the author and published in the *Geographical Review*, January, 1956.

waters" in these Arctic seas are regarded as extending in a wedge from the land-holdings of each state to an apex at the pole—each country laying claim to all of the land areas found within that sector of ice and water. The United States is the sole nation with large holdings that has not assumed this "right," and, in fact, challenges the USSR and Canada to such claims. (These three latter states are the only ones that acquire jurisdiction over any large areas of the Arctic Ocean under this plan, known as the *theory of polar sectorism*.)

Military defense measures in the Arctic regions—part of a worldwide strategic plan— grew out of the experience of World War II. That war, the first truly global conflict, saw fighting in several Arctic sectors: the North Atlantic and North Pacific Oceans, and in Northern Europe.

The speed with which developments in air and atomic warfare emerged during and after the war was largely responsible for giving to the basin of the Arctic Mediterranean the increased strategic importance it now holds, while the greater range and speed of aircraft (along with the destructive power of the new post-1945 weapons) increases the possibility of attack in the polar area as well as minimizes the effectiveness of defense preparations. Nevertheless, both the Soviet Union and the two American states are strengthening their positions in the North.

In accordance with the terms of international agreements compacted between the United States and several of the member nations of the North Atlantic Treaty Organization, there is a mutual exchange of data— meteorological, oceanographic, cartographic, military, etc.—in order that all of these nations can be in full possession of all of the facts that are known and used in the Arctic.

Should another world conflict break out, the land and seas of the Arctic Basin would certainly become the scene of major naval and air battles because it is from across "the pole" that any possible attack is expected to break. Canada, Siberia, and Alaska all face the prospect of becoming possible crush zones—in the jet air age.

14

Latin America

Latin America comprises the block of states that stretch from the Rio Grande River to Cape Horn. It encompasses all of the countries of the Western Hemisphere except the United States and Canada, both Anglo–American.

Ten of the independent Latin American countries are in South America, six are situated on the narrow intercontinental strip of land known as Central America, while to the north lies Mexico, on the North American continent and closest Latin neighbor of the United States. Three are island states within the West Indies' Archipelago.

The term "Latin" has been applied uniformly across this great area of nations because of their common heritage from two of the Latin states of Europe—Spain and Portugal. The Latin "veneer"—language, religion, customs —varies, and is "light or heavy" depending upon the degree of modification. Spain left the deepest imprint in Latin America for all of these nations—except Brazil, the largest, and Haiti, the smallest—were colonized by Spain. Brazil is linguistically Portuguese, Haiti is French—both languages borrowed from the mother country that settled the territory. In some of the countries, Indian dialects are more common than are the languages adopted from the European mother state. All are Roman Catholic.

Latin America is almost three times larger than the United States but the populations of the two areas are approximately equal.

THE TWO AMERICAS

The casual use of the label "American" when referring to the United States often leads people to forget that more Americans live outside than inside the bounds of that nation.

An interesting paradox is presented in the contrast found in the political structures of the two Americas, Anglo and Latin. The paradox was created by the dominant colonizing states, Britain and Spain (or Iberia). Spain, which, after many centuries of Moorish dominance, had cohered under the united effort to expel the Arabs from Iberia, transferred this idea of integration to the overseas colonies, administering Spanish America as a unit under officials who were as closely supervised from Spain as the contemporary means of communication permitted. Yet, with the passage of time, the Spanish Empire on the mainlands of Central and South America broke away—not as a unit, however, but as sixteen separate regional nuclei that later became as many sovereign states. Besides these countries of Spanish origin, there arose an independent Brazil and three dependent territories under the Dutch, British, and French (the Guianas).

Contrariwise, the colonies that later enlarged to become Anglo–America, and which, under the British, had been set up as several distinct and separate settlements, were left relatively free to rule themselves; each was completely distinct—and, it might be said, even hostile to each other. They formed, in the end, only *two large states* that incorporated into their domains not only the British lands, but French, Spanish, and Dutch territories as well. One of these two nations is still tied to the mother state by membership within the Commonwealth of Nations.

Other basic differences existed, and exist, between Latin and Anglo–America and help to distinguish them sharply from each other. One of these is found in the motives for settlement or exploration. To both continents came men who sought easy riches in the gold and other minerals, or in furs. To both came those who wished to spread the gospel of Christianity —or to escape religious intolerance and persecution. And the search for adventure was generously mixed in with such more practical reasons as the recouping of the royal treasury, and the clearance of prisons, or the cancellation of debts or jail terms.

In general, however, there was a basic difference in the class of people who first touched the shores of the two Americas: soldiers and plunderers made the first contacts for Spain, colonists looking for homes came to the territories north of the Rio Grande. However, the variant complexion of these two colonizing groups is what might have been expected in terms of the differing opportunities offered by the northern and southern continents. The Spanish explorers were fortunate enough to conquer lands where gold and silver were in relative abundance, and accessible; this naturally attracted a motley of men. There were no such known minerals in the lands settled by the North Europeans. Had there been, undoubtedly the migrants would have been more checkered in character.

Iberians preceded the Europeans of Northwest Europe by about a century in their settlement of the New World. When the English, Dutch, and French did begin, however, successful colonization proceeded at a much faster pace than in Latin America. There were two basic reasons for this. The first is found in the differing environments of the two regions. The Europeans of northwest Europe migrated westward *along similar lines of latitude* so that they settled in areas with relatively comparable environments to those they left—temperate, mid-latitude zones. Here it was comparatively easy to transplant not only their culture but all of the appurtenances of that culture, such as the methods of agriculture, the crops, and animals. The Iberians, on the other hand, *cut across the lines of latitude* to invade tropical or subtropical areas, in most instances very different from those at home. They were difficult environments, either too hot and wet, or topographically rugged. It was necessary, therefore, to initiate a new pattern of life. Under the Spanish, tropical plantation agriculture, with great numbers of native slave-laborers working under a feudal system, grew up.

The second reason lies in the pattern of settlement that took place—the two very different, but both quite suited to the lands within which they developed. Although many of the original thirteen North American colonies were laid out on the basis of huge tracts granted to a family or an individual or a group, these were broken down for the most part into plots of workable family size—relatively small—and given to the colonists. In the Spanish territories, on the other hand, the large or even huge estate was the pattern followed. This same structure of land grant and ownership has tended to persist. When new territories opened up in the North American West beyond Appalachia, the 160-acre grant or homestead became the typical pattern; in Latin America, the large "European" holding has endured.

In view of these contrasting patterns of land ownership, a paradox appears. Although it might well be supposed that the "small farmer" and democratic processes should naturally lead to an amalgamation of the indigene with the foreigner, in Anglo–America the Indian was eventually dispossessed of his lands and relegated to reservations. Restricted in area and isolated from the main body of the population, he has made no contribution (except for minor ones in the early colonial period) to the civilization and culture patterns of the Anglo–American nations. Canada and the United States reflect only European influences—modified to fit the American environment. In Latin America, on the other hand, there has been an amalgamation of European and Indian culture —in some instances, the Indian influence is dominant; in others, the Iberian. Language, religion, and architecture are undoubtedly the greatest contributions of the Spanish and Portuguese in Latin America. The Indian, however, is an equally dominant motif. Latin America is really Iberian–Indian.

Another interesting contrast is found in the pattern of settlement that the English- and Latin-speaking colonists took. Whereas most Americans in the United States are lowlanders, the majority of people in Latin America dwell in regions with elevations of a thousand feet and higher—often much higher, as the plateau dwellers of Peru, Ecuador, Bolivia, and Colombia. This is true because so much of Latin America is tropical; people move to the highlands to escape the heat. The basin of Latin America's greatest river, the Amazon, is almost empty as compared with the Mississippi Basin in the United States.

A further contrast is one that has not been imposed by man—namely, location. A study of a polar map reveals that Anglo–America is centrally located relative to the land masses, the populations, the industrial centers, and the markets of the world; most of Latin America is peripheral. Anglo–America is nodal; much of Latin America marginal and lying on the fringes of the commercial and political world.

In certain other aspects of location the two Americas are remarkably alike. Both face two oceans—the Atlantic and Pacific—as well as a polar sea. But whereas the North Atlantic and the North Pacific are the world's most travelled oceans, the South Atlantic and South Pacific are, by themselves, of minor importance in world trade. The same thing holds true of the polar waters: while the Arctic has become a "mediterranean" sea in the air age, the Antarctic remains, and must always remain, peripheral—because most of the southern hemisphere is only a desolation of water and, hence, cannot act as the home of man. Where men live, things become important!

Hemispheric Relations

Latin America and Anglo–America have many historic similarities. All were colonies of European states; most share a tradition of revolutionary independence; all occupy a location in the "New World."

On the other hand, as pointed out, there are differences among the states—differences in language, culture, and outlook; differences in political traditions and legal systems, the latter reflecting the varied European backgrounds from which these governmental structures were drawn.

The outlook of the United States and Canada is conditioned by an acceptance of responsibility toward world affairs. Latin America has been less concerned with global matters and the reaction to international emergencies is often delayed in the portions of the hemisphere "south of the border." There is a sense of remoteness among the Latins, based, to a certain extent, on sheer distance. To vast numbers of "Latin" Americans— who in many regions are far more Indian than Latin—the next state is as far away as are the countries on the other side of the universe. However, since World War II this has been somewhat changed. Active participation in the United Nations is evidence of this.

The United States has made many efforts—

historic and contemporary—to effect close relationships with the Latin American countries. Why are these states important to the United States?

The Latin American states are vital to American defense. In the most material sense, under international conditions where the world is divided into two opposed power blocs, the vast region between Texas and Tierra del Fuego represents 20 votes in the United Nations. Because of this, a close liaison is maintained by the United States' delegation with the representatives from Latin America on all issues. Secondly, a friendly Latin America means a safe border, not only along the Rio Grande but along the Caribbean and Pacific approaches to the strategic Panama Canal as well. Thirdly, in terms of military support, Central and South America represent not only manpower but, even more, highly strategic materials.

Beyond the need for mutual defense lies the economic importance of Latin and Anglo–America to each other. The United States buys some 44 per cent of the gross produce of Latin America. Sugar from Cuba, coffee from Colombia and Brazil, oil from Venezuela, tin from Bolivia, copper, nitrates, iron ore from Chile, and iron from Brazil are only some of the more obvious items of trade that flow in great streams to the United States. In turn, the Latins depend heavily upon the United States for many needed commodities, particularly manufactures.

Pan Americanism is a concept that had its roots both in the United States and in Latin America. In 1823, the Monroe Doctrine made clear that European powers did not have the right to intervene in American affairs or seize American territory. Three years later Simon Bolivar, the Great Liberator, called the first convention of American states—the Congress of Panama. The aim was both similar to and different from that of the Monroe Doctrine— namely, to form a confederation to protect the hemisphere from foreign attack *and* to settle inter-American disputes.

The first International Conference called by the United States met in Washington in 1889-90. The Commercial Bureau that was set up at this meeting developed, in 1910, into the Pan American Union. Subsequently, nine International Conferences have been convened.

At the Bogota Conference (1948) the Charter of the Organization of American States (OAS) was adopted. Twenty-one American nations regulate their international relations with each other on the basis of this organization, the stated purposes of which are: 1) to strengthen the peace and security of the area; 2) to prevent possible causes of difficulties and to ensure the pacific settlement of disputes that may arise among the member states; 3) to provide for common action on the part of those states in the event of aggression; 4) to seek the solution of political, judicial, and economic problems that may arise among them; 5) to promote, by cooperative action, economic, social, and cultural development. The Pan American Union is its Secretariat.

Another organization that promotes inter-American unity is the Inter-American Treaty of Reciprocal Assistance (the Rio Pact) signed in Rio de Janeiro in 1947. This treaty provided for collective action to maintain peace and security within the hemisphere and to defend the Americas against any aggression from without. The Rio Pact was really the fulfillment to Bolivar's dream. The treaty's enforcement measures to halt aggression were made binding on all parties by a two-thirds majority. However, no state is required to use armed forces without its consent.

Political Stability and Instability in Latin America

The most serious challenge to progress in Latin America and to hemispheric relations has been the unevenness of Latin American politics. Central America has been called the "Balkans of the Americas," and the violence and instability that has long been endemic among the Central American republics located at "the hemisphere's waistline" finds a repetitious counterpart on the continent to the south.

Political turmoil has been continuous from the days of the wars of independence up to the present moment.

Some of the political difficulties of the Western Latins stem from the paternalistic nature of the colonial systems. Spain ruled its dependencies in a manner that negated experience in self-government: the reins of government were held tightly in the hands of Spaniards sent from Iberia, preventing any direct contact of the Latin American states with other nations; the colonies were exploited for the benefit only of the colonizers; intrusion of thought from the outside was resisted by a system of strict censorship.

However, the American and French Revolutions acted like an inspiration to the Latins and, shortly thereafter, the struggle for sovereignty began. French Haiti was the first colony to declare its independence. In 1804, taking advantage of the struggles on the European continent, it broke away from France. During the next fifty years all of the territories that later formed the Latin American states attained liberty, except Cuba. Between the decline of Spanish power and the rise of United States influence, Latin America was organized into the 20 independent nations (plus the several European colonies).

Political freedom did not mean a clean break from the authoritarian traditions of the colonial regimes. The Iberian colonial powers had not undergone the social, economic, and political revolutions that had brought change to France and England and, consequently, the new countries, patterning themselves after the Iberian states, were in structure similar to the countries of Medieval Europe. For nearly 100 years they subsisted as backward agricultural countries dominated by a few large landowners and foreign companies. It was only with the spread of modern contacts and the bulge in export profits—during and after World War II—that forceful demands among the masses began to foment a change. The result has been internal political tension, strain, and even chaos.

International boundary disputes have also kept Latin America in a state of intermittent tension for a period of nearly 150 years. When it is remembered that, in proportion to the size of the continent, the inter-state boundaries are second in length only to those of Europe, frontier tension is not unexpected. A second reason for boundary friction lies in the fact that, while most of the boundary divisions had their origin in the Spanish provincial boundaries of the colonial period, none of these had been exactly delineated. Therefore, when the empire broke up into sovereign states, disputes naturally arose as the young countries laid claim to what they considered their rightful domains.

There are 37 international boundaries in Latin America (if the Panama Canal Zone is considered as a territory apart). Most of these have been delineated since the mid-nineteenth century, and many during the last five decades. S. Whittemore Boggs of the State Department wrote:

When one considers South America as a whole it is indeed astonishing . . . that so many boundaries were established by pacific means. It should be recalled that an extraordinary number of problems arose in establishing the boundaries, following upon a period in which the authority of the Old World was severed by means of force; that the attempt was made to fix the frontiers as far as feasible in accordance with the terms of an almost continuous stream of Spanish decrees and laws relating to administrative, judicial, and ecclesiastical jurisdictions which overlapped one another; that precision of definition of boundaries could not exceed the contemporary inadequate geographical knowledge of a vast new continent; and that no controversies are more disturbing to amicable relations between nations than those relating to boundaries. Not without reason is Brazil rather proud of the fact that all of its ten boundaries have been peacefully determined; and several of the remaining fifteen frontiers of the continent have likewise been established without recourse to armed conflict. The complexities of the problems involved, partly because little geography was known and a great deal of history was remembered, account for the large place that boundary-making occupies in the history of South America.[1]

---

[1] S. Whittemore Boggs, *International Boundaries, op. cit.*, pp. 74-5.

Population and People

Sixteen per cent of the land area of the globe, but only six per cent of its population, is found in Latin America. Today, however, the Latin American population is increasing more rapidly than that of any other major region in the world.

Four main groups of people make up the inhabitants of Latin America—Indians, Negroes, Europeans, and a variety of mixed races. Of the latter group the *mestizos* (mixed Indian and white) possibly make up the greatest number; they also comprise the largest part of the people as a whole. The next largest element in the population is the Indian who has contributed richly to the culture of the whole area. The Negroes, whose ancestors were brought from Africa as slaves, number many thousands; they are found primarily in coastal Brazil and the Caribbean countries. Those of Portuguese and Spanish ancestry form by far the largest body of Europeans although there are others who have come more recently as immigrants. These non-Iberian Europeans—and Asians—form substantial minorities. The mixture of races in Latin America has, in general, been a harmonious one.

Latin American society is comprised of two layers. The mass of the people live very simply; many are poor, and there is no substantial middle-class. The social structure of Latin America is that of a small group of wealthy individuals at the top with the vast majority living at substandards. Thus, there is a great inequity in the distribution of wealth. Further, in many countries the wealthy have not invested in such a way as to contribute to the prosperity and general welfare of the masses in the region.

The cultural and social schism between the two classes is as great as is the economic division. Not even a common religion brings them together for, so far as the native Indian is concerned, Roman Catholicism was superimposed upon ancient pagan beliefs and his religion is a weird mixture of Christianity and the worship of the pagan gods. In certain areas, Christianity is more of a veneer to the Indian than a basic belief.

The advantages of culture are as unequally shared. Only two or three Indians out of every ten can read and write; only in Costa Rica does literacy run higher. It is significant that in the latter state there is also a marked feeling of "civic awareness" among the general population. However, in Costa Rica the population is relatively non-Indian and homogeneous—*and* European—for the early Spaniards nearly wiped out the native people. Here, too, the Costa Rican of European ancestry works the land and inhabits the rural areas—a condition not generally obtaining in the other countries. Yet stratification remains, and the Costa Rican peasant is, culturally, "centuries away" from the officials who rule the state. As for the typical Indian of Latin America, he scarcely belongs to the same civilization as his compatriots of European ancestry.

Throughout all of Latin America social stratification remains rigid for the few hold the wealth; in all states except Costa Rica the great bulk of the productive land is in the hands of a few hundred families. The few have the education and ambition—and the few hold the power; everywhere the fissure between the rich and the poor is tremendous and thwarting; contrasts are abrupt. Therefore, in all of the countries of Latin America, the economic and social chasms have left the governments without underpinning.

Latin American Economy

Although political colonialism was thrown off over a century ago, the economic structure throughout much of the area is such that it might be termed *economic colonialism*. Such "colonialism" is epitomized in the economic dependence of some of the countries upon foreign corporation plantation agriculture and in the system of large landholdings. In the former instance, Central America is more affected than is the southern continent.

Nationalist sentiment, however, has increasingly demanded some measure of government control over foreign investment and the exploitation of resources. On the other side of the picture, there has developed a reluctance to invest on the part of foreigners unless the reasonable return and freedom from expropriation can be assured. The trouble of the United Fruit Company with the Guatemalan Government in 1954 is a case that illustrates both aspects of the problem of foreign investment brought out above; it also exemplifies the point made on economic colonialism.[2]

Latin America is predominantly agricultural. The great majority of Latin Americans are subsistence cultivators. Due, however, to the large proportion of Latin America that is tropical or subtropical, the area is valuable as a source of tropical agricultural products—commodities that cannot be raised in the midlatitude states where the greatest markets are located. Many of the products of agriculture find their way into world trade channels, therefore. However, commercially, many of the countries have one- or two-crop economies and are highly dependent upon fluctuations in price and demand on the world market—as coffee and bananas. The need is for greater diversification so as to lessen dependence on international trade.

The agricultural potential is still a long way from being fully developed. Several factors contribute to this condition. As with the development of minerals, transportation handicaps certain areas; in many places, due to the low population density, there is a labor shortage; further, there are no large local or national markets.

Many of the states of Latin America have rich and varied mineral resources awaiting development. It was the fabulous store of gold and silver in Mexico and Peru that attracted the Spanish *conquistadores* at the beginning of the colonial period. In the modern era, the best-known mineral ores are Mexican silver, Bolivian tin, Chilean nitrates, and Venezuelan oil; manganese and iron ore in Brazil, and iron ore in Chile and Venezuela are not as well

known but contribute no less to the rich reserves of mineral wealth. However, only Brazil, Argentina, Mexico, and Chile have begun both the development of the mineral potential *and/or* manufacturing; Venezuelan iron and oil are being developed with the aid of foreign capital.

Economically, Latin America makes a substantial contribution to world commerce. The mineral, animal, and agricultural riches—potential and actual—make Latin America one of the world's great sources for raw materials.

Communication

Inadequate communications have hampered economic development and political coherence in the Latin American states. Retarded development of transportation facilities results from conditions of political instability, lack of capital, and the physical geography of the area. The latter factor has been very important, for the physical features of the continent present many difficulties. The high Andes are a tremendous barrier to transportation. The Amazon rainforests are an even more formidable obstacle—if this is possible: swamp lands, hundreds of thousands of square miles of the most absolute tropical rainforests in the world, accompanied by excessive heat and high humidity, make difficult and expensive the building of communication lines. Further, the almost "empty" character of the region (in terms of human occupants) is another discouraging factor. Therefore, vast areas are devoid of any surface means of transportation except river boat. The plains' regions south of latitude 15 degrees and a few scattered coastal areas are the only places where anything approaching an adequate railroad and road net is to be found.

Central and South America fall far short of the integrated railroad systems that characterize both West Europe and the United States, therefore. There are, however, some transcontinental lines that cross both Central and South America. In the latter continent, between the La Plata estuary on the one hand and the Valparaiso and Lake Titicaca districts on the other, eastern spurs from the Atlantic connect

[2] See "News of the Week" section of the *New York Times,* Sunday edition, July 4, 1954, p. 4E, "United Fruit Company is a Vast Enterprise."

with those from the Pacific to give South America east-west lines in the southern half. In Central America, Mexico, Panama and Guatemala have ocean-to-ocean connections. Whereas in the past most railroad development was carried out by foreign investors, a number of states have now nationalized their rail lines.

In such a land of high mountains and steamy rainforests the advantages of air transport are immediately apparent, and air communication in Latin America is highly developed as compared with other types of transport—both nationally and internationally. The most extensive air development has occurred since 1940. Improved airports and airmail subsidies have been a part of this program.

One of the most ambitious undertakings of highway construction ever attempted any place in the world is in the process of completion in Latin America, namely, the Pan American Highway. Commencing at the Texan border town of Laredo, it will eventually connect all of the states in Central and South America by paved highway. Today it extends, interruptedly, southward across Mexico and into Central America, in about 800 miles of unconnected links. New blocks of the road are constantly being added but it will be several years yet before the through highway is completed.

The great river systems of South America provide a valuable supplement to the roads, and railroads, and airlines; and they make communication possible in some areas where penetration would otherwise be very difficult. The Amazon is navigable nearly all the way across the continent at its broadest width—for 2000 miles from the mouth to the foothill country of the Andes. There are, besides, hundreds of miles of tributaries that are navigated. The Uruguay–Paraguay–Parana–La Plata system is another water channel that permits navigation far into the interior, as do also the Orinoco of Venezuela and the São Francisco.

CENTRAL AMERICA

Central America comprises an area but slightly smaller than the combined territory of New England, New York, and Pennsylvania, yet the population (8 million) is not much greater than that of New York City alone! Located at the waistline of the hemisphere, it at once connects two continents and divides two oceans; hence, it is a crossroads of the Western Hemisphere.

Diverse in many ways, there are nevertheless more similarities than differences among the six little nations that occupy this narrow strip of intercontinental terrain; they rise from coastal littorals, where steamy jungles are bordered by banana and cacao plantations, to the rugged highlands important for their coffee groves. The cities of Central America are Spanish, a remnant of colonial days; the forests and the mountains are largely Indian; the great commercial plantations are generally foreign enterprises or in the hands of a few influential old families.

Central America has been called "the troublesome backyard" of the United States because the politics of this volcano-packed little territory have been almost as explosive as are the physical phenomena. In fact, Central America has long been considered the barometer of United States–Latin American relations: when harmony characterizes the relations between Central America and the United States, that condition generally obtains between the United States and the remainder of Latin America.

Central America is vital to the United States. Economic ties draw the two regions close—Central America is very dependent upon United States for markets and for the goods they buy. Secondly, geographic proximity makes these little countries strategic to the North American state; so long as the world remains divided and the United States has strong enemies, hostility south of the border would be intolerable. Thirdly—as mentioned before —there is Panama.

The Panama Canal and Panama

It is somewhat paradoxical that Panama, the first portion of the mainland in the Western Hemisphere to be colonized, has not—more

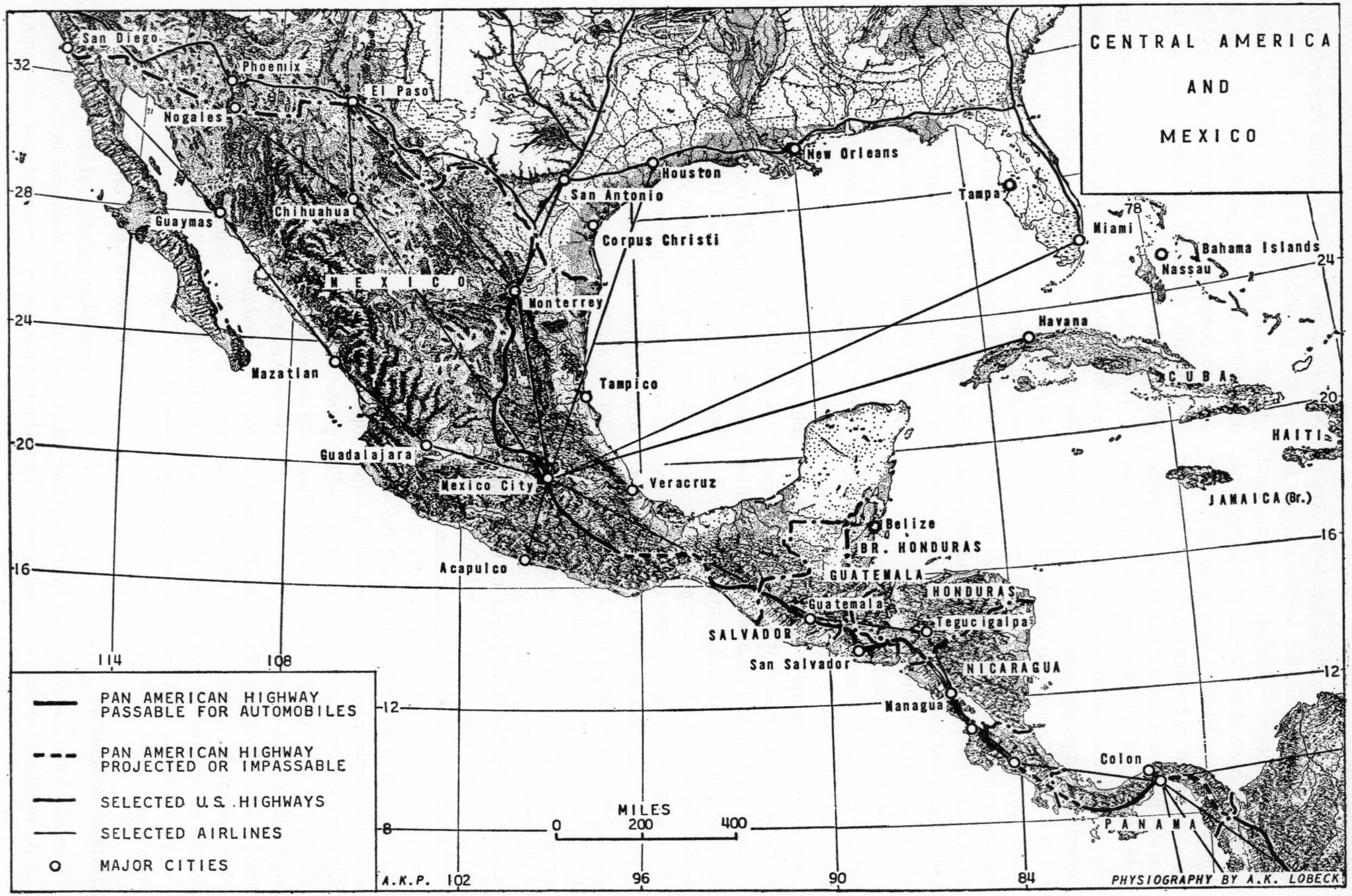

CENTRAL AMERICA
AND
MEXICO

PHYSIOGRAPHY BY A.K. LOBECK

MILES

0   200   400

A.K.P.

PAN AMERICAN HIGHWAY
PASSABLE FOR AUTOMOBILES

PAN AMERICAN HIGHWAY
PROJECTED OR IMPASSABLE

SELECTED U.S. HIGHWAYS

SELECTED AIRLINES

MAJOR CITIES

Figure 14.1

San Diego, Phoenix, Nogales, Guaymas, El Paso, Chihuahua, Mazatlan, Guadalajara, Mexico City, Acapulco, Monterrey, San Antonio, Corpus Christi, Houston, New Orleans, Tampico, Veracruz, Tampa, Miami, Nassau, Bahama Islands, Havana, CUBA, HAITI, JAMAICA (Br.), Belize, BR. HONDURAS, GUATEMALA, Guatemala, SALVADOR, San Salvador, HONDURAS, Tegucigalpa, NICARAGUA, Managua, Colon, PANAMA

M E X I C O

than 450 years after its discovery (1501)—been fully explored. Large areas are unknown except by aerial photography; its economy might be described as in a state of retardation, if not stagnation.

These conditions result largely from the fact that Panama, down through the centuries, has been a transit land. In Spanish colonial days the treasures of the Inca kingdom moved by mule train across the Panamanian jungle trail (known as the Camino de Oro), to the port of Portobelo on the Atlantic side, for transfer to the galleons that carried the treasure back to Spain—or to capture by a pirate ship. The California gold rush of 1849 brought another stream of travellers across the isthmus, this time prospectors. The deadly conditions of the tropical climate (made apparent in the toll among the transmigrants at this period) led to the construction of the Panama Railroad—transcontinental, but spanning the continent at a point only 50 miles wide. The third facet of Panama's role as a transit land came in 1914 with the opening of the Panama Canal by the United States.

The relations of the United States with Panama date back to 1903. Under the administration of Theodore Roosevelt, the United States signed an agreement with Colombia (of which Panama was then a part) for the right to construct a canal across the isthmus.

The Colombian Senate refused to ratify the agreement. Fearful lest an alternative route through Nicaragua be selected—and encouraged by the United States, which prevented Colombia from landing troops on the isthmus—Panama revolted and, on November 3 of the same year, declared itself a republic. Within two weeks the newly constituted state and the United States had signed a treaty for the building of a canal, creating the Canal Zone, then a strip extending across the isthmus five miles wide on either side of the Canal. The treaty granted the use of the Canal Zone to the United States *in perpetuity* and gave full authority over the area to the American state. For this control the United States paid Panama the sum of 10 million dollars in cash and promised an annuity of 250,000 dollars.

The 1903 treaty also gave the United States the right to intervene in political disputes that might interfere with the operation of the canal. The first such "interference" occurred in 1908 when there was trouble between the political parties in Panama; the United States later exercised this prerogative on several other occasions. However, other Latin American states have been opposed to such American intervention in Latin affairs, and, in 1931, when internal political strife broke out anew, the United States desisted from interfering and it has not done so since that date.

In 1936, the original agreement was modified in the United States–Panama General Treaty signed in Washington on March 2. The latter treaty "formalizes the legal and political relationships" of the two nations. It also increased the annuity to 450,000 dollars. Since that time further changes have been sought by Panama.

However, American power within the Canal Zone has decreased. After World War II, a political storm arose over the use of land for American bases on Panama territory. Acceding to Panamanian pressure, by 1947 all but 17 of these bases had been returned to Panama and the government in power agreed to permit the United States to keep the latter, most of which were radar outposts and fighter strips. However, so violent was Panamanian public reaction against this that the United States finally abandoned all bases within the republic.

The Canal Zone is, quite literally, an enclave of American territory in the Panamanian republic, and it binds the little state closely to the United States, historically and defensively. As for the effects upon Panama, that country is physically cut in two by the American-controlled zone and waterway; further, it has made the economy so dependent upon the Canal Zone that scarcely any other aspect of the country has been developed. More than one-fourth of the 800,000 people of the republic live in the two terminal canal cities of Colon and Panama City.

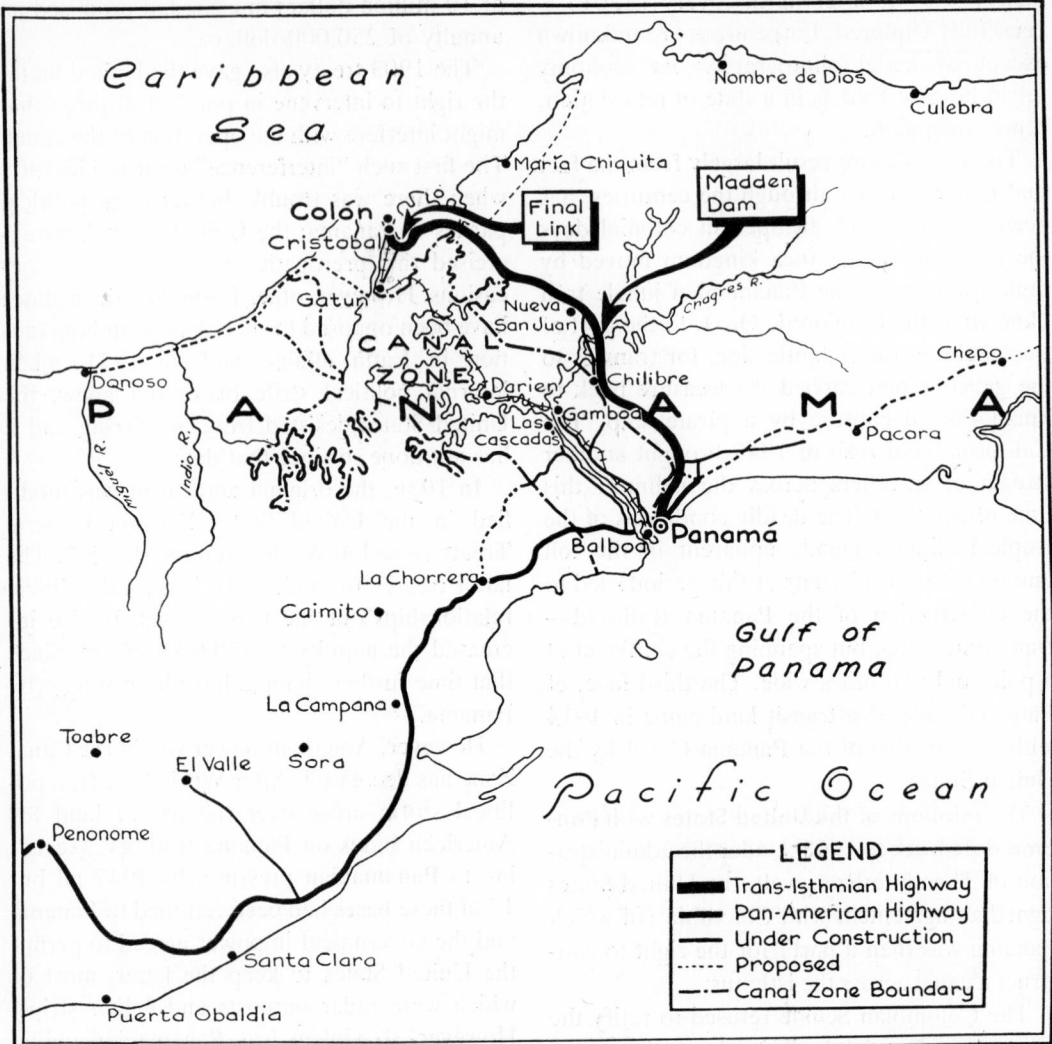

Figure 14.2. Panama Canal Zone. The New Highway Goes Outside of the Canal Zone but Helps Zone Traffic. (R. Lenz, cartographer. Courtesy *The Christian Science Monitor.*)

Until 1914 there were only two modes of transportation by which the Atlantic and Pacific coasts of the isthmus were connected—by boat via the canal and by train via the century-old railway (in many places only single-tracked). It became apparent to the United States during and after World War II that there should be highway connections between the two coasts, and finally, in 1949, such a highway was opened, American financed and con-

structed, at a cost of 10 million dollars. The highway, built for Panama without obligation to that state, must be maintained by Panama. Under the existing conditions of transport, quick movement of military personnel and equipment had not been possible. Further, both the canal and railroad were subject to damage or destruction and not easily repaired. Hence, from the point of view of security, the construction of the highway was imperative. At present, therefore, the area in the immediate vicinity of the canal is adequately integrated with communication facilities. Throughout the remainder of Panama, however, except for the Pan American Highway, there are no modern means of transportation available. Because of this, much of the country remains marginal.

The Panamanian economy is unbalanced. Bananas, cacao, and abaca make up two-thirds of the value of Panamanian exports, which, in 1952, totaled approximately 12.5 million dollars. Most of these exports are shipped out by the United Fruit Company (called the Chiriqui Land Company in Panama), described by some as "the most important single factor in the economy of Panama." Whether the statement is true or not, this colossal American organization has an annual gross payroll of 8 million dollars—one-fifth as great as the total annual budget of the state of Panama. It is, therefore, a huge business and economically very significant. It creates, however, an imbalance in the Panamanian economy because it makes the country too dependent upon the one enterprise.

The economy of the country has another interesting side—namely, its maritime interests. On the basis of registered tonnage, the Republic is the world's fourth largest maritime power—exceeded only by the United States, Great Britain, and Norway. And yet it owns not a ship; it has no shipyards and no ports. The only ports within the republic, outside of the Canal Zone, are two interior ports owned by the United Fruit Company, built and operated for a special purpose. Nevertheless, some 600 ships, totaling 4.5 million tons, fly the flag of this small Central American state.

How can such a circumstance obtain? The pre-World War II Neutrality Act gave the impetus that led to the building of this remarkable fleet. In 1940, United States' shipowners found the oceans zoned and many areas of the high seas barred to their ships so long as they were registered under the United States. Transferring registration to Panama, they were unrestricted in any waters. Many ships made the transfer, and it was perhaps to the advantage of the American government that they did—because American vessels could move throughout the globe unimpeded despite restrictions on United States' shipping. Ships from more than 30 countries now fly the Panamanian flag.

Panamanian populaion is a mixed one. About half the size of the state of Michigan, this Latin American republic is populated thinly by less than a million people. However, in keeping with its character as a crossroads, the population is a mixed one. The largest segment of the people are Indian, living, in the main, in the outlying districts, retarded socially and economically. Negroes from the British West Indian territories make up a substantial minority. They came as laborers at the time of the construction of the railroad about a century ago, and more arrived when the canal was dug. Many remained, and today this West Indian Negro presents Panama's major population problem. They were to have been repatriated at the end of the building projects, but nothing was ever done to return them to their West Indian homes and they remain in Panama as a distinct, unassimilated minority.

Other minorities are the East Indians and Chinese who, like the Negroes, remain a people apart, holding to the customs and languages of their homelands. Despite the distinctness of these four different racial populations, Panama has not been troubled with serious racial strife, as such, and racial discrimination is unlawful in the Republic.

The Strategic Canal

Particularly in an air and atomic-hydrogen age is the Panama Canal very vulnerable. Only adequate radar outposts, able to give warning to fighter aircraft, are an adequate defense of the waterway today. In the past, the canal was regarded as vulnerable from the Caribbean area, and it was as a defense outpost for the Canal Zone that the Virgin Islands were purchased, in 1917, by the United States from Denmark.

Geopolitically, the isthmus is linked to the Caribbean; historically, however, it was a part of South America. In terms of geology,

Panama is a part of Central America, and it is geology that gives it its tremendous geopolitical importance. Although an examination of a map of the whole of Central America might seem to indicate a number of other "crossings" between the Atlantic and Pacific realms, it is significant that no other transcontinental route has ever seriously competed with the Isthmus as the location for the connecting waterway. Even on land, there has been no competitor. This proves the superioriy of the isthmus location for the canal.

THE PLATEAU STATES: MEXICO, PERU, AND BOLIVIA

Less than 50 years after Columbus discovered the islands of the Caribbean, Spain had broken much of the power of the native rulers and had established itself in all parts of what later became Spanish America. By 1513, the Isthmus of Panama was spanned; eight years later the Spanish, gaining access to the Mexican Plateau via Veracruz, had subdued the resistance of the powerful Aztecs; in 1532 and 1533 the Incas of Peru had been crushed and two years later the whole of the central Andean Plateau had been taken.

On the new continents, the Spanish had thus conquered the two most powerful of the indigenous empires—the Aztec and the Inca. Both were plateau domains, and on the sites of these native centers the Spanish set up their two kingdoms, each ruled by a viceroy. Although it was seemingly obvious to them that there were two individual land masses that required separate administration, what was not at first apparent was the tremendous extent of territory set up under each of these political cores. But it was not long before a subdivision of the territories became necessary. The first political units were the *audiencias;* they presaged subsequent administrative subdivisions, most of which later became the nuclei for the independent states of Latin America.

Although relatively inaccessible, the two plateaus (the Mexican Plateau and the Altiplano) were attractive to the Spanish. In the first place, they found—ready for the taking—the rich reserves of gold and silver treasure that were stored by the Indians. In a matter of five or six years they had made away with this, in the meantime seeking the *sources* of the mineral wealth. Already skilled in mining, not even the most inaccessible mines proved too difficult for them; they had the mining techniques and the indigenes were conscripted to provide the labor. The Spanish were themselves more or less acclimated to the elevation of the plateaus coming, as they did, from the Spanish Meseta.

This latter feature was the second reason for the drawing power of the plateaus—on them the Spanish found natural conditions somewhat similar to those at home. Physiographically, all three were basin structures crossed by ranges of highlands; climatically, they were similar in being dry and dusty much of the year, and moist the rest of the time; all were characterized by a lack of tree vegetation; all experienced great differences in temperature between night and day. On the Peruvian and Mexican Plateaus, as on the Meseta, water shortage was an outstanding handicap.

Thirdly, the plateaus offered escape from the inhospitable tropical lowlands that bordered the coast—in Peru from arid tropical deserts, in Mexico from humid and malarial tropics. The Mediterranean coastal plains of Iberia were not, however, a counterpart of either of these zones, and in this the regions differed.

On these two plateaus then—one in North America, the other south of the Isthmus—Spain set up two centers from which control extended to include a large part of the Western Hemisphere. From the triangular plateau of Mexico the Spanish spread their power along the Pacific to encompass an area stretching from Lower California and the southern part of the present state of California approximately to the latitude of San Francisco and inland in the Rocky Mountains and plateau region until stopped by the Canyon of the Colorado; along the Gulf they spread eastward to where arid country becomes humid. All of these latter territories were later taken by the United

States. (Interestingly, the frontier between Mexican and United States territory, in the vicinity of the California–Arizona border, follows a low "saddle" that marks a break between the Rockies and the Sierra Madre Occidental—a passageway that comprises the major corridor between the Pacific Coast state and the more humid east.) Southward Spanish power effectively held nearly the same territory that is now Mexican. The Isthmus of Tehuantepec is really the "line of weakness"[3] in the south. It is a low break—tropical and forested —between highlands. The Mexican state of Chiapas lies south of this line.

Today the nuclear plateaus are still the core centers of the modern states of Mexico and Peru. Mexico City still remains the capital of the country, the plateau the ecumene of the nation. The Valley of Mexico, lying in the south central portion of the plateau, is the political, cultural, and social center as the plateau is the economic core. Outward from the plateau the bonds become weaker, transportation- and other-wise. Now, as historically, the narrow coastal littorals along both shores, and the desert to the north, have tended to be held by the power that controlled the plateau. Lower California, almost rent from the rest of the country, has always been a political sore spot.

Economically, the coastal regions make their valuable contributions. Along the east coast are the Mexican oil fields, with a production that generally places the country among the first ten oil producers—although near the bottom of the list; on the west coast, irrigation agriculture has developed along the eleven rivers that flow from the mountains into the sea.

The easiest approach to the plateau is from the west, from Acapulco to Mexico City. Here the topography slopes more gently up to the plateau than along either of the routes leading from Veracruz to the highland region. During Spanish colonial days the route across Mexico, via Acapulco, was much used for the transshipment of goods from the Spanish holdings in the east (Philippine Islands), and this route was utilized by the Spaniards in preference to either of the isthmus' passages farther south (Panama and Tehuantepec) for the portaging of Oriental goods from the Pacific to the Atlantic.

In Peru the economic core of the state still remains the plateau—but the political core has shifted. Since the *conquistadores* arrived from the sea, and since it was necessary to maintain connections with Spain, the capital was moved from the ancient Inca nucleus at Cuzco on the plateau to a site at the mouth of a river—running through absolute desert—on the shore, namely, Lima. Thus, the early Spanish political core and that of the modern state both are outside of the Peruvian ecumene. A route, one of the few that leads from the narrow coast to the plateau, extends inland from Lima.

As with Mexico, effective control diminishes with distance from the nuclear plateau. The plateau has an elongate shape, running, along interconnected valleys, from the Gulf of Guayaquil approximately through the northern third of Chile. Parallel with this, and along the coast, lies the desert which has tended to be politically subservient to the plateau powers. To this Peruvian Viceroyalty the remainder of Spanish South America was subject, the predominant role of high tableland in the production of precious minerals likely being the reason for the political ascendancy of the Peruvian puna.

The Charcas Valley, a part of the Viceroyalty of Peru, was made an audiencia; this later formed the nucleus of the state of Bolivia. From the plateau the Spanish worked down the inner side of the Andes along headwaters of the Parana into the tropical lands below so that the Spanish held, in addition to the highland kingdom of the Incas, the lowlands adjacent to both sides of the mountains. The tropical lands that extend along the eastern margin of the Andes are of minor importance as compared with other parts of the Andean states; they are sparsely populated and very difficult of access, particularly from the west.

Bolivia was unable to declare its independence until the power of Spain had been broken

---

[3] Whittlesey, *op. cit.*, p. 414.

in South America for it lay right next to the center of colonial power in Peru. Although the state suffers from a number of handicaps, the two outstanding geopolitical problems arise from the fact that the various regions of Bolivia are so contrasted physically (mountain and plateau, and inland tropical lowland) as to make the boundaries relatively indefensible; secondly, economically dependent upon the export of mineral products, the country has no seacoast and is therefore dependent upon foreign ports as outlets for the ores. A third interesting concomitant arises out of the strikingly contrasted and therefore ill-cohered regions; although the official capital, complete with capital buildings, was located at Sucre for many years, the governments—changing as various strong leaders seized power—operated "illegally" from La Paz.

Peru was the last South American state to declare its independence notwithstanding the fact that it had been the first to be conquered by the *conquistadores*. Two reasons lay behind this. In the first place, as the locale of the Viceroyalty, colonial military control was perhaps more absolute here than elsewhere. Also, as the governing center, the interests of the colony *and* Spain were more or less reciprocal and Peru undoubtedly became the recipient of many more political indulgences than the other territories.

The desert littoral of Peru is ameliorated by the fact that many rivers drop from the mountains into the sea, providing water for the irrigation of the alluvial fans of the rivers that, combined, form almost a piedmont plain along the shore. The Indians had practiced irrigation along ten of these rivers and the settlements formed natural points at which invasion of the area could take place. Lima, however, combined elements that not only made entry most favorable at that point but provided the most adequate facilities as a base of operations both for inland military maneuvers and for connections with Spain. It had a large irrigated hinterland; it had a route by which the central portion of the plateau was most easily accessible; and the harbor facilities were the best along the

coast. For access to portions of the upland farther north, as at Quito, and farther south, other routes were better.

NORTHWESTERN SOUTH AMERICA

Northwestern South America, comprising Colombia, Venezuela, and Ecuador, was known in colonial days as New Granada (then also including Panama).

The countries of the northern part of the continent are even more cut up by the mountainous terrain of the Andes than are those of the southern half. It was undoubtedly for this reason that New Granada disintegrated instead of cohering to form one state as it had been, administratively, under the Spanish. Today the airplane links together the segments of these topographically fragmented countries so that, in Colombia, no important part of the state is more than a day's journey from any other part. Motor highways also are very significant in integrating the parts.

All of the tropical Andean states of South America find their counterpart *in each other* in having a central upland with a cool climate, a tropical humid or tropical dry coast, and a humid tropical interior; and all—except Venezuela—in having the political and/or economic core, and hence the ecumene, in the highland regions. This is true of the states of the Northwest.

The Ecuador highlands, characterized by mountain swells with intervening valleys—of which the Quito Valley is the most important —hold the heaviest population of the small state as well as the political core. This section is relatively self-sufficient, and faces toward the interior. Further, all parts of it are well integrated, although along the Ecuador–Peruvian border, rough and difficult terrain have inhibited connections between the plateau areas of these vicinal states; this border has been the subject of dispute in the post-World War II period—a condition that likely results from the physical character of the border area which is one of tangled mountain topography. In contrast to the highlands, coastal Ecuador, centered around the Guayas lowland, with fertile

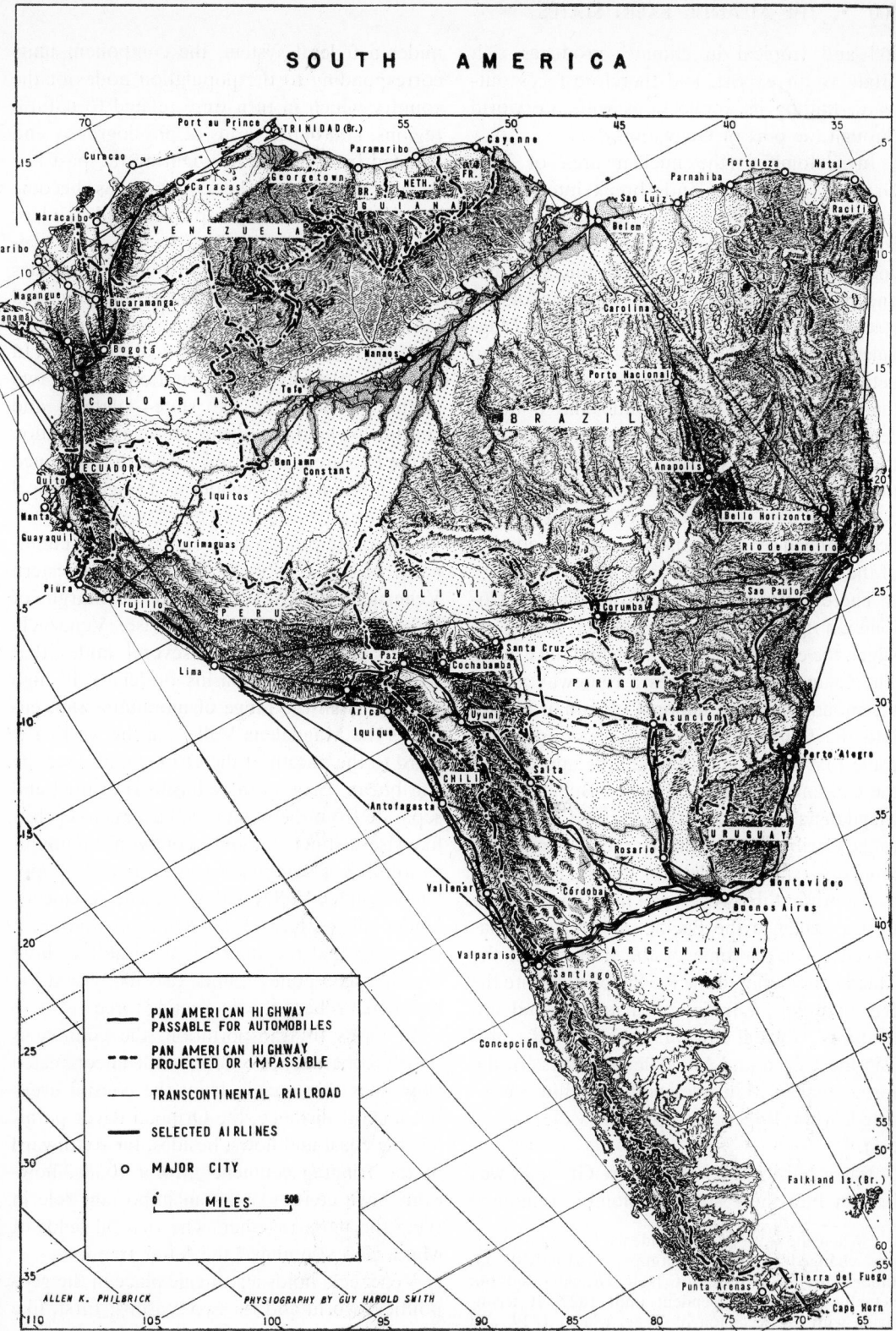

SOUTH AMERICA

Legend

— PAN AMERICAN HIGHWAY PASSABLE FOR AUTOMOBILES

-- PAN AMERICAN HIGHWAY PROJECTED OR IMPASSABLE

— TRANSCONTINENTAL RAILROAD

— SELECTED AIRLINES

○ MAJOR CITY

0 —— MILES —— 500

ALLEN K. PHILBRICK   PHYSIOGRAPHY BY GUY HAROLD SMITH

Figure 14.3.

299

soil and tropical in climate, produces rich products for export, and therefore faces outward, finding its connections with the world through the port of Guayaquil.

In Colombia (the nuclear area of New Granada[4]), the highlands break into several ranges, and the single coastline that characterizes the other Andean states becomes two coastal littorals—one on the Pacific side and one on the Caribbean. The ecumene of the state lies in the two great valleys of the Magdalena and Cauca Rivers which finger up between the three mountain ranges of the Colombian Andes. The economic and political center, therefore, lies in the bracing climate of the highlands, just as did the Spanish core—in the Bogota Basin, the one feasible focal area of New Granada. This nuclear basin had already been utilized by the Indians before the coming of the Spanish.

There are two obvious entries into the Colombian nucleus—the Magdalena River, on which the capital city is located, and the Cauca. The Cauca approach gives a routeway across the mountainous Ecuador–Colombian border into the Quito region, and it was along this route that one party of Spaniards approached the Colombian mountain heart. But the great Magdalena River outlet has turned Colombia to the Caribbean, and the Maracaibo area even more so—since the days of the Spanish Main to the present. However, rail lines now link the Cauca valley to the Pacific, and this link has served to divert some of the traffic from the Magdalena outlet to the Pacific port despite the fact that the latter lies on a narrow and unhealthful tropical littoral; two rail links also join the Cauca and Magdalena valleys. In the former valley Manizales and Madellín are located, while Bogota occupies the valley to the east.

For a half century after New Granada was broken into three states, Colombia remained

---

[4] When the wars of independence began the name was changed to Great Colombia (1819-1830) although the Viceroyalty of New Granada did not actually become independent until 1822. It terminated with the secession of Venezuela in 1829, and Ecuador in 1830.

under a federal system, the component units corresponding to the population nodes of the country which in turn were related to natural regions, laid out in terms of physiography and isolated from each other. During the past five decades, however, the country has become more unified due to improved and modern means of communication. It has been suggested that, had such transportation modes existed at the time when New Granada gained independence, the colonial state might never have divided into three political entities. (In Ecuador, the diverse orientation of the two major divisions of the state—plateau and coastal lowland—*and* the physical separation of the two areas, have several times threatened the continuance of Ecuador as a single political unit.)

The easternmost spur of the Andes culminates in the Caribbean lowlands of western Venezuela closely adjacent to the margin of Lake Maracaibo. Populationwise, Venezuela is also composed of the several nodes that stretch, in scattered basins of relatively high density, from the range of mountains that encloses the Magdalena Valley on the west eastward to the mouth of the Orinoco; all face the Caribbean. Each of these basins is distinct and separate from the others, and access to each is likewise distinct; the only common communication link is southward to the sparsely populated Orinoco Valley with which each connects. Under this pattern of distinct segmentation, it is strange that the state has been able to hold together as a political unit. It is likely that the Orinoco has been the integrating force.

In terms of transportation, the country is poorly cohered; railroads are all unconnected spur lines that run in from the coastal areas but a short distance; the Orinoco River parallels the coast and flows, besides, far southward of the fringing ecumene. Motor roads, however, have come to play an important role in tying the parts together. The rich oil fields of Maracaibo stimulated the latter trend.

Venezuela holds a strategic place in the geopolitical world and for two reasons. First, like the other Caribbean lands, the state faces upon the sea that controls the eastern entrance to the Panama Canal; in the second place, Venezuela has valuable mineral resources. From the oil wells, part of which lie under the waters of the tropical Lake Maracaibo, flows enough petroleum to make Venezuela the world's second largest producer and second largest exporter of this strategic fuel.

Oil has financed all of the modern innovations that have been introduced into the country in the past two decades (since the death of the Dictator Juan Vicente Gomez in 1935)— schools, transportation and communication facilities, health and sanitation programs, etc. Oil might be characterized as "a modern phenomenon superimposed upon an ancient land," for, until the death of Gomez, there had been little change for the European Venezuelan from the days of Spanish control. As for the Indians, they continue to live in much the same fashion as they did before the *conquistadores* invaded the country.

Both Columbus and Amerigo Vespucci saw Venezuela. Columbus discovered the outlet of the Orinoco, while Vespucci navigated along the coastal waters bordering the territory. Through the Venezuelan mountains and jungles the Spanish explorers tramped in their search for the gold of New Granada. To the cause of Latin American independence, Venezuela contributed the Great Liberator, Simon Bolivar, who, more than any other single South American, helped to shake loose the Spanish colonial yoke under which the colonies were chafing.

Lying entirely within the tropical zone (between 1° and 13° north latitude), the geographic factors that had kept the Indian population small and scattered before the coming of the *conquistadores* were the same that have, since that early pre-Spanish period, kept the population small and spotty. Much of the lowland region is tropical jungle or savanna grassland, plagued by seasonal extremes of alternate drought and excess precipitation. The highlands in the west, however, provide escape from the lowland tropics and, here, the other export items are produced—coffee and cacao;

in the grasslands, cattle are raised in large numbers.

World role. Although the population of the colony remained small, the Venezuelan dependency was one of the first to revolt against Spain. It will also be remembered that the first inter-American Conference was called by the Venezuelan, Simon Bolivar. Bolivar had not only a vision of an independent continent, but also of a unified New World. This, of course, has never been achieved. In fact, aside from Europe, it would be difficult to find an area of comparable size where *inter*-national friction has been as rife.

From this backward glance, it is apparent that Venezuela has taken an active role in the political affairs of not only Latin America but of the world, ever since the early part of the Spanish period.

SOUTHERN SOUTH AMERICA

The Andes form the natural frontier between the two southernmost Latin American countries, Chile and Argentina. The longest continuous mountain chain in the world, the Andes rise to spectacular heights in the southern part of the continent. However, the earliest waves of exploration sent Spaniards southward from the Altiplano into these lofty southern Andes and eastward into the Parana lowlands.

South of the broad shoulder of the Altiplano the Andes change configuration, becoming a confusion of mountain ranges, knots, and detached peaks. This region is known as the Plateau of Atacama. East of the puna and spreading through about 15 degrees of latitude, the Andes are a series of relatively parallel ridges separated by intermontane valleys, the latter lying at elevations sufficiently low to permit the growing of a number of mid-latitude crops wherever irrigation water is available. On the other side, the dry and desolate plateau sweeps down to the even drier desert of the Atacama lowland.

Across the 20,000-foot high wall of the Andean Cordillera, a few high passes permit movement between Chile and Argentina. One railroad, the TransAndean Railway, makes its way almost from one side to the other, across Uspallata Pass (the site at which is placed the famous "peace" statue of the Christ of the Andes).

So divisive is the character of the Andes in the south that, although the Spanish *conquistadores* early reached the lowland of Central Chile and there established a settlement, the colony was left quite to itself. Its political distinctness was given recognition by the establishment of a nearly independent captaincy-general. In the modern day, the barrier aspect of the mountainous frontier is evidenced in the antipodal orientation of the two states—Chile faces the Pacific, Argentina, the Atlantic. Although, when the captaincy-general of Chile was set up, Cuyo (a desert-oasis area on the eastern side of the Cordillera) was attached to Chile, this eastern region was later reassigned; at the establishment of a fourth viceroyalty in the La Plata area, Cuyo was made a part of the political district that was oriented around Buenos Aires—*a concession to the barrier character of the mountain system in the southern portion of the continent.*

Some boundary adjustments have had to be made between Chile and Argentina, but, in general, the Andean border has been a peaceful frontier, and whatever changes were made have been relatively minor. Both countries adhered to the decision of a British Commission that was brought in to settle the disputed border. It was upon the culmination of this boundary dispute—that nearly reached the fighting stage—that the statue "Christ of the Andes" was erected by the joint efforts of the two countries.

In the north, however, Chile fought a war with Peru and Bolivia over that portion of the nitrate territories that lay within Bolivia. According to the peace treaty that followed (1883), the Chilean boundary was moved northward from 24° to 17° 30′ south latitude. Since that time this, too, has been a peaceful frontier.

Stretching through 2600 miles of latitudinal extent, Chile is a land of stark contrasts. At no point more than 221 miles wide, it ex-

tends from the desert tropics into the sub-Antarctic zone. It is a land not only of contrasts but of paradoxes: along one side of its length, it presents (for its area) the longest coastline in the world, while along the other side, it is bordered by some of the highest mountains. A land that was minerally too poor to attract the attention of the *conquistadores*, today, whatever prosperity Chile has is to be attributed to its vast mineral deposits—nitrates, copper, iron, and manganese. Located, as one writer puts it, "at the farthest corner of the universe," it is more advanced in its social legislation than is any nation on the southern continent. A land of contrasts, its contrasts are largely geographically induced.

The country falls into three regions, each distinct from the other two in climate and topography as well as in adjustment. The northern 40 per cent is tropical desert—the Atacama, arid and mountainous. Yet here are the great mineral resources of the state; in an area where all of the necessities of life and work must be imported is found perhaps the greatest natural wealth of the country. Until World War I (when the process of taking nitrogen from the atmosphere was perfected), Chile had a monopoly on nitrates, necessary both in the manufacture of explosives and fertilizers. Today, although nitrates are still the second most important export, Chile contributes but a small fraction of the world's supply of this mineral. From the desert comes also a large part of the copper ore that makes Chile the world's second largest copper producer. Although the Atacama is a barren land that precludes normal habitation, it is this very aridity that is responsible for the formation of some of its vast mineral resources, namely, its nitrates.

South of the desert and reaching to the island of Chiloe is the subtropical portion of Chile—a diversified region topographically but relatively uniform in its climate. It resembles parts of Spain and is Mediterranean in character. Included is the Central Valley of Chile, the agricultural heart of the country as well as the industrial and population center. Here was the nuclear center of the early captaincy-general, and here is the ecumene and the political center of the present nation.

Below the island of Chiloe and stretching to the tip of Chile and the continent at Cape Horn is an islanded and fjorded territory, the third part of Chile—largely highland and heavily forested but with occasional mountain pastures that allow sheep to graze. It is a rainsoaked area with a marine climate that is productive of the dense belt of temperate trees. Except in the Magallanes area, population is sparse; here, the grazing country is somewhat better, and here the number of people increases. The whole southern third of the country is a frontier land, however, offering a rich resource of timber and waiting only to be developed.

Chilean "stock" is largely European with some mingling of Indian strains. Originally settled by the Spanish *conquistadores* and later by Spanish immigrants, the Iberian blood has been thinned by that of other Europeans who have come in during the past century—British, who settled largely along the coast, Germans who colonized the south, French and Italian in the urban centers, and, most recently, Irish and Swiss. Chile is, therefore, something of a melting pot.

The indigenes, who were there when the Spanish came, resisted both the intrusion of their lands by the foreigners and, when they were at long last subdued, assimilation. The Araucanian Indians, now numbering about 25,000, were the most defiant and it is only in very recent decades that they have ceased to make trouble. Today, still a distinct group who maintain their customs and ways of life, they are found in the wooded lake regions in the southern portion of the country. Most of the other Indian tribes have disappeared, and what remains of them are merely the strains of their blood in the racial mixing that took place.

Both topography and shape militate against Chilean coherence. Long and narrow (averaging about 110 miles in width), shelved between the Pacific Ocean and the Andean crests, the political divisions of the state are in the main characterized by provinces that com-prise the watershed of a short river, with the boundary lines located on the divides. Communications are difficult under such conditions of terrain and form, and it is significant that no railroads extend southward beyond Chiloe Island through the fragmented and mountainous territory of the marine region.

Chile has some 5600 miles of railway, half of which run north and south through the Central Valley and north across the desert to the Peruvian border. However, important as are these lines in cohering the northern three-fourths of the country, of even greater significance are those that run east and west, for Chile looks to the sea. Economically, the short spur lines that extend in from the coast are of tremendous importance.

The railroad connection between Chile and Argentina has been referred to. Reaching in from Buenos Aires via the Uspallata Pass and from Valparaiso–Santiago on the Chilean side, the two lines do not quite meet; the crest of the Andean ranges must be surmounted by motor roads.

Supplementing the lacy net of railways are the highways and air lines. Since 1940, Chile has been carrying on a program of highway construction to correct the deficiency in this aspect of the communications system. As to the airplane, regular air service connects Chile both with Peru and Argentina, and, from thence, with other parts of Latin America.

On the other side of the Andes stretches another elongate state, Argentina. Argentina reaches north and south from the wet and dry tropics of the Chaco through 2300 miles of latitude to Tierra del Fuego. It is the second largest of the Latin American states in area and population, and its more than a million square miles vary from deserts and hot scrub-forests to snow-covered mountains and fjorded coasts.

The Plata–Parana River, inlet to the Argentine, lies a long way offside from the main course that was followed by the Spanish conquerors, and it was further isolated from Spanish lands by the great intervening colony of the Portuguese (Brazil) whose long coast was vigilantly watched. And yet, contemporaneous with the conquest of Peru by Pizzaro, Spaniards moved up the Parana, exploring interior Argentina and attempting to establish a settlement at the site of Buenos Aires. This earliest attempt at Argentine colonization was as great a failure, however, as the setting up of the Viceroyalty in Peru was a success. The failure can be laid to geography because this part of South America was without domesticable animals, and food resources were so meagre as to barely support the few indigenes in the area. A further difficulty in establishing a settlement on the estuarial river mouth lay in the fact that the open coast (held on the north by the Portuguese) provided no natural defensive qualifications—against Portuguese or Indian.

The Spanish, therefore, moved up the river to the point where the Pilcomayo and Paraguay Rivers flow together to become the Parana. Here they established Asuncion. It is something of an anomaly, however, that, once the colony was established, it made connections with the *Altiplano* (to the government of which it was soon attached) rather than developing into a political division itself in the plains' area.

Within the next few decades the Spanish gradually moved *down river,* setting up a line of forts; and, finally, within about a generation, they established themselves on the estuary. In their early period, these settlements were given military aid from Asunción and the Altiplano, and they continued to be politically subject to the Viceroyalty on the plateau as was Asuncion.

This political "inversion"[5] was repeated economically; all goods that moved to Spain —and these goods duplicated rather than complemented the products of Iberia—were required *legally* to move via the Altiplano, the Pacific Ocean, the Isthmus and the Caribbean to Europe. Export could not take the shorter, more direct route downstream to Buenos Aires and across the Atlantic. This reversal of the natural order of things can be laid to the emphasis placed by the Spanish homeland

upon the importance of precious metals. It had several ill effects, slowing the growth of the plains' area, and encouraging lawlessness and smuggling.

Eventually the latter conditions led to the establishment of a Viceroyalty at Buenos Aires. The new administrative unit incorporated all of the river and plains' settlements *and much of the plateau* which had long been administratively paramount (*i.e.* the Charcas).

Climatically, Argentina divides into four major divisions. In the North are the wet and dry grasslands of the tropical *Chaco* with seasonal extremes of drought and wetness that make the land difficult even for the grazing of animals (although this is its major industry); *the West,* which stretches in deserts to the base of the Andes whence it sweeps to the extreme heights of the lofty mountains; *the Pampas,* occupying a central position in the country, arcuate about the La Plata estuary, and from which Argentina derives its strength and economic supremacy; and *Patagonia,* the windswept and semi-arid South.

All of the natural regions of Argentina— except the Pampas—are problem areas for the state. In the west, cultivation and habitation are possible only on oases; in the Gran Chaco the extremes of climate make the area difficult; while Patagonia (about the size of Texas) is another of the far corners of the earth—a plateau of high wind and meagre rain, scant vegetation, and a sparse population. Except in the north where irrigation makes possible the growing of fruit, sheep-raising is the major occupation—and from Patagonia comes most of the wool that Argentina exports in large quantities. But it is a hard land requiring a hardy people. From the Pampas, on the other hand—humid subtropical in climate and rich in fertile soils and natural nutritive grasses— come the flax, the corn, and the beef that go to Northwest Europe.

Spanish and Italian stocks comprise most of the 18 million people of Argentina. Notable settlements of Welsh, however are, found in Patagonia. Only about 20,000 to 30,000 Indians remain.

5 *Ibid.,* p. 430.

Physical coherence has not been achieved. Although Argentina grew into a political unit via the back door, so to speak, the nuclear area of the state lay in the estuarial mouth around which the ecumene of the present nation curls itself. Argentina is not well integrated in terms of communication. Throughout all of Patagonia only four or five spur rail lines run in from the coast to offer access to the ocean lanes that lead to the ecumene—and to the world trade routes. No railroad runs north and south through this vast territory. The west, too, is inadequately supplied with transportation, although railroads do spider out into the oases from the La Plata and even beyond to penetrate portions of the Andes. Likewise in the Gran Chaco spur rail lines reach from the river inland to feed the animal products southward, but the railroads are far apart. The ecumene, however, is webbed with a close net of railroads that fan in from all directions to Buenos Aires (and Rosaria) like closely spaced spokes of a wheel.

The La Plata inlet makes Argentina strategically important. Argentina is the soft underbelly of South America—the La Plata estuary permits intricate penetration from the Atlantic into all parts of the inner continent. What happens there, therefore, is highly significant to the rest of the world—more so than what happens in the Pacific Latin American countries.

BRAZIL: PORTUGUESE AMERICA

Portuguese South America is politically united. In contrast to the fragmentation into 16 states that characterizes Spanish-speaking America, that portion of the southern continent that was colonized by Portugal remained unified to eventually form the one huge independent state of Brazil. It occupies almost one-half of South America. Two-fifths of the Latin Americans are Brazilians.

A study of the map will indicate that geographic factors, at least in part, have been responsible for this continuing political coherence. The barrier mountains of South America lie *around* Brazil's borders, not within the

country; secondly, although Brazil falls naturally into two physical divisions—the plateau, and the Amazon Basin and coastal lowlands—due to the adverse climatic conditions of the Amazon country, the river lowland likely could not, within itself, form a favorable core area for a state.

Physical coherence is difficult, however. It is to be seen, therefore, that, whereas certain natural conditions favored political coherence, others worked against economic unity. Brazil is not well coordinated physically; the Amazon Basin, access to which is achieved by way of the river, is a land apart from highland Brazil. The only land connection between the two is via the difficult coastal strip; by ocean navigation the way is far easier. Within the Amazon lowland, river boat, or air communication focusing on Manaus, are the only means of tying the basin together. However, stream navigation is possible for over a thousand miles inland by ocean steamer because the flow of water in this tropical river is tremendous.

Portuguese penetration of the Amazon followed on the papal division of the unclaimed parts of the globe between Spain and Portugal. The papal allocation of territory placed the mouth of the river just within the Portuguese sphere. Given this lead, the basin was soon "conquered" by Jesuit missionaries. Through them, and because they were Portuguese, the entire river domain fell to Portugal.

The Amazon region is marginal to the ecumene of the modern state. The nuclear area, the ecumene, and the political center of Brazil, however, have always been in the coastal area and in the plateau hinterland. And from the coast and the plateau edge, the frontier of settlement has moved westward across the highlands. To the populous core area, the Amazon country is like an annex.

The early center of settlement was in the northeast coastal littoral where the tropical forest could be cleared, with relative ease, to make way for the sugar plantations. Slaves were brought from Portuguese Africa, and the interest of Portugal turned from the Orient and focused on the territories in the New World.

The pattern of plantation agriculture that developed in northeastern Brazil was very different from the type of horticultural agriculture that was typical of Portuguese Iberia, or from the plateau grazing and wheat-raising economy of the Spanish Meseta. Because of the importance of this northeastern area in settlement and agriculture, in the middle of the sixteenth century Bahia was made the capital of all Portuguese America. With this as the major center, the Portuguese set out to hold the entire coast. So successful were they in keeping other Europeans from setting foot on any of the territory southward from the mouth of the Amazon to the Rio de la Plata that the only portion of the continent left to the exploits of the ambitious Dutch, French, and British was that bit of country lying between the Amazon and the Orinoco River—what later came to be known as the Guianas. Today the coastal plateau area of the Rio–São Paulo district is the economic, political, and population core of the country, and hence, the ecumene.

The first challenge to the supremacy of the Bahia nucleus came with the disclosure of gold deposits and, later, diamonds in the interior plateau. Previous to the mineral discoveries, settlement in the Santos–Rio de Janeiro area had been held back by several aspects of the physiographic environment. In the first place, excellent as was the natural harbor on which the present capital is located, in the early colonial period, the harbor was not even backed by a river, but by a swampy littoral leading to the base of a forbidding plateau escarpment. No stream provided easy access to the interior. Second, although farther from the equator, these southerly coasts offered a climate not much more healthful than that found in the tropical northeast. Hence, the coastal settlements, offside from the major centers farther north, remained small and local. However, on the plateau above Santos, the highlands afforded a cooler, more healthful environment and, here, despite difficulty of access, there grew up a settlement (São Paulo) of mixed Indian and Portuguese. It thrust its explorations outward in all directions across the pla-

teau without regard for the papal demarcation line. The Paulistos (settlers of São Paulo) were among those who made the gold discoveries in the seventeenth century, and, the following century, diamonds.

Because of the concentrated mineral wealth found to the northeast of São Paulo, Minas Gerais was the first inland state to be established in Portuguese territory. Rio de Janeiro became the port of export for the minerals. On their plateau, the Paulistos developed an agriculture based, first, on coffee, and later, on cotton and oranges; Santos became the port for São Paulo.

Because of its minerals the Minas Gerais district attracted thousands of settlers of other European nationalities; later, coffee culture also drew many to Brazil. The territory from São Paulo northward developed as a focus of mining, agriculture, and settlement—and became known as "the Center." So strong did the Center become that, in 1763, the capital was moved from Bahia south to Rio de Janeiro, already the major port city of the Portuguese holdings. As for the Amazon, except for the brief two decades or so during which that tropical region held a monopoly on the world rubber market, the vast river lowland has added little except "area" to the state.

Since the Latin American state won its independence from Portugal in 1822, the country has been politically a unit. As stated, however, physically Brazil lacks coherence and whether or not the giant nation can, without this physical coherence, remain politically unified remains to be seen. One of the three rail nets of South America is Brazilian; it focuses on the ecumene and reaches its tentacles to the developed parts of the plateau. Where river traffic was formerly the means of connection to Amazonia, the Mato Grosso, and Goiaz, motor roads and airlines are making these great areas more accessible, and rail lines now reach across the plateau into Goiaz.

Present plans call for a Federal District to be located near the geographic center of the nation. When Brazil declared its independence, the constitution called for the establishment of a capitol at some central location within the domain, and Rio de Janeiro was described as the "temporary" seat of government. More recently plans were made for the setting up of a Federal District to be located in the interior state of Goiaz, thus relocating the seat of government on "a growing frontier and near some of Brazil's great mineral reserves," as well as closer to the geographic center. In 1957 the new capital, Brasilia, began to rise. A law passed by Congress provides for the transfer of the capitol from Rio de Janeiro to Brasilia in April, 1960.

Brazil is still a land in transition, with huge spaces that are not only unconquered but even unexplored. Whether all of this territory represents a frontier for pioneer settlement remains debatable. Mineral resources will eventually be exploited, wherever they are, if the demand is great enough. But whether the tropical lowlands can ever be regarded as a frontier land suitable for supporting millions of agricultural inhabitants is a moot question. At present Brazil is an exporter of iron, manganese, and coffee.

Although Brazil has large and ultra-progressive modern cities, vast areas are backward and very thinly populated. Three-fourths of the Brazilians are found within 100 miles of the coast. The population (of some over 55 million) is still small for the vast expanses of the state but is growing rapidly, both by natural increase as well as by immigration. In the two decades between 1920 and 1940, the population jumped by 40 per cent, between 1946 and 1955 by approximately one-third.

The Brazilians are a mixed "nation." During the colonial era, large numbers of Negroes were brought to Brazil to supply labor on the sugar, coffee, tobacco, and cotton plantations. They came as slaves—but they stayed to become a part of the "raw material" out of which the Brazilian "nation" was formed; the Portuguese, few in number, from the first intermarried with the Negroes and the Indians to create a new people.

Although social discrimination has characterized Brazilian society throughout its history, *racial tolerance* has persisted. In fact, in Brazil today there is going on perhaps the most interesting experiment in the mixing of races of any place on earth. By deliberate policy Brazil is attempting to absorb all of the diverse peoples, through miscegenation, to form a unique racial amalgam; the interfusion is quite advanced.

About one-half of the Brazilians are of European extraction of which the original and dominant stock is Portuguese; subsequent immigration brought in large numbers of Italians, Spanish, and Germans, and, to a lesser extent, other Europeans. From the intermarrying of the peoples of European stock with the indigenous Indians and the Negroes, there has resulted a large group of mestizos. According to a recent census, 63.5 per cent of the population listed themselves as white; 14.6 per cent, black; 21.2 per cent, of mixed blood; and 0.6 per cent, yellow (mostly Japanese). The remaining 0.1 per cent made no declaration as to color. Undoubtedly, the number of mixed bloods is actually far larger, many who declare themselves "white" actually having some mixture.

In areal distribution, a certain racial pattern can be discerned. The Indians are concentrated in the interior Amazon of northern and northeastern Brazil; the Negroes and mulattoes in the northern and central coastal states; the whites in the south. The prevalence of the "white" in the south is due to the influx, for decades of Europeans—Italians comprised about one-third of this inflow, and Portuguese were next in numbers, making up about 30 per cent.

Because of official policy on racial tolerance and miscegenation, Brazil has not been perplexed with minority population problems to any great degree.

A strategic consideration. The logistics of World War II, which necessitated the movement of men and material across the broad Sudan of Africa in order to supply the Mediterranean and Near Eastern theatres, brought Dakar (Senegal) to the attention of the world, and with it, the location of Atlantic South America relative to the rest of the nations of the globe. Americans have been wont to regard South America as *close,* because the northern continent shares the Western Hemisphere with the southern continent and the two are tied together by the thread of Panama. Likewise, Americans have regarded the South American location as peripheral to the rest of the world —and so it is. Yet, the eastern tip of Brazil is only 1800 miles from the port of Dakar on the African West Coast, *one-half as far distant as is Brazil's eastern bulge from the southern tip of Florida.*

Latin America protects the southern flank of the United States as well as the east and west approaches to the Panama Canal. For more than a century, Latin and Anglo–America have mutually recognized the value of friendly and close relationships. Seldom has this hemispheric unity been strained so as to undermine hemispheric security; never, until the infiltration of the political doctrines of the Nazis and Communists, has the security and unity of the hemisphere been seriously threatened from without.

15

Western Europe

The states of the Western Bloc are all a part either of the amphibious or of the insular group of nations that rim themselves, generally speaking, in a double layer around the periphery of the Communist heartland. A very significant part of these rimming countries is found in the West European, Mediterranean, and African territories. Like the United States, these states are continental and maritime, or maritime (if insular, as England).

Historically, the European portion of the amphibious rimland has been a zone of conflict. In the first place, much effort has been expended to "contain" Russia inside its boundaries and to prevent its emergence on the sea —hence, there has been conflict between the continental heartland and this maritime rim. Conflict has also recurred between some of the states within "the rim," particularly between France and Germany—to offset the strength of whichever state was most powerful.

Europe is a peninsula of peninsulas. A study of the eastern and central states of Europe would not make apparent the fact that Europe is merely a peninsula of Asia—for the USSR and the central European nations occupy the broad, generally unfragmented portions of this land mass that is "a continent by courtesy." But from the Baltic and Adriatic Seas westward, Europe is a peninsula of peninsulas. Large and small protuberances jut out from the mainland body, some without a noticeable natural break—as in the case of Denmark and French Brittany; others are separated on the landward side by mountains of considerable barrier proportions—as is true of some of the larger peninsulas, Italy and Spain for example. Although Scandinavia lacks a physical barrier to cut it off from the mainland across its base, it is, nevertheless, the most isolated of all of the peninsulas for its land connections are in polar areas, and those portions closest to the European ecumene are separated from the adjacent lands by water. Britain, an island state, has been no more apart from European affairs during the course of its history than have either Scandinavia or Iberia. Although, during certain epochs of the

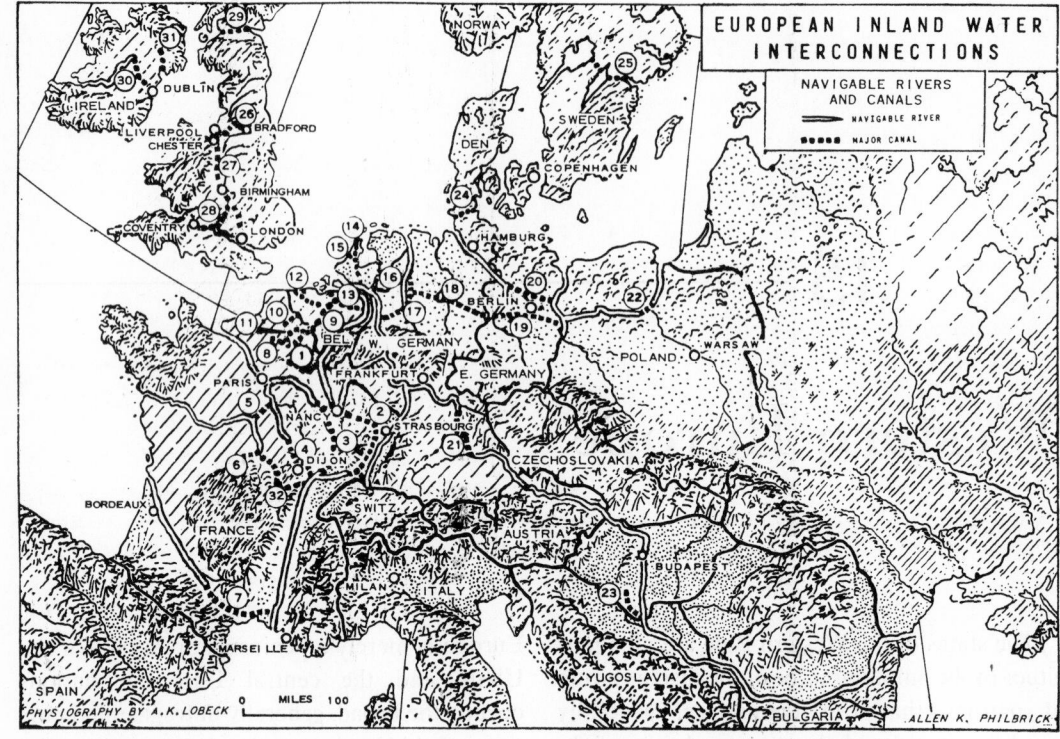

1 Aisne River to Meuse River
2 Doubs River to Strasbourg to Marne River
3 Saone River to Marne River
4 Saone River to Yonne River
5 Seine River to Loire River
6 Cher, Loire, Saone Rivers Canal
7 Garonne River to Rhone River
8 Somme River to Peronne
9 Somme River to Mons
10 Somme River to Lille
11 Oise River to Scheldt River
12 Ghent to North Sea
13 Anvers to Meuse River
14 Lek River to Amsterdam
15 Amsterdam to Velsen
16 Lek River to Swolle

17 Rhine River to Hamborn to Meppen on the Ems
18 Rhine-Ems C. to Elbe River
19 Potsdam to Frankfurt (Oder R.)
20 Elbe River to Oder River
21 Maine River to Danube River
22 Wisla River to Notec River
23 Danube River to Szekesfehervar
24 Kiel Canal
25 Gota Canal
26 Liverpool to Bradford
27 Chester to Birmingham to London
28 Avon River to Conventry
29 Firth of Forth to Firth of Clyde
30 Royal Canal
31 Newry Canal

Figure 15.1. Although Europe is greatly fragmented topographically, the continent has a maze of interconnecting waterways. Canals link all of the major rivers so that traffic and freight can move by inland water channels from the North Sea-Atlantic Ocean-Gulf of Finland in the north to the Black-Mediterranean Seas. This is economically advantageous to the European states for products carried by water transportation move more cheaply than do those carried by rail.

past, barriers have been partially overcome to bring the various peninsular states more closely into European affairs, the degree of participation has generally been conditioned by the effectiveness of physical barriers. Italy has functioned largely within the Mediterranean; Iberia in the Mediterranean and Atlantic. The great maelstrom of European entanglements has been *inside* the mountain and water rim—in France, Germany, Belgium, the Netherlands, and eastward into central Europe and the Balkan Peninsula where "gateways" or topographic alignment permit ready access.

Topography contributed to the evolvement of the present pattern of political states. The irregular shape of west Europe acted unfavorably toward the political unification of the whole. Topography was a second element that influenced the political pattern that developed. Although the physiography of the various west European states is far from simple, there is, nevertheless, an interesting correspondence between political and geographical units. Sweden and Norway are separated essentially along the crest of the Scandinavian Highlands, Spain and Portugal, at the place where the plateau breaks to slope to the sea; Denmark is peninsular, as is Italy. On three sides France faces water or mountain fronts while along the east, at the southern end, the Alps separate it from Italy and Switzerland; in the north, although the Rhine forms a barrier for some distance, in actuality, the limits of the Paris Basin are confined by the Vosges Mountains–Black Forest. Of the "low countries," which on the seafront are low and swampy, Belgium is separated from states to the southeast by the Ardennes.

Germany, too, is more or less of a natural unit, rising from the North Sea lowland through the Bavarian Mountains into the higher Swiss and Austrian Alps, and, at least in the southeast, separated from the Slav country by the blunt mountainous nose of Czechoslovakia. Natural features along the German boundary in the west have already been indicated; but on certain portions—as along the French–German border—large pieces of disputed territories have been held first by one, then by the other state, as Alsace–Lorraine and the Saar. Both are in areas where the natural boundaries are less clearly defined. Southern Jutland, merging from Denmark into the German plain, became a part of Germany, the frontier pushed back across the low, accessible peninsular waist.

Shape and topography together make physical coherence of western Europe difficult among certain areas. Shape has interfered with the physical unification of parts of the fragmented western portion of the continent because the peninsular prolongations lengthen transportation and communication lines; topography often either opposes easy communication or has raised the construction costs of communication connections. Disregarding the airplane (which, it is granted, nullifies physical barriers but has been a factor of consideration for only a decade or so), to pass from Denmark to the Scandinavian Peninsula requires the ferrying of all traffic—including trains—across the Kattegat; to go from the continent to England involves a double transshipment of goods and passengers; three rail lines only connect France and Iberia, two of them found at the two "ends" of the Pyrenees, the other crossing the mountains toward the lower southern terminus. In the case of the French–Spanish railroad connection that skirts the Mediterranean, the French line comes to a halt on the French side of a sort of no-man's land, French administered—wired off from French and Spanish territory by closely guarded high wire fences—and the Spanish line picks up on the other side. The fenced area, which is a very mountainous section, is "portaged" by taxi. Several good passes permit connections between northwestern Europe and the Mediterranean, but they are high passes involving the construction of numerous and long tunnels.

It is not surprising that west Europe—about one-fourth the size of the United States—is politically divided into nine distinct national units. The peopling and political division of that continent took place at a time when transportation and communication were slow and hard whereas the peopling and unification of the United States was rapidly carried out with the coming of the railroads about a half century after the American Union was organized.

Because of its shape—a series of land blocks—west Europe does not have defense in depth, nor do any one of the individual countries. The only states that are "defensible" are defensible-in-degree because of location or physical barriers. England, the Scandinavian Peninsula, Iberia, and Italy are relatively defensible because they are "insular" in character. Although Scandinavia, Iberia, and Italy are peninsular, the physical barrier aspect of their connections with the European land mass makes them "insular" on all sides, in actuality.[1] Successful invasion of Spain was made by the Arabs from the south, not across the land connections in the Pyrenees. With the great development and activity in the Soviet Arctic, the barrier aspects of tundra, bare rock, and snow in northern Scandinavia may break down; however, mountains and distance could take the defensive role. From the Finnish border, the Scandinavian landscape in the north is one of mountain behind mountain behind mountain dropping, at length, sheerly to the fjorded Norwegian coast.

France has some "defense" in the east in the physiographic character of the Paris Basin. Paris lies approximately in the center of a series of cuestas whose upturned edges appear as a hard rock outcrops, sloping gently toward Paris but dropping relatively sheerly on the east. This pattern repeats itself eastward. The defense of France in World War I rested, in part, on the defensive character of the cuesta formations; the Germans were delayed as the French held out first on one cuesta, then the next westward, etc. Some of the most famous land battles of that war were fought for possession of these ridge positions. In their quick breakthrough and overwhelming of France in World War II, the Germans completely bypassed the approach from the east and entered from the northeast near the Belgian border. This sector holds no topographic advantages, defensively speaking, to the French but sweeps down into the Paris lowlands through a corridor. The latter was the main area of German attack in World War I, also.

France, a united Germany, and Spain, all relatively compact, have more defense "in depth" than do the other Western European states which are elongated or tiny; but not even these countries are large enough to mire enemy forces. Due to their relatively small size and adjacence to each other, all of the west European states are highly vulnerable to one another and to the countries in the east. Unification in NATO, which coheres all of the states into one defense bloc, somewhat counteracts the element of small size, but a foe could never be defeated by "space" in west Europe as is possible in the USSR. Although Americans hope that such a contingency will never arise, the "last stand" in west European defenses lies *behind the Pyrenees* in Iberia.[2]

In location, however, west Europe is highly favored. Europe is situated at the center of the land masses of the globe, the exact point of centrality being within France. In terms of density of population, location is also advantageous. West Europe itself comprises one of the three major population nodes of the world; it is across the Atlantic from another such node —eastern United States—and is connected with the latter by the densest network of international communication and transportation lines found on the globe. These two latter areas also comprise the two greatest world market centers up to the present time; here the higher standards of living create a greater demand than elsewhere. In terms of ocean transportation, the west European industrial areas are closer to the potential markets of the densely populated East than is the industrial United States.

---

[1] Northern Italy less so, perhaps, than the others for northern Italy is strategically vulnerable from the Alps—even as it was in the days of Carthage when Hannibal succeeded in invading the peninsula, via the Alps, with the aid of elephants.

[2] The validity of such military planning is to be questioned, however. Iberia fell to Napoleon; its coasts are vulnerable, and modern aircraft can surmount the mountainous barrier. If France fell, it is to be doubted that Iberia could long be held against a strong attack.

Climatically, the location is beneficial. Except where they connect with east Europe, the west European states are surrounded by waters that are ice-free during all months of the year. Even along the Rhine, the number of days when river traffic is held up by ice is minimal. Location, the fragmented shape, and topographic alignment are responsible for the mildness of the climate; west Europe lies within the belt of the Westerlies which, north of approximately 40 degrees latitude, affect the area at all seasons of the year and, in the Mediterranean lands, during the winter season. This means a maritime influence that is moderating and moist the year around. The fragmentation—which cuts the west end of Europe into blocks of shallow depth so that distance from water is not great in any part—disperses the maritime influence rather generally. Topographic alignment, in general east and west and not transverse to the prevailing offshore winds, permits a deep penetration of the Westerlies. The climates—Mediterranean, marine, or modified-marine—are healthful and invigorating.

West Europe is located on the world's most travelled ocean—the Atlantic—as well as on one of the world's first historically important seas—the Mediterranean. Undoubtedly the shape and location of Europe gave to these two bodies of water their importance: *location,* because it provided a climate stimulating to the inhabitants; *shape,* because the character of Europe (particularly western and Mediterranean Europe) as a "peninsula of peninsulas" provided a seacoast that induced men to take up navigation. Europe has the advantage of both major and minor indentations; these have acted like "an invitation" to the sea. The peninsulas provided protected waters in the major indentations—great arms of the sea that were seas themselves—while the irregular coastlines, with their minor indentations, provided excellent harbor space on which have developed many great ports. The only coastline in west Europe that is conspicuously wanting in natural harbors is that along the east side of the Italian Peninsula. Estuarial river mouths—on the Elbe, Weser, Rhine, Seine, Rhone,

Thames, and others—also offered excellent sites for port development. Thus, Europe has had, in its sheltered waters, the necessary training grounds for navigation; and, facing the Atlantic, it has had unbarred access to the world oceans.

The maritime location, favorable from all aspects, developed maritime interests very early. Some of the world's first and greatest navigators were Europeans, as the Portuguese (who found the way around Africa and opened the sea route to the Spice Islands of the East) and all of the earliest circumnavigators of the globe. Maritime location and navigation led west Europeans to explore the globe and claim tremendous portions of the other continents for their states; the colonial powers of the world have always been west Europeans, except as we consider the new colonial powers of today, the USSR and China.

Maritime location, however, need not necessarily imply close contact with the sea; further, the maritime-land relationships of states may change with the passage of time. To take Spain as an example—in the past one of the greatest of sea powers, today it has few maritime interests; except for some fishing in offshore waters, it looks landward.

EASTERN VERSUS WESTERN EUROPE

The ethnic and political characteristics of east and west Europe are, in general, contrasted. The Western and Communist Bloc states face each other across a boundary that, if it were straightened, would run approximately from the head of the Adriatic Sea to the western entrance to the Baltic. East of this line lie Central Europe and the Balkans, and the USSR. The ethnic character of these lands has been pointed out: largely Greek Orthodox with some mingling of Roman Catholicism in the western portions; largely Slav, with a few intrusions—and outliers; in the east, a land successively run over by waves of Asian invaders, particularly in Russia, while Turkey is, as Whittlesey so aptly put it, an "interloper in Europe from the Steppes of nomadic Asia." West of this line there are no Slavs, Greek

Orthodoxy does not exist, and the only apparent Asian influence is the Moorish heritage left by the Arab invaders into Iberia; Roman Catholicism and several forms of Protestantism represent the religious beliefs.

Some geographic factors are likewise different. This line is significant not only as a divisive frontier on either side of which strongly-contrasting political ideologies and ethnic characteristics are found. It is also critical in marking a division between certain geographic aspects that are important to political geography. These geographic contrasts were pointed out: to the east, Europe is massive and continental, to the west maritime and peninsular; to the west, climate is moderate, to the east, relatively extreme with marked seasonal contrasts. A study of the map also discloses that the rivers of the west flow from the interiors to the deeply indented coasts that open onto world highways, whereas the rivers of the east lead into politically closed or landlocked seas; further, the rivers of the west are navigable the year around or closed but a few days annually by ice, whereas those of the east may be icebound for weeks and even months during the cold season.

Certain impacts of history have left contrasting impressions in these two broad areas. West Europe fell under the civilizing hands of Rome and Greece; the Inner Eastern lands were scarcely touched by these enlightening influences. Peninsular Europe was sedentary long before the tribes of the east had settled down. When, at length, west Europeans began to press eastward into Central Europe, it was done at the expense of modifying the culture of the central European peoples—hence the cultural distinctions between Central Europe and Russia. Secondly, these latter differences were heightened by the series of migrations and the long period of control of the Asians within the eastern state.

European civilization developed first in the Mediterranean. Civilization passed from east to west within the basin of the enclosed sea as one civilization succeeded and eclipsed the preceding in power and influence. Rome, in the west, extended its power and culture into barbarian northern Europe, and, as centuries passed, the center of culture shifted gradually from the Mediterranean to northwest Europe. The accomplishments in navigation of the southern Portuguese and Spanish helped to hasten the latter metastasis for, with the closing of Lisbon to the Dutch shipping merchants—who purchased the products of the East from the Portuguese and acted as distributors in the northern countries—other European nationalities, led by the Dutch, took to the high seas to bring back the spices from the Moluccas.

Northwest Europe, therefore, had already begun to look seaward—although not very far seaward for the first shipping was between Mediterranean and the Hanseatic League ports —when Columbus and others discovered the New World and led exploratory expeditions across the Atlantic and into the new lands. With the discoveries, the relocalization of power and culture became more complete. For reasons difficult to explain, such Mediterranean states as Venice never took part in the transoceanic navigation although Venetian ships had early ventured northward along the Atlantic coast. This meant a further relative decline in the Italian states—and a relative accretion of power and influence in the northern nations.

The discoveries meant a reorientation of outlook and interest for the European states in the North. Facing the Atlantic, the perspective and scope of operations of the west European states were enlarged to include much of the globe, and they began to look West. Britain and France held highly desirable locations relative to the new trade channels that opened up, but England was better able to exploit its favorable position because France was preoccupied with the defense of its European territories. The latter state was even forced to give up its first overseas empire. The Netherlands, likewise engaged, had also to accede some of its extracontinental holdings to England, namely, those in Africa.

GREAT BRITAIN

Lying off the northwest mainland of Europe, the British Isles are insular—and hence marginal to the European continent. The insularity of the Isles is reflected in the attitude of the British people toward their relationship to Europe: they invariably refer to "England and the continent"—a Britisher is British, not European. Marginal as is the location (and it was very marginal during the period when European culture faced south to the Mediterranean), for a thousand years of their early history, conquest after conquest swept the Isles to leave remnants of people and culture; and there were hundreds of years, following the earlier period, when England held territories on the mainland. However, during the more modern era, Britain has not only been free from invasion but has kept relatively free from entangling alliances on the continent as well.

Great Britain was organized from England. The Thames Basin was the nuclear center of Great Britain, and the southern half of the main island had been politically unified sometime before the discoveries in the New World were made. Just as overseas colonization was begun, Scotland was joined to England.

The physical character of the British Isles contributed to the development of the form of government—a loosely coherent structure of the component parts with wide powers of local autonomy. Each of the four parts—England, Wales, Scotland, and Ireland—comprises a distinct core. Ireland lies across stormy intervening seas; topographically, Scotland and England are quite distinct, as are Wales and England, an abrupt change in physiography marking the political separation. All four portions have lowlands (which constitute the ecumenes of the states) more or less surrounded by highlands.

The independence of the Scot is comprehensible in the physical aspect of the country. Although fully one-half of all of the Scots of the country reside in the central lowlands between or on the Firth of Forth and the Firth of Clyde, the people are essentially highlanders who, historically, feuded among themselves and warred against intruders. Scotland is a rugged mountainous land. The central lowland, which is the economic, political, and cultural center of the country, is a faulted block of the earth's crust bordered on both sides by highlands. The Scottish Highlands of the north are high, and deeply trenched by the river gorges that flow eastward to the sea; the west coast is fjorded, and the mountains drop abruptly to the sea in a fragmented coast. The northern third of the Scottish Highlands is separated from the southern portion by another graben that runs like a narrow split through the mountain core. South of the central lowland is the Southern Upland of Scotland, an area not as extensive or bold as the northern shield, but, like the latter, sparsely populated.

Wales, likewise mountainous, was brought into the Union through military conquest. The association of Wales and Scotland to England has been loose, and each has retained a considerable degree of local authority. Because of the "land" character of the frontiers, some peaceful penetration of Wales and Scotland has been possible, and the consolidation of Wales was accomplished without too much effort. But in the case of Scotland, which is larger, more rugged, and farther removed from England than Wales, consolidation was resisted by the highlanders long after association within the Union. The Irish, their island-state completely noncontiguous, were never completely won by the British state, and, in 1922, the greater part of Ireland became independent.

The "Emerald Isle" derives its name from the rain-soaked character of the island. Ireland, in form, is almost saucer-like, the central portion low and boggy, surrounded by higher edges, particularly in the north and northeast and in the south and southwest. Rainfall is so abundant and drainage so poor as to constitute a handicap, and Ireland has been a land of emigration—particularly in years of potato famine. There are fewer Irishmen in Ireland than there are in the United States. With few resources other than its soil—which makes up 95 per cent of the natural wealth—some thin seams of coal or lignite, and peat, Ireland is a hard land from which to wrest a living. The population tends to outrun the resources for even the soil, which is leached and poor, offers indifferent agricultural opportunities. The central portion provides year-round pastures, but the land is too wet for good haymaking. Animal husbandry is, however, the most profitable branch of Irish agriculture.

Today the island is divided into two political units—the Irish Free Republic and Northern Ireland, the latter with its own parliament, but also represented in the British Parliament. The political split was along religious lines, the Roman Catholic Free State (holding somewhat more than 80 per cent of the territory) and the Protestant North. Northern Ireland is content in its position within the British Union, but the Irish Free State continually agitates for a united and independent Ireland.

Such independence of spirit is somewhat contradictory to the best interests of the Irish in terms of economic realities for the island is remarkably dependent upon Great Britain for its markets and imports. Approximately 88 per cent of all Irish exports go to Britain and 70 per cent of all imports derive from there. Unification of the North and South would give an industrial base to the agricultural south.

The English plain is the most significant and distinct of the British lowlands. The English plain, broadest and, climatically, most favorable in the southeast, extends northward along the east coast to Newcastle and between the Welsh Highlands and the Pennine Range to the Liverpool–Manchester area in the west. The southeast is the sunniest corner of marine England. Here, a greater portion of the country is cultivated than in the moister sections.

England slopes off from the Pennines, Wales, and Cornwall to the broad English "downs" in the southeast. These lowlands face Europe, across the Channel and Strait, on two sides. In the South, they lie opposite the Paris Basin; in the southeast, they front the Rhenish Lowland. Both areas present important commercial possibilities. Both shores—English and the French–Belgian—provide easy access into the interior in the drowned river mouths which are the sites of great ports: London on the Thames; Portsmouth on the River Test; Rotterdam and Antwerp on the Rhine and Scheldt, respectively; LeHavre, and farther upstream, Rouen, on the Seine.

Because of the natural advantages of the southeast, the Thames region has taken the leadership in the British Isles—in political, agricultural, and commercial matters; this sector has also borne the shock of invasion and military bombardment, and taken the lead in the direction of foreign relations. It was the nuclear area of the state, and is the ecumene of Great Britain and of the Commonwealth. Locally, the ecumene has extended tendrils along the industrial arc of the Pennines and northwest to include the industrial and trade district of the Liverpool area. From here, the "lifelines" of the Empire and Commonwealth were—and are—bound to the nucleus of political and economic power.

In the past, before Great Britain became a world empire and before the commercial and industrial revolutions swept over the Isles to change the role of Britain, England must have resembled pastoral Australia of today, heavily a sheep-raising land. Animal industries are still important, but the economic base has broadened immeasurably. Britain cannot feed itself, but industrial products and specialized animal culture provide valued items of exchange.

Agriculture is basic but not dominant in England. England is not well-balanced with regard to the proportion of people engaged in agriculture compared to those in other industries. It has the lowest percentage of people in Europe in agriculture (about 7 per cent).

About 150 years ago, England was feeding itself. But several factors led to the relative and actual decline in cultivation: 1) the population increased, decreasing the percentage thus engaged; 2) with the industrial revolution and the development of industry, many rural workers came to the urban industrial centers to live and work; 3) the repeal of the Corn Laws influenced the drop in cultivated acreage. These laws had put high tariffs on imported grains, favored landowners and farmers, and pushed up the price of wheat. As manufacturing grew, however, a conflict developed over this import tax; manufacturers wanted a free flow of trade from the outside so that cheap wheat could come in, allowing lower wages to be paid to the factory workers. The repeal did not give protection to the farmer. But, since Britain moved on to an industrial base between 1840 and 1860, "free-trade" has been—and is—a good policy for the nation.

The dependence on outside sources for much of its food has placed the British Isles in a very precarious position. During World Wars I and II, when effective blockades threatened to starve the country out, natural pastures were plowed up to add to the cultivated acres, and the population was placed on a meagre and strict food-rationing system. Thus, while insularity has advantages for security, it also strictly circumscribes the boundaries (which are tight and cannot be expanded except across the water), and it holds disadvantages in time of war. After 1945, because of the fear instilled by the blockade, England for a time engaged in an agricultural program that aimed at near self-sufficiency.

The industrial revolution began in England. The first machines were British-invented. For a long while after the beginning of the industrial revolution, England held a monopoly on the machines and methods of modern manufacturing. Eventually, however, such knowledge became universal and other nations were soon developing manufacturing, inventing machines, originating methods, and competing for markets—and the lush day of English supremacy was past. British primacy and supremacy was based upon a local coal and iron ore supply, and priority in invention: England has produced more new ideas in the industries of iron and steel, cotton and wool, and shipbuilding than any other nation. Their early start gave them a good lead held until very recently.

As industry increased and commerce spread, Britain evolved a new system that partially discarded economic insularity but retained political insularity (from Europe). The system was based on industrial supremacy, exports to young countries, free trade, and commercial aids such as banking, a large merchant marine, insurance (marine), and trade promotion agencies. The system worked best up to World War I, after which, because of the drain on the economy and, more lately, changes within the political structure of the Empire, it had to be modified. But for many decades, the tight little Isle of Britain has been a base from which to operate in world economic—and political—affairs. Every Britisher has had his eye out for investments. Control of the sealanes made possible the transfer of armies and colonists to foreign shores until one-fourth of the world's lands and peoples were brought under the British flag. It also kept the ocean highways open to a vast swarm of merchant ships that brought to crowded England the essential foodstuffs and raw materials. Britain's destiny has been *upon the sea,* and sea power has been essential to its very existence.

Britain is no longer the world's "great" power. Britain still ranks among the great, and, when British diplomats speak, the world listens attentively. But a decline set in sometime during the second decade of the twentieth century. Some of the reasons for the decline have already been mentioned. There were not as many industrial and manufacturing secrets as before; other nations were catching up in industry; there was a rise in universal machine efficiency —the British techniques were copied and improved on; a "sick" coal industry; a wave of world-wide *economic nationalism* under which a number of countries began to think in terms of self-sufficiency—manufacturing their own cottons, pottery, and metallurgical goods; unrest in parts of the Commonwealth. The overall result was a decline in British exports.

Markets—and supplying food for its population—are perhaps Britain's outstanding economic problems. Thirty years ago cereals, meat, dairy products, tea, and citrus fruits flowed abundantly into British ports in exchange for coal, cotton and woolen goods, pottery, and "invisible" items—as service, insurance to all parts of the world, dividends on foreign investments, tourism. During World War II, Britain was forced to exchange some of its valuable foreign investments for war materials. The revenue it received from such investments declined; in 1938 overseas investments paid for 21 per cent of the imports, in 1952, only 2 per cent. In a world where demands for food products are increasing, this means, in addition, paying increasingly higher prices to supply basic needs.

The economic problems of Britain are not simple. To meet the economic emergency, British industry has gone through what might be termed a transmutation. Some of the older industries have been "retooled" to produce very modern products—lighter metal products, as aluminum instead of heavy metallurgy; manufactures of rayon, nylon, and other synthetic fabrics instead of cotton and wool; the production of aircraft and the like.

Resources and industry. The resources of Great Britain consist of cultivable soil, grasslands, coal, iron ore—and climate. Climate in Britain is a favorable resource; not unduly cold in winter nor hot in summer, no month without rain and with comparatively little snow, the climate is invigorating, and productive of permanent pastures that are highly suited to animal husbandry.

Coal is the one fuel resource that Britain has in substantial reserves, and the country ranks third in world coal production. But it is an increasingly expensive production for the output per man has been decreasing steadily. Nevertheless, Britain has coal supplies for perhaps 200 years. Iron ore is the only mineral found in quantity. Although it was tin and lead that attracted traders from the Mediterranean to Cornwall hundreds of years ago, tin, lead, and iron must now be imported along with such other industrial raw materials as copper, rubber, ferro-alloys, zinc, cotton, etc. The formerly rich Cleveland iron ore reserves that, with coal, gave England the industrial base on which to erect its steel industry, are now largely depleted and 40 per cent of the iron ore needs must be imported. These imported ores come notably from Sweden, Spain, and North Africa. The United Kingdom still ranks fourth in iron ore production despite declining resources, and third in steel production—despite the re-emphasis on newer metals and products.

Geopolitical considerations. The accomplishments of Great Britain—a relatively small nation of people living upon a restricted and rigidly defined land base—have never been matched. For several hundreds of years insularity, by keeping England out of European wars and entanglements, has accorded the island state long eras of peace while other European countries have exhausted their peoples and resources in war. Insularity also turned England toward seafaring, leading to fishing, commerce, exploration, conquest, and colonization. England has been, traditionally, a maritime nation. It thinks in terms of the sea.

Although just one of the component units within the British Commonwealth and on an equal footing (theoretically) with any of the others, as the nucleus from which the Empire grew and as the capital where the recognized head of Commonwealth government resides, Great Britain—and even more, England itself —is looked upon with deep affection by all Commonwealth peoples. It holds a special place within the union.

The regard in which England is held is demonstrated by the fact that when the name "Great Britain" is pronounced, there is a tendency to conjure up the picture of not only the Isles but of the whole bulwark of power represented by the Commonwealth. There is a tendency to infer, also, that the political ties that hold the parts of the Commonwealth together are close and binding. The ties are close and they are relatively binding;[3] however, they are not ties of authority but of affection. The Commonwealth is a loose union made up of states

[3] Although certain of the independent Commonwealth states—India, Pakistan, and the Union of South Africa—have at times been on the brink of breaking away from the Commonwealth, to date they have not. The long-standing ties are not lightly rent.

completely independent and sovereign in all matters. The only political "tie that binds" is the common recognition of the British Crown as the head of government and not even this is common to all of the participant states; India, in seeking association within the British family of nations, was disinclined to recognize the Crown. Hence, to keep India within the Commonwealth and from going the way of independence as did Burma, tradition was modified to permit that colony to come in under the terms it desired. This flexibility in governmental structure is perhaps the most significant quality that has held together the vast and farflung territories and peoples within the Empire. Canada, Australia, New Zealand, the Union of South Africa, India, Ceylon, Pakistan, and Southern Rhodesia all clung to the common association when afforded the opportunities of choosing their political way. It is the highest compliment British colonialism could have been paid. Only Burma chose independence.

Colonies, protectorates, and mandated lands spread across the globe complete the territorial domain of the Commonwealth. The peoples of these lands are being trained for eventual self-determination as they reach the stage of political maturity. By this highly politic method, the British Empire has been spared the convulsions which have torn the French Empire.

The territories of the Commonwealth constitute a defense front that girdles the globe. Although the dominions are not obligated in any sense to assist Britain or any of the other dominions, generally they stand together in time of real trouble. The territories of the Commonwealth also constitute a "chain of responsibility," and, as Kimble states, "great responsibility has a habit of begetting great trouble and Britain is no exception."[4] Great Britain had known revolt and dissent before the American colonies broke away, and it has known it since. Quite periodically, even within the confines of the Isles, Wales and Scotland have stirred restlessly, rebelliously; eventually, Ireland

wrenched itself free, and it continues to agitate for union with Northern Ireland. In the past decade, restiveness has displayed itself in an ominous fashion in parts of Africa—in the Union of South Africa where, because it feels the censure of other Commonwealth states, secession has at least been rumored; in Kenya, where a society of natives attempted to drive out the colonists by terrorist methods; in the English colonies of Central and West Africa.

Britain stands for the Commonwealth—*and* it stands alone. The Isles look small, lying off the northwest coast of Europe, and it is not generally realized that Great Britain (with the exception of West Germany) has the largest population among the Western European states and that it ranks ninth among the nations of the world. In spite of its economic difficulties resulting from the wars of this century, "Britain still occupies a key trading position in the world. Located off the highly industrialized continent of Europe and athwart the sealanes linking the two largest groups of mercantile-minded peoples, she still does the second largest carrying business in the world, and she builds three times as many merchant ships as the United States, her nearest competitor. And in keeping with her continuing commercial greatness, Great Britain remains the banker for more than one-fifth of the world; Australia, New Zealand, India, Pakistan, Ceylon, Southern Rhodesia, the Union of South Africa, Jordan, Libya, Burma, Iraq, Eire, and Iceland, as well as the colonies, continue to pay homage to the 'Old Lady of Threadneedle Street' and adhere to the sterling bloc."[5]

Transporation and Coherence

The connections of the imperial domain include all forms of modern transporation and communication. In fact, so scattered are the parts of the Commonwealth that there is scarcely a world transportation route or communications' line that does not begin, pass, or terminate on British territory. However, the major linking element is water, and all heavy commerce and the greater portion of other

[4] G. H. T. Kimble, "Great Britain," *Focus,* Vol. II, No. 7 (March 15, 1952), p. 1.

[5] *Ibid.,* p. 1.

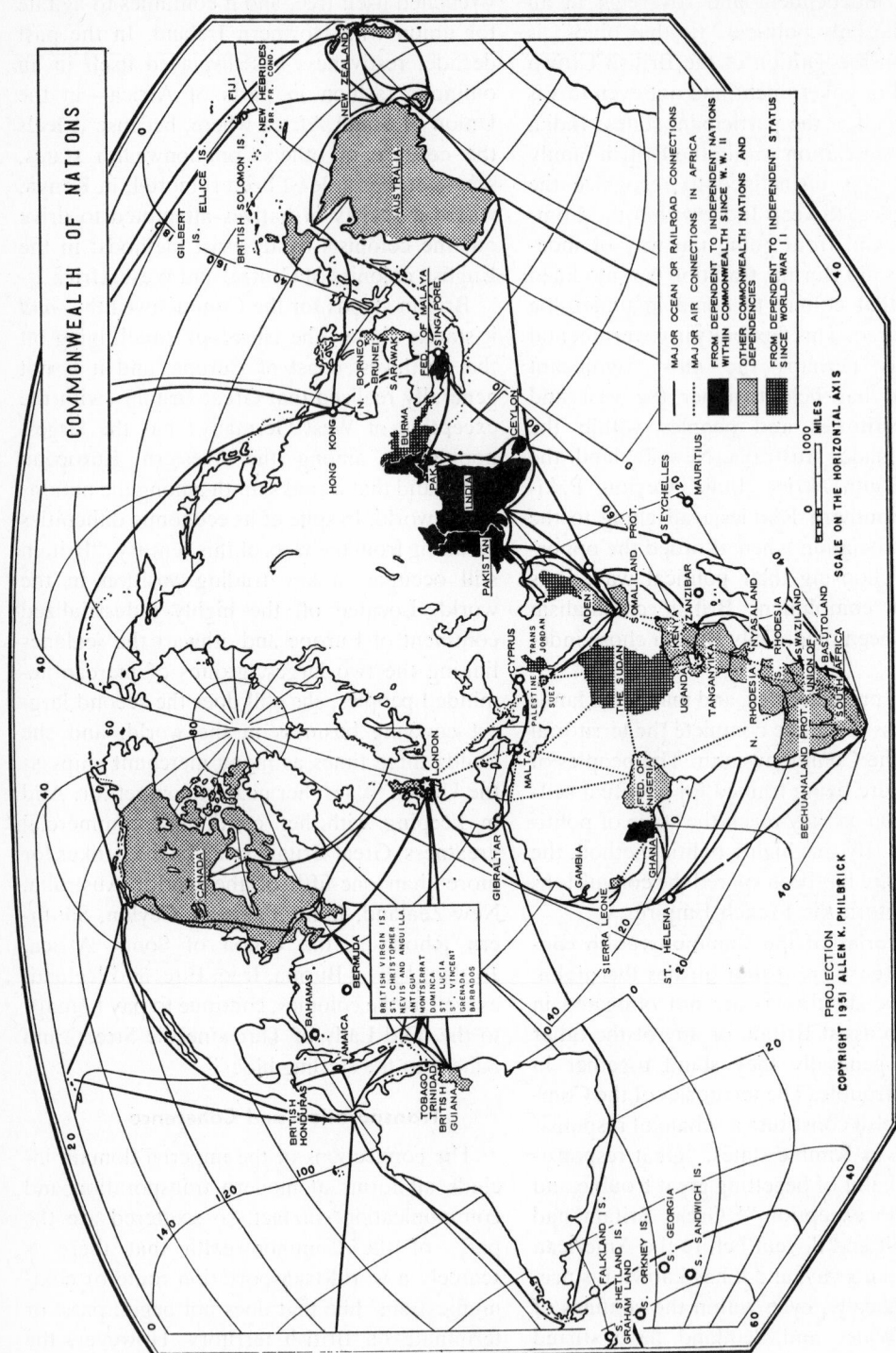

Figure 15.2. The Commonwealth of Nations and dependencies, scattered over the entire globe, are linked by an interconnecting system of airways and surface transportation—lifelines of the Commonwealth. A study of the map shows that the connecting links of surface transportation are all waterways except the railroad trajectory that stretches from Atlantic to Pacific across southern Canada.

freightage, passenger traffic, and mail pass along the oceanways between the several units. Rail lines comprise relatively insignificant cohesive links except for the transcontinental rail system across Canada. This long continental bridge connects, at the West Coast ports, with the elongate transportation trajectory across the Pacific to Australia and thus forms the intermedium by which the imperial waterways engirdle the globe.

Airlines comprise the next important transport medium, being second only to sea routes in the coalescing web. A number of the airways pass across the land, shortening the lines; others pass close along the coast rather than proceeding above non-British zones. Telephone, telegraph, and radio add lines of intricacy to the pattern of coherence. Over three-fifths of the imperial lands and about three-fourths of the people center around or lie on the peripheries of the Indian Ocean; only Canada, British Guiana, and West Indian and West African territories lie beyond. These, with Britain, are in the North Atlantic. Hence, the British "lifeline" is that ocean-and-sea route that passes between England and the East. To insure the integrity of this highly significant waterway, Britain secured control of certain strategic water passes and land positions along the route. The water passes are nodal points in the web of the Commonwealth where the lines that link its parts focus at a spot unusually and crucially strategic. Gibraltar, Suez, the Strait of Bab-el-Mandeb, the Strait of Malacca, and the Torres and Bass Straits are some of these knots, while among the land positions—or steppingstones—are Malta, Cyprus, the Socotra and Maldive Islands, and the tip of India. Those nodal areas that lie between the Atlantic and Indian oceans are the most critical.

The Strait of Gibraltar controls the western entrance to the Mediterranean. The control points at the Strait of Gibraltar are the Southern Pillar of Hercules in Spanish Morocco on the African coast, the Port of Tangier, a zone formerly administered by an International Commission, and "the Rock," a tiny bit of land hanging off the Spanish Peninsula. The Rock of Gibraltar fell to the English about 250 years ago (1704) when a combined Dutch and British fleet captured it from Spain. Since that date it has withstood many sieges, including the agitation of 1952-53, by Spain, for its return. From the moment it became British it has played a mighty role in the fortunes of Europe.

Gibraltar's history is strictly military. It goes back to 711 A.D. when the Moorish chieftain Tarik Ibn Zayid began the invasion of Spain. The Moors held Gibraltar for 727 years, Spain for 266 years, Britain for 248 years. Spain has tried to win it back at various times but has failed. One of these attempts was the Great Siege of 1779-1783 which lasted three years, seven months, and twelve days.

On the other side of the nine-mile strait are the two other "little Gibraltars," Spanish-owned and on the Moroccan shores. One of these is Ceuta, just across the Strait from Gibraltar and within sight of it. The other is Melilla. Spain captured these places centuries ago for reasons of strategy, and annexed them to Metropolitan Spain. Geographically they are part of Morocco just as, geographically, Gibraltar is part of Spain. Administratively, they were separated from the Spanish Moroccan protectorate and came under the jurisdiction of Metropolitan Spain.

"The Rock" surges up out of the Mediterranean in sheer walls—from a base only three miles long by three-fourths of a mile wide—to a crooked ridge running north and south and reaching a maximum elevation of 1,396 feet. Seemingly impregnable to military attack, it is very vulnerable from another viewpoint: the water supply, fresh fruits and vegetables, and the workers come from Iberia. Were an economic boycott imposed by Spain, Gibraltar would be dependent upon its rainwater reserves and fresh water supplies brought in by tankers; more drastic, the 12,000 Spaniards would be cut off. It would be difficult to replace these workers because the Rock has no accommodations for housing such numbers of additional inhabitants. The harbor on the Rock of Gibraltar is an important naval base capable of

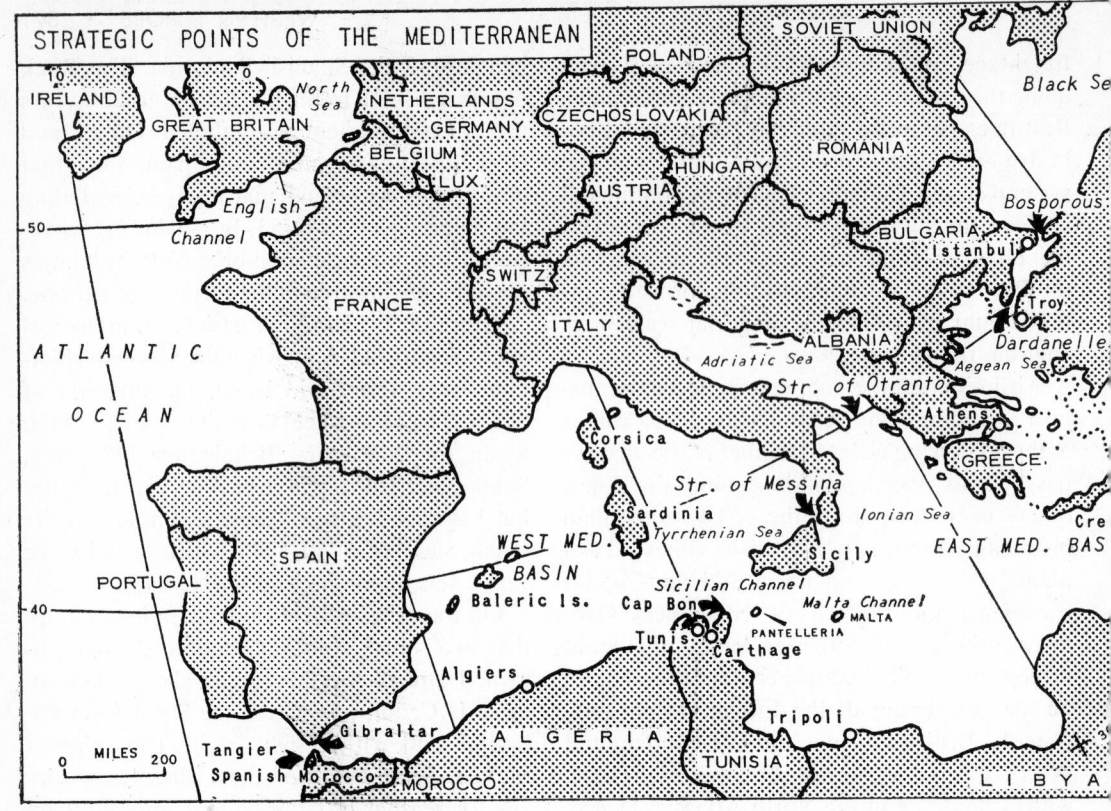

Figure 15.3.

bunkering twelve ships at a time without using any dock space for the purpose. Its dry docks can care for all but the largest aircraft carriers and within the solid rock are miles of tunnels used for a number of purposes including electronic detection.

Gibraltar may have lost some of its strategic value as a result of modern methods of warfare. Artillery, firing from Spain, could doubtless render the harbor and the airstrip impotent. But there is no doubting its value as a North Atlantic Treaty Organization base so long as the Spanish mainland remains friendly, or at least neutral. Gibraltar is still a major fortress of British—and Western—power. Like a sentinel, it guards the western Mediterranean entrance.

Malta is situated at the "waist" of the Mediterranean. Malta acts as another British control-point for another nodal area along the lifeline. On the southwest Tunisia overlooks the narrows, on the northeast, Italian Sicily; halfway between the shores lies the little, strategically placed Italian island of Pantelleria. There

are two water connections between the two basins of the Mediterranean—the broader pass already referred to as "the waist," and the Strait of Messina. The latter does not have either the commercial or geopolitical importance of the former because it lies offside the major searoutes; further, it is likely to be held by the one state that holds the two bordering shores.

Between Cape Bon and the closest point on Sicily, the span of water across the waist—80 miles in breadth—is sufficiently wide so that it is not possible to hold control of the narrows from either shore. And only as a base for British naval units can Malta serve to maintain a free passageway. The strategy of "the waist" is based upon naval strength. During relatively few periods in history have both shores been held by one power, and these corresponded to eras when a single authority extended its hegemony over much of the Mediterranean world. The Phoenicians controlled not only the south shore of Sicily but the islands of Pantelleria and Malta as well. When Carthage was

322

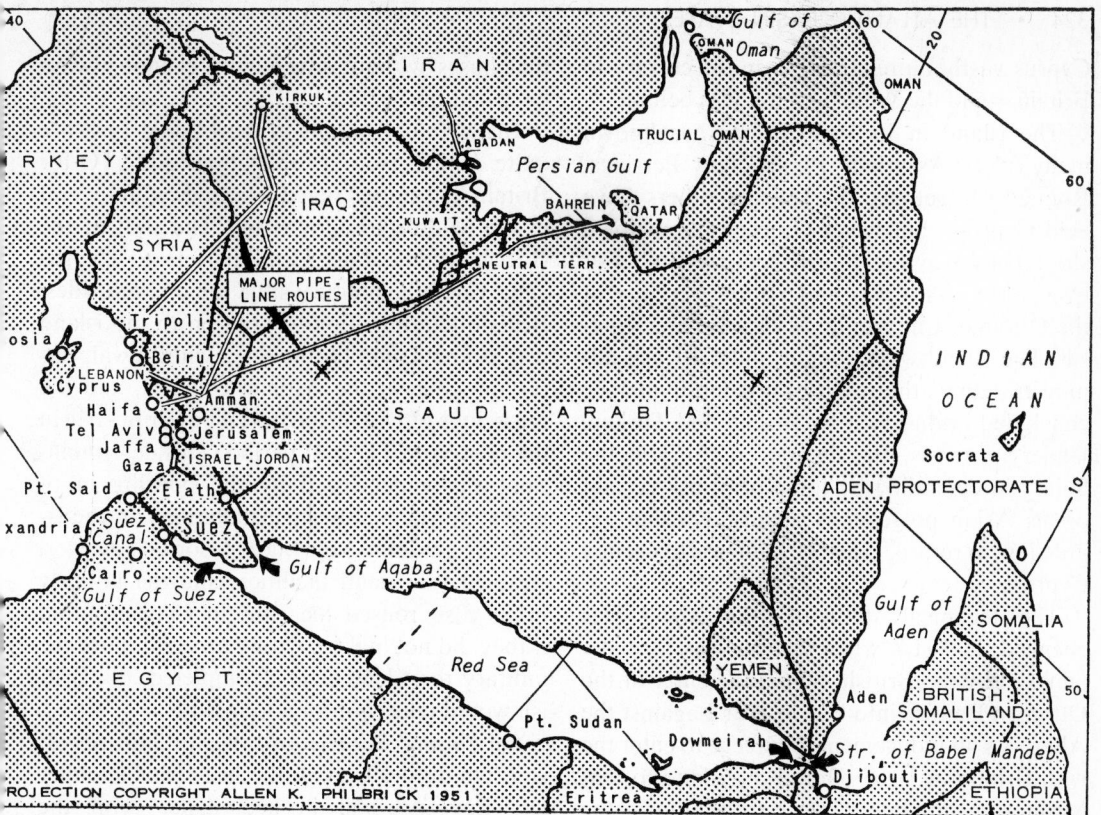

founded, its greatness rested upon sea power and not upon the land, for the Carthaginians were situated in a small area hemmed in by desert to the landward sides and facing the sea upon the others. When Carthage began to rise as a power in the Western Basin, it also held the south shore of Sicily, Pantelleria, and Malta, the latter islands inherited from the Phoenicians. Except for the Strait of Messina through which Greek trading cities in eastern Sicily maintained an open passage, Carthage controlled, for many decades, the traffic that passed between the two basins, and, within the Western Basin (which Carthage regarded as a Carthaginian sea), it destroyed any non-Carthaginian ships found upon the open waters. Even Rome was denied use of the Tyrrhenian Sea.

In due course, however, Carthaginian supremacy was overthrown by Rome. Sicily was taken as the first step to dominance. With Sicily in its grasp, Rome had sure access to and through "the waist" and, therefore, the right of passage within the Western Basin.

Malta has been held by the British since 1800. This small, critically situated island has been considered the "traditional key" to the passageway. Valletta, the capital and port, is a naval dockyard where the British Mediterranean Fleet units are refitted and repaired. Seventy-five per cent of the Maltese depend directly or indirectly upon the British armed forces on the island for their livelihood. Important, however, as Malta has been as the "key" to "the waist," it is very vulnerable to atomic attack; Libyan bases are necessary to "back up"—and they even top—Malta as a control-point.

Cyprus, near the eastern end of the Mediterranean, guards the Middle East for the British. Cyprus has, for some time, been the advance base of the British Air Command, and, with British evacuation of the Suez Canal Zone, it became the base of operations for the Middle East Command, transferred from Suez. It, too, is an important link along the lifeline. The evacuation of the Suez base at Ismailia and the loss of Palestine after World War II made

Cyprus vastly more strategic and necessary to Britain—and the West—than it was before.

The island in its long history has known many rulers; Assyrians, Phoenicians, Persians, Romans, Venetians, Turks, and others have held Cyprus—but never Greece, except for a short period in the fourth century B.C. For over 300 years it was under the suzerainty of the Ottoman Empire; in 1878 it became British. The island was brought under British administration as the result of a defense alliance concluded in that year by Britain and Turkey. Under its terms, Britain agreed to "join the Sultan in defending by force of arms" certain of his Asian possessions against Russian aggression; in return, Great Britain was to occupy Cyprus.

The technical status of the island was changed, in 1914, when Cyprus was formally annexed by the British—upon the entry of the Ottoman Empire into World War I against the Allies. As an inducement to Greece to enter the war, Britain in 1915 offered the island to that Mediterranean state. Greece turned down the offer. In the Treaty of Lausanne, July 24, 1923, Turkey recognized the annexation of Cyprus and renounced all rights and title to it; in 1925, it became a British Crown Colony.

Ever since Britain came into the island, *Enosis*—or union—with Greece has been demanded. Cypriots number about 450,000 of which approximately 90,000 are Turkish, the rest of Greek nationality. After the late 1940's, the demand for *Enosis* became more urgent, and Greece itself entered the struggle to back the demands of the Cypriot Greeks. Turkey, however, has been unwilling to see sovereignty pass to the Balkan state, both from strategic considerations and because of the substantial Turkish minority which opposes *Enosis* and has no ties with Greece. Britain has maintained that it cannot relinquish sovereignty over Cyprus any more than over Gibraltar at the other end of the Mediterranean. To the Greek offer that, if Cyprus were annexed to Greece, that state would be willing to lease bases on Cyprus to the British, Britain's diplomats have replied that "Britain's experience in Egypt has shown that bases without sovereignty cannot always be relied on."

Britain's obligations in the Middle East are quite distinct from its obligation to NATO for Britain has mutual defense treaties with several of the Middle Eastern states. The shift of the British Middle East Headquarters to Cyprus aggravated the political situation on both sides. British determination to hold on to the island was strengthened by the Suez withdrawal, unrest in some of the African colonies, and the recessions of British territorial power in Asia in the post-World War II period. This determination was underscored by the pouring in of money for new military installations on the island. The influx of Suez troops, however, strained the island facilities; and the military influx also roused the fear, in Cypriots, that if they did not make a strong protest before the military resettlement was completed, the British would take root for a long time.

An "open" Suez is an international necessity. On July 19, 1956 the last British soldier left Egyptian soil in accordance with the Anglo–Egyptian agreement of 1954. The British had been in the Canal Zone since 1882. In two world wars, the Suez base in the eastern deserts of Egypt had been the keystone of an effective system of defense for the Middle East, and it is in the context of the Middle East as a whole that the base and arrangements concerning it are of wide international importance— and not only as a nodal point along the lifeline.

The defense of the Middle East during the first and second world wars was made possible by base facilities in the Suez Canal area available before hostilities; and the successful liberation of Palestine and Syria in the First World War was organized from this base. In the Second World War the base facilities in the Suez Canal Zone, granted to Britain under the Anglo–Egyptian Treaty of 1936, were a vital factor in the defense of the Middle East and of Egypt itself, and also in the successful campaigns which resulted in the liberation of Cyrenaica, Tripolitania, and Syria. The base also served as the supply center both for the actions which preserved Iraq from Axis domination and for the resistance movements in Greece and Crete.

The security of the Middle East area is of vital concern not only to the countries lying within the region but to all of the countries in the world; the Middle East affords, strategically, the most important land bridge in the world (linking three continents—Asia, Africa, and Europe). Through it, via the Suez Canal and the civil airports at Cairo, Beirut, Bagdad, and Bahrein, pass the shortest sea and air routes linking Europe with Africa and Asia. Direct rail and/or road connections radiate from the Canal Zone westward to Libya and Tunisia, southward to the Sudan and East Africa, and eastward to Israel, Jordan, Lebanon, Syria, Turkey, Iraq, and Iran. The Canal Zone lies at the focal point of the area, across the land route between Africa, Asia, and Europe, and close to the important east-west international air routes, one of which passes through Cairo. The Canal itself provides the only easy means of transferring goods and people from the Mediterranean to the Persian Gulf and Indian Ocean, and naval forces from one sea flank of a Middle Eastern front to the other.

The 97.5 mile canal runs through Egyptian territory, was dug and financed by French businessmen, and, until October, 1954, was under the military supervision and occupation of the British. It is, therefore, an international project. It is the longest artificial waterway in the world.

The steamship age was just beginning when the canal was cut through, and even De Lesseps, the builder, did not realize the importance the canal would have. It handles twice the traffic of the Panama Canal; the only artificial waterway carrying greater tonnage is the Sault Ste. Marie connecting Lake Superior and Lake Huron. The canal, traversing the isthmus between Asia and Africa, is significant because it shortens the water route between Europe and the East. The old route, through the South Atlantic around the continent of Africa, was thousands of miles longer (about 5,000).

When the Suez was completed in 1869, it began to operate as a business enterprise under a 99-year lease from the Egyptian Government. At the termination of the lease the whole project was to revert to Egypt. With the passage of time Britain, as the world's greatest seapower and with many interests in the Middle East and Indian Ocean, gradually increased its influence in and around the Canal Zone so as to play, at length, the dominant role in its administration. By terms of a contract drawn up in 1888 at Constantinople by representatives of Britain, France, Germany, Austria, Spain, Italy, the Netherlands, Russia, and Norway, it was agreed that the canal must "always be free and open, in time of war and peace, to every vessel of commerce or war, without distinction of flag."

During World War I, the operation and defense of the canal were in the hands of the British military authorities. This gave Britain a control that it maintained until 1956. However, under the treaty of 1936 between Britain and Egypt—in effect until 1956—Britain gave up all claims in Egypt except control of the Suez and the right to maintain 10,000 troops and 400 planes in the Zone. The main provisions of the 1954 negotiations, leading to the complete withdrawal of Britain from Egyptian soil, were as follows:

(1) All British troops and uniformed technicians will be withdrawn from the canal zone within twenty months from the signing of a detailed agreement; . . .; (2) Egypt will assume responsibility for the base and will permit Egyptian and British commercial firms to maintain and operate some of the installations; (3) in the event of an armed attack on Egypt or any other Arab state or Turkey, Britain will be allowed to return; (4) in the event of a threat of attack on any of these nations, Egypt and Britain will immediately consult together; (5) The agreement will last for seven years.

Under Egyptian control, the terms of the contract (calling for the canal to be "free and open to every vessel") have been violated for the African state has refused, at times, passage to Israeli ships. This constitutes the use of the canal as a political weapon—a contingency against which the international agreements have guarded so carefully in the past and present.

The failure of the French–British attack of the fall of 1956 to wrest control of the canal from Egypt weakened the British–French position in the Middle East immeasurably. It, also, likely nullified the provision of the 1954 British–Egyptian negotiations which stipulated that Britain might return if Egypt were attacked. Thus Britain lost control of one of the key points along the lifeline; control rests now with Egypt.

The Strait of Bab-el-Mandeb is the constricted water outlet that connects the Red Sea with the Gulf of Aden. Perim Island and Aden—with the Port of Aden to the east—are British held, while the control points on the south are held by France (French Somaliland) and Abyssinia, the peninsula of Dowmeirah in Eritrea being the most strategic spot in the latter territory.

Singapore Island commands the Strait of Malacca, the narrows between the Malay Peninsula and Sumatra. Here, on this little island (27 miles long and 14 miles wide) situated at the southernmost tip of the great continent of Asia, the East and West really meet. It is one of the world's great crossroads. From it radiate cable lines to all parts of the globe; eight air lines, whose routes reach out in every direction, make it the air center of the Orient. Its great harbor, as well as its strategic location, make it a natural shipping center. Commercially, Singapore is the rubber and tin market of the world and, as such, has produced more dollar credits for the British than any other single market. It is, in brief, a "commercial middleman" in an Asian world where that role for Europeans is rapidly disappearing.

Singapore is a separate political entity, administratively not a part of the mainland of Malaya to which it is historically associated and on which it depends for its economic life. Further, although geographically it is a part of Malaya, its population is overwhelmingly Chinese; these Asians regard the island as a place of economic opportunity—but China as their home. Of the Island's 1 million inhabitants, less than 1 per cent are European, 8 per cent are Indian, 12 per cent Malayan, and 78 per cent Chinese.

Historically a key military and commercial center, Singapore was a strong fort and trading post known as Singapura (Lion City) during the thirteenth and fourteenth centuries. In the last quarter of the fourteenth century, however, it was destroyed by the Javanese, and, from then until early in the past century, it was only a collection of fishermen's huts. However, in 1819, exclusive rights on the island were acquired by the British from the Sultan of Johore by Sir Stamford Raffles. He suggested possession of the strategic island as a means of breaking the Dutch trade monopoly in the area. In 1824, British rights became sovereign, and, under Raffles, Singapore was made a free port—in a region of trade restrictions and monopolies. As such, the city grew in size and developed commercially. Trade between the East Indies and Malaysia and Europe passed through the Strait of Malacca. Control of the narrows could be largely contrived from the island; thus, Singapore became the British military headquarters of the Far East.

Singapore is the eastern key to the Indian Ocean; a fleet based in Singapore is able to effectively operate throughout the Indian Ocean, southeastward as far as New Zealand and northeastward to China as far as Hongkong. However, in the China Seas, France and the Netherlands have, in the past, cooperated with the British to keep the sea routes open.

FRANCE

France, the second largest country in west Europe and the second largest empire in the world, is an old geopolitical unit. This unitary aspect of the national state is due to the fact that, throughout their greatest extent, the boundaries lie along natural frontiers.

France faces on both the northern and southern seas. Hence, it has been a bridge across which various European strains have commingled. In the north, a gateway opens that permits access to the southwest border; from the Mediterranean, a passageway—in the

Rhone–Saone valley—strikes inland into the Paris Basin, and, eastward into the Rhineland. Between the seas, the lofty Pyrenees compact the state north to the compound mountain frontier formed by the Alps, Jura, Vosges, and Ardennes Highlands along the east. This latter frontier zone has been the most formidable for it is broken through in several places by lowland corridors: the Burgundy Gate between the Rhine and Rhone–Saone Basins, and the Sambre–Meuse Gateway edging along the Ardennes. Both have permitted French influence to penetrate into Teutonic lands, and, on the other side and more disastrously, Germans to repeatedly invade French lands to the very core of the nation.

France has a varied topography of mountains and highlands and plains. The lowlands, centered in the Paris Basin and spreading south to the Pyrenees and north to merge with the Flemish Lowlands of Belgium, were the nuclear area of the political state as they are today the center of economic activity. The upper and the lower basins of these plains, connected by the Poitou Gate, face different seas with varying opportunities. Hence, the interests and outlook of the people of the northern and southern sectors are different. The northern (Paris) basin is the agricultural heart of the country, and, with Algeria, provides most of the grain that makes France self-sufficient in breadstuffs (wheat); the southern (Aquitaine) basin, extending an arm between the Central Massif and the Pyrenees to the Mediterranean Sea, is largely a land of the vine.

The lowlands are traversed by four great rivers, the basins of which present markedly different characters. The Rhone–Saone drains into the tranquil Mediterranean and is the outlet of France to the Orient and North Africa. With the great port of Marseille near its mouth, the valley is a focus of routes that lead inland, from there, to all parts of France—and other parts of Europe as well. This valley and the southern lowland littoral are the only parts of France that are truly Mediterranean.

The Garonne–Gironde Basin (the Aquitaine) faces on the stormy Bay of Biscay. The climate of the lowland, however, is very favorable, combining Mediterranean and marine characteristics that make this one of the leading agricultural regions of France—and even of Europe—in range and yield. Bordeaux, at the head of the estuarial Gironde, is the port through which passes most of the trade with the French colonial possessions.

The Loire River is the least important of the four great French streams in terms of river and ocean transport. Up and down the coast, however—and even to the south of the Garonne— are very important French fisheries. Along the Loire is the famous "chateau" country of France with its equally famous vineyards and wineries.

The most important of French river systems is the Seine in the north. Draining the Paris Basin, its hinterland comprises the most important sector of all France. With a gentle gradient and a steady supply of water in the year-round but moderate rains of the marine region, the river system can be navigated by barges and river boats except in its extreme head-waters; further, its waters make connections, through canals that cut across the low divides, with every other major river system except the Garonne. Almost central, in the midst of the river, lies the Ile de la Cité, the political island in the heart of Paris.

The Paris Basin, near the hydrographic center of the Seine system, was the nucleus of the Duchy of France; regionally, it is known as the Île de France. Here, in the center of the Seine Basin, was the nucleus of the French *nation and empire* from the period of the Middle Ages—but not before. Although the Frankish kings (who moved with Germanic peoples into the French lowlands from the east) established Paris as their capital, these rulers were migratory and, during their reign, the Île de France did not have the importance it later assumed. The frontiers of this regional unit are approximately the same as were those of the territory of Hugh Capet, who, in 987, became King of France. Politically, it was like a French island surrounded by unfriendly powers—Norman, Burgundian, English, and others; physically, it had natural defensive aspects. Seldom did the power of Capet and his successors reach beyond the bounds of the Paris Basin; however, because of their position between the domains of the Dukes of Burgundy and Normandy—greatest rivals of the Capets —they were able to prevent a union between the two bordering states and, eventually, to emerge supreme.

The variegated physical environment has had marked effects upon the economic and political structure, and cultural differentiation, within the state. Interset around and among the river lowlands (which are the political, agricultural, and trade foci) are the highlands of France—the Pyrenees, the Central Massif, the Alps–Jura–Vosges–Ardennes, and the ancient remnant of the Armorican Massif in Brittany. The varying natural environments fostered exchange between lowland and lowland, lowland and highland. To carry on the exchange or to carry the products to the ports or international frontiers for exchange with foreign states, a network of roads and other interconnecting means of transportation have been built from the lowlands to take the easy passes across the highlands. Thus, a close network of communication was formed throughout the nation, though less intricately in the highlands.

The patchwork of topography led, also, to a cultural and political compartmentalism that has expressed itself in sovereignty or in attempts at independence at different periods and in differing degrees. Those areas that are physically most apart from the others—as Brittany (Armorica)—have maintained, up to the present, the greatest cultural distinctness. The old *provinces* of France were representative of these cultural and geographical alignments; the *departments,* which now subdivide and cut across the old political divisions without regard to ancient provincial affiliation, are purely administrative. They were, in fact, set up to break down the old "provincialism." In this they have been very successful, for, although the natural regions still reflect distinctions in culture, occupation, and produce,

France is one of the most highly integrated of political states—despite the strong individualism of Frenchmen (a French national trait).

Continental France is compact. France proper comprises more than continental France. Corsica and Algeria are an integral part of the metropolitan state. However, exclusive of the two latter political sub-divisions, France occupies a concise territory of 212,655 square miles inhabited by approximately 43 million people. Shape and even physiography have facilitated coherence for the rivers have intruded easy passageways in otherwise difficult terrain. The feeling of French nationality, which slowly evolved to become more dominant than the divisive regional loyalties, was actually consequent to political unification, occurring concomitantly with political expansion through the nineteenth century. The natural barrier frontiers to which the French people pushed their boundaries have facilitated and accentuated national cohesion.

Population and People

France, on a smaller scale, has been a melting pot of peoples as has the United States. Some of the French character undoubtedly derives from the blending of the ethnic stocks for fusion of the strongly contrasted types has gone on continuously and is spread widely across the country. On the other hand, in certain areas where fusion has been slight due to isolation, the characteristics of each of the three main European ethnic types stand out dominantly. The varied character of the population base may help to explain the lack of racial prejudice prevalent among French peoples—in French territories skin color has been less of an obstacle, socially and politically, than in any other of the colonial states except Portugal; mixed marriages are quite common —and accepted.

The 1954 census put the population of France at some 43 million, the highest in the nation's history. Previous to this, during the first half of this century, the population of France had remained relatively stable except for two drops that occurred during the decades of the two world wars. The downward trend was observed with considerable alarm. But it has been reversed, recently, as a result of a higher birth and a lower mortality rate. Population losses suffered during the war have been made up and the previous high—42 million in 1936—has been surpassed.

Certain features of the political and economic systems have acted to restrict the prosperity of the people. In the first place, during the current postwar period, prices have been very high, and, in comparison, wages and salaries low. Secondly, certain aspects of the population add to the burden. Just before the war there were 14.6 births for every 1000 persons; in 1947, there were 20.7. At present, as in 1936, children between the ages of 9 and 15 years make up 23 per cent of the population while at the opposite end, the number of persons 65 years or older also is increasing steadily, forming over 11 per cent of the total population. This increasing proportion of dependents has resulted in a great increase in the economic and social burden of the working population. Increase in the number of aged has also meant a heavier burden on the national budget; the Government in some cases (as in the case of the national railways) is paying as much in retirement pensions as it is in wages.

Thirdly, there is the instability of the French Government. Many observers have attempted to analyze and suggest remedies for this instability. France is one of the most democratic countries in the world—so much so that cabinets rise and fall with bewildering rapidity. This, of course, almost negates any constructive or decisive action because the next Government may reverse the decisions of the former.

The Empire

Not only at home but abroad in many parts of the vast and scattered Empire as well, the French Government is faced with critical problems. The French Empire embraces some 100 million people that are spread over an area of about 4.5 million square miles. The greater part of the overseas territories are in the big western bulge of the African continent where they have stretched, almost solidly, from French Equatorial Africa on the Congo through to the Atlantic and Mediterranean coasts.

France had cherished an ambitious plan, in the postwar period, to assemble the jigsaw puzzle of its empire into a Union with common citizenship for all of the millions of people. This plan was frustrated by the loss in Indochina and North Africa. In Tunisia and Morocco the French tried to direct the ascendant Moslem nationalism into channels that would eventually lead these dependencies into association with France along somewhat similar lines to that of Algeria. However, for half a decade, Tunisian and Moroccan nationalist forces agitated violently and with bloodshed for reforms that would lead eventually to independence. Since sovereignty has been accorded these two dependencies, Algeria, an integral part of France and the bastion of the Metropolitan state in Africa, has been rife with nationalism.

The huge overseas empire is a heavy burden on the nation. It is largely the realization that, without its overseas territories, Metropolitan France would likely lose status as a great power that makes the average Frenchman willing to bear the heavy tax load necessary to maintain the empire. Overseas France is a deficit operation; the war in Indochina cost nearly a billion dollars, plus French lives. Loss of North Vietnam was serious not only to France but to the West as well. However, the loss of parts of French North Africa was far more serious.

The North African territories are highly productive lands. They are in close proximity to France and have a climate that is very similar to that found in parts of the European state; further, they are rich in valuable mineral and manpower resources. Strategically, North Africa is essential to Western defense. Equally significant, North Africa holds many French colonials who have made it their home, in many cases for several generations. They live as minority groups in all of the three states—

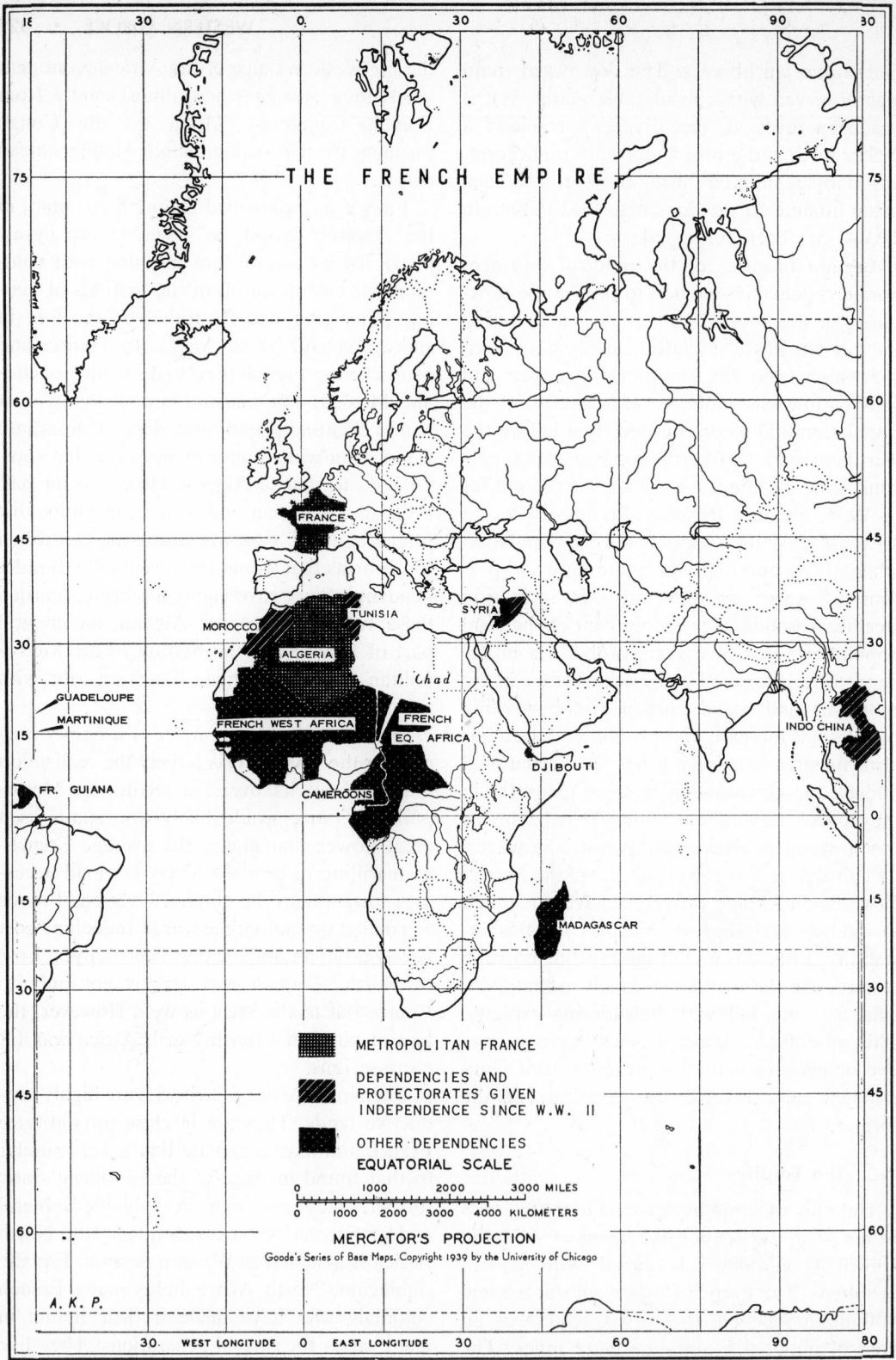

THE FRENCH EMPIRE

FRANCE

MOROCCO TUNISIA SYRIA
ALGERIA
L. Chad
GUADELOUPE
MARTINIQUE
FRENCH WEST AFRICA FRENCH
EQ. AFRICA
FR. GUIANA DJIBOUTI
CAMEROONS

INDO CHINA

MADAGASCAR

MUTROPOLITAN FRANCE

DEPENDENCIES AND
PROTECTORATES GIVEN
INDEPENDENCE SINCE W.W. II

OTHER DEPENDENCIES
EQUATORIAL SCALE

0   1000   2000   3000 MILES
0   1000   2000   3000   4000 KILOMETERS

MERCATOR'S PROJECTION
Goode's Series of Base Maps. Copyright 1939 by the University of Chicago

A. K. P.

30   WEST LONGITUDE   0   EAST LONGITUDE   30   60   90   80

Figure 15.4. Although France has lost valuable dependencies since the end of
World War II, the French Empire is still the second largest in the world. Most of the
French territories are in Africa, not widely scattered across the globe as are those
of the Commonwealth.

but large minorities comprising about one-eighth of the population. They have fought against separation from France but, on the other hand, refuse to leave the now independent territories where most of them live at a better standard than do the great majority of French at home. The Spanish in the department of Oran, Algeria, also make up a wealthy and large minority of Europeans.

The French Economy

The economy of France is balanced between agriculture and industry. Although agriculture no longer employs the majority of the population as was true a few decades ago, more than one-third of the working population are farmers, nearly twice as many Frenchmen as are engaged in industry. Agriculture still remains the backbone of the economy.

The agricultural production is highly varied, a reflection of the diversity of environments that characterizes France. France is ideal for the production of wheat, grown throughout the whole extent of the country but most concentrated in the northern half. Aside from the Soviet Union, France is the leading wheat producer in all of Europe. More than one-fifth of Europe's oats and sugar beets are produced in France, and France (excepting the USSR) is the outstanding European producer of the latter crop. Potato production is almost co-extensive with France; vine culture is more significant in the French economy than in that of any other country in the world. The vineyard areas are concentrated in the southern half of the country.

Productive as is French agriculture, the cultivation of the land is not as efficient as it might be. Many of the individual holdings are scattered and fragmented, and much of the work is still done without machinery other than the plow, spade, and hoe. However, since 1950, the amount of farm machinery used has noticeably increased.

French industry has a special character. Although France is relatively rich in mineral resources—ranking high among the nations of the world in iron ore reserves, having some of the largest deposits of bauxite, important supplies of potash and China clay, and notable supplies of coal and hydroelectric potential—the country is so seriously lacking in some of the vital minerals that, in competition with other great industrial powers such as the United States, the Soviet Union, and even Germany, France is greatly handicapped. Another difficulty lies in the fact that France does not have a great merchant marine to import the deficient raw materials; further, although some of the French colonies have important deposits of minerals, the mineral resources of the French empire are not on a par with those of the Commonwealth either in variety or quantity. Hence, industry in France is relatively more specialized than is that of the other industrial powers and tends to be of a sort that depends upon the skill and artistic creativeness of its workers rather than being characterized by practicability and mass production. Even the products of its heavy industry tend to have this character. In certain of its products of heavy manufacture—as locomotives and railroad equipment—France is outstanding.

The French coal reserves are scattered. French reserves of coal are large but mining of the fuel is difficult and costly because the seams are thin, broken, and tilted. The reserves of both Germany and Britain are greater than those of France and even the little Saar matches the coal supplies of the French state. The best industrial fuels are those in the north, adjacent to the Belgian border. With the Saar, France ranked fourth among the powers in world coal output—after the United States, the USSR, and Germany. Failing the Saar, the annual output is over 50 million tons, less than half the production of West Germany, less than one-fourth that of the United Kingdom, and about three-fifths that of Poland. Coal is one of the most pressing needs of France. Large amounts must be imported, part of which is coking coal for only a small proportion of the French coal is suitable for coking. Most of the industrial coals imported come from the German Ruhr.

Partly to compensate for the lack of easily

and cheaply obtainable coal, France has developed a large proportion of the hydroelectric potential. Aside from the USSR, only Italy exceeds France among European states in the amounts of waterpower produced, and only Italy and Norway have a greater hydroelectric potential. Even here, however, difficulties present themselves for the French power produced from water is dependent upon streams that have an irregular flow due to freezing in winter and the seasonality of precipitation; hence, stand-by thermal stations are necessary. The areas of greatest potential and production are naturally in the mountainous regions of the country—in the French Alps and Pyrenees, the Vosges, and in the Central Massif. The waterpower developed in these areas is drawing industries into the south as never before, particularly electrochemicals and electrometallurgy.

France, including Lorraine, has excellent iron ore; failing Lorraine, the iron ore is scattered. As long as France holds Lorraine, the other deposits will remain unimportant. The "minette" ores of Lorraine are France's most important mineral reserve and are, in fact, one of the world's largest and most significant deposits of iron ore. But the mineral content of the ore is not high—about 32 per cent—and the ores are phosphatic in character. Development of this important reserve awaited the discovery of the Thomas–Gilchrist process, in 1878, before they could be utilized.

Saar coal and Lorraine ore lie side by side— and adjacent also to Luxembourg and the Ruhr —this being one of the few choice regions of the earth where the basic mineral and fuel of heavy industry are found together. Transportation, however, is relatively costly due to the lack of adequate waterways. The ore and finished products that move out, and the coal that comes in, must be shipped almost entirely by rail. French iron ore output is third largest in the world while its steel production ranks fifth, the USSR, the United Kingdom, and Germany exceeding France in Europe.

The great bauxite reserves are found in southern France. Prior to World War II, this country led the world in the production of this clay. Since the war, France has fallen to fourth place, due not to a falling off in production but to the increased output of bauxite in other areas. Actually the French output of bauxite has more than doubled since the pre-war period (1938). France is the largest aluminum producer in Western Europe and, on a world basis, is exceeded only by the United States, the USSR, and Canada. The large and adjacent development of hydroelectricity has done much to stimulate the increase in aluminum production which requires huge amounts of electric power in the conversion of the bauxite (a clay) to an ore.

The potash reserves of France are located in southern Alsace. The potash deposits passed to France in 1919. Prior to that time, they had been a part of Germany and unexploited because of the huge deposits located in the Staszfurt–Magdeburg area of central Germany. Under the French the annual production of potash has reached approximately a million tons and France is the world's third largest producer.

French manufacturing shows a nice balance between heavy and light industry. Among the products of heavy industry for which France is outstanding, besides steel and aluminum, steel rails, locomotives, machine tools, and ships rank high, as well as automobiles. But it is perhaps in the light industries that France is more famous and luxury products of French manufacture are geopolitically important for the exchange value they possess. The British invented the modern industrial system and its first machinery; the United States gave industry the assembly-line of mass production; France has contributed its specialized products. Included are perfumes, fashions, textiles (cottons, wools, silk, silk velvets), accessories, jewelry, porcelain products and the like. The "magic" of the Paris—or French— label has drawn millions of dollars in currency to France for many decades.

France would like to equate its industrial strength with that of Germany, its historically aggressive neighbor to the east. There are, however, several reasons why the French nation is incapable of a production equal to that of the West German republic. First, France does not have the combined fuel and ore resources nor the transportation facilities (in terms of cheap water transport) to compete with Germany for technological leadership of continental Europe. While the state can produce almost every type of manufacture in small quantity, there are certain essential products which it is incapable of producing in quantity —machine and electronic products, in particular.

Further, the policy of established French industry is small production of high priced commodities catering not to a mass market but to a more restricted luxury market. Hence, French industrial productivity is low and the average Frenchman is unable to buy the many manufactured items, large and small, that would make life more pleasurable and easy— as can the average American who benefits from the mass production that is characteristic of American industry. The typical French industrialist is asocially minded.

In spite of the fact that there are some French enterprises that are very large scale, French manufacturing, as a whole, is small-scale, and the assembly-line, mass production methods of the American system could likely not be introduced with any great success.

Disputed Areas

Alsace–Lorraine. Although usually referred to as Alsace–Lorraine, there is no sound geographical or ethnic reason for regarding Alsace and Lorraine as a unit except that, historically, the ownership of both has been contested between France and Germany and both have alternately been held, first by one country, then by the other. Alsace was incorporated into the French domain in the seventeenth century, Lorraine during the eighteenth, but both lie outside of the naturally defined borders of the French state.

Alsace lies to the east of the north-south axis of the Vosges Mountains, looking away from France toward the Rhine and Germany. It is similar, structurally, to the area on the opposite bank of the Rhine within which Baden is located. Because of this eastward orientation, Germans have penetrated the province deeply to become so well established that the majority population is unmistakably German. Alsatians speak a language that is their own, showing a stronger flavor of guttural German than of French. On this majority basis the German nation stakes its claim to the territory. It is difficult to say just how the Alsatians felt about affiliation with one state or the other for there has never been a plebiscite held in Alsace to find out; political allegiance has been determined on the basis of force.

The same holds true for Lorraine although this province reflects equally French and German influences of nationality and language. In fact, culturally and linguistically, it forms a "marchland" between the two states; in this sector of the German–French frontier, the boundary between the two cultures is found at the zone of mixing *within* Lorraine. The Lorraine territory is a rich prize for either state because of the rich *minette* iron ores.

Alsace and part of Lorraine were taken by the Germans in 1871 and in the following way. Napoleon III in 1870, terminating the war with Mexico, had started trouble with Prussia over Luxembourg. Because Bismarck had shortly before imposed the Hohenzollern monarchy over the German states, Napoleon III was probably counting on the Austrian, Bavarian, and South German states joining him against the Northern Confederation. However, early in August, 1870, a united Germany retaliated by invading France. The result was the annexation by Germany of Alsace and about half of Lorraine.

Bismarck's annexation of these territories coincided with the discovery of iron ore in Lorraine. Unknowingly, however, the division was made short of the actual limits of the ore field and half of the ore remained in French hands. The late nineteenth century saw the vast expansion of German heavy industry based on Lorraine ore and Ruhr coal in Westphalia. The ore in the western Lorraine formed the base of a corresponding development of heavy industry in the Briey–Longwy district of France, using the Lens–Valenciennes coal.

In 1919, following the defeat of Germany, France regained the Alsace and Lorraine territories, thus adding to its own excellent reserves the German ore deposits with their great industrial potential. Undoubtedly, the political status of these two provinces will continue to be a thorny problem between France and Germany unless some mutual plan—as perhaps the Coal-Steel Community—can be worked out to bring about understanding between the two countries. The location of the ore and coal deposits in close proximity to the international frontier has, until the present, been a strategic disadvantage because it placed France's greatest centers of heavy industry in a vulnerable position. This same situation, particularly in association with the location of Ruhr coal, becomes just as strategically *advantageous* in terms of an international cooperative plan of mutual development. The French and German industrial developments in the German Ruhr and northeastern France are interdependent, for France is still dependent upon imports of the high-grade Ruhr coal and Germany upon the Lorraine ore. The location of the fuel and ore deposits makes this French–German zone a "natural" for the development of an international industrial "community"—if the political knots can be smoothed out.

The Saar. One of the major stumbling blocks to the build-up of the Western defense community in the post-World War II period was the bitterness of the Germans over the attachment of the Saar to France and the determination of the French to keep this tiny but highly strategic bit of land economically tied to the French state. The Saar problem goes back to Charlemagne. After his empire broke up (843 A.D.), the Saar area became and remained German for a thousand years except for two short intervals of French domination—from 1680 to 1697 under Louis XIV and between 1792 and 1815 under Napoleon I.

The peace conference that followed World War I almost floundered on the Saar question.

Clemenceau wanted outright annexation by France; Woodrow Wilson and Lloyd George opposed this. A compromise solution created a tiny "phantom" area—governed by a League of Nations Commission of five men; ownership of the coal mines (for which the Saar is important) went to France; and the area was tied to France in a customs union, French currency being made the legal tender.

The 976,000 Saarlanders are German in culture and language; economically, however, the Saar has long had close economic links with France. This has resulted in a dual nature, or tie, which goes far in explaining the pull and tug, first in one direction, then in the other, that has characterized recent Saar history. As in the case of Lorraine, the value of the Saar to France consists of its contribution to the industrial potential of the French state—as compared with that of Germany. With the Saar fields tied to the French economy, French coal production was about three-fifths and French steel production perhaps four-fifths that of Germany; without it, the latter is only about 55 per cent as great. The Saar is much more economically complementary to France than it is to Germany, for the coal and steel production of the Saar helped France to maintain a balance of production with the state to the east and an equilibrium of power within the Coal and Steel Community. Saar production, added to that of France, gave France 34 per cent (7 per cent of this was from the Saar) of the total production of the six nation community as against the German 35 per cent. With the Saar on the other side of the international boundary, a gross imbalance in the productive power of the two nations is created. The territory was transferred to the West Germans in January, 1957, by agreement between the leaders of the two interested powers.

Saarland comprises some 750 square miles of territory located at the point where France, Germany, and Luxembourg meet. The Saar River, which rises in Lorraine, flows northwestward near the French border and empties into the Moselle near Trier, gives the territory its name. It is a natural coal basin, highly industrialized, and one of the most densely populated areas in Europe. Ninety per cent of the population work in the mines or are dependent upon subsidiary industries for their living.

The territory was governed for fifteen years under the structure set up by the Paris Peace Conference. But, in 1935, with rising German nationalism becoming increasingly evident, a plebiscite—conducted under the terms of the Versailles Treaty—indicated a nine to one preference for German affiliation. Germany bought back the mines—as provided in the treaty—and, until the end of World War II, the Saar was a part of the German Reich. With the occupation of Germany by the four Allied Powers, the Saar fell within the French Zone, and, in 1946, the Basin was again set up as a special political unit. To the 1920-35 Saar Territory the French added a neck of land that extends up to the boundary of Luxembourg. Thus, the area of Saarland was about 1000 square miles and the frontier situation of the extended territory eliminated more than half of the French–German boundary between the Rhine and Luxembourg.

In 1949 Britain and the United States agreed to permit all of the coal mined in the Saar to be kept by France; this amounted to a "de facto" recognition that the Saar was to be economically tied to France. France has consistently indicated a desire to absorb the region economically; in this, Britain and the United States supported—while the USSR opposed—France. In 1950, France gave the title of "Republic" to the Saar, conceding broad powers of autonomy in return for control of the valley's rich coal mines for a 50-year period. At that time, in a treaty signed by France and the Saar, France promised this little border area full independence in 50 years. The pact granted greater freedom in internal matters, but left its foreign affairs and military security in the hands of the French. The effectiveness of the pact, however, hinged on the final settlement between Germany and the Allies—and Germany refused to recognize the pact.

The situation between France and Germany blew hot and luke-warm many times after 1950, fanning the old ashes of European disunity. One solution, agreed on in the fall of 1954 by the Governments of Mendes-France and Konrad Adenauer, would have given a "European" status to the Saar, and the territory would have been governed by a neutral Commissioner responsible to the Western European Union. Such Europeanization would have made the Saar independent of both France and Germany, at the same time encouraging French and German economic relations. A plebiscite, held in the Saar on October 23, 1955, rejected the plan, however. The Saar controversy, as stated, was finally solved with the return of the coal rich province to Germany, in January, 1957.

THE BENELUX COUNTRIES: BELGIUM, NETHERLANDS, AND LUXEMBOURG

Although the political borders of most of the West European states seem to have been suggested by the natural boundaries that now limit the territorial domains in many places, this was not the case in the Belgium–Netherlands frontier. It may have been more true in the past when the national states were taking form than it is today because natural barriers of a different sort—such as wide marshlands or dense forests—were then as divisive as are mountains at the present time.

The "low countries"—particularly Belgium—have been unfortunate in their location for they lie astride the major passageway between the great eastern expanse of the North European Plain and the smaller French counterpart in the Paris Basin and Aquitainia. At this lowland corridor, relatively broad as compared with other breaks in the mountainous terrain that lies between the Germanic and French lands, the North European Plain almost pinches out. Hence, historically, it has been one of the paths along which invading peoples have passed from one portion of the great lowland to the other.

Belgium lies very nearly at the "crossroads of Europe." Whereas such a crossroads location frequently brings prosperity, it just as frequently brings disaster. And for little Belgium, this situation at the crossroads has been perhaps the most unfortunate location in Europe for it lies between Germany, France, and England, West Europe's three great powers. The smooth, open lowland gateway facilitates and even invites passage. Many wars, that were not Belgian conflicts, have been waged on Belgian territory. Napoleon I fought his battle of Waterloo about 10 miles outside of Brussels; during World Wars I and II, Belgium became a shatter zone; and, in the last war, the Netherlands shared this fate with its little neighbor. For about 18 or 20 decades it has been the fate of Belgium to serve as the battleground for the opposing forces from the east and southwest. Belgium's chief defense lies in the alliances that it can make with stronger states and not in any inherent strength of its own.

One portion of Belgium is not lowland: the southeastern sector is a continuation of the adjacent highland country of France and Germany, the Ardennes. Physiographically and ethnically, the French frontier could have been drawn along the westward margins of these highlands and have done little injustice to the Belgian nation[6] for the state is divided, linguistically, culturally, and politically, into two parts—the Flemish lowlands, which are the nuclear area of the Belgian people, and the Ardennes, inhabited by a French-speaking population known as the Walloons. The Walloons are a community with independent traditions; and, although culturally and linguistically closer to France than to Belgium, they have oposed union with France also. The French language which is spoken is an archaic form.

The boundaries of Belgium were arbitrarily drawn. When the frontiers of Belgium were drawn, in 1831, at the formation of the Kingdom, they were obviously laid down arbitrarily and with little regard to the existing realities of physical and ethnic coherence. Belgium is not

even today a "nation" of people; the division, which coincides ethnically and physically, has at times threatened the unity of the state. After World War II, in spite of the great prosperity that characterized the economy, Belgium was seriously split within itself—and *along several lines*. There was, first of all, the basic, long-standing and dangerous division along linguistic lines between the French-speaking Walloons of the south and the Flemish-speaking Flemings in the north; there was, besides, a split between monarchists and republicans, and between socialists and conservatives. The division along linguistic lines has become increasingly sharp with the passage of years, and, of late, Flemish nationalism has asserted itself with growing intensity. More than once this— and the monarchy—have brought Belgian unity close to the breaking point.

Nationality develops slowly, and is facilitated by an environment that provides some degree of isolation from others and, hence, opportunity for unity. Belgium has had only a little over a hundred years in which to develop a feeling of nationality, and the state has been unfortunate in occupying a location that does not provide either a coherent or protected environment. Although the eight million population is about equally divided between Walloons and Flemish, the Flemish hold a slight majority. They are, however, largely of the middle and lower classes and much of the wealth and political control lies in the hands of the French-speaking peoples. Further, of the four Belgian universities, only the one at Ghent is Flemish. In 1950 and again in 1953, there were outbreaks of Flemish nationalism. It is not possible now to say whether these were merely temporary disturbances or whether they are forerunners of more serious internal trouble. Belgium is Catholic but singleness of religion seems to have had no effect upon lessening the divisive force of the separative factors.

Physically, Belgium falls into three regions that find relatively distinct expression in the economy. The physical regions of Belgium include the Flemish Plain, the Sambre–Meuse Valley, and the Ardennes. The Flemish low-

---

[6] On the other hand, without the Sambre–Meuse Valley and the Ardennes, Belgium would have been without its industrial coreland. Again, it must be re-emphasized, that frontiers, drawn with equity in terms of one element, may result in gross inequities in terms of others.

land is old, historic Belgium. Here the skilled manufacture of northern Europe had its beginning in the Flemish crafts, and, until the Industrial Revolution, it was Europe's dominant industrial district. It was a center for fine textiles during the Middle Ages; its cities belonged to the Hanseatic League, and, hence, were among European leaders in the initiation of European and world trade. Brugge, Ghent, and Antwerp had access to the sea by canal or river. Today the Flemish lowlands are still the textile center of the country as well as the agricultural core, but the Sambre–Meuse Valley has become the industrial heart of Belgium. The latter arose as a center of heavy industry after the Industrial Revolution. This region possesses good coking coal, workable iron ore, and lies within easy access to the Lorraine iron deposits. Steel, glass, cement, and lead and zinc products flow out from here. The Ardennes Plateau, in contrast, is the Belgian "back country." It is a rough, rolling-to-hilly country where sheep-raising is the major occupation, although agriculture is found in suitable areas.

Belgium may be characterized as an industrial nation—with a good base of agriculture. The cultivation is small-scale but painstaking, and it results in astonishing yields that usually surpass many times over the per-acre production of such crops as wheat, oats, and rye in other areas. It also produces some specialties of marked quality—flax fibre, tobacco, choice vegetables and fruits, the latter grown to a large extent for export.

Export trade is vitally necessary to the economy. For such trade, Belgium's location in the heart of industrial Europe is unexcelled—it is perhaps equalled, however, by that of the Netherlands for the two locations, commercially speaking, are quite comparable. An excellent system of communications links the country together. Per square mile, Belgium perhaps leads the world in railroad mileage; it has, further, access to hundreds of miles of internal canals and waterways. Its leading port, Antwerp, lies at the mouth of the Scheldt River, adjacent to the highly strategic outlet of the Rhine. Facing the North Sea and directly across from London, it lies right on the waterfront of the world's greatest ocean routes.

The one foreign possession of Belgium, the Belgian Congo, over 75 times larger than the mother country, is a treasure-trove of mineral wealth and tropical products.

The Netherlands has been somewhat less unfortunate in its location, history, and political life than has Belgium. In the beginning the Netherlands consisted of Holland, an area located to the southwest of the Zuider Zee—low, marshy, and with many islands. It was a frontier zone facing the North Sea. Slowly, through acquisition by war or marriage, bits of territory were added to Holland. Among these was a piece of land acquired in the fourteenth century that later was to become very important to the modern state; the cession was made by the Count of Flanders—namely, the Zeeland Islands, formed by the distributaries of the Rhine delta. Thus, the state acquired control of the outlet of this politically and commercially important river.

In the last quarter of the sixteenth century, seven provinces united to form a federal republic—Holland, Zeeland, Utrecht, Gelderland, Overijssel, Frisia, and Groningen. The lands of most of these territories were below sea level—which is the meaning of the English term "netherlands"—and dikes and windmills kept the land from being inundated by the sea.

A feeling of nationality developed early among the Dutch. The nuclear area of the state was in Holland but very early there was a feeling of unity among the peoples of the several provinces because of the strong Protestantism that developed among them. Religious unity was a strong factor in uniting the Dutch as a nation and in developing a feeling of national consciousness.

During the seventeenth century, after the republic had been established for some time and after Protestantism had become firmly entrenched throughout all of the state, some new territories were annexed. These lay to the south of the River Waal, the most southern of the Rhine distributaries. The new lands had been held by Spain and were Roman Catholic in religion. Thus was introduced into Protestant Netherlands a minority group that had divisive force; although Protestants now are in a majority, the Catholic minority is a large one composing about one-third of the total population.[7] From that time forward, language replaced religion as the cohering force. Although in the Middle Ages three languages had been spoken in different parts of the country, Frankish (a language derived from the Teuton invaders) gradually spread until it prevailed throughout the whole of the domain; from it modern Dutch, as well as literary Flemish, derive.

The Belgian–Netherlands boundary favored the Dutch. Belgium had remained under the authority of Catholic countries—Spain, Austria, and France—for a far longer time than any of the Dutch lands with which it had at one time been united under Spanish rule. In 1814, it was again reunited with the Netherlands, but so distinct, ethnically, were the Belgian people that the two states could not be welded into a satisfactory political unit, and, seventeen years later, the Kingdom of Belgium was set up. However, the dominantly Catholic lands that had been held by the Netherlands from the earlier period remained within the Dutch realm although they were ethnically closer to Belgium.

The political frontier between the Netherlands and Belgium, therefore, runs through the midst of a geographically and ethnically unified region, and southern Netherlands is more like Belgium than it is similar to the state to which it is attached. The boundary is unfortunate for Belgium and favorable to the Netherlands from still another point of view. As the frontier is demarcated, it cuts off the estuarial mouth of Belgium's one major river, the Scheldt, leaving the leading Belgian seaport politically cut off from the North Sea.[8] It also extends a prolongation of Dutch authority southward, in Limburg, between Belgian and German territory. This border line, obviously dictated by the Dutch, has been a source of friction between the two small states ever since it was drawn up.

The fight against the sea has been continuous. Although Holland has fought many aggressors, none has been as persistent as the sea; the Netherlands has, literally, been drawn from the seawaters to a large extent. Half of the total area of the Dutch domain lies about three feet below the flood level of the North Sea; and within this region are the two largest cities of the state, Rotterdam and Amsterdam. An important phase in the history of the Netherlands has been written in the constant struggle of man against natural forces—in this case, the sea.

The country is protected by an elaborate system of dikes and gradually, that large, shallow inland sea lying behind the protective dikes—the Ijsselmeer (or Zuider Zee)—has been made smaller. For more than a millennium the Dutch have been shutting off their fields and pastures—and creating new ones—by erecting artificial banks against the waves. By this process, the islands and mainland have been extended and broadened to the recession of marshland and sea. Today the seawalls are being greatly extended, for the work of dike construction did not go on uninterruptedly nor did the existing dikes always provide the needed protection against the tempestuous North Sea waters. In some years, particularly during the Middle Ages when the winter seas were unusually stormy, much of the hard-won land was inundated again. Countless times the pounding waves have broken the dikes and swept over the *polder* lands. As recently as January, 1953, the dikes in Zeeland were breached, and the sea overran some 400,000 acres of land with a loss of 1500 lives.

Thus, whereas in most parts of the world *land reclamation* refers to the "putting on" of water, in the Netherlands it means "taking it off." Even the rivers of Holland, in general, flow *above the level of the land.* Oil or gas

---

[7] Catholic Holland has a higher birth rate than does the Protestant portion of the state, and, hence, will become relatively stronger with the passage of time.

[8] This Scheldt River boundary exemplifies the geopolitical concept of the unity of both banks of a river; the frontier violates this principle.

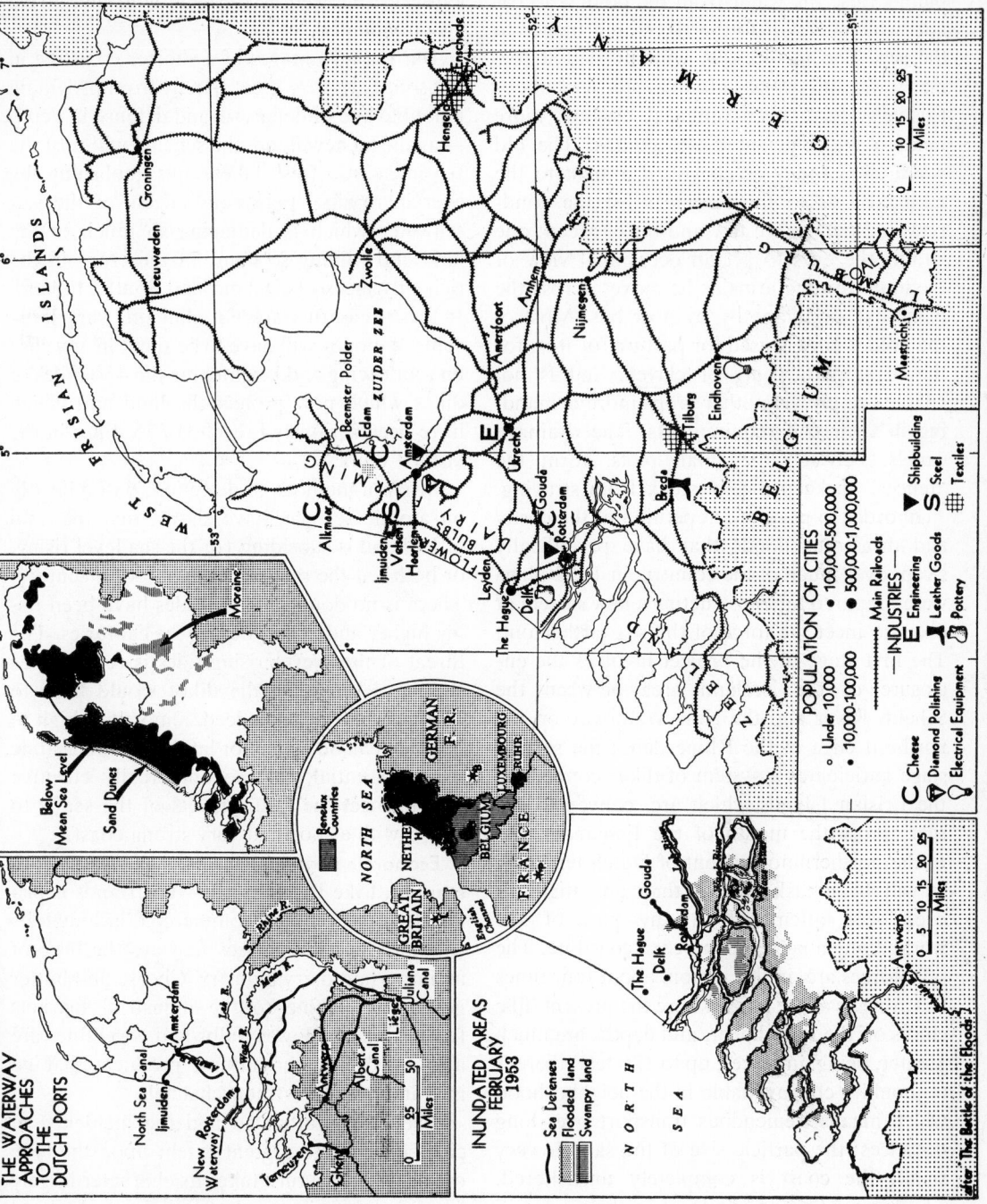

Figure 15.5. (Courtesy American Geographical Society. From Norman J. G. Pounds, "The Netherlands in Focus," *Focus*, IV.)

pumps raise the water from the polders to canals which carry it to the rivers and thence to the sea. The picturesque windmills, that formerly did this work automatically and unobtrusively, have been replaced by low, more modern and efficient diesel pumps. The old windmill is today as cherished a sight to the Hollander as to the foreigner for the wind-powered pumps are few and far between; one strains the eyes to get an occasional view of the long, turning arms as he moves across the plane-flat landscape by train or bus. Most of the polder land is used for pasture for it is, for the most part, peaty or clayey, and is not adapted to growing other crops more demanding in their soil requirements. The drainage canals, between the small plots, form the "fences" to keep the livestock from straying.

In order to prevent a repetition of the costly and disastrous floods that have periodically swept over much of the country, in 1952 plans were prepared for constructing a new system of dikes to meet the force of the sea farther out. The first stage of the project involves the enclosure of the Zeeland area between the Scheldt River and the New Waterway on the northern edge of the Rhine delta; the second stage anticipates a system of dikes connecting the Frisian Islands which arc, convex to the sea, across the mouth of the Ijsselmeer and to the northernmost extent of Dutch territory. It will be a task greater than any that has ever been attempted in any part of the world along a fierce open ocean coastline. The tidal forces are, in this region, about four times as strong as at the place where the present dike closes off the Ijesselmeer, and depths are much greater, being, in places, up to 120 feet; there is no boulder clay available in the neighborhood which means tremendous transport over long distances; the particle size of the sand is very small; the coast is completely unsheltered, which means long periods when the work will have to be interrupted owing to the fierce pounding of the northwest and southwest winds. At the main mouth of the River Meuse, which is also one of the mouths of the Rhine, a weir of great dimensions will be necessary because ice, as well as freshets, will have to be accommodated.

But the advantages of a shorter coastline in the south are very great. Apart from providing a double line of defense—and defense in depth —against a new flood, the scheme will turn the sea inlets into fresh lakes, thus abolishing the ever increasing, poisonous effects of the salt seawater which is damaging so much of the land and ruining so many of the crops in the rich provinces of Zeeland and South Holland. If these sea-arms are not shut off, very large sums of money will have to be spent in any case on reinforcing and heightening the 450 miles of dikes which now protect the land and which have been seriously breached 375 times in the last 70 years.

Modern methods of detection, based largely on atomic science, have shown that the land of Holland is subsiding (or the sea level rising, or both) at the rate of nearly a foot a century. There is no doubt that the tides have been rising higher and higher during the centuries. The threat of these ever rising tides is regarded as serious. Ultimately, the dikes would have to become very high—indeed, almost too high to be practical. So sooner or later a short coastline seems essential, for the only really effective way to meet the future threat of the sea is to face it with a short but very strong coast.

Economic power of the Netherlands is substantial. Like Belgium, the Netherlands is primarily industrial and commercial, although its soils produce the grasses that are the base of an important dairy industry. Cheese and butter go up the Rhine to the industrial markets farther inland; flower bulbs and vegetables are also important agricultural products that go into international trade channels.

The crops cultivated and the incidence of cities depends to a great extent upon the type of soil, which in turn takes its character largely from the elevation of the land above the level of the sea. Along the North Sea coast, except in those areas where the sea has broken through, is an almost continuous band of dune country. Anchored by vegetation, these sand hills break the impact of sea and winds alike.

The outer side of the dune country has little economic value except as a resort area, but along the inner side of the dunes—a region that is transitional between the dune lands and the polder country—is an area that is very favorable for the cultivation of such crops as vegetables, fruits, and flower bulbs. Hothouses and acres of carefully tended fields (actually horticulture) characterize this district. The famous tulip country of the Haarlem region is found here. This inner dune belt is also a district that is highly urbanized, for the soil here is more firm and, hence, more suitable as building sites.

The dune country is broken through by two rivers (the Scheldt and the distributaries of the Rhine) and by two artificial waterways—the New Waterway extending between Rotterdam and the sea via one of the Rhine outlets and the North Sea Canal which gives access to the sea from Amsterdam, a port located inland in the polder country along the southern shore of the Ijsselmeer.

The Netherlands coast, relatively straight and unindented, does not invite seafaring. However, fishing is a significant activity; and, resulting from control of the Rhine outlet, commercial activities have always been an important aspect of the Dutch economy.

Nederland means low country, and, east of the dune regions in the polder lands of Holland is perhaps the Netherlands "in its most typical form." The economic significance of these lands has already been referred to. They are largely used as pastures and from here come the famous Dutch dairy products, including the cheeses. Holland's two greatest cities and ports, Amsterdam and Rotterdam, are located in the polder region. Amsterdam, center of the colonial trade since the seventeenth century, is the economic core of the country. The warehouses lining the canals, bearing their legends of spices and other products of the East, bespeak the importance of Amsterdam, even today, as the center of what trade still filters in from the decimated empire; the banks, great business establishments, and the stock exchange reflect its importance as one of the most important financial centers in Europe. Rotterdam, on the other hand, located at the seaward terminus of the world's second greatest inland waterway, the Rhine, is Holland's leading port. Its trade, however, is international rather than national; it serves the needs of the Rhineland rather than acting as a Dutch port.

East and south of the polder lands is the Eastern Upland, a sandy area covered with scattered heath. Although called an upland, the elevation is inconsiderable even though it is above sea level. In the past this was largely a wasteland, very sparsely populated. Portions of the upland still lie waste but pressure for land has forced the use of this eastern region so that today it is a farming and grazing area. A recent development has been the discovery of oil in the southeast.

But industry and commerce are paramount in the Netherlands. Heavy industry produces a half million tons of steel—about one-third the requirements of the country. Steel production is based on Limburg coal (these reserves being an extension of the German coal fields) and imported Swedish ore. Shipbuilding has been a specialized skill of the Dutch for many centuries; today the industry concentrates on small craft, tugs, and tankers. Textiles, pottery, chemicals, bicycles and motor cars, rubber products, paper, and processed foods—as dairy products and the processing of tropical products—are other items of manufacture.

Because the population of only a little over 10 million does not provide a market large enough for the sale of all of its goods, the Netherlands is highly dependent upon export trade—and it has a higher per capita volume of foreign trade than does any European state except Belgium. Location is very favorable for foreign trade. The chief commercial and strategic advantage to the Netherlands accrues from its position as outlet to the important Rhineland hinterland, and *transit trade* is a significant item adding to the prosperity of the state. Rotterdam is the chief port on the delta. In Antwerp, Rotterdam has a strong competitor for Rhineland commerce, but certain handicaps give the Dutch port an advantage:

the river route via Antwerp is longer than that through the Lek distributary on which Rotterdam is located, less direct, and beset with the necessity of using canal navigation for part of the route and, hence, more difficult than the direct and broad channel of the Rhine River.

The Rhine is the most important river and waterway of Europe. Rhine traffic exceeds that of the Volga and even of the Upper Mississippi in the United States. Several factors combine to give it this significance: 1) the channel is deep and wide, and the flow even, due to the sources from which the water is drawn; 2) it is an international river that drains through Europe's most important districts of heavy industry—the two Low Countries, the German Ruhr, eastern France, and Switzerland —and empties into the North Sea which connects with the world's most commercial ocean, the Atlantic. The Rhine hinterland is far greater than the drainage basin of the river for canals connect it with other major European rivers so that it serves even the Danube–Black Sea countries; canals connect it also with the Marne River, and with the Rhone and, hence, the Mediterranean Sea. Outside of the Great Lakes of North America, there is no single fresh-waterway comparable to the Rhine.

The river has been a cohesive force in unifying people along its course, culturally and economically; but it has also been a perpetual international problem. From 1868 on, an international committee, known as the International Commission of the Rhine River, has functioned to establish the machinery for the international use of the river, encourage the development of the resources of the Rhine, and to regulate navigation. In order to stimulate the transit trade through its territory, the Netherlands has passed legislation that favored shipping, such as the establishment of a free port, partial support to navigation lines, and the facilitation of international banking.

Coal and steel products make up the bulk of the tonnage that passes downstream while iron ore, timber, and other requirements for the industrial centers move upstream—largely coming from or going to Germany. Although the Rhine rises in Switzerland (where the two major headwater streams unite into one, at Basel, Switzerland, before dropping down to the graben that separates the Vosges Mountains from the Black Forest), flows between France and Germany through part of its middle course, and enters the sea by way of Dutch territory, the Rhine is considered—and is—a German river because of the dominance of German trade in the river traffic. It is well that the outlet lies under the authority of a small state, for this gives an international guarantee of the common use of its waters. Other world powers would never permit the seizure of the outlet by a major power, such as Germany, that might dictate the use of the Rhine waters as did Russia those of the Danube for a brief interim in the recent postwar years.

Like Belgium, the Netherlands has had an overseas empire that was many times greater than the mother country—the tropical East Indies and Surinam. However, since the termination of World War II, rising nationalism resulted in the independence of all of the fabulous Indies' possessions except Western New Guinea. Thus, the Netherlands was shorn of most of its colonies; in area, they were more than 60 times greater than the Netherlands. Although Indonesia is, according to the Dutch, within the structure of the Netherlands Union, the Indonesians have repudiated the tie.

A geopolitical evaluation of the Netherlands. Several factors contribute to the strength and, on the other side, lack of power of this little country, historically and in the present era. Among the factors that contribute toward its strength is the successful economy based on a mixture of agriculture, manufacture, and commerce; for a small country, the economy is characterized by variety and vigor. Aiding the well-rounded development are three physical aspects of location. In the first place, climatically, the Netherlands is highly favored for it lies within the region of marine climate, which means mildness of temperature at all seasons of the year as well as adequate, year-round precipitation largely in the form of rain. Secondly, it faces the sea, having direct frontage on what has become the world's most travelled ocean. This very early induced the Dutch to engage in maritime activities—fishing, commerce, and exploration—which led, in turn, to the acquisition of a huge overseas empire that, through the tropical products and mineral resources, added to the variety and wealth of the resources and products of the state and served as well as an outlet for excess population. Thirdly, its location in the heart of industrial Europe and at the mouth of the Rhine gives the little state an international importance that is difficult to assess. But, taking advantage of its location close to industrial markets, it developed a specialized agriculture—horticulture and dairying—that catered to the needs of the adjacent urban agglomerations; and, as stated before, it played its position as the outlet of the Rhineland by developing trade, and passing laws and engaging in policies that would capitalize on the economic opportunities for the Dutch as well as be beneficial to the Rhine countries.

On the other side, however, certain limitations characterize the Netherlands, particularly accentuated since World War II. The first and most insistent of these problems is the pressure of an expanding population on a limited land area. Even prior to the war, this was a major problem; but, since the loss of the East Indies, the major outlet for excess population has been closed off. In fact, a large proportion of the Dutch in Indonesia returned to Holland as refugees after conditions became intolerable for them in the East. The absorption of these colonists posed a very real problem for the home state. The Netherlands has a higher density of population than any other country in the world. Further, it is a population that is increasing rapidly; between 1930 and 1950, the population increased by one-fourth (from eight to ten million).

A second problem (not inherent, however, as is the population problem) is that posed by the loss of the greater part of the empire. Part of the hardships attendant upon Indonesian independence have been alluded to above. Another aspect is that of the relative impoverish-

ment of the national economy and, therefore, a decline in the prosperity of the state. Thirdly, the loss of the empire has reduced the Netherlands to "just another small country." Productive the home state will remain, and products, resulting from industries inherent in the capacity of the state itself to produce, will continue to flow into world trade channels—as bulbs, vegetables, cheeses, hams, and chocolate. However, politically speaking and on a global scale, the Netherlands is of small importance—except as it acts as keeper of the Rhine outlet.

Luxembourg is a vest pocket Grand Duchy of about 300,000 people and 998 square miles in size. For three-quarters of a century its economy has been based on steel, an industry that developed on local iron ore and German coal. Today, the Luxembourg ores are facing exhaustion and, to maintain the production, 50 per cent of the mineral needs are being supplied by imports from Sweden. So heavily industrial, and so small, is the country that it can furnish neither its basic needs nor a market for its products. Eighty per cent of the national requirements are supplied from without; and 90 per cent of its production goes into international trade channels. Although the total production seems small, about 1.5 per cent of the world total, this tiny steel-camp is, nevertheless, a strategic spot lying in the midst of Europe's most important district of heavy industry.

GERMANY

Examination of a series of historical maps of Germany, of the critical periods during the past half century up to the present days, shows the reduction, resurgence, and even greater reduction of a strong, aggressive, industrial power with a prewar area of 181,693 square miles (minus Austria and Czechoslovakia) to a divided country, the largest piece of which constitutes West Germany, 94,892 square miles in area and 49 million in population. Germany was partitioned into anywhere from four to ten pieces, depending on the point of view. There were four occupation zones—

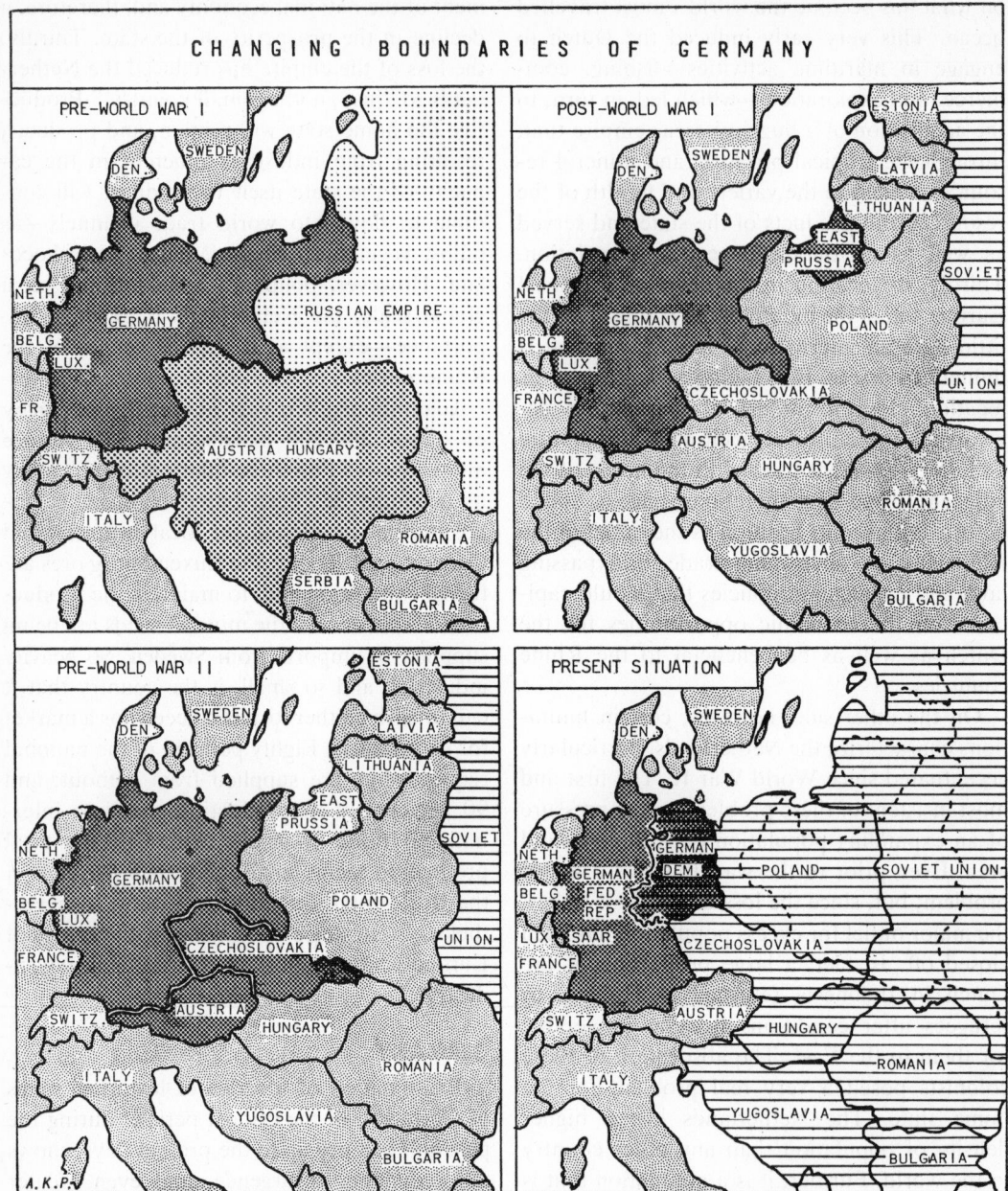

Figure 15.6. The Changing Boundaries of Germany. From 1871 until the outbreak of World War I, the frontiers of Germany remained relatively stable—a period of over four decades. Since then, boundary change—resulting from aggressive expansion by the Germans and consequent attrition imposed by her enemies—has been perhaps the outstanding reality for the state.

British, French, Russian, and American; Berlin, within the Soviet Zone, was placed under a separate jurisdiction—a joint administration of the four occupying powers—and eventually the city split into two zones (East and West) because of the inability of the administrators to agree; Poland received eastern Germany up to the Oder–Neisse Rivers, an area of 47,000 square miles and, in addition, part of East Prussia; the USSR absorbed the strategic northern portion of East Prussia adjacent to the Lithuanian SSR and fronting on the Baltic Sea; the Saar became economically tied to France; and the Sudeten lands, granted to Hitler at Munich in 1938, were returned to Czechoslovakia. With the unification of the three western zones into an independent state in the summer of 1955, it still left two Germanys—the German Federal Republic (West Germany) and the German Democratic Republic (East Germany), *plus* a shadowy Germany that the German people are not going to forget even though Germans have been removed from the territories and the lands no longer bear the German name, namely, the region east of the Oder–Neisse line and East Prussia. Although it is generally assumed that only the two republics are involved in the re-unification issue, ultimate aims on German re-unification, as far as the Germans are concerned, include the re-incorporation of at least the Polish-held lands. It can be expected that German political and economic policy will be oriented along those lines that best favor such re-incorporation of territory.

A contest for Germany has gone on intermittently since 1945. The reason for the struggle between the West and the East becomes apparent enough by a further examination of the map of Europe; Germany, in its location and geopolitical power, is the key to Europe. It is a borderland of the Western world—as in the past, the farthest frontier of the West against Slav (and, at present, Communist) penetration. Should war break out between the two great power groups, Germany would inevitably become a battleground. From the geopolitical point of view, Germany's geographical location is distinctly unfavorable to the Germans, for the state is situated in the midst of Europe on a border zone between two great areas of not only differing but antagonistic ideologies, and with little protection of natural frontiers. Although in the past Germany has been a very militant and aggressive nation, with the most modern means of warfare it could never stand alone. It must be allied with one group or another—or take an avowedly neutral stand which would automatically withdraw the weight of its power from the Western Bloc, and thus, serve to strengthen the other side. Thus, although it is true that, as a nation, it could not stand alone, it has nevertheless emerged as the European *pivot* around which the balance of power may turn.

The idea of a neutral role for Germany arose relatively recently—after it became apparent to the Soviets that, first, West Germany could not be drawn into the Communist Bloc, and, secondly, could in no other way be kept out of the Western Alliance of which it is now a part. After the granting of independence to Austria and the neutralization of that state whose political interests were also with the West, all indications in Soviet policy with regard to Germany have pointed to the Soviet's acceptance of unification of the two Germanys under some form of neutralization.

Certain European countries have been historically neutral, as Sweden and Switzerland. Because of their geographical locations or rugged topography, it may be that they can hope to preserve their neutrality even during possible conflicts to come, at least to the extent that has been possible in the past. During World War II, they were spared occupation and the use of their domains as battlegrounds but they were forced to make certain concessions to the Germans—in Sweden, the right to use Swedish air routes within certain limited areas, and, in Switzerland, the manufacture of precision instruments that the Germans needed. Swedish and Swiss neutrality is based on the hope, as Adenauer stated it, "that their countries would not be of crucial importance to the belligerent states."

But neither of these conditions holds true for the Federal Republic. The strategic location, skilled labor, highly developed industries, and wealth of important natural resources make that state a desirable ally—or coveted territory. Neutrality for Germany—even as for Austria—would be a "paper neutrality" that would mean nothing were war to break out.

So long as Germany remains partitioned there can be no lasting peace in Europe. Control of a united Germany would likely mean control of Europe; each power group has, therefore, sought reunification on terms that would ally the state with its side—or bring it within its eventual control. The diplomacy of Conrad Adenauer has kept the nation on a conservative path that, while it ties the German state to the West, at the same time assures the nation the most complete autonomy and sovereignty. However, the West Germany of today is largely the work of this one man, and there is great apprehension that, when Adenauer leaves the political scene, his political structure may prove to have been a frail stack of blocks. As long as Germany remains divided, the magnetic draw of Soviet Zone commerce and the lost Eastern lands may prove to be stronger than the ties of amity with the West; further, commercially at least, the Communist group of states has, perhaps, a good deal more to offer a neutral Germany than has the West. Moreover, were the Soviets able to induce the Germans to accept unity *and neutrality,* West European unity would be gravely disarranged —and might collapse completely. The military frontier of the West, with all that is involved in the transfer of air bases and depots, would be moved westward to the line of the Ardennes and the Rhine; German industrial strength and manpower would be lost to the West. In brief, without Germany, effective Western unity is impossible. The West would, indeed, be relegated to a toehold on the fringelands of Europe.

The stakes in the East-West struggle over Germany are very great. The stakes include the actual and potential economic and military strength of the German state, *and* the effect an allied or uncommitted Germany would have upon both the Western Alliance and the power of the Communist Bloc. German unity, which depends upon the stance that Germany takes in the international political structure, is, by its very nature, a "patriotic" question. Any German party that opposed unification—if a convincing offer were made—would be risking its future; it is likely that the patriotic moderation that now characterizes Germany would be replaced by an extreme nationalism among some of the political groups. Historians have never fully interpreted—nor agreed in interpreting—why the Germans, a people as mixed as Americans, developed such an acute awareness of nationality. About a century and a half ago, there were over 300 recognized political units within what came to be called Germany.

The post-World War II position of Germany resembles that of post-World War I Belgium or eighteenth century Poland—the former state a buffer zone located in the lowland corridor between opposing power blocs, the latter apportioned among neighboring countries. However, Germany will not accept the role that these two states did. Frontiers are always a provocative issue, and they are involved in the German question in the long view, for, due to the Potsdam Agreement, large tracts of former German territory are in Polish hands. Even the unification of the East and West sectors will undoubtedly not be accepted by Germany as a final settlement of its territorial problems.

With the amputation of the Soviet zone of occupation from the rest of Germany by the Soviets there were created two Germanys. The two Germanys epitomize—as do divided Korea and Indochina—the East-West power struggle: the German Federal Republic in the West and the People's Democratic Republic in the East. The governmental structure of each state partakes of the character of the power bloc with which it is allied.

The Federal Republic, with its capital at Bonn, occupies an area a little more than half the size of prewar Germany. The German Federal Republic still remains the largest state between the Atlantic and the Soviet frontier.

Within West Germany are comprehended the mines and factories of the Ruhr, the farmlands of Bavaria, and the North Sea ports of Bremen and Hamburg, all thriving as never before. Although eight million refugees from the lost territories were forced upon West Germany during the first post-war years, causing an almost unbearable economic burden, today West German industrial production has nearly reached that of Hitler's Reich in 1938. Coal from the Federal Republic feeds the furnaces of France, Belgium, and Luxembourg; and German steel is the base of Italian manufacture.

West Germany is the economic leader among European nations. The economic recovery of the Federal Republic has been rapid and consistent. The currency reform of June 20, 1948, uncovered the true condition of impoverishment of the country as a result of war damage, inflation, the dissolution of the German economic unit, the influx of refugees, etc. Dismantling alone, according to the Bremen Committee of Research, took 45 per cent of the industrial capacity (1945) in the Soviet Zone, 33 per cent in East Berlin, 67 per cent in West Berlin, and 8 per cent in the Western zones occupied by the three Western powers.

Economic recovery began with the establishment in March, 1948, of the Bank Deutscher Lander, and, three months later, the currency reform. Displaced persons, previously a burden, no longer constitute a drag on the national economy; they have become indispensable to the economic upsurge. Coal and steel output has increased steadily—toward the middle of the decade of the 1950's, steel mills were working up to 80-90 per cent of capacity and they were still unable to fill all orders; the output of Ruhr coal had reached 128 million tons and coal exports had risen from 24.7 to 28.4 million tons in the twelve-month period. German hard coal production made up more than 50 per cent of the total output of all five of the other members of the Coal and Steel Community.

Shipbuilding is another industry that has made an impressive recovery; West Germany ranks second only to Great Britain among the shipbuilders of the world. By the late months of 1956, West Germany had rebuilt its merchant fleet to three-fourths of its total World War II capacity, and the Lufthansa airline again began functioning.

The Ruhr is one of the greatest coal basins and industrial centers in the world. The importance of *the Ruhr* to the German economy is best perceived by noting its contribution to the prewar state; close to 70 per cent of the total German output of coal (bituminous and anthracite) and steel was produced in this area. The Ruhr district has no exact boundaries, but, in general, it lies between the Ruhr and Lippe Rivers, bounded on the west by the Rhine and extending eastward to Dortmund. It is a very small area—about 50 miles in east-west extent and less from north to south. Within this small space, however, live six million people concentrated in urban industrial centers; within it, also, is a steel capacity almost as great as that of all of Great Britain, and coal mines with a capacity of well over 125 million tons a year.

Before the war (while Germany still held German Silesia and the Saar) the Ruhr coal deposits constituted about 73 per cent of the total reserves; now they probably comprise 90 per cent of the coal of West Germany. Although the Ruhr was "the arsenal" for the Kaiser and Hitler, it is of even more significance to West Germany for its industrial output represents 93 per cent of all of the coal mined in the Republic and 80 per cent of all of the steel manufactured; further, the contribution of coal-tar derivatives enlarges the raw material resources of the Western Republic. It contains 14 cities of over 100,000 population, seven of which—Duisburg, Oberhausen, Mülheim, Essen, Bochum, Gelsenkirchen, and Dortmund—constitute one virtually continuous urban development of 2.5 million residents. It is, as might be expected, not self-sufficient in food; less than 4 per cent of the population in the area is engaged in agricultural pursuits as compared with 27 per cent for all of Germany (prewar figures).

In 1938 Ruhr coal production represented

10 per cent of the coal mined throughout the world and 22 per cent of European output. Although production has not yet reached that of the peak prewar years, there is no reason to doubt that the output of the Ruhr will again attain its former importance and likely exceed it. Sixty-eight per cent of the Ruhr reserves are of excellent coking quality (bituminous) and another 5 and 7 per cent are anthracite and semi-bituminous, respectively—the two latter coals being less suitable for coking but usable in forges and the like. Gas-coal normally represents about 20 per cent of the coal production; its high volatile content makes it best suited for the manufacture of gas but some of it is also mixed with bituminous and processed into coke. The gas and other by-products of the coke industry are used as valuable raw materials in the chemicals industries for the production of such products as nitrogen fertilizers, explosives, solvents, dyes, and plastics. Germany was perhaps the pioneer among nations in the important fields of chemicals and synthetics.

Although iron ore deposits within Germany are extensive, the ore is of inferior quality. With present technological methods of smelting, it is not possible to exploit the West German ores economically. Only 20 per cent of national needs are filled from local sources. The low grade and high phosphorus Lorraine ores (30-35 per cent iron content), which were acquired by Germany in 1871, were unusable until the invention of the Thomas–Gilchrist method of smelting ore (1878). From that time on, however, Lorraine supplied a major portion of the iron ore consumed in the Ruhr area. Of Germany's total iron ore production in 1913, over 73 per cent was supplied from Lorraine and another 25 per cent from Luxembourg which, at that time, was joined in a customs union to Germany. However, the Treaty of Versailles, in 1919, withdrew both of these territories from German control. In the years preceding World War II, 20 per cent of the Ruhr iron requirements were locally supplied, 60 per cent came from Sweden, 10 per cent from Lorraine, about 5 per cent from Spain and her colonies, and the remainder from varied sources. Sweden, at present, continues to be the major source of supply for ore for the Ruhr industries. Before the war, 95 per cent of the scrap requirements—which are the raw material for the best steel—were supplied from German sources. The imported scrap came mainly from adjacent states—France, Belgium, Luxembourg.

In addition to coal, the Ruhr area also has small deposits of iron ore, lead, and zinc. Western Germany, besides having this rich fuel-mineral industrial area, has, in other parts of the domain, sizable reserves of lead and zinc, manganese, salt, limestone, and clay.

The German Democratic Republic is, territorially, not quite half as large as the Federal Republic and has about one-third as many people. In area, East Germany comprises 41,535 square miles, in population, over 18 million. It is heavily agricultural, lacking the basic ore for heavy industry. However, the vast lignite, potash, and salt beds of the former German state are located in the East, as well as some coal, together forming the base of the German chemical industries. After the United States, East Germany is the largest producer of potash. It has not yet attained prewar capacity, however, which was considerably larger than the present output in the United States. Uranium has been discovered and is being exploited under Russian management.

Since the days of the Hanseatic League, the German lands have held an important place in world wide commerce. German Hanseatic League ships plied the North and Baltic Seas, and Leipzig was the center of an important fair to which traders came from as far as the Mediterranean lands. It was late when Germany entered the race for industrial markets; but since the turn of the century, except for the periods of war and reconstruction, this state has led all other countries on the European continent in volume of trade. The location, that geopolitically is unfavorable to the state, economically is eminently desirable. Germany faces the ice-free North Sea (unrestricted vestibule to the Atlantic and world trade routes), is linked with no less than nine European countries by a fine web of navigable waterways that includes the Rhine and Danube (international rivers), and the Elbe and Weser; has easy lowland access to the continent, east and west, via the European plain; and easy passes give ingress to Switzerland, Czechoslovakia, and France.

The force that gives German industry its vitality is trade—for neither the Federal nor Democratic republics are self-sufficient and division has accentuated this condition by removing from the West some of the most productive agricultural lands, and, from the East the industrial district (Silesia) that provided many of its requirements. Prewar Germany was able to supply only 70 per cent of its food requirements because less than one-fourth of its area was suitable to cultivation. Today West Germany is barely able to supply 60 per cent of its needs. In the north the plain is generally wet and sandy; where farming is carried on continuously, extensive fertilization is required and such crops as potatoes and rye do best. South of the plains' region is an area of ancient, complex mountain terrain, generally infertile and difficult to cultivate. However, here, and extending up into the Bavarian country in the south (that blends in the Bavarian Alps with the Alps of Switzerland), are some remarkably fertile pockets and valleys where fine crops of sugar beets and grains, grapes, and other fruits are produced. The south is also dairy country.

Waterpower and forests are two of the other resources of Germany. More than one-fourth of the total German domains are covered with some of the finest stands of timber in Europe, kept in continuous production by a careful program of management and reforestation. Developed waterpower produces more than three million horsepower annually. The largest projects are located on the upper reaches of the Rhine and Danube, but stations are scattered throughout Germany on the lesser rivers as well.

Undoubtedly the greatest asset of the German nation is its people—resourceful, energetic, intelligent. Ten years after suffering defeat in a war that almost pulverized some of its major industrial and commercial centers, the German people have risen to challenge Britain for second place economically, after the United States, in the Western Bloc. Shorn of all of their colonial holdings after World War I and of more than half of the territorial domain after the more recent struggle, West Germany is beginning *to exploit the advantages of being deprived of colonies*—and the experiment places colonialism in an incongruous position. One of the values set upon dependent territories has been the commercial advantages to the mother state, for the colonies have been viewed as potential markets for manufactured goods and sources of raw materials. In the present nationalistic mood prevalent among colonial and formerly colonial peoples, the West German trade leaders have found markets—*because* of the very fact that they are a non-colonial nation. Also in their favor is something that did not exist in prewar days, namely, a liberal enough trade and colonial policy on the part of the mother countries to permit other nations to engage in colonial trade. This situation constitutes a challenge to colonial powers and also points up a lesson or two. The West Germans are already making such progress on the international scene that their vigor and foresight may compensate for the loss of the colonies.

The above discussion indicates the great complexity of the whole German problem—involving recovery, independence and the re-establishment of Germany within the community of nations, reunification, international alignment, etc., not only in the area of international politics but in national and international economies as well. Fear of economic competition by the West European industrial states, the fear of France that the rise of German power may lead to renewed aggression, fear of the spread of Communism, fears of many and contradictory sorts have both aided and delayed the final emergence of Germany as an independent state in its prewar dimensions.

The Soviet stand on Germany seems also to be based on fear—and ambition. The Russians have made German reunification dependent on demilitarization and neutralization *within the framework of an "all European security pact"* that would annul the NATO. This would eject the United States from Europe.

16 ————————————————————————

The European Neutrals

Neutrality is always a variable. The neutrals of Europe include the Scandinavian states, Switzerland, and Austria—democratic countries that, because of size, location, or necessity, follow "the middle course" rather than definitely aligning themselves with one or the other side of the politically polarized world. This policy of neutrality has been characteristic of all of these states for many decades in all cases except Austria, and is quite a different neutrality than that found in the other portion of the neutral area—that is, in South Asia and North Africa. In the latter region, the middle course is essentially *non-commitment* rather than positive and constructive neutrality. This holds more or less true even in the case of India despite the efforts that the leaders of that state are making to maintain peace between the West and the Communist worlds.

The Scandinavian countries have traditionally held to policies of neutrality and have attempted to stay out of the recurring conflicts of Europe. Although national aspirations and ideologies are unmistakably with the West, the Scandinavian states have an uncomfortable awareness that close by are strong and aggressive nations that can, with ease, overpower them. This results in an understandable caution. Nevertheless, they have found it increasingly difficult to maintain a neutral role during the past two decades. Norway and Denmark, invaded by Germany in 1940, learned the bitter lesson that neutrality was no assurance of escape from the disaster of war. In the post-1945 period of the cold war these two states, with Sweden, were faced with the necessity of deciding whether or not to remain aloof; and the two countries that had suffered invasion decided to throw in their lot with the Atlantic Pact powers; Sweden held to neutrality. All three nations, however, have continued to serve the cause of peace through their continuing and effective efforts to maintain or bring about concord in the troubled world. Bunche, the American who achieved a temporary cessation of the Israel–Arab conflict in 1948, succeeded Bernadotte, a Swede who was assassinated in his attempts at conciliation in the

Near East; in the United Nations the most staunch advocates of peace have been the Scandinavians—and the Indians.

Belief in "doctrinaire neutrality" is widespread in Sweden and of long standing. Not since 1814, when Napoleon's ex-Marshal Bernadotte (founder of the present Swedish dynasty) took Norway from Denmark in a short war that ended in the Treaty of Kiel, have the Swedes started an aggressive war. The Swedo-Danish conflict was short; and, although it took more gunpowder to convince the Norwegians that they should acquiesce to joining the Swedes, the latter struggle was still more brief.

Before that time, however, Sweden had been quite prominent on the battlefields of continental Europe. Most of their major conflicts were with Russia. During the seventeenth and eighteenth centuries, Sweden was one of the great European powers holding a number of colonial territories, won by war, beyond the Baltic. In time, however, these possessions fell away from Sweden in the same manner in which they were acquired. Since then and for over 140 years Sweden has held to the policy of "settlement without war." It was this policy that made it possible for Norway to gain independence in 1905 without bloodshed. During World War II, neutrality was conditioned less by emotions than by physical facts: Sweden had no choice but to remain neutral. With Denmark and Norway overrun by the Nazis, Sweden was completely hemmed in; the only possible course was to deal with Germany, for the last exit to the outside (through the USSR) was closed to Sweden when the Germans invaded the eastern Slav nation. Swiss neutrality was compromised in the same manner during the war as was Swedish neutrality. The Swiss traded precision instruments and other highly strategic goods for German coal—because there was no alternative but to play along.

During the past decade, however, the reach of the Western powers has lengthened, somewhat changing the situation. It is likely that, if Denmark and Norway can be protected under the Atlantic Pact (and hence defended), so can

Sweden. And yet Sweden straddles the neutrality fence. What are the other facts behind this policy?

They are geographic, in the main. In the first place, Polish-Swedish trade has always been high. This is a natural condition not only because of the physical proximity of the Baltic state to Sweden but also because Sweden is an almost coalless country, and, from Poland have come—and does come—the needed fuel. In exchange Sweden ships iron ore, roller bearings, and wood pulp, all strategic materials. Materially, neutrality has paid off—for those European states that have found it possible to maintain this policy—in social and economic benefits.

Part of the neutral role, however, was dropped recently by Sweden when these nationals embraced the Charter of the United Nations, accepting it at full face value. This at least puts a new interpretation on the traditional Swedish stand. Nevertheless, while accepting without reservations the principles of international cooperation and security, and rejecting isolationism, the Swedish Government still adheres to the policy of *freedom from alliances outside the Scandinavian bloc of nations.* At the same time, it recognizes that, should war center around Sweden again, neutrality would be possible only so long as Swedish territory was not important to the contending states. Further, neutrality is possible only under the operation of such treaties as the Atlantic Pact. This is recognized by all of the self-determined neutrals. *Tidningen,* a Stockholm newspaper, wrote, in 1950: "organized collaboration between the western powers . . . creates the necessary balance of power in the world. Only in the shelter of such a balance can a country like Sweden try to be neutral."

Although there is a great deal of cooperation between the Scandinavian states in many fields, there is no military cooperation. For example, Sweden sent no arms' aid to Norway or Denmark during the days of their occupation, yet so much Swedish aid—in money, food, "haven"—was given that, at least as far as Norway was concerned, Swedish assistance kept that population from almost literally "going under." In the Korean conflict, Sweden again refused to send arms or troops; but they expended more money than did most of the United Nations' countries in the hospital that they erected and in the continuous medical services they have provided and still provide at their own expense. Their contributions are of a pacific nature.

Sweden has become the most prominent European neutral. Many of the Western states resented the Swedish concessions allowed the Germans during the war, and resent, as well, the postwar policy of non-participation in NATO. However, the Swedish people are united in backing the Government in its determination to prevent Scandinavia from becoming a point of friction between the political ideologies and economic conflicts of the West and the Communist worlds. Perhaps the greatest contribution that these three little Scandinavian countries (whose combined population totals only about 10 million) can render is to continue to set an example, and to help the greater powers negotiate, for peace.

SCANDINAVIA

Seemingly marginal to the centers of world population and world affairs, in the air age the Scandinavian location has become strategically significant. Scandinavia lies along the edges of the Arctic seas, and has the potential of a great air and submarine base. Its ragged coastline, with the thousands of islands and skerries forming a "guard" to the inland waterway, and the deep, penetrating, and protected fjords that finger for tens of miles into the Norwegian coast, provide unsurpassed submarine shelters. The value of Arctic location and the fjorded harbors are further enhanced by the fact that for 12 months of the year the whole of the Norwegian coast is ice-free for the Gulf Stream, which sweeps the 2,125 miles of the peninsular length, and the westerly winds give Norway a climate usually characteristic of more southerly latitudes. North Cape, Norway's most northern point, lies at 71.5 degrees north latitude. The polar circle is passed at 66.5 degrees, and yet, because of the influence of the warm Gulf Current flowing from the Florida Coast across the Atlantic and sliding, in part, past North Cape, the temperatures remain mild and the fjords open.

As an air and sea base the influence of Scandinavia is further enhanced in that it is extended outward. Reference to a polar map will reveal some of the relationships of Scandinavia with other areas. For example, if a circle, with a 2000-mile radius (the distance within the range of the modern heavy bomber carrying fissionable weapons) and centered on Oslo, is drawn it will encompass *all* of Europe (including all of European and some of Asiatic USSR) and the Mediterranean coasts, Atlas Africa plus northern Libya and the northern coast of Egypt, Turkey, the North Pole, Iceland, and Greenland.

As pointed out before when discussing the Arctic lands, recent Soviet interest in Scandinavia has centered on the Norwegian-held islands of Svalbard, 400 miles poleward of the northernmost tip of Scandinavia. Tracing another circle of the same 2000-mile radius but centered this time on Svalbard, the land thus surrounded would include all of Europe poleward from La Rochelle on the French coast, the head of the Adriatic, Black, and Caspian Seas; all of northern Siberia (except the Chukchi Peninsula); northern Alaska, and all of the fragmented coast and islands of northern Canada (bringing in also the mouth of Hudson Bay), the northern tip of Labrador and all of Greenland. The first circle puts Suez within range, while the second places the bombers almost upon the shores of Lake Baikal in the innermost Soviet lands. If the two circles are meshed, it is to be seen that all of the European *and* Mediterranean lands and the northern portions of the Asiatic and North American continents are included.

A second aspect of Scandinavian location likewise epitomizes the strategic significance of these states. Scandinavia is in a position to control Europe's three northern waterways: the Arctic route around the head of the peninsula to the Soviet ports of Archangel and Mur-

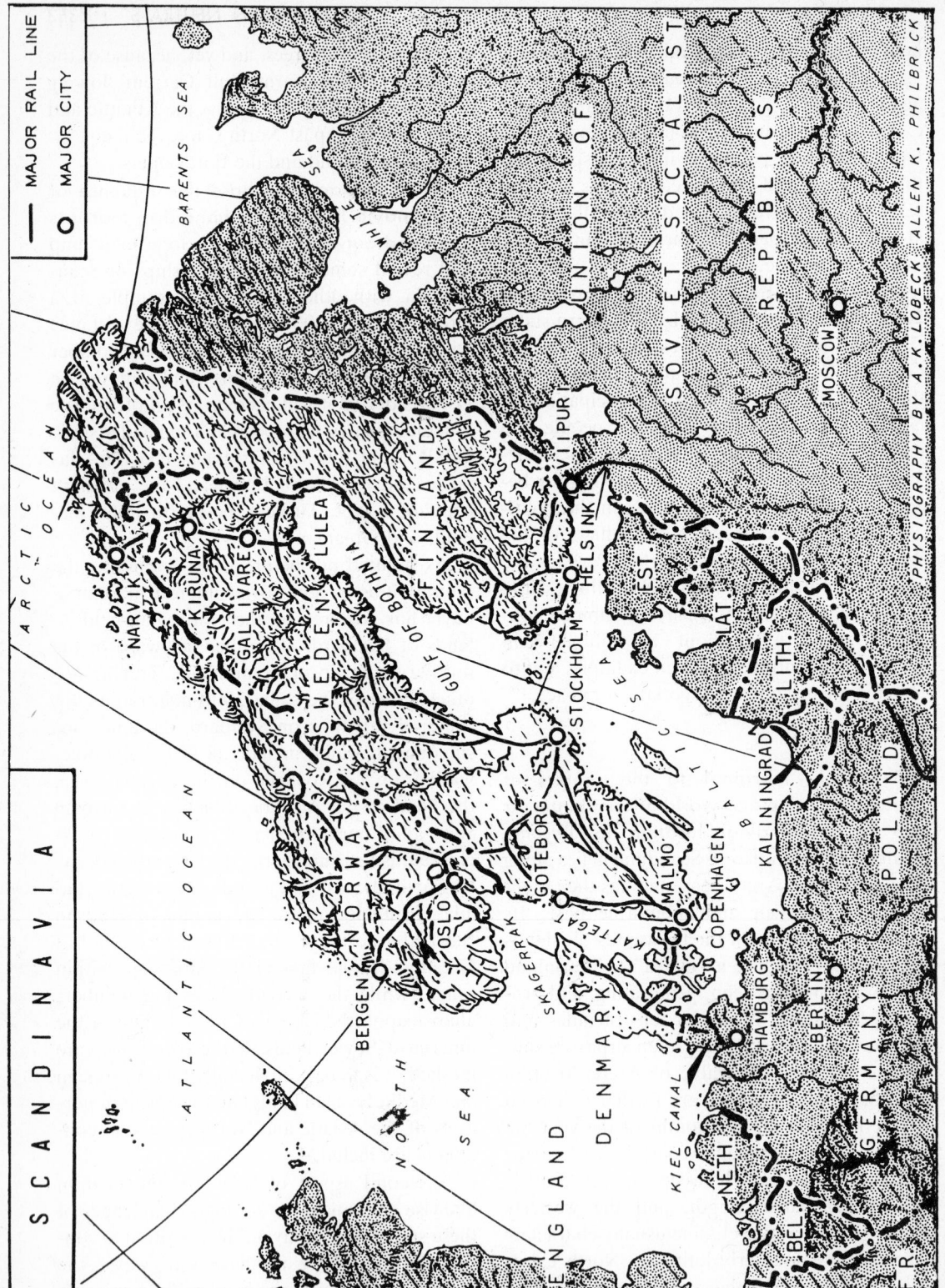

mansk (the latter Russia's only year-round, ice-free port outside of the politically constricted Black Sea area), the northern entrance to the North Sea, and the Kattegat and Skagerrak, bottlenecks to the Baltic and the Gulf of Finland.

Norway

Extending along the western and northern sides of the Scandinavian Peninsula, Norway is Europe's outpost of the Arctic; nevertheless, on the west, it faces mild oceans. It has a rugged topography and an irregular coastline, for during the Ice Age mountain glaciers descended from the heights to grind out valleys and gorge-like fjords. The salt water inlets of these glacial valleys cut deeply into the land like a maze of great watery fingers set between sheer mountain walls, the latter rising abruptly from the level of the sea to great heights. The fjords and the skerry guard provided the protected waterways that *invited* the Norsemen to early take to the seas—even as the land (72 per cent of which is composed of mountain, forbidding plateau, and glaciers) compelled them to look to the waters.

The 1700 miles of coast is translated into an actual shoreline 12,000 miles long by these bights and bays and fjords. Sogne Fjord, largest of the fjords, penetrates 122 miles inland from the sea to slash a gash into the middle of the country; Vest Fjord, which terminates inland beyond the port of Narvik as Tys Fjord, comes within four miles of the Swedish border.

Norway is a frugal country. Mountains, fjords, waterfalls, forests, and the sea describe this northern country. Farms are nestled along the base of mountains or climb up the slopes to, at times, almost perch on a steep mountain side; or they cluster in numbers along a rare but green and fertile valley stretching beside a fjord between the towering peaks. Seldom, however, do such valleys occur. Only four per cent of the land is cultivable, and the most productive areas lie in the south. Farming is very intensive, and, since three-fourths of the arable land is in pasture (natural or cultivated), large quantities of foodstuffs must be imported. About one-third of the population is engaged in farming—and dairying, the latter the most profitable branch of Norwegian agriculture and accounting for 75 per cent of the value of farm produce.

Another 24 per cent of Norway is forested, and forestry and wood products have always been important in the Norwegian economy. Seventy-two per cent of the land is waste, however, and hence, the land has "thrown" many of its people to the sea to earn a living. Fishing has long been one of the most important sources of national income as has also the Norwegian Merchant Marine.

Mineral wealth is varied but, except for pyrites and copper, the reserves are small and mineral fuels are generally lacking. However, in the well-distributed rainfall, in the permanent snowbeds of the mountains, and in the waterfalls and rapids of the streams is a huge potential for waterpower. Whatever industry has grown up has been developed on hydroelectricity, and hence, such manufactures as electrochemicals and electrometallurgy are important in Norway. The ores, usually in a partly refined state, are imported.

Shape and topography make coherence within the country difficult. Long and narrow, throughout most of its attenuated length Norway is little more than a fjorded, mountainous coast backed by more mountains that are buttressed, in turn, by the plateau. Some 125,000 square miles in size—and therefore about 2.5 times greater in area than England—it has a population of only 3.3 million people, a total national population less than half that of the city of New York, less than the population of Chicago. Despite a sparse and greatly scattered population, Norway is a "nation" of people who hold intense feelings of loyalty to their mountainous and fjorded homeland.

Denmark

Denmark and Sweden are very different from Norway. Denmark (16,575 square miles in area, or about the size of the state of Ohio) is a flat to rolling country of well-kept farms, fields of grain, and pastures of beautiful cattle.

The most prominent physiographic feature is no more than a glacial terminal moraine that forms the north-south backbone of the peninsula.

Denmark is the smallest of the three Scandinavian countries, the southernmost, and the one most closely situated to the rest of Europe. And yet, through its policies, it has managed to stay remarkably clear of European affairs. It is peninsular and insular, for, in addition to the mainland of Jutland, the country also consists of a number of Baltic islands on the largest of which (Sjaelland) Copenhagen, the capital, is located.

The country has only one land boundary, common with Germany; the other borders face on the sea—the Skagerrak separates the state from Norway, the Kattegat from Sweden. These were not always the frontiers, however. At one time, the Danes held the territory that lay on the shores of both the Kattegat and Oresund; at Helsingor (facing the narrowest point of the channel separating Denmark and Sweden) one can look across the water to the opposite shore and see the heavy fort that, with the Kronberg Castle in Denmark (Elsinore of Shakespearean fame), controlled the passage of all vessels going into and out of the Baltic waters and exacted toll. This central position between the North and Baltic Seas meant that, in an earlier era, the Danes played a very active role in European affairs.

As constituted today, Denmark provides the stepping stones between the European plains and Sweden. Except for two short water crossings that are traversed by ferry, the connections are by land.

It will be remembered that early in the eleventh century England was conquered by the Danes and ruled by them as long as Canute the Great and his successor lived. Late in the fourteenth century, all of Norway and the Norwegian holdings of Iceland, Greenland, and the Faroe Islands were taken over. During the fourteenth and fifteenth centuries the location of Denmark between the two centers of Hanseatic trade (the North and Baltic Seas) become very significant and, as a result of Danish

control of the passages between these two seas, the "toll," previously referred to, was imposed —and not lifted until 1857.

Denmark's location, controlling the water narrows between east and west Europe, is somewhat comparable to that of Belgium at the narrows of the European plain. Like Belgium, in later years Denmark tried to maintain a policy of neutrality. Although small, Denmark's integrity was more or less guaranteed because no great power was willing to see this strategic bit of European territory fall into the hands of a powerful state; further, it was more set apart from the main currents of European communication and flow than was Belgium. At the same time, it has occupied the position of a buffer state, to a degree at least.

The dissolution of the Danish Empire began in the early nineteenth century. In 1814 Norway disentangled itself from Danish rule. Iceland maintained the Danish ties; they became, however, decreasingly close until, in 1944, that island became an independent republic. The Faroe Islands attempted separation in 1946 but complete independence has not yet materialized. Only Greenland remains an outright possession.

An important slice of Danish territory was lost for good to Denmark at the end of World War I when Holstein was aceded to Germany and southern Schleswig voted, under a plebiscite, to likewise be attached to the German state. Historically, Schleswig–Holstein had been Danish; but Danish power, in the middle of the nineteenth century, was not great enough to hold securely all of its lands as far south as the Elbe River (where the Jutland Peninsula terminates), and, in 1864, following a defeat by Germany and Prussia, these lands became German. With Germany's defeat following World War I, a reappraisal was made of the ownership of these lands with the end result as stated above. The Kiel Canal, dug through the lower portion of the neck of the peninsula through German territory, provides a short water channel between the Baltic and North Seas. This has had the effect of taking away some of the importance of Copenhagen. The

Helsingör narrows has sometimes been called the Gibraltar of the North, however.

In proportion to its size and population (4.5 million) the foreign trade of Denmark is large. The country normally ranks about fifteenth among the world's trading nations. Possessing no natural resources—other than its soil—as do most other nations, Denmark is highly dependent upon the products of its farms. Even here, however, Denmark is handicapped for the marine climate does not permit a wide variety of crops to be raised. Pastures and feed crops for the animal industries lead, and, from the animals' industries, butter, bacon, condensed milk, poultry, and eggs flow into the international trade channels.

Without any natural mineral base on which to establish manufacturing, *demand* became the base on which industry was erected. At present about one-fourth of the country's exports consist of industrial goods other than agricultural or fish products. Proximity to Europe's industrial market centers and ease of access account in part for the large amount of export trade. Another factor lies in the high quality of Danish produce; Danish dairy products command highest prices on the world market. (The high quality rests in large part in the standards imposed by the cooperatives.)

Sweden

Physiographically, Sweden is intermediate between Denmark and Norway. It is monotonously level in the southwest to rolling in the southeast; north of Stockholm the land is level to rolling to hilly while inland along the Norwegian border and in the far north, it becomes mountainous and rugged. Vegetation is also varied. Scattered trees become more numerous to the east in the southern lobe and as one goes northward to a certain limit in the Far North where trees again almost disappear because of the cold. The Central Lake District is a beautiful land of lakes and trees; the best and greatest trees are found here although forests exist over large parts of all of the peninsular state.

Sweden is a varied land, then, with soft contours in the south—a region of farms and grassland becoming more wooded, more rolling in the Central district, and in the North, a land of pines and mountains—and, at last, of scrubs and shrubs and bare rock, in places even of tundra. This northland area is the home of the Lapps.

Sweden is called the Aristocrat of Scandinavia by many Europeans. The term has a dual application. It applies to the people because they are so formal, and to the natural base of the country, for Sweden has an abundance of natural resources as compared with the other two Scandinavian countries. It has fertile soil and level land—about all Denmark possesses, and in which Norway is so impoverished; it has forests—of which Denmark has none and Norway some, though less than Sweden; it has water for power—potential and developed—of which Denmark has none but in which Sweden is exceeded by Norway; it has minerals—iron and copper especially—and is generally richer in mineral ores than Norway; Denmark has none. Nearly seven per cent of the known iron ore reserves of the world are found in Sweden. By comparison, it has been estimated that the USSR, with its vast territories, has only 11 per cent of the total world iron reserves.

Sweden occupies the eastern and larger portion of the Scandinavian peninsula. Although about the size of California, by European standards Sweden is fairly large, comprising 173,436 square miles of territory and extending north and south through a distance of 1000 miles (or about 15 degrees of latitude). Aside from the USSR only Germany, Spain, and France in Europe are larger; and yet, Sweden's population numbers but 6.5 million.

Like Norway, Sweden is one of the most northerly countries in the world. It stretches from 55 degrees north latitude past the Arctic Circle to beyond 70 degrees north. One-seventh of the country, including several towns of considerable size as well as important industrial and mining developments, lies beyond the Arctic Circle. Although its bounds neither reach as far poleward as do those of Norway nor face on the Arctic seas, the climate of Sweden is more continental than that of its peninsular neighbor; facing the Gulf of Bothnia and the Baltic Sea, it is affected not by oceanic but by continental influences, and, during the winter, Swedish ports are closed by ice for several months.

Because of its continental orientation—facing as it does upon land-enclosed waters instead of upon the broad oceans—the Swedes have not taken to the sea to the same degree that have the Danes and Norwegians; also, because the land base is richer, the sea has not seemed so inviting. Hence, Sweden is continental not only in climate but in outlook and economy as well.

The economy of Sweden is varied. Sixty per cent of Swedish territory is covered with forests, and Sweden's geography is unexcelled for forestry operations. Including flumes and man-made channels, there are 20,000 miles of timber-floating waterways—twice the mileage of the state's railroads. Moreover, the rivers flow in a southerly direction which means that the mouths are the first to thaw—preventing a piling up of logs in a jam behind an overflowing and ice-filled outlet (as happens in so many places). In winter, snow and frozen ground aid the hauling of logs to waterside. Timber, pulp, paper, and fibre board constitute 40 per cent of Sweden's exports; in addition, matches, furniture, and other wood products go out.

The mineral resources of Sweden have been referred to. Central Sweden produces the iron and copper ores that are used by privately owned industries in the manufacture of iron and steel and metal products. Sweden's Arctic Northland (from near the towns of Gallivare and Kiruna) supplies the ore that is exported. It goes out through two ports, Luleå (Swedish port on the Gulf of Bothnia) and Narvik, Norway, on Vest Fjord (the latter facing on the North Sea and the Atlantic). The Arctic ore has a high iron content but is also phosphatic. For this reason and because of its distant location, the only Swedish plant that uses this Arctic iron in the manufacture of iron and steel and steel products is located at Luleå and is a government owned operation. About 30 per cent of the country's exports are comprised of basic iron and steel and steel products—as mining machinery, cargo vessels, and tankers; ball and roller bearings make up another 20 per cent of Swedish exports. Only 10 to 15 per cent of the country's exports come from agriculture and fishing.

Lacking coal, Swedish industry depends heavily upon imported raw fuels—from Europe and the United States. Due to the lack of coal many plants use wood for fuel. This is also the reason for the use of charcoal in the iron and steel business as well as for the large production of high quality steel products (as razor-blade steel, mining drills, and bearings).

Transportation facilities adequately cohere the Swedish domain internally and internationally. Physical coherence is less difficult within Sweden than in Norway; further, Sweden is well connected with its Scandinavian neighbors. Main rail lines run between Stockholm and Oslo, Norway; between Stockholm and Göteborg, Swedish port facing the Kattegat and the Skagerrak; between Stockholm and Malmö, port city on the southwest tip of Sweden and connected by ferry with Copenhagen and, hence, to the European mainland. (Passenger trains ferry across the Kattegat between Copenhagen and Malmö.) By this latter route, Stockholm has through rail service to the capitals of Europe. Lines also run from Sweden to Trondheim, Norway; an electric line —the Ore Railroad—passes from the Kiruna and Gällivare ore fields to the Norwegian port of Narvik; and a rail line extends northward from Stockholm to the Finnish frontier where it connects with the Finnish rail system. All parts of Sweden are well served by railroads except in the mountainous interior and the extreme north. This is in contrast with Norway which, north of Bodö, has only a difficult combination of bus and rail or coastal steamer service. The best connections between Narvik and Oslo are via the Swedish railways. Canals and rivers are also important in Sweden, particularly in the south.

Scandinavian People and Population

The Scandinavian countries are not plagued with troublesome minority problems as are many of the European states. This is due in part to the fact that Scandinavia is set apart in location from the main flow of European affairs as well as to the barrier character of the boundaries that separate each of the Scandinavian states from the others: the water boundaries make complete the segregation of the Danes from Norway and Sweden; in the case of the two latter nations, the natural mountain barrier (that forms the divide between the two states) extends the full length of the frontier and is, further, almost devoid of population.

Although composed of three independent countries, the states of the Scandinavian triad are, ethnically and culturally, closely associated. All are Nordic—and the Scandinavians are the most purely Nordic peoples of any nationalities thus classed. They apparently developed from a common stock that is thought to have entered Scandinavia by way of Sweden (where the purest types exist). In Norway the most purely Nordic types are found away from the seacoast and in some of the interior and hidden valleys. The greatest mixing—and hence, the least pure of the Nordics—are found in Denmark. Here the strain was more modified because of proximity to other Europeans.

The distinctions between the three Scandinavian peoples, however, were noted centuries ago. As early as the seventh and ninth centuries Danes and Norwegians were recognized as distinct from each other. Segregation undoubtedly influenced this differentiation, and geography furthered the segregation.

Geography, too, is responsible for the population distribution pattern that is found in Scandinavia today. Sweden's six million people are largely agglomerated in the rich farming and industrial lands that extend southward from a line that runs approximately from Göteborg to Stockholm. The Norwegians fringe the coastal areas of the state, leaving the rest of the country largely barren of people—density is highest around the Oslo fjord. The Danes are concentrated in the eastern half of the country (including insular Denmark)—because west and northwest Denmark tends to be less fertile and, hence, less capable of supporting large populations. As a matter of fact, one-fifth of the people of Denmark are congregated in the capital city of Copenhagen. In these areas, too, are the ecumenes of the states.

The Scandinavian histories have been closely intertwined. Although natural barriers have produced three distinct Scandinavian "nations," proximity has concurrently led to intimate associations, in both the past and in the present. Reference was made to the fact that the Swedish coast, opposite Denmark, was held by the latter state during the Middle Ages. "Sea power," which was built on the wealth and importance of Copenhagen, made possible this early supremacy by Denmark in Scandinavia. However, as populations grew in adjacent lands—particularly in Sweden and Germany—Denmark was unable to maintain this position, and political infraction by the Swedes gradually usurped the lands on the Scandinavian peninsula that now form Sweden.

Although Denmark, Sweden, and Norway cooperate closely on matters of common interest to the three states, there has been no tendency toward confederation among them; they have wished to remain sovereign and independent. However, with few exceptions, their associations have, historically, been mutually helpful, and have reflected a high degree of respect and tolerance for each other.

This cooperation and their community of thought in international affairs has been pointed out; but the concord of the Scandinavian countries is perhaps no place so much in evidence as in intra-Scandinavian affairs. When Norway became sovereign, it was agreed that the long common frontier betwen that state and Sweden should be without guard or fortification. Scandinavian nationals pass from one Scandinavian country to the other without passports.

FINLAND

The term *Scandinavia* generally refers to three countries—Norway, Sweden, and Denmark—but there are some grounds for the inclusion of Finland as well, for Finland is culturally—and by blood ties—closely related to the Scandinavian states, particularly Sweden.

The Finns originated as a Mongol group, the Finno-Ugrians, who migrated northward from the lower reaches of the Volga River. Therefore, fundamentally, they are of a different racial stock than are the Swedes and Norwegians. But they have been in Finland a long time—from before the period when the Magyars migrated into the Danubian lowlands—and there has been a mixing of the Asian stock with the European Slav and the Scandinavian (relatively more with Scandinavian than with Slav blood). Although high cheek bones and a stocky build at times reveal very definite traces of the Mongoloid background, more prominent perhaps are Scandinavian qualities, such as blue eyes and blond hair.

This dualism in Finnish racial stock and culture stands out very strongly on a regional basis; Finns who live in the interior contrast physically with the Finns who reside along the periphery of the peninsula where the racial type is quite Scandinavian—tall, blond, and Nordic. Inland from the Baltic fringe, the Finnish type has both the stocky stature and the broad head of the Mongoloid. High cheek bones, however, characterize all of the Finns.

The long period of Swedish dominance and contact gave the Finns their "nordic" physical character, and their cultural Scandinavian flavor; by religion they are Lutheran, a further tie with the Nordic peoples. The years of Swedish association also inculcated the ideals of the democratic West so that, basically, in culture, politics, and economy the Finns look West.

However, in the nineteenth century, the Russians interposed themselves on the Finnish scene, and the Russian contacts have complicated the ethnic and economic structures. So deeply, however, has the Scandinavian imprint been laid upon the Finnish people that the cen-

tury of pre-World War I and post-1939 Russian dominance has not even blurred this obvious orientation toward the West. *Neutrality* is a necessity, however, for Finland is actually within the sphere of the Russian; they can do nothing but cooperate with the Soviets and along the lines dictated by the latter.

Independence from Russia came with the downfall of the Czarist regime. The 1920 boundaries incorporated into Finland the Petsamo district in the far north (including the port of Petsamo) and the Oland Islands. Finland asked for possession of the latter territories (then Swedish) on the basis that without them the Finnish coast was vulnerable. Sweden, however, could have put forward a similar claim, and the Swedish claim was backed by the fact that the Oland Islanders are of Swedish nationality. Nevertheless, the Swedes accepted the League of Nations decision that gave the islands to the Finns. An international convention prevents Finland from fortifying the islands, however.

Between 1939 and 1944, as a result of the two wars fought between Finland and the USSR, the Russo–Finnish frontier was drastically modified. The Petsamo area, with the Finnish nickel mines and ice-free port, became Russian—bringing the Soviet border up against that of Norway and cutting Finland off from the Arctic Seas; much of Karelia was lost to the USSR. Very significantly, the whole of the Lake Ladoga area, including the highly important city of Viipuri, fell to the Soviets and the port of Hango and the Porkkala Peninsula were leased to the USSR, giving that state domination over the major control points on the northern shores of the Gulf of Finland. (The southern shores became exclusively Soviet when Estonia was incorporated into the USSR as an SSR.) In a magnanimous gesture after the first Geneva Conference in the summer of 1955, Porkkala Peninsula was returned to the Finns, apparently for propaganda purposes.

The ecumene of Finland is the small portion of the Baltic littoral that extends from Tampere and Turku eastward to and perhaps past

Helsinki. (It formerly extended east to include Viipuri and the Ladoga area which was the part of Finland most developed industrially.) Within this small space the great majority of the population live while the remainder of the more than 130,000 square miles is very sparsely peopled—a land of marshes, lakes, trees, and poor soils. In the Far North are the Lapps, about a thousand in number and a minority group that causes no problems. The other minority group—the Swedes—are a peaceful part of the population but politically and economically powerful far beyond their numbers.

The resources of Finland are circumscribed. Forests, Finland's greatest natural resource, cover about two-thirds of the country; waterpower is its only other resource, for farmlands are poor and meagre in area. Essentially without minerals or fuels (other than waterpower) of any kind, Finnish industry has been concerned in the main with the production of lumber, pulp, and paper.

THE MOUNTAIN STATES OF AUSTRIA AND SWITZERLAND

In May, 1955, Austria was accorded independence by a treaty (signed in Vienna by the four occupying powers) that also stipulated a neutral status for the country and a quittance of the land by the soldiers of the occupying forces. Just previous to this signing, Pravda (official news organ of the Soviets) had advised Austria to follow the way of neutrality, in the pattern of Swiss neutrality.

At the present time Switzerland and Austria are the only neutrals, aside from the Scandinavia, found in Europe. How do the two countries compare?

Both are Alpine states and transit lands that hold strategic passes through the mountains that lie between northern and Mediterranean Europe. Austria is the larger in area as well as in population, and natural resources are likewise greater. However, Switzerland is economically one of the strongest states in Europe.

The differences between Austria and Switzerland are not so much distinctions of natural endowment as of history. The Swiss economy was designed after the Western pattern, in a setting of world trade and with a determination to support itself within the small domain. Austria, on the other hand—while an empire —organized its economy in terms of a regional pattern that included the domination of surrounding lands and peoples. It built a cosmopolitan capital, Vienna, that looked beyond the confines of Austria—northward to Czechoslovakia and southward into and beyond Hungary—for support. When the empire fell away, therefore, little Austria was left with a huge city that contained from one-third to one-half of the entire Austrian population; 80 per cent of the industrial development was in Czechoslovakia, for Bohemia had been developed as the Austrian industrial core; its best farm lands (in the Danubian lowland) were in Hungary and Yugoslavia, while its imperial port of Trieste was Yugoslav. With its function as a diplomatic world-capital reduced by the disintegration of empire, Austria entered into a period of great difficulty.

In time sequence, the Swiss mountaineers were just beginning to make a bid for independence when Austria was expanding its territory through the absorption of adjacent lands. By the time that Switzerland had finally established a constitutional form of government and won international recognition of its status of neutrality, Austria had reached the height of its imperial glory. The last 75 years have seen Switzerland move steadily ahead along democratic, self-reliant lines whereas the Austrian Empire started into a decline that ended in complete disintegration after the Axis defeat in 1918.

Austria entered its independent, neutral way —with the signing of the Vienna treaty (1955) —with about the same status it held a millenium ago: a small country of Germanic peoples thrust into Slav and Magyar territory. Whether the Austrians will fill again the role they held in the past remains to be seen. They were the wedge of the West that stood between the Slavic East and the non-Slav West; *and,* they were a core around which a large part of the West and Southern Slavs were oriented—

westward, and, thereby, drawn *away from* the more logical eastern (ethnic) orientation. Vienna, key city on the Danube, could well act as a center from which to again capture and fulfill both functions in the future.

Switzerland

Modern Switzerland had its political beginnings more than 650 years ago. The world's oldest existent democracy, Switzerland began in a loose federation of states made up of the three forest "cantons" of Uri, Schwyz, and Unterwalden. The people of these cantons first convened on the shores of Lake Lucerne (in 1291) to establish a system of local government in opposition to the one set up by the Hapsburgs. The Swiss cantons had obtained "charters" from the Holy Roman Emperor to organize such a federation "for mutual safety and protection." The shift of the main route of travel between northern and southern Europe across the Alps—from the St. Bernard passes at the western end to the St. Gotthard in Switzerland—placed the cantons in a position not only to carry on trade themselves but to benefit from whatever foreign commerce funneled through the passes.

The beginnings of Swiss neutrality. The ancient confederation was active in European affairs—wars included. However, when the Holy Roman Empire was shaken by civil war (the Thirty Years' War, 1618-1648), the Swiss stayed out of the conflict and, in 1648, withdrew from the empire. This was the first major step taken by the Swiss to disentangle themselves from the turbulent affairs of the states around them, and it was the first step toward a policy of national neutrality.

Swiss neutrality was formally and internationally recognized after the termination of the Napoleonic wars at the beginning of the nineteenth century—through the Congress of Vienna in 1815. By that agreement the European powers acknowledged the key position of the Alpine passes, and made Switzerland the guardian of these strategic communication routes—placing control in the hands of a weak power whose neutrality all states have recog-nized and helped to maintain. Since that time, nearly 150 years ago, Switzerland has been a neutral.

Though resources are limited, the Swiss economy is strong. Less than half the size of the state of Maine (16,944 square miles), the Swiss environment has had little to offer in the way of natural resources except impressive beauty. Three-fourths of its domain is covered with young and rugged mountains bereft of mineral resources; only a small proportion of the country is suitable for farming. Topographically broken up into fragmented valleys separated from each other by mountain ranges over a large part of the country, physical integration posed a problem. Switzerland was, nevertheless, one of the first ten countries in the world to construct railroads, and today, it has one of the densest rail nets—and undoubtedly the most efficient—on the globe. Without coal but replete with hydroelectric potential, the railroads were electrified and today 98 per cent of the Swiss rail mileage is run by electricity.

Using its scenery and railroads—and establishing one of the finest systems of hotels in the world—the Swiss capitalized on the tourist attractions that their little mountain state provided. Tourism is a big business in Switzerland. Whatever industries developed grew out of Swiss skill in handicrafts—wood carving, watch and toy making, etc.—and today the manufacture of precision instruments (which require a high degree of skill in manufacture but a minimum of raw materials) characterizes Swiss industry. The country is unable to feed itself, but its mountain pastures are utilized for the raising of large numbers of dairy cattle and dairy products are important items entering international trade channels.

It is in its location that Switzerland is geographically and politically important. The state lies at one of the strategic crossroads of the continent, surrounded by several of Europe's leading nations—Germany, France, Italy, and Austria. In Switzerland rise the headwaters of the Rhine, a number of the major tributaries of the Danube, and the Rhone—all

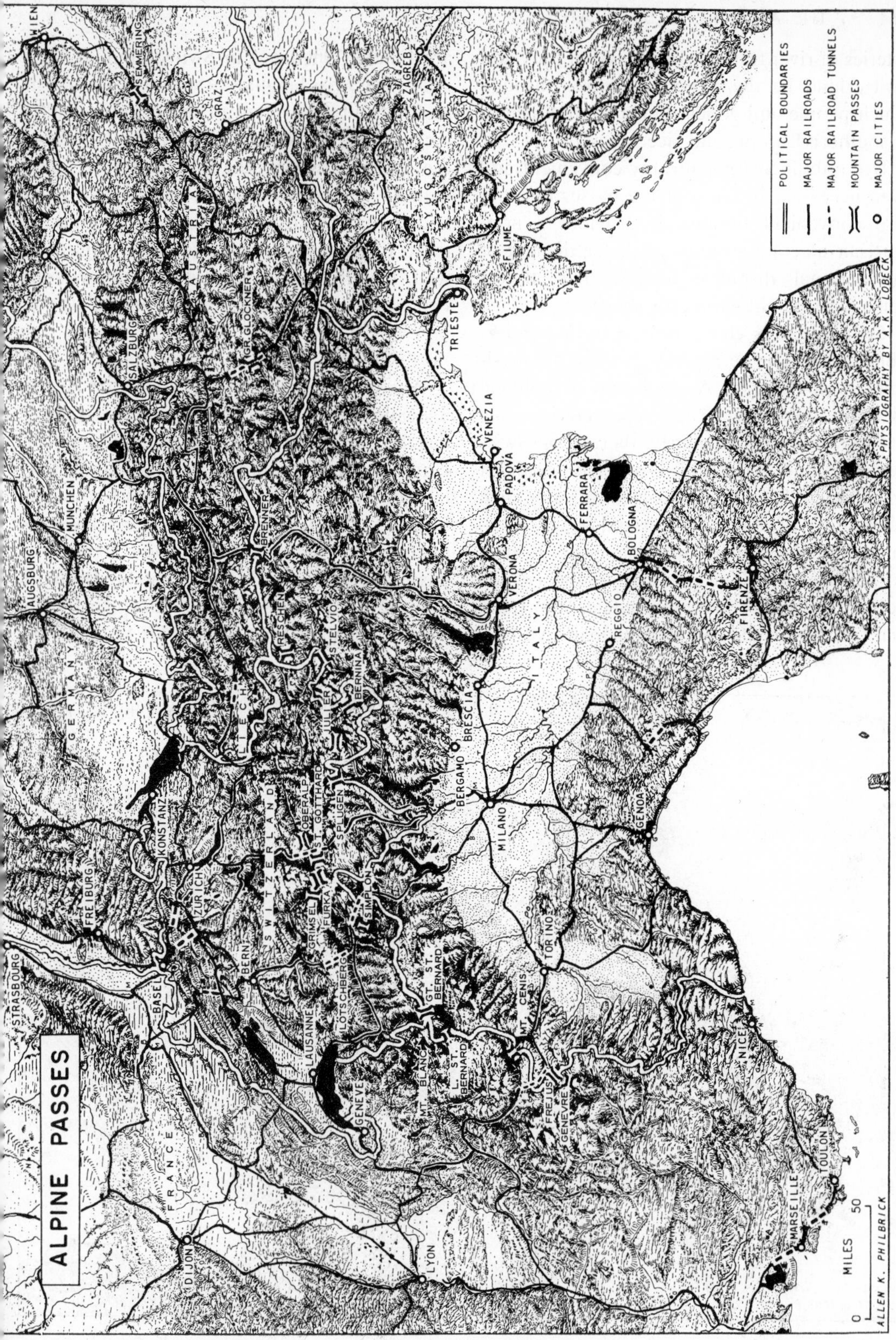

ALPINE PASSES

POLITICAL BOUNDARIES
MAJOR RAILROADS
MAJOR RAILROAD TUNNELS
MOUNTAIN PASSES
MAJOR CITIES

PHYSIOGRAPHY BY A. K. LOBECK

ALLEN K. PHILBRICK

MILES
0   50

Figure 16.2.

arteries of river traffic, while between Italy and Switzerland lie the mountain passes through which people and goods funnel from northern to southern Europe, and vice versa.

Not only is Swiss neutrality convenient and even necessary because of the passes but it is also convenient because it provides a non-partisan meeting ground for the settlement of international disputes. Geneva has almost come to represent *efforts for peace.*

Switzerland is characterized by a remarkable unity. The territorial domain is, physically, well cohered. A singleness of political ideology and policy also characterizes the country, and yet, peculiarly, there is no Swiss language and no national religion—both of which might have been expected to foster such community of ideas. Switzerland speaks German, Italian, French, and Romansh—French is the majority language close to the French border, Italian in those areas adjacent to Italy, and German in the southern plateau. All four

are official languages in Switzerland. If there is a single Swiss language it would be Romansh, and yet but 1 per cent of the people speak it whereas 71 per cent speak German (found on the plateau where the population is most densely agglomerated), 22 per cent French, and 6 per cent Italian. Many Swiss speak all three of the latter languages and English as well. In religion, 56 per cent of the Swiss are Protestant and 42 per cent Roman Catholic.

Austria

Austria too occupies a location that is strategically significant in that, within its territory, lies the Alpine Brenner Pass that leads, via the Isarco River, from northern Europe to the lowland of the Italian Po. Lying farther to the east, however, this Austrian gap does not have the commercial significance of the three Swiss passes (St. Gotthard, the Great St. Bernard, and the Simplon) which also drop to the Po Valley. (The Little St. Bernard is farther west,

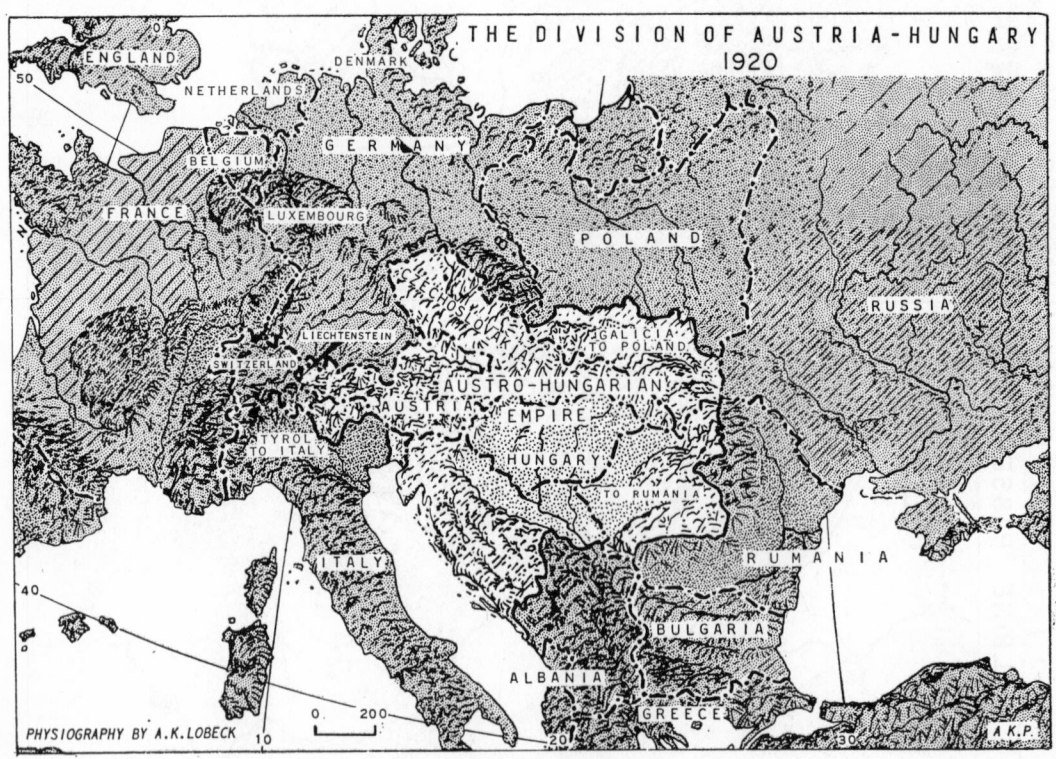

Figure 16.3.

also leading to the Italian lowland and lying between France and Italy.)

One or two other aspects of Austrian location ought to be pointed out—aspects of location that have developed as a result of the post-World War II situation. Occupied Austria was the tie for the West between the Western military forces in Germany, Italy, Yugoslavia and Austria; the unified, neutral Austria severs this physical link. Further, Austria (a Germanic state) is a helpless little country poised dangerously along the Communist fringe—unless guarantees of neutrality are sincere.

Post-empire Austria (as reconstituted by the Vienna Treaty) has had a political existence of only 37 years, and during those less than four decades the country was occupied by the Nazi Germans for seven years and by the four post-World War II occupying-powers for ten. Thus, for only 20 years has modern Austria been politically responsible for itself.

Although occupying the same space, the present independent Austria is far better off than the post-World War I Austria; that state for many years subsisted at near-starvation level. Developments in Austrian oil resources by the Nazis and Russians, and American Marshall Plan aid have done much to modernize and equip the mountain state despite Soviet dismantling in the Eastern zone of occupation. Today Austria is a relatively viable state. There seems no reason that, given time (and neutrality should do this), Austria cannot develop a strong economic structure. Particularly will this be true if a normal flow of trade opens up between Austria and the adjacent Communist states, for Austrian trade channels, most naturally, via the Danube River—*i.e.* within the territory that comprised the former empire. Vienna is the logical focus—economically, financially, and culturally—for the whole of the Danube Basin. An Austria separated from these natural trade outlets is likely to be unable to exist without subsidy.

THE MEDITERRANEAN—
AFRICAN WORLD

17

The Mediterranean

GEOPOLITICAL CONSIDERATIONS

Times, diplomacy, and tactics may vary but the place of the Mediterranean in European history, strategy, and control endures. The civilization of the West began its development along the littoral of this 2200-mile waterway known as the Mediterranean—"the Middle Sea"; and mastery of the *medi-terranean* area was an important phase of the history of the Phoenicians, Greeks, Persians, Carthaginians, Romans, and other peoples, who, in one era or another, held extended authority over the waters of this inland sea and the nations along its shores.

Down through the centuries the means of wielding this ascendency was the ship. The oar-driven galley, the sailing vessel, and the steamer followed each other successively; today the warship, the air base, and the airplane carrier are the significant factors in maintaining control over the seas of the Mediterranean and its connective waterways.

In the modern era it has been the vital concern of Great Britain to control the Mediter-

ranean. During the constant modulations in British policy attendant on the effort of preserving a favorable balance of power, British seapower in the Mediterranean has been a great asset. When the Suez Canal opened a waterway through the "Middle Sea," thereby shortening the route to the East and Australia–New Zealand, the Mediterranean–Red Sea passageway became the lifeline of the Empire, and thereafter, about one-half of Britain's naval strength was utilized for the protection of the inland water route.

The United States has intermittently been in and out of the Mediterranean for a century and a half. The first action was taken against the Barbary pirates who were preying on merchant ships; the navy of the young state brought the Moslem corsairs to terms. From that time forward until the Spanish–American War, the United States kept some ships more or less constantly in the Mediterranean, using, by arrangement with Spain, a base in the Balearic Islands for many years. Following the First World War, the United States again maintained a small force in the Mediterranean until the

366

growing isolationist sentiment forced the American vessels to return home.

Until the outbreak of World War II, however, the United States had no particular interest in the Mediterranean aside from maintaining the status quo which, largely, was merely backing British policies. Since the end of World War II, however, the United States has been in the Mediterranean in force, maintaining a Mediterranean fleet to supplement that of the British, and, besides, stationing air force contingents on bases, at the strategic locations, leased from states bordering the sea. Not only is the American state committed to assuming many of the duties which the British can no longer keep up but the United States, as leader of the Western Bloc, has definite policies which make control of the Mediterranean a requirement. These bear upon Soviet ambitions to expand their sphere of influence in Europe and the Middle East and to obtain access to the ocean trade routes unhampered by frozen seas or by a politically controlled Dardanelles (*i.e.* politically controlled by a state other than the Soviet Union).

The Mediterranean area was regarded by the Ancients as the center of the world; today, it is one of the few geopolitical "key" areas. Plagued by such provocative problems as intense and violent nationalism, open border clashes, national rivalries, political change and innovation, and economic difficulties, much of the region is obviously at a turning point. It must either go forward into a newer, more liberal and concordant way or risk submersion in anarchy, warfare—and, possibly, as an aftermath, Communism.

Among the lands facing the Mediterranean that can be considered as within the Western sphere are Iberia, Italy, Greece, and Turkey; the remainder, aside from Albania, are neutral —except French Algeria, a dependency that, because of its political affiliation with France, should be Western. It is, in sentiment, allied with the neutral group, however, and, because of strong feelings of nationalism and anti-Westernism it is not as dependable to the West as might be desired.

HISTORICAL SUMMARY

The Mediterranean is unique as an element of man's physical environment and as a center of human advancement. Though geologically young, the Mediterranean is old historically. In this basin was an ancient cradle of civilization and a nursery of human progress; the first cultures of the Old World grew up in the Nile and Asian river valleys. These civilizations could not fail to influence the more backward peoples that lived to the west, and the contacts, through trade and migration, were along two main thoroughfares: the land bridge of Asia Minor and the Mediterranean Sea.

Invited by the favorable environment, there arose in the basin a succession of maritime commercial states—Crete, Phoenicia, Greece, Carthage, and Rome. Continuous intercourse back and forth across the water bound the peoples of the basin together economically and led likewise to an interchange of ideas. The result was that, aided by the similarity of landscape and climatic environment, Mediterranean culture took on an essentially uniform character and something of a *Mediterranean civilization* arose. Particularly did the pattern of land use develop along nearly identical lines.

In time sequence the first mature civilization rose at the eastern end of the Mediterranean, in Crete, Phoenicia, and Greece. It progressed from there to Italy. Rome, in its prime, reached out to conquer North Africa and the barbarians of northern Europe. During the Middle Ages, Italian Genoa and Venice were the great rival ports of trade. Milan, situated at the foot of St. Gotthard Pass, was a city of wealth and power, while the trading and financial center of Florence, under the Medici, became the leader in the Renaissance movement that carried Europe from Medievalism into the modern period. It was in the basin of the Mediterranean, and particularly in the cities of Venice and Florence in Italy, that the Renaissance had its first and greatest expression. This movement was not only cultural, as is so often regarded, but economic in character as well.

For nearly 2000 years the Mediterranean

was dominant. During all that time European civilization faced south. The end of this brilliant period of Mediterranean supremacy came as the control of the spice trade slipped from the hands of the Turks at the beginning of the sixteenth century. Hitherto the products of the East had flowed by caravan through Egypt or by way of Baghdad and Aleppo (the route of the Fertile Crescent) to the Levantine ports. Here they were met by the galleys of the Italian cities and transported westward. By the early sixteenth century, however, practically no spices were arriving at the ports of the eastern Mediterranean. All of them were being carried in Portuguese vessels by way of the ocean route around Africa and thence to Lisbon, to be picked up there and distributed by the ships of the Hanseatic League. Dominance, thereafter, moved westward to the two countries of the Iberian Peninsula, Mediterranean lands that faced also upon the Atlantic. The Portuguese and Spanish together opened up the highways of ocean transport and, following discovery and exploration, they took possession of new lands far and wide. At one period in history the newly discovered and still unknown lands of the entire globe were divided equally between Spain and Portugal. A line drawn by the Pope designated the territories of each. Portugal was the first Atlantic seapower.

In time Iberia, too, declined. Portugal, with the dying out of the royal line, came under Philip II of Spain and Spanish interests were pushed to the elimination of those of the Portuguese. Though it had its illustrious days, Spanish colonial history is notable not only for the dimensions of its reach but also for its swift ebb after attaining a glorious climax. Spain went into eclipse, through bankruptcy, at the defeat of the Armada by England.

Progress moved north, and, for a time the by-passed Mediterranean became a backwater in the affairs of the world. Though in the first half of the nineteenth century a revival of Mediterranean commerce manifested itself, it was only with the opening of the Suez Canal that the sea returned to a place of great prominence as a route of trade. The states that bordered the sea, however, remained in relative obscurity. Only within less than a half-century have there been indications of their recovery.

THE MEDITERRANEAN ENVIRONMENT

The physical scene of Mediterranean lands has an identifiable character. Physiographically, the Mediterranean environment is a region of alternating, fragmented littoral plains and projecting headlands, backed by lofty mountain ranges toward the continent and fronted by the waters of the inland sea. Large Mediterranean coastal plains are a rarity. Only the Po Valley in Italy, the Ebro in Spain, the coastal regions of southern France and European Turkey have level areas of any extent. Greece, dissected by mountains and fringed with multitudes of islands, is a jumble of ranges and valleys and promontories thrust into the sea so that the coast is an alternation of forbidding cliffs and deep indentations. Off shore, the islands are the tops of submerged ranges that are a continuation of the mountains of the mainland. The end of the Turkish peninsula is also fragmented and rugged, but fingering up toward the plateau are fertile valleys that widen toward the sea.

Mediterranean lands are typified by a particular climate. All around the Mediterranean Basin the climate has the same characteristics —except in Egypt and Libya, which are located beyond the reaches of the Mediterranean effects and are tropical deserts. The climate has two seasons, a cool winter with rain and a hot, dry summer. Rarely does the temperature drop to freezing, for mountain barriers on the northern and eastern sides shut out the cold winds from continental interiors. Even during the winter, the proportion of sunny days is high. Summer is a period of drought broken by occasional thunder showers, of brilliant sunshine, hot south winds, and, in selected places, of dust storms out of the Sahara that may even blow across the sea. This dry season parches the lands so that the grass and other vegetation is brown and scorched, fields are bare and often plowed in readiness for the planting of wheat and barley with the oncoming of the wet season, or lie fallow. Precipitation, averaging between 15 and 35 inches, varies considerably from place to place and from year to year, but is dependable for the growing of winter crops. Only by careful use and conservation, however, are the people of the Mediterranean able to maintain a water supply that satisfies even the minimum requirements.

In Mediterranean lands, man has better exploited the possibilities offered him by nature than in most regions. The two factors of topography and climate have, in turn, acted to shape Mediterranean life throughout the ages. Three types of agriculture are carried on side by side: the growing of winter grains using natural precipitation; terracing and the raising of tree crops whose roots reach down to subsoil water and live through the drought period; and irrigation agriculture.

In few regions of the world has topography and soil, climate and even the sea itself had a more direct bearing on human development. In turn, it can be said also that there are few areas where man has worked so closely with nature to make a garden of wasteland. The development of the techniques of Mediterranean agriculture took centuries. Through trial and error and the interchange of ideas, there slowly unfolded the now familiar form of horticultural cultivation that characterizes Mediterranean lands today.

Because the environment is meagre for the large population that is found everywhere in the Mediterranean Basin, and, also, because the sea invites, fishing and commerce have become important occupations.

This, then, is the environment that characterizes all of the states described as Mediterranean. They surround the inland sea and include all nations bordering its shores (*except Libya and Egypt*—deserts—and African).

THE IBERIAN PENINSULA: SPAIN AND PORTUGAL

No explanation of the political partition of the Iberian Peninsula into Spain and Portugal is to be found in the ethnographic composition of the two countries. The peoples are closely similar for all Iberians are of very old Mediterranean stock, and though this unity has been modified by the invasion and colonization by the Viking, Moor, Jew, and other aliens, the basic character of the people has little changed.

Lying between Europe and Africa, the peninsula was long the battleground of Islam and Christianity. The turmoil subsided earlier in Portugal than in Spain, and, welded together by six and a half centuries of struggle against the foreign Moorish civilization inflicted upon them by the Moslem invaders from North Africa, the people of the compact little land were early bound into social and political unity. Two hundred years before neighboring Spain was liberated and unified, the African Moors had been ejected from Portugal and the area emerged as a national state.

While the Portuguese were slowly tracing the outline of coastal Africa in their ships, the Spanish were duplicating the experiences of their western neighbor in expelling the foreigners and creating a nation. Eventually Spain was reconquered by the Christians, who began in the north and moved southward. In 1492 they expelled the Jews whom, for economic and religious reasons, they would not tolerate in the country; 17 years later, in 1509, they had driven out the Moors.

The Arabs had occupied Spain for 800 years and, during this long period, they greatly influenced the economy of the country for they brought with them to Iberia techniques of agriculture far superior to those practiced in Europe at the time, and several new crops—the orange, the fig, and many vegetables. They also introduced irrigation agriculture to Spain.

The early division of Iberia into two sovereign and distinct nations can be explained only in historical terms. However, once the dual nationality had been created, geographic factors tended to perpetuate the political division. That geography should influence the promotion and maintenance of national separatism is the more logical when one considers that within Spain itself "patriotism is a local thing—reflecting the geographical division of the country; a man says he is a Galician, an Asturian, a Castilian, and Andalusian; he rarely thinks of himself as a Spaniard."[1] Dialects and even languages differ from one locality to another for Spaniard is separated from Spaniard by physical barriers, by custom, by classes of society. Only the forced collective action, against the Moorish invaders, of the half dozen little realms (of which Castile and Aragon were the most important) brought about coalescence into a nation—a unity that has precariously endured to the present. Portuguese separateness and eventual independence arose in part as a result of its physical seclusion on the coastal edge of the tableland. The two states are separated by the rough mountain country that features the plateau margin on the west.

The geology and physiography of Iberia have much influenced the orientation of Spain and Portugal. The boundary between Spain and Portugal lies along a zone where "it becomes easier to go downhill to the west coast rather than uphill and across the plateau to the Spanish centers."[2] Portugal slopes to the sea— and hence faces the Atlantic. The coastal location is enhanced by the navigability of the lower reaches of the Douro and Tagus rivers. Thus the Portuguese are naturally sea-minded. This is borne out in the facts that, historically, the Portuguese were among the first great navigators of Europe, and, at present, the important place fishing holds in the economy of the country.

Spain, largely plateau, is oriented landward. Though it had a brilliant career as an exploring and colonizing nation, this was but an episode, relatively short-lived, because the potential of Spain as a seapower is weak. With few exceptions the coasts offer meagre opportunity for modern harbor developments, and the Castilians (plateau dwellers) show little aptitude for the water. Recently, however, there has been a revival of interest in trade. At present, the Spanish merchant marine amounts to little over one per cent of the world's total.

The Iberian Peninsula lies between the Mediterranean Sea and the Atlantic Ocean, and, cut off from the rest of Europe by the lofty Pyrenees and from Africa by Gibraltar, it lies between these two continents and acts as a land-bridge between them. From the Atlantic, the peninsula dominates an important means of access to Europe and Africa and commands the entry into the Mediterranean through the Straits of Gibraltar. Mountains make Iberia a natural fortress. The peninsula's only land boundary with Europe lies along the crests of the Pyrenees Mountains which extend from one coast to the other. Elevations rise above 11,000 feet; passes are few and narrow and, hence, the mountains are an effective barrier —one of the most absolute on the globe.

Iberia owes its strategic value to geography. For many decades Great Britain has had a major interest in this critically located peninsula, and, since World War II the United States has become as greatly concerned. By agreements concluded with the two Iberian states—with Portugal in 1951, and with Spain in 1953—the United States secured the use of naval and air bases. One of these, the Rota Naval Port and Air Station on Spain's southern coast, lies only 68 miles distant from British-held Gibraltar. Strategically, this base is ideally situated for it dominates the approaches to Gibraltar and the Mediterranean. In addition to this highly valuable base are a number of other facilities for air fields.

Giving support and defense-in-depth to the American-leased bases in Spain are four in Portugal—two on the mainland, two offshore in the mid-Atlantic: 1000 miles west of Lisbon lie the Portuguese Azores. Since the commencement of the air age, they have become very significant to the West for they are situated on the North Atlantic air route between Iberia and the United States.

Politically, the islands are not a colony but a province within the governmental structure of the mainland state. With the signing of the treaty between the United States and Portugal, the Azores became a global crossroads; every commercial American plane that flies from

---

1 Bowman, *The New World, op.cit.*, p. 215.
2 Samuel Van Valkenburg, *Europe*, 2nd edition (New York: John Wiley & Sons, Inc., 1952), p. 437.

Lisbon or North Africa to the United States stops at these tiny islets. In strategic importance, they rival Hawaii; they are an aerial gateway to Europe and Africa. For nearly five centuries these islands have been a "way station" in the Atlantic, and during World War II, the United States Air Transport Command was based there; in case of another conflict, they undoubtedly would take on even greater significance than they have had in the past.

The alliances with the Iberian states mean much more than defensive depth for Europe. One of the criticisms raised against the United States by other Western nations for the Iberian build-up has been that it looked like a "retreat to the Pyrenees." But for the United States it means the setting up of rearguard defenses to keep the Strait of Gibraltar open and the American Sixth Fleet "operational" in the eastern Mediterranean. The defense line on the Pyrenees is little more than geographical. There is nothing on the Spanish side of the mountains to compare with the paved roads and railways of France. But, because of the effectiveness of the highland barrier (and given modern weapons and craft), it is believed that a relatively small force could defend the mountain line, and, at the same time, have immense striking power outside of Iberia.

Portugal

Portugal is the governing center of the world's fourth largest colonial empire. Smaller in size than Indiana (35,414 square miles) and lying inconspicuous and isolated along the western margin of the Iberian Peninsula, Portugal holds dependencies that are scattered nearly half way around the globe. Despite the loss of great portions of its holdings to more recent empire builders and to the nationalist sentiment that led to the independence of Brazil in 1822, Portugal still retains a significant part of the territories that Pope Alexander VI, in 1494, awarded to it when he portioned the unclaimed lands of the world between the two Iberian states.

Portugal, therefore, is not small. Parts of the empire are made up of tiny islets lying off the shores of four continents. For four centuries they have been important as supply and shelter stations for ships—more recently valuable as air bases. Parts of the empire consist of pinpoints of land hanging along the edge of states that are acutely sensitive to such intrusive dots of foreign political control—as India and China. The largest portions are found in the two great African colonies of Mozambique and Angola, to be valued in terms of undeveloped but important resources.

The islands include the Azores and the Cape Verde Islands in the Atlantic, and eastern Timor, a part of the East Indies and lying just north of Australia. The importance of the Azores to the Western nations has already been mentioned. Timor was occupied by Japan during World War II, but is now back in Portuguese hands.

Macao, Goa, Diu, and Damão, and Mormugão are remnants of the day when tiny specks of land were occupied here and there along the trade routes of the world, by the seafaring nations, to act as waystations and trading centers for the merchant ships. Macao, almost clutching for a hold on the south coast of China, is valuable to both the Chinese and the West for it acts as a center of smuggling and information between the Communists and the outside as well as a listening post. Goa, Diu, Damão, and Mormugão huddle precariously between India and the sea. Portugal has held these specks of land for four centuries and they are an integral part o the empire. Mormugão has one of the finest harbors along the Indian peninsula, and the 700,000 inhabitants of the Portuguese colonies are said to be somewhat better off economically than their Indian neighbors. In recent months the national status of one of these tiny colonies, Goa, became a critical issue between India and Portugal. India, newly independent and sensitive to anything that resembles colonialism, smarts under the Portuguese hold on these four bits of the Indian subcontinent. The majority of the population of the colonies are Roman Catholic and Portuguese citizens, desirous of remaining politically attached to Portugal; India, however, feels that Goa is rightfully a part of the Indian domain. Emotional feeling in the matter has run high on both sides, and violence has occurred.

In terms of size and economic value, the two large holdings on the African continent— Mozambique and Angola—are the most significant. Located on the east and west side of Africa, they hold British Rhodesia and the rich mining areas of the upper Congo (Belgian Congo) between them like a nut between the two halves of a shell, for the harbors of the Portuguese territories serve as the outlets for the valuable ores of these two highly important mineral areas. Agricultural and animal products go out from the British veldt also.

Portugal, the nucleus of this farflung empire, is a little country of only 8.5 million people. They are a homogeneous people, and, as compared with Spain, relatively prosperous, although 65 per cent are illiterate. Basically, Portugal is agricultural for over three-fifths of the population makes their living by cultivating the land; fishing is also important. Industries are largely limited to the making of wine, the processing of olive oil and cork, and fish-canning.

Political difficulties kept the country unstable for about a generation. In 1910 an armed revolt upset the monarchy, and, for a period of 16 years, a succession of uprisings against any would-be rulers kept the country in a state of chaos until General Carmona established order in 1926. Although Portugal has an elected president, the government is run by a dictator, Salazar.

Under Salazar the state is stable politically as well as economically, but there are a number of problems that face the small nation. First, although dominantly agricultural, Portugal is not self-sufficient in food; the shortage, however, can be made up through exchange because Portugal has some important exports—wine, sardines, and cork leading. Secondly, although Portugal has deposits of coal, iron, kaolin, tungsten, lead, and manganese (most of them in relatively small reserves), modern industry is non-existent.

Thirdly, of all of the colonial powers of the world, this state has done less to develop and exploit the potential of its dependencies than any other. Only the holdings of Britain, France, and Belgium are greater; the area of the overseas possessions of Portugal are 23 times greater than that of the mother country. The empire could, therefore, do much to increase the prosperity of the state; it remains, however, almost untouched. The population of the colonies exceeds that of Portugal, approximating 20 million as compared with the 8.5 million of the European nation.

Many people other than the Portuguese speak the Portuguese tongue; it is the official language not only throughout the colonial territories but also in Brazil, a former colony, where 70 million people show this former tie with the little Iberian state.

Spain

The colonies of Spain are only one-sixth the size of those of Portugal. What remains of the former world empire is found scattered from northwest Africa to Spanish Guinea (Rio Muni on the coast, Fernando Po, and four other small islands). Rio de Oro, the largest of these possessions, lies south of Morocco in the Sahara Desert. The total population of the holdings is but 1.5 million and, since three-fourths of the colonial territories lie within the desert of Africa, they are not, relatively, of much value. It is difficult to realize that Spain, whose discovery of the New World opened up a whole unknown hemisphere to Europeans, whose empire surpassed the proportions of any the world has ever seen, whose civilization at one time was worldwide—the remnants of which are found in all of the many and widely scattered Spanish-speaking lands of the present day—is now one of the most retarded and isolated of nations. Although Spain is much larger, much more richly endowed, and more varied than the little state to the west, it is nevertheless one of the poorest countries in Europe.

Spain scarcely seems a part of Europe. So divisive are the barrier-Pyrenees that the peninsula is largely cut off from influences of the continent. Three rail lines cross the Spanish–French frontier, but the value of these connections is lessened by the fact that, due to differences in rail gauge, transshipment of goods and people must take place at the frontier. There is isolation also within Spain. The interior Meseta, which covers about one-half of the Spanish domain, is isolated from the valley and coastal regions by mountains that make access to the plateau difficult, and the plateau itself is cut up by mountain ranges that separate one portion from another.

Because of the plateau location, the ameliorating effects of the surrounding waters upon the climate are largely absent and Spain has a continental climate—characterized by extremes of temperature and a small and uncertain rainfall—throughout all of its territory except along the Basque coast in the north and the Mediterranean lowland littorals. The Meseta (interior plateau), over most of which the precipitation averages between 12 and 16 inches a year, is suitable only to dry farming or grazing. Here wheat and cattle are the major products of agriculture; barley and rye take the more marginal areas and, in the better watered regions of the north, apples, green pastures, and trees become important. In the Mediterranean regions, the olive tree, and, where irrigation is used, rice, grapes, citrus, figs, almonds, and a variety of vegetables are grown. However, like Portugal, Spain is not self-sufficient in food.

Iberian mineral resources are concentrated in Spain. From the days of the Phoenicians, Carthaginians, and Romans, the Spanish deposits have been known. The famous Rio Tinto reserves of the southwest have been mined for their copper since 1240 B.C. Mines of lead and silver exist, and Spanish deposits of coal are estimated to be almost equal to those of the Saar although production is only one-third that of the latter territory. In the north, between Santander and Bilbao, is one of Europe's important iron reserves, rivaling those of Germany. The small production of about three million tons annually is exported chiefly to

Great Britain and Germany; it is also the basis for a small Spanish industry in iron and steel. Mercury is secured from the Almaden mines in south central Spain and smaller deposits occur in several other regions; Spain supplies nearly half of the mercury requirements of the world. Potash deposits, constituting Spain's leading chemical resource, are the second largest in the world, ranking next to those of Germany; they are four times as great as those of the United States. Zinc, lead, and wolfram are also present in sizeable quantities adding to the variety of the mineral resources.

For the size and variety of the ore deposits, Spanish industrial development is small. The industry that has developed is largely in the north near or on coal or water power, the latter developed in the Cantabrian Mountains. Textile manufactures lead, with food-processing, paper, leather, and tobacco factories ranking next. The refinement of petroleum has begun and is to reach a capacity of three million tons of crude petroleum annually.

Raw materials and labor are not lacking for industry; rather, fuel and transportation seem to be the limiting factors. Compared with the potential offered in the raw materials of the state—mineral, vegetable, and animal—industry is still in its infancy. Coal production does not supply the needs; hydroelectricity, normally insufficient, becomes a critical deficiency in years of abnormal precipitation. The output of electric current may vary as much as 50 per cent from one year to the next. In 1953, many plants in Madrid and Valencia had to shut down for three days a week during the late summer and fall due to lack of electric power. Transportation facilities limit industry as much as do fuels. They focus on Madrid like the spokes of a wheel to the hub, but the roads and railroads are both insufficient in number and in poor repair, making them inefficient and even dangerous.

These several obstructing elements hamper industry and increase the costs, which, in turn, present obstacles to export trade. The principal exports are olive oil, wines, oranges, ores, and nuts; Britain and the United States are the chief markets for these products.

Despite the diversity and richness of its agricultural and industrial base, Spain's economy is chronically frail, and, politically, the state is weak. The structure and internal policies of the government are in part to blame. Until there is a more liberal policy adopted in the economy such that private investment—both domestic and foreign—is encouraged *and,* until there is a liberalization in religious matters, Spain cannot rise out of the economic and social depression into which it has settled. Roman Catholicism is the state religion, and the restrictions against Protestants, who number only about 20,000 out of 28 million, are oppressive in the extreme.

Spain has political stability, but it is a stability imposed by prohibition and authority; the governmental and economic structures seem rigid and unable to change to meet new conditions and demands. Although American money has been put into the country to help pay for raw materials and equipment for industries and for the partial renovation of the railroads, it is unlikely that the alliance can or will have any effect in bringing about the political, economic, and social reforms that are so urgently needed.

ITALY

Geography did not intend that Italy should be a great power. Although disputes have arisen along the land frontiers to the north, the boundaries are naturally marked and quite concise. Expansion in almost any direction would mean leaping beyond a substantial physical barrier to territory disjointed from the Italian domain—or, at least, separated by obstructions. In other words, areally Italy is about as restricted by its boundaries as are such island nations as Japan and Britain. Secondly, the natural endowment is not particularly rich; Italy lacks the major fuel and mineral resources for a modern industry. Any industry that has developed has done so at great effort and is largely based on imported raw materials—that is, aside from light industries as winemaking, glass, etc. Even agriculture is handicapped. Although most of the country has a Mediterranean climate with moist winters and hot, dry summers, except for the winter-grown cereals and such deep-rooted crops as grapes and the olive tree, cultivation over the greater part of the land requires irrigation—and in the southern half it is essential. Most of the hills of peninsular Italy lie bare and brown in the sun, supporting no vegetation. Undoubtedly a part of this barren aspect is the result of the indiscriminate cutting of vegetation, over-grazing, and the like, for centuries. But it has raised the problem of erosion, intensified by the fallowing that is practiced in the growing of winter grains.

Land hunger and poverty, concomitants of over-population, are the foremost problems facing Italy. The condition of the peasant farmer has been an ancient and recurring problem for this Mediterranean state. Until just after World War I, the pressure generated by too many people on too little land was partially relieved through emigration. The total number of persons departing for other countries is still large, but, proportionally, it is not great enough; emigrants equal but one-fourth the annual population increase.

Italy, 120,000 square miles in area, is about the same size as the British Isles. On this constricted space live 47 million people. Of these, one-half derive their living from the land—a land that is but 21 per cent plains, 79 per cent being either mountainous or hilly. For centuries the farmers have been making things grow in the valleys and on the mountainsides, utilizing every little bit of available space. So intense is the cultivation in Italy that the word "manicured" perhaps describes it most accurately.

The time comes, however, when even the most intensely worked soil is incapable of supporting more people—under existing methods. This is the case in Italy where the population is rising rapidly. For the past 50 years, however, this increment has been largely associated with the development of industry—in Milan and Turin in the north and Rome and Naples along the peninsula; in the central and southern portions of the country the increase is less marked. But, in the urban manufacturing areas as in the rural districts, the essential need is to create more work for industrial development has not been sufficient to take care of the steadily mounting population numbers.

The political, economic, and social problems are, at present, greatest in the south—coincident, roughly, with the area that extends from Naples and Foggia down through Sicily. It is as if this region, which for centuries has been backward, neglected, and downtrodden, is now being roused to demand a better life. A 12-year plan, started in 1950, was initiated by the Government to redistribute the land and reduce the number of landless peasants. Southern Italy has the highest population density in Europe.

Italy, being geologically young, is naturally poor in mineral resources. Although there are small deposits and a limited production of zinc, lead, iron, and coal, only mercury, waterpower, sulphur, and marble are found in appreciable quantities. Lacking coal (except for some small deposits on Sardinia), Italy must import this fuel or substitute others. It is well supplied with waterpower potential, but this is almost entirely confined to the north where the mountain streams from the Alps supply the power. An interesting development and one with great promise is that of the generation of the thermoelectricity produced by tapping the live steam from volcanoes. It is looked upon as a cheap and probably permanent source of energy. Explorations for petroleum are being carried on, mostly in the Po Valley along the foothills of the Apennines. Although this oil was known as early as 1860,[3] production of crude petroleum supplies only one per cent of the national needs. Shale containing oil exists both in the north and in Sicily. Due to American competition, Italy (Sicily), which formerly held a near monopoly in native sulphur, today supplies but four per cent of

this chemical. It still ranks as a major world producer of mercury, however.

Possessing only thermal and hydroelectric power as assets and lacking the mineral and vegetable resources that are requisite for a major development in manufacture, Italy has nevertheless established an important industry. Italian heavy industry equals that of the Saar. The metallurgical industries produce such items as automobiles (Fiat), motor boats, roller bearings, sewing and calculating machines, and typewriters. Textiles, produced from the natural fibres of silk, cotton, and wool, as well as the synthetics, rayon, and staple fibre, are important, and chemicals, of which sulphuric acid leads, are produced.

In 1951 the volume of industrial output was 36 per cent higher than in 1938, providing an outlet for the absorption of a portion of the excess population. The great number of Italian manufacturing concerns are small, however, and handicrafts are a vital part of the industrial economy of the country. Among these glassmaking ranks high. Although the number of small establishments far exceeds that of the large manufacturing plants, huge state owned and private monopolistic corporations dominate every major field of production. This concentration of industrial power has meant also a concentration of wealth in the hands of the few, and little of the benefit of industry has sifted down to the masses.

Industry focuses in the North. The heavy metallurgical industries and silk textiles, concentrated in Turin and Milan in the Po Basin, are unequalled in any other part of Italy. Although Rome, which was the nuclear center of the state, remains the political, religious, and cultural center of Italy, the Po Valley is the ecumene. Here the most important agriculture and industry, the densest population, and the heaviest transportation net are found. It is—and is likely to remain—the geographical core of the state. Within this focus of economic life, Milan is the industrial and commercial giant; it is unrivaled, in the production of goods for peace or war, by any other Italian city.

The Po Valley is sharply separated from

---

[3] Wallace E. Pratt and Dorothy Good, *World Geography of Petroleum* (New York: The American Geographical Society, 1950), p. 265.

the rest of the country by the mountain arc that makes up the northern third of the Apennines. In no European state are the contrasts more distinct between regions than are those found in the Po—with its more stimulating semi-continental climate, and broad, well-watered valley lowland, and agricultural and industrial production—and the peninsular Mediterranean lands of southern Italy, relatively dry and largely upland.

A concomitant to the dissimilarity of physical and economic orientation has been the development of a diversity of interests and outlook between the people of the north and south —even the cohering and fusing effects of a common language and religion have been unable to obliterate these regional differences. However, this divergence is not in any way divisive politically—at least in itself. In fact, the dual orientation has strengthening qualities because each compensates for the weaknesses of the other. The Italians are a "nation," loyal to the national ideal.

The Italian Empire

The colonial empire of Italy—vast, nearly a million square miles in area—was largely desert, and hence, wasteland. It was comprised of territory in northeast Africa and included Libya, Eritrea, and Italian Somaliland. Although Libya was considered more valuable than the other two colonies, it lies within the confines of the Sahara; only a narrow fringe along the Mediterranean is anything better than pure desert. These territories were residua that other colonial powers had not bothered to claim up to the time that Italy, at a late date, decided to take part in the scramble for an empire. They held prestige value for Italy, and, also, were strategic in location in that all lay along the Mediterranean–Red Sea–Gulf of Aden waterway. The strategic aspect was less apparent at the time of acquisition than it became later on—and, at all periods of Italian holding, was somewhat nullified by British control of strategic Mediterranean focal areas. Despite the marginality of the colonies, Italians emigrated to these lands, and, during the

period of Italian ownership, the dependent lands were rather remarkably developed considering their potential.

With Italy's defeat in World War II, the colonies were taken from that state. After a brief period of British administration under the United Nations, Libya was given independence, on December 24, 1951. Following a simulated plebiscite—verbally carried out because of the illiteracy of the inhabitants— Eritrea was incorporated into Ethiopia; Somaliland was made a trust territory, under Italy, for a 10-year period after which political independence is to be granted to the Somali peoples. The Italian domain, therefore, is confined to the peninsula and the two large islands of Sicily and Sardinia—for to Albania went the island of Saseno, small but strategic, in the narrows that control the entrance to the Adriatic Sea; to the Greeks the Dodecanese Islands[4] in the Aegean; and, to China, Italy's former concession in Tientsin. The final disposition of the Trieste Territory has already been discussed.

The design of empire laid out by Mussolini was, in part, to open up lands into which Italians might move; Abyssinia offered the greatest potential for colonization. Italian rule here, however, was short lived. With colonial holdings wiped out and immigration barriers more stringent than before in many areas, Italy must rely more on an intensification of the development of its own resources—and on a revised social program—to adjust its people to the domain.

Geopolitical Considerations

The movement of Italians over frontiers into adjacent countries has created some notable minorities of Italians in these states. France has perhaps the largest minority group of Italians of any of the Old World countries. Fortunately, no frontier difficulties have developed

---

[4] There was no justification for the annexation of the Dodecanese Islands by Italy in the first place, however. They were first occupied by the Italians following the cessation of the Italo–Turkish conflict of 1912, and, at that time, Italy had promised to evacuate them within a short period.

that have not been settled by the two states. There have, however, been exchanges of territory across the Italo–French frontier, and, recently, some border differences have occurred.

In 1915, prior to the entrance of Italy into the war against Austria–Hungary, the latter nation offered Italy a part of the Southern Tyrol (where Italians made up a significant majority of the population). By entering the war upon the side of the Allies, however, Italy obtained, under the treaty of St. Germain, the whole of the drainage basin of the Adige River, and the Italian boundary was aligned close to the crest of the Central Alps cutting across the Brenner Pass. By this treaty the vitally strategic mountain passage, between the Upper Danube and Lombardy, is shared by both states. This cession of territory brought within Italian borders large minorities of Austrian Germans, however. They strongly resisted the transfer and have, at times, caused trouble in the area by their agitation for reincorporation with Austria. Farther eastward the frontier was placed so that the rocky peninsula of Istria, with the ports of Trieste and Fiume, fell under Italian control—in accordance with the post-World War I policy of taking away from Austria all non-Germanic lands and from Hungary those that were non-Magyar. Italians quickly moved into the new Istrian territory, particularly the urban areas, so that the cities became largely Italian while the rural districts remained Slav. The creation of the new state of Yugoslavia soon raised the problem of that Slav state claiming territory inhabited by a majority of Slavs—and thus the Trieste problem began.[5]

Italy has been described as the key to Mediterranean traffic. Its position is at the center of the basin and, with such a location, its function of control of the inland sea is fundamental. In the last war, because of Italy (which shut the Eastern Mediterranean Basin off from the Western), Allied ships were obliged to go all the way around Africa, costly both in time and money.

---

[5] Still not happily "settled."

GREECE

Greece is located at the tip of the Balkan Peninsula. Washed on three sides by seas and indented by many inlets and bays, Greece has one of the longest coastlines in Europe. The land frontiers across the north are also long—and on the other side lie Albania, Yugoslavia, Bulgaria, and, on the northeast, Turkey. But location, topography, and coastal frontiers have turned the Greeks to the sea.

The domain of Greece is fragmented in topography and ragged in outline. A rugged mountain country, it is the most barren and sterile of all of the European Mediterranean lands. Four-fifths of the area is made up of mountain chains and spurs. The Pindus, a series of long, continuous ranges, run southeast through central Greece. East of the Pindus the topography is one of basins separated by southeast and eastward trending promontories. The principal plains are those of Thessaly in the eastern portion of the peninsula. To the south lies the Peloponnesus, separated from the mainland by the Corinth Canal cut through a narrow isthmus to sever the former peninsula from the continent, but giving passage between the Aegean and Ionian Seas. The many islands in the bordering waters make up nearly one-sixth of the total area of Greece.

The domain of Greece includes Macedonia and Thrace, fringelands stretching along the northern Aegean to European Turkey. Thrace and Macedonia run against the trend of the Balkan structures and are a series of river plains separated by mountain spurs that tail off into the sea. Greek Thrace adjoins its Turkish counterpart which continues as a triangular lowland to the Sea of Marmara. At this spot where Europe and Asia attach are two great crossroads of the Old World: one, the most ancient historical seaway; the other, the land-bridge between Europe and Asia—a continuation of the route of the Fertile Crescent that fingers out on the European side along a number of river lowlands to give access through the Balkans to north and west Europe.

Greece, like Italy, has become a land of

emigration. On an area about the size of North Carolina (51,182 square miles) live about eight million people. Thus, Greece may appear to be a nation but sparsely peopled. However, only 15 per cent of Greece is cultivated and, on this amount of land, 60 per cent of the population live as peasants. As in Italy, population pressure and poverty are the foremost problems confronting the nation. The per capita income is one of the lowest in Europe, and Greece is in as difficult a position economically as perhaps any state in the world.

Therefore, induced by the meagre environment and invited by the sea with which he is so familiar, since ancient times the Greek has gone out as a navigator and colonist into and beyond the bounds of the Aegean. Today he is the shipper of the Mediterranean; in an earlier day, he traded throughout the Black Sea area and settled in every port of the Levant. Thus it was that the Greek became an integral part of the life of coastal Turkey, and thus it was that Greek colonists, forming minority—and at times, majority—groups with Irredentist sentiments, have become a geopolitical problem during the twentieth century.

In the first quarter of the twentieth century the major problem of Hellenic minorities was that of the Greek colonists in Turkey. In numbers of about one million, they were found in the coastal lowlands of the Anatolian peninsula, particularly in and around the city of Smyrna where, alone, nearly half a million Greeks were living. In fact, Smyrna was Greek. To the newly organized Moslem Republic of Turkey this large and compact minority of foreign Christians constituted an enigma—solved by the forced repatriation of Greeks from Turkey and Moslems from Greece. This took place between 1922 and 1925. Practically all of the repatriated Greeks settled in western Thrace and adjoining portions of Macedonia. Although absorption of so large a group of immigrants into the economy of Greece was a severe strain, the repatriates were a rich addition to the country. The largest proportion were agriculturists who brought with them Turkish techniques of cultivation and new

plant species far superior to those of Greece. Today this section of the country is the leading producer of tobacco—Turkish variety—the state's outstanding export item. Many skilled artisans were also in the group—silkweavers and carpetmakers.

In the contemporary post-World War II period, the Greek majority on Cyprus has created a very tense international situation in its—and the Greek—demands for the cession of that island, by the British, to Greece.[6]

In Macedonia and Thrace the Greeks base their claim to the entire territory eastward to the Maritza River on ethnic grounds and historical association. However, although the Aegean littoral is undoubtedly Greek in the majority, farther inland Slavs and Bulgars make up the great weight of the population. And it is on this basis that Bulgaria has agitated for Macedonian independence, or association with Bulgaria, over a period of decades.

The Turkish–Greek boundary was set up by the Treaty of Lausanne in 1923. Circumstances that led up to the allocation of territory in Thrace derived both from the Balkan Wars of 1912-13 and from World War I. Greek victory in the former struggle netted Greece large gains of territory in Macedonia and in the northern portions of Thessaly and Epirus, but Greek ambitions in Thrace were not realized. In 1919, however, due to the expulsion of the pro-German ruler from Greece and to the fact that the Hellenic state had entered the war on the Allied side, the victorious Allies were inclined to be generous to the Greeks—who hoped to acquire territory all the way to the Maritza, possibly even to the Straits. The justification for Greek claims was based both on the historic past and on the large numbers of Greek nationals living in western Thrace; the Greeks were the single largest national element in the population although they did not make up the majority of the population. The historical base—that Greek culture was very important in Constantinople—was even less well founded. The decision of the Western Powers to draw the frontier along the Maritza,

---

[6] Against the wishes of the Turkish minority.

and not farther east, was prompted largely by the rapid political and military revival of Turkey under Mustapha Kemal (Ataturk). He expelled the Greek population from the western part of the Anatolian Peninsula, defeated French efforts to incorporate Cilicia into Syria, and pushed his authority over European Turkey as far as the Maritza so as to reincorporate Eastern Thrace into the Turkish state. There appear to be good reasons for the setting of the Turkish–Greek boundary along the line as drawn. Less equitable does the Bulgarian–Greek boundary delineation appear to be. In consideration of the large numbers of Bulgarian Macedonians, it is reasonable that the Slav state should have been given an outlet to the Aegean.

Within Greece, the population are found scattered widely over two regions with differing geographical environments. The two differentiated areas are the blocky peninsular portion of Thessaly and Epirus, Macedonia, and Thrace, and the maze of fringing and ragged peninsulas and islands that make up the southern half of the country. No Greek can live far from the water. In the north, he may be as much as 50 miles from the sea but, in the south, the fragmented character of the land creates an environment that is maritime and Aegean. The outlook of the Greeks in these two regions is rather different, as is also the character of the people; the southern and insular Greeks are of the Mediterranean type while those of the more continental north have been somewhat Slavonized.

Agriculture remains the backbone of the Greek economy. Mountain barriers, however, isolate one small plains' region from another, particularly in southern Greece. Of the cultivated area more than 60 per cent is over 750 feet above sea level with the result that most of the land farmed is steep, rocky, and cut by gullies. The holdings of the Greek farmer are small and fragmented. American economic aid has done much to help the Greeks alleviate problems of land reclamation through drainage, erosion and flood control, irrigation and soil conservation, and spectacular results have been made in the reclamation of alkali lands through rice production. Thousands of acres of such areas, which had been considered useless since before the time of Christ, are being sweetened by the steady flow of fresh river water poured in to irrigate the grain. Always a large importer of rice, the rice produced on these reclamation projects should at least meet the cereal requirements of Greece.

The main crops, produced in valleys that nestle between or among mountains, are tobacco, wheat, grapes, and olives. Tobacco provides Greece with its leading trade item and makes up from 50 to 60 per cent of Greek exports, representing 13.5 per cent of the total value of Greek agricultural produce.

Greek industrial development has lagged. Beneath the bare and rocky hills of Greece are minerals which, if properly developed, can contribute much toward national solvency and prosperity. Although not rich in natural resources as compared with many countries, minerals are one of the few assets Greece possesses. Fourteen basic ores, in quantities and qualities worth mining, are known to exist. They include among others iron, lead, zinc, lignite, magnesite, chromite, manganese, bauxite, and emery.

By constructing a series of new power plants, Greece, for the first time in its history, is able to produce electricity from its own resources, water and lignite; previously, oil had to be imported for this purpose. Mines, not operated in years, have been reopened during the last decade. One fuel resource, virtually untouched until recent years, is lignite. Since 1950, this has been the single most important development in the mining field. The largest reserve is at Ptolemais, in Macedonia, about 26 miles from the Yugoslav border. These lignite mines have been termed the "fuel bin" of the nation. Another recent undertaking has been the revival of chromite extraction at Domokos in central Greece; near Lavrion, at the tip of the peninsula of Attica, important deposits of zinc and lead, yielding by-products of silver and iron pyrites, are being worked. The latter is the locale of the famous silver mines that supplied Athens with wealth over 2000 years ago.

Though Greek rehabilitation has been slow, industry produces electricity, textiles, metals (bauxite and copper manufactures), chemicals, foodstuffs and brewed goods, cigarettes, and leather. The Athens–Piraeus district is the major center of industrial development.

Fishing is an important occupation in Greece. It is, also, probably one of the most ancient—although the Mediterranean Sea falls short of some of the requirements of a great fishing ground. A speciality in the warm waters of the Aegean and along the African coast of the eastern Mediterranean is sponge gathering. Greeks bring up 80 per cent of the Mediterranean take, and, before the war, supplied over 50 per cent of the world's sponges. Synthetic sponges are cutting into this industry, however.

When Greece and Turkey joined NATO in March, 1952, the action extended the defense line of the Western Powers into the Mediterranean. The formation of the Balkan Alliance some time later, between Greece, Turkey, and Yugoslavia, further strengthened the West in the Near Eastern area. However, the Cyprus question has sorely tried this alliance; and the reinstitution of diplomatic relations between Yugoslavia and the states of the Communist Bloc caused Western observers to wonder just how significant the Balkan Alliance would be if faced with a real test. It is too early yet to know. Greek action over Cyprus, already discussed, has created an unforeseen situation; it may possibly weaken Western strength in the eastern Mediterranean.

TURKEY

After having long been considered the oppressor of nations and, later, "the sick man of Europe," Anatolia has emerged as a relatively strong state and a dependable ally of the West. Turkish membership in NATO, the defense pacts of Turkey with Pakistan and Iraq, and the Baghdad Treaty has drawn into the Western Community three Moslem countries that might logically have been associated with the uncommitted states. Turkey does not aspire to leadership among Islamic powers. In fact, the Turks have shown no desire to make foreign alliances on the basis of religious sympathies, and the Turkish–Iraqi and Baghad agreements have caused bitterness among other Arab peoples who consider these alliances a betrayal of the Arab cause. The purpose behind the Western-sponsored pacts is to carry out the American–British plan to set up a bulwark of Middle East states as a barrier to the southward extension of Soviet influence.

Historical Background

The Ottoman Empire had its beginning as a consequence of the early Mongol invasions and conquests of Central Asia. These events of history forced a small group of people to leave their Central Asian homelands as fugitives and migrate to safer regions. They entered the tablelands of Anatolia and took up residence among the Seljuk Turks who were already established there. The migrants formed the nucleus of the group that later became known as the Ottoman Turks.

The Ottoman Turks established a small state traditionally under Osman I (1288-1326), and, beginning with Orkhan I (1326-59), expanded to organize an empire on both sides of the Dardanelles. For 600 years the Ottoman Empire ruled large parts of southeast Europe, North Africa, and the Middle East. The Turks were a minority in these territories, but they held authority over millions of people not only hostile to the Turks but mutually hostile as well for they differed among themselves in religion, language, and way of life. At its greatest extent, the Sultanate included—besides the Anatolia and the Constantinople area —Syria, Egypt, Iraq, the Barbary states, the Balkan states, and portions of Russia and Hungary.

The collapse of the Empire—which had been feeble, heavily in debt, and decadent for a long time—came in 1918 with the Allied victory. According to the terms of the treaty that followed, the Arab countries of the Ottoman Sultanate were made mandates of the League of Nations; in the other parts of the

Empire occupation troops were stationed. Only Anatolia, a barren and semi-arid peninsula, remained to Turkey. Even on to this territory invasions were made, by the Greeks. Most of the islands that lay off the Turkish coast were taken away from the country, with the exception of those that lay within three miles of the Anatolian coast. These remained under Turkish suzerainty.

The Republic was declared in 1923. However, a fighting spirit manifested itself almost immediately. Under Ataturk a local resistance was organized so that, by 1923, the Greeks had been expelled, the occupation forces of the British, French, and Italians had withdrawn, the Sultan had been deposed and a republic declared. The Treaty of Lausanne in the same year recognized the independence of the Turkish national state. In place of the extensive and heterogeneous empire of the past, the Republic was characterized as a relatively small country of some 296,000 square miles populated by a homogeneous people. The bounds of the domain encompass an essentially natural unit (except perhaps for the European annex across the Dardanelles) comprised largely of the Anatolian peninsula eastward to its roots in the Armenian knot.

Under Ataturk many reforms were initiated. The Caliphate was abolished. Replacing the sacred law code of Islam and the religious courts with the Swiss civil code, the Italian criminal code, and the commercial code of the German Republic, a legal structure was set up that gave Turkish citizens, men and women, democratic rights characteristic of West European nations. Women's status in society was changed radically; polygamy became illegal; and the fez, the turban, veils, and religious costumes disappeared. The Latin alphabet replaced the Arabic, the language in which Turkish had been written for a thousand years. The latter innovation, introduced to wean the conservative faction away from old customs and thought, cut off much of the literature of the past from future generations.

Not only were the political, legal, and social structures of the state revolutionized and westernized but the economy as well. Economic well-being predicated modernization, and Ataturk set out to industrialize the state. However, there are few large private fortunes in Turkey, and the upper-class Turk usually has little surplus capital to invest in industry (even if he were interested in doing so). This lack of private capital for investment retarded the growth of industry, and led to the establishment of state controlled enterprises. The latter trend tended to aggravate the existing situation for it discouraged the investment of such capital as might have been available.

The Turkish revolution, peacefully contrived, was, however, a remarkable feat; within the period of three decades an Eastern autocracy of the most absolute character was transformed into a democracy that is essentially like those of the states of the West.

The Geographic Character of Anatolia

Natural barriers separate Turkey from its neighbors on all borders. Being peninsular, the country is surrounded on three sides by water. It is, further, buttressed on three sides by mountains, for, a short distance inland from the northern and southern shores, the rugged mountains that mark the plateau edge rise up with great abruptness from the littoral—the Pontus Ranges in the north, the Taurus in the south; at the eastern end, the Anti-Taurus, trending northeast-southwest across the plateau, blend with the great mass of crumpled mountains that ties the Anatolian, Iranian, and Little Caucasus ranges into the Armenian Knot. Although a prolongation of Anatolia, these lofty highlands, as the source of the Tigris–Euphrates system, are oriented southward and not toward Turkey. Because of this, the region has been one of many border difficulties.

The greater part of Turkey is high plateau and relatively inaccessible. The smaller part is comprised of the Mediterranean–Black Sea littoral plains, generally narrow and stringing along the margin of most of the peninsula. The lowlands are relatively accessible—from the sea; and the western end of the peninsula, with

TURKEY AND THE OTTOMAN EMPIRE
LIBYA (Tripoli)
Turkish Vilayet..........1835
To Italy..........1912
Independent..........1951
ALGERIA
Turkish dependency..........1519-1710
To France..........1830
TUNISIA
Turkish dependency..........1575-1871
To France..........1871
Independent..........1956
EGYPT
Turkish dependency..........1517
British occupied..........1882
British protectorate..........1914-1922
Independent..........1922
SYRIA-LEBANON
Turkish dependency..........1512-1920
French mandate..........1920
Independent states..........1920
PALESTINE-TRANS JORDAN
Turkish dependency..........1512-1920
British mandate..........1920
Independent..(ISRAEL:JORDAN)....1945
IRAQ
Turkish dependency...between....1520-1566
to....1920
British mandate..........1920
Independent..........1945
FALLING AWAY OF THE EMPIRE
TURKEY..........Since..1921
INDEPENDENT..........1699-1913
TO AUSTRIA-HUNGARY. 1699-1718 1772-1775
TO RUSSIA..........1783-1829
TO FRANCE..........1830,1871
TO BRITAIN..........1878-1882
TO ITALY..........1912
OTHER INDEPENDENT COUNTRIES
EMPIRE BY 1481
EMPIRE BY 1683
ALLEN K. PHILBRICK
PHYSIOGRAPHY BY A.K.LOBECK
0 MILES 100
PORTUGAL
SPAIN
FRANCE
SWITZERLAND
ITALY
CZECHOSLOVAKIA
UNION OF SOVIET SOCIALIST REPUBLICS
ARAL SEA
CASPIAN SEA
SEA OF AZOV
BLACK SEA
ROMANIA
YUGOSLAVIA
ALBANIA
GREECE
ISTANBUL
TURKEY
SYRIA
IRAQ
IRAN
LEBANON
JORDAN
ISRAEL
SAUDI ARABIA
PERSIAN GULF
RED SEA
EGYPT
LIBYA
TUNISIA
ALGERIA
MOROCCO
LIGURIAN SEA
TYRRHENIAN SEA
ADRIATIC SEA
IONIAN SEA
AEGEAN SEA
MEDITERRANEAN SEA
B.
GR.
BLACK SEA
BOSPORUS
USKUDAR
SEA OF MARMARA
AEGEAN SEA
GELIBOLU
DARDANELLES
ANCIENT TROY

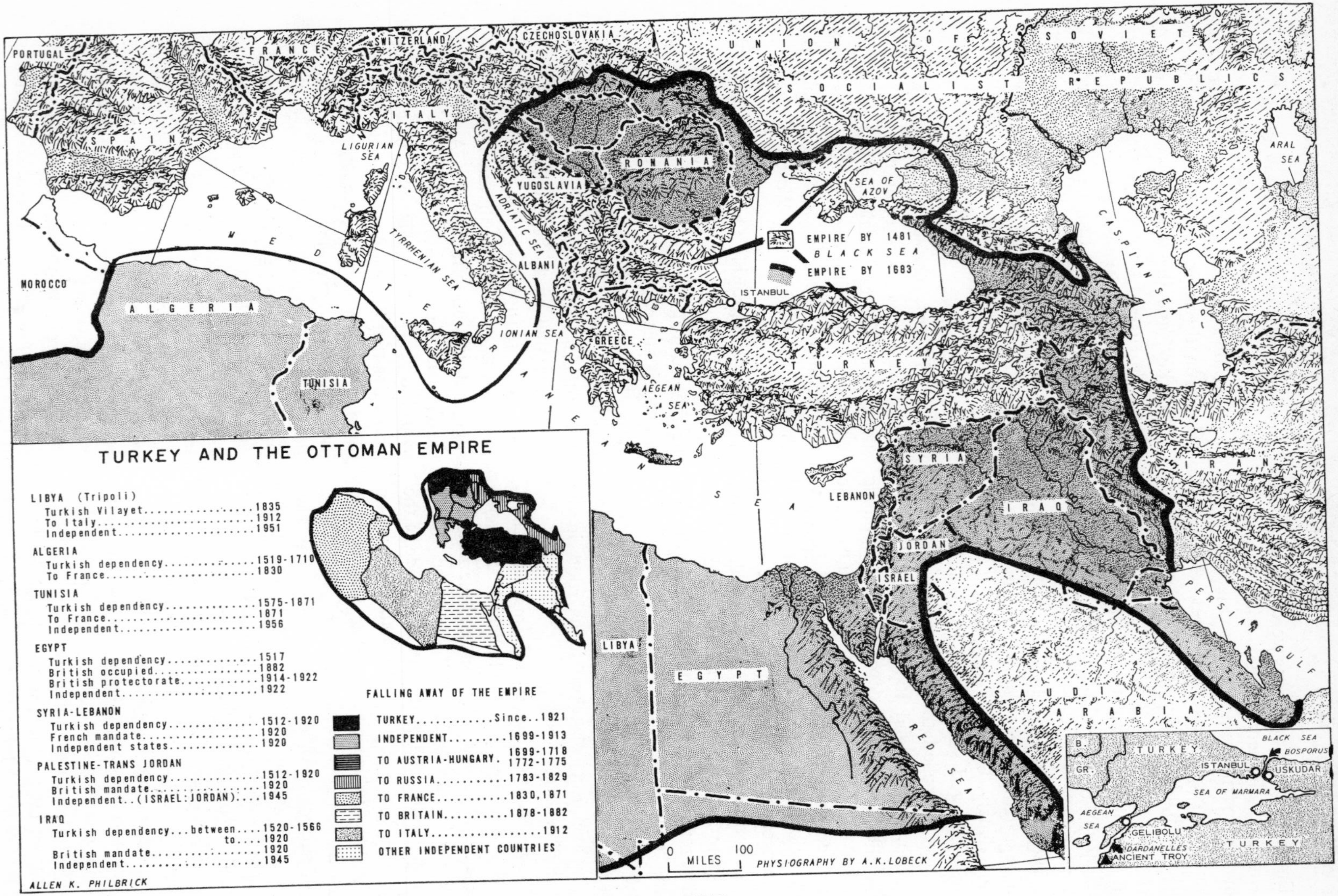

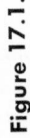

Figure 17.1.

its wider valleys, more extensive plains, and fragmented shores, offers the easiest approach. It is along this littoral that most of the great cities of the past grew up, as Troy on the Hellespont (Dardanelles). From this side, also, the interior is most easily reached.

Thus, despite natural barriers, Turkey— where most populous and productive (*i.e.* in the lowland plains)—is pregnable, its position not one of great strength but of weakness. It is the naval might of the British and American fleets in the Mediterranean that guarantees the integrity of the state—not its impregnability.

Because of the two strikingly different physiographic environments, Turkey falls also into two broadly contrasted climatic regions. In the lowland littoral, broadest in European Turkey and at the western end of the peninsula, Mediterranean climate and culture obtain; the plateau is arid to semi-arid and with continental extremes. The natural—but generally poor— steppes of the latter area are suitable largely for pasture or dry farming; in the plains along the sea are the major agricultural regions.

From ancient times pastoralism has been important in Anatolia. Although still a relatively primitive industry in Turkey, livestock provide the Turkish farmer with many of his needs—draft animals, milk and meat, mohair and wool for clothing, skins and hides for many purposes. The industry supplies, as well, a surplus of animal products for export—live animals, angora wool, mohair, hides and skins, cheese and butter—and products, such as wool, for the home industries (among which rugmaking is perhaps the best known).

Historic and traditional as is pastoralism, the Turkish economy is predominantly agricultural and four-fifths of the people are cultivators. Since there are few large landholders and few landless peasants, Anatolian agriculture has a strong base. Turkey, with an estimated population of 21 million and an area of nearly 193 million acres, is one of the least densely populated countries of the Middle East. Seventy-three per cent[7] of the total area

---

[7] This figure, though taken from an official Turkish source, seems high.

is considered cultivable; of this, less than 20 per cent is in field or tree crops; the rest is pasture. About one-third of the cultivated land lies fallow annually. The possibilities for increasing the cropland are, therefore, obviously great if these estimates are correct.

Wheat has been the most important crop in both acreage and value. It accounts for one-half of the cereal area which in turn occupies about nine-tenths of the cultivated cropland. About half as much land is devoted to other cereals as is planted to wheat. Today Turkey is a surplus wheat area whereas in the days before the revolution it was necessary to import this grain.

Along the coastal regions bordering the Mediterranean and Aegean Seas and in some portions of the narrow Black Sea plain, very intensive farming is carried on, and here are grown the most important exports. Cotton and tobacco hold first place among the exports of the country and, among countries exporting Oriental tobacco, Turkey ranks first. Like wheat, the production and acreage of cotton have been greatly expanded. It feeds a steadily increasing textile industry.

Turkey's mineral potential is not known for the country has been incompletely explored. However, among the known mineral and fuel reserves are coal, copper, chromite, manganese, iron, salt, and sulphur. Turkey is rich in coal, large deposits being found along the Black Sea coast near Zonguldak. This is high-grade bituminous coal, and the output is used almost entirely to supply the iron and steel industry whose ores are shipped from the plateau. Since 1951, Turkey has exported coal. One of the world's leading producers of chromite, Turkey's contribution to international trade in this metal is significant. In 1951, Turkey was the world's leading producer; in 1952, with a production higher than that of the previous year, 70 per cent of the ore mined was shipped to the United States (a state deficient in this metal). In the southeast, the Turks are drilling for oil. The possible occurrence of this resource brought a change in the policy of state enterprise that has dominated the mining industries since the Republic was founded: foreign investors and mining specialists were invited in.

Besides strategic considerations—largely in terms of the location of the country—the contribution that Turkey makes to the Western Bloc is indicated in part by its international trade. Since 1945 West Europe and the United States have replaced the Central European nations as its leading customers. The largest proportion of Turkish exports go to Germany and the United States (26 and 21 per cent, respectively). At present, agricultural products make up over 90 per cent of the exports but the increasing amount of mineral ores now being shipped is a trend to be noted. For Western European states this trend is significant; it makes possible the obtaining of important materials formerly secured from the dollar area.

Problems of the Republic

Turkey is faced with a number of difficult problems. An unfavorable import-export balance affects the well-being of the economy. Although Turkey has increased its exports by some 30 per cent since 1938, imports have risen by 185 per cent. The disproportion between imports and exports has created a condition of instability in the economy that can be countered only by greater productivity and greater export. Here, however, the nation is faced with an enigma; lacking foreign exchange for imports of raw material and parts, certain industries—notably the woolen, rubber, and metalworking operations—are faced with difficulties. Production has dropped, and, as a consequence, labor has been thrown out of employment and had to seek work elsewhere. On the other hand, the criticism has been raised that Turkey has over-extended its industrialization and development efforts with reference to available capital, resources, and manpower; and, further, that the efforts lack necessary coordination. These conditions have led to a reluctance on the part of foreign countries to send materials into Turkey.

A second problem—and one that undoubtedly lies, in part at least, at the base of the unproductivity of Turkey—is that of inadequate transportation. Turkey is underdeveloped, and must remain so until the means of communication are improved. Aside even from defense considerations, this is one of the weakest aspects of the country's development. In some regions, pack animals are the only available means of transporting either goods or people. Not even light vehicles (as light wagons) can get about in certain areas.

In the late 1940's a road and railroad construction program was laid out, and agreements made with the United States for the loan of capital for building and aid in the supervision and training of personnel connected with this work. Three types of roads make up the net that will eventually integrate even the most remote parts of the state. These are the national system of highways, the provincial routes, and the village roads. One of the planned highways spans the entire east-west length of northern Asia Minor. Two others are equally important from a commercial and strategic standpoint. One is to extend from the Thracian border in European Turkey along the west and south coasts of the country. At the port of Iskenderon, near Antioch and the Syrian frontier, this route connects with the second road that angles northeastward from the Mediterranean Sea, across the Taurus Mountains and the plateau to Erzurum, and from there to the Soviet boundary. The latter project requires tunneling.

To build a road system that will serve a territory approximately the size of Texas may not seem to be a stupendous task to an American. Actually the problem confronting Turkey is in a way comparable to that faced by the United States in attempting to unite its domain about the time of the nineteenth century, for thousands of Anatolian villages are as isolated from each other and from the rest of Turkey as was the West Coast of the United States from the Atlantic core at that early period of American history.

Strategic Considerations

Straddling the 17-mile stretch of water that separates Europe and Asia, and thus lying between the East and the West and close to Africa, Turkey and the historic Bosporus are the pivot of the Old World.

Anatolia projects out from the mainland of Asia as a lofty and solid block of plateau, 1000 miles long and at its broadest part 350 miles in width. It thrusts forward out of Arab Asia into Europe, reaching across the Straits to lay hold on a small piece of territory on that continent —seemingly, in both a physical and symbolic sense, to try to grasp the West. Because of its location the state has a dual character. It is Eastern *and* Western—involved with the East in its relations with Russia and the remainder of Islam; involved with the West by its purposeful adoption of Western ways and technologies, and its association through the several alliances.

The collision of the Russians and the Turks is historic. Whether, as has been suggested by some observers, this is due to an "inevitable tendency" for adjacent peoples living in contrasting environments to clash, or whether, as seems more likely, it is a concomitant of geography—*i.e.* the struggle for control of the Black Sea and its hinterland through the Straits —supremacy over Constantinople has been sought by both nations for several hundred years. A second focus of the Turko–Russian clash has been along the 367-mile land frontier between the two countries.

The importance of the Straits led the Byzantine Empire to place its capital, Constantinople, on this water and land crossroads, and, for a millenium, the city was one of the leading centers of the Christian world—becoming the traditional core of Orthodox Catholicism. It was captured by the Turks in 1453 from which time, until 1933, it served as the capital of the Turkish Empire and center of the Mohammedan world.

Russia entered the scene of European politics late, and not until the Turkish Empire had already begun to recede was the Slav nation able to offer a challenge to the Ottoman state. The decline of the latter nation began with the failure of the siege of Vienna in 1683. However, although 13 wars have been fought between Russia and Turkey between 1677 and the present, and although Turkish territory has been lost to the Russians, the latter were never able to establish control of the Dardanelles. Since the middle of the fifteenth century Turkey has held jurisdiction over this strategic waterway—since the end of World War I with the consent and surveillance of the Western powers. The land boundary of the Russo–Turkish frontier was established (1878) following the Crimean War and the Congress of Berlin when Kars, the last section in that area to be transferred, was acquired by the Russian state.

The problem of Mosul and its oil reserves was a big issue in setting up the Iraq–Turkish frontier following World War I. The racial composition of the region added complications. Of the 800,000 inhabitants of the contested border zone, the Kurds predominated, but numbers of Arabs, Christians, Turks, Yezidis, and Jews also lived in the area. As demarcated in 1927 the British-favored Brussels Line, which allotted the Mosul area to Iraq, was adopted. Turkey, however, was to have 10 per cent of the oil royalties received by Iraq for a period of 25 years. Turkish nationals on the Iraq side of the frontier were permitted repatriation, if they so desired.

The Turkish–Syrian border did not involve the ethnic problems that had complicated the Iraq settlement. Turks had not settled in Syria in any numbers. In Syria, therefore, the Turk was more or less of an alien and merely an administrator, and hence, no drastic social or economic adjustments were involved in transferring the Turk from Syrian soil to his own land.

The plateau is the political center of the New Turkey. The plateau, we have noted, was the nuclear area of the Ottoman Turk. Although economically less important than the plains and despite the relative inaccessibility of the plateau, when the Republic was declared the capital was moved from the ancient and strategically located city on the Bosporus, Constantinople (now Istanbul), to Ankara in the midst of the bleak upland. Here, spreading out over the plains around the base of an ancient Hittite citadel, it epitomizes the New Turkey. Its situation, on the stump of an old volcano, dominates the surrounding country while the modern character of this capital symbolizes the new era in Anatolia. Istanbul, however, remains the guardian of the Dardanelles and Bosporus as well as the chief commercial center of the country.

Turkey and the Dardanelles

In the summer of 1946 the USSR brought the age-old problem of the Straits out into the open once more with a note to Turkey demanding a part in the defense of the waterway and a revision of the Montreux Convention. A "part" in the defense meant permitting Soviet military bases along the Dardanelles. The note also requested that the matter of defense and administration be decided by the Black Sea nations, *i.e.* the USSR, Turkey, Rumania, and Bulgaria.

The demand prompted the United States and Britain to focus new attention on Turkey, and particularly on modern Turkey's inherited problem—the Straits. Both realized that the Convention governing the control of the Straits (contracted in Montreux, Switzerland, in 1936) needed revision but, likewise, both nations protested to Russia that the problem was of international, worldwide proportion rather than of mere local implication and interest. Progress toward a satisfactory solution did not materialize. The USSR continued to press demands and even took steps toward the accomplishment of its desire. Therefore, in the spring of 1947, the United States made some very direct moves aimed at stopping the Russians, *i.e.* the loan of money and technical aid to Greece and Turkey, key areas in the defense of the eastern Mediterranean.

The Dardanelles, from ancient days up to the present, has been a zone of contest between conflicting powers. The issue in the current era remains much as in former times, the only differences being those of participants and of scope as time and history and technolo-

gical advancement progress. A new element has recently been added to the picture, however—namely, the active interest of the United States. Thus has the problem moved from a purely local setting in the eastern Mediterranean to one of European proportions to, finally, one of international (meaning worldwide) implications.

The historical geography of the Straits. Narrow corridors, as restricted passageways of travel and transit, have always been contested areas, areas that stand out as spots with tumultuous histories. As shown above, the Straits' question is not a new problem. The importance of the Dardanelles is illustrated by the number of wars that have been waged for its control; in succession Trojan, Greek, Roman, Byzantine, and Ottoman Turk have fought for possession of the narrow straits and control of the trade of the Black Sea basin. Russia, since the days of Peter the Great (1672-1725) and Catherine II (1729-96), has reached out for the Straits as a warm water outlet for trade and power. Mastery of the Mediterranean has always hinged on control of its several constricted passageways—of which the Dardanelles is one.

However, but half of the picture is seen if merely the "straits" aspect of the Dardanelles is emphasized, for this area is also an isthmus acting as a landbridge between two continents. Over this landbridge peoples have passed from the prehistoric, early post-glacial times.

In the proto-historic movement of peoples by land, they migrated around and across the Marmara region in practically all directions. Following this period of intense movement, there was a long era of respite during which the peoples of the Aegean had a chance to find themselves—after the utter disintegration and intermingling that took place during the intrusion of the foreigners—and there followed the renascence that has been characterized "Greek Civilization." With this progress in culture, the importance of the Marmara region as merely a land corridor ceased, and the Greeks commenced to use the searoute through the Straits and the Marmara into the hospitable

Black Sea. These waters they exploited extensively.

The function of the Marmara as a seaway was not entirely a new one even for the Greeks. Legends of Argonautic exploration of the Straits–Marmara–Black Sea area in the thirteenth century, B.C., give accounts of at least two details which experience has confirmed. One is the incidence of the "blue wandering rocks" at the north entrance of the Bosporus, shrouded in mist, and perilous to navigators of the frail boats of the Greeks and Phoenicians. These "rocks" are now known to be the ice floes that drift, at times, from the Black Sea into the Bosporus. The other is the local use of fleeces for the collection of gold from the silt of the torrential Armenian streams —the "golden fleeces" of Greek legend. (They appear to be a rude anticipation of the modern "grease process" for collecting gold.)

It was only after the Milesian and Megarian explorations of the eighth and ninth centuries that regular use began to be made of the Straits and the wealth of Asia Minor, and that of the Don and Dnieper country began to be exploited by adventuresome seamen. Trade in furs, gold, and grain began to be carried on.

The bountiful production of grain in the fertile black lands of the steppe to the north and east of the Black Sea had economic, and later political, implications for the Greek city-states. Freedom of transit for Pontus grains into the Aegean became a primary necessity to the Greek way of living throughout its Golden Age. One of the conditions of political supremacy of any one, or league, of the city-states over its neighbors was the stranglehold on the food supplies of the rest—by the possession of strategic bases of control on the Dardanelles and the Bosporus (or alliances with those states that held control).

Strategic sites on the thresholds to the straits or along the narrows functioned in the early regulation of the traffic even as they do today. Particularly was one city, located at the southern end of the Dardanelles, important in this control for many years. This was Troy. Other cities acting as important controls to the traffic of the Straits were Sestos and Abydos located on either side of the narrows of the Dardanelles. Cyzicus with its twin harbors and island screen to cover its shipping nearly half way over, and Chalcedon and Byzantium at the Bosporus mouth, were all likewise influential in regulating trade. Though the through-trade was the more important, ferry towns also had their share of the spoils, a middleman's share. But it was Troy that for so long was master of all ships desiring to enter the Propontis for trade, and it was this exploitation of the strategic location, with the resultant levying of tolls and other exactions, that finally incited the Greeks to war on the Trojans.

Homeric Troy was a great commercial center because of its command of the Black Sea route. The narrow straits presented difficulties to sailing vessels because of the strong current that flows from the Black Sea to the Mediterranean; besides, the channel is narrow and winding and, during the winter, is apt to be swept for days at a time by a dreaded etesian wind. With wind and tide against them, sailing vessels would be held up at the entrance to the Straits where, besides, Troy controlled the only sources of fresh water. "The Trojan war is thus resolved into an early struggle for freedom of navigation."[8]

A period of prosperity for the Greek cities set in after the fall of Troy. Troy itself had declined for the site was not possessed of other advantages. Further, the situation at the north end of the Straits on the Bosporus is vastly superior to that at the southern extremity. Here is the great crossing of the north-south seaway with the east-west land route—the overpass between two continents. It is the route that runs from Western Europe and the Danube Basin (via the Maritza valley) to Adrianople, crossing the Bosporus, and following the Sakarya Valley into the heart of Anatolia. It is the route of the present Orient Express, the Berlin-to-Baghdad railroad, that connects northwest Europe with major cities in southern Asia. Istanbul commands this crossing-point.

[8] "Constantinople and the Straits," *Geographical Review*, Vol. 8, No. 3 (September, 1919), p. 193.

The Marmara[9] region played no more than a passive role in the struggles between the Greek and Persian forces. "It had common interests of its own, but little political cohesion; it was a no-man's-land between an Asiatic empire and a more or less Hellenized Europe, patrolled by Athenian seapower."[10] The Propontis had become a miniature Aegean. In whatever measure any one power dominated one side of this lakeland, it was drawn by local hostilities or friendships into local complications on the other, but political unity went no further.

The Marmara region owes its first significance as a regional state and the first recognition of its strategic and political value to one of the officers of Alexander's army, Lysimachus. Evidently sent to rule this area, he set up the capital where it could function in the dual capacity of protecting the region and embarrassing Macedonia's enemies—at a new site a little to the north of the Isthmus of Gallipoli. It was named Lysimachia. It occupied a double seafront which gave the city control of the Marmara and of the northern Aegean. So strategically was this city located relative to the grain routes of the Black Sea and to some of the important routes of the Aegean and Mediterranean that Lysimachus was well on the way to establishing an empire. Contemporaries of Lysimachus dismantled the city, however, and thus destroyed his power. From that time on until the Roman era various European and Asian powers held the Straits but for no long period of time.

The entrance of Rome into the eastern Mediterranean profoundly affected the position and fortunes of the Marmara. Previous to this intervention, the principal Roman road connecting Italy with Anatolia was a southern route extending from Durazzo, opposite the heel of Italy, to Salonika past the ruins of Lysimachia to the Hellespont[11] ferry. This was the Ignatian Way of the period of about 167 B.C. By that route the Hellespont ferry offered a shorter way to Asia Minor than did the Bosporus.

Adrianople was the first Roman imperial city founded within the Marmara region. It lay on the European side, inland, at the confluence of the Hebros River with its principal northern tributary. But located as it was, it could not prevent the use of the narrows by the Goths who were ravaging the Greek cities of Pontus Asia, the Marmara, and even of the Aegean. In the face of this, the closing of the Straits became urgent, and an arsenal was required, together with a fortress which would have timber and metal resources available. The European side had none and so a new city, Nicomedia, rose rapidly on the Asiatic side at the head of the Gulf of Ismid. The Straits were patrolled from the harbor of this city.

Constantine's plan for retrieving the situation was more effective than was his predecessors'. In choosing the site for his capital, there were several almost irreconcilable considerations to be taken into account: 1) if the New Rome was to defend the Empire as a whole, it must be as near as possible not only to the Danube frontier and to the northwestern trunk-road by which Aquileia and Milan were to receive and give reinforcements, but to the Euphrates frontier as well; 2) if it was to be a great population center, it must be fed—so it must stand on the seaboard within reach of the grains of Egypt and of the Propontic steppe area; 3) it must be able to protect these supplies in transit as well as stop searaiders out of the North, so it must be a naval arsenal with direct access on the Pontus and also, as direct as might be, to the Levant; 4) in case of interruption to the flow of resources from overseas, it must have local supplies and a local reserve of men as it must command the Thracian grainlands and highlands as Lysimachia and Adrianople had done, but without the risk of isolation which had hampered both of these—and it must not merely stand in a big garden, it must be a palace and a *citadel;* 5) it must be essentially Greek for it was to dominate the sentiments as well as the interests of the Greeks, but it

---

[9] Known to the Ancients as the Propontis.

[10] J. L. Myres, "The Marmara Region: A Study in Historical Geography," *The Scottish Geographical Journal*, XL, May, 1924, p. 140.

[11] Dardanelles.

must also be a New Rome, unprejudiced by memories.

The capital was located on the one great harbor of the Bosporus (now known as the Golden Horn) and was called Constantinople. Its history is a witness to how well it has fulfilled the demands made upon it as the site of the Eastern Capital of the Roman Empire.

The power of the Byzantine Empire was finally broken by the Ottoman State. The latter established itself not merely in Asia Minor, but on the very frontier of the Marmara region itself, obstructing the main avenue between the Byzantine capital and its richest and most prosperous hinterland. It was left for the Ottoman Turks, the main aggressors, to reorganize the Empire—much in the old way—after they had occupied the city. The Turks swept across the Hellespont and Marmara in 1391 and the Bosporus in 1453. For about three centuries the Turks held undisputed dominion over the Straits. It was not until the dream of Russian expansion began to take form that the power of the Ottoman Turks started to waver and diminish. Though Turkey on several occasions, in the two centuries following Czar Peter's seizure of the Sea of Azov, successfully asserted itself and for the greater share of the time was in actual control of the waterway, the recurrent challenges by Russia weakened its position. It also had the further (and possibly more important) effect of focusing European attention upon the Straits. This had far-reaching consequences.

Peter the Great was the first Czar to understand the full implications of the lack of an ice-free port for Russia. Although the strategic value of the Straits had been appreciated in a rudimentary sort of way previous to Peter, no one had taken the initiative of solving the problem of icelocked harbors until his time. He started the southern expansion of Russia by establishing arsenals on the shores of the Sea of Azov and by founding the Russian navy. Later rulers, particularly Catherine the Great, pushed this southward development. Never once, since the death of Peter the Great, has Russia swerved from its purpose of obtaining for its navy and merchant marine a politically free outlet from the Black Sea to the Mediterranean. But it was due to the conquest of the north shores of the Black Sea, by Catherine II, that the monopoly of trade in that region, held until then by outsiders, was broken.

The Political Geography of the Straits

Although politics blended with "Straits'" history before the time of Peter the Great, it was not until the advent of the Russians into the Straits' problem that the question began to take on an acute political aspect. During the two centuries following the intrusion of Russia, that state and Turkey went to war several times over the matter.

Immediately after Peter had made himself master in the Sea of Azov in 1699, Turkey took a stand that had previously not been disputed, *i.e.* the navigation of the Black Sea was "an inviolable and sacred possession"[12] of the Sublime Porte. But Turkey was already a decadent power and, despite this action, could offer no continuously effective resistance to Russia's aggressive and growing maritime ambitions. It had to grant free navigation of the Black Sea and passage through the Straits.

The concessions extorted by Peter the Great were not permanent, however. At the peace of Belgrade in 1739, Russia was again forced to concede Turkey exclusive rights on the Black Sea, and Russia was forbidden to build any naval vessels. This condition, too, was of brief duration, however, for, in 1774, Catherine II, by the Treaty of Kutchuk–Kainarji, once more secured full rights to navigation on the Black Sea and through the Straits.

When Bonaparte invaded Egypt in 1798, an alliance to resist French aggression was made between Russia and Turkey to allow Russian naval vessels to pass through the Dardanelles. This treaty was amplified in 1805 by an agreement which provided that no armed vessels of any power except Turkey and Russia should be permitted to enter the Black Sea.

---

[12] Vice-Admiral Hollweg, "The Dardanelles Problem," *Living Age*, Vol. 315, November 18, 1922, p. 385.

The question, originally, was one between Russia and Turkey alone for the seapowers of Western Europe were too fully engrossed in their own difficulties to be bothered about the Dardanelles. A little later, however, as signs of friendship between Napoleon and Czar Alexander appeared to be developing, England took a hand in this Middle Eastern question. England, at this time, concluded a treaty with Turkey which was designed to deprive Russia of its power in the Black Sea. Also in the treaty, however, was the clause restricting naval vessels of all other countries, including England, from entering the Dardanelles. By this British intervention in the question of the Straits, the issue was converted from a purely Turkish–Russian affair to a European issue.

Since then, Russia has sparred with several combinations of European powers over the Dardanelles and Bosporus. In 1833, Russia compelled Turkey to sign a treaty that virtually made it a Russian protectorate (Treaty of Hunkiar–Skelessi). Russian vessels were permitted free passage through the Straits and English vessels excluded. The Russian success was of short duration, however, for France sided with England, and Russia had to submit the matter to an international conference and to recognize that the question of the Straits was a European problem. Two London Conferences followed in 1840 and 1841. These aimed to deprive Russia for all time of its privileged position, as well as to make Turkey merely a "helpless doorkeeper of the Straits under the pretense of protecting her."[13] The Paris Treaty, ending the Crimean War, expressly declared that the preservation of the Turkish Empire was demanded by the common interests of European powers. Fearing Russia, Turkey readily accepted protection. The treaty further stated that the Black Sea should constitute an area of neutral waters and that no naval vessels were to be allowed upon it. All Russian arsenals and shipyards were destroyed thereby causing Russian seapower and the whole Russian Black Sea policy to suffer. In 1870, Russia sent a letter to all the powers denouncing the

Paris Treaty. This resulted in a threat of war from England. A conference followed in which both Bismarck of Germany and the United States backed Russia. Following the Russo–Turkish war of 1878, Russia tried to secure certain special privileges by a secret codicil to the Treaty of San Stephano. England ordered its navy to the Dardanelles. The Berlin Congress followed. Though Bismarck again supported Russia, he could not prevent the Dardanelles question from being treated as a European problem.

All treaties applying to the Straits were so drafted as to be capable of several interpretations. Their common purpose, however, was to enforce England's desire to keep the Russian navy out of the Mediterranean, and thus to limit the Russian fleet to modest proportions. In order to attain this objective, England was willing to renounce her right to conduct naval operations in the Black Sea. The weakness of Turkey, which the Great Powers perpetuated for political reasons, was utilized to the utmost.[14]

In anticipation of an Allied victory over Turkey during the First World War, a series of secret agreements were entered into by England, France, Italy, and Russia. In accordance with the terms, Russia was to receive Constantinople and the Straits, with free port rights reserved for Britain and France. In March, 1915, Britain, France, and Russia signed an agreement by which, in case of victory, Russia was also to be given complete control of the Bosporus and one side of the Dardanelles while France and England were to be conceded certain trade guarantees in the region of the Straits. Under the Sykes–Picot Agreement of May, 1916, Russia was to receive northeast Asia Minor from Turkey. These secret commitments were never carried out because the Russian Revolution led to the withdrawal of Russia from the war.

After World War I, the Peace Treaty of Lausanne (1923) set up, under the auspices of the League of Nations, an International Straits' Commission to insure freedom of passage and navigation of the Dardanelles–Bosporus–Black Sea Area. The European and Asian shores of

---

13 *Ibid.*, p. 385.

14 *Ibid.*, p. 386.

the Straits were demilitarized and the Straits were opened to all commercial vessels of the world as well as to warships of any nation (with certain reservations).

In 1936, the Montreux Convention considerably altered the powerless position of Turkey and enabled that state to regain all rights to fortify the zone. It also recovered supervision of the Straits and gained full control in case of belligerency.

At the Berlin Conference, Great Britain and the United States agreed with the Soviet Union that the Montreux Convention did not conform to the existing conditions and the question was to be subjected to direct negotiation between the governments of the Big Three and Turkey. Russia made four proposals for the revision of the Convention: a) the Straits should always be open to the passage of all merchant ships of all nations and to the passage of warships of Black Sea powers; b) passage through the Straits for warships not belonging to Black Sea powers should not be permitted except in cases especially provided for; c) the establishment of a regime of the Straits as the sole seapassage leading from the Black Sea to the Mediterranean Sea should come under the competence of Turkey and other Black Sea powers; and d) Turkey and the Soviet Union, as the powers most interested and capable of guaranteeing freedom to commercial navigation and security in the Straits, should organize joint means of defense of the Straits for the prevention of the utilization of the Straits by other countries for aims hostile to the Black Sea powers.

The governments of Great Britain and the United States expressed general agreement with the first three points as principles for discussion, but the American government took exception to the last two. It claimed that the control of the Straits was a matter of concern not only to the Black Sea powers but also to other nations including the United States. Thus did the Straits' question cease to be merely a problem of the European continent and enter the arena of global politics.

The United States stands against a joint Russo–Turkish defense of the Straits, favoring Turkish jurisdiction. Should the Straits become the object of attack, the United States has recommended that the matter be referred to the Security Council of the United Nations. Theoretically this is the position that the United States has taken; practically, the American nation has undertaken to protect the integrity of the Dardanelles–Bosporus waterway. The loans to Greece and Turkey, direct from the United States to their respective governments, and the continuous presence of the United States fleet in Mediterranean waters, confirm this.

THE MEDITERRANEAN AND THE MIDDLE EAST

In a number of countries across the globe radical changes in the social, political, and economic structure are taking place—as in Asia and Africa. But in few areas on the earth is there such a striking picture of a new society emerging from the remnants of the old as in the Middle East and North Africa. The rise of Israel, the decline of French influence in North Africa, American oil enterprise in Arabia, and the ending in Egypt of the monarchy and British influence have brought, as an almost unavoidable concomitant, a mutation in the seemingly changeless, inert, poverty-ridden, and exploited world of the Arab. A summary of Middle Eastern conditions presents a rather dark picture for global concord. Throughout most of the Arab lands there has been crisis, confusion, and turbulence; this is one of the world's very critical regions. Two of the most turbulent areas have been the Atlas countries and the Israeli–Arab frontier regions, African and Asian territories lying within the Mediterranean realm.

The Arab world resents Israel. Regarded *"as a creation by outsiders,"* the Arab peoples have protested recognition of the Jewish state. Basically, the outstanding objections are: 1) the Arab nations do not want to accept Israel as a Jewish national state because they regard Palestine territory as essentially Arab; 2) there is the fear that Israel may, in time, come to economically dominate the Arab world itself—

at least the Asian states that lie adjacent. The Arab countries, in clinging to the patterns of the past, have been retarded technologically, economically, politically, and socially.

The refugee problem has accentuated Arab animosity toward Israel. At the outbreak of hostilities, many of the Arabs living in Israel fled that state and went into the adjacent Arab countries, notably Jordan and the Gaza strip, a small remnant of old Palestine now administered by Egypt. The United Nations' truce line of 1949 cut the latter territory off from the Jewish state. Since that time it has been disputed, and intermittent fighting has occurred along the boundary frontier. Dispute over the Gaza area is comprehensible for, historically, the Jews lay claim to it as a part of their ancient homeland, Palestine; historically, also, the Arabs regard it as a part of their traditional lands, and look upon the Israelis as intruders—even if from way back. The strip is only 26 miles long, fronting the Mediterranean, and but four to eight miles in width. It is, however, a less desolate region than are many of the Middle East outposts for there are many wells and springs to water the land. Hence, both Egypt and Israel desire the territory.

Another critical area lying between Israeli and Arab territory is the Gulf of Aqaba, a thin blue slit of water stretching up from the Red Sea along one side of the Sinai Peninsula and bounded by Egypt and Saudi Arabia on the east and west; the bit of land lying around the head of the gulf is shared by Jordan and Israel. For half a decade Egypt has blockaded the gulf to Israeli ships and limited the effective rights of the Jewish state to their territorial waters—in this instance defined as a five mile strip fronting the Israeli shore. These waters, located in the north, are sealed off from the Red Sea by the territorial waters of Egypt, Saudi Arabia, and Jordan. Blockade of the gulf is achieved through Egyptian control of the small island of Tiran located in the straits about 150 miles south of the head of the gulf. Egypt occupied the island in 1950 and, through batteries stationed on Tiran and the adjacent Egyptian coast, has controlled the waters of the gulf—refusing navigation to Israeli shipping.

Egyptian activities have caused tension in the eastern Mediterranean to grow. The signing of the agreement for the sale of Czechoslovak arms to Egypt late in 1955 sounded another dangerous threat for it heralded the possible beginning of an arms' race in an area already highly explosive. Further, it appeared to cut the lines more sharply. By aligning—at least through trade pacts—some of the neutral Arab states with the Communist Bloc countries, a new element was introduced—*i.e.,* the East—West struggle became identified with a controversy that, to that time, had been confined to Israel and Egypt (at least on the surface).

Egyptian seizure of the Suez Canal also inserted a highly explosive element into Mediterranean affairs,[15] and control of the Canal has been an international issue ever since. The problem arose with the withdrawal of the British from the Canal Zone. Seizure of the Canal was one of the achievements that brought popular support to the revolutionary council of officers that replaced Farouk upon his forced abdication; it also rallied the other Arab states around Egypt. Soviet backing of Egyptian claims in this crisis not only sharpened the East—West power struggle but afforded an "in" for the Soviets—the implications of which are difficult to foresee.

As has often been true in the past, events in the Arab world have erupted not in one area but in several. There have been equivalent conditions in all of these crisis areas—that is, tension between contrasting cultural groups and intense nationalism. Nationalism, which appears to have spread by suggestion from the East, across southern Asia, and into the Middle East, has mounted in intensity as the Arabs have tried to grope their way out of political dependency toward emerging and but only partly resolved relationships with other states. Among the most seething and frenzied of the problems has been the critical situation in North Africa where the demands of Moslems

---

[15] See pages 324–326.

in Morocco, Algeria, and Tunisia were accompanied by barbaric acts of violence—and met with reprisals by the French. The bloody agitation in Tunisia and Morocco brought independence to those areas, but Algeria remains turbulent as the Arab nationalists seek to force control from the French, and the latter are equally determined to maintain their authority in this North African territory—held for over 125 years and regarded as part of Metropolitan France.

For hundreds of years before the French entered the scene, the North African states were ruled by despotic monarchs who held absolute authority over a stagnant society. Individuals had no existence of their own, for the concept of freedom for the individual was never a part of Arab thinking. Being historically a migratory people, security could be found only within the group and in unchanging traditions.

The entrance of the French into North Africa marked the beginning of a new era. Algeria, Morocco, and Tunisia were developed along Western lines by European initiative and money. The resulting industry attracted many of the indigenous people to the cities. But, uprooted from their familiar surroundings and way of life, detribalized, and, finding their dwelling in shanty-towns (*bidonvilles*) on the edges of the European centers, or in ancient *medinas,* they were faced with the problem of adjusting from the old to the new. Frustrated, this portion of humanity, in the crowded native quarters of the greater cities such as Casablanca, Rabat, Marrakech, Meknes, and Fez, has formed a "culture medium" in which many sorts of extremism have flourished. It was in the medinas and *bidonvilles* of the urban centers of northern Morocco that nationalism was most intense and, from here, that it spread abroad throughout the Atlas territories. The contrasts of living are overwhelming (as is true throughout all of the Middle East). There is not only the contrast between the European and the poverty-stricken Arab, but between the wealthy Arab and the masses, the former still living in feudal splendor.

In their drive for national determination, the Arab states of Atlas Africa received moral support from other Middle Eastern countries, particularly Egypt. Not only were "calls to revolt" broadcast over the Cairo radio, but the independent Arab states to the east have given these Moslem nationalists *voice* at the United Nations and throughout the world—and, with it, an inspirited feeling of obvious destiny.

The nexus among the Arab states is the mutual bond of Islam. In many respects, however, Morocco, Tunisia, and Algeria are much closer to Europe than to the other Arab lands (although Europeans have little prestige among these Moslems).

The crisis in North Africa has been very difficult for the French. Not only has it been necessary to attempt to meet Arab demands, but the "colonists"—who oppose any liberal policy toward the indigenes—have had to be appeased. Further, the French have tried to work out agreements with the nationalists that would satisfy them and, at the same time, keep this valuable portion of the empire closely associated with Metropolitan France. In 1950, the French North African problem was "a cloud" no greater than "a man's hand"; since that time, Arab nationalism has burst upon the political scene in a storm that has wrenched two of the dependencies from French control.

MEDITERRANEAN NORTH AFRICA

Mediterranean Africa has, historically, had its fate decided by circumstances which derived from outside of the country. The history of Barbary is a result much less of geographical conditions than of human influence. It is thought that even prehistoric North Africa did not escape invasions.

The Berbers, one of the two groups of people known as the *indigenes,* originally settled here. They are a stock with somatic traits that relate them to the inhabitants of Southern Europe from where they are thought to have migrated at an early date. Wherever the Berbers have remained pure from foreign penetration, very characteristic types are recognizable.

Two great and ancient civilizations, those

of Phoenicia and Rome, established themselves in Mediterranean Africa. Phoenician influence was felt as early as 1101 B.C., when the Phoenicians of Tyre founded Gabes on the east coast of what is now Tunisia and some time later located colonies on the Moroccan coast. In 803 B.C., Carthage was founded. Within three centuries this city had taken over the ventures of the previous Phoenician settlements and made itself supreme, throughout the western Mediterranean, by a network of trading centers and naval supremacy. Beginning in the third century B.C., Carthage fought a series of wars with Rome (the Punic Wars), the last of which resulted in the complete destruction of the Phoenician city (149-146 B.C.).

At first Rome was content with occupying the former Punic lands. Gradually, however, the Italian state attempted to establish good relations with the Berbers, and the kingdoms along the sea were rapidly drawn under Roman influence. In general, however, Roman jurisdiction spread slowly, and only in 45 B.C. did Caesar set up a new province in these African territories. By the fifth century, the Roman Empire was breaking up, and Vandals and other barbarians from the East moved in and settled on the northwest coast. However, remnants of the advanced civilizations of Roman Africa—which was limited only to the "Mediterranean" sections—are still strikingly evident in the ruins of aqueducts and colosseums (larger than the one in Rome) and in the relics of Christianity that indicate that at one time the Berbers—at least large parts of them—were Christian.

The Islamic conquest of North Africa has had the most marked effects. Little is known of the history of North Africa from the time that the Vandals (in the fifth century) passed across the area to the conquest by the Moslem Arabs in the seventh century. So complete was the Islamic conquest of Barbary that it erased the imprint—except for ruins—of the former conquerors. North Africa is today Moslem in religious and social structure; the political framework of the French was a relatively superficial superstructure built upon a solid and unchanged base of Islam so far as the native people were concerned—Arab and Berber alike. The Jew and the Christian European are the only non-Moslems. Arabic is the language of the people, as it is in all Islamic countries west of Persia, except Turkey.

The conquering of North Africa by the Moslems was but one episode in a series of Barbary conquests; it was not the last, but it was the most complete. Not only was it a physical conquest of territory and people, but a spiritual, social, and political conquest as well. Later, the French took Barbary and, to an extent, subdued the tribes—yet, in no sense, did they actually conquer the people. Islamic North Africa is a proud and haughty land that despises the Christian European—as it despises the Jew.

The first entry of the French into North Africa was in 1830 when they obtained a foothold in Algeria in order to suppress piracy. Four years later, they declared Algeria a French Colony; however, 17 years of warfare were necessary to subdue the tribes and bring the territory under effective French control. Tunisia came under French administration when the Sultan of Tunis shifted his loyalties from Turkey to France. Not until 1912, however, did the Sultan of Morocco accept French "protection," and then only because of the pressing of German claims in Moroccan territory. Just south of and around Gibraltar, a small zone that had come under Spanish influence became attached to Spain (Spanish Morocco—or the Riff), while Tangier was internationalized.

The great historic regions of North Africa are a result of both history and nature. In general, the natural regions run east and west across almost the entire extent of the French territories. There is the Mediterranean littoral lying between the mountains and the sea, deeper in places as the plain pushes inland between the ranges, narrower in others as the highlands come close to the sea, playing out in some areas particularly toward the east where mountains drop sheerly into the Mediterranean. The second region, the Atlas, trend from west to east in two great ranges—the Little and the Saharan Atlas—highest, broadest, and most complex in Morocco where the Middle and Anti-Atlas flank two sides of the High Atlas. In northeast Tunisia, the Atlas lose themselves in the sea to continue, across the "waist," in Sicily. South of the mountains the Sahara takes hold.

In general, the distribution of the several peoples takes a parallel pattern; the Arabs are in the north, the Berbers, generally, in the mountains and along the valleys to the south. The Berber–Arab distribution developed as a result of the Berber retreat, into and beyond the mountains, before the Arab invaders. Erecting little stone villages on relatively impregnable hills or mountaintops, or building mud or stone *casbahs* surrounded by great walls, they tended to live in distinct districts; the Berbers and the Kabyles[16] occupy the Atlas and sub-Atlas country while the Arabs, the other major ethnic stock, are found generally in the plains of the north and west. In the cities and in the rural areas north of the Atlas, there is a mixing zone of Arab and Berber. Desert people occupy the sub-Saharan lands. The Atlantic façade of Morocco is the only region that does not fall within this pattern.

The Riff coast, extending for 200 miles along the Mediterranean, has been the great highway of ancient cultures; but, since only open roadsteads give access to the sea, it has never been important in maritime activity. Further, the coastal area is shut off from the interior, except at either end, by the Riff and Jebel highlands. The narrowness of the Mediterranean at the western end encouraged intercourse between Spain and the Riff ports; but this coastal contact did not permit the Spanish to penetrate inland.

The historic value of the straits' coast has been more in its land than maritime aspect. The coast facing Gibraltar almost touches Europe—this is as close as Africa gets to the northern continent; it, also, dominates one of the great crossroads of the world. To the Ancients, *the Straits* of Gibraltar had no significance for no one ventured beyond the "Pillars of Hercules" which, to them, marked the end of the world. Likewise, during the Middle Ages, the water passageway had no strategic value for the Mohammedans and Mediterraneans rarely ventured beyond the gates. When, in the fifteenth and sixteenth centuries, the Atlantic and its approaches attained hitherto unparalleled importance, the Mohammedans in the West took no part in the development, but limited their activities to piracy. Thus, they merely functioned to jeopardize the busy trade route over which they might have had control. For the Moroccans, the Gibraltar coast was, first and foremost, the way to Spain—which, from the tenth to the fifteenth centuries, the Moslems followed in their conquest of Iberia.

Although the Atlantic coast provides frontage for over 250 miles on the ocean—a long façade that leads inland to the very heart of Morocco—the shore is one of the most hostile to maritime activity that can be found in the world. It runs "dead straight and almost shelterless" from north to south, indented only by mediocre harbors and poor estuaries. In fact, the west coast of Morocco is like a great breakwater for the ocean—"the great Atlantic swell crashes onto the coastal platform, and spreads out in mighty waves which burst into foam on the shore. It has been for centuries Morocco's best rampart."[17] Thus, Morocco has been unfortunate in most of its water frontage; in the North, the country is isolated by its coast, and, to an even greater degree, by the highlands; along the West, by the Atlantic. Hence, the limited shore facing Gibraltar has played a preponderant role in Moroccan history.

Aspects of the Physical Geography and Economy

The Atlantic side is the best watered of any portion of North Africa. Inland, on the dry

---

[16] The Kabyles, a group closely related to the Berbers, are the Atlas peoples—and earliest inhabitants—of Algeria.

[17] Henri Terrasse, *History of Morocco* (Casablanca: Editions Atlantides, 1952), p. 3.

plateau toward the Atlas (as around Marra-kech), irrigation water from the mountains or wells provides moisture for more scattered cultivation. In the Fez–Meknes area, agriculture turns the countryside into an "Eden" as compared with all but a few of the irrigated portions of Morocco. Contrasts between the Atlantic and Mediterranean coastal plains and the rest of Morocco are striking.

The Mediterranean plains, which, in general, are broken and fragmented by intervening highland areas, are, in Algeria, very productive. Cultivation runs up to the mountains in most regions; grain fields, citrus and olive orchards, and vineyards rise and fall, cresting the high hilltops and covering the valleys with green. The Oran district, and that area surrounding Algiers, are particularly lush. The cultivation is typically "Mediterranean" (already described).[18] Although the "Tell" of Algeria is one of the most highly productive regions in the French empire, cultivation is, at present, not as extensive as it was in Roman days and there is room for the expansion of agriculture. The best lands in the Atlantic and Mediterranean plains are in the hands of French and Spanish settlers or of large native landowners. As one travels through the countryside, the "visage" of the land tells one whether the cultivation is European or wealthy Arab, or that of the small landowner; both the character of the land (which, in general, is very rocky) and the agricultural methods unfold the story.

The folded Atlas are a part of the same great chain of folded mountains found across the waters in southern Europe. In general, the highlands consist of two systems of mountains (complex with many ranges) that enclose a high plateau. The plateau development is most pronounced in Algeria and Tunisia; in Morocco, the mountains are much more complex and rugged, and, except in the east, the intermontane plateau almost plays out.

The Atlas country vegetation varies with the rainfall pattern. Northern slopes are wooded, becoming more dense with distance north or

increased elevation; southern slopes are relatively bare with the effects of aridity more marked southward, with the slopes of the Saharan Atlas, overlooking the desert, as arid as the desert itself. The high plateau is steppe-land with a long grass (alfa grass) as the major vegetation—used for pasture and exported for the manufacture of paper.

As stated before, the Atlas country is Berber country. The typical scene is the Berber village, built of local material—stone or baked clay—rising almost indiscernibly from the crest of a hill or mountain, the terraced cultivation—at times pitiably meagre—covering the adjacent slopes or valleys. In places the black tent of the nomadic Arab spreads out on the mountain pastures or in the foothill country. Added to the Mediterranean crops is the Barbary fig—acting as garden, fence, wall, etc.—especially in the Northern Atlas and the drier coastal lowlands. Infrequent fertile valleys may run through the rocky terrain in green ribbons of semi-tropical character, becoming gradually less lush as the valley penetrates the highlands more deeply. South of the Atlas, the only life found is along "wadi" or other oases where water makes existence possible. The great proportion of French North Africa is desert for Algeria reaches down beyond the center of the Sahara. Everything south of the Saharan Atlas Ranges is barren country—except, as stated, for the occasional oases. This is generally not realized.

The mineral wealth of Barbary North Africa is considerable, and, under the French, development has been extensive. Morocco is the world's largest producer of phosphate, Tunisia ranks second, and Algeria fourth. Together they mine about one-third of the phosphate of the world. Morocco has the fifth largest output of manganese; lead and zinc, and a variety of other minerals are also exploited although in minor quantities. Coal is scarce—Morocco has but two small mines in the east, close to Oujda, and Algeria but one, some distance to the south. Fuel is therefore a problem.

Industry is little developed and North Africa

---

[18] See pages 360–369.

is largely agricultural and pastoral. However, such industries as cement manufacture (which is very important), and certain of the metallurgical industries, as processing of zinc, lead, and phosphates, are quite significant. They mark a beginning in industry and constitute an important source of revenue for the state. The area, however, does not have a large industrial potential as such, and can be expected to remain, in the main, agricultural.

Population and People

Morocco, with an area of 155,000 square miles, has a population of 8.5 million (density, 54 per square mile); Algeria, 846,124 square miles in size, has 8.9 million inhabitants (density, 11 per square mile); Tunisia, 60,165 square miles in area, has 3.5 million people (density, 58). These figures, however, do not tell the full story because in all three countries there are vast spaces—particularly in Algeria —that are uninhabited or nearly so. In general, population is very unevenly distributed. Some areas, as urban centers like Casablanca, are over-populated in terms of work potential; others are under-populated in terms of resources.

North Africa is vital to the West. Morocco's position at the Mediterranean entrance is comparable to that of Turkey on the Dardanelles and Egypt on the Suez. Hence, its place within the strategy of the West becomes apparent.

Ever since the French proclaimed a protectorate over Morocco in 1912, however, nationalism has been directed against the Europeans in all three of the Barbary states, and particularly in Morocco. Because of the importance of Algeria to the French economy—known as "little France in Africa"—that dependency was made an integral part of the metropolitan state —a device to satisfy Algerian ambitions. However, although Algerians are French citizens theoretically with rights equal to any other Frenchman, in practice, this is not the case. There is discrimination economically, politically, and socially; Algeria of the north is French, not Algerian.

The ascendant minority problem of North Africa has been that of the ruling minority— who are foreigners. A second minority group —and one that, under Moslem rule, was constantly persecuted—is the Jewish. The *mellahs* to which they were restricted by the Moslems still exist—in a former day, they were ghettos of the worst sort. Today the *mellah* is found in every Moroccan city, usually a slum district of shacks that is almost indescribable in its misery. In urban centers, new *mellahs* and *medinas* were being constructed by the French authorities—modern and clean, but carefully holding to certain aspects of the traditional ways of the Moroccans and Jews so that the people would not be averse to moving into them. It was a slow and expensive task; and, with ever more of the rural people crowding into the cities, one that seemed to grow greater, instead of less, with the years. These projects were still uncompleted when Morocco and Tunisia gained independence. Under the French, the Jews did not constitute a minority problem. A third and troublesome minority problem in Morocco has been found along the border where Spanish and French Morocco and Algeria meet: Riffan Moroccans, entering from the Spanish territory, have stirred a great deal of strife, so that the area has been a very uneasy zone.

Barbary Africa is not Africa. Atlas Africa is Mediterranean, not African. Although the Barbary states sit on the northwest corner of the continent, and therefore would appear to be geographically and culturally a part of Africa, they are Mediterranean. Physiographically, also, the Atlas lands are linked with the north for, structurally, the Atlas country is the only area of folded terrain in Africa; it is completely different from any other portion—a part of the great system of folded mountains that continue into Europe, interrupted only by subsidence at Gibraltar and the "waist." More important, Atlas Africa is separated by the great expanse of Sahara from all other parts of the tropical continent. Whereas Egypt has had connections with the south along the Nile waterway since ancient times, and Libya is desert and has always had connections southward, the Barbary states have historically faced the Mediterranean and been separated from contact with the rest of Africa. Ethnically, too, North Africa is Mediterranean for its people, Berbers, Arabs, and Jews, are of non-African derivation.

THE MARE MEDITERRANEAN: ITS IMPORTANCE

The Mediterranean, more than any other inland water body, is characterized by a multiplicity of straits and subsidiary seas—formed by the active subsidence of this intercontinental area. The ancients considered all of these extensions of the Mare Mediterranean as a part of the main water body and pushed their fishing and trading vessels through and into all of them. Of all of these sectors of the Mediterranean, "the Straits" has been perhaps the most critical and recurrently significant.

Since the first civilizations of the Mediterranean grew up, men and nations have sought control of this important midland sea and its strategic water passes and inland extensions. During both World Wars I and II, control of these waters had critical and decisive effects upon military strategies and logistics, and upon the final outcome of the conflicts. During World War I, the Dardanelles Campaign was a failure because tactical difficulties were not well handled, and further operations in the Mediterranean were not given serious consideration until late in the war. When they eventually were resumed as secondary campaigns, they brought the collapse of Bulgaria and the capitulation of Turkey, and these successes were instrumental in accomplishing the surrender of Germany. The first critical clash between the Eastern and Western victors of the last war came in the Mediterranean area—when the Soviet Union sought to take control of Greece.

Although control of the Mediterranean is contingent upon control of the sea, the assertion of naval superiority is not merely a matter of ships. It depends strongly, also, on air bases and harbor facilities.

Maritime states have always turned to naval rather than military build-up to maintain security for their territories and obtain control of certain significant areas. In this strategy, the Mediterranean has played a critical role for the Middle Sea furnishes access to three continents and joins two oceans. Through Gibraltar the Euro–American world of the Atlantic opens up; the Adriatic arm cuts a passage to the Balkans and Central Europe; the Straits of the Dardanelles give access to the rich Ukraine of the USSR and the Danubian countries; and, through the Suez–Red Sea outlet, the shortest approach to East Africa, South and East Asia, and the Pacific islands is afforded. This is the reason why, in all the history of war, the Mediterranean has been an essential center of traffic. At the present time, this inland sea has even more significance than it had in the past, for the Mediterranean is a shortcut and a control center that is indispensable strategically and economically.

Thus, Anglo–American policy, since World War II, has been directed toward blocking the southerly expansion of the Soviets wherever possible. This blockade has taken the form of maintaining naval fleets in the Mediterranean, of establishing air bases and maintaining aircraft in the area, of further developing naval facilities, and, above all, of backing the countries along the Mediterranean, that have been threatened by Russian interference, diplomatically and defensively.

IN RETROSPECT—TO GAIN PERSPECTIVE

Rome ruled over the Mediterranean basin so long as other peoples were prevented from breaking through and settling upon the shores. Eventually this happened—and the Roman Empire became divided into West and East, with Rome ruling in the western Mediterranean, the Byzantine Empire in the eastern.

Religion sundered the unity of the Mediterranean basin. Weakened by the division, Rome was unable to prevent the Moslems from sweeping, in the seventh century, across North Africa, across Gibraltar into Spain, and, in the East, eventually into the Balkans. Penetration across all of southern Europe by Islam was not accomplished, however, and that part of

Europe between Iberia and the Balkans remained Christian. *Thus were the first lines of distinction drawn between the African and European Mediterranean—lines of religion;* and the sea acted like a defensive ditch to segregate the antithetical forces of Christianity and Islam.

With the division of the Mediterranean into two rival commercial and political realms, the "middle sea" never regained the former glory it once held. Mediterranean Africa became, *not* a part of the continent of Africa *but of Moslem Asia*—and for a millenium this has held true.

18 ————————————————————

The Middle East

The Middle East lands radiate outward from Suez in four directions—westward across half of Africa, eastward to the edges of the plateau that looks down upon the Indus Valley, northward to the Taurus ranges of Turkey; and southward across Arabia and half way across the Sahara. They begin beyond the delta of the Nile in Libya and extend almost to India, embracing the vast crescent of lands that includes the countries of Egypt and Libya, Saudi Arabia, Israel, Lebanon, Syria, Jordan, Iraq, Iran, Afghanistan, and a number of sheikdoms. Areally, Turkey is also a part of the Middle East, but, because of its pro-West alignments and affiliation with Europe, it is often regarded as European.

This is a vast region with a population of more than 50 million and an area covering nearly 2.5 million square miles—of deserts and steppes, plateaus and mountains inhabited by nomads and cultivators and city dwellers of many nationalities, people who are largely (though loosely) linked by a common language and religion. The population is predominantly Moslem, Israel and Lebanon excepted. Near the western fringe of the Middle East where three continents meet, Islam and Zionism collide, the rival interests of great Western powers clash, Arab nationalism and even the slightest hint of Western colonialism ride head on, and the world's two power blocs contend for influence. Most of it is within the Arab world.

For countless centuries the Middle East has been a tholepin of history. Across the Middle East lands the Persians extended their empire; across the Fertile Crescent and Iran marched the Macedonian Alexander in his triumphal conquests; much later, across much the same region the German Kaiser of pre-World War I days dreamed of extending German interests by means of the Berlin-to-Baghdad railroad. One of the main passages for the migrations of peoples in the Eastern Hemisphere has been the arid tracts of the Middle East.

As time has spanned the years of many centuries the Middle East has wielded a profound spiritual influence on peoples and history. Here was the cradle of three of mankind's great religions—Judaism, Christianity, and Islam. From the heart of desert Arabia the Moslem armies, under the impulse of Mohammed the Prophet, initiated their conquest of Mesopotamia (Iraq) and Egypt in the seventh century—to spread the faith *by the sword* until, today, the followers of Mohammed are diffused from Gibraltar across North Africa and southern Asia to Pakistan and Indonesia and even beyond. Islam stands at the gateways of communication throughout all of this area—Gibraltar, Suez, the Dardanelles, Bab-el-Mandeb, and the Straits of Malacca—in some instances controlling them. It also dominates the areas in the Middle East that contain more than half of the oil of the world. The strategic value of this oil—added to location—greatly enhances the importance of the Middle East.

Today, the Middle East is the center of Islam, a faith that imposes a distinctive way of life upon its followers. This suggests—and correctly—that the Moslems of the Middle East are linked by tradition, custom, and religion westward with the 20 million Moslems of North Africa and eastward with the more than 150 million Mohammedans of south Asia: in India–Pakistan are some 100 million Moslems; in Indonesia, some 70 million; China contains about 20 million "followers of the faith," and the Philippines number some very militant and virile of Islamic followers; Russia, too, has many. In certain portions of southern Europe isolated fragments of Islam are found, as in the Balkans where the Turks left their stamp; southern Spain, likewise, bears the imprint of the era of Arab dominance—in the Moorish character of the architecture. Throughout the entirety of the Middle East and North Africa, the Arabic language and Moslem traditions are important cultural and political links.

However, national rivalries have hindered these states, in the past, from cohering into a bloc that would permit them to develop their power to its full tremendous potential. United they constitute a formidable group in international politics. The vital strategic passages that they hold (or overlook) could become barriers to communication or roadways for military aggression. The oil constitutes a strategic source of energy upon which the European powers depend not only for fuel for their navies but also for most of the other oil needs. Even within the United Nations the Middle East states wield a power previously little expected. That the Moslem world has not commanded the regard and deference that it might rests upon the fact that the several states within it have not acted in concert. It is divided and, hence, relatively impotent. However, in its renewable oil contracts it holds a weapon of strategy that it uses.

A further weakness lies in the fact that many of the Islamic states are socially decadent and politically petrified. Among a great proportion of the Moslems *tribal rule,* such as prevailed in the days of the Old Testament, still prevails—absolute authority even to the power of life or death. Afghanistan—and native authority in Africa—is still largely tribal with the tribal chiefs paying obeisance to the religious head who also heads the government. Saudi Arabia, Yemen, and other countries on the great desert peninsula, are still *pre-feudal states* governed by ruling practices that reach back several thousand years. In Iran, a democratic Shah finds his hands tied, his innovations in land reform, industrial and communications development and the like largely nullified because of the power of individual tribal chieftains. The social injustice is unmatched in any other part of the world.

IMPORTANCE OF THE MIDDLE EAST

The economic importance of the Middle East stems largely from its petroleum reserves—a source of energy that is vital to the mechanized civilization of the West. The Middle East, itself backward and largely unmechanized, uses little of this fuel.

But important as is oil, perhaps a greater significance derives from the strategic location of the Middle East. At the point of contact of Asia, Africa, and Europe, it is at once a land of transit and a zone of mixing. Despite the air age, the water narrows that traverse its lands are among the world's half dozen critical pas-

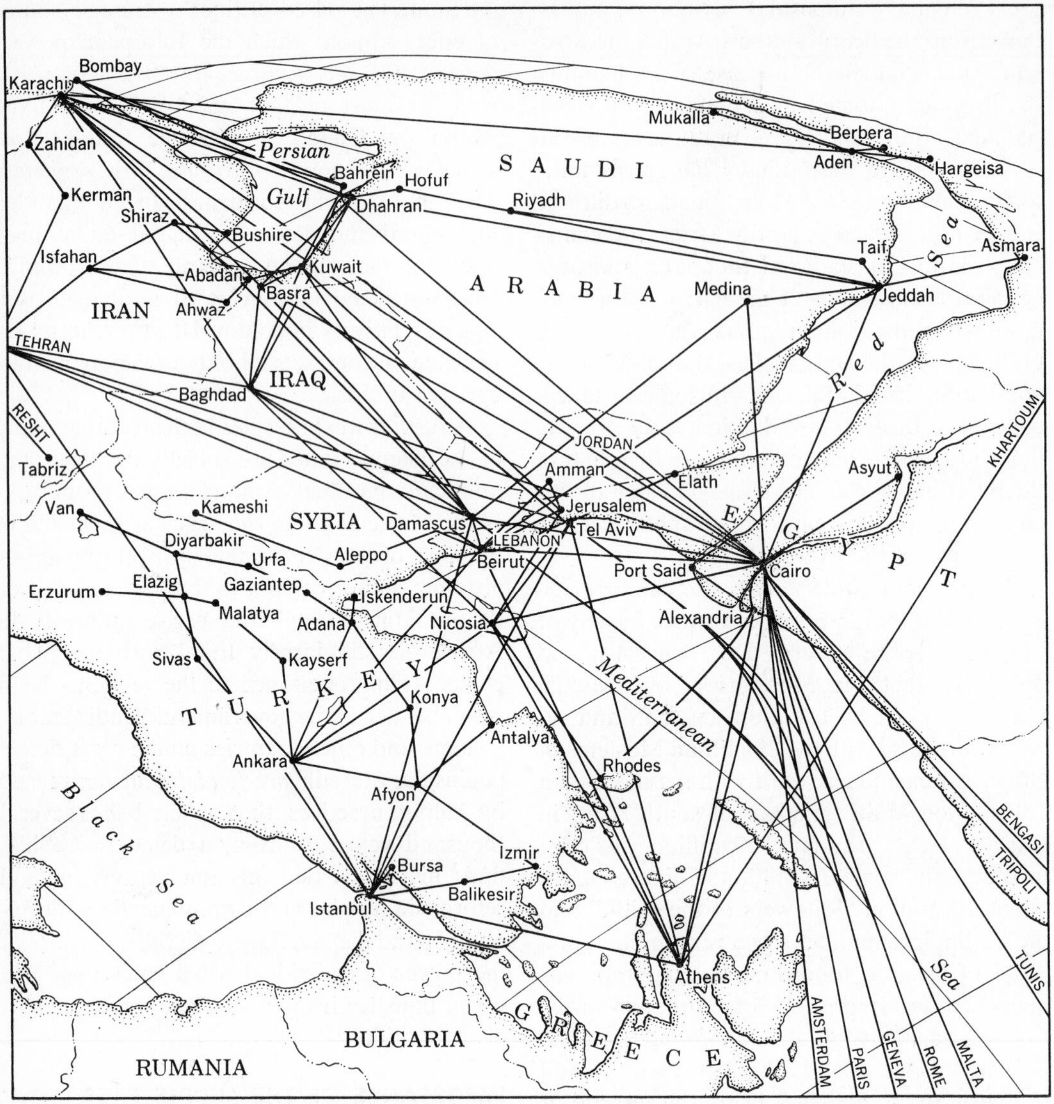

Figure 18.1. The Middle East is focal in the air-transport system of the Afro-Eurasian world. (Courtesy Arabian American Oil Company.)

sages—Suez and the Dardanelles literally control the second most important searoute on the globe, the Mediterranean—Indian Ocean waterway. Its ports supply strategic naval bases; its territories provide equally strategic air fields. It has been said that without the Mediterranean, Europe could not be held; without the Middle East, the Mediterranean could not be held.

MIDDLE EAST UNREST

Marshal Lyautey, pacificator of French Morocco, once said that the extended world of the Moslem was like a "drum": no matter where it is tapped, it resounds all over. This was never more true than in the post-World War II period.

The turbulent restlessness of the Middle East can be traced to a number of factors, but

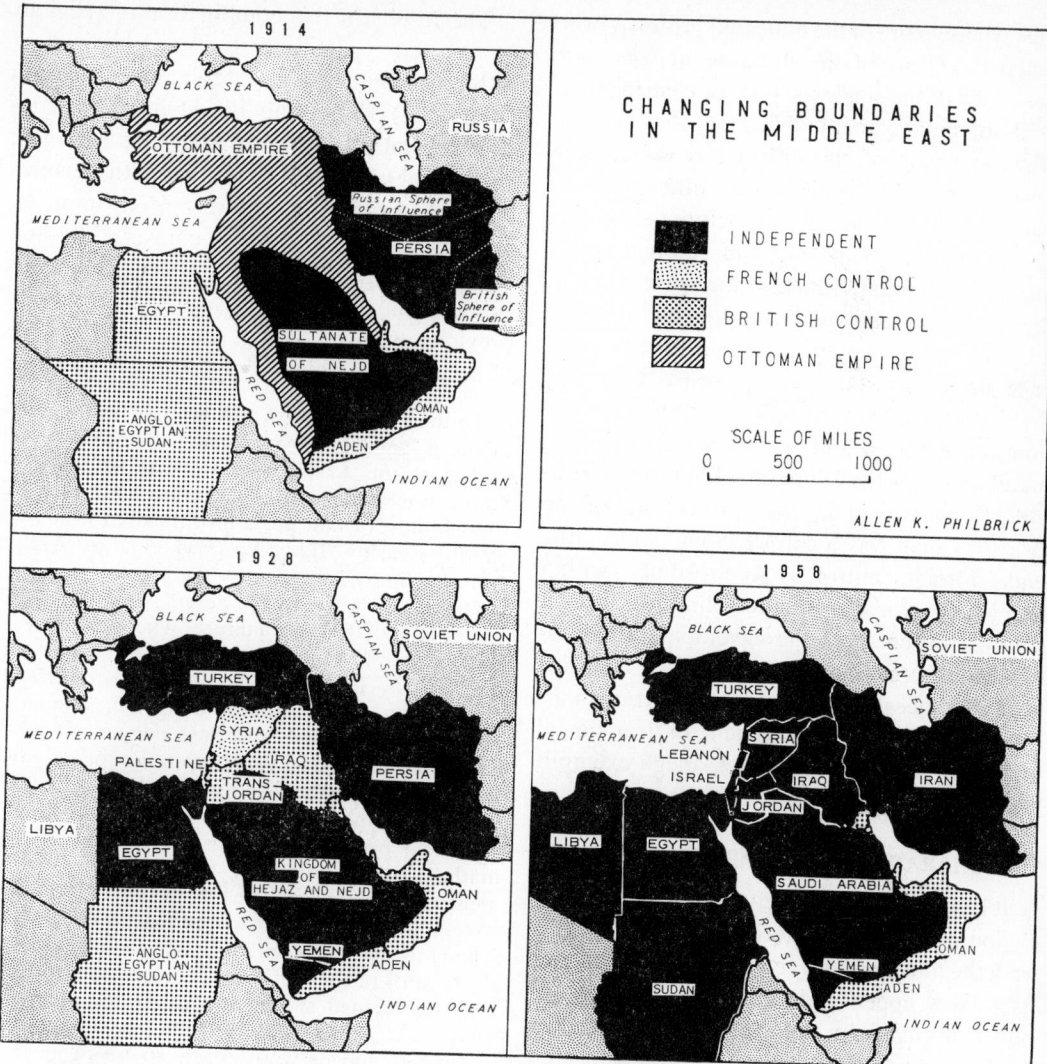

Figure 18.2. Although basic boundaries have not been erased, 1958 saw two new countries form through the federation of already existing states—namely, the formation of the United Arab Republic, initially by Egypt and Syria; and the counterfederation of the two Hashemite kingdoms of Iraq and Jordan into the Arab Federation. The capital of the latter state will alternate between Bagdad and Amman, with King Faisal as head of state. Nasser is to be the president of the United Arab Republic; Cairo, the capital. In February, 1959, Yemen joined the Republic.

the basic answers lie in a compound of history the parts of which are interrelated: first, in the decline of the power of Imperial Britain which, for 200 years had exerted a profound influence upon the affairs of the world and the maintenance of order. The reasons for this recedence of British power are found in the two world wars and the economic crises that have attended Great Britain in the inter- and post-war period.

The second reason lies in the fervent nationalism of the former colonial world which includes the Islamic states. This rise of Arab nationalism is, in part, inherent in the Middle

East where many of the educated groups—who shape the ideas of the illiterate masses—are possessed of the single purpose of clearing their lands of any remnant of foreign domination. However, part of the disquiet is due to the reverberating nationalism from other parts of Islam that have recently (but before the Middle East) been emancipated from colonial status into full sovereignty. Part of the answer lies in the *residue of colonialism*—for all of these areas have been under European rule or influence until yesterday, so to speak. Iran was divided into spheres of influence; Syria, Lebanon, Israel, Iraq, and Jordan were territories mandated after the fall of the old Ottoman Empire; Egypt was under the "protection" of the British; Libya was a colony. Some still writhe under foreign control, as Aden; some—with a repugnance for the slightest hint of foreign control—resent even the development of economic resources by outsiders lest it be some form of concealed colonialism. The Iranian attitude toward the development of Iranian oil under the premiership of Mossadegh exemplified this.

THE CHARACTER AND IMPACT OF ISLAM

It has been appropriately remarked that "the Bedouin is the raw material of Islam." Today, as in the first era of the movement, Islam makes its greatest appeal and receives its greatest support from the poor and illiterate masses of the Arab world—and the wealthy and educated *tend to perpetuate the Moslem way of life in all of its restrictive extremes because of the power that continues to reside in the hands of the latter classes.*

Mohammed addressed his teachings first to the Bedouins of Arabia, but the fervor of the new faith was soon to extend beyond the peripheries of Arabia, a land that was readily converted to Islam. In the indoctrination of other peoples, it was the Bedouin who flourished the sword of the conquering fanatic—inspired by Mohammed's promise that to die in combat for the faith was assurance of a superior paradise. In all likelihood, he coveted the abundance of the Fertile Crescent also.

The results of this combination of religious fervor and violence was the Islamization, within a century after Mohammed's death (632 A.D.), of not only the whole of the Middle East but all of North Africa, as well, *and* the conquest of southern Spain with penetrations into France. During this era of unprecedented expansion the Arabs converted to their faith, language, and even physical characteristics, greater numbers of foreigners than any previous or later group, including even the Greek, Roman, English, and Russian Slav.

To their empire the Arabs brought a religion—Islam; a language—Arabic; and their own blood—that of the Arabs. The Islamization of their realm was pervasive; its Arabization, less so, though most of that portion of the area which we call the Near or Middle East has remained Arabic from the time of conquest to the present.

One thing, however, the desert Arabs could not bring, and that was a culture. Their gift in this respect was to assimilate, not to originate; and their legacy to the world came down through assimilation. They settled among the conquered peoples, intermarried, absorbed elements of other cultures—Persian, Indian, Syrian, Egyptian—and the result was a civilization which at its zenith shone as a light of the mediæval world.

Arabic became the language of learning. In mathematics, astronomy, geography, medicine, alchemy, architecture; in the arts of oration and romantic poetry (always opposed by puritanical Islam) Moslems of many backgrounds became the savants of the world.

Islam reigned supreme, and Arabic as a language conquered also. But the leaders of the empire no longer were Arabs so much as they were mixtures of Persian, Syrian, Egyptian, and other strains. The Arab of the desert had been absorbed and vanquished racially when he settled down, though his religion and language had first conquered the peoples among whom he came. The Arab himself remained pure only in the great bowl of Arabia, inaccessible as always to outside influence.[1]

The Islamic Empire reached the height of its glory under Caliph Harun al-Rashid (786-809 A.D.) of Baghdad. Today little of the brilliance of this Islamic era remains except in such remnants of culture as the architecture—mosques, as the Umayyad Mosque in Damascus, and the

---

[1] Harry B. Ellis, "Battlefield of Empires," *Christian Science Monitor,* November 16, 1954.

Moorish palace of the Alhambra in Granada, Spain; in the widespread prevalence of the Moslem religion, and the almost equally widespread use of the Arabic language. Fabled Baghdad is today (like the other cities, medinas, and casbahs of the Mohammedan World) an agglomeration of mud dwellings surrounded by mud walls.

The reasons for the decline and eventual fall of the Islamic Empire are multiple. Foremost among the causes for the recession was the growing disunity within the empire itself; Islam was reft into several factions. Centers of Islamic control shifted from Arabia (where the faith had its inception—this was more of a religious than a temporal center of power, and so it still remains today) to Damascus (under the great Umayyad dynasty) to Baghdad (under the Caliphate of Harun al-Rashid). The differences and rivalries between religious and political factions continued to widen, particularly between the Shiite and Sunni Moslems, a division growing out of caliphate succession and marked by ravage and killing. These two factions remain the two powerful and rival sects of Islam today. The Shiites are the followers of Ali, the cousin and son-in-law of Mohammed.

Thus, the structure of empire fell apart, and, in its place, there arose a number of dynasties representing areas that had formerly been provinces of the Islamic Empire. The invasion of the Middle East by the Christian Crusaders and by the hordes of the Mongol Genghis Khan furthered the dissolution of the empire. To the present day the power of the Arab has never been recovered, but it was written that the religious faith he professed should triumph over the conquerors. Both the Seljuk Turks and the Mongols (in the eleventh and thirteenth centuries respectively) attempted to demolish the power of the Mohammedan caliphs; instead, they came to accept the teachings of Islam and to champion the faith.

Under the Ottoman Empire of the Turks, Islam again overran and conquered all of the Middle East, North Africa, and much of southern Europe. Suleiman the Magnificent (1520-1566 A.D.), with his empire centered on the Bosporus at Constantinople, ruled over a domain that spread from the Hungarian Basin and the Russian Crimea to Mesopotamia and around the south Mediterranean to include North Africa. Later, portions of the Caucasus, Persia, and the Arabian Peninsula also fell to the Turks.

For about four centuries the Arabs were prostrate under the Moslem Turks "whom they had Islamized" and the predominately Arab Middle East was a Turkish realm. Not until the beginning of the nineteenth century did the Arabs begin to stir, and only in the post-World War II period has nationalism become a strident cry.[2]

RESOURCES OF THE MIDDLE EAST

Since Biblical times, the Middle East has been a crossroads of the strategy and commerce of the world as well as being an important center for the *diffusion of learning and religion*. In modern times, the region has assumed a new significance as a focal area of sea, land, and air traffic and economic activity.

The whole of the Middle East is essentially a vast desert interspersed with fertile oases that are intensively cultivated. Rivers have given rise to the largest of these oases—as Mesopotamia ("land between the rivers") in Iraq and the Nile oasis. Some coastal littorals are also in the nature of oases—as coastal Israel, Lebanon, and Syria, and certain sections of Libya in Cyrenaica and Tripolitania. Here, however, cultivation is not entirely dependent upon irrigation (as in true oases) but is also possible in the winter when Mediterranean lands are under the influence of the shifting Westerlies which bring rain.

Because of the vast areas of arid and semiarid land, a large proportion of the population are engaged in a nomadic pastoralism. Such nomadic herdsmen are known in the Middle

[2] This section on the *Character and Impact of Islam* has been drawn very largely from the writings of Harry B. Ellis, a Christian Science Monitor correspondent who has travelled in and written extensively on Arabia in recent months.

East as Bedouins. In all of these countries there are sharp differences in outlook—and usually deep-seated and inherent antagonisms—between the sedentary oases dwellers and the Bedouin nomads. Not until the nineteenth century was any one ruler in any territory able to impose centralized control over both the Bedouin and the oases dwellers. That ruler was Mohammed Ali of Egypt.

Britain has been the most powerful of the European powers in the Middle East. British modern interest in this area goes back to the days of its early trade with India in the eighteenth century. With the settlement of Australia and New Zealand and the development of commercial interests in the East during the nineteenth century, it became vital to Britain to defend the Middle East as a part of the lifeline of supply and communication for the Empire.

The strategic importance to the West of the Middle East has already been pointed out. It lies in four main factors: the Suez Canal, which shortens searoutes by thousands of miles; the military bases in the area—especially naval and air; the oil supplies; and the commercial airports which are fundamental links in the routes to the Far East, South Africa, and Australia. Economically, the importance of the Middle East lies in oil reserves, in the chemical products of the Dead Sea, and in the commercial produce of the oases (notably Egyptian cotton and, to a lesser degree, dates).

The Oil of the Middle East

No natural resource is as involved in international affairs as is oil. In the Middle East, oil is intricately entangled with many of the problems that perplex Western diplomats. Over 60 per cent of the petroleum reserves of the world are estimated to be in the area. (By comparison, the United States has possibly 25 per cent of the world's oil, South America about 10 per cent, and the Soviet Union 6 per cent.) However, of the total world production, the Middle East produces only 18 per cent as yet, whereas the United States accounts for but slightly less than 50 per cent of the present

total—a very disproportionate amount in view of the distribution of known reserves. However, Middle Eastern production is steadily mounting; in the past five years Middle East output nearly doubled, causing a relative decline in the production of the United States.

The oil basin lies all around the Persian Gulf—in Iran, Iraq, Kuwait, and Arabia, extending into Israel and Egypt (in smaller amounts).

The Iranian output up to 1951 was the largest in the Middle East. Production of Persian oil began in 1911. At the outbreak of World War I, the British government obtained controlling interest in the Anglo–Iranian Oil Company in order to assure a supply of oil for its Navy. During the four-year period of the war, production expanded rapidly as it did also in the inter-war period that followed; at the Iranian port of Abadan the Anglo–Iranian Oil Company had erected the world's largest oil refinery. The largest single source of revenue of the Government of Iran came from oil royalties which, in 1949, amounted to 54 million dollars. Dissatisfaction over the royalty rate, and rising nationalism—that, in Iran, expressed itself in anti-British sentiment—led Iran to nationalize its oil industry in April, 1951. Nationalization eventually shut down practically every aspect of the oil industry for, with the expulsion of British technicians, there were no trained personnel to supervise its functioning. Thus, for four years (from 1951 to 1955) nothing but storage supplies of Iranian oil reached the world market; nationalization threatened to deprive Great Britain and Western Europe of its most important source of this vital fuel. How to meet this sudden decline in oil became an immediate problem. It was done by pushing production in the other Mid-Eastern fields, and the slack was picked up.

With the unseating of Mossadegh as Premier, concessions for the development of the oil industry were given over to eight foreign companies (in 1955) who were to serve as *operators* of the industry and buy oil from Iran for sale elsewhere. British, Dutch, French, and

American companies[3] are participating in this enterprise. But, whereas Iranian production formerly led in the Middle East, today it ranks fourth exceeded by Kuwait, Saudi Arabia, and Iraq.

The northernmost of the oil-producing structures of the Middle East are those of Iraq. Kirkuk lies at the center of this oil basin, a field that extends northward to Mosul and south to Palkana. Kirkuk—with its large reserves, its refinery, and as one terminus of the pipelines that run the oil to the Mediterranean ports in Syria, Lebanon, and Israel—is the core of Iraq's large oil industry. In 1953, surpassing the 100-million ton mark, Iraq became the world's sixth largest producer.

The development of Iraq oil is largely in the hands of the Iraq Petroleum Company. Under British management, it operates on behalf of an international group. The Anglo–Iranian Oil Company, Royal Dutch Shell, the Near East Development Corporation, and the Compagnie Françaises des Petroles each holds a 23.75 per cent interest. The Near Eastern Development Corporation is controlled equally by Standard Oil of New Jersey and Socony Vacuum, and a small number of the Iraq Petroleum Company's shares (five per cent) are in private hands.

The technical problems of production and transport of the large quantities of oil from Kirkuk have now been largely solved. Two pipelines, with an annual capacity of eight million tons, terminate at the Lebanese port of Tripoli; a new 30-inch pipeline, completed in 1952, terminates at Baniyas, Syria. It has an annual capacity for transporting 14 million tons of oil. Another pipeline runs to Haifa, Israel, but it is idle as a result of the Israeli–Arab conflict.

The proven oil reserves of Iraq are almost as great as those of Arabia but, until a new royalty agreement was drawn up and signed in 1951, production was hardly one-third as great.

[3] Companies represented are Anglo–Iranian Oil, Royal Dutch Shell, Compagnie Françaises des Petroles, Standard Oil of New Jersey, Standard Oil of California, Socony Vacuum, Gulf Oil, and the Texas Company. (53 per cent of Anglo–Iranian Oil belongs to the British Government.)

The new agreement stipulated an annual increase of royalties to the Iraqi Government from 15 million pounds sterling in 1951 to 59 million in 1955. This of course speeded production by the company.

Arabian oil is an American development. The right to develop oil on a royalty basis from the eastern portion of the country of Saudi Arabia was granted to Americans, in 1933, by King Ibn Saud. In September of that year the first group of American oil surveyors began explorations under a contract signed four months previously. Operations began in the Damman Dome and the first wildcat well came in in 1935; but not until three years later was a really important oil strike made. From then on, however, developments under the Arabian–American Oil Company (Aramco, a subsidiary of the Standard Oil Company) have boomed. The concessions today include a string of nine proven fields that lie scattered for 280 miles along or near the eastern coast of the peninsula. Explorations are constantly being carried on, and the chances of finding new fields are held to be very good. A promising region, as yet unprospected, is the Rub'al Khali (translated Empty Quarter), a desolate area of sand desert located in the southern part of Saudi Arabia, in size, almost as large as Texas.

Arabian production averages about one million barrels of crude oil daily, but this output is not considered indicative of the potential that is suspected. Production has been held down because of a shortage of refineries and construction materials for added installations. The Abqaiq field is the most important at present, accounting for more than half of the Arabian production. Single wells there produce the phenomenal amount of 10 to 15,000 barrels of oil daily. (An output of 5,000 barrels is usual.) Ain Dar, to the southwest, is the next larger producer.

Dhahran is the "nerve center" of the Arabian oil industry and is the headquarters for the oil company. However, the refineries are at Ras Tanura on the coast through which oil goes out by tanker. A pipeline, completed in December, 1950 and sending oil from the Arabian fields

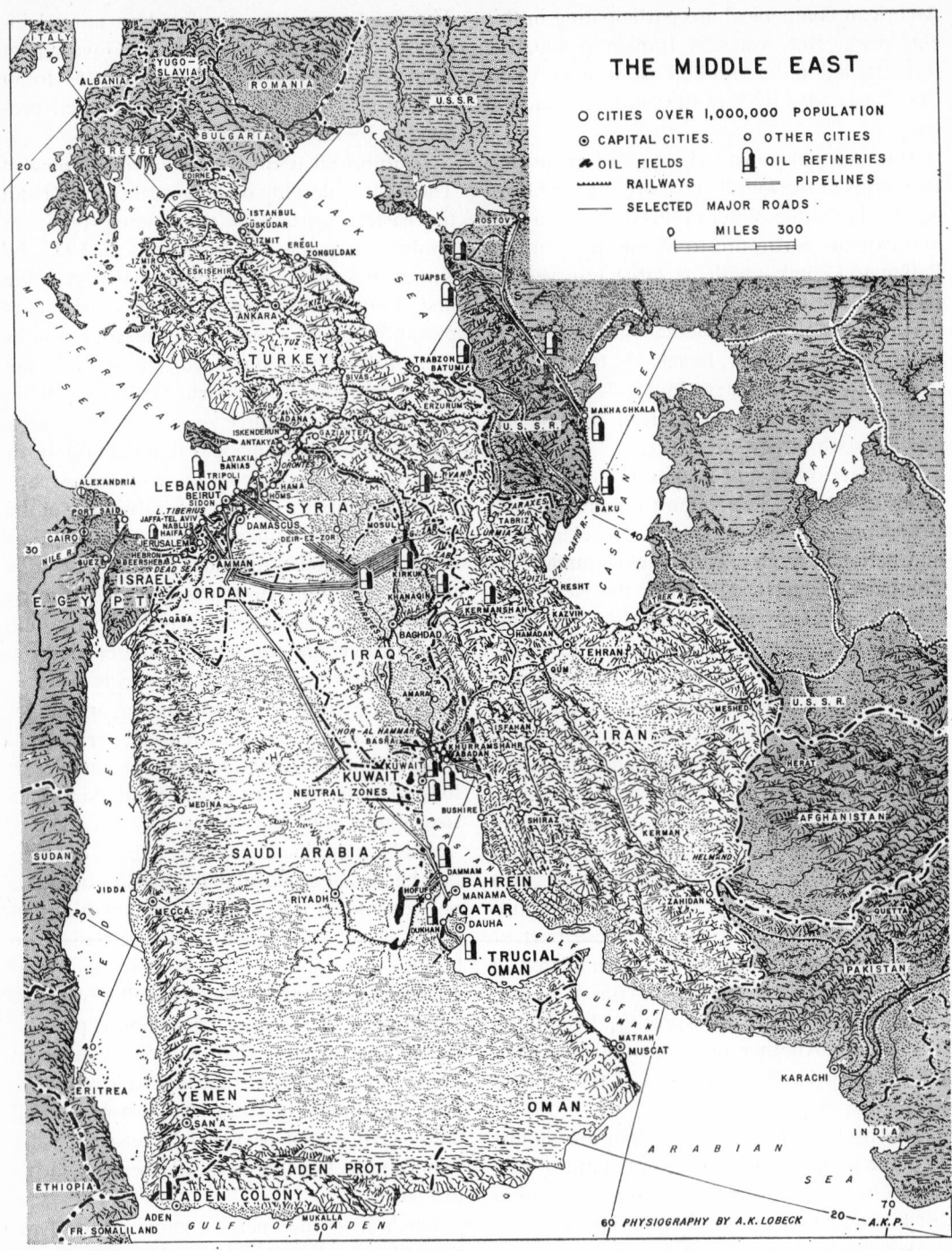

Figure 18.3. Physiography, surface transportation, and oil facilities of the Middle East. Note the way in which cities and transportation lines follow the base of mountains, string along the intermontane valleys or, in the case of truck and railroad routes, stretch between places where water is available. This is the typical pattern of population settlement and movement in arid lands.

across 1200 miles of desert to Port Sidon in Lebanon, on the Mediterranean, eliminated the 3,000 mile trip via the Persian Gulf, Red Sea, and Suez Canal by tanker. It has a capacity of over 300,000 barrels of oil daily. Pipelines also carry the oil from the fields to the refineries at Ras Tanura and Bahrein Island.

Politically under Britain, the oil of the Bahrein Islands is exploited largely by American interests. The Bahreins (five small islands in the Persian Gulf offshore from Dhahran) and Kuwait are smaller areas in the Persian Gulf area that have attracted the Western nations because of their oil reserves. Long ago the Bahrein Islands were under the suzerainty of Iran, but after 1880 they were ruled by Arab sheiks who, under an agreement with Britain, placed them in the protective custody of the British. The main island, only 25 miles long by 10 miles wide, is one of the smallest rich spots on earth—famed formerly for its pearls, now for oil. The whole of the island is (in the words of geologists) an elongated oil dome. Production averages about 11 million barrels annually.

Kuwait is thought to have the single largest oil reserve in the world. Kuwait, a tiny sheikdom in the extreme northeast of the Arabian peninsula—a territory less than 2000 square miles in area inhabited by less than 125,000 people—is the locale of another of the oil rich reserves of the Middle East. Estimates place the Kuwait reserves at 11 billion barrels. It is a comparatively new field, discovered only in 1938; but in 1951 this tiny area was producing 205 million barrels of oil. The Kuwait Oil Company (owned equally by an Anglo–Iranian subsidiary and Gulf Exploration Company of the United States) is the third largest of the oil-producing giants of the Middle East. By itself, it was the fifth largest producer in the world in 1951, exceeded only by the United States, Venezuela, the USSR, and Saudi Arabia.

Oil places in the hands of the Arab nations a tremendous geopolitical weapon with which to wield power. The significance of the Middle East oil reserves is found not only in their own tremendous potential (estimated at about three-fourths of the world's) but also in the rapid increase in production relative to the output of other areas. So significant are the reserves that Middle East diplomacy is almost synonymous with oil diplomacy. That the Arabs realize they hold a powerful weapon is evidenced in the increasingly larger royalty demands that they make—and get—from the foreign concessionaires. Oil has meant *revenue,* and can mean increasing prosperity and social betterment in all of the countries concerned if the royalties are well used. The trouble is—and it spells *trouble*—that the wealth has rolled into the coffers of the rulers and, except in Iraq and Kuwait, little has been used to improve the condition of the masses.

Britain and the United States have the most important interests in this area—the United States in Saudi Arabia, Britain in Iran and Kuwait; France is only a minor investor in Middle East oil. The British and French investments are government controlled (Anglo–Iranian Oil and the Compagnie Françaises des Petroles) while the American are private.

STRATEGIC CONCERNS

The strategic factors of the Middle East—oil and location—have been pointed out as well as the potential power that this region holds for both the West and Communist Blocs. These lands lie to the south of Moscow, to the south of the Black and Caspian Seas—lands of deserts and hills that hide oceans of oil. Beyond the Mediterranean and centrally located near the western side of the Arabian Peninsula are Mecca and Medina, holy cities of the Moslems, the former the religious capital of Islam. Closely adjacent are Suez and the Red Sea, for more than eight decades passageways that represented European sway and power in the Middle East. Russia, from the first attempts under Peter the Great, has never been able to penetrate this ring of Western influence and control.

A résumé of the British position of influence in the Middle East is perhaps appropriate at this point. In 1914 the Middle East was still almost wholly under Ottoman rule. Prior to

1914, British policy aimed at the neutralization of the whole area between the Dardanelles and the Persian Gulf in order to ensure the security of India. For this reason Britain took a leading part in the coalitions of Powers that defeated the attempts of Napoleonic France and Czarist Russia to dominate the area.

France had established close connections with the Middle East in the second half of the nineteenth century, and had been interested from much earlier times in the Christian communities in Lebanon and the Holy Places. As early as 1888, the international importance of the Suez Canal had been recognized in the Suez Canal Convention of December 22 (signed by Austria–Hungary, France, Germany, Great Britain, Italy, the Netherlands, Russia, Spain, and Turkey). Articles VIII and IX made the defense of the Suez a special concern of all the signatory Powers, who were to advise and consult with Egypt (or, failing Egypt, Turkey) on the measures which were needed to maintain the freedom and security of navigation of the Canal. Article XIV stated that these obligations were not limited to the period of validity of the Suez Canal Company's concessions.

Up to 1914, Britain had special relationships only with the fringes of the Middle East. Cyprus was occupied by Britain at the time of a serious Russian threat to the integrity of the Ottoman Empire; the port of Aden was occupied as a counter to Napoleon's aggressive ambitions and to secure the sea communications with India; Egypt was occupied in 1882 in order to suppress a rebellion against the Khedive and to stop the killing of Europeans. The latter occupation was continued until 1922 for the purpose of ensuring the neutrality of Egypt and the freedom of the Suez Canal in the face of, firstly, French and, later, German threats to the area. In the Persian Gulf the strong and long established British influence had been instrumental, through a series of treaties with the coastal Sheikdoms,[4] in virtually ridding the area of piracy and the slave trade, and had supported the Sheiks of Kuwait

and Mohammerah, at the head of the Gulf, in maintaining their independence against the claims of the Ottomans (supported by Germany) and the Persians.

As pointed out, with the waning of British power, the United States has participated more and more actively in the affairs of the Mediterranean and the Middle East in support of the continuance of the "policy of neutralization" of the whole area that had, up to 1914, been almost the sole responsibility of the British. The invention of the airplane—and the concomitant involvement of all parts of the globe in almost any international troubles regardless of how localized—*and* the extensive American oil interests in the Middle East undoubtedly influenced the American participation.

PROBLEMS OF THE MIDDLE EAST

Since before the days of Moses, land distribution has been one of the recurrent problems of the Middle East. One attempt to resolve this difficulty is found in the Old Testament, in the 25th Chapter of Leviticus, where Moses ordered that every 50th year be a "year of Jubilee" when bonded servants should be freed and land, sold under the duress of economic hardship, should be returned to the former owners or their families.

The land problem is particularly acute in an area of desert, such as the Middle East, where *the availability of water is the one critical factor that determines the usability of the land.* New land distribution regulations and new land distribution programs could bring needed economic relief to the peasants, a large proportion of whom are landless and barely subsist under conditions of dire poverty. Only a few of the Moslem states have initiated such programs, however; Egypt, Iran, Syria, and Iraq have made the most forceful attacks on this prevalent condition. Under the military government in Egypt, the breaking up of Egypt's great landed estates is probably the greatest economic change that has occurred in the Valley of the Nile in a millenium and more.

Poverty and illiteracy are two other enigmas but they are largely concomitants of

---

[4] In particular the General Treaty of Peace concluded in 1820.

other more basic problems. Among the latter are, first, the archaic social and political restrictions of the Islamic religion many of which (as the veiling of women) were unknown in Mohammed's day. A whole series of "evils" attends some of these hard held customs. Secondly, there is the economic backwardness of the Arab lands, including an almost complete lack of development of any of the natural resources other than land for agricultural and pastoral purposes.

Jewish–Arab antipathy is another vexious problem. This too reaches back to the dawn of recorded history. Both groups are Semitic; both, in the distant past, were pastoral. Abraham, a nomadic pastoralist of Ur in Chaldea, led a band of his people into the "promised land" and usurped the grazing grounds of other pastoral nomadic peoples. In time, many of the Jews became sedentary. From earliest times an antipathy has existed between the cultivator and the pastoralist; from the time when these two ways of life began to exist side by side, the pastoralist has regarded the sedentary inhabitant as an encroacher on his rightful grazing lands, and has, consequently, preyed upon him. The antipathy is a natural one, for the pastoral nomad is destructive of the natural landscape (of the vegetation and, hence, of the soil itself through erosion) whereas the cultivator preserves and builds.[5] As a whole, the Middle East —and Atlas North Africa—were, in the past, covered with a much more lush vegetation; the early *Arab,* nomad and predator on man, beast, and vegetation, literally laid waste the land. Much bitterness is still expressed in the Barbary lands over the wanton destruction of the natural flora by these invaders.

The Israeli dispossession of the Arabs— after the latter had fled their Palestine homes in 1948 at the setting up of the "homeland" for Jews—and the influx of Jews from all parts of the world to fill the lands that had shortly before been Arab, intensified the antagonism of the two groups into feelings of hate and bitterness. Since 1948, Jewish–Arab animosity has been the Middle East's most immediate problem, and the homeless Arab refugee its embittered manifestation.

Religious beliefs undoubtedly accentuated tribal and cultivator-pastoralist hostilities; although both peoples are monotheistic, in other aspects the religions are quite antithetical in the tenets of conduct to which they hold. Further, for centuries in Arab lands under Moslem rule, the Jew has suffered unremittingly.

It is not easy to analyze completely the reasons underlying Jewish–Arab antagonisms. They are multiple, and it is to be doubted that any political solution between Israel and the Arab states will remove all of the deeply ingrained antipathy. It is there—and it must be faced and dealt with as best it can.

Lack of capital is still a problem in many parts of the Middle East. In those countries rich in oil, if royalties were rightly used, this condition would not obtain. But, aside from oil, most of the Middle East is poor in resources.

Water is the most apparent and persistent problem of all. Water (or the lack of water) in this sun bathed desert or near desert spells the difference between life-giving productivity or arid wasteland. Nature imposes rigid limitations, and hence, geographic conditions are at the base of many of the international disputes. Many clashes arise over the waters of rivers.

Where water is available, the question is: How can available water resources be developed and properly used for increased production? Equally important—and at the same time something of an anomaly—is the control of floods and the draining of swampy lands in this arid country. And, along the same thought, how can water be stored for irrigating the vast areas of *potentially rich farm land*—that awaits only water to produce? Lastly, how can water resources be efficiently used for the creation of power for industry?

Further problems that confront the Middle East are the settlement of the nomadic tribes— now that modern civilization is moving in. How

---

[5] This antipathy was marked and violent in the American early West; recall the rivalry between the ranchers and the "nesters."

can the peasants be trained to make the most effective use of the cultivated land?

THE ARAB LEAGUE

For a decade the political power of the Middle East has resided to a degree in the Arab League, a loose alliance of eight countries—Egypt, Iraq, Jordan, Lebanon, Libya, Saudi Arabia, Syria, and Yemen. These states are linked by three factors: a common religion, Arab nationalism, and, most strongly, opposition to the new Israeli state. These ties have endured the acrid dynastic rivalries among these states and the vying ambitions and discord over many issues. Although the League has made a great pretense of power, its influence is actually minor.

The Arab League was conceived, in 1944, by Egypt and became an actuality under the initiative of the British who at that time controlled six of the charter member states. Britain was hopeful that it would serve as a useful instrument of British influence. It was this for a short time after the signing of its charter in 1945; however, it has been used largely as a means through which Cairo has gained Middle East support for its foreign policy.

According to Doty,[6] although the charter states had the objective of coordinating the political, economic, social, and cultural activities of the member nations, the League's actual accomplishments "have been kept to a minimum by the provision that all binding decisions must be approved unanimously." The membership itself is so disparate as to make unanimity virtually impossible except in the most noncontroversial resolutions. Most apparent discordances are found between Lebanon and the other nations—Lebanon being half-Christian and very Westernized, and between Saudi Arabia and Yemen *and* the rest of the states—the two former being "absolute monarchies in a purely Asian Islamic pattern," the rest, somewhat more liberal. Further dividing the membership into camps has been the ambition of

Iraq to federate with Syria, Lebanon, and Jordan in the formation of a large and potentially quite powerful Middle East state. Such a coalition was vigorously opposed by both Saudi Arabia and Egypt—Egypt fearing a political rival in the Levant, Saudia Arabia opposing it because of the long standing feud between the royal families of Saudi Arabia and the Hashemite line of Jordan and Iraq.

Of the ties, perhaps stronger than either religion or nationalism, is the common feeling of resentment against the establishment of Israel as a Jewish state. Under Abdel Rahman Azzam Pasha of Egypt (first Secretary General of the League), the Arab League became the center of opposition efforts to deter the establishment of the Jewish state. When diplomatic efforts failed to stop it, the League made attempts to raise a coordinated army of the Arab states to take military action. This too was relatively unsuccessful, and the failures led to acrimonious accusations against each other. However, anti-Israeli sentiment has remained a common bond among the Arab League states, if only for limited periods and for limited action.

Since the signing of the Charter a decade ago a number of alliances, compounded by League member states with non-member nations—agreements that in two instances, at least, have stepped beyond the Arab–Moslem line—have further fractured the shaky unity of the Arab League. The latest such defense alliance (and reinforcing the former alliances) is the Middle East Treaty Organization (METO) signed in November, 1955, between Iran, Iraq, Turkey, Pakistan, and Great Britain. This pact, which links four of the largest and potentially strongest Moslem countries with the West, is opposed not only by the other Arab nations but by the USSR as well. The Arab League states looked upon this Iraqi move as treason to the Arab cause; the USSR, recognizing it for what it was —a defense line to block any Russian moves toward the south—registered not only diplomatic protests but threats of possible recrimination against Iran as well. (The Soviet threat against Iran was based on an old treaty signed

---

[6] Summarized from the Robert C. Doty analyses of Arab League activities, Sunday editions of *The New York Times,* January 23 and 30, 1955.

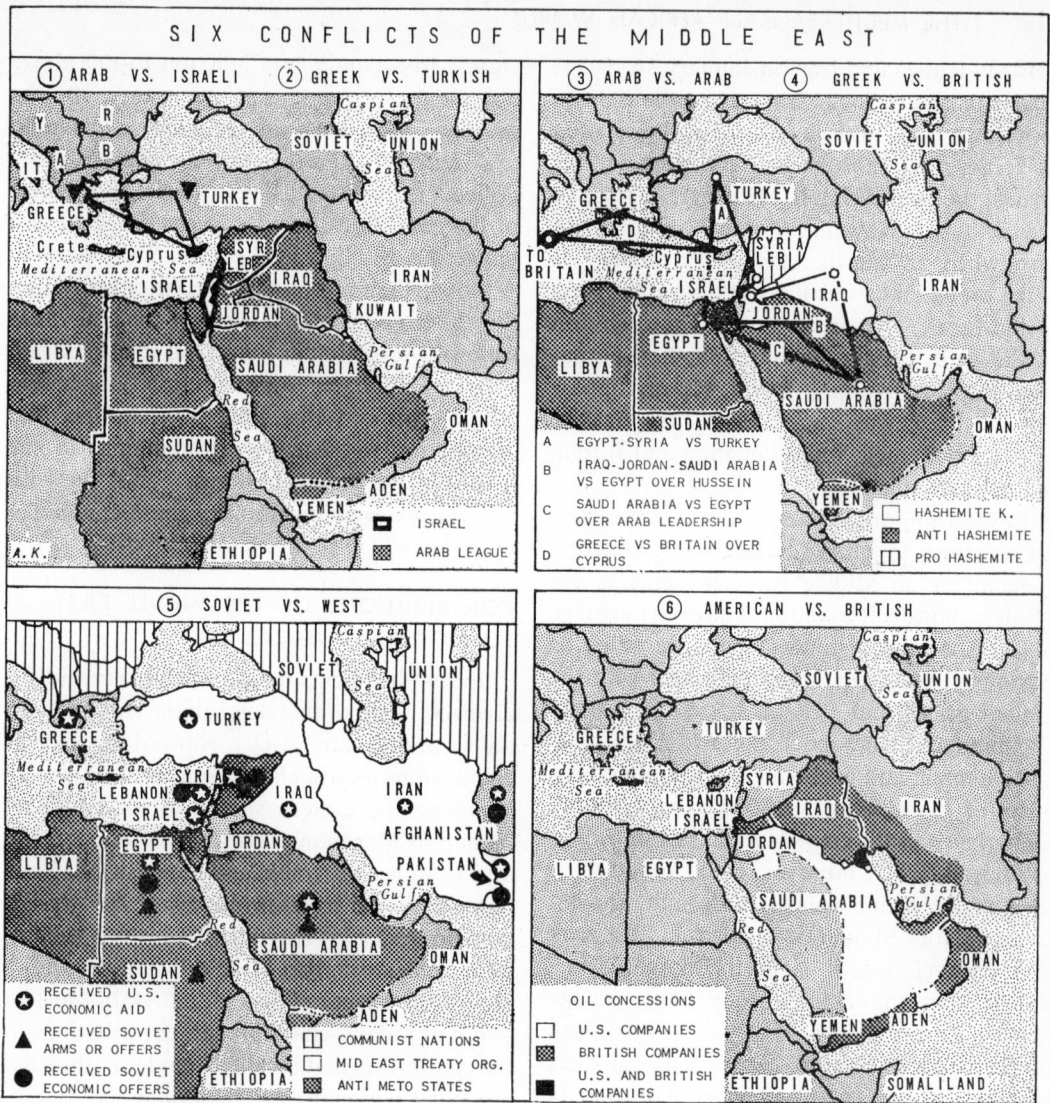

Figure 18.4. The Middle East is a zone of pressures and contention. Six major conflicts are to be discerned, but within some of these conflicts are inner strivings that further complicate the situation. Basic and seemingly irreversible is the hostility of Arab to Israeli; only slightly less, that of the Greek to Turk. Within the Arab World, where one might logically expect unity to exist, discord marshals the states into a near-confusion of alignments, re- and cross-alignments. Within the pro- and anti-Hashemite conflict, which very basically aligns the countries as indicated above, are the following cross-conflicts: a) between Egypt and Arabia for Arab leadership; b) the Arabian-Iraq backing of Jordan over Hussein; c) Syria-Egypt first, against Turkey and, more lately, joining forces in the United Arab Republic; d) the move, by Iraq and Jordan, to unite as a counter to the new political alignment headed by Nasser. Within the Greek-Turkish antipathy, which is historic and today finding expression in the trouble over Cyprus, there is also the conflict between the Greeks and British—NATO allies—over the same island. The struggle between the Soviets and the West is likewise basic, but that between American and British economic interests runs counter, as is the case with the conflicts within the Arab League, to connate attachments. So many are the cross-currents that run through the Arab World that, like the borders that divide these political states, conditions are fluid and subject to quick and unpredictable change.

between Russia and Iran on January 16, 1921. Under that pact Soviet troops had the right to move into Iran "in the event of Iran being used as a base for hostile military preparations against the Soviet Union." However, a rider to the treaty stipulates that Moscow has this right only when a "considerable armed attack" is being prepared by members of a loyalist group to the former Czarist regime.) The desertion of the Arab League by Iraq split League nations into two groups—Egypt, bitterly opposing the Pact, was backed by Saudi Arabia, Syria, and Yemen, while Lebanon and Jordan did not take sides.

How strong are the actual ties that bind the METO states together? Religion is a cohering element for all Middle Eastern members are Moslem; however, traditions and even language differ. The most significant bond, however, is obviously the desire, commonly held with the United States and Britain, to try to contain Communism. How much the Soviet offensive —diplomatic and economic—has nullified the effect of the alliance cannot yet be assessed. Only time and the course of events can prophesy this. METO, however, could never serve as a really strong defense line militarily because the four Middle Eastern powers are weak and undeveloped; it is in the psychological impact that the alliance may have, in the Middle East, that it is regarded as important by the Western powers. Nor can this alliance be taken to signify any great modification in the attitude of Middle Eastern neutrality—so far it can only be taken as, *perhaps, a wavering* in neutrality. There are forces here that are antipodal to both Communism *and* the West, and the natural and expected role is one of neutrality;—or, at the most, participation in the defense plans of the West because of the economic and defense benefits directly derived therefrom. The participation of the British in the Pact was an attempt to increase security and stability in the Middle East. Iran and Iraq have vacillated from pro-West to strongly anti-West sentiments several times in the half decade.

Neutrality is difficult for the Middle East states. In seeming contradiction to the above statement regarding the neutrality of the Middle East states, *oil, geographic location, and Arab–Israeli antagonisms make neutrality difficult* to maintain; the strategic importance of the geopolitical factors places this area in a dangerous position in the East–West conflict. Although their logical stand is one of neutrality, they have neither the power nor the coherence sufficient to maintain this stand if challenged. (*History* militates against close association with European states, while Moslem doctrines are opposed to the tenets of communism. Some question the latter, however; and, as with METO, exigency could alter these traditional attitudes.)

CONTRIBUTIONS OF THE MIDDLE EAST TO MODERN CIVILIZATION

Early Phoenician maps, which portrayed the civilized world of that day (about 1600 B.C. to the second century A.D.), showed the ancient civilizations as stretching from the Nile Valley up along the eastern shores of the Mediterranean to Macedonia and eastward across the arid stretches of Arabia and the oasis of Mesopotamia to the farthest reaches of the Persian domain in distant Kashmir. As history has unfolded the story, this Middle Eastern world— almost the exact outlines of the Arab–Moslem world of today—made greater contributions to the civilization that is called "modern" than did any other region in any era of time.

Many ethnic groups had intermingled here since the earliest of the nomadic pastoralists settled in Mesopotamia to cultivate the land in sedentary fashion and evolve a *civilized culture*. One group overpowered another for control of the fertile valley, and each in turn left a rich cultural heritage to the culture that took its place. Persian astronomers sought the heavens for answers to their questions, and Egyptian engineers erected the tombs of the Pharaohs; the sculptors of Assyria carved friezes on their temples—friezes that were to leave in stone a perpetual record of the history of its peoples and religion—while the mathematicians of Sumeria evolved a system for telling time by minutes and hours; in Babylonia the cuneiform script was "laying the foundation for the modern alphabet, and Hebrew writers were recording the ancient prophecies, made by word of mouth, for the "children of Israel."[7]

At the base of these civilizations—*sedentary* as opposed to the migratory way of life of the primitive nomadic pastoralists—was the cultivator, who tilled the soil and depended upon it for all the sustenance of his living.

His life and religion were bound by the soil, and to insure prosperity he made libations to the gods of fertility and observed the rites of spring. His lands prospered and his husbandry developed wheat, barley, oats, cotton, and alfalfa. Choice fruits—nuts, figs, olives, and dates—originated in his orchards. He bred swift Arabian horses and camels and fine sheep. He cultivated rare oranges from the Orient that were introduced to him through the western world. He used methods of cultivation that have survived the centuries.

From their home port of Beirut, Phoenician ships handled the commerce of the world, carrying the cedar of Lebanon and the spices of Arabia to the Greek city-states and sailing west to the edge of the Mediterranean for tin from the mines of Spain. Oils and wines from Israel were sold in the marketplaces of Tyre and Egyptian produce found buyers in Carthage.

Two thousand years have altered this world. Erosion, dust storms, and constant cultivation have swept away the topsoil and robbed the land of its fertility. As agricultural productivity waned, the centers of trade moved westward to Europe. The Middle East slipped gradually into decline.[8]

The plunder and destruction of the Mongols further despoiled the land until once fertile areas were left near wastelands.

The desiccating work of nature and man, combined with the rigidity of the social system imposed when the Islamic faith became prevalent, caused the whole of the Middle East to lapse into sterility. Only now, as the bonds of subjection by foreign powers are being released and modern ideas seep—or sweep—in, is the area beginning to emerge. Its renascence is an almost terrifying phenomenon—and yet, it should be thrilling for all through the Middle

East (and extending westward through North Africa even to the Atlantic) the shackles of the past are being burst.

EGYPT

Egypt is more Middle Eastern than African. Due to the land link with Asia at Suez and the divisive deserts that lie around the African three-quarters of its borders, Egypt has, in a sense, been more a part of the Middle East than of Africa. Here, in the valley of the Nile, was nurtured one of the world's great civilizations that, with other Middle East cultures of the Ancients, mothered the later civilizations of the Mediterranean. It will be recalled that when Mediterranean culture came to represent world culture, not only one shore or two shores but the entire periphery of the Mediterranean was involved and there was no distinction made between the northern and southern littorals. During this early period of Mediterranean control, when Egypt, Phoenicia, Greece, Carthage and others rose within the basin of the middle sea, no one power was able to extend its authority across all of the basin from Suez to Gibraltar. This accomplishment awaited the rise of Rome—and the fall of Carthage.

It is likely that no land has seen as much history as has Egypt—and borne it so well. An endless flood of events has moved across its open borders and up and down the ancient Nile without sundering the historical continuity or changing the pattern of its life. In fact, in few places on the earth would the men of the era that existed three milleniums before the birth of Christ feel more at home in the modern world than in Egypt (Cairo excepted). For *Egypt is*—and has been from the first day of its historical beginning—*the Nile;* and a pattern of life—regulated by the river and the evenness of its seasonal flow, and based on irrigation agriculture in a protected but isolated river valley—has developed and been maintained for 6,000 years. Cultivation of the soil has played the leading role in the unfolding of Egypt. Agriculture has been responsible not only for the growth of the valley into a center of world culture in ancient times, but also for

---

[7] Editorial, *Foreign Agriculture*, Vol. XIII, No. 9 (Sept., 1949), p. 195.
[8] *Ibid.*

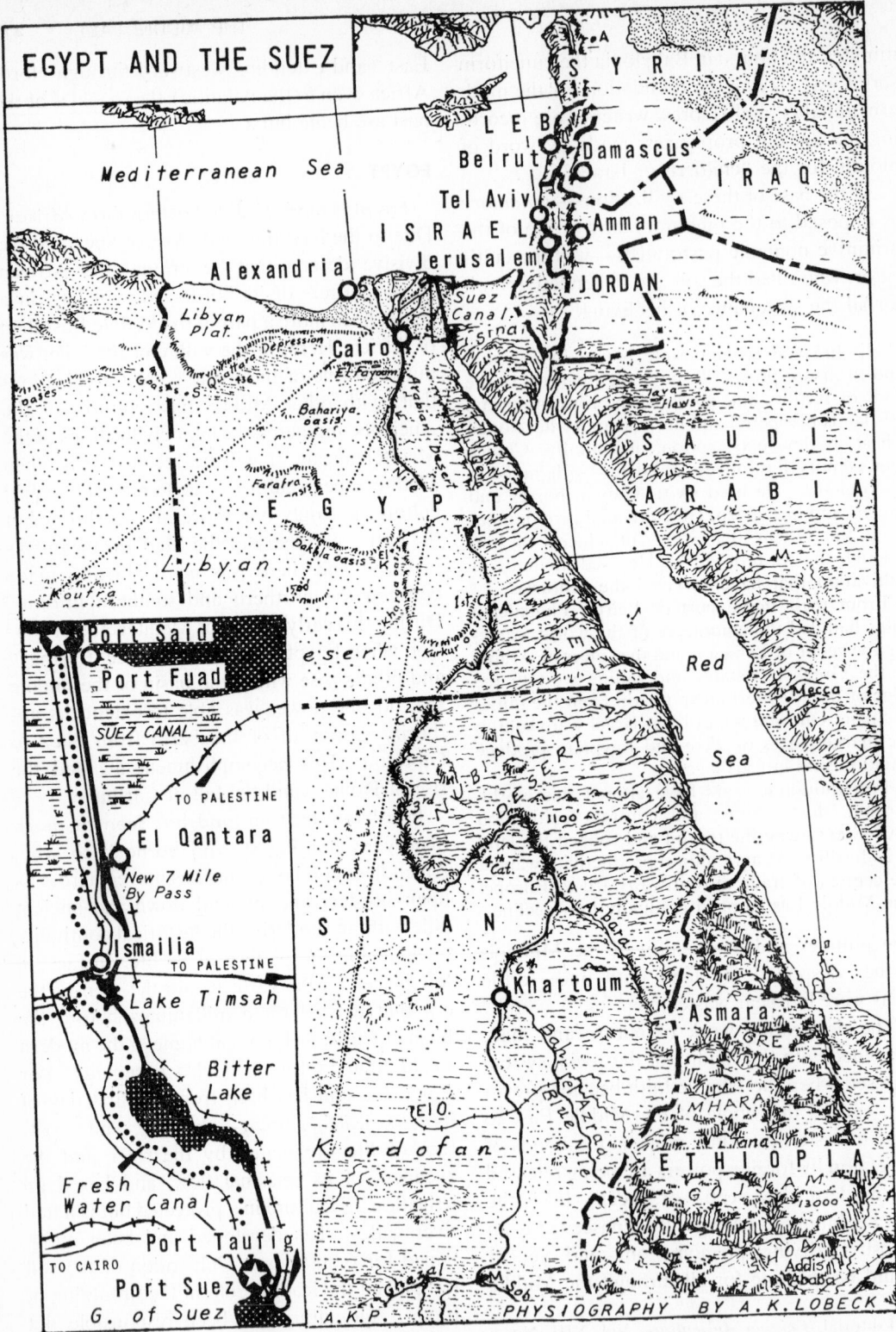

Figure 18.5. The Suez Canal lies entirely within Egyptian territory. One hundred and three miles long, it includes four miles of approach channels added after the completion of the original canal. The Suez has no locks and is open at both ends to the seas.

its transition into a national entity in the modern era.

Agriculture is the wide and solid base on which the entire national economy of the nation rests. It accounts for a major portion of the national income and for an even greater share of the total value of the exports. Some 80 per cent of the population is dependent upon agriculture for a living. These are the fellahin, the cultivators of the soil.

Egypt in the Modern Era

In the last century, Egypt, under the nominal suzerainty of the Ottoman Empire, enjoyed a considerable degree of autonomy under the rule of the sultans' Khedives. At various times certain nations obtained, by treaties concluded with the Turkish sultans, "capitulatory rights" in Egypt. The British obtained such rights as far back as 1675. The essence of these rights was found in the immunity accorded to nationals of the treaty powers who were, a) to a great extent removed from the application of the local law, and b) removed from the jurisdiction of the local tribunals.

The opening of the Suez Canal in 1869 placed Egypt in a geographical position of very special importance. However, economically, the state was not well off, and, by 1877, the finances of Egypt had become entirely chaotic. In 1882, there occurred in Egypt a nationalist revolt during which the Egyptian Government was unable to protect the lives or property of foreigners. After other European powers had declined to intervene, British troops were landed to help the Egyptian Government restore order. It is from this period that the British military occupation of Egypt dates, and from this time that the British Government took upon itself a certain measure of supervision over the Government of Egypt.

The Sudan becomes a condominium. In 1883, the Sudan—which had been part of Egyptian territory exploited by the Egyptians chiefly as a source of slaves—rebelled under the leadership of the Mahdi. By 1885, it had asserted its independence. However, in 1896 operations were undertaken by a joint force of the Egyptian and British armies under the command of General Kitchener for the recapture of the Sudan, and the power of the Mahdists was successfully broken in 1898 at the battle of Omdurman. Following this defeat, a condominium was set up jointly by Britain and Egypt.

The Condominium Agreements placed the administration of the Sudan in the hands of a Governor-General who was nominated by the British Government and appointed by the Khedive of Egypt.. The whole administrative machinery derived its authority from the supreme powers vested in the Governor-General, and the higher administrative posts of the Sudan Civil Service were held almost exclusively by British subjects. Until the unfortunate events of 1924 (to which reference is made later), numbers of Egyptians were employed in the lower administrative posts as well as in technical posts and in the police forces, and Egyptian military forces as well as British were always stationed there; Egyptian and British flags flew side by side at the Palace at Khartoum. With the development of the country, more and more Sudanese were employed in the administration, and Sudanese soldiers formed an increasingly important part of the troops maintained in the country for defense purposes.

The Suez Canal Convention was signed in October, 1888 and became fully effective by a Franco–British declaration in 1904. Under this convention the duty of protecting the Canal was entrusted in the first place to the Egyptian Government and to the Ottoman Government in the second.

The role of the British in Egypt has been a changing one. When Turkey entered the war in 1914, the British Army was still in occupation of Egypt and consequently was exercising a controlling influence in a territory nominally under the suzerainty of an enemy country. The British Government, therefore, declared Egypt a British protectorate, and Turkish suzerainty was declared at an end. By the treaty of Lausanne, in 1923, this act was confirmed.

Meanwhile, a movement for independence

had been growing in Egypt, and negotiations for a treaty, which had begun between the British and Egyptian Governments in 1920 and 1921, ended in a unilateral declaration by the British Government in 1922 recognizing the independence of Egypt under the rule of a King, the successor of the Khedives. In 1923 an Egyptian constitution was adopted on the basis of a constitutional monarchy and a parliamentary regime on a democratic basis. The United Kingdom retained certain rights, however—among them, the prerogative to keep a British Army of occupation in Egypt and to retain a certain number of British officials in the administration.

This arrangement remained in force until the signature of the 1936 treaty. The first of its three major conditions provided for the *implementation* of the alliance (concluded under the treaty) whereby, in time of war, menace of war or an international emergency, the King of Egypt was bound to furnish to the British Government on Egyptian territory all the facilities and assistance in his power, including the use of the ports, airports, and communications, and was responsible for taking all the necessary legislative measures to render this assistance effective (Article 7). The second was the provision for the maintenance of British troops on Egyptian territory in the vicinity of the Suez Canal for the defense of the Canal until such time as both parties should agree that the Egyptian Army was in a position to guarantee the Canal's entire security (Article 8). Certain detailed provisions were included as to immunities granted to the British forces, and the physical conditions governing their presence until the British occupation of Egypt was terminated. The third provided for the administration of the Sudan (Article 11).

During the era of the 1950's, Egypt assumed complete control of all Egyptian territories and affairs. The 1936 treaty was abrogated after World War II due to the ever increasing pressure of Egypt for the complete withdrawal of all British troops from Egyptian soil. In 1951, after 69 years of occupation, Britain withdrew from Egypt and the latter became a sovereign state, acknowledging the authority of no other nation over any of its affairs—internal or external. Only in Suez did British troops remain, and these were finally withdrawn from the Canal Zone, upon the demands of Egypt, in 1955.

The withdrawal of all foreign influence from all of its territories and the concomitant acquisition of complete control of the Suez placed Egypt in a position of strategy comparable only to Turkey as the "keeper" of the Dardanelles. In the case of the Dardanelles, Turkey is the guardian of the straits through, it might be said, "the courtesy" of the great Western powers; in the case of the Suez Canal, Egypt acknowledges no such a position of subjection to foreign interference.)

Egypt becomes a republic. Another decisive chapter in Egyptian history—and one fraught with the potential of tremendous change—was written, in 1952, when a military coup dethroned and exiled King Farouk; and a year later, on June 18, 1953, when the monarchy (reaching back thousands of years to the Pharaohs) was overthrown and a republic proclaimed. Since that time a military junta has ruled the country. Under the new Government, Egyptian foreign and domestic policy have taken new trends. For long years in the past, the international policy of Egypt was largely limited to seeking a position of leadership in the Middle East and to soliciting Arab support to the cause of British withdrawal from the Canal Zone. Following the change of government, Egypt became aware of its position as the dominant Moslem state in northern Africa.

As the British finally withdrew from Suez, bringing to a close a 70-year struggle for national independence, Egypt's scope of interest widened to include all of the Middle East states and even European countries on the opposite shore of the Mediterranean. In the United Nations, it has united with other Arab states and other former colonies in giving overt support to nationalist yearnings. On the whole, Egypt maintains a policy of uncommitment in the East–West struggle.

Problems of the Egyptian Republic

Wealth and politics in the Kingdom of Egypt were largely the concern of the aristocrats, the landowners, the industrialists (these three groups comprising only 5 per cent of the population but holding 95 per cent of the national wealth) and a small group of Egyptian intellectuals. The great mass of 20 million Egyptians—illiterate and extremely poor—have been generally apathetic about both governmental affairs and economic matters on a national scale: so engrossed has the *fellahin* been in his struggle to make a bare subsistence for himself and his family that he has not had the time or energy to feel either resentment at the inequitable distribution of wealth or even much interest.

The military government of the Republic has ruled with as absolute authority as did the monarchy that preceded it; but the suggestion is that the Egyptians are being groomed for participation in government, and that this will take time. An immediate attack was made upon the major domestic problem facing the country —that is, land tenure; and one of the first acts of the military government was to wipe out the *pasha* class. The land reform program included the distribution of some of the former royal lands; in total acreage, however, very little land has actually been distributed.

The problem of land tenure is as old as Egypt itself. In the ancient past all of the land was divided into thirds—one-third belonged to the Pharaoh, another third to the gods (but held in trust by the high priests who benefited from the "charge"), the final third to private owners. In the early years of the Christian era, the Egyptian monarchs took over all of the land directly as a private royal domain, wiping out private and priest-held lands. They supervised the cultivation of about half of the lands themselves, leasing the remainder to the tax-collectors who, in turn, leased land to the *fellahin.*

Until the beginning of the nineteenth century this system of land tenure obtained throughout the Nile Valley of Egypt. With the ascent to the throne of Mohammed Ali (founder of the royal family that ruled until 1953), the tax collecting middlemen were eliminated and the domain again became a private reserve of the royal family. Title deeds were abolished and the commerce in Egyptian produce became a royal monopoly. The peasants were permitted to stay on the land as long as they conducted themselves in harmony with the wishes of the king. Revolt arose, however, leading, in 1858, to the Land Law. Under this law the *fellahin* could own the land they worked—provided they paid the king a stipulated amount for each acre. The king, however, remained the largest landowner; and, to keep the most fertile soil of the Nile Valley in the hands of the family, he granted huge estates—tax-free—to members of the nobility.

The *right* of landownership has been in effect for about a century, but the condition of land tenure has not greatly changed from what it was almost from the beginning. In 1945, 29 per cent of the population owned 87 per cent of the land, the top .05 per cent holding 37 per cent of all agricultural land. To correct this evil, the military government has redistributed 125,-000 acres of land; this is but a tiny start that scarcely begins to touch the land-tenure problem.

In addition to the two reforms mentioned above, other programs have been initiated. West of the Nile delta vast projects for the reclamation of barren lands have been started, factories for the production of civilian and military goods (small arms) were constructed, social service work has begun and plans for the construction of the ambitious and costly High Dam, to the south of Aswan, are complete. (Financially, this may prove impossible to carry through, however.)

The Nile River

Quite appropriately, Egypt has been called the Valley of the Nile. Egyptian life—plant, animal, human—depends almost entirely upon the waters of that river and upon the extremely fertile soil it has built up in its extensive delta and valley over many milleniums. As in the days of the Pharaohs, all along the 4000-mile course of the river from Lakes Victoria and Tana in the rain drenched plateaus and mountains of East Africa, the silt laden waters seep deeply into the parched soils of the valley and delta.

In Egypt and in Sudan to the south, life and *The River* are one and the same. Only by damming the Nile and irrigating the soil can the *fellahin* grow food and cotton, and survive. Like a great long ribbon of green the Nile Valley stretches across the largely irrecoverable desert; on either side of the river bed extend the green fields, but, just beyond, rise the arid valley walls above which the desert stretches out endlessly in all directions. The contrasts are dramatic and sharp. Were it not for the Nile, most surely the Libyan and Nubian—Arabian deserts would close in and choke off all signs of life. Of Egypt's 386,000 square miles, only 3 per cent is inhabited and cultivated; 95 per cent of the inhabitants reside in the Nile Valley; the remaining people occupy oases to the west of the valley or are nomadic pastoralists. Without the Nile flow—pouring billions of cubic yards of water across the arid wastes—the fertile Nile Valley of Egypt and the million acre Gezira of Sudan would desiccate into desert.

The Nile is an international river. One branch (the White Nile, providing the steady year-round flow of water) rises in Lake Victoria and flows northward through Uganda and Sudan before reaching Egypt; another branch (the Blue Nile, and the one that furnishes the mud laden floodwaters of summer) emerges from Abyssinian Lake Tana, flowing northwestward to join the White Nile in Sudan; a third major tributary likewise rises in the highlands of Abyssinia and joins the Nile in Sudan. The waters of the Nile reach Egyptian soil, therefore, only "by courtesy" of Sudan and Ethiopia.

Population and People

Few countries have so homogeneous a population as Egypt. The *fellahin,* constituting 82 per cent of the people, is Hamitic in type and Moslem in religion. His blood strain is very pure although there has undoubtedly been some slight mixing with Arab blood in the north and Negro in the south.

Another element in the population is that of the Coptic Christian, descended from early Egyptians who accepted Christianity. The Patriarch of the Coptic Church is headquartered at Alexandria. The Coptic Christians, formerly cultivators like the Moslem *fellahin,* have tended to be drawn to the urban areas to become merchants, traders, moneylenders, artisans, and the like. They make up the second largest element of the population, but are, in general, a nondissident minority.

The remainder of the population is comprised of perhaps half a million Bedouins and foreigners, among whom Jews, Syrians, Greeks, Turks, and other Mediterranean peoples make up the major portion. The homogeneity of the population—racially and ethnically—is a strong unifying factor. Further uniting the nation is the Arabic language which all speak.

SUDAN

The concern of the Egyptians in Sudanese politics can well be understood because an unfriendly regime, south of Egypt's border, could cut off the flow of waters that supplies the system of dams, barrages, and canals on which the fertile valley relies. Friendly relations with Ethiopia are also necessary for, as stated, from here originate the seasonal and silty floods. Inevitably, the economic welfare of Egypt is very closely tied up with Ethiopia and Sudan.

But Egypt's interest in Sudan does not lie wholly in the assurance of a supply of water. Egypt, with a population of 20 million (and increasing constantly), is faced with the problem of food shortages. Cotton is supreme not only in the agriculture but in the total Egyptian economy, and often occupies land where food should grow; it is the greatest export, in value exceeding the next largest export (rice) by 7.5 times. In cotton production, Egypt normally ranks about fifth in the world. To raise and export this cotton, Egypt must import food.

Sudan, which has a surplus, could be the source.

Egypt would like to have Sudan politically attached to itself. But, according to an agreement reached between Britain and the Moslem state in 1953, the Sudanese were to determine their own status—whether independent or associated with the other African state, or linked to the Commonwealth of Nations. At first, it appeared that Sudanese sentiment favored unification with Egypt but, in the late summer of 1955, a new element—really an ancient element become vocal—appeared to oppose such a move.

The Sudan is a vast territory of a million square miles, touching Egypt on the north and black Africa—Kenya, Uganda, and the Belgian Congo—on the south. The north is arid or semi-arid, the south, lush tropical savannah or forest. Ethnically and racially the two portions of the country differ sharply; the northern Sudanese are largely Moslem Arabs strongly influenced by Egyptian culture, whereas those of the south are pagan Negroes. Enmity between these two groups is of longstanding and complicates greatly the problem of autonomy and unity within the territory. Since the Arab north is the stronger of the halves, it was supposed that the nation might decide to draw closer within the sphere of influence of Egypt, also Arab and Moslem. However, the dissident forces of the south were strong enough to prevent this. Late in December, 1955 Sudan declared its independence and, on January 1, 1956, Egypt and Britain recognized that status.[9]

LIBYA

Three territories were combined to form the new state of Libya—Cyrenaica, Tripolitania, and Fezzan—making it the largest of Africa's independent states. The Emir of Cyrenaica became king of all Libya but, due to disagreement as to the location of the capital, two capital cities were designated: Tripoli, where the Na-

tional Assembly meets to make the laws for the desert state, and Bengasi, where the King conducts the affairs of his subjects. Both cities are located in the narrow but well watered and fertile littoral, Mediterranean in climate, where about three-fifths of the million or so inhabitants reside.

The greater part of Libya is desert, however. There the population is made up largely of nomadic or semi-nomadic tribes, or oases dwellers who cultivate wheat, barley, and dates under irrigation. Despite the restrictive environment, a variety of products is exported— some wheat, vegetable oils, salt, sponges (taken off the northern shore), tobacco, and esparto grass.

Libya was the "pride" of Italy's African empire. About 680,000 square miles in area, the domain stretches across the 800 miles of territory between Egypt and Tunisia and the boundaries dip deeply southward into the desert. During World War II, the hot sandy wastes of the Libyan Desert were the locus of battles between the Allied and Axis forces.

The history of Libya is very ancient. Although this is one of the world's newest countries, its importance commercially goes back over 3000 years to the Phoenicians and Greeks. Roman ruins attest to the occupance of the Libyan sands by Romans, and, succeeding the Romans, Vandals from the Balkans; later, Arabs from the East invaded the territory. The population of the present era is largely Moslem Arab although there are minorities of Italians and Jews. Under the new state structure Italians are not citizens, excluded from the franchise which is limited to Libyan males who have attained their majority (21).

Many international observers doubted the wisdom of creating an independent Libya. The three great tribal groups, although all Arab and Moslem, still show their mutual hostility and jealousy in such little things as the dual capital.

A united Libya was purely an Italian innovation. The desert touches the sea at the Gulf of Sidra separating Cyrenaica and Tripolitania, two countries that have always gone separate

---

[9] The new state was given added recognition as a sovereign entity when, on February 6, 1957, the Security Council of the United Nations voted to admit it to the international organization.

ways. In fact, the two peoples are oriented in opposite directions; historically, Cyrenaica is linked to Graeco–Egypt, and Tripolitania to Phoenician Carthage. Despois stated that the desert divide between Tripolitania and Cyrenaica "is without dispute one of the most decided frontiers, natural or human, to be found anywhere in the world." Fezzan lies inland, separated from both of the other two centers. To pull such widely separated components into a single political whole is truly a Herculean task. In area, Libya is comparable to Britain, France, Italy, and Spain put together—although its population is but a tiny fraction as great (679,350 people).

Another reason that made observers doubt the wisdom of the independence move was the effect that the giving of such sovereignty might have in arousing nationalistic ambitions in adjacent Arab states—dependencies that have a greater natural potential for the constitution of a state *and* that have had more contact with modern methods of government than any of the three Libyan groups. How much the rise of nationalism in French North Africa was influenced by Libyan independence is impossible to estimate, but it was likely quite significant.

SAUDI ARABIA

From the dim past, varying reasons have caused men to beat a path to Arabia. In the ancient world, while the valley civilizations of the Middle East were still emerging, nomadic tribes with their flocks were already finding their way back and forth between the lands of Arabia and those of the Fertile Crescent in a seasonal cycle—even as they do today—in search of pasture. Since the seventh century, the call to the faithful to make a journey to the Holy City of Mecca before death has drawn thousands upon thousands of pilgrims from all parts of the Moslem world to the religious center. In the modern era, however, it is oil that draws the world to the arid wastes of Arabia.

With the oilmen came the appurtenances of Western culture. While the Bedouin tribes still rove over the desert with their camels and sheep, and Moslem pilgrims continue to make the holy pilgrimage, railroads, and metalled roads now cross the arid surfaces and airplanes span the tortuous distances. Riyadh, inland capital of the kingdom, now connects by rail with the Persian Gulf oil port of Damman—an accouterment of modernity in a still ancient land.

Except for the incidence of water, Arabia is irremediable desert. It has been said that oil and water don't mix. But in Arabia they seem to have blended quite well—for the oil explorations have uncovered not only sources of oil but new reserves of water as well. Whenever water is "struck," new settlements spring up and, if the supply is large enough, cultivation begins; oil is beginning to alleviate the age-old problem of water shortage. Rainfall in Saudi Arabia averages about three inches and there are no permanent streams; the country, over a half million square miles in extent, is a plateau of rock, or gravel, or sand dunes. It needs water.

Arabia is a paradoxical land, perhaps because it is entering a period of transition. The extremely modern aspect of the Western oil industry stands in startling and almost unbelievable contrast to the indigenous modes of adjustment. Nomadic tribal peoples and sedentary cultivators both carry on their way of life as in Biblical times, and the age-old tradition of slavery—long outlawed from other parts of the world—is practiced "openly and extensively," according to a United Nations report. But the oil industry is as modern as any in the world, and the innovations introduced with oil wealth are working some startling changes among the Arabs.

The Boundary Problems of Saudi Arabia

Many of the boundaries that mark the frontiers between the national domains of the Middle East pass across such bleak and arid wastelands that they do not—and have not—posed any great problems except in a few instances. This is largely true of the boundaries of Libya and Egypt. At times, however, the prevalent nomadic way of life raises controversies. A rather vexatious boundary problem arose along the frontier between Iraq and Saudi Arabia. It was solved in an unusual way (except in instances of temporary division lines)—*i.e.* by the establishment of *Neutral Territories* between the Arabian–Iraq and Arabian–Kuwait frontiers.

These territories were set up in 1922, by the Treaty of Mohammerah, as a combined effort on the part of the Arab rulers to diminish border raiding.

The Neutral Territories are, economically, unimportant, the coastal territory being largely composed of a salt marsh that is usually dry but which, during rainy periods, becomes impassable. However, the Neutral Territories lie between, and separate, two great oil basins. Oil interests in the area have gained concessions for exploration of the liquid fuel because there is a strong possibility that petroleum deposits might well underlie those intermediary regions also. Explorations are still in progress.

THE STATES OF THE SYRIAN–PALESTINE MANDATES: LEBANON, SYRIA, ISRAEL, AND JORDAN

The countries located at the eastern end of the Mediterranean Sea—Syria, Lebanon, Israel, and Jordan—are, geographically, really one region. Three of them have coastlines on the Mediterranean, and range from a dry subtropical climate along the littoral into desert in the east; Jordan becomes, for Israel, the counterpart of the Syrian desert for Syria and Lebanon. Both desert regions—really one—blend into the equally arid wastes of Iraq. All share the life-giving waters of the Jordan River; and, generally speaking, no natural frontiers separate one state from the other—their regions merge. All, except Jordan (which is desert, or semi-arid at best), produce the same crops—citrus, vines, olives, cereals (wheat and barley, particularly)—typically Mediterranean, while their desert or semi-arid lands are the homes of wandering herdsmen or oases dwellers practicing irrigation agriculture.

Historically, too, they have been closely linked. All have been transit lands, for they lie on the trade routes that connect three continents. All have been closely associated as an area—as they are today (except for the modern Jewish state). Christ and his disciples moved from Jerusalem (Israel and Jordan) to Damascus and Aleppo (in Syria) to Bethlehem (Jordan); further back, in Old Testament days, Lot chose the northern area of the fertile Jordan Valley and the adjacent coastal plain—in the vicinity of Tyre and Sidon of Phoenicia (now Lebanon)—while Abraham chose the less desirable lands of Canaan to the south (Palestine). All were part of the Turkish Empire, administratively divided into the two vilayets of Aleppo and Damascus (major administrative provinces) and the three sanjaks of Beirut, Jerusalem, and Petit Liban (Smaller Lebanon), subdivisions of the vilayets. At the end of World War I, the territory was mandated to two European powers—France having jurisdiction over Syria (later, when independence was granted, Syria and Lebanon), while Palestine and Transjordan were mandated to the British. At the close of World War II, all became independent, sovereign nations.

Lebanon

Lebanon was carved from Syria, by the French, to form a separate state. In a glorious past, Lebanon was the Phoenicia of the ancient world—a trader nation that conquered the eastern basin of the Mediterranean and established the colony of Carthage halfway across the North African continent. It carried its products, including fruit and grain and the famed and fragrant *cedars of Lebanon,* far and wide throughout the Mediterranean realm. The ancient ports were Tyre and Sidon. Today, as then, the small state serves as the "vestibule" to the Mediterranean and the Western world—through the modern ports of Beirut and Tripoli.

Perhaps this "vestibule" character accounts for the diversity of its people which, ethnically, form two groups; about 55 per cent of the Lebanese are Christian, 45 per cent Moslem. In Syria and Jordan, in contrast, the populations are Moslem; in Israel all but 10-15 per cent are Jewish: the Israeli minority group are Moslem. The official language of Lebanon is Arabic, but (due to French occupation) great numbers are fluent in French and English as well.

Representation in the government is on the basis of religion. The President of the Lebanese Republic must be Christian (because it is the majority group)—and not only Christian but a Maronite Roman Catholic. This Catholic group, strongest of the Christian groups in Lebanon, is the reason for the creation of Lebanon as a political entity separate from Syria. To constitute a better state, the French took three sections of Moslem Syria and added to the Christian state, hence the mixed religious population.

The head of Parliament must be Moslem, and, since there are two sects of Moslems in Lebanon, this post and that of premier (who presides over the Cabinet) are divided between them; the head of Parliament must belong to the Shiist sect while the Premier is of the Sunni branch of Islam. Members of Parliament are also selected on the basis of religion. The five states of Lebanon are divided into counties, each usually being quite solidly either Christian or Moslem; where counties have a mixed population, the religious groups are represented proportionately to their numbers. There has been a movement to change this practice of representation on the basis of religion, however.

Of the Middle East states, Lebanon is the least involved in the Israel–Egypt tension. It is, however, as anti-Israeli as any other. Economic reasons are partly the reason for this because the ports of Lebanon and Israel compete as outlets for the Middle East. As an outlet for Middle East oil—Tripoli and Sidon are terminal points for pipelines extending from the Iraqi fields—Lebanon is strategically important to the West.

Syria

Since the last foreign troops departed, Syria has guided its own political destiny. Modern Syrian political history has, to date, been a stormy one despite the fact that the country is largely Moslem.

An area of 72,000 square miles and population of over 3.5 million, give it a density of about 50 people per square mile. Compared to some areas—as the Nile Valley—this would not constitute a high pressure upon the land if the people were evenly distributed, but they are not. Syria is largely desert, and most of the Syrians live in the fertile northern and western portions of the state where the Euphrates and other streams provide water for agriculture; the rest of the people are pastoralists. However, in favored places where water is available, as on the alluvial fan of the Barada River at the foot of the Anti-Lebanon Mountains (Damascus occupies this site), irrigated oases may be found.

The major problems faced by the new state are relics of the past: 1) how to solve the problem of land tenure, and 2) how to develop to the fullest the agricultural potential under a system of independent landowners and farmers. In 1950 Syria adopted a new Constitution which included a provision (Article 22) for the fuller utilization of the nation's land resources on the basis of "social justice and for the benefit of the people." This was the first land reform provision to be written into a constitution in the Middle East.

Boundary Problems of the Former Mandate States

Circulation and irrigation are often paramount considerations in the laying down of boundaries in arid and semi-arid regions. To illustrate the importance of such factors in boundary setting in the Middle East, Syria is worth examining in some detail. In the delineation of the Syrian–Iraqi frontier several considerations had to be taken into account, most important of which were *circulation, water rights, and the details of the "native lands and habits."* A League of Nations commission that was appointed to make a study of the boundary area "considered circulation." One of its tasks, writes Jones, "was to recommend whether the mountains known as Jebel Sinjar, divided by the existing delimitation, should be given entirely to one or the other country. The commission was unanimous that the mountains should be allocated as a unit. The majority, relying on observations of the trails and the movement of caravans, recommended allocation to Iraq. A minority report held that the flow of traffic towards Iraq from the Jebel Sinjar was in part forced by the *de facto* boundary that had been in use for some years.

"The existing delimitation of the Iraq–Syria boundary required the line to cross the Euphrates at the city of Abu Kemal. An international boundary through a city is certain to hamper circulation. In this case, a *de facto* boundary was in use, eight kilometres downstream. The commission recommended the legalization of this *de facto* line."[10]

In the case of water supply in the boundary area, the commission reported as follows:

Both parties, to justify their claims to a particular locality, have repeatedly pleaded the absolute necessity of being able to use certain wells. There can be no doubt that full use of a pasture cannot be made without a good water-supply. We would point out, however, that the drilling and maintenance of the wells are at present left to the nomads. Each tribe, possessing only very rudimentary equipment, at present does no more than what is strictly necessary, and that in the most primitive way, to provide for its water-supply for a short period ahead.

. . . we are convinced that, at small expense, the present system of wells could be improved and supplemented. . . .

We therefore consider that the present distribution of wells and springs should not be allowed to influence the position of the frontier.[11]

Considerations of details of native lands and habits were reported on, in part, by the Commission.

Climatic conditions in these regions vary to an extent which is unknown in temperate climates— the rainfall in certain parts of Mesopotamia was only one-sixth of normal last winter—and may oblige the nomads, as was the case this year, to prolong, shorten or change completely their usual itinerary. In these circumstances, we have acquired the conviction that it is practically impossible to draw a frontier which does not cut

the route of migration of at least some of these tribes.[12]

As a whole, the boundaries of Syria have been relatively peaceful although some conflict between migratory natives is almost unavoidable. *"Intergovernmental" consultations*—as in the case of the Iraq–Saudi Arabian boundary where the Neutral Territories were set up—are the best means of dealing with such tribal conflicts. Only in the case of the Israeli–Syrian border have frontier wrangles flaired into fighting.

The latter disputes were in connection with the Huleh Marshes, a desolate and mosquito-infested swampland about 150 square miles in area, near the frontier where Lebanon, Israel, and Syria meet. Both Syrians and Israelis have had visions of draining the region, putting in irrigation canals, and cultivating the area. As early as 1914 two Syrian investors secured from the Turkish Government "a concession to improve and farm the Huleh swamps." After Palestine was mandated to the British after World War I, the concession remained in force. But, in 1934, it passed into the hands of the Palestine Land Development Company; and, when Israel became a state, this little Huleh knob was transferred to Keren Kayemeth Le Israel.

During the Arab–Palestine War of 1948, Syria occupied the Huleh area and withdrew only upon the agreement of Israel to keep troops out and carry on a "normal life." The region was demilitarized. Three years later, when reclamation of the region was started by the Jews, Syria sent a protest to the United Nations claiming that the reclamation work constituted a violation of the "normal life" provision of the agreement. The United Nations asked that the reclamation work be suspended but Israel refused with the result that Syria sent troops to the border, and Israel and Syria fought a little war over the Huleh marshes.

Work has gone ahead on the Huleh project as well as on the diversion of the Jordan River. According to Israel, these projects are being carried out in such a way that they can be inte-

---

10 Jones, *op. cit.*, p. 22.

11 League of Nations, *Mandates: Report of the Commission Entrusted by the Council with the Study of the Frontier Between Syria and Iraq, sup. cit.*, p. 38.

12 *Ibid.*

grated into an Arab–Israeli *Jordan Valley Authority*. At present water from both the river and the swamps is diverted to irrigate the arid Israeli lands of Galilee in the north and the Negev Desert in the south. If a joint Arab–Israeli project can be worked out for the diversion and use of Jordan waters, both lands will profit enormously. So bitter, however, is the feeling of the Arab states against the Jewish nation that no agreements have been possible although months of technological planning and diplomatic endeavors have sought to make the Authority a reality. The diversion of Jordan waters is perhaps the bitterest (and most tangible) controversy between Israel and its eastern and northern neighbors—Lebanon, Syria, and Jordan.

The Jordan River is far more of an Arab river than it is Israeli. The Jordan rises in Lebanon, flows southward through Galilee for a distance of perhaps 35 miles before becoming the boundary between Jordan and Israel. This length of frontier is short—possibly 15 miles. The river then enters the domain of the state of Jordan, and, in Jordan territory, flows into the Dead Sea, *three-fourths of which lies within the Arab state*. Only the southwestern quarter lies within Israel. The disconcertion of the Arab countries is understandable. In an area where water is the critical element of the environment and where the Jordan River is the major surface source of that life-giving element, rivalry for water rights becomes the major source of friction. It has always been so.

Israel

Border conflict has been the outstanding characteristic of Israeli relations with the Middle East countries since its inception as a state. The Israeli record is one of an aggressive people pressing for territories which they feel are traditionally theirs. The Jews have a just historic claim, but the claim of the Arab peoples is equally just. Numerically, the Arabs far outnumbered Jews in Palestine on May 15, 1948, when the Jewish state (in the historic Holy Land) was proclaimed; but the historic claims of both peoples have become lost in the confusion of ethnic groups for millennia. It has been a zone of intermingling of Jew and Arab. Religious differences run deep, however, and so, generally, do the traditional ways of life. When Palestine was a mandate, there were but 80,000 Jews in Palestine (which was larger than contemporary Israel).

The Zionist colonization of Palestine began with immigration from Russia in 1882. Fifteen years later, the first Zionist Congress was called, and the World Zionist Organization was founded (1897); out of a total Palestine population of 650,000, only 50,000 were Jews. Then, in 1917, came the controversial Balfour Declaration affirming British approval of a Jewish National Homeland in Palestine. This provided the political basis for the Zionist movement.

So much blame has fallen on the British for what has seemed to be flagrant reneging of the Balfour Declaration that it is well to study briefly some of the British statements relative to this famous document. However, a brief history of the area during the 1914-18 period is necessary first.

The Allies of World War I, in order to secure Arab assistance against the Turks (allies of Germany), promised that, in return for Arab support, they would assist the Arabs to obtain sovereignty over their lands if and when the Ottoman yoke was broken. This, then, was a pledge of Allied support to the Arab cause which the Balfour Declaration appeared to contradict. The Balfour Declaration contained the words: "His Majesty's Government view with favor the establishment of a National Home for the Jewish People . . ." How was this to be interpreted? The Churchill Memorandum of 1922 attempted to clarify the British intention when it defined the Balfour Declaration as meaning "not the imposition of a Jewish nationality upon the inhabitants of Palestine as a whole but the further development of the existing Jewish community with the assistance of Jews in other parts of the world, in order that it may become a center in which the Jewish people as a whole may take, on grounds of religion and race, an interest and pride."

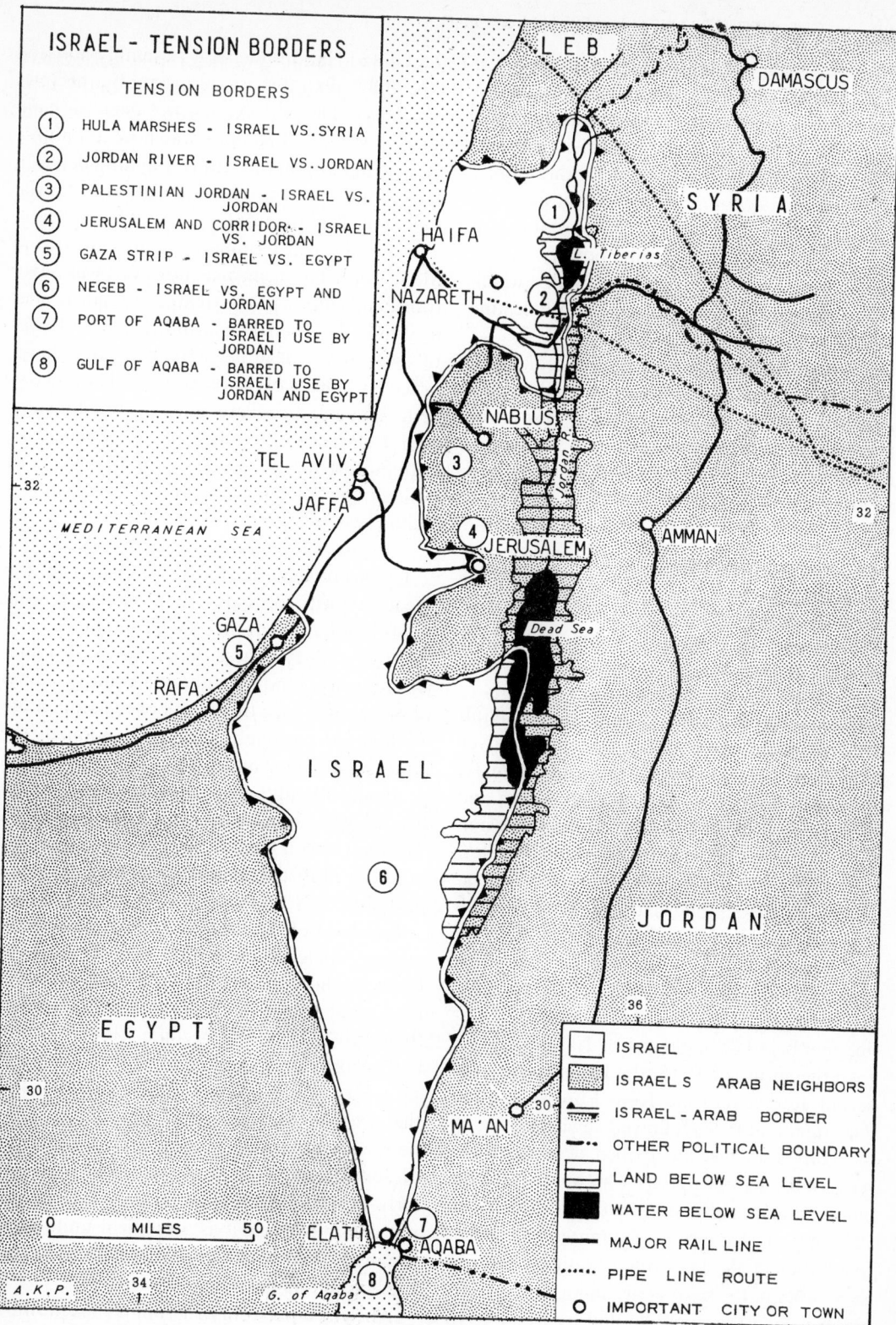

Figure 18.6.

427

Again, when a Zionist delegation appeared at the Peace Conference in 1919, the American Secretary of State (Mr. Lansing) asked for a definition of the phrase, "a Jewish national home." Dr. Weizman replied that "the Zionist organization does not want an autonomous Jewish Government, but merely to establish in Palestine, under a mandatory power, an administration, not necessarily Jewish, which would render it possible to send into Palestine 70,000 to 80,000 Jews annually."

The British mandate for Palestine took effect in 1923. According to a statement made by the British Government, Britain undertook three tasks in the mandated territories which included what is now both Jordan and Israel: 1) to promote the well-being and development of the people of Palestine; 2) to facilitate the establishment in Palestine of a national home for Jewish people and Jewish immigration into Palestine while ensuring that the rights and position of other sections of the population were not prejudiced; 3) to prepare the people of Palestine for self-government.

During the mandate period, Jewish–Arab strife mounted, in part due to conflict over Jerusalem's Holy Places, but, increasingly, over Arab protests of Jewish immigration and purchase of land. In 1937 the Peel Commission of Britain recommended the partition of Palestine into Jewish and Arab sections with Jerusalem placed under international control. Both groups rejected the plan. Two years later the British issued the White Paper restricting Jewish immigration to 75,000 for the following five years. By 1940, Jewish residents in Palestine numbered 450,000 out of 1,500,000.

In the spring of 1945, the British refused to permit Jewish refugees from Europe to enter Palestine, and there followed Jewish rioting in the Holy Land as the British detained those refugee Jews (on Cyprus) who were above the number permitted under the quota. Finally, in February, 1947, Britain submitted the Palestine problem to the United Nations, and, in September of the same year, announced the decision to end the mandate and by May, 1948 to withdraw all troops. In November of 1947,

the United Nations General Assembly adopted a partition plan that was accepted by the Jews but rejected by the Arabs; the next problem facing the United Nations was how to enforce the partition upon the Arabs. Fighting between Israel and its four Arab neighbors—Syria, Lebanon, Jordan and Egypt—that lasted about a year and a half terminated in an armistice in May, 1949. This armistice, however, was never translated into a peace treaty; instead, border hostilities between Israel and the three larger of these states have been frequent and sharp.

The problems of the partition and boundary-setting negotiations are too detailed to enter into. Reference to Figure 18.6 indicates the location of the boundary as set up after years of conflicting claims for territory. The Jewish Republic was proclaimed on May 15, 1948, the first Jewish national state in 1878 years.

Upon proclamation of the Jewish state, the great majority of Palestinian Arabs, fearing Jewish reprisals, left their lands and homes and fled the country. These people are still homeless refugees, literally without a country. Israel has refused to take them back or to compensate them for the properties they abandoned; the Arab states, poor and with critical population problems already, do not feel they can accept the refugees as nationals into their countries. They have been United Nations' wards, housed in camps in Jordan and the Gaza area, and supported by UN funds.

Problems of the New Israel. The major economic problems facing the new Israel have been: 1) how to absorb the large numbers of immigrant Jews—many of them destitute when they arrive; 2) how to become self-supporting, and to provide its citizenry with an adequate supply of goods and services at prices within the reach of the average income. Israel is not now self-supporting. Without the contributions of Jews in other parts of the world—particularly those in the United States—Israel could not continue to exist as a political unit. There are many who doubt that this small nation can ever be self-supporting.

About 80 per cent of Israel is mountainous or desert. In the past much greater portions of the country were both cultivated and covered with a natural growth of vegetation than is true today. This gives the people hope that large areas of what is now wasteland may be made productive. Reclamation of land through drainage and irrigation is contributing additional arable land.

The Negev Desert is the site of one of the most extensive projects of reclamation through irrigation. Israel does not have a large domain to begin with; it is only 7,951 square miles in area, about the same size as New Jersey. The Negev Desert occupies from one-third to one-half of the entire national territory and for this reason much effort is being expended in its development. Archeology indicates that several thousands of years ago various stretches of the Negev were cultivated.[13] Today one of the major national efforts is to find and bring water into the Negev. In July, 1955, the first pipeline was opened. This project carries water from the Yarkon River into the desert.

During the first seven years of the existence of Israel, the area under irrigation more than tripled. Irrigation will make cultivation possible the year around and in desert places, whereas under the natural precipitation only the cultivation of winter grains or deep-rooted crops, such as the grape and olive, are possible.

The mineral resources, which have largely lain untouched since the days of Solomon, are again being exploited. The Dead Sea yields valuable salts—potassium, magnesium chloride, and bromine. The central Negev produces phosphate, and this desert area is expected to furnish copper and other minerals, also.

The population of Israel numbers about 1.8 million of which 200,000 are Arabic. But this doesn't tell the whole story—or even the half. Thirty months after the state was proclaimed, Israel absorbed half a million new inhabitants (in the United States an equivalent

[13] Man-made water systems existed in the Negev in ancient times. About 1000 cisterns and some dams, constructed some 2000 years ago by the Nabataeans, still remain and actually are being put to use again to aid in developing new agricultural settlements.

Figure 18.7. Yarkon Pipeline. (R. Lenz, cartographer. Courtesy *The Christian Science Monitor.*)

figure would be 105 million). As its main purpose, the Jewish state was established as a haven for all of the "catastrophic" Jewish emigrants everywhere; its doors are open to everyone of Jewish extraction.

Sixty-one nationalities are represented in this tiny state for three-quarters of the Jews have come from other parts of the world. Israel is a "Babel" of tongues, although Hebrew is the official language. Religion is the common tie and the inspiration that accounts for the zeal of the Zionists. Yet even in religion—though they are all Jews—the Israelis are often wide apart for they have lived separately for so long, in association with other peoples and cultures, that their beliefs and customs have become modified. This is reflected in the politics of the state. There are the extreme orthodox who advocate a theocratic state and the very liberal—holding the Old Testament to be a record of the history and tradition of the Jewish people, and not a basis for religious philosophy—who prefer a secular form of government.

Israeli imports equal six or seven times the value of the nation's exports. With such an imbalance, it is easy to see how—without loans, gifts, or investment from abroad—the state cannot continue to exist. The modern "promised land" is a harsh and austere country that offers a challenge economically and socially as a political experiment—and also geopolitically because the small Jewish nation, completely surrounded by the Moslem Arab lands of the Middle East, is a political anomaly for the whole world.

Jordan

To understand the unsettled character of the internal politics of Jordan and the role of this Hashemite Kingdom in the Middle East, it is necessary to know something of the involved political setting within which this state was created on April 1, 1921. A glance at the map reveals that the irregular Jordanian boundaries could not have been drawn for economic reasons. They must have been drawn for exigencies of an entirely different nature.

Jordan is more than 80 per cent desert—over which still roam nomadic Bedouin tribes. The remainder of the domain, semi-arid, is under-developed and incapable of feeding and supporting the 1.3 million inhabitants of the state.

However, out of the history—ancient and modern—of this territory have emerged several legacies which not only make Jordan compellingly interesting to students of Middle Eastern affairs but which also make the Hashemite realm pivotal in determining the way in which Middle Eastern affairs may turn. These include the presence, within its lands, of many of the places holy to Christendom, Jordan's Arab Legion, strongest and best-trained Moslem army in the Middle East, and, the 350-mile frontier shared commonly with Israel.

Jordan, along with other mandated states, was carved out of the old Ottoman Empire by the British after World War I. The Arabian prince, Abdullah, son of King Hussein of Hejaz, was named Emir of Trans-Jordan under the British Mandate. For several hundred years previous to this, the desert tribesmen of this territory had had little interference from the Ottoman Turks although the latter were nominally their rulers. However, this condition of tranquillity was abruptly terminated by the World War I battles between the German-supported Turks and the British-supported Arab army from Hejaz, led by Prince Feisal and Lawrence of Arabia. As an aftermath of this desert fighting, Feisal was set up in Damascus as the ruler of Arab Syria—in fulfillment of an earlier promise made to Hussein of Hejaz, father of Feisal.

However, within a short period of time, France had assumed a mandate, similar to that of the British mandate in Palestine, over Syria and Lebanon, and, after some disagreements with the Arab king, removed him from the Syrian throne. At this juncture, Abdullah entered the picture. He appeared in Trans-Jordan, with a large force of tribesmen from Hejaz, avowedly to march northward and recapture the Damascus throne for his younger brother, Feisal. To prevent the outbreak of fighting among their principal Arab allies, the French and British stepped in—and dissuaded Abdullah from carrying out his purpose by offering him the Emirate of Trans-Jordan. The establishment of Feisal upon the throne of Iraq and the creation of Trans-Jordan as a separate political entity gave rise to the close dynastic ties between Jordan and Iraq, both ruled by Hashemite princes. Saudi Arabian–Hashemite antagonism, a major factor in Middle East politics for three decades, resulted from the ejection of Hussein of Hejaz by Ibn Saud in 1924. (The first break in this rivalry came during the April–May crisis of 1957 when King Saud of Arabia offered troops for the protection of the integrity of Jordan's borders during the national political emergency.)

In 1946 Trans-Jordan became politically independent. The state, when it first obtained sovereignty, occupied territory that lay eastward of the Jordan River—hence, the name of the Emirate, Trans (across)-Jordan. In

November 1947, the United Nations partitioned Palestine, on the western side of the
Jordan River, into a Jewish and an Arab state,
and two years later, as a result of the war with
Israel, Abdullah annexed the greater part of
the largest of the three portions of Arab Palestine, the section that lay along the west bank
of the Jordan River. The Jordan of today was
thus created by the unification of Arab Palestine with Trans-Jordan.

This annexation added about 2000 square
miles of territory to the state—about one-
fifteenth of the total area—but it trebled the
population which increased from an estimated
400,000 to over a million. The population of
Palestinian Jordan was composed of two
groups—nearly half a million destitute refugees who fled Israel at the outbreak of hostilities and the Palestinian Arabs who had lived
west of the Jordan River before partition. Both
groups have been dissident factions within the
state that formerly had a homogeneous Bedouin population. The Palestinian Arabs are
better educated than the Bedouin Jordanians,
and have become dominant and vociferous in
the government; the refugees have simply
added to the burden of the state by making the
population a full third larger, and by remaining
a group that the economy has been unable to
absorb. The homogeneity and tranquillity of
Jordan disappeared with the annexation of this
Palestinian territory and it was a fanatic from
this region who was responsible for the assassination of Abdullah in 1951.

This acquisition led also to the division of
Jerusalem between Israel and Jordan—the old
city falling to the Arab state. Thereby, all hope
of constituting Jerusalem as an international
zone disappeared. Jerusalem is a city that is
holy to the peoples of three religions, Moslems,
Jews, and Christians, and its possession was
therefore greatly desired by both Arabs and
Jews. Christians throughout the world had
hoped for its internationalization.

Abdullah, while he lived, was a power within
the Arab world despite the fact that he ruled
over an impoverished and indigent state. His
prestige stemmed largely from that fact that,
as a member of the Hashemite line, he was
directly descended from Mohammed. During
his reign he had visions of a Greater Syria—
that is, the union of Iraq, Jordan and Syria into
one large Arab nation. In this he was opposed
by Saudi Arabia and Egypt. He also was the
one ruler—and, therefore, Jordan the one
Arab state—that even considered the acceptance of Israel as an entity. For this he was mis-
trusted by the other Arab countries and made
some powerful enemies among them. This
willingness for rapprochement with Israel has
been the cause of disaffection among the Palestinian Arabs—who are extremely hostile to the
Jewish state.

Five years later, it was the power of the
Palestinian Arabs within the government that
forced young King Hussein to dismiss Glubb
as head of the Arab Legion and to embrace an
anti-Western policy; and it was the power and
pressure of these same Palestinian Arabs that,
eventually (1957), caused the government
crisis from which Hussein emerged, at least
temporarily, in the ascendancy.

IRAQ, IRAN, AND AFGHANISTAN
Iraq

Iraq was the first of the Arab League states
to break the Arab ranks and link itself to the
defense of the West. This occurred in February 1955, when Iraq signed a mutual security
pact with Turkey whose membership in NATO
indirectly tied Iraq with the Western powers.
Despite protests and accusations from the other
Arab League countries, this bond with the West
was made more firm when, in late fall of the
same year, Iraq entered into the Middle East
Treaty Organization, a defense agreement in
which Iran, Turkey, Pakistan, and Britain are
also members.

After World War I Iraq was detached from
Turkey and made a British mandate. In 1930,
a treaty was signed between the two states,
running until 1955, which made Iraq independent but gave Britain the right to use two
air bases and maintain troops on Iraq soil.
British ground forces were withdrawn from
Iraq in 1948, and, the succeeding year, Britain

drew up a new mutual defense pact with the Middle East state. Rioting in Baghdad followed the announcement of the proposed agreement, and the treaty was never signed—on the grounds that it did not give recognition to the aspirations of the state.

Three years later, Iraq requested that the 1930 treaty be revised and, in the same year, asked that the royalties on oil be raised. There were even suggestions that Iraq might follow Iran's lead and nationalize oil. A pro-British Premier, who controlled 80 per cent of the votes of the Parliament, took a firm hand, however, and blocked all attempts to press for the nationalization of the petroleum industry.

While it is evident from this account that Iraq has held some anti-West (British) feelings that might have been expected to hold the country to a strictly neutral course, there are other reasons why Iraq might well loosen its close ties with some of the Arab League states. One of these lies in the fact that Jordan and Iraq are ruled by kings from the same royal family—the Hashemite—a family that has traditionally been a strong rival of the ruling house of Saudi Arabia. Hence, antagonisms have existed between Iraq and Jordan on the one hand, and Saudi Arabia on the other. Another lies in the fact that Iraq has had dreams of uniting itself with three of the other Arab League states to form a large Moslem state that would be viable and strong. Both Arabia and Egypt oppose such a move—Arabia for historic reasons, Egypt because it fears being replaced as the strongest Arab state in the Middle East.

Iraq has all of the ingredients (inherently needed in the Middle East) for prosperity and geopolitical importance. In the first place, the country is strategically located not only in relation to the historic Fertile Crescent, but also in relation to the contemporary geopolitical situation. Flanking Iran, Arabia, and Kuwait (locale of over half of the world's oil reserves), Iraq commands—and could well be a part of— the Soviet access to the Persian Gulf. Further, a combination of fertile land and available water for irrigation has made Iraq one of the garden spots and bread baskets of the Middle East. The cultivated portions of the country lie in a long valley bounded by mountains. This topographic setting, combined with a climate that provides sun and heat in quantity the year-round, makes Iraq a veritable natural hothouse where almost anything can be grown—provided water is put on the land.

Probably few areas on earth have been associated with so great a volume of authentic history and lengendary myth as the fertile *Mesopotamia* that comprises the valley of the Tigris and Euphrates Rivers where the prosperous kingdoms of the Sumerians, Babylonians, and Assyrians once lay—their records dating back more than four millennia before the birth of Christ. The story of Iraq "has been written in the rich allu-mud of the Tigris and Euphrates" ever since the Sumerians first began building highly advanced irrigation works nearly 6000 years ago. Water was thus provided for the land to the east of the Tigris, and the giant hydraulic system nurtured the first of the world's highly developed civilizations.

The three great kingdoms rose in succession, "a sequence of human progress interrupted by periods of stagnation and decay."[14] In time, Iraq became the center of Islamic culture (under the Abbasid Khalifs). Shortly thereafter, however, decay set in—and the desiccating effects of winds and floods aided in laying waste the "works" that provided Iraq with its controlled flow of water, and, therefore, with life and prosperity; the destruction spread by the Mongol invaders (1258) helped to finish the work of despoilation. Two centuries later the Turks entered and conquered Iraq and, from that day until this, few remnants remain to mark the prosperity and glory of the ancient world of *the land between the rivers*. Only where natural conditions permitted life and cultivation to go on, as in the south around Basra, did the valley continue to bloom like a garden.[15]

---

[14] Samuel Van Valkenburg, "Iraq," *Focus,* Vol. IV, No. 5 (January, 1954), p. 1.

[15] The Garden of Eden is supposed to have been in Mesopotamia.

Iraq is almost entirely a pure desert land. As "Egypt is the Nile," so Iraq is "the valley of the two rivers." Only in the north and northeast, in the vicinity of the mountains that separate Iraq from Iran and Turkey, is the natural precipitation sufficient to raise crops without irrigation. Southward the rainfall averages about five inches annually. Without water control, the rivers continue to be the affliction and the benefaction of the people. They alone provide life-giving water to the fertile alluvial soil (the fertility of which is renewed by the flood waters of the Tigris and Euphrates which, like the Nile, are heavily laden with silt); on the other hand, every three years or so, the rivers flood the land causing destruction and loss of life.

The Iraqi domain, 175,000 square miles in area, is divided between fertile but desert river valley (Mesopotamia), upland steppes, and mountains. It supports a sparse 5 million inhabitants of which 99 per cent are followers of Islam. The first problem facing the country is the reclamation of the land and the redevelopment of the hydraulic system. The second—and one that prevails in all of the Middle East Moslem lands—is that of land tenure; most of the arable acres are under the control of the tribal chiefs (sheikhs) and the owners of the water pumps. Land distribution must be a concomitant of water control to raise the standard of living. A third problem (and one in seeming contradiction of the two above) is that of the increasing salinity of the land as a result of excessive irrigation.

Iraq is a poor country that has suddenly become wealthy—wealthy on the royalties from the oil, 50 per cent of which flow into the Government treasury. With this money notable changes are being made in the country as the problems of the land are concertedly attacked. If the program of land, water, mineral, and industrial development are continued and a judicious program of landownership can be worked out, the living conditions of the 5 million people should be remarkably improved within a relatively short time.

Iran

As in Iraq, Iranian nationalism, epitomized in anti-British and anti-West sentiment, has resolved in a defense pact with Britain and the West. Vehement nationalism and assertive independence are not new phenomena in Iran for many times in the past 2500 years Persian nationalism has been affirmed—often at the expense of other peoples. On the other hand, the integrity of the Persians has as often been tread upon, and it is undoubtedly in this that the outburst of extreme nationalism of the past five years is to be understood.

For several decades, the political status of Iran—though independent—might be described as one of "semi-colonial." Reference has already been made to the buffer status of Iran. Iranian history cites a long series of examples to indicate that little has been gained in contacts with peoples outside of their own borders. Though this history goes back to the times of the invasions of Alexander the Great and the Roman Empire, to Genghis Khan and Tamarlane, it has been the foreign invasions and the influences of the twentieth century which have nurtured the roots of nationalism.

During World War I, Iran was a battlefield for the British, Russian, and Turkish troops. Shortly before that, in 1907, the country was divided into spheres of influence—British in the south, Russian in the north—with a neutral zone in between. In World War II, Iran served as a vital link in the allied supply line to the Soviet Union, even though Iranians, in the main, were spectators in the great conflict. Foreign troops, stationed within the country during that war, boded ill to the state in several ways. They were a factor in bringing on near crippling inflation; Soviet troops quartered in the northern province of Azerbaijan not only refused to withdraw from the country after the war but backed a Communist revolt which set up a pro-Soviet regime in that area. United Nations action—supported strongly by the United States—finally forced the Soviet troops out, and the Azerbaijan regime collapsed. But to many Iranians this was another example of what to expect from foreigners; so tread on has Iran been by the pressures of the Great Powers that Lenin's characterization of Iran as a "semi-colonial country" seems appropriate. Nationalization of the oil was a reaction to the humiliations suffered by a proud people at foreign hands in modern times. However, the geographic realities of the country—the strategic location and the oil reserves—make it impossible for Iran to remain outside of the main body of contemporary history.

However, nationalism in Iran was more than a protest to the influence of foreigners within the country. As in East and South Asia, the rest of the Middle East, and North Africa, Iranian nationalism was as well a protest against unbearable social and economic conditions within the national structure—an inaudible cry, however, as the discontent was diverted into the nationalist movement. What are the fundamentals of Iranian life and environment that are significant to the geopolitics of the current period?

The details of the natural environment are basically the same as those that characterize the rest of the Middle East except in one aspect. Iran is a high plateau surrounded by mountains, and, despite the fact that waters bound it on the south and partially on the north (the Caspian Sea), it is an arid land where life is possible only as water for irrigation is available. The population distribution pattern demonstrates the extreme dependence on sources of water—other than rain. Towns and cities string along the base of mountains or in intermontane valleys where the added elevations of the highlands wring out enough moisture from the winds to produce streams that flow into the lowlands. And Iran is not blessed with a "Nile" or any rivers comparable in volume or dependability to the Tigris and Euphrates in Iraq. Cities lie on alluvial fans—where the streams descend out of the mountains and onto the plains; even so, most of these population centers suffer for lack of water during the warmest and driest part of the year. Only along the north-facing, narrow littoral and adjacent slopelands ringing the southern

end of the Caspian Sea is natural rainfall adequate for cultivation and the maintenance of sedentary life. Further, the elevation, aided by the plateau character of the country, makes Iran quite bitterly cold during the winter months as compared with other Middle East lands.

Of the total area of the state, about 30 per cent is economically usable. Of this, 15 per cent is grazing land, 10 per cent is cultivated, the rest is in upland forests; the bulk of the country is barren desert or mountains. Yet, on the one-fourth of the land devoted to cultivation and pastoralism, over 80 per cent of the population (which numbers 16.5 million) make their living—for they are farmers or graziers in the main. Water is the fundamental problem, and 80 per cent of the water used for irrigation is ground water, secured by the laborious *kanat* system.

Aside from oil, Iran is not well supplied with either other fuels or minerals. Some deposits of coal, iron, lead, and copper occur, but they are small, scattered, and inadequately served by transportation facilities, making exploitation difficult and costly.

Iran is poorly cohered. Because of the scattered nature of the population distribution, it is difficult to unify the "nation" except through extensive and good means of communication. However, the transportation system is completely inadequate to modern needs. Few roads are passable the year around, and there is but one through railway, the Trans-Iranian, which runs from the Persian Gulf to the Caspian via Tehran.

Since Iran has been a crossroads of conquest, its population is naturally a mixed one. The majority are of Indo–European stock. Most of these people speak Persian with an admixture of Arabic. Semitic and Mongolian blood is found in considerable amounts, and in the northwest corner of the country—in and adjacent to Azerbaijan—are an influential minority group of Turki-speaking people who comprise about one-fourth of the total population. They are a distinct group, with their own language, customs, and traditions; related peoples are found in Iraq, the USSR, and Turkey.

The Iranians are Moslem, adhering to the Shiite sect of the Islam world. Religion is a cohering factor, but, as in several other Middle East states, tribal rivalries and the jealous guarding of prerogatives on the part of sheikhs, makes it difficult for the central government to unify the country under a central authority. The Western oriented and progressive Shah (Reza Pahḷavi), who favors land distribution, modernization of the country, technical aid from the West, etc., has had strong opposition from tribal peoples and leaders—the latter feeling their rule over and income from the people slipping away as modern innovations replace ancient customs. The tribesmen themselves are noted for their love of independence and resentment of government interference.

Boundaries of Iran. The difficulties of fixing boundaries in areas where migratory peoples move seasonally over wide territories (irrespective of national frontiers) or where a frontier separates a people united by common language, traditions, and the like, have already been pointed out. Both of these conditions have repeatedly arisen in the Middle East. In discussing the placing of the boundary on the Turkish–Iranian frontier, Colonel Ryder wrote: "The fixing of a frontier was . . . repugnant to the finer feelings of the Kurds,"[16] a tribal people who occupy the mountain regions of northwest Iran and adjacent highland areas in Iraq and Turkey.

This boundary, about 1200 miles in length and long a subject of dispute, was not fixed until 1913-14. However, the border "assumed more or less its present position early in the 17th century."

Portions of the Iran–Iraq frontier had been disputed for over a century by Iran and Turkey. When Iraq became independent, the disputes were passed on to Iraq from the Ottoman Empire. Both Turkey and Iraq laid claim to all of the broad estuary and delta of the Tigris–Euphrates Rivers (that is, the Shatt-al-Arab),

Iraq claiming all the territory to the farther, or eastern, bank on the Iranian side; Iran, on the other hand, maintained that the boundary should be traced along the thalweg or chief navigable channel. In disputing this, Iraq claimed that the whole of the river course should lie within Iraqi territory since this was the sole outlet to the sea for Mesopotamia whereas Iran had a long coast on the Persian Gulf.

In the Treaty of Erzerum (1848), compacted between Iran and Turkey under pressure from Britain and Russia, Article II carried the following provision:

The State of Turkey also firmly undertakes that the town and seaport of Mohammarah, and the Island of Al Khizr, and the anchorage place, and also the lands of the eastern bank, *i.e.* of the left side of the Shatt-al-Arab, which are in the possession of tribes admittedly attached to Persia, shall be in the possession of the State of Persia in full sovereignty. Moreover, Persian ships shall have the right to navigate the said river in full liberty, from the point where it flows into the sea to the point of juncture of the frontiers of the two parties.

Ratified in Constantinople in 1848, the Treaty still left the demarcation of the frontier unclear, and it was not until 1914 that a Turko–Persian commission determined the boundary with the aid of England and Russia.

The demarcation of the Iranian–Afghan frontier resulted in an allocation of territory that was unfortunate to both states. The greatest injustice was done to Afghanistan within whose domain the whole of the Seistan Basin should logically lie. In the ancient past Seistan, like Mesopotamia, was one of the bread baskets of the arid Middle East, crisscrossed by a wonderful system of canals that provided the water to make this fertile but extremely arid region one of high productivity. As in Mesopotamia, the destruction of invaders and the subsequent desiccation left it an area of almost complete desolation except in those parts where irrigation could be easily achieved.

The Seistan Basin lies along the southern third of the frontier, at the point where Afghanistan and Iran touch the northwestern point of

---

16 C. H. D. Ryder, "The Demarcation of the Turco-Persian Boundary in 1913-14," *Geog. Jr.*, Vol. 66, September, 1925, pp. 234-35.

Baluchistan (Pakistan). For a distance of about 50 miles, the Iran–Afghan frontier runs through the Hamun-i-Helmund, the large but shallow lake within the Seistan Basin, and into which the Afghan river, the Helmund, drains. According to Boggs, Iran and Afghanistan, somewhat before 1940, "negotiated a convention providing that the water of the Helmund River 'from the Kamal Khan dam on' . . . be divided evenly between the two countries. A joint commission" determines "the quantity of water available in the autumn of each year" and so regulates "its flow that one-half goes to Iran and one-half to Afghanistan."[17]

Afghanistan

In the swirl of history that has moved across Persia (Iran) and Afghanistan, the two plateau states have been crossroads of invasion and commerce, havens for trespassing peoples, and, in the modern period, buffer zones for the great powers. The history of Afghanistan is the history of the typical buffer state—up to the present moment; a buffer, historically, between Russia and Britain[18] (in India); at present, between the USSR and the West. Even the problems of setting the boundaries were, in the case of the northern and southern frontiers, "the joint concern" of the British and the Russians rather than of the Afghans.

The boundary definition of Afghanistan was associated with its "buffer" role. The Persian–Afghan boundary was established between 1903-05, that along the Russian border somewhat earlier (1895). "Afghanistan itself did not require the delimitation and demarcation of exact boundaries, but was involved in setting definite limits to its territory as a buffer state."[19]

Afghanistan, even more than Iran, is a country of *tribes,* so independent and possessing so much local authority that Afghanistan can scarcely be called a "nation" either in terms of

political coherence or people. "When two tribes in the region of the Indian–Afghan frontier are unable to agree upon a line to be established and maintained, the laying down of a boundary line by oath is a method which seldom failed, once they agreed to use it."[20]

A. H. McMahon, who served on the boundary commission that laid out the Afghan–Baluchi frontier, reported in these words the scale of operations needed to lay out a boundary—a character of Asian boundary demarcation in many cases:

The Baluch–Afghan Boundary Commission started in March, 1894, and by June, 1896, succeeded in laying down the boundary line to Persia. The length of this line from the Gomal to Persia is over 800 miles, and it took us nearly two full years to complete it.

. . . We had an escort of 150 infantry and 60 cavalry. Our whole party, including escort, survey party, office establishment, and tribal chiefs and followers, amounted to about 1000 men and 600 animals, *i.e.* camels, horses, and ponies. The Afghan commissioners, who subsequently joined us, brought an escort and camp following amounting to much the same number as ours.[21]

In 1747, Afghanistan became an independent country ruled by a king with authority over all of the tribes within the domain. Previous to that date, Afghanistan was composed of numerous tribes under Arab or Mongol control or, at times, divided between the various surrounding peoples—Indians, Persians, and Uzbeks. Despite the establishment of central government, tribal control remained strong.

Afghanistan is a Moslem state, and one in which Islamic customs and the law of the Koran have been and are the ruling tenets of life. Like Korea, because of the numerous invasions on its territories, Afghanistan was long a hermit nation; until 1921 no outsiders were welcomed within the Afghan frontiers for all foreigners were looked upon with suspicion. In that year, however, the ruling monarchs, who had travelled in Europe and become ac-

---

[17] S. Whittmore Boggs, *International Boundaries* (New York: Columbia University Press, 1940), p. 146.

[18] However, twice Russia affirmed that Afghanistan lay outside of its zone of influence.

[19] Boggs, *op. cit.,* p. 141.

[20] *Ibid.,* p. 145.

[21] Sir A. Henry McMahon, "The Southern Borderlands of Afghanistan," *Geog. Jr.,* Vol. 9, April, 1897, p. 393.

quainted with modern ideas of life and dress and democracy, attempted to introduce some modifications to the strictly Moslem traditions that held Afghanistan; they abolished the veil, instituted compulsory education for women, and the like. In this tradition bound land, such innovations so suddenly imposed were not accepted, and the king and queen had to abdicate the throne.

In 1921, in a treaty compacted with Britain, Afghanistan opened the frontiers of the country to foreign visitors. From that date changes began to take place, and since the end of World War II the Afghan people and government have been desirous of technical aid for the improvement of agriculture and the livestock industry and the development of industry based on the natural resources of the country. However, the Afghans are only now beginning to break away from old customs that have stultified progress in the land. Afghanistan is just now learning the use of the wheel! The changes can scarcely be called a social "revolution"—such as was the change that took place in Turkey under Ataturk—but surely revolutionary changes are beginning to appear in the practices of agriculture and animal husbandry.

Except for the mountain areas and the steppelands adjacent to the mountains, Afghanistan is a barren, desert country. However, a number of important rivers that have their sources in the lofty highlands of the north provide the water necessary for the establishment of several significant oases. The Kabul Valley—watered by the Kabul River, the only Afghan stream that finds its way eventually to the sea—is the richest and most productive, as well as the most densely populated, of such river oases. It is scarcely a valley, for it lies on the plateau of 5-6000 feet elevation; but, drained by the river which waters the alluvial soils and surrounded on all sides by lofty mountains, it gives the appearance of a valley. Kabul, the capital, lies here and here the historic route that passes through the Khyber Pass to the Indus Valley originates.

Other Afghan rivers provide water for all forms of life. The Amu Darya, in the north, forms the Russo–Afghan border for a distance of 480 miles and then turns northward flowing through Russian Turkestan into the Aral Sea. The Murghab, after a course of 360 miles, loses itself in the sands of the Oasis of Merv (Russian Turkestan). The Hari-Rud waters the fertile plain of Herat before likewise disappearing in the deserts of Russian Turkestan (in the Oasis of Tejend). The Helmand, the only river whose entire course lies within the country as pointed out before, flows into the Hamun-i-Helmand in the Seistan Basin after coursing from the Hindu Kush mountains across 600 miles of the Hazara (mountainous region in central Afghanistan) and the southwestern deserts.

The population, estimated variously at 7 to 12 million, is a very disparate one. The racial origin of the Afghans is uncertain, and, certainly, the numerous invasions and consequent residua have greatly modified the original stock. Aryan, Semitic, Mongol, and other racial characteristics are clearly discernible among the present Afghans.

The most turbulent of the tribal peoples have been the *Pathans* of the northeast Khyber Pass region, "keepers" of the 30-mile gorge that serves as the gateway to India; their tribal lands today are split between Pakistan and Afghanistan. They claim to be the remnants of the ten lost tribes of Israel carried into captivity by Nebuchadnezzar; they are a Semitic group calling themselves the Beni Israel.

The *Hazaras,* occupying the central portion of the country, are Mongoloid in character with yellowish skin and sparse beards, relics of the Genghis Khan army. In the north, adjacent to Turkestan, are the Turkomen, and, in the west, the Tadjiks of Persian origin while in the mountains northwest of Kabul are the Kaffir, a fair-skinned and blond-haired tribe that has recently accepted the Islam faith. In addition to these five groups there are the nomadic Baluchis, migratory pastoralists wandering with their flocks across the deserts of the south.

Beside Pushto (or Pkhtu), the official Afghan and Pathan language, almost all of the tribes speak Persian; in the north, the second language is Turkoman. There are fewer than a thousand foreign residents in Afghanistan, most of them in the city of Kabul. Less than 10 per cent of the people reside in the five cities of over 10,000 population. The great proportion are agriculturalists who live in small villages or are semi-nomadic pastoralists. Probably one-half of the population is pastoral, and fully three-fourths of the country is suitable for grazing. Sheep are the base of the Afghan economy, and animal products—as karakul—are the major items of export.

Afghanistan is known to have a number of minerals. These could be exploited for the benefit of the economy if financial and technical aid were available. Both have been offered by both the United States and the USSR, but Afghanistan, desiring to remain neutral in the present world situation—and perhaps still somewhat suspicious of inquisitive foreigners—suspended American explorations for oil along the northern frontier, and, previously, rejected a Russian note protesting these explorations as "interference in Afghanistan's internal affairs." Later, in 1953, however, the country permitted Soviet geologists to come into the Turkestan area to continue the oil ex-

plorations; two years later the Afghans established economic ties with the USSR. The display of unfriendliness toward Western powers followed the support by the latter states of Pakistan in the *Pushtoonistan* independence move.[22]

Afghanistan plays a lone hand in international politics. However, sharing a long boundary with the Soviet Union, and due to the fact that the northern portion of Afghanistan faces inward to Turkestan rather than outward, trade relations are naturally close between the two states. That the Soviets regard Afghanistan as important to itself is demonstrated in the fact that the USSR maintains the largest diplomatic staff in that country. Except as the gateway to Pakistan and India from Turkestan and the west through the historic Khyber and Bolan Passes, Afghanistan has little strategic importance to the rest of the world; geographic isolation makes it relatively inaccessible to any of the great powers except the USSR, and its natural resources—whatever they may be—are largely unprospected and undeveloped.

[22] See pages 487 and 489.

19

Africa: Continent in Ferment

Africa, one of the last frontiers of the globe, presents the West with a series of challenges of unparalleled complexity and increasing urgency. It challenges Western conceptions of national freedom and human liberty, of race, of religion, of culture, of economic development, and of peaceful progress. It challenges the inhabitants—Africans, Arabs, Asians, and Europeans—to find the will and the way to live together in harmony, for already they share a homeland there in association with one another.

In the north, Britain, Egypt, and the Sudan were engaged in a struggle that involved national dignities and international security. In Algeria, France has contended with the same forces of Arab nationalism that gained sovereignty for Tunisia and Morocco, and for the new African country of Libya. In the south, a constitutional crisis has endangered the stability of the strongest independent nation of Africa, endangered the unity of the peoples of Dutch and English descent (the white—and minority—but ruling group), sparked the

embers of racial intolerance, and embittered the relations of Europeans, native Africans, and Indians. In the west, African dependencies have moved rapidly toward independence, while in Central and East Africa the concept of colonialism has been turned and twisted in eccentric circles in the attempt to find a solution satisfactory to native and European.

Africa epitomizes the challenge of the earth at its most primitive and at its richest. Nearly half of the world's gold, one-third of the chrome, three-fourths of the cobalt, almost all of the industrial diamonds, and a large portion of the uranium lie beneath the surface of African soils; further, nine-tenths of the columbium (used for making high-temperature alloys important to jet engines, gas turbines, etc.), and one-fifth of the world's copper, tin, and manganese come from African mines; iron ore exists in unsurveyed deposits.

With regard to food and raw materials (aside from minerals) the grounds for evaluation are a little less sure. At first glance, the potentialities seem great. Africa produces about nine-tenths of the world's palm kernels, three-fifths of the cacao, one-third of the sisal fibre, three-fourths of the peanuts (for oil), and nearly one-tenth of the wool and cotton. Yet, in spite of this seemingly large output, prewar statistics show that Africa exported only three per cent of the raw materials (vegetable and animal) of the world, and its exports remain at about the same level today.

The production indicates, however, that Africa, which a century ago was virtually unknown, is awakening; a storehouse of strategic materials, it is being drawn into world affairs. However, rising with the increasing economic momentum is the problem of Africa's native peoples. Left far in the background during the progress of mankind, 150 million Negro natives (among the most primitive inhabitants of the globe) are beginning to apprehend their potentialities and possible opportunities, and to demand their rights—and challenge the Western colonial powers as never before. The native is not the primitive he was 50 years ago; further transforming the ethnic picture has been the transmutation of the racial stock by immigrant Europeans and Asiatics. Particularly in the north and east—and southward to the Cape of Good Hope—East meets West, and both meet Africa.

Despite all of these factors, Africa is still the most colonial of continents. Today, however, the African wants the foreigner out of his land. In almost all parts of the continent, the demand for self-determination has arisen, and, in almost every part of colonial Africa, aside from the Belgian and Portuguese territories, nationalism is a growing flood. There have been many evidences of this—the Mau Mau in Kenya, racial strife in the Union, the pressing for independence in several areas, as Algeria and Nigeria.

HISTORY OF THE CONTINENT

Only Libya, Ethiopia, Liberia, Egypt, Sudan, Morocco, Tunisia, Ghana, and the Union of South Africa are independent. These nine countries occupy less than one-third of the land area and have less than one-third of the people of Africa. There remains, therefore, nearly 8.5 million square miles of area with inhabitants numbering up to 125 million still under colonial domination.

Geopolitically, the human element of Africa has been relatively unimportant in the past. Africans comprise but seven per cent of the world's population. They have taken only a passive role in world affairs. However, the geopolitical significance of the continent of Africa—to Europe and Asia, and, in fact, the world—has been conspicuous. At present, not only is the human factor acting with more telling effect, but the locational relationships of Africa to Europe and Asia have become enhanced as perhaps never before in history, and, economically, Africa is replacing India–Southeast Asia as a raw materials source for Britain and other Western states.

The navigation ventures of the Iberians wrought a fundamental change in the geopolitical character of the Mediterranean and Africa. Although divided by religion after the Islamic conquests of the African, Asian, and Iberian lands peripheral to it, the Mediterranean Sea had remained the center of world trade; the commerce of the Mediterranean—which was the focus of that world—flowed along the sea. And, as contacts with the Orient opened up near the end of the thirteenth century—whereby the Mediterranean sea route connected with the overland caravan trails from the East—the Mediterranean remained the commercial waterway.

However, as the circum-African ocean routes replaced the caravan-Mediterranean trade lines, the status of the Mediterranean Sea *and area* underwent a complete transformation. The sea, North Africa, and Southern Europe went into a decline, and Africa south of the Sahara assumed a geopolitical significance hitherto unforeseen. Immediately, the nations engaging in the Indies' trade—*Atlantic* European powers that had accrued strength concomitant with the recession of Mediterranean states *and* as the ocean trade routes became paramount—seized control points along the African coast, on or offshore, for the protection of their shipping lines. Thus was coastal Africa laid claim to and spottily settled as trading posts and fuel and provision stations were set up. The interior, difficult to penetrate and having no part in this contest for world trade dominance, remained unknown and largely unclaimed.

The final scramble for African territory took place in the last 80 years. The "dark continent" was a comparatively new venture in colonial conquest. Until the latter part of the nineteenth century, European holdings in Africa continued to be coastal trading posts or ports where ships might take on fuel and food. However, the conquest of the continent began in the sixteenth century, and it was the coastal explorations of the Portuguese that were the first of the many that finally put Africa under the domination of Europeans. The remnants of the very extensive holdings of the Portuguese are the islands of the Azores, Madeira, Cape Verde, St. Thomas, and Principe; and Portuguese Guinea, Angola, and Mozambique—a total area of 796,000 square miles and a population of nearly 10 million.

No holdings remain to the Dutch in Africa today. The Dutch began acquiring territory when, at the closing of the port of Lisbon to their ships, they started to make the long trip to the East Indies to bring back the spices themselves. Previous to this, they had acted as distributors of Oriental goods for the Portuguese. Needing a waystation on the route to the East, in 1652 the Dutch established a colony on the Cape of Good Hope. They also engaged in trade in Africa—as a matter of fact, it was a Dutch ship that brought the first slaves to the colony of Virginia in 1619.

Although the Dutch almost drove the Portuguese out of Africa, they eventually lost all of the extensive territories they at one time held—in 1814 selling the Cape Colony, the remaining possession, to the British as part of the peace settlement following Napoleon's defeat. This left large numbers of Dutch nationals within British territory, however, and when slavery was abolished throughout the British Empire

in 1833, several thousand rebellious Boers (Dutch settlers) left Cape Colony, trekked inland to the Veld, and set up the Orange Free State, Natal, and later, the Transvaal Republic. Natal was annexed by the British in 1845. In 1867 and 1884, diamonds and gold were discovered in the Dutch-settled territories and, when a great influx of British settlers moved in, conflict developed betwen the Dutch and British leading to the Boer War at the end of the century (1899-1903). The British were victorious, and in 1910 the Dutch and British settlers joined to form the Union of South Africa as a Dominion within the Commonwealth of Nations. The historical background of the Union of South Africa gives a clue to the friction that has developed in the present decade and helps, also, to explain the *apartheid* policy of the Dutch, now in power in the Union's Parliament. No holdings remain to the Dutch in Africa today.

Early official British interest on the continent was almost entirely concerned with protecting the trade route to India. The dispossession of the Dutch and the acquisition of as many islands and good harbors along the west coast as was possible were prompted by this policy. When the Suez Canal was opened in 1869, Britain was just as active in securing control points along the Mediterranean–Red Sea waterway as it had been in obtaining territory in east and west Africa when the route rounded the Cape.

Nongovernment agencies in Britain, however, became interested in Africa itself—scientific societies, missionaries, explorers, trading companies. Mungo Park explored the Niger River area for a British scientific society; David Livingstone and others worked in East and Central Africa; and Cecil Rhodes led the activities of the British South Africa Company in the south central area.

The extension of British interests in the Mediterranean (for the protection of the water route) led Britain to establish or enlarge protectorates over Aden, the Sultanate of Zanzibar, and Egypt. With the assumption of virtual control over the foreign affairs of Egypt (1882), Britain found it necessary to extend its influence up the Nile—into the Sudan and Uganda—at the same time that Cecil Rhodes was pushing British influence up from the south. This suggested to British empire-builders the possibility of a vast British domain extending from Egypt to the tip of the continent on the south—the only gap in British territory lay between Rhodesia and Lake Victoria. This was closed, after World War I, when the German East African dependency of Tanganyika became a British mandate. Space does not allow a recital of the history of British African acquisitions further than has been given. A glance at the political map reveals, however, that the British holdings on the continent are second only, in area, to those of the French. In area, they constitute nearly three million square miles and over one-fourth of Africa's people (50 million).

France, too, early became interested in trade with the East and, hence, in establishing waystations as control points along the route. Between 1640 and 1700, the French established themselves on Madagascar, on the outlet of the Senegal River in the west, and on the Ivory Coast. There was little official interest in these undertakings, however, and the settlements were merely forts and trading posts through which slaves and ivory flowed out to the world.

It was not until after its defeat by Germany in 1870-71 that France turned seriously to the building of an empire in Africa. Then, from the Barbary Coast, they pushed south to link up with the Guinea Coast holdings. De Brazza carried out extensive explorations in Equatorial Africa and, from there, the French spread their control into the Lake Chad district. From their tiny foothold in Somaliland in the east they pushed westward to the Upper Nile. At the latter point, however, they were stopped and forced to withdraw by Kitchener (British). Thus, the French ambition to extend a continuous empire, from the Senegal River in the west across the broad part of Africa to Somaliland in the east, was frustrated.

They emerged with the largest territorial holdings in Africa but, to the present, these territories have not been the source of wealth that have the British and Belgian colonies, due to the fact that so large a part of the French empire lies within the Sahara. Recent geologic exploration, however, suggests that there are mineral, petroleum, and even water potentials hitherto unknown. Further work is necessary to reveal the extent and value of these resources.

The Dutch, British, and Portuguese empires developed largely as a result of attempts to control the sea lanes. Not so with the French Empire in Africa; it is a land domain. Its "lifeline" is the great net of caravan trails, the main line of which extend from Algiers across the Sahara to Timbuktu, with branches reaching east to the Lake Chad district, south to the Ivory Coast, and west to Senegal. Today, busses and automobiles travel these routes, and the planned railroads have been extended to Colomb–Bechar (southward from Algiers) and from the Dakar–St. Louis district eastward to Koulikoro—but from there on the desert trail takes over. As with the projected Cape-to-Cairo Route of the British, the airplane, run on scheduled flights to the main centers of all of the French African territories, may cut down on some of the extensive plans for surface transportation.

Shortly after the expulsion of the Moors from Spain that Iberian state reached across the Strait of Gibraltar to acquire territory. It laid hold on three points on the shore of what became Spanish Morocco—Melilla, Ceuta, and Alhucemas Island. Spain went no further than this out of respect for the papal line of demarcation and because its energies were taken up with activities in the New World. In the final scramble for territory in Africa during the last quarter of the nineteenth and early part of the twentieth centuries, Spain took possession of Rio de Oro in order to curb French expansion, and later extended its holdings in North Morocco. Except for the strategic value of Spanish Morocco, the African colonies of Spain have been of little worth. They included, besides those mentioned, the Canary Islands and Rio Muni on the Guinea Coast. The total area was some over 136,000 square miles, Rio de Oro being the largest; the total population numbers only about 1.5 million, two-thirds of these people living in Spanish Morocco. In 1956, Spanish Morocco was given its independence; Ceuta and Melilla, however, remained part of the territory of Metropolitan Spain.

The Germans, like the Dutch, were dispossessed of all of their African holdings. Although as early as 1861 the German State of Brandenburg founded trading posts on the Gold Coast, it was not until after the unification of the German states under Bismarck that that nation began to acquire an empire. Twenty years later, however, Germany had annexed Togoland, the Cameroons, Southwest Africa, and Tanganyika. It held these until the close of World War I when the colonies were divided among Britain, France, and Belgium as spoils of war. The Cameroons and Togoland were divided between Britain and France; Southwest Africa became a mandate of the Union of South Africa, and Tanganyika of Britain; and Ruanda–Urundi was attached to the Belgian Congo.

Not until the second half of the last century did the European powers embark on a large-scale colonization venture in Africa. When it did start in earnest, around the 1880's, it became a free-for-all among England, France, Belgium, Germany, and Italy. Little Belgium, under Leopold II, took a leading part in getting the movement started and came in for a sizable share along with England and France. On the whole, the colonization of Africa was a scheme on the part of the European states to occupy the continent and divide the spoils. After 1870, European territorial claims changed in pattern from a rim of small coastal holdings to a mosaic of colonies, protectorates, and dependencies that spread over the vast unexplored interior like a veritable patchwork quilt. Only a few native states retained even a shadow of autonomy.

NATURAL FEATURES

Not only is Africa the most colonial of continents, it is also the most tropical—undoubtedly the political status resulting, at least in part, from the latitudinal position. Bisected north and south by the equator, the great proportion of this huge triangular mass of land is either tropical forest, or savannah, or desert. Only the extremities of the continent—Cape Province and the Mediterranean slopes and plains—lie outside of the equatorial zones; these are dry subtropical in climate.

Africa is a block plateau. Seemingly there are no obstructions to communication into the interior for there are no real mountains other than the folded Atlas. However, the plateau edge drops abruptly to the shore or to a narrow littoral plain, and all but one of Africa's great rivers fall into sea, often in a series of rapids that must be portaged if the river is to be navigated. Thus, the physical structure of the continent has helped to keep Africa the "dark" (unknown) area that it was for ages. Disease, tropical rivers bordered by tangled jungle that made penetration beyond the water courses difficult, and the primitive peoples all had a defensive character in warding off intrusion. Fact *and* fancy kept men out of interior Africa and held the European to the fringes and accessible portions. The great interior remained within the realm of the almost unknown until very recently.

Today Africa is not the fearsome continent that it was in the past. There are still many "dark" aspects to Africa—as the living conditions of and discrimination against many of the natives, the strife between European and native, and native and Asian, the unknown extent of the resources, etc. Perhaps the airplane, and World War II—when logistics required the movement of men and supplies from Dakar across the Sudan to Khartoum and hence northward to Egypt or Aden or some other spot in the Middle East—spearheaded a more rapid unfolding of Africa than any other factor. World War II and the ensuing cold war gave impetus to the geologic exploration for mineral resources and the opening up of new mining ventures.

PEOPLE AND POPULATION

In terms of the human element, Africa falls into three major divisions—the Arabs, the Negroes, and the Europeans. The Arabs occupy the North, but they have spread their religion southward so that, ethnically, the Saharan peoples and the northern Sudanese are related to them, having adopted the Moslem faith. Negro Africa extends along the Guinea Coast and southward perhaps from the 12 or 15 degree parallel of north latitude. It coincides broadly with tropical Africa. Europeans form a dominating minority throughout Negro and Arab Africa.

This division has mixed elements of both racial and ethnic factors, however, for the Arabs are "white," as are also the Egyptians and Ethiopians although their skin color is darker than that ordinarily associated with the word Caucasian. These peoples belong to the Hamitic and Semitic groups of the white race. In terms of the indigenes, a color line and an ethnic line—the two practically synonymous— can be drawn; this would pass (with some minor adjustments) approximately along the same parallel of north latitude. The North is white Africa, the South, black Africa, the North is Moslem and Christian, the South, generally, pagan. However, scattered unevenly across both sections is the Caucasian European, making up but a tiny fraction of the total population.

Africa's population is increasing—and, with the beginning of industry, the increment can be expected to go higher. The African population is very unevenly distributed. Parts of the continent—the limited fertile portions—are already overcrowded, as the Nile Valley in Egypt (one of the most densely populated areas in the world), the coastal regions of Mediterranean North Africa, Cape Province and Natal, and portions of the Guinea Coast and Nigeria. In some of these areas the agricultural population runs to several hundred per square mile. In some of the fertile and densely populated belts (as well as in many other regions of Africa), soil erosion and over-grazing are an acute and growing threat; fires, set by the natives to clear the land, are destroying both the soil and the vegetation.

The underdeveloped areas of Africa are largely in the equatorial central portion—the tropical "black belt." About 150 million people inhabit black Africa, which is all colonial, except for Ethiopia and Liberia, and controlled by four European powers—Britain, France, Belgium, and Portugal.

COLONY EVALUATION

The French territories. In French Africa— largest of European colonial holdings in area but predominantly desert—people and resource development are largely in the coastal districts or spottily distributed where conditions are favorable. French Equatorial Africa has scarcely been touched; it is one of the least developed colonies on all the continent. However, in Senegal and the French Niger River area, extensive projects of redevelopment and rehabilitation of the Negroes have made a good start. Sufficient geologic explorations have not been made to determine the mineral and water resources of the French territories. At present, except for some gold exported from Equatorial Africa, the exports of the French colonies consist of agricultural products and the value of the exports is not great. Dakar and St. Louis on the southern half of the big bulge of Africa, have isolated locations relative to the rest of the continent and to the Mediterranean due to the great desert hinterland that extends in back of them. Nevertheless, locationally, Dakar may be very strategic—as during the last war when it served as the port of entry through which allied soldiers and supplies funneled eastward to the battle zones in and around the Mediterranean. Of greatest value of the French African colonies is Algeria, strategic in location with reference to Europe and the Mediterranean, and with mineral and agricultural resources that are also very significant.

In the Niger River country of the Sudan the French find promise for agricultural develop-

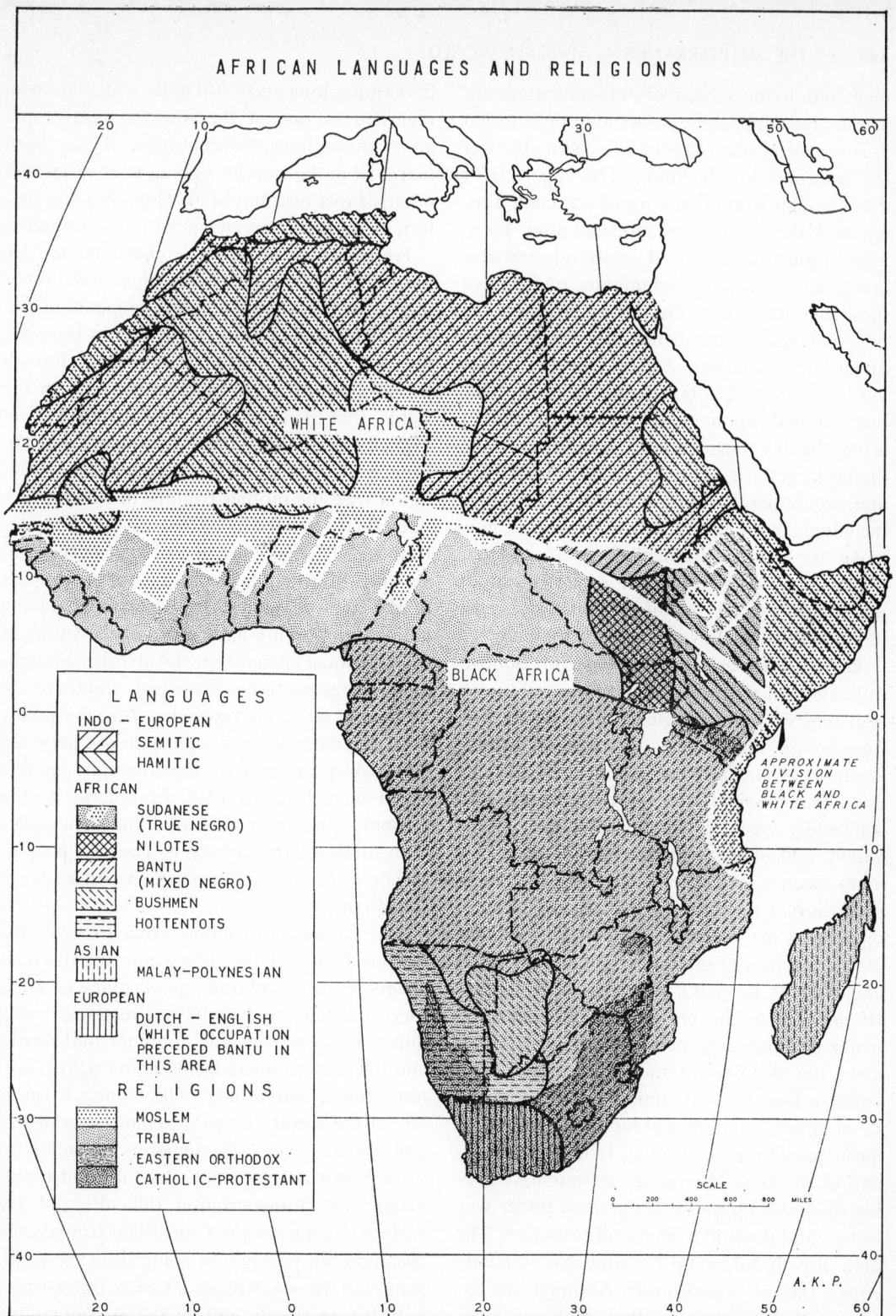

AFRICAN LANGUAGES AND RELIGIONS

WHITE AFRICA

BLACK AFRICA

APPROXIMATE
DIVISION
BETWEEN
BLACK AND
WHITE AFRICA

LANGUAGES
INDO - EUROPEAN
  SEMITIC
  HAMITIC
AFRICAN
  SUDANESE
  (TRUE NEGRO)
  NILOTES
  BANTU
  (MIXED NEGRO)
  BUSHMEN
  HOTTENTOTS
ASIAN
  MALAY-POLYNESIAN
EUROPEAN
  DUTCH - ENGLISH
  (WHITE OCCUPATION
  PRECEDED BANTU IN
  THIS AREA
RELIGIONS
  MOSLEM
  TRIBAL
  EASTERN ORTHODOX
  CATHOLIC-PROTESTANT

SCALE
0 200 400 600 800 MILES

A. K. P.

Figure 19.1. Africa has been referred to as the "Dark" Continent. However: 1) nearly half of the continent is populated largely with peoples of Caucasoid stock; 2) the populations of about half of the continent hold to one of the great religions of the world—not tribal religions.

ment and, in the Sahara, of obtaining minerals. These areas appear to be opening up a bright era in a period when France as a colonial power has been steadily declining. The Niger River development is in the nature of a French Tennessee Valley Authority; modeled after TVA, it will transform semi-arid grasslands and arid desert into a thriving community of irrigated farmlands. It is located in the region where the Niger makes its big bend into the northern Sudan and southern Sahara, in the Niger "Delta." Over 27,000 native farmers have been settled upon some 100,000 acres of fertile, freshly irrigated land. Already it is one of the largest rice-growing centers in Africa, and, where desert once obtained, other crops, including cotton, peanuts, corn, fruit, etc., now make the desert productive. Modern techniques have doubled the per acre rice output until it now exceeds that of the famed rice bowl of the Mekong Valley of southern Vietnam.

Recent discoveries in the Algerian Sahara indicate that that vast desert may hold mineral reserves comparable to those of the Belgian Congo. The geologic survey of the Sahara has just begun. Early indications are that mineral—and possibly water—resources may be sufficiently great to expand settlement, cultivation, and industry in the interior. The Colomb–Bechar area, in western Algeria, holds promise of large mining and industrial developments. Coal reserves, estimated to contain 20 million tons of good coking fuel, are being exploited at Kanadsa just west of Colomb–Bechar. Up to the present this has been the major resource exploited in the Sahara. However, the deposits of manganese, lead, and copper close by will undoubtedly mean the development of a major industrial center in and around Colomb–Bechar. In the region bordering the Atlas Mountains, an extensive geological and geophysical program is under way to find and develop existing oil resources. The area already taken up by concessions nearly equals that of France itself. Although the extent of the resources of these Saharan territories have not been proven, indications are that they are very large. The Sahara, nearly

2500 miles long and 1800 miles wide, has been regarded as one of the world's great empty areas throughout the centuries. It has been marginal in the extreme. These discoveries and others, however, may somewhat alter the pattern of economic ascendency on the continent.

French colonial policy is characterized by hindsight. The French policy of assimilation of native peoples should perhaps be mentioned in brief. This policy finds expression in the relative lack of racial prejudice among the French people both at home and abroad, and in the status that is eventually anticipated for all French colonial territories; the intention of the French is to integrate the dependencies into a union with the mother country in which every individual shall be a citizen of the "Greater France." Theoretically, the policy is excellent; actually, it has not been carried out in the spirit of the avowed policy. In Algeria, where the natives supposedly have attained the status of full and equal citizenship with all other Frenchmen, representation is not equal, and there are numerous other discrepancies. Had the policy been effectuated as designed it is likely the North African (at least, the Algerian) trouble might have been avoided. France, up to the present, appears to have used hindsight rather than foresight in carrying its colonial peoples through the transition from dependence to sovereignty.

The Belgian Territories. Area for area the Belgian Congo is the richest unit in Africa. It covers nearly a million square miles of territory, and has great variety of resources: rich mines of copper, tin, gold, uranium, and cobalt; and tropical products including oil palms, cotton, coffee, and rubber. The Congo River is one of the world's largest streams, in both size and volume, with a tremendous potential for waterpower development. But falls and rapids make river transportation difficult, and the early navigator on the Congo had to make no less than ten portages in going from the headwaters to the sea. Roughly, half of the territory is lush forest land, and, in the mesopotamian stretches of the Middle Congo are great areas of as fertile soil as can be found in Africa.

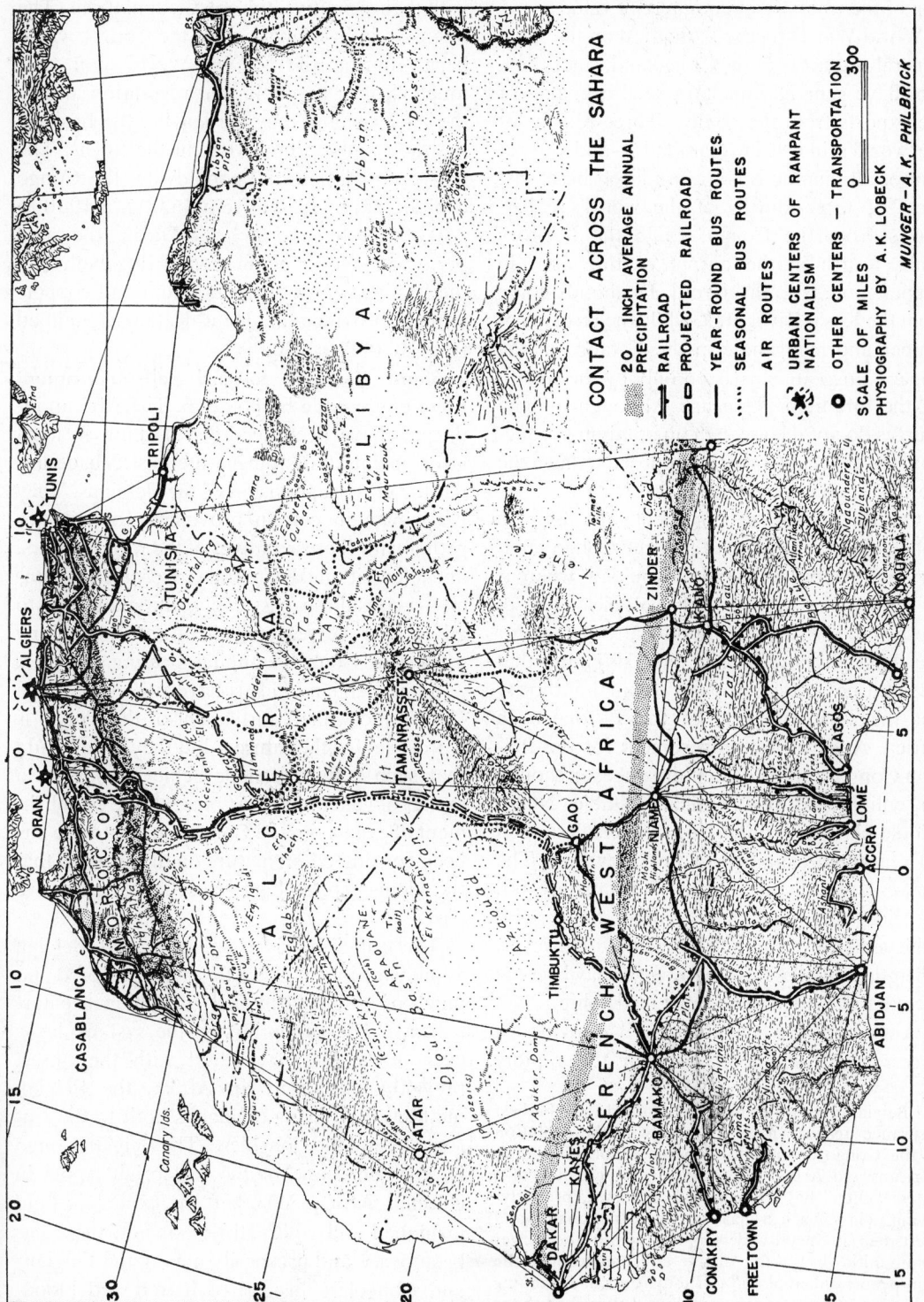

Figure 19.2. (Courtesy Edwin S. Munger, American Universities Field Staff.)

Profuse as are the forests, only a small proportion of the trees are of commercial value.

World War II focused attention on the great mineral resources of the Congo and, since then, ores have generally made up well over half of the exports from the colony. Three-fourths of the world's industrial diamonds—and 63 per cent of all diamonds—are produced here; just short of three-fourths of the world's cobalt comes from the Congo, while the territory ranks fourth in the output of tin, sixth in copper, and seventh in gold. Diamonds come from the Kasai River area, while the reserves of copper and manganese in the Katanga of the upper Congo are surpassed only by the wealth of the uranium deposits. Although official sources do not release data on uranium production, the Belgian Congo is supposed to have the world's leading reserves.

On this disturbed continent, the Belgian policy of moderation has kept the Congo territory politically stable and untroubled, whereas in all of the surrounding colonies—except those of the Portuguese—political strife and/or racial hatreds have created tense situations that threaten not only European colonial authority but the very existence of the European in Africa. And yet, self-government for the Belgian Congo is still a distant dream, even though an enlightened, economically stable Negro middle-class is springing up—where less than 50 years ago cannibalism was prevalent. The natives are content; and the Belgians are full of pride over what they consider to be solid achievements in running the colony. However, when this middle-class matures, it may become the core of Congo nationalist leadership.

A new native "bourgeoisie"[1] provides a necessary steadying element in the rapidly mushrooming cities and industrialized districts with their primitive, uprooted populations. The intensive industrialization of the Congo, which began during the Second World War, has touched off a psychological revolution among the Africans and they are leaving the bush by the thousands to find work in the towns. The native population of Leopoldville, the Congo capital, had increased from 46,000 in 1940 to 250,000 by the end of 1954. During the same period, the Negro population of Elizabethville, the leading center of the uranium and copper-mining province of Haut–Katanga, jumped from 30,000 to 130,000.

Slight gestures toward self-government have been made by Belgium. The African indigenes have been accorded a share in local government affairs during the past decade under the close supervision of the Belgians. They participate in certain provincial councils together with representatives of the white settlers, and a few sit on the Central Government Council—a consultative assembly whose task it is to advise the Governor-General of the colony during the Council's annual meeting.

Some Belgian officials have suggested that a "black-and-white" parliament of the Congo is a prospect for the future—but they usually add that such a thing can be achieved only in a matter of generations. At present, the establishment of even a limited Congolese electorate has been considered premature on the grounds that the Congo is "still too close to its primitive past."

The criticism has been made that Belgian administration in the Congo has savored too much of an old fashioned "enlightened paternalism." The supporters of the system, however, reply that, compared with the unrest prevailing elsewhere in Africa, the Belgian methods are paying dividends both to the Europeans and the Congolese. The Belgian Congo is, currently, one of the few bright spots in colonial Africa. Whether the policy is "old fashioned and paternalistic" or not, there has been peace and prosperity among the Belgians and Congolese instead of hatred and bloodshed.

---

[1] Belgian authorities have maintained that the best insurance against violent outbreaks in the evolution of the Congo community (composed of 12 million Africans and 70,000 Europeans) is the creation of a native "elite," based on a well-organized, property-owning class. Such a class of Negro merchants and craftsmen is steadily developing within the larger communities where the "native city," adjacent to the European residential and office quarters, is becoming a significant business center with well-furnished shops and comfortable hotels.

Physical unity, in terms of transportation connections within the colony and to the oceans, has been a problem for the Belgian Congo. One rail line connects the industrial districts in the Upper Congo with Leopoldville and, hence, to the Atlantic; this is entirely within Belgian territory. Another more direct route crosses Angola (Portuguese) to Benguella, while connections with the Indian Ocean have had to take a circuitous route through Northern and Southern Rhodesia and Mozambique to the Portuguese port of Beira. A new line (that involves ferrying Lake Tanganyika), completed in 1956, connects the Lake Tanganyika–Kabalo (on the Congo) line with the Upper Congo industrial areas and provides an Atlantic-to-Indian Ocean route that cuts off hundreds of miles of travel. Although the territory is webbed with a network of rivers, transportation via river and rail facilities involves such an amount of transshipment that costs are considerably raised. Further, such shipment is slower. "Portage" railroads have been constructed along those stretches of the Congo River where falls and rapids make navigation impossible.

Good communications are vital to the successful development of the Congo but enormous difficulties have to be overcome to provide suitable roads and railroads. Jungles and rugged terrain have to be surveyed; materials for construction must be brought in from long distances. Plans have been made for the building of about 3000 miles of main highways to be completed by 1960. The most important of these new arterial roads will join Bukavu (north of Lake Tanganyika) to Stanleyville, 400 miles away to the northwest. This road will cut in half the present rail and water route needed to link the two towns. The existing transport route requires three transshipments from rail to barge and back before reaching Bukavu. The new road, which will have to pass through mountains nearly 5,000 feet high before plunging down into steamy jungles, is to be hard surfaced and over 25 feet wide. The Congo River—navigable for more than 1,000 miles from Leopoldville to Stanleyville—and

its tributaries, however, will for long remain the main means of transport in the colony. Large 600-ton barges can use these waterways easily and thus provide cheap transport.

The British Territories. In the early part of 1948 two events occurred in British Africa which had deep significance for its future. An African mob advanced against the Governor's Castle at Christiansborg, in the Gold Coast, and was stayed only with bloodshed that spread throughout the countryside; and, secondly, the Smutz Government fell in the Union, giving way to the Nationalist Party with its program of *apartheid*. In the first case, the process of handing over a greater share of government to Africans in the Gold Coast colonies was accelerated. Today, as Ghana, the Gold Coast is independent. In the second case, at the southern end of the continent all hope for a more liberal native policy was submerged, and, since then, it has been difficult to see any probability of its revival in the near future.

Throughout the British colonies in other parts of Africa the task of orderly evolution was rendered more difficult by the violence of these opposing political trends in the west and south, although British colonial policy has changed. The "old colonialism" was abandoned for a policy that anticipates eventual sovereign status within Commonwealth for all dependent territories. The postwar years have seen an accentuation of political strife and race conflict in East and Central Africa, more particularly in the colonial territories of Kenya, Uganda, and Tanganyika where the discord has been most intense. The causes of the disputes are more apparent than are the remedies. Among the reasons for the conflict are the fact that the colonists have carried with them into the new lands their political traditions and inherited freedoms, and have attempted to transplant them *per se*. These frequently run counter to the policies of the Civil Service Governments attempting to establish their order and influence. Secondly, the ultimate responsibility for policy lies not in the colonial governments but with the distant Government of Great Britain. The whole situation—political, economic, and social—has been complicated by the presence and rapid increase of an Asian minority which migrated from India. Had this third population element not been present, the situation would not be nearly as complex. A further reason for conflict lies in the early errors that were made in preempting the land for white occupancy, particularly near Nairobi in Kenya. This has left a resentment that has never been overcome. Although readjustments of territory have been made—as in 1932 when large additions were made to native reserves—agitators do not hesitate to keep resentment alive. Lastly, the granting of independence in other British areas throughout the world—as the winning of freedom by Burma, sovereignty to India (which local Asians in Africa interpreted as having been "wrested" from Britain), the rapid political progress in West Africa, and the change in the whole colonial policy of the Commonwealth—reacted upon the small core of Africans who lead the masses of inert natives.

The northern territories (Kenya, Uganda, and Tanganyika) have a combined area of some 700,000 square miles and an African population of about 20 million, scattered irregularly in tribal units. The European population numbers about 50,000 of which only a small proportion are on the land. The Asians (artisans and clerical workers largely) total approximately half a million. Kenya has the largest European population, numbering perhaps 30,000. Both Asians and Africans are increasing very rapidly, the latter group having doubled itself in the past 30 years.

As in most other parts of Africa, many of the European and Asian colonists are African-born, consider Africa their homeland, and have never seen either Europe or India. However, the Asian still turns to India for support and political strength; as for the European, he looks south to the Union of South Africa and not to Britain, for the mother country is pursuing a colonial policy of eventual self-determination for these territories that, in the eyes of the colonist, can only mean the ultimate repudiation of his influence in Africa. Both Asian and European have become apprehensive of the future, but it is the European who is in the most difficult position.

The entire history of modern Africa has been told in the last 50 years. Until well into the last quarter of the nineteenth century, in general, the indigenous people had had no contact with the outside world or its civilization. They had experienced only the horrors of the slave trade and the occasional contact with explorers. They had neither the plow nor the wheel, they had no written language, no alphabet, no universal tongue. Although they were few in number as compared to the large spaces that they inhabited, they were constantly at war, one tribe with another; their animals were disease ridden; and they lived primitively, governed by the traditions of the tribe and the fantasies of the witch doctors. There were no roads or permanent structures, and only the crudest forms of Iron Age implements of agriculture and industry had been evolved. Superstition substituted for religion, the witch doctor for medical services; there were no schools; only in rare instances did trade and barter exist. In no area had there developed any form of representative government other than that exercised by the elders and tribal chiefs, the clan leaders, and warrior organizations. Although Europeans and Asians had established themselves in the coastal littorals, the great interior hinterland remained unknown and untouched. Populations were almost static because wars and disease offset the natural increase.

Africa, in the past half century, has been changed almost beyond recognition. In the British, Belgian, and French North African territories, African achievements have undoubtedly been more remarkable than in any other area of colonization within an equivalent period of time. Today, Africa, although still colonial, is a continent of young countries relatively well equipped with modern roads, railroads and other means of communication, with towns, hospitals, schools, and scientific services; and, as industry has developed the resources, some of the amenities of modern civilization have been provided along with the basic needs of the indigenes. A new economy was imposed upon the subsistence economy that had obtained; tribal wars were ended, and the population began to mount rapidly. The largest proportion of Africans are still living in native reserves and are agriculturalists, and the native economy as yet is but little above the subsistence level. However, slowly the people are acquiring better methods of animal husbandry and soil cultivation.

The rival claims of African, Asian, and European do not present easy solutions. The European, who believes that his control and leadership are needed in Africa for a long time —and who desires to keep some hold over the strategic resources and territories of the continent—has been reluctant to let go. He has, also, been unwilling to accede any of the trusteeship to the Asians who, in British territories, regard themselves as equal members of the Commonwealth with the Europeans.

The first practical experiment in racial partnership is being made in the new Federation of Rhodesia and Nyasaland. The total area of the Federation is over 485,000 square miles, consisting of Southern Rhodesia, Northern Rhodesia, and Nyasaland. This is larger than the whole of the Union of South Africa, larger than the combined area of the American states of Texas, California, and New York. As yet the Federal territory is sparsely populated, numbering about seven million of whom Europeans comprise 215,600; Africans, 6.7 million; Asians, 14,200; and mixed nationalities, 10,-000.

Although the whole of the Federation lies within the tropics, the elevation of the greater portion of it is such that nearly all of it is favorable for European settlement. Under the federal system, the three component units will continue to hold the same political status as formerly. Southern Rhodesia is described as a self-governing colony; Northern Rhodesia and Nyasaland are protectorates administered by the Secretary of State for the Colonies on behalf of the United Kingdom Government. Northern Rhodesia, however, has a considerable degree of self-government.

The Federation has a Governor General appointed by the Queen. There is a Cabinet presided over by a Prime Minister. Members of the Cabinet are taken from the Federal Assembly of 35 members, made up as follows: 26 elected members (of European or Asian extraction) of whom 14 are from Southern Rhodesia, 8 from Northern Rhodesia, and 4 from Nyasaland; 6 African members of whom 2 are elected from each component unit; and 3 European members "charged with special responsibilities for African affairs" of whom one is elected in Southern Rhodesia and the other two appointed, one each by the Governors of Northern Rhodesia and Nyasaland.

Although this is a representative form of government, the European preponderance should be noted—representation of the two races is wholly out of proportion to their numbers, leaving governmental control, literally, in the hands of the white population. A similar experiment—but ethnic, not racial—has been carried on in Algeria by France. Here, too, the same discrepancy of representation is found, freely admitted—and, in some instances, severely criticized—by the French. The unequal representation in government personifies the European fear of submergence by the native. Any representation of the indigenes in government is considered as a step ahead, and through this multiracial policy the British hope to stem the spread of terrorism, found in the northern territories, into Central Africa.

The economic potentials of the Federation are considerable; mining is the mainstay of the economy, and minerals make up the greater proportion of exports. In 1952 the combined external trade of the three territories totaled 850 million dollars of which slightly over half represented exports. These exports include copper, zinc, lead, and tobacco from Northern Rhodesia; tobacco, asbestos, gold, textiles, and chrome ore from Southern Rhodesia; tobacco and tea from Nyasaland. In copper output, Northern Rhodesia ranks fifth in the world, while in asbestos production Southern Rhodesia holds third place (*i.e.* of known production).

The Federation of Rhodesia and Nyasaland

has no seacoast, and hence, like the Belgian Congo, is dependent upon foreign ports for the shipment of its goods. The railroad systems of the two Rhodesias connect with each other as well as with the Belgian Congo in the Katanga region from which some Belgian ore is shipped, southward with the Union of South Africa and, hence, with the ports of Durban and Capetown; and, westward, with the Portuguese lines, at Umtali, with Beira. Northern Rhodesia has just one line of railway, its position determined by the mining enterprises in the territory, and running north-south to almost bisect the state. In all, the Rhodesias have 2500 miles of railway; but a new line, in the process of construction, will connect the Rhodesian railroads with the fine Portuguese port of Lourenço Marques. Only the southern part of Nyasaland is served by railroads and these connect with Beira. Main roads, which are in the process of modernization, connect all the main centers of the Federation, while secondary roads serve the rural areas.

The Central African Federation is a very critical experiment. Its success or failure, which must be measured very largely in terms of the welfare and progress of the native population, will be a definitive chapter in modern African history and would be most likely to influence the course of events in East Africa and even in the Union of South Africa. At this point some concessions are in order. One must frankly admit that the federation of Southern Rhodesia, Northern Rhodesia and Nyasaland places power in the hands of the white population which could be used against the interests of the native population. On paper and in the minds of its really enthusiastic supporters, it purports to initiate an effort to associate natives and Europeans in the government of the Federation and to set in train developments which in the indefinite future will give equality to civilized men of both races. Many of the natives who stubbornly resisted federation to the bitter end did so in the conviction that federation actually increased the chances that, in spite of the announced program of multi-racial cooperation, a rigid rule of white over black will ultimately be established. Most native leaders are openly distrustful of federation. Their fear is that the economic improvements promised by federation will mean more European immigrants, more overcrowding and less land for the natives, more taxes, more pressure to leave their inefficient land to work for the white man,

without any really substantial improvement in their political and economic status.[2]

Nor are the fears of the natives without foundation. The settlers in Southern Rhodesia came from the Union and from the first they have accepted the "segregationist assumption" that African and white should live in separate areas. Although the doctrines and policies of segregation are not as extreme as are the *apartheid* policies of the Afrikaners in the Union of South Africa, belief in separation is largely prevalent among the English settlers in Rhodesia. Ideas from the south and north continually flow into Central Africa, and federation does not imply that this area is immune to *apartheid* policies or terrorism.

There has been talk of federation, also, among the three states of East Africa. But, while reasons for unification are perhaps as strong as in Central and South Africa, the objections to such federation are not as easy to surmount. South Africa was unified as the aftermath of war; the Central African Federation resulted from the predominance of English settlers over the Dutch, fear that the immoderation of the south would spread, British prestige, and the absence of a coherent Indian group.

In East Africa each of the three racial groups—African, Indian, and European—represents a strong force politically and territorially. In Uganda the natives are disinclined to give further concessions to Europeans or Indians, either "on the land or under the law"; and, further, historic treaties and calculated policy have, in effect, given to Uganda the promise that native rights will be held paramount. In Kenya, so effective has been the terrorist policy of the Mau Mau that under federation the Europeans would be forced to grant "damaging political and economic concessions," whereas in Tanganyika, "influential Indian opinion is convinced that it would be folly at the present juncture to give up the special bargaining power provided by the separate status of Tanganyika as a mandated territory." According to a prominent Indian leader the correct

2 Cornelis W. Keiwiet, "African Dilemmas," *Foreign Affairs*, Vol. 33, No. 3 (April, 1955), p. 454.

policy for Indians is "to resist closer federation between Uganda, Kenya, and Tanganyika in order not to obscure the special claim, not merely of local Indians but also of India, to settlement and opportunity in East Africa." A number of the Indians living here regard the East African territories as a natural area to provide space for expansion for Indians in the future. India, in turn, acts as the spokesman for the Indians in East and South Africa. Although there is a difference of opinion among observers regarding what India might or might not do about East Africa as a pioneer area for Indians, Keiwiet states: "In spite of her present neutralism, there is a latent and implicit imperialism in India that could be shocked into action not only over Kashmir or Pakistan or the exigencies of her economic development but also over Indian 'nationals' in Africa. Active and hostile action over these issues is not thought to be inconsistent with India's general emphasis upon pacifism or neutralism."[3]

In none of the territories of East, Central, or South Africa are there any real signs that the three racial groups "will follow the patterns of miscegenation and assimilation" that fused the peoples of Latin America into new social hybrids. From the inception of the Portuguese and Spaniard into South and Central America there was "enough of the hospitality of church, home and blood to obscure any hard line of separation between Europeans, Africans, and the native Indians." In Africa, the opposite situation prevails; there is an inhospitality of church, home, and blood—and this separation of the races creates some of the most severe of the existing problems in the Dark Continent.[4]

Particularly in Kenya do the Europeans understand that improved relations with the natives are necessary to their very existence in the Colony. Since, in general, East Africa has less natural wealth than either the South or Central portions—at least Uganda and Kenya—federation is even more of a necessity in these territories. But it is difficult to say whether unification will result from the current moves toward a new policy or not. Since it is a key area in the Western defense system, such cohesion would be highly desirable. Kenya and Uganda are British protectorates; Tanganyika, formerly a German colony, is a Trust Territory.

Tanganyika is the richest of the three East African territories. Still primarily an agricultural country, its wealth coming from its great exports of sisal (in which it leads the world), the mineral resources of the Trust Territory are still largely untouched because of the lack of transportation facilities. From what is known of the reserves of ore, they vastly exceed those of Kenya and Uganda (another reason for federation for the industrial potential of Tanganyika would complement the economies of the two protectorates). The 1940 discovery of the great diamond field of Shinyanga resulted in Tanganyika's being allocated a quota of 10 per cent of the world's diamond sales. Coal fields and iron ore beds lie only 35 miles apart—a proximity that usually leads to the establishment of heavy industry. In the southern part of Tanganyika are major deposits of lead. Kenya's resources are few and the white settlers in the latter colony regard federation in a favorable light. They would like to see the Trust Territory integrated into the Commonwealth domain.

Tanganyika is the largest of all of the United Nations' Trust Territories. But, aside from this fact of size and the fact of natural resource wealth, Tanganyika still looms important in Africa today. This importance springs from the political experiment that is being implemented in that territory—namely, the innovative concept of "seven-seven-seven." This would give equal representation to each of the three races in the Legislative Council. The plan calls for seven Europeans to represent the 15,000 Europeans; seven Indians, the 72,000 Asians, and seven Africans, the 7.5 million Negroes. Although this does not give equal representation on the basis of population numbers, numerically, the representatives of the three races are

---

[3] *Ibid.,* p. 456. (Summarized and quoted from Keiwiet.)

[4] *Ibid.,* p. 456. (Summarized and quoted from Keiwiet.)

equal, and in no other multi-racial area in Africa is such equal representation of races even considered as a government policy. Racial relations within the Territory are unusually good; there is no segregation of races in urban areas and whites and non-whites travel together. Tanganyika appears to be moving more surely toward the goal of a workable society of many races, creeds, and colors than perhaps any political unit in Africa.

In the Union of South Africa is found perhaps the world's most involved racial situation. Here, there is not only the three-cornered problem of white versus Negro versus Indian, but great complexity is added by the Colored (or mixed blood) *and* the division among the white minority, the latter split sharply along national, ethnic, political, and even economic lines. The 2.5 million Europeans are divided numerically about 60-40 between Afrikaans-speaking (Boers) and English-speaking (Britishers) people; the non-European elements, numbering about 10.5 million, form a majority more than four times greater than the ill-cohered Europeans. Of the non-Europeans over 80 per cent are native African, the Colored comprise about one million, Indians 250,000. Political power lies within the hands of the Europeans with the Afrikaners majority presently in power—and since 1948. Under their policy of *apartheid,* interracial and inter-European relations have constantly deteriorated.

Apartheid may be defined as the separation of the races—residentially, socially, politically. Segregation "on a grand scale" was lately begun in the Johannesburg area when 50,000 native urban dwellers were forcibly uprooted from their homes in native suburbs (formerly set aside for the Negroes) and moved into new villages, lying at greater distances from Johannesburg, and constructed for the purpose. One of the leading principles of the *apartheid* doctrine is that the "Reserve" is the home of the African. The concept embodies the idea that, although the native may move to the white man's cities to work, he must regard himself as merely a temporary dweller there; and further, he must expect no benefits to accrue to himself, other than wages, from such work and residence.

At any given time, 4,000,000 to 5,000,000 Africans are outside the reserves. The soil of the reserves is badly eroded, through over-grazing by cattle and the ubiquitous goats which strip the last bit of grass from the unprotected land. Since it is quite impossible for these areas to support the native population, anywhere from 50 to 80 per cent of the men are away working in the gold and diamond mines, industry, domestic service, etc. There is, of course, a fairly large detribalized group of Africans who have no footing in the reserves at all. But most Africans who come to the cities or mines do so for periods of service—nine to fifteen months in the mines, and less regular terms in other employment—leaving their families in the reserves to till the small plot of land which is a kind of old age insurance.

This practice of migratory labor has struck at the roots of the African's tribal and family institutions and shattered his traditional sanctions of behavior without putting others in their place.[5]

The African compares favorably with Europeans as an industrial worker and, as the industrial revolution (now taking place in the Union) progresses, he is being drawn, in constantly greater numbers, into manufacturing plants. In reality, the *apartheid* program of racial segregation is having an adverse effect upon the economy—and this is likely to become more marked as industrial development progresses. Africans make up 28 per cent of the work force in business and finance, 50 per cent in manufactures, 87 per cent in mining, and 92 per cent in agriculture. Serious uncertainties to the economy have been created by the recently initiated policy of total segregation.

There are some who believe that the South African industrial revolution will "carry his cause" for the Negro. But, whereas even half a decade ago, certain concessions—as better housing, wages, education, etc.—might have satisfied them, today African leaders are unwilling "to wait for such long processes to operate. Today, African leaders are demanding equality, a highly explosive concept in South

---

[5] Gwendolen M. Carter, "Can Apartheid Succeed in South Africa?" *Foreign Affairs,* Vol. 32, No. 2 (January, 1954), pp. 297-98.

Africa and one which almost no European is prepared to grant."[6] At times the Indians in South Africa have contributed funds to the Negro campaign for bettered status; however, there is a natural basis for antipathy between the Indian and the African because, economically, their interests clash. Hence, the continuance of mutual assistance is problematic.

The antagonisms of Afrikaner and Britisher weaken the position of the European minority. Most attitudes of the minority European population toward the majority Negroes and mulattoes are based on fear, and are not difficult to understand. Nor are the attitudes of most of the politically vocal non-Europeans difficult to comprehend. Less easy to fathom are the antagonisms of the two European factions: the Afrikaners of Dutch ancestry, who are the majority white faction and largely Nationalist in political alignment; and the English-speaking people of British descent.

It was 300 years ago that the Boers settled in the territory that now comprises the Union. Severed from political ties with the Netherlands by the British, they migrated from their original settlements in Cape Province into the Veld country when the British came in. Their deep feeling of racial consciousness arose from a close and long association with the native people who opposed their northward migration; Dutch antagonism for the British deepened as, with the discovery of diamonds and gold, the territories to which they had migrated were opened by the British government to floods of English prospectors from Cape Province and the British Isles. The majority whites, the Boers were forced (after losing the Boer War to England) to unite with the English in the formation of a Dominion which became a part of the British Commonwealth. From that period onward, the Afrikaners, as they more lately became known, have striven to achieve political ascendency in the state—accomplished in 1948 (when the Smuts Government fell and Malan was elected Prime Minister) and held since that time.

Because of the dual character of the European population, the Union of South Africa has two capitals—the administrative capital, Pretoria in the Transvaal, and Capetown in Cape Province, the legislative capital; two official languages, English and Afrikaans; two flags— the British Union Jack and the Boer tricolor, orange, white, and blue; and two national anthems—*God Save the Queen* and *Die Stem van Suid Afrika* (*The Voice of South Africa*). The English South Africans have been concerned, since the Nationalists came into power, lest the day come when their rights will be curtailed.

South Africa is about one-sixth the size of the United States. The Union is comprised of the Cape of Good Hope, Natal, The Orange Free State, and the Transvaal—the latter two provinces largely Boer, the two former, in the majority British. Most of the more than 472,-000 square miles of territory are high, dry, rolling country; the grassland of the Veld (meaning *grassy plain*) covers much of the central plateau which falls abruptly to the narrow littoral in the Drakensberg Escarpment. Between the plateau edge and the ocean the precipitation increases, and here lush semi-tropical forest and grasslands prevail.

Although farming and grazing were the most important economic activities in the early days of European settlement, today manufacturing and the mining industries bring in the greatest proportion of the national income. However, wool earns three times as much for the Union as do diamonds despite the fact that South Africa is the world's leading producer of the gem variety. (The Belgian Congo has the leading output by weight, but only about five per cent of the Belgian Congo production is of gem quality; South Africa, although producing less by weight, leads in value owing to the higher proportion of gem stones.)

Gold mining is the outstanding economic activity of the Union. The Union of South Africa produces between one-third and one-half of the world's gold from mines in the Transvaal and the Orange Free State. Uranium, extracted from the gold tailings, may in time prove more important than the gold ore itself. In 1953, nine mines in the Transvaal and six

---

[6] *Ibid.,* p. 298.

in the Orange Free State were constructing uranium extraction plants. Besides diamonds, gold, and uranium, South Africa has important deposits of copper, manganese, and chrome— all important strategic ores—as well as coal, iron ore, and limestone in close proximity to serve as the bases of heavy industry. As recently as mid-1954, a great new coal reserve was discovered in northwest Transvaal. Except for coal and iron ore, located in west central Natal, and diamonds and copper in the extreme northwestern portion of Cape Province, all of the minerals are highly concentrated between Postmasburg in the north central part of Cape Province, near Kimberley in the Orange Free State, and northward through the Transvaal to the northern border.

The industrial revolution of South Africa began with the discovery of gold and diamonds. Today manufacturing brings in most of the national income. Small plants, constructed during World War I when the Union was cut off from its source of manufactured goods, have expanded into a large and varied industry that not only makes South Africa self-sufficient in manufactures but provides goods for export. The mining areas in the Transvaal, the Orange Free State, and Natal (Northwest) are the leading centers of heavy industry, producing iron and steel and steel products especially; the lighter, consumer industries—which include leather goods, clothing, textiles (wool), wine and brandy, and sugar—are concentrated in Capetown, Port Elizabeth, and Durban. Machinery is also manufactured in the latter ports.

The agricultural products reflect the climate. Along the east coast, sugar cane, pineapples, and wattle predominate; on the plateau, tobacco, alfalfa, wheat, fruits, and vegetables grow in the irrigated districts whereas on the natural precipitation, barley, rye, oats, and maize are raised; in the better watered regions of Cape Province citrus fruits and grapes are predominant. On the grasslands, animal industries are very important, with sheep as the chief livestock. The semi-arid uplands of the state produce fine merino wool in quantities second only to the Australian output; in more humid regions, dairy and beef cattle become more important. The backbone of all of this production is the native labor—the industrial and mining forces drawn from Africa's "black millions"—bound by racism, and kept in menial and inferior positions by the *apartheid* policy of the Boer-dominated government.

History in Africa is out of joint. The most liberal mind may contemplate its dilemmas and see no clearly right road. They could not be resolved at a single blow by violence nor by a single act through decree. Here men are the prisoners of one another, products of an historical process that brought them together without softening their differences or dissolving them into each other. As matters actually stand, the best that anybody who has observed the history of mankind can say is that those societies prosper best where all who live within them have some reason for hope and faith in the future.[7]

_____
[7] Keiwiet, *op. cit.,* p. 457.

WESTERN AND NEUTRAL LANDS OF ASIA AND THE PACIFIC

20

East Asian Offshore Islands and the Pacific

Asia is the world's largest continent and well over half of mankind make their homes upon its surfaces. It is easy to forget that Asia extends through 165 degrees of longitude—nearly half of the way around the globe; that Indonesia (if set over northern Eurasia) would string from London into the heart of Siberia; that Britain would fit comfortably into a corner of India just as the whole of Europe could be eased into a corner of Asia. The countries of South and Southeast Asia and of the East are large countries, and they stretch across a very wide area; each has a high degree of individuality, and may contain many different peoples; most have a cultural history far more ancient than that of the West and religions older than Christianity—and culture and religion have left their mark upon the peoples and the countries.

No land mass in the world could be more various in its scenery than that of South and East Asia—desert country, jungle country, towering highlands, and fertile plains. And yet, despite the variety, the countries of East and South Asia are bound together by many common elements. By Western standards they are comparatively undeveloped, subsisting by agriculture rather than industry; because of their low standards of living, they are all burdened with high rates of illiteracy; they all support relatively large populations whose increase is a threat to even the present standards of living.

Despite the age of their cultures, many of the Asian states are regarded today as new countries. In this sense, the most recent are the Federation of Malaya, North and South Vietnam, and Cambodia; among the oldest are Thailand, China, and Nepal, which have been sovereign nations for a very long time. India, Pakistan, Ceylon, Burma, Indonesia, and the Philippines all have gained independence since the end of World War II; Formosa became the

"Republic of China" when Chiang Kai-shek and his nationalist army took refuge on that island in 1949; Singapore, North Borneo, Sarawak, and Brunei are administered by Britain.

All of the countries represent peoples who have undergone profound and even revolutionary changes in political and social environment within a relatively short time. All are countries which have spent most of their time in modern history as political and/or economic dependencies of the great Western powers. All are emerging nations. In some states, the emergence has been from dependent to independent status; in others, it has been the change from one type of political structure to another vastly different; in all, there has been *an emergence into* a changed and changing world *with a sharpening of self-consciousness in respect to that emergence*.

In many of these countries, the alterations in political and social structure have been *superimposed* (at times arbitrarily) upon cultural patterns that have remained almost unaltered for centuries. This has created inner as well as outer conflicts. Modern techniques and new ideas are being embraced; there is still, however, much of the old. All are inhabited by what the Westerners loosely refer to as "colored" peoples—although the color of many, like the Arabs, is merely the deep burn of the sun. Most of the people harbor a deep suspicion for the European and, despite the close ties with the Western nations, have much more in common with each other than with any European allies. All of the countries and territories in the area are faced with much the same problems: how to improve their standard of living and keep their growing populations fed; how to modernize their economies—and close the gap between the Asian level of technology and that of the West.

THE ATTITUDE OF THE EAST TOWARD THE WEST

In the turbulent flux of history, dissimilar peoples usually adopt dissimilar methods of adaptation and readjustment because of the conditioning of their past experiences. Today, many of the Asian peoples draw back from the advice and assistance of Western nations because of their recent colonial associations with these states; but these Asian nations will likely achieve a political, economic, industrial, and even social revolution despite this seeming independence. However, science and technology have made the peoples of the world inexorably interdependent, it is the psychological and the cultural barriers that prevent the development of greater understanding and closer ties.

No nation has been exempt from racial pride and cultural arrogance, "*but these,*" remarks an Indian (the Vice-Chancellor of the Benares Hindu University since 1939), "*have become dangerous in western nations who have been the political masters of the world in recent times.*" The Asian point of view is, at least in part, expressed in these words of Sir S. Radhakrishnan. Continuing, he comparatively reviews Asian and European historical achievement and, while so doing, gives Westerners an insight into the attitude of the Asian intellectual toward the West—thus providing the latter peoples with a penetrating look at themselves "as others see us."

Herodotus opens his history with a vivid antithesis of Europe and Asia and ends it with an account of the defeat and discomfiture of Persia at Salamis and Platea when Europe was rid of the Asiatic intruder. Yet the Persian Empire of the 5th century B.C. with its vast stretch of territory and wealth of ideas was no mean achievement.

The period between the fall of Rome and the rise of modern Europe is described as the dark ages. Whatever it may have been for Europe, it was not specially dark for Asia. Across these centuries, the spirit of the Buddha moves, linking together, in a spiritual fellowship the countries of the east from Ceylon to the furthest isles of the Japanese Archipelago. In China, the Tang dynasty, famous for its poets and pilgrims, ruled from 618 to 907 A.D. The work of Indian teachers and the Chinese pilgrims forms an epic comparable to the feats of the most daring explorers. It was in this period again that the disciples of the Prophet conquered Syria, Egypt, North Africa and later Spain. For four centuries while the European mind was deep sunk in ignorance and sloth, Herbert Fisher writes, in his History of Europe, the intellectual leadership of the western world belonged to the peoples of Islam. The Arabs, whose learned men read Greek and commented on Aristotle, stirred the reviving Latin races into intellectual life.

All this may or may not be but it is asserted with confidence that Asia has been lacking in the two fundamental features of modern life, political organization and scientific spirit. This country has known even in the pre-Buddhistic times the three main forms of government which are still preserved in our political life, vital Kingships, Orthodox republics and federal governments. The monarch who planted trees and dug wells along the roadways, built rest houses and founded hospitals, who sent missionaries to different parts of the world, who preached the law of piety, who proclaimed a better way of conquest than that of the sword, who enjoined respect for other faiths than one's own, is not antiquated even for political wisdom.

Again, Asia is not all astrology and magic. The world owes to Asia the rudiments of agriculture, the discovery of metals, the art of writing. A historian of Science, Dr. Sarton, relating the achievements of Greek science observes, "The foundations of Greek science were wholly oriental, and however deep the Greek genius, it is not certain that it could have built anything comparable to the actual achievements without these foundations." Even in the matter of applied science, Asia's influence has been considerable. One can only mention a few examples, cotton and silk, printing and gun powder.

Any student of history knows that European civilization was not much superior to the Islamic or the Chinese or the Indian till three centuries ago. Our recent past, however, has been feeble and dull. Intellectual life slackened. Memory took the place of research. We repeated old texts. Industrious imitation of the works of a previous age was our art and literature. Echoes of the past were heard, correct in form but void of meaning. When we walk through the inland parts of Asia where European influence has not penetrated, we find squalid towns, deserted villages, insanitary dwellings, neglected fields. While Asia's development was arrested, Europe forged ahead by the application of science to industry, agriculture and warfare. This gave European nations an immeasurable superiority which they used to bully and exploit the weaker peoples of Asia and Africa. The world has no pity for the weak. Their very weakness presents too great a temptation to the strong who aspire for wealth and power. Countries which preferred a gentler destiny were subjugated. Subjection is the greatest evil not because it deprives us of our material wealth but because it degrades our mind and corrupts our character.

Contact with the west has served as a great corrective, a valuable discipline. It stirred in us a passionate longing for freedom. India treating courageously the ideas of her rulers, accepting whatever is valuable in their technique was never, deep in her soul, subdued. Despite an outward submission to her fate, she lived her own inward life divinely certain of her own destiny. The overlordship of tangible things, the occupation of territory did not give a purchase on the soul . . . The human mind even under a heavy pressure of national degradation is still a mighty vehicle to the operation of which there is no assignable limit. Asia produced leaders who spoke on behalf of their countries with firmness and dignity. The names of Zaglul Pasha, Mustafa Kamal, Sun Yatsen, Chiang Kai-shek, Gandhi, Nehru leap to our minds.

Nations are not born or reborn in a day. We have to prepare ourselves for a new world both mentally and morally. We must emancipate our minds from the tyranny of custom. If our first duty is to remember the past, our next duty is to forget it. We must realize that there can be no liberty without social justice. We must remove glaring contrasts of wealth and poverty, disease and illiteracy, exploitation of men and women and for this great task of an economic and social revolution we require imagination and unselfishness as well as scientific and technical skill.

All this belongs to the equipment of civilization, which is different from the purpose of civilization.[1]

EAST AND SOUTH ASIA IN WORLD ECONOMY

The power of any country, as well as the standard of living, depends upon the natural resources, potential and actual. To say that the states of East and South Asia have unexploited reserves of raw materials and potential sources of power is to say very little; the people of these areas will receive no benefit from them until the natural potential has been put to some productive use.

It is obvious that some of the natural wealth has been utilized for a long time. It was the riches of the East that attracted to the Orient every trading ship, from the argosies of Vasco da Gama to jet planes. Much effort—largely European—has gone into the development of the area more lately, and a great flow

---

[1] Sir Sarvapalli Radhakrishnan, "The Spirit of Asia," from a talk broadcast over All-India Radio, New Delhi, India.

of products has come from it. Even so, the East remains, as a whole, very little developed. In industry, scarcely any country except Japan and India has even made a beginning except in isolated instances. This is one of the reasons that the standards of living remain so low. Other factors that explain the great poverty and backwardness of the people are the pressures of population upon the land, the high rates of illiteracy, and the almost complete lack of technical skills. Most basic of the causes of poverty and retardation, however, is the primitive level of the cultivation.

This factor is particularly critical because East and South Asia are predominantly agricultural; except in the urban areas, *people live off the land*. Yet techniques of cultivation throughout the entire area are about the same as they were two thousand years ago. The bullock draws the handmade wooden plow, the rice paddies—or fields of dry crops—are planted and hoed and reaped by hand, the grain is husked by primitive means and winnowed; only the regularity of the seasonal rains, the intensive use of fertilizer, and the long hours of work can account even for the modest returns. Over very large areas jungle and desert continue to bar cultivation.

Not all of the land cultivated is in food crops, and, hence, Asia makes a considerable contribution to world economy. In exchange for such imports as manufactured goods, East and South Asia supply the world with the bulk of its tea, rubber, jute, and spices, one-third of the vegetable oils, and two-thirds of the world's tin. Significant as such products are, their value will always depend upon world markets the fluctuations of which are largely beyond the control of the Asian states.

Most of these countries wish to follow the example of the Western and Communist worlds, and industrialize. It is wasteful and expensive for any state to import goods for which it has the basic materials to manufacture and which it can learn to manufacture more cheaply for itself. Industrialization will provide many of the amenities of modern living. But few of these states, in their hurry to rush into industrialization—which to many seems to offer the way to a better life—understand that, before any widespread program of industrial development can be put in operation, a great deal of planning and effort, redeployment and investment is necessary. Construction of a factory is not enough. Cheap sources of energy have first to be assured, and effective communications established; skills and techniques must be mastered, and a new industrial labor force brought into being. It is often necessary to move populations, construct housing, and provide the public facilities necessary for urban living—all without the disruption of the vital food production. It is frequently forgotten that the Industrial Revolution *was a revolution indeed*—and that it has taken the Western world two centuries to carry it forward to the present state.

The political sympathies of the Asian states are varied. Within this area which stretches, for the most part, along the east and southern periphery of the Soviet Union, are nations that align themselves with all three of the power blocs of the world. China, North Korea, and North Vietnam, all Communist states, have already been discussed. The greater number of countries form the larger proportion of the neutral bloc. Here, too, are some few states that stand with the West forming, with the islands and countries of the Pacific, the forward line of Pacific defense—Japan, Formosa, the Philippines, Malaya, Singapore, Siam, Pakistan, Australia, and New Zealand.

Asia is a continent in ferment and in the process of awakening. Great forces are pulling at the peoples of this continent. One of these forces is international Communism; another is the meaning and capacity of the democracy of the West; the third force, the nationalism and neutralism of Asia itself, exerts a profound influence. Which way the balance of forces moves in Asia is perhaps the decisive factor in the political world of our time.

JAPAN

Certain geographic realities have influenced the geopolitical course that Japan has taken. First, Japan is insular—it is a group of 2000 or more islands. This has meant that the Japanese people have been navigators, putting to sea from their island base. Japan, therefore, is a maritime state interested in commerce and fishing. The insular location also gave the Japanese isolation and protection—and hence they developed a culture of their own, and self-sufficiency; under the protection of the surrounding waters, they were spared invasion and war. Never during historic times, except when the Mongols of Kubla Khan landed on Kyushu in 1274 and 1281 (only to be driven off by the winds which were wrecking their ships), was Japan invaded until American forces entered the islands in 1945. Insular location has, therefore, been an advantage; however, *it has also proven disadvantageous because it provided no room for expansion.*

A second geographic reality is the location of the island state along the fringe of Asia. Because of this position, Japan has historically had ties with the eastern continent. Further, this location has meant that Asia was the only area to which Japan could logically expand.

Thirdly, the Japanese Islands are mountainous. The mountain structure is extremely significant within Japan's geographical base. Only one-fourth of the country is plainsland and, of this lowland area, two-fifths is swampland; a mere one-sixth of the domain is cultivable. Due also to the mountain structure of the islands, there are sharp differences in the physical geography. Within the more obvious differences between highlands and lowlands are sharp local variations—as in soil, vegetation, and climate; the north-south alignment of the mountains also creates local differences. This regional fragmentation and diversity aggravates the problems of the country.

Superimposed upon these physical differences is a homogeneous people. Not even between the northern and southernmost islands, Hokkaido and Kyushu, are the differences very marked. The inhabitants of the Japanese Islands have been molded into a coherent social unit—they are a nation, a single people.

The fact of population explosion is a further reality. For approximately two centuries previous to 1832, Japan had a fairly static population because the society was such (feudalistic) that a larger number of people could not be supported. Such practices as infanticide, birth control, and the like were used to hold down the increase. Since 1870, however, when changes in the ruling house initiated social and economic changes as well, the population has increased rapidly; since that date the number of Japanese has more than doubled, increasing from 40 million to well over 85 million persons —and it is still growing. A large proportion of the increase has been absorbed by industry. But population densities, on arable lands and in urban centers, are among the highest in the world. Insularity, location, *and* population pressure have combined to foster the policy of aggression on other Asian peoples that has characterized the Japanese state for the past half century.

A seventh reality is the importance of agriculture in Japan. The cultivation is tied to the lowlands, to paddy-rice culture, and to supplementary crops; and it is so intensive a type of hand cultivation as to be horticultural in character. Agriculture forms the base of the Japanese economy.

Superimposed upon the agricultural base is a modern industry. The industrialization of Japan, which marked a dynamic change in the structure of the economy, didn't "fit" very well because the domain is inadequately supplied with the basic raw materials of heavy manufacture (another reason for the imperialistic expansion into resource-rich Manchuria and Korea). Japan is dependent on the outside for much of its industrial ores although the state is supplied with coal for fuel. However, despite the agricultural base of the economic structure and the inherent weakness for industry, Japan is the only Asian state that can be called industrial. For the area and resources, the achievements of Japan are noteworthy. The Island Empire has been—and undoubtedly will be again—a leading power in Asia as well as a world power to reckon with. India and China, both nations with a far greater areal, resource,

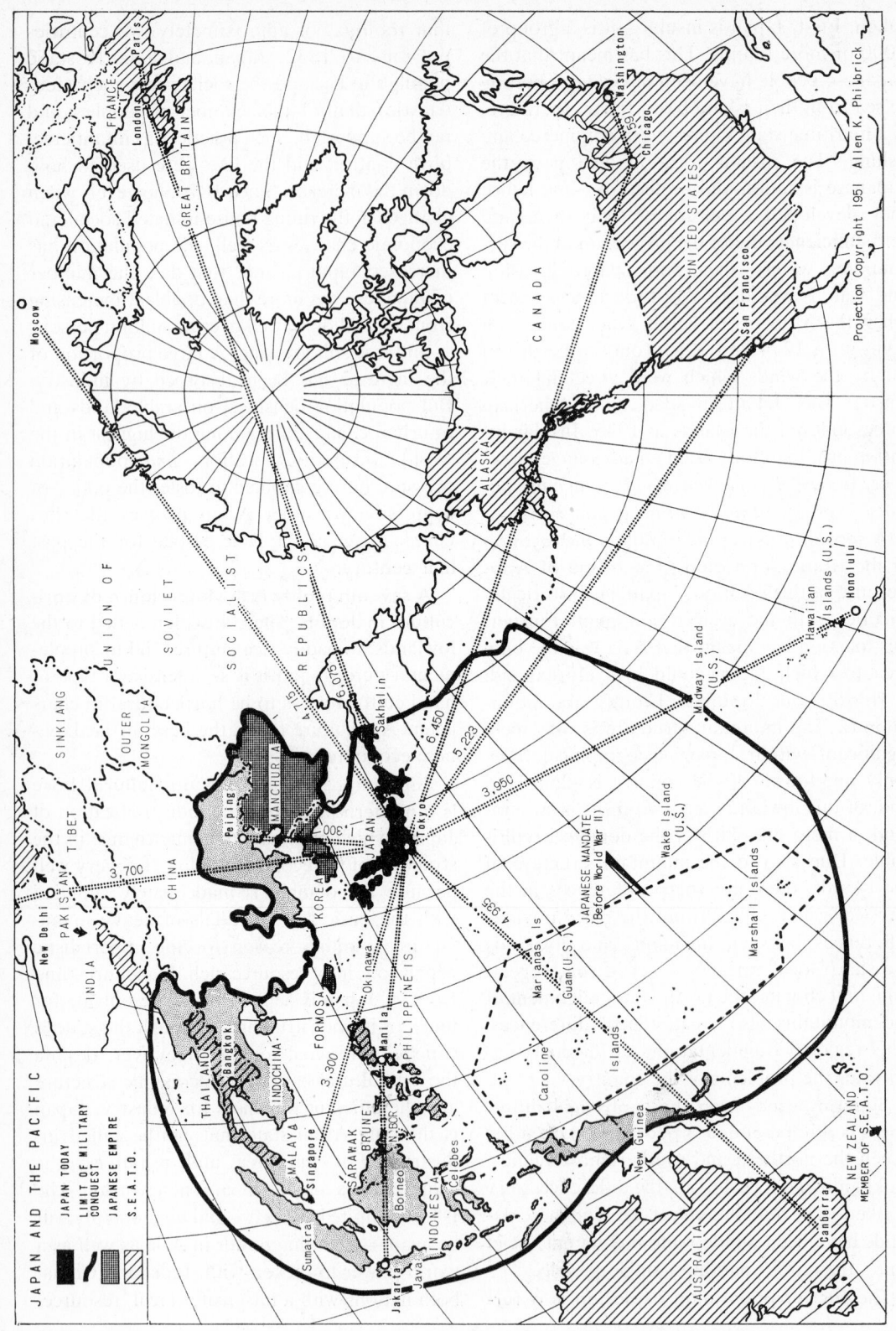

Figure 20.1.

JAPAN AND THE PACIFIC

JAPAN TODAY

LIMIT OF MILITARY
CONQUEST

JAPANESE EMPIRE

S.E.A.T.O.

Projection Copyright 1951 Allen K. Philbrick

and population base, will likely, in the foreseeable future, eclipse Japan as leading world powers, however. War in Japan and the postwar American occupation of Japan are two other realities that have made a tremendous difference on several aspects of the Nipponese state.

Geopolitical Considerations

The Treaty of San Francisco concluded with Japan on September 8, 1951 limited Japan to the four large islands of Honshu, Shikoku, Kyushu, and Hokkaido plus some 500 islets—a narrow domain 1300 miles long with a total area of 142,427 square miles. Postwar Japan is but a fraction as large as was the pre-1940 empire. The puppet state of Manchukuo is now Manchuria, a part of China; Korea is independent; the Kuriles and Karafuto (southern Sakhalin Island) have been returned to the USSR; Formosa is under Nationalist China; the islands of the Ryukyus and other Pacific Islands (former mandates of the League of Nations) are in American hands; fishing rights, which formerly had extended almost worldwide, were restricted to the home waters after the war. Except for the re-extension of Japanese fishing rights beyond these limits—notably southward toward and into Australian waters—the bounds of Japanese territory remain today as set by the treaty.

Although small, Japan occupies a strategic location. The Japanese islands enclose the shore of East Asia from Khabarovsk almost to Shanghai, controlling the Pacific approaches to Vladivostok (Russia's major Asian port) and Korea, and commanding the approaches to the Yellow Sea and, hence, North and Central China. Only the British Isles, commanding the approaches to much of Western Europe and to the North Sea, occupy a somewhat comparable position.

Under the security treaty, the United States is committed for an indefinite time to the defense of Japan. For the United States, the islands are a part of the first line of Western defense in the Asian area; and in the building-up of these Pacific defenses, the United States maintains bases on the Japanese archipelago.

The political role of Japan in Asia has been important. Considered a part of "Free Asia"—a name frequently used to designate Asian allies of the West as against the Communist and neutral states—Japan has recently swung more and more toward neutrality. Some Japanese visualize the role of the state as a bridge between the West and the East. The more logical ties and the historic associations have been with Asians. "Asia for the Asians," lately chanted by the Chinese, was first a Japanese slogan—a phrase designed to "make friends and influence" Asian peoples and, also, to gain acquiescence to the entrance of the Japanese armies when they invaded the French and Dutch colonial territories during the war, displacing the European authorities. Trade ties have also been heavily Pacific and Asian.

But Japan, with the only highly industrialized economy in Asia, is having difficulty regaining prewar markets and finding new ones. Japan depends on imports for a fifth of its food and for almost all of its industrial raw materials; and it needs to export in order to attain a viable balance, now unfavorable, to the island nation. In terms of volume, Japan's exports are only about half what they were before the war, and trade is more imbalanced, partly because imports are relatively more expensive. The Japanese are failing, to the extent of over a billion dollars annually, to sell enough goods abroad to pay for what they buy in foreign markets.

Before World War II Japan sold huge quantities of textiles in Asia, including the countries of China and Manchuria. Trade with the two states normally accounted for over one-third of Japanese foreign commerce; nearly all Japanese textile products were exported to the Asian mainland by 1939, and, of the total exports, more than three-fourths went to the Asian mainland or the adjacent islands of Indonesia. From these countries the state was able to purchase large amounts of food, cotton, and other materials. These are Japan's logical markets. Further, China is now a power in the East, and Japan must reckon with that giant state.

Therefore, aside from any position which the Japanese government may take regarding relations with Communist China, an important segment of opinion throughout Japan favors the establishment of relations with that new and powerful nation.

The eventual disposition of the Ryukyu Islands constitutes a problem for the United States. One problem resulting from World War II that yet remains to be solved is the disposition of the chain of islands—rugged and overpopulated—that stretches southward from Japan in the arc of the Ryukyus. The islands were first brought to the attention of the United States over a hundred years ago by Commodore Perry. This naval officer, noting the advantages that the islands provided for ship refitting stations, recommended that the United States attempt to secure a foothold there. The suggestion was turned down. American public interest was awakened in the archipelago, however, in the spring and summer of 1945 when American forces, island-hopping toward Japan, suffered large losses of life in establishing themselves on some of the islands of the Ryukyus and Bonins (Okinawa and Iwo Jima, especially). Following the fall of Okinawa, the Ryukyus as well as the Bonins (all Japanese Islands between northern Formosa and the 29 degree parallel of north latitude) were placed under provisional American jurisdiction. This is still their status. The future of these islands must necessarily be given serious consideration by the United States and the West; and a wide variety of factors enters into such a consideration.

The strategic location of the islands makes them of interest to the United States. Extending in an arc from southern Kyushu to Formosa, they enclose, with Japan and Formosa, the entire coast of East Asia and control, thereby, all of the outlets to the Pacific. In area (1291 square miles) about equal to Rhode Island, they extend for a distance of 500 miles north and south off the Chinese mainland. Okinawa, the largest island, comprises one-third of the total area; it would be easily defended for it is buttressed by other island outposts, and it is situated in such a manner that island air bases lie within close "striking distance" to the major target areas of the Asian east coast—from Vladivostok to the Si Kiang.

Ethnically, racially, and historically, however, the Ryukyus are allied to Japan. The languages are related; racially, the two peoples are undoubtedly the result of the blending—but in varying proportions—of racial strains common to both nationalities. In religion, however, they are unlike for only a small proportion of the Ryukyuans became Buddhist or Shintoist, the great majority holding to ancient animistic forms of religion.

Although, historically, the islands were for a long period under the dual domination of both Japan and China, the Japanese antedated the Chinese in the Ryukyus, penetrating the islands early in the twelfth century. About the fourteenth century Chinese influence began to be felt, but it was an influence that touched largely the upper classes. It was a cultural (art and literature) and political impact (i.e. the Chinese political patterns were introduced). However, both states exacted tribute from the Ryukyuans—simultaneously; and, even after Japan placed the southern islands under their "protection," the Chinese continued to collect tribute. In 1871 Japan, against the protests of China, formally annexed the archipelago.

Economically, the Ryukyus are not well off, and economic considerations must also guide the Ryukyuans in determining their political sympathies; further, the cost of continuing the American occupation also enters in. The islands have a population of 917,000, which means an average density of 709 persons per square mile. However, when the realities of the economy are considered, the density rises much higher. Agriculture forms the economic base, and 75 per cent of the Ryukyuans are cultivators; further, less than one-third of the island area is arable and, at present, only one-sixth is worked. Farms are miniature—about two acres in size—and barely provide a subsistence level of living.

While under Japanese suzerainty, many of the people were forced to emigrate to other areas, and they went chiefly to the Japanese Mandated Islands, Hawaii, or Peru. Following American occupation, the Ryukyuans were repatriated from the Mandated Islands (which became Trust Territories of the United States under the United Nations). This raised the population by about 132,000 persons. Although some 36,000 find employment (nine per cent of the working population) with the American occupation forces, the problem of livelihood is serious. The Ryukyuans, much as they appreciate the American aid in dollars that has been put into the islands, desire to be restored to Japan. This has been officially indicated at least twice.

The Potsdam and Cairo Declarations, the Japanese Instrument of Surrender, and the Peace Treaty with Japan give the United States the legal right to be in the Ryukyus. The Potsdam Agreement (July 26, 1945) limited Japanese authority to the four main islands of the Japanese archipelago and whatever minor ones the Allied Powers might designate. The Cairo Declaration (December 1, 1943) stipulated that the Allies intended to take from Japan those territories which it had gained "by violence and greed"—but the Ryukyus were not named specifically. When the Instrument of Surrender was signed by Japan on September 2, 1945, Japan concurred to the terms of the Potsdam Agreement.

Article III of the Peace Treaty treats specifically of the Ryukyus along with all of the other Japanese islands between latitude 29 degrees north and Formosa. On signing that article, Japan agreed to accept any American proposal submitted to the United Nations to place the islands under the Trusteeship of the United States, with the latter state as "the sole administering authority." The Article further provided that, pending such a proposal to the world group, the American state would be permitted to "exercise the powers of administration, legislation, and jurisdiction" over the lands and peoples of the archipelago. Japan, the United States, and 47 United Nations members signed the Peace Treaty on September 8,

1951; Russia, the other Communist states, and some few isolated countries did not.

The United States has not, to date, presented to the United Nations any proposal for the further disposition of the Ryukyus; and, it is likely that, if the United States submitted a proposal to the United Nations for a *strategic trusteeship* over the island arc, the Soviet Union would not concur. A settlement of the status of the Ryukyus is necessary if for no other reason than to maintain American prestige in Asia. If a trusteeship were established, it is likely that most Asians would look upon the move as imperialistic, making small distinction between trusteeship and outright annexation. Three courses appear open to the United States: 1) administer the islands, as now, while awaiting a general Far Eastern settlement; 2) annex or hold as trust territories only the southern islands of the group—which are most suitable to strategic purposes—and return the northern portion to Japan; 3) return the entire archipelago to Japan and lease bases from that state. The latter choice appears to be the best solution.

FORMOSA

Formosa, "the Other China," is a big mountainous island lying off the southeast China coast and separated from it by the 90-mile stretch of the Formosa Strait; it is 13,885 square miles in area and has a population of about eight million. A study of a map shows Formosa's strategic location with reference to the Chinese mainland and the western Pacific Islands. Particularly would it have strategic significance to the West if the island (and the Pescadores) were in the hands of an enemy. However, the question arises whether its significance is such to warrant the use of armed forces (and risk of a major war) to defend or reoccupy it. In event of another conflict, will the West need Formosa? Further—and this question is moral—should the United States, as an anticommunist power, "help to maintain a center of anticommunist resistance in China?"

These questions have, intermittently, been the subject of heated debates, particularly in government circles in the United States, ever since the Nationalist regime of Chiang Kai-shek fled to Formosa at the conquest of the Chinese mainland by the Communists. Here, the Nationalist Chinese set up what they regard as the legitimate Government of China, thereby creating another of the political anomalies of the post-World War II period—a country divided against itself, as are also Germany, Korea, and Vietnam. Populated with Chinese but under Japanese role since 1895, it was returned to China at the close of the war in 1945. It has been known by another name, for the Manchus who took it in 1683 named the island Taiwan ("terraced fields"). There was little development under the 250-year rule of the Chinese; on the other hand, Japan, within the five decades of its authority, wrought important changes in the island economy. The sugar industry was developed so that the home islands of Japan found their sugar requirements largely met from Formosa. Several hundred miles of railroads and fine highways were constructed; the irrigated acreage of rice was extended; hydroelectric dams for the production of power, an aluminum industry, and a cement plant went up.

Economically, however, the island is neither big enough nor its resources great enough to be very significant in global terms. The critical character of Formosa today lies in its location —strategic to Western defense plans—*and* in the attitude of the Chinese Communist and Nationalist governments toward the island. In the latter aspect, Formosa holds an importance far beyond its natural or even strategic significance.

The situation, as constituted, is delicate; Formosa was returned *to China* at the end of the war—not to a regime in power. Official recognition ordinarily is accorded any government—regardless of the ideology that the policies of that government represent—so long as that government holds effective control of the state. However, because the Western nations have feared Communism and the intent of Communist states, recognition of Communist China (more effectively cohering and controlling Chinese territory than at any period in modern history) has been withheld by most democratic nations, and the Nationalist regime has retained official recognition and a seat in the United Nations. This attitude of much of the West toward Communist China is inconsistent with past policy, also, for recognition was accorded to almost every other Communist state (excepting only North Korea and North Vietnam)—and efforts have even been made to make one such state an ally of the West, namely, Yugoslavia.

Acquisition of Formosa by Communist China is a matter of prestige—a quality highly valued by the Chinese and by all Asians smarting under previous domination of alien Europeans. The Nationalists are not merely interested in defending Formosa and the Pescadores and thus in maintaining the islands as their headquarters and domain; they view the islands as bases for a Nationalist counterattack against the Chinese mainland—with, it is hoped, United States support. While there is general agreement between the United States and Nationalist China on the strategic significance of Formosa and the Pescadores, there is a difference in point of view as to just how to deal with the over-all problem of China. Also entering into the American tactical and diplomatic approaches to the Chinese question are the attitudes of the Western allies of the United States, and their policies relative to China.

The problem of Formosa is very complex, therefore, for wrapped up in it is the whole enigma of the two Chinas. The basic aspiration of the Nationalists is an eventual return to the mainland—although they have carried out their strategy in line with the West's desire for peace because they recognize they can return to China only from within the setting of the whole Far Eastern situation.

THAILAND

Perhaps the most pro-West state of the Asian mainland is Thailand (land of the Thai —"free"—people), formerly called Siam. Thailand has long been independent. But, although it has maintained national integrity, it has had an uneasy independence because it lies within the area of the South China Sea—a region which can properly be called a "sensitive" portion of the globe both historically and in the present period.

The sovereignty of Siam as a state was formally guaranteed by the Franco–British agreement of 1896 and the London Convention of 1904, the latter likewise defining the respective spheres of influence of Britain and France on either side of the valley of the Menam River. Thus, its boundaries have been held sacrosanct. But, although it was immune from attack, the effect of these agreements was to convert Siam into a buffer state, and in this capacity it found its geopolitical role for many decades. With the independence of Burma and Indochina, the two European powers are no longer in a position to implement this policy—and it is likely that Thailand would prefer to find its security in regional alliances of its own choosing and in the United Nations.

A community of interests already binds Thailand close to its near neighbors—Malaya, South Vietnam, Cambodia, and Burma: namely, fear that they may in time be subjected to pressures from the two Asian giants on either side, India and China. Although Thailand experienced invasions from Burma in the past, at present China is held in greater distrust than is India due to the fact that one-fifth of the population of Thailand is Chinese. This Chinese minority is, moreover, more aggressive economically than are the indigenous Thai, and control a large share of the retail and import trade of the country; they are, also, a distinctive minority group, maintaining Chinese customs and showing little inclination to merge with the Siamese. Although the entrance of the Chinese into Thailand has been simply a natural drift of people southward, this alien group has and does cause a thorny problem, economically and legally. A further danger of these Chinese to the state is similar to that experienced in Malaya where local Chinese have been pressured by Communist Chinese infiltrators to sabotage the tin and plantation rubber industries.

Less than 25 years have elapsed since Thailand ceased to be an absolute monarchy. Since then frequent *coups d'etat* have indicated the unstable character of the more liberal government. The governments of Thailand have not always been good when judged abstractly, but the state has survived and no major revolutions have occurred to upset the general even tenor of Siamese life. Nor has the state been colonial —under the authority of another nation. This may account for the lack of "fence straddling" in the present critical period; Thailand is openly on the side of the West.

On the other hand, it is interesting to note that Thailand "is far more a politicohistorical phenomenon than a cultural one, and not one entirely prescribed by physical geography"; the Thai peoples are not confined within the limits of the state, and non-Thai peoples make their home in Thailand. Further, although the Menam lowland forms the core of the country, the plain spreads into Cambodia and blends with the Malayan Peninsula. Its boundaries, therefore, are not physical, and they have little or no "historical precedent." They are boundaries recently created by the "political manipulation" of outside powers. British and French rivalry has kept this state from being further carved up because neither of these two great powers could have taken more without incurring the protests of the other. "Political and cultural nationalism is new to the individualistic Thai peoples, and its rise among them may well provoke further boundary issues."

The stability of the economy offers a significant parallel to the political constancy. Thailand is a producer of surplus rice—in an area that is typically in need of food. Further, nearly three-fourths of its peasant farmers— which compose about nine-tenths of the population—own their own land, a high proportion in any part of the world. Nine-tenths of the cultivated acreage is planted to paddy rice. This monoculture is one of the weaker aspects of the economy, particularly when the predominant crop is the major export commodity —and hence dependent upon the fluctuations of the world demand. Rubber is the next important crop and, usually, the third important export; tin, mined in the southern extension of the country in the Malayan Peninsula, ranks between rice and rubber as Thailand's second greatest item of trade. The state normally places fifth in the output of tin concentrates and fourth among world producers of natural rubber.

Political change is the order of the day in Asia, and Thailand is not exempt. Thailand is still a monarchy, but acquaintance with modern technology and democratic institutions has aroused at least the beginnings of a desire for modifications. The time, however, has been too short to achieve realization as yet; Thailand might be termed a benevolent dictatorship —oriented toward the West and Western ideas.

Before the Indochinese stalemate that resulted in the partition of Vietnam into two parts, that French territory had been regarded as the front line, in South Asia, against the further spread of Communism. Today, Thailand and Malaya are the front line of resistance to the movement. Thailand is a relatively isolated and small outpost of freedom—but in an area where the West needs to maintain and build its strength.

MALAYA AND SINGAPORE

Malaya, like Indonesia, is a major producer of rubber and tin. One-third of the total output of the tin and rubber of the world comes from Malaya; in tin production it ranks first, while it is second only to Indonesia in its exports of natural rubber. Because of the value of these two strategic materials and because of its location Malaya is highly significant. It commands, with Sumatra, the Straits of Malacca, and reinforces the position of Singapore, vital outpost of the West in the Far East.

Politically Malaya, until 1948, was composed of three parts. The Straits Settlements (of which Singapore was the capital) consisted of a number of isolated tracts that included the important islands of Penang and Singapore as well as considerable portions of the mainland. The Federated Malay States, occupying the largest area, was made up of native states under British direction. The third sector was made up of some of the native states also under British direction but not associated with the Federation. They were called the Unfederated Malay States.

In February, 1948, after long consultations between the British Government, the Malay rulers, and representative groups of the people of Malaya, the governmental organization was changed to form the Federation of Malaya and Singapore. The new Federation under British protection was composed of all of the former territories except Singapore which became a Crown Colony; the seat of government of the Federation of Malaya is Kuala Lumpur. Singapore shares with the Federation certain common services and technical advisors, and Civil Service was made interchangeable.

Eight years after the establishment of the Federation, Malaya took another big step toward independence (February, 1956). At a London Conference between Malayan representatives and British authorities, an agreement was concluded under which the Federation of Malay States, as a member of the Commonwealth of Nations, took full control of all government functions on August 31, 1957. Until that date Great Britain conducted Malayan external affairs and defense. Under the Federation, Malaya has become not only a geographic but a political unit as well.

Thus was accomplished the political aim for Malaya, i.e. self-government within the Commonwealth of Nations—equal membership among the independent nations. There were some unusual difficulties involved in working out a federal form of government that would not prejudice the interests of the Malay States, however, and, since Malaya is a country of several races (Malays, Chinese, and Indians), the rights of all had to be protected. This latter aspect made it necessary to work out a formula for Malayan citizenship. A common citizenship with the Malayans is offered to immigrant races but is not automatically acquired; it must be applied for.

The Federation of Malaya[2] is 50,850 square miles in area, about four-fifths jungle; the population is estimated at 5.3 million people, including 2.6 million Malayans, 2 million Chinese, and 578,300 Indians and Pakistanis. Singapore is only 217 square miles in size and has an estimated population of about a million people, of which 800,000 are Chinese, 125,000 Malayans, and 74,000 Indians and Pakistani. The city of Singapore is one of the world's leading entrepôt ports, the major outlet for Malayan tin and rubber, and a guardian of the British sea routes. It grew out of a dream of Sir Stamford Raffles, who visioned its situation, at the apex of the peninsula that commands the Straits of Malacca, as the primary focus for all eastern trade. Although he did not live to see it—for at that period it was merely a coastal village and base point for traders and pirates—his dream came true.

The Chinese of Malaya have not been, until recently, a troublesome minority. However, since the end of World War II, the outstanding problem for the British in Malaya has been the sabotage of the rubber and tin industries by local *Communist* Chinese and infiltrators. Their aim was to create economic chaos, and they struck at the heart of the economy. Rubber trees were slashed so that plantations became armed camps; laborers in the tin mines were intimidated. For a decade the problem has been a very serious one, and progress of any kind—political, economic, or social—has been extremely difficult for Malaya has had to give first attention to its ceaseless fighting of Communist terrorism.

Malaya and Singapore are a "halfway house" on the sea route between China and India. They also lie midway between the other countries of the Indochinese peninsula and the East Indies. As a convenient market center for the whole area, Malaya held a significant place in Eastern trade long before Europeans navigated the Indian waters. However, because the indigenous people were, in the main, fishermen and cultivators from earliest times, the trade of the region was organized by non-Malayans—foreigners.

For a millenium Indians dominated the scene. Later, for a time, Arab influence was supreme in Malacca, a great trading port on the western side of the peninsula. From them the Malayans learned of the teachings of Mohammed, and today nearly all of the Malayans are Moslem. Not long after the Portuguese arrived in the East, they took Malacca (1511) which they held until driven out by the Dutch in 1641. Both Dutch and Portuguese attempted to maintain a monopoly on trade. To break the Dutch monopoly the British acquired Penang in 1795, and, in 1819, Singapore, and at these two points established free ports.

Because of its location, Singapore became the focal point of trade in the region. The city expanded rapidly. Malayans from other parts of the peninsula and Chinese were attracted to the southern peninsula tip, and, as its trade grew, Singapore became the mart of the Indian Ocean. It remains equally strategic and economically significant today.

Malayan tin and, later, plantation rubber—achieving sudden importance with the invention of the internal combustion engine and the pneumatic tire—made the economy of Malaya boom. Malayan standards of living are higher than are those of most tropical and Asian states.

Because of their enterprise, the Chinese have become a thorny problem in a number of South Asian and Pacific territories. In a number of places, Chinese control the retail trade and hold much of the economic power. They are well equipped to become colonists for they are ingenious, shrewd, economical, and hard working, but they are not missionaries. They are not interested in exploration for exploration's sake, nor are they generally concerned with the welfare or progress of the lands to which they travel. Their object is to make money, and for this the Chinese will live cheerfully in the poorest conditions and work tirelessly. They have a talent for trade, but they

---

[2] Nine Malay states—Perak, Selangor, Negri Sembilan, Pahang, Johore, Kedah, Perlis, Kelantan, and Trengganu—and two British settlements—Penang and Malacca—form the Federation.

are workers as well as traders and shopkeepers. It was the Chinese who led the way in the development of the flourishing tin industry long before the British arrived in Malaya.

Singapore and Malaya have recently both experienced an upsurge of nationalism and Communist pressure. Having been accorded the privileges of self-government, Malaya is now satisfied. But Singapore (almost one hundred per cent Chinese), one of the main remnants of the British Empire in the East, is seeking political concessions, and is vocal in its demand for independence.

The future of the two tropical areas is very significant not only to Britain and the Commonwealth but to the West as well. The Malayan Federation and the great free port and entrepôt of Singapore earn hundreds of millions of dollars in export and re-export trade every year; their strategic value has been assessed. They have remained the only two dependent British possessions in Asia, of first importance, that were not sovereign. Despite this, pressures for independence were not great until recently. As with the other Asian colonies of Britain—which have already achieved independence—Singapore will eventually be granted sovereignty within or without the Commonwealth, according to the desires of the people.

Although, for most of the past decade, Malaya has been the more turbulent of the two areas, recently the Federation has been far more stable than Singapore. The basic population element in the troublous Singapore situation is the Chinese. As previously indicated, four-fifths of the population of the island colony are Chinese—and of these, 50 per cent are young. The greater part of the Chinese stock was born in Singapore, but the rise of Communist China to a position of world power has aroused a latent racial and national allegiance among them so that today most of the Chinese are pro-Peking. The Chinese desire self-rule so as to orient Singapore toward China while the Communists among them would like to see the colony become a Communist community. Other Asians also want independence although along democratic and non-communist lines.

THE PHILIPPINE REPUBLIC

President Roosevelt's signature in March, 1934, to the Tydings–McDuffie Bill limited American rule over the 7,000 or more islands of the Philippines, and created a new political unit, the Commonwealth of the Philippines. The Tydings–McDuffie Act made the Philippines a self-governing commonwealth; full sovereignty was to follow 10 years later. However, World War II intervened, and independence had to be delayed until 1946. July 4, 1946, American Independence Day, marked the beginning of the Philippine Republic.

The American domain had enlarged greatly by pushing out its frontiers; now it was giving up one of its richest possessions to satisfy Philippine leaders and American business interests. The signing had an additional meaning to the Philippine people besides mere independence for *they traded certain economic advantages for political ambitions;* they gave up one of the richest tariff-free markets in the world for the right to manage their own affairs. Nominally they had had near autonomy—for the United States had treated the islands like an indulgent godfather and actually the Filipinos had had no grievances against the American nation.

Until the end of World War II, the Philippine Islands constituted not only the most unusual but also the most distant territory under American jurisdiction. Undoubtedly distance played a part in the evolution of the policy of control. From the first days as an American dependency, the Filipinos were tutored for self-government and the foundations for independence carefully laid; from 1916 on, the Islands had had a major voice in their own administration. In status, although a part of the Union, the islands were not a state, territory, colony, or naval base, but "a non-incorporated territory"; the people were citizens *not* of the United States but "of the Philippine Islands of the United States." They held most of the rights and privileges of American citizens but few of the responsibilities. They paid no federal or income taxes; they made their own laws (in all cases in which American laws did not specifically include the islands, local law prevailed), issued their own currency and postage stamps, and even made their own schedule of import duties.

The Spanish left a deep imprint upon the islands. The history of the islands might be said to have begun in 1521 with the discovery of the archipelago by Magellan, a Portuguese navigator in the services of the king of Spain. Shortly thereafter, Spain laid claim to the island group; they were named the "Philippines," after Philip II of Spain, by a Spanish exploring party that visited the islands 21 years after their discovery. Spanish domination lasted from 1565 to 1898 when, following the Spanish–American War, the islands became a United States possession. Spanish impressions upon the Philippines were lasting, however, one of the most significant being religious; the majority of Filipinos are Roman Catholic. The Philippine Republic is the only Christian state among all of the Asian nations. Two ties, therefore, bind the Philippines to the West: religion and the deep feeling for the democratic way of life and government.

The Philippines are tropical isles located 7000 miles westward from American shores. The Philippine archipelago lies 500 miles off the southeast coast of Asia, and nearly all the way across the Pacific Ocean from the United States. In area (115,600 square miles) it is about the size of Italy. It has more than 7000 islands, of which only 11 are relatively large, many of the rest being mere rock fragments projecting above the sea. The archipelago stretches north and south for 1,100 miles reaching approximately from 5 to 22 degrees north latitude. The islands are, therefore, tropical in climate. Rice, corn, and yams are among the major food crops cultivated, while agriculture produces abaca (Manila hemp, a rope fibre), copra and coconut oil, sugar, and tobacco for export.

When the Philippine Islands became a Republic, their new status was one of mixed blessings. With political sovereignty came the many problems of economic independence. Decreased production and reduced exports resulted from the war; some resulted from conditions inherent in the rural economy, as the prevalence of tenancy, insufficient capital and credit, and antiquated methods of farming. Moreover, the new government did not take immediate measures to lessen the problems—hence, they worsened as time passed. Added to the economic problems was the difficult situation presented by a dissident minority—the Hukbalahaps (Huks) who engaged in raiding and acts of violence in an attempt to spread dissension.

Democratic development in the Philippines has been bound up with economic stability. As late as 1950, the Island Republic was almost facing disaster. Since that time major steps have been taken to root out the Philippine troubles and the Republic is beginning to lift itself out of its socio-economic distress. This is significant not only to the welfare of the Philippine government and peoples but to the United States and the West; the peoples of South Asia, particularly those in the newly sovereign states, have looked to the Philippines for some indication of whether Western concepts of politics and economics will work in Asia.

When independence was accorded the Philippines, the United States rose in the regard of the Asian states. Some of this, however, was counteracted by the lopsided provisions of the Philippine Trade Act of 1946 —the act that established duty-free trade between the United States and the Philippine Republic until 1954. Impartial on the surface, the trade agreements permitted American products to flow into Philippine markets in unlimited quantity whereas island exports to the mainland were rigidly restricted. Further, American businessmen and capital were given the same rights in the archipelago as Philippine businessmen and capital—a provision that necessitated changing the Philippine Constitution.

Greatly improved, the economy still is not strong. The gravest economic problem facing the Philippine Islands is caused by the rapidly expanding population. Each year it increases by more than half a million persons. In the last two decades the population of the country, which is now somewhat more than 20 million, has expanded by 48 per cent. This means that, to hold the standard of living even at the present level, production must increase by an equal amount. Tenantry is a major weakness in the economic structure—a hangover from the days, before the turn of the century, when Spain ruled the islands. Vast Spanish-owned estates, employing large numbers of tenant peasants, was the order of the day; wealth was concentrated in the hands of a few and there was not, as yet, an appreciable middle class. Another weakness lies in the lack of diversity found in the products produced and exported by agriculture—this commercial production forming the base of the economy; further, these exports and, hence, the prosperity of the state are vulnerable to price fluctuations in the world market.

The international trade of the Philippines is continuously on the deficit side; only exchange and import controls *and* the continuing high level of American expenditures in the islands have kept the problem from becoming too serious. The duty-free trade period—extended to 1974—is coming to an end in less than 20 years; at that time all "favored treatment" to the Philippines by the United States will be ended.

It is estimated that, at the present time, only three-fifths of the arable land is cultivated; large forest resources spread over the islands have been scarcely touched; revision of the land tenure system could do much to inject life into the peasant cultivation and also bring fuller employment. These are internal problems that require time to solve—and they are problems that are very similar (although different in context and, therefore, manifestation) to those faced in all of the newly independent states of South Asia. The desire *to be given time* to solve their economic and social problems is largely the source of Asian neutrality.

Although the mineral resources of the Philippines are not as great as are those of Indonesia, they are nevertheless considerable. Gold ranks first, ordinarily accounting for about 85 per cent of the ores mined; in 1935, Philippine production was greater than that of Alaska while in 1953, the islands ranked eighth among the gold producers of the world. Iron, chromium, manganese, coal, oil, lead, zinc, and other minerals are known to exist, but the mining industry is still in its infancy, and reserves are not large.

The Philippine Islands lie a bit aside from the major lines of communication in the East—and particularly those that connect the East and West—and hence the islands are not as strategically important as are certain other areas in the East. This is not to say that they are not needed among the defense links in the Western Pacific; their vital role was demonstrated during World War II. It is, however, in their over-all productiveness that they perhaps find their important value.

The ethnic structure of the Philippine Islands is complex. In the first place, there are a number of "tribes" that differ culturally from each other, and that vary, in stage of culture, all the way from relatively primitive groups (as the Pygmies) to those that have adopted quite modern elements. Secondly, they differ in religion. The great majority of the 20 million people are Christian—about 90 per cent. The Christian tribes include the Visayas, inhabitants of the central group of islands and numbering about seven million, and the four million Tagalogs in the Manila region on Luzon —a dominant group who have developed a literature and have contributed government leaders. Their dialect is the official language of the Republic despite the rivalry of the outnumbering Visayas to displace Tagalog with their language. Pagan peoples number about one million while Moslems make up a relatively small minority but they are a domineering people. In the past (at the time when the islands were acceded to the United States), they were a very troublesome group. Eighty-seven native languages and dialects are spoken throughout the islands. About four million Filipinos speak English which, with Spanish, has long been one of the two official languages of business and government.

The Catholic Church has taken an influential part in the affairs of the Philippine Islands, particularly at the time of Spanish domination. During the period when the United States had authority, the Church was less ascendant. However, in the 1953 presidential elections, the Catholic Church once more took on a dominant role—which may be a portent for the future.

OCEANIA, THE PACIFIC WORLD: THE TRUST TERRITORIES

The islands known as the Trust Territories of the Pacific Islands were taken by Japan from Germany during World War I, and, later, mandated to the Asian state by the League of Nations. Under the Trusteeship Agreement of 1947 they were removed from Japanese jurisdiction, and the United States was designated as the "sole administering authority," with the right to establish military bases and fortifications on the island (a provision not included in the Mandates Agreement). The Trust Territory includes a great sweep of islands reaching west and north, across three million square miles of the Pacific Ocean, from the Philippines to Hawaii. It includes the some 2100 islands of Micronesia grouped in three great archipelagoes—the Marshalls, the Carolines, and the Marianas. These islands are the home of about 55,000 natives.

Micronesia was taken during the war from Japan by United States forces—at Kwajalein, Saipan, and Peleliu. Held officially in trust for the United Nations, they were designated a "strategic area in the custody of the American nation" with the power to close Micronesia to other nations as it deems necessary. The United Nations Charter clause that assigned these islands to the United States, while it repudiates nineteenth century colonialism (in theory), gives formal recognition to the principle of *international accountability for dependent peoples.*

They were, during the first years as a Trust Territory, administered by the United States Navy. However, gradually naval authority has been replaced by civil administration. No attempt has been made to disrupt the political customs of the islands; in fact, the United Nations Trusteeship Council has consistently encouraged the Micronesians to develop regional organs of self-government, and several regional legislative bodies are now functioning—in Palau and the Marshall Islands.

In the last fifty years, the islands have been held by no fewer than four alien powers—Spain, Germany, Japan, and the United States. The greatest changes have come about under the Americans who are attempting to broaden the economic base (by the introduction of poultry, new crops, and processing of agricultural products), to increase the literacy and educational opportunities of the natives, and to improve health through the introduction of medical facilities.

Unlike the Ryukyus, the status of the Micronesian archipelagoes likely should remain what it is. Economically, the islands are of no value to any nation for they are relatively infertile and unproductive, being coral islands in the main. Strategically, however, they hold great significance; by way of example, it will be remembered how important to the United States Navy was the atoll of Kwajalein during the Pacific war—its protected waters could harbor a great fleet safely within its coral ring. So scattered are the single islands—even within each of the archipelagoes—that self-determination in terms of the formation of a modern state is out of the question. They must remain a trust territory under some nation that will not abuse its responsibility—as did Japan during the inter-war interim. Were the "protection" of these islands dropped by the United States without the replacement of some other United Nations-approved status, there would undoubtedly be an immediate claim laid to Micronesia by an imperialistic power.

AUSTRALIA AND NEW ZEALAND

In international diplomacy, Australia has been one of the most active states. It now has a complex web of diplomatic contacts linking it particularly with all parts of the Eastern Hemisphere (except with Communist China, which Australia refuses to recognize). It was Australia that proposed the Colombo Plan, under which certain of the nations of the West extend financial and technical aid to Asian countries; it is a member of the Manila Pact (SEATO) under which both Australia and New Zealand have made binding military commitments that link them with Asian nations and the United Kingdom, the United States, and Canada in the defense of Free Asia against Communism; it is linked with the United States and New Zealand in the Anzus Council, another defense agreement that came into effect in April, 1952.

"Distance" no longer guarantees Australian security. Formerly located on the periphery of world affairs, Australia found itself in the near center of a global conflict during World War II. When a Japanese force was turned aside just a few hundred miles off Queensland, in May, 1942, it marked the first time in the 162-year history of Australia that invasion had threatened the "country down under." For the first time the Australians realized the difficulty of defending a *state that was a continent*—with a population numbering but a little more than eight million. In terms of defense, the vast expanses of territory became a liability. The security of the past is gone, and Australia has become increasingly anxious to take action that would implement the defense of Oceania and Southeast Asia.

Australia lacks manpower. World War II also brought industry to Australia—at the same time that nearly a million and a half men and women went into the armed forces. The withdrawal of such a large proportion of the population nearly stripped the country of its manpower, and the labor shortage has been difficult to adjust; although the men in uniform returned, the economy had expanded to such a degree (beyond that of 1939) that Australia has felt a chronic shortage of manpower. Australia's number one problem is a population problem—but it is the antithesis of the population problem found in most other parts of the world: Australia doesn't have enough people.

The country, therefore, began a drive to attract *selected* immigrants, hoping to raise the population to 10 million by 1960.

Australia has held to a policy of "white nation." Nearly 100 per cent of the Australians are of British stock. In the first postwar drive for immigrants, Australia tried to attract the British and Americans, urging Australians to sponsor relatives and friends by guaranteeing them jobs and temporary living quarters. Britishers began arriving in 1947 but the influx was not great or rapid enough to meet the government's goal. Most of the Americans who came soon left again to return to the States. The Australians have always been uncomfortably conscious of the fact that the people who want most to come in and settle have been those with lower standards of living than the Australians. The White Australian Policy was "designed to maintain an Anglo–Saxon standard by keeping out the colored races." Further, to keep out white Europeans who were considered unwanted, rigid tests were adopted by the Immigration Department.

The double problem posed by the need for population increases and the fact that the British and Anglo–Americans were not filling the quota meant that a new policy was needed. There remained only one course that Australia could take—namely, to consult with the International Refugee Organization; the state agreed to take 12,000 displaced persons from Germany "as long as the refugees anxious to make the trip were available." The first incomers were North Europeans—Latvians and Estonians; later, as ethnic selection became less rigid, along with the Baltic peoples came Poles, Hungarians, Austrians, and Russians; and, still later, southern Europeans also. Thus, the population of Australia began to assume a new and different character.

The Australian aborigines, a separate race of people—the Australoids—are rapidly disappearing. When white settlement began in 1788, the Australoids were estimated to number 300,000; today there are only 60,000 or less; in some of the states they are already extinct, as in Victoria and Tasmania. Contact with the White and the impact of Western civilization upon the highly complex social life of the native have been such as to largely destroy it; the skill and morale of the aborigine, who was accustomed to existing under conditions that would likely prove disastrous for most Whites, have been undermined. Every advance made by Australia—as the development of a railroad, highway, or air line—has hastened the extinction of this unique group of people. They have not been a troublesome minority to deal with for they have not resisted the gradual occupance of the continent by the White; neither, however, have they aided, in any de-

gree, in relieving the shortage of manpower, except in the north where they have gone on to the large estates as workers.

Geography

Australia is a continent nearly three million square miles in area—inhabited with a population not much greater than the size of the city of New York! This seems like a very small population, but, because of the physical characteristics, the total carrying power is not great. The United States is only a little larger than Australia, but the central portion of the American state is a food-producing region of tremendous

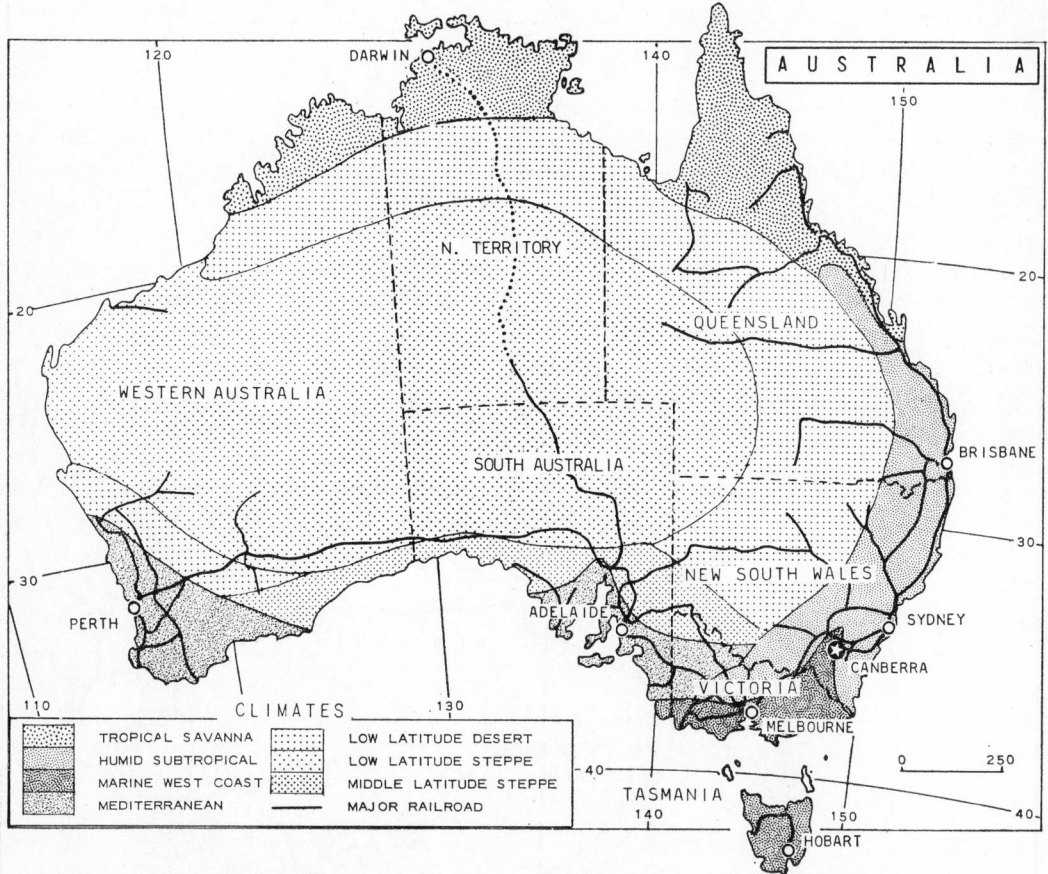

Figure 20.2. Climatic regions of Australia. Notice the large proportion of the continent that is almost uninhabitable because of aridity. Eastern Australia is the most important portion of the country—the Australian ecumene. Here is the greatest area having a climate favorable to permanent habitation and utilization, and here also are found the greatest proportion of the population, industry, agriculture, and transportation facilities. (See map on the next page.)

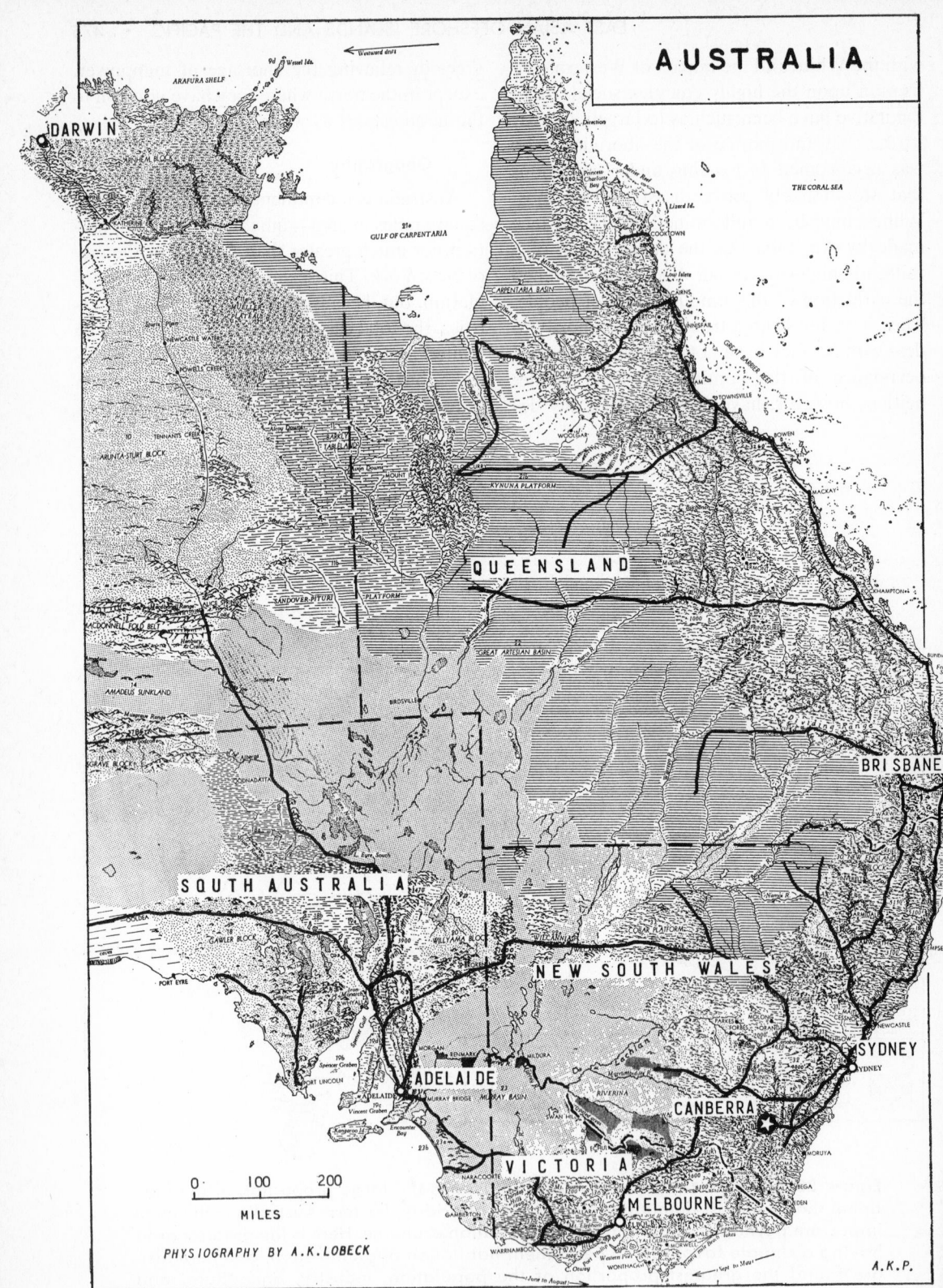

Figure 20.3.

476

capacity, whereas Central Australia is largely an unproductive desert. Hundreds upon hundreds of miles of flat, baked, and barren wasteland, broken only by xerophytic brush vegetation or areas of desolate rock, comprise this immense heartland of the continent.

The habitable portion of the state is made up of the tropical grassland area that runs across the north, and the narrow littoral strip along the east coast over to and including the Murray–Darling Basin which extends inland for a considerable distance and reaches eastward to the Eastern Highlands. By-passing the territory fronting on and extending back from the Great Australian Bight, another habitable portion reappears, in patches, along the southwest and western coast. The "green belts" of Australia are given over largely to wheat ranches or the raising of animals, particularly sheep and cattle.

Landholdings are large; and the small farmer is almost unknown. Recently a Commission was set up by the Government to study the problem of large landholdings. The report favored a "policy of subdivision," particularly in the cattle lands. It stated that "large areas of land held cheaply are not conducive to production. The experience of history is that any commodity, inclusive of land, becomes the subject of waste and abuse if in too cheap and plentiful supply." In remote areas, however, the Commission recommended that large holdings be permitted to obtain.

These statements by the Commission are in themselves a commentary on the policy of land acquisition and holding that has obtained throughout the history of the state. Some of the largest ranches individually owned cover tracts of more than 10,000 square miles in area. In the past, such huge properties could be permitted, for, under the uncertain conditions of weather and transportation, plenty of elbow room was considered essential to obtain sufficient pasture. Thus, the large holdings and the benevolent attitude of the colonial government developed.

Today, however, things have changed. Railroads and motor vehicles tap the interior (not as much as needed, however), airlines are covering an increasing proportion of the continent, and communities are being established. The Commission recommends, therefore, that "in the future, wherever practicable, holdings be limited to carry a maximum of 6000 to 10,-000 head of cattle, according to regions defined." Additional grants of land would be made "conditionally upon progressive development of the land."

The exports of both Australia and New Zealand are agricultural or animal products; their imports largely manufactured goods. Both are outstanding exporters of wool, dairy products, and meat—commodities of little bulk and high value. What industries as have developed—aside from the manufacture of dairy products—are for home consumption.

21

South Asia

INDIA AND PAKISTAN

India and Pakistan are independent states within the Commonwealth of Nations, granted sovereignty in August, 1947. Political independence was an event of economic and religious as well as political significance and was the British answer to the demand of the 92 million Indian Moslems that they be given a homeland of their own.

The basis for the partition of territory lay in the religious majority represented in an area—i.e. whether Hindu or Moslem. The only other religious groups that are found in any significant numbers at all comparable to the Hindus and Moslems are the Christians and Sikhs, the latter a sect particularly strong in the northwest; their numbers were incorporated into the Hindu and Moslem states.

Of the two predominant religious groups, the Hindus were the most westernized. The Moslems had developed a deep distrust of the British after the mutiny. Therefore, among the Indians, it was the Hindus who were the leaders in business and commerce, the professions, industry, and modern education. "This factor of uneven economic development . . . provided some . . . basis for fears of 'Hindu imperialism.' " Further, on a purely historic basis, what Indian nationalism as existed "was markedly Hindu in temper." Under such circumstances the Moslems felt that they would at best occupy an unequal place with the Hindus under an independent India. A further factor adding to the situation was that of population proportions as represented by the two religious groups—Moslems made up only one-fifth of the total, hence they would be a minority people. The only course left to the British, if they were to make India sovereign, was to accede to the separatist demand. By June, 1947, "partition" had been accepted by all parties although with reluctance on the part of some.[1]

The Moslem separatist bid was made for "areas in which Moslems were numerically in

[1] O. H. K. Spate, "The Partition of India and the Prospects of Pakistan," *The Geographical Review*, January, 1948, p. 5.

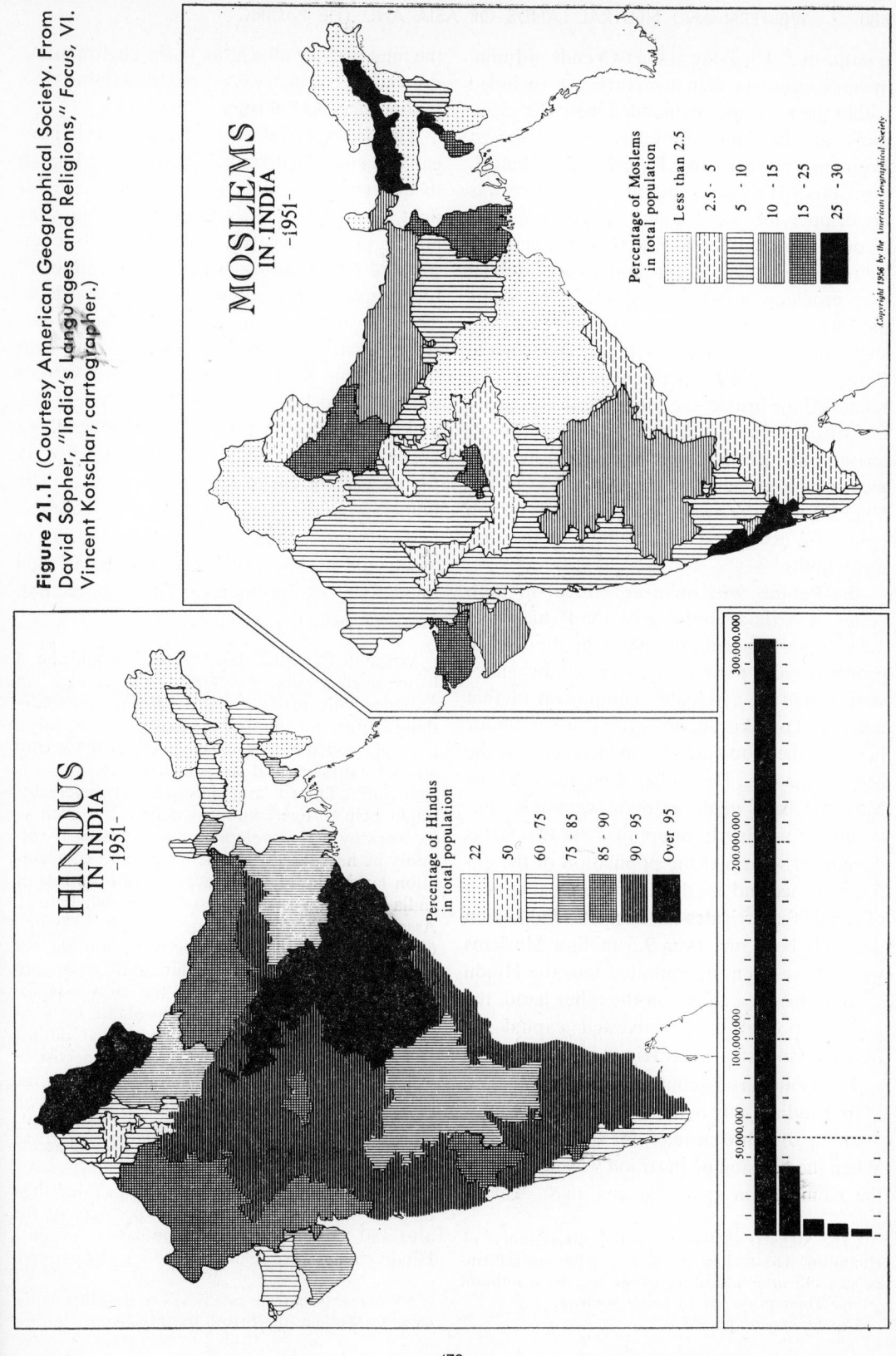

Figure 21.1. (Courtesy American Geographical Society. From David Sopher, "India's Languages and Religions," *Focus*, VI. Vincent Kotschar, cartographer.)

MOSLEMS
IN INDIA
–1951–

Percentage of Moslems
in total population

Less than 2.5
2.5 – 5
5 – 10
10 – 15
15 – 25
25 – 30

Copyright 1956 by the American Geographical Society

HINDUS
IN INDIA
–1951–

Percentage of Hindus
in total population

22
50
60 – 75
75 – 85
85 – 90
90 – 95
Over 95

a majority." These lay at the two ends of India, in the Northwest and in the Northeast. Included within the territories demanded were the provinces of the Sind, Baluchistan, Northwest Frontier Province, the Punjab, and Bengal. Over the first three of the provinces there was no dispute for the Moslem majority ranged "from 71 per cent in the Sind to 97 per cent" in Baluchistan. It was in the Punjab and Bengal that problems arose, for, although Moslems did form a majority in both regions, they were slight majorities—only 57.1 per cent in the Punjab and but 54.7 per cent in the east. To render ethnic justice, therefore, these two provinces had to be partitioned. The allocation of territory in the Punjab was rendered more complex by the presence of large numbers of the Sikhs,[2] an aggressively vocal religious group politically associated with neither of the majority faiths.[3]

The Punjab was an area critical to both states. As a food-surplus area, the Punjab held a particularly significant place in the Indian economy; any parts of it obtained by either state would be a valuable component of that country. To Pakistan, however, it was vital for here was the economic and financial core of the Moslem people. The Indian Congress and the Moslems both made extreme demands. Between the varying frontiers that the two states demanded were half the population of the entire province and nearly all of the great system of canals that irrigates the Punjab. Had Indian demands been met over 9.5 million Moslems would have been incorporated into the Hindu state in this area alone; on the other hand, the greatest proportion of invested capital—in trade and industry—was Hindu.

The Boundary Commission was comprised of four Indians—two Moslems and two Hindus —and a British chairman, Sir Cyril Radcliffe. When the decision on partition was to be made the Commission split two and two—leaving the final work of allocation to the chairman. As drawn, the boundary is criticized as doing "less than justice" to Pakistan.

The problem of drawing the frontiers in Bengal was somewhat simpler than in the Punjab in the sense that there was no powerful dissident third group (as the Sikhs) to confuse the ethnic issue. However, other elements complicated the division—namely, the realities of topography and communication in the delta. The map indicates the division of the various Bengal districts on the basis of religion. It is to be noted that eight sections in the southwestern part of the delta have non-Moslem majorities and that to the west of the Hooghly River these are emphatic. The same situation holds directly to the east of the delta and in Assam. The boundary, as drawn, was criticized as "curious" and perhaps "impractical," and, according to Spate, the premiers of both states envisioned immediate readjustments. These have not, however, been made to date.

Without Calcutta, East Bengal would be a badly overcrowded and almost purely agrarian province with small possibility of developing anything better; but the inclusion of Calcutta within it would rob the port of most of its hinterland and all its power and raw-material resources except jute. Transit and free-port arrangements might help to overcome this defect, but even so its working and development would almost certainly be hampered. Another important consideration lay in the fact that access from the rest of India to Assam is possible only through Bengal. Assam had one Muslim[4] majority district (Sylhet, 60.7 per cent) but as a whole was about 41 per cent Hindu, 34 per cent Muslim, and 24 per cent aboriginal hill tribesmen. It is the only province with really large areas of land available for agricultural expansion without high capital outlay, and for 2 or 3 decades there has been a persistent squatter migration of Muslim families from the adjoining and badly overcrowded Dacca Division of Bengal, which led to some friction between the provincial governments. Ownership of, and access to, Assam are thus of great importance.

Muslim demands were more exaggerated than in the Punjab, amounting to 75 per cent of the area and 83 per cent of the population, whereas Hindu claims were relatively modest, 50 per cent

---

[2] The Sikhs (and Jains) are the "Protestants" of Hinduism. The former began as a religious-reformist sect but after a century or so became a militant group. Their pride lies in being soldiers.

[3] Spate, *op. cit.,* pp. 7-8.

---

[4] Whereas American practice is to transliterate the word to Moslem, the British use Muslim.

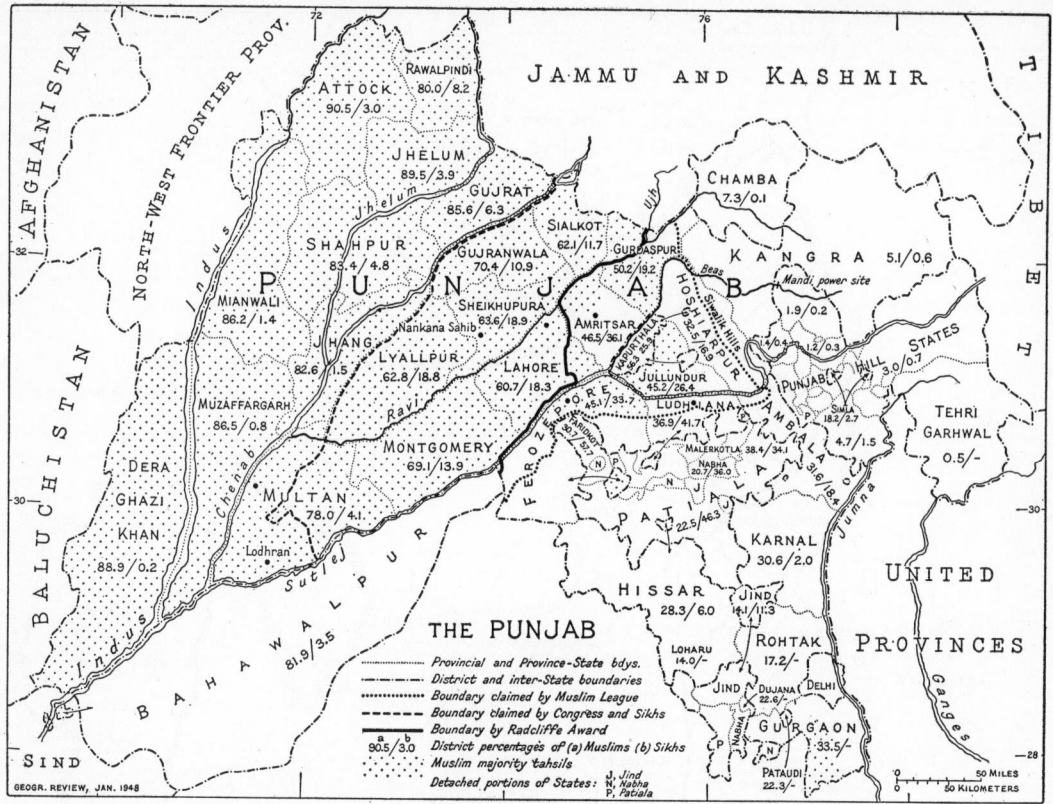

Figure 21.2. (Courtesy American Geographical Society. From O. H. K. Spate, "The Partition of India and the Prospects of Pakistan," *The Geographical Review,* XXXVIII.)

and 47 per cent respectively. Both obviously included large minorities, the Muslims taking in no less than 67 per cent of the non-Muslim population.[5]

The maps indicate the differential claims as well as the final allocation of territory. Again, the ultimate decision rested with Sir Radcliffe for the equally divided Boundary Commission was unable to reach agreement.

At the time of partition the status of Hyderabad and Kashmir, the two largest states of pre-1947 India, were undecided. Within approximately two years, however, Hyderabad had been drawn into the Indian Union. Hindu in population but with a Moslem ruler (and a 12 per cent Moslem minority), Hyderabad had sought to join Pakistan. The state was com-

pletely surrounded by Indian territory, however, and landlocked as well, having to rely on Indian ports and transportation facilities for its outlets to the sea. Although, theoretically, each of the princely states (not incorporated into one or the other of the new states) had the right of choosing which nation it would join, India imposed a stringent economic blockade on Hyderabad, and, as a means of inducement, sent troops to the borders of the country. The end result was that Hyderabad allied itself with India.

The Kashmir problem remains unsettled. So delicate has been the situation in Kashmir that fighting between Indian and Pakistani troops has occurred a number of times within the borders of that area. According to the formula for partition, Kashmir (77 per cent Moslem) should have gone to Pakistan. (Kashmir, since

---

[5] Spate, *op. cit.,* p. 12.

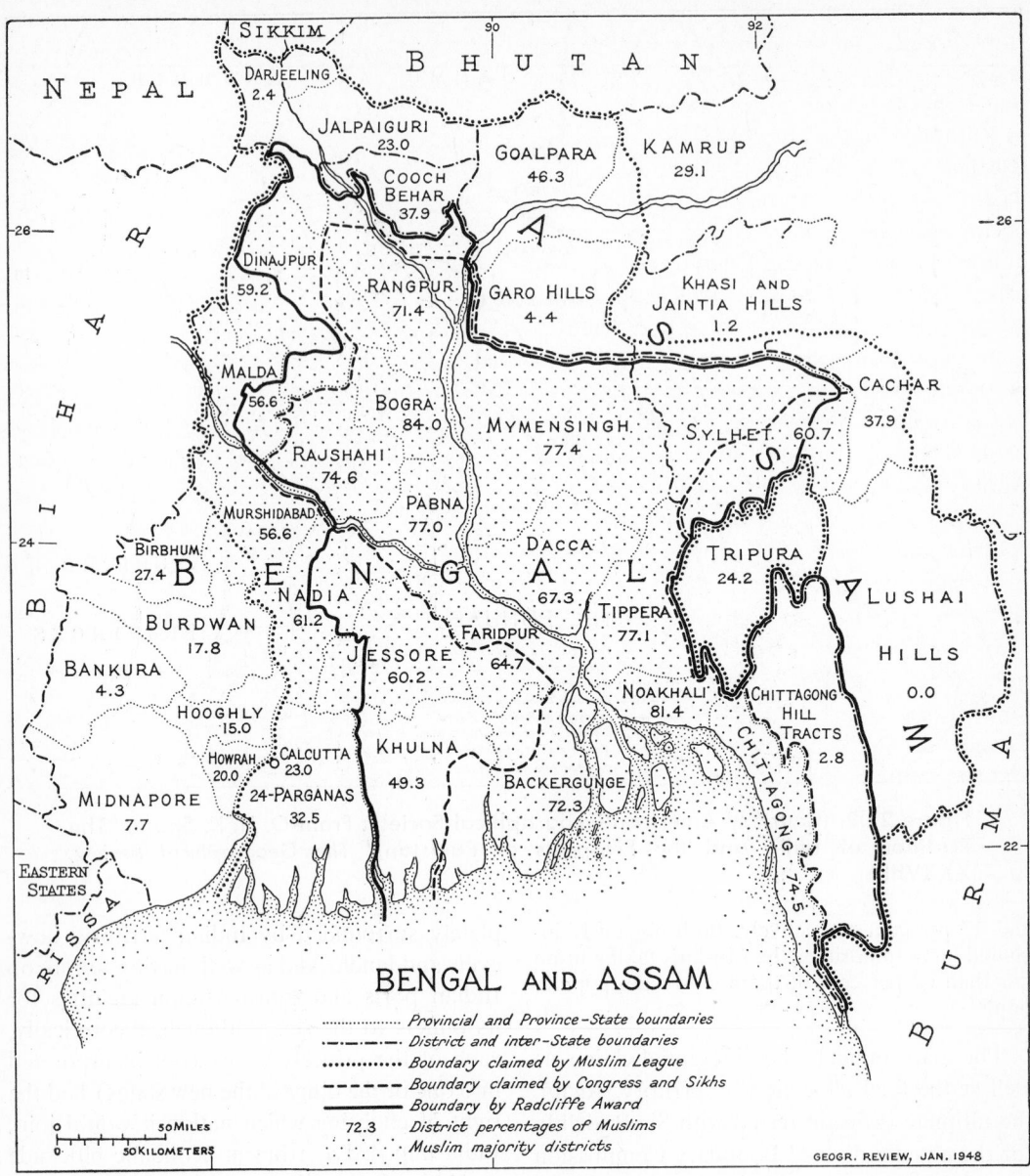

Figure 21.3. (Courtesy American Geographical Society. From O. H. K. Spate, "The Partition of India and the Prospects of Pakistan," *The Geographical Review,* XXXVIII.)

British domination was extended over the state, has included the Hindu state of Jammu and the Buddhist state of Ladakh as well.) However, as in the case of Hyderabad, the ruler of Kashmir represented the minority group—in this case the Hindu and, hence, he was pro-Indian, apparently feeling that the democratic and modern reforms he planned for Kashmir would be possible only under the secular rule of India. The Moslem element, on the other hand, indicated that they would choose Pakistan.

A further complication to the Kashmir

problem—and a very basic one—lies in the stubborn fact that the breadbasket of Pakistan is dependent upon the rivers of Kashmir, rivers that form the headwaters of the Indus and rise in Kashmir. On the other side, India feels that Kashmir was legally united with India in 1947 when, on the 25th of October, the Maharajah, fleeing Moslem mountain tribesmen to Jammu, announced that he ceded Kashmir to India and asked for Indian troops. Although the United Nations has stepped in and continuously attempted to bring about a solution, their only accomplishment has been the establishment of cease-fire lines. A plebiscite is scheduled to be held. However, India insists on maintaining, within Kashmir, more troops than Pakistan is willing to permit for the plebiscite—and so the stalemate continues.

Ladakh, the easternmost province of this disputed territory, is at present one of the most strategic spots in all of Asia. Ladakh lies at the juncture of three nations—India, China, and Pakistan. Its status still is undecided—*i.e.* as to whether it will join India or Pakistan— and the attitude of Communist China toward Ladakh is also not quite clear. Ladakh is Buddhist, its Lama subordinate to the one at Lhasa in Tibet; further, the men (one-third of whom enter into a monastery to lead a religious life) are educated in Tibet. The ties with the Chinese are therefore strong and, very frequently, Ladakh is referred to as "Little Tibet." This designation is not only religious and ethnic, but social and economic as well, for the two provinces are closely associated economically.

Before 1950, Ladakh was a significant focus of trade for Central Asia, and merchants from India and adjacent Asian centers had their headquarters at Leh, capital of Ladakh. However, after the Communists came to power, the latter have progressively sealed off the border between Tibet and Ladakh until today only a trickle of trade funnels through between Leh and Chinese Turkestan. This decreasing trade causes economic hardships to the people of the Kashmiri province. It is likely that this frontier zone should be in the hands of a strong neutral power able to defend the integrity of the strategic frontiers.

The Two Republics

As allocated, Pakistan received about one-fourth of the domain of all India and one-sixth of its population. Pakistan comprises two completely separated pieces of territory. Eastern Pakistan is the smaller portion composing but one-seventh of the country but containing four-sevenths of the population. This portion of the domain is by far the most productive—in a region where the pressure of population on the land results in less than half an acre of cultivated area per capita. (In the west, the per capita average is about 1.2 acres.) A further disparity between area and population distribution is focused in the fact that in the Ganges delta region there is almost no chance of extending the cultivated acreage; in the west, any such extension of agricultural land depends on an extension of irrigation.

An independent Pakistan, set up to resolve the national dilemma, does not solve that problem. Although, with partition, there followed one of the greatest mass migrations of people in the history of the world, there are still many Moslems living in India and many Hindus and other non-Moslems in Pakistan; it has been estimated that fully one-third of all of the Moslems of Old India remain in India. In Pakistan the educational and economic standing of non-Moslems is very disproportionate to their numbers.

The allocation of natural resources between the two states was very unequal. The areal distribution of resources rendered their apportionment quite disparate. In terms of agricultural opportunities, Pakistan is capable of less crop diversification than is India, but, because of the smaller population, is better able to feed its population. In area allocation, out of a total of 280–285 million cultivated acres in all India, Pakistan received some 42–44 million (about one-seventh); irrigated land in all India was represented by 60–65 million acres, and of this, some 19 million acres (or approximately one-third) fell to Pakistan. However, great as is the disparity in agricultural resources, it is not as glaring as the inequality of the mineral reserves of the two Republics. Pakistan is almost devoid of mineral ores whereas India has an excellent mineral base for the heavy industry that had already developed in the territory that fell to her, and has, as well, all of the mica. Fuel resources are markedly deficient in the Moslem state, hydroelectricity representing the only national source of energy.

The two outstanding raw materials of Pakistan are jute and cotton—both agricultural products and production of the former fluctuating widely from year to year. In terms of fibres, Pakistan is well supplied. Of the forest reserves of all India, Pakistan received about one-eighth, largely located in Eastern Pakistan where are found the forested Chittagong Hills, the "tidal" Sundarbans, and the Madhupur Jungle which has some scrub forests. The great portion of the industrial development that took place under the British was within those areas that fell to India. Spate quotes the following figures (taken in part from the *Eastern Economist*) regarding the distribution of industrial establishments at the time of partition:

. . . cotton mills, India 857 and Pakistan 15; jute mills, 111 and 0; sugar mills, 176 and 15; iron and steel works, 36 and 0; cement and lime works and potteries, 57 and 8; paper mills, 19 and 0; glassworks, 112 and 5. This does not include small factories and workshops making light consumption goods such as hosiery and knitwear, electrical fittings, rugs and shoes and leather goods, or the handicrafts in wool, leather, silk, embroidery, and gold and silver of cities like Lahore. In these, Pakistan is not so badly under-represented; . . .

Nor is there much prospect of industrialization, except in agriculturally based lines such a cotton ginning and milling, flour, food processing, and jute milling in Eastern Pakistan, though here are serious difficulties, . . . For heavy industry the resources are almost pitifully slight.[6]

The problems of partition have been many. Under the British, India was developing its industry but foreign trade still consisted largely of agricultural products, in a raw or semi-

processed form, exchanged for manufactured goods. With partition, the regions productive of the exportable surplus food and the agricultural raw materials for the factories fell almost entirely to Pakistan, leaving "India with 96 per cent of the industrial enterprises, a farm production largely dependent on the vagaries of the monsoons, and a population of nearly 350 million—reportedly increasing by about 4 million a year."[7]

On the other hand, in normal years, Pakistan can feed its people. But it is physically divided, and, as a further liability, has to look largely to Indian industry for an outlet for its jute and even other lesser raw materials. In turn, Pakistan has traditionally received its sugar, coal, cotton goods and most of its processed consumer goods from what is now India. Economically, the two states are almost reciprocal and, in the past, were tightly interknit. A decade of independence finds both nations faced with almost the same problems—and in almost as great a degree—as confronted the newly founded states in 1947. The problem of integrating the several million refugees has not entirely been solved; India is recurrently faced with food shortage, Pakistan with an unstable economy (due to its weak base); rivalry and threatened feuds between the two nations over the unsettled status of Kashmir; problems of national defense and security; maintenance of law and order; minority issues. Besides these mutual problems, each state has its own peculiar difficulties most of which relate, however, to the above.

Indian–Pakistani antagonisms extend in many directions. The Hindu–Moslem problem of old India that gave rise to partition was not really a religious question for the Moslem minority did not fear religious persecution by the Hindus. It was one built rather on a latent alienation that was rooted in history, culture, economics, and politics. The Moslems have been in India since about 1000 A.D. They came as conquerors—to convert the peoples of

---

[6] *Ibid.*, p. 22.

[7] Doris Detre Rafler, "India and Pakistan—The Problems of Partition." *Foreign Agriculture,* Vol. XIII, No. 12 (December, 1949), p. 272.

the peninsula to Islam. Moslems (wherever found the world over) are a dynamic group, sensitive to the group allegiance of peoples around them; they feel—and deeply—that if people are not *with* them, they are *against* them. Although in the past the Moslems desecrated the temples of the Hindu and other religious groups, there were no major conflicts (such as have occurred in the post-World War II period) until the last century, actually; and, until 1874, there were no major Hindu–Moslem riots. But the situation was nevertheless latent throughout the years.

In character, the Hindus and the Moslems are quite antipodal. An Islamic society is a very solid, unified, irresilient, and intolerant group whereas the Hindus are loose knit, tolerant, and flexible. *There is a center to Hinduism but no periphery; Islam, however, is sheared off.* The innate teachings of the two religions create this basic difference in the character of the Hindu and the Moslem.

However, in many other ways they are not so far apart—for all were Indian. Seventy-five per cent of the Moslems of the subcontinent were of the same stock as the Hindus (*i.e.* Indian converts or descendants of Indian converts). Further, in addition to the line of cultural divergencies along the religious base, *cultural division was (and is) provincial:* Moslems in different parts of the subcontinent differ almost as much from each other as do Hindus and Moslems in the same district—at times, more. Culturally, therefore, they are not so far apart. Religiously, the schism is somewhat comparable to that of the Protestant and Catholic: impartial Indians (as the Parsees) point to the fact that the present great strife— and post-World War II wave of intolerance— parallels the former period of Roman Catholic–Protestant contention, intolerance, and persecution.

Economically, the rift was wide. In general, the Moslems were more backward and less educated than the Hindus—a condition that obtains the world over wherever large segments of Mohammedans are found, whether as a majority or minority group. Nor was Indian wealth in the hands of the Moslem; it was largely Hindu. Such wealth as the Moslems held was usually that of the landlord; but tenants could be either Hindu or Moslem and there was no discrepancy of treatment on the basis of religion. On the other hand, moneylenders were Hindu and, as is true of most Oriental moneylenders, were typically extortioners; but, the Hindu debtor suffered as much from the Hindu lender as did the Moslem.

Impartial Indians have expressed the feeling that, politically, the latent and potential antagonisms were played upon. According to non-Moslem and non-Hindu observers, religious antagonisms were exploited to "divide and conquer" the people. Whether there is any justification in this accusation hurled against the British is questionable—but anticolonial sentiment (nationalist sentiment) is deep enough in all Indians to interpret the growing religious strife—that culminated in separation —in this manner. And this alone is geopolitically significant. According to Professor P. E. Dustoor (a Parsee) of Delhi University, India, the development of the Moslem League, which was born about 1905, was concurrent with the commencement of the nationalist movement— and the British at that time "seduced the Moslems away from the nationalist movement." The rioting since Gandhi's death (August, 1947) is the *end* of the chapter of Hindu–Moslem strife, not the beginning. Active rioting, however, began a year earlier. At that time Jinna set aside a "direct movement day" which called for the massacring of Hindus in Calcutta —because Nehru had started an interim government without including the Moslems.

When partition took place, that event acted as the signal for the paying off of old debts— and was a kind of revenge for what had been happening throughout all of the years of Hindu–Moslem association. The rioting was not very widespread; most of it was concentrated within the Punjab.[8]

---

[8] Summarized and quoted from a talk (unpublished) presented by Professor Dustoor to a meeting of the Seattle Chapter of the Institute of Pacific Relations, attended by the writer.

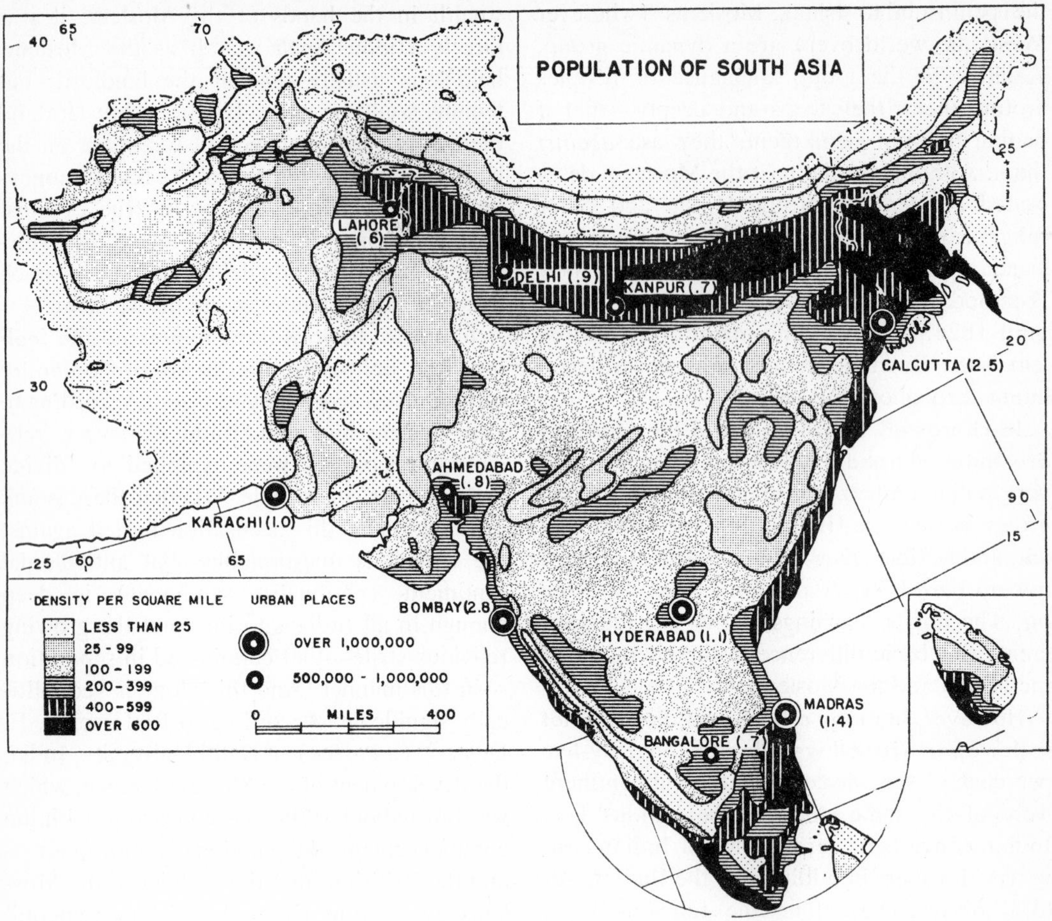

Figure 21.4.

Pakistan

Pakistan, 365,907 square miles in area and 83 million[9] in population, is numerically the world's largest Moslem state. Although a theocratic state, it leans in foreign policy toward the Western camp. During its decade of independence, it has had grave problems in setting up a democratic form of government. For six years a Constituent Assembly tried vainly to write a Constitution and finally was dissolved in October, 1953, by the Governor General (Ghulam Mohammed) appointed by the British Crown under the Indian Independence Act. In the absence of a Constitution, the Independ-

[9] United Nations "Monthly Bulletin of Statistics," April, 1957.

ence Act is Pakistan's law; and, since 1953, the country has been ruled by decree.

The political difficulties experienced by Pakistan are not surprising. In the first place, physical coherence is impossible for the state is formed of two parcels of land separated from each other by 2000 miles of intervening Indian territory. Western Pakistan, the largest of the parts territorially (though having less than half of the people) contains the capital, Karachi, and is politically dominant. Although strongly cohered in terms of religion, West Pakistan is badly torn by regional contention. East Pakistan, comprised of the single province of East Bengal—much smaller but holding the majority of the population and industry—is restive under what appears to the East Pakistanis as political domination by the minority in the West. At one time, they demanded a separate state.

The most dissident group of West Pakistan is the Pathan. The Pathans have recurrently demanded the formation of a separate, independent state to be known as Pushtoonistan (or Pakhtoonistan). The continuing feud between India and Pakistan over Kashmir has aided the Pathans in securing certain concessions, the latest being subsidies from both Afghanistan and Pakistan to maintain peace. Fourteen per cent of Pakistan's 1954 national budget was allocated for the preservation of law and order in the Northwest Frontier Province, largely Pathan in population and the territory demanded for the new Pushtoon state. However, the latter (if demands of the Pathans were acceded to) would comprise not only most of the Northwest Frontier Province but parts of the Punjab as well.

By nationality the Pathans are traditionally Afghan.[10] Their tribal lands and people, now partly in Afghanistan and partly in Pakistan, were split by the British in creating the Durand Line as a "militarily strategic border between British India and Afghanistan." The Pathan territories contain the famous Khyber Pass. The Afghans have backed the claims of the Pathans against Pakistan—although they have said nothing about conceding the Pathan-claimed Afghan territory to the group. Kabul, the Afghan capital, lies within this area. In fact, the Afghan government has had no notion of adding the Pathan-claimed territory on the plateau to Pushtoonistan, maintaining that the Afghan Pathans have no such feeling of independent nationalism as do those in Pakistan. However, Afghanistan has insisted that the future status of the Pakistan area—wherever Pathans make up 60 or more percent of the population—be decided by plebiscite.

The legal position of Afghanistan is that that country cannot recognize "as valid and binding Pakistan's jurisdiction over an area of which they were deprived by the British." Further,

they point out that the Pushtoonistan dispute not only seriously embitters relations between the two Moslem states, but creates a condition of internal instability within Pakistan itself. At times the controversy has become so tense that diplomatic relations between the two states concerned have been on the verge of breaking. The disputed area is a very strategic piece of territory—particularly to Afghanistan—for through here and across Pakistan's domain, lies landlocked Afghanistan's only easy passage to the sea. Should diplomatic relations be suspended and the channeling of goods to and from Afghanistan across Pakistan territory be brought to a halt, conditions could become so serious as to have far wider than local consequences.

The difficulties of maintaining order among the Pathans are not new. The British were plagued with trouble from the time of the adoption of the Durand Line. Finally, to attain some peace in the Khyber area, the British gave the Pathans sovereignty in local affairs and paid them a subsidy apparently in payment to the Afridi tribes—historic guardians of the strategic mountain pass, and most powerful of the Pathan tribes—for use of the Khyber route. Today the Afridis exert great influence among the other Pathan peoples. It was at the suggestion of Afghanistan in July, 1949, that the Pathans first made their declaration of independence from Pakistan and sought a sovereign political status.

The prospects for Pakistan. Pakistan was founded out of an apprehension of Hindu dominance. Hence, rather than viewing itself as a companion state of the Indian nation, it sees itself as a counterpoise to it. Perhaps not wisely constituted as a sovereign state, Pakistan is beset with the economic difficulties that its restricted and divided domain imposes upon it; economic instability has increased despite the aid that the United States has provided. Pakistan is allied with the West through several pacts. Some observers, however, report that neutralism is almost as prevalent among the general Moslem public as it is in India and that, were it not for the fact that the Pakistan econ-

---

[10] Historically, they claim to be the descendants of the ten lost tribes of Israel, however.

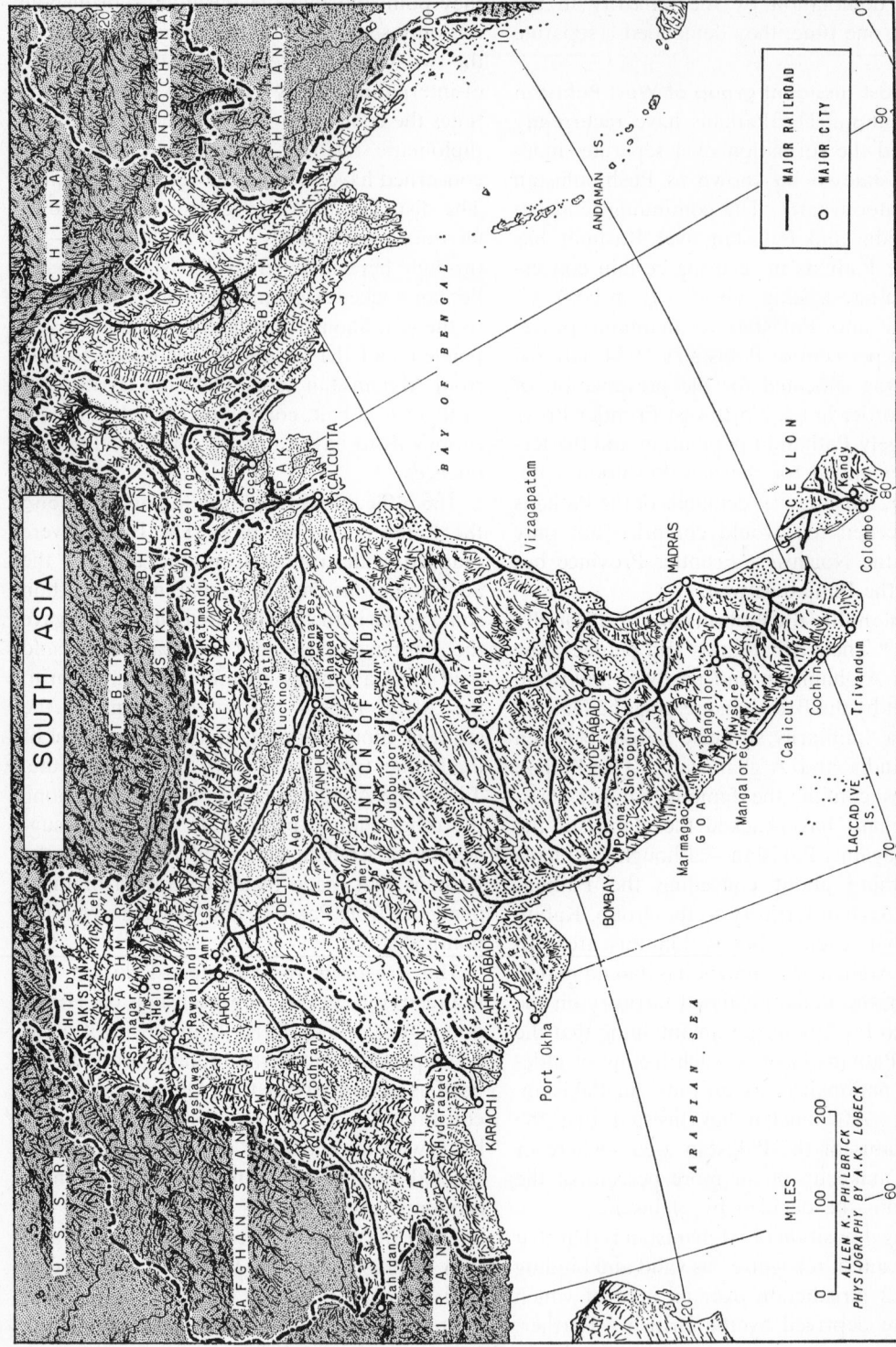

Figure 21.5. Note the way in which transportation is held within the mountain walls that surround India-Pakistan. In no place do railroads reach beyond the borders into other states except for one small spur just across the frontier of Iran.

omy is so unsoundly dependent upon American assistance, Pakistan too would be within the neutral camp. The solving of Pakistani differences with India would likely have the effect of drawing the nation closer to neutralism and farther away from the West. One of four South Asian Moslem states to be aligned through military pacts with the West, Pakistan—with the other three Islamic nations (Turkey, Iraq, and Iran)—is looked upon as a renegade by other Mohammedans.

The Dominion of India

India is a "Babel" of tongues and peoples. Formerly it was said that, despite the differences in culture and religion, somehow India had made Indians out of all of the people that live there. However, since partition, a surge of nationalist feeling has stirred among a number of the linguistic or religious minorities that go to make up India's 365 millions. The upshot of this outcry for sovereignty was the recasting of the provinces of India into new and fewer component political divisions.

The State Reorganization Commission was appointed in 1952 following a policy laid down by the All India Congress Committee, and in recognition of the wishes of large numbers of Indians. The purpose was twofold, namely, to "arrest the growing fragmentation of Indian unity" and to meet the demand for "linguistic redistribution." Two major changes have been made in India's political map since the British agreed to separatism: 1) the Punjab and Bengal were divided by the British between the Hindus and the Moslems; 2) in 1950, the Indian Government again redrew the internal frontiers after incorporating many small, princely states within the Union.

The last census listed 845 languages and dialects in India, of which 15 languages are major, spoken together by about 90 per cent of the population and all classified as a "mother tongue." The first official recognition to the demand for linguistic redistribution was accorded in 1953 when Madras State was divided into two provinces—Andhra, of northeast Madras and representing the Telegu-speaking

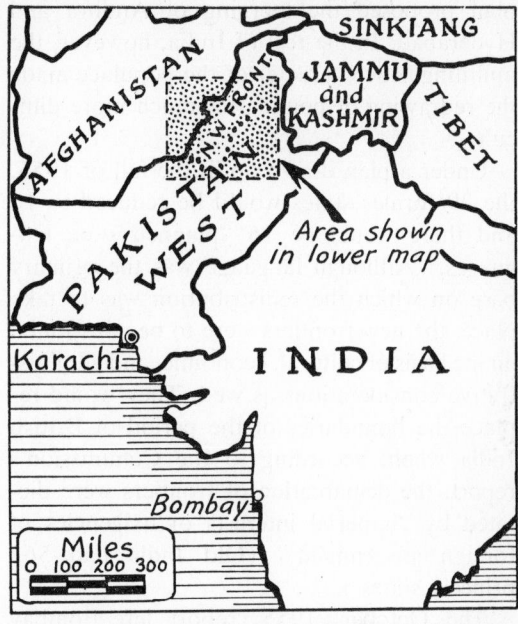

Figure 21.6. Pushtoonistan. The lower map is an enlargement of the shaded area in the upper map. The territory involved lies between the Afghan frontier and the dashed line in the east and south. (R. Lenz, cartographer. Courtesy *The Christian Science Monitor*.)

peoples, and the rest of Madras, retaining the name of the former state and remaining to the Tamil-speaking Madras. Although this division was thought to take care of the linguistic demands of the South, two months later a new plan proposed the merging of Andhra and Hyderabad. In the rest of India, however, the multilinguistic character of the populace made the redrawing of boundaries much more difficult.

Under a plan drawn up in the fall of 1955, the 29 former states would be reduced to 16 and there would be 16 "planned state languages." Although language was the primary base on which the redistribution was to take place, the new frontiers were to be constituted on the basis of cultural, economic, and administrative considerations as well. They would replace the boundaries of the period of British India when, according to the Commission's report, the demarcation of frontiers were dictated by "imperial interests or exigencies of foreign government." (Old India had 562 princely states.)

The October, 1955, report left Bombay State intact—to the disappointment of three groups; the Marathis wanted a Marathi-speaking state *including Bombay;* the Gujeratis wanted the northern portion of Bombay set aside to form a Gujerati-speaking state also including Bombay; disappointed, also, were the Punjabi–Sikhs who desired a solely Punjabi-speaking unit. In November, readjustments were made in these two areas. The Punjab, instead of being carved up, however (as demanded by the Sikhs), was enlarged. Bombay State was divided into three components. Maharahshtra, comprising southern and central Bombay with its Marathi-speaking people, made up the first. Vidarbha, a province of Marathi-speaking people in Central India, was incorporated into Maharahshtra. Gujerat (composed of northwestern Bombay, the Cutch, and Sourashtra) was constituted in the north to meet the demands of the Gujerati-speaking group. The city of Bombay was made an independent state because incorporation in either of the newly created states would seriously cripple the other. Announcement of this latter decision set off riots in the Bombay area. A study of the linguistic map and of the old and new political maps will make clear the changes that were made. The new arrangement was thought to go far toward satisfying the demands of the various linguistic groups.

However, by February, 1956, disorders resulting from the change of boundaries seriously raised the question of the wisdom of redrawing the Indian political map along language lines, and the Congress Party (in power) "decided to abandon its immediate efforts to create a group of purely linguistic states and to work, instead, toward the creation of fewer, and larger, states that would cross language lines and would . . . themselves be multi-lingual . . . The wide diversity of ethnic and language groups in India certainly suggests that a logical form of government would be a relatively loose federation with large powers residual in at least semi-autonomous units. Regional demands, such as those of the Sikhs, . . . could thus be met."[11]

The divisions previously suggested were opposed by Nehru and others of his party for two reasons. In the first place, it was felt desirable "to break down regional barriers rather than to perpetuate them"; secondly to strengthen the economy, a "strong centralized government" is a necessity. "Cohesiveness in India has always been relative. One element in unity was a strongly centralized Indian Civil Service under British rule. The rule has disappeared but the framework of the service remains. An even stronger unifying element was opposition to that British rule. That factor has necessarily disappeared. There is, therefore, some danger of real fragmentation. . . ."[12] India, a vast area as large as Europe (1.2 million square miles) and as variegated, is Asia's largest democracy.

Many problems face an independent, democratic India. They include illiteracy, need for land reform, primitive means of agriculture, uncertainty of precipitation coupled with inadequacy of irrigation works, an abyssmally low standard of living for the great masses of people. Most of these problems still remain, and, compared with the rapid changes that

---

[11] *New York Times Ediorial:* "Problems in India," February 12, 1956. See map on page 502.
[12] *Ibid.*

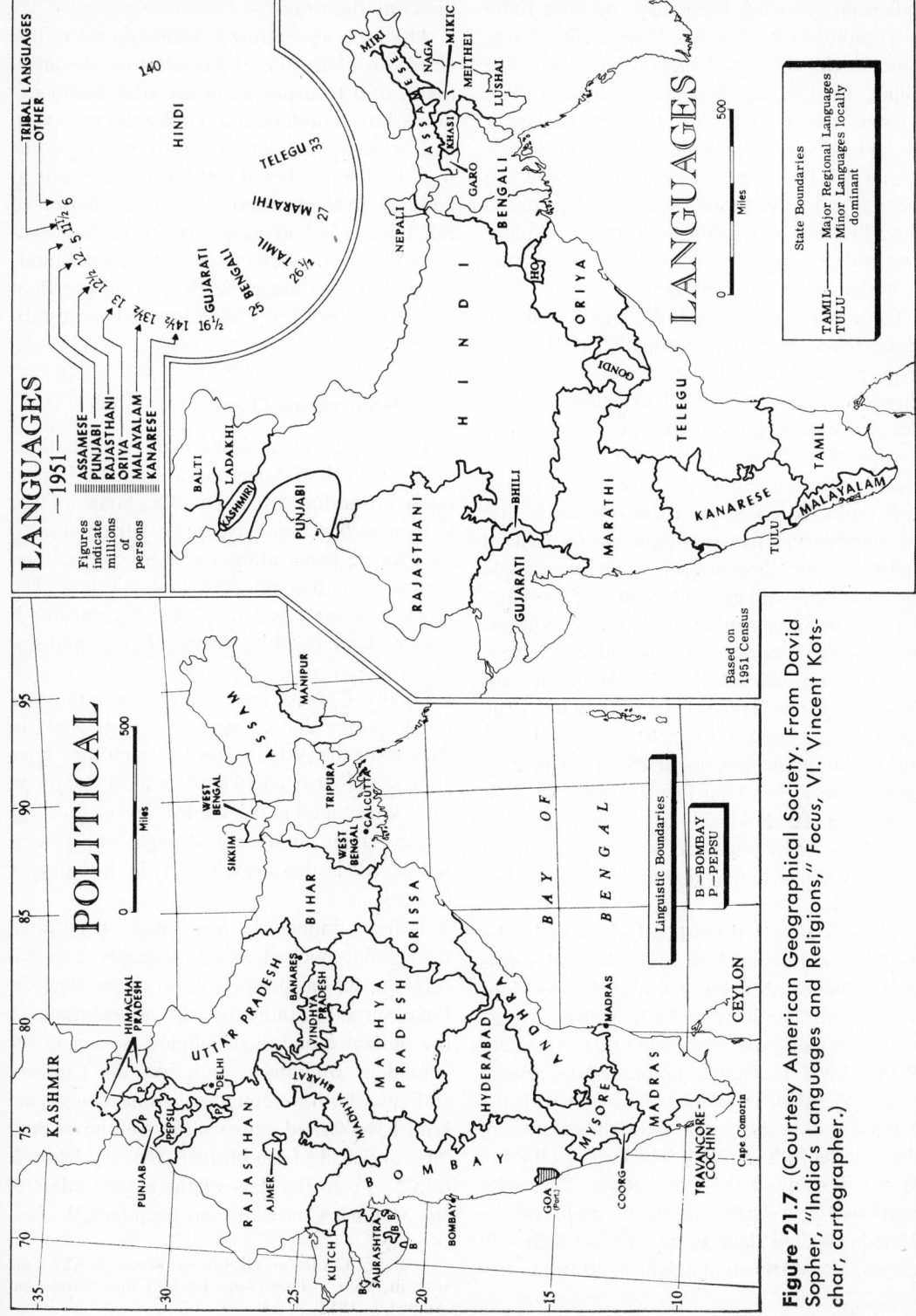

Figure 21.7. (Courtesy American Geographical Society. From David Sopher, "India's Languages and Religions," *Focus*, VI. Vincent Kotschar, cartographer.)

491

China has undergone under the Communists, Indian progress has been slow; because India is a democracy, progress necessarily moves more slowly than in a dictatorial nation like China. Yet the state has moved ahead. Indian leaders are pledged to the establishment throughout all India of a "viable *socialistic* economy." It is felt that only in this way can the tremendous economic dilemmas be worked out. This, however, requires "centralized planning and a strongly centralized administration" or it cannot be accomplished.[13]

For many generations India has repeatedly faced food shortages. Annually, a relatively large proportion of its moderate foreign exchange has had to be used to obtain grain—rice and wheat—to feed the people. Tenantry is a problem, most of the land being in the hands of feudal landlords who have exacted high rents. To effect the rural revolution that was necessary, a five-year plan was introduced in 1951. Since three-fourths of India's people live in villages and go out to cultivate the land, a drastic improvement in rural living conditions and practice was necessary in order to have a firm base on which to build a democratic industrial society. Today land reform has gone forward so well that India has at least begun the evolutionary movement toward a healthy rural society based on farmers who till their own lands. The landlords from whom land has —and is—being alienated, are being compensated. About a billion dollars have been thus expended.

Since water is the critical element in the environment of much of India, irrigation has been given high priority under the development plan. The increase in irrigated acreage, as completed by the end of the first Five-Year Plan (April 1, 1956), amounted to several million acres of land. In association with the extension of irrigation has been the erection of dams along India's rivers. The largest (Bhakra Dam) is rising in the Sutlej River, 225 miles north of New Delhi, in the foothills of the Himalayas. The dam, to be 750 feet high, will exceed Hoover Dam in height (700 feet), now the world's highest. An American engineer is directing the work.

Although agriculture is receiving the major emphasis industry, hydroelectric development, and transportation are also being extended and modernized. Under the first plan, hydroelectric production was to be doubled as was also the number of new railroad cars added annually to the transport system. Extension of rail lines is not as necessary to the improvement of the communication systems as is modernization for, under the British, an excellent network of rail lines had already been established.

India versus China

India and China, as the two largest nations of the East, both have had a dramatic impact upon bordering Asian peoples. Some of the influences of China have already been alluded to; Chinese penetration was more cultural and commercial than religious and political. The great Chinese "religion," Confucianism, is rather a code of ethics than a religious philosophy and, hence, its impact was cultural. Commercially, Chinese influence is seen in the economic power that Chinese emigrants wield in various of the Asian states to which they have gone as colonists and where, in most instances, they have obtained a control over trade far beyond their numerical strength. In places, retail trade is almost exclusively in the hands of Chinese.

Indian influence has also penetrated throughout much of Asia, and deeply. The cultural impact has been great, for at one time the East "turned to India for arts and techniques"; the influence of Indian religion is seen in the spread of Buddhism; and, like the Chinese, Indians who have emigrated from their homeland have settled across all of Southeast Asia "to corner all of the business that the Chinese don't." From the days of the early traders of the Malabar Coast, this has been true.[14]

---

[13] *Ibid.*

[14] James Cameron, "Nehru vs. Mao—A Key Contest in Asia," *The New York Times Magazine,* August 7, 1955, p. 13.

The East has always been deeply conscious of India—more so in some ways than of China, which always loomed, but never expanded. So, when 1947 came—the great punctuation mark of Asian resurgence—India emerged most resoundingly as the first truly "liberated" land, the first major unit of the continent to achieve complete independence, and moreover to do it peacefully, in exactly the way that the great leader Gandhi had planned and prophesied. The impact on all Asia of India's independence was tremendous; it did two things at once: it produced a swing of unexpected respect and affection toward Britain, who had kept her word, and it consolidated the new India as a huge moral force.

That aspect of it did not immediately appear. Had India joined a "bloc" of one kind or another, her influence would have been merely that of the bloc; she would never have achieved her unique position of today. However, she joined nothing (her membership in the Commonwealth is considered irrelevant and superficial) and, what was more, made a great song about joining nothing. Further, she denounced people who did. "Alliances and engagements always bring war nearer," says Nehru, time after time, and all over Asia the heads nod gratefully, *relieved to have their own indecisions sanctified by Asia's man of reason.*

The appeal of India is negative. Nehru is far from being a negative man, but the force he represents is the peculiarly Asian one of negation. Do nothing, lest you be led into committing sin—that is what the old Taoists used to say . . .

The appeal of China is positive, intensely so. It is, of course, the elementary appeal of revolution to the anxious and dispossessed, . . . its really powerful attraction is not in its Marxism but in its terrific Asianism. Everybody appreciates that, whatever else Mao Tse-tung may have done, he took a great, amorphous corrupt, bickering, hopeless mass of negligible humanity and turned it, within five years, into a major world power—and every single member of the vast Asian community can identify himself somehow vicariously with that supremely successful revolution.[15]

The social and cultural heritage of most Asian peoples has been taken, in part at least, from either China or India. Today there are no Asian states—other than the Soviet Union which incorporates millions of square miles of the Asian mainland but which is actually European—that can compare in either size (of area and population) and resources to India and China—to act as the leaders, or guardians,

and set an example to the newly emerging sovereign entities. Inasmuch as both India and China rose concurrently into a place of importance in the political world (it was only two years after India achieved independence that Mao consolidated the Communist hold on China),[16] it was to be expected that both would have a deep influence upon the smaller, but also emerging nations.

The similarities of the rise to power of India and China are striking, but the dissimilarities are equally conspicuous. Both used the five-year plan to accomplish a rapid economic change and development. These "plans" were entered upon only one year apart, India's preceding that of China. Internally, both nations had the same purposes in view. It is in the *means to the ends* that the two nations differ. Communist China "chose the system whereby political liberty was subordinated entirely to the harsh necessities of expansion"; democratic India "proposed to advance to self-sufficiency within a framework of political liberty accepted by the West."[17] A further contrast is found in the immediate goals. India chose the harder, longer way of building from the bottom—attempting first to raise the living standards of its masses by bringing improvements in agriculture; China moved directly into a major effort of industrialization, and, as in the USSR, the needs of the masses must wait until the Communist leaders feel secure in the strength of their industrial might. Perhaps the social need was greater in India. At any rate, 60 per cent of the investments of India's first Five-Year Plan went into agriculture.

CEYLON

Another independent state of the Commonwealth of Nations—a "drop" of a nation—was created when British India was carved up and Ceylon became sovereign. The smallest of the new states spawned by the departure of the

---

15 *Ibid.,* p. 13.

16 This political emergence was likewise contemporary with that of the other former colonial dependencies of Asia now sovereign, as Ceylon, Burma, Indonesia, etc.

17 Cameron, *op. cit.,* p. 58.

British from the subcontinent, it too has assumed the role of a neutral. However, like the Scandinavian states and India, Ceylon is not merely negatively neutral but positively and aggressively so; the island state has grasped every opportunity to act as mediator and, several times, has acted as spokesman for several of the newly created countries of former British India. Like Geneva in European Switzerland, Ceylon's Colombo has at times acted as a lever to keep the *status quo* in the East. The capital city has been a center to which representatives of the governments of South Asian countries have come to discuss problems of common interest and concern—as the Colombo Plan and the Colombo Conference; the term "Colombo Powers" further confirms this role.

The neutral functions of Ceylon and Switzerland are, however, differently interpreted by the two states; whereas the Ceylonese actively participate as mediators and conciliators the Swiss, in a sense, stand aside from all international questions—not participating, but merely maintaining the neutrality of the state and *permitting* their territory (usually Geneva) to be used as the site of international conferences. Swiss neutrality is passive; Ceylonese neutrality is active and positive. The Swiss attitude of neutrality, like that of many of the South Asian states, must be characterized as one of negation. Whether Ceylon, however, will ever have the geopolitical importance in Asia that Switzerland does in Europe is questionable because Ceylon's location is not of critical importance. However, the forceful role its leaders have taken has thrust the tiny state into a position of much greater diplomatic prominence than would normally be merited in terms of size and strength.

Culturally—in religion and language—Ceylon relates closely to India off whose southeast coast it hangs like a detached appendage. In religion it is Hindu and Buddhist; in language, although English is still the most common means of communication—a remnant of the British—Ceylon plans to gradually replace this with Tamil and Singhalese, the languages of the two ethnic groups who predominate on the island.

BURMA

When on January 4, 1948, at exactly 4:20 A.M., Burma (officially known as the Union of Burma) became a free and independent state, the imaginations of many Western peoples were fired. Burma was the first of the colonial Asian states to receive complete independence in the post-World War II period. It was a country that called to mind the Oriental past; here was Kipling's Burma with its temples and monuments, the pagodas and the stupas of the Buddhists—the "old Moulmein pagoda lookin' lazy at the sea." Any names connected with this little known land were wont to be romanticized despite the fact that American soldiers had hacked their way through Burmese jungles during the Pacific war. The people—the Burmese, the Chins, the Kachins, the Mons, the Shan, the Karens—were almost legendary, so far apart did they appear to be from the West.

Today the picture that is called to mind is different. In Burma, Western people now see striving, pulsing, *human,* and turbulent men with desires and feelings like themselves struggling, along with the other groups in Asia, for self-expression, for autonomy, for freedom from any form of colonialism. Much of the romance is gone, and today the West sees them realistically—perhaps too realistically, for acquaintance during the last decade and a half has destroyed the aura of unreality that previously enhanced the view but largely shrouded the people (as was the case with the Africans) from our vision. The strife, widely publicized, reveals ordinary, normal people—with differing customs, yes, but in nature very like all the rest of mankind.

Among Asian states Burma is—and has been—economically one of the most thriving; its people are well fed, it is under-populated, and it has an exportable surplus of food. However, almost from the day of independence, it has been torn by civil war that has threatened its economic and political future as a sovereign state. For the Burmese, independence has not come up to expectations; it brought an end to nearly a century and a quarter of foreign rule, but it also brought chaos, bloodshed—and a badly-damaged economy.

Background to Burmese Problems

Texas-size Burma has a population of some 18 million people (about twice the density of the Lone Star State). A recent census listed 126 native languages and dialects classified into 11 principal language groups; however, two-thirds of the inhabitants claim Burmese as their mother tongue and 70 per cent of the remainder speak Burmese well. Hence, linguistically, the picture is not too complex.

The people who inhabit Burma belong to the Mongolian race. The Burmese are, however, more closely allied ethnically and culturally to the Thais and Indo-Chinese people than to the Indians or the Chinese. This is true despite the fact that for over a century Burma was a province of British India, and, secondly, has long common boundaries with both China and India. Geographic barriers isolate Burma from the two large states and, because of the effectiveness of these physical barriers, Burma has not been a transit land nor has it received its principal cultural stimuli from either the Hindus or Chinese. A wall of mountains shuts Burma off from India; with no railroads and no usable roads crossing these ranges, Burma can be reached from India only by the sea. During World War II, two roads were hacked across the barrier frontier to facilitate logistics but they have since fallen into disrepair and are no longer serviceable to modern means of transport. Between China Proper and Burma lies the tangled and rugged topography of mountainous Yunnan Province. Further isolating Burma from foreign contacts are the mangrove swamps which extend almost unbroken along the Arakan and Tenasserim coasts.

The country is a land of longitudinal mountains and valleys. Along the west lie the Naga–Chin–Arakon Yoma, rugged in the north and rising to heights of 10 to 20,000 feet. To the east is the Shan Plateau, 2000 to 4000 feet in elevation and dropping abruptly to the central plain in an almost unbroken scarp; the plateau is cut through and drained by the Salween River. The central plain, valley of the Irrawaddy and Sitang Rivers, is broken by interruptions of hills—the Pegu in the south, the Kachin in the north; it tails off like the string of a kite in the long southward extension of Malayan Tenasserim.

There are five dominant ethnic groups in Burma. In this environment of strongly contrasting physiography are at least five dominant groups of indigenous people plus a number of Indians and Chinese, the latter making up the largest foreign element of the population. Burmese form the overwhelming majority, comprising about 70 per cent of the population; the Karens are Burma's largest minority group and make up from 10 to 15 per cent of the people. They are also the most dissident minority. The Burmans are thought to have entered the peninsula about 900 A.D., although the earliest inscriptions date only from the eleventh century. Previous to their entry into the present Burmese territory, Indians had penetrated the valley as far north as Prome, and Arab trading vessels had touched the mouth of the Irrawaddy.

Native history is a story of petty states waging wars and conquests on each other. However, in the latter part of the sixteenth century, much of Burma was united under one kingdom. This soon fell apart again, however, and not until the middle of the eighteenth century did there rise another leader strong enough to establish his rule over the whole of the land. This state lasted from 1752 to 1885 at which time the British obtained control of the territory. The capitals of the various native Burmese kingdoms (as Prome, Pegu, Pagan, Amarapura, and Mandalay) were all located in the interior of the country; Rangoon, the political core of British Burma, was located on the sea on an outlet of the Irrawaddy. The selection of this location for the colonial capital reflected the dependence of the British upon seapower.

European interest in Burma was long delayed. Burma's isolated location and the disturbed political conditions had discouraged any but a minor interest in the country on the part of European states until long after the latter were well established in other parts of Southeast Asia. The Portuguese were the first of the Europeans to trade with Burma, but colonial ambitions caused the British and French to take sides in the native quarrels fairly early. Britain, in control of India, followed events in Burma closely and on three occasions—in 1824, 1852, and 1885—found provocation for interference. In the latter year, the last portions of independent Burma were incorporated into the British Empire.[18]

British control brought an influx of Indians into Burmese territory. This immigration had far-reaching consequences for English law legalized the dispossession of the Burmese of their land; it was estimated that by the beginning of World War II, the chettiars (the Hindu professional moneylenders) had alienated up to 40 per cent of the cultivated area from the natives. They charged high rents and lent money at usurious rates of interest, at times as high as 50 per cent. Many Burmese felt that one of the greatest injustices of the British regime was the leniency shown toward uncontrolled lending of money and the accompanying dispossession of the Burmese of their lands. Alien moneylenders of foreign dress and customs, the chettiars had always been disliked by the Burmese and part of the popular support for the land nationalization program, instituted by the Socialist-minded government of the new Union of Burma, was based on this antipathy for the Hindu moneylender and landowner. Indian–Burmese racial strife at times became quite violent.

The Karen–Burmese antagonism is an an-

cient antagonism. Before the coming of the British, the Karen were a minority people greatly misused by the more numerous Burmese and often enslaved. However, during the British colonial era, the Karens were a favored group. They differ in language and custom from the majority Burmese, and are Baptist Christian as opposed to the Buddhist Burmese. They live in the southeastern part of the country, in the hill lands out and south of Moulmein, and are simple, easy-going, sturdy peasants, numbering about two million. Most of the Burmese troops recruited by British were drawn from the Karens.

The longstanding Burmese–Karen antagonisms revealed themselves with renewed intensity shortly after the wartime occupation of Burma by the Japanese when Burmese massacred the entire population of an isolated settlement of pro-British Karens who had fought alongside the British against the Nipponese invaders. Recalling this massacre and the years of oppression under the Burmese before the days of the British, in 1948 (the first year of Burma's independence) the Karens rose up in revolt and revenge against the Burmese, demanding an independent state of their own. They made up one element of the triangle of Burmese nationals who waged a civil war against the constituted government of the new state. For six tragic years the revolt dragged on, and only in 1954 did Karen opposition appear to be drawing to an end—and then only because most of the fighting men had been killed.

Seeking at first independence, as their strength diminished the Karens decreased their demands to autonomy for their group with minority rights to include "special schools and a special administration." However, it is unlikely that the Burmese, now in command of the situation within the country, will grant any such privileges to the Karens lest other minorities (as the Chins, Kachins, and Shans) make like demands and "the Union" be dissolved. On the other hand, the Karen leaders remain apprehensive lest the role of their people—less educated than the Burmese and also more retarded

---

[18] The British conquered South Burma in 1852 at which time the country was still undeveloped in a modern sense. It was easy, therefore, for the British to acquire monopolies on sea and river traffic, railroads, rice exports, the timber reserves including the valuable export timber, on teak, and, in time, on the mineral resources—oil, copper, and tin—British investors made an enormous amount of money in Burma.

in other lines of development—become that of a servile people.

The other major opponents to the Government in power have been two opposing and unilateral factions of Communists—the Reds and the Whites. Although, theoretically, the two Communist factions were followers of Trotsky and Lenin, actually loyalty to one or the other group has meant loyalty to the Burmese leader of that particular faction. Burmese Communism arose on the eve of World War II as a result of widespread nationalist resentment against the domination of the Burmese economy by foreigners, chiefly British and Indian. The pre-war numerical strength was never accurately known because, previous to the war, the Communists operated underground. Although the two factions were unilateral, nevertheless the common cause (opposition to the Government) made their cause "one," and this was true also of the Karens. However, the three forces were opposed to each other, and hence, although the civil struggle continued for over half a decade, there was little danger of the government forces being defeated.

Burma's civil strife has abated, but the country is faced with a population problem (really a minority problem) that has a potential for bursting forth at any moment—the Karens, the Shans, the Chins, and the Kachins all uneasy under their union with the Burmese who form an overwhelming majority. All but the Karens, however, are pretty well submerged within the Burmans. Communism *within the country* is still a problem—all the more so because the Shan plateau (the large eastern lobe of Burma) pushes hard into Communist China. Across this plateau ran the famed Burma Road of World War II, a logistical lifeline for the West running between Lashio in Burma and Yunnan in China.

Burma is, normally, a surplus area for food and mineral products. Before the past war, Burma was the world's largest exporter of rice, supplying surpluses to food deficient India, Japan, and Indonesia; it will again be a leading rice surplus area. Its extensive natural resources of timber and minerals once sent teak and oil, rubies, jade, and tungsten into world trade channels; undoubtedly they will again.[19] The Socialist Government of the Union of Burma aims at ultimate and complete nationalization of land and industry.

Politically, Burma is a weak spot. Offered independence or dominion status within the Commonwealth of Nations, as were the other new states constituted from the Indian Empire, the Burmese rejected affiliation within the Commonwealth in order to chart their own course as a nation. However, independent Burma has been unable to avoid the anarchic undercurrents left in the wake of colonialism, Japanese occupation, war, and internal ethnic antagonisms. Like Malaya and Vietnam, Burma is a weak spot in South Asia; and Siam, the other of the states of the peninsula of Indochina, is weak or strong according to the success of its peninsular neighbors in the current world struggle for power and allies.

INDONESIA

In the strong tide of nationalism that swept across Asia after World War II, Western influence in the East waned rapidly—and almost every colonial dependency was torn with rebellions and revolutions, some by civil war. The Dutch East Indies is one of the territories that has run the full gamut of revolution, civil war, and internal dissension in this struggle for independence and sovereign national status and unity.

Several European powers contested for the Spice Islands. In the distant days when the Portuguese and Spanish were opening up the ocean trade lanes, these were the famed Spice Islands of the East, the coveted prize that several nations vied for: the Portuguese, Spanish, Dutch, and English competed for the archipelago, and the Spice Islands were the subject of much international strife. In that day the prizes of trade were the spices—pepper, cloves, cinnamon, mace, and nutmeg—just as today

---

[19] Chinese jade is really Burmese jade; it becomes "Chinese" after these Oriental craftsmen have carved the stone into Chinese design. But Burma has for centuries been China's source of this semi-precious stone.

are oil, tin, rubber, and uranium. So "cut-throat" was the competition in the early days of trade that merchant ships were equipped not only for commerce but for battle as well. The period of competition was ended in 1683 when the Dutch took over complete control of the islands; concurrently, the name was changed from Spice Islands to Moluccas.

The Portuguese were the first to lay claim to the East Indies—although this claim was not uncontested. Pope Alexander VI's partition between Spain and Portugal of the unclaimed areas of the world was agreed to, with minor changes, by the rulers of the two Iberian states. The line, drawn "370 leagues west of the Cape Verde Islands" and extending from pole to pole, designated that all of the newly discovered lands east of that line were in the Portuguese sphere, all to the west of the line within the sphere of Spain. Magellan, who had visited the islands as a seaman, maintained that the Spice Islands were within the Spanish half of the world and he proposed to sail west to the islands to prove it. He was in error; the islands lay well within the Portuguese zone of the influence and, hence, were Portuguese possessions.

However, in 1600 the Portuguese were ejected from Amboina (center of the Portuguese political and commercial control in the Moluccas) by the Dutch East Indies Company which sent out a Dutch governor to rule the islands and built a fort to secure control. A period of English and Dutch competition for the valuable isles then set in which continued during the first portion of Dutch dominance; for a five-year period, Britain actually held the Isles. In general, however, Dutch administration continued unbroken for nearly 300 years —interrupted only for the half decade during the Napoleonic era. Not until the Japanese occupation in 1942 was Dutch authority replaced.

The nationalist movement began in the Indies about the turn of the century. At this period, nationalist manifestations were also rising in other parts of Southeast Asia. Although the Dutch found it necessary to make some concessions to the Indonesian nationalists during the two decades preceding World War II, anticolonialism did not become a serious threat to the Dutch until the war years when the Japanese occupied the islands (1942-1946). This occupation gave the movement impetus in two ways. First, under the Japanese administrators who, with the help of Indonesian "quislings," were able to extend their authority throughout most of the sprawling archipelago, and who propagated the "fiction" of Indonesian independence; secondly, with the evacuation of Japanese troops, quantities of weapons fell into the hands of the islanders making it feasible for them to resist the reinstatement of Dutch authority.

Immediately following the surrender of the Japanese to the Allies, and before the Dutch could return to the Indies, the Indonesian nationalists proclaimed their independence from the Netherlands (August 17, 1945) and the establishment of the Republic of Indonesia (consisting of the three most important islands of the archipelago, Java, Madura, and Sumatra). The proclamation of the Republic precipitated war between the Netherlands and Indonesia—a war that terminated only in 1949 with the Netherlands' recognition of the sovereign status of Indonesia. Independence, however, did not bring internal peace to Indonesia, and there is still trouble also between the Netherlands and the Republic regarding the status of Dutch New Guinea, "Irian," as the Indonesians call it.

Indonesia stretches for 3000 miles east and west through the island-dotted seas that connect the Indian and Pacific Oceans. The islands lie at once off the southeast coast of Asia and the north and northwest coasts of Australia, and are important to each continent. Generally, the islands are regarded as a part of Asia; ethnically, they are racially allied to the Malayans, and, in religion, are largely Moslem.

Politically, the East Indies were divided among four colonial powers previous to the setting up of the Republic. The greater portion was Dutch, and the Netherlands' territories stretched from Sumatra to the Australian mandate of New Guinea. This same territory is now all incorporated into the Republic of Indonesia with the exception of the western half of the island of New Guinea, still held by the Dutch; the British own three small enclaves of territory in northwestern Borneo—Sarawak, Brunei, and North Borneo; the Portuguese still retain a tiny foothold (of their once extensive East Indian holdings) in eastern Timor, while, as inferred, the eastern half of New Guinea is under Australian administration.

"The wealth of the Indies" is not a new tale; it is a very old one. The European powers were rivals for the rich spice trade, the eastern terminus of which lay in the Moluccas. As colonial power in the East Indies, the Netherlands held a strategically located archipelago of islands that compounded a domain 58 times vaster than that of the mother country, a population that was nearly nine times greater, and a base of natural resources that exceeded those of the Netherlands by many times over. The products of the Indies literally poured into the European state—or the profits from the products. Normally, the Indies are one of the world's two leading producers of both tin and natural rubber, while the oil reserves on Sumatra and Borneo are the most important in the Far East. Although spices—the "riches" for which the islands first gained their fame—have declined in relative importance (both as other areas have increased their contributions of spices, and as the spices of the Indies are forced to compete with other East Indian products)—the Moluccas are still the chief suppliers of mace and nutmeg, and also send pepper and cloves into world trade channels; sugar, rubber, tobacco, copra, kapok, and tea, other plantation crops, add to the flow of tropical products that these valuable islands produce.

Java, lush and volcano studded, and nearby Madura, although together not comprising the greatest areas by any means, nevertheless contain two-thirds of the population. These two islands form the economic and political ecumene of the Republic; here is Batavia, former capital of the Dutch colony and political center also for the new state, now under the Indonesian name of Jacarta; here is the center of production for all of the East Indian tropical plantation crops except rubber and tobacco. West of Java is Sumatra, larger, wilder and more primitive, and, likewise, less densely populated. It contains only about eight to nine million inhabitants as opposed to Java and Madura's 50 million. But here is the center of the rubber and tobacco plantations and here is a part of Indonesia's oil reserve. Off the northeastern Sumatran coast lie the three tin islands—Bangka, Billiton, and Singkep—a rich resource area among the few tin reserves of the world. From these western islands (Java, Sumatra, and the adjacent small ones) have, in normal times, come most of the exports of the archipelago.

To the north of the central portion of the main island arc lies large Borneo, yielding petroleum, gold, diamonds, and spices; and, east of Borneo are the original Spice Islands of the Moluccas. Bali, east of Java, and art and culture center from ancient times, is a little world in itself, economically not very important except as an attraction for tourists. New Guinea, terminating the island chain in the east, remains undeveloped and inhabited by primitive folk. It was because of the distinctness of New Guinea—ethnically (it is Melanesian) and economically—that the Dutch justified their retention on the western half of the large island.

Emergence of the Political Structure of the State

When independent Indonesia began to function as a political entity, it was known as the United States of Indonesia and was a *federal republic* of 16 states. The largest of these states was the Republic of Indonesia comprised of two separated portions of Java and most of Sumatra. The other component units were states that had been organized by the Dutch before independence, and had been made components of the new nation in the Constitution that was drafted before the Dutch transferred sovereignty to the Indonesians.

Immediately upon attaining independence, however, a series of adjustments and revolutionary changes were begun—not the least of which was the merging of the smaller states into increasingly larger units. The uniting of the East Java state with Jacarta and West Java was the first of such moves but, within a short period of time, all of the 16 autonomous units were incorporated into the "Republic" except East Indonesia (the Spice Islands) and East Sumatra. This reduced the number of component units to three and, thus, radically changed the structure of the state. The question was whether the federal structure would have to be altered.

Although within the country there are several strong factions all seeking control of the Government—the Masjumi (a Moslem political party), the Nationalists, the Communists, and the Socialists—there are no basic differences among them on the principle of national unity. The federal system that was formulated at the time of independence was makeshift, for it was an inheritance from the structure of states that the Dutch had set up in the process of cutting up the Jogjacarta Republic. Political tradition in Indonesia is unitary for the 300 years of Dutch authority were built on a policy of direct rule with strong centralized control. It was quite logical, therefore, that the new state should follow along somewhat similar lines, even though the physical fragmentation would suggest decentralization.

The contrast between Dutch and British colonial administration makes an interesting study, particularly in the light of post-colonial events. British policy has favored "principles of progressive decentralization." In other words, British administration was more in the nature of a trusteeship than of direct control, leaving a progressively increasing amount of authority in the hands of the colonial peoples. This left a tensility that proved valuable, especially under the pressures of mounting nationalism so that, when nationalism climaxed in political independence, India was able to emancipate itself from colonial status into four sovereign states through constitutional processes and not via the convulsions of revolution. Undoubtedly the lack of resilience in Dutch administration influenced the postwar course of events in unhappy Indonesia, for the Indonesians had no training in government. Today the Republic of Indonesia is a unitary republic, and is, in no sense, a federal system. However, although the many component parts have been welded into a single state, the nation is far from unified.

Problems of the republic are multiple. The Indonesians are faced with more critical dilemmas today than they were on the day when the Dutch tricolor was lowered from the palace of the Governor General in 1949. Lack of unity among its people is the foremost of the problems. Nationalism, fervent during revolutionary period, has become negative.

Of the nearly 80 million people of Indonesia some three million are Chinese. A minority group that is resented, these Chinese pose a further knotty problem for the new Republic in the status of *dual nationality* that they claim—*i.e.* while accepting Indonesian citizenship, they still regard themselves as citizens of the Chinese Republic, and so does China. Under proposed legislation, it has been suggested that the Indonesian Government declare that it will not recognize the principle of dual citizenship for Indonesian citizens; this, however, would not alter the situation for the Chinese state holds to the principle. The basic reason for Indonesian resentment of the Chinese residents lies in the fact that these nationals occupy a strong position as middlemen in the economy of the country.

The issue of the political status of two portions of the Dutch East Indies still faces the Republic—*i.e.* of Dutch New Guinea and the "Spice Islands." The Dutch retained control of New Guinea, moving the headquarters of the Dutch Empire from Batavia to Hollandia, New Guinea. Because Dutch New Guinea was a part of the East Indies, Indonesia feels it should be a part of the Republic; the Netherlands maintains, on the other hand, that New Guinea is primitive and not prepared for independence. It represents the last remnant of the former great empire in the East. In November, 1955, the Indonesians lost their petition in the

United Nations trying to force the Netherlands to negotiate with them over the Republic's claim.

The Moluccas have continued to agitate for separation from Indonesia. As with the Karens in Burma, the Ambonese of the Moluccas were the group from which the major portion of native troops (in the employ of the Dutch) were drawn. Since sovereignty was granted, the people of the Spice Islands have sought separate political status. By 1950, the issue of whether the Southern Moluccas were to be counted in or out of the Republic had become urgent. In the fall of that year Indonesian troops captured the capital (Amboina) of the Moluccas—also the rebel stronghold—and thus, temporarily, had the situation under control. For five years martial law held the islands in subjection; then, in 1955, the trouble broke out again.

The key to the Southern Moluccas is Amboina; from here, on April 25, 1950, the self-styled Republic of the South Moluccas was pronounced. As the shock troops of the Dutch (in keeping control over all parts of the Indies), the Ambonese had been loyal to the Dutch, and the Dutch often referred to this area as the thirteenth province of Holland. Relations between the Dutch and Ambonese were close and friendly. The Spice Islanders have no desire to be incorporated into Indonesia. They want independence. Many of the natives have left the Moluccas to migrate to Holland. A further aspect of the Moluccan problem is religious; in contrast to the greater part of Indonesia which is Moslem, the Moluccas are 60 per cent Christian, the result of the missionary activities of, especially, the Dutch Reformed Church. The Indonesians are wont to liken this attempt at severance of political ties to the attempted secession of the South from the Union of the United States. They do not expect to give up the territories. Not only does Indonesia want these islands within the Republic because of the former unitary character of the Indies and not only is the problem a case of a "minority nationalism in conflict with majority nationalism" but strategically, the Moluccas are valuable for they form a buffer chain of islands facing Dutch-held New Guinea. Both Irian and the Moluccas are thorny issues facing an uncertain future at the present moment.

THE COLOMBO PLAN

It has been stated before that the neutral states of the world do not form a bloc in the sense that they are closely allied with each other through pacts and treaties (see pages 124–131). However, segments have united to form alliances—economic, defensive, etc.— that include members of the neutral states but that also usually extend beyond the neutrals to include states from one or the other of the two power blocs. The Colombo Plan is such an alliance.

Under this alliance 17 Asian and Western nations are associated in a mutual attempt to improve economic conditions in Southeast Asia through technical aid. Originating in 1950 among the governments of Australia, Canada, Ceylon, India, New Zealand, Pakistan, and Great Britain, within five years it had extended its membership to include also Burma, Indonesia, Nepal, Thailand, Vietnam, Cambodia, Laos, the United States, Japan, and the Philippines. Nine of the members are "aid-receiving" countries—India, Pakistan, Ceylon, Indonesia, Nepal, Cambodia, Vietnam, Laos, and Burma; the rest (with the exception of the Philippines and Thailand which are "observer nations") are "donor" states. One of the main features of the organization is the exchange of technological skill and knowledge among the member countries.

The Bandung Conference. In January, 1955, five of the Colombo powers—Pakistan, India, Ceylon, Burma, and Indonesia—were instrumental in setting up the conference of 29 Asian and African states in what came to be known as the Bandung Conference. The meeting was held in Bandung, Indonesia, in April, 1955. Although described as being significant for what it didn't accomplish, certain results followed this meeting of Asian and African states. It is well to look at some of them.

Among the participating states indicated in

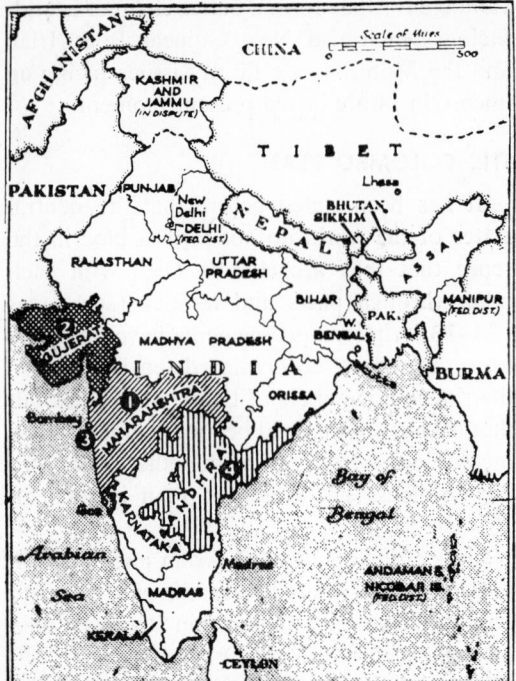

Figure 21.8. Revision proposed for Indian States: Bombay would be split into Maharashtra (1), Gujerat (2), and the city of Bombay (3). Under the altered plan, Hyderabad and Andhra would be merged in a new state (4). (Courtesy *The New York Times*.)

Figure 21.9, it will be noted that no Western nations attended; none were extended an invitation. This was the first time that Asian and African nations had assembled without the participation of any of the Western States—and perhaps more significantly—this was the first time that many of these states (many of which are small, former colonies) have had an opportunity to express themselves in a large international gathering *and be heard*. Over half of the populations of the world were represented at this meeting although, areally, the representation was less significant (12 per cent). In scale of population representation only a meeting of the Assembly of the United Nations can rank with the Bandung Conference.

It was remarkable that the Conference met at all for there was no precedent for it. In a sense, it was the "coming-out party" of the

Asian and African peoples—peoples that, for the entire interim between the beginning of the period of exploration to the postwar decade, had been political dependents of European powers. Until that conference these peoples had been represented in international gatherings by foreigners; at Bandung they took their places as equal citizens of the world to speak for themselves. It marked the end and the beginning of two eras for the Afro-Asian states and was, therefore, significant—significant in a way not objectively discernible in the results accomplished.

In terms of geographic delineation, no clear pattern of participants emerged—other than that only Asian and African peoples were taking part. The inclusion of these peoples was not complete, however. What was common to all of the participating states—and therefore worth noting—was that all of the countries had spent most of the modern era as political and/or economic dependents of the great Western powers; further, there was scarcely a state represented that had not, within a relatively recent period, experienced profound and, in some cases, revolutionary mutations, socially, economically, and politically. In some, these changes marked emergence from a colonial to a sovereign status; in others, they represented a scrapping of old political structures for new and markedly different ones. In all of these states, economic and social problems are so critical that "internal" matters should be—and are—the first concern. All of the participants were manifestly conscious of their new position.

Adherents of all three power forces were there—pro-West, pro-Communist and Communist, and neutrals. This mixed representation is one of the reasons that the conference ended without any major tangible accomplishments, for the most powerful representatives of all three factions pulled in three directions—India, China, and, among the pro-West, notably Pakistan and the Philippines. Because of their previous status as colonial dependencies, colonialism in all forms was denounced including the *"colonial" status of the Soviet satellites*.

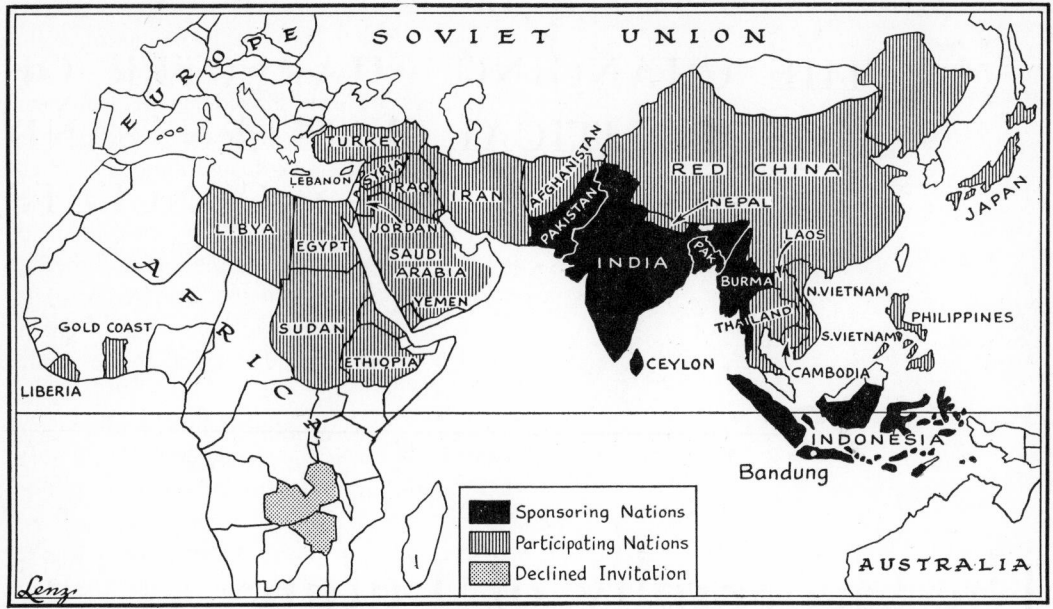

Figure 21.9. The Bandung Conference. (R. Lenz, cartographer. Courtesy *The Christian Science Monitor.*)

Since the Conference—and it would appear as an aftermath of Bandung—anticolonialism has flared in the United Nations. Now that these peoples have been given an opportunity to speak out, they are likely to become increasingly vocal. This *growing vociferousness of the small state* is a new aspect in international politics that has not appeared in the past; always the big nations have run the show. Now the little states are upsetting "the best laid plans of mice and men." Only time will tell whether it is all to the good. At any rate, it means a reorientation of foreign policy for all of the great powers.

An interesting sidelight on the conference is brought out in the fact that English was the official language. French, Chinese, and other languages could be used—provided the speakers furnished translators to transpose their words into English. In view of the highly anti-colonial, anti-West tone of the Conference, at times—even among the neutrals—this is particularly interesting, and perhaps significant. It is, of course, a by-product of colonialism itself, and illustrates the deep impression that the culture of the West already has made in certain areas. Twenty-nine languages were represented at Bandung.

THE CHANGING CHARACTER OF GEOPOLITICAL PATTERNS AND CONCEPTS

22

The Geography of Future World Politics

THE EVOLUTION OF THE SUPRA-NATIONAL ORGANIZATION

Human organizations—whether of a social, political, or economic nature—have progressed from smaller to larger units over the several millenia which mankind has recorded. As man advanced in social living, and as population increased and became disseminated more widely and thickly over the globe, increased organization has generally been a concomitant. The family gave way to the clan, the clan to the tribe, the tribe to the state; custom became solidified in law. Politically, there has been a relinquishment of some of the powers by the smaller to the larger unit in each case. States, representing the organization of peoples into countries, has been the major pattern of political life for centuries. There are, however, certain areas that have only begun to advance out

of the tribal state into the higher form, as in parts of the Middle East and Africa. In general, however, the increase from smaller to larger components has been a pervasive trend, and is apparent in every facet of human living.

The political world, today, is apparently advancing out of the stage of the national state—sovereign and independent—and into a higher and enlarged form of political living. Aspects of this extra-national organization have been making their appearance for a long time on a temporary basis; nations have made pacts, treaties, and alliances for defense against common foes, economic exchange of goods, etc., as they have seen the inadequacy of acting alone. The largest of such temporary joint efforts were undoubtedly made during World Wars I and II when two opposing political blocs, each comprised of a number of states commonly allied, arrayed themselves against each other. Unified land and sea commands, under chosen leaders, were elements new to such alignments, signifying a relinquishment of national authority within limited areas and effort. The opposing forces took in such a large portion of the nations as to make the first war the most devastating and widespread contest-at-arms in the history of mankind up to that time; the second, vastly more destructive and comprehensive than the former conflict, was of truly global proportions.

The 1914-18 war has fallaciously been called World War I when, in actuality, it was not a *world* war at all. Granted that more nations participated in the contest than in any previous encounter, action was still areally confined to campaigns in the Middle East, Northwest Europe, Greece, Turkey, Italy, and extensive operations at sea. The most notable aspects of that conflict were the submarine blockade of the British Isles, which brought near disaster to the peoples of that small island group, and the long and deadly siege of France and Belgium. Although populations suffered due to blockades, etc., World War I was still a war of the battlefield—a contest between soldiers, sailors, and aviators, and civilian populations felt little direct impact from the military operations themselves.

Nevertheless, a new epoch in warfare began with World War I. It was the first war in which nations engaged in battles in the air, in which the submarine was a truly effective weapon, and in which radio was used, the latter greatly improving communications; it was the first truly mechanized war due, first of all, to the "development of precision manufacture and mass production," and, secondly, to the invention of the internal combustion engine. These innovations were as far-reaching in their effects as were "the first bow, the Romans' siege engines, the introduction of gunpowder or the rifled gun and the shell."[1]

The 1939-45 war differed greatly from the previous one; it involved such vast areas as to make it *global*—practically all of Europe and the Mediterranean, the northern half of Africa, the Pacific theatre reaching from the North American Aleutians south to and including Australia, and, from the Aleutian and Hawaiian islands westward to include Far and Southeast Asia were battle zones. Secondly, it was "a war of movement."[2] Thirdly, in this conflict, the domains and populations of the warring states were the major objectives; and air warfare was *the effective weapon* that forced the surrender of the foes—Germans and Japanese.

"The cloud of controversy about strategic bombing, the oceans of ink spilt . . . by those who do not yet understand that they have lived through a revolution in human affairs, can not obscure the fact that one of the major belligerents, Japan, surrendered unconditionally with her armies intact before a single Allied soldier had set foot on her soil, primarily—not solely, but primarily—owing to air bombardment, and was brought to the point of that decision, as we now know, before the first atomic bomb was dropped."[3]

With the cessation of the First World War, a reaction against war set diplomats of some of the involved powers to organize the *League of Nations.* Isaiah Bowman, writing, in 1921, in *The New World,* analyzed the attitude and the political mood of the postwar period that led to the evolvement of that unprecedented international organization.

. . . the World War showed that science and human cooperation have made it possible to conduct war to the point of self-destruction, that in a world war there is no such thing as a victorious power—all alike suffer irreparable losses. The damage that war does cannot be made good by the aggressor even if we take all that the aggressor has. This is another way of saying that war has been developed to the point where it has passed beyond human control.

If these things be true, we must look at war and international relations from an entirely new point of view . . . the reduction or elimination of war is certainly an aim that ought to be tested. . . .

---

[1] Vannevar Bush, *Modern Arms and Free Men* (New York: Simon and Schuster, 1949), p. 10.

[2] Sir John Slessor, *Strategy for the West* (New York: William Morrow and Company, 1954), p. 12.
[3] *Ibid.,* pp. 12-13.

So far as it is the last resort of reason, war is a discredited institution. It obtained many good things for us in the past and it may yet obtain good things for the human race. It gave us many of the institutions of civilization, and to the people of the United States, for example, it brought national liberty. But peace has done vastly more. It has given us our body of law. It has permitted the growth of institutions. It has enabled man to test his life and relationships by reason and justice rather than by force. We should not look to history for the lessons of war, because war has become a new thing in scope and purpose and its possibilities of destruction are now limitless, whereas war in the past had a limited effect . . .[4]

But the League of Nations as an instrument for peace and international justice was not structurally strong enough to carry out its aims or to inhibit the aggressive policies of certain strong powers. As time went on, it became less effective; Japan refused the League of Nations' Commission on Mandates the right to see that the provisions of the mandate agreements were carried out; Germany ignored it when Nazi power became strong. In one sense, therefore, it failed; in another, it did not for its failures pointed the way toward other attempts at international organization of a supra-national character. Failure of the League—if it shall be so characterized—did not deter the growth of the supra-national idea. The inter-war period of reaffirmed nationalism was perhaps not characterized by any noticeable movement from the national to the supra-national concept—but it was a period of incubation.

After the world had undergone a second global conflict, the supra-national idea germinated quickly and in three facets of international relations—defense, economics, and politics. NATO and the Warsaw Pact both illustrate the supra-national approach to defense—albeit, they are both illustrations f the old, old alliance system. A number of economic integration plans, particularly in Europe, have been suggested, and some very effectively put into operation. All involve the relinquishment of certain national powers into the hands of the supra-national organization. These have already been discussed—Benelux, the Schumann

Plan, the Coal and Steel Community, etc. (see Chapter VIII). The prosperity of Europe depends upon such economic integration—an integration that would resemble that of the United States where, as among the 48 states, trade barriers do not exist, and raw materials and manufactured goods can move freely between contrasting regions.

The current political offspring of the supra-national idea on a worldwide scale is the United Nations. Its birth represented, essentially, a reiteration by statesmen that war must be eliminated. To eliminate international conflict, some international organization that would represent world opinion and pressure appeared to be the only instrument capable of attaining the objective. The United Nations functioned during and after World War II—in a worldwide capacity since the war terminated.[5] But, although the years intervening between 1945 and the present have been characterized by quiescence of generalized warfare, this period has not been one of peace. It has been an era of cold war and localized military engagements—in Korea, Indochina, North Africa, the Middle East, Hungary.

THE CHARACTER OF WAR

The precise distinctions between the conditions of peace and war became blurred during the cold war. It is likely that "for some years to come the world will go on, as now, in this sort of curious twilight between war and peace, in which force must have an influence far more permeating than it had in what used to be regarded as normal conditions of 'peace,' and influence which must be exercised primarily with

---

[4] Bowman, op. cit., pp. 4-5.

[5] It is interesting to note here the circumstances under which the *United Nations* was conceived. The name was suggested by President Franklin D. Roosevelt, and was first employed by 26 states meeting in Washington, in 1942, "to draft a *Declaration by United Nations."* These nations pledged their support to continue the war against the Axis Powers; until 1946, the United Nations was a wartime alliance. Although the international organization today represented in the United Nations was drawn up at San Francisco in 1945, "the foundations" of this world organization were chartered at Dumbarton Oaks Conference in Washington the year before. Hence, in its "conception," the United Nations was not exactly global.

the object of preventing the outbreak of what we used to understand by 'war.' "[6]

Essentially, war is "a conflict of wills." Too often contemporary history has seen states aggress upon the rights and territories of other nations simply because they desired something, or didn't want something to happen, or tried to force some other state to accept their will. War "is a projection of policy, a continuation of diplomacy by other means." Further, nations do not engage in military conflict unless they are moderately certain that they can be successful. That raises the next question regarding war, in the words of Marshal Foch, "*de quoi s'agit il?*" (what is the point?)[7]

War is followed by peace; the conflict is not itself the primary objective—but rather the peace that is subsequent to the war. This is a point frequently forgotten as war becomes the all pervading aim. The phrase coined during World War II, "winning the peace," embodied this concept. However, most of the combatants, while glibly pronouncing the words, forgot the meaning. The World War II recriminatory disarmament terms[8] bear this out. They laid the grounds for future wars, not future peace. War "means not merely forcing an enemy to lay down his arms and accept terms, but *being successful in creating world conditions more favorable . . . than if there had never been a war.*"[9]

As cultures have grown and flowered into civilizations with greater enlightenment and "spread," as human associations have evolved into progressively more extensive relationships, so war has advanced from the contest of individual combatants with weapons that were relatively inextensible—to conflicts in which weapons became so extensible as to include guided missiles and hydrogen bombs dropped from great heights. The "battlefields and sieges" of the eighteenth century—"wars in which armies knocked off and went into winter quarters, 'will messieurs the enemy fire first, and all that sort of thing,'"[10]—were characterized by fighting done by mercenaries and professional soldiers. In the total war of the mid-twentieth century—in which land, sea, and air were all battlefields, in which all of the populations of the combatant states were involved (and, all too frequently, the domains and nationals of neutral states)—the fighting spread across the globe. So ravaging have the weapons of war become that "war has abolished itself"[11] —or else has the potential for the very destruction of mankind and his civilizations. To avert that destruction, it is not enough to abolish the use of a weapon of war[12]—as advocated for the atomic bomb. War itself must be discarded.

However, abrogation of war does not infer immediate disarmament. Only from strength —physical strength—can nations, looking toward peace, deal with those states that look toward aggression. Wars in the future will likely take the pattern that the conflicts of the post-World War II period have had—that is, they are likely to be "relatively small, localized affairs." Contests of strength between major powers on a widespread scale will be avoided, if possible. The world may "be entering upon an era of 'Crimean' wars." The actual conflict of the past decade has been the cold war. The "minor wars of the future" (the Koreas and the Crimeas) "if they come, should be regarded as what they will be, *tactical episodes in the real world war of our time,* which it will be to our interest to isolate and keep localized."[13] This is not to say, however, that such local wars (as the several Arab-Israeli conflicts) will not burst into a general conflagration.

[6] Slessor, *op. cit.,* pp. 7–8.

[7] *Ibid., pp.* 8-9 (summarized and quoted).

[8] As the occupation of Germany by the four Powers that led to the eventual division of Germany into East and West; the absorption of German territory, east of the Oder–Neisse Rivers by Poland, and of East Prussia by the USSR and Poland, to cite only one instance.

[9] Slessor, *op. cit.,* p. 10.

[10] *Ibid.,* p. 11.

[11] *Ibid.,* p. 16.

[12] By tacit agreement—because of its lethal character—poison gas is not used, but its rejection did not eliminate war: it simply led to the invention of different but even more deadly and destructive weapons, as the hydrogen bomb.

[13] Slessor, *op. cit.,* pp. 64-65.

Should a local conflict catch fire and most of the nations again take up arms, what would such a war be like? Taking a cue from the 1939-45 war and the developments in weapons since the termination of that conflict, the conclusion must be drawn that armies in the field will play an ever lessening role while air power —and likely atomic and hydrogen weapons— become the menace of the future. Since this would be true—and again adding together clues from World War II and armament developments—no nation would be able to hold out against air attacks for the length of time that Germany did—five years. They would be knocked out or crippled in a matter of days or weeks—provided *atomic warfare* was waged. With jet planes, instruments of detection, satellites, guided missiles and bombers, and hydrogen and atomic bombs, no spaces would be vast enough and no critical centers so deeply hidden as to prevent destruction or detection. The vital spots of the combatant domains would soon be demolished.

STRATEGY AND TACTICS FOR LASTING PEACE

Because of the destructiveness of the new weapons and the fear of annihilation, the two major power blocs have for more than a decade waged a cold war—in the midst of which local conflicts have sputtered and exploded continuously. However, for the major powers during the era of the cold war the emphasis—or contest—has shifted from the military to the economic and political. The military build-ups of both sides brought this about—for only from strength can a nation talk and bargain. Without the power to back up its words, no state or block of states can negotiate in the world as it exists today.

It is a platitude that the building of strong defenses must lead to war; diplomacy is powerless unless it deals from strength. Until the international organization—whether it be the United Nations or some other world federative assembly—commands the force and influence necessary to induce the great powers to comply

with its decisions, group coalitions (as represented in NATO, for example) must be the keepers of the peace and integrity of nations. Unity among the free nations is necessary.

In strategy, simple containment is not enough. "It would be entirely misleading to describe our policy and purpose as being no more than the preservation of the *status quo*." The West is "inevitably on the defensive."[14] However, attack, at times, "is the soul of defense,"[15] and may become a necessary tactic. Tactics and strategy should not be confused. Attack should be avoided if possible—but circumstances may not always permit this. ". . . thus far and no farther"—words spoken by statesmen of the West and backed up by force—has represented the strategy of the free world since 1950. ". . . strategy must be flexible and the main emphasis—of the defensive policy—[be] adapted to meet the changing threat." Whatever offensive is taken in the current era, it "must be mainly one of ideas . . . the real offensive in this new war is in the field of foreign policy and diplomacy in their fullest sense, the art of the statesman and the business of the foreign ministries and state departments . . . 'For us, many of the weapons of peace lie unexploited. Certainly we must deal forcefully with force, but we shall gain more in the long run by dealing with facts.' " If the opposition can be proven wrong, then " 'their cause will decay and the foundations of . . . power will begin to crumble.' . . . It is a world-wide strategy of two main fronts, economic and political, closely connected and supplemented by a vigorous and imaginative offensive in the field of ideas, what we know as psychological warfare . . . [Our] objective must be to provide economic elbow room for backward peoples to develop freely along their own lines";[16] to provide for the fullest economic development and integration within the community of free nations; and, to allow—and recognize the right of —the opposing states to develop and trade,

---

[14] *Ibid.,* p. 57.
[15] *Ibid.,* p. 121.
[16] *Ibid.,* pp. 59, 71-73.

with equal rights, within the world of nations. Peace agreements following a war—or periods of peace—that recognize that all nations have the right to develop their national potential and that the *peace must benefit the enemy as well as the ally* will further the cause of peace and, concomitantly, act to abolish war and contention.

There can be no such thing as "national strategy" any longer. "Strategy today is world strategy and it is no more possible to shape it merely to suit the limited interest of one particular country than it is to confine a typhoon to a potato patch."[17]

Military defense is still a necessity. That defense means largely air defense. Although the point was made that, in atomic air warfare, no spaces will be great enough to assure security, nevertheless even the air must have defense in depth—space enough to make the weight of its impact felt, *i.e.* spaces that contain resource reserves, supply centers, space for distributed bases to pack a punch. Hence, it is a truism that power, of whatever sort, still requires large area and, hence, defense in depth.

THE NEED FOR THE "VOLUNTARY SUBORDINATION OF NATIONAL POLICY"[18]

International Law

". . . a secure world order is impossible without world law," stated A. H. Feller, general counsel and director of the legal department of the United Nations. But how can such law be had? Modern international law has existed for about three centuries. It has a complex structure for it is "made up of rules embodied in treaties between states and of customary rules applied by foreign offices of governments and national and international courts. There has never been a legislature to make or an executive to enforce these rules. To the average man international law hardly exists . . . Is international law really law?

"International law is a fragmentary and primitive system." This is not surprising since international law has been built up, bit by bit, "through the actions of sovereign states in a disordered world." But what is surprising is that *sans* legislative or executive action, and notwithstanding its unsystematic and sporadic evolution, there is such a body of law, and that it is viable.[19, 20]

The notion that if it isn't enforceable it isn't law acquired a gloss of academic respectability in the last century. In the final analysis this sort of thinking holds that law only exists at the end of a policeman's club. The experience of mankind and particularly of our own country teaches a different lesson. There have been many communities plentifully endowed with legislatures, codes of law and law enforcement officers which have been as disorderly and anarchic as the international community. Contrast the lofty supremacy of the United States Supreme Court, which commands implicit obedience with only a single marshal at its command even though it gives judgment against powerful corporations, great states, the Federal executive and even the laws enacted by the Congress itself.[21] Law is not just the rule enforced by the policeman; it is the rule obeyed by the citizen, and obeyed because of the necessities of his own existence in an organized society.

Both in theory and in practice, nations consider themselves bound by the rules of international law. Sometimes they will break the rules, just as individuals do in their own communities. But even the most flagrant law breaker among the nations will not deny that there is an international law; it will argue either that there is no rule to govern the case or that the rule means something different. Read nearly any exchange of diplomatic correspondence and you will see a legal argument— each party contending that the law is on its side. Even in the midst of a world war or the most intense ideological struggle, the nations still cling

---

17 *Ibid.*, p. 47.
18 *Ibid.*, p. 43.

19 A. H. Feller, "We Move, Slowly, Toward World Law," *New York Times Magazine, New York Times,* June 5, 1949.
20 For further discussion, see J. L. Brierly, *The Law of Nations* (London: Oxford University Press, 1955), Chapters VIII and IX, pp. 273-326.
21 It is true that the Supreme Court has but one marshal. However, to be truly realistic, it is necessary to call to mind that, under the Supreme Court, there are the lower Federal courts, such as the Federal District Courts and the Courts of Appeals, each with their own marshals.

to at least the profession that they are bound by the rules of international law.[22]

. . . . . .

. . . international law has been developing since its inception. Its early preoccupation was with the status of diplomatic representatives and territorial waters, and later with the rules of warfare and neutrality. In this century there was much law making, through treaties, to cover new situations —international trade and commerce, aerial navigation, the control of the narcotics traffic, telecommunication, arbitration and judical settlement of disputes. After 1922 the Permanent Court of International Justice added a solid body of doctrine through numerous decisions. The system has developed, but often too slowly, usually erratically, and twice in this century a world war has interrupted its progress just when it was gathering greater headway.[23]

It is not possible to say that any individual organization will have the necessary authority to enforce international law.[24, 25] The founders of the League of Nations thought their institution would solve the problem. The San Francisco Conference on International Organization, meeting in 1945, instituted the United Nations in the hope that there would be a world body with more power than the League, and more effective. For the first five years the United Nations made many recommendations on critical issues of conflict and peace. During the second five-year period, however, it became increasingly ineffective—frustrated by the deadlock in the Security Council. Nevertheless, during this period, it carried out some notable

actions—as, the creation of the *United Nations Emergency Force* and the waging of a war to stop aggression in Korea.

Nationalism and Neutralism

The historic role of the United States has been isolation—an isolation made possible by a physically-framed separation. "It allowed us the luxury of standing apart from our principal allies, particularly from Great Britain and France, which had direct interests and commitments all over the world. Standing apart, we could support them and we could refuse to support them, we could approve and we could criticize what they did. We could measure all claims on our support, particularly in the colonial and dependent areas of Asia and the Middle East, by our own ideological standards."[26]

Such isolationist policies—expressed in neutrality of action—are not possible for Americans today, or for few other people. Strong nationalism is evidence of political immaturity. Genuine though it may be, and deep as may be the need of some of the less politically mature nations to give their entire attention and thinking to the mutation of social and political matters and the development of the national economy (withdrawing—or taking the role of onlooker—in world affairs), no state can really remain outside of world politics. In the case of a major conflict, granted that any particular domain was spared the shattering impact of battles and attacks, all countries "would in the long run share the fate of the rest of civilization, in a greater or lesser degree. And it is a fallacy to suppose that any free nation can pull its full weight in the world or have any real freedom of action outside the coalition of free peoples, still more that it can effectively influence for good or ill the policy of either camp." Their very freedom of action is guaranteed by the coalition of states that is preserving the peace. "Neutralism today is . . . a form of escapism, the attitude of the ostrich."

However, this does not imply that every

---

[22] The trouble with international law is not that it isn't law; the weakness lies in its decentralized nature. "If the system is to furnish a secure foundation for the world community it must be developed until its content approximates that of national legal systems."

[23] Feller, *op. cit.*

[24] ". . . law does not destroy violence unless it is bound up with an organized and stable society. On the other hand, no society can be stable unless it is founded on justice and the rule of law." (Feller, *ibid.*, p. 37)

[25] It may be that the structure of the League of Nations and the United Nations has been wrong— representation solely on a national basis. It has been advocated by some that the world organization adopt a federal system with representation on both a population and national basis—as in most national legislatures. For a further discussion, see J. L. Brierly, *op. cit.*, pp. 91-117.

[26] Walter Lippmann, *Isolation and Alliances: An American Speaks to the British* (Boston: Little, Brown and Company, 1952), p. 35.

nation, regardless of size or location, must declare its partisanship in the present power struggle; the neutrality of some, as those countries hanging precariously along the edges of the Communist center, is understandable. Full participation in the Western defense community would jeopardize the integrity of their domains. Some states, as the newly constituted sovereign entities in Asia and Africa, are too "young" and feel, yet, too insecure in their new found independence to enter boldly on one side or the other. Some, however, are carried along by the NATO states as "passengers who enjoy the pleasures of the voyage without working their passage"—*i.e.* sharing all of the benefits of protection that NATO provides, but sharing none of the responsibilities. Another general conflict would be a "war of continents between two conflicting creeds far more fundamentally antagonistic than Christendom and Islam in the Middle Ages. In such a war there would be no neutrals; . . ."[27]

The Supra-National Concept

No nation can "go it alone"; isolation is unrealistic. The progressive step in the evolution of political organizations is the supra-national organization constituted by sovereign states through the "voluntary subordination of national policy" to a common international policy and purpose—embodying concepts similar to those embodied by the League of Nations and the United Nations.

In any association, whether it be a military or economic coalition of a limited number of nations or an organization on a grand scale that is worldwide, the forces within it should be balanced, as far as possible. General Omar Bradley[28] advocated a balance in terms of the *ability* of each participating member nation—that ability measured in national resources, character, and experience—not in terms of each nation attempting to reflect a microscopic reproduction of the larger league. In all likelihood, the application of this tenet to the great powers would be moderate if it had

any application, for on the great states would rest global obligations. In the two world organizations that have made their appearance to date, and in NATO, the principle has had so little application as to scarcely exist.

All sorts of political prejudices and traditions, vested interests and national prides come into play. And one may look around him today and see several examples of small nations trying, quite vainly, to have their own army, navy, and air force all complete as though there were no such thing as NATO in existence. That is the antithesis of the sound strategic principles of co-operation and economy of force, and someday we may learn to think really internationally in this respect, but it looks as though we may have to put up with the antithesis for some time to come.

There are some who are impatient of military alliances and yearn for the creation of a world police force to maintain the rule of law between the nations. We can share their aspirations without agreeing that anything on these lines is anything but a pipe dream in the present state of the world. The history of the Military Staff Committee of the United Nations Organization should be enough to prove that a world police force is a chimera without a world government—the political horse must come before the military cart. We must be patient enough to work towards our goal by limited advances.[29]

The United Nations. The powers and the limits of the General Assembly and the Security Council appear to be the two factors that have rendered the United Nations relatively impotent—and to an increasing degree—as time has gone on, and the weaknesses show up in varying manifestations. As constituted, the United Nations can recommend and also, within certain specific areas, impose action; the International Court of Justice can pass judgments[30] and the Security Council may impose action.[31] The impact of the General Assembly lies largely in the moral censure it can levy through its resolutions.[32] More specifically, it is the *veto* that has nullified Security Council ac-

---

[27] Slessor, *op. cit.*, p. 44 (last two paragraphs summarized from this reference).

[28] From a speech delivered in Chicago, 1949.

[29] Slessor, *op. cit.*, pp. 48-49.

[30] See Articles 36 and 38 of the Statute of the International Courts of Justice, Charter of the United Nations.

[31] See Articles 24-26 and 94 of the Charter of the United Nations.

[32] See Articles 10 and 12 of the Charter of the United Nations.

tion wherever the interests of the East and West collide because unanimous approval by the five Permanent Members is required. In all of the other functioning bodies of the United Nations, majority rule holds. During the years since the inception of the United Nations, the veto has been invoked within the Security Council upwards of a hundred times. The General Assembly is empowered to make recommendations upon all matters within the scope of the Charter except where a dispute is being debated in the Security Council.

The United Nations was created as an international instrument to keep the peace, and the Great Powers, working through the Security Council, theoretically would function as the police force to enforce justice. Such a structure was based on the premise of the concert of action by the large states in whom this extra authority resided. But it didn't work out that way as time went on. During the first half decade the Soviet Union refrained from taking an aggressive role; further, it even gave silent consent to United Nations action in "intra-Free World disputes." The change in policy came in January, 1950 when, in differences arising over the China issue, the USSR walked out of the organization. Upon the return of the Russian delegates to the Council, Soviet policy became more aggressive and less permissive, to the end that the Western states were forced

. . . to rely more and more on regional defense alliances against new aggressions; the attitudes of the Asian and Arab neutralists, together with Soviet interference in such issues as Palestine, further diminished the area of effective United Nations action. This was particularly so in the case of Indochina and Formosa, since Communist China, despite its prominent connection with both disputes, had been barred from membership by the United States.[33]

The upshot has been that the United Nations has tended to become an arena in which the two great power blocs play power politics. This trend has been decried by the positively neutral nations, such as the Scandinavians and Indians.

It has also been used as a sounding board by many of the others, notably the Arab states. However, to say that the United Nations is becoming powerless to act is not to imply that the United Nations is no longer a dominant influence in world affairs. It is; the two phrases are not parallel. This is true despite the fact that the partition of Trieste was negotiated in London—in the face of the 1947 agreement of the Security Council "to make itself responsible for the independence and territorial integrity of the Free Territory of Trieste." The Kashmir problem has been repeatedly brought back to the Security Council and no effective action taken. The Palestine question has recurrently arisen, without enough power within the United Nations to enforce upon the involved states the partition and cease-fire agreements. Moreover, Western powers have relied increasingly upon mutual defense pacts for security.

The role—or the power—of the international organization appears to be changing. It is passing out of the hands of the Security Council and into the General Assembly; and it is by indirect means that the United Nations effects its power or impact—not by direct action. In this change the United Nations—and the world leaders—are confronted with circumstances of the greatest significance. As the power wielded by the Security Council has declined and shifted, the functions and powers of the General Assembly have also gradually changed. Originally, it was the body of the United Nations where opinions were exchanged and the air cleared, so to speak. Its purpose was primarily one of recommendation. The body that was to function in the actual execution of decisions was the Security Council. However, as indiscriminate and contradictory use of the veto paralyzed Security Council action, it became inevitable that the authority would be taken over by the Assembly. Today, the Assembly is no longer merely a "debating society." And this directs attention once again to the concept of international law and the evolutionary process by which that law is built up and becomes an *effective body of jurisprudence.*

---

[33] Thomas J. Hamilton, "Revising United Nations Charter Will Be No Easy Task," *New York Times,* April 19, 1955, p. E5.

In debates and discussions, there is residual an important organic process. This is the evolution of new concepts in the field of international law. The Assembly is not, strictly speaking, a "law-making body." As the Secretary General has pointed out, its decisions and the compacts reached under them are actually enforced only through the accession of sovereign states. And for this reason, the development of changes in the international legal pattern has been necessarily slow. But the means of achieving that development are at hand in the Assembly. Out of its deliberations there can come, eventually, a modified and better framework, in law, for the whole field of international relationships.[34]

As the power of the United Nations has gradually shifted from Security Council to General Assembly, another concomitant phenomenon has developed: the Great Powers are losing the initiative. This is particularly confounding to the Western Bloc nations who regard the United Nations as the association of states most likely to "contain Communism" within its present bounds—since the purpose of the United Nations is, first and foremost, to provide peace and security to all nations (and, in the view of the West, the current threat to that security comes from the Eastern Bloc). American "control" of the United Nations has been compared to the prewar domination of the League of Nations by Great Britain. This control is now slipping—along with the power of the other great nations that sit on the Security Council. Many diplomats regard this as one of the most important trends in United Nations history.

A further coefficient of the growing importance of the General Assembly is the growing "voice" of the little state. It is largely out of this—and the use to which these formerly almost unheard countries are lending their voices—that the United Nations retains the force it does. Among these less powerful states are many former colonies and neutral countries. And to these newly sovereign and neutral states—as well as to any that incline towards neutrality—this new voice has great appeal. (It must also be remembered that in the Gen-

eral Assembly, size and power have no bearing on the vote—each member nation casts one ballot; each state holds a "power" equal to that of every other member country.) The neutralist force in the United Nations is not a new phenomenon. With India and the Scandinavian states in the van, the members of this group have performed a very positive function as intermediaries between parties of the two great power blocs.

But while neutralism may—and does—act as a positive force to reduce tensions within this international organization, anticolonialism is negative. The French North African crisis of the summer and fall of 1955, British–Greek disagreement on the Cyprus matter, and the Dutch–Indonesian dispute over New Guinea, brought out a new wave of anticolonial feeling that thrust these explosive issues into the debates of the General Assembly. Discussion of the North African situation led to a temporary boycott of the General Assembly by the French. Since the Soviet Union does not view the Communist satellites as "dependencies," and since Russia has never regarded itself as a colonial state (Russian acquisitions of foreign territory were always contiguous to territory already Russian and quickly absorbed—albeit, by force—into the body politic), the whole of the vindictive of anticolonial antagonism falls upon the West European countries.[35]

The Soviet Union has tried to *use* the surge of anticolonialism in the General Assembly as well as to use all of the other of "the great divisions of the noncommunist world," as Walter Lippmann so tersely characterized this Soviet maneuver. These great divisions include, among others, Europe and the Moslem world, the two Germanys, the Arab world and Israel, India and Pakistan. On the latter issue, Russia

---

[34] *New York Times* editorial, September 18, 1955.

[35] The loud and critical voice of the Soviets against colonialism by Western nations and its seeming sympathy with the anti-colonial reactions of former or present Western dependencies, apparently convinced many of the colonial or former-colonial peoples that Russia was not imperialistic. Soviet military action within Hungary, in the fall of 1956, placed the relationship of Soviet and satellite in its true perspective, however.

took definite sides despite the fact that the Security Council—on which the USSR has a permanent seat—is pledged to settle the issue through a plebiscite—and, hence, be impartial.

Colonialism is a subject on which the three great Western powers—Great Britain, France, and the United States—are divided. Debate on such matters lies within the province of United Nations action, the Charter specifically providing that:

Members of the United Nations which have or assume responsibilities for the administration of territories whose peoples have not yet attained a full measure of self-government recognize the principle that the interests of the inhabitants of these territories are paramount, and accept as a sacred trust the obligation to promote to the utmost, within the system of international peace and security, . . . the well-being of the inhabitants of these territories, and, to this end:
  a. to insure . . . their political, economic, social, and educational advancement, their just treatment . . .;
  b. to develop self-government . . ." etc.[36]

In other words, it is the obligation of the United Nations to protect the rights of non-self-governing territories, as colonies. However, the United Nations rejection of a resolution to urge Dutch–Indonesian talks on West New Guinea and the action taken to remove some of the pressure on France in the Moroccan crisis both reflected a cautious reluctance in that world body to take up such matters. The trend is, nevertheless, to use the United Nations in achieving self-government for colonial areas. The success depends upon the good faith of the metropolitan governments.[37]

An appraisal of United Nations influence. In what does the strength of the United Nations rest? It lies, undoubtedly, in the universal respect and support that it can command. In the words of Henry Cabot Lodge, Jr., United States Representative to the United Nations since 1953:

The key lies in the single word: influence.

This influence is of several kinds, including the day-to-day work of the diplomats who use the U.N., in the words of the Charter, as "A center for harmonizing the actions of nations." This is the essential U.N. function which the founders foresaw, and which will always play a great part in settling disputes peacefully.[38]

The Need for a Supra-National Organization

History has repeated itself, but it has also advanced. It is necessary only to go back a few hundred years to appreciate these advances —and the most conspicuous feature of human history is the *progression of progress*. The historic panorama is characterized by depth and continuity as well as advancement. The "depth" is provided by areas in which man has moved forward—social, moral, scientific, political, economic, philosophic, and the like; the continuity results from building on the past and the progression. Seldom has the continuity been broken either by extreme retrogression or progression—*i.e.* by a leap ahead beyond the bounds of all contemporary thought and conditions.

The historical development of man's social and political relations has already been alluded to—from the family unit to the tribal to the national to the international. As man has moved slowly but steadily into the larger arena of human association, he has erected legal structures to protect his society. The extra-national relationships of the state have grown ever more complex. Any number of areas are torn by dispute; talk of disarmament conflicts with the reality of multiplying defense pacts and increasing the build-up for defense; the Great Powers of the world are put to confusion by the outspoken attitude of small states and the militant show of resentment by colonies, former dependencies, and mandates. In short, international relations are highly explosive, making even the most immediate future un-

---

[36] Charter of the United Nations, Chapter XI, "Declaration Regarding Non-Self-Governing Territories," Articles 73-74.

[37] A further trend has been the broadening scope of the United Nations organs and activities. Illustrative are the actions taken relative to Human Rights, Genocide, the Status of Women, UNESCO, UNRWA, etc. (see *Everyman's United Nations*, New York: United Nations, December 31, 1955).

[38] Henry Cabot Lodge, Jr., "Appraising the U.N.'s Influence," *The New York Times Magazine*, September 18, 1955, p. 14.

certain. At such a period when the diplomacy, if not the temper, of international relations is in turmoil, there is a need, as never before, for "a center" where the aims and desires of nations can be harmonized. Some sort of supranational organization has become essential to the continuance of civilized society—even to the continuance of human life itself. This must be the next stage of political progress.

GEOGRAPHY AND THE WAY OF THE FUTURE

The Changing Dimensions of the Globe

Though the roundness of the earth was proven nearly 500 years ago, only the advent of aircraft drove home the true significance of the concept "round." As land obstacles were erased by flight man found it possible to follow the shortest routes, without deviation, between two points—the courses of the great circle. Man's realization of a "round" globe brought also into focus the geographic relationships of one area to another—*i.e.* "west" may be "east," depending on where one lives. The Far East lies west of the United States, but it is to the east of Europe, and the USSR, and Africa; and, while the United States lies west of Europe, Asians look east to see the nearest American shores.

With the coming of the airplane the conceptions of global dimensions changed, too. People living in eastern United States are no longer 3500 miles away from London or Paris, but 12 to 15 flying hours distant; no longer nearly 7000 miles removed from Peking, but hours and minutes away. This changed conception of space, from linear measurement to measurement in terms of time, has forced every state on the globe to consider the vast size of the earth on a much smaller scale. Truly, in physical terms, all men—and states—are today neighbors, whether friendly or hostile. Behind these changed concepts of distance lie the changing patterns of international policy among nations: security pacts—and counter pacts—by blocs of states, in their efforts to make themselves defensible in a small and uneasy world.

The influence of changing transportation technology upon military geography and, hence, upon political geography must be alluded to, at least. Until the days of the frigate, land-based powers held advantages over maritime states; and the land-based states that could most rapidly extend their might, in greatest force, became dominant. This was the value of the Roman roads, and the Paris location of Louis Capet. As technology evolved improved sailing vessels, worldwide mobility came to those nations that had ships in numbers—and there was a concomitant rise of maritime powers.[39] However, seapower can only fully dominate the edges of land masses, not the interiors of large continents.

The railroad, the next major innovation in transportation, during the past hundred years has allowed land-based states to recapture mobility[40]—at least on a limited scale. Railroads provided the means of handling military logistics within a land area—and with somewhat greater speed than was possible on water. Germany took full advantage of the railroad for military purposes—as did the USSR.

It will be recalled that reference was previously made to the role played by railroads in the peopling and unification of the United States. The introduction of the railroads had a like effect upon the unification of the German territories; without the railroad, it is probable that there would have been no German state as known from 1870 to the end of World War II. The motor car brought the road again into prominence as a transportation medium and further increased land-mobility.

During the last quarter century, the airplane has become the medium to revolutionize transportation. No longer is geographic distance measured in miles. It is calculated in "transit time." The support area for air power must, of necessity, be an industrialized complex with large and varied reserves of mineral resources, or resources that have value as exchange items so that the necessary materials may be bought.

---

[39] See Alfred T. Mahan, *op. cit.*
[40] See Sir Halford Mackinder, *op. cit.*

The global misconceptions of men in high places resulted in some great diplomatic and strategic mistakes in the past. The isolation policy of the United States, for example, was based upon a two dimensional view of the world which placed the Americas in a secure position of insularity, surrounded by vast and impenetrable seas. Such errors in geography stemmed from a failure to see the world as "round." Even the present generation does not appear to have quite grasped the meaning of this fundament or always to have acted upon it when geographical intelligence and wisdom were important. On the opposite side, despite the decreasing dimensions of the globe coincident with the great conquest of the air, this generation of the earth has been forced to a new appreciation of the size of the globe—the immensity of the world was underlined as people followed the arduous movement of ocean convoys, the air and ship transport of relatives, during World War II, to all parts of the globe —Port Moresby and Sidney, Dakar and Murmansk, Basra and Aden, Iwo Jima, Calcutta, and Corregidor. These were geography "lessons, driven home under the hard impact of war."[41]

No nation can afford to underrate the importance of the physical aspects of the world in the determination of national policies, internal or international. NATO, for example, is a grand alliance of nations physically knit by long lines of sea communication—the realities of geography must be considered and overcome before that body can even function; raw materials, abundant in some parts of the globe and deficient in others, must be mined and produced in locus, and then transported to industrial and consumption centers—the geography factor again a preeminent one; the shutting down—or destruction—of oil installations or pipelines, as on Bahrein Islands and across Syria during the Suez fighting between British–French forces and Egypt, closed off the source of supply in one area, and the deficiency had to be met by increased production and ship-ment from other regions—else the British Navy would have been unable to operate at full force, and the air service would have been handicapped; the stockpiling of strategic and critical mineral and fuel reserves—*all reflect the pervasiveness of the geographic factor in war and peacetime.* "It was not the battle fleet that was the real backbone of British seapower in our palmy days, nor the greyhounds of the Atlantic; it was the freighters, the tramp steamers and tankers, cargo ships of all types and sizes all over the world—the 'dirty British coaster with the salt-caked smoke stack' of Masefield's poem"[42]—that brought the foodstuffs and minerals to England's door and, thus, to feed the factories. These activities characterize the relationship of geography to political and economic affairs.

However, not always do the politician and diplomat think within the framework of geography. Too often persons in government are more interested in public reactions to policies advocated than to their consonance with the physical setting. History records manifold instances of the disparity between political action—internal and international—and geographic and scientific reality. As a matter of fact, going a step farther, political geography— and geography in general—has often been perverted to justify national ambitions. German geopolitics, Soviet policy toward the satellite countries, Italian actions in Dalmatia and Abyssinia (to name only three of the most blatant examples) reflect this perversion of geography for the furtherance of such aims. And geography has been used a countless number of times to justify diplomatic and political moves that were often inflammatory from the moment of their inception—the creation of the Polish Corridor; the Nazi following of the "folk" into the Sudeten; the promulgation of the doctrine, by a whole line of German thinkers, that posited the necessity of state expansion for survival. Put to such use—to justify the means to the end of an aggressive intention—geography has, at times and in cer-

[41] Fitzgibbon, *op. cit.,* p. 3.

[42] Slessor, *op. cit.,* p. 93.

tain states, acquired an infamous name and fallen into disrepute.

The Concept of "the Hemispheres"

Americans, when speaking of the American sphere, are prone to refer to it as "this hemisphere," as if there were the only one hemisphere in which the United States were located. But the global relationships of the United States—and other nations—will be better understood if it is realized that this country—and every country—makes up a part of many hemispheres—not merely one. The globe can be divided into innumerable hemispheres, for the word "hemisphere" simply means a half sphere or, as used in geography, half of the terrestrial globe. Since the earth is essentially a sphere, this means that any plane passing through the globe so as to bisect it would divide it into hemispheres. The center plane distinguishes one hemisphere from any other. Certain hemispheres are more easily comprehended than others, however, perhaps because the traditional hemispheres, for one reason or another, have proved useful as divisions of the world.

The traditional hemispheric views are the eastern and the western, the northern and southern. How valid are they? The eastern and western hemispheres probably became thus designated for one or all of the following reasons: 1) as the exploration of the earth unfolded, the major outlines of the land mass of Afro–Eurasia (the Eastern Hemisphere) first became known, and only later those of the Americas (the Western Hemisphere); 2) great oceans separated the Old World from the New, each half seemingly a world in itself, and the latter lying to the west of those countries that actually made the discoveries; 3) the general acceptance, in 1884, of the Greenwich Meridian as the Prime Meridian and of the International Date Line, which together nearly (though not exactly) divide the globe into the east and the west hemispheres as we know them.

The concepts of "eastern" and "western" have been significant, historically and politically, in the international relations between states. The Monroe Doctrine[43] was predicated on the idea of an eastern and western "half," the one set apart from the other by effective separators—the oceans were regarded as barriers. But important as these concepts have been in the semantics of history and politics, the so-called eastern and western hemispheres actually have no political, geographic, or economic validity. In the first place, the nomenclature is misleading for, as stated before, though the New World lies to the west of Europe, it is situated to the east of Asia. If the Asians had made the first explorations, the western hemisphere could equally well have become known as the "eastern" for it is quite as much east of Asia as it is west of Europe. In fact, the concepts of "eastern" and "western" hemispheres are unfortunate for they suggest limiting or dividing lines, extending north-south (meridians), that separate one part of the world from another. Such a view presents a world "partitioned" where, in reality, unity exists. It splits land masses, which are the home of man, and leads to such thinking as "hemispheric isolation" and "hemispheric solidarity." Further, the economic (and therefore strategic) centers of world production overlap these conventional hemispheres and refute the reality and validity of the hemispheric view.

Today nations must be oriented not hemispherically but globally. The Marshall Plan, the Point Four Program, the Atlantic Pact, SEATO, two world wars with the so-called western hemisphere supplying material and manpower to the eastern, and, last but not least, the United Nations, all contradict the old

---

[43] Interestingly enough, the term "western hemisphere" was not used by President Monroe in his message to Congress in 1823 when he presented the Monroe Doctrine. The phrases "the American continents" and "this hemisphere" were, seemingly, synonymously employed. He had the non-intervention of Czarist Russia in mind and it is certain that he did not consider any part of Siberia as within "this hemisphere." An examination of the "western hemisphere," however, will reveal that the easternmost portions of the Soviet domain are included within it.

idea of hemispheric thinking. As a matter of fact the western hemisphere, if it retreated into absolute isolation, would be greatly handicapped. In the present complex structure of the modern world, where man has become highly dependent upon "things" produced by machines (and both the "things" and machines dependent, in turn, upon a large and sure supply of a great variety of raw materials, particularly minerals), the western hemisphere would find itself in an untenable position politically, economically—and, militarily, in case of war. Though the United States acted as an arsenal for the Western world in the three latest conflicts, some of its most strategic raw materials have to be imported from the continents of the eastern hemisphere, notably from Africa. Today, the commercial oceans do not divide peoples from each other; they link them together. Water transportation is cheaper, though slower, than land, and availability of cheap water transportation as against expensive overland haulage frequently determines whether or not a resource will be exploited. Likewise, the airplane nullifies the old idea that oceans "divide."[44]

The only hemispheres whose common boundary has any geographic validity are the northern and the southern. With the divisive plane passing through the equator, seasons on opposite sides are antipodal, the one hemisphere having summer during the period when the winter season holds in the other. What of these two hemispheres? What of the southern? It is mostly water—and icecap—even more so than the western. At present, political geography stops essentially at 60 degrees south latitude *because beyond that parallel is a realm of water, or snow and ice, and, hence, it is beyond the periphery* of most of man's habitations, activities, and strife.[45] Much of the southern hemisphere is significant for what it doesn't have. Even excluding Antarctica, the land areas (26 per cent of a world total that includes neither the Greenland or the Antarctic icecaps) are marginal in location, and restricted in population (nine per cent of mankind). This relative unimportance is exemplified in the effect that political occurrences in South America have upon the politics of the rest of the world. Despite the many local disturbances that are constantly stirred up within and between nations, the political climate of the rest of the globe remains almost oblivious to them. They happen too far away from the center of things—from man's world—and too few people are involved. The preeminence of Europe and the Near East, on the other hand, stems not alone from the size of the populations and the economic productiveness but also from the central location.

In the air age, it is the northern hemisphere that is the important hemisphere. It includes North America, part of South America, all of Europe and Asia, and three-fourths of Africa.[46] With the exception of the land hemisphere (which is centered on France), this is by far the most significant; significant because here man—and his activities—are concentrated. It has a circular relationship; that is, all of the land masses are closely associated within a closed circle and tied together at the top—at the pole. Populations and states are, therefore, in close adjacence—not far apart, separated by unnavigable seas—but united, by air time-distance. Hence, happenings in one area affect other regions acutely. With the advent of aircraft and the realization of the navigability of the great ocean of air, the earth has become a

---

[44] Actually oceans may have the effect of binding nations and peoples together, *e.g.* the Atlantic Pact, the Mediterranean Pact, and, to take an unofficial organization, the Institute of Pacific Relations which has chapters in every country that faces on the Pacific Ocean. Further, Seattle and San Francisco look west, not east. Within the bounds of this country, and connected to the rest of the nation by rail and air, nevertheless their interests and contacts look west to the Orient and north to Alaska.

[45] Only in Antarctica are nations striving for footholds, and these are mainly for economic reasons that are at present minor (fishing rights). Though some minerals are known to be present, it is highly unlikely that any exploitation will take place in this climatically marginal region until deposits of like minerals play out in the more accessible areas. This will occur in the foreseeable future.

[46] Sixty-seven per cent of the area and 68 per cent of the population of Africa are included.

limited globe on which political occurrences in any part may affect the welfare of the United States and large segments, or all, of the rest of the world. These changes have had the effect of drawing the world together, of making it "one." Looking at weight of land area and weight of population, it is to be seen that nine-tenths of the land and over nine-tenths of the people of the globe are in the northern hemisphere. Here is where man lives, each human in close proximity to every other one; weight of land and population are disproportionately concentrated in the northern half of the globe, and, hence, nations and peoples are here intimately associated.

The Significance of the Shrinking Globe

The Magellan expedition was the first to circumnavigate the globe. It took a few days less than three years (from August, 1519, to July, 1522) to accomplish this miracle in the conquest of space. Thomas Cavendish, in the *Desire,* traveled around the earth (1586 to 1588) in two years and 50 days; and Nellie Bly, a newspaper woman (using a combination of the fastest means of land and sea transport) girdled the globe in only a little over 72 days. She started on November 14, 1889 and returned January 25, 1890. But this record speed was decimated when, in 1933, the first solo airplane[47] sped around the earth, consuming the miles in seven days, 18 hours, 49.5 minutes. This was not non-stop, however. Each time an expedition or person cut days—or hours and minutes—from the period that was necessary to encircle the globe, the time-distance was thereby cut and the globe took on smaller dimensions.

The earth today is a "limited" globe. No longer can men, in the old sense, speak of dark unknown places in one part of the world or another. Ice-breakers push their prows into the floes and icebergs of the Arctic and Antarctic to unfold the secrets, and helicopters, set loose from their decks, aid in the research; planes span deserts and wet tropics and Arctic regions and mountains, photographing deep and formerly hidden mysteries, and aircraft carry equipment and supplies into the most remote sections of the world; submarine and sonic devices probe the obscurities of the ocean depths. No longer does the designation, the "known world" apply, for all of the world, generally speaking, is known and all parts, because of the swift character of communication and transportation, lie in close adjacence the one to the other. The fuzzywuzzy of fearsome Melanesia, the dark skinned indigene of "darkest Africa," the Moroccan Berber or the Algerian Kabyle living in his stone casbah in the remotest mountain retreats are all in contact with at least some of the appurtenances of modern cultures. They comprehend (though they may not understand how) that sickness is allayed by the needle that injects something into the arm; they see the television and hear the radio as they walk the boulevards of "eastern towns" or, in their own (often primitive) homes, they switch a knob and the news of the world flashes across their consciousness; trucks roll by on asphalt roads, planes drone overhead, and they sense the din and the power of the technology and science of Western man.

Now man lives in a little and constricted world. Though the spherical character of the globe was proven by Columbus, it is only "now," with the inventions of radio and television and aircraft, that this fact has been driven home—the fact of the three dimensional world that grows ever smaller as time-distances shatter the distances implied in the "miles" of linear space.

Geography as a "Weapon" of Planning

No nation possesses a monopoly of geographic wisdom. It is to be hoped, however, that the mistakes of the past will serve as guides in making decisions in the present and future. The United Nations, for example, appears to

---

[47] This solo flight was made by Wiley Post, and he covered 15,596 miles in this round-the-world trip. However, his was not the first plane to span the globe. In 1924, four United States Army Air Corps men, flying four Douglas Cruiser biplanes, flew around the world, leaving from and returning to Seattle. Two planes returned after 175 days of flight, covering from 26,345 to 27,553 miles (the figures vary on the distance traveled).

have learned more about the relationship of politics to geography than had the League of Nations. It is now recognized that geographical sense and geographical wisdom are weapons in the peacetime and wartime planning of every nation—and maps are some of the most potent of the geographical tools.

The advent of the airplane and the acceptance of the concept of the round globe together effectively refuted the specious platitude, "East is east and west is west, and never the twain shall meet." They, therefore, have led to the discard of distorted views of the world—such as those presented by the cylindrical Mercator projection which essentially has, for centuries, obscured from men the true relations of one part of the globe to another. A knowledge and comprehension of the physical relationships between all countries is prerequisite to the understanding of international relations, especially in an air age—and the map is an essential and inevitable tool that must be used for the discernment of these relationships.

It took a world conflagration like World War II, and the subsequent cold war and little wars, to bring home to the peoples of the earth the full geographic implications of a round world, and, through difficult experience, mankind was freed to learn that the earth is a globe. Such teachings in geography have a permanent value and utility in forcing mankind to realize the "oneness" of the earth and its three dimensional character; they have helped men to de-velop more accurate conceptions of direction, distance, place, and size than they ever held before. The human race has, at long last, become geography, travel, and map minded. And the map maker has come into his own as never before. It is perhaps ironic that war should be responsible for the advance in the cartographic coverage of the world. And yet, since the dramatic days in 1939 when the second period of German aggression began, the political map of the world has had to be revised, at times almost daily, and large parts of the globe, formerly known in only the most superficial and sketchy manner, have been mapped in detail through either aerial photography or cartography, or both.

Without the perception of distance, of the relationship of region to region, and a knowledge of where places are, without an appreciation for all of the other primary elements of geography, planning for peace or war, nationally or internationally, becomes blind. All states are nextdoor neighbors, in a manner of speaking—economically, politically, and socially dependent upon one another, close in time and movement, less remote in this present world (that shrinks almost daily as new inventions devour space) than in the day when maritime transportation was the only means of communication between lands isolated from each other by oceans. These geographic realities must be reflected in the world politics of the future.

Bibliography

Air Navigation, Air Science 3, VII. AROTC Handbook.

Bailey, Thomas A., *A Diplomatic History of the American People.* New York: Appleton-Century-Crofts, Inc., 1950.

Balzak, S. S., V. F. Vasyutin, and Y. G. Feigin, *Economic Geography of the USSR.* New York: The Macmillan Company, 1949.

Berle, Adolf A., "Latin America Moves Slowly Toward Stability," *The New York Times Magazine* (October, 1955).

Bishop, Dwight R., "Agricultural Production in Asia and the Middle East," *Foreign Agriculture,* XIX (May, 1955), pp. 92-93, 101-104.

Boggs, S. Whittemore., *International Boundaries.* New York: Columbia University Press, 1940.

———, "Problems of Water-Boundary Definition: Median Lines and International Boundaries Through Territorial Waters," *Geographical Review,* Vol. 27 (1937), pp. 445-56.

Bowles, Chester, "India Revisited: 'Spectacular Progress,'" *The New York Times Magazine* (April 3, 1955).

Bowman, Isaiah, *Geography in Relation to the Social Sciences.* New York: Charles Scribner's Sons, 1934.

———, "Foreword," *International Boundaries* by S. Whittemore Boggs. New York: Columbia University Press, 1940.

———, *The New World.* Yonkers-on-Hudson: World Book Company, 1921.

Brierly, J. L., *The Law of Nations.* London: Oxford University Press, 1955.

Burck, Gilbert., "The Boom That Made Canada," *Fortune* (August, 1952), pp. 91-99.

Burleson, Mrs. A. S., "Wandering Islands of the Rio Grande," *National Geographic Magazine,* Vol. 24 (1913), pp. 381-86.

Burpee, Lawrence J., "From Sea to Sea," *Canadian Geographical Journal,* Vol. XVI (1938), pp. 3-32.

Bush, Vannevar, *Modern Arms and Free Men.* New York: Simon and Schuster, Inc., 1949.

Cameron, James, "Nehru vs. Mao—A Key Contest in Asia," *The New York Times Magazine* (August 17, 1955).

Carlson, Lucile, "The Mining District of Kiruna Stad, Sweden," The Scientific Monthly, LXXIV (February, 1952), pp. 76-83.

———,"Narvik and Lulea: Swedish Ore Ports," *The Journal of Geography,* LII (January, 1953), pp. 1-13.

———, "Svalbard and International Politics," *The Geographical Review,* XLVI (January, 1956), pp. 123-125.

Carter, Gwendolen M., "Can Apartheid Succeed in South Africa?" *Foreign Affairs,* XXXII (January, 1954), pp. 296-309.

Chen, Ta, *Population in Modern China.* Chicago: The University of Chicago Press, 1946.

Claude, Inis L., Jr., *Swords Into Plowshares.* New York: Random House, Inc., 1956.

Davis, Kingsley, "Demographic Fact and Policy in India," *The Milbank Memorial Fund Quarterly,* XXII (July, 1944), pp. 256-278.

————, "Future Migration into Latin America," *The Milbank Memorial Fund Quarterly*, XXV (January, 1947), pp. 44-62.

————, *The Population of India and Pakistan*. Princeton: Princeton University Press, 1951.

Determinants and Consequences of Population Trends. New York: United Nations, 1953.

Doty, Robert C., (Analyses of Arab League Activities) *New York Times* (January 23 and 30, 1955).

Ebenstein, William, *Today's Isms*. Englewood Cliffs, N.J.: Prentice-Hall, Inc., 1957.

(Editorial.) *Foreign Agriculture*, XIII (September, 1949), p. 195.

(Editorial.) *New York Times* (September 8, 1955).

Ellis, Harry B., "Battlefield of Empires," *Christian Science Monitor* (November 16, 1954).

Espenshade, Edward B., Jr. (ed.), *Goode's World Atlas*. Chicago: Rand McNally & Company.

Everyman's United Nations. New York: United Nations, 1955.

Fairgrieve, James, *Geography and World Power*. London: University of London Press, 1941.

Feller, A. H., "We Move, Slowly, Toward World Law," *The New York Times Magazine* (June 5, 1949).

Fitzgerald, Walter, *The New Europe*. New York: Harper and Brothers, 1945.

Fitzgibbon, Russell H., *Global Politics*. Berkeley, California: The University of California Press, 1944.

Freeman, Otis, *Geography of the Pacific*. New York: John Wiley and Sons, Inc., 1951.

Goodrich, Leland M., and Edvard Hambro, *Charter of the United Nations, Commentary and Documents*. Boston: World Peace Foundation, 1949.

Grey, Arthur L., Jr., "The Thirty-eighth Parallel," *Foreign Affairs*, XXIX (April, 1951), pp. 482-487.

Hamilton, Thomas J., "Revising the United Nations Charter Will Be No Easy Task," *The New York Times* (April 15, 1955), E5.

Hanson, E. P., "The Amazon: A New Frontier," *Headline Series*, No. 45. New York: Foreign Policy Association, 1944, pp. 5-88.

Harris, Chauncy D., "U.S.S.R. Resources: I—Heavy Industry," *Focus*, V (February, 1955).

Hartshorne, Richard, "The Functional Approach to Political Geography," *Annals* of the Association of American Geographers, XL (June, 1950), pp. 95-130.

————, *The Nature of Geography*. New York: The Association of American Geographers, 1939.

Hill, A. V., "Health, Food and Population in India," *International Affairs*, XXI (January, 1945), pp. 40-52.

Holdich, Sir Thomas Hungerford, *Political Frontiers and Boundary Making*. London: Macmillan & Co., Ltd., 1916.

Hollweg, Vice Admiral, "The Dardanelles Problem," *Living Age*, CCCXV (November 18, 1922), p. 384-387.

Jones, Stephen B., *Boundary Making*. Washington, D. C.: Carnegie Endowment for International Peace, 1945.

Keiwiet, Cornelius W., "African Dilemmas," *Foreign Affairs*, XXXIII (April, 1955), pp. 445-457.

Kennan, George F. "America and the Russian Future," *Foreign Affairs*, XXIX (April, 1951), pp. 351-370.

Kimble, G. H. T., "Great Britain," *Focus*, II (March 15, 1952).

Kish, George, "Yugoslavia," *Focus*, I (March 15, 1951).

Koenig, Ernest, "Planning in Czechoslovak Agriculture," *Foreign Agriculture*, XVI (September, 1952), pp. 157-158.

Laws, J. B., "A Minor Adjustment in the Boundary Between Tanganyika Territory and Ruanda," *Geographical Journal*, Vol. 80 (1932), pp. 244-247.

League of Nations, *Mandates: Report of the Commission Entrusted by the Council with the Study of the Frontier Between Syria and Iraq*. Geneva: League of Nations, 1932 (Publication No. C.578.M.285.1932.VI).

————, *Covenant of the League of Nations*.

Lengyel, Emil, *The Soviet Union*. New York: Oxford University Press, 1951.

Lie, Trygve, "Trygve Lie Appraises the Future of the United Nations," *The New York Times Magazine* (May 8, 1948).

Lippmann, Walter, "Geography and the Ideological Conflict," *New York Herald Tribune* (June 21, 1951).

————, *Isolation and Alliances: An American Speaks to the British*. Boston: Little, Brown and Company, 1952.

Lodge, Henry Cabot, Jr., "Appraising the U.N.'s Influence," *The New York Times Magazine* (September 8, 1955).

Lorimer, Frank, "Population Movements in Imperial Russia and in the Soviet Union," *Compass of the World*, edited by Hans W.

Weigert and Vilhjalmur Stefansson. New York: The Macmillan Company, 1947, pp. 443-460.

Lower, Arthur R. M., *Colony to Nation*. Toronto: Longmans, Green and Company, 1946.

Mackinder, Sir Halford, *Democratic Ideals and Reality*. New York: Henry Holt and Co., 1919.

———, "The Geographical Pivot of History," *The Geographical Journal,* XXIII (1904), pp. 421-444.

———, "The Round World and the Winning of the Peace," *Foreign Affairs,* XXI (July, 1943), pp. 595-605.

Mahan, Alfred Thayer, *The Influence of Sea Power Upon History*. New York: Little, Brown and Co., 1890.

Martin, H. H., "Fisheries of the Future," *Conservation of Natural Resources,* edited by Guy-Harold Smith. New York: John Wiley and Sons, Inc., 1950.

McCune, Shannon, "The Thirty-eighth Parallel in Korea," *World Politics,* I (January, 1949), pp. 223-232.

McMahon, Sir A. Henry, "The Southern Borderlands of Afghanistan," *Geographical Journal,* IX (April, 1897), pp. 393-415.

Minerals Yearbook. Washington, D.C.: U.S. Government Printing Office.

Munro, Keith, "Now Canada Comes of Age," *The New York Times Magazine* (March 30, 1952).

Myres, J. L., "The Marmara Region: A Study in Historical Geography," *The Scottish Geographical Journal,* XL (May, 1924), pp. 129-150.

Niles' Weekly Register, XIV (February 27, 1819), p. 4. (Published in Baltimore, Maryland.)

Notestein, Frank W., "Fundamentals of Population Change in Europe and the Soviet Union," *Compass of the World,* edited by Hans W. Weigert and Vilhjalmur Stefansson. New York: The Macmillan Company, 1947, pp. 429-442.

———, "The Population of the World in the Year 2000," *Journal of the American Statistical Association,* XL (September, 1950), p. 335-345.

Ofner, Francis, "Israel Waters Its Waste Places," *Christian Science Monitor,* March 24, 1955, p. 9.

Our Southern Partners. Department of State Publication 5604, Inter-American Series 49 (December, 1954).

"Past and Future Growth of World Population: A Long-Range View," United Nations' *Population Bulletin,* No. 1, Document No. St/SOA/Series N/1 (December, 1951), pp. 1-12. New York: United Nations.

Porter, K. H. (ed.), *National Party Platforms*. New York: The Macmillan Co., 1924.

Pratt, Wallace E., and Dorothy Good (editors), *World Petroleum Geography*. New York: American Geographical Society, 1950.

"Pressing Scientific Problems of the North." New York: The Arctic Institute of North America, 1957.

"Problems in India," *New York Times* (February 12, 1956).

Rafler, Doris Detre, "India and Pakistan—The Problems of Partition," *Foreign Agriculture,* XIII (December, 1949), pp. 272-277.

Romulo, Carlos P., "What the Asians Expect of Us," *New York Times Magazine* (June 19, 1955).

Ryder, C. H. D., "The Demarcation of the Turco-Persian Boundary in 1913-14," *The Geographical Journal,* LXVI (September, 1925), pp. 227-242.

Shabad, Theodore, *Geography of the USSR*. New York: Columbia University Press, 1951.

———, *New York Times* (May 15, 1955), p. 26.

Simmons, Ernest J., *USSR: A Concise Handbook*. Ithaca, N.Y. Cornell University Press, 1947.

Slessor, Sir John, *Strategy for the West*. New York: William Morrow & Company, 1954.

Smith, Guy-Harold (ed.), *Conservation of Natural Resources*. New York: John Wiley & Sons, 1950.

Smith, J. Russell, and M. Ogden Phillips, *Industrial and Commercial Geography*. New York: Henry Holt & Company, 1946.

Smith, W. Bedell, "The United States and the Dardanelles," *Current History,* XII (January, 1947), pp. 76-77.

Snow, Edgar, "The Rover Boys Rule Burma," *The Saturday Evening Post,* CCXX (May 29, 1948), pp. 26-27 f.

Spate, O. H. K., "The Partition of India and the Prospects of Pakistan," *The Geographical Review,* XXXVIII (January, 1948), pp. 5-29.

Spencer, Joseph E., *Asia, East by South*. New York: John Wiley & Sons, Inc., 1954.

Spykman, Nicholas John, "Frontiers, Security, and International Organization," *The Geographical Review,* XXXII (1942), pp. 436-447.

————, *The Geography of the Peace.* New York: Harcourt, Brace & Co., 1944.

Steiner, H. Arthur, "The Relation Between Geography and Politics," *Global Politics,* edited by Russell H. Fitzgibbon. Berkeley, California: The University of California Press, 1940.

Stern, Peter M., "Alaska," *Focus,* IV (September, 1953).

————, "Poland," *Focus,* III (November, 1952).

Sun, K. K., *La Chine de Demain.* Paris, 1946.

Terrasse, Henri, *History of Morocco.* Casablanca: Editions Atlantides, 1952.

Toynbee, Arnold J., "What Makes A Great Power Great," *The New York Times Magazine* (May 29, 1955).

"United Fruit Company Is a Vast Enterprise," "News of the Week" section of *The New York Times* (July 4, 1954).

United Nations, *Charter of the United Nations.*

————, *Demographic Yearbook, 1949-50.* New York: United Nations, 1951.

————, *Demographic Yearbook, 1955.* New York: United Nations, 1956.

————, "Monthly Bulletin of Statistics," April, 1957.

"USSR—Summary of Basic Economic Information," International Reference Service, U.S. Department of Commerce, VII (December, 1950).

Van Royen, William and Oliver Bowles, *The Mineral Resources of the World.* Englewood Cliffs, N.J.: Prentice-Hall, Inc., 1952.

Van Valkenburg, Samuel, *Europe.* New York: John Wiley & Sons, 1952.

————, "Iraq," *Focus,* IV (January, 1954).

Volin, Lazar, "Russian Agricultural Potential," *Foreign Agriculture,* XVII (October, 1953), pp. 175-180.

————, "The New Battle for Grain in Soviet Russia," *Foreign Agriculture,* XVIII (November, 1954), pp. 194-199.

————, "Twenty Years of Soviet Agrarian Policy," *Foreign Agriculture,* XXI (January, 1957), pp. 9-10, 21.

von Grunebaum, Gustav E., *Unity and Variety in Muslim Civilization.* Chicago: University of Chicago Press, 1955.

Wambaugh, Sarah, *A Monograph on Plebiscites, with a Collection of Official Documents.* Publication of the Carnegie Endowment for International Peace. New York: The Oxford University Press, 1920.

Wassan, R. Gordon, "Are the Russians As Well Off as They Were Under the Czar?" *U.S. News World Report* (March 16, 1951), p. 33.

Weigert, Hans W. and Vilhjalmur Stefansson (editors), *Compass of the World.* New York: The Macmillan Company, 1947.

Whittlesey, Derwent, *The Earth and State.* New York: Henry Holt & Company, 1939.

Index

Abyssinia, 376
Aden, 441
  location, 437–438
Afghanistan, 183, 431, 435, 436–438
  as a buffer state, 29, 436
  location 437–438
Africa, 325, 401, 439–456
  Belgium, 443, 446, 448–449, 450
  British, 441, 449–456
  French, 442, 444, 446, 447 (map), 450
  Germans in, 443
  importance of, 114–115
  Moslems in, 394
  nationalism, 422
  Netherlands, 441
  population and people, 41, 46, 49, 51, 444, 445 (map)
  Portuguese, 441
  resources, 56
  Spain in, 442–443
  transportation, 86, 442, 447 (map), 449
Africa, East, 452–454
Africa, North, (see North Africa)
Africa, South, 453 (see Union of South Africa)
Agriculture, 58
  control of, 66
  plantation (see Plantation agriculture)
Airplane, and the shrinking globe, 73–74, 515, 518, 520
  as integrative medium, 86
Air power, 73
Air transportation, 72–73, 106
  and international law, 106
  open vs. closed sky, 106
Alaska, 247, 262–266
  statehood, 266
  strategic value, 266
Albania, 187, 202, 206, 212–213, 376, 377
Aleutian Islands, 264, 266
Algeria, 82, 329, 331, 393, 394, 396–398
Alps Mountains, 363 (map)
Alsace, 79, 311, 333–334
Aluminum, 67
Amazon, 305
  resources, 56
Anatolia, 378, 387
Andes Mountains, 301–302
Anglo-America, 247–283, 284–286, 308
  compared to Latin America, 284–286
  relations with Latin America, 286–287
Angola, 82, 371, 372
Antarctica, 72
Antimony, 67
Anzus, 474
Apartheid, 449, 452, 454–456
Aqaba, Gulf of, 130, 392
Arabia (see Saudi Arabia)
Arab Federation, 403
Arab League, 130–131, 412, 414, 431
Arabs, 312, 369
  Arab-Israeli conflict, 351, 391–392, 411, 413 (map), 424–428, 427 (map), 513
  Palestinian, 428, 431

Arab World, 392–393
  impact, 414–415
  location and extent, 414
Arctic, The, 141, 181–182, 275–283, 280–281 (map), 312, 353–354
Arctic Mediterranean, 26, 72, 279–283, 280–281 (maps)
  Northwest Passage, 279
  Svalbard, 282
  Theory of Polar Sectorism, 282–283
Arctic Ocean, centricity of, 36 (see also Arctic Mediterranean)
Argentina, 301–305
Armenia, 143
Asia, 325, 401, 457–477
  and Communism, 218, 460
  continentality of, 27
  and democracy, 218–219
  East, 217–244, 220 (map), 457–466
  nationalism, 219, 460
  neutralism, 219, 460
  population, 41, 46, 49
  South, 351, 457, 478–503, 488 (map)
  Southeast, 240–244, 241 (map), 457
  and the West 458–459
Asia Minor, 367
Assyria, 36
Athens, 36, 380
Atlantic Ocean, 342
  geopolitical role of, 72
Atlantic Pact, 352 (see also North Atlantic Treaty Organization)
Atomic Energy Community, 116–118
Audiencia, 296
Australia, 77, 316, 319, 473–477, 475 (map), 476 (map)
  location, 32, 35
  population, 41, 46, 51
  problems, 474, 477
  resources, 56
  size, 475
Austria, 77, 351, 361, 363 (map), 364–365
  neutrality, 126, 128, 361
Austria-Hungary, 361, 364 (map), 377
Azerbaijan, 143
Azores, 370, 371

Bab-el-Mandeb, 321–323
Babylonia, 36
Bagdad Pact, 380 (see Middle East Treaty Organization)
Bahrein Islands, 409
Balfour Declaration, 426
Balkan Alliance, 116, 380
Balkan States, 311, 377, 190–191, 197–206, 210–216
  boundaries, 184–85
  cohesive and disruptive forces, 202–203
  corridors, 185, 186 (map), 187
  ethnic structure, 187, 188 (map), 189–191, 198–199, 204–206, 213–215
  minorities, 48, 195

Balkan States (*cont.*)
  Moslems in, 206
  problem areas, 213–216
  relief, 184–187
  religion, 191
Baltic Republics, 151, 153, 169
  and Russia, 152 (map), 169
Bandung Conference, 129, 501–503, 503 (map)
Belgian Congo, 56, 82, 372, 443, 446
  resources and power, 56
Belgium, 82, 311, 335–337, 340, 443
  as a crush area, 33 (map), 127, 335–336
  as a Colonial power, 80–82, 337
Benelux, 116, 335–337, 506
Berlin, 345, 347
Berlin Conference, 391
Bessarabia, 151, 198, 199
Black Sea, 378, 389, 390
Bogota Conference, 287
Bolivia, 296, 297–298
  tin, 65
Bosporus, 34, 140, 387 (*see* The Straits)
Boundaries, 11–12, 89–108, 311, 403 (map), 424–426, 435, 438
  allocation, 99–102
  barrier, 11, 26
  complex, 98–99
  cultural, 11, 96–97
  defense of, 11
  definition of, 90, 107
  delimitation, 99, 102–103
  demarcation, 99, 103–104
  desert, 11
  ethnic (*see* Boundaries, cultural)
  function of, 104–105
  geometric, 97–98
  inter-realm, 106–107
  justification for, 11
  lake, 93–94
  land, 29
  mountain, 11, 95–96, 184–185
  natural, 11, 90–97
  ocean, 92–93 (*see also* Territorial waters)
  physical (*see* Boundaries, natural)
  river, 11, 90–92, 215–216, 342
  surveillance, 105–106
  water, 29, 90–95 (*see also* Boundaries, lake; ocean; river)
  zonal, 89–90
Bowman, Isaiah, 16, 23–24
Brazil, 303, 305–308
  iron, 65, 307
  problems, 78, 305, 307
  size, 37, 307
British Empire, 17, 441, 499
Buffer States, 30, 32, 127, 335–336, 433, 467
Bulgaria, 187, 200–202, 204, 210–211, 377
Burma, 82, 319, 468, 494–497
  and neutralism, 130
Byzantine Empire, 389

Cable, 73
California, Lower, 297
Cambodia, 240, 244
Cameroons, 443
Canada, 277–279, 319
  Arctic, 277–279
  boundaries, 29, 97, 103, 256
  and Britain, 271, 272, 273
  coherence, 272–274, 278
  economy, 275–276
  French Canadians, 273
  location, 265, 276
  nationalism, 271–272

Canada (*cont.*)
  population and people, 41, 46, 272–275
  problems and problem areas, 78, 276
  size, 37, 271
  transportation, 278
  and United States, 271, 272, 274, 275, 276–277
Cape Verde Islands, 371
Capital, The, 77–78
  accessibility to, 77
Carinthia, 11, 205
Carpathian Mountains, 184, 185
Carthage, 367, 394, 415, 422
Catherine the Great, 148
Catholicism, 143, 146, 313, 316, 338, 471
  Greek Orthodox, 143, 146, 313
  Roman, 143, 313, 316, 338, 471
Central African Federation, 451–452, 453
Central America, 284, 285, 291–296, 292 (map)
  communications, 292 (map)
  location, 286, 291
  and United States, 291
Central Europe, 183–210, 311
  boundaries, 96, 184–185
  as a buffer zone, 32
  cohesive and disruptive forces, 202–203
  ethnic structure, 187, 188 (map), 191
  minorities, 195
  religion, 191
Ceylon, 82, 319, 493–494
Chaldea, 36
Chile, 297, 301–303
  location, 27
  shape, 38 (map)
  transportation, 38 (map), 301, 303
China, 76, 183, 313, 371, 376, 468, 500
  boundaries, 219–221
  capital, 77
  climate, 223
  coherence, 224–226
  domain, 219, 227–228
  economy, 229–232
  ecumene, 224
  and India, 492–493
  location, 27, 28, 32, 35, 219, 221–222
  Nationalist, 227–228 (*see* Formosa)
  nuclear area, 76
  population and people, 40, 49–50, 225–227
  relief, 220 (map), 222, 223–224
  and Russia, (USSR), 149, 232
  size, 37, 219, 222–223
  trade of, 121
  transportation, 224–225
Chromium, 67
Climate, 25–26, 68
  and development, 26
  and effect upon state relations, 76
  and habitability, 26
  polar, 26
  and population, 58
  tropical, 26
Coal-Steel Community, 116, 117 (map), 506
Collectives, 140
Colombia, 293, 298, 300
Colombo Plan, 474, 501–503
Colonialism, 80 (table), 81 (map), 101 (map), 125, 404, 513, 514
  burden of, 83
  effects in Asia, 217–218, 404
  problems of, 83
Colonial Possessions, 57, 80 (table), 81 (map)
  and resources, 57
Colonial Powers, 68–70, 80 (table)
Colonies, 79–84
  involvement in wars, 79
  value of, 9

Columbus, 36
Commonwealth of Nations, 79–82, 315–316, 319–326, 320 (map), 331, 449, 451, 453, 470
  coherence, 319–321, 320 (map)
  dependencies, 319
  ecumene, 316, 318
  population, 41–42, 47
  structure of, 79
  transportation, 319–321, 320 (map)
Communication, 68
  in an air age, 72–73
  and the annihilation of distance, 71
  facilities, 68
  as an implement of government, 73
  as an integrative medium, 70, 84–85
  as an element of power, 73–74
Communism, 468, 470
  frontiers of, 216
  future of, 123
  and the land problem, 58
  method of, 122
Communist Bloc, 106–107, 118–124, 345, 351, 380, 460
  cohesive factors, 120–122
  definition of, 118, 123–124
  location of, 120–121, 122
  population, 43, 50
  sources of strength, 118–119
  sources of weakness, 118–120
Communist Organization of Economic Cooperation, 121
Congo, 446, 448
  resources, 56 (see also Belgian Congo)
Conservation, international, 67
Constantinople, 385 (see also Istanbul)
Copenhagen, 356
Copper, 68
Crete, 367
Crush Zone, 183 (see Buffer States)
Cyprus, 321, 323–324, 378, 380, 513
  location, 35, 70
Cyrenaica, 324, 405, 421, 422
Czechoslovakia, 31 (map), 183, 195–196, 203–204, 205, 208–209, 311, 345, 349, 392

Damão, 371
Danube River, 215–216, 349, 362, 365, 387
Dardanelles, 34, 140, 147–148, 150, 367, 380, (see The Straits)
Denmark, 309, 311, 351, 355–357, 359
  empire, 356
  location, 356
Determinism, geographic, 14
Diu, 371
Dodecanese Islands, 376
Domain, 75–76 (see State, The, concept of territoriality)

East Asia (see Asia, East)
East Germany (see Peoples Democratic Republic)
East Indies, 342 (see Indonesia)
Eastern Europe, 137–216 (see Europe, eastern)
  population, 167–172, 187–192
Eastern Hemisphere, 517
Economic Factors, 55–74
Ecuador, 298
Ecumene, 76–77
Egypt, 324, 353, 392, 410, 411, 415–421, 416 (map), 422, 441 (see United Arab Republic)
  location, 70. 397
  and Suez, 397, 416 (map), 417
Emigrations, 51–54 (see Migrations)
  and over-population, 52

England, 70, 312, 315, 318, 390
  capital, 77
  constituent units, 78
  ecumene, 76–77
  nuclear area, 76
  population, 48
  territorial interests, 79–82
Eritrea, 376
Estonia, 151, 169, 360
Ethiopia (see Abyssinia)
Ethnic Integrants, 44, 187–192
  language, 44
  religion, 44
Euratom (see Atomic Engery Community)
Euromarket (see European Economic Community)
Europe, 309, 325, 401, 513, 518
  defense of, 312
  location, 34, 312–313
  a maritime continent, 27
  population, 41, 46, 47, 48
  shape, 309, 311–312, 313
  topography of, 311
  transportation, 310 (map), 311, 313
Europe, Western, 309–350, 310 (map), 387
European Atomic Energy Commission (see Atomic Energy Commission)
European Defense Community (EDC), 112
European Economic Community (Euromarket), 116–118
European Payments Union, 118
Exploitable Areas, 57, 71, 109

Fairgrieve, James, 21
Far East, 468 (see Asia. East)
Federation of Malaya (see Malaya)
Fertile Crescent. 368. 377, 432
Finland, 151. 360–361
  location, 32
  and neutralism. 126, 128
  and Russia, 360
Finno-Ugrian. 360
Fisheries, 93. 95
  in international affairs, 93–95
Foreign Policy, 87–88, 509–510
  and the State. 87
Formosa. 227–228. 465–466 (see China)
France. 309. 311, 312, 326–335, 349, 376, 410, 442. 468. 514
  capital, 77
  as a colonial power. 79. 82
  component units, 78, 328
  economy, 331–333
  ecumene. 76–77
  empire, 82, 314, 329–331, 330 (map)
  as a Great Power, 8
  location. 28, 326–327
  nuclear area, 76
  population and people, 40, 328
  problem areas. 77
  relief, 327–328
  shape, 38–39 (map), 328
  territorial interests, 79–82
  transportation, 38–39 (map)
French North Africa, 329 (see North Africa; Algeria)
Frontiers (see Boundaries)
Frontier Zones (see Boundaries, zonal)

Gaza, 130, 392
Geography, 3, 514–516
  definition of, 5
  function to political geography, 2

Geography (*cont.*)
  political (*see* Political geography)
  as a weapon of planning, 22, 519–520
Geopolitical Maturity and Immaturity, 84–85
Geopolitics, 14, 16–23
  American, 22–23
  contributions to geopolitical thought, 22
  English, 21–22
  of Fairgrieve, 21
  German, 14–18
  of Haushofer, 16–18
  of Kjellen, 16–17
  of Mackinder, 18–21, 22
  of Mahan, 22–23
  of Spykman, 21–22
  versus the concept of the status quo, 17
Geopolitik (*see* Geopolitics)
Georgia, USSR, 143
German Democratic Republic, 348–349 (*see* Peoples Democratic Republic)
German Federal Republic (West Germany), 333, 343, 345, 346–348
Germany, 18, 309, 311, 331, 333, 334, 342, 343–350, 356, 473
  boundaries, 311, 344 (map), 343–345
  as a Colonial Power, 78–79, 349
  location, 345
  partitioning of, 343, 344 (map), 346, 513
  problem areas, 79
  and Russia, 345, 346, 350
Ghana, 82, 84, 449
Gibraltar, 321–323, 370, 371, 395
  location, 35, 70
Global Relationships, 517
Globe, The, 520
  changing centricity on, 35
  diminishing dimensions of, 35, 515–519, 520
Goa, 371, 372
Goiaz, 306, 307
Gold Coast, 84 (*see* Ghana)
Government, 86–88
  and habitat, 86
Granada, New, 298, 300, 301
Great Britain, 309, 315–326, 374, 378, 467, 469–470, 473, 497, 514
  component units, 315–316, 318
  defense, 29
  economy, 316–318
  as a Great Power, 8, 295, 317
  location, 29, 314, 318
  as a maritime state, 27
  and the Mediterranean, 366–367, 391
  in the Middle East, 406, 410, 411, 426, 428, 431
  as a sea power, 22 (*see also* Lifeline, British)
  and Suez, 324–326, 366, 392, 410, 417–418
Great Lakes, 342
  as boundaries, 93, 94 (maps)
Great Lakes Waterway, 65, 70
Greece, 324, 325, 367, 415, 422
  location, 28
Greenland, 353, 356
Guam, 269
Guianas, 306

Habitat and Government, 86
Hanseatic League, 368
Hashemite, 430, 432
Haushofer, Karl, 16–18
  geopolitik of, 16
  and Hitler, 17, 18
  and the Monroe Doctrine, 18
  interest in Pacific area, 17
  source of ideas, 17–18

Hawaii, 247, 266, 267–269
  Mahan concept of, 23
  statehood, 266–267
"Heartland" Theory, 18–22
  definition of, 20
  theory of Mackinder, 18–21
  variations, 21–22
Hellespont, 383 (*see* Dardanelles)
Hemispheres, 517–518
Hindu, 478–485, 479 (map), 481 (map), 482 (map), 484
History, contributions to political geography, 5
Holland, 337 (*see* The Netherlands)
Holy Roman Empire, 362
Hongkong, 227, 228–229
Human Groups, 6–7, 54–55
  achievements of, 6
  differences in initiative, 7
Humboldt, Heinrich von, 14
Hungary, 32, 53, 183, 196–198, 209, 361 (*see* Austria-Hungary)

Iberia, 296, 309, 311, 312, 368, 369–374
  location, 28
  strategic importance, 370–371
Iceland, 353
Île de France, 76
Immigrants, 51–54 (*see* Migrations)
India, 319, 371, 478, 483, 489–493
  British in, 485
  and China, 492–493
  languages of, 489–490, 491 (maps)
  location, 35
  and neutralism, 126–127, 128–129, 494
  partition of, 478–486, 493, 481 (map), 482 (map)
  population, 49–50, 53, 478–483, 479 (map), 486 (map)
  size, 489, 492
India-Pakistan, 478–486, 479 (map), 481 (map), 482 (map), 513
Indochina, 82, 183, 214 (map), 240–244, 329, (*see also* Vietnam)
  civil war and partition, 242–244
  French in, 240, 242
  history, 240–242
Indonesia, 82, 342, 343, 497–501
  as a neutral, 129
  tin, 65
Industrial Revolution, effects upon population, 50
Industry, 55–68
  and power, 66, 67–68
  and transportation, 68
Inter-American Treaty of Reciprocal Assistance (Rio Pact), 115, 287
International Relations, 87–88, 509–510
  function of political geography, 5
Iran, 150, 183, 431, 433–436
  as a buffer state, 433
  nationalism in, 433, 434
  and neutralism, 126
  oil, 406–407
Iraq, 324, 380, 407, 431–433 (*see* Arab Federation)
Ireland, 315
Ireland, Northern, 316
Irish Free Republic, 316
Islam, 369, 404–405 (*see* Moslems)
  character and impact, 404–405, 414–415
Islamic Empire, 404–405
Israel, 325, 391, 405, 407, 423, 426–430, 427 (map)
  boundaries, 427 (map), 430
  Israeli-Arab conflict, 351, 391–392, 411, 413 (map), 424–428, 427 (map), 513
  migration into, 53, 426, 428

Istanbul, Turkey, 34 (*see* Constantinople)
Istria, 11 (*see* Trieste)
Italy, 76, 309, 311, 312, 374–377
    capital, 77 (*see* Rome)
    as a Colonial Power, 79, 376–377, 421
    ecumene, 77
    land problem, 58, 374–375
    location, 28
    nuclear area, 76
    population, 374–375
    territorial interests, 79–81
Iwo Jima (Bonine Islands), 270

Japan, 374, 460–465, 462 (map)
    location, 27, 29, 462 (map)
    as a maritime state, 27
    and neutralism, 129
    population, 48
    and the United States, 263, 264, 270
Jerusalem, 431
Jordan, 392, 423, 428, 430–431 (*see* Arab Federation)
Jordan River, 425, 426, 427 (map), 431

Kant, Immanuel, 14
Karafuto, 463
Kashmir, 481, 483, 512
Kenya, 82, 449, 450
Khyber Pass, 437, 487
Kiev, 144, 169
Kjellen, Rudolf, 16–17
Korea, 183, 232–240
    boundaries, 233–234, 238–240
    compared to Vietnam, 232–233
    location, 233–234
    political, 235–240
    the two Koreas, 237–240
Kowloon, 227, 228–229
Kurile Islands, 463
Kuwait, 409, 432

Ladakh, 483
Lakes, as boundaries, 93–94 (maps)
Land resource, 56–58
    distribution, 57–58
    and industrial resources, 58
    and international relations, 58
    and power, 58
    problems, 58
Lapps, 89–90, 361
    migrations of, 52
Latin America, 284–308
    coherence within, 290–291
    communications, 290–291
    compared to Anglo-America, 284–286
    economy, 289–290
    population and people, 46, 48, 49, 51
    relations with Anglo-America, 286–287
    stability and instability, 287–288
    and the United States, 286–287, 308
Latvia, 151, 169
Lausanne, Treaty of, 324, 378, 381, 390, 417
Law, 86–87
    and environment, 66
    international, 509–510
    interplay of law and region, 66–67, 86
    and resources, 66–67
    and the State, 86–87
League of Nations, 390, 424, 473, 505, 506, 510
Lebanon, 405, 407, 411, 423–424
Lebensraum, 15, 18 (*see* Ritter)
Leningrad, 147, 180

Liberia, 44, 440
    race, 44
Libya, 82, 353, 376, 405, 421
Lifeline, British, 319–326, 322 (map), 366, 516
List, Friedrich, 14, 15–16
Lithuania, 151
    population, 48
Location, 25–36, 55
    astronomical, 25–26
    central vs. peripheral, 32–34
    effect upon state relations, 76
    as a factor in history, 35
    insular, 28
    maritime vs. continental, 26–27, 28–30, 313, 398
    strategic, 34–35
    vicinal, 29–32
London, 77
Lorraine, 79, 311, 333–334
Luxembourg, 335, 343

Macao, 227, 229, 371
Macedonia, 213–214, 377, 378, 379, 388
Mackinder, Sir Halford, 18–21, 22
    concept of Germany's role, 20
    "Heartland" concept, 16
    place of United States in political pattern, 20
    concepts of World-Ocean and World-Island, 19
Madagascar, 442
Magellan, 35
Magnesium, 68
Magyars, 360
    migrations of, 53
Mahan, Alfred Thayer, 22
    concept of sea power, 22–23
Malacca, Strait of, 321, 326, 468
Malaya, 326, 468–470
    tin, 65
Malta, 321, 323
    location, 35, 70
Mandates, 79–84, 100 (map), 424, 428, 431, 443, 465, 473, 506
Manganese, 65, 67
Manifest Destiny, policy of, 248–249
Manila Pact, 115–116
Maracaibo, Lake, 301
Marmara, Sea of, 387
Marshall Plan, 118
Median line, 93, 94 (map)
Mediterranean, 35, 322 (map), 378, 380, 383, 386, 388, 392
    agriculture, 369
    Arctic, 26 (*see* Arctic Mediterranean)
    centricity of, 35–36
    climate, 368–369
    culture, 367, 415
    environment, 368–369, 397–398, 423
    and Europe, 366
    geopolitical considerations, 366–367
    and Great Britain, 366–367, 391
    history, 367–368
    relief, 368, 369
    Sea, 398
    strategic points of, 322 (map)
    and the United States, 366–367, 391, 398
    waterway, 68, 70
Mesopotamia, 36, 405, 432, 435
Mexico, 292 (map), 296–297
    boundaries, 29
Micronesia, 473
Middle East, 324, 367, 391–393, 400–438, 402 (map), 413 (map)
    boundaries, 403 (map), 424–426, 427 (map), 435, 438
    and Britain, 406, 410, 426, 428, 431

Middle East (*cont.*)
  and Communism, 121, 402 (map), 409
  and France, 410
  and Islam, 400
  location and extent, 400–402
  nationalism, 402–404
  neutralism, 410, 414
  oil, 71, 130, 406–409, 408 (map)
  resources, 405–409
  strategic importance, 401–402, 406, 409–410
  and the United States, 407–409, 410
Middle East Treaty Organization (Bagdad Pact), 115, 380, 412, 414, 431
Migrations, 51–53
  and border policies, 52–53
  effect of, 51
  of Europeans to other areas, 51
  inter-continental, 53
  intra-continental, 51, 53
  mass, 51
  and minority problems, 54
  population growth and decline, 51–53
Minerals, 58–66
  as expendable resources, 58
  need for international cooperation, 67, 68
  in international politics, 65
  localization of, 59–64 (maps), 65
  occurrence, 65, 68
  and power, 65
  rate of use, 65
  and transportation, 65
  in vogue, 65, 66
Minorities, 54
Mississippi River, 70, 342
Moluccas, 497–501 (*see* Indonesia)
Molybdenum, 68
Mongols, 405
  migrations of, 52
Monroe Doctrine, 18, 517
Montreux Convention, 140, 386, 391
Mormugão, 371
Morocco, 82, 321, 329, 393, 394, 396–397
  and Gibraltar, 321, 323
  location, 35
Morocco, Spanish, 321, 442–443
Moscow, 77, 145 (map), 169, 179
Moslems, 53, 422, 469, 478–485, 479 (map), 481 (map), 482 (map), 484, 513
  in Africa, 394, 399, 421
  in India-Pakistan, 478–485, 479 (map)
  migrations of, 53
  Moslem-Jewish conflict, 351, 391–392, 411, 413 (map), 424–428, 427 (map), 513
Mosul, 385
Mountains, 301–302, 312, 370, 371, 372
  as boundaries, 95–96 (*see* Boundaries, mountain)
Mozambique, 82, 371, 372

"Nation," 192
Nationalism, 435, 470, 498, 510–511
  Asian, 219, 435, 461
  Canada, 271–272
  Middle East, 402–404
Nationality, 75, 192
Netherlands, the, 68, 311, 335, 337–343, 339 (map), 497
  boundaries, 331, 338
  as a Colonial Power, 82
  Empire, 342–343 (*see* Belgian Congo; Indonesia; New Guinea)
  location, 337
  territorial interests, 80–82, 314

Neutralism, 352–353, 361, 410, 414, 422, 461, 494, 510–511, 513
Neutral States, 107
  Asian, 128–131, 219, 460
  definition of, 124–125, 127
  European, 127–128, 351–365
  location of, 125
  Middle East, 130–131
  strength of, 125–126
  weakness of, 125
Neutral Territories, the, 423, 425
New Granada (*see* Granada, New)
New Guinea, 82, 342, 498, 500, 513, 514
New Zealand, 319, 473, 474, 477
  location, 32, 35
Nickel, 65
Nietzsche, Friedrich Wilhelm, 14
Nigeria, 84
Nile River, 367, 405, 419–420
Nitrates, 302
North Africa, 351, 393–398
  and Communism, 121
  and Islam, 369, 399, 404, 405
  people and population, 130
North America, 247–267, 270–283, 296–297
  population, 47, 51
North American Arctic, 264 (map), 265–266, 277–279, 279–283, 281 (map)
  significance of, 279
North Atlantic, 36, 68, 69 (map)
  centricity of, 36
North Atlantic Treaty Organization (NATO), 112, 115, 312, 350, 353, 380, 431, 506, 508, 511, 516
Northern Hemisphere, 518
Northern Rhodesia (*see* Rhodesia)
Northern Sea Route, 141, 280 (map)
North Sea, 349
Northwest Passage, 72, 279, 281 (map)
Norway, 295, 311, 351, 352, 355, 359
  location, 28, 353, 355
Nuclear Area, 76
Nyasaland, 451 (*see also* Central African Federation)

Oceania, 473–477
  population, 51
Oceans, 92–95
  as boundaries, 92–93
  concept of closed and open seas, 92
Oceanways, 68–70, 69 (map)
  as integrative media, 86
Oder-Neisse Line, 345
Oil (*see* Petroleum)
Organization of American States (OAS), 287
Ottoman Empire, 324, 380–381, 382 (map), 389, 405, 417, 435

Pacific Area, 462 (map), 473–477
  defense, 472
  geopolitical role of, 72, 462 (map)
  United States in, 465
Pakistan, 82, 319, 380, 478, 483–489
  and India (*see* India-Pakistan)
  population, 53, 479 (map), 481 (map), 482 (map), 486 (map)
Palestine, 324, 391 (*see* Israel)
Panama, 291–295, 298, 308
  and the United States, 293–295
Panama Canal, 291–296, 292 (map), 301, 308, 325
  location, 35
  strategic importance, 287, 293, 295, 296
Panama Canal Zone, 247, 288, 294 (map), 295

Panama, Isthmus of, 296
Pan American Highway, 291, 295
Pan American Union, 287
Pan-Slavism, 151
Paris, 77
Paris Basin, 311, 312, 327–328
Paris Treaty, 390
Passes, Alps, 311, 362, 364, 377
Pathan, 487
Peace, 508–509
Peoples Democratic Republic (East Germany), 345, 346, 348–349
Persia (see Iran)
Peru, 296, 297, 298
Petrograd (see Leningrad)
Petroleum, 174–175, 181, 407
  as a political weapon, 71
Philippines, 82, 84, 247
  from colony to independence, 84
Phoenicia, 367, 415, 423
Plantation Agriculture, 57
  and politics, 57
  Plebiscite, 356, 487
Poland, 183–216
  boundaries, 192–195
  buffer state, 30 (map), 32
  economic and political structure, 206–207
  location, 32
  partitions of, 147, 193 (map), 194 (map)
  people and population, 48, 192–195
  relief, 192
  and Russia, 192, 194
Polar Sectorism, Theory of, 282–283
Political Areas, 6–7, 10–11
  in space, 10
  in time, 10
Political Geography, principles of, 2–133
  of Isaiah Bowman, 23–24
  definition of, 2–12
  in England, 22
  function of, 4, 5
  in Germany, 14–18
  of Greeks, 13
  growth of, 13–23
  primary factors of, 2–133
  role of, 12
  of Romans, 13
  static and dynamic elements, 6, 12
  in the United States, 22–23
Political Maturity and Immaturity, 84–85
Political Science, function to political geography, 6
Polynesians, 11
Population, 40–54 (see Population, under various countries)
  age distribution (table), 47
  climatic distribution, 40–41, 58
  composition, 43
  continental patterns, 41, 42 (map)
  density-effects policy toward immigrants and emigrants, 53–54
  dynamics of, 44–51, 54
  effectiveness, 43
  emigration, 52
  growth potential, 43
  and industrialization, 50
  and international tension, 40
  and manpower, 54
  migration, 51–54
  and power, 40, 42, 43, 58
  size, 43
  trends, 44–51
Portugal, 68, 82, 305, 311, 313, 368, 369, 371–372, 497

Portugal (cont.)
  as a colonial power, 82, 371–372
  location, 371
  strategic value, 370–371
Potsdam Agreement, 346
Power, 8–9
  concept of in a bipolar world, 109–133
  equation of, 8
  geography of, 9
  military, 131, 509
  national, 9
  obligations of, 9
  and resources, 58
Powers, 8–9
  colonial, 68–70
  Great, 8–9, 67, 131, 514
Problem Areas, 78–79
Propontis, 388 (see Sea of Marmara)
Prussia, 345
Punjab, 480–481, 481 (map), 490
Pushtoonistan, 438, 487, 489 (maps)
Pyrenees, 312, 370, 371, 372

Race, 44
  definition, 44
  and national policy, 44
  and population structure, 44
Radio, 73
  as integrative medium, 86
Ratzel, Friedrich, 14, 15–16
  laws of growth of states, 15
Raw materials, 67
  critical, 67
  essential, 67
  strategic, 67
Religion, 44
  in Africa, 444 (map)
  distribution, 191 (map), 479 (map), 400–401
  in Europe, 191 (map)
  Greek Orthodox, 143, 146
  in India, 478–480, 479 (map)
  Moslem, 191, 202, 400–401, 479 (map)
  Roman Catholicism, 143, 191 (map)
Resources, 6, 55–68
  control of, 67
  inequable distribution, 55–56
  and law, 66–67, 87
  potential and actual, 55
  and power, 55, 56, 58
  and the stage of the arts, 55–56
  time element in use, 56
Resources, Extractive, 58–66
Rhine River, 30, 311, 337, 341, 342, 343, 349
  as an international boundary, 311, 342
  and laws, 66
Rhodesia, 319, 372, 451–452 (see Central African Federation)
Rio de Janeiro, 306, 307
Rio de Oro, 442
Rio Grande River, 91 (map), 92, 256
Ritter, Karl, 14, 15
  and geographic determinism, 14
Rivers, as boundaries, 90–92, 91 (map)
Roman Empire, 109, 398
Rome, 76, 367, 388, 415
Roosevelt, Theodore, recognition of importance of geography to state planning, 22
Rotterdam, Netherlands, 339 (map), 341
  location, 341, 342
Ruanda-Urundi, 443
Ruhr, 331, 347–348
  second (see Silesia)

Rumania, 32, 198–200, 204, 209–210
  boundaries, 198–199
  and Russia, 199–200
Russia, 150, 309, 355, 433 (see USSR)
  and China, 149
  expansion of, 109
  and Japan, 149
Russian nationalities, 144, 146
  Belo, 144, 167, 169, 170
  Great, 144, 167–169
  Little, (see Ukraine, nationality)
Ruthenes, 168 (see Ukraine, nationality)
Ryukyu Islands, 270, 463, 464–465, 473
  location, 35, 464
  and the United States, 464–465

Saar, 11, 331, 334–335, 345, 347
  boundaries, 11, 334–335
Sahara, 72, 442, 447 (map)
St. Lawrence Waterway, 275
St. Petersburg (see Leningrad)
Sardinia, 375, 376
Saudi Arabia, 412, 422–423, 430
  oil, 407–409
Sault Saint Marie Canal, 325
Scandinavia, 309, 312, 351, 353–361, 354 (map),
  494
  location, 28, 353, 355
  and neutralism, 127–128
Schleswig-Holstein, 356
Schuman Plan, 506 (see Coal-Steel Community)
Scotland, 315
Sea power, 68
  of Britain, 22, (see Lifeline, British)
  Mahan concept of, 53
  United States as a, 8, 22–23, 295, 391
Serbia, 204 (see Yugoslavia)
Shape, 38, 39
  attenuated, 38
  advantages of compactness, 38–39, 328
  fragmented, 38, 311
  protuberant, 38, 252, 309
  and transportation, 38–39
Siam, (see Thailand)
Siberia, 26, 139, 181, 280 (map)
  location, 26, 72, 139, 283
  movement into, 51
  population, 41
Sicily, 376
Sierra Leone, 44
Silesia, 207, 347
Size, 6, 36–38, 55
  of ancient state, 36
  as a concomitant to power, 37
  effect upon state relations, 76
  of modern state, 36
  relation to power of state, 37–38
  is relative, 37
  and the stage of the arts, 37
Slavs, 361, 378
  differentiation among, 189–191
  Eastern, 167, 168, 190
  Southern, 168, 190
  spread of, 142–143, 189
  Western, 168, 190
Socotra Islands, British, 70
  location, 35, 70
Somalia, 376
Somaliland, British, 70, 84
  Italian (see Somalia)
South America, 284, 296–308, 299 (map), 305,
  308, 406, 518
  location, 286

South America (cont.)
  population, 49, 51
  transportation, 290, 295, 299 (map)
South Asia, (see Asia, South)
Southeast Asia, (see Asia, Southeast)
Southeast Asia Treaty Organization (SEATO), 115,
  474
Southern Hemisphere, 518
Southern Rhodesia, (see Rhodesia)
Southwest Africa, 443
Southwest Asia, (see Middle East)
Soviet Union, (see Union of Soviet Socialist Republics)
Space, 6
  components, 25
  factors, 24–39
  and power, 25
  in time, 24
Spain, 68, 77, 296, 297, 309, 311, 338, 368, 372–
  374, 442, 471, 473, 497
  as a Colonial Power, 79, 372, 442–443
  location, 27
  strategic importance, 370–371
  territorial interests, 79–81
Sparta, 36
Spice Islands, (see Moluccas), 313
Spykman, Nicholas John, 21
  geopolitics of (see Geopolitics, of Spykman)
State, The, 6–8, 75–88
  components of, 8
  and the concept of territoriality, 75–76
  continental, 29
  domain, 75–76
  and foreign policy, 87
  growth of, 15
  and the Laws, 86–87
  maritime, 29
  planning, 22
  structure, 76–86
State Farm, 140
State Planning, 22, 519–520
  relation to geography, 22
Steel, 67
Straits, The, 147–148, 385, 386–389, 389–391, 397
  (see Bosporus; Dardanelles; Sea of Marmara)
  location, 384, 386–387
  and Russia, 147–148, 201
  and Turkey, 140, 148, 397
Sudan, 82, 417, 421
Sudbury, Ontario, 65
Sudeten, 11, 345
Suez Canal, 130, 321, 324–326, 353, 366, 368, 392,
  397, 406, 409–410, 417, 441
  and Britain (see Britain and the Suez)
  control of, 66
  and Egypt (see Egypt, and Suez)
  location, 35, 70
Sumatra, 326, 468
Supra-National Organization, 504–506, 509–515
Surinam, 342
Svalbard, 282, 353
Sweden, 311, 345, 351, 352, 355, 357–359
  location, 28
  and neutralism, 126, 352, 353
  population, 46
Switzerland, 311, 345, 349, 351, 361–364, 363 (map)
  location, 29
  as a neutral, 127, 361, 362, 364, 494
Syria, 324, 405, 407, 423, 424–426 (see United
  Arab Republic)

Tanganyika, 443, 449, 450, 453–454
Tangier, 321, 394

Telegraph, 73
  as an integrative medium, 86
Territorial Base, effect upon state relations, 76
Territorial interests, 79–84
Territorial waters, 92–93
Thailand, 466–468
Thames River, 76
Thrace, 377, 378
Tibet, 183
Timor, 371
Tin, 65, 67
Togoland, 443
Topography, 55
  effect upon state relations, 76
Trade, 71
  barriers, 71
  basis for, 68
  international, 109–110
Transjordan, 423 (see Jordan)
Transportation, 68–71, 72–74, 518
  air, 72–73, 106
  in an air age, 72–73
  and the annihilation of distance, 71
  as an element of power, 73–74
  as an implement of government, 73
  and industry, 68
  as integrative media, 70, 84–85
  ocean, 68–70, 69 (map)
  and shape, 38–39
Treitschke, Heinrich von, 14
Trieste, 214–215, 361, 376, 512
  minority problems, 54
Tripolitania, 405, 421, 422
Troy, 36, 383, 387
Trust Territories, 79–84, 465, 473
Tungsten, 67
Tunisia, 82, 329, 393, 394, 397
Turkestan, Russian, 150, 181
Turkey, 324, 353, 377, 378, 380–391, 382 (map)
  405, 431, 435
  boundaries, 385
  location, 384, 386–387
  and Russia, 385, 390
  and The Straits (see Straits, and Turkey)
  territorial interests, 79–81, 276 (see Ottoman
    Empire)

Uganda, 449, 450
Ukraine, 151
  nationality, 146, 167, 168
  size, 36
Union of South Africa, 44, 319, 449, 454–456
  race, 44, 454–456 (see Apartheid)
Union of Soviet Socialist Republics (USSR), 17, 21,
  77, 137–282, 312, 331, 345, 352, 353, 357, 360,
  367, 386, 392, 412, 513
  agriculture 149, 164–167
  Arctic, 141, 181–182, 280 (map), 282, 312
  boundaries, 96, 141, 153–160
  and Britain, 149
  canals, 180–181
  capital, 77
  climate, 139–141, 165, 183
  constituent units, 160–161
  economy, 163–164
  ecumene, 166 (map)
  expansion of, 145 (map), 148–151
  and Germany, 345, 350
  history, 142–153
  industry, 172–173, 178–182
  location, 26, 32, 137, 138
  minerals, 65, 164, 175–178, 182
  and neutralism, 127

Union of Soviet Socialist Republics (USSR) (cont.)
  Northern Sea Route, 141, 280 (map)
  outlets to sea, 138–139, 140–141
  political structure, 160–161
  population and people 41, 48, 161–163, 162
    (map), 167–172
  as a power, 8, 110, 131
  power resources, 172–175
  problem areas, 78
  regional planning, 161
  relief, 138–139, 183
  religion, 168
  resources, 56, 164–167, 406
  satellites, 118
  serfdom, 146–147, 148
  size, 36, 37, 137–138
  time variable affecting mode of adjustment, 10
  trade, 182
  transportation, 86, 149, 151
  Turkestan, 150, 181
Uniscan, 118
United Arab Republic, 403
United Kingdom, (see Great Britain)
United Nations, 425, 428, 433, 453, 465, 473, 510,
  511–514, 518
United States, 18, 247–270, 331, 350, 370, 473, 510,
  514, 518
  American Arctic, 264 (map), 265–266
  boundaries, 29, 97, 99, 103, 256
  capital, 77
  and Central America, 291–296
  coherence within, 252–253, 311–312
  communication, 252–253
  constituent units, 77
  dependent territories, 80, 262–270
  domain, 254–256, 255 (map)
  ecumene, 77, 253 (map)
  expansion of, 109, 255 (map), 254–256
  and foreign relations, 87–88, 247, 260–262
  growth of, 247–249
  industry, 65, 257–259
  and Latin America, 308
  location, 25, 27, 28, 251–252
  and the Mediterranean, 366–367, 391
  minerals, 65, 67–68, 256–259, 406
  nuclear area, 76, 254
  Pacific interests, 267–270, 465
  and Panama, 293–295
  and policy of Manifest Destiny, 248–249
  population and people, 41, 46, 249–251, 312
  problem areas, 79
  as a Great Power, 8, 23, 131, 259–260, 295
  resources, 256–259
  resource use, 56, 256–257
  size, 252
  Pacific strategy, 269, 270
  time variable in the mode of adjustment, 10
  transportation, 252–253, 311–312

Venezuela, 298, 300–301
  location, 27
  oil, 301
Versailles Treaty, 335
Vienna, 361, 362, 365
Vienna Treaty, 361, 365
Vietnam, 242–244, 329, (see Indochina)
  compared to Korea, 244
  seventeenth degree parallel, 242, 244
  the two Vietnams, 242–243
Virgin Islands, location, 295
Volga River, 180, 342

Wake Island, 269
Wales, 315
War, 505–508
  and boundaries, 99
  cold, 111 (map)
  and peace, 508–509
  relation to geography, 3
Warsaw Pact, 122
Washington, D. C., 77
Wei Ho Valley, 76
Western Bloc, 106–107, 110–118, 309, 351, 458–459
  cohesive factors in, 112–114, 115–118, 261 (map)
  defense, 329, 334, 380, 412
  defined, 110, 112
  disruptive factors in, 112–113
  future of, 118
  location of, 110–112, 114
  role of dependent territories in, 114–115

Western Europe (see Europe, Western)
West German Republic (see German Federal Republic)
Western Hemisphere, 517
  location, 35
  movement into, 51
West Indies, population, 51
Whittlesey, Derwent, 23

Yalta Agreement, 149
Yemen, 412 (see United Arab Republic)
Yugoslavia, 77, 187, 204–206, 211–212, 361, 377, 380

Zanzibar, 441
Zionist Movement, 426

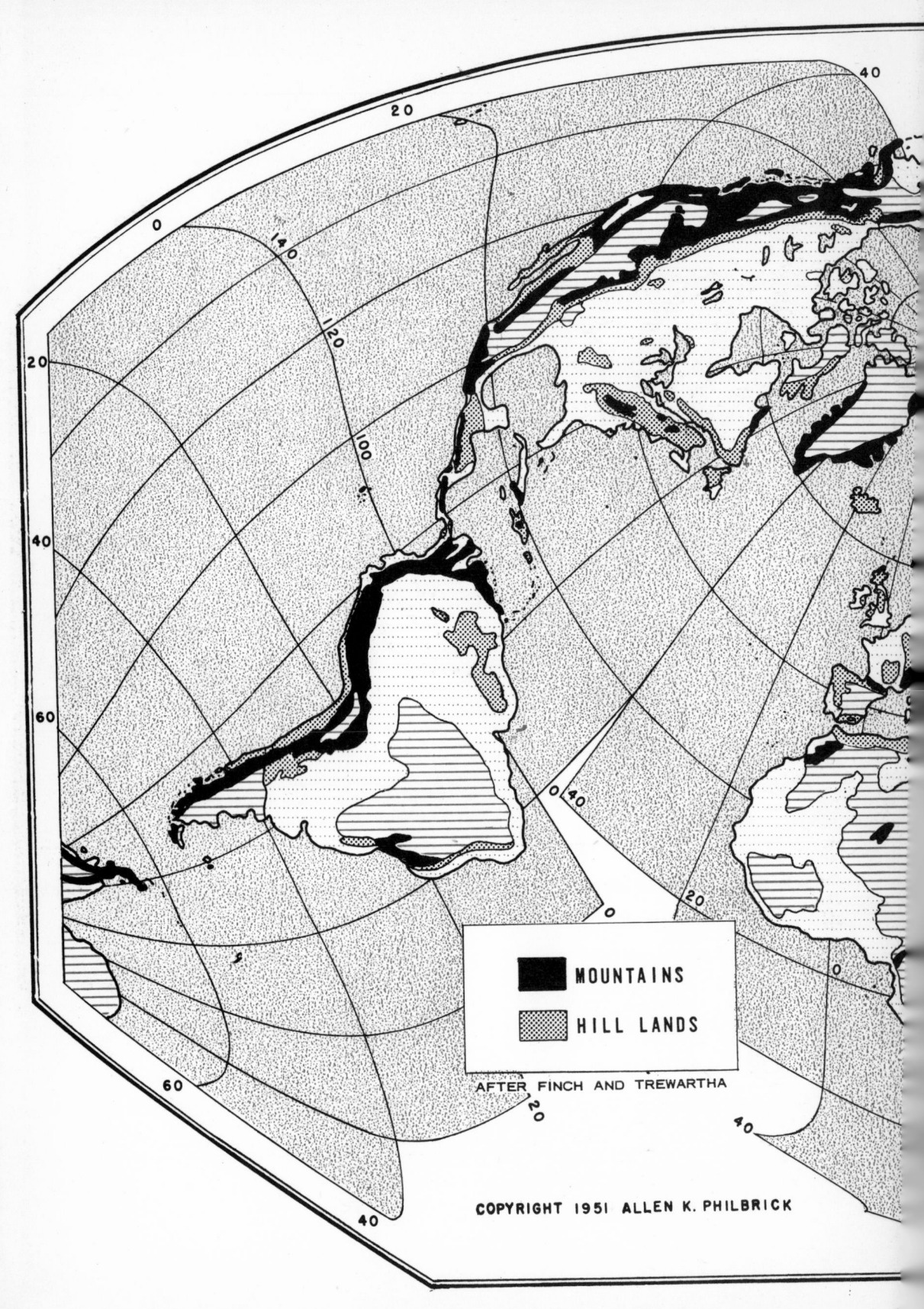

MOUNTAINS

HILL LANDS

AFTER FINCH AND TREWARTHA

COPYRIGHT 1951 ALLEN K. PHILBRICK